NORTHERN
CALIFORNIA
HANDBOOK

INCLUDING SAN FRANCISCO • WINE COUNTRY
BIG SUR • YOSEMITE • REDWOOD COAST

SECOND EDITION

NORTHERN
CALIFORNIA
HANDBOOK

INCLUDING SAN FRANCISCO • WINE COUNTRY
BIG SUR • YOSEMITE • REDWOOD COAST

SECOND EDITION

KIM WEIR

WITH A FOREWORD BY URSULA K. LE GUIN

MOON
PUBLICATIONS INC.

NORTHERN CALIFORNIA HANDBOOK
SECOND EDITION

Please send all comments, corrections, additions, amendments, and critiques to:

**NORTHERN CALIFORNIA HANDBOOK
C/o MOON PUBLICATIONS, INC.
P.O. BOX 3040
CHICO, CA 95927-3040, USA**

Published by
   Moon Publications, Inc.
   P.O. Box 3040
   Chico, CA 95927-3040, USA

Printed by
   Colorcraft Ltd.

Printing History
   1st edition June 1990
   2nd edition January 1994
      Reprinted — February 1995
      Reprinted — July 1995

Library of Congress Cataloging-in-Publication Data

Weir, Kim, 1953-
   Northern California Handbook/Kim Weir.—2nd ed.
      p.   cm.
   Includes bibliographical references.
   ISBN 0-918373-84-0 :
   1. California. Northern—Description and travel—Guide-books.
   I. Title.
   F867.5.W44   1990
   917.94—dc20   89-13581
                                  CIP

Printed in Hong Kong

Front cover: "Big Sur Spring Sunset" © 1990 by Tom Killion

True places are not found on maps.

—HERMAN MELVILLE

ACKNOWLEDGMENTS

Once again I am indebted to my editor, Taran March, the queen of syncopated syntax, for her patience and persistence. This is one wild white whale of a book, more than enough to sink a lesser mortal. Ms. March's intelligence, "heart," and personal integrity continue to give her what she needs to give me what I need: direct and honest response.

My everlasting thanks also to Ursula K. Le Guin, for writing "World-Making" in the first place, and for allowing me to remake it as a foreword to this book. I have yet to find or devise a better brief statement of my own fledgling philosophy of "conscious travel," a journey with as many inner steps as outer. I offer my gratitude also to Ms. Virginia Kidd, for her patience and support in obtaining permissions.

At the top of my thank-you list, too, is Publisher Bill Newlin, for his genuine efforts to "make it work" so I can complete my longer term task—telling the entire California story in travel book form. Welcome aboard, Mr. Newlin. As Walt Whitman would say: "Oh Captain! my Captain! Our fearful trip is done." At least one book has weathered the rack. Let's hope we'll all still be cheering after the next book is made, and the next one after that.

The crew is so large. As always, I reserve a special category of gratitude for the many Moon Publications authors who have helped me learn the ropes, particularly Jane King, Steve Metzger, and Bob Nilsen. This time out, I also want to thank Tim Moriarty, both for his diligent research and for his own written contributions to the San Francisco chapter. (Though the world seems to be transforming itself at warp speed these days, I still hope we can manage to make this a long-term association.) I offer my appreciation, too, to Michelle Bonzey, for her help in updating sections of both the Wine Country and North Coast chapters, and to Ed Aust, Taran March, and Gary Thompson for their contributions to this book's editorial content.

I am also grateful to Carey Wilson and Dirk Walls, for diligently finding the right place for endless editorial additions, and to Sheri Wyatt for checking text continuity. My thanks, too, to Asha Johnson and Don Root for copyediting this tome, a monumental task. I am also indebted to Mark Arends for proofreading, and for housesitting, especially the important work of taking care of faithful dog Sarah, four cats, and a jungle of house plants while I was on the road.

Snapping off a fascinating photograph would be the best way to express my gratitude to the production crew at Moon Publications. Words, however, will have to suffice. I particularly appreciate Nancy Kennedy for her meticulous layout work. I'm thankful as always to Art Director David Hurst, for his keen sense of balance, design, and overall visual aesthetics as well as his patient attention to all those picayune graphic details.

Special thanks to Bob Race, Brian Bardwell, and former Moon employee Louise Foote, for such fine work on the maps, and to Bob Race for his original artwork on the leading page of each chapter. Based on my stick-figure drawings, I'm still amazed that he could translate them into visual images—and so beautifully.

Thanks, too, to Marketing Director Donna Galassi, as well as promotion and sales wizards Julie Mason and Leslie Parmenter, for doing everything possible to help us all make a living in this business.

I am also grateful to other underappreciated workaholics at Moon Publications, particularly front-office phone answerers, financial fact-finders, maniacal shipping clerks, and desktop publishing technology fiends, for mastering endless repetitive yet complex tasks with rare error and nary a whimper. That's dedication.

My special thanks to photographer friends and sympathizers who have contributed their work to this work, including Ed Aust, Todd Clark, Wes Dempsey, Dave Hurst, and Bob Nilsen, not to mention the City of San Francisco Arts Commission and the California Department of Parks and Recreation. I also thank Tom Killion for his fine cover woodblock, and Philip Right for a fabulous full-color peek into the mysterious heart of a North Coast redwood grove.

Reaching back into my past, I am still indebted to many of my environmental studies instructors at the University of California at Santa Barbara and to my biology professors at California State University, Chico—particularly Doug Alexander, Wes Dempsey, Roger Lederer, Rob Schlising, and Tom Rodgers—for teaching me to see the living world. As I recall, that subject was never included on any class syllabus.

Arriving in the present, I also extend my heartfelt thanks to Fred Sater, media relations manager for the California Office of Tourism. I appreciate his personal encouragement and support, not to mention that refreshing sense of humor. I am also grateful for so many gracious introductions to travel industry pros at chambers of commerce and visitors bureaus throughout California. Their contributions and thoughtful suggestions have greatly improved this book's practical focus and (I hope) its overall usefulness.

—Kim Weir

CONTENTS

MAPS

MAP SYMBOLS AND ABBREVIATIONS

▬▬▬ FREEWAY	N.R.A. NATIONAL RECREATION AREA	▬ ▬ ▬ INTERNATIONAL BORDER
▬▬ MAIN HIGHWAY	S.R.A. STATE RECREATION AREA	▬ ▪ ▬ ▪ ▬ STATE BORDER
▬ SECONDARY ROAD	S.R. STATE RESERVE	▪▪ ▪ ▬ ▪ ▪ ▪ REGIONAL BORDER
▬ ▬ ▬ UNPAVED ROAD	R.P. REGIONAL PARK	▪ ▪ ▬ ▪ ▪ ▬ COUNTY BORDER
▪ ▬ ▪ ▬ ▪ FOOT TRAIL	S.P. STATE PARK	═══ BRIDGE
▬▬( )▬▬ TUNNEL	N.P. NATIONAL PARK	▬▬▬ RAILROAD
⬡ INTERSTATE HIGHWAY	C.P. COUNTY PARK	⌐ ⌐ GATE
⬡ U.S. HIGHWAY	S.H.P. STATE HISTORIC PARK	↟ WATERFALL
⬡ STATE HIGHWAY	S.B. STATE BEACH	▲ MOUNTAIN
○ LARGE CITY	C.B. CITY BEACH	■ POINT OF INTEREST
○ MEDIUM CITY	G.C. GOLF COURSE	⬬ WATER
○ SMALL TOWN	C.G. CAMPGROUND	

IS THIS BOOK OUT OF DATE?

As mentioned elsewhere in this book, this being California, most things change faster than traffic lights. Though every effort was made to keep all current facts corralled and accounted for, it's no doubt true that *something* (most likely, a variety of things) will already be inaccurate by the time the printer's ink squirts onto the paper at presstime.

Due to this unfortunate fact of life in the fast lane of travel writing, comments, corrections, inadvertent omissions, and updated information are always greatly appreciated. Just remember this: whatever you divulge may indeed end up in print—so think twice before sending too much information about your favorite hole-in-the-wall restaurant, cheap hotel, or "secret" world's-best swimming hole or hot springs. Once such information falls into the hands of a travel writer, it probably won't be a secret for long. Address all correspondence to:

Northern California Handbook
c/o Moon Publications
P.O. Box 3040
Chico, CA 95927

ABBREVIATIONS

AAA = American Automobile Association
a/c = air conditioning
Ave. = Avenue
AYH = American Youth Hostel
B&B = bed and breakfast
BLM = Bureau of Land Management
d = double occupancy
Dr. = Drive
F = Fahrenheit
Hwy. = Highway
I = Interstate
Ln. = Lane
MC = MasterCard
mph = miles per hour
Mt. = Mount

OP = out of print
OW = one way
pp = per person
Pt. = Point
Rd. = Road
Rt. = Route
RT = roundtrip
RV = recreation vehicle
s = single occupancy
St. = Street, Saint
TDD = Telecommunications Device for the Deaf
TTY = teletype
UC = University of California
WW I = World War I
WW II = World War II

WORLD-MAKING

by Ursula K. Le Guin

It's a happy but humbling experience, after finishing a book the size of Northern California Handbook, *to discover that someone has already said it all, and in many fewer words.*

Kim Weir

We're supposed to be talking about world-making. The idea of making makes me think of making new. Making a new world: a different world: Middle Earth, say, or the planets of science fiction. That's the work of the fantastic imagination. Or there's making the world new: making the world different: a utopia or dystopia, the work of the political imagination.

But what about making the world, this world, the old one? That seems to be the province of the religious imagination, or of the will to survive (they may be the same thing). The old world is made new at the birth of every baby, and every New Year's Day, and every morning, and the Buddhist says at every instant.

That, in every practical sense, we make the world we inhabit is pretty well beyond question, but I leave it to the philosophers to decide whether we make it all from scratch—mmmm! tastes like a scratch world! but it's Bishop Berkeley's Cosmo-Mix!—or whether we patch it together by a more or less judicious selection of what strikes us as useful or entertaining in the inexhaustible chaos of the real.

In either case, what artists do is make a particularly skillful selection of fragments of cosmos, unusually useful and entertaining bits chosen and arranged to give an illusion of coherence and duration amidst the uncontrollable streaming of events. An artist makes the world her world. An artist makes her world the world. For a little while. For as long as it takes to look at or listen to or watch or read the work of art. Like a crystal, the work of art seems to contain the whole, and to imply eternity. And yet all it is is an explorer's sketch-map. A chart of shorelines on a foggy coast.

To make something is to invent it, to discover it, to uncover it, like Michelangelo cutting away the marble that hid the statue. Perhaps we think less often of the proposition reversed, thus: To discover something is to make it. As Julius Caesar said, "The existence of Britain was uncertain, until I went there." We can safely assume that the ancient Britons were perfectly certain of the existence of Britain, down to such details as where to go for the best woad. But, as Einstein said, it all depends on how you look at it, and as far as Rome, not Britain, is concerned, Caesar invented *(invenire,* "to come into, to come upon") Britain. He made it be, for the rest of the world.

Alexander the Great sat down and cried, somewhere in the middle of India, I think, because there were no more new worlds to conquer. What a silly man he was. There he sits sniveling, halfway to China! A conqueror. Conquistadores, always running into new worlds, and quickly running out of them. Conquest is not finding, and it is not making. Our culture, which conquered what is called the New World, and which sees the world of nature as an adversary to be conquered: look at us now. Running out of everything.

The name of our meeting is Lost Worlds and Future Worlds. Whether our ancestors came seeking gold, or freedom, or as slaves, we are the conquerors, we who live here now, in possession, in the New World. We are the inhabitants of a Lost World. It is utterly lost. Even the names are lost. The people who lived here, in this place, on these hills, for tens of thousands of years, are remembered (when they are remembered at all) in the language of the conquistadores: the "Costanos," the "Santa Claras," the "San Franciscos," names taken from foreign demigods. Sixty-three years ago, in the *Handbook of the Indians of California,* my father wrote:

> The Costanoan group is extinct so far as all practical purposes are concerned. A few scattered individuals survive. . . . The larger part of a century has passed since the missions were abolished, and nearly a century and a half since they commenced to be founded. These periods have sufficed to efface even traditional recollections of the forefathers' habits, except for occasional fragments.

Here is one such fragment, a song; they sang it here, under the live oaks, but there weren't any wild oats here then, only the California bunch-grasses. The people sang:

> I dream of you,
> I dream of you jumping,
> Rabbit, jackrabbit, and quail.

And one line is left of a dancing song:

> Dancing on the brink of the world.

With such fragments I might have shored my ruin, but I didn't know how. Only knowing that we must have a past to make a future with, I took what I could from the European-based culture of my own forefathers and mothers. I learned, like most of us, to use whatever I could, to filch an idea from China and steal a god from India, and so patch together a world as best I could. But still there is a mystery. This place where I was born and grew up and love beyond all other, my world, my California, still needs to be made. To make a new world you start with an old one, certainly. To find a world, maybe you have to have lost one. Maybe you have to be lost. The dance of renewal, the dance that made the world, was always danced here at the edge of things, on the brink, on the foggy coast.

BOB RACE

INTRODUCTION
CALIFORNIA AS MYTH

California is a myth—a myth in the sense of a traditional tale told to impart truth and wisdom, and in the fanciful sense of some extravagant storybook fiction. Californians happen to like the quirky character of the state they've chosen to live in. Whether or not they realize it, California as myth is exactly why they're here—because in California, even contradictions mean nothing. In California, almost everything is true and untrue at the same time. In California, people can pick and choose from among the choices offered—as if in a supermarket—or create their own truth. Attracted to this endless sense of creative possibilities—California's most universal creed, the source of the ingenuity and inventiveness the state is so famous for—people here are only too happy to shed the yoke of tradition, and traditional expectations, that kept them in harness elsewhere.

Californians tend to think life itself is a California invention, but "lifestyle" definitely is: people come to California to have one. Coming to California, novelist Stanley Elkin observes, "is a choice one makes, a blow one strikes for hope.

No one ever wakes up one day and says, 'I must move to Missouri.' No one chooses to find happiness in Oklahoma or Connecticut." And according to historian Kevin Starr, "California isn't a place—it's a need." Once arrived in California, according to the myth, the only reason to carry around the baggage of one's previous life is because one chooses to.

But it would be naive to assume that this natural expansiveness, this permission to be here now, is somehow new in California. It may literally be as old as the hills, oozing up through the rocks and soil like psychic black gold. Native peoples, the first and original laid-back Californians, knew this. Busy with the day-to-day necessities of survival, they nonetheless held the place in awe and managed to honor the untouchable earth spirits responsible for creation. The last remembered line of an ancient Ohlone dancing song—"dancing on the brink of the world"—somehow says it all about California.

As a place, California is still a metaphor, for Shakespeare's "thick-coming fancies" as well as for those awesome mysteries that can't be

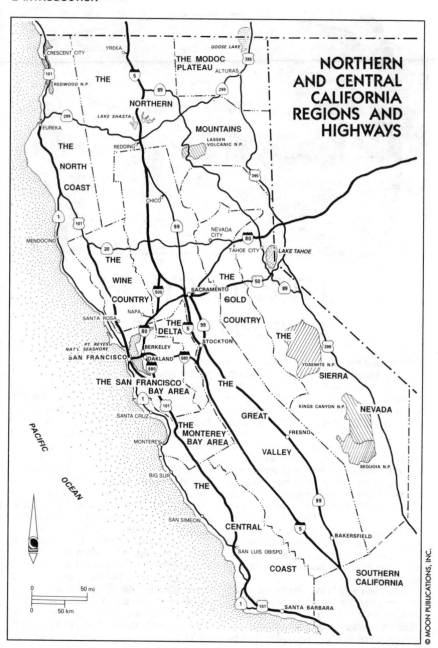

NORTHERN AND CENTRAL CALIFORNIA REGIONS AND HIGHWAYS

CRESCENT CITY
YREKA
GOOSE LAKE
THE MODOC PLATEAU
ALTURAS
REDWOOD N.P.
THE
NORTHERN
LAKE SHASTA
EUREKA
MOUNTAINS
LASSEN VOLCANIC N.P.
THE
NORTH
COAST
REDDING
CHICO
MENDOCINO
NEVADA CITY
TAHOE CITY
LAKE TAHOE
THE
WINE
COUNTRY
SACRAMENTO
THE
GOLD
COUNTRY
SANTA ROSA
NAPA
THE
DELTA
STOCKTON
THE
PT. REYES NAT'L SEASHORE
BERKELEY
SAN FRANCISCO
OAKLAND
YOSEMITE N.P.
SIERRA
THE SAN FRANCISCO BAY AREA
KINGS CANYON N.P.
NEVADA
SANTA CRUZ
THE
MONTEREY
BAY AREA
THE
GREAT
FRESNO
MONTEREY
BIG SUR
VALLEY
SEQUOIA N.P.
PACIFIC
OCEAN
SAN SIMEON
CENTRAL
SAN LUIS OBISPO
BAKERSFIELD
COAST
SOUTHERN CALIFORNIA
SANTA BARBARA

MOON

0   50 mi
0   50 km

© MOON PUBLICATIONS, INC.

grasped by the five senses. People come here to sort it all out, to somehow grasp it, to transform themselves and the facts of their lives—by joining in the dance.

CALIFORNIA AS EUROPEAN MYTH

Native peoples had many explanations for how the land and life in California came to be, almost as many stories as there were villages. But it's a stranger-than-fiction fact that California as a concept was concocted in Europe, by a Spanish soldier turned romance writer.

The rocky-shored island paradise of California, according to the 1510 fictional *Las Sergas de Esplandian* by Garci Ordonez de Montalvo, overflowed with gold, gems, and pearls, was inhabited by griffins and other wild beasts, was "peopled by black women, with no men among them, for they lived in the fashion of Amazons" under the great Queen Calafia's rule. With such fantastic images seared into the European imagination, it's no wonder that Cortes and his crew attached the name California to their later territorial claims from Baja California north to Alaska.

While California is still a destination of the imagination and a rich land indeed, its true wealth is (and always was) its breathtaking beauty, its cultural creativity, and its democratic dreams.

THE MYTH OF NORTHERN AND SOUTHERN CALIFORNIA

The primary political fact of life here is that California is one state. Technically indisputable, this fact is nonetheless widely disputed. Californians themselves generally view the state as two distinct entities: Northern California, centered in sophisticated San Francisco, and the continuous sprawl of Southern California south of the Tehachapi Mountains, its freeways spreading out from its Los Angeles heart like the spokes of a bent and broken wheel.

Northern California's mythic soul is represented by nature in all its contradictions—the rugged outdoors and the rugged individualist struggling for survival, the simple beauty of humanity in nature as well as more complicated relationships that result from humanity's attempts

to change and control nature's inherent wildness. The collective and personal histories of Northern California suggest secessionism, rebellion, and the high-technology innovations largely responsible for today's global culture. Northern California is also about human awareness in nature, and a modern consciousness seemingly sprung fully formed from nature worship: holistic health and get-in-touch-with-yourself psychological trends; mandatory physical fitness, as if to be ready at a moment's notice to embark upon ever more challenging outdoor adventures; natural foods and a regionally focused appreciation of fresh produce and fine wines. Life in Northern California is defined by outdoor-oriented, socially responsible narcissism—and symbolized by an upwardly mobile young professional couple nudging their new, energy-efficient four-wheel drive onto well-engineered highways leading out of the city and into the wilderness.

According to the Southern California myth, style is more important than substance. This is the land of the American dream made manifest, where the sun always shines—on the degenerate and deserving alike, the ultimate in California-style social democracy—and where even the desert itself is no limitation since, thanks to the wonders of modern engineering, water can be imported from elsewhere. In Southern California, image is everything. Life itself is defined by humanity—by an artificial environment of pavement and plastic manufactured by human need and vanity, by the worship of physical beauty in human form, and by the relentless search for the ultimate in hedonistic diversion and novelty. An engineered Eden ruled by Midwestern social and political mores, Southern California worships everything new—from new beliefs and ideas and commercially viable images transmitted via its own film and media industries to art and innovation for their own sakes—and rarely questions the intrinsic value of cosmetic change. The main moral question in the southstate is not "Is it important?" or "Is it right?" but: "Is it new?"

Even if freeway graffiti in Northern California says U.S. Out of Central America and, in Southern California, No Fat Chicks, Surf Nazis Only, and The Past Ends Here, in other ways the two ends of the state are becoming one. Despite regional chauvinism, southstate-style growth, with all its attendant problems, is fast becoming a fact of life in the north; within several decades, almost as many people will live in Northern California as in the south. In all parts of the state, growth is away from major cities and into the suburbs—a fact that is influencing political trends as well. Northern California, traditionally more liberal than Southern California, is becoming more Republican, while the southstate's increasing concerns over health and environmental issues are liberalizing urban political trends. Though Northern California politicians tend to openly oppose any increased water shipments to Southern California, most are much quieter about supporting water engineering feats designed to meet the needs of the northstate's own suburban growth.

Californians themselves still see most statewide social, political, and "style" differences in terms of north versus south regionalism. The time-honored historical idea of politically splitting California into two separate states (an idea quite popular in the north) still comes up regularly. But the actual facts about modern-day California suggest a different reality—that life here is (and will be continue to be) defined by the conflicting cultures of minority-dominated urban areas, more conservative Sun Belt suburbs created by "white flight," and declining, truly rural resource-based communities.

CALIFORNIA AS "FIRST IN THE NATION"

California's most obvious "first" is its population. Number one in the nation now—with more than 30 million people—at current growth rates, by the year 2005 California's population will be nearly 40 million, and by 2030, almost 50 million. (Or more. The state has been growing so rapidly during the past decade, largely due to legal and illegal immigration, that deomographers can't keep up.) California is also number one in construction-related business contracts and leads the nation in number of millionaires. But despite the crush of its urban population, California usually makes more money in agriculture than any other state, and produces (and consumes) most of the country's wine. The land has its own firsts-and-bests, since California boasts the highest point in the contiguous U.S. (Mt. Whitney) and the lowest (Death Valley). California is also home to

the world's largest living thing, the Sequoia big tree, the world's tallest, the coast redwood, and the world's oldest, the bristlecone pine.

Common wisdom in the U.S. holds that "as California goes, so goes the nation." As with most California legends, there is at least some truth to this. California is quite often the national trendsetter, from fads and fashions in political or social beliefs to styles in cars and clothes. In its endless pursuit of style, California searches for its identity, for some explanation of itself. California is constantly inventing and reinventing its own mythology.

The Free Speech Movement, the philosophical foundation supporting both civil rights and anti-Vietnam War activism, took root in California. But so did the New Republicanism (best represented by Richard Nixon, Ed Meese, and Ronald Reagan), a reactionary trend toward social control which arose at least as an indirect result. California is usually first in the nation for new religious and spiritual trends, too, from New Age consciousness to televangelism.

California is the birthplace of the motel, the climate-controlled shopping mall, suburban sprawl, and a lifestyle almost entirely dependent upon cars and elaborately engineered highway and freeway systems. But California is also first in the nation in car thefts and in marijuana cultivation. It's home to the back-to-the-land culture and spawning ground for the philosophy of bioregionalism, too, decrying all things homogenized, unnatural, unnecessarily imported, and plastic. For every action in California, there is also a reaction.

CONTEMPORARY CALIFORNIA FACTS AND FANCY

Among common misconceptions about the state is the one the rest of the world tenaciously clings to—that everyone in California is laid-back, liberal, blond, rich, and well-educated.

California As Laid-back

California may be casual, but it's not exactly relaxed. Despite the precedents set by native peoples and early Californios (those of Spanish descent born in the pre-American period), most of the state's modern residents are hardly content to live in leisure. In their frantic rush to accumulate, to stay in style, to just keep up with the state's sophisticated survival code and incredible rate of change, Californians tend to be tense and harried. And now that Californians have remembered—and reminded the rest of the world—that rest and relaxation are necessary for a well-rounded life, people here pursue recreation with as much vengeance as any other goal. Just sitting around doing nothing isn't against the law in California, but it's definitely déclassé.

California As Liberal

If people in California aren't particularly laid-back, they aren't particularly liberal either. After all, California created both Richard Nixon and Ronald Reagan. Though Democratic legislators predominate in California's Senate and Assembly, even in the state's representation in the U.S. House of Representatives, at last report the state still has a Republican governor (and has supported Republicans in that office since the departure of "Governor Moonbeam," Jerry Brown). Yet in 1992, California was first in the nation to elect two women—both Democrats, Barbara Boxer and Diane Feinstein—to fill both of its U.S. Senate seats, outdoing all other states, cities, and municipalities in paying homage to "the year of the woman." And California overwhelmingly supported Governor Bill Clinton, a Democrat, in the 1992 presidential election.

Occasional flamboyant public figures and long-standing double-edged jokes about the land of "fruits and nuts" aside, predicting the direction in which political winds will blow here is difficult. Until recently, pollsters detected a steady trend toward increasing identification with the Republican party among the state's voting-age population. Generally speaking, the political labels of Democrat and Republican mean little in California. People here tend to vote on the basis of enlightened economic interest, personal values, and "political personality."

But if the New Republicanism is quite comfortable in California, so is the orthodoxy of no orthodoxy. Traditional values, political and social, are discarded as easily as last year's fashions. (Californians don't oppose tradition so much as they simply can't find the time for it.) The state's legendary liberalness is based on the fact that, like social voyeurs, Californians tolerate—some would say encourage—strangeness in others. Rooted in the state's rough-and-tumble gold

Despite cultural myths to the contrary, not everyone in California is blond, tan, and living at the beach.

rush history, this attitude is almost mandatory today, considering California's phenomenal cultural and ethnic diversity.

California As Blond

Despite the barrage of media and movie images suggesting that all Californians are blond and tan and live at the beach, not much could be further from the truth. Though Caucasians or "Anglos" predominate, ethnically, California's population has represented almost every spot on the globe since the days of the gold rush. Blacks, Asians, and those of Hispanic descent predominate among the state's diverse minority population—and by the turn of the century, according to demographic projections, California's collective "minority" populations will become the majority. (This has already occured in school classrooms.)

By the year 2000, California's Asian population (now representing almost 10% of the total) will grow by more than one million, its Hispanic population (now approximately 26%) by almost three million. Blacks in California will remain at a fairly stable population level, demographers project, about seven percent of the population, as will Native Americans at around one percent.

But no matter what color they started out as, people in Paradise are getting a bit gray: by the beginning of the next century, retirees will be California's fastest-growing age group. The Golden State's stereotypical golden glow of youth is definitely on the wane.

California As Rich

Though California is the richest state in the union, with a bustling economy of nation-state status and an average per-capita personal income of $18,753, the gap between the very rich and the very poor is staggering—and shocking to first-time visitors in major urban areas, since the despair of homelessness and poverty is very visible on city streets.

Recent interpretations of U.S. census data suggest that California is becoming two states— or at least two states of mind. One California is educated, satisfied, and safe. The other is young, uneducated, immigrant (many do not speak English), restless, and impoverished. The ranks of the upper-income professional class (household income $50,000 or above) increased almost 10% between 1980 and 1990, to 33%—a phenomenon partly attributed to greater numbers of working women. (It's also striking to note that 18% of all U.S. households with an annual income of $150,000 or more are in California.) During that same decade, the state's middle-income households shrank from 35% to 33%, and the number of low-income households also declined, from 41% to 34%. But the numbers of the actual poor increased, from 11.4% to 12.5%.

Contradicting the Skid Row-alcoholic image of street life, almost one-third of the homeless in California are under age 18. But almost more disturbing is California's unseen poverty. Not counting those who are turned away because there isn't enough to go around, over two million people—almost one in every 10 Californians— regularly require food from public and private charitable organizations just to survive; on any given day in the Golden State, a half-million people stand in line to get a free meal at a soup kitchen or commodity pantry. Minors, again, are California's largest class of hungry people. Current statistics suggest that one in every four children in the Golden State lives in poverty.

California As Well-educated

California has long been committed to providing educational opportunity to all citizens—a commitment expressed in public financing for the nine (soon to be 12) campuses of the prestigious University of California, the 19 California State University campuses, and the 106 independent California community colleges. But due to the obvious educational impacts of increased minority immigration—80 separate languages are spoken at Los Angeles schools, 40 at Hollywood High alone —and the unofficial reality of socially segregated schools, uneven early educational opportunities are a fact of life even in well-intentioned California. And the situation is worsening, since California now spends annually $900 less per public school student than the national average.

These facts, coupled with increasingly stringent entrance requirements at both University of California and California State University campuses, have led critics such as former Assemblymember (now Senator) Tom Hayden of Santa Monica to suggest that California's current public education policies are creating a "de facto educational apartheid." Though California's two-year community colleges are providing more four-year college preparation courses and are increasingly encouraging students to transfer to state universities, most minority groups in California are vastly underrepresented even in public universities.

The state's current budget crisis has meant significant cuts in public financial support for education. Fees for public universities are increasing rapidly (by 40% for the University of California in 1992 alone). Just to keep pace with current and anticipated demand, the University of California needs three new campuses, the California State University system needs five, and the California Community Colleges need 28.

Overall trends in education, economics, and employment patterns suggest that California is evolving into a two-tiered society dominated by an affluent and well-educated Anglo-Asian "overclass." Those who make up the underclass and who compete for relatively low-paying service jobs will increasingly be immigrants or the functionally illiterate. According to Bill Honig, former state superintendent of public instruction, about 60% of California's public school students leave school without being able to read well enough to compete in California's increasingly complex, technology oriented job market.

THE LAND: AN ISLAND IN SPACE AND TIME

California's isolated, sometimes isolationist human history has been shaped more by the land itself than by any other fact. That even early European explorers conceived of the territory as an island is a fitting irony, since in many ways—particularly geographically, but also in the evolutionary development of plant and animal life—California was, and still is, an island in both space and time.

The third-largest state in the nation, California spans 10 degrees of latitude. With a meandering 1,264-mile-long coastline, the state's western boundary is formed by the Pacific Ocean. Along most of California's great length, just landward from the sea, are the rumpled and eroded mountains known collectively as the Coast Ranges.

But even more impressive in California's 158,693-square-mile territory is the Sierra Nevada range, which curves like a 500-mile-long spine along the state's central-eastern edge. Inland from the Coast Ranges and to the north of California's great central valley are the state's northernmost mountains, including the many distinct, wayward ranges of the Klamaths—mountains many geologists believe were originally a northwesterly extension of the Sierra Nevada. Just east of the Klamath Mountains is the southern extension of the volcanic Cascade Range, which includes Mount Shasta and Lassen Peak.

This great partial ring of mountains around California's heartland (with ragged eastern peaks reaching elevations of 14,000 feet and higher) as well as the vast primeval forests that once almost suffocated lower slopes, have always influenced the state's major weather patterns—and have also created a nearly impenetrable natural barrier for otherwise freely migrating plant and animal species, including human beings.

But if sky-high rugged rocks, thickets of forest, and rain-swollen rushing rivers blocked migration to the north and east, physical barriers of a more barren nature have also slowed movement into California. To the south, the dry chaparral of the east-west Transverse Ranges and the northwest-southeast trending Peninsular Ranges impeded northern and inland movement for most life forms. The most enduring impediment, however, is California's great southeastern expanse of desert—including both the Mojave and Colorado deserts—and the associated desert mountains and high-desert plateaus. Here, only the strong and well-adapted survive.

EARTHQUAKES, VOLCANOES, AND PLATE TECTONICS

Perched along the Pacific Ring of Fire, California is known for its violent volcanic nature and for its earthquakes. Native peoples have always explained the fiery, earth-shaking temperament of the land quite clearly, in a variety of myths and legends, but the theory of plate tectonics is now the most widely accepted scientific creation story. According to this theory, the earth's crust is divided into 20 or so major solid rock (or lithospheric) "plates" upon which both land and sea ride. The interactions of these plates are ultimately responsible for all earth movement, from continental drift and landform creation to volcanic explosions and earthquakes.

Most of California teeters on the western edge of the vast North American Plate. The adjacent Pacific Plate, which first collided with what is now California some 250 million years ago, grinds slowly but steadily northward along a line more or less defined by the famous San Andreas Fault (responsible for the massive 1906 San Francisco earthquake and fire as well as the more recent shake-up in 1989). Plate movement itself is usually imperceptible: at the rate things are going, within 10 million years Los Angeles will slide north to become San Francisco's next-door neighbor. But the steady friction and tension generated between the two plates sometimes creates special events. Every so often sudden, jolting slippage occurs between the North American and Pacific plates in California—either along the San Andreas or some other fault line near the plate border—and one of the state's famous earthquakes occurs. Though most don't amount to much, an average of 15,000 earthquakes occur in California every year.

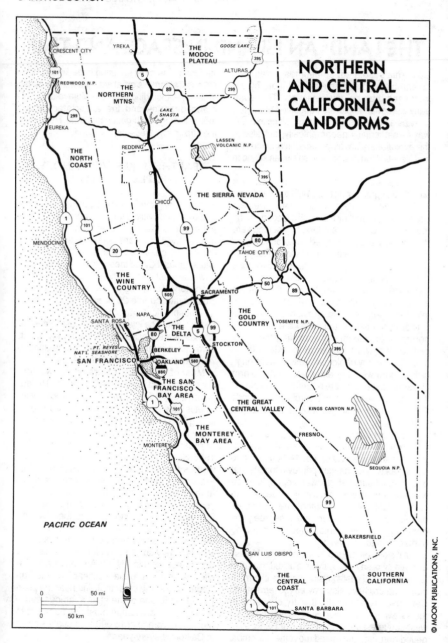

NORTHERN AND CENTRAL CALIFORNIA'S LANDFORMS

THE MODOC PLATEAU

THE NORTHERN MTNS.

REDWOOD N.P.

THE NORTH COAST

LASSEN VOLCANIC N.P.

THE SIERRA NEVADA

THE WINE COUNTRY

THE GOLD COUNTRY

YOSEMITE N.P.

PT. REYES NAT'L SEASHORE

THE DELTA

THE SAN FRANCISCO BAY AREA

THE GREAT CENTRAL VALLEY

KINGS CANYON N.P.

THE MONTEREY BAY AREA

SEQUOIA N.P.

PACIFIC OCEAN

THE CENTRAL COAST

SOUTHERN CALIFORNIA

CRESCENT CITY, YREKA, GOOSE LAKE, ALTURAS, EUREKA, LAKE SHASTA, REDDING, CHICO, MENDOCINO, TAHOE CITY, SACRAMENTO, NAPA, SANTA ROSA, BERKELEY, STOCKTON, SAN FRANCISCO, OAKLAND, MONTEREY, FRESNO, SAN LUIS OBISPO, BAKERSFIELD, SANTA BARBARA

0   50 mi
0   50 km

© MOON PUBLICATIONS, INC.

CALIFORNIA CREATION:
WHEN WORLDS COLLIDE

California as land was created by the direct collision, starting some 250 million years ago, of the eastward-moving Pacific Plate and the underwater western edge of the North American Plate—like all continents, something like a floating raft of lighter rocks (primarily granite) attached to the heavier, black basalt of the earth's mantle. At first impact, pressure between the two plates scraped up then buckled offshore oceanic sediments into undulating ridges of rock, and an eventual California shoreline began to build.

But the Pacific Plate, unable to follow its previous forward path against such North American resistance, continued on its way by first plunging downward, creating a trough that soon began filling with oceanic basalts, mud, and eroded sediments from what is now Nevada. Sinking (or subducting) still further beneath the North American Plate, some of these trench sediments slipped into the hot core (or athenosphere) beneath the earth's lithosphere and melted—transformed by heat into the embryonic granitic backbone of the Sierra Nevada and other metamorphic mountains that slowly intruded upward from the inner earth.

Approximately 140 million years ago, the northern section of what would later be the Sierra Nevada started to shift westward along the east-west tectonic fault line known as the Mendocino Fracture, the genesis of the Klamath Mountains. The Pacific Ocean, sloshing into the area just north of the infantile Sierra Nevada, brought with it the sediments which would create California's northeastern Modoc Plateau—a high-plains landscape later transformed by volcanic basalt flows and "floods."

Some 60 million years ago, California's modern-day Sierra Nevada was a misshapen series of eroded ridges and troughs sitting on the newly risen edge of the continent. The violent forces generated by continuing plate confrontation, including sporadic volcanism and large-scale faulting, pushed the state's mountains slowly higher. Remaining ocean sediments later rose to create first the Coast Ranges, as offshore islands some 25 to 30 million years ago, then eventually an impressive, 450-mile-long inland sea which, once filled with sediment,

gradually evolved into the marshy tule wetlands recognizable today as California's fertile central valley.

Though California's creation has never ceased—with the land transformed even today by volcanic activity, earthquake shifts, and erosion—the landscape as we know it came fairly recently. Approximately 16 million years ago, the Sierra Nevada stood tall enough (approximately 2,000 feet above sea level) to start changing the continent's weather patterns: blocking the moisture-laden winds that had previously swept inland, desiccating the once-lush Great Basin. Then, one million years ago, the Sierra Nevada and other fault-block ranges "suddenly" rose to near their current height. By 800,000 years ago, the mountains had taken on their general modern shape—but fire was giving way to ice. During the million-year glaciation period, particularly the last stage from 100,000 to 30,000 years ago, these and other California landforms were subsequently carved and polished smooth by slow-moving sheets of ice. Vestigial glaciers still remain in some areas of the Sierra Nevada and elsewhere.

Though vegetation typical of the late ice age has largely vanished and mastodons, saber-toothed cats, and other exotic animals no longer stalk the land, the face of the California landscape since those bygone days has been transformed most radically by the impact of humanity—primarily in the past century and a half. Building dams and "channeling" wild rivers to exploit water, the state's most essential natural resource; harvesting state-sized forests of old-growth trees; hunting animals, to the edge of extinction and beyond, for fur and pelts; digging for, and stripping the land of, gold and other mineral wealth; clearing the land for crops and houses and industrial parks: all this has changed California forever.

FROM FIRE TO ICE:
THE CALIFORNIA CLIMATE

California's much-ballyhooed "Mediterranean" climate is at least partially a myth. Because of extremes in landforms, in addition to various microclimatic effects, there are radical climatic differences within the state—sometimes even within a limited geographic area. But California

Some 60 million years ago, today's dramatically rugged Sierra Nevada was little more than a misshapen series of eroded ridges and troughs.

WES DEMPSEY

as a whole does share most of the classic characteristics of Mediterranean climates: abundant sunny days year-round, a cool-weather coast, dry summers and rainy winters. California, in fact, is the only region in North America where summer drought and rainy winters are typical.

Between the coast and the mountains immediately inland, where most of the state's people live, temperatures—though cooler in the north and warmer to the south—are fairly mild and uniform year-round. Due to the state's latitudinal gradation, rain also falls in accordance with this north-south shift: an average of 74 inches falls annually in Crescent City, 19-22 inches in San Francisco, and less than 10 inches in San Diego. When warm, moist ocean air blows inland over the cool California Current circulating clockwise above the Equator, seasonal fog is typical along the California coast. Summer, in other words, is often cooler along the coast than autumn. (Just ask those shivering tourists who arrive in San Francisco every June wearing Bermuda shorts and sandals.)

Inland, where the marine air influence often literally evaporates, temperature extremes are typical. The clear, dry days of summer are often hot, particularly in the central valley and the deserts. (With occasional freak temperatures above 130° Fahrenheit, Death Valley is aptly named.) In winter, substantial precipitation arrives in Northern California—especially in the northwest "rain belt" and in the northern Sierra Nevada—with major storms expected from October to May. In the High Sierra, the average winter snowpack is between 300 and 400 inches; California's northern mountains "collect" most Pacific Ocean moisture as rain. Wrung out like sponges by the time they pass over the Sierra Nevada and other inland mountains, clouds have little rain or snow for the eastern-slope rainshadow.

CALIFORNIA FLORA: BLOOMING AT THE BRINK

"In California," observed writer Joaquin Miller, "things name themselves, or rather Nature names them, and that name is visibly written on the face of things and every man may understand who can read." When explorers and settlers first stumbled upon California's living natural wonders, they didn't "read" landforms or indigenous plants and animals in the same way native peoples did, but they were quite busy nonetheless attaching new names (and eventually Latin terminology) to everything in sight. From the most delicate ephemeral wildflowers to California's two types of towering redwoods, from butterflies and birds to pronghorn, bighorn sheep, and the various subspecies of grizzly bear, the unusual and unique nature of most of the territory's life-forms was astonishing. California's geographical isolation—as well as its dramatic extremes in landforms and localized climates—was (and still is) largely responsible for the phenomenal natural divergence and diversity originally found here.

THE CALIFORNIA DROUGHT: WATER, WATER ANYWHERE?

At one time, California was a wet land indeed. Scientists studying ancient sediments underlying San Francisco Bay—shell and soil deposits dating back some 4,500 years—have discovered that as recently as 200 years ago twice as much fresh water flowed down the state's major rivers. To arrive at this conclusion, researchers compared past sediment salinity levels to present (non-drought) levels after adjusting for the impact of modern water diversions.

But California, historically and prehistorically, has also been quite dry. The state's recent water crisis, a devastating six-year drought, has been accompanied by great ecological stress in natural areas, and by mandatory water rationing almost everywhere. (Some of California's most expensive residential communities, including towns in Marin County and the central coast near Santa Barbara, have become known as places where the affluent live but can't flush their effluent.) The drought may—and may not—have ended with 1992-93's twice-normal precipitation. If California's most recent drought is actually over, this climatic phenomenon has tied this century's drought longevity record, set between 1929 and 1935 during the Great Depression.

To some extent, dry years are natural in California. Depending on who you talk to, drought occurs within various cyclical patterns: multiyear droughts are almost predictable every 200 years, every 50 years, and some say every 25-30 years, with shorter dry-year cycles in between.

And the drought pattern's larger cycles may be unbelievably long. Paleontologists from Reno's Desert Research Institute reported in 1992 that preliminary tree-ring evidence at Lake Tahoe suggests a drought some 5,000 or 6,000 years ago that lasted at least 300 years, perhaps as long as 1,000 years. Other work indicates that, as recently as the 1400s or 1500s, 30- to 40-year droughts were not uncommon.

Former President Ronald Reagan, while still governor of California and embroiled in a battle over expanding redwood parks, unwittingly expressed the old-and-in-the-way attitude about the state's resources with his now-famous gaffe, widely quoted as: "If you've seen one redwood, you've seen 'em all." (What Reagan actually said was: "A tree is a tree—how many more do you need to look at?") But his philosophy, however expressed, is the key to understanding what has happened to California's trees, other native flora, and animal species.

Even today, the variation in California's native plant life is amazing. Nearly 5,200 species of plants are at home in the Golden State—symbolized by the orange glow of the California poppy—and over 30% of these trees, shrubs, wildflowers, and grasses are endemic. (By comparison, only 13% of plant life in the northeastern U.S., and one percent of flora in the British Isles, are endemic species.) In fact, California has greater species diversity than the combined totals of the central and northeastern U.S. and adjacent Canada—an area almost 10 times greater in size.

But to state that so many plant species survive in California is not to say they thrive. The economic and physical impacts of settlement have greatly stressed the state's vegetative wealth since the days of the gold rush, when the first full-scale assaults on California forests, wetlands, grasslands, and riparian and oak woodlands were launched. The rate of exploitation of the state's 380 distinct natural communities has been relentless ever since. Half of the state's natural terrestrial environments and 40% of its aquatic communities are endangered, rare, or threatened.

Some of the state's most notable natural attractions are its unique trees—entire forests nearly toppled at the edge of extinction. California's *Sequoiadendron giganteum,* or giant sequoia, grows only in limited surviving stands in the Sierra Nevada—saved as much by the brittleness of its wood as by the public outcry of John Muir and other enlightened 19th-century voices. But the state's remaining virgin forests of *Sequoia sempervirens,* the "ever-living" coast redwoods, are still threatened by clearcutting, a practice which also eliminates the habitat of other species. The same conservation-versus-economic expediency argument also rages over the fate of the few remaining old-growth outposts of other popular timber trees. Even trees without notable economic value are threatened by compromises imposed by civilization. Among these are the ancient bristlecone pines near the California-Nevada border—the oldest living things on earth, now threatened by Los Angeles smog—and the gnarled yet graceful valley oak. An "indicator plant" for the state's most fertile loamy soils, even the grizzled remaining veterans not plowed under by agriculture or subdivision development are now failing to reproduce successfully.

And while the disappearance of trees is easily observed even by human eyes, other rare and unusual plants found only in California disappear, or bloom at the brink of eternity, with little apparent public concern. A subtle but perfectly adapted native perennial grass, for example, or an ephemeral herb with a spring blossom so tiny most people don't even notice it, are equally endangered by humankind's longstanding laissez-faire attitude toward the world we share with all life.

Only fairly recently, with so much of natural California already gone for good, have public attitudes begun to change. No matter what Ronald Reagan says, and despite the very real economic tradeoffs sometimes involved, most Californians—and usually the state's voters—strongly support conservation, preservation, and park expansion proposals whenever these issues arise—this despite the fact that budget cutbacks threaten to close or curtail sevices at some state parks.

CALIFORNIA FAUNA: A LONELY HOWL IN THE WILDERNESS

The Golden State's native wildlife is also quite diverse and unique. Of the 748 known species of vertebrate animals in California, 38% of freshwater fish, 29% of amphibians, and nine percent of mammals are endemic species; invertebrate variation is equally impressive. But with the disappearance of quite specific natural habitats, many of these animals are also endangered or threatened.

One notable exception is the intelligent and endlessly adaptable coyote, which—rather than be shoved out of its traditional territory even by suburban housing subdivisions—seems quite willing to put up with human incursions, so long as there are garbage cans to forage in, swimming pools to drink from, and adequate alleys of escape. Yet even the coyote's lonely late-night howl is like a cry for help in an unfriendly wilderness.

OVER CALIFORNIA

Audubon would die
or kill every bird he ever saw
to be up here, goose-eyed,
looking down over California.

We're following the flyway
south, out of season, battling
head winds, angling cross-valley
and bayward, to root

(not nest) at the home-opener.
If this were an Audubon spring
we'd have crashed long ago,
sent back to earth by flocks

of northbound waterfowl
blackening the sky, fouling the prop.
But in our age, only a few
late skeins stitch the air going home.

After years of drought, water's
what we notice of earth:
the smooth–flowing leveed Sacramento
we follow, man–made ponds
near mansion ranch homes. A refuge
at Colusa and Graylodge, but few
other wetlands or marshes
to beckon flocks down from long flights.

The plane yaws west at the Buttes
as if guided by natural law,
still on course and on time
for the bay and the ballgame—

baseball, Audubon
just missed out on, though we guess
he would've cheered a few teams:
Cardinals, Blue Jays, Baltimore Orioles.

—Gary Thompson
(for Richard Collins)

WES DEMPSEY

Not yet endangered in the Golden State is the state flower, the California poppy

The rapid slide toward extinction among California's wild things is perhaps best symbolized by the grizzly bear, which once roamed from the mountains to the sea, though the wolf, too, has long since vanished from the landscape. The San Joaquin kit fox, the desert tortoise, and the California condor—most surviving birds maintained now as part of a zoo-based captive breeding program—are among many species now endangered. Upward of 550 bird species have been recorded in California, and over half of these breed here. But the vast flocks of migratory birds (so abundant they once darkened the midday sky) have been thinned out considerably, here and elsewhere, by the demise of native wetlands and by toxins.

The fate of the state's once-fabled fisheries is equally instructive. With 90% of salmon spawning grounds now gone due to the damming of rivers and streams, California's commitment to compensatory measures—fish hatcheries and ladders, for example—somehow misses the point. Now that humans are in charge of natural selection, the fish themselves are no longer wild, no longer stream-smart; many can't even find their way back to the fisheries where they hatched out (in sterile stainless steel trays).

However, some California animals almost wiped out by hunters as well as habitat elimination and contamination are now starting out on the comeback trail. Included among these are native elk and the antelope-like pronghorn populations, each numbering near 500,000 before European and American settlement. Also recovering in California is the native population of bighorn sheep—probably never numbering more than 10,000—that now clambers over craggy high peaks in small groups collectively totaling about 5,000. Among marine mammals almost hunted into oblivion but now thriving in California's offshore ocean environments are the northern elephant seal and the sea otter.

Until recently, California's predators—always relatively fewer in number, pouncing from the top of the food chain—fared almost as poorly as their prey, preyed upon themselves by farmers, ranchers, loggers, and hunters. Though the grand grizzly hasn't been seen in California for more than a century, California's black bear is still around—though increasingly tracked and hunted by timber interests (for the damage the bears inflict on seedling trees) and poachers out to make a fast buck on gall bladders popular in Asian pharmacology. Of California's native wildcats, only the rare (and rarely seen) mountain lion and the spotted, smaller bobcat still survive. The last of the state's jaguars was hunted down near Palm Springs in 1860.

THE HISTORY OF THE GOLDEN DREAM

Europeans generally get credit for having "discovered" America, including the mythic land of California. But a dusty travel log tucked away in Chinese archives in Shenshi Province, discovered in the 19th century by an American missionary, suggests that the Chinese discovered California—in about 217 B.C. According to this saga, a storm-tossed Chinese ship—misdirected by its own compass, apparently rendered nonfunctional after a cockroach got wedged under the needle—sailed stubbornly for 100 days in the direction of what was supposed to be mainland China. (The navigator, Hee-li, reportedly ignored the protests of his crew, who pointed out that the sun was setting on the wrong horizon.) Stepping out into towering forests surrounding an almost endless inlet at the edge of the endless ocean, these unwitting adventurers reported meetings with red-skinned peoples—and giant red-barked trees.

Conventional continental settlement theory holds that the first true immigrants to the North American continent also came from Asia—crossing a broad plain across the Bering Strait, which existed until the end of the ice age. Archaeologists agree that the earliest Americans arrived more than 11,500 years ago, more or less in synch with geologists' belief that the Bering "bridge" disappeared some 14,000 years ago. Circumstantial support for this conclusion has also come from striking similarities—in blood type, teeth, and language—existing between early Americans and Asians, particularly the northern Chinese. But new discoveries have thrown all previous American migration theories into doubt.

In 1986, French scientists working in Brazil discovered an ancient rock shelter containing stone tools, other artifacts, and charcoal that was at first carbon-dated at approximately 32,000 years old. (A subsequent announcement, that the discovery was actually more than 45,000 years old, shocked archaeologists.) Wall paintings suggest that cave art developed in the Americas at about the same time it did in Europe, Asia, and Africa. Preliminary evidence of very early human habitation (possibly as long ago as 33,000 years) has also been found in Chile.

So the question is: if migration to the Americas was via the Bering Strait, and so long ago, why hasn't any similar evidence been discovered in North America? Some suggest that signs of human habitation farther north have been erased by glaciation. But no one really knows. One thing is certain: most archaeologists would rather be buried alive in a dig than be forced to dust off and reexamine the previously discredited "Thor Heyerdahl theory" of American settlement: that the first immigrants sailed across the Pacific, landed in South America, then migrated northward.

CALIFORNIA'S FIRST PEOPLE

However and whenever they first arrived in California, the territory's first immigrants gradually created civilizations quite appropriate to the land they had landed in. "Tribes" like those typical elsewhere in North America did not exist in California, primarily because the political unity necessary for survival elsewhere was largely irrelevant here. Populations of California native peoples are better understood as ethnic or kinship or community groups united by common experience and shared territory.

Though no census takers were abroad in the land at the time, the presettlement population (some 500 groups speaking 130 dialects) of what is now California is estimated at about 250,000—a density four to eight times greater than early people living anywhere else in the United States. Before their almost overnight decimation—due to settlement, and attendant disease, cultural disintegration, and violence—California's native peoples found the living fairly easy. The cornucopia of fish, birds, and game, in addition to almost endlessly edible plant life, meant that hunting and gathering was not the strict struggle for survival it was elsewhere on the continent. Since abundance in all things was the rule, at least in non-desert areas, trade between tribal groups (for nonlocal favorite foods such as acorns, pine nuts, or seafood and for nonlocal woods or other prized items) was not uncommon. Plants and animals of the natural

Ishi walked out of the Stone Age and into the Industrial Age with dignity and without fear.

world were respected by native peoples as kindred spirits, and a deep natural mysticism was the underlying philosophy of most religious traditions and associated myths and legends.

Most California peoples were essentially nonviolent, engaging in war or armed conflict only for revenge; bows and arrows, spears, and harpoons were used in hunting. The development of basketry, in general the highest art of native populations, was also quite pragmatic; baskets of specific shapes and sizes were used to gather and to store foods and for cooking in. Homes, boats, and clothing were made of the most appropriate local materials, from slabs of redwood bark and animal hides to tule reeds.

Time was not particularly important to California's first immigrants. No one kept track of passing years, and most groups didn't even have a word for "year." Attention was paid, however, to the passage of the moons and seasons—the natural rhythm of life. Many native peoples were seminomadic, moving into cooler mountain regions in summer where game, roots, and berries were most abundant, then meandering down into the foothills and valleys in autumn to collect acorns, the staff of life for most

tribes, and to take shelter from winter storms.

But there was nowhere to hide from the whirling clouds of change that started sweeping into California with the arrival of early explorers and missionaries, or from the foreign flood that came when the myth of California gold became a reality. Some native peoples went out fighting: the 19th-century Modoc War was one of the last major Indian wars in the United States. And others just waited until the end of their world arrived. Most famous in this category was Ishi, the "last wild man in America" and the last of his Yahi people, captured in an Oroville slaughterhouse corral in 1911. Working as a janitor as a ward of the University of California until his death five years later from tuberculosis, Ishi walked from the Stone Age into the industrial age with dignity and without fear.

FOREIGNERS PLANT THEIR FLAGS

The first of California's official explorers were the Spanish. Though Hernando Cortés discovered a land he called California in 1535, it was Juan Rodríguez Cabrillo—actually a Portuguese, João Rodrigues Cabrilho—who first sailed the coast of Alta California ("upper," as opposed to "lower" or Baja California, now part of Mexico) and rode at anchor off its shores.

But the first European to actually set foot on California soil was the English pirate Sir Francis Drake, who in 1579 came ashore somewhere along the coast (exactly where is still disputed, though popular opinion suggests Point Reyes) and whose maps—like others of the day—reflected his belief that the territory was indeed an island. Upon returning to England, Drake's story of discovery served primarily to stimulate Spain's territorial appetites. Though Sebastián Vizcaíno entered Monterey Bay in 1602 (18 years before the Pilgrims arrived at Plymouth), it wasn't until 1746 that even the Spanish realized California wasn't an island. It wasn't until 1769 and 1770 that San Francisco Bay was discovered by Gaspar de Portola and the settlements of San Diego and Monterey were founded.

Though the Spanish failed to find California's mythical gold, between 1769 and 1823 they did manage to establish 21 missions (sometimes with associated presidios) along the Camino Real or "Royal Road" from San Diego to Sonoma.

And from these busy mission ranch outposts, maintained by the free labor of "heathen" natives, Spain grew and manufactured great wealth.

But even at its zenith, Spain's supremacy in California was tenuous. The territory was vast and relatively unpopulated. Even massive land grants—a practice continued under later Mexican rule—did little to allay colonial fears of successful outside incursions. Russian imperialism, spreading east into Siberia and Central Asia, then on to Alaska and an 1812 outpost at Fort Ross on the north coast, seemed a clear and present danger—and perhaps actually would have been, if the Russians' agricultural and other enterprises hadn't ultimately failed. And enterprising Americans, at first just a few fur trappers and traders, were soon in the neighborhood.

As things happened, the challenge to Spain's authority came from its own transplanted population. Inspired by the news in 1822 that an independent government had been formed in Baja California's Mexico City, young California-born Spanish ("Californios") and independence-seeking resident Spaniards declared Alta California part of the new Mexican empire. By March of 1825, when California proper officially became a territory of the Republic of Mexico, the new leadership had already achieved several goals, including secularizing the missions and "freeing" the associated native neophytes (not officially achieved until 1833), which in practice meant that most became servants elsewhere. The Californios also established an independent military and judiciary, opened the territory's ports to trade, and levied taxes.

During the short period of Mexican rule, the American presence was already prominent. Since even Spain regularly failed to send supply ships, Yankee traders were always welcome in California. In no time at all, Americans had organized and dominated the territory's business sector, established successful ranches and farms, married into local families, and become prominent citizens. California, as a possible political conquest, was becoming increasingly attractive to the United States.

General John C. Frémont, officially on a scientific expedition but perhaps acting under secret orders from Washington (Frémont would never say), had been stirring things up in California since 1844—engaging in a few skirmishes with the locals or provoking conflicts between Californios and American citizens in California. Though the U.S. declared war on Mexico on May 13, 1846, Frémont and his men apparently were unaware of that turn of events and took over the town of Sonoma for a short time in mid-June, raising the secessionist flag of the independent—but very short-lived—Bear Flag Republic.

With Californios never mustering much resistance to the American warriors, Commodore John C. Sloat sailed unchallenged into Monterey Bay on July 7, 1848, raised the Stars and Stripes above the Custom House in town, and claimed California for the United States. Within two days, the flag flew in both San Francisco and Sonoma, but it took some time to end the statewide skirmishes. It took even longer for official Americanization—and statehood—to proceed. The state constitution established, among other things, California as a "free" state (but only to prevent the unfair use of slave labor in the mines) This upset the balance of congressional power in the nation's anti-slavery conflict and indirectly precipitated the Civil War. Written in Monterey, the new state's constitution was adopted in October of 1849 and ratified by voters in November.

DREAMING THE NEW GOLD DREAM—THEN AND NOW

California's legendary gold was real, as it turned out. And the Americans found it—but quite by accident. The day James Marshall, who was building a lumber mill on the American River for John Sutter, discovered flecks of shiny yellow metal in the mill's tailrace seemed otherwise quite ordinary. But that day, January 24, 1848, changed everything—in California and in the world.

As fortune seekers worldwide succumbed to gold fever and swarmed into the Sierra Nevada foothills in 1849, modern-day California began creating itself. In the no-holds-barred search for personal freedom and material satisfaction (better yet, unlimited wealth), something even then recognizable as California's human character was also taking shape: the belief that anything is possible, for anyone, no matter what one's previous circumstances would suggest. Almost everyone wanted to entertain that belief. (Karl Marx was of the opinion that the California gold rush was directly responsible for delaying the Russian revolution.) New gold dreamers—all colors and creeds—came to California, by land and by sea, to take a chance on themselves and their luck. The luckiest ones, though, were the merchants and businesspeople who cashed in on California's dream by mining the miners.

Due to the discovery of gold, California skipped the economically exploitive U.S. territorial phase typical of other western states. With almost endless, indisputable capital at hand, Californians thumbed their noses at the Eastern financial establishment almost from the start: they could exploit the wealth of the far West themselves. And exploit it they did—mining not only the earth, but also the state's forests, fields, and water wealth. Wild California would never again be the same.

Almost overnight, "civilized" California became an economic sensation. The state was essentially admitted to the union on its own terms—because California was quite willing to go its own way and remain an independent entity otherwise. The city of San Francisco grew from a sleepy enclave of 500 souls to a hectic, hell-bent business and financial center of over 25,000 within two years. Other cities built on a foundation of prosperous trade included the inland supply port of Sacramento. Agriculture, at first important for feeding the state's mushrooming population of fortune hunters, soon became a de facto gold mine in its own right. Commerce expanded even more rapidly with the completion of the California-initiated transcontinental railroad and with the advent of other early communications breakthroughs like the telegraph. California's dreams of prosperity became self-fulfilling prophecies. And as California went, so went the nation.

The new land of opportunity—always a magnet for innovation, never particularly respectful of stifling and stodgy tradition—has continued to dictate terms to the rest of the country throughout its more modern history. Even with the gradual arrival of what the rest of the world could finally recognize as civilization, which included the predictable phenomenon of personal wealth translated into political power, California's commitment to prosperity and change—sometimes for its own sake—has never waned.

From the founding of the Automobile Club of Southern California in 1900 to the construction of Yosemite's Hetch Hetchy Dam (to slake San Francisco thirst) in 1923; from the establishment of the first Hollywood movie studio to the 1927 transmission, from San Francisco, of the first television picture; from the completion in 1940 of the world's first freeway to opening of Disneyland in 1955; from the 1960s Free Speech Movement, the rise of Black Power, and Cesar Chavez's United Farm Workers Union to the Beat poets, San Francisco's Summer of Love and the oozing up of New Age consciousness; from California's rise as leader in the development of nuclear weapons and defense technology to the creation of the microchip and personal computer: California history is a chronicle of incredible change, a relentless double-time march into the new.

"All that is constant about the California of my childhood," writes Sacramento native Joan Didion in an essay from *Slouching Towards Bethlehem*, "is the rate at which it disappears."

CALIFORNIA GOVERNMENT: THE BEST THAT MONEY CAN BUY

California's political structure is quite confusing, with thousands of tax-levying governmental units—including special districts, 58 county governments, and hundreds of cities both large and small—and a variety of overlapping jurisdictions. Based on the federal principle of one person, one vote and designed with separate executive, judicial, and legislative (Assembly and Senate) branches, the game of state-level California government is often quite lively, almost a high form of entertainment for those who understand the rules. The use and abuse of public resources is the ultimate goal of power-brokering in the Golden State, affecting statewide and local economies (as well as the private sector) and creating (or abandoning) commitments to social justice and various human rights issues most Californians hold dear.

The popularity of unusually affable, charismatic, and highly visible California politicians, from Ronald Reagan to Jerry Brown, would suggest that Golden State politics generally take place in the entertainment arena. Nothing could be further from the truth. Though Californians are committed to the concept of public initiatives and referenda on major issues—politicians be damned, basically—most decisions affecting life in California are made in the time-honored behind-the-scenes tradition of U.S. politics, with back-room deal-making conducted something like a poker game. In order to know the score, you have to know the players and what cards they hold.

Those in the know contend that the California Legislature, considered the best state-level legislative body in the nation as recently as 1971, has steadily been careening downhill, in terms of effectiveness and ethics, ever since—largely due to "juice," or the influence of lobbyists and special interest money. According to veteran *Sacramento Bee* political reporter and columnist Dan Walters: "Votes are bought, sold, and rented by the hour with an arrogant casualness. There are one-man, one-vote retail sales as well as wholesale transactions that party leaders negotiate for blocs of votes."

In the meantime, serious political problems either remain serious or get worse. As a result of California's most recent "tax rebellion," which resulted in the passage of Proposition 13 (the Jarvis-Gann Initiative), local property tax revenues have been restricted while the number of state-mandated programs cities and counties must offer continues to increase—a situation causing economic crisis for many rural communities. But urban areas have their problems too—increasing poverty and homelessness, for example, plus the need for major new public works projects as the state's "infrastructure" ages and starts to sag and snap. The quality of all public services has deteriorated since the 1960s, partly from the strain of an ever-increasing population with ever-increasing demands, and ever-diminishing economic and political resources. Environmental problems are also increasing.

Since the 1970s, California has slowly but surely moved from "first" to "worst" in educational quality (as measured by public investment per student and by class size) and in environmental quality (as measured by overall air pollution, the continued decline of endangered and threatened species, and loss of wetlands and old-growth forests). And health care in California is clearly in crisis, with almost 20% of the population uninsured—an increase of 50% since the 1980s.

Statewide, jails and prisons are as overcrowded as courtrooms and "repeat crime" is on the rise: a staggering 76% of convicts released from California prisons are rearrested within three years. In addition to drug-related and gang violence, even East Coast-style organized crime is increasing. And, the near-impossibility of adequately educating the state's fast-growing, multiethnic population has sent the public school system into a tailspin. Ethnic resentments are also growing elswhere: witness the recent political success of California's English-only official language initiative.

For some reason, polls indicate that Californians increasingly distrust their politicians. From his years observing the species from the 19th-century Washington, D.C., press gallery, Mark Twain offered this fitting summary, a quote from a fictitious newspaper account in his novel, *The Gilded Age:* "We are now reminded of a note we received from the notorious burglar Murphy, in which he finds fault with a statement of ours that he had served one term in the penitentiary and one in the U.S. Senate. He says, 'The latter statement is untrue and does me great injustice.'"

It came as no surprise in 1992 when California became one of the first states in the nation to pass a "term limitations" law, restricting its Assembly members to maximum six-year terms in office and limiting the terms of governor, state senators, and other constitutional officers to eight years. An all-new Legislature is expected by 1998. And the initiative, put before the voters as Proposition 140 in 1990, also cut the Legislature's operating budget by $70 million, about 38%. It has been upheld as constitutional by the the state supreme court.

THE GLITTER OF THE GOLDEN STATE ECONOMY

If the lure of gold brought pioneers to California, the rich land, resources, and the state's "anything goes" philosophy kept them here. The Golden State has essentially become a nation-state—an economic superpower, the fifth-largest (or sixth or seventh, depending on the comparison data) economy in the world. A major international player in the game of Pacific Rim commerce, California's cry is usually "free trade," in contrast to the philosophy of high-tariff trade protectionism so strong elsewhere in the United States. And with so much financial clout, California is often the tail that wags the dog of U.S. domestic and foreign economic and political policy. No one ever says it out loud, but California could easily secede from the union, only too happy to compete as an independent entity in the world market.

The economic spirit of the northstate, suggested philosopher George Santayana in a 1910 Berkeley speech, is best summed up by the immense presence of nature in Northern California—nature in tandem with engineering and technology. Now that the roughshod, rough-and-tumble days of man against nature are no longer widely condoned, Californians increasingly expect technology to respect nature's standards. In Northern California particularly, information is the cleanest industry of all. It seems no coincidence that both the microchip and the personal computer were born here.

Agriculture has long been an economic mainstay in California. ("The whole place stank of orange blossoms," observed H.L. Mencken on a Golden State visit.) Though most Southern California citrus groves have long since been paved over for parking lots and shopping malls (those disturbed by California's proclivity for bulldozing the past in the name of progress have coined a verb for it: "to californicate") agriculture in Northern California and pockets of Southern California is still going strong. Because of the large size and concentrated ownership of farm and ranch lands, helped along by public subsidies of irrigation engineering projects, agriculture in California has always been agribusiness. In its role as agricultural nation-state, California produces more food than 90% of the world's nations, an $18 billion annual business.

But California, northern and southern, is industrious in all ways. Travel and tourism is a major industry—now promoted, since California has started to lose ground in the tourist sweeps to other Western states—with annual revenues in the $28 billion range. Growth itself is a growth industry in California, with all aspects of the construction trade generating an average $30 billion in business annually. Revenues gen-

SANTA CRUZ SEASIDE COMPANY, JIM AEDER

Commercial tourism attractions and diversions, such as the historic Giant Dipper roller coaster at the Santa Cruz Beach Boardwalk, represent one facet of California's immense recreation and travel industry.

erated by California's top 100 privately held companies—including Bechtel Group, Hughes Aircraft, USA Petroleum (and other oil companies), Twentieth-Century Fox Films (and other media giants), Purex Industries, Denny's Inc., Raley's, both the AAA-affiliated Automobile Club of Southern California and the California State Automobile Association, and a long string of agricultural cooperatives as well as health- and life-insurance companies—usually exceed $70 billion annually.

A U.S. capital of finance and commerce, the state is also the world's high-technology headquarters. Helped along by state-supported University of California labs and research facilities, California has long been a leader in the aerospace and weapons development industries. Including military bases and research, testing, and surveillance sites, some 80 outposts of nuclear weaponry are—or were—based in California.

ALL THAT GLITTERS IS NOT GOLD

Like naysayers on the federal level, pundits have suggested for some time that all that glitters is not gold in California—that past decades of prosperity, and the assumption that it would last indefinitely, ignored major structural changes occuring in the state's economy and sociopolitical effectiveness. And when the Golden State's budget crisis hit in the late 1980s, as a major downturn began, it seemed clear that they were right.

By late 1991, California's economic performance had "slipped" to the national average, and both public budget woes and the prospect of looming long-term deficits led to the loss of the state's prized AAA bond rating by Standard & Poor's. By late 1992, the state's 10%-plus unemployment rate—the highest in the nation—reflected a still-declining economic picture.

Even California agriculture, the state's longtime economic mainstay, is facing increasingly hard times due to the conversion of agricultural land to urban uses, to increasing restrictions on and competition for publicly subsidized water supplies—previously all but free to farmers—and to rising public alarm over the environmental side effects of modern agricultural practices.

Other recent events—including the long-term drought, closure of 11 military bases, and the dramatic decline of defense-related industry, especially in California—have also tarnished the state's economic luster. The issue the Golden State is just beginning to come to terms with, like the rest of the nation, is the impact of "economic restructuring," or the loss of high-paying jobs in an increasingly competitive world economy.

And though California has traditionally led the U.S. out of depressions and recessions, this time it looks like it will be the other way around—with a stronger overall U.S. economy increasing the demand for California goods and services.

Other trend watchers suggest that ultimately California will diminish its economic relationships with the East Coast and other parts of the U.S., seeking still stronger ties with its Pacific Basin trading partners.

In other words, in its economic choices as in all other things, California will continue to go its own way.

THE PEOPLE

Everyone is moving to California and vicinity, it seems. According to *American Demographics,* the geographic center of the U.S. population moves 58 feet farther west and 29 feet to the south every year. (Recent bad times in California suggest that this trend may be slowing temporarily.) Nonetheless, some people consider Californians among the most obnoxious people on earth, and this is not necessarily a new phenomenon.

To some, the state is a kind of cultural purgatory, settled (in the words of Willard Huntington Wright) by "yokels from the Middle West who were nourished by rural pieties and superstitions." Others consider, and have always considered, Californians as somehow inherently unstable. "Insanity, as might be expected, is fearfully prevalent in California," Dr. Henry Gibbons stated before San Francisco's local medical society in 1857. "It grows directly out of the excited mental condition of our population, to which the common use of alcoholic drink is a powerful adjunct." The general outside observation today is that if Californians aren't talking about themselves (and about accomplishing their latest career, financial, fitness, or psychospiritual goals), they talk about California. New Englander Inez Hayes Irwin defined those afflicted with Californoia in her 1921 book *Californiacs:*

> *The Californiac is unable to talk about anything but California, except when he interrupts himself to knock every other place in the face of the earth. He looks with pity on anybody born outside of California, and he believes that no one who has ever seen California willingly lives elsewhere. He himself often lives elsewhere, but he never admits that it is from choice.*

There may be more than a shred of truth in this, even today; pollsters say one out of every four Californians would rather live elsewhere—for the most part, either in Hawaii or Oregon. But many who live and work in California are not native Californians. This is almost as true today as it ever was; fully one-third of contemporary Californians were born somewhere else. Somehow, California's amazing cultural and ethnic

CALIFORNIA'S IDENTITY CRISIS: TWO STATES? OR THREE?

California's secessionist spirit has been stirred again in recent years, with at least some parts of California demanding that the Golden State be split into two states—perhaps even three.

As shocking as the idea of redrawing the state's borders may seem, it's actually a political tradition, one proposed over 20 times since original statehood. Curious to contemplate these days, though, is the fact that disaffected, dry, and down-and-out Los Angeles first pushed the idea. Envying San Francisco's economic and political power and angry about the lack of state support for civic improvements and services, in 1851 the south proposed the creation of a new Southern California political entity, the state of Colorado.

That separatist effort was ultimately defeated by the outbreak of the Civil War, just as in this century, in the far north, the state of Jefferson was deep-sixed by the bombing of Pearl Harbor and U.S. involvement in World War II. But political traditions die hard, so Californians are at it again. The rebellion is still Jeffersonian, still rooted in the north. This time, Assemblymember Stan Statham snatched up and carried the rebel flag, with his original legislative proposal to create America's 51st state, Northern California. (Regional chauvinists subsequently suggested the name "Superior California.")

Though mainstream pundits shook their heads in tolerant disbelief, a number of counties in Central and Northern California put the issue before the voters, as an advisory measure, in June 1992. It passed in 27 out of 31 counties.

Why? The two ends of California have been feuding with each other all century, at least socially. Northern California residents tend to view Southern California as a nightmare of overcrowding and escalating crime, a collective freeway-maddened multitude only too happy to bleed the north of its water and other natural resources.

"We are deadly serious," Statham has stated. "I will predict that there will be more than one California by the year 2000. . . . It's being compared to the breakup of the Baltic states. We're trying to do something revolutionary here."

Statham has formed the Assembly Select Committee to Divide California, a group determined to draft formal split-state legislation by sometime in 1993, then put the proposition before all California voters. At last report these lawmakers were promoting a three-state division—Northern California, Central California (including San Francisco), and Southern California.

Why three states?

Regional chauvinism is more complicated than simple north-versus-south hostility, as it turns out. San Francisco would rather fall into the ocean than admit any kinship at all with Los Angeles (and vice versa), but most rural communities don't care to associate with either city.

Should California actually succeed in its current drive toward political separatism, quite distinct cultural identities will need to be formalized for both (or all) the new Californias. Even discussing that possibility has created surprising new expressions of public humor. In Northern California, suggests *Sacramento Bee* writer J.D. Lasica, Chico is clearly most suited to become state capital, with Jerry Brown as governor. Appropriate for the north state's motto: "It's *our* water, dammit!" State song? "Stuck in Lodi Again." After chowing down on traditional northstate cuisine (grilled rattlesnake with a beer chaser), for recreation natives will just go out and polish their gun racks or perhaps tend family gardens of Humboldt County loco weed (marijuana), the state flower.

Disneyland is the obvious candidate for the capital of Southern California, with Bart Simpson residing in the governor's mansion. The south's official state bird? The pink plastic flamingo. (State animal: Spuds MacKenzie.) "I think I'm gonna hurl!" is the southstate's official motto, with smog alerts the most appropriate (and patriotic) recreational pursuit.

In all seriousness, however, the political power of Southern California far outweighs the impact of even unanimous alliances forged farther north. And the southstate has no intention of releasing its claim to Northern California water supplies.

It's unlikely that much will change. California will continue to be the state in a state of perpetual identity crisis—the state that loves to hate itself.

---

diversity is the source of both its social stability and its self-renewal.

Perhaps due to misleading portrayals of California's past, in the media and the movies as well as the history books, a common misconception is that the impact and importance of California's ethnic populations is relatively recent, a post-World War II phenomenon. But many peoples and many races have made significant contributions to California culture and economic development since the days of the gold rush—and since the decimation of native populations.

Blacks and Hispanics, despite attempts (official and otherwise) to prevent them from dreaming the California dream, were among the first to arrive in the gold fields. The Chinese, who also arrived early to join the ranks of the state's most industrious citizens, were relentlessly persecuted despite their willingness to do work others considered impossible (including the unimaginable engineering feat of chiseling a route over the forbidding Sierra Nevada for the nation's first transcontinental railroad). And when the state's boom-bust beginnings gave way to other possibilities, including farming, ranching, and small business enterprises, California's minorities stayed—helping, despite the realities of subtle discrimination and sometimes overt racism, to create the psychological pluralism characteristic of California society today.

DOING THE DREAM: PRACTICALITIES

California is crowded—both with people trying to live the dream on a permanent basis and with those who come to visit, to re-create themselves on the standard two-week vacation plan. Summer, when school's out, is generally when the Golden State is most crowded, though this pattern is changing rapidly now that year-round schools and off-season travel are becoming common. Another new trend: "mini-vacations," with workaholic Californians and other Westerners opting for one- to several-day respites spread throughout the year rather than traditional once-a-year holidays. It was once a truism that great bargains, in accommodations and transport particularly, were widely available during California's non-summer travel season. Due to Northern California's mild coastal temperatures and winter sports possibilities, this is no longer true. But the early spring and autumn are still often the best times to travel.

Because Northern California is such a land of contrast and contradiction, the most enjoyable way to travel here is California style: spontaneously. Unfortunately, for those traveling on the cheap or who have a strong need to know where they'll be staying, and for those with special needs and specific desires, some of the surprises encountered during impulsive adventuring may be unpleasant. If the availability of specific types of lodgings (including campgrounds) or eateries, or transport, prices, hours, and other factors are important for a pleasant trip, the best bet is calling ahead to check details and/or to make reservations. (Everything changes rapidly in California.) For a good overview of what to see and do in advance of a planned trip, including practical suggestions beyond those in this guide, also contact the chambers of commerce and/or visitor centers listed. Other good sources for local and regional information are bookstores, libraries, sporting goods and outdoor supply stores, and local, state, and federal government offices.

BEING HERE:
ATTITUDE AND ATTRACTIONS

Whenever you arrive and wherever you go, one thing to bring along is right attitude—bad attitude, strangely enough, being a particular problem among American travelers (including Californians) visiting California. One reason visitors become annoyed and obnoxious is because (often without realizing it) they started their trip with high, sometimes fantasy-based expectations—akin, perhaps, to being magically cured of all limitations at a Lourdes-like way station along life's freeway—and, once arrived in California, reality disappoints. Even the Golden State has traffic jams, parking problems, rude service people, and low-lifes only too happy to make off with a good time by stealing one's pocketbook—or car. Be prepared.

Visitors also bring along no-fun baggage when they go to new places and compare whatever they find with what they left behind "back home." This is disrespectful. The surest way to enjoy California is to remain open-minded about whatever you may see, hear, do, or otherwise experience. It's fine to laugh (to one's self) at California's contradictions and cultural self-consciousness—even Californians do it—but try to view new communities, from sophisticated San

KIM WEIR

For the best advice on what to do and why, strike up a conversation with the local folks.

Francisco to the most isolated and economically depressed backwater, from the perspective of the people who live and work there. Better yet, strike up conversations with locals and ask questions whenever possible. These experiences invariably become the best surprises of all—because nothing, and no one, is ever quite what they first appear to be in California.

Conduct And Custom

Smoking is a major social sin in California, often against the law in public buildings and on public transport, with regulations particularly stringent in urban areas. People sometimes get violent over other people's smoking, so smokers need to be respectful of others' "space" and smoke outdoors when possible. If smoking hasn't been banned outright, most restaurants in California offer nonsmoking and smoking sections; smoking is not allowed on public airplane flights (though nervous fliers can usually smoke somewhere inside—or outside—airline terminals). Many bed and breakfasts in California are either

entirely nonsmoking or restrict smoking to decks, porches, or dens; if this is an issue, inquire by calling ahead. Hotels and motels, most commonly in major urban areas or popular tourist destinations, increasingly offer nonsmoking rooms (or entire floors). Ask in advance.

English is the official language in California, and even English-speaking visitors from other countries have little trouble understanding California's "dialect" once they acclimate to the accents and slang expressions. (Californians tend to be very creative in their language.) When unsure what someone means by some peculiar phrase, ask them to translate into standard English. Particularly in urban areas, many languages are commonly spoken, and—even in English—the accents are many. At least some foreign-language brochures, maps, and other information can usually be obtained from city visitor centers and popular tourist destinations. (If this is a major concern, inquire in advance.)

Californians are generally casual, in dress as well as etiquette. If any standard applies in most situations, it's common courtesy—still in style, generally speaking, even in California. Though "anything goes" just about anywhere, elegant restaurants usually require appropriate attire. (Shirts and shoes—pants or skirt too, usually—are required in any California restaurant.) To show gratitude for services rendered in the service trade, a tip is usually expected. In expensive restaurants or for large groups, an automatic tip or gratuity may be included in the bill. Otherwise, depending on the quality of the service and other factors, 15-20% is the standard gratuity for the service trade, from waitresses and waiters to barbers, hairdressers, and taxi drivers. Also tip porters at airports and hotel bellboys and porters: $.50 and up per bag. If he helps with baggage or parks the car, also tip the hotel doorman. Unless one stays for several days, the standard practice is not to tip the chambermaid.

By law, public buildings in California are wheelchair-accessible (at least partially so). The same is true of most major hotels and tourist attractions; even national and state parks, increasingly, are attempting to make some sights and campgrounds more accessible for those with physical disabilities. But private buildings, from restaurants to bed and breakfasts, may not be so accommodating. Those with special needs should definitely inquire in advance.

The legal age for buying and drinking alcohol in California is 21. Though Californians (as they say) tend to "party hearty," public drunkenness is not well-tolerated. Drunken driving—which means operating an automobile (even a bicycle, technically) while under the influence—is definitely against the law. California is increasingly no-nonsense about the use of illegal drugs, too, from marijuana to cocaine, crack, and heroin. Doing time in local jails or state prisons is not the best way to do California.

Shopping

Most stores are open during standard (8-5 or 9-5) business hours and often longer, sometimes seven days a week, due to the California trend toward two-income families and ever-reduced leisure time. This trend is particularly noticeable in cities, where shops and department stores are often open until 9 p.m. or later, and where many grocery stores are open 24 hours. Exploring shopping malls—almost self-sustaining cities, with everything from clothing and major appliances to restaurants and entertainment—is the typical California trend, but cities (large and small) with a viable downtown shopping district often offer greater variety in small-business shops and services. Also particularly popular in California are flea markets and arts-and-crafts fairs (the former usually held on weekends, the latter best for handcrafted items and often associated with the Thanksgiving-through-Christmas shopping season and/or special events). California assesses a 7¼% state sales tax on all nonfood items sold in the state, and many municipalities levy additional sales tax.

Entertainment, Events, Holidays

Not even the sky's the limit on entertainment in California. From air shows to harvest fairs and rodeos, from symphony to opera, from rock 'n' roll to avant-garde clubs and theater, from strip shows (male and female) to ringside seats at ladies' mud-wrestling contests, from high-stakes bingo games to horse-racing—anything goes in the Golden State. Most communities offer a wide variety of special, often quite unusual, annual events (listed by region, city, or town elsewhere in this guide).

Official holidays, especially during the warm-weather travel season and the Thanksgiving-Christmas holidays, are often the most congested and popular (read: more expensive) times to travel or stay in California. Though most travel destinations are usually jumping, banks and many businesses close on the following major holidays: New Year's Day (January 1); Martin Luther King, Jr.'s Birthday (January 15, usually observed on the following Monday); Presidents' Day (the third Monday in February); Memorial Day (the last Monday in May); Independence Day (July 4); Labor Day (the first Monday in September); Veterans Day (November 11); Thanksgiving (the fourth Thursday in November); and Christmas (December 25).

Outdoor Recreation

With its tremendous natural diversity, recreationally California offers something for just about everyone. Popular spring-summer-fall activities include hiking and backpacking; all water sports, from pleasure boating and water-skiing to sailing, windsurfing, and swimming; whitewater rafting, canoeing, and kayaking; mountain and rock-climbing; even hang gliding and hunting. Winter activities popular in Northern California include both Alpine and Nordic skiing, snowshoe hiking, sledding and tobogganing, and just plain playing in the snow. Among Northern California's most popular year-round outdoor sports: bicycling, walking and running, and coastal diversions from beachcombing to surfing (only for the hardy). The most likely places to enjoy these and other outdoor activities are mentioned throughout this book.

And where do people go to re-create themselves in the great outdoors? To Northern California's vast public playgrounds—almost endless local, regional, and state parks as well as national park and forest lands. For more information on the national parks, monuments, and forests (including wilderness areas) mentioned throughout this book, contact each directly. For those who plan to travel extensively through national parks and monuments, a one-year Golden Eagle Passport, which provides unlimited park access for the holder and family for $25, can be obtained from: **National Park Headquarters**, U.S. Dept. of the Interior, 18th and C Streets NW, Washington, D.C. 20240. Those age 62 or older qualify for the Golden Age Passport, $20, which provides free access to national parks, monuments, and recreation areas, and a 50% discount on RV fees. Dis-

ON JOHN MUIR'S TRAIL

I could give up this life
of children and fuss
because there's still a John Muir
trail I retreated down
that insane sixties summer I was
trapped between boy and man.

I would carry my life
again in the green canvas pack
and hike Muir's high granite trail
from lake to barely-touched lake,
lonely and learning to live
in someone else's world.

I should step from this mirror
of my responsibly-shaved face
to face John Muir's white-bearded
stare at the camera. It says:
he blazed his own mountain way
away from family and Martinez farm

with abandon.

—Gary Thompson

abled travelers are eligible for the $20 Golden Access Passport, with the same privileges. No similar program is available for state park and recreation areas, where the per-vehicle day-use fee is usually $5 (sometimes $6-7 for popular beach areas). Campgrounds in some national parks and monuments in California can be reserved in advance by calling another toll-free Mistix number, tel. (800) 365-CAMP, at least eight weeks in advance.

Information about state parks, beaches, and recreation areas is also scattered throughout this guide, though a complete listing (including available facilities) and campground reservation forms and other information can be obtained by contacting: **California Dept. of Parks and Recreation,** P.O. Box 942896, Sacramento 94296-0838. A complete *Official Guide to California State Parks* map and facilities listing is available for $2 (send check or money order to the attention of the Publications Section). Also available, and free: a complete parks and recreation publications list (which includes a mail order form).

The parks and recreation people also put out a quarterly "Special Events in California State Parks," primarily as a media press release—but if you'll be spending a great deal of time in the state parks, or would like to plan your stays around special events, if you ask nicely perhaps they'll send you one. Also available through the state parks department is an annually updated "Sno-Park" guide to parking without penalty while playing in the snow. Free to AAA members is the annual *Winter Sports Guide* for California, which lists prices and other current information for all downhill and cross-country ski areas.

For general information and fishing and hunting regulations (usually also available at sporting goods stores or bait shops where licenses and permits are sold), contact **California Dept. of Fish and Game** headquarters at 1416 9th St., Sacramento 95814 (License Section: 3211 S St., Sacramento 95816), tel. (916) 445-7613.

ACCOMMODATIONS AND FOOD

Camping Out

Due to many years of drought, and the accompanying extreme fire danger, all California national forests, most national parks, and many state parks now ban all backcountry campfires. Some areas even prohibit portable campstoves, so be sure to check current conditions and all camping and hiking or backpacking regulations before setting out.

California state parks offer excellent campgrounds. In addition to $8-14-per-night developed "family" campsites, which usually include a table, fire ring or outdoor stove, plus running water, flush toilets, and hot showers (RV hookups, if available, are extra), some state campgrounds also offer more primitive "walk-in" or environmental campgrounds, usually for $7 per night, and/or very simple hiker-biker campsites, $3 per night. Group campgrounds are also available (and reservable in advance) at many state parks. Special discounts are available for the disabled, for some honorably discharged disabled veterans, and for senior adults. Most of California's state park campgrounds are described and listed elsewhere in this book, but for a complete listing and other current information (including advance campground reservation forms), contact: **California Dept. of Parks and Recreation,** P.O. Box 942896, Sacramento 94296-0001, tel. (916) 445-6647.

Reservations for state park campgrounds are handled through a concessionaire and should be made at least two weeks in advance of a planned trip—theoretically it's possible one business day in advance, if space is available—but no more than eight weeks in advance. (If you plan to camp over the Memorial or Labor Day weekends, or the July 4th holiday, be sure to make reservations as early as possible.) Camping reservations can be made either by mail (request an application form in advance) or by telephone (with credit card payment or "deferred payment" by personal check, if received in time). In addition to camping fees, a reservation fee is also charged. To get more information or to reserve campsites, contact: **Mistix,** P.O. Box 85705, San Diego 92138-5705, or, within California, call toll-free (800) 444-7275 (444-PARK) or the TTY number for the hearing impaired, (800) 274-7275. To make state campground reservations or to request information from out of state, call (619) 452-1950.

For anyone planning to camp extensively in national forest campgrounds, purchasing U.S. National Forest Service "camp stamps" in advance (at national forest headquarters or at ranger district stations) is a good idea; these prepaid camping coupons amount to a 15% discount on the going rate. (Most national forest campgrounds are first-come, first-camped; even camp stamps don't guarantee a campsite.) Senior adults, disabled persons, and those with national Golden Age and Golden Access recreation passports pay only half the standard fee at any campground and can purchase camp stamps at half the regular rate as well. To purchase camp stamps by mail—in denominations of $.50, $1, $2, $3, $5, and $10—send your request with check or money order to: **Camp Stamps,** USDA Forest Service, P.O. Box 96090, Washington, D.C. 20090-6090. Some popular national forest campgrounds can be reserved in California by calling Mistix toll-free at tel. (800) 283-CAMP.

For information about campgrounds (and reservations, if applicable) in national parks and monuments in California, see relevant entries elsewhere in this guide. (Some popular campgrounds can be reserved through Mistix, tel. toll-free 800-365-CAMP.) To obtain a *California Visitor Map* of other federal campgrounds ($1), contact: **Bureau of Land Management,** California State Office, 2800 Cottage Way, Sacramento 95825, tel. (916) 978-4754. In addition, Pacific Gas and Electric offers camping and picnicking facilities for public use; for its free "Guide to PG&E Recreation Areas" map-guide, contact: **Pacific Gas & Electric Company,** Land Department, 77 Beale St., San Francisco 94106, tel. (415) 972-5552. Many private campgrounds are available throughout Northern California. Members of the American Automobile Association (AAA) should pick up a free current copy of the *Campbook for California and Nevada,* which lists (by city or locale) a wide variety of private, state, and federal campgrounds.

For A Cheap Stay:
AYH Hostels, YMCAs, YWCAs
One of the best bargains around, for travelers of all ages, are the American Youth Hostel outposts scattered throughout Northern California—located in the heart of the redwoods, in the center of the Tahoe area ski scene, in various spots along the coast, and elsewhere (also listed separately throughout this guide). Most hostels, affiliated with the International Youth Hostel Federation, offer separate dormitory-style accommodations for men and women (and couple or family rooms, if available), kitchens or low-cost food service, and/or other common facilities. At most hostels, the maximum stay is three nights; most are also closed during the day, which forces hostelers to get out and about and see the sights. Fees in Northern California are in the $9 and up range for AYH members, usually several dollars more for nonmembers. Since most hostels are quite popular, especially during summer months, advance reservations—usually secured with one night's advance payment, but call first—are essential. Guests are expected to bring sleeping bags, sleepsacks, or sheets; mattresses, pillows, and blankets are provided.

For more information on Northern California hostels, including how to become a member of American Youth Hostels (International Youth

Hostel Federation), contact: **AYH, Golden Gate Council,** 425 Divisadero St., Suite 307, San Francisco 94117, tel. (415) 863-9939; and **AYH, Central California Council,** P.O. Box 28148, San Jose 95159, tel. (408) 298-0670. (For travelers heading south after seeing and doing the northstate, contact the AYH's **Los Angeles Council** at tel. 213-831-8846 and the **San Diego Council** at tel. 619-239-2644 or 234-3330.)

There are other reputable hostels in Northern California, some independent and some affiliated with other umbrella organizations. A good bet, for example, is the **American Association of International Hostels,** 1412 Cerrillos Rd., Santa Fe, NM 87051, tel. (505) 988-1153, which has more than 30 affiliated hostels nationwide. (See also the "San Francisco" chapter.)

Particularly in urban areas, the **Young Men's Christian Association** (YMCA) often offers housing, showers, and other facilities for young men (over age 18 only in some areas, if unaccompanied by parent or guardian), sometimes also for women and families. **Young Women's Christian Association** (YWCA) institutions offer housing for women only. For more information, contact: **Y's Way International,** 356 W. 34th St., New York, NY 10001, tel. (212) 760-5856; and/or YWCA, 726 Broadway, New York, NY 10003, tel. (212) 614-2700. Life being what it is these days, though, many of these facilities are primarily shelters for the destitute and the homeless; don't steal their beds unless absolutely necessary. Another low-cost alternative in summer is on-campus housing at state colleges and universities.

Hotels, Motels, Bed And Breakfasts

California, the spiritual home of highway and freeway living, is also the birthplace of the motel. Motels have been here longer than anywhere else, so they've had plenty of time to clone themselves. As a general precaution, when checking into a truly cheap motel, ask to see the room before signing in (and paying up); some places look much more appealing from the outside than from the inside. Mid-range and high-priced motels and hotels are generally okay. In addition to the standard California sales tax, many cities and counties—particularly near major tourism destinations—add a "bed tax" of 5-18% (or higher). To find out the actual price you'll be paying, ask before making reservations or signing in.

Unless otherwise stated, rates listed in this guide do not include state sales tax or local bed taxes.

Predictably reliable, on the cheaper end of the accommodations scale, are a variety of "chains" common throughout Northern California. To obtain a complete listing of motel locations and current information, contact: **Allstar Inns,** P.O. Box 3070, Santa Barbara, CA 93130, tel. (805) 687-3383; **Budget-Host Inns,** P.O. Box 10656, Fort Worth, TX 76114, tel. (817) 626-7064 or toll-free (800) BUD-HOST for reservations; **Days Inn of America, Inc.,** 2751 Buford Hwy. NE, Atlanta, GA 30324, toll-free tel. (800) 325-2525; **E-Z 8 Motels,** 2484 Hotel Circle Place, San Diego, CA 92108, tel. (619) 291-4824; and that all-time budget favorite, **Motel 6,** 14651 Dallas Parkway, Dallas, TX 75240, tel. (505) 891-6161 for reservations and information.

For members of the American Automobile Association (AAA), the current *Tourbook for California and Nevada* (free) includes an impressive number of rated motels and hotels, from inexpensive to top-of-the-line, sometimes also recommended restaurants, for nearly every community and city in Northern California.

The hot new trend in California is the bed-and-breakfast phenomenon. Many guides and listings are available in bookstores, and AAA also publishes its own (free to members) *Bed & Breakfast* guide for Northern and Central California plus Nevada. Unlike the European tradition, however, with bed and breakfasts a low-cost yet comfortable lodging alternative, in California these inns are actually a burgeoning small business trend—usually quite pricey, in the $50-150 range (sometimes cheaper), more of a "special weekend getaway" for exhausted city people than a true accommodations bargain. In some

A NOTE ON PRICES

With a few possible (inadvertent) exceptions, accommodation rates and other prices listed in this book were accurate as of press time. To "translate" these prices into the future, assume annual increases of 5-10%, though in many cases actual cost increases may be smaller (or nonexistent), and unexpected discounts may be offered due to the current uncertain state of the California economy.

areas, though, where motel and hotel rooms are on the high end, bed and breakfasts are quite competitive.

The Land Of Fruits And Nuts And California Cuisine

One of the best things about traveling in California is the food: they don't call the Golden State the nation's breadbasket for nothing. In agricultural and rural areas, local "farm trails" guides are commonly available (ask at local chambers of commerce and visitor centers), and following the seasonal produce trails offers visitors the unique pleasure of gathering up (sometimes picking your own) fresh fruits, nuts, and vegetables direct from the growers. This fresher, direct-to-you trend is also quite common in most urban areas, where regular farmers markets are *the* places to go for fresh, often exotic produce and farm products. For a complete listing of Northern California farmers' markets and direct-to-you growers, write the **California Dept. of Food and Agriculture,** Direct Marketing Program, 1414 K St., Suite 320, Sacramento 95814, and request a current copy of the *California Farmer-to-Consumer Directory.* To find out what's in season where, call toll-free (800) 952-5272.

Threaded with freeways and accessible on-ramp, off-ramp commercial strips, Northern California has more than its fair share of fast-food eateries and all-night quik-stop outlets. (Since they're so easy to find, none are listed in this guide.) Most communities have locally popular cafes and fairly inexpensive restaurants worth seeking out. (Ask around.) Genuinely inexpensive eateries often refuse to take credit cards, so always bring some cash along just in case.

The northstate is also famous for its "California cuisine," which sometimes means consuming tastebud-tantalizing, very expensive food in very small portions—almost a cliché—while oohing and ahhing over it throughout the meal. But culinary creativity is quite real, and worth pursuing (sans pretense) in many areas. Talented chefs, who have migrated outward from major cities, usually prefer locally grown produce, dairy products, meats, and herbs and spices as basic ingredients. To really "do" the cuisine scene, wash it all down with some fine California wine.

OTHER PRACTICALITIES

Visas For Foreign Visitors

Foreign visitors to the U.S. are required to carry a current passport and a visitor's visa plus proof that they intend to leave (usually a return airplane ticket is adequate). Also, it's wise to carry proof of one's citizenship, for example, a driver's license and/or birth certificate. To be on the safe side, photocopy your legal documents and carry the photocopies separately from the originals. To obtain a U.S. visa (most visitors qualify for a B-2 or "pleasure tourist" visa, valid for up to six months), contact the nearest U.S.

California's love of good food is perhaps rooted in its agricultural tradition.

embassy or consulate. Should you lose the Form I-94 (proof of arrival/departure) attached to your visa, contact the nearest local U.S. **Immigration and Naturalization Service** (INS) office or contact headquarters: 4420 N. Fairfax Dr., Arlington, VA 22203, tel. (703) 235-4055. Contact the INS also for a visa extension (good for a maximum of six months). In order to work or study in the U.S., special visas are required; contact the nearest U.S. embassy or consulate for current information. To replace a passport lost while in the U.S., contact the nearest embassy for your country. Canadian citizens entering the U.S. from Canada or Mexico do not need either a passport or visa, nor do Mexican citizens possessing a Form I-186. (Canadians under age 18 do need to carry written consent from a parent or guardian.)

Time

California, within the Pacific Time Zone (two hours behind Chicago, three hours behind New York), is on Daylight Savings Time (a helps-with-harvest agricultural holdover), which means clocks are set ahead one hour from the first Sunday in April until the last Sunday in October. Without this seasonal time adjustment, when it's noon in California it's 10 a.m. in Hawaii, 8 p.m. in London, midnight in Moscow, and 4 a.m. (the next day) in Hong Kong.

Business Hours, Banking, Money

Standard business hours in California (holidays excepted) are Monday through Friday 9 a.m.-5 p.m., though many businesses open at 8 a.m. or 10 a.m. and/or stay open until 6 p.m. or later. Traditional banking hours—10 a.m. until 3 p.m.—are not necessarily the rule in California these days. Particularly in cities, banks may open at 9 a.m. and stay open until 5 or 6 p.m., and may offer extended walk-up or drive-up window hours. Many banks and savings and loans also offer Saturday hours (usually 9 a.m.-1 p.m.) as well as 24-hour automated teller service. Before traveling in California, contact your bank for a list of California branches or affiliated institutions.

For the most part, traveling in California is expensive. Depending on your plans, figure out how much money you'll need—then bring more. Most banks will not cash checks (or issue cash via automatic tellers) for anyone without an account (or an account with some affiliated insti-tution). Major credit cards (especially Visa and MasterCard) are almost universally accepted in California, except at inexpensive motels and restaurants—and are often mandatory for renting cars or as a "security deposit" on bicycle, outdoor equipment, and other rentals. The safest way to bring cash is by carrying traveler's checks. American Express travelers checks are the most widely recognized and accepted. For U.S. travelers who run short of money, ask family or friends to send a postal money order (buyable and cashable at any U.S. Postal Service post office); ask your bank to wire money to an affiliated California bank (probably for a slight fee); or have money wired office-to-office via Western Union, toll-free tel. (800) 325-6000 (800-225-5227 for credit-card money transfers; 800-325-4045 for assistance in Spanish), with the surcharge depending on the amount sent.

International travelers, avoid the necessity of wiring for money if at all possible. With a Visa, MasterCard, or American Express card, cash advances are easily available (get details about applicable banks before leaving, however). But if you must arrange for cash from home, a cable transfer from your bank (check on corresponding California banks before leaving), a Western Union money wire, or a bank draft or international money order are all possible. Make sure you (and your sender) know the accurate address for the recipient bank—to avoid obvious nightmarish complications. In a pinch, consulates may intervene and request money from home (or your home bank) at your request—deducting their cost from funds received.

Measurements, Mail, Communications

Despite persistent efforts to wean Americans from the old ways, California and the rest of the union still abide by the British system of weights and measures (see measurements chart in the back of this book). Electrical outlets in California (and the rest of the U.S.) carry current at 117 volts, 60 cycles (Hertz) A.C.; foreign electrical appliances require a converter and plug adapter.

Even without a full-fledged post office, most outback communities have some official outpost of the United State Postal Service, usually open weekdays 8-5, for sending letters and packages and for receiving general delivery mail. Basic postal rates within the U.S. are $.19 for postcards, $.29 for letter mail (first ounce); for international mail, rates from the U.S. are $.40 for postcards, $.50 for letters (the first half ounce). For mail sent and received within the U.S., knowing and using the relevant five- or nine-digit zip code is important. Mail can be directed to any particular post office c/o "General Delivery," but the correct address and zip code for the post office receiving such mail is important—especially in cities, where there are multiple post offices. (For zip codes and post offices, call the number listed in the local phone book or toll-free 800-332-9631.) To claim general delivery mail, current photo identification is required; unclaimed mail will be returned to the sender after languishing for two to four weeks. At larger post offices, **International Express Mail** is available (delivery to major world cities in 48-72 hours).

Telephone communication is easy in California. Local calls are often free (or inexpensive) from many motel and hotel rooms, but long-distance calls will cost you. Collect and person-to-person operator-assisted calls are usually more expensive than direct-dial and telephone company (such as AT&T) credit-card calls.

What To Bring

Generally speaking, bring what you'll really need—but as little of it as possible. A good rule of thumb is: select everything absolutely necessary for your travels, then take along only half. Remember, you'll be bringing back all sorts of interesting tokens of your trip, so leave space. Remember, too, that camera equipment is heavy; bring only what you'll really use. (Try carrying your packed luggage around for 15 or 20 minutes if you need motivation to lighten the load.) Standard luggage is adequate for most travelers, especially those traveling by bus or car, but a backpack—or convertible backpack-suitcase—may be more useful for those covering ground on foot. For any traveler, a daypack may also come in handy, for use on day hikes and for toting home travel trinkets.

In characteristically casual California, clothing should be sensible and comfortable. Cotton and other natural fibers are preferable because they "breathe" in California's variable climate; cotton is the basic California fiber—quite versatile, too, when layered to meet one's changing needs. Dark or bright colors, knits, and durable clothing will keep you presentable longer than more frivolous fashions (though laundry services and coin-operated laundromats are widely available). Even for summer travel, always bring a sweater or light jacket, since summer fog can cool temperatures near popular coastal destinations, and nights are cool even in the foothills. A heavier jacket is advisable even for summers in the Sierra Nevada. Winter weather in mountainous regions can be quite severe, so pack accordingly; coats are advisable anywhere in Northern California during winter. Those planning to participate in California-style high life should pack some dress clothes, of course, but the most universally necessary thing to bring is a decent (preferably broken-in) pair of walking shoes.

SERVICES AND INFORMATION

Services

Even backwater areas of Northern California aren't nearly as primitive as popular mythology would suggest. Gasoline, at least basic groceries, laundry facilities of some sort, even video rentals are available just about anywhere. Backwoods outposts are not likely to have parts for exotic sports cars, however, or 24-hour pharmacies, hospitals, and garages, or natural foods stores or full-service supermarkets, so any special needs or problems should be taken care of before leaving the cities. It's often cheaper, too, to stock up on most supplies (including outdoor equipment and groceries) in urban areas.

General Information

Consumers can receive free California travel-planning information by writing the **California Office of Tourism**, P.O. Box 1499, Sacramento, CA 95812-1499, or by calling toll-free (800) 862-2543. The office has published an ambitious barrage of information under "The Californias" theme. That concept is being discarded as of late 1993 in favor of a new, more unified approach: Golden California. Obtain a free packet of information by writing: Golden California, P.O. Box 9278, Van Nuys 91409, or by calling toll-free (800) 862-2543 (U.S. only). Traditionally included among California's free publications are nine comprehensive consumer guides, a listing of regional attractions, lodging options, and local chambers of commerce and visitors bureaus; a "California Visitors Map"; "Bed &

Breakfast Inns"; and slick, visually enticing events, ethnic events, and ski magazines.

Future state-sponsored publications will include the *Golden California Visitors Guide*, the *Golden California Travel Planner's Guide*, and the *Golden California Magazine*, the latter distributed free to travelers at the state's borders.

Most major cities also have very good visitor centers and often offer accommodations reservations and other services; some offer information and maps in foreign languages. (For international travelers, another good source is the **U.S. Travel and Tourism Administration**, most helpful at its 10 overseas offices but located in the U.S. at 14th St. and Constitution Ave. NW, Washington, D.C. 20230, tel. 202-377-4003.) In rural areas of Northern California, chambers of commerce are something of a hit-or-miss proposition, since office hours may be minimal; the best bet is calling ahead for information. Asking locals—people at gas stations, cafes, grocery stores, and official government outposts —is often the best way to get information about where to go, why, when, and how. Slick city magazines, good daily newspapers, and California-style weekly news and entertainment tabloids are other good sources of information.

Special Information

The **Council on International Educational Exchange** (CIEE) Travel Services, with an office in the Bay Area at 919 Irving St. (between 10th and 11th avenues), San Francisco 94122, tel. (415) 566-6222, sells the International Student Identity Card (good for various discounts on everything from travel arrangements to arts and entertainment) and offers information on low-cost travel, work-study programs, and other deals. Another good source for similar information and services is **Let's Go Travel Services**, affiliated with Harvard Student Agencies, Thayer Hall, Harvard University, Cambridge, MA 02138, tel. (617) 495-9649.

Reliable information sources for disabled travelers include the **Society for the Advancement of Travel for the Handicapped**, 26 Court St., Penthouse, Brooklyn, NY 11242, tel. (718) 858-5483, and the **American Foundation for the Blind**, 15 W. 16th St., New York, NY 10011, toll-free tel. (800) 232-5463. Tour companies include **Directions Unlimited**, 720 N. Bedford Rd., Bedford Hills, NY 10507, toll-free (U.S.)

tel. (800) 533-5343; **Flying Wheels Travel,** 143 W. Bridge St., P.O. Box 382, Owatonna, MN 55060, toll-free tel. (800) 535-6790; and **Whole Person Tours,** P.O. Box 1084, Bayonne, NJ 07002- 1084, tel. (201) 858-3400.

Senior adults can benefit from a great many bargains and discounts. A good source of information is the "Travel Tips for Older Americans" pamphlet published by the U.S. Government Printing Office, tel. (202) 275-3648, available for $1. The federal government's Golden Age Passport offers free admission to national parks and monuments and half-price discounts for campsites and other recreational services. Discounts are also frequently offered to seniors at major tourist attractions and sights as well as for many arts and entertainment activities in Northern California. Another benefit of experience is eligibility for the international **Elderhostel** program, 75 Federal St., Boston, MA 02110, tel. (617) 426-7788, which offers a variety of fairly reasonable one-week residential programs in California. For information on travel discounts and other membership benefits of the U.S.'s largest senior citizen organization, contact the **American Association of Retired Persons,** 1909 K St. NW, Washington, D.C. 20049, toll-free tel. (800) 227-7737. Despite the name, anyone age 50 and older—retired or not—is eligible for membership.

Maps

The best all-around maps for California, city and country, are those produced by the **American Automobile Association,** which is regionally organized as the California State Automobile Association (CSAA) in Northern and Central California, and as the Automobile Club of Southern California in the southstate. The AAA maps are available at any local AAA office, and the price is right (free, but for members only). In addition to its state map, AAA has urban maps for most major cities, plus regional maps with at least some backcountry routes marked (these not necessarily reliable, however; when in doubt about unusual routes, ask locally before setting out). For more information about AAA membership and services in Northern California, contact: California State Automobile Association, 150 Van Ness Ave., P.O. Box 1860, San Francisco 94101-1860, tel. (415) 565-2012 or 565-2468.

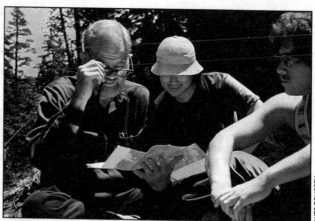

Especially along forest trails, a decent map may be your best friend.

WES DEMPSEY

Also excellent for general travel are **Thomas Bros. Maps,** particularly the "California Road Atlas & Driver's Guide" and the various, very detailed spiral-bound book-style maps in the "Thomas Guide" street atlas series—the standard block-by-block reference (constantly updated) since 1915 for anyone spending much time in major urban areas in either Northern or Southern California. These various maps are available at any decent travel-oriented bookstore, or contact: Thomas Bros. Maps, 550 Jackson St., San Francisco 94133, tel. (415) 981-7520 or toll-free (800) 432-8430.

When it comes to backcountry travel—where maps quickly become either your best friend or arch enemy—the going isn't nearly as easy. U.S. Geological Survey quadrangle maps in most cases are reliable for showing the contours of the terrain, but U.S. Forest Service and wilderness maps—supposedly the maps of record for finding one's way through the woods and the wilds—are often woefully out of date, with new and old logging roads (as well as disappearing or changed trail routes) confusing the situation considerably. In California, losing oneself in the wilderness is a very real, literal possibility. In addition to topo maps (carry a compass to orient yourself by landforms if all else fails) and official U.S. maps, backcountry travelers would be wise to invest in privately published guidebooks and current route or trail guides for wilderness areas; the Sierra Club and Wilderness Press publish both. Before setting out, compare all available maps and other

information to spot any possible route discrepancies, then ask national forest or parks personnel for clarification. If you're lucky, you'll find someone who knows what's going on where you want to go.

Aside from well-stocked outdoor stores, the primary source for quad maps is: **U.S. Geological Survey,** 345 Middlefield Rd., Menlo Park, CA 94025, tel. (415) 853-8300; an index and catalog of published California maps is available upon request. For a complete listing of available relevant national forest and wilderness maps, contact: **U.S. Forest Service,** Pacific Southwest Region, Public Affairs, 630 Sansome St., San Francisco 94111, tel. (415) 705-2869. (If you walk in off the street, bring adequate cash or personal check; the office can't make change and doesn't take credit cards.) For basic information and very basic maps for California national parks (be specific), contact: **U.S. National Park Service,** Interpretation Division, 450 Golden Gate Ave., San Francisco 94102, tel. (415) 556-3535. (For better information, contact each park directly or consult guidebooks and maps.) The **Sierra Club Book Store,** 730 Polk St., San Francisco 94109, tel. (415) 923-5600, carries an incredible selection of maps to national parks, forests, and wilderness areas, plus a good line of guidebooks. Another good bet is **Wilderness Press,** 2440 Bancroft Way, Berkeley 94704, tel. (510) 843-8080, or its two affiliated **Map Center** stores, one at the same address in Berkeley, tel. 841-6277, and another in Santa Clara at 63 Washington St., tel. (408) 296-6277.

Not necessarily practical for travelers are the beautiful yet utilitarian maps produced by **Raven Maps & Images,** 34 N. Central, Medford, OR 97501, tel. (503) 773-1436, or (for credit card orders) toll-free (800) 237-0798. These beauties are big, and—unless you buy one for the wall and one for the road—you'll never want to fold them. Based on U.S. Geological Survey maps, these shaded relief maps are "computer-enhanced" for a three-dimensional topographical feel and incredible clarity—perfect for planning outdoor adventures. Raven's "California" map measures 42 by 64 inches and costs $20. New is "Yosemite and the Central Sierra," 34 by 37 inches, $15. And wonderful for any California-lover's wall is the three-dimensional, five-color "California, Nevada, and the Pacific Ocean Floor" digital landform map, which offers three aerial oblique views: now, five million years ago, and five million years in the future. Fabulous. All Raven maps are printed in fade-resistant inks on fine quality 70-pound paper and are also available in vinyl laminated versions suitable for framing.

HEALTH AND SAFETY

Emergencies, Medical Care, And General Health

In urban areas and in many rural areas, 24-hour walk-in health care services are readily available, though hospital emergency rooms are the place to go in the event of life-threatening circumstances. (In most places in California, call 911 for any emergency; in medical emergencies, life support personnel and ambulances will be dispatched.) To make sure health care services will be readily provided in the event of emergencies, health insurance coverage is almost mandatory; carry proof of coverage while traveling in California.

To avoid most health and medical problems, use common sense. Eat sensibly, avoid unsafe drinking water, bring along any necessary prescription pills, and pack an extra pair of glasses or contacts (if you wear them), just in case. Sunglasses, especially for those unaccustomed to sunshine, as well as sunscreen and a broad-brimmed hat, can help prevent sunburn, sunstroke, and heat prostration. Drink plenty of liquids, too, especially in hot weather.

No vaccinations are usually necessary for traveling in California, though here as elsewhere very young children and seniors should obtain vaccinations against annually variable forms of the flu virus; exposure, especially in crowded urban areas and especially during the winter disease season, is a likelihood.

As in other areas of the United States, the AIDS (Acquired Immune Deficiency Syndrome) virus and other sexually transmitted diseases are an increasing concern. In mythic "anything goes" California, avoiding promiscuous sex is the best way to avoid the danger of AIDS and venereal disease—though AIDS has also been proven to be transmitted via shared drug needles and contaminated-blood transfusions. (All medical blood supplies in California are now screened for evidence of the virus.) Sexually speaking, "safe sex" is the preventive key phrase, under any circumstances beyond the strictly monogamous. This means always using condoms in sexual intercourse (some sources suggest lubricants containing nonoxynol-9, which may guard against garden variety venereal disease and diminish the AIDS virus); oral sex only with some sort of barrier precaution; and no sharing sex toys.

City Safety

Though California's wilderness once posed a major threat to human survival, in most respects the backcountry is safer than the urban jungle of modern cities. Tourism officials don't talk about it much, but crimes against persons and property are a reality in California. To avoid harm, bring along your street-smarts. The best overall personal crime prevention includes carrying only small amounts of cash (inconspicuously, in a money belt or against-the-body money pouch); labeling (and locking) all luggage; keeping valuables under lock and key (and, in automobiles, out of sight); being aware of persons and events, and knowing where you are, at all times; and avoiding dangerous, lonely, and unlighted areas after daylight hours, particularly late at night and when traveling alone. (If you're not sure what neighborhoods are considered dangerous or unsafe, ask locals or hotel or motel personnel—or at the police station, if necessary.)

Women traveling alone—not generally advisable, due to the unfortunate fact of misogyny in the modern world—need to take special care to avoid harm. For any independent traveler, self-defense classes (and/or a training course for carrying and using Mace) might be a worthwhile investment, if only to increase one's sense of personal power in the event of a confrontation with criminals. Being assertive and confident, acting as if you know where you are going (even when you don't), are also among the best deterrents to predators. Carry enough money for a phone call—or bus or taxi ride—and a whistle. When in doubt, don't hesitate to yell and scream for help.

General Outdoor Safety

The most basic rule is: know what you're doing and where you're going. Next most basic: whatever you do—from swimming or surfing to hiking and backpacking—don't do it alone. For any outdoor activity, be prepared. Check with local park or national forest service officials on weather, trail, and general conditions before setting out. Correct, properly functioning equipment is as important in backpacking as it is in hang gliding, mountain climbing, and sailing. (When in doubt, check it out.)

Among the basics to bring along for almost any outdoor activity: a hat, sunscreen, and lip balm (to protect against the sun in summer, against heat loss, reflective sun, and the elements in winter); a whistle, compass, and mylar "space blanket" in the event of becoming lost or stranded; insect repellent; a butane lighter or waterproof matches; a multipurpose Swiss Army-type knife; nylon rope; a flashlight; and a basic first-aid kit (including bandages, ointments and salves, antiseptics, pain relievers such as aspirin, and any necessary prescription medicines). For hikers and backpackers and other outdoor adventurers, bring plenty of water (or water purification tablets or paraphernalia for long trips), at least minimal fishing gear, good hiking shoes or boots, extra socks and shoelaces, "layerable" clothing adequate for all temperatures, and a waterproof poncho or large plastic garbage bag. (Even if thunderstorms are unlikely, any sort of packable and wearable plastic bag can keep you dry until you reach shelter.) The necessity for other outdoor equipment, from campstoves to sleeping bags and tents, depends on where you'll be going and what you'll be doing.

Poison Oak

Poison oak (actually a shrub-like sumac) is a perennial trailside hazard, especially in lowland foothill areas and mixed forests; it exudes oily chemicals that cause a strong allergic reaction in most people, even with only brief contact. (Always be careful what you're burning around the campfire, too; smoke from poison oak, when inhaled, can inflame the lungs and create a life-threatening situation in no time flat.) The best way to avoid the painful, itchy, often long-lasting rashes associated with poison oak is to avoid contact with the plant—in all seasons—and to immediately wash one's skin or clothes if you even suspect a brush with it. (Its leaves a bright, glossy green in spring and summer, red or yellow in fall, poison oak can be a problem even in winter—when this mean-spirited deciduous shrub loses its leaves.) Learn to identify it during any time of year. Once afflicted with poison oak, never scratch; oozing skin only spreads it. Drying, cortisone-based lotions and other medications can help control the discomfort, but the rash itself goes away only in its own good time.

Lyme Disease And Ticks

Even if you favor shorts for summer hiking, better plan on long pants, long-sleeved shirts, even insect repellent. The weather may be mild, but there's an increasing risk—particularly in California coastal and foothill areas, as in other states—that you'll contract Lyme disease, transmitted by ticks which thrive in moist lowland climates.

A new ailment on the West Coast, named after its 1975 discovery in Old Lyme, Connecticut, Lyme disease sufferers are often misdiagnosed as having afflictions such as rheumatoid arthritis. Lyme is already the most common vector-transmitted disease in the nation, caused by spirochetes transmitted through blood, urine, and other body fluids. (Current research indicates it has often been wrongly diagnosed.) Temporary paralysis, arthritic pains in the hands or arm and leg joints, swollen hands, fever, fatigue, nausea, headaches, swollen glands, and heart palpatations are among the typical symptoms. Sometimes there's an unusually circular red rash that appears first, between three and 30 days after the tick bite. Untreated, Lyme disease can mean a lifetime of suffering, even danger to unborn children. Treatment, once Lyme disease is discovered through blood tests, is simple and 100% effective if recognized early: tetracycline and other drugs halt the arthritic degeneration and most symptoms. Long-delayed treatment, even with extremely high doses of antibiotics, is only about 50% effective.

Outdoor prudence coupled with an awareness of possible Lyme symptoms even months later, are the watchwords when it comes to Lyme disease. Take precautions against tick bite: the sooner ticks are found and removed, the better your chances of avoiding the disease. Tuck your pants into your boots, wear long-sleeved shirts, and use insect repellent around all clothing openings as well as on your neck and all exposed skin. Run a full-body "tick check" daily, especially checking hidden areas like the hair and scalp. Consider leaving dogs at home if heading for Lyme country; ticks they pick up can spread the disease through your human family.

Use gloves and tweezers to remove ticks from yourself or your animals—never crush the critters with your fingers!—and wash your hands and the bitten area afterwards. Better yet, smother imbedded ticks with petroleum jelly first; deprived of oxygen, they start to pull out of the skin in about a half hour, making it easy to pluck them off without tearing them in two and leaving the head imbedded.

TRANSPORT

By Bicycle
Northern California is great fun for cyclists, especially for those who hanker after a little backroads sightseeing while huffing and puffing uphill. But since cycling on public roadways usually means competing with car traffic, brightly colored bicycle clothing and accessories, reflective tape, good lights, and other safety features are advisable. Always wear a helmet. Various good cycling guides are available (see "Booklist"), but free referral information on publications endorsed by the California Association of Bicycling Organizations (CABO) is available from **Caltrans, Dept. of Transportation and Planning,** Attn. Rick Blunden, P.O. Box 1499, Sacramento 95807, tel. (916) 322-9015. Ask here, too, about the two district cycling guides available for Northern California—and request a

copy of the California Highway Patrol's cycling safety booklet. **Bikecentennial,** P.O. Box 8308, Missoula, MT 59807, tel. (406) 721-1776, is a nonprofit national organization that researches long-distance bike routes and organizes tours for members. Their maps, guidebooks, route suggestions, and Cyclist's Yellow Pages can be helpful.

By Bus
Most destinations in the northstate are reachable by bus, either by major carrier or in various combinations of national and local bus lines. (And if you can't get exactly where you want to go by bus, you can usually get close.)

Greyhound/Trailways is the universal bus service. Obtain a current U.S. route map by mail (see below), but check with local Greyhound offices (listed elsewhere in this guide) for more detailed, localized route information and for information about Reno-Lake Tahoe "casino service" and other local specials. Greyhound offers discounts for senior adults and disabled travelers, and children under age 12 ride free when accompanied by a fare-paying adult (one child per adult, half-fare for additional children). The **Ameripass** offers unlimited travel on both Greyhound and Trailways for various periods of time (but is usually more economical for long-distance trips with few stopovers). For international travelers, inquire about the **International Ameripass.** For more information, contact: Greyhound Lines, Inc., Customer Service, 901 Main St., Dallas, TX 75202, tel. (214) 744-6500.

By Train
An unusually enjoyable way to travel the length of California and the West Coast, or to head west over the Sierra Nevada or across the great desert, is by train. In recent years, service has expanded greatly. For **Amtrak** train travel routes (including some jogs between cities in California actually by Amtrak bus), current price information, and reservations, contact a travel agent or call Amtrak toll free at (800) USA RAIL (872-7245). For the hearing impaired, Amtrak's toll-free TTY number is (800) 523-6590 or 91; in Pennsylvania only, (800) 562-6960. A current "California Amtrak Timetable" is usually available through the state Office of Tourism (see "General Information," above).

A good deal for international travelers (though the U.S. rail system is much more limited than most nations') is the Amtrak **USA Rail Pass,** similar to the Eurailpass and valid anywhere in the U.S., though the two-week **Western Regional Rail Pass** is generally a better bargain for those traveling only in the West. Purchase these passes outside the U.S. or through U.S. travel agents (passport required), or contact: Amtrak International Sales, 400 N. Capitol St. NW, Washington, D.C. 20001. Domestic travelers, inquire about the **All-Aboard America** discount fare schedule, as well as children's, active military's, veterans', seniors', and disabled travelers' discounts.

Most other train travel in California is primarily a tourist diversion, but one enjoyable exception is the *Northcoast Daylight* run from Willits to Eureka (see "The North Coast").

By Automobile

This being California, almost everyone gets around by car. The one notable exception is San Francisco, where it's quite possible to live, work, and see the sights on public transit. (Many San Franciscans don't even own cars, and if they do, may roll them out of the garage only on weekends.) Urban freeway driving in California, due to congestion and Californians' no-nonsense get-on-with-it driving styles, can inspire panic even in native drivers. If this is a problem, plan your trip to skirt the worst congestion—by taking back roads and older highways and by trying neighborhood routes (but only if you know something about the neighborhoods).

A good investment for anyone traveling for any length of time in California is a membership in the American Automobile Association (see "Services and Information" above) since—among many other benefits—a AAA card entitles the bearer to no-cost emergency roadside service, including five gallons of free gas or towing, if necessary. To check on current road conditions before setting out, call Caltrans toll free at (800) 427-ROAD.

Though every municipality has its own peculiar laws about everything from parking to skateboarding or roller skating on sidewalks, there are basic rules everyone is expected to know and follow—especially drivers. Get a complete set of regulations from the state motor vehicles department, which has an office in all major cities and many medium-sized ones (or write: **California Dept. of Motor Vehicles,** 2415 1st Ave., Sacramento 95818). Foreign visitors planning to drive should obtain an International Driver's License before leaving (they're not available here); licensed U.S. drivers from other states can legally drive in California for 30 consecutive days without having to obtain a California driver's license.

Among driving rules, the most basic is observing the posted speed limit. Though many

This being California, almost everyone gets around by car.

CALIFORNIA DEPARTMENT OF PARKS & RECREATION

CALIFORNIA ON WHEELS

California's public officials, at least in urban areas, continue to make every effort to offer viable alternatives to automobile travel, but Golden State residents and their cars are almost inseparable. Part of the Western myth, after all, is the freedom to move, to go anywhere at the drop of a hat. Given the state's vast size and the great distances between destinations—and despite widespread awareness about the evils of air pollution, global warming, and excess energy consumption—California's love affair with wheels is a basic fact of life.

So, what's a visitor to do?

Those who arrive by air and who prefer to travel by public transportation can reach most areas of California—with careful advance planning—by train and/or by bus. (See relevant regional chapters for specific information.) Travelers can also tour by bicycle, an option most feasible for the very fit and flexible, requiring conscientious back-roads route mapping and careful planning.

Most people who arrive without their own wheels, however, soon choose to rent some, either a car or, for longer trips to more obscure destinations, a recreational vehicle.

All major national car rental agencies are well represented in San Francisco, where most Northern California visitors first arrive, both at the airport and downtown. (For specifics, see "Just the Facts" in the San Francisco chapter, as well as "By Automobile" under this chapter's Transport section.) Lower-cost statewide and local agencies are also abundant and usually reliable. Consult the telephone book yellow pages for a complete listing; if in doubt about a given company, contact local visitor bureaus and chambers of commerce. And if you'll be arriving during the holidays or at other peak travel times, it's prudent to reserve rental vehicles well in advance.

Flat rate (daily or weekly) and unlimited mileage rentals are generally the best deal, since a California-style day trip can easily pass the 300-mile mark. If planning a trip or trips to outlying areas, it is usually much less expensive to start from—and return your rental vehicle to—agencies located in major urban areas. Renting a car in a small, remote city with the idea of ending your adventure back in San Francisco or Oakland may make perfect sense; but the associated "drop-off fee"—essentially an inconvenience penalty imposed by the rental company, concerned about getting that car back in their shop—can range to $500 and more, a definite drawback.

Recreational vehicles (RVs), including four-wheel drives and pickup trucks with campers, are substantially more expensive to rent than cars, and are usually available only through specialized agencies and RV sales dealers.

Compared to European rates, California vehicle rentals are expensive. Once comfortable with one's vehicle and familiar with California driving customs and laws, a special bonus for European and other international travelers is the price of gasoline—still remarkably inexpensive in the U.S., averaging $1.20 per gallon. Though this fact of life may soon change, since higher taxes on energy resouces may be included in President Bill Clinton's new national economic policy, for the time being at least travel by car is cheaper here (at least in terms of personal costs) than almost anywhere else in the world.

California drivers ignore any and all speed limits, it's at their own peril should the California Highway Patrol be anywhere in the vicinity. The statewide speed limit for open highway driving is 55 miles per hour, though certain freeway sections are posted for 65 mph; speed limits for cities and residential neighborhoods are substantially slower. Another avoidable traffic ticket: indulging in what is colloquially known as the "California stop," slowing down then rolling right through stop signs without first making a complete stop.

Once arrived at your destination, pay attention to parking notices and tow-away warnings, also the color of the curb: red means no parking under any circumstances; yellow means limited stops only (usually for freight delivery); green means very limited parking; and blue means parking for the disabled only. In San Francisco (the hilly city) and similar locales, always turn your front wheels into the curb (to keep your car from becoming a rollaway runaway) and set the emergency brake.

Driving while under the influence of alcohol or drugs is a very serious offense in California—aside from being a danger to one's own health and safety, not to mention those of innocent fellow drivers. Don't drink (or drug) and drive.

Renting a car in California usually won't come cheap, though bargains are sometimes available through small local agencies. The car rental agencies serving most major cities (and airports) include: **Alamo,** toll-free tel. (800) 327-9633; **Avis,** tel. (800) 331-1212; **Budget,** tel. (800) 527-0700; **Dollar,** tel. (800) 800-4000; **Hertz,** tel. (800) 654-3131; **National,** tel. (800) 328-4567; and **Thrifty,** tel. (800) 367-2277.

By Airplane

Airfares change and bargains come and go so quickly in competitive California that the best way to keep abreast of the situation is through a travel agent. Another good information source on domestic and international flight fares: the travel advertisements in the weekend travel sections of major urban newspapers. Super Saver fares (booked well in advance) can save fliers up to 30-70% and more. Peak travel times in and out of California being the summer months and the midwinter holiday season, book flights well in advance for June-August and December travel. The best bargains in airfares are usually available from January to early May.

Bargain airfares are often available for international travelers, especially in autumn and spring. Charter flights are also good bargains, the only disadvantage usually being inflexible departure and return-flight dates. Most flights from Europe to the U.S. arrive in New York; from there, other transcontinental travel options are available. Reduced-fare flights on major airlines from Europe abound.

BOB RACE

SAN FRANCISCO
LIFE ON THE EDGE

"When I was a child growing up in Salinas we called San Francisco 'The City,'" California native John Steinbeck once observed. "Of course it was the only city we knew but I still think of it as The City as does everyone else who has ever associated with it."

San Francisco is The City, a distinction it wears with detached certitude. San Francisco has been The City since the days of the gold rush, when the world rushed in through the Golden Gate in a frenzied pursuit of both actual and alchemical riches. It remained The City forever after: when San Francisco started, however reluctantly, to conceive of itself as a civilized place; when San Francisco fell down and incinerated itself in the great earthquake of 1906; when San Francisco flew up from its ashes, fully fledged, after reinventing itself; and when San Francisco set about reinventing almost everything else with its rolling social revolutions. Among those the world noticed this century, the Beatniks or "Beats" of the 1940s and '50s publicly shook the suburbs of American complacency, but the 1960s and San Francisco's Summer of Love caused the strongest social quake, part of the chaos of new consciousness that quickly changed the shape of everything.

Among its many attributes, perhaps most striking is The City's ability, still, to be all things to all people—and to simultaneously contradict itself and its own truths. San Francisco is a point of beginning. Depending upon where one starts, it is also the ultimate place to arrive. San Francisco is a comedy. And San Francisco is a tragedy.

As writer Richard Rodriquez observes: "San Francisco has taken some heightened pleasure from the circus of final things. . . . San Francisco can support both comic and tragic conclusions because the city is geographically *in extremis,* a metaphor for the farthest flung possibility, a metaphor for the end of the line." But even that depends upon point of view. As Rodriquez also points out, "To speak of San Francisco as land's end is to read the map from one direction only—as Europeans would read or as the East Coast has always read it." To the people living on these hills before California's colonialization, before the gold rush, even before there was a

San Francisco, the land they lived on represented the center, surrounded on three sides by water. To Mexicans extending their territorial reach, it was north. To Russian fur hunters escaping the frigid shores of Alaska, it was south. And to its many generations of Asian immigrants, surely San Francisco represented the Far East.

The precise place The City occupies in the world's imagination is irrelevant to compass points. If San Francisco is anywhere specific, it is certainly at the edge: the cutting edge of cultural combinations, the gilt edge of international commerce, the razor's edge of raw reality. And life on the edge is rarely boring.

THE LAND: NATURAL SAN FRANCISCO

Imagine San Francisco before its bridges were built: a captive city, stranded on an unstable, stubbed toe of a peninsula, one by turns twitching under the storm-driven assault of wind and water, then chilled by bone-cold fog.

The city and county of San Francisco—the two are one, duality in unity—sit on their own appendage of California earth, a political conglomeration totaling 46.4 square miles. Creating San Francisco's western edge is the Pacific Ocean, its waters cooled by strong Alaskan currents, its rough offshore rocks offering treachery to unwary sea travelers. On its eastern edge is San Francisco Bay, one of the world's most impressive natural harbors, with deep protected waters and 496 square miles of surface area. (As vast as it is, these days the bay is only 75% of its pre-gold rush size, since its shoreline has been filled in and extended to create more land.) Connecting the two sides, and creating San Francisco's rough-and-tumble northern edge, is the three-mile-long strait known as the Golden Gate. Straddled by the world-renowned Golden Gate Bridge, this mile-wide river of sea water cuts the widest gap in the rounded Coast Ranges for a thousand miles, yet is so small that its landforms almost hide the bay that balloons inland.

Spaniards named what is now considered San Francisco Las Lomitas, or "Little Hills," for the landscape's most notable feature. Perhaps to create a romantic comparison with Rome,

popular local mythology holds that The City was built on seven hills—Lone Mountain, Mt. Davidson, Nob Hill, Russian Hill, Telegraph Hill, and the two Twin Peaks, none higher than 1,000 feet in elevation. There are actually more than 40 hills in San Francisco, all part and parcel of California's Coast Ranges, which run north and south along the state's coastline, sheltering inland valleys from the fog and winds that regularly visit San Francisco.

City On A Fault Line

The City has been shaped as much by natural forces as by historical happenstance. Its most spectacular event involved both. More than any other occurrence, San Francisco's 1906 earthquake—estimated now to have registered 8.25 on the Richter scale—woke up residents, and the world, to the fact that The City was built on very shaky ground. California's famous, 650-mile-long San Andreas Fault, as it is now known, slips just seaward of San Francisco. In the jargon of tectonic plate theory, The City sits on the North American Plate, a huge slab of earth floating on the planet's molten core, along the San Andreas earthquake fault line. Just west is the Pacific Plate. When earth-shaking pressure builds, sooner or later something has to give. In San Francisco, as elsewhere in California, a rumble and a roar and split-second motion announces an earthquake—and the fact that an interlocking section of the earth's crust has separated, a movement that may or may not be visible on the earth's surface. San Francisco's most recent major quake, on October 17, 1989, was a reminder that The City's earthquake history is far from a finished chapter.

City In A Fog

San Francisco's second-most-famous physical feature is its weather—mild and Mediterranean but with quite perverse fog patterns, especially surprising to first-time summer visitors. When people expect sunny skies and warm temperatures, San Francisco offers instead gray and white mists, moist clouds seemingly filled with knife-sharp points of ice when driven by the wind.

Poets traditionally call forth all nine muses to honor the mysteries of fog. Scientists are much more succinct. Summer heat in California's central valley regions creates a low-pressure weath-

SAN FRANCISCO

er system, while cooler ocean temperatures create higher atmospheric pressure. Moving toward equilibrium, the cool and moist coastal air is drawn inland through the "mouth" of the Golden Gate and over adjacent hills, like a behemoth's belly breath. Then, as the land cools, the mists evaporate. So even during the peak fog months of July and August, wool-coat weather dissipates by midafternoon—only to roll back in shortly after sundown. Due to microclimates created by hills, certain San Francisco neighborhoods—like the Mission District, Noe Valley,

and Potrero Hill—may be quite sunny and warm when the rest of the city still shivers in the fog.

San Francisco Weather
The coast's strong high-pressure system tends to moderate San Francisco weather year-round: expect average daytime temperatures of 54-65° F in summer, 48-59° F in winter. (Usually reliable is the adage that for every 10 miles you travel inland from the city, temperatures will increase by 10 degrees.) September and October are the warmest months, with balmy days near

70 degrees. The local weather pattern also prevents major rain storms from May through October. Despite the water-rich imagery associated with the San Francisco Bay Area, the region is actually semiarid, with annual (non-drought) rainfall averaging 19-20 inches. Snow is a very rare phenomenon in the region.

HISTORY AND CULTURE:
HUMAN SAN FRANCISCO

At its most basic, the recorded history of San Francisco is a story of conquest and curiosity. The region's original inhabitants, however, were generally content with the abundant riches the land provided quite naturally. Probably the descendants of mysterious nomads who first crossed the Bering Strait from Asia to the North American continent some 20,000 or more years ago, California's native peoples were culturally distinct. The language groups—"tribes" doesn't serve to describe California Indians—living north of the Golden Gate were classified by anthropologists as the Coast Wiwok people. Though the barren and desolate site of San Francisco attracted few residents, the dominant native population throughout the greater Bay Area was called Costanoan ("coast people") or Ohlone by the Spanish, though the people called themselves Ramaytush.

In precolonial days, the region was the most densely populated on the continent north of Mexico, with a population of 10,000 people living in 30 or more permanent villages. Though each village considered itself unique, separated from others by customs and local dialect, the Ohlone intermarried and traded with other tribes and shared many cultural characteristics. Though dependent on shellfish as a dietary staple, the Ohlone also migrated inland in summer and fall to hunt game, fish, and collect acorns, which were valued throughout California for making bread and mush. Thousands of years of undisturbed cultural success created a gentle, gracious, unwarlike society—a culture which quickly passed away with the arrival of California's explorers and colonizers.

Early Explorations
Discoveries of dusty manuscripts, ancient stone anchors, and old coins now suggest that Chinese ships were the first foreign vessels to explore California's coastline, arriving centuries before Columbus bumbled into the new world. The Portuguese explorer Cabrillo (Cabrilho) was the coast's first official surveyor, though on his 1542 voyage he failed to discover the Golden Gate and the spectacular bay behind it. In 1579 the English privateer Sir Francis Drake took the first foreign step onto California soil, quite possibly near San Francisco, and claimed the land for Queen Elizabeth I. (Where exactly Drake landed is a subject of ongoing controversy and confusion. For a further discussion, see "Point Reyes National Seashore" in the following chapter.) And even Drake failed to see the Golden Gate and its precious natural harbor, perhaps due to the subtle subterfuge of landforms and fog.

The Arrival Of Spain,
Mexico, Russia, And America
Some 200 years after Drake, the Spanish arrived—a scouting party led by Gaspar de Portola, searching for Monterey Bay farther south, missed its mark altogether and instead discovered San Francisco Bay in 1769. After Monterey was secured, Captain Juan Bautista de Anza was assigned the task of colonizing this new territorial prize. With 35 families plus a lieutenant and a Franciscan priest, de Anza set out on the grueling trip from Sonora, Mexico, arriving on the peninsula's tip on June 27, 1776, just one week before the American revolution. The first order of business was establishing a military fortress, the Presidio, at the present site of Fort Mason. And the second was establishing a church and mission outpost, about one mile south, on the shores of a small lake or lagoon named in honor of Nuestra Senora de los Dolores (Our Lady of Sorrows). Though the mission church was dedicated to Saint Francis of Assisi, it became known as Mission Dolores—and "San Francisco" was attached to the spectacular bay and the eventual city that grew up on its shores.

Though Spain, then Mexico, officially secured the California territory, underscoring ownership by means of vast government land grants to retired military and civilian families, the colonial claim was somewhat tenuous. By the 1830s, Americans were already the predominant residents of the settlement at Yerba Buena Cove (at the foot of what is now Telegraph Hill), the earliest version of San Francisco. Yerba Buena was first a trading post, established by William Anthony Richardson, an Englishman who married the Presidio commandant's daughter. In the early 1800s, Russian fur hunters established themselves just north along the coast, at the settlement of Fort Ross. They sailed south to trade. English, French, and American trading ships were also regular visitors—with the Yankees arriving in ever greater numbers, even by land, by the 1840s, spurred on by the nation's expansionist mood and the political dogma of "Manifest Destiny!" The official annexation of the California territory to the United States, when it came in mid-1846, was almost anticlimactic. After the 13-man force at the Presidio surrendered peacefully to the Americans, the citizens quickly changed the name of Yerba Buena to that of the bay, San Francisco—a shrewd business move, intended to attract still more trade.

The World Rushes In: The Gold Rush

Events of early 1948 made the name change all but irrelevant. San Francisco could hardly help attracting more business, and more businesses of every stripe, once word arrived that gold had been discovered on the American River in the foothills east of Sacramento. Before the gold rush, San Francisco was a sleepy port town with a population of 800, but within months it swelled to a city of nearly 25,000, as gold seekers arrived by the shipload from all over the globe. Those who arrived early and lit out for the gold fields in 1848 had the best opportunity to harvest California gold. Most of the fortune hunters, however, arrived in '49, thus the term "forty-niners" to describe this phenomenal human migration. (For more on the gold rush, see "The Gold Country" chapter.)

As cosmopolitan as the overnight city of San Francisco was, with a surprisingly well-educated, liberal, and (not so surprisingly) young population, it was hardly civilized. By 1849 the ratio of men to women was about ten to one, and saloons, gambling halls, and the notorious redlight district—known as the Barbary Coast—were the social mainstays of this rootless, risk-taking population. Though early San Francisco was primarily a tent city, fire was a constant scourge. The city started to build itself then burned to the ground six times by 1852, when

San Francisco was recognized as the fourth-largest port of entry in the United States. And though eccentricty and bad behavior were widely tolerated, unrestrained gang crime and murder became so commonplace that businessmen formed Committees of Vigilance to create some semblance of social order—by taking the law into their own hands and jailing, hanging, and running undesirables out of town.

More Barbarians And Big Spenders

By the late 1850s, the sources for most of California's surface gold had been picked clean. Ongoing harvesting of the state's most precious metal had become a corporate affair, an economic change made possible by the development of new technologies. The days of individualistic gold fever had subsided, and fortune hunters who remained in California turned their efforts to more long-lasting development of wealth, often in agriculture and business.

The city, though temporarily slowed by the economic depression that arrived with the end of the gold rush, was the most businesslike of them all. A recognizable city and a major financial center, no sooner had San Francisco calmed down and turned its attentions to nurturing civic pride than another boom arrived—this time silver, discovered in the Nevada territory's Comstock Lode, a crop requiring capital, heavy equipment, and organized mining technology. This was a strictly corporate raid on the earth's riches, with San Francisco and its bankers, businesses, and citizenry the main beneficiaries. Led by the silver rush "Bonanza Kings," the city's nouveau riche built themselves a residential empire atop Nob Hill and set about creating more cultured institutions.

Confident California, led by San Francisco, believed the future held nothing but greater growth, greater wealth. That was certainly the case for the "Big Four," Sacramento businessmen who financed Theodore Judah's dream of a transcontinental railroad, a development almost everyone believed would lead to an extended boom in the state's economy. (For more on the state's railroading history, see "Sacramento and Vicinity.") Soon at home atop Nob Hill with the city's other nabobs, Charles Crocker, Mark Hopkins, Collis Huntington, and Leland Stanford also set out to establish some political machinery—the Southern

Pacific Railway—to generate power and influence to match their wealth.

Bad Times And Bigotry

But the transcontinental railroad did little to help California, or San Francisco, at least initially. As naysayers had predicted, the ease of shipping goods by rail all but destroyed California's neophyte industrial base, since the state was soon glutted with lower-cost manufactured goods from the East Coast. A drought in 1869, a major setback for agricultural production, and an 1871 stock market crash made matters that much worse.

Legions of the unemployed, which included terminated railroad workers all over the West, rose up in rage throughout the 1870s and 1880s—attacking not those who had enriched themselves at the expense of the general populace but "outsiders," specifically the Chinese who had labored long and hard at many a thankless task since the days of the gold rush. Mob violence and the torching of businesses and entire Chinese communities, in San Francisco and elsewhere, wasn't enough to satisfy such open racist hatred. Politicians too bowed to anti-Chinese sentiment, passing a series of discriminatory laws that forbade the Chinese from owning land, voting, and testifying in court, and levied a special tax against Chinese shrimp fishermen.

A near-final bigoted blow was the federal government's 1882 Oriental Exclusion Act, which essentially ended legal Asian immigration until it was repealed during World War II. (For more information, see also "Angel Island State Park" in the following chapter.) San Francisco's Chinese community, for the most part working men denied the opportunity to reunite with their families, was further damaged by the Geary Act of 1892, which declared that all Chinese had to carry proper identification or face deportation. The failure of American society to support traditional Chinese culture led to rampant crime, gambling, and prostitution—acceptable diversions of the day for bachelors—and a lawless reign of terror by competing tongs who fought to control the profits. Only the gradual Americanization of the Chinese, which minimized tong influence, and the disastrous events during the spring of 1906 could change the reality of Chinatown. But the year 1906 changed everything in San Francisco.

The World Ends: Earthquake And Fire

By the early 1900s, San Francisco had entered its "gilded age," a complacent period when the city was busy enjoying its new cosmopolitan status. San Francisco had become the largest and finest city west of Chicago. The rich happily compounded their wealth in downtown highrises and at home on Nob Hill and in other resplendent neighborhoods. The expanding middle class built rows of new Victorian homes, "painted ladies" that writer Tom Wolfe would later call "those endless staggers of bay windows," on hills far removed from the low life of the Barbary Coast, Chinatown, and the newest red-light district, the Tenderloin. But the working classes still smoldered in squalid tenements south of Market Street. Corruption ruled, politically, during the heyday of the "paint eaters"—politicians so greedy they'd even eat the paint off buildings. The cynical reporter and writer Ambrose Bierce, sniffing at the status quo, called San Francisco the "moral penal colony of the world." But the city's famous graft trials, a public political circus which resulted in 3,000 indictments but shockingly little jail time, came later.

Whatever was going on in the city, legal and otherwise, came to an abrupt halt on the morning of April 18, 1906, when a massive earthquake hit. Now estimated to have registered 8.25 on the Richter scale, the quake created huge fissures in the ground, broke water and gas mains all over the city, and caused chimneys and other unstable construction to come tumbling down. The better neighborhoods, including the city's Victorian row houses, suffered little damage. Downtown, however, was devastated. City Hall, a shoddy construction job allowed by scamming politicians and their contractor cohorts, crumbled into nothing. Though a central hospital also fell, burying doctors, nurses, and patients alike, the overall death toll from the earthquake itself was fairly small. Sadly for San Francisco, one of the fatalities was the city fire chief, whose foresight might have prevented the conflagration soon to follow.

More than 50 fires started that morning alone, racing through the low-rent neighborhoods south of Market then into downtown, raging out of control. The flames were unchecked for four days, burning through downtown, parts of the Mission District, and also demolishing Chinatown, North Beach, Nob Hill, Telegraph Hill, and Russian

WELLS FARGO BANK HISTORY ROOM

The scene at 18th and Howard streets after the 1906 earthquake: not everything was lost to fire.

Hill. The mansions along the eastern edge of Van Ness were dynamited to create an impromptu firebreak, finally stopping the firestorm.

When it was all over, the official tally of dead or missing stood at 674, though more recent research suggests the death toll was more than 3,000, since the Chinese weren't counted. The entire city center was destroyed, along with three-fourths of the city's businesses and residences. With half of its 450,000 population now homeless, San Francisco was a tent city once again. But it was an optimistic tent city, bolstered by relief and rebuilding funds sent from around the world. As reconstruction began, San Francisco also set out to clean house politically.

Modern Times

By 1912, with San Francisco more or less back on its feet, Mayor James "Sunny Jim" Rolph, who always sported a fresh flower in his lapel, seemed to symbolize the city's new era. Rolph presided over the construction of some of San Francisco's finest public statements about itself. These included the new city hall and Civic Center, of course, but also the 1915 world's fair and the Panama Pacific International Exposition, a spectacular 600-acre temporary city designed by Bernard Maybeck to reflect the "mortality of grandeur and the vanity of human wishes." Though the exposition was intended to celebrate the opening of the Panama Canal, it was San Francisco's grand announcement to the world that it had not only survived but thrived in

the aftermath of its earlier earthquake and fire.

During the Great Depression, San Francisco continued to defy the commonplace, dancing at the edge of unreal expectations. Two seemingly impossible spans, the Golden Gate Bridge and the Bay Bridge, were built in the 1930s. San Francisco also built the world's largest man-made island, Treasure Island, which hosted the Golden Gate International Exposition in 1939 before becoming a U.S. Navy facility.

No matter how spectacular its statements to the world, San Francisco had trouble at home. The 1929 stock market crash and the onset of the Depression reignited long-simmering labor strife, especially in the city's port. Four longshoremen competed for every available job along the waterfront, and members of the company-controlled Longshoremen's Association demanded kickbacks for jobs that were offered. Harry Bridges reorganized the International Longshoremen's Association, and backed by the Teamsters Union, his pro-union strike successfully closed down the waterfront. On "Bloody Thursday," July 5, 1934, 800 strikers battled with National Guard troops called in to quell a riot started by union busters. Two men were shot and killed by police, another 100 injured; the subsequent all-city strike, the largest general strike in U.S. history, ultimately involved most city businesses as well as the waterfront unions. More so than elsewhere on the West Coast, labor unions are still strong in San Francisco.

Other social and philosophical revolutions, for iconoclasts and oddballs alike, either got

WALKING ON WATER ACROSS THAT GOLDEN GATE

SAN JOSE CONVENTION & VISITORS BUREAU

the Golden Gate Bridge

Nothing is as San Francisco as the city's astounding **Golden Gate Bridge,** a bright, red-orange fairy pathway up into the fog, a double-necked lyre plucked by the wind to send its surreal song spiraling skyward. The bridge stands today as testimony to the vision of political madmen and poets, almost always the progenitors of major achievements. San Francisco's own **Emperor Norton**—a gold rush-era British merchant originally known as Joshua A. Norton, who went bankrupt in the land of instant wealth but soon reinvented himself as "Norton I, Emperor of the United States and Protector of Mexico"—was the first lunatic to suggest that the vast, turbulent, and troublesome waters of the Golden Gate could be spanned by a bridge. The poet and engineer **Joseph Baermann Strauss,** a titan of a man barely five feet tall, seconded the insanity, and in 1917 he left Chicago for San Francisco, plans and models in hand, to start the 13-year lobbying campaign.

All practical doubts aside, San Francisco at large was aghast at the idea of defacing the natural majesty of the Golden Gate with a manmade monument; over 2,000 lawsuits were filed in an effort to stop bridge construction. California's love of progress won out in the end, however, and construction of the graceful bridge, designed by architect Irwin F. Morrow, began in 1933. As Strauss himself remarked later: "It took two decades and 200 million words to convince the people that the bridge was feasible;

then only four years and $35 million to put the concrete and steel together."

Building the Golden Gate Bridge was no simple task, rather, an accomplishment akin to a magical feat. Some 80,000 miles of wire were spun into the bridge's suspension cables, a sufficient length to encircle the earth (at the equator) three times, and enough concrete to create a very wide sidewalk between the country's West and East coasts was poured into the anchoring piers. Sinking the southern support pier offshore was a particular challenge, with 60-mile-an-hour tidal surges and 15-foot swells at times threatening to upend the (seasick) workers' floating trestle. Once the art-deco towers were in place, the *real* fun began—those acrobats in overalls, most earning less than $1 an hour, working in empty space to span the gap. Safety was a serious issue with Strauss and his assistant Clifford Paine. Due to their diligence, 19 men fell, but landed in safety nets instead of in the morgue, earning them honorary membership in the "Halfway to Hell Club." But just weeks before construction was completed, a scaffolding collapsed, its jagged edges tearing through the safety net and taking nine men down with it.

When the Golden Gate Bridge was finished in 1937, the world was astonished. Some 200,000 people walked across the virgin roadbed that day, just to introduce themselves to this gracious steel wonder. At that time, the bridge was the world's longest and tallest suspension structure—with a single-span, between-towers distance of 4,200 feet—and boasted the highest highrises west of New York's Empire State Building. Its total length was 1.7 miles, and its 746-foot-tall towers were equivalent in total height to 65-story buildings. Even now the bridge's grace is much more than aesthetic. As a suspension bridge, the Golden Gate moves with the action of the immediate neighborhood. It has rarely been closed for reasons of safety or necessary repairs, though it *was* closed, in 1960, so French President Charles de Gaulle could make a solo crossing. Even in treacherous winds, the bridge can safely sway as much as 28 feet in either direction, though standing on a slightly swinging bridge of such monstrous dimensions is an indescribably odd sensation.

Perhaps the best thing about the Golden Gate Bridge, even after all these years, is that people can still enjoy it, up close and very personally. Though the bridge toll is $3 per car (heading south), for pedestrians it's a free trip either way. The hike is ambitious, about two miles one-way. For those who don't suffer from vertigo, this is an inspiring and invigorating experience, as close to walking on water as most of us will ever get. (But it's not necessarily a life-enhancing experience for the seriously depressed or suicidal. The lure of the leap has proved too tempting for over 900 people.) Parking is available at either end of the bridge.

And though the Golden Gate Bridge is the Bay Area's most royal span, credit for San Francisco's propulsion into the modern world of commerce and crazy traffic actually goes to the **Bay Bridge** spanning San Francisco Bay between downtown San Francisco and Oakland/Berkeley. Completed in 1936, and built atop piers sunk into the deepest deeps ever bridged, the Bay Bridge cost $80 million to complete, at that time the most expensive structure ever built. And in recent history, the Bay Bridge has made front-page and nightly news headlines. The whole world watched in horror when part of the bridge collapsed amid the torqued tensions of the 1989 earthquake, a rush-hour event. There were deaths and injuries, but fewer casualties than if the quake had come during peak commuter traffic. Despite the quake, the bridge still remained structurally sound, and the more critically necessary repairs have been made.

their start in San Francisco or received abundant support once arrived here. First came the Beatniks or "Beats" in the 1950s, poets, freethinkers, and jazz aficionados rebelling against the suburbanization of the American mind. The Beats were followed in short order by the 1960s, the Summer of Love, psychedelics, and rock groups like the still-living Grateful Dead. More substantial, in the '60s, the Free Speech Movement heated up across the bay in Berkeley, not to mention anti-Vietnam War protests and the rise of the Black Panther Party. San Francisco has managed to make its place at, or near, the forefront of almost every change in social awareness since, from women's rights to gay pride. And in the 1980s, San Franciscans went all out for baby boomer consumerism; young urban professionals have been setting the style for quite some time. But there are other styles, other trends. You name it, San Francisco probably has it.

San Francisco As Destination

Still shaking from its 1989 encounter with local earthquake faults, in 1990 San Francisco was declared the number one United States *and* international travel destination in *Condé Nast Traveler*'s annual Top 10 reader's survey. Since tourism is the city's top industry these days, that reprieve from public fears must come as a big relief. All earthquake anxieties aside, it's not difficult to understand San Francisco's appeal. The city offers almost everything, from striking scenery and sophisticated shopping to fine hotels and restaurants. Even budget travelers can arrive, and stay, with exceptional ease, at least compared to elsewhere in California. And the city's multiethnic cultural, artistic, and entertainment attractions are among its most undervalued treasures.

Downtown San Francisco, which serves as the city's corporate and financial headquarters as well as tourist central, is a world of skyscraping office towers and imposed isolation. Surely it's no accident that the city's homeless live here. But the most authentic spirits of San Francisco live elsewhere, out in the neighborhoods, where in recent years the people have seceded from the city as The City. So do get out—out past the panhandlers and the polished glass buildings, past the pretty shops and the prettier shoppers—to see San Francisco.

Even out in the neighborhoods, though, San Franciscans have started to suspect that things aren't quite as wonderful as they once were. Their beloved city suffers from the same problems as other major cities, from staggering demands on urban services and shrinking revenues to worsening traffic problems, astronomical housing costs, and business flight.

But at last report—and despite some some notable historical lapses—the city's deepest traditions, liberalism and tolerance, are still going strong. And freedom is still the city's unofficial rallying cry.

THE LAY OF THE LAND

In other times, San Francisco neighborhoods and districts had such distinct ethnic and cultural or functional identities that they served as separate cities within a city. It wasn't uncommon for people to be born and grow up, to work, to raise families, and to die in their own insular neighborhoods, absolutely unfamiliar with the rest of San Francisco.

For the most part, those days are long past. Since its inception the city has transformed itself, beginning as a sleepy mission town then a lawless gold-rush capital that gradually gained respectability and recognition as the West Coast's most sophisticated cultural and trade center. The process continues. The city's neighborhoods continue to reinvent themselves, and California's accelerated economic and social mobility also erase old boundaries. Just where one part of town ends and another begins is a favorite San Francisco topic of disagreement.

The following guide to the local lay of the land introduces the unusual diversity of San Francisco, including the sights and some unusual or unusually entertaining features. For more information about major attractions, see "Delights And Diversions" below. For complete practical information, including how to get around town and where to stay and eat, see the concluding sections of this chapter.

DOWNTOWN AND VICINITY

In San Francisco, "downtown" is a general reference to the city's hustle-bustle heart. Knowing just where it starts and ends is largely irrelevant, so long as you understand that it includes **Union Square,** much of **Market Street,** and the **Civic Center government and arts buildings. The Financial District** and the **Waterfront** are also included. Six or seven blocks directly west of the Civic Center is the **Alamo Square Historic District,** one among other enclaves of gentrified Victorian neighborhoods in the otherwise down-and-out **Western Addition,** which also includes **Japantown.** Though purists will no doubt quibble, for reasons of proximity these are included with downtown. And while more "uptown" parts of the **South of Market Area** (SoMa) are essentially downtown too, as are **Nob Hill** and **Chinatown,** those areas are covered in more depth elsewhere below.

Around Union Square

Named after rallies supporting Union forces that were held here during the Civil War (California eventually spurned the Confederacy), San Francisco's Union Square is parking central for downtown shoppers, since the square also serves as the roof of the multilevel parking garage directly below. (A better bargain, though, is the Sutter Street Garage, 330 Sutter.) The landmark **Westin St. Francis Hotel** flanks Union Square on the west (see "Luxury Hotels" under "Accommodations: Staying in Style," below), the bar a time-honored retreat from nearby major stores like **Saks Fifth Avenue, Neiman-Marcus, I. Magnin,** and **Macy's,** as is the Rotunda at Neiman-Marcus. A relatively new thrill for shoppers is the eight-story circular escalator ride up to **Nordstrom** and other stores at the **San Francisco Centre** at 5th and Market, completed in

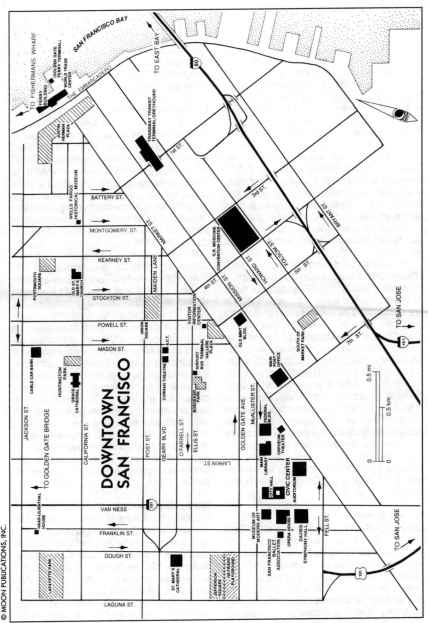

© MOON PUBLICATIONS, INC.

the late 1980s with the hope of attracting suburbanites and squeezing out the homeless.

The neighborhood offers still more shopping. The rectangle formed by Sutter, Kearny, Geary, and Stockton to the east of Union Square—bisected by Post and Grant—offers an unabashed selection of astounding and expensive stores, from **Cartier, Dunhill,** and **Tiffany** to **Bullock & Jones** and **Wilkes Bashford.** Increasingly prominent are the area's (expensive) art galleries. But there's nothing quite like **Gumps** at 250 Post, the elegant specialist in one-of-a-kind and rare wares, where even the furniture is art. Even if you're just looking, don't miss **F.A.O. Schwartz** at Stockton and O'Farrell, full of adult-priced toys. **Kinderzimmer** at 250 Sutter is a wonderland of imported unusual toys, from stuffed animals and dolls to musical instruments. And—hungry or not—never miss a trip to the **Candy Jar,** the truffle-lover's Achilles' heel at 149 Grant.

Also take a stroll down traffic-free, two-block **Maiden Lane,** a one-time red-light district stretching between Stockton and Kearny, chock full of sidewalk cafes and shops. **Robinson's Pets** is one of the world's most elegant (and photogenic) pet stores, featured in Alfred Hitchcock's *The Birds.* (Pick up some doggie popcorn and other tempting treats.) Just across the way is the **Circle Gallery,** most ogled for its architecture. Designed in 1949 by Frank Lloyd Wright, the building with its spiral interior is an obvious prototype for his more famous Guggenheim Museum in New York. At the **Brooks Camera** shop on the corner of Kearny, head upstairs to the free **Joseph Dee Museum** to peek at the old camera collection, including the special Nixon memorial spy camera (a model used in the Watergate break-in). From Kearny, stroll north to Post then east a half block to the **Crocker Galleria** and still more shopping.

The Tenderloin

Stretching between Union Square and the Civic Center is **The Tenderloin,** definitely a poor choice for a casual stroll by tourists and other innocents. A down-and-out pocket of poverty pocked these days by the city signposts of human misery—drug dealing, prostitution, pornography, and violent crime—the densely populated Tenderloin earned its name around the turn of the century, when police assigned to patrol its mean streets received additional hazard pay. (The extra cash allowed them to dine on the choicest cuts of meat.) The Tenderloin's historic boundaries are Post, Market, Van Ness, and Powell. In reality, however, the city's designated theater district (with accompanying cafes and nightspots), many newly gentrified hotels, even the St. Francis Hotel and most Civic Center attractions fall within this no-man's land, which is especially a no-woman's land. More realistic, better-safe-than-sorry boundaries are Larkin, Mason, O'Farrell, and Market, with an extra caution also for some streets south of Market (especially 6th) as far as Howard. As a general rule, perimeters are safer than core areas, but since this is San Francisco's highest crime area, with rape, mugging, and other assaults at an all-time high, for tenderfeet no part of the Tenderloin is considered safe—even during daylight hours.

But the area has its beauty, too, often most apparent through the celebrations and ministries of the Reverend Cecil Williams and congregation at the renowned **Glide Memorial United Methodist Church** at 333 Ellis, tel. (415) 771-6300, which sponsors children's assistance and other community programs, from basic survival and AIDS care to its crack cocaine conference. And some neighborhoods are cleaning up considerably, the indirect influence of commercial redevelopment and large numbers of Asian immigrants, many from Cambodia, Laos, and Vietnam. The annual **Tet Festival** celebrates the Vietnamese New Year. The Tenderloin also supports a small but growing arts community. Ask local shopkeepers and restaurant or hotel personnel about the safety of specific destinations, if in doubt, and travel in groups when you do venture any distance into the Tenderloin.

Market Street And The Financial District

Basically, the Financial District features San Francisco's tallest, most phallic buildings, perhaps suggesting something profound about the psychology of the global capitalist thrust. When rolling into town on the river of traffic, via the Golden Gate Bridge or, especially, Oakland's Bay Bridge, this compact concentration of law offices, insurance buildings, investment companies, banks, brokerages, and high-brow businesses rises up from the sparkling waters like some fantastic illusion, the greenback-packed Emerald City of the West Coast. Even if wandering on foot and temporarily lost, to get back downtown one merely looks up and heads off toward the big buildings.

The actual boundaries of the Financial District, built upon what was once water, Yerba Buena Cove, are rather vague, dependent upon both personal opinion and that constant urban flux of form and function. In general the district includes the entire area from the north side of Market Street to the Montgomery Street corridor, north to the Jackson Square Historic District. Market Street is anchored near the bay by **Justin Herman Plaza** and its either-loved-or-hated **Vaillancourt Fountain,** said to be a parody of the now-demolished freeway it once faced. Above and behind the plaza is the astounding and Orwellian **Embarcadero Center** complex, the high-class heart of the Golden Gateway redevelopment project. Here is the somewhat surreal **Hyatt Regency Hotel,** noted for its 17-story indoor atrium and bizarre keyboard-like exterior, as well as the **Park Hyatt Hotel.** But the main focus is the center's four-part shopping complex, **Embarcadero One** through **Embarcadero Four,** between Clay and Sacramento. Inside, maps and information kiosks can help the disoriented.

For a hands-on lesson in the **World of Economics,** including the chance to pretend you're president of the U.S. or head of the Fed, stop by the lobby of the Federal Reserve Bank at 101 Market, weekdays 9-4:30, to play with the computer games and displays. The **World of Oil** in the Chevron USA Building, 555 Market (at 2nd), open weekdays 9-3:30, is a small museum with industry-oriented facts, including a computerized "Energy Learning Center." Also worth wandering through is the **American Indian Contemporary Arts Gallery** on the second floor at 685 Market, featuring authentic arts and crafts from many native U.S. cultures plus a gallery gift shop. **Robert Frost Plaza,** at the intersection of Market and California, is a reminder that New England's poet was a San Francisco homeboy.

Heading up California Street, stop at the **Bank of California** building at 400 California for a tour through its basement **Museum of the Money of the American West,** everything from gold nuggets and U.S. Mint mementos to dueling pistols. **Bank of America** at California and

Kearny and **Wells Fargo Bank** at 420 Montgomery also feature historical displays. The 1905 Merchants Exchange at California and Montgomery is now **First Interstate Bank,** but the bygone boat-business days are remembered in the Exchange Hall with ship models and William Coulter marine paintings. For a look at more modern mercantile action, climb to the visitors gallery for a bird's-eye view of the action at the **Pacific Coast Stock Exchange** at Pine and Sansome, the largest in America outside New York City.

People were outraged over the architecture of the **Transamerica Pyramid** at Montgomery and Washington, the city's tallest building, when it was completed in 1972. (For a look around, take a free ride up to the 27th floor, where the "viewing area" is open to the public during business hours—well worth it for sunny-day views of Coit Tower, the Golden Gate Bridge, and Alcatraz.) But now everyone has adjusted to its strange winged-spire architecture. Popular during Friday lunch hours in summer are the free "Music in the Park" concerts at Transamerica's Redwood Park, featuring jazz, blues, bluegrass, a cappella and choral singers.

Designated these days as the **Jackson Square Historical District,** the section of town stretching into North Beach across Washington Street was once called the **Barbary Coast,** famous since the gold rush as the world's most depraved human hellhole. Pacific Street was the main thoroughfare, a stretch of bad-boy bawdy houses, saloons, dance halls, and worse —like the "cowyards," where hundreds of prostitutes performed on stage with animals or in narrow cribs stacked as high as four stories. Terms like "Mickey Finn," "Shanghaied," and "hoodlum" were coined here. Local moral wrath couldn't stop the barbarity of the Barbary Coast —and even the earthquake of 1906 spared the area, much to everyone's astonishment. Somewhat settled down by the Roaring '20s, when it was known as the International Settlement, the Barbary Coast didn't shed its barbarians entirely until the 1950s. And now it's quite tame, an oddly gentrified collection of quaint brick buildings.

On The Waterfront

San Francisco's waterfront, its docks and wharfs just a remnant of bygone booming port days, stretches some six miles along the wide, sea-wall-straddling **Embarcadero** that runs from Fisherman's Wharf in the north to China Basin south of the Bay Bridge. The area is much improved, aesthetically, now that the up-in-the-air Embarcadero Freeway is gone—damaged by the 1989 earthquake, then razed. Just south of Broadway is the city's only new pier since the 1930s; 845-foot-long **Pier 7** is an elegant public-access promenade for dawdlers and fisherfolk, complete with iron-and-wood benches, iron railings, and flanking colonnades of lampposts, the better for taking in the nighttime skyline. At the foot of Market Street is the **Ferry Building,** completed in 1898, formerly the city's transport center. One more witness to dockside urban development trends, the Ferry Building is largely office space today, including the **World Trade Center,** though the building still features its 661-foot arcaded facade, triumphal arch at the entrance, and temple-style clocktower echoing the Giralda tower of Spain's Seville cathedral. Across from the updated 1889 **Audiffred Building** at 1 Mission is city-within-the-city **Rincon Center,** incorporating the former Rincon Annex Post Office, which was saved for its classic New Deal mural art. Note, too, the **36,075-pound brass screw** from a World War II tanker at 100 Spear Street, introducing the waterfront exhibits inside. More than elsewhere in the city, except perhaps Nob Hill, the ironies of Financial District art are indeed striking.

The **Waterfront Promenade** just south, a seawall walkway favored by office brownbaggers and midday joggers, replaces the waterfront's old piers 14 through 22. A very long block south of Rincon Center is **Hills Plaza,** a new commercial-and-apartment development with a garden plaza, incorporating the shell of the old Hills Brothers Coffee building. Farther south along the Embarcadero are more new developments also housing restaurants, including **Bayside Village** and the world-renowned drug rehabilitation program **Delancey Street.** Beyond, in China Basin, is the new **South Beach Marina Pier,** a public fishing pier with a good skyline view of the South Beach Marina.

The Theater District

With so many fine theaters scattered throughout the city, it's something of a New York affectation

to insist on that designation downtown. But San Francisco, a city that has loved its dramatic song and dance since gold-rush days, definitely insists. Poetry readings, lectures, opera, and Shakespeare were integral to the 1800s arts scene. And superstar entertainers of the era made their mark here, from spider-dancer Lola Montez and her child protégé Lotta Crabtree to Lillie Langtry, opera star Luisa Tetrazzini, actress Helena Modjeska, and actor Edwin Booth. These days the concentration of upscale Union Square hotels downtown roughly duplicates the theater district boundaries. **Geary Street** near both Mason and Taylor is the official center, with the 400-block of Geary serving as home turf to the **American Conservatory Theater (A.C.T.)** repertory company and its **Geary Theater** (perhaps renovated by the 1994 season, after recent earthquake damage) as well as the **Curran Theater,** noted for its Broadway road shows. Other neighborhood venues include the **Cable Car Theatre** at 430 Mason, the **Golden Gate Theatre** at 25 Taylor, and the **Marines Memorial Theater** at 609 Sutter, all good bets for off-Broadway shows. Unusual small theaters include the **Theatre on the Square,** sharing space with the Kensington Park Hotel at 450 Post and the **Plush Room Cabaret** inside the York Hotel at 940 Sutter.

Just down a ways, beyond the theater district per se, at 661 Geary is the odd **Blue Lamp** bar—note the blue lamp, a classic of neo-neon art—once just a hard-drinkers' dive, now a campy, hipsters', hard-drinkers' dive, most interesting late at night when the neighborhood gets a bit scary. Clubbers seem to *love* that adrenaline rush. But the real reason to come here is live music, just-starting band badness. Just a few blocks away, near Union Square at 333 Geary, is another world entirely—**Lefty O'Doul's,** a hofbrau-style deli and old-time bar stuffed to the ceiling with baseball memorabilia. Lefty was a local hero, a big leaguer who came back to manage the minor-league San Francisco Seals before the Giants came to town.

The Civic Center And Vicinity

Smack dab in the center of the sleaze zone is San Francisco's major hub of government, the Civic Center, built on the one-time site of the Yerba Buena Cemetery. (See cautions mentioned under "The Tenderloin" above, which also apply to almost any section of downtown Market Street after dark.) A sublime example of America's beaux arts architecture, the center's **City Hall** was modeled after St. Peter's Basilica at the Vatican, in the belle epoque style, complete with dome and majestic staircase. Renaissance-style sculptures state the city's dreams—the not necessarily incongruous collection of Wisdom, the Arts, Learning, Truth, Industry, and Labor over the Van Ness Avenue entrance, and Commerce, Navigation, California Wealth, and San Francisco above the doors on Polk Street.

Across Van Ness is **War Memorial Opera House,** the classical venue for the **San Francisco Ballet Company** as well as the **San Francisco Opera,** *the* place for society folk to see and be seen during the September-to-December opera season. Twin to the opera house, connected by extravagant iron gates, is the **Veterans Memorial Building,** with the **Museum of Modern Art** on the third and fourth floors, noted for its impressive impressionist collection and changing special exhibits, great bookstore, and cafe. The cramped quarters here mean that only a minute part of the collection is on display at any one time—a situation which will change when the museum relocates in 1995 as part of the south-of-Market **Yerba Buena Gardens** redevelopment project. The **Louise M. Davies Hall** at Van Ness and Grove, which features North America's largest concert hall organ, is the permanent venue for the **San Francisco Symphony.** If in the neighborhood, performing arts aficionados should definitely head west one block to the weekdays-only **San Francisco Performing Arts Library and Museum** at Grove and Gough.

The Civic Center branch of the **San Francisco Public Library,** on McAllister between Larkin and Hyde, is worth a browse, especially for researchers interested in its third-floor **History Room and Archives.** Free volunteer-led City Guides tours are headquartered here, and some depart from here (see "Walking Tours" under "Delights and Diversions"). **Civic Center Plaza,** across Polk from the library, is home to many of the area's homeless and also forms the garden roof for the underground **Brooks Hall** exhibit center and parking garage. In the hallways of the city's **Civic Auditorium** are two free museums, the third-floor **Boxing Museum** and the **Police Museum** on the fourth floor.

City Hall, centerpiece of San Francisco's Civic Center

United Nations Plaza stretches between Market Street and the Federal Building at McAllister (between 7th and 8th), commemorating the U.N.'s charter meeting in 1945 at the War Memorial Opera House. On Wednesdays and Sundays the plaza bustles with buyers and sellers of fish and unusual fruits and vegetables when the **Heart of the City Farmer's Market,** tel. (415) 558-9455, is in bloom.

In addition to the area's many cafes, restaurants, and nightspots (see "City Fare" for more individual listings), the **California Culinary Academy** at 625 Polk Street (at Turk) is noted for its 16-month chef's training course in Italian, French, and nouvelle cuisine. For the curious, the academy is also an exceptionally good place to eat wonderful food at reasonable prices. The academy operates a bakery and cafe, the basement **Academy Grill** buffet, tel. (415) 771-1655, the **Careme Room,** tel. 771-3536, a glass-walled dining hall where you can watch what goes on in the kitchen, and the somewhat more formal, Mediterranean-style **Cyril's,** tel. (415) 771-3500. Call for hours and reservation policies, which vary. Also in the trendy Polk Gulch area is the **Sierra Club** headquarters and retail store at 730 Polk.

The Western Addition

Attracting the Pacific Heights population, the **Upper Fillmore Street** area between Jackson and California is noted for its late-night trendiness, and quite refined **Sacramento Street** between Lyon and Spruce is the city's best boutique boulevard. But most of the Western Addition—the area west of Van Ness Avenue, south of Pacific Heights, and north of Haight-Ashbury—is depressed and depressing. Settled in turn by Jewish, Japanese, and African Americans, the area is remarkable primarily because so many of its 19th-century Victorians survived the 1906 earthquake, though some subsequently declined into subdivided apartments or were knocked down by the wrecking ball of redevelopment. The Western Addition's remaining Victorian enclaves are rapidly becoming gentrified. The most notable—and most photographed—example is Steiner Street facing **Alamo Square** (other pretty "painted ladies" with face-lifts stretch for several blocks in all directions), though country-like **Cottage Row** just east of Fillmore Street between Sutter and Bush is equally enchanting. (For an exceptional selection of African-American literature, **Marcus Books** is nearby, at 1712 Fillmore.) Much of the Western Addition south of Geary, considered "The Fillmore," is composed of heavy-crime, low-income housing projects. Those who otherwise are without hope can hoof it over to **St. Dominic's Catholic Church** at Bush and Steiner, one block west of

Fillmore, and take their case before the patron saint of lost causes, St. Jude.

Fillmore Street also creates the western border of **Japantown** or Nihonmachi, an area encompassing the neighborhoods north of Geary, south of Pine, and stretching east to Octavia. This very American variation on Japanese community includes the old-style, open-air **Buchanan Mall** between Post and Sutter, and the more modern and ambitious **Japan Center,** a three-block-long concrete mall on Geary between Fillmore and Laguna. It's inaccessibly ugly from the outside, in the American tradition, but offers intriguing attractions inside, like karaoke bars and the **Kabuki Hot Spring** communal bathhouse on the ground floor. For Japanese-language films, head to the **Kokusai Theater** at 1746 Post.

NOB HILL

Snide San Franciscans say "Snob Hill" when referring to cable car-crisscrossed Nob Hill. The official neighborhood name is purported to be short for "Nabob Hill," a reference to this high-rent district's nouveau riche roots. And Robert Louis Stevenson called it the "hill of palaces," referring to the grand late-1800s mansions of San Francisco's economic elite, California's railroad barons most prominent among them. Known colloquially as the "Big Four," Charles Crocker, Mark Hopkins, Collis Huntington, and Leland

the much-photographed Victorian-style houses that look out on Alamo Square

SAN FRANCISCO CONVENTION AND VISITORS BUREAU

SAN FRANCISCO NEIGHBORHOODS AND DISTRICTS

© MOON PUBLICATIONS, INC.

Stanford were accompanied by two of the "Irish Big Four" or "Bonanza Kings" (James Fair and James Flood, Nevada silver lords) as they made their acquisitive economic and cultural march into San Francisco and across the rest of California. (For more about the state's railroading history, see "Sacramento and Vicinity.")

Only one of these original homes stands today—James Flood's bearish, square Connecticut brownstone, now the exclusive **Pacific-Union Club** (or the "P-U," in local vernacular) at 1000 California Street; the rest of the collection was demolished by the great earthquake and fire of 1906. But some of the city's finest hotels, not to mention an exquisite Protestant place of worship, have taken their place around rather formal

Huntington Park. Huntington's central memorial status atop Nob Hill is appropriate enough, since skinflint Collis P. Huntington was the brains of the Big Four gang and his comparatively simple home once stood here.

Facing the square from the corner of California and Taylor is the charming, surprisingly unique red-brick **Huntington Hotel** and its exceptional **Big Four** bar and restaurant. The **Mark Hopkins Hotel** ("the Mark," as it's known around town) was built on the spot of Hopkins' original ornate Victorian, at 1 Nob Hill (corner of California and Mason). Take the elevator up to the **Top of the Mark,** the bar with a view that inspired the city's song, "I Left My Heart in San Francisco," and perhaps its singer Tony Ben-

cable car gripman

S. F. CONVENTION & VISITORS BUREAU, MARK GIBSON

nett as well. Straight across the street, facing Mason between California and Sacramento, is the famed **Fairmont Hotel,** an architectural extravaganza built "atop Nob Hill" by James Fair's daughter Tessie (the lobby recognizable by American TV addicts as the one in the series "Hotel"). Good views can be had from the Fairmont's highest point, too. One of the world's finest, the **Stanford Court Hotel** at California and Powell, occupies the land where Leland Stanford's mansion once stood, strictly a geographical connection. For an artistic rendering of local nabobery, though, stop for a peek at the Stanford's new lobby murals.

The **Bohemian Club** on the corner of Taylor and Post is a social club started by some of California's true bohemians, from Jack London, Joaquin Miller, and John Muir to Ambrose Bierce, Ina Coolbrith, and George Sterling. Though for old-time's sake some artists are invited to join, these days this very exclusive all-male club has a rank and file composed primarily of businessmen, financiers, and politicians. In July of each year, these modern American bohemians retreat to the Russian River and their equally private **Bohemian Grove** all-male enclave for a week of fun and frolic (see "The Bohemian Grove" in the Russian River chapter).

Hobnobbing With Spirit:
Grace Cathedral
At the former site of Charles Crocker's mansion is **Grace Cathedral,** facing Huntington Park from Taylor Street, an explosion of me-

dieval Gothic enthusiasm inspired by the Notre Dame in Paris. Since the lot *was* cleared for construction by a very California earthquake, Grace Cathedral is built not of carefully crafted stone but steel-reinforced concrete.

Most famous here, architecturally, are the cathedral doors, cast from Lorenzo Ghiberti's *Gates of Paradise* from the Cathedral Bapistry in Florence, Italy. The glowing rose window is circa 1970 and comes from Chartres. Also from Chartres: Grace Cathedral's spiritual **Labyrinth,** a roll-up replica of an archetypal meditative journey in the Christian tradition. Since Grace is a "house of prayer for all people," anyone can walk the Labyrinth's three-fold path, just part of the cathedral's multifaceted **Quest Center for Spiritual Wholeness** program directed by the Reverend Lauren Artress. The Labyrinth is open to the public the first Sunday of every month 1-3 p.m., and the third Wednesday, 5:30-8 p.m. Usually on Wednesdays there is also live vocal accompaniment. Music, in fact, is another major attraction at Grace Cathedral, from the choral evensongs to pipe organ, carillon, and chamber music concerts. Mother church for California's Episcopal Diocese, Grace Cathedral hosts endless unusual events, including **St. Francis Day** in October, in honor of St. Francis of Assisi, the city's patron saint, and the interconnectedness of all creation. All God's creatures, large and small—from elephants and police horses to dressed-up housepets, not to mention the women walking on stilts—show up to be blessed. For more information about Grace

Cathedral's current calendar of odd and exhilarating events, call (415) 776-6611. And while you're in the neighborhood, take a peek into the modern **California Masonic Memorial Temple** at 1111 California, with its tiny scale model of King Solomon's Temple and colorful mosaic monument to Freemasonry.

Nob Hill's Invention And The Cable Car Barn

Not just material wealth and spiritual high spirits are flaunted atop Nob Hill. Technical innovation is, too, and quite rightly, since this is where Andrew Hallidie launched the inaugural run of his famous cable cars, down Clay Street. A free stop at the **Cable Car Barn** at Mason and Washington, tel. (415) 474-1887, open daily 10-6, tells the story. No temple to tourist somnambulism, this is powerhouse central for the entire cable car system, which is energized solely by the kinetic energy of the cables. Electric motors turn the giant sheaves (pulleys) to whip the (underground) looped steel cables around town and power the cars. The idea is at once complex and simple. Feeding cable around corners is a bit tricky; to see how it works, hike down to a basement window and observe. But the "drive" mechanism is straightforward. Each cable car has two operators, someone working the grip, the other the brake. To "power up," heading uphill, the car's "grip" slides through the slot in the street to grab onto the cable, and the cable does the rest. Heading downhill, resisting gravity, the brake gets quite a workout. Also here: a display of historic cable cars plus a gift shop on the mezzanine.

CHINATOWN

The best time to explore Chinatown is at the crack of dawn, when crowded neighborhoods and narrow alleys explode into hustle and bustle, when the scents, sounds, and sometimes surreal colors compete with the energy of sunrise. Due to the realities of gold-rush-era life and, later, the Chinese Exclusion Act of 1882, this very American variation on a Cantonese market town was for too long an isolated, almost all-male frontier enclave with the predictable vices—a trend reversed only in the 1960s, when more relaxed immigration laws allowed the possibility of families and children. The ambitious and the

educated have already moved on to the suburbs, so Chinatown today (the country's most densely populated neighborhood except for Harlem in New York) is home to the elderly poor and immigrants who can't speak English. It's still the largest community of Chinese anywhere outside China and Hong Kong. And it's still a cultural and spiritual home for the Bay Area's expanding Chinese community. Even those who have left come back, if only for a great meal and a Chinese-language movie.

To get oriented, keep in mind that Stockton Street is the main thoroughfare. Grant Avenue, however, is where most tourists start, perhaps enticed away from Grant's endless upscale shops and galleries by the somewhat garish green-tiled Chinatown Gate at Bush, a 1969 gift from the Republic of China. As you wander north, notice the street-sign calligraphy, the red-painted, dragon-wrapped lampposts, and the increasingly unusual roofscapes. (Despite the color on Grant, the in-between streets, Sacramento, Clay, Washington, Jackson, and Pacific, along with the fascinating interconnecting alleys between them, represent the heart of Chinatown.) Grant goes the distance between Market Street and modern-day Pier 39. This happens to be San Francisco's oldest street, originally little more than a rutted path in 1834 when it was dubbed Calle de la Fundación (Foundation Street or "street of the founding") by the ragtag residents of the Yerba Buena pueblo. The name was changed to Dupont by mid-century, in honor of an American admiral, a move that also recognized the abrupt changing of California's political guard. But by the end of the 1800s, "Du Pon Gai" had become so synonymous with unsavory activities that downtown merchants decided on another name change, this time borrowing a bit of prestige from Ulysses S. Grant, the nation's 18th president and the Civil War's conquering general.

Since traffic is horrendous, parking all but impossible, and many streets almost too narrow to navigate even sans vehicle, walking is the best way to see the sights. If you haven't time to wander aimlessly, taking a guided tour is the best way to get to know the neighborhood. (See "Walking Tours" below.)

Chinatown Sights

At the corner of Grant and California is **Old**

Saint Mary's Church, the city's Catholic cathedral from the early 1850s to 1891, still standing even after a gutting by fire in 1906. On Saint Mary's clock tower is sound maternal advice for any age: "Son, Observe the time and fly from evil." (Saint Mary has a square, too, a restful stop just east and south of California Street, where there's a Bufano sculpture of Dr. Sun Yat-sen, the Republic of China's founder.) Also at the Grant/California intersection is the **Ma-Tsu Temple of the United States of America,** with shrines to Buddha and other popular deities.

Grant Avenue between California and Broadway, with its many restaurants and tourist shops, is always bustling. Of particular interest is the unusual and aptly named **Li Po Bar** at 916 Grant, a watering hole honoring the memory of China's notoriously romantic poet, a wine-loving warrior who drowned while embracing the moon—a moon mirage, as it turned out, reflected up from a river. Head down narrow, cobbled Commercial Street for some cultural education. **The Chinese Historical Society of America** at 650 Commercial St., tel. (415) 391-1188, open Tues.-Sun. afternoons noon-4 p.m., is the nation's only museum specifically dedicated to preserving Chinese-American history. Chinese contributions to California culture are particularly emphasized. Some unusual artifacts in the museum's collection: gold-rush paraphernalia, including a "tiger fork" from Weaverville's tong war, and an old copy (handwritten) of Chinatown's phone book. Admission is free, but donations are appreciated. **The Pacific Heritage Museum,** 608 Commercial (at Leidesdorff), tel. 399-1124, is housed in the city's renovated brick 1875 U.S. Mint building, featuring free rotating exhibits of Asian art and other treasures, open weekdays 10-4. To place it all in the larger context of California's Wild West history, head around the corner to the **Wells Fargo History Room** at 420 Montgomery.

Portsmouth Square—people still say "square," though technically it's been a plaza since the 1920s—on Kearny between Clay and Washington is Chinatown's backyard, offering an astounding look at everyday local life, from the city's omnipresent panhandlers to neigborhood-specific early-morning tai chi and all-male afternoons of checkers, *go,* and gossip, life's lasting entertainments for Chinatown's aging bachelors. Across Kearny on the third floor of the Fi-

nancial District Holiday Inn is the **Chinese Cultural Center,** which has a small gift shop but otherwise caters mostly to meeting the needs of the local community (see "Information" below).

The actions and attractions of Chinatown's heart are increasingly subtle, from the Washington Street **herb and herbalist shops** to **Ross Alley**'s garment factories and **fortune cookie company.** You can buy some instant fortune, fresh off the press—keeping in mind, of course, that fortune cookies are an all-American invention. (The "adult" messages aren't all that spicy, perhaps just enough to elicit titters from adolescents.) Intriguing, at 743 Washington, is the oldest oriental-style building in the neighborhood, the three-tiered 1909 "temple" once home to the Chinatown Telephone Exchange, now the **Bank of Canton.** But even **Bank of America,** at 701 Grant, is dressed in keeping with its cultural surroundings, with benevolent gold dragons on its columns and doors, and some 60 dragons on its facade. Also putting on the dog is **Citicorp Savings** at 845 Grant, guarded by grimacing temple dogs.

Both Jackson and Washington streets are best bets for finding small and authentic neighborhood restaurants. **Stockton Street,** however, especially between Broadway and Sacramento and especially on a Saturday afternoon, is where Chinatown shops. Between Sacramento and Washington, **Waverly Place** is referred to as the "street of painted balconies," for fairly obvious reasons. There are three temples here, open to respectful visitors (donations appreciated, picture-taking usually not). **Norras Temple** at 109 Waverly is affiliated with the Buddhist Association of America, lion dancing and all, while the fourth-floor **Tien Hau Temple** at 123 Waverly primarily honors the Queen of Heaven, she who protects sojourners and seafarers as well as writers, actors, and prostitutes. The **Jeng Sen Buddhism and Taoism Association,** 146 Waverly, tel. (415) 397-2941, perhaps offers the best general introduction to Chinese religious tolerance, with a brief printed explanation (in English) of both belief systems.

For a delightfully detailed and intimate self-guided tour through the neighborhood, bring along a copy of Shirley Fong-Torres' *San Francisco Chinatown: A Walking Tour,* which includes some rarely recognized sights, such as the **Cameron House** on Sacramento, a youth center named in honor of Donaldina Cameron (1869-1968), who helped young Chinese slave girls escape poverty and prostitution. This marvelous and readable introduction to San Francisco's Chinese community also covers history, cultural beliefs, festivals, religion and philosophy, herbal medicine (doctors and pharmacists are now licensed for these traditional practices by the state of California), Chinese teas, and Chinese food—a very good introduction, from ingredients, cookware, and techniques to menus and restaurant recommendations.

Chinatown Shopping

To a greater extent than, say, Oakland's Chinatown, most shops here are aware of—and cater to—the tourist trade. But once you have some idea what you're looking for, bargains are available. Along Grant Avenue, a definite must for gourmet cooks and other kitchen habitués is **The Wok Shop** at 804 Grant (at Clay), tel. (415) 989-3797, the specialized one-stop shopping trip for anything essential to Chinese cooking. **China Bazaar Discount Imports,** 826-832 Grant, tel. 982-9847, may also have what you're looking for, since this place sells almost everything available elsewhere, usually at reasonable prices. The **King Wah Goldsmith** in the China Trade Center, 838 Grant, tel. 433-7070, is a good stop for jewelry-sized jade. (Also well worth a stop here: **Kitemakers of China,** for silk dragon kites and windsocks.) The **Ten Fu Tea Company,** 949 Grant (at Jackson), tel. 362-0656 or toll-free (800) 543-2885, features over 50 varieties of teas, the prices dependent on quality and (for blends) content. There's a private area in back where you can arrange for instruction in the fine art of a proper tea ceremony. (Notice, on the wall, a photo of former President George Bush, who didn't quite get it right when he tried it.) For unusual gifts, silk shirts, high-quality linens and such, **Far East Fashions** at 953 Grant, tel. 362-0986 or 362-8171, is a good choice.

Ever hankered after a handkerchief-sized ideogram of your own name? This and other samples of Chinese brush art are available at the **I Chong Art Gallery** at 661 Jackson (at Kearny), tel. (415) 788-3366, which offers other Chinese fine art works and elegant furnishings. Best for Chinese books is **East Wind Books,** down in the basement at 1435 Stockton, with an English-language outlet at 633 Vallejo, around the corner.

NORTH BEACH AND VICINITY

For one thing, there isn't any beach in North Beach: In the 1870s the arm of San Francisco Bay that gave the neighborhood its name was filled in, creating more land for the growing city. It *is* often sunny here, though. Those absolutely determined to get sand in their shoes on a North Beach outing can head northeast to Aquatic Park, near Fort Mason and the San Francisco Maritime National Historic Park.

For another, San Francisco's spaghetti-Western, Italian-American quarter has also long since lost its beatniks and bohemians, some seduced into Haight-Ashbury hippiedom by the Summer of Love, all priced out of the neighborhood. Quite a number of American poets and writers grubbed out some kind of start here: Gregory Corso, Lawrence Ferlinghetti, Allen Ginsberg, Bob Kaufman, Jack Kerouac, Gary Snyder, Kenneth Rexroth. By the 1940s, North Beach as "New Bohemia" was a local reality. It became a long-running national myth.

Otherwise sound-asleep America of the 1950s secretly loved the idea of the alienated, manic "beat generation," a phrase coined by Jack Kerouac in *On the Road.* The Beats seemed to be everything no one else was allowed to be—mostly, *free.* Free to drink coffee or cheap wine and talk all day, free to indulge in art, music, poetry, prose, and more sensual thrills just about any time, free to be angry and scruffy and lost in the forbidden fog of marijuana while bopping along to be-bop. But Allen Ginsberg's raging *Howl and Other Poems,* published by Ferlinghetti and City Lights, brought the wolf of censorship—an ungrateful growl that began with the seizure of in-bound books by U.S. Customs, and got louder when city police filed obscenity charges. The national notoriety of an extended trial, and Ginsberg's ultimate literary acquittal, brought busloads of Gray Line tourists. And the Beats moved on, though some of the cultural institutions they founded are still going strong.

Nowadays, North Beach is almost choking on its abundance—of eateries, coffeehouses, tourist traps, and shops, a fact that may pop to mind if you're trying to find a parking place. Public transit is the best way to get around in North Beach.

Adding to neighborhood stresses and strains —and to the high costs of surviving—is the influx of Asian business and the monumental increase in Hong Kong-money property investment, both marching into North Beach from Chinatown. Old and new neighborhood residents tend to ignore each other as much as possible, in that great American melting-pot tradition. (Before the Italians called North Beach their home turf, the Irish did. And before the Irish lived here, Chileans did. In all fairness, Fisherman's Wharf was Chinese before the Italians moved in. And of course Native Americans inhabited the entire state before the Spanish, the Mexicans, the Russians, and the Americans.) Like the city itself, life here makes for a fascinating sociology experiment.

What with territorial incursions from Chinatown, the historical boundaries of North Beach increasingly clash with the actual. Basically, the entire valley between Russian Hill and Telegraph Hill is properly considered North Beach. The northern boundary stopped just short of Fisherman's Wharf, now pushed back by rampant commercial development, and Broadway was the southern boundary—a thoroughfare and area sometimes referred to as the "Marco Polo Zone" since it once represented the official end of Chinatown and the beginning of San Francisco's Little Italy. The neighborhood's spine is diagonally running Columbus Avenue, which begins at the Transamerica Pyramid at the edge of the Financial District and ends at The Cannery near Fisherman's Wharf. Columbus Avenue between Filbert and Broadway is the still-beating Italian heart of modern North Beach.

North Beach Sights

Piazza-like **Washington Square,** between Powell and Stockton, Union and Filbert, is the centerpiece of North Beach, though, as *San Francisco Chronicle* columnist Herb Caen has pointed out, it "isn't on Washington Street, isn't a square (it's five-sided) and doesn't contain a statue of Washington but of Benjamin Franklin." (In terms of cultural consistency, this also explains the statue of Robert Louis Stevenson in Chinatown's Portsmouth Square.) There's a time capsule beneath old Ben; when the original treasures (mostly temperance tracts on the evils of alcohol) were unearthed in 1979, they were replaced with 20th-century cultural values, including a bottle of wine, a pair of Levi's, and a poem by Lawrence Ferlinghetti. In keeping with more modern times, Washington Square also features a statue dedicated to the city's firemen, yet another contribution by eccentric little old Lillie Hitchcock Coit. Its twin towers lighting up the whole neighborhood come nightfall, **Saints Peter and Paul Catholic Church** fronts the square at 666 Filbert. Noted for its rococo interior and accompanying graphic statuary of injured saints and souls burning in hell, the Saints also offers daily mass in Italian and (on Sundays) in Chinese.

Two blocks northeast of Washington Square is the **North Beach Playground,** where bocce ball is still the neighborhood game of choice (just as October's **Columbus Day Parade** and accompanying festivities still make the biggest North Beach party). Just two blocks west of the square are the stairs leading to the top of **Telegraph Hill,** identifiable by **Coit Tower,** Lillie Coit's most heartfelt memorial to the firefighters. (More on that below.)

For an overview of the area's history, stop by the free **North Beach Museum** on the mezzanine of the Eureka Federal Savings Bank at 1435 Stockton St. (near Green), tel. (415) 391-6210, open during banker's hours, for its occasionally changing exhibits of artifacts and photographs.

The North Beach "experience" is the neighborhood itself, the coffeehouses, the restaurants, the intriguing and odd little shops. No visit is complete without a stop at Lawrence Ferlinghetti's **City Lights Bookstore,** on the neighborhood's most literary alley at 261 Columbus, tel. (415) 362-8193. City Lights is the nation's first all-paperback bookstore and a rambling ode to the best of the small presses; its poetry and other literary programs still feed the souls of those who need more nourishment than what commercial bestsellers can offer.

You can shop till you drop in this part of town. And much of what you'll find has something to do with food. Just about anything necessary to outfit an Italian kitchen is available at **Figoni Hardware Co.,** 1351 Grant Ave., tel. (415) 392-4765 (or in the old phone number style: EXbrook 2-4765), a bar, hotel, and restaurant supplier but also the long-established neighborhood stop for fishing tackle and sporting goods, building and plumbing supplies, and shovels and vegetable seeds. For Italian ceramics, **Biordi Italian**

S. F. CONVENTION & VISITORS BUREAU, DAVID WEINTRAUB

Coit Tower sits atop Telegraph Hill like a beacon—or a firehose.

Imports at 412 Columbus, tel. 392-8096, has a fabulous selection of art intended for the table (but almost too beautiful). For a price—and just about everything is pricey—the folks here will ship your treasures, too.

While you're wandering, you can easily put together a picnic for a break in Washington Square. The city's oldest butcher shop is sawdust-floored **R. Iacopi & Co. Meats,** 1460 Grant (at Union), tel. (415) 421-0757, *the* place to stop for traditionally cured *pancetta* and prosciutto. Head to **Molinari's** on Columbus for cheeses, sausages, and savory salads, and to the Italian and French **Victoria Pastry Co.** at 1362 Stockton St. (Stockton and Vallejo), tel. 781-2015, for cookies, cakes, and unbelievable pastries. (Other good bakery stops nearby include **Liguria Bakery** at 1700 Stockton, tel. 421-3786, famous for its *focaccia,* and, for French bread, the **Italian French Baking Co. of San Francisco** at 1501 Grant, tel. 421-3796.) If you didn't load up on reading material at City Lights—for *after* you stuff yourself but before falling asleep in the square—stop by **Cavalli & Company** at 1441 Stockton, tel. 421-4219, for Italian newspapers, magazines, and books.

Telegraph Hill And Coit Tower

The best way to get to Telegraph Hill—whether just for the view, to appreciate the city's "hanging gardens," or to visit Coit Tower—is to climb the hill yourself, starting up the very steep stairs at Kearny and Filbert or ascending more gradually from the east, via either the Greenwich or Filbert steps. Following Telegraph Hill Boulevard as it winds its way from Lombard, from the west, is troublesome for drivers. Parking up top is scarce; especially on weekends you might sit for hours while you wait—just to park, mind you. A reasonable alternative is taking the No. 39-Coit bus.

Lillie Hitchcock Coit had a fetish for firemen. As a child, she was saved from a fire that claimed two of her playmates. And as a teenager she spent much of her time with members of San Francisco's all-volunteer Knickerbocker Engine Company No. 5, usually tagging along on fire calls, eventually becoming the team's official mascot and allowed to play poker and smoke cigars with the boys. Started in 1929, financed by a Coit bequest, and completed in 1933, Coit Tower was to be a lasting memorial to the firemen. Some people say its shape is like the nozzle of a firehouse, others suggest more sexual symbolism, but the official story is that the design by Arthur Brown was intended to look "equally artistic" from any direction. Coit Tower was closed to the public for many years, due to the damage caused by vandalism and water leakage. After a major interior renovation, the tower is now open in all its original glory, so come decide for yourself what the tower symbolizes. Or just come for the view. From atop the 180-foot tower, which gets extra lift from its site on top of Telegraph Hill, there's a magnificent 360-degree view of the entire Bay Area, boosted still more by the coin-op telescopes here. Coit Tower, tel. (415) 362-0808, is open daily 10-

6, until 9 p.m. in summer. Admission is free, technically, but there is a charge for the elevator ride to the top: $3 adults, $2 seniors, $1 for children ages 6-12.

The real reason to visit Coit Tower, though, is to appreciate the marvelous Depression-era Social Realist interior mural art in the lobby, recently restored and as striking as ever. (At last report seven of the 27 total frescoes, those on the second floor and along the narrow stairway, weren't available for general public viewing, since quarters are so close that scrapes from handbags and shoes are almost inevitable. You can see these murals too, however, on the Saturday guided tour.) Even in liberal San Francisco many of these murals have been controversial, depicting as they do the drudgery, sometimes despair, behind the idyllic facade of modern California life—and particularly the lives of its agricultural and industrial workforce. Financed through Franklin Roosevelt's New Deal-era Public Works Art Project, some 25 local artists set out in 1934 to paint Coit Tower's interior with frescoes, the same year that Diego Rivera's revolutionary renderings of Lenin and other un-American icons created such a scandal at New York's Rockefeller Center that the great Mexican painter's work was destroyed.

In tandem with tensions produced by a serious local dock worker's strike, some in San Francisco almost exploded when it was discovered that the new art in Coit Tower wasn't entirely politically benign, that some of it suggested something less than total support for pro-capitalist ideology. In various scenes, one person is carrying *Das Capital* by Karl Marx, and another is reading a copy of the Communist-party *Daily Worker;* grim-faced "militant unemployed" march forward into the future; women wash clothes by hand within sight of Shasta Dam; slogans oppose both hunger and fascism; and a chauffered limousine is clearly contrasted with a Model-T Ford in Steinbeck's Joad-family style. Even a hammer and sickle made it onto the walls. Unlike New York, even after an outraged vigilante committee threatened to chisel away Coit Tower's artistic offenses, San Francisco ultimately allowed it all to stay—everything, that is, except the hammer and sickle.

Another Telegraph Hill delight: the intimate gardens along the eastern steps. The **Filbert Steps** stairway gardens are more formal, in a landscaping sense, lined with trees, ivy, and garden flowers, with a few terraces and benches near The Shadows restaurant. Below Montgomery Street, the Filbert stairway becomes a bit doddering, unpainted tired wood that leads to enchanting **Napier Lane,** one of San Francisco's last wooden-plank streets and a Victorian survivor of the city's 1906 devastation. (Below Napier the stairway continues to Sansome Street.) The brick-paved **Greenwich Steps** wander down to the cliff-hanging old Julius Castle restaurant, then continue down to the right, appearing to be private stairs to the side yard, weaving past flower gardens and old houses to reach Sansome. If you go up one way, be sure to come down the other.

Russian Hill

Also one of San Francisco's rarer pleasures is a stroll around Russian Hill, named for the belief that Russian sea otter hunters picked this place to bury their dead. One of the city's early bohemian neighborhoods and a preferred haunt for writers and other connoisseurs of quiet beauty, Russian Hill today is an enclave of the wealthy. But anyone can wander the neighborhood. If you come from North Beach, head up—it's definitely *up*—Vallejo Street, where the sidewalks and the street eventually give way to stairs. Take a break at **Ina Coolbrith Park** at Taylor, named in honor of California's first poet laureate, a woman remarkable for many accomplishments. A member of one of Jim Beckwourth's westward wagon trains, she was the first American child to enter California by wagon. After an unhappy marriage, Coolbrith came to San Francisco, where she wrote poetry and created California's early literary circle. Many men fell in love with her, the ranks of the hopelessly smitten including Ambrose Bierce, Bret Harte, and Mark Twain. (She refused to marry any of them.) Librarian for both the Bohemian Club and the Oakland Free Library, at the latter Coolbrith took 12-year-old Jack London under her wing, her tutelage and reading suggestions his only formal education. Up past the confusion of lanes at Russian Hill's first summit is **Florence Street,** which heads south, and still more stairs, these leading down to Broadway—the original route, which shows why the city eventually burrowed the new *under* the hill. Ina Coolbrith's last home on Russian Hill still stands at 1067 Broadway.

San Francisco Brewing Company

To see the second summit—technically the park at Greenwich and Hyde—and some of the reasons why TV and movie chase scenes are frequently filmed here, wander west and climb aboard the Hyde-Powell cable car. Worth exploration on the way up: **Green Street, Macondray Lane** just north of Jones (which eventually takes you down to Taylor Street), and **Filbert Street,** San Francisco's steepest driveable hill, a 31.5-degree grade. (To test that thesis yourself, go *very* slowly.) Just over the summit, as you stare straight toward Fisherman's Wharf, is another wonder of road engineering: the **Crookedest Street in the World,** the one-block stretch of Lombard Street between Hyde and Leavenworth. People do drive down this snake-shaped cobblestone path, a major tourist draw, but it's much more pleasant as a walk.

North Beach Hangouts, Nightlife

Caffe Greco at 427 Columbus, tel. (415) 397-6261, is the best of the neighborhood's new coffeehouses. But head to what was once the heart of New Bohemia, the surviving **Caffe Trieste** at 601 Vallejo (at Grant), tel. 392-6739, for that classic beatnik bonhomie, complete with opera and Italian folk songs on the jukebox and jazz or opera concerts on Saturdays at 1 p.m.—always a crowd pleaser. Also-been-there-forever **Vesuvio Cafe,** across Kerouac Alley from City Lights bookstore (look for the mural with volcanoes and peace symbols), 255 Columbus Ave., tel. 362-3370, is most appreciated for its upstairs balcony section, historically a magnet for working and wannabe writers (and everyone else, too). It was a favorite haunt of Ginsberg and Kerouac, an in-town favorite for Welsh poet Dylan Thomas, and Francis Ford Coppola reportedly sat down at a back table to work on *The Godfather.* A painting depicts *Homo beatnikus,* and there's even an advertisement for a do-it-yourself beatnik makeover (kit including sunglasses, a black beret, and poem). **Spec's 12 Adler Museum Cafe,** across from Vesuvio at 12 William Saroyan Place (once Adler Alley), tel. 421-4112, is also a treasure trove-cum-watering hole of eclectic seafaring and literary clutter, open daily after 4:30 or 5 p.m.

Another righteous place to hide is **Tosca** at 242 Columbus, tel. (415) 391-1244, a late-night landmark with gaudy walls and comfortable Naugahyde booths where the hissing of the espresso machine competes with Puccini on the jukebox. Writers of all varieties still migrate here, sometimes to play pool in back. But you must behave yourself: Bob Dylan and Allen Ginsberg got thrown out of here for being unruly. **Malvina's** is a good bet, too, especially for early-morning pastries with your coffee, though this long-time North Beach mainstay is now in new quarters at Union and Stockton, tel. 861-2228. For truly odd atmosphere, stroll into the boat-like **Lost and Found Saloon** at 1353 Grant Ave., tel. 397-3751, once the popular Coffee Gallery.

A fairly inexpensive hot spot, with wonderful turn-of-the-century ambience as well as hearty beers and ales, is the **San Francisco Brewing Company** at 155 Columbus, tel. (415) 434-3344. But **The Saloon** across from Caffe Trieste at Grant and Fresno Alley (1232 Grant), tel. 989-7666, is the city's oldest pub, circa 1861, a bit scruffy but still hosting what's happening after all these years (blues and rock, mostly).

Serious social history students should also peek into **The Condor Bistro,** at Columbus and Broadway, tel. (415) 781-8222, the one-time Condor Club made famous by stripper Carol Doda and her silicone-enhanced mammaries.

The place offers a memory of the neighborhood's sleazier heyday. The new Condor, a bar and dance club, features the old blinking-boobs sign installed in state near the bar, Carol Doda's infamous performance-space piano still hanging from the ceiling, and a memorial stripper museum. (The official-seeming historical plaque out front is just a gag.) Other neighborhood perversion palaces, survivors of the same peepshow mentality, are becoming fewer and farther between, in any event not really all that interesting.

Famous for over a half century and counting, **Finocchio's** at 506 Broadway (at Columbus), tel. (415) 982-9388, is home to a long-running revue of female impersonators. Perhaps destined for an equally lasting run is infamous "Beach Blanket Babylon" at **Club Fugazi,** 678 Green St. (at Powell), tel. 421-4222, song-and-dance slapstick of a very contemporary high-camp cabaret style, where even favorite Broadway tunes end up brutally (and hilariously) twisted. Thematic and seasonal changes, like the Christmas revue, make this babbling Babylon worthy of return visits—especially to see what they'll create next in the way of 50-pound decorative headdresses.

FISHERMAN'S WHARF

There was a time when San Francisco's fishing industry and other port-related businesses were integral to both the city's cultural and economic life. That day is long gone. Fisherman's Wharf, which extends from the breakwater at Pier 39 to the municipal pier just past Aquatic Park and the maritime museum, has largely become a carnival-style diversion for tourists. Originally, though, the Chinese pulled ashore their catch here, followed in time by Italian fishermen who took over the territory. After World War II the city's fishing industry declined dramatically, the result of both accelerated pollution of San Francisco Bay and decades of overfishing. In between the shopping centers, arcade amusements, and oddball museums, there is a small fishing fleet struggling to survive.

Commercial Attractions

Fisherman's Wharf's main attractions are quite attention-grabbing. **Pier 39** offers San Francisco schlock par excellence, not to mention some

unusual shops, like the Disney store and a boutique for southpaws. It also offers an experiential tour through local history with the high-speed, emotional, and sensate cravings of the TV-and-computer culture in mind: **San Francisco Experience,** on the second level, tel. (415) 982-7559, open daily, with shows every half hour, 10-10. When the earthquakes of 1906 and 1989 are shown, you'll get to experience *that,* too, thanks to jiggling seats, surround sound, and computerized projectors and strobe lights. And in case you've missed it in your other San Francisco forays, fog machines will make you some. Admission $6 adults, $3 children. Absolutely free, though, is time spent watching the lolling **sea lion** population, a fairly recent invasion force. Also enjoyable, especially in December or at other times during the mid-November-to-June season, is fresh **Dungeness crab.** You can pick out your own, live or already cooked, from the vendor stands, or head for any of the more famous Italian-style Fisherman's Wharf seafood restaurants: **Alioto's, Castaglione's, Sabella's,** and **Scoma's,** among others.

If you're in the mood for still more entertainment, Fisherman's Wharf offers a wacky variety. **Ripley's Believe It Or Not Museum** at 175 Jefferson St. (near Taylor), tel. (415) 771-6188, features both bizarre and beautiful items and replicas collected during Robert L. Ripley's global travels. Open from 9 a.m. to midnight in summer, short hours otherwise. Admission fee. Nearby is the **Guinness Museum of World Records,** 235 Jefferson, tel. 771-9890, open 9 a.m. to midnight in summer, shorter hours at other times, essentially a collection of models, photographs, and video displays about the world's tallest, largest, fastest, smallest, shortest, longest everything. Admission fee. Also in the neighborhood is the **Wax Museum of Fisherman's Wharf,** 145 Jefferson, tel. 885-4975 or toll-free (800) 439-4305, a wacky, zoo-like collection of the graven images of almost anyone you can think of, from patriots to poets. Admission fee. The affiliated **Medieval Dungeon** on Jefferson at Mason (same phone numbers as the wax museum) is a bloody treat for those who haven't yet worked out their own inhumane or sadistic instincts, chock full of simulated horrors and tortures, from skull crushers and guillotines to spiked coffins. Hands-on exhibits are a particular thrill for do-it-yourselfers. Open the

S.F. CONVENTION & VISITORS BUREAU, KERRICK JAMES

Balclutha, *one of the Hyde Street historic ships berthed at the San Francisco Maritime National Historic Park*

same hours as the wax museum: Sun.-Thurs. 10-10, Fri. and Sat. until 11. Admission fee. Comparatively speaking, the **Haunted Gold Mine** nearby has little to offer.

You can also shop till you drop—at elegant **Ghirardelli Square,** 900 North Point (Beach and Larkin), a complex of 50-plus shops and restaurants where you also get one of the best hot fudge sundaes anywhere, or **The Cannery** at Beach and Leavenworth, another huge theme shopping center, this one offering outdoor street artist performances as well as the worthwhile **San Francisco International Toy Museum** (second floor, admission fee) and the new **Museum of the History of San Francisco.** Time-honored for imports and the occasional bargain is the multi-store **Cost Plus** at Taylor and North Point.

Historic Ships And Simple Pleasures

Quieter, less commercial pleasures are also available along Fisherman's Wharf—a stroll through **Aquatic Park** perhaps or, for some fishing, out onto the **Municipal Pier.** And in addition to shoving off on boat tours of San Francisco Bay—including the don't-miss experience of **Alcatraz**—this area features some fascinating seagoing attractions, all part of the **San Francisco Maritime National Historical Park.** To get oriented, first stop by the park's **National Maritime Museum of San Francisco** in Aquatic Park at Beach and Polk, tel. (415) 556-3002, open daily 10-5, free admission. The double-decker building itself is like an art deco ocean

liner. Washed ashore inside are some excellent displays, from model ships and figureheads to historic photos and exhibits on fishing boats, ferries, and demonstrations of the sailor's arts. The affiliated **J. Porter Shaw Library,** tel. 556-9870, housed in Building E at Fort Mason along with the park's administrative offices, holds most of the Bay Area's documented boat history, including oral histories, logbooks, photographs, and ship-building plans.

Not easy to miss at the foot of Hyde Street are the **Hyde Street Pier Historic Ships,** an always-in-progress collection also part of the national park, tel. (415) 556-6435 or 556-3002, small admission fee. Here you can clamber across the decks and crawl through the colorfully cluttered holds of some of America's most historic ships. Tagging along on a ranger-led tour, offered hourly from 11 to 4, complete with summertime "living history" adventures, is the best way to get your feet wet. And don't miss the chance to sing sea shanties, raise sails, watch the crews "lay aloft," or participate in the Dead Horse Ceremony—wherein the crowds heave a horse doll overboard and shout "May the sharks have his body, and the devil have his soul!" Fun, too, is the champagne-and-sunset brigantine bay cruise ($35). Call for current events.

The Hyde Street fleet's flagship is the three-masted 1887 **Balclutha,** a veteran of twice-annual trips between California and the British Isles via Cape Horn. Others include the side-wheel **Eureka,** the world's largest passenger ferry in her day (built to ferry trains), the oceangoing tugboat *Hercules,* the British-built, gold rush-era paddlewheel tug *Eppleton Hall,* the scow schooner *Alma,* the three-masted lumber schooner *C.A. Thayer,* and the behemoth *Jeremiah O'Brien,* the last unaltered World War II liberty ship, tied up at Fort Mason. Also among the collection at Pier 41 is the **U.S.S. Pampanito,** a tight-quarters Balao-class World War II submarine that destroyed or damaged many Japanese vessels and also participated in the tragic sinking of the Japanese *Kachidoki Maru* and *Rayuyo Maru,* which were carrying Australian and British prisoners of war.

THE MARINA DISTRICT, COW HOLLOW, AND PACIFIC HEIGHTS

The neat pastel homes of the very respectable **Marina District,** tucked in between Fort Mason and the Presidio, disguise the fact that the entire area is essentially unstable. Built on landfill, in an area once largely bay marsh, the Mediterranean-style Marina was previously the 63-acre site of the Panama-Pacific International Exposition of 1915—San Francisco's statement to the world that it had been reborn from the ashes of the 1906 earthquake and fire. So it was ironic, and fitting, that the fireboat *Phoenix* extinguished many of the fires here, part of the disproportionate damage caused by the 1989 earthquake.

The Marina's main attractions are those that surround it—primarily the neighborhood stretch of San Francisco's astounding shoreline **Golden Gate National Recreation Area,** which includes the **Fort Mason** complex of galleries, museums, theaters, and nonprofit cultural and conservation organizations. (For more information on the park and its many facets, see "Golden Gate National Recreation Area" below.) If you're in the neighborhood and find yourself near the yacht harbor, do wander out to see (and hear) the park's wonderful **Wave Organ,** powered by sea magic. (The siren song is loudest at high tide.) Then wander west toward the Golden Gate Bridge on the **Golden Gate Promenade,** which meanders the three-plus miles from Aquatic Park and along the Marina Green—popular with kite fliers and well-dressed dog walkers—to Civil War-era **Fort Point.** (Be prepared for wind and fog.) The truly ambitious

can take a hike across the bridge itself, an awesome experience.

Exhausted by nature, retreat to more sheltered attractions near the Presidio, including the remnants of the spectacular Panama-Pacific International Exhibition of 1915, the Bernard Maybeck-designed **Palace of Fine Arts,** and the indescribable **Exploratorium** inside, fun for children of all ages and considered the country's finest science museum by no lesser authority than *Scientific American.* See "Museums and Buildings" and "The Presidio and Fort Point," both below, for more area information.

Separating the Marina District from high-flying Pacific Heights is the low-lying neighborhood of **Cow Hollow,** a one-time dairy farm community now noted for its very chic **Union Street** shopping district, an almost endless string of bars, cafes, coffeehouses, bookstores, and boutiques stretching between Van Ness and Steiner. Not to be outdone, the Marina boasts its own version, **Chestnut Street,** still primarily a neighborhood pleasure, since local trendsetters now tend to favor upper **Fillmore Street** near the Heights and outer **Sacramento Street,** near Presidio Avenue. (The fashion fates are fickle.) **Pacific Heights** proper is the hilltop home pasture for the city's well-shod blue bloods, its striking streets, Victorian homes, and general architectural wealth well worth a stroll. Pick up a copy of the Convention & Visitors Bureau "Pacific Heights Walking Tour" pamphlet to get started, or take a guided tour (see "Walking Tours" below).

THE AVENUES

The Richmond District And Vicinity

Originally called San Francisco's Great Sand Waste, then the city's cemetery district before all (or most) bones were dug up and shipped south to Colma in 1914, today the Richmond District is a middle-class ethnic sandwich, built upon Golden Gate Park and topped by Lincoln Park and the Presidio. White Russians were the first residents, fleeing Russia after the 1917 revolution, but just about everyone else followed. A stroll down **Clement Street** and its multiethnic eateries and shops should bring you up to speed on the subject of ethnic diversity. The area between Arguello and Park Presidio is colloquially called "New Chinatown," noted for its good, largely untouristed Asian eateries and shops. And the gold-painted onion domes of **Russian Holy Virgin Cathedral of the Church in Exile,** a Russian Orthodox church at 6210 Geary Blvd., and the Byzantine-Roman Jewish Reform **Temple Emanu-El** at Arguello and Lake (technically in Pacific Heights) offer inspiring architectural reminders of earlier days. The contrast is ever-present: elderly Russians still park themselves on the playground benches at pretty **Mountain Lake Park** near the Presidio while other residents enjoy performances at the small **Asian American Theater Company** at 403 Arguello, tel. (415) 751-2600, one of the country's finest. Highlights of the Richmond District include the **University of San Francisco** atop Lone Mountain, an institution founded by the Jesuits in 1855 (complete with spectacular **St. Ignatius** church), and the **Neptune Society Columbarium** just off Anza near Stanyan at 1 Lorraine Ct., tel. 221-1838, the lone remnant of previous cemetery days. With its ornate neoclassical and copper-roofed rotunda, the building offers astounding acoustics, best appreciated from the upper floors or during occasional musical events staged here. The building is open to the public Tues.-Sat. 10 a.m.-noon.

Seacliff is an exclusive seaside neighborhood nestled between the Presidio and Lincoln Park, a once-rural community where famed California photographer **Ansel Adams** was raised. **Land's End** west of Seacliff is the city's most rugged coastline, reached via footpath from Lincoln Park and the Golden Gate National Recreation Area. **China Beach,** just below Seacliff, was probably named for Chinese immigrants trying to evade Angel Island internment by jumping ship, all a result of the Exclusion Act in effect from the 1880s to World War II. During the Civil War this was the westernmost point of the nation's anti-slavery "Underground Railroad." You can swim here—facilities include a lifeguard station plus changing rooms, showers, restrooms—but the water's brisk. Northeast is **Baker Beach,** considered the city's best nude beach.

The neighborhood's main attraction, though, just beyond Lincoln Park's Municipal Golf Course, is the **California Palace of the Legion of Honor,** on Legion of Honor Drive, tel. (415) 750-3600 or 863-3330, built in honor of American soldiers killed in France during World War I, and unfortunately closed for renovation and earthquake-proofing until sometime in 1994. Established by French-born Alma de Bretteville Spreckels, wife of the city's sugar king, this handsome hilltop palace is a 1920 French neoclassic, from the colonnades and triumphal arch to the outdoor equestrian bronzes. Intentionally incongruous, placed out near the parking lot in an otherwise serene setting, is George Segal's testimony to the depths of human terror and terrorism: the barbed wire and barely living bodies of *The Holocaust.* Also here are some original bronze castings from Rodin, including *The Thinker* and *The Shades* outdoors, just part of the Legion's collection of over 70 Rodin originals. Inside, the permanent collection was exclusively French, originally, but now includes the M.H. de Young Museum's European collection—an awesome eight-century sweep from El Greco, Rembrandt, and Rubens to Renoir, Cézanne, Degas, Monet, and Manet. Take a docent-led tour for a deeper appreciation of other features, including the Legion's period rooms.

Special events include films, lectures, and painting and music programs, the latter including Rodin Gallery pipe organ concerts as well as chamber music, jazz, and historical instrument concerts in the Florence Gould Theater. The Legion of Honor also features a pleasant cafe and a gift shop, and is open—when it *is* open again, sometime in spring 1994—Wed.-Sun. 10-5, extra hours for special events. Small admission fee, though the museum is free the first Wednesday of every month, also 10 a.m.-noon on the first Saturday of the month. Get here by car from the entrance to Lincoln Park at 34th and Clement, or come by bus. For the fit and fresh-air loving, an alternative route is on foot—following the meandering **Coastal Trail** north from Cliff House or south from the Golden Gate Bridge.

The Sunset District

Most of San Francisco's neighborhoods are residential, streets of private retreat that aren't all that exciting except to those who live there. The **Sunset District,** stretching to the sea from south of Golden Gate Park, is one example, the southern section of the city's "Avenues." In summertime the fog here at the edge of the continent is usually urelenting, so visitors often shiver and shuffle off, muttering that in a place called "Sunset" one should be able to see it. (To appreciate the neighborhood name, come any-time *but* summer.) The golden gates, both the city and national parks, offer delights and di-versions at the fringe. For beach access and often gray-day seaside recreation, from surfing and surf fishing to cycling, walking, and jog-ging (there's a paved path), follow the **Great Highway** south from Cliff House and stop any-where along the way.

Stanyan Street at the edge of the Haight and east of Golden Gate Park offers odd and at-tractive shops, as does the stretch of **9th Av-enue** near Irving and Judah. Just south of the park at its eastern edge is the **University of California at San Francisco Medical Center** atop Mt. Sutro, the small eucalyptus forest here reached via cobblestone Edgewood Ave. or, for the exercise, the Farnsworth steps. From here, look down on the colorful Haight or north for a bird's-eye view of the **Richmond District,** the rest of the city's Avenues.

Stern Grove at Sloat Blvd. and 19th Ave. is a wooded valley beloved for its Sunday con-certs. Just off Sloat is the main gate to the **San Francisco Zoo,** which offers an Insect Zoo, a Children's Zoo, and the usual caged collection of primates plus lions, tigers, and bears. (Mealtime for the big cats, at the Lion House at 2 p.m. every day except Monday, is quite a viewing treat.) Large **Lake Merced** just south, accessible via Skyline Blvd. (Hwy. 35) or Lake Merced Blvd., was once a tidal lagoon. These days it's a freshwater lake popular for canoeing, kayaking, nonmotorized boating (rent boats at the Boat House on Harding), fishing (large-mouth bass and trout), or just getting some fresh air.

The Lake Merced area offers one of the newer sections of the **Bay Area Ridge Trail,** a hiking route (signed with blue markers at major turning points and intersections) which one day will total 400 miles and connect 75 parks in nine Bay Area counties. (For more information, and to obtain printed guides to the trail, contact the Bay Area Ridge Trail Council, 311 California St., Suite 300, San Francisco 94194, tel. 415-391-0697.) Farther south still is **Fort Funston,** a one-time military installation on barren cliffs, a fa-vorite spot for hang gliders. East of Lake Merced is **San Francisco State University,** one of the state university system's best—noted for its

Sutro Library and **American Poetry Archives** —and the community of **Ingleside,** home of the 26-foot-tall sundial.

HAIGHT-ASHBURY

Aging hippies, random hipsters, and the hope-lessly curious of all ages are still attracted to San Francisco's Haight-Ashbury, once a com-mercial district for adjacent Golden Gate Park and a solid family neighborhood in the vicinity of Haight Street. The Golden Gate's block-wide **Panhandle** (which certainly resembles one on a map) was intended as the park's carriage en-trance, helped along toward the desired ambi-ence by neighboring Victorian-age Queen Annes. Once abandoned by the middle class, however, Haight-Ashbury declined into the cheap-rent paradise surrounded by parklands that became "Hashbury," "hippies," and head-quarters for the 1967 Summer of Love.

Drawn here by the drum song of the com-ing-of-age Aquarian Age, some 200,000 young people lived in subdivided Victorian crash pads, on the streets, and in the parks that summer, cul-turally recognizable by long hair, scruffy jeans, tie-dyed T-shirts, granny glasses, peace signs, beads, and the flowers-in-your-hair style of flow-ing skirts and velvet dresses. Essential, too, at that time: underground newspapers and unre-strained radio, black-lights and psychedelia, in-cense, anything that came from India (like gurus), acid and mescaline, hashish, water-pipes, marijuana and multicolored rolling pa-pers, harmonicas, tambourines, guitars, and bongo drums. A Volkswagen van was helpful, too, so loads of people could caravan off to anti-Vietnam-War rallies, to wherever it was the Grateful Dead or Jefferson Airplane were play-ing (for free, usually), or to Fillmore West and Winterland, where Bill Graham staged so many concerts. It was all fairly innocent, at first, an innocence that didn't last. By late 1967, cultural predators had arrived: the tourists, the national media, and serious drug pushers and pimps. Love proved to be fragile. Most true believers headed back to the land, and Haight-Ashbury became increasingly violent and dangerous, especially for the young runaways who arrived (and still arrive) to stake a misguided claim for personal freedom.

"The Haight" today is considerably cleaner, its Victorian neighborhoods spruced up but not exactly gentrified. The classic Haight-Ashbury head shops are long gone, runaway hippies replaced by runaway punks panhandling for quarters (or worse). But Haight Street and vicinity is still hip, still socially and politically aware, still worth a nostalgic stroll. The parkside Upper Haight stretch has more than its share of funky cafes, coffee shops, oddball bars and clubs, boutiques, and secondhand stores. You can even go bowling, at **Park Bowling Alley,** 1855 Haight, tel. (415) 752-2366. And if this all seems stodgy, amble on down to the Lower Haight near the Western Addition, an area fast becoming the city's new avant-garde district.

Haight-Ashbury Sights

Aside from the commercial versions, there are a few significant countercultural sights in the Upper Haight, like the old Victorian **Dead House** at 710 Ashbury, where the Grateful Dead lived and played their still-living music (and possibly where the term "deadheads" first emerged for the Dead's fanatic fans), and the **Jefferson Airplane**'s old pad at 2400 Fulton. Definitely worth a stop, for organic juice and granola, art to meditate by, and for New Age computer networking, is **The Red Victorian** at 1665 Haight (near Belvedere), also a fascinating bed and breakfast complex that successfully honors The Haight's original innocence. Do climb on up the steep paths into nearby **Buena Vista Park,** a shocking tangle of anarchistically enchanted forest, just for the through-the-trees views.

Otherwise, the scene here is wherever you can find it. **Bound Together** at 1369 Haight St., tel. (415) 431-8355, is a collective bookstore featuring a somewhat anarchistic collection: books on leftist politics, conspiracy theories, the occult, and sexuality. **Pipe Dreams** at 1376 Haight, tel. 431-3553, is one place to go for Grateful Dead memorabilia and quaint drug paraphernalia, like water pipes and bongs, but **Distractions** at 1552 Haight, tel. 252-8751, is truest to the form. In addition to the Dead selection—and don't ignore that "Closes early for Dead shows" sign on the door—you can also snoop through head shop supplies, an ample variety of Tarot cards, and Guatemalan clothing imports. The **Mascara Club** at 1408 Haight, tel. 863-2837, also honors the dead, but as in Frida Kahlo mania: Day of the Dead shrines and other Mexican religious icons, voodoo dolls, votive candles. **Bones of our Ancestors** at 622 Shrader, tel. 221-2427, sells magic crystals; **Forma** near Cole at 1715 Haight, tel. 751-0545, specializes in nostalgic toys and unusual sculptures.

Style is another Haight Street specialty. **Ameba** at 1732 Haight, tel. (415) 750-9368, is the most innovative, featuring both the bold and bizarre, everything designed locally and also available in toddler sizes. (What tyke could resist wearing the image of thousands of sperm, or Charlie Manson's maniacal mug?) Though secondhand clothing stores here tend to feature higher prices than elsewhere, two of the best are the **Buffalo Exchange** at 1555 Haight, tel. 431-7733, and **Aardvarks** at 1501 Haight, tel. 621-3141. For old-style music bargains—and actual *albums,* including a thousand hard-to-find ones—head to **Recycled Records** at 1377 Haight, tel. 626-4075. For thousands of used CDs and tapes, try **Reckless Records** at 1401 Haight, tel. 431-3434.

Shops of interest in the Lower Haight include **Deviant,** 473 Haight St., tel. (415) 554-0360, *the* place to find censored or banned comics and magazines. **The Naked Eye** at 533 Haight, tel. 864-2985, specializes in impossible-to-find videos. **Used Rubber U.S.A.** at 597 Haight, tel. 626-7855, makes very durable, very hip, high-style handbags out of otherwise unrecycled car tires. (A bit expensive.) Well respected in the neighborhood for more organic personal decoration is **Erno's Tattoo Parlor,** 152 Fillmore, tel. 861-9206. Shop the Lower Haight, too, for stylish used clothing stores with better pickings, lower prices, and zero crowds.

Haight-Ashbury Bars And Nightlife

A laid-back bar popular with young and old is **The Gold Cane** at 1569 Haight St., tel. (415) 626-1112, serving the cheapest drinks in town. More typical of modern Haight is **John Murio's Trophy Room,** 1811 Haight, tel. 752-2971, full of self-styled hippies and punks as well as unusual combinations of leather jackets, long hair, and tattoos. The crowd often shifts back and forth between here and the **Nightbreak,** 1821 Haight, tel. 221-9008, better for dancing and up-close-and-sweaty performances by the best local bands. Until recently, when groups started to catch on at the Nightbreak, in no time at all they ended up across the street, opening for a nationally known group at the **I-Beam.** But the I-Beam is no more, gone along with the street's ability to attract big talent. In its place is **The Quake,** 1748 Haight, tel. 668-6006, usually charging a cover for live music and dancing. (For big names, head to the Kennel Club—see below.) **Martin Macks** at 1568 Haight, tel. 824-0124, is cleaner and quieter, a bit more upscale than the usual Haight bar scene, with at least 10 imported beers on tap. Dressier and pricier—there's even a dress code—is the **Achilles Heel** at 1601 Haight, tel. 626-1800, a Victorian pub with Old World-decor and stained glass lamps. Somehow the Achilles sticks out like a sore thumb in this otherwise down-at-the-heels neighborhood.

Wilder by far are the bars and clubs in the Lower Haight. No matter what the weather, **Mad Dog in the Fog,** 530 Haight, tel. (415) 626-7279, is packed every night, the very mixed clientele attracted by the English pub-style dart boards as much as the live music. Serious drinking is the main agenda at loud and boisterous **The Toronado** across the street at 547 Haight, tel. 863-2276. **Tropical Haight** at 582 Haight, tel. 558-8019, is a high-concept venue for blues, jazz, and salsa. **Nickie's Haight Street BBQ** at 460 Haight, tel. 621-6508, serves BBQ by day, red-hot DJed dance music by night, everything from hip-hop and salsa to world beat and the music of Islam. (And the bar jumps, too.) Perhaps a tad too self-conscious for this very natural neighborhood is the **Noc Noc** at 557 Haight, tel. 861-5811, an artsy environment simultaneously inspired by "The Flintstones" cartoons and "Star Trek" reruns. For genuine cultural inspiration, though, that now-gone mural of former President George Bush shooting up at **The Kennel Club** was a classic. But the Kennel, six blocks off Haight at 628 Divisadero, tel. 931-1914, still opens its doors for nationally known live shows and dancing. The two-tiered black bleachers that ring the inside walls also make this a great place to just sit and watch. On Thursday and Saturday nights, it's called **The Box,** *the* high-energy hot spot for gays and lesbians.

THE MISSION DISTRICT

Vibrant and culturally electric, the Mission District is one of San Francisco's most exciting neighborhoods. The fact that most tourists never discover the area's pleasures is a sad commentary on our times. To the same extent people fear that which seems foreign in America—a nation created by foreigners—they miss out on the experience of life as it is. And the country becomes even more hell-bent on mandating social homogenization despite ideals and rhetoric to the contrary.

On any given day in the Mission District, especially if it's sunny, the neighborhood is busy with the business of life. The largely Hispanic population—Colombian, Guatemalan, Mexican, Nicaraguan, Peruvian, Panamian, Puerto Rican, Salvadorean—crowds the streets and congregates on corners. Whether Mission residents are out strolling with their children or shopping in the many bakeries, produce, and meat markets, the community's cultural energy is unmatched by any other city neighborhood—with the possible exception of Chinatown early in the morning.

The natural hospitality of the Mission District is partly climatic. Before the arrival of the Spanish, the Bay Area's Ohlone people *(Ramaytush* was what they called themselves) established their largest settlement here in the sheltered expanse later known as Mission Valley. Largely uninhabited until the 1860s, the valley attracted a large number of Irish immigrants and became one of the city's first suburbs. Most of the Mission District was spared the total devastation otherwise characteristic in the fiery aftermath of the 1906 earthquake, so some of San Francisco's finest Victorians are still area standouts.

The Mission's ungentrified modern attitude and relatively low rents have also created a haven for artists, writers, social activists, and politicos. The Latino arts scene is among the city's most powerful and original. This is San Francisco's "New Bohemia," a cultural crazy quilt where artists and assorted oddballs are not only tolerated but encouraged. Businesses catering to this emerging artistic consciousness are becoming prominent along Valencia Street, already considered home by the city's lesbian community.

more is appreciated. (The best time to arrive, to avoid busloads of tourists and the crush of school children studying California history, is before 10 a.m.) This is the sixth mission established in California by the Franciscan fathers. Founded earlier, in 1776, the modest chapel and outbuildings came to be known as **Mission Dolores,** the name derived from a nearby lagoon and creek, Arroyo de Nuestra Senora de los Dolores or "Stream of Our Lady of Sorrows."

And how apt the new shingle proved to be, in many ways. Inside the mission's walled compound, in the peaceful cemetery here—near the vine-entwined tombstones of pioneers and prominent citizens, like California's first governor under Mexican rule, Don Luis Antonio Arguello, and San Francisco's first mayor, Don Francisco de Haro—is the "Grotto of Lourdes," the unmarked grave of over 5,000 Ohlone and others among the native work force. Most died of measles and other introduced diseases in the early 1800s, the rest from other varieties of devastation. After California became a state, the first U.S. Indian agent came to town to take a census of the Native American population. It was an easy count, since there was only one, a man named Pedro Alcantara who was still grieving for a missing son.

The sturdy mission chapel—the small humble structure, not the soaring basilica adjacent—survived the 1906 earthquake due largely to its four-foot-thick adobe walls. Inside, the painted ceilings are an artistic echo of the Ohlone, whose original designs were painted with vegetable dyes. And the simple altar offers stark contrast to the grandeur next door. For a peek at the collection of mission artifacts and memorabilia, visit the small museum.

Mission District Murals
The entire Mission District is vividly alive, with aromas and sounds competing everywhere with color. And nothing in the Mission District is quite as colorful as its mural art. There are over 200 murals in and around the neighborhood, ranging from brilliantly colored homages to work, families, and spiritual flight to boldly political attacks on the status quo. **The Mexican Museum** at Fort Mason, tel. (415) 441-0445 or 441-0404 (recorded information), offers a self-guided mural map for $2, or you can take a walking tour (at last

Mission Dolores

Technically, the Mission District extends south from near the Civic Center to the vicinity of Army Street. Dolores or Church Street (or thereabouts) marks the western edge, Alabama Street the eastern. Mission Street is the main thoroughfare (BART stations at 16th and 24th), lined with discount stores and pawnshops. Main commercial areas include 16th Street between Mission and Dolores, 24th Street between Valencia and York, and Valencia Street—the bohemian center of social life, lined with coffeehouses, bars, bookstores, performance-art venues, and establishments serving the lesbian and women's community.

Mission Dolores
With the Mission District's return to a predominantly Hispanic ethnic attitude, a visit to the city's oldest structure seems especially fitting. Completed in 1791, Mission San Francisco de Asis at Dolores and 16th streets, tel. (415) 621-8203, is open daily 9-4. A donation of $1 or

report, scheduled for first and third Saturdays of every month at 1:30 p.m.) with well-informed guides from the **Precita Eyes Mural Center,** a charming gallery at 348 Precita Ave. (just south of Army), tel. 285-2287.

Start with some **"BART art,"** at the 24th Street station, where Michael Rios' columns of humanoids lift up the rails. On Mission near 24th is the **Mexican Culture Center,** tel. (415) 863-7058, a community cultural and sociopolitical center marked outside by a mammoth mural, inside by its **Galeria Museo** collection of folk art and folklore exhibits. Particularly impressive, if you can't enjoy the Mission's entire outdoor art collection, are the murals eight blocks down, off 24th Street on the fences and garage doors along **Balmy Alley,** and also at the **Flynn Elementary School** at Precita and Harrison (near the mural center). For fans of Frida Kahlo, artist and wife of Diego Rivera, there's a new mural in her honor at 14th and Natoma. Stop too at the nonprofit **La Galeria de la Raza** at 2851 24th St. (at Bryant), tel. 826-8009, featuring some exciting, straight-ahead political art attacks, and the affiliated **Studio 24** gift shop adjacent, with everything from books and clothing to religious icons and Day of the Dead dolls.

East of the Mission District proper and southeast of the SoMa scene is gentrifying (at least on the north side) Noe Valley-like **Potrero Hill,** known for its roller-coaster road rides (a favorite spot for filming TV and movie chases scenes) and the world-famous **Anchor Brewing Com-**

pany microbrewery and its Anchor Steam beer, 1705 Mariposa St., tel. (415) 863-8350, tours available. And if you drive to Potrero Hill, detour to the **"Poor Man's Lombard"** at 20th and Vermont, which has earned the dubious honor of being the city's second twistiest street. *This* snake-like thoroughfare is not festooned with well-landscaped sidewalks and flowerbeds, but instead an odd assortment of abandoned furniture, beer bottles, and trash. Not yet socially transformed is the south side of the hill, close to once-industrialized, now poverty, drugs, and violence-ravaged **Bayview-Hunters Point,** the neighborhoods left behind when World War II-era shipbuilding ceased.

Other Mission District Sights

If you're curious about how the West's most historic britches evolved, stop by **Levi Strauss & Co.** at 250 Valencia St., tel. (415) 565-9153, for a free tour (Weds. only, at 10:30 a.m. and 1 p.m., reservations required—and make them well in advance). This, Levi's oldest factory, was built in 1906 after the company's original waterfront plant was destroyed by the earthquake and fire. The company is the world's largest clothing manufacturer, and most of its factories are fully automated. But here you can hear the riveting story of how Levi's 501's were originally made, and see it, too. Skilled workers cut, stitch, and assemble the button-fly jeans, as in the earlier days of the empire that Bavarian immigrant Levi Strauss built. During the boom days of

Mission District mural

the California gold rush, miners needed *very* rugged pants, something that wouldn't bust out at the seams. Strauss stitched up his first creations from tent canvas; when he ran out of that, he switched to sturdy brown cotton "denim" from Nimes, France. Levi's characteristic pocket rivets came along in the 1870s, but "blue jeans" weren't a reality until the next decade, when indigo blue dye was developed.

Other area apparel attractions include **Clothes Contact** at 473 Valencia, tel. (415) 621-3212, a store selling fashionable vintage clothing for $6 per pound. (Consumer alert: those big suede jackets in the back weigh more than you might imagine.) Worth poking into, too, is the **Community Thrift Store** at 623 Valencia, tel. 861-4910, a fundraising venture for the gay and lesbian Tavern Guild—an expansive, inexpensive, and well-organized place, with a book selection rivaling most used bookstores. (The motto here is "out of the closet, into the store.") For the latest word on feminist and lesbian art shows, readings, performances, and other events, stop by the nonprofit **Women's Building** just off Valencia at 3543 18th St., tel. 431-1180. **Old Wives Tales** at 1009 Valencia, tel. 821-4675, has a fairly complete selection of lesbian and feminist books, though cooperatively run **Modern Times Bookstore** at 968 Valencia, tel. 282-9246, is the source for progressive, radical, and Third World literature, magazines, and tapes. **La Pajarita** ("The Paper Bird") at 3125 16th St., tel. 861-2209, is also a fascination, the place to stop for newspapers, books, and magazines from the Spanish-speaking Americas and France, along with an intriguing selection of African, Caribbean, French, Latin, and salsa-style music.

And if you're down on your luck, head over to **Lady Luck Candle Shop** at 311 Valencia, tel. (415) 621-0358, a small store selling some pretty big juju, everything from high-test magic candles and religious potions (like St. John the Conqueror Spray) to Lucky Mojo Oil and Hold Your Man essential oil. **Good Vibrations** at 1210 Valencia, tel. 550-0827, home of the vibrator museum, is a clean, user-friendly, liberated shop where women (and some men) come for adult toys, and to peruse the selection of in-print erotica, including history and literature.

More common in the Mission District are neighborhood-style antique and secondhand

stores of every stripe. Bargains abound, without the inflated pricetags typical of trendier, more tourist-traveled areas.

Mission District
Entertainment And Nightlife

The Roxie, 3117 16th St., tel. (415) 863-1087, is the neighborhood's renowned repertory film venue, with a full schedule of eclectic and foreign films as well as special programs, including live audience interviews with filmmakers. Most of the Mission's coffeehouses, bars, and clubs are equally entertaining. **Cafe Picaro** at 3120 16th St., tel. 431-4089, is an unpretentious new bohemian coffeehouse-cum-used bookstore (read or buy) and restaurant. For better food (vegetarian) and flashier hairstyles, head to **The Beano** at 878 Valencia St., tel. 285-2728, another artist-type coffee and talk shop. **Radio Valencia** at 199 Valencia, tel. 826-1199, puts a musical spin on the coffeehouse scene, serving up the latest releases from a broad range of genres along with an occasional record release party. Beer and wine served, too.

Bars and clubs offer everything. **Doctor Bombay's** at 3192 16th St., tel. (415) 431-5255, is dim and diminutive, the clientele quite happy to talk the night away while downing the good doctor's award-winning specialty drink, the melon-flavored Pixie Piss. Across the street is the **Albion**, 3139 16th, tel. 552-8558, a popular corner bar complete with pool table and degenerative art—home-away-from-home for a hip but friendly, artsy crowd. Occasional live music. When the intellectual conversations at Doctor Bombay's and the Albion become unbearable, an alternative is **The Clubhouse** at 3160 16th, tel. 621-5877, a fun dance and live music venue, once a San Franisco firehouse. **Esta Noche** at 3079 16th, tel. 861-5757, is the red-hot Latino answer to the almost-all-white gay bars in the Castro.

Athens by Night at 811 Valencia St., tel. (415) 647-3744, is the place to go for live Greek music (Friday and Saturday nights) and belly dancers. **The Zan Zibar** (formerly the Crystal Pistol), 842 Valencia, tel. 695-7887, attracts all persuasions—old, young, gay, straight—who dance with happy abandon on the tiny back-room dance floor. **The Chameleon** at 853 Valencia, tel. 821-1891, is an unbearably smoky dive with a lizard motif and bizarre felt paintings on the walls, popular with punk throwbacks in tattoos and torn second-hand clothing. Many are willing to fork over the $3 cover charge for the live alternative bands. Way down at 901 Valencia is **La Rondalla,** tel. 647-7474, the most festive bar around, what with the year-round Christmas lights, smoke-stained tinsel, and revolving overhead disco ball. (Quite decent traditional Mexican food is served in the restaurant.)

El Rio at 3158 Mission St., tel. (415) 282-3325, features live music, from rock to world beat, as well as stand-up comedy. There's usually a steep cover charge, and drinks are also expensive. But the outdoor deck, shuffleboard set-up, and pool tables make this an excellent warm-weather hang out. Next door is **Cesar's Latin Palace,** also known as the All-Star, 3140 Mission, tel. 648-6611, where people soak up live salsa bands and dance the samba.

CASTRO STREET AND VICINITY

The very idea is enough to make America's righteous religious right explode in an apoplectic fit, but the simple truth is that San Francisco's Castro Street is one of the safest in the entire city—and that's not just a reference to sex practices.

This tight-knit, well-established community of lesbian women and gay men represents roughly 15% of the city's population, and 35% of registered voters. Nationally and internationally, the Castro District epitomizes out-of-the-closet living. (There's nothing in this world like the Castro's Gay Freedom Day Parade—usually headed by hundreds of women on motorcycles, the infamous Dykes on Bikes—and no neighborhood throws a better street party.) People here are committed to protecting their own and creating safe neighborhoods. What this means, for visitors straight or gay, is that there is a *response*—people get out of their cars, or rush out of restaurants, clubs, and apartment buildings—at the slightest sign that something is seriously amiss.

Who ever would have guessed that a serious revival of community values in the U.S. would start in the Castro?

Actually, there have been many indications. And there are many reasons. The developing cultural and political influence of the Castro District became apparent in 1977, when openly gay Harvey Milk was elected to the San Francisco Board of Supervisors. But genuine acceptance seemed distant—never more so than in 1978, when both Milk and Mayor George Moscone were assassinated by conservative political rival Dan White, who had resigned his board seat and wanted it back. (White's "diminished capacity" defense argument, which claimed that his habitual consumption of high-sugar junk food had altered his brain chemistry, became a national scandal but ultimately proved successful. He was sentenced to a seven-year prison term.)

So, while Castro District community values are quite strong and getting stronger, the ambience is not exactly apple-pie Americana. People with pierced body parts (some easily visible, some not) and dressed in motorcycle jackets still stroll in and out of leather bars. And shops can be somewhat unusual, like **Art Lick Gallery** —noted for scintilating contemporary art installations and painted furniture—**Condomania**—a reference not to housing units but to high-class condoms that come in all colors, flavors, and textures—and **Does Your Mother Know,** a seriously homoerotic greeting card shop on 18th Street.

Castro Sights
The neighborhood's business district, both avant-garde and gentrified Victorian, is actually quite small, stretching for three blocks along Castro Street between Market and 19th, also a short distance in each direction from 18th and Castro—all included, geographically, in what was once recognizable as **Eureka Valley.** (Parking can be a problem, once you've arrived, so take the Muni Metro and climb off at the Castro Street Station.) Some people also include the gentrifying **Noe Valley** (with its upscale 24th Street shopping district) in the general Castro stream of consciousness, but the technical dividing line is near the crest of Castro Street at 22nd Street. Keep driving on Upper Market Street and you'll be winding up into the city's geographic center. Though the ascent is actually

easier from Haight-Ashbury (from Twin Peaks Boulevard just off 17th—see a good road map), either way you'll arrive at or near the top of **Twin Peaks,** with its terraced neighborhoods, astounding views, and some of the best stairway walks. More challenging is the short but steep hike to the top of **Corona Heights Park** (at Roosevelt), also noted for the very good **Josephine D. Randall Junior Museum,** tel. (415) 863-1399, a youth-centered natural sciences, arts, and activities center open Tues.-Sat. 10-5.

Down below, **A Different Light,** 489 Castro St., tel. (415) 431-0891, is the city's best gay and lesbian bookstore, with literature by and for. Readings and other events are occasionally offered; call for current information. A fabulous resource in nearby Noe Valley is the nonprofit **Small Press Traffic Literary Arts Center,** 3599 24th St. (at Guerrero), tel. 285-8394, open Tues.-Sat. noon-6 p.m. and specializing in hard-to-find small press books, noncommercial samples of the printer's art, and literary magazines. Lectures, readings, and writers' workshops are also offered.

Truly classic and quite traditional is the handsome and authentic art deco **Castro Theater** at Castro and Market, tel. (415) 621-6120, still a favorite city venue for classic movies and film festivals. **Cliff's Variety** at 479 Castro, tel. 431-5365, is another classic, a wonderfully old-fashioned hardware store where you can buy almost anything, from power saws to Play-doh. Also stop by **The Names Project** at 2362 Market, tel. 863-1966, a museum-like memorial to those felled by AIDS, including the famous AIDS Memorial Quilt, each section created by friends and family in honor of someone who has died. Adjacent (in the same building) is **Under One Roof,** tel. 252-9430, a cool and classy little gift shop with Act Up votive candles, art work, T-shirts, and more. All money earned goes to support some 50 AIDS service organizations.

Castro District Nightlife

Many of San Francisco's 200-plus gay bars are in the Castro District. Those in the know say the best way to find just the scene you're looking for is to wander. **The Cafe,** once known as Cafe San Marcos, 2367 Market St., tel. (415) 861-3846, is the Castro's best lesbian bar, also attracting some heteros and gay men. From its balcony overlooking Market and Castro, you can get a good overview. Also featured: indoor

Small Press Traffic
• Literary • Arts • Center •

patio, pool table, and loud music. Alas, the comfortable lounge chairs have been replaced by ordinary bar stools. **Cafe du Nord** is underground, quite literally, at 2170 Market, tel. 861-5016, featuring cheap drinks and good bar snacks along with smoke and only moderate pretense. The food's good, too. **Josie's Cabaret & Juice Joint** at 3583 16th St., tel. 861-7933, is the place to go for healthy relaxation and pure juice intoxication. There's usually a cover charge for the show—the best local and national gay and lesbian performers, from cabaret acts to stand-up comedy.

SOUTH OF MARKET

Known by old-timers as "south of the slot," a reference to a neighborhood sans cable cars, San Francisco's South of Market Area was a working- and middle-class residential area—until all the homes incinerated in the firestorm following the great earthquake of 1906. Rebuilt early in the century with warehouses, factories, train yards, and port businesses at China Basin, these days the area has gone trendy. In the style of New York's SoHo (South of Houston), this semi-industrial stretch of the city now goes by "SoMa." As is usually the case, the vanguard of gentrification was the artistic community: the dancers, musicians, sculptors, photographers, painters, and graphic designers who require low rents and room to create. Rehabilitating old warehouses and industrial sheds here into studios and performance spaces solved all but strictly creative problems. Then came the attractively inexpensive factory outlet stores, followed by eclectic cafes and nightclubs. The construction of **Moscone Convention Center** as part of the Yerba Buena Gardens redevelopment project, which will one day include the city's Museum of Modern Art, sealed the neighborhood's fate. Even near the once-abandoned waterfront just south of the traditional Financial District boundaries, avant-garde construction like **Number One Market Street,** which incorporates the old Southern Pacific Building, and **Rincon Center,** which encompasses the preserved Depression-era mural art of the Rincon Annex

CLEAN UP YOUR ACT AT BRAINWASH

No doubt the cleanest scene among SoMa's hot spots is BrainWash at 1122 Folsom, tel. (415) 861-FOOD and 431-WASH, a combination cafe, smart bar, night-club, laundromat, and loosely affiliated upstairs gym facility. The brainchild of UC Berkeley and Free Speech Movement alumnus Susan Schindler, BrainWash ain't heavy, just semi-industrial, a reformed warehouse from the beamed ceilings and neon to the concrete floor. The decor here includes cafe tables corraled by steel office chairs with original de-coupaged artwork on the seats. (Admit it. Haven't you always wanted to sit on Al-bert Einstein's face?) At last report, some tables were also plugged into the Bay Area's new coffeehouse-to-coffeehouse computer net-working system—intellectu-al discourse gone electronic. BrainWash also features a small counter/bar area, and bathrooms for either "Readers" (lined with *Dirty Laundry Comics* wallpaper) or "Writers" (with walls and ceiling of green chalkboard, chalk provided for generating brainwashable graffiti). Since literary urges know no boundaries in terms of gender, of course both are open to both basic sexes. And others.

The small cafe at BrainWash offers quick, simple fare—salads, spinach and feta turnovers, pizza, and decent sandwiches (vegetarian and otherwise)—plus pastries and decadent pies, cakes, and cookies. Try a BrainWash Brownie, either double chocolate or double espresso. There's liquid espresso too, of course, plus cappuccino and latte, fresh unfiltered fruit or carrot juice, teas, beer, and wine. Or try a smart drink, "Designer Mood Cocktails" like Fast Blast, Sidewinder, and Quantum Punch containing L-phenylalanine and various other chemicals and ingredients purported to enhance one's intelligence. But be smart about it. Smart drinks are for adults only—even then with notable exceptions, such as pregnant women, lactating women, and people with Parkinson's and other diseases—and a smart person never drinks more than three in any eight-hour period.

Behind the cafe (and glass wall) is the Brain-Wash washhouse, a high-tech herd of washers and dryers ($1.50 per load for a regular wash load, $3 for a jumbo washer, and a quarter for 10 minutes of dryer time). Ask about the laundromat's wash-and-fold and dry-cleaning services. Upstairs is a combination theater and personal fitness center, also Neuroti Records (a record store). The whole shebang here is open daily 7:30 a.m.-11 p.m. (until 2 a.m. on Friday and Saturday nights). "Last call" for dryers is 10 p.m. nightly. Call ahead to make sure, but live music is usually scheduled after 9 p.m. on Tues.-Thurs. and Friday or Saturday nights, jukebox available otherwise. BrainWash also sponsors community events, such as the "Take The Dirty Shirt Off Your Back" benefit for the STOP AIDS Project. The place can also be rented for private parties.

So come on down, almost anytime, for some Clorox and croissants.

Post Office, have added a new look to once down-and-out areas. Land values are shooting up in areas where previously only the neighborhood homeless did that, and the starving artists have moved on to the Lower Haight and the Mission District. In SoMa, the strictly eccentric is now becoming more self-consciously so.

SoMa Sights

Actually closer to the waterfront and Financial District, the **Jewish Community Museum** at 121 Steuart Street, tel. (415) 543-8880, features changing, usually exceptional exhibits on Jewish art, culture, and history. The **Telephone Pioneers Communications Museum** at the corner of Natoma and New Montgomery, tel. 542-0182, offers electronic miscellany and telephone memorabilia dating to the 1870s. Across from the Moscone Center is a major presence in San Francisco's art scene, the **Ansel Adams**

Center at 250 4th St., tel. 495-7000 or 495-7242, with five galleries dedicated to the photographic art, one set aside exclusively for Adams' own internationally renowned black-and-white works. Less serious is **The Cartoon Art Museum** on the fifth floor of the San Francisco Print Center Building, 665 3rd St., tel. 546-3922, which has recently doubled in size and chronicles the history of the in-print giggle, from cartoon sketches and finished art to toys and videos. Open Wed.-Fri. 11-5, Sat. 10-5. In the foyer is **Explore Print!** formerly The Printing Museum of Northern California, tel. 495-8242, open weekdays 9-5, on Saturday and at other times by appointment, with several interactive video displays and other exhibits on printer's ink through the ages.

The Greek revival **Old U.S. Mint Museum** at 5th and Mission, tel. 744-6830, open weekdays 10-4, is a fabulous free museum housed in San Francisco's old federal mint building, the great gray "Granite Lady" circa 1874, responsible for stamping some of the finest coins of the realm from raw California gold and Nevada silver. One of the city's best museums, this one tells the California money story from gold mining and stamp mills to coin-making. Coin collectors, *do* stop in at the Treasury Department's numismatic shop.

SoMa Shopping

Shop-and-drop types, please note: serious bargains are available throughout SoMa's garment district, the city's largest industry, a wholesale business of $5 billion annually. Most of the manufacturing factories are between 2nd and 11th streets, and many have off-price retail outlets for their own wares. And you won't necessarily shop in comfort, since some don't have dressing rooms and are as jam-packed as the post office at tax time. Major merchandise marts, mostly for wholesalers, are clustered along Kansas and Townsend streets. Some retail discount outlets for clothing, jewlery, and accessories are here, too, also along Brannan Street between 3rd and 6th streets. If at all possible, come any day *but* Saturday, and always be careful where you park. The parking cops are serious about ticketing violators.

Yerba Buena Square, 899 Howard St. (at 5th), is an off-price factory mall. **Six Sixty Center** at 660 3rd St. (at Townsend) offers 20 discount outlets under one roof. Some of the best places have to be hunted down, however. **Esprit Direct** at 499 Illinois (at 16th) is a warehouse-sized store offering discounts on San Francisco's hippest women's and children's wear. (Try lunch at adjacent Caffe Esprit.) **Lilli Ann,** 2701 16th St., sells both clasic and contemporary women's wear at near-wholesale prices. For activewear, leotards and leggings to T-shirts, try **San Francisco City Lights Factory Outlet** at 333 9th St. (between Harrison and Folsom). **ACA JOE** at 148 Townsend specializes in men's casual wear, but women like the sweats here, too. Neighborhood anchor **Gunne Sax** at 35 Stanford Alley (between 2nd and 3rd, Brannan and Townshend) has a huge selection, over 25,000 garments (including dress-up dresses), best bargains way in the back. **Simply Cotton** at 610 3rd St. specializes in manufacturer-direct women's wear, and **Harper Greer for the Larger Woman** at 580 4th St. offers wholesale-priced fashions for women size 14 and larger.

Since shopping outlets open, close, and change names or locations at a remarkable rate, consult the "Style" section of the Sunday *San Francisco Examiner-Chronicle,* which lists discount centers and factory outlets in SoMa and elsewhere around town.

SoMa Clubs And Nightlife

Many of the restaurants in the South of Market Area (see "City-style Chow" below) do double-duty as bars and club venues. You won't go far before finding something going on. The classic, for people who wear ties even after work, is **Julie's Supper Club** at 1123 Folsom, tel. (415) 861-0707, though the **M&M Tavern** at 198 5th St., tel. 362-6386, is also a genuine institution, the place to find most of the *Chronicle* or *Examiner* staff, even during the day. The **Southside,** 1190 Folsom, tel. 431-7275, is a popular watering hole for celebrities, models, people who look like extras from the defunct "Dallas" TV series, and Financial District escapees.

The best blues, jazz, rhythm and blues, and zydeco club in town is **Slim's** at 333 11th St., tel. (415) 621-3330, the cutting edge for conscious yuppies, pretty steep cover. Before braving the line, fill up at the **20 Tank Brewery** across the street at 316 11th, tel. 255-9455, a lively brewpub run by the same microbrewery folks who brewed up Triple Rock in Berkeley.

The **Caribbean Zone** at 55 Natoma, tel. (415) 541-9465, has a mezzanine cocktail lounge created from an airplane fuselage, so you can sit and down a few while porthole-window television screens and sound effects simulate takeoff (and crash landings). The point of **Club DV8** (don't think about it too hard) at 540 Howard, tel. 957-1730, is unclear, but people tend to take the attitude too seriously. With a cave-like contempo ambience and three dance floors, this is one of those clubs where people are all officially deviant but somehow the same, wearing pale complexions and too much black. Cover. Artistically and genetically expansive, in a punkish sort of way, is the **DNA Lounge** at 375 11th St., tel. 626-1409, serving up dancing nightly after 9, cover on weekends.

But don't miss the **Paradise Lounge** at 1501 Folsom, tel. (415) 861-6906, marvelously maze-like and sporting several bars, two separate live stages, and a smoke-filled upstairs pool hall. Also upstairs is **Above Paradise,** featuring acoustical music and poetry readings. And all of this adventure is included for one reasonable cover charge.

Since SoMa in the 1970s was a nighttime playground for the bad-boys-in-black-leather set, the gay bar scene here is still going strong. The *original* gay bar is **The Stud** at 399 9th St. (at Harrison), tel. (415) 863-6623, formerly a leather bar, now a dance bar. For dancing in the gay, country-western style, try the **Rawhide II** at 289 7th St., tel. 621-1192. But the hottest younger-set gay nightclub in the neighborhood, some say in the entire city, is the **End Up** (also known as Club Uranus and Dekadance) at 955 Harrison, tel. 543-7700, famous for serious dancing—"hot bodies," too, according to an informed source—and, for cooling down, its large outdoor deck.

AN OPEN-MINDED GUIDE TO NIGHTCLUBBING IN SAN FRANCISCO

First, ask the basic questions: Who am I? What am I doing here? Where do I belong? To go nightclubbing in San Francisco, at least *ask* the questions. The answers don't really matter; your political, social, sexual, and musical preferences will be matched somewhere. Rave, techno, acid, house, fusion, industrial, world beat—whatever it is you're into, it's out there, just part of the creative carnival world of San Francisco nightclubbing. Everything goes, especially cultural taboos, leaving only freewheeling imaginations and an unadulterated desire to do one thing and only one thing—dance with total abandon. In the city, heteros, gays, lesbians, blacks, whites, Asians, and Latinos all writhe together, unified in a place where all prejudice drops away: the dance floor.

The hottest dance clubs come and go considerably faster than the Muni buses do, so the key to finding the hippest, most happening spot is to ask around. Ask people who look like they should know, such as young fashion junkies working in trendy clothing shops, used-record stores, or other abodes of pretentious cool. If you're seeking one of those infamous and illegal "warehouse" parties, then look for small invitational flyers tacked to telephone poles or posted in the above-mentioned and other likely places (particularly in the Haight, lower Haight, and Castro neighborhoods). The flyers announce a party and list a phone number to call. When you call up—ooh, the intrigue—you'll get directions to that night's secret dance locale. Warning: these roving nonlicensed dance clubs tend to put on quite crowded parties, very expensive to boot.

Throbbing together with hundreds of other euphorics, experiencing ecstasy en masse, may be the closest we'll ever really get to living in one united world. Still, San Francisco nightclub virgins tend to avoid their initiation, somehow intimidated by the frenzied cosmic collision of electrifying lights, thumping dance tunes, and sweat-drenched bodies. But be not afraid. There are answers to even the three most common worries:

Worry: I can't dance. *Answer:* It wouldn't matter even if you could. The dance floors are so crowded, at best it's possible only to bounce up and down.

Worry: I'm straight (or gay) and the crowd seems to be predominantly gay (or straight). *Answer:* Since the limits of gender and sexuality are hopelessly blurred in San Francisco, and since nobody would care even if they weren't, just dump your angst and dance.

Worry: I'm afraid I'll look like a fool (feel out of place, be outclassed, fall down, throw up, whatever). *Answer:* As we said, nobody cares. You're totally anonymous, being one of over 725,000 people in town. And no matter what you do, nobody will notice, since narcissism in San Francisco's clubs is at least as deep as the Grand Canyon.

—*Tim Moriarty*

DELIGHTS AND DIVERSIONS

WALKING TOURS

San Francisco is a walking city par excellence. With enough time and inclination, exploring the hills, stairways, and odd little neighborhood nooks and crannies is the most rewarding way to get to know one's way around. Helpful for getting started are the free neighborhood **walking tour pamphlets** (Pacific Heights, Union Square, Chinatown, Fisherman's Wharf, and more) available at the Convention & Visitors Bureau Information Center downstairs at Powell and Market (see "Information" under "Just the Facts" below). Also helpful: books like Adah Bakalinsky's *Stairway Walks in San Francisco,* Michelle Brandt's *Timeless Walks in San Francisco: A Historical Walking Guide,* and any of Margot Patterson Doss's time-honored on-foot guidebooks, like *A Walker's Yearbook: 52 Seasonal Walks in the San Francisco Bay Area.*

Even with substantially less time there are excellent options. Free or low-cost walking tours are offered by a variety of local nonprofit organizations. Quite unusual commercial tours are also available, most ranging in price from $15 to $40 per person, more for all-day tours.

Free And Inexpensive Walking Tours
The City Guides walking tours offered by Friends of the San Francisco Public Library, headquartered at the Civic Center public library, (call 415-557-4266 for a recorded schedule of upcoming walks: what, where, and when), include many worthwhile neighborhood prowls. Most walks include local architecture, culture, and history, though the emphasis—Waterfront by the Full Moon, Pacific Heights Mansions, the Beaux Arts City, the Gold Rush City, Victorian San Francisco, Haight-Ashbury, Mission Murals, Japantown—can be surprising. City Guides are free, but donations are definitely appreciated.

Heritage Walks are sponsored by the Foundation for San Francisco's Architectural Heritage, headquartered in the historic Haas-Lilienthal House at 2007 Franklin St., tel. (415) 441-3004, and include architectural walking tours of Chinatown, Pacific Heights, and the Presidio.

Friends of Recreation and Parks, headquartered at McLaren Lodge in Golden Gate Park, Stanyan and Fell streets, tel. 221-1311 (for upcoming hike schedule), offers guided flora, fauna, and history walks through the park from May through October, Saturdays at 11 a.m. and Sundays at 11 a.m. and 2 p.m., group tours also available. **Precita Eyes Mural Center,** 348 Precita Ave. (near Folsom), tel. 285-2287, offers fascinating two-hour mural walks through the Mission District on the first and third Saturdays of the month starting at 1:30 p.m., $3 adults, $2 seniors, and $1 students. No reservations necessary. In addition to its self-guided Mission murals tour, the **Mexican Museum** at Fort Mason, tel. 441-0445 or (for recorded information) 441-0404, sponsors docent-led tours of San Francisco's Diego Rivera murals. The **Chinese Culture Center,** tel. 986-1822, offers both a culinary and cultural heritage walking tour. (See "Information" below for more about this organization.)

Commercial Walking Tours
Frisco Productions offers very entertaining walking tours, along with bus tours and other specialties, with exceptional information always enhanced along the way by period-costumed actors and actresses. (For more information, see "Time-Tripping with Mr. Frisco.") **Helen's Walk Tours,** P.O. Box 9164, Berkeley 94709, tel. (510) 524-4454, can also be a bit theatrical—a personal touch provided by very personable Helen Rendon, tour guide and part-time actress. Tour groups usually meet "under the clock" at the St. Francis Hotel (Helen's the one with the wonderfully dramatic hat) before setting off on an entertaining two-hour tour of Victorian Mansions, North Beach (want to know where Marilyn Monroe married Joe DiMaggio?), or Chinatown. Other options: combine parts of two tours into a half-day Grand Tour, or, if enough time and interested people are available, other neighborhood tours can be requested. Make reservations for any tour at least one day in advance.

Adah Bakalinsky, author of the ever-popular *Stairway Walks in San Francisco,* is happy to share her knowledge with small groups on guided weekday two- to three-mile walks. For information, send a self-addressed stanped envelope to **Stairway Walks,** 101 Lombard St., Apt. 606, San Francisco 94111.

Dashiell Hammett Literary Tours, tel. (707) 939-1214, are led by Don Herron, author of *The Literary World of San Francisco and its Environs.* The half-day tours wander through downtown streets and alleys, on the trail of both the writer and his detective story hero, Sam Spade. Usually offered from May through August. Other literary themes can be arranged. Early risers will appreciate the early-morning Union Square, Chinatown, and Barbary Coast tours, as well as the *Maltese Falcon* murder site tour offered by writer John McCarroll through **A.M. Walks,** tel. (415) 928-5965. A bit more specialized are **Antique Amblings,** tel. 435-5036, exploring the city's neighborhood antique shops (six different tours), and **Roger's High Point Walking Tours,** tel. 742-9611, including unusual adventures like trips through the Cable Car Barn, to the top of Lombard Street, and over the Golden Gate Bridge. **Bella Passeggiat—Beautiful Walks in San Francisco,** tel. 648-8159, offers a four-hour Art in the Park Tour to the Asian Art and M.H. de Young museums (gourmet picnic included), an Alamo Park Victorian Home tour (complete with afternoon tea and scones), and other cultural heritage walking tours.

Cruisin' the Castro, historical tours of San Francisco's gay mecca, tel. (415) 550-8110 (best hours: 5-8 p.m.), are led by local historian Ms. Trevor Hailey and offer unique insight into how San Francisco's gay community has shaped the city's political, social, and cultural development. Everyone is welcome; reservations are required. Tours are offered Tues.-Sat., starting at 10 a.m. at Harvey Milk Plaza (brunch at the Elephant Walk Restaurant), continuing through the community's galleries, shops, and cultural sights, then ending at the Names Project (home of the AIDS Memorial Quilt) at 1:30 p.m.

Culinary Walking Tours

No matter where else you walk off to, don't overlook San Francisco's fabulous food tours—most of which focus on Chinatown. **Wok Wiz Chinatown Walking Tours,** headquartered at the Holiday Inn, 750 Kearny St., Suite 800, tel. (415) 355-9657 or 981-5588 (reservations required), are already a local institution. The small-group Wok Wiz culinary and historical adventures are led by founder Shirley Fong-Torres, her husband Bernie Carver, and other tour leaders, usually starting at 10 a.m. at the Holiday Inn on Kearny and ending at 1:30 p.m. after a marvelous dim sum lunch (optional). Stops along the way include Portsmouth Square, herb, pastry, and tea shops (where the traditional tea ceremony is shared), a Chinese open-air market, a fortune cookie factory, and a brush-paint artist's studio. Along with taking in the sights along Chinatown's main streets and back alleys, visitors receive a fairly comprehensive history lesson about the Chinese in California, and particularly in San Francisco. Wok Wiz also offers an "I Can't Believe I Ate My Way Through Chinatown!" tour, with an exclusive emphasis on Chinese foods and food preparation, and a shorter (90-minute) "Yin Yang" history tour of Chinatown. (Special group tours can also be arranged.) Serious food aficionados will probably recognize Fong-Torres, well-known for her articles, books, and Chinese cooking television appearances. She is also the author of several books, including *San Francisco Chinatown: A Walking Tour* and the *Wok Wiz Chinatown Tour Cookbook.*

There are other food-lover tour options. Combining two cross-cultural tidbits of folk wisdom— "You never age at the dinner table" (Italian) and "To eat is greater than heaven" (Chinese)— Ruby Tom's **Glorious Food Culinary Walk Tours,** tel. (415) 441-5637, stroll through both North Beach and Chinatown, separately or on the same tour. Special walking tours include North Beach Bakeries (an early morning slice of life), North Beach Nightbeat (complete with cabaret, theater, or jazz entertainment), and Lanterns of Chinatown (a stroll under the night-

Lanterns of Chinatown (a stroll under the night-lit red lanterns followed by a hosted banquet). Ruby Tom is a graduate of the California Culinary Academy. She is an award-winning chef herself and conducted and organized the first professional chefs exchange between the People's Republic of China and the city of San Francisco. **Chinatown Discovery Tours,** tel. 982-8839, conducted by San Francisco native Linda Lee, also walk visitors through Chinatown's past and present; tours include a traditional Chinese luncheon or dinner. Call for reservations and current schedule.

OTHER TOURS

Tours By Land
A Day in Nature, tel. (415) 673-0548, offers very personalized half-day or full-day naturalist-guided tours (groups of just one to four people) of North Bay destinations like the Marin Headlands, Muir Woods, and the Napa Valley wine country, complete with gourmet picnic. **Artfocus** at 2616 Jackson St., tel. 921-4111 or 567-3225, specializes in Bay Area art—with tours of museums, selected galleries, and fine art publishors. Reservations required. **Sketchbook Tours,** tel. 668-8444, feature picturesque introductions to San Francisco history and cityscapes by local artist Jessica Hart (materials and instruction provided). **Pro Photo Tours,** tel. (510) 945-7549, offers day-long photography tours of San Francisco and vicinity, technical instruction and composition advice included along with history and other topical asides.

Some tour companies aim to entertain visiting businesspeople. **Business Outdoor Adventures (BOA),** headquartered in San Jose, tel. (408) 997-7280 or toll-free (800) 888-7088, does it all, from bungee jumping and hot-air ballooning to fishing, hang gliding, horseback riding, and whitewater rafting. Perhaps in honor of that great American myth of the Wild West, **Great Guns Shooting Tours,** tel. (510) 284-1890, provides the whole works, from transportation to ammo and weapons.

The Gray Line, tel. (415) 558-9400, is the city's largest tour operator, commandeering an impressive fleet of standard-brand buses and red, London-style double-deckers. What you'll get is pretty much what it sounds like, a narrat-ed tour touching on the basics, in San Francisco proper and beyond. Unlike other companies, though, Gray Line offers its city tour in multiple languages: Japanese, German, French, Italian, and Spanish. Much more personal is the **Great Pacific Tour Company,** tel. 626-4499, which offers four different tours in 13-passenger minivans, half-day city or Marin County trips plus full-day Monterey Peninsula and Napa/Sonoma wine country tours (foreign-language tours available). **Tower Tours,** tel. 434-8687, also offers a 25-person Yosemite trip, and six-person tours are offered by **Quality Tours,** tel. 994-5054. Other firms create quite personalized, special-interest tours with reasonable advance notice; contact the Convention & Visitors Bureau for a complete listing (see "Information" under "Just the Facts" below).

Near Escapes, tel. (415) 921-1392, caters not so much to tourists as to local folks, certainly anyone curious about what is (or was) *really* going on—at scenes like Bay Area lighthouses, the Colma cemetery, and Haight-Ashbury during the Summer of Love. Other tours include the statues of Golden Gate Park, Sausalito houseboats, Halloween-season mortuaries, and edible plant hikes; particularly popular are tours of a chemical manufacturing plant and an auto factory. To keep up with Near Escapes, you can subscribe to the newsletter, $10 per year.

Tours By Sea
For winter whalewatching, usually January through April, nothing beats an ocean-going adventure with Oakland's **Whale Center,** tel. (510) 654-6621, or the **Oceanic Society** based at Fort Mason in San Francisco, tel. (415) 474-3385 (reservations required, $50 pp). Oceanic Society expeditions are multifaceted, however. Only scientific researchers and trusted volunteers are allowed *on* these cold granite islands, but the Society's **Farallon Islands Excursion** takes you as close as most people ever get. The Farallons, 27 miles from the Golden Gate, are part of a national wildlife and marine sanctuary now protected as a UNESCO Biosphere Reserve, since these nutrient-rich coastal waters are vital to the world's fisheries, to the health of sea mammal populations, and to the success of the breeding seabird colonies here. And you'll see some birds, perhaps tufted puffins or rhinoceros auklets. The 85-foot Oceanic Society

TIME-TRIPPING WITH MR. FRISCO

We always think we know who and where we are. Time-wise, it's the modern world, the last gasp of the 20th century. The signs are all here. We're strolling down a San Francisco sidewalk, a word-bound bunch of writers and editors trying to ignore the crush of humanity, the blare of business as usual, the thigh-high smog. We're off on an adventure, a **Frisco Productions** tour of the Barbary Coast. We're following this energetic and gleeful fellow in a felt fedora, Mark Gordon, as he holds forth about the minutiae of the city's unusually colorful and wicked past, including almost every horrible or hilarious thing people here ever did to one another.

The city has always loved its difference, or deviance, depending upon your point of view, Gordon explains. It's in the rules. Always has been. (And San Francisco has always had some unusual rules, like the law that states it's illegal—six months and/or a $500 fine—to offer a cigarette to a snake.) In the beginning, during the gold rush, there was a rule that said no policemen could enter the brothels or bars after dark. "So, in San Francisco, the inmates were genuinely running the asylum," he's saying. "At one time there were over 700 speakeasies in the city. You couldn't get busted unless you were really dumb—like one of the Hearsts."

Then—whoa! where are we?—suddenly we've time-tripped. The 1990s have disappeared altogether, replaced by the mid-1800s. Here, along the 400 block of Bush Street, the one-time site of the city's theater district, is famed opera singer Luisa Tetrazzini (you know, the one they named that chicken dish after). And she sings for us, right there on the sidewalk, in front of God and everybody. Even after all these years, can she *ever* belt out a tune.

It keeps happening. There in Trinity Alley, near Cafe Pacifica at 333 Bush, is the place that infamous gentleman bandit Black Bart, the poet ("PO8") of the placers, was finally nabbed. "Hi, Charley. (Bart's real name was Charles Bolton.) Howya doin'? Say, was that old rumor true—that in exchange for your promise never to rob Wells Fargo again, the company gave you an old-age pension?" Absolutely not, he says, refusing to reveal more about his mysterious life. Seeing we're futuristic fellow travelers, he instead wants to know about the negative reviews posterity has given his poetry, about his literary lynching. "Is it true," he asks, "what that cranky old misanthrope Ambrose Bierce once said, that 'an editor is a person who drinks out of the skull of authors'?"

KIM WEIR

famed 19th-century opera singer Luisa Tetrazzini (actress Kate Doyle) and Mr. Frisco himself, Mark Gordon

Time for lunch, and perhaps some fine red wine. We touch down at The Cypress Club, a contemporary take on an old-school speakeasy serving both unbelievably good food and indescribable atmosphere. Then we're off again. Back at the Palace Hotel, it's not really a surprise when we encounter none other than Lillie Hitchcock Coit, a delightful little old lady, the eccentric one they named that phallic, firehose nozzle-shaped tower after. She regales us with mere allusions, veiled references to just why the firemen of San Francisco loved her so much, and why her parties at the Palace were so scandalous.

Then—pop!—the party's over. We denizens of the 20th century are out on the streets once again, forced to find our own way through the past, present, and future.

And so it goes when San Francisco visitors embark on a time-tripping tour with Frisco Productions' own Mr. Frisco, Mark Gordon, and his ever-expanding entourage of actors, entertainers, singers, and such. You can count on being fully informed—

Gordon and his crew love San Francisco, down to the last oddball detail—and you can also count on being endlessly entertained.

Mark Gordon and company have also created a stationary entertainment venue: **Jake Finnegans's Rendezvous Club,** something of a white Cotton Club West, open to the general public by October 1993. Expect to drink your alcohol from coffee mugs and to be entertained by Mayor "Sunny Jim" Rolph, by illicit horse racing on the radio, by Gershwin show tunes, and by dancing the varsity drag and the Charleston. To get into this 1927 speakeasy, an authentic re-creation of "the era when San Francisco was the wettest dry town in the United States," you need to know the password: "Jake sent me."

Frisco Productions walking tours include the two-and-a-half-hour **Barbary Coast/Wild West Tour,** which requires some fairly vigorous walking but no steep-hill climbing. (As on all tours, just *who* might appear en route, historically speaking, depends upon the size of the group and other factors. It'll be a surprise.) The **Film and Fiction Tour** usually begins on Nob Hill across from the apartment building where Kim Novak lived in Hitchcock's *Vertigo,* the same street where Steve McQueen did his own stunt driving in *Bullitt.* Gordon also explains how Coit Tower, off in the distance, was incorporated into the *Thin Man* movie series. Frisco Productions even offers its own **Historic Bar Crawl** nightlife tour (drinks not included in the price, so you don't need to crawl unless you truly want to).

In addition to its walking tours, Frisco Productions provides actor-enhanced bus adventures, equally entertaining and more accessible for those with physical limitations. (Walking is included, to a degree, even on some of these tours, however. Call for details.) If it's at all possible—and it's easier in the off-season—Gordon allows, even encourages, groups to design their own tours. He and his entertainment troupe even do special parties. But the regular group tours are plenty enticing. In addition to motorized versions of the Barbary Coast and Bar Crawl adventures, Frisco offers **The Moving Feast,** a half-day epicurean exploration of "the city that knows how to chow"—featuring tastes of everything from sourdough bread to beer, along with an education in how green goddess salad dressing, peach melba, and hangtown fry came to be. The **Hollywood in San Francisco Tour** visits the town's Hollywood hot spots, with almost no tidbit of movie trivia left unturned. Two different versions of Frisco's **Sentimental Journey** tour explore San Francisco in the more innocent swing-era 1930s and '40s, while the **Frisco Crime Tour** is a factual comedic romp. The **"Amazing Grace" Great Cathedral Tour** takes a look, inside and out, at some of San Francisco's most amazing architecture, including the only full-scale copy of Ghiberti's *Gates of Paradise.* And during the holidays, don't miss the **Christmas Lights and Stories Tour.**

At last report, the Film and Fiction and the Barbary Coast walking tours cost $18 per person, $25 (sans booze) for the Bar Crawl. The price for group bus tours is $16.50 per person, with a 25-person tour minimum, bus *not* included. (For groups that don't want to be bothered with the task, Frisco Productions can arrange bus transportation, at extra cost.) The per-person fee for The Moving Feast food tour is $26.50, eats and drinks included.

Call Frisco Productions at tel. (415) 681-5555 for current information and advance reservations (necessary) or to request a tour schedule. Since you'll often get the answering machine—Mark Gordon is one busy guy, but good about returning calls—just leave your name, address, and phone number.

boat carries 70 passengers and two naturalists, and the trip takes eight or nine hours, shoving off at 9 a.m. (Saturdays and Sundays only) from the San Francisco Yacht Club. Don't miss this trip. Contact the nonprofit Oceanic Society for other excursion options.

The **Red & White Fleet,** with boats and ferries at both Pier 41 and Pier 43⅓, tel. (415) 546-BOAT or toll-free in California (800) BAY CRUISE, offers the justifiably popular **Alcatraz Cellhouse Tour** with ferry ride and walking tour (see "Touring the Real Rock" for more information). For advance charge-by-phone ticket reser-vations, call 546-2700. New through Red & White is the half-day daily **Fisherman's Wharf to Muir Woods Tour,** which includes a high-speed ferry ride to Tiburon then luxury van transport to Marin County's Muir Woods within the Golden Gate National Recreation Area. After a self-guided walk in the redwoods and extra time in Tiburon, passengers return by ferry to San Francisco. (You can catch a later ferry if you want more time.) Fares: $24 adults, $12 children (under age four free). Red & White's other tours include a 45-minute **Golden Gate Bay Cruise** with interesting audio narration—including personal

TOURING THE REAL ROCK

Visiting Alcatraz is like touring the dark side of the American dream, like peering into democracy's private demon hold. At Alcatraz, freedom is a fantasy. If crime is a universal option—and everyone behind bars at Alcatraz exercised it—then all who once inhabited this desolate island prison were certainly equal. Yet all who once lived on The Rock were also equal in other ways—in their utter isolation, in their human desperation, in their hopelessness.

Former prison guard Frank Heaney, born and raised in Berkeley, is now a guide for the Red & White Fleet's exclusive "Round the Rock" Alcatraz tour. When he started work as a correctional officer at age 21, Heaney found himself standing guard over some of America's most notorious felons, including George "Machine Gun" Kelly, Alvin "Creepy" Karpis, and Robert "The Birdman of Alcatraz" Stroud. Heaney soon realized that the terrifying reality of prison life was a far cry from Hollywood's James Cagney version.

The job was psychologically demanding, yet often boring. There was terror in the air, too. Inmates vowed—and attempted—to "break him." But he ignored both death threats and too-friendly comments on his youthful appeal. Guards were prohibited from conversing with the inmates—one more aspect of the criminals' endless isolation—but Heaney eventually got to know Machine Gun Kelley, whom he remembers as articulate and intellectual, "more like a bank president than a bank robber." Creepy Karpis,

Ma Barker's right-hand man and the only man ever personally arrested by FBI Director J. Edgar Hoover, was little more than a braggart. And though the Birdman was considered seriously psychotic and spent most of his 54 prison years in solitary confinement, Heaney found him to be "untrustworthy" but rational and extremely intelligent. Many of Frank Heaney's favorite stories are collected in his book *Inside the Walls of Alcatraz,* published by Bull Publishing and available at Pier 41, at the Alcatraz gift shop, and elsewhere.

Others who remember The Rock, both guards and inmates, are included on the "Alcatraz Cellhouse Tour," an "inside" audio journey through prison history provided by the Golden Gate National Park Association and offered along with Red & White Fleet tours to Alcatraz.

Among them is Jim Quillen, former inmate, who on the day we visit is here in person. He leans against the rusted iron doors of Cell Block A. His pained eyes scan the pocked walls and empty cells, each barely adequate as an open-air closet. Quillen spent the best years of his life on Alcatraz. "Ten years and one day," he says in a soft voice. "The tourists see the architecture, the history—all I see are ghosts. I can point to the exact spots where my friends have killed themselves, been murdered, gone completely insane."

And that's the main reason to visit Alcatraz—to explore this lonely, hard, wind-whipped island of exile.

THE RED & WHITE FLEET

The Red & White Fleet offers an exclusive Round the Rock tour of infamous Alcatraz.

The ghosts here need human companionship.

There is plenty else to do, too, including the a ranger-guided walk around the island, courtesy of the Golden Gate National Recreation Area (GGNRA), and poking one's nose into other buildings, other times. National park personnel also offer lectures and occasional special programs. For current information, call the Golden Gate National Recreation Area at (415) 556-0560, stop by the **GGNRA Visitors Center** at the Cliff House in San Francisco (tel. 556-8643), or contact the nonprofit, education-oriented Golden Gate National Park Association, tel. 776-0693. (For more information about the recreation area in general, see that section elsewhere in this chapter and also "Point Reyes National Seashore.")

If you're coming to Alcatraz, contact the **Red & White Fleet,** Pier 41, Fisherman's Wharf, San Francisco 94133, tel. (415) 546-BOAT for general information. To make charge-by-phone ticket reservations—advisable, well in advance, since the tour is quite popular, attracting over one million people each year—call 546-2700. At last report, roundtrip fare was $8.50 per adult, $4 per child, plus a $2-per-

ticket reservation surcharge if you reserve your ticket by phone. (Be sure to be there 30 minutes early, since no refunds or exchanges are allowed if you miss the boat.) The entire audio-guided walking tour take more than two hours, so be sure to allow yourself adequate time. (The audio tape is available in English, Japanese, German, French, Italian, and Spanish.) If at all possible, try to get booked on one of the early tours, so you can see the cellblocks and Alcatraz Island in solitude, before the rest of humanity arrives. Pack a picnic (though snacks and beverages are available), and bring all the camera and video equipment you can carry; no holds barred on photography. And wear good walking shoes, as well as warm clothes (layers best), since it can be brutally cold on Alcatraz in the fog or when the wind whips up. Due to the island's ruggedness, with moderate to strenuous climbing, there is limited access for wheelchairs and strollers. For those with limited mobility who can't "do" the Alcatraz tour in person, a special interactive computer program can take you there anyway.

—Tim Moriarty and Kim Weir

interviews with Golden Gate Bridge workers, earthquake survivors, and former Alcatraz inmates and guards—in five languages: English, German, Japanese, Mandarin, and Spanish. Fares: $15 adults, $11 seniors and juniors (ages 12-18), $8 children (under age four free). Popular, too, through Red & White is the family-oriented **Marine World Africa USA** ferry trip to Vallejo and back, the entire roundtrip package (including admission) $36 for adults, $20.50 for children.

The **Blue & Gold Fleet** based at Pier 39, tel. (415) 781-7890 for general information, tel. 781-7877 for schedule information, offers a narrated year-round (weather permitting) **San Francisco Bay Cruise** that passes under both bridges, around Alcatraz, and within view of other sights in just over an hour. Fare: $14 adults, $7 senior, active military (in uniform), and children (under age five free when riding with paying adult). Group rates and charters also available.

Hornblower Dining Yachts at Pier 33, tel. (415) 394-8900, offers big-boat on-the-bay eating adventures, from extravagant nightly dinner dances and weekday lunches to Saturday and Sunday champagne brunch. Special events, from whodunit murder mystery dinners to jazz

cocktail cruises, can be especially fun. Hornblower's **Monte Carlo Cruises,** tel. 433-4FUN for ticketing and reservations, tel. 434-6800 for group reservations, have a creative new concept underway, with their Las Vegas-style casino gaming tables (proceeds go to charity). But at last report, as far as gambling goes, the experience was closer to amateur night at a PTA fundraiser. Nonetheless, the MV *Monte Carlo's* small-party lunch, dinner, and singles dinner dance cruises (the latter complete with karaoke singing) are all part of an enjoyable bay cruise. Probably the best deal going, and the perfect fresh-air ending to a night on the town (especially in clear, mild weather), is the $15 Friday and Saturday night **Moonlight Cruise,** featuring fabulous views from the open-air top deck. The night cruise departs at 11 p.m. and returns by 1 a.m., hors d'oeuvres, snacks, and desserts provided (beverage service available).

Tours On Your Own

If you have a car, taking the city's **49 Mile Scenic Drive** is a good way to personally experience the entirety of San Francisco. The route is a bit tricky, though, so be sure to follow the map and directions provided by the Convention & Visitors

Bureau—and never try this particular exploration during rush hours or peak weekend commute times.

With enough time, design your own tour or tours, starting with the neighborhood and district information included in this chapter. Or, using a variety of special-interest books and other resources, design a tour based on a particular theme—such as "literary haunts," "bars throughout history" (best as a walking tour), "stairway tours," "musical high notes" or "theatrical highlights," even "steepest streets."

The **Steepest Streets Tour** is a particular thrill for courageous drivers and/or suicidal cyclists. (However you do this one, take it slow and easy.) As far as vertical grade is concerned, those all-time tourist favorites—Mason Street down Nob Hill to the Mark Hopkins, and Hyde Street to Aquatic Park—don't even register in San Francisco's top ten. According to the city's Bureau of Engineering, **Filbert Street** between Leavenworth and Hyde and **22nd Street** beween Church and Vicksburg are the city's most hair-raising roadways, sharing a 31.5% grade. Coming in a close second: **Jones** between Union and Filbert (29%, plus a 26% thrill between Green and Union). So a good way to start this sidetrip is by shooting down Filbert (a one-way, with the 1100 block a special thrill) then straight up intersecting Jones. It's a scream. For more cheap thrills, try **Duboce** between Buena Vista and Alpine (a 27.9% grade) and between Divisadero and Alpine then Castro and Divisadero (each 25%), **Webster** between Vallejo and Broadway (26%), **Jones** between Pine and California (24.8%), and **Fillmore** between Vallejo and Broadway (24%). Whether or not you travel all these streets, you'll soon understand *why* hard-driving local cabbies burn out—their brakes, that is—every 2,000 miles or so.

A worthy variation is the **Most Twisted Streets Tour,** starting with one-way **Lombard Street** between Hyde and Leavenworth, a route touted as "The World's Crookedest Street," with eight turns within a distance of 412 feet. But San Francisco's truly most twisted is **Vermont Street** between 20th and 22nd streets, with six fender-grinding turns within a distance of 270 feet. Better for panoramic views in all directions is **Twin Peaks Boulevard,** with 11 curves and six about-face turns in its one-mile descent.

GOLDEN GATE NATIONAL RECREATION AREA

One of San Francisco's unexpected treasures, the Golden Gate National Recreation Area (GGNRA) starts in the south along Sweeney Ridge near Pacifica, then jumps north to a narrow coastal strip of land adjacent to Hwy. 1, taking in Thornton Beach, Fort Funston, the Cliff House, and other milestones before it pauses at the pilings of the Golden Gate Bridge. The GGNRA also includes Alcatraz Island, one of the nation's most infamous prison sites, and Angel Island, "Ellis Island of the West" to the Chinese and other immigrant groups, though it is administered by the state. Converting from military to domestic purposes, and slated for formal inclusion in the GGNRA by late 1995, is the historic Presidio, 1,446 acres of forest, coastal bluffs, military outposts, and residences adjacent to the Golden Gate Bridge. But that's just the beginning. Vast tracts of southern and western Marin County headlands, north of the bridge, are also included within GGNRA boundaries, making this park a true urban wonder. Much of the credit for creating the GGNRA, the world's largest urban park, goes to the late Congressman Phillip Burton. Established in 1972, the recreation area as currently envisioned includes more than 36,000 acres, a cooperative patchwork of land holdings in excess of 114 square miles, and is also the most popular of the national parks, drawing more than 20 million visitors each year.

The opportunity for **urban hiking,** on the San Francisco side, and **wilderness hiking,** throughout the Marin Headlands, is one major attraction of the GGNRA. Get oriented to the recreation area's trails at any visitor center (see below), or sign on for any of the GGNRA's excellent guided hikes and explorations. The schedule changes constantly, depending upon the season and other factors, but the following represent a sample of what's available on the San Francisco end of the Golden Gate Bridge: the Sutro Heights Walk, the Presidio's Mountain Lake to Fort Point Hike and Main Post Historical Walk, and the Point of the Sea Wolves Walk. National park service rangers also lead other guided tours through the Presidio, including its Natural History of the Presidio hike. A particularly spectacular section of the GGNRA's trail system is the 2½-mile trek from the St. Francis Yacht Club to Fort Point and the Golden Gate Bridge, part of the still-in-progress **San Francisco Bay Trail,** a 450-mile shoreline trail system, which will one day ring the entire bay and traverse nine Bay Area counties. (For more information, see below.) For the very ambitious, there are current hiking options: following the GGNRA's **Coastal Trail,** for example, allows hikers to walk from San Francisco to Point Reyes National Seashore in Marin County. And once on the north side of the Golden Gate, possibilities for long hikes and backpacking trips are almost endless.

Special GGNRA events are also well worth it, from the Story of the Golden Gate Bridge tour and Family Fun at Muir Woods theater workshop to presentations at one-time defense installations: Women on Military Posts, and Songs and Sounds of the Civil War (Fort Point); Seacoast Defense (Baker Beach); and Rockets to Rangers—Nike Site 88 (Marin Headlands).

San Francisco-side GGNRA Sights

The GGNRA includes the beaches and coastal bluffs along San Francisco's entire western edge (and both south and north), as well as seaside trails and walking and running paths along the new highway and seawall between Sloat Boulevard and the western border of Golden Gate Park. Where now there are condos along the O'Shaughnessy Seawall, farther north, the famed amusement park Playland at the Beach once stood.

The original **Cliff House** near Seal Rocks was one of San Francisco's first tourist lures, its original diversions a bit on the licentious side. That version, converted by Adolph Sutro into a family-style resort, burned to the ground in 1894, soon replaced by a splendid Victorian palace and an adjacent bathhouse, also fire victims. Ruins of the old **Sutro Baths** are still visible among the rocks just north. Aptly named **Seal Rocks** offshore attract vocal sea lions.

The current Cliff House, across the highway from Sutro Heights Park, dates from 1908 and still attracts locals and tourists alike. The views are spectacular, of course, which explains the success of the restaurants, the Phineas T. Barnacle pub-style deli, and the Ben Butler Room bar. The stairway outdoors leads down the cliff

to the GGNRA **Cliff House Visitor Center,** tel. 556-8642, open daily 10-5, a good stop for information, free or low-cost publications and maps, and books. Also down below is the **Musee Mechanique,** a delightful and dusty collection of penny arcade amusements (most cost a quarter) from nickelodeons and coin-eating music boxes to fortunetelling machines, and the very odd **Camera Obscura & Hologram Gallery.** The gallery's "camera" is actually a slow revolving lens that reflects images onto a parabolic screen—with a particularly thrilling fractured-light image at sunset.

Wandering northward from Cliff House, Point Lobos Avenue then El Camino del Mar lead to San Francisco's **Point Lobos,** the city's westernmost point. There's an overlook, to take in the view. Nearby is the **USS *San Francisco* Memorial,** part of the city's namesake ship. Also nearby is **Fort Miley,** which features a 4-H "adventure ropes" course. But the most spectacular thing in sight (on a clear day) is the postcard-pretty peek at the Golden Gate Bridge. You can even get there from here, on foot, via the **Coastal Trail,** a spectacular city hike that skirts **Lincoln Park** and the **California Palace of the Legion of Honor** before passing through the **Seacliff** neighborhood, then flanking the **Presidio.** From **Fort Point** at the foot of the Golden Gate, the truly intrepid can keep on trekking—straight north across the bridge to Marin County, or east past the yacht harbors to **Fort Mason** and the overwhelming attractions of Fisherman's Wharf.

For some slower sightseeing, backtrack to the Presidio's hiking trails and other attractions (like the **Presidio Army Museum** at Lincoln and Funston) or spend time exploring the coast. At low tide, the fleet of foot can beach walk (and climb) from the Golden Gate Bridge to Baker Beach and farther (looking back at the bridge for a seagull's-eye view). Though many flock here precisely because it is a de facto nude beach, the very naked sunbathers at **Baker Beach** usually hide out in the rock-secluded coves beyond the family-oriented stretch of public sand. Near Baker Beach is the miniature **Battery Lowell A. Chamberlin** "museum," a historic gun hold, home to the six-inch disappearing rifle. Weapons aficionados will want to explore more thoroughly the multitude of gun batteries farther north along the trail, near Fort Point.

THE PRESIDIO AND FORT POINT

A national historic landmark and the oldest active military installation in the U.S., San Francisco's **Presidio** is currently facing reincarnation as a national park. Now that Congress has decided to close this treasure, the nation's most beautiful military installation, the Golden Gate National Recreation Area (GGNRA) stands to gain some of the choicest real estate in the city by 1995. Though Congress may allow the Sixth Army headquarters to stay on, by mid-1993 the Presidio's next life had yet to be determined with any precision. Among other proposals for putting the buildings here to good public use, it's quite possible that this will become the new environmental headquarters for the United Nations. In April 1993, the Presidio became home to the U.S. headquarters for Mikhail Gorbachev's **Gorbachev Foundation.**

The Presidio's 1,446 acres lie directly south of the Golden Gate Bridge along the northwest tip of the San Francisco Peninsula, bordered by the Marina and Pacific Heights districts to the east and Richmond and Presidio heights to the south. To the west and north a coastal strip of the Golden Gate National Recreation Area frames the Presidio, which boasts some 70 miles of paths and trails of its own winding along cliffs and through eucalyptus groves and coastal flora. The 1,600 buildings here, most of them eclectic blends of Victorian and Spanish-revival styles, have housed the U.S. Army since 1847.

Founded by the Spanish in 1776 as one of two original settlements in San Francisco, the Presidio had a militaristic history even then, for the area commands a strategic view of San Francisco Bay and the Pacific Ocean. The Spanish garrison ruled the peninsula for the first 50 years of the city's history, chasing off Russian whalers and trappers by means of the two cannons now guarding the entrance to the Officer's Club. After 1847, when Americans took over, the Presidio became a staging center for the Indian wars, a never-used outpost during the Civil War, and more recently, headquarters for the Sixth Army Command, which fought in the Pacific during World War II.

Today the Presidio is open to the public, and visitors may drive around and admire the neat-as-a-pin streets with their white, two-story wood Victorians and faultless lawns or trace the base's history at the **Presidio Army Museum** (one of the oldest buildings, originally the hospital) located near the corner of Lincoln Blvd. and Funston Avenue, tel. (415) 561-4115. Pick up a map there showing the Presidio's hiking trails, including a six-mile historic walk and two ecology trails. Museum hours are Tues.-Sun. 10 a.m.-4 p.m., admission free.

Ranger-led GGNRA guided tours include the **Natural History of the Presidio,** an exploratory lesson in the San Francisco Peninsula's geology, geography, and plant and animal life, featuring an enchanted forest and the city's last free-flowing stream; **Presidio Main Post Historical Walks;** and the **Mountain Lake to Fort Point Hike.**

For more information about the Presidio and scheduled events and activities, call the **Presidio Resource Center,** tel. (415) 556-0865 or 556-1874. To submit suggestions and proposals for the Presidio's transition into domestic service, contact:

For More Information

For information on the GGNRA included elsewhere in this chapter, see also "Touring the Real Rock," "The Presidio and Fort Point," "Fort Mason" immediately below, and "The Avenues," above. For more information on the Marin County sections of the GGNRA, see "Point Reyes National Seashore" and "Angel Island State Park" under "Eastern Marin and Vicinity" in "The San Francisco Bay Area" chapter.

For current information about GGNRA features and activities, contact: **Golden Gate National Recreation Area,** Fort Mason, Building 201, San Francisco 94123, tel. (415) 556-0560. Check on local conditions, events, and programs by calling the GGNRA's other visitor centers: **Cliff House,** tel. 556-8642; **Fort Point,** tel. 556-1693; **Marin Headlands,** tel. 331-1540; and **Muir Woods,** tel. 388-2596. For current details about hiking and other activities at the Presidio, contact the **Presidio Resource Center,** tel. 556-0865. To receive a subscription to the quarterly and very complete **"ParkEvents"** calendar of GGNRA events, join the nonprofit **Golden Gate National Park Association,** same Fort Mason address, tel. 776-0693, an organization that actively supports educational programs as well as park conservation and improvement. Fees range from $15 per year for students and seniors, $25 for an individual, and $35 for a family to $100 for "participating" members. Association members also receive the

National Park Service, Presidio Planning Team, Building 277, Crissy Field, Presidio of San Francisco, San Francisco 94129, tel. 556-8600.

More businesslike in design but in many respects more interesting than the Presidio, **Fort Point** off Lincoln Blvd. is nestled directly underneath the southern tip of the Golden Gate Bridge and worth donning a few extra layers to visit. Officially the Fort Point National Historic Site since 1968, the quadrangular red-brick behemoth was modeled after South Carolina's Fort Sumter and completed in 1861 to guard the bay during the Civil War. However, the fort was never given the chance to test its mettle, as a grass-roots plot hatched by Confederate sympathizers in San Francisco to undermine the Yankee cause died for lack of funds and manpower, and the more palpable threat that the Confederate cruiser *Shenandoah* would blast its way into the bay was foiled by the war ending before the ship ever arrived.

Nonetheless, military strategists had the right idea situating the fort on the site of the old Spanish adobe-brick outpost of Castillo de San Joaquin, and through the years the fort-that-could was used as a garrison and general catchall for the Presidio, including a stint during WW I as barracks for unmarried officers. During the 1930s, when the Golden Gate Bridge was in its design phase, the fort narrowly missed being scrapped but was saved by the bridge's chief design engineer, Joseph B. Strauss, who considered the fort's demolition a waste of good masonry and designed the somewhat triumphal arch that now soars above it.

Fort Point these days enjoys a useful retirement as a historical museum, open daily 10-5, admission free. While the wind howls in the girders overhead, park rangers clad in Civil War regalia (many wearing long johns underneath) lead hourly tours, 11 a.m.-4 p.m., through the park's honeycomb of corridors, staircases, and gun ports. Cannon muster is solemnly observed at 1:30 and 2:30 p.m., and two slide shows are also offered, at 11:30 a.m. and again at 3:30 p.m. A fairly recent addition is the excellent exhibit and tribute to black American soldiers. At the bookstore, pick up some Confederate money and other military memorabilia. For more information about tours and special events, call Fort Point at (415) 556-1693.

quarterly **"The Park"** newsletter, which includes current news and feature articles as well as upcoming, members-only events—such as tours of Presidio architecture, moonlight hikes to the Point Bonita Lighthouse (and elsewhere), and candlelight after-hours tours of Fort Point and other installations.

Useful publications and guidebooks published by the Golden Gate National Park Association, available for under $10 each at GGNRA visitor center bookstores and elsewhere (such as the National Park Store on Pier 39 at Fisherman's Wharf), include the comprehensive 100-page *Park Guide* plus *Alcatraz: Island of Change; Fort Point: Sentry at the Golden Gate;* and *Muir Woods: Redwood Refuge.* Also widely available is "The Official Map and Guide to the Presidio," $2.50, a very detailed multicolored map jam-packed with historical and other information.

For a free map of the entire San Francisco Bay Trail, and/or detailed maps of specific trail sections ($3 each), contact the **San Francisco Bay Trail Project,** c/o the Association of Bay Area Governments, P.O. Box 2050, Oakland 94604. About 200 of the Bay Trail's 450 total miles of trails are completed, with planning and/or construction of the rest underway. To volunteer trail-building labor or materials, to help with fundraising, or to lead guided walks along sections of the Bay Trail, call (510) 464-7900. Also of interest to area hikers: the **Bay Area Ridge Trail,** tel. (415) 391-0697 for information, a 400-mile ridgetop route which one day will skirt the entire bay, connecting 75 parks.

FORT MASON

Headquarters for the Golden Gate National Recreation Area—see above for detailed information—Fort Mason is also home to the **Fort Mason Center,** a surprisingly contemporary complex of one-time military storage buildings at Marina Boulevard and Buchanan Street, now holding a variety of unusual nonprofit arts, humanities, educational, environmental, and recreational organizations and associations. Since the 1970s, this shoreline wasteland has been transformed into an innovative multicultural community events center—perhaps the country's premier model of the impossible, successfully accomplished. Several pavilions and the Conference Center host larger group events, though smaller galleries, theaters, and offices predominate. The variety of rotating art exhibits, independent theater performances, poetry readings, lectures and workshops, and special-interest classes is truly staggering—everything from martial arts, group psychodrama, and conscious caregiving training by the Zen Hospice Project to mature drivers safety seminars and meetings of the San Francisco Tesla Society.

And no one will ever starve out on these seemingly desolate piers, since one of the country's best vegetarian restaurants, the San Francisco Zen Center's **Greens** in Building A-North, tel. (415) 771-6222, along with its **Tassajara Bakery II** outpost, tel. 771-6330, also call Fort Mason home. For some entertainment after an evening meal, see what the **San Francisco Folk Music Center/Plowshares Coffeehouse** has on tap. Folk musicians from all over the U.S. come here (Building C, Room 225, tel. 441-8910) for bluegrass, Cajun, Acadian, and Irish Celtic performances. Building C, Room 225, tel. 441-8910,

Other permanent Fort Mason residents include the **African American Historical & Cultural Society** in Building C, Room 165, tel. (415) 441-0640, a cultural and resource center featuring a library, museum, speaker's bureau, and monthly lecture series. **The Mexican Museum,** Building D, tel. 441-0404 or 441-0445, is the first American institution devoted exclusively to exhibitions of, and educational programs about, Mexican-American and Mexican art. The permanent collection here includes 9,000 items from five periods, including pre-Hispanic and contemporary Mexican art, though the rotating exhibits tend to attract more public attention. Some recent examples: "Burning Desire: The Art of the Spray Can;" a retrospective on the surrealist Leonora Carrington; the Nelson A. Rockefeller Collection of Mexican Folk Art; Day of the Dead installations; and traveling Frida Kahlo and Diego Rivera shows.

FORT MASON CENTER

Exhibits at **The Museo Italo Americano** in Building C, tel. 673-2200, foster an appreciation of Italian art and culture. Definitely worth a detour is the **San Francisco Craft & Folk Art Museum,** Building A-North, tel. 775-0990, which features surprising rotating exhibits of American and international folk art, from **"Improvisation in African-American Quiltmaking"** and **"Classical Chinese Furniture"** to **"Hand Bookbinders of California."** Museums at Fort Mason Center charge very nominal admission fees, if any.

Relatively new, open only since 1989, is Fort Mason Center's 440-seat **Cowell Theater,** a performance space that hosts events from the Asian Pacific Performing Arts Festival and Theatre Flamenco to guest speakers and unusual video, musical, and theatrical presentations. Among its showstoppers is the **Magic Theatre,** Building D, tel. (415) 441-8001, internationally recognized as an outstanding American playwrights' theater, performing original plays by the likes of Sam Shepard and Michael McClure as well as innovative new writers. Other Fort Mason performing arts groups include **Life on the Water,** tel. 885-2790 or 776-8999, **Make*A* Circus,** Building C, tel. 776-8477, and—for young people—the **Performing Arts Workshop,** tel. 673-2634, and the **Young Performers' Theatre,** tel. 346-2610.

The Fort Mason Art Center, Building B, tel. (415) 561-1840, is the place for instruction in fine arts and crafts; for the 12-and-under set, it's the **San Francisco Children's Art Center,** Building C, tel. 771-0292. The **National Poetry Association,** Building D, tel. 776-6602, is committed to the creative marriage of poetry and filmmaking. One of the most intriguing galleries here is the **San Francisco Museum of Modern Art Rental Gallery,** Building A-North, tel. 441-4777, representing over 600 artists and offering, in addition to rotating exhibits, the opportunity to rent as well as buy works on display. The **Blue Bear School of Music,** Building D, tel. 673-3600, **California Lawyers for the Arts,** Building C, tel. 775-7200, and **Media Alliance,** Building D, tel. 441-2557, are among Fort Mason's other arts-oriented organizations. But do stop by the Friends of the San Francisco Public Library's **Book Bay Bookstore** in Building C-South, tel. 771-1076, to see what's on sale.

At the far eastern edge of Fort Mason Center, berthed at Pier 3, is the **S.S. *Jeremiah O'Brien*,** tel. (415) 441-3101, the world's last unaltered World War II-era Liberty ship, open for bow-to-stern tours weekdays 9-3, weekends 9-4. On the third weekend in May, this massive ship also shoves off for unforgettable day-long bay cruises (call for current information).

In addition to the attractions mentioned above, Fort Mason expansion plans include the establishment of a marine ecology center, another theater, more exhibit space, and another good-food-great-view restaurant. All in all, it's not surprising that Fort Mason is being studied by the Presidio's national park transition team, and even by other nations, as a supreme example of how urban eyesores can be transformed into national treasures. For more complete information, including a copy of the group's monthly **"Fort Mason Center" newsletter** and current calendar of events, contact the **Fort Mason Center Foundation,** Building A, Fort Mason Center, San Francisco 94123, tel. (415) 441-5706, Mon.-Sat. 9-5. For recorded information 24 hours a day, call 441-5705.

GOLDEN GATE PARK

Yet another of San Francisco's impossible dreams successfully accomplished, Golden Gate Park was once a vast expanse of sand dunes. A wasteland by urban, and urbane, standards, locals got the idea that it could be a park—and a grand park, to rival the Bois de Boulogne in Paris. Frederick Law Olmsted, who designed New York's Central Park, was asked to build it. He took one look and scoffed, saying essentially that it couldn't be done. Olmsted was wrong, as it turned out, and eventually he had the grace to admit it. William Hammond Hall, designer and chief engineer, and the park's green-thumbed godfather, Scottish gardener John McLaren, achieved the unlikely with more than a bit of West Coast ingenuity. Hall constructed a behemoth breakwater on the 1,000-acre park's west end, to block the stinging sea winds and salt spray, and started anchoring the sand by planting barley, then nitrogen-fixing lupine, then grasses. Careful grading and berming, helped along in time by windrows, further deflected the fierceness of ocean-blown storms.

"Uncle John" McLaren, Hall's successor, set about re-creating the land on a deeper level. He trucked in humus and manure to further transform sand into soil, and got busy planting more than one million trees. That was just the beginning, of course. In and around walkways, benches, and major park features there were shrubs to plant, flowerbeds to establish, and pristine lawns to nurture. McLaren kept at it for some 55 years, dedicated to creating a park for the everlasting enjoyment of the citizenry. He bravely did battle with politicians, often beating them at their own games, to nurture and preserve "his" park for posterity. He even fought with groundskeepers who tried to keep people off the lush lawns and attempted to hide despised-on-principle statues and other graven images with bushes and shrubs. But in the end he lost this last battle. To his eternal shock, surely, after McLaren died the the city erected a statue in his honor.

McLaren's Legacy

Much of the park's appeal, still, is its astounding array of natural attractions. The botanic diversity alone, much of it exotic, somehow reflects San Francisco's multicultural consciousness— also transplanted from elsewhere, also now as natural as the sun, the moon, the salt winds, and the tides.

The dramatic Victorian **Conservatory of Flowers** on John F. Kennedy Drive, tel. (415) 558-3973, was imported from Europe and assembled here in 1878. This is a showcase jungle of tropical plants, though the conservatory is also noted for its seasonal botanic displays. Open daily 9-5, until 6 p.m. from March through September. Nominal admission; free the last half-hour of every day, all day on major holidays and on the first Wednesday of each month. But **Strybing Arboretum and Botanical Gardens,** Martin Luther King Jr. Drive, tel. (415) 221-1311, features the park's most exotic and rare plants. Noted here is the collection of Australian and New Zealand plant life, along with exotics from Africa, the Americas, and Asia. Several gardens are landscaped by theme, such as the New World Cloud Forest. The Asian Garden, with its serene Moon-viewing Pavilion, is a worthy respite when the Japanese Tea Garden is choked with tourists. Quite a delight, too, is the Garden of Fragrance—a collection of culinary and medicinal herbs easily appreciated by aroma and texture, labeled also in Braille. Any plant lover will enjoy time spent in the small store. Admission to the arboretum is free, and it's open daily—weekdays 8 a.m.-4:30 p.m., weekends 10-5. Guided tours are offered on Saturdays and Sundays from May through October, on a weekly changing schedule; call for tour times and meeting places. Next door is the **San Francisco County Fair Building,** site of the annual "fair"—in San Francisco, it's a flower show only—and home to the Helen Crocker Russell Library, some 12,000 volumes on horticulture and plants.

The **Japanese Tea Garden** on Tea Garden Drive, tel. (415) 558-4268, a striking and suitable backdrop to the Asian Art Museum, is an enduring attraction, started (and maintained until the family's World War II internment) by the full-time Japanese gardener Maokota Hagiwara and his family. Both a lovingly landscaped garden and teahouse concession—the Hagiwaras invented the fortune cookie, first served here, though Chinatown later claimed this innovation as an old-country tradition—the Tea Garden is so popular that to enjoy even a few moments of the intended serenity, visitors should arrive early on a weekday morning or come on a rainy day. The large bronze "Buddha Who Sits Through Sun and Rain Without Shelter," cast in Japan in 1790, will surely welcome an off-day visitor. The Japanese Tea Garden is most enchanting in April, when the cherry trees are in bloom. Open daily 9-4, nominal admission, free on major holidays and on the first Wednesday of every month.

Also especially notable for spring floral color in Golden Gate Park: the **Queen Wilhelmina Tulip Garden** on the park's western edge, near the restored (northern) **Dutch Windmill,** and the **John McLaren Rhododendron Dell** near the Conservatory of Flowers. The very English **Shakespeare Garden,** beyond the Academy of Sciences, is unusual any time of year, since all the plants and flowers here are those mentioned in the Bard's works.

But even the **San Francisco Zoo,** Sloat Boulevard at 45th Avenue, tel. (415) 753-7080, has its botanical attractions. The main reason to come, though, is to commune with animals in captivity. The zoo is open daily 10-5, and admission is free on the first Wednesday of every month.

The Asian Art Museum

Golden Gate Park is a magnet for museums. Though current plans call for this museum's relocation to the current site of the downtown library by early in the 21st century, San Francisco's Asian Art Museum is now housed in a wing of the park's de Young Museum. But the Asian Art Museum may one day be called the American Museum of Asian Art—and may one day be a worldwide wonder. It's already astounding. The original art in the collection was given to San Francisco in 1966 by the late philanthropist Avery Brundage, former U.S. diplomat, but that collection has expanded greatly. It now includes examples of Asian masterpieces from India, Tibet, Nepal, Mongolia, Korea, Iran, and other Eastern cultures, these accompanying vast collections of Chinese and Japanese art. The Asian Art Museum includes more than 12,000 objects, spanning 6,000 years of history and representing more than 40 Asian cultures; the total collection is so large that only about 10% can be displayed at any one time. Among the treasures here: the oldest known dated sculpture of Buddha, from China, circa A.D. 338 in Western time;

North "Dutch" Windmill—west end of Golden Gate Park

earthenware animals from the Tang Dynasty; and an astounding array of jade. Special changing exhibits include themes such as "A Playful Art: Composite Paintings," a display of miniature Indian paintings, and "Beauty, Wealth, and Power: Jewels and Ornaments of Asia." Call for current exhibit schedule.

The Asian Art Museum, on Tea Garden Drive, tel. (415) 668-8921, is open Wed.-Sun. 10-5. Admission is free the first Saturday of each month from 10 a.m. to noon, and on the first Wednesday from 10 a.m. to 8:30 p.m. Otherwise, it's $6 adults, $3 seniors, free for those age 18 and younger, which includes admission to the adjacent M.H. de Young Museum. Call for information about docent-led tours.

The California Academy Of Sciences

At home on the park's Music Concourse, across from the de Young and the Japanese Tea Garden, the California Academy of Sciences is a multifaceted scientific institution, the oldest in the West, founded in 1853 to survey and study the vast resources of California and vicinity.

The Academy includes a **Natural History Museum** with dioramas and exhibits like Wild California and African Safari. A surprisingly realistic waterhole exhibit, and the "Life Through Time" exhibit, offer a 3.5 billion-year journey into the speculative experience of life on earth. At the **Hohfeld Earth & Space Hall** the neon solar system tells the story of the universe and the natural forces that have shaped—and still shape—the earth. Especially popular with children is the **"Safe-Quake"** simulation, a "you are there" experience which imitates two of the city's famous earthquakes. But there's more. The **Wattis Hall of Human Cultures** specializes in anthropology and features one of the broadest Native American museum collections in Northern California, with an emphasis on cultures in both North America and South America. The **Far Side of Science Gallery,** 159 original Gary Larson cartoons, gives a hilarious perspective on humanity's scientific research. The **Gem and Mineral Hall** contains some real gems, like the 1,350-pound quartz crystal from Arkansas. The **Discovery Room for Children,** tel. 750-7155, or tel. 750-7156 for group reservations, is a hands-on exploration of everything —especially suitable for children, also ideal for the physically handicapped, blind, and deaf.

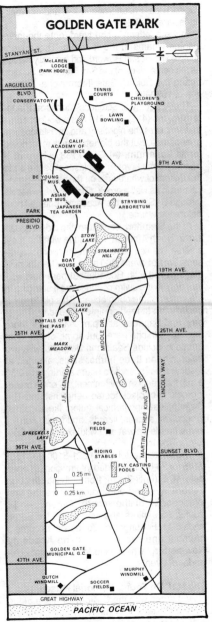

GOLDEN GATE PARK

© MOON PUBLICATIONS, INC.

(Open Tues.-Fri. afternoons 1-4, and on weekends 11 a.m.-3:30 p.m.)

In the academy's courtyard, note the intertwining whales in the fountain. These were sculpted by Robert Howard and originally served as the centerpiece of the San Francisco Building during the Golden Gate International Exposition of 1939-40.

The Academy of Sciences' **Morrison Planetarium,** tel. (415) 750-7141, is a 65-foot dome that simulates the night sky and its astronomical phenomena. But the planetarium is most noted for its **Laserium,** tel. 750-7138, where blue beams from a krypton gas laser slice the air to the rhythm of whatever's on the stereo—classical music as well as rock. (Tickets are available through BASS or at the Academy, one-half hour before show time.)

At the **Steinhart Aquarium,** the oldest aquarium in North America, commune with the most diverse live fish collection in the world, representatives of over 1,000 species. The stunning glass-walled Fish Roundabout here puts visitors right in the swim of things, as if standing in the center of the open ocean. This place is especially fun at feeding time—Tuesday, Thursday, and Saturday at 2 p.m. Altogether there are 189 exhibits here, but some of the most dramatic include Seals and Dolphins, with two dolphins and three harbor seals, also fun at feeding time (every two hours starting at 10:30 a.m.); the Penguin Environment, an entire breeding colony of black-footed penguins; and The Swamp, featuring tropical critters like alligators, crocodiles, snakes, lizards, and frogs. Fun for some hands-on wet and wild exploring is California Tidepool.

The academy, tel. (415) 221-5100 (tel. 750-7145 for 24-hour recorded information), is open daily 10-5 (until 7 p.m. from July 4th through Labor Day), and admission is free the first Wednesday of the month. Otherwise: $6 adults, $3 seniors and students, $1 children ages 6-11. For ongoing information, become a member and subscribe to **"The Academy Newsletter,"** which includes a complete calendar of events.

The M.H. De Young Memorial Museum

Now merged with the California Palace of the Legion of Honor into the jointly operated **Fine Arts Museums of San Francisco,** the park's

M.H. de Young Museum, tel. (415) 750-3600, is one of the city's major visual arts venues. The museum, with its Spanish-style architecture, honors San Francisco newspaper publisher M.H. de Young. The de Young's specialty is American art, from British colonial into contemporary times, and the collection here is one of the finest anywhere. Examine the exhibits of period paintings, sculpture, and decorative and domestic arts; the 20th century American realist paintings are almost as intriguing as the textile and modern graphic arts collections. (Most of the ciy's very contemporary American art is part of the San Francisco Museum of Modern Art collection; for more information, see "Civic Center and Vicinity," under "The Lay of the Land" above.) Also included in the de Young's permanent collection are traditional arts of the Americas, Africa, and Oceania, housed in new galleries. Come, too, for changing special exhibits, like "Beyond the Java Sea: Art of Indonesia's Outer Islands." For current information on exhibits, call 863-3330; for information on becoming a museum member, call 750-3636.

Typically open Wed.-Sun. 10 a.m.-4:45 p.m., the museum is open 10-9 on the first Wednesday of the month, when admission is free. The de Young also offers free admission 10 a.m.-noon the first Saturday of each month. At other times: $6 adults, $3 seniors, free for those under age 18. Admission includes access to the Asian Art Museum. Call about docent-led tours.

Park Activities, Events, And Information

Kennedy Drive from 19th Avenue to Stanyan is closed to automobile traffic every Sunday; enjoy a walk or bike ride (bicycle rentals on Stanyan). **Golden Gate Carriage, Ltd.,** tel. (415) 761-8272, offers horse-and-buggy park tours daily, weather permitting, from 11:30 a.m. to 6 p.m., with five different itineraries and fares from $5 to $60. **Friends of Recreation and Parks,** tel. 750-5105, offers free guided tours throughout the park from May through October. But even more active sports fans won't be disappointed. Golden Gate Park action includes archery, baseball and basketball, boating and rowing, fly-casting, football, horseback riding and horseshoes, lawn bowling, model yacht sailing—there's a special lake for just that purpose—plus polo, roller-skating, soccer, and tennis. In addition to the exceptional **Children's Playground,** there are two other kiddie play areas.

Free **Golden Gate Band Concerts** are offered at 2 p.m. on Sundays and holidays at the park's Music Concourse. The **Midsummer Music Festival** in Stern Grove, Sloat Boulevard at 19th Avenue, is another fun, and free, park program. Scheduled on consecutive Sundays from mid-June through August, it's quite popular, so come as early as possible. (For exact dates and program information, call the park headquarters, listed below.) A variety of other special events are regularly scheduled in Golden Gate Park, including **A La Carte, A La Park,** San Francisco's "largest outdoor dining event," a benefit for the San Francisco Shakespeare Festival, which offers an annual schedule of free public performances. (Shakespeare in the Park comes in August.) This gala gourmet fest, with themed pavilions, showcases the wares of Bay Area restaurants and Sonoma County wineries, the talents of celebrity chefs, and a wide variety of entertainment. A La Carte, A La Park, tel. (415) 383-9378 for information, is usually scheduled in late summer, over the three-day Labor Day weekend.

To save money on visits to multiple park attractions, purchase a **Golden Gate Cultural Pass** for $10 from the park office or downtown at the visitor information center at Hallidie Plaza. For more information about park events and activities (maps are $2; other items are free), contact **Golden Gate Park Headquarters** in ivy-covered **McLaren Lodge** on the park's east side at Fell and Stanyan, tel. (415) 556-2920, open weekdays 10-5, or contact directly each of the attractions and museums listed above. The **San Francisco Recreation and Park Department,** tel. 666-7200, also provides schedules of park activities and recreation opportunities.

Light meals and snacks are available at various concessions or at **Cafe de Young** inside the de Young Museum; at the **Academy of Sciences;** and at the **Japanese Tea Garden** teahouse (fortune cookies and tea). There is also great choice in restaurants near the intersection of 9th Avenue and Irving, or along Haight and Stanyan streets.

To reach the museums and the tea garden via public transportation, board a westbound #5-Fulton bus on Market Street, climbing off at Fulton and 8th Avenue. After 6 p.m. and on Sundays and holidays, take #21-Hayes to Fulton and 6th. Call 673-MUNI for other routes and schedule information.

MUSEUMS AND BUILDINGS

San Francisco's major public museums, including the **Asian Art Museum,** the **M.H. de Young Memorial Museum,** and the **California Palace of the Legion of Honor** (closed for renovation until spring 1994), have been covered in depth elsewhere in this chapter, along with most worthwhile smaller museums. Among these, the don't-miss list includes the **Old Mint** in SoMa at 5th and Mission, the **Cable Car Barn** at Mason and Washington (for a quick visual comprehension of how it all works), and the **Names Project AIDS Memorial Quilt** display in the Castro. (See "The Lay of the Land" for more about all of these destinations.)

Sophisticated Child's Play: The Exploratorium

Another major city attraction is also a museum, one ostensibly designed for children. But this is no mass-marketed media assault on the senses, no mindless theatrical homage to simple fantasy. The truth is, adults also adore the Exploratorium, **"A Museum Of Science, Art, And Human Perception"** inside the Palace of Fine Arts and a wonderfully intelligent, fact-oriented playground built around the mysterious natural laws of the universe. According to *Scientific American,* this is the "best science museum in the world." *Good Housekeeping* says it's the "number one science museum in the U.S." Either way, this place is definitely worth some time. At home in the Marina District at 3601 Lyon St. (Bay and Lyon), the Exploratorium was founded in 1969 by physicist and educator Dr. Frank Oppenheimer, the original "Explainer," but one whose research career was abruptly ended during the blacklisting McCarthy era. Brother of J. Robert Oppenheimer, who was father of the atomic bomb, Frank Oppenheimer's scientific legacy was nonetheless abundant.

The Exploratorium includes over 700 three-dimensional exhibits delving into 13 broad subject areas: animal behavior, language, vision, sound and hearing, touch, heat and temperature, elec-

EXPLORATORIUM

tricity, light, color, motion, patterns, waves and resonance, and weather. What is learned here can rarely be taught in the classroom. Here everything can be *experienced*, from a touch-sensitive plant shrinking from a child's probing hand, and infinite kaleidoscopic reflections of oneself from mirrors joined at 60-degree angles, to the light-and-color images of Bob Miller's "Sun Painting," or the tactile computerized fingerpainting in Richard Greene's "Light Strokes." On the waterfront, the wave-activated voice of the San Francisco Bay is brought to you by the "Wave Organ," an astounding creation by Peter Richards and George Gonzales. As Oppenheimer himself said: "Explaining science and technology without props is like attempting to tell what it is like to swim without ever letting a person near the water." But just as art is a science, science is also art. It's all a question of perception, of how the mind understands its own workings. So in addition to its revolutionary science curriculum, the Exploratorium features a crew of visual and performing artists-in-residence who continue to create many of the exhibits as well as special programs.

Other special museum programs include "Sleepover Science" overnight stays, field trips, multicultural and community outreach science programs, and high school-aged "Explainer" employee training programs. The ultimate—and the first—truly participatory science museum, the Exploratorium has influenced the establishment of hundreds of other children's and/or science museums in the U.S. and abroad. Looking to the future, the Exploratorium plans to expand its science education efforts even further—through the development of a Center for Public Exhibition, a Center for Teaching and Learning, and a Center for Media and Communication. To keep up with what's happening, subscribe to the **"Exploratorium Quarterly"** newsletter: $18 annually for an individual, $24 for institutions, and $36 for foreign subscriptions.

For more information, call the Exploratorium at tel. (415) 563-7337 (for prerecorded information: tel. 561-0360; for film schedule: tel. 561-0315; for performances: tel. 561-0361). The Ex-

ploratorium is open Tues.-Sun. 10-5, Wed. until 9:30 p.m. On the first Wednesday of each month, admission is free. Otherwise: $7 adults, $5 students (with ID), $3.50 seniors, $3 children ages 6-17, free for under age 6. Admission to the **Tactile Dome,** tel. 561-0362, reservations strongly advised, is $7 per person, which includes museum admission. Stock up on educational toys, games, experiments, and oddities—the hand-held pinscreen an all-time favorite—at the **Exploratorium Store,** tel. 561-0390, or toll-free (800) 359-9899 for mail orders. Especially worth purchasing, for teachers and brave parents alike, is the ***Exploratorium Science Snackbook,*** which includes instructions on how to build home or classroom versions of over 100 Exploratorium exhibits.

Other Worthwhile Buildings

For visitors with more time, or who have a particular interest in historic buildings, San Francisco certainly has its share. Many are privately owned, however, and can only be appreciated from the outside, on walking tours. (See above.) The **Haas-Lilienthal House,** 2007 Franklin at Jackson, tel. (415) 441-3004, is a handsome and huge Queen Anne Victorian, a survivor of the 1906 earthquake and the city's only fully furnished Victorian open for regular public tours. Tours are conducted on Wednesdays and Sundays; call for times. Admission $4 adults, $2 for seniors and children. The very unusual 1861 **Octagon House,** 2645 Gough at Union St., tel. 441-7512, is owned by the National Society of Colonial Dames of America; it's now restored and fully furnished in colonial and federal period antiques. Open only on the second and fourth Thursdays and the second Sunday of each month, closed in January and on holidays. Call to request special tour times. Donation greatly appreciated.

THE PERFORMING ARTS

San Francisco's performing art scene offers everything from the classics to the very contemporary, kitsch, and downright crazed. Find out what's going on by picking up local publications or calling the San Francisco Convention & Visitors Bureau information hotlines (see "Information" under "Just the Facts" below).

Tickets for major events and performances are available through the relevant box offices, mentioned below.

Low-income arts lovers, or those deciding to "do" the town on a last-minute whim, aren't necessarily out of luck. **TIX Bay Area** on Stockton Street at Union Square offers day-of-performance tickets to local shows at half-price. Payment is cash and traveler's checks only, no credit cards. Call (415) 433-7827 for details. A full-service **BASS** ticket outlet as well, TIX also handles advance full-price tickets to many Bay Area events. No telephone orders or reservations accepted, so show up Tues.-Sat. noon-7:30 p.m. To charge BASS arts and entertainment tickets by phone or to listen to recorded calendar listings, call (510) 762-BASS. Another helpful information source: KUSF 90.3 FM's **Alternative Music and Entertainment News (AMEN)** information line, tel. (415) 221-2636.

Other ticket box offices and brokers include the **City Box Office** at Sherman Clay & Co., 141 Kearny, tel. (415) 392-4400, **Entertainment Ticketfinder**, tel. 756-1414 or toll-free (800) 523-1515, and **St. Francis Theatre and Sports Tickets,** a service of the Westin St. Francis Hotel, tel. 362-3500.

Classic Performing Arts

The **San Francisco Ballet,** according to the *New York Times,* is "a truly national ballet company," one of the nation's oldest classical dance companies. The ballet troupe's regular season, with performances in the Civic Center's War Memorial Opera House, runs from February through May, though holiday season performances of the *The Nutcracker* are a long-running San Francisco tradition. For tickets, call (415) 621-3838. The opera house also hosts visiting performances by The Joffrey Ballet and The Kirov Ballet, among others.

The smaller **Herbst Theatre** inside the War Memorial Veteran Building, tel. (415) 552-3656 for box office information, offers smaller dance and musical productions, including performances by the **San Francisco Chamber Symphony** and the **San Francisco Early Music Society.**

The **San Francisco Opera** season runs September through December, a total of 10 productions with big-name stars. Since this is *the* San Francisco social scene, tickets are expensive and quite hard to come by; call (415) 864-3330. Generally more accessible is the **San Francisco Symphony,** which offers a September-through-June regular season in **Louise M. Davies Hall** downtown in the Civic Center, plus July pops concerts. For tickets, call 431-5400. Davies Hall, reopened in 1992 after a two-year, $10 million accoustic renovation, is also a venue for other performances, including some programs of the West's only major independent music conservatory, the **San Francisco Conservatory of Music,** tel. 759-3475 for tickets. The conservatory's annual **Chamber Music West Festival** in late May and early June is usually staged at various sites, including **Hellman Hall** at 19th and Ortega in the Sunset.

San Francisco Theater

Wherever you find it, pick up a free copy of the quarterly *Stagestruck: Theatre in San Francisco* magazine, for its current and comprehensive show schedules. For Broadway shows, the **Curran Theatre** at 445 Geary, tel. (415) 474-3800 or, for tickets, tel. (510) 762-BASS, is the long-running standard, though the **Golden Gate Theatre** at 6th and Market, the **Orpheum** at 8th and Market, and the **Marines Memorial Theatre** at Sutter and Mason (same phone numbers for all) are other popular mainstream venues for comedies, musicals, and revues. The **Lamplighters Music Theatre** at the Presentation Theatre in the Western Addition, Turk at Masonic, tel. (415) 752-7755, specializes in musicals.

The repertory **American Conservatory Theater (A.C.T.),** normally at home at the venerable **Geary Theatre,** 415 Geary (at Mason), tel. (415) 749-2200 or 749-2228 (box office), has been performing its big-name-headliner contemporary comedies and dramas at the **Stage Door Theater** at Mason and Geary and at the **Theatre on the Square,** 450 Post, pending major earthquake repairs. Evening performances Tues.-Sun., plus Wed. and weekend afternoon matinees.

San Francisco is also home to a number of small, innovative theaters and theater troupes, including the **Magic Theatre, Cowell Theater,** and **Young Performers Theatre** at Fort Mason and the **Asian American Theatre** in the Richmond District, mentioned in more detail in "The Avenues" section above. The **Actors Theatre of San Francisco,** 533 Sutter (between Powell

POETIC AMUSEMENTS

There's probably only one thing better than reading a good poem in a quiet room by yourself. And that's listening to an impassioned poet reading a poem out loud in a small coffee-scented cafe full of attentive writers, lawyers, bikers, teachers, computer programmers, divinity students, musicians, secretaries, drug addicts, cooks, and assorted oddball others who all love poetry and are hanging onto every word being juggled by the poet behind the microphone. The only thing better than *that* is to read your own poems at an open-mike poetry reading.

One of the wonderful things about San Francisco and vicinity is that this kind of poetic melee takes place in some cafe, club, or bookstore almost every night, for those who know where to look. No one revels in the right to free speech like Bay Area denizens, and open poetry readings are as popular as stand-up comedy in many cafes and clubs, with sign-up lists at the door. Bring your own poetry, or just kick back and listen to some amazing musings.

The following suggested venues will get you started. Since schedules for local poetic license programs do change, it's prudent to call or otherwise check it out before setting out. Current open readings and other events are listed in the monthly tabloid **Poetry Flash,** the Bay Area's definitive poetry review and literary calendar, available free at many bookstores and cafes, or write to them at P.O. Box 4172, Berkeley 94704.

IN SAN FRANCISCO

Cafe Babar, 994 Guerrero St., tel. (415) 282-6789, Thursdays at 8 p.m.

Cafe Francisco, 2161 Powell St., tel. 397-2602 or 397-8010

Elbo Room, Valencia at 17th St., Fridays at 9 p.m.

Exit Cafe, 1777 Steiner St., tel. 929-7117, Tuesdays at 7 p.m.

Paradise Lounge, 1501 Folsom St., 2nd Floor, tel. 861-6906, Sundays at 8 p.m.

3300 Club, 3300 Mission St. (29th and Mission), tel. 826-6886.

IN THE EAST BAY

Coffee Mill, 3363 Grand Ave. in Oakland, tel. (510) 465-4224, Thursdays at 7 p.m.

La Val's, 1834 Euclid Ave. in Berkeley, tel. (510) 843-5617, Tuesdays at 7:30 p.m.

—Ed Aust

and Mason), tel. (415) 296-9179, usually offers unusual plays. Other progressive dramatic theaters include SoMa's **Climate Theatre,** 252 9th St. (at Folsom), tel. 626-9196, and the **Phoenix Theatre** at 301 8th (at Folsom), tel. 621-4423. Another innovator, in the entire realm of performance art, is **Theater Artaud,** 450 Florida St. (at 17th), tel. 621-7797. **Theatre Rhinoceros,** 2926 16th St., tel. 861-5079, is America's oldest gay and lesbian theater company.

The long-running **Eureka Theatre Company,** now located at 340 Townsend, tel. (415) 243-9899, is "San Francisco's most politically astute theatre," according to the *Village Voice,* noted for its provocative presentations. At last report, however, this theater company's status was uncertain. **Intersection for the Arts,** 446 Valencia St., tel. 626-2787, the city's oldest alternative arts center, presents everything from experimental dramas to performance and visual art and dance. One-time "new talent" like Robin Williams, Whoopi Goldberg, and Sam Shepard are all Intersection alumni. Theatrically speaking, at least in its new San Francisco digs, the new kid on the block is **George Coates Performance Works,** 110 McAllister, tel. 863-8520 or 863-4130, its innovative music-theater presented also at acclaimed U.S. and international festivals.

Theater As Circus

Worth seeing whenever the group is in town is the much-loved, always arresting, and far from silent **San Francisco Mime Troupe,** a decades-old institution true to the classic Greek and Roman tradition of theatrical farce—politically sophisticated street theater noted for its complex simplicity. In addition to boasting actor Peter Coyote and the late rock impressario Bill Graham as organizational alumni, and inspiring the establishment of one-time troupe member Luis Valdez's El Teatro Campesino, the Mime Troupe was repeatedly banned and arrested in its formative years. In 1966, the state Senate Un-American Activities Committee charged the group with the crime of making lewd performances, the same year troupe members were arrested in North Beach for singing Christmas carols without a permit. More recently, the Mime Troupe has won a Tony Award and three Obies.

A tad more family-oriented, "the kind of circus parents might want their kids to run away to," according to Jane Pauley, is the **Pickle Family Circus,** another exceptional city-based theater troupe. Watch local newspapers for announcements and advertisements of coming performances; tickets available through BASS.

Bizarre cabaret-style **"Beach Blanket Babylon,"** playing at Club Fugazi in North Beach at 678 Green St. (at Powell), tel. (415) 421-4222, is the longest-running musical revue in theatrical history, the performance heading toward its 20th anniversary. The storyline is always evolving. Snow White, who seems to seek love in all the wrong places, was recently encountering characters like Anita Hill and Judge Clarence Thomas.

Other Performing Arts
"Eclectic" is the word used most often to describe the **Audium** at 1616 Bush St., tel. (415) 771-1616, perhaps the ultimate performance of sound, certainly the only place like this in the world. Some 136 speakers in the sloping walls, the suspended ceiling, and the floating floor all create an unmatched aural experience. Regular performances are on Friday and Saturday nights at 8:30 p.m.; tickets go on sale at 8 p.m. Children under age 12 not allowed.

Special events abound year-round. With a little help from The Gap Foundation, along with KJAZ Radio and the *San Francisco Business Times,* for example, the **San Francisco Museum of Modern Art,** at Van Ness and McAllister tel. (415) 863-8800 (until 1995), offers its new, extended-hours "Third Thursday at the Modern" evening of live jazz-and-art-and-lecture fusion. In summer, after-hours lectures are offered every Thursday, along with short "spotlight" tours, and live jazz is offered on the third Thursday of the month. Call for current information.

MORE ARTS AND ENTERTAINMENT

A selection of entertaining bars, nightclubs, and other neighborhood diversions is included under "The Lay of the Land." To keep abreast of the ever-changing arts and entertainment scene, consult local newspapers, especially the weeklies for their calendar sections and the Sunday *Examiner-Chronicle*'s pink "Datebook" section. For other ideas, see "Information" under "Just the Facts" below.

Art Galleries
The downtown area, especially near Union Square and along lower Grant Avenue, is rich with art galleries and arts-related specialty shops. Others are mentioned elsewhere above, under their respective district or neighborhood. The free *San Francisco Arts Monthly,* available around town and at the visitor information center downtown, includes a complete current listing of special gallery tours, exhibits, and art showrooms. Very useful, too, is *The San Francisco Gallery Guide,* published every two months by The William Sawyer Gallery, 3045 Clay St., tel. (415) 921-1600; it includes goings-on at galleries large and small as well as information about current shows at major Bay Area museums. The nonprofit **San Francisco Art Dealers Association,** 1717 17th St., San Francisco 94103, is also a good source for fine arts information, since the 30 or so well-respected member galleries are included by invitation only. Usually in July, the association sponsors its public "Introductions" program, with member galleries featuring works by new visual-arts talent. Member galleries are also open into the evening hours the first Thursday of each month, as part of its "First Thursday" gallery program.

Real Food, Real Art, Real Radio
San Francisco's **Real Food Company** delis and stores—at 1001 and 1023 Stanyan St., 2140 and 2164 Polk St., plus 1240 Sutter and 3939 24th St., and elsewhere in the Bay Area—are the most predictable places to pick up free **San Francisco Open Studios** artists' listings, detailed maps, and resource directories. Or stop by Bay Area bookstores, art-supply stores, and selected galleries such as **Somar Gallery** at 934 Brannan, which also displays examples of individual artists' work. The Open Studios concept offers direct-to-you fine arts, plus an opportunity to meet the artists and often see how and where they work. The Bay Area's Open Studios experience, sponsored by California Lawyers for the Arts and local businesses, usually scheduled

on consecutive Saturdays and Sundays from late October to mid-November, feature over 500 local artists who open their studios or personally share their work with the public. You can come just to schmooze, of course, but these working artists will eat better if you buy. For more information, call (415) 861-9838.

A similar open-air event in spring, held on consecutive May weekends in various local parks, features many of the same artists and is sponsored by the cooperative **Artists Guild of San Francisco**, tel. (415) 822-6110.

And a real treat for radio fans is a Saturday afternoon spent in the audience of the weekly two-hour KQED **"West Coast Weekend"** news and features show, which covers whatever's going on. Live and lively interviews with artists, entertainers, musicians, playwrights, theater directors, and other principals in the local, national, and international arts scenes are a staple for the show, which comes to you each week from Fort Mason's **Life on the Water** studio. For more information, call (415) 553-2213 or 553-2215.

Comedy

Campy *Bar None,* staged at the York Hotel's **Plush Room**, 940 Sutter, tel. (415) 885-2800, is the city's longest-running comedy, a murder mystery where the entire cast is suspect and the audience must investigate. But the equally funny *Party of One* at the **New Conservatory Theater,** 25 Van Ness (at Market), tel. 861-8972, is the city's longest-running original, a musical comedy about being single.

Bay Area Theatresports (BATS) performances in the **Playroom Theatre,** 450 Geary, tel. (415) 824-8220, are hilarious and improvisational, often team efforts, with the "scripts" for instant plays, movies, and musicals often created from audience suggestions. Similar in style but specializing in pulp-fiction stories—adventure, romance, horror, and the like—the **Pulp Playhouse,** tel. 922-9375, plays at various around-town venues, including the New Conservatory Theatre.

The **National Theatre of the Deranged,** tel. (415) 441-7808, inspired by The Committee, always welcomes audience participation as it

rewrites the news. At last report, the Deranged were playing Monday nights at the famed stand-up comedy venue **The Improv,** 401 Mason St., tel. 441-7787. The hottest yuckspot in town, some say, is **Cobb's Comedy Club** at The Cannery on Fisherman's Wharf, tel. 928-4445. Other venues include the **Punchline Comedy Club** at 444 Battery, tel. 397-7573, and the **Holy City Zoo** at 408 Clement, tel. 386-4242.

Films And Film Series

The **San Francisco International Film Festival,** Northern California's longest-running film festival, is scheduled annually, usually from late April into May. This cinematic celebration includes 60 or more films from dozens of countries, showing (at last report) at the AMC Kabuki 8 Theaters in Japantown and at Berkeley's Pacific Film Archives. For current program and price information, call (415) 567-4641. The city has all sorts of noteworthy festivities focused on film, including the 15-year-old **Lesbian & Gay Film Festival,** usually held at the Castro Theater in late June, which has apparently survived attacks by Senator Jesse Helms on its National Endowment for the Arts funding.

But in San Francisco, going to the movies is always entertaining. If you don't mind the (outdoor) neighborhood horror show, the **Strand** downtown near the Civic Center, at 1127 Market between 7th and 8th, tel. (415) 621-2227, shows unusual foreign films, sometimes double and triple features, from noon on. Cheap, too.

Classic theaters with friendlier neighborhoods, these most likely to host foreign, revival, and other film festivals, include grand and Moorish **The Alhambra,** 2330 Polk St., tel. (415) 775-2137; the 1930s **Castro Theater** near Market at 429 Castro St., tel. 621-6120, where you get live organ music during interludes, Hollywood classics, contemporary films, and clever double bills; and the very hip **Roxie** near Valencia at 3117 16th St., tel. 863-1087, specializing in independent, oddball, and trendy films, sometimes showing silent flicks accompanied by organ. At the **Red Victorian Movie House** near the

in independent, oddball, and trendy films, sometimes showing silent flicks accompanied by organ. At the **Red Victorian Movie House** near the same-named Victorian in the Haight, 1659 Haight St., tel. 668-3994, count on art films, revivals, interesting foreign fare—and California-casual couches for comfort.

Hole-in-the-wall **Artists Television Access (ATA)** at 992 Valencia, tel. (415) 824-3890, offers truly underground, experimental, and radical political films from unknown, independent filmmakers. Other good movie theater bets: the **New York Theater,** 2789 24th St. (at Bryant), tel. 647-8181; the **Lumiere** at 1572 California (at Polk), tel. 885-3200; the **Clay,** 2261 Fillmore, tel. 346-1123; and the **Bridge** a few blocks west of Masonic at 3010 Geary Blvd., tel. 751-3212. To see what's playing at a glance, or for a complete mainstream movie round-up, consult movie listings in local newspapers (see "Information" under "Just the Facts" below).

Playing Pool
South Beach Billiards in SoMa at 270 Brannan St., tel. (415) 495-5939, is a one-time licorice factory converted into a pretty hip pool palace. In addition to the 30-something eight-foot tables covered in burgundy felt, there's a nine-foot antique table available in a private suite, also an indoor bocce ball court. Microbrewery ales on tap. Also gentrified and comfortable even for absolute beginners is **The Great Entertainer** at 975 Bryant, tel. 861-8833, once a paint warehouse, now the West Coast's largest pool hall. Most of the tables in the 28,000-square-foot hall (half is designated nonsmoking) are nine feet long. Private suites are available. Also here: snooker, shuffleboard, and Ping-Pong (table tennis) tables.

EVENTS

San Francisco events are even more kaleidoscopic than the city's arts scene, an almost endless combination of the appropriate, inappropriate, absurd, inspired, and sublime. Museums, theaters, neighborhood groups, and other cultural institutions usually offer their own annual events calendars. Even most shopping centers sponsor a surprising array of entertainment and events. That said, consider the seasonal events selection offered below as merely a sampling, and consult local newspapers for more complete information on what's going on.

Spring Events
The big deal in March, and quite the party, is the annual **Bammies,** the Bay Area Music Awards ceremony in the Civic Auditorium, tel. (415) 974-4000. Expect everything to be Irish and/or green at the city's annual **St. Patrick's Day Parade** and all-day street party, tel. 661-2700, both events attracting plenty of politicians. Otherwise, people start warming up to the attractions of the great outdoors by attending the *Chronicle*'s **Great Outdoors Adventure Fair,** an exposition on everything and anything to do with recreation, tel. 777-7120.

St. Stupid's Day Parade on April 1 is a no-holds-barred celebration of foibles and foolishness. Show up in April with your bonnet for Union Street's **Annual Easter Parade,** tel. (415) 441-7055. Japantown's big **Cherry Blossom Festival,** tel. 563-2313, usually includes a parade and other cultural festivities. And outdoor life comes back to the bay with a bang as both **baseball season** and **yachting season** start up again. The latter's **Opening Day on the Bay** is quite the sight. Also in April, head for the Concourse Exhibit Center and the **Whole Life Expo.**

In May, the Mission District hosts two major events: the **Cinco de Mayo Parade & Festival,** a two-day party scheduled as close to May 5 as possible, and the later **Carnaval San Francisco.** For more information on both, call the Mission Economic & Cultural Association at tel. (415) 826-1401.

Summer Events
Of course there's always more going on in summer. The Haight celebrates its long-gone Summer of Love in June with the **Haight Ashbury Fair,** tel. (415) 661-8025. Among the arts, crafts, and other wares, you can probably count on plenty of tie-dyed items, prism-cut glass, and other hippie-style creations. But everyone's in a street-party mood, so June (sometimes late May or early July) also features the **New North Beach Fair,** the **Union Street Spring Festival Arts and Crafts Fair,** and **Jazz and All That Art on Fillmore,** the latter celebrating the cultural and musical heritage of what was once a largely black neighborhood. Call 346-4446 for

information on all three events. Also in June is the **Ethnic Dance Festival,** tel. 474-3914, and the start of Golden Gate Park's **Stern Grove Midsummer Music Festival,** tel. 252-6252, Sundays at 2 p.m. (It ends in late August.) Show up, too, for the **Kitemakers Annual Father's Day Kite Festival** on the Marina Green, tel. 956-3181. Usually also late in June, coinciding with the film festival, comes the annual **Lesbian-Gay Freedom Day Parade and Celebration,** tel. 864-3733, one huge gay-pride party usually led by Dykes on Bikes and including cross-dressing cowboys (or -girls), gay bands and majorettes, cheerleaders, and everyone and everything else. Act Up and other groups also deliver a more serious message—about the rising death toll from AIDS and its (so far) disproportionate impact on the gay community.

In inimitable American style, **Independence Day** is celebrated in San Francisco with costumes (prizes for Most Original Uncle Sam and Best Symbol of America), ethnic food, multicultural entertainment, comics, and nighttime fireworks at Crissy Field, tel. (415) 556-0560. Also in July: **Comedy Celebration Day** in Golden Gate Park, tel. 777-7120, and the annual **KQED International Beer Festival,** tel. 553-2200. Musically speaking, major annual music celebrations start up around this time. Both the **Midsummer Mozart Festival** in Herbst Theatre, tel. 552-3656, and the **San Francisco Symphony Pops Concerts,** tel. 431-5400, end in August. Golden Gate Park's annual **Summer Festival of Performing Arts,** tel. 474-3914, runs into September.

The **San Francisco Shakespeare Festival** is staged in Golden Gate Park from August into October, tel. (415) 666-2221. Also in August: the **San Francisco Fair,** a flower show in Golden Gate Park, tel. 753-7090; the **Ringling Brothers Barnum and Bailey Circus** at the Cow Palace, tel. 469-6000, and Fort Mason's **Pacific States Crafts Fair,** tel. 896-5060. Or head to Japantown for the **Nihonmachi Street Fair,** tel. 922-8700.

Autumn Events

Usually in mid-September is the Japantown **Festival of the Viewing of the Moon,** an arts and crafts street fair, tel. (415) 346-4446. But don't miss the annual **Bay Area Robot Olympics** at the Exploratorium, tel. 563-7337, and the **LEAP Sandcastle-Building Contest**

for Architects in Aquatic Park, tel. 775-5327. Also in September: the Mission District's **Festival de las Americas,** tel. 826-1401, **Opera in the Park,** tel. 864-3330, and the **San Francisco Blues Festival** at Fort Mason, tel. 826-6837. Also show up in September for the **Folsom Street Fair,** tel. 431-6197, with entertainment, arts, crafts, and more.

If you're feeling nostalgic for the farm come October, plan on attending the city's international **Great Halloween & Pumpkin Festival,** more arts and crafts, tel. (415) 346-4446. Another possibility is the **Grand National Livestock Exposition Rodeo and Horse Show** at the Cow Palace, tel. 469-6000. Or bless your pet (or cow or horse) at Grace Cathedral's **St. Francis Day** service, tel. 776-6611. During **Fleet Week,** unless the military has been mothballed in its entirety, the U.S. Navy puts down the plank for the public, and also welcomes ships from around the world. A major cultural blowout is the **Columbus Day Celebration and Parade** in North Beach, tel. 434-1492. Also scheduled in October is the **German Fest** in the Civic Auditorium, tel. 397-1085, the **Castro Street Fair,** tel. 467-3354, Fort Mason's **Fall Antiques Show,** tel. 921-1411, the annual **Jazz in the City Festival,** tel. 864-5449, and the **Antique Tribal Art Show and Sale,** tel. 889-5187. To finish off the month in absolutely absurd style, on Halloween head for the **Exotic Erotic Ball,** tel. 864-1500. Alternatively, the best street show is in the Castro and Mission districts.

November events include the **San Francisco Bay Area Book Festival,** tel. (415) 861-BOOK, the **San Francisco International Auto Show** at Moscone Center, and the start of holiday festivities all over town.

Winter Events

Most December events reflect seasonal traditions, and the major arts performances are quite popular, so get tickets well in advance. The **San Francisco Ballet** performs *The Nutcracker,* tel. (415) 861-1177 for subscribers, 621-3838 for box office, and the **American Conservatory Theater** presents *A Christmas Carol,* tel. 749-2228. The **Crosby Croon-Alike Contest** takes place at Pier 39, tel. 981-8030, with finalists belting out "White Christmas."

In January San Francisco hosts the **Martin Luther King Birthday Celebration,** tel. (415)

771-6300. Also this month comes the **San Francisco Sports and Boat Show** at the Cow Palace, tel. 931-2500. In February of alternate years, the **California International Antiquarian Book Fair** is held in San Francisco, tel. 495-0100. (When it's not here, it's in Los Angeles.) But the main event, sometimes in January, sometimes in February, is the city's **Chinese New Year Celebration,** complete with parade and throngs of people, a very American tradition. For current information, contact the Chinese Chamber of Commerce, tel. 982-3000.

SHOPPING

Whether the addiction is neighborhood boutique hopping or spending days in major-league malls, San Francisco is a shopper's paradise. To seek something specific, study the current *San Francisco Book,* published by the San Francisco Visitors & Convention Bureau, for mainstream shopping destinations. To pursue shopping as social exploration, wander the city's neighborhood commercial districts. (Be sure to take advantage of museum and arts-venue gift shops, which usually feature an unusual array of merchandise. Secondhand and thrift shops can also be surprising. Some suggestions are included under the districts section of this chapter.) To shop for one's consumer identity—covering as much ground, and as many shops, as possible without having any particular result in mind—visit the city's mall-like marketplaces.

The uptown **Union Square** area is an upscale shoppers delight. Major San Francisco shopping palaces include the new nine-story **San Francisco Shopping Centre** a few blocks from Union Square at 5th and Market, astonishing for its marble and granite elegance and its spiral escalators and retractable atrium skylight. Also in the neighborhood is the **Crocker Galleria** between Post and Sutter, Kearny and Montgomery, a glass-domed wonder (complete with rooftop gardens) modeled after the Galleria Vittorio Emmanuelle in Milan. Another major downtown commercial attraction is the **Embarcadero Center,** designed by John C. Portman, Jr., an eight-block complex (between Clay and Sacramento, Drumm and Battery) with three plaza-style levels and four main buildings plus the

THE GREENPEACE STORE
890 NORTH POINT, SAN FRANCISCO
OPEN DAILY 10-10   474-1870

Hyatt Regency and Park Hyatt hotels, not to mention five office towers.

The three-square-block **Japan Center** in the Western Addition's Japantown, designed by Minoru Yamasaki, adds up to about five acres of galleries, shops, restaurants, theaters, hotels, and convention facilities. **Chinatown** is famous for its ethnic commercial attractions, and adjacent **North Beach** also has its share.

But nearby **Fisherman's Wharf,** along the northeastern waterfront, is becoming shopping central. **The Cannery** at Beach and Leavenworth, one block east of the Hyde Street cable car turnaround, is a brick-and-ivy behemoth. Once the world's largest fruit cannery, the building is now home to collected cafes, restaurants, shops, galleries, a comedy club, a jazz club, even the new Museum of the City of San Francisco, which features City Hall's original Goddess of Progress (or at least her head) and a section of a 13th-century Byzantine mosaic ceiling once part of William Randolph Hearst's globetrotting acquisitions program. **The Anchorage Shopping Center,** bounded by Jefferson, Beach, Leavenworth, and Jones, is very contemporary, very nautical, with some unusual shops—like **The Spy Factory,** specializing in bulletproof vests, Pepsi-can safes, and other forms of personal protection, and **Victorian Greetings,** for stylized stationery and gifts—and some equally unusual events. The annual **San Francisco International Accordion Festival,** honoring that North Beach invention, the piano accordion, takes place here, usually in October. (Highlights include the Lady of Spain-a-Sing and the Ms. Accordion San Francisco Pageant.)

Perhaps most famous of the Fisherman's Wharf shopping destinations, though, are 45-acre, carnival-crazy **Pier 39** along the waterfront, with over 100 shops and endless family amusements, and the one-time chocolate factory **Ghirardelli Square,** with stylish shops and restaurants and some great views.

Vaulted glass and Renaissance marble, the **Stonestown Galleria** on Highway 1 at Winston Drive near San Francisco State University and Lake Merced offers all sorts of sophistication—and the luxury, in San Francisco, of free parking.

SPORTS AND RECREATION

Though in mid-1992 it appeared that indecisive San Francisco had all but sacrificed its major league baseball team to covetous St. Petersburg, Florida, the **San Francisco Giants** are still here, playing ball in the blustery cold winds of Candlestick Park, tel. (415) 467-8000. Fans are chastened but still fickle these days; seats are usually available. (To betray the city's baseball heritage, zip across the bay to the Oakland Coliseum and the **Oakland A's**

games, tel. 510-430-8020.) The city has had better luck with its **San Francisco 49ers** football team, tel. (408) 562-4949 for information, tel. (415) 468-2249 for tickets, made famous by the long and legendary career of ex-49ers quarterback Joe Montana.

Sart Franciscans are big on participatory sports. Some of the city's most eclectic competitive events reflect this fact, including the famous *Examiner* **Bay to Breakers** race, tel. (415) 777-7773, attracting 100,000-plus runners, joggers, and walkers, most wearing quite creative costumes—a phenomenon that has to be experienced to be believed. (Request registration forms well in advance.)

San Francisco's outdoor and other recreational opportunities seem limited only by one's imagination (and income): hot-air ballooning, beachcombing, bicycling, birdwatching, boating, bowling, camping, canoeing, kayaking, hang gliding, hiking, horseshoes, fishing, golf, tennis, sailing, swimming, surfing, parasailing, rowing, rock climbing, running, sailboarding. Golden Gate National Recreational Area and Golden Gate Park, discussed in detail above, are major community recreation resources.

For a current rundown on sports events and recreational opportunities, or for information on very specialized activities, consult local newspapers and magazines, the telephone Yellow Pages, and the very helpful folks at the San Francisco Convention & Visitors Bureau (see "Information" under "Just the Facts" below).

ACCOMMODATIONS: STAYING IN STYLE

San Francisco is not exactly an inexpensive city. A first-time visitor's first impression might be that no one is expected here unless they arrive with a bankroll so hefty that a Rolls-Royce—or flatbed truck—is also required, just to roll it around town. But first impressions never last. The rest of us are indeed welcome, especially when it comes to accommodations and eateries (more about eating out below).

San Francisco offers two hostels affiliated with American Youth Hostels (and Hostelling International, formerly the International Youth Hostel Federation) in addition to other hostels and quite inexpensive options. Some definitely dirt-cheap choices for an overnight are in pretty seedy areas—not usually the best bets for women—though budget travelers with city savvy, street smarts, and well-honed self-preservation skills may want to consider establishments in questionable neighborhoods. (In the context of truly low-budget accommodations, "European-style" generally means "the bathrooms are in the hallway.") City-style motels offer another world of possibilities. Some reasonably priced ones are scattered throughout the city, though Lombard Street (west of Van Ness) is the place to go for overwhelming concentrations of motel choice. The city also supports a wide variety of bed-and-breakfast inns, with ambiences ranging from Haight-Ashbury-style funk to very proper Victoriana.

In general, San Francisco offers great choices in the mid-range hotel market. The biggest bedding-down phenomenon is the "boutique hotel" trend, still going strong into the 1990s. Many of these attractive and intimate hotels—old-timers and aging grand dames now renovated and redecorated for the modern carriage trade—are well located, near visitor attractions as well as public transit. Lack of convenient off-street parking is rarely a drawback, since most offer some sort of valet parking arrangement. Very good to exceptional restaurants—and room service—are often associated with boutique hotels. When travel is slow, most notably in winter, off-season and package deals can make these small hotels (and others) genuine bargains. Do check around before signing in. Also check at the visitor center on Market Street, since some establishments offer special coupons and other seasonal inducements. Many boutique and fine hotels also offer substantial discounts to business travelers and to members of major "travel-interested" groups, including the American Automobile Association (AAA) and the American Association of Retired People (AARP).

If you can afford the prices ("tariffs," actually), consider a stay at one of the city's four- or five-star hotels. Some of the city's finest hotels are also among its most historic, survivors—at least in part—of the great 1906 earthquake and fire.

Reservation Services

If you're unable to make an accommodations choice well in advance, or if you'd rather let someone else do the detail work, contact a local reservations service. **San Francisco Reservations,** 22 2nd St., 4th Floor, San Francisco 94105, tel. (415) 227-1500 or toll-free (800) 677-1550, offers a no-fee reservations service for over 200 hotels, most of these in San Francisco, and keeps current on discounts, specials, and packages. The company offers preferred rates for business travelers at some of the city's finest hotels, including many of the boutiques. With one call, you can also take advantage of their free best-deal airline ticketing and car rental reservations service. Call 8-8 Mon.-Sat., 9-5 on Sunday. **Discount Hotel Rates/Golden Gate Lodging Reservations,** 1030 Franklin St., Suite 405, San Francisco 94109, tel. 771-6915 or toll-free (800) 423-7846, also no-fee, represents over 200 hotels in San Francisco and beyond. Subject to room availability, the firm offers rates at quality hotels for 10-60% less than posted rates. **Lodging San Francisco,** 421 North Point, San Francisco 94133, tel. 292-4500 or (800) 356-7567, specializes in boutique hotel accommodations, including family and "romance" packages.

Bed & Breakfast International, P.O. Box 282910, San Francisco 94128-2910, tel. (415) 696-1690 or toll-free (800) 872-4500, offers referrals to a wide range of California bed and breakfasts—everything from houseboat and home stays to impressive Victorians and country-style inns—especially in San Francisco, the

Napa-Sonoma wine country, and the Monterey Peninsula. Rates: $50-175 per night (with two-night minimum). Similar, and often without the mandatory two-night stay, is **Bed and Breakfast San Francisco,** P.O. Box 420009, San Francisco 94142, tel. 931-3083 or (800) 452-8249. Definitely different is **Boat & Breakfast USA,** Pier 39, P.O. Box HM-2, San Francisco 94133, tel. 291-8411 or (800) BOAT-BED, offering various overnight accommodations ($115 and up) on private yachts in San Francisco, Oakland, and Sausalito.

HOSTELS AND OTHER VERY INEXPENSIVE STAYS

Hostels And Low-Budget Accommodations

The **San Francisco International AYH Hostel** at Fort Mason, Bldg. 240, San Francisco 94123, tel. (415) 771-7277, is a local institution—one located right on the bay and part of the city's urban national park, the Golden Gate National Recreation Area. Close to the "Bikecentennial" bike route and the cultural attractions of the Fort Mason complex, San Francisco International is also within an easy stroll of Chinatown and downtown (you *could* take the cable car) as well as Fisherman's Wharf and Ghirardelli Square.

The hostel itself is one of AYH's largest—and finest—offering a total of 160 beds, clean rooms, and strict enforcement of the one-chore-a-day rule. Popular with all age groups, families. Lock-out daily, 10 a.m.-4:30 p.m., 2 a.m. curfew. Lots of lounge space, big kitchen, plenty of food storage, laundry facilities, linen rentals, and pay lockers for baggage. Family rooms are available. Wheelchair accessible. Parking available; the ride board here is quite helpful for travelers without wheels. Guests can also participate in AYH-sponsored hikes, tours, and bike rides—including the biggest annual event, **The AYH Great San Francisco Bike Adventure** in June, California's largest cycling event (not a race), sponsored by the *San Francisco Chronicle*. Anytime, reservations are essential for groups, and always advisable for others—especially in summer, when this place is jumping. Rates: April-Sept. $13 pp, Oct.-March $12 pp, AYH members and nonmembers. Five-day minimum stay. To reserve by mail, send one night's deposit (address above) at least three weeks in advance; by phone (above) or fax (771-1468), call at least 48 hours in advance and confirm with a major credit card (Visa, MC).

Near all the downtown and theater district hubbub is the **AYH Hostel at Union Square,** between Geary and O'Farrell at 312 Mason St., San Francisco 94102, tel. (415) 788-5604, another good choice for budget travelers. This hotel-style hostel offers double and triple rooms—most share a bathroom—and amenities from kitchen and laundry facilities to baggage storage, linen rentals, and vending machines. Check-in 7 a.m.-midnight, no lockout. Family rooms available. Groups welcome, by reservation only. Reservations are essential for everyone June-Sept. (advisable at other times). Rates for AYH members $14, for nonmembers $18. Reserve by phone (above) or fax (788-3023) with major credit card (Visa, MC) and at least 48 hours notice. Ask about the best nearby parking.

Among other decent low-budget stays is the non-AYH **International Network Globe Hostel** South of Market just off Folsom at 10 Hallam Pl., tel. (415) 431-0540, a fairly large, lively place with clean four-bed hotel rooms, private sundeck, community lounge, laundry room, continental breakfast and dinners served. The Globe is specifically for foreign guests, usually students, but these can also include Americans who present passports with stamps verifying their own international travels. Open 24 hours, no curfew, $15 pp (key deposit extra). Also in the area and strictly for international travelers ("operated by students for students" and affiliated with the American Association of International Hostels) are two other SoMa budget outposts, the **European Guest House** at 761 Minna (between 8th and 9th Streets), tel. 861-6634, and the affiliated **San Francisco International Student Center** at 1188 Folsom (near BrainWash), tel. 255-8800, both offering dorm-style accommodations as well as private rooms and all other basic amenities, from $11 pp per night.

Hostel-style accommodations north of Market include the **San Francisco Globetrotter's Inn** at 225 Ellis St. (Ellis and Mason, one block west of Powell), tel. (415) 346-5786 (tel. 673-4048 to reach guests), with daily rates of $12 per night (shared) or $24, weekly rates $75. The very large San Francisco **YMCA Hotel,** 220 Golden Gate Ave., tel. 885-0460, is in an unappealing area two blocks north of Market at Leavenworth, with adequate rooms for women and men (double locks on all doors), plus pool, gym, and the city's only indoor track—a plus for runners, since you won't want to run through the neighborhood (for fun, anyway). Room rates, including breakfast: $32-45. Hostel beds are $16, available for members only.

Another "Y" option is the men-only **YMCA Chinatown** closer to downtown, between Stockton and Grant at 855 Sacramento St., tel. 982-4412. Nearby at 615 Broadway is the **Sam Wong Hotel**, 615 Broadway, tel. 781-6836, clean rooms but just the basics, singles or doubles with bath $30-35. Inexpensive in Chinatown for women only—primarily a boardinghouse—is the **Gum Moon Women's Residence** on the corner of Stockton at 940 Washington, tel. 421-8827.

Close to Nob Hill is the very nice **San Francisco James Court International Hostel Hotel** at 1353 Bush St. (between Polk and Larkin), tel. (415) 771-2409, with European-style accommodations and basic amenities plus kitchen, from $25 pp per night (double occupancy). The **Mary Elizabeth Inn** a few blocks away at 1040 Bush (between Jones and Leavenworth), tel. 673-6768, is a women's residence, part of a mission program sponsored by the United Methodist Church. Tourists are welcome when space is available. Facilities include private rooms (shared baths) with linen service, laundry facilities, sundeck and solarium, and two meals daily (except Sunday). An even better bet, though, for a longer visit in San Francisco is the **Harcourt Residence Club** at 1105 Larkin, tel. 673-7720, where a stay includes two meals a day, Sunday brunch, access to TV. Unlike most other residence hotels, this one attracts international students, a younger clientele. Weekly pp rates: $130-200.

A good budget bet in the Mission District/Upper Market is Accommodations International's **18th Street Guest House** at 3930 18th St. (between Noe and Sanchez), tel. (415) 255-0644, a 1910 Edwardian with 12 rooms (four have private baths) offering a bed-and-breakfast-style hostel stay for $14 s, $28 d (discounts available for long-term guests). Amenities include continental breakfast, a library, abundant tourist and travel information, color TV, full kitchen, and access to a large landscaped yard complete with hammock and barbecue. Truly unusual in San Francisco,

pets are allowed (call first). Good access to public transit (BART and Muni buses). Storage available if you'll be returning.

GOOD INEXPENSIVE HOTELS

Pensione International at the gentrifying edge of the Tenderloin just east of Hyde St. at 875 Post St., tel. (415) 775-3344, offers quite attractive rooms for $30-40 ($55-65 with private bathroom), breakfast included. A good choice, too, is **The Ansonia** at 711 Post, tel. 673-2670, which features nice rooms, laundry, and breakfast and dinner (except on Sunday). Rates: $35-60, depending upon the bathroom arrangement. Weekly rates, too, and student rates for one month or longer.

Perhaps the epitome of San Francisco's casual, low-cost European-style stays is the **Adelaide Inn** at 5 Isadora Duncan (quite near the theater district, off Taylor between Geary and Post), tel. 441-2261 or 441-2474. Reservations are advisable for the 16 rooms with bathrooms in the hall, rates $32 s, $42 d and up, including continental breakfast. Another budget gem is in the Chinatown area, the **Obrero Hotel**, also a Basque restaurant at 1208 Stockton, tel. 989-3960, just a dozen cheery bed-and-breakfast rooms with bathrooms in the hall, full breakfast included for $40-45. A family-style Basque feast (extra) is served at 6:30 p.m. Another best bet is the **Grant Plaza Hotel,** 465 Grant Ave. (between Pine and Bush), tel. 434-3883 or toll-free (800) 472-6899, with rates $37-65. Group rates available. Unpretentious and reasonably priced (private bathrooms) is the **Union Square Plaza Hotel** at 432 Geary (between Powell and Mason), tel. 776-7585, $45-60.

Nicer Inexpensive Hotels
A few blocks north of the Civic Center between Hyde and Larkin, in a borderline bad neighborhood, is the justifiably popular **Hotel Essex,** 684 Ellis St., tel. (415) 474-4664 or toll-free (800) 44-ESSEX in California, (800) 45-ESSEX from elsewhere in the U.S., small rooms with private baths, even telephones, some with TV. Free coffee. Especially popular in summer—when rates are slightly higher—with foreign tourists, particularly Germans. Rates: $40-60. Weekly rates, too.

SOME HIP SAN FRANCISCO STAYS

Every city has its style, reflected in how things appear, of course, but mostly in how they feel. The following establishments offer just a sample of that inimitable San Francisco attitude.

The Phoenix Inn at 601 Eddy St. (on the corner of Eddy and Larkin at the edge of the Tenderloin), San Francisco 94109, tel. (415) 776-1380 or toll-free (800) CITY INN, is more than just a 1950s motel resurrected with flamingo pink and turquoise paint. It's a subtle see-and-be-seen art scene, first attracting rock 'n' roll stars and now attracting almost everybody—*the* place in San Francisco to spy on members of the cultural elite. A partial list of the Phoenix Inn's 1991-92 celebrity bookings, for example, includes Linda Ronstadt, Emmylou Harris, Laurie Anderson, Sinead O'Connor, the Cowboy Junkies, even Chubby Checker, Bo Didley, and Etta James. Just-plain-famous folks like Faye Dunaway, John Kennedy, Jr., Dan Rather, and Alexander Cockburn can also be spied from time to time. Like the hot, on-site Caribbean-style restaurant, **Miss Pearl's Jam House,** even the swimming pool here is famous, due to its 1990 Francis Forlenza mural, "My Fifteen Minutes—Tumbling Waves," the center of a big state-sponsored stink over whether it violated health and safety codes (since public pool bottoms are supposed to be white). "That's how it is up at Eddy and Larkin, where the limos are always parkin'," according to the inn's complimentary *Phoenix Fun Book,* a cartoon-style coloring book history illustrated by *Bay Guardian* artist Lloyd Dangle. (Also as a service for guests the Phoenix sporadically publishes its own hippest-of-the-hip guide to San Francisco, *Beyond Fisherman's Wharf.*)

Accommodations at the Phoenix—the inn named for the city's mythic ability to rise from its own ashes, as after the fiery 1906 earthquake—are glass-fronted, uncluttered, pool-facing '50s motel rooms upscaled to ultramodern, yet unostentatious with handmade bamboo furniture, tropical plants, and original local art on the walls. Phoenix services include complimentary continental breakfast from Miss Pearl's Jam House (room service also available), the "Phoenix Movie Channel" on in-room cable, with 15 different made-in-San Francisco movies (plus a film library with 20 "band on the road" films), and a complete massage service, including Swedish, Esalen, Shiatsu, even poolside massage. In addition to complete concierge services, the Phoenix also offers blackout curtains, an on-call voice doctor (for lead vocalists with scratchy throats), and free VIP passes to SoMa's underground dance clubs. Regular rates: $84 s, $89 d, and $125 for each of the three suites. Rates for the arts, corporate, and government clientele start at $69. The "special winter rate" for regular customers—subject to availability—also starts at $69, with the fourth night free.

THE PHOENIX INN

The pool at the Phoenix Inn is considered a work of art: My Fifteen Minutes—Tumbling Wave *by New York artist Francis Forlenza.*

Awesomely hip, too, is the **Hotel Triton** on Grant, in the heart of the city's downtown gallery district. The one-time Beverly Plaza Hotel just across from the Chinatown Gateway has been reimagined and reinvented by Bill Klimpton, the man who started the boutique hotel trend in town in 1980. The Triton's artsy ambience is startling and entertaining, boldly announcing itself in the lobby with sculpted purple, teal, and gold columns, odd tassle-headed, gold brocade "dervish" chairs, and mythic Neptunian imagery on the walls. Rooms are comfortable and contemporary, with custom-designed geometric mahogany furniture, sponge-painted or diamond-patterned walls, original artwork by Chris Kidd, and unusual tilework in the bathrooms. Each guest room reflects one of three basic configurations: a king-size bed with camelback upholstered headboards, similar double beds, or oversized daybeds that double as a couch. Other basics: soundproof windows, same-day valet/laundry service, room service, color TV with remote (also cable and movie channels), and direct-dial phones with long cords. Modem hookups can also be arranged. Basic rates: $125, $165 for junior suites. A nice feature of this and other Klimpton-owned hotels, too, is the fully stocked honor bar—unusual in that items are quite reasonably priced. For more information or reservations, contact: Hotel Triton, 342 Grant Ave., San Francisco 94108, tel. (415) 394-0500 or toll-free (800) 433-6611.

Affordable style is apparent and available at other small San Francisco hotels, including Klimpton's Prescott Hotel, home to Wolfgang Puck's Postrio Restaurant. But there's nothing else in town quite like Haight-Ashbury's **Red Victorian Bed and Breakfast Inn,** a genuine blast from San Francisco's past. This 1904 survivor is red, all right, and it's a bed and breakfast—but except for the architecture it's not very Victorian. The style is early-to-late Summer of Love. Downstairs is the Global Village Bazaar, a New Age shopper's paradise. (The Global Family also offers a coffeehouse, computer networking services, a meditation room, and a gallery of meditative art with calligraphic paintings to help you program yourself, subliminally and otherwise, with proper consciousness.) Everything is casual and *very* cool—just two blocks from Golden Gate Park and its many attractions.

Upstairs the Red Victorian's 18 guest rooms range from modest to decadent, with sinks in all rooms; some have private baths, others share. (If you stay in a room that shares the Aquarium Bathroom, you'll be able to answer the question: "What happens to the goldfish when you flush the toilet?") The Summer of Love Room features genuine '60s posters on the walls and a tie-dyed canopy over the bed. The Peace Room has an unusual skylight, though the Skylight Room beats the band for exotica. Or get back to nature in the Japanese Tea Garden Room, the Conservatory, or the Redwood Forest Room. Expanded continental breakfast (with granola and fresh bakery selections) and afternoon popcorn hour are included in the rates, which range from $55-125 (slightly higher in summer, two-night minimum on weekends). Spanish, German, and French spoken. No smoking, no pets, and leave your angst outside on the sidewalk. Well-behaved children under parental supervision are welcome. Make reservations for a summer stay well in advance. For more information, contact: The Red Victorian Bed and Breakfast Inn, 1665 Haight St., San Francisco 94117, tel. (415) 864-1978.

The **Sheehan Hotel** near Union Square, 620 Sutter St. at Mason, tel. (415) 775-6500 or toll-free (800) 848-1529 in the U.S. and Canada, is a real find, a surprisingly elegant take on economical downtown accommodations. Rooms have cable TV and phones; some have private baths, others have European-style shared baths (these the bargains). Other facilities include an Olympic-size lap pool, a fitness and exercise room, a downstairs tearoom and wine bar. Discount parking is available. Basic rooms are $45-95 (more expensive with private bathrooms), breakfast included. Inviting for families, too, since children under age 12 stay free with parent or parents. Close to shopping, art, BART, and other public transport.

A relative of The Phoenix Inn, **The New Abigail Hotel** at 246 McAllister St., tel. (415) 861-9728 or toll-free (800) 243-6510, offers spruce British-style charm and antiques, even down comforters, all just a hop, skip, and a jump from City Hall, the Civic Auditorium, and nearby arts venues. On-site pub-style restaurant. Regular rates: $59-79, with discounts for artists, government employees, and groups, plus other deals when the town slows down. Another good deal in the area is the **United Nations Plaza Hotel** at 45 McAllister, tel. 625-5200, rooms $60-65, family plan available.

Between Union Square and Nob Hill is the quite charming **Cornell Hotel,** 715 Bush St. (at

Powell), tel. (415) 421-3154 or toll-free (800) 232-9698, all rooms nonsmoking. Rates: $55-85, though the one-week special package rate may be a better bet. Noteworthy for its antiques, comfort, and fresh flowers is the small **Golden Gate Hotel** nearby at 775 Bush St. (between Powell and Mason), tel. 392-3702 or toll-free (800) 835-1118, with rooms $55-90 (16 rooms have private bathrooms, the other seven are less expensive), complimentary breakfast and afternoon tea included. **The Amsterdam Hotel,** also between the theater district and Nob Hill, between Bush and Sutter at 749 Taylor St., tel. 673-3277 or toll-free (800) 637-3444, features clean, comfortable, spacious rooms, some with contemporary private bathrooms, others with just a sink (shared hallway bathroom), all with color TV and cable, radio, and direct-dial phones. Attractive Victorian lobby, complimentary breakfast. Rates: $44-49 without bath, $59-70 with private bath. Quite convenient to the theater scene is the **Pacific Bay Inn** at 520 Jones St. (at Geary), tel. 673-0234 or toll-free (800) 343-0880 in California, (800) 445-2631 elsewhere in the U.S., an 84-room old-time hotel gone contemporary, with fresh decor and high ceilings. Rates: $55-75, including complimentary continental breakfast and all the basic amenities.

BOUTIQUE HOTELS NEAR UNION SQUARE AND NOB HILL

San Francisco's bouquet of European-style boutique hotels is becoming so large that it's impossible to fit the flowers in any one container. The following sampling offers an idea of the wide variety available. Most of the city's intimate and stylish small hotels are included in the annual *San Francisco Convention & Visitors Bureau Lodging Guide,* listed among all other accommodations options by area, and not otherwise distinguished from more mainstream hostelries. Two clues to spotting a possible "boutique": the number of rooms (usually 75-150, rarely over 200) and the price range ($80-150, with rooms and suites sometimes $200-250 or higher).

But there are remarkable specials, at least sometimes. One cluster of very nice small hotels near Union Square offers a fascinating bargain special, the "Midnight Check-in" plan. If you're willing to chance a last-minute, midnight-or-later reservation at **Hotel Diva, Hotel Union Square, Hotel Metropolis,** or the **Kensington Park Hotel,** you can stay in an exceptional room (subject to availability) at half-price, and wake up to good coffee and croissants in the morning. The offer is good seven days a week (but not in conjunction with other specials), one-night maximum, first-come, first-served; room inquiries accepted after 11:30 p.m. (same day stay), no advance reservations accepted. Call each hotel directly (see below) or central reservations at tel. (415) 202-8787 or toll-free (800) 553-1900 to inquire about this special and other deals (including government or corporate rates) featured at any of the four establishments.

Aside from saving money, what's the big appeal? **Hotel Diva** right across from the Curran and A.C.T. theaters at 440 Geary (between Mason and Taylor), tel. (415) 885-0200, is a chrome-faced contemporary Italian classic, awarded "Best Hotel Design" honors by *Interiors* magazine. Special features include a complete business center—with computers, modems, you name it—daily newspaper, complimentary breakfast delivered to your door, meeting facilities, and a 24-hour fitness center. Rates: $115-135 (plus a special $88 government travelers' discount rate), superior suites $135, Villa Suite $300. Monday through Friday, Diva offers complimentary limousine service to downtown. Cable cars roll right by the six-floor **Hotel Union Square** at 114 Powell St., tel. 397-3000, one of the city's original boutiques, with an art deco lobby and rooms decorated in a blend of contemporary California and old-brick San Francisco. Multiple amenities, including continental breakfast. Wonderful rooftop suites with gardens. Rates: rooms $99-129, suites from $135. The one-time Elks Lodge No. 3 is now the **Kensington Park Hotel,** just steps from Union Square at 450 Post St., tel. 788-6400, noted for its parlor lobby with original handpainted Gothic ceiling and warm Queen Anne floral decor. All the amenities, including financial district limo service. Rates: $110 for most rooms, $160 corner suite, $350 for the Classic Royal Suite. (Inquire about hotel/theater packages, since Theatre On The Square is also located here.) Open just in time for the increasingly frugal '90s, the new **Hotel Metropolis** at 25 Mason, tel. 775-4600, offers 105 very vivacious Arts & Craft rooms (some suites) and amenities: continental breakfast, a business center, and a fitness and massage center. Rates: $85-135.

Fairly reasonable, near the theater scene, is the cheerful and colorful **Hotel Bedford** at 761 Post St., tel. (415) 673-6040 or toll-free (800) 227-5642, a 17-story 1929 hotel featuring florals and pastels. There's a cafe adjacent, but don't miss the tiny mahogany-paneled **Wedgwood Bar** just off the lobby, decorated with china gifts from Lord Wedgwood. Rates: standard rooms $84-89, deluxe rooms $104-109, suites $155. Another good choice in the vicinity is **The Raphael Hotel** at 386 Geary, tel. 986-2000, toll-free (800) 821-5343, with rates $84-120. Also close to the theaters is the 1913 **Savoy Hotel** at 580 Geary, tel. 441-2700 or toll-free (800) 227-4223, a taste of French provincial with period engravings, imported furnishings, even goose-down feather beds and pillows. Amenities include continental breakfast, afternoon sherry and tea. Downstairs is the **Brasserie Savoy.**

Closer to Nob Hill and Chinatown is nine-floor **The Hotel Juliana** at 590 Bush St., tel. (415) 392-2540 or toll-free (800) 372-8800 in California, (800) 382-8800 elsewhere in the U.S. Rooms and suites offer pastel charms and the romantic ambience of a small hotel in Paris or Rome with many amenities, including the convenience of on-site **Vinoteca Restaurant,** eclectic and Italian. Rates: rooms $114, junior suites $140, and executive suites $150. Also within an easy stroll of Nob Hill: the elegant art deco **York Hotel,** 940 Sutter St., tel. 885-6800 or toll-free (800) 227-3608 in the U.S. and Canada, the usual three-star comforts, limousine service, complimentary breakfast. Rates: $95-175.

The **Villa Florence Hotel** at 225 Powell St., tel. (415) 397-7700 or toll-free (800) 243-5700 in California, (800) 553-4411 elsewhere in the U.S., features a 16th-century Tuscany/Italian Renaissance theme, and American-style European ambience. Colorful and comfortable guest rooms—soundproof walls and windows, a good idea above the cable cars and so close to Union Square—with in-room coffeemakers and all basic amenities. The hotel features a beauty salon as well as California-Italian **Kuleto's Restaurant** and antipasto bar. Rates: rooms $119, junior suites $139, deluxe suites $189. For an all-American historical theme, consider the newly renovated **Monticello Inn** at 127 Ellis

(between Powell and Cyril Magnin), tel. 392-8800 or toll-free (800) 669-7777, cool blue-and-white colonial-style lobby with Chippendale reproductions and wood-burning fireplace, early American room decor with soundproof walls and windows, refrigerators, honor bars, other amenities. Complimentary continental breakfast in the lobby. Rates: rooms $114-119, suites $144-165.

Between Union Square and Nob Hill is **The Orchard Hotel,** 562 Sutter (between Powell and Mason), tel. (415) 433-4434 or toll-free (800) 433-4434 in California, (800) 433-4343 in the U.S. and Canada, furnished in European antiques. You'll find a bowl of fresh apples in your room, fresh-squeezed orange juice in the morning. Room rates are $99-130 (weekend specials sometimes available), suites from $195. Also fairly reasonable by boutique hotel standards is **The San Francisco Carlton Hotel,** 1075 Sutter (at Larkin), tel. 673-0242, toll-free in California (800) 792-0958, in the U.S. and Canada (800) 792-0958, comfortable rooms with Queen Anne-style chairs and blue and beige decor. Rates: rooms $92-102, the Sir Edmund Hillary Suite $200.

Moving into San Francisco's trend-setting strata, the gleeful **Hotel Triton** on Grant is the talk of the town—and other towns as well, attracting celebrities galore as well as comparisons to New York's Paramount and Royalton hotels. (For more information, see "Some Hip San Francisco Stays.") The city has more classical class, of course. The four-star **Prescott Hotel** at 545 Post St., tel. (415) 563-0303 or toll-free (800) 283-7322, elegantly combines earthy Americana—most notable in the lobby—with the feel of a British men's club. Rooms and suites come complete with paisley motif, over-stuffed furniture, and every imaginable amenity, from honor bar and terry robes to shoe shines and evening wine and cheeses. Not to mention room service—courtesy of Wolfgang Puck's downstairs **Postrio Restaurant,** where hotel guests also receive preferred dining reservations (if rooms are also reserved well in advance). Services for guests on the Club Level include express check-in (and check-out), continental breakfast, hors d'oeuvres from Postrio, personal concierge service, even stationary bicycles and rowers delivered to your room on request. Rates for rooms and suites: $155-525.

Among other exceptional small hostelries in the vicinity of Union Square is wheelchair-accessible **The Regis Hotel** at 490 Geary St., tel. (415) 928-7900 or toll-free (800) 827-3447 in the U.S. and Canada, furnished with French and English antiques and offering exceptional service. Rates: $115-205, with discounts for AAA members (inquire about other specials). Another best bet, and a bargain for the quality, is the **Chancellor Hotel** on Union Square at 433 Powell, tel. 362-2004 or toll-free (800) 428-4748, elegant rooms within walking distance of just about everything. (Or hop the cable car.) Rates: $90-114. Truly exceptional is **The Donatello,** a block west of Union Square, 501 Post St. (at Mason), tel. 441-7100 or toll-free (800) 227-3184 in the U.S. and Canada, noteworthy also for its restaurant. Rates for four-star amenities: $155-220. Quite refined, too, with the feel of a fine residential hotel, is the **Campton Place Hotel, Kempinski San Francisco,** just north of Union Square at 340 Stockton St., tel. 781-5555 or toll-free (800) 235-4300 in California, (800) 426-3135 in the U.S. and Canada. All the amenities, on-site restaurant. Rates: $180-300.

BOUTIQUE HOTELS ELSEWHERE

North of Market, at the edge of the Financial District at 191 Sutter (between Montgomery and Kearny), is the **Galleria Park Hotel,** tel. (415) 781-3060 or toll-free (800) 792-9639, its striking art nouveau lobby with crystal skylight still somehow overshadowed by the curvaceous, equally original sculpted fireplace. Attractive rooms with soundproof windows and walls, meeting facilities, on-site parking, rooftop park and jogging track, athletic club access. Adjacent restaurants include **Brasserie Chambord,** for country French fare, and acclaimed **Bentley's Seafood Grill,** noted by *Gourmet* magazine for its fresh seafood and oyster bar.

The Embarcadero YMCA south of Market near the Ferry Building now shares the waterfront building with the **Harbor Court Hotel,** 165 Steuart St., tel. (415) 882-1300 or toll-free (800) 346-0555, a fairly phenomenal transformation at the edge of the financial district and a perfect setup for business travelers. Oversized, Old World creature comfort instead of dereliction and destitution is the theme these days, from plush

rooms rich with amenities to the renovated YMCA recreational facilities right next door—multiple floors, including basketball courts, aerobics classes, a pool, even stationary bicycles with a view, plus a whirlpool, a steam room, and a dry sauna. The building's Florentine exterior has been beautifully preserved, as have the building's original arches, columns, and vaulted ceilings. And now that the Embarcadero Freeway is gone, bay views are superb. Room rates: $130, bay-view rooms $140, $195 for the penthouse (the former martial arts studio, now featuring a Louis XVI-style bed and 18-foot ceilings). Amenities include TV, radio, direct-dial phones with extra-long cords, complimentary beverages, a business center, Financial District limo service, and same-day valet laundry service. Affiliated Victorian saloon-style **Harry Denton's** restaurant here has predictably good food and becomes a lively dance club/bar scene after 10 p.m. Adjacent and also worthwhile is the **Hotel Griffon,** 155 Steuart St., tel. 495-2100 or toll-free (800) 321-2201 in the U.S. and Canada, with amenities like continental breakfast and morning newspaper, fitness center. Rates: $115-270.

The Tuscan Inn two blocks from Pier 39 at Fisherman's Wharf, 425 Northpoint St., tel. (415) 561-1100 or toll-free (800) 648-4626, features Italianate lobby with fireplace, a central garden court, and 220 rooms and suites with modern amenities. Rates: rooms $168-175, one-bedroom suites $195. Also here: a convenient Italian trattoria, **Cafe Pescatore,** specializing (at lunch and dinner) in fresh fish and seafood, pastas, and pizzas baked in a wood-burning oven. Open for breakfast also.

Near Civic Center cultural attractions (see also "Inexpensive" categories above, and "Some Hip San Francisco Stays") is the exceptional small **Inn at the Opera,** 333 Fulton, tel. (415) 863-8400 or toll-free (800) 423-9610 in California, (800) 325-2708 elsewhere in the U.S., featuring complimentary breakfast, morning limousine service, excellent on-site restaurant. Rates: $110-225.

The Sherman House in Pacific Heights, west of Van Ness and south of Lombard at 2160 Green St., San Francisco 94123, tel. (415) 563-3600, is among the city's finest small, exclusive hotels. The ambience here, including the dining room, exudes 19th-century French opulence. Rates range $235-750 per night.

CITY-STYLE BED AND BREAKFASTS

With most of San Francisco's European-style and boutique hotels offering breakfast and other homey touches, and many of the city's bed and breakfasts offering standard hotel services (like concierge, bellman, valet/laundry, and room service), it's truly difficult to understand the difference.

The 22-room **Chateau Tivoli** townhouse at 1057 Steiner St., San Francisco 94115, tel. (415) 776-5462 or (800) 228-1647, is an 1892 Queen Anne landmark with an astounding visual presence. "Colorful" just doesn't do justice as a description of this Alamo Square painted lady. The Tivoli's eccentric exterior architectural style is electrified by 18 historic colors of paint, plus gold leaf. Painstaking restoration is apparent inside, too, from the very Victorian, period-furnished parlors to exquisite, individually decorated guest rooms, each reflecting at least a portion of the city's unusual social history. (Imagine, under one roof: Enrico Caruso, Aimee Crocker, Isadora Duncan, Joaquin Miller, Jack London, opera singer Luisa Tetrazzini, and Mark Twain. Somehow, it *is* imaginable, since the mansion was once the residence of the city's pre-earthquake Tivoli Opera.) Chateau Tivoli offers two suites and five rooms, all with private baths, two with fireplaces. Rates: $80-200. Onetime home to Archbishop Patrick Riordan, the **Archbishop's Mansion** at 1000 Fulton (at Steiner), tel. 563-7872, is also exquisitely restored, with comfortable rooms and suites in a French Victorian mood, some with fireplaces and in-room spas, all with phones and TV. Full breakfast. Rates: $100-285.

Also close to the Civic Center arts scene is **The Inn San Francisco**, 943 S. Van Ness Ave., San Francisco 94110, tel. (415) 641-0188 or toll-free (800) 359-0913, a huge, renovated 1872 Italianate Victorian with 22 guest rooms, double parlors, and a sun deck. The five bargain rooms here share two bathrooms. Most rooms feature private baths; all include TV, radio, telephone, and refrigerator; some have a hot tub or in-room spa tub; two also have a fireplace and balcony. Rates: $75-175. Not far away is **The Grove Inn** near Alamo Square at 890 Grove St., San Francisco 94117, tel. 929-0780, a restored Italianate Victorian with 19 rooms (some

share baths) and real-deal rates of $40-45 s, $55-75 d. Off-street parking available for a small fee. Complimentary breakfast. The **Alamo Square Inn** at 719 Scott St., tel. 922-2055 or (800) 345-9888, is another neighborhood possibility, offering rooms and suites in an 1895 Queen Anne and an 1896 Tudor Revival, a range of amenities, and rates $85-250.

Petite Auberge near Nob Hill and Union Square at 863 Bush St., San Francisco 94108, tel. (415) 928-6000, is an elegant French country inn right downtown, featuring Pierre Deux fabrics, terra-cotta tile, oak furniture, and lace curtains. All 26 guest rooms here have private bathrooms; 16 have fireplaces. The "Petite Suite" has its own entrance and deck, a king-size bed, fireplace, and Jacuzzi. Two doors down is the affiliated **White Swan Inn,** 845 Bush, tel. 775-1755, with parlor, library, and 26 rooms (private baths, fireplaces, wet bars) decorated with English-style decorum, from the mahogany antiques and rich fabrics to floral-print wallpapers. Both inns serve full breakfast (and morning paper), afternoon tea, even homemade cookies, and provide little amenities like thick terry bathrobes. All rooms have TV and telephone. Ask about the Celebration Package. Rates: Petite Auberge, $105-215, White Swan, $145-250.

Close to the Presidio and Fort Mason in Cow Hollow is the **Edward II Inn**, 3155 Scott St. (at Lombard), San Francisco 94123, tel. (415) 922-3000 or toll-free (800) GREAT-IN, an English-style country hotel and pub offering 24 rooms and six suites, all with color TV and phone, some with shared bathrooms, suites with in-room whirlpool baths. Continental breakfast, or grab a bite at **Scott's Seafood** (the pub). Rates: $70-85 for regular rooms, up to $175 for suites. Peaceful and pleasant amid the hubbub of North Beach is 15-room **Millefiori Inn** at 444 Columbus Ave., San Francisco 94133, tel. 433-9111, offering continental charm all the way to breakfast, which is served either indoors or out on the patio. On-site restaurant, too. Rates: $65-95, a good deal. Also in North Beach is the French country **Washington Square Inn**, 1660 Stockton St., tel. 981-4220 or toll-free (800) 388-0220, featuring 15 rooms (most have private baths), continental breakfast, and afternoon tea. Rates: $85-180.

Near Lafayette Park in Pacific Heights and something of a cause célèbre is/are **The Mansions** at 2220 Sacramento St., San Francisco

94115, tel. (415) 929-9444, an elegant bed-and-breakfast-style hotel composed of two adjacent historic mansions. The 28 rooms and suites here are opulent and feature telephones, private bathrooms, and numerous amenities. Stroll the Bufano sculpture gardens, play billiards, or attend nightly music concerts and recitals. The Mansion Magic Concert is a big hit on weekends. Full breakfast served every morning, in the dining area or in your room, and dinners are also available. Rates: $74-225.

LUXURY HOTELS

In addition to the fine hotels mentioned above, San Francisco offers an impressive selection of four- and five-star luxury hotels. The air in these establishments is rarefied indeed. (Sometimes the airs, too.) Many, however, do offer seasonal specials. Business-oriented hotels often feature lower weekend rates.

The Ritz, The Palace, The St. Francis
Peek into the new **Ritz Carlton, San Francisco** at 600 Sutter (between California and Pine) to see what a great facelift an old lady can get for $140 million. Quite impressive. (For more information, see "Puttin' on the Ritz.")

Equally awesome—and another popular destination these days for City Guides and other walking tours—is that grande dame of San Francisco hostelries, the 1909 **Sheraton Palace Hotel,** newly renovated and resplendent downtown at 2 New Montgomery St. (at Market), San Francisco 94105, tel. (415) 392-8600 or toll-free (800) 325-3535. Wander in, under the metal grillwork awning at the New Montgomery entrance, across the polished marble sunburst on the foyer floor, and sit a spell in the lobby to appreciate the more subtle aspects of this $150 million renovation. Then mosey into the central **Garden Court** restaurant. The wonderful lighting here is provided, during the day, by the (cleaned and restored) 1800s atrium skylight, one of the largest leaded-glass creations in the world. Some 70,000 panes of glass arch over the entire room, a best bet for Sunday brunch. Note, too, the 10 (yes, 10) 700-pound crystal chandeliers. New **Maxfield's** restaurant is now at home in the hotel's former **Pied Piper Bar,** which has moved—along with its famous Max-

PUTTIN' ON THE RITZ

Serious visiting fans of San Francisco, at least those with serious cash, tend to equate their long-running romance with a stay on Nob Hill, home base for most of the city's ritzier hotels. And what could be ritzier than the Ritz?

The Ritz-Carlton, San Francisco, 600 Stockton at California St., tel. (415) 296-7465 or toll-free (800) 241-3333, is a local landmark, San Francisco's finest remaining examples of neo-classical architecture. At the financial district's former western edge, and hailed in 1909 as a "temple of commerce," until 1973 the building served as West Coast headquarters for the Metropolitan Life Insurance Company. Expanded and revised five times since, San Francisco's Ritz has been open for business as a hotel only since 1991. After painstaking restoration (four years and $140 million worth), this nine-story grande dame still offers some odd architectural homage to its past. Witness the terra-cotta tableau over the entrance: the angelic allegorical figure ("Insurance") is protecting the American family. (Ponder the meaning of the lion's heads and winged hourglasses on your own.)

The Ritz offers a total of 336 rooms and suites, most with grand views. Amenities on the top two floors ("The Ritz-Carlton Club") include private lounge, continuous complimentary meals, and Dom Perignon and Beluga caviar every evening. All rooms, however, feature Italian marble bathrooms, in-room safes, and every modern comfort, plus access to the fitness center (indoor swimming pool, whirlpool, training room, separate men's and women's steam rooms and saunas, massage, and more). Services include the usual long list plus morning newspaper, child care, VCR and video library, car rental, and multilingual staff. Tariffs: $185-500. (The Ritz-Carlton's "Summer Escape" package, when available, includes a deluxe guest room, continental breakfast, valet parking, and unlimited use of the fitness center—all for $185 per night, including tax, single or double occupancy. Additional nights are $155.) The Ritz-Carlton also provides full conference facilities. **The Courtyard** restaurant here offers the city's only al fresco dining in a hotel setting—like eating breakfast, lunch, or dinner on someone else's well-tended garden patio. (Come on Sunday for brunch—and jazz.) Adjacent, indoors, is somewhat casual **The Restaurant.** More formal, serving neoclassical cuisine, is **The Dining Room.**

Until he retired in 1993, Arnold Batliner washed coins at the St. Francis Hotel.

field Parrish mural—but is still a Palace fixture. To sign up for a City Guides tour (free), contact the hotel directly at tel. 546-5026.

In addition to plush accommodations (rooms still have high ceilings), the Palace offers complete conference and meeting facilities, a business center, and a fitness center—the latter up on the roof. The swimming pool up here, under a modern vaulted skylight, is especially enjoyable at sunset; spa services include poolside whirlpool and dry sauna. Rooms: $180-260, suites: $350-1500.

Another beloved San Francisco institution is the **Westin St. Francis Hotel** directly across from Union Square at 335 Powell St. (between Post and Geary), tel. (415) 397-7000 or toll-free (800) 228-3000, a recently restored landmark recognized by the National Trust for Historic Preservation as one of the Historic Hotels of America. When the first St. Francis opened in 1849 at Clay and Dupont (Grant), it was considered the only hostelry at which ladies were safe, and it was also celebrated as the first "to introduce bedsheets to the city." But San Francisco's finest was destroyed by fire four years later. By the early 1900s, reincarnation was imminent when a group of local businessmen declared their intention to rebuild the St. Francis as

"a caravansary worthy of standing at the threshold of the Occident, representative of California hospitality." No expense was spared on the stylish 12-story hotel overlooking Union Square —partially opened but still under construction when the April 18, 1906 earthquake and fire hit town. Damaged but not destroyed, the restored St. Francis opened in November of 1907; over the entrance was an electrically lighted image of a phoenix rising from the city's ashes. Successfully resurrected, the elegant and innovative hotel attracted royalty, international political and military leaders, theatrical stars, and literati.

But even simpler folk have long been informed, entertained, and welcomed by the St. Francis. People keep an eye on the number of unfurled flags in front of the St. Francis, for example, knowing that these herald the nationalities of visiting dignitaries. And every long-time San Franciscan knows that shiny old coins in their pockets most likely come from the St. Francis, thanks to the hotel's long-standing policy of washing them—to avoid soiling ladies' white gloves—a practice that continued until the very recent retirement of octogenarian Arnold Batliner. Meeting friends "under the Clock" means the Magneta Clock in the hotel's Powell Street lobby, this "master clock" from Saxony a fixture since the early 1900s.

Both the Tower and Powell Street lobbies have been freshened up by 1991 restorations, including three 40-foot *trompe l'oeil* murals by Carlo Marchiori depicting turn-of-the-century San Francisco, new inlaid marble floors, a central carpet, and gold-leaf laminate to the ornate woodwork in the Powell Street lobby. In-progress restoration of the original building's Colusa sandstone facade will be finished by 1997.

After additions and renovations, the St. Francis today offers 1,200 luxury guest rooms and suites (request a suite brochure if you hanker to stay in General D. MacArthur's suite, Queen Elizabeth II's, or Ron and Nancy Reagan's) plus fitness and full meeting and conference facilities, a 1,500-square-foot ballroom, five restaurants (including elegant **Victor's** atop the St. Francis Tower), shopping arcade, and valet parking. Rates: rooms $160-315, suites $300-1600. But subject to availability, discounts of up to 40% are offered with advance reservations in summer (usually through September).

Inquire about other specials, and about the hotel's Executive Traveler and Japanese Guest Services programs.

Other Downtown Luxury Hotels

The Four Seasons Clift Hotel is a five-star midsize hotel downtown at 495 Geary St. (at Taylor), tel. (415) 775-4700 or toll-free (800) 332-3442, offering every imaginable comfort and service, including free Financial District limo service, transport to and from the airport (for a fee), and a good on-site restaurant. Rates: rooms $190-300, suites $315-1200.

Also within easy reach of downtown doings: the sleek, modern, four-star **Pan Pacific Hotel, San Francisco,** (formerly The Portman) one block west of Union Square at 500 Post St. (at Mason), tel. 771-8600 or toll-free (800) 533-6465, offering Rolls-Royce shuttle service to the Financial District and regular room rates of $185-310, suites $335-1500. The Pan Pacific is business oriented—there are three phones with call waiting in each room, personal computers are delivered to your room upon request, and notary public and business services are available—but it's also luxurious. Bathrooms, for example, feature floor-to-ceiling Breccia marble, artwork, mini-screen TV, and telephone. The The "Pampering Weekend" special starts at $139 and includes breakfast in your room or at the on-site **Pacific Grill** restaurant.

Other worthy downtown possibilities include the contemporary Japanese-style **Hotel Nikko** at 222 Mason, tel. (415) 394-1111 or (800) NIKKO-US, with room rates of $225 and up; the **San Francisco Hilton on Hilton Square,** 1 Hilton Square (O'Farrell and Mason), tel. 771-1400 or toll-free (800) HILTONS, the city's largest with almost 2,000 rooms and suites ranging in price from $165 to $2000-plus; and the 1,000-room **Parc Fifty Five Hotel** (formerly the Ramada Renaissance) at 55 Cyril Magnin St. (Market at 5th), tel. 392-8000 or toll-free (800) 338-1338, with rooms $170-255, suites $350 to over $1000.

The exquisite **Mandarin Oriental San Francisco** is housed in the top 11 floors of the First Interstate Center in the financial district, 222 Sansome, tel. (415) 885-0999 or toll-free (800) 622-0404, 160 view rooms (even the bathrooms have a view), all the amenities, and wonderful **Silks** restaurant. Rates: rooms $245-390, suites

$475 and up. The **Hyatt Regency San Francisco** at 5 Embarcadero Center (Market and California), tel. 788-1234 or toll-free (800) 233-1234, is most famous for its 17-story lobby, an atrium, and its rotating rooftop restaurant, **The Equinox.** Rates: rooms $149-268, suites from $325. (There are Hyatts all over San Francisco, including the nearby Park Hyatt on Battery plus those at Union Square, Fisherman's Wharf, and out at the airport in Burlingame; a toll-free call can reserve a room at any and all.) Other quite comfortable hotel choices near the financial district include the **San Francisco Marriott** south of Market and just north of the Moscone Convention Center at 55 4th St., tel. 896-1600 or toll-free (800) 228-9290, with room rates $185 and up, and the nearby **ANA Hotel San Francisco** (formerly Le Meridien Hotel), 50 3rd St., tel. 673-6040 or toll-free (800) 543-4300, with rooms $155-240.

Nob Hill Luxury Hotels

Some of the city's finest hotels cluster atop Nob Hill. Since judgment always depends upon personal taste, despite official ratings it's all but impossible to say which is "the best." Take your pick.

The Huntington Hotel, across from Grace Cathedral and Huntington Park at 1075 California St. (at Taylor), tel. (415) 474-5400 or toll-free (800) 652-1539 in California, (800) 227-4683 from elsewhere in the U.S., is the last surviving family-owned fine hotel in the neighborhood. And it's a beauty, a destination in and of itself, every room and suite (one-time residential apartments) individually designed and decorated, every service a personal gesture. Stop in just to appreciate the elegant lobby restoration. Dark and clubby and open daily for breakfast, lunch, and dinner, **The Big Four Restaurant** off the lobby pays pleasant homage to the good ol' days of Wild West railroad barons —and often serves wild game entrees along with tamer continental contemporary cuisine. Rates: rooms $160-245, suites $310-640. Inquire about The Huntington's small-group business and meeting facilities and about "Romance Packages," if available, with extra pampering and extra low rates.

Top-of-the-line, too, is the romantic, turn-of-the-century **Fairmont Hotel and Tower,** 950 Mason St. (at California), tel. (415) 772-5000 or toll-free (800) 527-4727, noted for its genuine grandeur and grace. The Fairmont offers 595 rooms (small to large) and suites, all expected amenities, and five on-site restaurants. For a panoramic Bay Area view at Sunday brunch, the place to go is the **Crown Restaurant** on the top of the Tower. Locally loved, too, however, are **Mason's,** for its French-style American classics, and **The Squire Restaurant and Wine Cellar,** which specializes in seafood. **Bella Voce** offers good ol' American fare for breakfast, lunch, and dinner (the Bella Voce Opera Singers accompany dinner), and the **Tonga Restaurant** serves Chinese cuisine. The Fairmont also offers full conference and business facilities (20 meeting rooms) and the **Nob Hill Club** (extra fee) for fitness enthusiasts. Rates: rooms $150-290, suites $450-2000.

The big news these days at the five-star **Stanford Court Hotel,** 905 California St. (at Powell), tel. (415) 989-3500 or toll-free (800) HO-TELS-1, is the 120-foot-long, sepia-toned lobby mural honoring San Francisco's "diversity," historically speaking. On the west wall, for example, are panels depicting the hotel's predecessor, the original Leland Stanford Mansion, with railroad barons and other wealthy Nob Hill nabobs on one side, Victorian-era African Americans on the other. Other panels depict the long-running economic exploitation of California places and peoples, from Russian whaling and fur trading, redwood logging, and the California gold rush (with Native Americans and the Chinese looking on) to the 1906 earthquake and fire framed by the construction of the transcontinental railroad and California's Latinization, as represented by Mission Dolores. Stop in and see it; this is indeed the story of Northern California, if perhaps a bit romanticized.

The hotel itself is romantic, recognized by the National Trust for Historic Preservation as one of the Historic Hotels of America. The Stanford Court features a decidedly European ambience, from the carriage entrance (with beaux arts fountain and stained-glass dome) to guest rooms decked out in 19th-century artwork, antiques, and reproductions (not to mention modern comforts like heated towel racks in the marble bathrooms and dictionaries on the writing desks). Opulent touches in the lobby include Baccarat chandeliers, Carrara marble floor, oriental carpets, original artwork, and an 1806 antique grandfather clock once owned by Napoleon Bonaparte. Guest services include complimentary stretch limo service, both for business and pleasure. Rates: rooms $195-305 (substantially lower on Fri. and Sat. nights), suites $450-2000. (The hotel was recently sold by Stouffer, so inquire about any new hotel policies and features that may have resulted from this ownership change.) Even if you don't stay, consider a meal (breakfast, lunch, and dinner daily, plus weekend brunch) at the hotel restaurant: **Fournou's Ovens,** tel. 989-1910 for reservations, is considered one of San Francisco's best.

And don't forget the **Mark Hopkins Hotel,** now the Mark Hopkins Inter-Continental, another refined Old California old-timer. Hobnobbing with the best of them at 1 Nob Hill (California and Mason), tel. (415) 392-3434 or toll-free (800) 327-0200, the Mark Hopkins features 391 elegant guest rooms (many with great views) and all the amenities, not to mention the fabled **Top of the Mark** sky room, still San Francisco's favorite sky-high romantic bar scene. The French-California **Nob Hill Restaurant** is open daily for breakfast, lunch, and dinner. Rates: rooms $180-305, suites $375-1400.

CITY-STYLE CHOW

San Franciscans love to eat. For a true San Franciscan, eating—and eating well—competes for first place among life's purest pleasures, right up there with the arts, exercising, and earning money. (There may be a few others.) Finding new and novel neighborhood eateries, and knowing which among the many fine dining establishments are currently at the top of the trendsetters' culinary A-list, are points of pride for long-time residents. Fortunately, San Franciscans also enjoy sharing information and opinions—including their restaurant preferences. So the best way to find out where to eat, and why, is simply to ask. The following listings should help fine-food aficionados get started, and will certainly keep everyone else from starving. See also restaurant mentions under "The Lay of the Land," "Delights and Diversions," and "Accommodations: Staying in Style," above.

UNION SQUARE AND NOB HILL

A well-kept secret, perhaps downtown's best breakfast spot, is **Dottie's True Blue Cafe** at 522 Jones St., tel. (415) 885-2767, an all-American-style coffee shop serving every imaginable American standard plus new cuisine, such as (at lunch) grilled eggplant sandwiches. Open daily for breakfast and lunch only, 7 a.m.-2 p.m. But those in the know say you haven't "done" the city until you've ordered breakfast—specifically, the 18 Swedish pancakes—at **Sears Fine Food,** 439 Powell (at Post), tel. 986-1160, a funky, friendly old-time San Francisco cafe. Another area classic, if for other reasons, is **John's Grill** at 63 Ellis (just off Powell), tel. 986-0069, with a neat neon sign outside and *The Maltese Falcon* memorabilia just about everywhere inside. (In the book, this is where Sam Spade ate his lamb chops.) This informal eatery ode to Dashiell Hammett serves good continental-style American fare, plus large helpings of Hammett hero worship, especially upstairs in Hammett's Den and the Maltese Falcon Room.

A veritable institution downtown and still Kon-Tiki after all these years is **Trader Vic's** at 20 Cosmo Place (off Taylor), tel. (415) 776-2232,

where the exotic decor is almost more of a draw than the food. Local fans prefer the various Chinese barbecued meat and fish selections; you can even order takeout.

For inexpensive and excellent seafood, dive into the **Brasserie Savoy** at the Savoy Hotel, 580 Geary St., tel. (415) 474-8686, also offering a taste of French provincial decor at continental breakfast, lunch (weekdays only), dinner, and late supper.

For northern-style dim sum, not far from Union Square is the innovative **China Moon Cafe,** 639 Post St., tel. (415) 775-4789. The menu here changes every few weeks, so there are always new variations on time-honored themes. Buddha buns, for example, are filled with Chinese black mushrooms and curried vegetables. The **Corona Bar & Grill** at 88 Cyril Magnin (at Ellis), tel. 392-5500, is high-concept, upscale, and south-of-the-border, the fare here featuring surprises like chile rellenos stuffed with a nut mixture, smoked salmon and watercress tacos, and chicken enchiladas with corn and shiitake mushrooms. Open for lunch and dinner daily, with light meals always available on the bar menu. Great brunch spot on Sunday. Also worth searching for downtown is **Cafe Claude** at 7 Claude Ln. (between Grant and Kearny, Bush and Sutter, just off Bush), tel. 392-3505, an uncanny incarnation of a genuine French cafe, from the paper table covers to the cafe au lait bowls. Quite good food, plus live jazz on Tues., Thurs., and Fri. nights.

A good choice downtown for pasta is **Kuleto's,** a comfortable trattoria-style Italian restaurant and bar inside the Villa Florence Hotel, 221 Powell St., tel. (415) 397-7720, popular for power lunching and dinner, also open for peaceful, pleasant breakfasts.

Better yet, though, is **Ristorante Donatello** at 501 Post St. (in the same-named hotel, at Mason), tel. 441-7182, justifiably famous for its Northern Italian regional dishes. This premier San Francisco restaurant, where the separate dining rooms are small and intimate and dressing up is de rigueur, puts on a show as good as, or better than, almost anything else in the neighborhood.

People should at least pop into Wolfgang Puck's northern outpost, **Postrio,** inside the Prescott Hotel at 545 Post St. (at Mason), tel. (415) 776-7825, to appreciate the exquisite ribbon-patterned dining room designs by Pat Kuleto. The food here is exceptional, of course, most entrees representing Puck's interpretations of San Francisco classics. Since the restaurant is open for breakfast, lunch, and dinner, try hangtown fry and some house-made pastries at breakfast, perhaps a pizza fresh from the wood-burning oven or Dungeness crab with spicy curry risotto at lunch. Dinner is an adventure. Great desserts. Make reservations well in advance, or hope for a cancellation.

Famous among Frisco foodies, not to mention its long-standing national and international fan club, is **Masa's** next to the Hotel Vintage Court at 648 Bush St., tel. (415) 989-7154, one of the city's finest dinner restaurants and considered by many to be the best French restaurant in the United States. Masa's serves French cuisine, with a fresh California regional touch and a Spanish aesthetic. Reservations accepted three weeks in advance. Very expensive.

Fleur de Lys at 777 Sutter, tel. (415) 673-7779, is another local legend, a fine French restaurant that also transcends the traditional, nothing too heavy or overdone. Very elegant, equally expensive. Open Mon.-Sat. for dinner. Reservations.

Some of the city's finest hotels, on Nob Hill and elsewhere, also serve of the finest food. (See the "Accommodations" section, above.)

THE FINANCIAL DISTRICT AND EMBARCADERO

One of the hottest haute spots for young white refugees from the Financial District is the very casual, very good **Gordon Biersch Brewery and Restaurant** along the Embarcadero, at home in the old brick Hills Brothers Coffee roastery in the shadow of the Bay Bridge, just off Steuart at 2 Harrison St., tel. (415) 243-8246, open from 11 a.m. daily. The German-style beer here is certainly a draw; three styles (Pilsner to Bavarian dark) are created on the premises, as is the surprisingly good food, far from the usual brewpub grub and getting better all the time. Most people here, though, seem attracted by the pheromones wafting through the barn-sized bar. Considering the vigor of this 20-to-30-something singles scene, and considering that no one is immune in the Age of AIDS, there is really only one major oversight here: at least in the women's restroom, no condom dispensers in sight. (Gordon Biersch also has outposts in Palo Alto and San Jose.) **Harry Denton's** across from Rincon Center and inside the Harbor Court Hotel at 161 Steuart St., tel. 882-1333, is a great bar, restaurant, and club, usually crowded as a sardine can after 5 p.m. Again, the food here is quite good. To hold a conversation, sink into a booth in the narrow dining room above the bar scene; to take in the great scenery (now that the Embarcadero Freeway is gone) head for the back room (also a dance floor Thurs.-Sat. nights). Harry Denton's is open daily for lunch and dinner.

Another relative newcomer is **Etrusca** at 121 Spear St., tel. 777-0330, featuring fine Northern Italian cuisine in an atmosphere of Carrara marble and Etruscan artifacts. **Asta's** at 101 Spear (Rincon Center), tel. 495-2782, is named after a star of the *Thin Man* movies (that little rat-like one, the short-haired terrier) and rises to the art deco occasion. The mood is strictly 1930s supper club, the food both traditional and inventive (post-post-deco) American. Lively bar, live jazz on Thursday and Saturday nights; the Saturday night "supper club" includes dinner and dancing. Open weekdays for lunch, Tues.-Sat. nights for dinner.

True history buffs might also try art deco **Circolo** at 161 Sutter, tel. (415) 362-0404, an unstuffy but upscale place for pizza, pasta, and Northern Italian at the one-time site of San Francisco's famous Old Poodle Dog restaurant. The history here goes far beyond the place or decor. It's actually about the old restaurant name, an evolutionary precursor of the city's multiethnic cultural and culinary confusions (and creativity). As the story goes, the name of an early gold rush-era restaurant, Poulet D'Or ("Golden Chicken"), got mangled into Poodle Dog, which lived on through many incarnations and reincarnated again in the 1980s as the *Old* Poodle Dog.

(What's the point? Perhaps just that the love of gold, chicken, dogs, and good restaurants will live on forever, at least in San Francisco. Or something like that.)

One of San Francisco's great little restaurants is **Square One,** 190 Pacific Avenue Mall (off Walton Park near the waterfront, at Front St.), tel. (415) 788-1110, serving contemporary California-style cuisine in a very contemporary atmosphere. Open for lunch on weekdays, for dinner nightly. Informal, reservations a must.

Bentley's Seafood Grill & Oyster Bar near the Crocker Galleria at 185 Sutter St., tel. (415) 989-6895, is like the United Nations of seafood, featuring the flavor and flair of almost any ethnic tradition somewhere on the menu. Lemon-juice purists can have it their way, too, especially at the oyster/seafood bar. Open Mon.-Sat. for lunch and dinner, Sunday for brunch. **Aqua,** 252 California St., tel. 956-9662, is also in the seafood swim of things, its reputation making a global splash among well-heeled foodies nationwide. Entrees include basil-grilled lobster, lobster potato *gnocchi,* and black-mussel soufflé. Open weekdays for lunch, Mon.-Sat. for dinner. **Le Central** at 453 Bush St., tel. 391-2233, is another power-lunching place par excellence, a New York-style Parisian bistro.

Sol y Luna across from the Pacific Stock Exchange at 475 Sacramento St., tel. (415) 296-8191, is noted for its multinational new cuisine, *entradas, ensaladas, tapas,* and *sopas* in intriguing combinations. Great people-watching spot at lunch. For people-watching of a different sort though, the place to go is **Delancey Street** at 600 Embarcadero, tel. 512-5179, real radical chic, a sociopolitically progressive place where the restaurant staff is comprised of Delancey's drug, alcohol, and crime rehabilitees. The daily changing menu is ethnic American, everything from matzo ball soup to pot roast. And there's a great view of Alcatraz from the outdoor dining area. Open for lunch, afternoon tea, and dinner.

An inexpensive stop for good dim sum, **Cafe Pacifica** at 333 Bush St., tel. (415) 296-8203, is a Japanese-owned franchise operation that does it well, inexpensively. **Yank Sing** at 427 Battery, tel. 362-1640, is popular with the Financial District crowd and noteworthy for the shrimp dumplings in the shapes of goldfish and rabbits. (There's another one at 49 Stevenson Street.)

A very good choice for Cantonese is Hong Kong-style **Harbor Village** at 4 Embarcadero Center, tel. (415) 781-8833, serving everything from dim sum to Imperial banquets. Open daily for lunch and dinner. Far from *modesto* straight upstairs (on the third level), behind those old olive-wood doors, is splendid **Splendido,** tel. 986-3222, a very fine, contemporary Mediterranean-style retreat for cost-conscious fine food fanatics. Everything here is fresh and housemade, from the breads and seafood soups to the pastas and unusual pizzas. Exceptional entrees include grilled swordfish and guinea hens roasted in the restaurant's very busy woodburning oven. Good wine list; save some space for dessert. Open for lunch and dinner daily; the bar serves appetizers until closing (midnight). For some boisterous Greek after-dinner sing-alongs (with plenty of Ouzo as voice lubricant), head for **Santorini,** also at 4 Embarcadero, tel. 397-2056.

CIVIC CENTER AND VICINITY

Miss Pearl's Jam House at the Phoenix Inn, that motel-like entertainment/arts mecca on the corner of Eddy and Larkin, tel. (415) 775-5267, serves up Caribbean-style California cuisine in a quirky, very hip atmosphere—the kitsch kicked into high gear by odd decorative details. (Look closely at that countertop.) Jumpin' joint, mon, most of the time; some claim to see Jah when live music is on tap. ¡Salud! at 500 Van Ness, tel. 864-8500, is a gussied-up, gringo-style Mexican retreat where Harry's American Bar & Grill used to be. If the mesquite-grilled meats and homemade tamales aren't enough for you, try some Geko—the private-label house beer, complete with lizard decal—an imaginative margarita, or one of the multitude of imported tequilas.

Tommy's Joynt at 1101 Geary (at Van Ness), tel. (415) 775-4216, is a neighborhood institution, a hofbrau-style bar and grill boasting bright paint, a bizarre bunch of bric-a-brac, beers from just about everywhere, and a noteworthy pastrami sandwich. Farther north along Polk Gulch (roughly paralleling fairly level Polk Street, from Post to Broadway) are abundant cafes, coffeehouses, and avant-garde junque and clothing shops. Worthwhile eateries include **Polk Street Beans,** 1733 Polk (at Clay), tel.

776-9292, a funky Eurostyle coffeehouse serving good soups and sandwiches, and **Mayes Restaurant**, 1233 Polk, tel. 474-7674, a remarkably reasonable Italian and seafood restaurant that's been in business in San Francisco since 1867.

Tucked inside the Inn at the Opera, and definitely another change-up, is **Act IV**, 333 Fulton St., tel. (415) 553-8100, a class act noted as much for its romantic charms as its very fine Northern Italian fare—a fitting finale for opera fans who have plenty of cash left to fan (this place is on the expensive side). Act IV definitely deserves a sitting ovation. You can offer yours nightly (until 10:30 p.m. on Fri. and Sat. nights) for dinner or Mon.-Sat. until 10:30 a.m. for breakfast. Call to see if lunch is being served.

Max's Opera Cafe at 601 Van Ness, tel. (415) 771-7300, also pitches itself to the neighborhood's more theatrical standards. Like Max's enterprises elsewhere, you can count on being served huge helpings of quite tantalizing all-American standards. At least at dinner, you can also count on the wait staff bursting into song, maybe opera, maybe a Broadway show tune. Open daily for lunch and dinner, until late (1 a.m.) on Friday and Saturday nights for the post-theater crowds. A bit different, in the same building, is **Monsoon**, tel. 441-3232, serving upscale Southeast Asian/Chinese fare in simple, eclectic elegance. Also new in the neighborhood, and just as popular with opera and symphony fans as neighborhood clubbers, is **Christopher's Cafe**, in Jeremiah Tower at 690 Van Ness Ave., tel. 346-8870. Christopher's serves an intriguing blend of California, Southwestern, Asian, even Cajun cuisines, including exceptional side dishes. Open for dinner nightly, for lunch weekdays only.

The **Hayes Street Grill** at 320 Hayes (at Franklin), tel. (415) 863-5545, is a very busy bistro, serving some of the best seafood in town. Open weekdays for lunch, Mon.-Sat. for dinner. Smoke-free **Zola's** at 395 Hayes (at Gough), tel. 864-4824, is a stylish yet casual nouveau Mediterranean restaurant. Dinners only, Mon.-Sat., reservations advised. Sometimes more like a moveable feast for fashion, judging from all the suits and suited skirts, the **Zuni Cafe** at 1658 Market, tel. 552-2522, is an immensely popular restaurant and watering hole, noted for its Italian-French country fare in a Southwestern

ambience. (Expensive.) Still yuppie central, though, even after all these years, is somewhat immodest, barn-sized **Stars** at 150 Redwood Alley (between Golden Gate and McAllister), tel. 861-7827, strictly reservations-only beyond the bar. Perhaps more palatable for just plain folks, open for breakfast, lunch, and dinner, is adjacent **Stars Cafe**, 555 Golden Gate, tel. 861-4344, something of a discount sandwich and salad outlet for Stars. Daily changing menu, great desserts. The Hayes Street area features other attractive small cafes as well.

Crustacean at Chelsea Square, 1475 Polk St. (Polk at California), tel. (415) 776-CRAB, is another one of those cutting-edge eateries enjoyable for ambience as well as actual eats. This place serves exceptional Euro-Asian cuisine (specialty: roast crab) and looks like a fantasy home to those particularly crunchy critters, with underwater murals and giant seahorses, not to mention handblown glass fixtures and a 17-foot wave sculpture. Open for dinners only, nightly after 5 p.m.; valet parking, full bar, extensive wine list. Reservations preferred.

Some folks swear that sophisticated **La Fiammetta** near Japantown at 1701 Octavia St., tel. (415) 474-5077, serves some of the best, most authentic Italian in town, from the tender *gnocci* with prawns, tomatoes, and almonds to the *pansoti* (homemade old-fashioned cheese ravioli). **Cafe Kati** near Japan Center at 1963 Sutter, tel. 775-7313, is one of those casual neighborhood places serving surprisingly good food. **Iroha Restaurant**, 1728 Buchanan Mall (Post St.), tel. 922-0321, is a great stop for noodles and Japanese standards.

CHINATOWN

The best way to find the best restaurants in Chinatown is to go where the Chinese go. Some of these places may look a bit shabby, at least on the outside, and may not take reservations—or credit cards. Since the prices at small family-run enterprises are remarkably low, don't fret about leaving that plastic at home.

For spicy Mandarin and the best pot stickers in town, try **The Pot Sticker** at 150 Waverly Place, tel. (415) 397-9985, open daily for lunch and dinner. Another Hunan hot spot is **Brandy Ho's** at 217 Columbus (at Pacific), tel. 788-

7527, and also at 450 Broadway (at Kearney), tel. 362-6268, open daily from noon to midnight. The **Far East Cafe,** 631 Grant Ave., tel. 982-3245, is a dark place lit by Chinese lanterns, a great choice for Cantonese. Another possibility is the tiny turn-of-the-century **Hang Ah Tea Room** off Sacramento St. at 1 Hang Ah St., tel. 982-5686, specializing in Cantonese entrees and lunchtime dim sum. Inexpensive and locally infamous, due largely to the rude waiter routine of Edsel Ford Wong (now deceased), is three-story **Sam Wo** at 813 Washington St. (at Grant), tel. 982-0596, where you can get good noodles, *jook* (rice gruel), and Chinese-style doughnuts (for dunking in your gruel).

New in Chinatown and a good bet for inexpensive dim sum is **J & J Restaurant** at 615 Jackson St., tel. (415) 981-7308, set up teahouse style—almost always packed, almost always noisy—and offering the options of tray selection or ordering off the menu. Open midday only, 9 a.m.-3 p.m. The real thing (good, inexpensive, and busy) is three-floor **Royal Jade** at 675 Jackson, tel. 392-2929, where whatever you point to on the tray is what you'll get. (It's a good idea to know what you're ordering.) Open until 3 p.m. For vegetarians, **Kowloon Vegetarian,** 909 Grant Ave., tel. 362-9888, open daily 9-9, serves over 80 meatless selections, including 20 types of vegetarian dim sum and entrees like sweet and sour pork or curried pork (soy bean and gluten substituting for meat). But probably the best place around for vegetarian is the upstairs **Lotus Garden New Vegetarian Restaurant** at 352 Grant, tel. 397-0130, open Tues.-Fri. for lunch, Tues.-Sun. for dinner (5-9).

Great Eastern Restaurant at 649 Jackson (between Grant and Kearny), tel. (415) 986-2500, is a relaxed family-style place serving good food at great prices. A best bet here (the waiters are telling the truth) is the fixed-price seafood banquet.

NORTH BEACH AND RUSSIAN HILL

In And Around Jackson Square
"Like the Flintstones on acid," one local food fan says of the almost indescribable style of the **Cypress Club** in Jackson Square at 500 Jackson St., tel. (415) 296-8555. This popular new restaurant near the Financial District is named

after that nightclub in Raymond Chandler's *The Big Sleep.* Snide types say: "Très L.A." Others have called doing lunch or dinner here "like sitting under a table" (those huge columns *could* be table legs) or "like going to a very expensive, very garish, catered carnival."

This is what a visit to phantasmagorical Cypress Club is like: you enter through a copper door, then push past the blood-red velvet speakeasy curtain. Curvaceous copper sectional "pillows," something like overblown landscaping berms, frame the dining room and separate the booths. At table, you sink into plush burgundy mohair seats or pull up a clunky chair, then relax under the familiarity of the WPA-style Bay Area mural wrapping the walls near the ceiling. (Finally, something seems familiar.) Then you notice the odd polka-dotted light fixtures. If the atmosphere is stimulating, so is the food, American fare reinvented. Desserts match the decor, tantalizing "architectural constructs." The wine list is quite remarkable—and safe, since the 14,000-bottle wine cellar is downstairs in an earthquake-proof room. The Cypress Club is open daily for dinner, Mon.-Sat. for lunch, and on Sunday for brunch.

And if that's not enough otherworldly ambience, around the corner and down an alley at 56 Gold St. is **Bix,** tel. (415) 433-6300, a small supper club and bar with the feel of a 1940s-style film noir hideout. Another possibility, quite new, is **Alto Gradimento** at 290 Pacific, tel. 398-6498, an Italian trattoria serving the classics in casual yet fine continental style (even pouring the house wine from porcelain pitchers). Open weekdays for lunch, Mon.-Sat. for dinner.

At home in a classic Jackson Square red brick Victorian, family-owned **Ernie's** at 847 Montgomery St., tel. (415) 397-5969, is a San Francisco institution. Absinthe was on the menu here in 1936, but Ernie's is famous for its classic, now quite contemporary French cuisine. And serious San Francisco movie buffs will recognize the bar, certainly the Tiffany stained-glass insets, from Alfred Hitchcock's *Vertigo*. The city's only Mobil-rated five-star restaurant, Ernie's has updated its ambience, too, banishing the bordello-red color scheme in favor of blond silk. In addition to dinner nightly, since 1991 Ernie's has again been serving lunch (Tuesday through Friday). Instead of abundant à la carte selections, diners can opt for the stunningly good, three-course, daily changing, prix fixe lunch menu, just $15. Wonderful wine list (and helpful sommelier).

Tommy Toy's Haute Cuisine Chinoise in the Montgomery-Washington Tower at 655 Montgomery St., tel. (415) 397-4888, serves up classical Chinese cuisine with traditional French touches, called "Frenchinoise" by Tommy Toy himself. The restaurant itself is impressive enough, patterned after the reading room of the Empress Dowager of the Ching Dynasty, the rich decor including priceless Asian art and antiques. Open for dinner nightly, for lunch weekdays only, reservations always advisable.

North Beach Proper

Farther north in North Beach proper there are almost endless cafes and restaurants, historically the perfect out-of-the-way area to eat, drink real coffee, or just while away the hours. These days, North Beach is a somewhat odd blend of San Francisco's Beat-era bohemian nostalgia, new-world Asian attitudes, and other ethnic culinary accents. An example of the "new" North Beach: the **New Sun Hong Kong** restaurant at the sometimes-harmonic, very cosmopolitan cultural convergence of Grant, Broadway, and Columbus (606 Broadway), tel. (415) 956-3338. Outside, marking the building, is a three-story-tall mural depicting the North Beach jazz tradition. But this is a very Chinatown eatery, open from early morning to late at night and specializing in hot pots and earthy, homey, San Francisco-style Chinese fare.

Also here, of course, are some of old San Francisco's most traditional traditions. The **Washington Square Bar and Grill,** for example, 1707 Powell St., tel. (415) 982-8123, is an immensely popular social stopoff for the city's cognoscenti—a place which also serves outstanding food with your conversation. The live jazz, too, is often worth writing home about. Purported to be the oldest Italian restaurant

around, **Fior D'Italia** at 601 Union St., tel. 986-1886, is legendary for its ambience—including the Tony Bennett Room and the Godfather Room—and its historic ability to attract highbrow Italians from around the globe. (In all fairness, the food is mostly fair.) Also famous is **Amelio's** at 1630 Powell, tel. 397-4339, serving expensive and excellent continental fare in an ambience oozing with Old World intimacy. Dinners only, reservations definitely advisable.

For exceptional food with a more elevated perspective, two dress-up restaurants on Telegraph Hill are appropriately romantic: **Julius' Castle** at 1542 Montgomery St., tel. (415) 362-3042, for French and Italian, and **The Shadows,** 1349 Montgomery, tel. 982-5536, for nouveau continental and French. Not that far away (along the Embarcadero), renowned for its fine food and flair, is the one and only **Fog City Diner,** 1300 Battery St. (at Lombard), tel. 982-2000. Though this is the original gourmet grazing pasture, Fog City has its imitators around the world.

But the real North Beach is elsewhere. **Campo Santo** next door to Tosca at 240 Columbus Ave., tel. (415) 433-9623, is yet another cultural change-up, Latin American kitsch kicking up its heels with campy Day of the Dead decor. The food is lively, too, from mahimahi tacos to crab-stuffed quesadillas. Open Mon.-Sat. from lunchtime through dinner (until 11 p.m.). For genuine neighborhood tradition, though, head to stand-up **Molinari's** at 373 Columbus, tel. 421-2337, a permanent fixture since 1907, a good deli stop for fresh pastas, homemade sauces, hearty sandwiches, and tasty sweet treats. Or stop off for a meatball sandwich or cappuccino at landmark **Mario's Bohemian Cigar Store** near Washington Square at 566 Columbus, tel. 362-0536, where the inexpensive sandwiches, frittata, and cannelloni are the main menu attraction. But most folks sip their cappuccino or Campari while watching the world whirl by, or while watching each other watching.

"Rain or shine, there's always a line" at very-San Francisco **Little Joe's** 523 Broadway, tel. (415) 433-4343, a boisterous bistro where the Italian food is authentic, the atmosphere happy, and everyone hale and hearty. The open kitchen is another main attraction. For faster service, belly up to a counter stool and watch the chefs at work. Classic, too, especially with the lots-of-food-for-little-money set, is the **U.S. Restaurant** at 431 Columbus, tel. 362-6251.

Exceptional **Basta Pasta** at 1268 Grant Ave., tel. (415) 434-2248, serves very reasonably priced, very good food, from veal and fresh fish to perfect calzone fresh out of the wood-burning oven. Surprisingly fine (and equally inexpensive) is **Caffe Roma,** 414 Columbus, tel. 391-8584, where the patio out back is a big draw on sunny days. Prohibition-era **The Gold Spike** at 527 Columbus, tel. 421-4591, also serves wonderful Italian fare. (Friday is crab *cioppino* night.) For pizza, *the* place to go is **North Beach Pizza,** 1499 Grant (at Columbus), tel. 433-1818, where there's always a line, and it's always worth standing in. **Caffe Macaroni** at 59 Columbus, tel. 956-9737, is also a true blue—well, red, white, and green—pasta house in the Tuscany tradition, intimate and aromatic. And *friendly.*

The big choice at dinners-only **Ristorante Castellucci,** 561 Columbus, tel. (415) 362-2774,

is whether to order from the Argentinian or the Italian side of the menu. (If it helps at all, those in the know say the *risotto al porcini* is the best thing San Francisco has to offer.) Exceptional for Afghan fare (and a real treat for vegetarians) is **The Helmand** at 430 Broadway, tel. 362-0641. Equally unusual in the neighborhood is very German **Beethoven Restaurant** at 1701 Powell (at Union), tel. 391-4488, informal and very good.

Off the tourist track and a good choice for breakfast, brunch, and lunch is **Caffe Freddy's** at 901 Columbus, tel. (415) 922-0151, where even the art is created in-house. Another good hiding place, serving up imaginative homestyle American food in time-honored Southern style, is **Susie Kate's** at 2330 Taylor St., Chestnut at Columbus, tel. 776-5283. Just a glance tells you Norman Rockwell has been here. And how often in San Francisco—in all of California, for that matter—do you see Mason jars of pickled corn relish on the tables? Count on almost everything to be tasty, from the egg bread French toast, house-made sausage, and fresh biscuits and sticky buns at Sunday brunch to lunch or dinner specialties like chicken and dumplings, barbecued pork loin, and wonderful black bean chili. Open Tues.-Fri. for lunch, Tues.-Sun. for dinner, and Sun. for brunch.

Russian Hill

A bit off the beaten path and beloved by San Franciscans is the relaxed **Le Petit Cafe** on Russian Hill at 2164 Larkin St. (corner of Green and Larkin), tel. (415) 776-5356, a neighborhood restaurant famous for its house-baked pastries, egg dishes, and coffee at breakfast and weekend brunch (this place is brutally busy; come *late*, after 1 p.m., for brunch), wholesome lunches, and excellent, very reasonably priced dinners. Entrees include Italian torte (pizza), fettuccini, and daily chicken, fresh fish, and hand-rolled pasta specials. Such a deal. Determined tourists can get here from Market Street and vicinity by cable car, too: take the Hyde/Powell route all the way to Green then walk one block to Larkin.

If you're coming that way anyway, another neighborhood possibility is the **Hyde Street Bistro,** 1521 Hyde St., tel. (415) 441-7778, one of those sophisticated little places where San Franciscans hide out during tourist season, not too trendy, plenty quiet, with quite decent Austrian

---

THE SAN FRANCISCO FOOD? IT'S SOURDOUGH BREAD

As mentioned elsewhere, if only in passing, San Francisco has a long roster of culinary inventions—from the all-American Chinese fortune cookie (invented in the Japanese Tea Garden) and "Italian" fish stew, or cioppino, to hangtown fry and peach melba. But nothing is more San Francisco in the food department than sourdough French bread, a much-loved local specialty. Dating from gold-rush days, when yeasts and shortenings were scarce, breads were leavened by fermented "starters" of flour, water, and other live ingredients, this bacteria-enhanced souring ingredient then added in small amounts to bread dough. With each new batch of bread, some dough some was pinched and put aside as the next generation of leavening. And on and on, down through time. Since sourdough bread connoisseurs believe that a good starter, and the bread line it creates, can only improve with age, a bakery's most prized asset is its own unique variety. It's no surprise, then, that during the great San Francisco earthquake and fire of 1906, many of the city's bakers risked their lives to rescue their starters. Such heroic acts are directly responsible for the time-honored tastes of the city's best breads.

and Italian food. Appreciate the breadsticks. **Ristorante Milano,** 1448 Pacific Ave., tel. 673-2961, is a happy, hopping little Italian restaurant with pastas—do try the lasagna—fresh fish, and sometimes surprising specials. New and not far away, at the one-time site of Lord Jim's and Henry Africa's, is **Johnny Love's,** 1500 Broadway (at Polk St.), tel. 931-6053, a bar and grill offering classic American fare (open daily) and separate dinner and bar/late night menus.

FISHERMAN'S WHARF AND GHIRARDELLI SQUARE

The Mandarin in Ghirardelli Square, 900 North Point, tel. (415) 673-8812, was the city's first truly palatial Chinese restaurant, also the first to serve up spicy Szechuan and Hunan dishes. The food here is still great. Stop by at lunch for off-the-menu dim sum (including green onion pie, spring rolls with yellow chives, and sesame shrimp rolls), served 11:30 a.m.-3:30 p.m. daily, or come later for dinner. Another class act here is **Orltalia,** tel. 749-5288, a clever culinary combination of Italian and oriental cuisines. And it's definitely not a typical tourist haunt: most of the folks eating here arrive without cameras, and dressed for the predictable post-dinner drop in temperature.

You won't go far wrong for seafood at the square's **McCormick and Kuleto's,** tel. (415) 929-1730, which features its own Crab Cake Lounge and 30-50 fresh specialties every day. Also much loved at Ghirardelli Square: **Gaylord,** tel. 771-8822, serving astounding Northern India specialties with a side of East Indies decor.

Even out here in the midst of tourist central, several entries in the pretty-cheap-but-good department mean budget-conscious foodies won't starve. Notorious as the tourist bar that introduced Irish coffee, the Victorian-style **Buena Vista** at 2675 Hyde St. (at Beach), tel. (415) 474-5044, is a great spot to share a table for breakfast or light lunch. And the waterfront views are almost free. Another good choice is **Little Rio Cafe and Pizzeria** at 2721 Hyde, tel. 441-3344, where the multicultural specialties emphasize both Brazil and Italy. Open daily for lunch and dinner. **Vicolo Pizzeria** in Ghirardelli Square, tel. 776-1331, is a good choice for designer pizzas. Even better, especially for deep-dish Chicago-style pizza, is **Pizzeria Uno** at 2323 Powell St. (at Bay), tel. 788-4055, open daily for lunch and dinner.

PACIFIC HEIGHTS, THE FILLMORE, AND THE MARINA DISTRICT

Technically on Russian Hill but a real deal for foodies who don't care one whit about the frills is the **San Francisco Art Institute Cafe** at 800 Chestnut St. (at Jones), tel. (415) 771-7020, where you can get a great lunch for $5 or less, along with one of the city's best bay views. The atmosphere is arty and existential, with paper plates and plastic utensils just to remind you that this *is* for students. Everything is fresh and wholesome: Southwestern black bean/vegetable stew, white bean and escarole soup, even house-roasted turkey sandwiches. Good breakfasts, too. Open Mon.-Sat., 9 a.m.-3 p.m.

Perhaps San Francisco's most famous, most fabulous vegetarian restaurant is **Greens** at Fort Mason (Building A), tel. (415) 771-6222, where the hearty fare proves for all time that meat is an unnecessary ingredient for fine dining—and where the views are plenty appetizing, too. Open for lunch and dinner Tues.-Sat, Sun. for brunch; reservations always advised. The bakery counter is open Tues.-Sun. from 10 a.m. to mid or late afternoon.

The casual **Chestnut Street Grill** at 2231 Chestnut St. (at Scott), tel. (415) 922-5558, serves interesting sandwiches and other light fare at lunch and dinner. For coffee and tasty pastries, an outpost of that Berkeley intellectual original **Peet's Coffee and Tea** is just down the block at 2156 Chestnut, tel. 931-8302. Another possibility is **Java Bay** at 2056 Chestnut, tel. 922-JAVA, where the ambience is as electric as the coffee combos—especially the Kuban Latte, a triple espresso spiced up with orange. For an all-American taste treat, stop off at **Beppie's Pie Shop,** 2142 Chestnut, for country-style breakfasts, light entrees at lunch and dinner, and Beppie's famous deep-dish pies.

Pane e Vino at 3011 Steiner St. (at Union), tel. (415) 346-2111, is a justifiably popular neighborhood trattoria, unpretentious and unwavering in its dedication to serving up grand, deceptively simple pastas. Also tastefully understated is **Pietro's Ristorante,** at home in an alley at 1851

Union St. (at Laguna), tel. 563-4157, old-style ambience with comforting contemporary pastas, fresh fish, and daily specials at dinner. And if you tire of privacy, head over to **Perry's** at 1944 Union, tel. 922-9022, one of the city's ultimate see-and-be-seen scenes, also a great burger stop.

Angkor Palace at 1769 Lombard St., tel. (415) 931-2830, has a vivid stunning decor of polished wood and Cambodian antiques, but the food is the real attraction. Not to mention the moderate prices. Start with the shrimp and whitefish soup, perhaps a curry dish, then work your way through the barbecued prawns and stuffed chicken legs. **Scott's Seafood,** 2400 Lombard, tel. 563-8988, serves some of the city's best, though the **Marina Cafe** at 2417 Lombard, tel. 929-7241, can also be counted on for fresh seafood as well as pastas. The **Curbside Cafe** at 2417 California, tel. 929-9030, specializes in flavorful delights from all over—France, Morocco, Mexico, and the Caribbean—and people kill for Curbside's crab cakes.

The Elite Cafe at 2049 Fillmore, tel. (415) 346-8668, is close to being just what it sounds like, a clubby pub serving far-from-pub grub, somehow quite appropriate to the neighborhood. The **Fillmore Grill** down the way at 2301 Fillmore, tel. 922-1444, is a classic American-style bar that also happens to serve great food, from rib-eye steak to pastas and fresh fish; it's party time here on weekend nights. **Pacific Heights Bar and Grill** at 2001 Fillmore, tel. 567-5226, also packs in the Pacific Heighters, especially after 4 p.m. or so, when waves of oysters—mostly raw, served on the half-shell—are sucked down with abandon.

Intimate, expensive, and very San Francisco is **The Sherman House** at 2160 Green St. (between Fillmore and Webster), tel. (415) 563-3600, the converted mansion of Leander Sherman, now an exclusive small hotel attracting inordinate percentages of celebrities and stars. There are four tables in the dining room, four more in the solarium, and a large before-dinner Second Empire salon. Open Mon.-Sat. for breakfast and lunch, for dinner nightly, and for brunch on Sunday. Valet parking. Reservations essential. **The Mansions** at 2220 Sacramento, tel. 929-9444, serves wonderful food in a Victorian dining room, complete with unusual entertainment.

For regular people planning a special night out, though, **Oppenheimer** at 2050 Divisadero, tel. (415) 563-0444, is a better choice, a tiny bistro offering simpler yet substantial pleasures. Another surprise is **Chateau Suzanne** at 1449 Lombard, tel. 771-9326, serving healthy and absolutely elegant French-Chinese entrees. Open Tues.-Sat. for dinners only, reservations advised.

Close to Japantown and adjacent to the Majestic Hotel, a one-time family mansion, the **Cafe Majestic** at 1500 Sutter St. (at Gough), tel. 776-6400, is widely regarded as one of San Francisco's most romantic restaurants, sedate yet far from stuffy, like a small European hotel. The Edwardian-style decor is ornate yet relaxed, pale green and apricot with potted palms. On top of that, you get good, reasonably priced food and friendly service. The cuisine here at lunch and dinner is Californian and European, emphasizing Italian and Spanish fare. Better yet, the Majestic serves breakfast on weekdays, brunch on weekends. Lunch is served Tues.-Fri., dinner nightly. Reservations wise.

THE RICHMOND, SEACLIFF, THE SUNSET

A fixture in the midst of the Golden Gate National Recreation Area and a favorite hangout at the edge of the continent, the current incarnation of **The Cliff House** at 1090 Point Lobos Ave., tel. (415) 386-3330 or 387-5847, is also a decent place to eat. As close to fancy as it gets here is **Upstairs at the Cliff House,** an Old San Francisco-style dining room. Decidedly more casual at this cliff-hanging complex are both the **Seafood and Beverage Company** and the **Phineas T. Barnacle** pub.

But unusual, exceptional Far Eastern and ethnic fare is a Richmond restaurant specialty. The 100-plus restaurants lining Clement Street represent this fairly new phenomenon, with South American, Mexican, Italian, even Russian restaurants and delis also represented as part of the culinary cultural mix.

The modern **Fountain Court** at 354 Clement St., tel. (415) 668-1100, is a notable in the city's "new Chinatown," a wonderful, inexpensive stop for northern-style dim sum and other Shanghai specialties. One of the few San Francisco restaurants serving spicy, sweet Singapore-style fare is **Straights Cafe** at 3300 Geary, tel. 668-1783, a light, airy, white-walled rendition complete with interior palm trees. Another is the **Singapore-Malaysian Restaurant** at 836 Clement (at 9th Ave.), tel. 750-9518, a casual cafe serving all kinds of stir-fry and open daily for lunch and dinner. Also quite inexpensive: the **Taiwan Restaurant,** 445 Clement (at 6th), tel. 387-1789.

Fairly new and quite good for Indonesian is **Jakarta** at 615 Balboa St. (between 7th and 8th avenues), tel. (415) 387-5225, also airy and light, featuring a very extensive menu of unusually well-done dishes plus an eye-catching array of artifacts, musical instruments, and shadow puppets. Another local favorite is simpler **Bali Restaurant** at 3727 Geary (at Arguello), tel. 221-9811.

Some say inexpensive, unusually good **Khan Toke Thai House,** 5937 Geary (at 23rd Ave.), tel. (415) 668-6654, is San Francisco's best Southeast Asian restaurant. Open daily for dinner only, reservations accepted. Another reliable neighborhood choice is the **Bangkok Cafe,** 2847 Geary (at Collins), tel. 346-8821.

For the whole Lebanese experience, including a belly dancer on some nights, make yourself at home at **The Grapeleaf,** 4031 Balboa St. (at 41st), tel. (415) 668-1515, a casual and charming retreat from everyday reality. For Moroccan, and more belly dancing, try **El Mansour** at 3121 Clement (near 32nd Ave.), tel. 751-2312. For all kinds of shish kebobs, **Kasra Persian Cuisine** at 349 Clement (at 5th Ave.), tel. 752-1101, is a very good choice.

Absolutely wonderful, for its multicultural Latin influences, is **Alejandro's Sociedad Gastronomica,** 1840 Clement (at 19th), tel. (415) 668-1184, a lovely tile-trimmed dining room serving pre-Colombian art and artifacts, strolling guitarists, and stylish Spanish, Mexican, and Peruvian specialties. A good choice for country French is tiny, welcoming **Cafe Maisonnette,** 315 8th Ave., tel. 387-7992. People rave about the rack of lamb. Monthly changing menu. **Cafe Riggio** at 4112 Geary, tel. 221-2114, is as much appreciated for its antipasto and world-class calamari as everything else, right down to the homemade *cannoli* at dessert.

Bill's Place at 2315 Clement, tel. (415) 221-5262, is an all-American burger joint (presidential portraits on the walls, a Japanese-style garden) where the creations are named in honor of local celebrities. Guess what you get when you order a Carol Doda burger: two beefy patties with an olive sticking out smack dab in the middle of each. **Tia Margarita** at 300 19th Ave. (at Clement), tel. 752-9274, is a long-running family cafe serving more than just American-style Mexican. A better bet for all-American vegetarians is the **Clement Street Bar & Grill** at 708 Clement (at 8th Ave,), tel. 386-2200, where grilled seafood and California-style pastas are culinary best bets.

Things are more than a bit gentrified in Presidio Heights. Just a few blocks south of the Presidio is **The Magic Flute Garden Ristorante,** 3673 Sacramento St., tel. (415) 922-1225, a sunny French country atmosphere with Italian and other continental specialties. Folks also sing the praises of nearby **Tuba Garden,** 3634 Sacramento, tel. 921-TUBA, a cozy Victorian open just for lunch and brunch, serving up Belgian waffles, homemade blintzes, and such.

Out at the edge of the Sunset District, assemble everything for a memorable picnic from the delis and shops along Taraval. Neighborhood eateries are equally interesting, an eclectic ethnic blend. **Leon's Bar-BQ** in an oceanside shack at 2800 Sloat Blvd., tel. (415) 681-3071, is a great stop for chicken and ribs. (There's another in the Fillmore.) **Brother's Pizza** at 3627 Taraval (near 46th), tel. 753-6004, isn't much to look at, but the pizzas (try the pesto special), pastas, and calzone overcome that first impression in a big hurry. Cafeteria-style lunch at **Stoyanof's Cafe & Restaurant** at 1240 9th Ave., tel. 664-3664, is a veritable Greek feast, especially enjoyable, if it's sunny, out on the decks in back. At dinner, count on a different menu, good Macedonian entrees. **Casa Aguila** at 1240 Noriega (near 19th), tel. 661-5593, specializes in authentic Mexican fare from Cuernavaca, very generous portions. **El Toreador Fonda Mejicana** at 50 W. Portal, tel. 566-8104 or 753-9613, is another good Mexican food choice.

Just down the way is **Cafe for All Seasons,** 150 W. Portal, tel. (415) 665-0900, for California-style cuisine. Great for neighborhood-style French is **La Creme** at 2305 Irving (24th and Irving), tel. 664-0669, known for downtown-quality food at Sunset prices (very reasonable). Friendly service and lots of fun, too.

HAIGHT-ASHBURY AND VICINITY

Campy as all get out, what with those murals and all, **Cha Cha Cha** just a hop or skip from Golden Gate Park at 1805 Haight St., tel. (415) 386-5758, is a hip *tapas* bar featuring unforgettable entrees such as grilled chicken paillard in mustard sauce, shrimp in spicy Cajun sauce, and New Zealand mussels in marinara. (One of the most popular places around, so it's sometimes hard to find a place to park yourself.) A real high for breakfast or lunch is **Ozone** at 1654 Haight, tel. 255-0565, a sophisticated yet simple atmosphere for continental-style American fare, quite down to earth. Ethereal, though, is the gray-and-white cloudscape on the walls.

On any afternoon, most of the restaurants and cafes lining the Haight will be filled to the gills with desperate young hipsters chowing-down on brunch specials or self-medicating with food to cure party-related hangovers. **Hell's Kitchen,** 1793 Haight St., tel. (415) 255-7170, offers an eclectic, inexpensive menu in an *Electric Kool-Aid Acid Test* atmosphere. Higher consciousness cafe fare is served up at **The Red Victorian,** 1665 Haight, tel. 894-1978, a high-concept, blast-from-the-past-and-future bed and breakfast and computer networking center. For monstrously generous omelettes and a hearty side of potatoes—full breakfast for under $6—slide on into **All You Knead** at 1466 Haight, tel. 552-4550. You'll get just that. **Dish** at 1398 Haight, tel. 431-3534, is all-American and always reliable, from the chops and chicken to the fish.

Always popular for pizza: **Cybelle's,** with two neighborhood outlets, one at 1535 Haight St., tel. (415) 552-4200, the other at 203 Parnassus, tel. 665-8088. Some neighborhood experts swear, however, that nothing beats **Escape from New York Pizza,** 1737 Haight, tel. 668-5577. (There's another Escape at 508 Castro, tel. 252-1515.)

For good, reasonably priced nouvelle American fare and knotty pine New England atmosphere, try the **Ironwood Cafe** inside a Victorian at 901 Cole St. (just one block east of Haight), tel. (415) 664-0224, the ever-changing menu featuring entrees from baked sea bass and chicken to pastas. If you're lucky, fresh nectarine and peach pie will be on the dessert menu. Open for lunch weekdays only, for dinner Mon.-Sat., closed Sundays.

A Oh at 701 Cole St., tel. (415) 668-6620, serves authentic West African cuisine, quite good, quite reasonable. Service can be slow, since everything is cooked with painstaking care. The famous **Tassajara Bread Bakery** at 1000 Cole, tel. 664-8947, affiliated with a Zen monastery (as well as a second bakery outlet at Fort Mason) is one of the city's best, well worth a stop for poppy seed cake and pastries. Other possibilities: **Bakers of Paris** at 1605 Haight, tel. 626-4076, for croissants, and **Beau Seventh Heaven,** 1448 Haight, tel. 626-4448, an interesting French-Russian outpost.

The area referred to as "the lower Haight" is an avant-garde enclave sandwiched between seedy Western Addition and the Fillmore projects, with nary a tourist attraction in sight. Without the homeless, runaways, and drug dealers notable in the upper Haight, this several-block area has become a fairly happy haven for artists and low-end wannabes, as well as for the cafes, bars, and restaurants they inhabit. (Great people-watching.) **Ground Zero** at 783 Haight St., tel. (415) 861-1985, has leopard-skin tables, elevated window seats, and a long black vinyl couch perfect for sucking down a latte or cold beer while having an intellectual conversation. A bit more boisterous, with sunny-day sidewalk tables, too, is the **Horse Show Coffee House,** 566 Haight, tel. 626-8852. Both of these establishments are plugged into computer-networking SF Net.

The Beehive refers to the big hair bouffants of the 1950s (and the B-52s) as well as the elaborate mural on the walls here, a funky hole-in-the-wall where drag queen waiters serve very cheap eats. But most of the neighborhood's bars serve fairly decent food during the day and into the evening, from the **Mad Dog in the Fog** English-style pub to the painfully hip **Noc Noc.** Particularly off the wall, in the spirit of the neighborhood, is **Spaghetti Western,** 576 Haight, tel. 864-8461, an earring-heavy reinterpretation of our collective cowboy heritage. Lots of food for the money. (And it's cheap.)

THE MISSION DISTRICT AND THE CASTRO

The Mission District is known for its open-air markets. One of the best is **La Victoria Mexican Bakery & Grocery** at 2937 24th Street. Buy some homemade tamales, some fruit, and a few *churros* (Mexican sugar-dipped doughnuts) and have a feast at the children's park (between Bryant and York on 24th) while studying the murals. Other ethnic bakeries worth poking into for impromptu picnic fixings include **Pan Lido Salvadoreno** at 3147 22nd St., tel. (415) 282-3350, and **Panaderia Rosita** at 5488 Mission St., tel. 333-3090. An ethnic change-up, serving great sandwiches, is **Lucca Ravioli Company**, 1100 Valencia, tel. 647-5581.

Among the Mission's inexpensive neighborhood joints is **Casa Aguila** at 1240 Noriega St., tel. (415) 661-5593, with an endless (and endlessly fascinating) menu and great *carne asada* selections. Of the hundreds of Mission District taquerias, **La Cumbre** at 515 Valencia, tel. 863-8025, is still king of the monster burrito. You can count on yours being stuffed to maximum capacity with beans, rice, and chicken or beef. For something more exotic, **Taqueria El Farolito** at 2779 Mission, tel. 824-7877, adds meat fillings including *lengua* (tongue) and *cabeza* (head). Or head for other good neighborhood eateries, including **El Tazumal**, 3522 20th St. (at Mission), tel. 550-0935, noted for very inexpensive, very good Mexican and Salvadorean food, and **Los Jarritos**, 901 S. Van Ness Ave., tel. 648-8383, where the "little jars" add color to an already colorful menu of Jalisco specialties. At **Los Guitarras**, 3200 24th St. (at S. Van Ness), tel. 285-2684, you get guitar music with your supper.

The line between the Mission and Castro districts, like distinct geographical and sociopolitical divisions elsewhere in the city, is often blurred. **Pozole** at 2337 Market St., tel. (415) 626-2666, has an almost religious, south-of-the-border folk feel, what with the candlelit shrines, skull masks, and festive colors. But the food here isn't a literal cultural interpretation—especially comforting when one recalls that *pozole* was human flesh specially prepared as fight fuel for Aztec warriors.

Fina Estampa, a nondescript Peruvian outpost at 2374 Mission St., tel. (415) 824-4437, features exceptional seafood, chicken, and beef entrees (humongous portions), good service. The **Flying Saucer** at 1000 Guerrero, tel. 641-9955, where the daily changing menu is beamed over onto the wall, is a happy landing for mostly French culinary creativity—like an interplanetary marriage between Berkeley's Chez Panisse and the Zuni Cafe in a neighborhood burger stand. Three nightly seatings.

Saigon Saigon, one more stop along The Mission's restaurant row (between 16th and 24th streets), 1132 Valencia at 22nd, tel. (415) 206-9635, serves an astounding array of Vietnamese dishes, from majestic rolls and barbecued quail to Buddha's delight (vegetarian). Open for lunch on weekdays, for dinner nightly.

Manora at 3226 Mission, tel. (415) 550-0856, is an attractive, tiny, and inexpensive Thai restaurant that's been around for years. It's still great, from the jumbo prawns and sautéed beef to chicken curry in coconut milk. Both restaurant and *tapas* bar, **Esperpento** across the way at 3295 Mission, tel. 282-8867, is a great place for surprising Catalonian entrees as well as very good, sophisticated Spanish finger foods. Fairly inexpensive. Open Mon.-Sat. for lunch and dinner. **Cafe Nidal** at 2491 Mission, tel. 285-4334, is a long-standing neighborhood stop for falafels and other inexpensive Middle Eastern specialties, but **Cafe Istanbul** at 525 Valencia, tel. 863-8854, also serves up the Fat Chance Belly Dancers on Wednesday and Saturday nights.

A neighborhood classic in the coffeehouse/coffee shop genre is very unpretentious **Cafe Picaro**, 3120 16th St. (at Valencia), tel. 431-4089, a combination bohemian cafe—sandwiches, pasta, seafood—and used-book store. The better-coiffed local intelligentsia tend to head for **Cafe Beano**, 878 Valencia, for the vegetarian specials. It's hard to see what's so new about American-style **New Dawn Cafe** at 3174 16th St., tel. 553-8888, a self-consciously funky place with antique toys and other secondhand distractions deliberately set into every nook and cranny.

For real cheap eats in the Castro, head to **Azteca Tacqueria** at 235 Church St., tel. (415) 255-7330, where a spicy two-fisted burrito will make a meal for less than $4. Also inexpensive, for locally famous burgers and renowned French fries, not to mention excessive neon and Marilyn Monroe memorabilia, is **Hot'n' Hunky** at 4039 18th St., tel. 621-6365.

Depending on what you order, though, you can eat well quite reasonably at many neighborhood cafes and restaurants. Very Castro is **Cafe Flore** at 2298 Market St., tel. (415) 621-8579, a popular gay hangout and cafe, serving up omelettes and crepes, salads and good sandwiches, and current information about what's going on in the neighborhood. (Great for people-watching, especially out on the plant-populated patio.) Another popular Castro destination is **The Bagdad Cafe,** 2295 Market St., tel. 621-4434, offering a healthy take on American-style fare, plus great salads. Missed by most tourists but quite popular for brunch is the **Patio Cafe** at 531 Castro (near 18th), tel. 621-4640. Nearby, and wonderful for succulent seafood, is the **Anchor Oyster Bar** at 579 Castro, tel. 431-3990.

It's Tops at 1801 Market, tel. (415) 431-6395, looks like a classic American greasy spoon—the decor hasn't changed since 1945—but the surprise is just how good the pancakes and other breakfast selections are. **Sparky's Diner** at 242 Church St., tel. 626-5837, got lost somewhere in the 1950s, style-wise, but the breakfast omelettes, burgers, and salads are certainly up to modern expectations.

The atmosphere at informal **Le Piano Zinc** at 708 14th St. (between Market and Church), tel. (415) 431-5266, is California-style art deco. This intimate cafe serves exceptional, innovative California-style French. Open daily from breakfast until 11 p.m. (Reservations wise at dinner.) There's a small takeout counter, too, and anything here can be prepared to go. In the same league but Victorian in style is **Ryan's,** 4230 18th St., tel. 621-6131, serving contemporary, creative American fare.

SOUTH OF MARKET

The area South of Market, or SoMa, San Francisco's answer to New York City's SoHo style, is post-hippy, post-hip, post-just about everything. Anything goes. Reality here ranges from street people chic and chichi supper clubs to only-those-in-the-know-know-where-it's-at dance clubs. Exploring the neighborhood—many areas are considered unsafe after dark, though they become safer when everyone else (in groups) is doing it—offers the same stunning cultural contrast as those encampments of the homeless in front of the White House.

Post-punk, politically correct, and pretty darn dirt cheap, **Limbo** at 297 9th St. (9th and Folsom), tel. (415) 255-9945, is a deconstructed diner serving healthy, classically inexpensive food, including good salads, sandwiches, veggie specialties, and tremendous desserts. This place is as electric as it is eclectic, so that uncannily fa-

miliar yellow plastic "M" out front may or may not mean anything. Also good and pretty cheap is the fast-as-your-laundry-cycle fare at **Brain-Wash** (see "Clean Up Your Act at BrainWash"). The burgers at **Eddie Rickenbacker's,** 133 2nd St., tel. 543-3498, are considered by connoisseurs to be close to the best, though there are other good bets, from the salads and soups to fish dishes. For those stirred to the soul by the world burger beat, the top stop is **Hamburger Mary's** at 1582 Folsom, tel. 626-1985, a cleaned-up bikers' bar easily mistaken for a downhome junque store. Also a possibility (if only for the great view of the railroad tracks) is **Caffe Esprit** along the waterfront in China Basin, 16th and Illinois, tel. 777-5558, serving Caesar salads and grilled salmon sandwiches in addition to great burgers. Sometimes you wait a while.

The design-and-dine fashion district crowd is attracted in spades by the appetizers at the **Ace Cafe,** 1539 Folsom, tel. (415) 621-4752. Dessert here is no slouch either, of course, especially that concoction of pine nuts, poppy seeds, and chocolate known as the Happy Sandwich. An area old-timer is understated, healthy **Eddie Jacks** at 1151 Folsom, tel. 626-2388 or 626-8862, also a taproom-style bar featuring live entertainment. One of the best places to eat in SoMa, though, is **The Acorn,** that red awning amid the auto garages and welding shops between 8th and 9th at 1256 Folsom, tel. 863-2469, open just for breakfast, lunch, and (3-5 p.m.) afternoon tea. Exceptional pastries and desserts are the norm. Everything else in this homecooking yet sophisticated haven changes daily, but is predictably no-nonsense. Good taste, honest food.

Marked by the big tomato, no-fuss **Ruby's** at 489 3rd St., tel. (415) 541-0795, is a fine Mediterranean cuisine scene in upscaling SoMa, disguised by a plain old storefront. Take your pick from pastas, pizzas, unusual specials. A fairly new kid in the neighborhood is exceptional **Fringale,** 570 4th St., tel. 543-0573, a light, airy, and inexpensive contemporary French/American bistro. Very good food, remarkably reasonable prices, a place well worth looking for. Open for lunch weekdays, for dinner Monday through Saturday.

Strictly for carnivores, sometimes overrun by conventioneers, the charming **Market Roastery** in the one-time Keystone Room at 68 4th St.

(between Mission and Market), tel. (415) 777-1200, serves manly hunks of meat. It's good meat, too, usually spit roasted to perfection. The "world famous Market Roastery chicken" is a real deal, too. But you can settle for less, from salads to sandwiches. Come nightfall, live jazz is also on tap. Open weekdays for lunch, Tues.-Sat. for dinner. A long-running neighborhood classic is the **Cadillac Bar and Grill** at 1 Holland Court (just off Howard, between 4th and 5th streets), tel. 543-8226, best known as a Corona beer-crazed yuppie bar but actually one of the best places around for unusual, excellent mesquite-grilled Mexican food.

Star-watching is always a favorite SoMa pastime, which means seeking out the trendiest places. Some like to do it at **Embarko** in South Beach, 100 Brannan, tel. (415) 495-2021, which also serves good food. Very mod **Undici** at 374 11th St., tel. 431-3337, serves good

Southern Italian specialties, like roasted chicken and sautéed spinach, in San Francisco's elegant post-Mediterranean answer to villa-style ambience. Pretty new, too, is **Ristorante Ecco** at 101 S. Park, tel. 495-3291, a trattoria-style California/Italian place with peachy sponge-painted walls quite popular with the young professional crowd. Great desserts. Straight across the park is Ecco's slightly older sibling, the **South Park Cafe,** 108 S. Park, tel. 495-7275, a very intimate French-style bistro whipping up espresso and croissants in the morning, more elaborate creations at both lunch and dinner. Open daily for breakfast, lunch, and dinner. But the area has its sociocultural flagships, such as **Julie's Supper Club** back at 1123 Folsom, tel. 861-0707, a restaurant and nightclub/bar known for its combination of space-age-meets-the-'50s supper club style and Old West saloon atmosphere.

JUST THE FACTS

INFORMATION

The clearinghouse for current visitor information is the **San Francisco Convention & Visitors Bureau,** P.O. Box 429097, San Francisco 94142-9097, tel. (415) 391-2000. Contact the SFCVB to receive current information on accommodations, events, and other travel planning particulars. For $2 postage and handling, request a copy of the SFCVB's semiannual *The San Francisco Book,* which contains very thorough information about sights, activities, arts, entertainment, recreation, shopping venues, and restaurants. (And then some.) It's worth the money to request in advance, if you'll be in town awhile.

To obtain visitor information once in town, stop by the SFCVB's **Visitor Information Center** downtown at Hallidie Plaza, downstairs (below street level) at 900 Market St. (Market and Powell). Official visitor pamphlets, maps, booklets, plus brochures about local businesses (including current accommodations bargains and various coupon offers), are freely available. In addition, multilingual visitor center staffers are available to answer questions. (You need to be quite specific about what you're interested in, since the folks here will seek what you need

from their voluminous behind-the-counter information stockpile.) The Visitor Information Center is open weekdays 9 a.m.-5:30 p.m., Saturdays 9-3, and Sundays 10-2. (Closed Thanksgiving, Christmas, and New Year's Day.)

The Visitor Information Center also offers a free, 24-hour, updated-weekly **Visitor Hotline** in five different languages. To find out what's going on in town, from entertainment and arts attractions to major professional sports events, just dial the city's multilingual "tele-itinerary." To get the news in English, call (415) 391-2001; in French, tel. 391-2003; in German, tel. 391-2004; in Japanese, tel. 391-2101; and in Spanish, tel. 391-2122.

The **Redwood Empire Association** at 785 Market St., 15th Floor, tel. (415) 543-8334, open weekdays 9-5, offers an impressive amount of information: brochures, maps, and pamphlets on member towns, counties, attractions, accommodations, and eateries—in San Francisco and vicinity and north to the Oregon border.

Available free at hotels, restaurants, and some shops around town is the small magazine-style *Key: This Week San Francisco,* chock full of the usual information plus a very thorough current arts, entertainment, and events section. An interesting source for local happenings, including

restaurants and clubs currently considered hot spots, is *Frisko* magazine. Though focused primarily for permanent Bay Area residents, *San Francisco Focus* magazine also offers regular food and entertainment columns, plus in-depth feature articles about the real world of San Francisco and environs.

Even more real: *The San Francisco Bay Guardian* and *SF Weekly* tabloid newspapers, along with the *East Bay Guardian,* available almost everywhere around town. The *Guardian's* motto (with a hat tip to Wilbur Storey and the 1861 *Chicago Times,* as interpreted by Editor/Publisher Bruce Brugmann)—"It is a newspaper's duty to print the news and raise hell"—is certainly comforting in these times, and the paper also generates some decent news/feature reading along with comprehensive arts, entertainment, and events listings. The *Weekly* also offers what's-happening coverage and—to its everlasting credit—Rob Brezsny's "Real Astrology" column, the best New Age innovation since karma. The *Express,* with its roots on the other side of the Bay Bridge, is usually the best easily available source for what's going on in Berkeley, Oakland, and environs.

Several tabloids focus exclusively on the local music scene, including *BAM* (the Bay Area Music Magazine), found in all Tower Records stores. The big *Whoop* is available in assorted hipster stores; *The Press* emphasizes the Northern California music scene (centered, of course, in San Francisco).

While roaming the city, look for other special-interest and neighborhood-scope publications. To keep absolutely current with the local restaurant scene, pick up a copy of *The Food Paper,* San Francisco/Bay Area edition, published quarterly by Gault Millau, Inc. (available at select locations around town or call toll-free 800-532-3781 for subscriptions). *City Sport* magazine will get you up to speed on recreation, sports, and outdoor diversions. The *CenterVoice,* downtown's monthly, covers the performing and visual arts. The *Bay Times* is a fairly substantive gay and lesbian bi-weekly. For more comprehensive events information, pick up a copy of *The Sentinel,* a weekly, and/or its main competition, the *Bay Area Reporter.* Widely read throughout the Sunset and Richmond districts is *The Independent.* Other popular neighborhood papers include the award-winning, hell-raising, multilanguage *Tenderloin Times,* the *North Mission News,* and the *Noe Valley Voice.*

The city's major dailies are universally available, at newsstands and in coin-op vending racks. The morning paper is the *San Francisco Chronicle,* most appreciated for its columnists—especially "The Sackamenna Kid" Herb Caen, whose good-humored snooping into everyone's business makes for readable community news, at least when he's not lamenting the hopelessly lost good ol' days. The afternoon/evening *San Francisco Examiner,* run by pretty clued-in William Randolph Hearst III, often offers more in-depth news and much more interesting writing. The two papers aren't competitors in the usual sense. They share printing facilities (and classified ads) and also combine forces every week to produce the humongous Sunday paper. That edition's pink "Datebook" section is packed with readable reviews, sometimes taciturn letters from demanding or demented Bay Area readers, and the most comprehensive listing of everything going on in the coming week. San Francisco's major non-English and ethnic newspapers include the Chinese-language *Centre Daily News,* the *Irish Herald,* and the black community's *Sun Reporter.*

Bookstores, Libraries

San Francisco is a well-read city, judging solely from the number of booksellers here. Perhaps most famous is that bohemian bookshop of lore in North Beach, **City Lights,** 261 Columbus Ave., tel. (415) 362-8193, with especially impressive small press and poetry sections. The **Sierra Club Bookstore** near the Civic Center at 730 Polk St., tel. 923-5600, offers a great selection of outdoor, ecology, nature, and travel books. **A Clean, Well Lighted Place for Books** is nearby and also well worth a stop, at 601 Van Ness Ave., tel. 441-6670. (Theater aficionados, take a side trip to **Drama Books** just south of Market at 134 9th St., tel. 255-0604.) Also in the same general neighborhood: **Fantasy Etc.** (for fantasy books) at the edge of the Tenderloin, 808 Larkin, tel. 441-7617, and the **European Book Company** at 925 Larkin, tel. 474-0626.

Probably the best downtown San Francisco stop for travel and maps is **Rand McNally** in the financial district at 595 Market St., tel. (415) 777-3131. Worthwhile elsewhere is **The Complete Traveler** at 3207 Fillmore, tel. 923-1511, and the always fascinating **Thomas Brothers' Maps** at 550 Jackson St. (in Jackson Square), tel. 981-7520. Two good Union Square-area antiquarian bookshops include **Jeremy Norman & Co., Inc.,** at 720 Market, tel. 781-6402, and **John Scopazzi,** 278 Post St., tel. 362-5708.

Some unusual specialty or neighborhood bookstores include the **San Francisco Mystery Bookstore** in Noe Valley (near the Mission District) at 199 Grove St., tel. (415) 282-7444, and **Marcus Bookstore** in the Western Addition, 1712 Fillmore St., tel. 346-4222, specializing in African-American books. Foreign-language book specialists include **Eastwind Books and Arts, Inc.** near Chinatown, 633 Vallejo St. and 1435-A Stockton St., tel. 781-3329 and 781-3331, respectively; **Kinokuniya** at Japan Center, 1581 Webster St., tel. 567-7625; and in the Richmond—for Russian—both **Russian Books,** 332 Balboa, tel. 668-4723, and **Znanie Bookstore,** 5237 Geary, tel. 752-7555.

Bookstores are also covered in individual districts under "The Lay of the Land" above. Keep in mind, too, that museums and other major sights offer impressive, sometimes special-interest selections of books and gifts. San Francisco also boasts quite a number of good general-interest new and used book stores.

And if you don't feel obliged to buy what you need to read, the **Civic Center Library Building** downtown between McAllister and Larkin, tel. (415) 557-4400, is a good place to start becoming familiar with the local public library system. A complete listing of neighborhood branches is listed in the white pages of the local phone book, under "Government Pages—SF City & County —Libraries."

Consulates, Passports, Visas, Etcetera

San Francisco is home to some 70 foreign consulates, from Argentina, Botswana, and Brazil to Indonesia, Malta, the Philippines, and what was once Yugoslavia. For a complete listing, contact the San Francisco Convention & Visitors Bureau (above). The **Australian Consulate** is downtown at 1 Bush St., 7th Floor, tel. (415) 362-6160 (in emergencies: tel. 330-7347); the **British** at the corner of Sutter and Sansom streets, 1 Sansome, Suite 850, tel. 981-3030 (emergencies: tel. 561-9346); the **Canadian,** 50 Fremont, Suite 2100, tel. 495-6021; the **French,** 540 Bush St., tel. 397-4330 (emergencies: tel. 425-6172); and **German,** 1960 Jackson, tel. 775-1061 (emergencies—allowed only 9 a.m.-11 p.m.—tel. 885-3494). The **Hong Kong Economic and Trade Office,** essentially the consulate here, is at 180 Sutter St., 4th Floor, tel. 397-2215. The **Irish** consulate is at 655 Montgomery St., Suite 930, tel. 392-4214, and the **Italian,** 2590 Webster St., tel. 931-4924. The **Japan Information Center** and consulate is at 50 Fremont, Suite 2200, tel. 777-3553, and open weekdays 9-5 (closed at lunch, noon-1 p.m.). The **Mexican** consulate is located at 870 Market St., Suite 528, tel. 392-5554, the **New Zealand Travel Council** at 550 Irving St., tel. 665-5503, and the **Spanish** consulate at 2080 Jefferson St., tel. 922-2995. The **Commission of the European Communities** is downtown at 44 Montgomery St., Suite 2715, tel. 391-3476.

For passports and visas, the **U.S. Department of State Passport Agency** is located downtown at 525 Market St. (at 1st St.), Suite 200 (lobby level), tel. (415) 744-4444 for recorded information (let it ring) or tel. 974-7972. Open weekdays 8-4. For Customs information and inquiries, contact the **U.S. Customs Office,** 555 Battery St. in the Financial District, tel. 705-4440.

For help in locating a foreign-language translator, or for information about San Francisco's foreign-language schools, contact the Convention & Visitors Bureau, which maintains a current listing of member public and private schools.

Other Helpful Information Contacts

For current **weather** information, call (415) 936-1212. For current San Francisco **time,** call that old-time favorite POPCORN (tel. 767-2676). For current **road conditions** anywhere in California, call 557-3755 or toll-free (800). The *San Francisco Chronicle* sponsors the free **Cityline,** tel. 512-5000, the number to call for a prerecorded summary of news, sports, stocks, entertainment, and weather information.

The **International Visitors Center** is located downtown in the financial district, at 312 Sutter St., Suite 402, tel. (415) 986-1388. This nonprofit organization promotes international understanding and friendship; foreign visitors are welcome to visit headquarters and to participate in the "Meet Americans at Home" program. Call the **Traveler's Aid Society,** tel. 255-2252, for advice and assistance for travel-related dilemmas.

The **Chinese Culture Center** on the third floor of the Chinatown Holiday Inn, 750 Kearny (at Washington), 3rd Floor, tel. (415) 986-1822, is the community clearinghouse for educational and cultural programs, including classes, lectures, workshops, and very current events—from the arts and upcoming performances to festivals. While **Japan Center** or Japantown in its entirety is the center of Japanese-American cultural life, the **Japanese Cultural and Community Center** is here, too, located at 1840 Sutter St., tel. 567-5505.

The **Alliance Française de San Francisco** at 1345 Bush St., tel. (415) 775-7755, is an international cultural center committed to promoting French culture and language, with facilities including a cafe, library, school, theater, and satellite television services. The **Booker T. Washington Community Center** in the Richmond District at 800 Presidio Ave. (at Sutter St.), tel. 921-4757, sponsors a variety of educational, recreational, scouting, and sports activities of specific interest to the black community. **La Raza Information Center,** sharing space with a translation service at 2588 Mission, tel. 826-5855, is useful for Latino community information, though clear across town at Fort Mason, the **Mexican Museum,** tel. 441-0445, offers assistance, too, including a self-guided tour map of the Mission District ($2). Call the **Jewish Community Information and Referral** at tel. 777-4545 for just about everything, from synagogue locations to special-interest community events. For **Senior Citizen's Information** and referrals, call 626-1033.

The **Women's Building of the Bay Area** is also in the Mission, at 3543 18th St. (just off Valencia), tel. (415) 431-1180, and serves as the region's central clearinghouse for feminist and lesbian arts, entertainment, and other information. This is the place to contact for a variety of nonprofit women's services (and for advice about where to go for others). **The Names**

Project, 2362 Market St., tel. 863-1966, is a nonprofit group dedicated to preserving the memory of those lost to AIDS, efforts that include the creation of the world-renowned AIDS Quilt. Berkeley's **Gay Switchboard and Counseling Services,** tel. (510) 841-6224, is very helpful for lesbians and gays spending time in San Francisco as well, since information about everything from local clubs and current community events to service referrals is offered in addition to counseling.

For special assistance and information on the city's **disabled services,** contact the **Mayor's Office of Community Development** (Attn. Disability Coordinator), 10 United Nations Plaza, Suite 600, San Francisco 94102, tel. (415) 554-8925 or TDD 554-8749, or the very helpful local **Easter Seal Society,** tel. 752-4888. To understand the ins and outs of disabled access to local public transit, request a copy of the *Muni Access Guide,* Muni Elderly & Handicapped Programs, 949 Presidio Ave., San Francisco 94115, tel. 923-6142 weekdays or 673-MUNI anytime.

Being Prepared:
Clothing, Local Customs

San Francisco's weather can upset even the best-laid plans for a frolic in the summertime California sun. For one thing, there may not be any sun. In summer, when most visitors arrive, San Francisco is enjoying its city-wide natural air-conditioning system, called "fog." When California's inland areas are basting in blast-furnace heat, people here might be wearing a down jacket to go walking on the beach. (Sometimes it *does* get hot—and "hot" by San Francisco standards refers to anything above 80° F.) Especially during the summer, weather extremes even in the course of a single day are normal, so pack accordingly. Bring warm clothing (at least one sweater or jacket for cool mornings and evenings), in addition to the optimist's choice of shorts and sandals, and plan to dress in layers so you'll be prepared for anything, quite comfortably. The weather in late spring and early autumn is usually sublime—balmy, often fog-free—so at those times you should bring *two* pairs of shorts (but don't forget that sweater, just in case). It rarely rains from May through October; raingear is prudent at other times.

Most buildings in San Francisco as well as public transit facilities should be accessible to people in wheelchairs or those with other physical limitations; many hotels, restaurants, and entertainment venues will make special accommodations, given some advance notice.

All of San Francisco's public buildings, and many restaurants, are nonsmoking. Others have no-smoking sections, or permit smoking only in the bar. Most motels and hotels have nonsmoking rooms, and many have entire floors of nonsmoking rooms and suites.

Unless otherwise stated on a restaurant menu, restaurants do not include a gratuity in the bill. The standard tip for the wait staff is 15% of the total tab, though truly exceptional service may merit 20%. The average tip for taxi drivers is 15%. It's also customary to tip airport baggage handlers and hotel porters (with $1 per bag, one-way, an acceptable standard), parking valets, and other service staff. When in doubt about how much, just ask someone.

Safeguarding Your Self

San Francisco is a reasonably safe city. Definitely unsafe areas, especially at night, include the Tenderloin, some areas south of Market Street, parts of the Western Addition, and parts of the Mission District (including, at night, BART stops, a favorite hangout and exit route for street drug dealers and other unsavories). For the most part, drug-related gang violence is confined to Hunter's Point, Sunnyvale, and other severely impoverished areas. The increase in the overall numbers of the homeless and the panhandling population, particularly notable downtown, is distressing, certainly, but most of these people are harmless lost souls.

Definitely *not* harmless is the new national crime craze known as "carjacking," also on the rise in San Francisco. As the scenario usually goes, you're sitting in your car at an intersection or at a parking garage when an armed stranger suddenly appears and demands that you get out. Though there have been highly publicized cases involving successful driver heroism, the best advice is: don't try it. If a criminal demands that you get out of your car or give up your car keys, do it. Losing a car is better than losing your life. Though there is no sure-fire prevention for carjacking, locking all car doors and rolling up windows is often suggested. Another good idea:

avoid dubious or unfamiliar neighborhoods.

If your own vehicle isn't safe, keep in mind that no place is absolutely safe. As elsewhere in America, women are particularly vulnerable to assaults of every kind. At night women traveling solo, or even with a friend or two, should stick to bustling, yuppie-happy areas like Fisherman's Wharf and Union Street. The definitely street-savvy, though, can get around fairly well in SoMa and other nightlife areas, especially in groups or by keeping to streets where there is plenty of benign human traffic. (You can usually tell by looking.) Sadly, in general it is still true that female travelers are safest if they confine themselves to main thoroughfares.

SERVICES

Post Offices, Banks, Currency Exchanges, Etcetera

San Francisco's main **U.S. Postal Service** office is south of Market downtown, at 7th and Mission streets, tel. (415) 621-6838, general delivery zip code 94101, and open Mon.-Fri. 9-5 and Sat. 9 a.m.-1:30 p.m. (For help in figuring out local zip code assignments, and for general information and current postal rates, call 550-6500.) Regional post offices are also scattered throughout San Francisco neighborhoods. Some branches are open extended hours, such as 7 a.m.-6 p.m. weekdays, or with some limited Saturday hours, and some have after-hours open lobbies, so customers can purchase stamps via vending machines. Public mailboxes, for posting stamped mail, are available in every area. Stamps are also for sale in major hotels (usually in the gift shop) and, increasingly, even in major grocery stores.

Branches of major national and international banks are available in San Francisco; most offer automated cash-advance facilities, often accessible through various member systems. Mugging while banking is a potential disadvantage of getting cash from an automated teller. Always be aware of who is nearby and what they're doing; if possible, have a companion or two with you. If the situation doesn't feel "right," move to another location—or do your banking inside.

Most currency exchange outlets are located either downtown or at the San Francisco International Airport (SFO). **American Foreign Ex-**

change **Brokers** at 315 Sutter St., 2nd Floor, tel. (415) 391-9913 (also at 124 Geary, tel. 391-1306, and at Pier 41 at Fisherman's Wharf, tel. 249-4667), charges no commissions on currency exchanges, and has fairly convenient hours: weekdays 9 a.m.-6 p.m, Sat. until 3 p.m. (The Pier 41 office is open both Sat. and Sun. 10-4.) **Bank of America Foreign Currency Services** is located at 345 Montgomery St., tel. (415) 622-2451, and open Mon.-Thurs. 9-4, on Fri. until 6 p.m., and Sat. 9-1. Another possibility is the **Bank of America** at the Powell Street cable car turnaround, Powell and Market, tel. 622-4498 (same hours). **Thomas Cook Currency Services, Inc.,** 75 Geary, tel. 362-3452, is open weekdays 9-5, Sat. 10-4. To exchange currency at the airport, head for the International Terminal, where both **Bank of America,** tel. 742-8079, and **Thomas Cook,** tel. 583-4029, offer currency exchange for both in- and out-bound travelers daily 7 a.m.-11 p.m.

For cardmembers, the **American Express Travel Agency** is another possibility for check cashing, traveler's-check transactions, and currency exchange. There are four San Francisco offices. The one located inside the Sheraton Hotel at Fisherman's Wharf, 2500 Mason St., tel. (415) 788-3025, is open daily 10-6. Another, downtown at 237 Post St., tel. 981-5533, is open weekdays 9-5 and also Sat. 10-5. In Northern California the American Automobile Association (AAA) is known as the **California State Automobile Association** (CSAA), and the San Francisco office is located near the Civic Center at 150 Van Ness Ave., tel. 565-2012. The CSAA office is open weekdays for all member inquries and almost endless services, including no-fee traveler's checks, free maps and travel information, and travel agency services.

San Francisco's major hotels, and most of the midrange boutique hotels, have a fax number and fax facilities; some offer other communications services. For telex and telegrams, **Western Union** is south of Market at 210 3rd St. (at Howard), tel. (415) 495-7301, open for business Mon.-Sat. 8 a.m.-10 p.m., Sun. 8-6. You can also arrange to send a telegram (24 hours a day) if you have a credit card, by calling toll-free (800) 227-5899.

Emergency Assistance: Safety And Health

In any emergency, get to a telephone and dial 911—the universal emergency number in California. Depending upon the emergency, police, fire, and/or ambulance personnel will be dispatched. Runaways can call home free, anytime, no questions asked, by dialing the toll-free **Runaway Hotline,** tel. (800) 843-5200. Other 24-hour crisis and emergency hotlines include: **Helpline,** 772-HELP; **Rape Crisis** (operated by Women Against Rape, or WAR), tel. (415) 647-7273, the number to call in the event of any violent assault; **Suicide Prevention,** tel. 221-1423; **Drug Line,** tel. 752-3400; **Alcoholics Anonymous,** tel. 661-1828; **Narcotics Anonymous,** tel. 621-8600, and **Poison Control,** tel. 476-6600.

The San Francisco Police Department sponsors several Japanese-style *kobans* or police mini-station neighborhood kiosks, in case you need law enforcement assistance (and are lucky enough to be nearby, when they're open, when you do). One is situated in the tourist-thick cable car zone at Market and Powell, the **Hallidie Plaza Koban,** staffed Tues.-Sat. 10 a.m.-6 p.m. The **Chinatown Koban** is on Grant between Washington and Jackson, open daily 1-9 p.m., and the **Japantown Koban** at Post and Buchanan is staffed Mon.-Fri. 11 a.m.-7 p.m.

San Francisco General Hospital on Potrero Hill at 1001 Potrero Ave. (at 22nd St.), tel. (415) 206-8000 (911 or 206-8111 for emergencies), provides 24-hour medical emergency and trauma care services. Another possibility is **The Medical Center at the University of California, San Francisco,** 505 Parnassus Ave. (at 3rd Ave.), tel. 476-1000. (There's a **dental clinic** nearby, too, tel. 476-1891 or 476-5814 for emergencies). Convenient for most visitors is **Saint Francis Memorial Hospital** on Nob Hill, 900 Hyde St., tel. 775-4321, which offers no-appointment-needed clinic and urgent care medical services as well as a Center for Sports Medicine, tel. 474-4525, and a physician referral service, tel. 775-4441. Other drop-in medical clinics include **Access Health Care,** downtown at 26 California St. (at Drumm), tel. 397-2881.

For nonemergency referrals, call the **San Francisco Medical Society,** tel. (415) 567-6230, and the **San Francisco Dental Society,** tel. 421-1435. The independent **Medical and Dental Referral Service,** tel. 673-3189, is sponsored by Bay Area Physicians for Human Rights. (At this point in time, in America those rights don't include affordable universal health care, so inquire in advance about fees.) The **Haight-Ashbury Switchboard,** tel. 431-1714, provides medical and legal referrals as well as housing and ride-sharing information (recorded).

TRANSPORTATION: GETTING TO AND FROM TOWN

At least on pleasure trips, Californians and other Westerners typically drive into the Bay Area. The only routes into San Francisco by land: via Hwy. 101 from the north and across the fabled Golden Gate Bridge ($3 toll to get into the city, no cost to get out); via I-80 from Oakland/Berkeley across the increasingly choked-with-traffic Bay Bridge ($2 toll to get into the city, no cost to get out); and from the south (from the coast or from San Jose and other South Bay/peninsula communities) via Hwy. 1, Hwy. 101, or I-280. Whichever way you come and go, avoid morning and afternoon/evening rush hours at all costs. The Bay Area's traffic congestion is truly horrendous.

San Francisco And Oakland Airports
The **San Francisco International Airport (SFO),** tel. (415) 721-0800, is about 15 miles south of the city via Hwy. 101, perched on a point of land at the edge of the bay. (That's one of the thrills here: taking off and landing just above the water.) Each of the three terminals—North, Central (or International), and South—has two levels, the lower for arrivals, the upper for departures. San Francisco's is the fifth-busiest airport in the U.S., seventh in the world, with 80 gates for shuffling some 32 million passengers per year. Over 40 major scheduled carriers (and smaller ones, including air charters) serve SFO. There's protected parking for 7,000 cars, best for short-term car storage.

San Francisco International has its quirks. For one thing, its odd horseshoe shape often makes for a long walk for transferring passengers; there's no "people mover" and people seem to avoid the second-floor intraterminal bus. (In all fairness, though, since SFO is primarily an origin/destination airport, for most travelers this isn't a problem.) With such a high volume of air traffic—an average of 1,260 flights per day—delays are all too common, especially when fog rolls in and stays.

People complain, too, that the airport always seems to be under major construction. A $1.7 billion dollar expansion project, begun in 1992 and scheduled for completion by 1995, is now underway. (A new international terminal is just part of the program.) A major ($512 million) remodel was completed in the late 1980s, with some pleasant consequences—like the permanent **"Images of Mexico"** cultural display, with masks and such, in the South Terminal connector (beyond the security check). And there are outstanding changing exhibits along United's North Terminal connector. Upstairs in the International Terminal is an **AT&T Communications Center,** open 8 a.m.-10 p.m., with special phone facilities to allow callers to pay the attendants (multilingual) in cash and a six-person conference room set up for teleconferencing (fax, too). Other airport facilities include restaurants (the **Bay View Restaurant** in the South Terminal, the **North Beach Deli** in the North), the South Terminal's **California Marketplace** (where you can get some wine and smoked fish or crab to go with that sourdough bread you're packing), and the North Terminal's **Author's Bookstore,** where titles by Bay Area and California writers are prominent.

Due to its excellent service record and relatively lower volume, many travelers prefer flying into and out of efficient, well-run **Oakland International Airport** just across the bay, tel. (510) 577-4000, with fairly easy public transit connections from downtown San Francisco in addition to very convenient shuttle service (see below).

Airport Shuttles, Taxis
If flying into and out of SFO, avoid driving if at all possible. (To paraphrase that old advertising jingle, "Leave the headaches to someone else.") Airport shuttles are abundant, fairly inexpensive, and generally reliable. Most companies offer at-your-door pick-up service if you're heading to the airport (advance reservations usually required) and—coming from the airport—take you right where you're going. The usual fare, depending upon the company, is $8-10 per person (one-way), for SFO/San Francisco service. (Inquire about prices for other shuttle options.) The blue-and-gold **SuperShuttle** fleet, with some 100 vans coming and going all the time, tel. (415) 558-8500 *to* the airport, tel. 871-7800 *from* the airport, is always a good bet. When

you arrive at SFO, shuttle vans (no reservation needed) to the city are available on the upper level of all terminals at the outer island. To arrange a trip to the airport, call and make your pick-up reservation at least a day in advance. (And be ready when the shuttle arrives. They're usually on time.) Group, convention, and charter shuttles are also available, and you can pay on board with a major credit card. (Exact fare depends on where you start and end.) Usually cheapest ($7, children $3), with shuttles running every 20 minutes, is **SFO Airporter,** tel. 495-8404, with nonstop runs between the airport and the Financial District or Union Square. (No reservations required, either way.) **Francisco's Adventure,** tel. 821-0903, specializes in Spanish-speaking tours as well as shuttle service from the city to and from SFO and the San Jose airport. **EZ Way Out Shuttle Service,** located in Hayward, tel. (510) 887-6226, provides door-to-door and hotel service throughout the Bay Area to and from SFO and both Oakland and San Jose airports. **Oakairporter** in Oakland, tel. (510) 568-RIDE or toll-free (800) 534-ABUS, offers 24-hour, daily shuttle service between San Francisco city and the Oakland International Airport. (Wheelchair-accessible vehicles are available upon request.) A company specializing in shuttle service between most Bay Area suburban communities and SFO, and hourly door-to-door service between any location in San Francisco and the Oakland Airport, is **Bayporter Express, Inc.,** tel. (415) 467-1800 or toll-free (800) 287-6783. **Marin Airporter** in Larkspur, tel. (415) 461-4222, provides service every half-hour from various Marin communities to SFO daily, 4:30 a.m.-11 p.m., and from SFO to Marin County 5:30 a.m.-midnight.

San Mateo County Transit (SamTrans), tel. toll-free (800) 660-4287 for route information, offers extensive peninsula public transit, including express and regular buses from SFO to San Francisco. And it's cheap, too (less than $1). Buses leave the airport every 30 minutes from very early morning to just after midnight; call for exact schedule. Luggage limits for the express bus—carry-on only—makes the regular bus, a 10-minute-longer ride, the only option for heavily laden travelers.

Taxis, of course, are another option. From SFO to San Francisco, the cost will be $25-30. **Standard San Francisco taxi fare,** which ap-plies also to around-town trips, is $2 for the first mile, $1.50 per additional mile (plus tip, usually 15%). Among the 24-hour taxi companies available: **DeSoto Cab Co.,** tel. (415) 673-1414, **Luxor Cab,** tel. 282-4141, **Veteran's Taxicab Company,** tel. 552-1300, and **Yellow Cab,** tel. 626-2345.

By Bus And By Train
The **Transbay Terminal** just south of Market St. between 1st and Fremont, 425 Mission St., tel (415) 495-1551 or 495-1569, is the city's regional transportation hub. On the second floor there's an information center, with displays, maps, and fee-free phone lines for relevant transit systems. **Greyhound** is here, tel. 558-6789, with buses coming and going at all hours. **Golden Gate Transit** buses to and from Marin County and vicinity; the East Bay's **AC Transit,** buses, tel. 839-2882; and **San Mateo County Transit (SamTrans)** buses from as far south as Palo Alto, tel. toll-free (800) 660-4287, also connect at the Transbay Terminal. Shuttle buses also take passengers across the bay to the **Amtrak** station at 1707 Wood St. (at 17th St.) in Oakland, tel. (510) 654-4613 or toll-free (800) USA-RAIL, where you can make train connections both north and south. (For more information on Northern California Amtrak train and bus connections, see "Oakland," "San Jose And Vicinity," and "Sacramento Practicalities.")

Primarily a regional commute service, **CalTrain,** tel. (415) 557-8661 or toll-free (800) 558-8661 within Northern California, runs south to Palo Alto and the Amtrak station in San Jose, with further connections (by bus) to Santa Cruz. The San Francisco CalTrain depot is at 4th and Townsend streets.

Ferry Transport
Since the city is surrounded on three sides by water, ferry travel is an unusual (and unusually practical) San Francisco travel option. And historically, before the construction of the Golden Gate Bridge in 1937, it was the *only* way to travel from the North and East bay areas. Nowadays, the ferries function both as viable commuter and tourist transit services. (See "Delights And Diversions" for more about ferry tours and other oceangoing entertainment.) The **Blue & Gold Fleet** is docked at Fisherman's Wharf, Pier 39, tel. (415) 781-7877, and offers roundtrip (two-way) service daily from the Jack London

Waterfront in Oakland and Alameda's Gateway Center to San Francisco's Ferry Building and Pier 39 (four departures both morning and evening). One-way fare is $3 on weekdays, $3.50 on weekends, including AC Transit and Muni transfers. A discount coupon book (10 roundtrips for $25) is also available. **Golden Gate Ferries** at the foot of Market Street, headquartered in the Ferry Building, tel. 332-6600, specializes in runs to and from Sausalito (adults $3.50) and more frequent large-ferry (725 passenger capacity) trips to and from Larkspur ($2.20 adults on weekdays, $3 on weekends). Family rates available, and the disabled and seniors (over age 65) travel at half fare.

The very busy **Red & White Fleet** at Fisherman's Wharf, Pier 41 and Pier 43½, tel. (415) 546-BOAT or toll-free (800) BAY CRUISE, offers daily service (departing from San Francisco at Pier 43½) between the city and both Sausalito and Tiburon in Marin County, one-way fare $4.50 adults. (Commute ferries from these communities, on weekdays, arrive at and also depart from the Ferry Building.) Red & White also runs ferries to Angel Island from both San Francisco (Pier 43½) and Vallejo (Vallejo Ferry Terminal), daily in summer, weekends only otherwise, roundtrip fare $8 adults from San Francisco, $10.50 from Vallejo. Daily ferry service to Vallejo departs from and returns to Pier 41 regularly, one-way adult fare $7.50, though limited commute service also connects at the Ferry Building. The Alcatraz ferries also depart and return from Pier 41, the $8.50 adult roundtrip fare including Red & White's audio tour. (For more information about the Alcatraz adventure, see "Touring the Real Rock.") The company also offers special ferry-and-bus tour packages to Marine World Africa USA in Vallejo, and to Muir Woods (via Tiburon), in addition to its audio-narrated Golden Gate Bay Cruise.

TRANSPORTATION: GETTING AROUND TOWN

San Francisco drivers are among the craziest in California. Whether they're actually demented, just distracted, insanely rude, or perhaps intentionally driving to a different drummer, walkers beware. The white lines of a pedestrian crosswalk seem to serve as sights, making people easier targets. Even drivers must adopt a heads-up attitude. In many areas streets are narrow, vertical grades awesome. And finding a parking place requires psychic skills. So while many people drive into and out of the Bay Area's big little city, if at all possible many use public transit to get around town.

But some people really want to drive in San Francisco. Others don't *want* to, but need to, due to the demands of their schedules. A possible compromise: if you have a car but can't stand the thought of driving it through the urban jungle yourself, hire a driver. You can hire a chauffeur, and even arrange private sightseeing tours and other outings, through companies like **WeDriveU, Inc.,** 60 E. 3rd Ave. in San Mateo, tel. (415) 579-5800. Other local limousine companies may be willing to hire-out just a city-savvy driver; call and ask.

Though those maniacal bicycle delivery folks somehow manage to daredevil their way through downtown traffic—note their bandages, despite protective armor—for normal people cycling is a no-go proposition downtown and along heavy-traffic thoroughfares. Bring a bike to enjoy the Golden Gate National Recreation Area and other local parks, though it may be easier to rent one—from rental outlets along Stanyan at the eastern edge of Golden Gate Park, like **Lincoln Cyclery** at 722 Stanyan, tel. (415) 221-2415, or, out in the avenues just a few blocks from the Presidio, **Presidio Bike Shop,** 5335 Geary, tel. 752-2453.

Car Rental Agencies

Some of the least expensive car rental agencies have the most imaginative names. **Bob Leech's Auto Rental** near the airport in South San Francisco, 435 S. Airport Blvd., tel. (415) 583-2727 or toll-free (800) 325-1240, specializes in new Toyotas, from $20 per day with 150 fee-free miles. (You must carry a valid major credit card and be at least 23 years old; call for a ride from the airport.) Family-owned **Reliable Rent-A-Car** downtown at 349 Mason, tel. 928-4414, rents new cars with free pick-up and return for a starting rate of $19 per day ("any car, any time"). That all-American innovation **Rent-A-Wreck,** between Hyde and Leavenworth at 555 Ellis, tel. 776-8700, rents out midsize used cars for $29 each day with 100 fee-free miles, or $159 per week with 700 free miles, $.20 per mile above those limits.

The more well-known national car rental agencies have desks at the airport, as well as at other locations. Though car rental fees are usually higher than those quoted above—rates are determined by vehicle make and model, length of rental, day of the week (sometimes season), and total mileage—special coupon savings or substantial discounts through credit card company or other group affiliations can lower the cost considerably. If price really matters, check around. Consult the telephone book for all local locations of the companies listed below.

Avis Rent-A-Car is downtown at 675 Post St., tel. (415) 885-5011 or toll-free (800) 331-1212, and **Budget Rent-A-Car** is at 321 Mason, tel. 875-6850 or (800) 527-0700. Downtown, **Dollar Rent-A-Car** is opposite the Hilton Hotel at 364 O'Farrell, tel. 771-5300 or (800) 800-4000, and **Enterprise** is at 1133 Van Ness Ave., tel. 441-3369 or (800) 325-8007. **General Rent-A-Car,** nationwide toll-free tel. (800) 327-7607, has an office near the airport, tel. 244-0555, plus downtown rentals desks at both the Holiday Inn in Chinatown/Financial District, 750 Kearny, tel. 433-6600, and the Mark Twain Hotel at 345 Taylor, tel. 441-8802. For **Hertz** rentals downtown, call 771-2200 or (800) 654-3131, or stop by the shop at 433 Mason. **Thrifty Rent-A-Car** is located at 299 Ellis St., tel. 673-6675 or (800) 367-2277.

For a transportation thrill, all you wannabe easy riders can rent a BMW or Harley-Davidson motorcycle for $60 a day (and up), plus insurance and cash or credit deposit, from **Dubbelju Tours & Service,** 271 Clara St., tel. (415) 495-2774 or 495-2803. Weekly and winter rates available. Open Mon.-Sat. 9 a.m.-1 p.m. or by appointment. German spoken.

And to get out of town for next to nothing, if you're carrying good-driver references, consider serving as a destination driver. The **Auto Driveaway Company** at 330 Townsend, tel. (415) 777-3740, offers an impressive array of destinations. You must be at least 21, with a valid U.S. driver's license and the means for a substantial cash deposit ($250-300, refunded when you deliver the car).

Parking Regulations And Curb Colors

If you're driving, it pays to know the local parking regulations as well as rules of the road—it'll cost you if you don't.

Curbing your wheels is the law when parking on San Francisco's hilly streets. What this means: turn your wheels *toward the street* when parked facing uphill (so your car will roll into the curb if your brakes and/or transmission don't hold), and turn them *toward the curb* when facing downhill.

Also, pay close attention to painted curb colors; the city parking cops take violations fairly seriously. **Red curbs** mean absolutely no stopping or parking. **Yellow** means loading zone (for vehicles with commercial plates only), half-hour time limit; **yellow and black** means loading zone for trucks with commercial plates only, half-hour limit; and **green, yellow, and black** means taxi zone. **Green** indicates a 10-minute parking limit for any vehicle, and **white** means five minutes only, effective during the operating hours of the adjacent business. As elsewhere in the state, **blue** indicates parking reserved only for vehicles with a state of California disabled placard or plate displayed. Pay attention, too, to posted street-cleaning parking limits, to time-limited parking lanes (open at rush hour to commuter traffic), and avoid even a quick-park at bus stops or in front of fire hydrants. Any violation will cost $20 or more, and the police can tow your car—which will cost you $100 or so (plus daily impound fees) to retrieve.

Parking And Parking Garages

If you're driving, you'll need to park. You also need to *find* parking, all but impossible in North Beach, the Haight, and other popular neighborhoods. San Franciscans have their pet parking theories and other wily tricks—some even consider the challenge of finding parking a sport, or at least a game of chance—but it's not so fun for visitors, who usually find it challenging enough just to find their way around. It's wise to park your car (and leave it parked, to the extent possible) then get around by public transit. Valet parking is available (for a price, usually at least $15 per day) at major and midsize hotels, and at or near major attractions, including shopping districts.

Call ahead to inquire about availability, rates, and hours at major public parking garages: **Fisherman's Wharf**, 665 Beach (at Hyde), tel. (415) 673-5197; **Downtown**, 833 Mission St., tel. 982-8522; **Downtown**, Mason and Ellis, tel. 771-1400 (ask for the garage); **Moscone Center,**

255 3rd St., tel. 777-2782; **Chinatown,** 733 Kearny (underground, near Portsmouth Square), tel. 982-6353; **Union Street,** 1910 Laguna, tel. 563-9820.

And good luck.

Public Transport: Muni

Though California's public budget crunch has also started crunching San Francisco—affecting levels and quality of services, and leading to some transport fare increases—the city's multifaceted **San Francisco Municipal Railway or Muni,** headquartered at 949 Presidio Ave., tel. (415) 673-Muni weekdays 7 a.m.-6 p.m., Sat.-Sun 9-5, is still the locals' public transit mainstay. One of the nation's oldest publicly owned transportation systems, Muni is far from feeble, managing to move almost 250 million people each year.

The city's buses, light-rail electric subway-and-surface streetcars, electric trolleys, and world-renowned cable cars are all provided by Muni. It costs $3 to ride the cable car. (It's odd that people stand in long lines at the Powell and Market turnaround, since it actually makes much more sense—no waiting, unless there's absolutely no space available—to grab on at Union Square or other spots en route.) Otherwise, regular Muni fare is $1 ($.25 for seniors and youth, children under age five free), exact coins required, and includes free transfers valid for two changes of vehicle in any direction within a two-hour period. If you'll be making lots of trips around town, pick up a multi-trip discount **Muni Passport** (which includes cable car transit), available for sale at the Muni office, the Convention & Visitors Bureau information center downtown, at Union Square's TIX outlet (see "The Performing Arts" under "Delights and Diversions" above), at the City Hall information booth, and at the Cable Car Museum. A one-day pass costs $6, a three-day pass $10, and a seven-day pass $15. Monthly passes are also available, $32.

Muni route information is published in the local telephone book yellow pages, or call for route verification (phone number listed above). Better yet, though, for a thorough orientation, are various Muni publications, most of which are available wherever Muni Passports are sold (and usually at the Transbay Terminal). A good overview and introduction is provided (free) by

"The Muni Guide" pamphlet and the very useful, seasonally updated **"TimeTables,"** which lists current route and time information for all Muni transit. Especially useful for travelers is Muni's **"Tours of Discovery"** brochure, which lists popular destinations and possible tours with suggested transit routes (including travel time) and optional transfers and side trips. But the best all-around guide, easy to carry in pocket or purse, is the official annual **"Muni Street & Transit Map"** ($1.50), available at bookstores and grocery stores in addition to the usual outlets. The Muni map explains and illustrates major routes, access points, frequency of service, and also shows BART and Muni Metro subway stops, along with the CalTrain route into San Francisco. As a city map, it's a good investment, too.

San Francisco's **Muni buses** are powered by internal-combustion engines, and each is identified by a number and an area or street name (such as #7 Haight or #29 Sunset). Similarly numbered local **trolleys** or streetcars are actually electrically operated buses, drawing power from overhead lines, and are most notable downtown and along the steepest routes. The summers-only **Historic Trolley Festival** is actually a do-it-yourself party, achieved by climbing aboard Muni's international fleet of vintage electric streetcars (F-Market) that start at the Transbay Terminal and run along Market Street to and from Castro.

The **Muni Metro** refers to the five-line system of streetcars or light-rail vehicles, often strung together into trains of up four cars, that run underground along Market Street and radiate out into the neighborhoods. Metro routes are identified by letters in conjunction with point of destination (J-Church, K-Ingleside, L-Taraval, M-Oceanview, and N-Judah). Some of the newer 1990s Metro streetcars will be "articulated," meaning that they bend in the middle, something like an accordion.

Historic Transport: The Cable Cars

With or without those Rice-a-Roni ads, Muni's cable cars are a genuine San Francisco treat. (Don't allow yourself to be herded onto one of those rubber-tired motorized facsimiles that tend to cluster at Union Square, Fisherman's Wharf, and elsewhere. They are not cable cars, just lures for confused tourists.) San Francisco's cable cars are a national historic landmark, a system called "Hallidie's Folly" in honor of inventor Andrew S. Hallidie when these antiques made their debut on August 2, 1873. The only vehicles of their kind in the world, cable cars were created with the city's challenging vertical grades in mind. They are "powered" by an underground cable in perpetual motion, and by each car's grip-and-release mechanism. Even though maximum speed is about nine mph, that can seem plenty fast when the car snaps around an S-curve. (They aren't kidding when they advise riders to hold on to their seats.) After a complete $67.5 million-dollar system overhaul in the early 1980s, 26 "single-enders" now moan and groan along the two Powell Street routes, and 11 "double-enders" make the "swoop loop" along California Street. (New cars are occasionally added to the city's collection.) To get a vivid education in how cable cars work, visit the reconstructed Cable Car Barn and Museum.

Public Transport: BART

The Bay Area's space-age, 71-mile **Bay Area Rapid Transit** or BART system headquartered in Oakland, tel. (510) 464-6000, calls itself "the tourist attraction that gets people to the other tourist attractions." Fair enough. Heck, it is pretty thrilling to zip across to Oakland and Berkeley underwater in the Transbay Tube. And at least as far as it goes, BART is a good get-around alternative for people who would rather not drive. There isn't yet much BART service on the San Francisco side of the Bay, with eight (underground) BART stations in San Francisco, the line ending at Daly City. But the system takes you to Oakland/Berkeley, then north to Richmond, south to Fremont, or east to Concord. (BART Express buses extend transit service to other East Bay communities.)

A variety of publications can be helpful, including the annual **"All About BART"** (with fares, travel times, and other details), **"Fun Goes Farther on BART,"** and the **"We Stop Where You Shop"** BART guide to major Bay Area shopping centers. BART trains operate Mon.-Fri. 4 a.m.-midnight, Sat. 6 a.m.-midnight, and Sun. 8 a.m.-midnight. Exact fare depends upon your destination, but it'll be $3 or less. For a special $2.60 "excursion fare," you can tour the whole system; just don't walk through the computerized exits, or you'll have to pay again before you get back on. Tickets are dispensed at machines based at each station. (Change machines, for coins or dollar bills, are nearby.) If you don't have a current Muni map, check out each station's color-keyed wall maps that show destinations and routes.

BOB RACE

THE SAN FRANCISCO BAY AREA

"Everything in life is somewhere else, and you get there in a car," observed the late American essayist E.B. White. And so it is, for the most part, once outside San Francisco with one's sights set on the wilds, scrambling through the suburbia that fringes the bay on all sides.

Worth exploring in its almost endless urbanism, the Bay Area also has its own wildness and wayside pleasures. As White also said: "I would feel more optimistic about a bright future for man if he spent less time proving that he can outwit Nature and more time tasting her sweetness and respecting her seniority." The San Francisco Bay Area offers ample opportunity for both.

THE PENINSULA

Sticking out into the Golden Gate like an aristocratic nose is the city and county of San Francisco, the northern tip of the San Francisco Peninsula. South along the San Mateo County coastline is **Daly City,** its hillside neighborhoods almost immediately recognizable as the inspiration for folksinger Malvina Reynolds's "Little Boxes" lyrics: "And they're all made out of ticky tacky and they all look just the same." (Inspiring in an entirely different sense, even quite accessible from SFO, is Daly City's **Full Moon Cafe** on Grand Street. Outside are fresh trout in aquariums. Inside, expect authentic Chinese fare in huge portions—at very reasonable prices). Smaller communities, including **Pacifica** and **Half Moon Bay,** pop up alongside the string of state beaches that continue down the coast as far as the northern elephant seal refuge at Año Nuevo. Just inland from the coast is a small nugget among the parks collected into the Bay Area's Golden Gate National Recreation Area, Sweeney Ridge near San Andreas Lake. There are also various state and local parks.

South from the city along the shores of San Francisco Bay is **Brisbane** (which merges with Daly City) and undeveloped San Bruno Mountain County Park, then a stretch of the San Francisco Bay National Wildlife Refuge and a slew of bayside communities stretching into Santa Clara County and the high-tech Silicon Valley suburbs that spread out from **San Jose.**

South from San Francisco along the peninsula's inland spine is **Colma,** an incorporated city inside Daly City where the dead outnumber the living by more than 2,000 to one, due to Colma's cemetery industry. Among this city of the dead's most famous residents are Ishi, gunfighter Wyatt Earp, riveted blue jeans creator Levi Strauss, sculptor Benjamin Bufano, and baseball batting champ Lefty O'Doul (whose gravestone lists his statistics and this comment: "He was here at a good time and had a good time while he was here").

After the one-time dairy town of **Millbrae** comes down-to-the-bayshore **Burlingame** (the West's first community dedicated to the country-club lifestyle) and very highbrow **Hillsborough,** founded in 1851 by a deserter from the British Navy, just north of **San Mateo.** San Mateo spreads into **Belmont,** which collides with **San Carlos** and the outskirts of **Redwood City,** named for its brisk 1800s business as a redwood-lumber port. **Atherton,** nearby **Menlo Park,** and economically depressed **East Palo Alto** all stand in the intellectual shadow of **Palo Alto,** home of California's prestigious Stanford University and the contentious Hoover Institution.

THE SAN MATEO COASTLINE: FROM PACIFICA SOUTH

The unstable wave-whipped coast south of San Francisco is all buff-colored bluffs and sandy beaches faced with rough rocks. Often foggy in summer, with birdwatching and whalewatching drawing the crowds in winter, the San Mateo County coastline is usually superb for great escapes from late summer into autumn. Though wetsuit-clad surfers brave the snarling swells in gale-force winds, swimming is dangerous even on serene sunny days due to treacherous undertows. Many of the region's beaches are officially accessible as state beaches or local beach

parks; others are state owned but undeveloped, or privately owned. Almost 20 miles of this 51-mile-long coastline are included as part of the San Mateo Coast State Beaches, starting with Daly City's **Thornton Beach** (popular for fishing and picnicking) in the north and ending at tiny **Bean Hollow State Beach** just north of Año Nuevo in the south. Though campgrounds are available inland, seaside public camping is possible only at **Half Moon Bay State Beach.** For more information contact: **San Mateo State Beaches,** 95 Kelly Ave., Half Moon Bay 94019, tel. (415) 726-6238. For more information on public-transit access to the San Mateo coast, call **SamTrans** at toll-free (800) 660-4287.

Pacifica

The self-proclaimed Fog Capital of California, Pacifica is a sometimes dreary place with (sunny day) good views, good food, and *attitude.* Come here in late September for the annual **Pacific Coast Fog Fest,** tel. (415) 346-4446, which features a Fog Calling Contest (almost everyone's a winner), the Phileas Fogg Balloon Races, high-octane alcoholic "fogcutters" (if drinking, *don't* drive off into the fog), plus a fog fashion show.

At **Sharp Park State Beach** along Beach Blvd. (reached from Hwy. 1 via Paloma Ave., Clarendon Rd., or streets in between) is the Pacifica Pier, popular for fishing and winter whale-watching. Migrating gray whales are attracted to the abundant plankton at the end of the community's sewage outfall pipe (the treatment plant is the building with Spanish arches). Some old salts here say the great grays swim so close to the pier you can smell the fish on their breath.

Farther south is sort-of secluded **Rockaway Beach,** a striking black-sand beach in a small rectangular cove where the coast has backed away from the rocky bluffs. Hotels and restaurants cluster beyond the rock-reinforced parking lot.

South Of Pacifica

Long and narrow **Montara State Beach** offers rock-and-sand beachcombing, and hiking. The state's tiny **Gray Whale Cove Beach** here is a concession-operated clothing-optional beach, open for all-over tans only to those 18 and over. Just south of Montara proper is the cypress-strewn **Moss Beach** area,

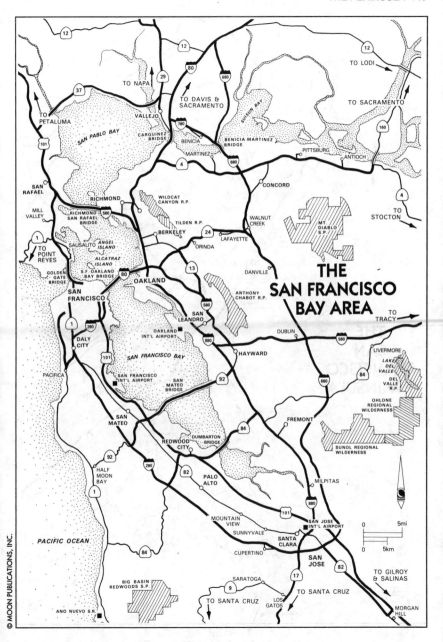

THE
SAN FRANCISCO
BAY AREA

© MOON PUBLICATIONS, INC.

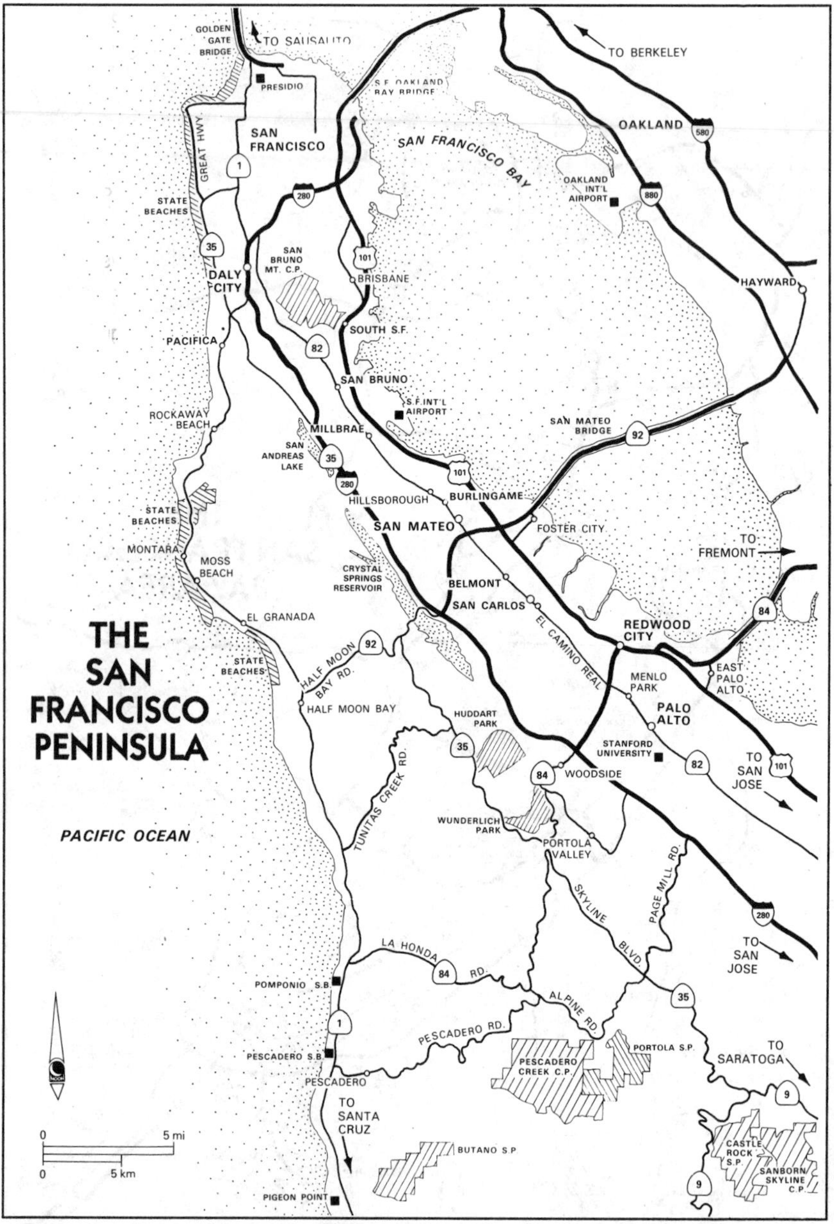

THE SAN FRANCISCO PENINSULA

GOLDEN GATE BRIDGE

TO SAUSALITO

TO BERKELEY

PRESIDIO

S.F. OAKLAND BAY BRIDGE

OAKLAND

580

SAN FRANCISCO

GREAT HWY

SAN FRANCISCO BAY

1

280

STATE BEACHES

35

DALY CITY

SAN BRUNO MT. C.P.

BRISBANE

101

Oakland Int'l Airport

880

HAYWARD

PACIFICA

82

SOUTH S.F.

ROCKAWAY BEACH

SAN BRUNO

S.F. INT'L AIRPORT

MILLBRAE

35

SAN ANDREAS LAKE

San Mateo Bridge

92

STATE BEACHES

280

MONTARA

MOSS BEACH

HILLSBOROUGH

BURLINGAME

101

SAN MATEO

FOSTER CITY

TO FREMONT

EL GRANADA

CRYSTAL SPRINGS RESERVOIR

BELMONT

SAN CARLOS

EL CAMINO REAL

REDWOOD CITY

STATE BEACHES

HALF MOON BAY RD.

92

MENLO PARK

EAST PALO ALTO

84

THE SAN FRANCISCO PENINSULA

HALF MOON BAY

TUNITAS CREEK RD.

HUDDART PARK

35

STANFORD UNIVERSITY

PALO ALTO

82

TO SAN JOSE

101

PACIFIC OCEAN

84

WOODSIDE

WUNDERLICH PARK

PORTOLA VALLEY

SKYLINE BLVD.

PAGE MILL RD.

280

TO SAN JOSE

LA HONDA RD.

84

POMPONIO S.B.

ALPINE RD.

35

TO SARATOGA

1

PESCADERO RD.

PESCADERO S.B.

PESCADERO CREEK C.P.

PORTOLA S.P.

9

PESCADERO

TO SANTA CRUZ

BUTANO S.P.

CASTLE ROCK S.P.

SANBORN SKYLINE C.P.

9

PIGEON POINT

0   5 mi

0   5 km

© MOON PUBLICATIONS, INC.

named for the delicate sea mosses that drape shoreline rocks at low tide.

Best for exploration from November through January are the 30 acres of tidepools at the **James V. Fitzgerald Marine Reserve** (open daily sunrise to sunset), which stretches south from Montara Point to Pillar Point and Princeton-by-the-Sea. At high tide, the Fitzgerald Reserve looks like any old sandy beach with a low shelf of black rocks emerging along the shore, but when the ocean rolls back, these broad rock terraces and their tidepools are exposed. For area state park information call (415) 726-6203, or for information on low-tide prime time at the Fitzgerald Reserve, call 728-3548; for more about docent-led guided tours, contact the Coyote Point Museum, tel. 342-7755.

Nearby, along Hwy. 1 in Montara, is **McNee Ranch State Park** and Montara Mountain, with hiking trails and great views of the Pacific. Next south is **El Granada,** an unremarkable town except for the remarkable music showcased here on a regular basis by the **Bach Dancing & Dynamite Society, Inc.,** the longest-running venue for jazz greats in the Bay Area. Begun in 1958 when jazz fanatic Pete Douglas started allowing musicians to hang out at his house and jam, public concerts blast off every Sunday (except around Christmas and New Year's) in a baroque beatnik beachhouse technically in Miramar. The family lives downstairs; upstairs at "the Bach" is the concert hall and deck, though guests are free to amble down to the beach and back at all times. Admission isn't charged, but a contribution of $10-15 or so is the usual going rate for Sunday concerts.

The Dancing & Dynamite Society has become so popular that Friday night candlelight dinner concerts cosponsored by local businesses or other supporters are also offered (reservations and advance payment required). For $5 anyone can join the society and receive its newsletter and calendar of coming attractions. For more information, contact: Bach Dancing & Dynamite Society, P.O. Box 302, El Granada 94018, tel. (415) 726-4143.

Area Accommodations

Inexpensive and incredibly pleasant for a coast overnight is the AYH **Point Montara Lighthouse Hostel** on Hwy. 1 at 16th St., P.O. Box 737, Montara 94037, tel. (415) 728-7177. It's quite popular so reservations (by mail only) are advisable. Rates are $9 for AYH members, more for nonmembers, extra for couple or family rooms in the new, wheelchair-accessible annex. (For more information, see "Near Santa Cruz.")

Fairly new in the neighborhood is **The Goose and Turrets Bed and Breakfast** at 835 George St., P.O. Box 937, tel. (415) 728-5451, a huge 1908 Italian-style seaside villa that dates back to the Bay Area's early bohemian days, when the adventurous and/or artistic rode the Ocean Shore Railroad from San Francisco to the arts colony and beach here. The five guest rooms are just part of the pleasure of this 6,000-square-foot home, which features great windows on its west wall. All rooms have private bathrooms and little luxuries, German down comforters and English towel warmers, with rates $80-95. French spoken. Breakfast is a four-course feast; tea and treats are served in the afternoon. And the family geese—Mrs. Goose and Mr. Turrets—*will* pose for photos when not busy announcing guests' arrivals.

The new English-style **Seal Cove Inn,** 221 Cypress Ave., Moss Beach 94038, tel. (415) 728-7325, is another find, an elegant and romantic inn overlooking the Fitzgerald Marine Reserve. The 10 guest rooms here each feature wood-burning fireplaces, refrigerators, TV, and ocean views; some have private decks. For small group meetings, there's even a conference room. Rates: $160-225. Motels (not many are inexpensive) pop up here and there along the coast.

Area Food

Traditional in Moss Beach is the straightforward Italian fare at **Dan's Place** on Virginia St. overlooking the Fitzgerald Reserve, tel. (415) 728-3343, open for lunch and dinner. The old **Moss Beach Distillery** in Moss Beach, at Beach and Ocean, tel. 728-5595, is now a romantic cliffside restaurant, very good for seafood, ribs, lamb, and veal. Fresh fish is the specialty at **The Shore Bird** in Princeton-by-the-Sea just down the coast at 390 Capistrano Rd., tel. 728-5541. Open for both lunch and dinner. **Barbara's Fish Trap** at 281 Capistrano Rd., tel. 728-7049, open daily for lunch and dinner, offers great Half Moon Bay views, fishnet kitsch decor, and fish selections that are a cut above the usual. Try the garlic prawns.

HALF MOON BAY

Known until the turn of the century as Spanish-town, Half Moon Bay was a farm community specializing in artichokes and Brussels sprouts and settled by Italians and Portuguese. Down and out during the early 1900s, things picked up during Prohibition when the area became a safe harbor for Canadian rumrunners. Fast becoming a fashionable Bay Area residential suburb famous for its pumpkins, Half Moon Bay also offers a rustic Main Street with shops, restaurants, and inns, plus pseudo-Cape Cod cluster developments along Hwy. 1.

New in the area is the **Burleigh Murray Ranch State Park,** still largely undeveloped, a former 1,300-acre dairy ranch now open to the public for day use. You can take a hike up the old ranch road, which winds up through the sycamores and alders along Mill Creek. About a mile from the trailhead is the ranch's most notable feature, the only known example of an English bank barn in California. This century-old structure relied on simple but ingenuous design, utilizing slope ("bank") and gravity to feed livestock most efficiently. Especially for those who can't remember even the basics of farm life, other outbuildings are also worth a peek. To get here, turn east on Higgins-Purisima Road from Hwy. 1 just south of Half Moon Bay. It's about two miles to the parking area (marked, on the left).

There's a Portuguese **Chamarita** parade and barbecue held here seven weeks after Easter. Over the July 4th weekend is the community's **Coastside County Fair and Rodeo.** But come to the very popular **Half Moon Bay Art and Pumpkin Festival** in October for pumpkin-carving and pie-eating contests, also the Great Pumpkin Parade. For more area events and other information contact the **Half Moon Bay/Coastside Chamber of Commerce** in the Caboose at 225 S. Cabrillo Hwy., P.O. Box 188, Half Moon Bay 94019, tel. (415) 726-5202.

Accommodations And Food

Reservations through Mistix, tel. (800) 444-7275, are usually required from March through October to guarantee a tent or RV campsite at the year-round **Half Moon Bay State Beach camground** (hot showers and all), though space is often available on non-weekend autumn days. Motels in Half Moon Bay tend to be on the pricey side. A nice mid-range choice is the **Harbor View Inn,** actually north of town in El Granada, tel. (415) 726-2329, with rooms from $64-74 (cheaper from January through mid-March). There's also a Best Western, the **Half Moon Bay Lodge,** on Hwy. 1 about 2½ miles south of the Hwy. 92 junction, tel. 726-9000, with rates from $96.

But the in thing in Half Moon Bay is inns. Much loved is the **Mill Rose Inn** bed and breakfast in "old town," 615 Mill St., Half Moon Bay 94019, tel. (415) 726-9794 or toll-free (800) 829-1794, a romantic Victorian with frills and fireplaces, spa, English gardens, excellent breakfasts. Rooms are $175-275, with reduced midweek rates. Another local favorite is the restored **San Benito House** country inn at 356 Main St., tel. 726-3425, with 12 rooms on the upper floor (two share a bath) for $59-121, upstairs sauna, redwood deck with flowers and firepit, plus a downstairs restaurant and saloon. The **Old Thyme Inn** at 779 Main St., tel. 726-1616, is $65-135 (less on weekdays) and includes some rooms with two-person whirlpools. For special occasions or extra privacy, the Garden Suite

Old Thyme Inn

features a private entrance ($210 per night on weekends and holidays, otherwise $145). The atmosphere here is very English, in a casually elegant style, with individually decorated rooms, some featuring fireplaces and/or in-room whirlpool tubs. Especially delightful for gardeners is the herb garden here, with over 80 varieties (true aficionados are allowed to take cuttings). Expect such things as homemade scones and marmalade with breakfast, possibly even French cherry flan. Another historic local favorite is **The Zaballa House,** almost next door to the San Benito House, 324 Main St., tel. 726-9123 or toll-free (800) 77-BNB4U, Half Moon Bay's oldest surviving building, circa 1859, now featuring four upstairs and five downstairs guest rooms, all with private bathrooms, several with double in-room whirlpool tubs, and four with fireplaces. Ask about the Halloween night special—quite reasonable, especially if you opt to stay overnight in "haunted" Room #6. Otherwise, rates are $60-150. Actually, seasonal specials (April Fool's Day and "Spring Fling," for example) and midweek rates can be real bargains at both The Old Thyme Inn and The Zaballa House.

Fairly new in the neighborhood is the contemporary **Cypress Inn** three miles north of Hwy. 92, just off Hwy. 1 at 407 Mirada Rd. (exit at Medio Ave.), Miramar 94109, right on the beach and just a few doors down from the Bach Dynamite & Dancing Society, tel. (415) 726-6002 or toll-free (800) 83-BEACH. The inn's motto is "in celebration of nature and folk art," and the distinctive rooms—each with an ocean view and private deck, fireplace, and luxurious private bath—do live up to it, whether you stay in the Rain, Wind, Sea, Sky, Star, Sun, or Moon rooms. For a special treat, head up into the Clouds (the penthouse). Gourmet breakfasts, afternoon tea, winetasting, and hors d'oeuvres included. Masseuse available too, by appointment. Room rates: $135-250. North of Half Moon Bay, too, is the **Pillar Point Inn** overlooking the harbor in Princeton-by-the-Sea, 380 Capistrano Rd. (P.O. Box 388, El Granada 94018), tel. 728-7377, all rooms with fireplaces and other modern amenities. Rates from $160 (lower on weekdays).

The **Half Moon Bay Bakery** at 514 Main, tel. (415) 726-4841, is also a stop on the local historic walking tour. The bakery still uses its original 19th-century brick oven and offers sand-wiches, salads, and pastries over the counter. Also quite popular are the **Pasta Moon** cafe, 356 Main St., tel. 726-5125, and the **San Benito House** restaurant downstairs at 356 Main, tel. 726-3425, noted for its French and Northern Italian country cuisine at dinner. Simpler but excellent lunches (including sandwich selections on homemade breads) served also. Open Thurs.-Sun. only, call for reservations. Excellent Sunday brunch.

FROM SAN GREGORIO SOUTH

On the coast just west of tiny **San Gregorio** is San Gregorio State Beach, with the area's characteristic bluffs, a mile-long sandy beach, and a sandbar at the mouth of San Gregorio Creek. San Gregorio proper is little more than a spot in the road, but the back-roads route via Stage Rd. from here to Pescadero is pastoral and peaceful.

Inland **Pescadero** ("Fishing Place") was named for the creek's once-teeming trout, not for any fishing traditions on the part of the town's Portuguese settlers. Both **Pomponio** and **Pescadero state beaches** offer small estuaries for same-named creeks: a small lagoon at Pomponio and the adjoining 584-acre Pescadero Marsh Natural Preserve; Pescadero Marsh is a feeding and nesting area for over 200 bird species as well as a successful blue heron rookery. (To birdwatch—best in winter—park at Pescadero State Beach near the bridge and walk via the Sequoia Audubon Trail, which starts below the bridge.) Rocky-shored **Bean Hollow State Beach** (it's a half-mile hike in) is better for tide-pooling than beachcombing, though there is a short stretch of sand, also picnic tables.

For a longer coast walk, head south to the **Año Nuevo** reserve, the point named by Vizcaino and crew shortly after New Year's Day in 1602. No matter what time of year it is—and the rare northern elephant seals who clamber ashore here are an item only in winter and spring—stop for a picnic and stroll Año Nuevo's three-mile-long beach.

Accommodations

The cheap place to stay in the area is the AYH **Pigeon Point Lighthouse Hostel** five miles south of the turnoff to Pescadero and just off Hwy. 1 via Pigeon Point Rd., tel. (415) 879-0633, with basic but quite adequate facilities in bunk and family rooms, plus on-the-cliffs hot tub, good tidepooling. Popular, reservations are usually essential. Rates are $9 for AYH members, $12 for nonmembers. (For more information, see "Near Santa Cruz.")

If the hostel is full, the campground at **Butano State Park** probably will be too—at least on Fridays, Saturdays, and holidays from May through September. Reached from Pescadero via Cloverdale Rd. (or from near Gazos Beach via Gazos Creek Rd.), park facilities include 21 family campsites, 19 walk-in sites, and a handful of backcountry trail camps. Reserve main campsites through Mistix, tel. (800) 444-7275, during the high season (otherwise, it's usually first-come, first-camped). Trail camp reservations must by made in advance through headquarters, P.O. Box 9, Pescadero 94060, tel. (415) 879-0173. For more comfortable comforts, the Spanish-style **Rancho San Gregorio** bed and breakfast at 5086 La Honda Rd. (Rt. 1, Box 54), San Gregorio 94074, tel. 747-0722, is a best bet, with just four attractive rooms (three have woodstoves; all have private baths). Many of the veggies and fruits served at breakfast are home-grown. Great hiking nearby. Rates: $80-125 on weekends, $65-90 on weekdays. Or head south along the coast. The **New Davenport Bed and Breakfast Inn** on Hwy. 1 about nine miles north of Santa Cruz, tel. (408) 426-4122, is a colorful oceanview hideaway with artist owners and beach access. Rates: $55-105.

Food

In Pescadero down-home **Duarte's Tavern,** 202 Stage Rd., tel. (415) 879-0464, is most noted for its artichoke soup and delicious olallieberry pie, not to mention the ever-changing fresh fish specials scrawled across the menu chalkboard. Open daily for breakfast, lunch, and dinner, reservations wise (especially in summer) for dinner and Sunday brunch. Nondescript **Dinelli's** in Pescadero, tel. 879-0106, is great for Greek-American fare. Near Pescadero is the **Phipps Ranch,** where berries, dried beans, baby lettuce, squash, and other local produce are available in season. (San Mateo County's "Coastside Harvest Trails" map lists other regional produce stands.)

Down the coast toward Santa Cruz, the **New Davenport Cash Store,** tel. (408) 426-4122, *is* a store, an arts and crafts gallery, but also an inexpensive eatery with healthy food (whole grains, salads, soups) in the Americanized Mexican tradition. Great desserts. Bed and breakfast rooms upstairs.

OTHER SAN MATEO PARKS: NORTH

Because the lupine-loving mission blue butterflies were wiped out elsewhere in the Bay Area, **San Bruno Mountain County Park** exists. Their last remaining habitat (on one east-facing slope) is now protected from development. San Bruno is a great almost-in-the-city hiking park also fine for picnics. Its trails are most enjoyable during the spring wildflower bloom, but the views are fabulous on any unfoggy day. Bay Area Mountain Watch and Friends of Endangered Species offer free group walks to butterfly and ancient Native American village sites.

To get here from San Francisco, head south on the Bayshore Freeway (Hwy. 101), take the Cow Palace-Brisbane exit, and follow Bayshore Blvd. past Geneva Ave. to Guadalupe Rd., turn right at Guadalupe and climb to the saddle, turn left at the park sign, follow Radio Rd. uphill all the way, and park near the telecommunications towers. For more information about San Bruno Mountain and other county parks, contact: **San Mateo County Parks and Recreation,** 590 Hamilton St., Redwood City 94063, tel. (415) 363-4020.

Down the bayshore at **Coyote Point County Park,** popular for fishing, sailboarding, swimming, and picnicking, is one of the best environmental science centers in the Bay Area: Coyote Point Museum for Environmental Education, tel. (415) 342-7755. Superb educational displays include the bay ecosystems exhibit and the world's largest bee tube. Special events scheduled year-round. Open Wed.-Fri. 10-5, weekends 1-5 p.m., small admission. If you've got some time and bikes on board, start from Coyote Point or the parking lot near the San Mateo Fishing Pier (at the eastern end of Hillsdale Boulevard) to explore the eight-mile **Bayfront Path,** a paved bicycling and walking trail, which heads south along the bay, meanders through area sloughs, then loops back to (and through) Foster City and Marina Lagoon. Leave early to avoid afternoon winds; pack a picnic if you'll be making a day of it. For a map of this and other bikeways in the area, call the San Mateo Department of Public Works, tel. 377-3315. For park information, call 573-2592. To the northwest, where Skyline Blvd. branches off from scenic I-280, is **Junipero Serra County Park,** with hiking and nature trails, playgrounds, picnicking, great views.

Sweeney Ridge just east of Hwy. 1 near Pacifica, and south of **Sharp County Park,** is a fairly new segment of the Bay Area's extensive Golden Gate National Recreation Area. The ridge offers great hiking and 360-degree views of San Francisco Bay and the Pacific, the same vantage point that Gaspar de Portola stumbled upon during his expedition to find Monterey Bay in 1769. From the Pacific coast side, the GGNRA trailhead up to Sweeney Ridge is near the Shelldance Bromeliad Nursery at 2000 Cabrillo Hwy. (Hwy. 1), on the left facing the hill. From the east, hike in from the trailhead just off Sneath Ln. from Skyline Boulevard. (However you arrive, wear good hiking boots or shoes and bring a sweater or jacket.) For more information, call (415) 666-7201.

Narrow **San Andreas Lake** and **Crystal Springs Reservoir** mark the route taken by the discouraged Gaspar de Portola expedition of 1769 (which he described as "that small company of persons, or rather say skeletons, who had been spared by scurvy, hunger, and thirst").

The lakes also mark the route of the San Andreas Fault. Due to chain-link fences and the hum of the freeway, modern-day adventurers will be disappointed with a hike along the San Andreas Trail, but the connecting Crystal Springs Riding and Hiking Trail to the south is worthwhile.

Worth it, too, is a moment of reverent reflection at the **Pulgas Water Temple** at the reservoir's south end just off Canada Rd., a monument to the elusive and liquid god of California progress. This circular Greek-style classic designed by architect Willis Polk marks the spot where the once-wild waters from behind Hetch Hetchy Dam in Yosemite are taken into custody by the San Francisco Water Department, originally established by gold-rush czar William Bourn in the 1860s as part of his Spring Valley Water Works. The old company is also enshrined here, near the two major reservoirs it built to provide water for up-and-coming San Francisco.

Also off Canada Rd. is Bourn's 17-acre **Filoli Mansion** and grounds, one of several mansions he built as temples to his wealth. This one was named from a condensation of his personal motto: FIght, LOve, LIfe. (Nighttime soap opera fans will recognize Filoli as Blake Carrington's "Dynasty" mansion.) This creation of San Francisco architect Willis Polk is filled with priceless furnishings from around the world. Almost more impressive, though, are Bourn's acres of formal gardens—best on a sunny day in spring. Open from mid-February through mid-November, mansion and garden tours are

Redwood groves as well as beaches are typical of the peninsula.

SANTA CRUZ COUNTY CONFERENCE & VISITORS COUNCIL

offered by Friends of Filoli, moderate admission fee, children under age 12 not allowed (and no one allowed even in the gift shop without reservations). For more information about tours and to make reservations, call (415) 364-2880.

South of Lower Crystal Springs Reservoir are two distinct parks connected via trails. **Huddart County Park,** almost 1,000 acres of cool canyons with second-growth redwoods, Douglas firs, and foothill oaks, offers a short trail system with ties to the Crystal Springs Trail to the north and the Skyline Trail that heads two miles south to **Wunderlich County Park,** with its own 25-mile trail system. To get to Huddart, take Hwy. 84 west to Kings Mountain Rd. in Woodside (stop off at the historic Woodside Store) and continue along Kings Mountain for two miles. From Wunderlich, the Skyline Trail continues south to Sky Londa. Across the Junipero Serra Freeway (I-280) and accessible via Edgewood Rd. is **Edgewood County Park,** a wonderful patch of open space threaded with trails, with abundant wildflowers from spring into summer.

OTHER SAN MATEO PARKS: SOUTH

Five miles inland from Año Nuevo State Preserve is **Butano State Park,** which offers 20 miles of excellent if strenuous hikes among redwoods, plus picnicking, camping, and summer campfire programs. For more information, call (415) 879-0173. Another worthy redwoods destination is **San Mateo Memorial County Park** eight miles east of Pescadero (via Pescadero Rd.), which features a nature museum, 200-foot-tall virgin trees, creek swimming, camping, and trails connecting with surrounding local and state parks. Adjacent **Pescadero Creek County Park** includes the steelhead trout stream's upper watersheds, 6,000 acres of excellent hiking. (The Old Haul Road and Pomponio trails link Pescadero to nearby Memorial and Portola parks.)

Just to the north outside La Honda (though the entrance is off Pescadero Rd.) is 867-acre **Sam McDonald County Park,** with rolling grasslands and redwoods, trails interconnecting with Pescadero Park, even a Sierra Club hiker's hut for overnights (call 415-327-8111 to reserve). To the southeast via Alpine Rd. and Portola State Park Rd. is **Portola State Park,** tel. 948-9098, rugged redwood terrain between Butano and Skyline ridges with backcountry hiking, a short nature trail, museum and visitor center, picnicking, and camping. Reservations through Mistix, tel. (800) 444-7275, are usually necessary from April through September for year-round family campsites (reserve trail camp through park headquarters).

In addition to public parks, the Midpeninsula Regional Open Space District administers other parkland, primarily preserves and limited-use areas perfect for hikers seeking even more seclusion in San Mateo and Santa Clara counties. Among these: **Purisima Creek Redwoods** southeast of Half Moon Bay; **Mount El Sereno** south of Saratoga; the **Long Ridge Preserve** near Big Basin; and the rugged chaparral **Sierra Azul-Limekiln Canyon Area** near Lexington Reservoir. For more information and maps, contact: Midpeninsula Regional Open Space District, Old Mill Office Center, Building C, Suite 135, 201 San Antonio Circle, Mountain View 94040, tel. (415) 949-5500.

For detailed information about sights, restaurants, and lodging in the region, contact any of the following chambers of commerce: the **San Mateo County Convention and Visitors Bureau,** 601 Gateway Blvd., South San Francisco 94080, tel. (415) 952-7600; the **Burlingame Chamber of Commerce,** 306 Lorton Ave., Burlingame, tel. 344-1735; the **San Carlos Chamber of Commerce,** 1250 San Carlos Ave., Suite 303, P.O. Box 1086, San Carlos 94070, tel. 593-1068; and the **Belmont Chamber of Commerce,** 1380 Civic Ln., P.O. Box 645, Belmont 94002, tel. 595-8696.

PALO ALTO

Characteristic of the San Francisco region, most Peninsula and South Bay communities offer up culture in surprising, usually delightful ways. In Palo Alto, hometown of Stanford University, cultural creativity is concentrated and condensed and always accessible—making this a choice destination when climbing down out of the hills. This is the place, after all, where the Silicon Valley computer revolution started—where, in the 1930s, Bill Hewlett and Dave Packard, founders of modern-day **Hewlett-Packard,** started their spare-time tinkering with electronic bells, whistles, and other gadgetry in a garage on Addison Avenue. (Their first creation was the audio oscillator, a sound-enhancing system first used by Walt Disney in *Fantasia,* which catapulted them into the corporate big leagues.)

Considered one of the Bay Area's best places to live, modern-day Palo Alto is an island of very contemporary and sophisticated affluence perhaps best summed up by the meditative classical-folk-jazz music of locally based **Windham Hill Records,** sounds people either love or dismiss as yuppie Muzak. Adjacent to Palo Alto is the predominantly black and Hispanic city of **East Palo Alto,** a newly independent, separate community with no banks, no shopping centers, few services, and a downward-spiraling economy.

The northernmost city in Santa Clara County, Palo Alto is not a typical tourist destination, which is in itself a major attraction for those tired of prepackaged community charm. For more information, including a current listing of member restaurants and accommodations, contact: **Palo Alto Chamber of Commerce,** 2450 El Camino Real, Suite 100, Palo Alto 94306, tel. (415) 324-3121. For local public transportation options, depending upon which way you're heading, contact: **CalTrain** (CalTrans), which serves the peninsula and San Francisco, tel. toll-free (800) 558-8661; **San Mateo County Transit (SamTrans),** tel. toll-free (800) 660-4287; or **Santa Clara County Transit,** tel. (415) 965-3100.

STANFORD UNIVERSITY

Once known as The Farm, the 9,000-acre campus of modern-day Stanford University was formerly Leland Stanford's Palo Alto stock farm, his spacious spread for thoroughbred racehorses. Some people now refer to Stanford as The Idea Farm, since this is the place that spawned birth control pills, gene splicing, heart transplants, the IQ test, the laser, the microprocessor, music synthesizers, and napalm—among other breakthroughs of the civilized world. Royalties from on-campus inventiveness earn private Stanford University over $5 million each year.

Though Stanford has a renowned medical school, a respected law school, and top-drawer departments in the sciences, most famous here is the **Hoover Institution on War, Revolution, and Peace,** which started out in 1919 to delineate and demonstrate "the evils of Karl Marx" with an original collection of five million World War I-related documents contributed by 40 governments. Critics of the Hoover Institution, both on-campus and off, suggest that the organization has become too ideological—tainting Stanford University's otherwise legitimate claims to intellectual objectivity—to stay on campus in the hallowed Hoover Tower and should establish headquarters elsewhere.

Next most famous on campus: the run-amok **Stanford University Marching Band,** a self-perpetuating autocracy still blamed by embarrassed alumni for "the Play" in 1982, when winning Stanford lost The Big Game to arch nemesis UC Berkeley across the bay with just four seconds remaining. When not getting trampled by football players for being in the wrong place at the wrong time, the Stanford band never marches (members say they don't know how) but instead swarms onto the field during half time and jostles into formations like Gumby's head, Ronald Reagan's nose, Jimmy Carter's hemorrhoids, the Death Star from *Star Wars,* and more mundane symbols like chainsaws and computers.

Keeping in mind the university motto—*Die Luft der Freiheit weht,* "the wind of freedom blows"—like other institutions in California, Stanford has all but been blown over recently, its prestige toppled by hard times. The 1989 Loma Prieta earthquake hit hard, damaging significant buildings, including the Stanford University Art Museum, the Memorial Church, and buildings surrounding the quad. Then, administrative scandals involving overbilling, and misappropriation, of some $480 million in federal research funds brought the rest of the roof down. Financial crises and cutbacks loom. Legal scholar and new university President Gerhard Casper, wooed from the windy city's University of Chicago, is expected to get Stanford's academic house in order again.

Stanford Sights

The sprawling Spanish-style campus, designed by Central Park's landscape architect Frederick Law Olmstead, is much too large to tour on foot. A good place to start is the campus **quadrangle,** where between-class undergraduate students mill around (some perhaps still proudly wearing T-shirts announcing the student body's unofficial motto: Work, Study, Get Rich). Get a campus map and other information on the second floor of the **Tresidder Student Union,** tel. (415) 723-4317 for general information, tel. 725-ARTS for special event tickets, or contact **Stanford University Guide and Visitor Service,** Building 170, Stanford 94305, tel. 723-2560, then set out by bike or on the free Marguerite Shuttle. Comprehensive student-guided tours are offered daily, except holidays and quarter breaks. For a tour of the **Hoover Observation Tower and Archives** (small fee), call 723-2053. Free one-hour **general campus** walking tours are fairly comprehensive; call 723-2560. Reservations are required for groups of 10 or more. (Tours leave from the Serra Street quadrangle entrance.) Finely focused tours of the **Stanford Linear Accelerator Center,** home of the quark, are led by graduate students; call 926-2204 for information and appointments. For unguided good times, try the hiking trails through the campus's wooded west end—or, for birdwatching, head out to the **Baylands Nature Preserve** outside Palo Alto at the end of Embarcadero Rd., tel. 329-2506.

The **Stanford University Art Museum** (on Museum Way near the hospital), tel. (415) 723-4177, is well worth a visit—at least when it's open. Closed for reconstruction and major repairs in the wake of the Bay Area's devastating 1989 earthquake, the majority of the museum's Rodin sculpture collection is temporarily on display at the downtown San Jose Museum of Art, at last report until 1993 or 1994. (Call for current information.) Under normal conditions, the Stanford University Art Museum is free and open to the public on weekends 1-5 p.m., and Tues.-Fri. 10-5. If you're in the neighborhood, stop anyway. The museum's best is outside on the lawn, in the **B. Gerald Cantor Rodin Sculpture Garden,** the most complete collection of Auguste Rodin original bronze-cast sculptures anywhere outside Paris. Included here are *The Martyr, The Thinker,* and the chaotic eight-ton *Gates of Hell,* flanked (as Rodin intended) by both *Adam* and *Eve.* The 20 outdoor sculptures can be enjoyed anytime, 24 hours a day, but the best place to start the Rodin tour is inside the Rodin Gallery, where an early version of *The Burghers of Calais, The Kiss,* and other examples of his most delicate touch are (usually) displayed.

That brawling bad boy of American letters is showcased in the Stanford Library's **Charles D. Field Collection of Ernest Hemingway,** which includes first editions, translations, stories and poems, published and unpublished letters, even galley proofs. (While a student at Stanford, another American literary lion—double-dropout John Steinbeck—got a "C" in freshman English. He later said college was a waste of time.)

OTHER AREA SIGHTS

Take a guided one-hour **walking tour** of Palo Alto, either **downtown** or **Professorville,** both areas included on the National Register of Historic Districts (tel. 415-324-3121 for further information). Usually departing on Saturdays at 10 or 11 a.m., the downtown tour covers Ramona street and architectural gems like William Weeks' Cardinal Hotel and Birge Clark's shops, plus Spanish colonial revival courtyards by Pedro de Lemos. The 1932 U.S. post office at 380 Hamilton was the first to sidestep the formal federal style. "Professorville" describes the collection of historic homes bordered by Addison, Cowper, Embarcadero, and Emerson, characterized by brown shingle-style houses built between the

1890s and 1920s. A standout is Bernard May-beck's "Sunbonnet House" at 1061 Bryant.

Other Palo Alto community attractions include the **Cultural Center** at 1313 Newell Rd., tel. (415) 329-2366, a de facto art museum with child- and family-oriented features as well as rotating exhibits and performances, and the **Junior Museum** at 1451 Middlefield Rd., tel. 329-2234, the first children's museum in the nation, this one emphasizing science and the arts. More children's "firsts" here: the **Children's Theatre,** 1305 Middlefield Rd., tel. 329-2216, a theatrical arts program started in 1932 with youngsters doing it all, from the writing and staging to lighting, sound, and set design, and the nearby public **Children's Library** at 1276 Harriet St., tel. 329-2516, which includes 18,000 books plus an adjacent "Secret Garden," a favorite for storytellers.

It's also fun to just stroll around downtown. Especially along University and Hamilton avenues, notice the town's nine **surreal outdoor murals** by Greg Brown. Some of Palo Alto's best attractions are its bookstores, from **Megabooks** at

Printers Inc. Bookstore

444 University Ave. (good used books) and The **Stanford Bookstore** just down the street to **Chimaera Books and Records** at 165 University, noted for its great selection of new and used poetry. **Bell's Books** at 536 Emerson is a Palo Alto classic, a time-honored book emporium stacked floor to ceiling with both new and used volumes. **Printers Inc.,** at 310 California Ave., tel. (415) 327-6500, is a coffee house and bookstore all in one.

Did you know that the number of Barbie dolls sold in the United States since 1959 is five times greater than the number of Americans born since then? That obscure 1991 *Harper's* magazine statistic surely comes as no surprise to fans. And the history of Barbie and cohorts is about American conceptions of the feminine ideal, and fashion, as much as it is about dolls. For those who have looked elsewhere in vain, the **Barbie Doll Hall of Fame** is right here in Palo Alto. This 16,000-piece private shrine to the American cultural value of human physical perfection—best symbolized by plastic Ken, Barbie, Skipper, and related dolls manufactured by Mattel Toys—is located at 325 Waverly Ave., tel. (415) 326-5841, open Tues.-Sat. 1:30-4:30 p.m., also Sat. mornings 10:30-noon, $2 adults, $1 children.

Menlo Park near Palo Alto is home to the West Coast lifestyle-establishing institution of *Sunset* **magazine** and the Lane Publishing Company at 80 Willow Rd., tel. (415) 321-3600; *Sunset's* "Laboratory of Western Living" offices are open for free tours on weekdays (excluding holidays) at 10:30 and 11:30 a.m. as well as 1, 2, and 3 p.m.; the gorgeous gardens are open weekdays 9 a.m.-4:30 p.m. Also in Menlo Park, at 345 Middlefield Rd., tel. 329-4390, is the **U.S. Geological Survey map center,** open for tours by appointment. And for earthquake information, call the survey office at 329-4025.

The **Foothill College Electronics Museum** on the college campus at 12345 S. El Monte Rd., tel. (415) 948-8590, is amusing, full of radios, telephones, and other communications technology. Open Thurs. and Fri. 9 a.m.-4 p.m., Sat. and Sun. 1-4:30 p.m., $2 adults, $.50 children.

PALO ALTO PRACTICALITIES

Area Accommodations

Best for an inexpensive summer stay in Palo Alto is **Stanford University,** at its on-campus residence halls (call 415-723-3126 for information and reservations), generally available from mid-June to mid-September.

Southwest of town is the wonderful AYH **Hidden Villa Ranch Hostel,** a woodsy and rustic ranch-style cabin setup on 1,500 acres at 26870 Moody Rd. in Los Altos Hills, tel. (415) 949-8648, open only September through May. Rates: AYH members $7-10, nonmembers $10-13. (Popular, so call ahead.) Also available—and not that far for those with a car—is the AYH **Sanborn Park Hostel** in Saratoga. See "San Jose and Vicinity."

Ever-faithful **Motel 6** is another possibility, at 4301 El Camino Real, Palo Alto 94306, tel. (415) 949-0833, almost always full—call well in advance for reservations—and expensive by Motel 6 standards: rooms $35 s, $41 d. Other motels abound along El Camino Real; the **Town House**

Motel at 4164 El Camino Real, tel. 493-4492, is among the most reasonable, with rooms for $39-50, though there's also the **Co-Z 8** at 3945 El Camino Real, tel. 493-3141, with rates $36-42, and the **Crystalodge Motel** at 3339 El Camino Real, tel. 493-2521, $34-45. Also good bets in the medium-budget range: the **Coronet Hotel,** actually a motel, 2455 El Camino Real, tel. 326-1081, with room rates $39-46, and the very nice **Sky Ranch Motel** across from one of the Hyatts, 4234 El Camino Real, tel. 493-7221 or toll-free (800) 255-4759, $40-50. Nearby are the two local Hyatt hotels: the **Hyatt Rickeys** at 4219 El Camino Real, tel. 493-8000, with rates $115-170, and the **Hyatt Palo Alto** at 4290 El Camino Real, tel. 493-0800, room rates $104-144. As evidence that the Bay Area empties in droves on weekends, rooms at both these luxury establishments are cheapest on Fri. and Sat. nights, as low as $69 s or d.

A better bargain, usually, is the **Best Western Creekside Inn,** 3400 El Camino Real, tel. (415) 493-2411, with rates $69-87. Better motels quite close to campus include the **Holiday Inn Palo Alto,** 625 El Camino Real, tel. 328-2800, with room rates usually $98-150, and the **Stanford Terrace Inn,** 531 Stanford Ave., tel. 857-0333, rooms $95-190. The exquisite **Garden Court Hotel** downtown at 520 Cowper St., tel. 322-9000, runs $150-400.

Homier and usually more reasonable is the **Cowper Inn** bed and breakfast at 705 Cowper St., tel. (415) 327-4475, 14 rooms in a turn-of-the-century Victorian within walking distance of downtown and the university, nice continental breakfast. Rooms (two share a bath) are $55-98 s or d, $10 each extra person. Quite reasonable, too, is the **Hotel California,** a bed and breakfast establishment at 2431 Ash St., tel. 322-7666, with rates $45-58. **The Victorian on Lytton,** 555 Lytton Ave., tel. 322-8555, is an elegant Victorian, circa 1895, with an English country garden, 10 guest rooms, in-room continental breakfast service, and afternoon tea and cookies, port, and sherry. Also serving up a taste of history, minus most of the frills, is Palo Alto's historic **Cardinal Hotel** downtown at 235 Hamilton Ave., tel. 323-5101, with rates in the $40-60 range. Even if you don't stay, do stop by for a look—noting in particular the automobile included in the exterior terra-cotta, a very unusual artistic flourish. Though some distance away,

unusual and unusually enjoyable is a stay at the tranquil **Mercy Center** at 2300 Adeline Ave., tel. 340-7474, in Burlingame north of Palo Alto, an ecumenical retreat run by the Sisters of Mercy, where silence is the rule. Individuals can stay in dorm rooms when space is available. (Popular for group retreats, so call ahead to check current rates and to make reservations.) For more information about accommodations and restaurants in the greater Palo Alto area, contact either the **Menlo Park Chamber of Commerce,** 1100 Merrill St., Menlo Park 94025, tel. (415) 325-2818, or the **Los Altos Chamber of Commerce,** 321 University Ave., Los Altos 94022, tel. 948-1455.

Inexpensive Student-style Food

The University Avenue area offers a generous choice in fairly cheap eats. For gourmet pizza, including cornmeal crusts and dozens of topping choices, head to **Vicolo Pizzeria** at 473 University Ave. (at Cowper), tel. (415) 324-4877, where you can even buy by the slice. Open daily for lunch and dinner. **Liddicoats** at 340 University Ave., tel. 321-8411, is a food-court-style conglomeration of over a dozen takeout stands and ethnic eateries, well worth a stroll. **Pudley's Burger Saloon** at 255 University Ave., tel. 328-2021, is a boisterous town-gown place with quite good burgers. Probably healthier is **The Good Earth** natural foods franchise at 185 University, tel. 321-9449, with good earthy muffins, omelettes, and breakfast shakes served until 11 a.m., also burgers (vegetarian, turkey, or beef) and tasty sandwiches (like the Key Largo shrimp), homemade soups and salads, fresh fish specials, and hearty entrees like walnut mushroom au gratin and Malaysian cashew chicken. (Good desserts, too.)

A little farther afield is one of two local **Hobee's,** at 4244 El Camino Real, tel. (415) 856-6124, locally famous for its coffeecake, omelettes, burgers, sandwiches, and such. No reservations, so prepare to wait. (The other Hobee's is at the Town & Country Village shopping center on El Camino Real.) Popular for pizza is **Franky, Johnny, and Luigi's Too** at 939 El Camino Real in Mountain View, tel. 967-5384.

More Expensive Fare

For quite respectable seafood, try **Pearl's Oyster Bar** at 535 Ramona St., between University and Hamilton, tel. (415) 328-2722, both a bizarre oyster bar, as if transplanted from somewhere in the South Pacific, and a New Orleans-style sit-down restaurant, open for lunch weekdays, Mon.-Sat. for dinner. There's an **Il Fornaio** inside the Garden Court Hotel at 520 Cowper St., tel. 332-9000, a chic California-style franchise born at a baker's school in Milan and noted for its good breakfasts, Northern Italian specialties. Always a good bet for a bit of that Northern Italian ambience, the first in the area and still one of the best, is wonderful **Osteria,** a trattoria at 247 Hamilton Ave., tel. 328-5700.

L'Escale in the Stanford Shopping Center on El Camino Real, tel. (415) 326-9857, is cozy and accommodating, a small place noted for its good French fare at lunch and dinner. Also in the same shopping complex, for those who appreciate astounding portions of good American food served with (at least at dinner) a song, is an outpost of **Max's Opera Cafe,** tel. 323-6364. (In nice weather, head for a patio table.) Also a prime stop for meat eaters is **MacArthur Park,** housed in a historic building at 27 University Ave., tel. 321-9990, where oak- and mesquite-grilled meats, fowl, and fish are the specialty. The **Gordon Biersch Brewery** at 640 Emerson St., tel. 323-7723, is a New Age brewery restaurant ("brewpub" doesn't quite fit) serving ethnically interesting variations on the California cuisine theme. Good for French food is New Orleans-style **Chantilly II** at 530 Ramona, tel. 321-4080. For elegant and up-scale California cuisine with a Vietnamese flair, head for Los Altos and **Beau Sejour,** 170 State St., tel. 948-1388.

Actually, for fine dining, the surrounding communities offer some excellent choices—including, in Los Altos, **Chef Chu's** at 1067 N. San Antonio Rd. (at El Camino Real), tel. (415) 948-2696. Very organic, in the innovative California cuisine category, is the **Flea St. Cafe** at 3607 Alameda de las Pulgas (near Santa Cruz Ave.) in Menlo Park, tel. 854-1226, worth a special trip for Sunday brunch. For Thai food, not far away is **Siam Garden** at 1143 Crane St. (between Oak Grove and Santa Cruz Ave.), tel. 853-1143. **Carpaccio** at 1120 Crane, tel. 322-

1211, is Northern Italian, in a California kind of way, from the exceptional entrees right down to the oak-oven pizzas.

For fine Spanish dining, some of Northern California's best, put on formal dining duds and head for the ritzy Portola Valley suburbs and the spectacular **Iberia Restaurant,** 190 Ladera-Alpine Rd., tel. (415) 854-1746. Sunday brunch here is quite special.

Events And Entertainment

For a university town, Palo Alto is somewhat straight-laced, more spit-polished than scruffy, but there's life here nonetheless. Pick up the free local *Metro* weekly around town for its calendar section and reviews of upcoming events. Another good source of information, particularly for university events, is the *Stanford Daily,* which lists events daily but provides a more comprehensive look at what's coming up in its "Friday Daily" section. Even better for what's happening is the *Stanford Weekly*. In May the **Palo Alto Film Festival** showcases the work of Bay Area filmmakers. **TheatreWorks** here is one of the Bay Area's best repertory theater companies, with performances usually staged in the Lucie Stern Center Theater at 1305 Middlefield Rd., tel. (415) 329-2623. Though there are plenty of movie theaters and nightclubs around, particularly enjoyable are the offbeat movies shown at **The New Varsity** at 456 University Ave., tel. 323-6411, a combination movie palace, bar, and cafe at home in an old downtown hotel. Reservations advisable. Also much appreciated locally is the **Stanford Theatre** at 221 University Ave., tel. 324-3700, a nonprofit enterprise dedicated to the memory of Hollywood's "golden age," famous, too, for its $5 double features. (Come early or stay late to appreciate the performance on the pipe organ.)

And of course, being a college town, Palo Alto and environs has its fair share of bars and nightclubs. A bit different, for those on the prowl, is the **British Banker's Club** at the Old City Hall and public library at the Menlo Center in Menlo Park, tel. (415) 327-8759, a convincing Edwardian bar with 25-foot ceilings, stained glass, even library books.

SAN JOSE AND VICINITY

Once thickly forested in oaks, even within recent memory the vast Santa Clara Valley was one continuous orchard of almonds, apples, apricots, peaches, cherries, pears, and prunes where blossom snow fell from February into April. Unofficially known as Silicon Valley—in honor of the computer chip, the U.S. defense industry, and local entrepreneurial innovators like Apple Computer—these fertile soils now grow houses, office buildings, and shopping malls—all tied together by frightening freeways.

Sunny San Jose, more or less in the middle of it all though aptly described as "all edges in search of a center," is the biggest city in the Bay Area, actually the largest in Northern California. Though such a sprawling suburban enclave doesn't *feel* like a city, it is—with lively, sophisticated arts and entertainment and other attractions. San Jose, in fact, was California's *first* city—not counting mission settlements and other early outposts of empire—and was the state's first capital following American territorial occupation. What is now San Jose State University was California's first normal school, the only one in the state for many years.

Though others in the Bay Area taunt San Jose for its all-too-contemporary concrete and its apparent lack of community, the area has many merits—one being a good sense of humor. Palo Alto has enshrined the memory of Ernest Hemingway as has Oakland with its native-born Gertrude Stein, but San Jose honors the badly written novel. Launched by professor Scott Rice, San Jose State University's **Bulwer-Lytton** ("It was a dark and stormy night . . .") **Fiction Contest** attracts 10,000 or more entries each year for its Worst Possible Opening Sentence competition. Among recent entries: "She was like the driven snow beneath the galoshes of my lust" (Larry Bennett, Chicago); "We'd made it through yet another nuclear winter and the lawn had just trapped and eaten its first robin" (Kyle J. Spiller, Garden Grove); and (1985 award winner by Martha Simpson of Connecticut) "The countdown stalled at T-minus 69 seconds, when Desiree, the first female ape to go up in space, winked at me slyly and pouted her thick, rubbery lips unmistak-

ably—the first of many such advances during what would prove to be the longest and most memorable space voyage of my career."

But when it comes to bad writing, there's endless talent out there. And San Jose attracts it. (Look for Penguin's *It was a Dark and Stormy Night: The Final Conflict* for a current compilation). Here's the winner from the 1990 competition, penned by Linda Vernon of nearby Newark:

"Dolores breezed along the surface of her life like a flat stone forever skipping along smooth water, rippling reality sporadically but oblivious to it consistently, until she finally lost momentum, sank and, due to an overdose of fluoride as a child, which caused her to suffer from chronic apathy, doomed herself to lie forever on the floor of her life as useless as an appendix and as lonely as a 500-pound barbell in a steroid-free fitness center."

And the tragedy probably happened on a dark and stormy night.

DOWNTOWN SAN JOSE

Tired of being mocked all these years as the city without a heart, San Jose is determined to obtain both heart and soul. The city's decrepit downtown—more or less defined as the plaza area near San Carlos and Market streets—is being swept clean of derelicts and the otherwise down-and-out, typical of the Bay Area gentrification trend. Nowadays new office buildings, hotels, and cleaned-up urban shopping and residential neighborhoods are taking the place of flophouses and run-down liquor stores.

As a friendly destination for families and businessfolk alike, the new downtown San Jose is astounding. The unofficial and striking centerpiece is the towering 541-room **Fairmont Hotel,** part of the city's Silicon Valley Financial Complex, which includes a 17-story office tower, an apartment complex, and a retail pavilion. The central **Park Plaza,** the original center of the Pueblo of San Jose, on Market Street, is almost like the Fairmont's private front lawn, with walkways and benches and dancing-water fountain. Not far away is the city's downtown **San Jose**

San Jose's Fairmont Hotel is the unofficial centerpiece of downtown redevelopment.

McEnery Convention Center, a 425,000-square-foot, $140 million project that augments existing convention facilities and the **Center for Performing Arts.** Other hotels—including the new **Holiday Inn Park Center Plaza,** facing the convention center, the **San Jose Hilton and Towers** adjacent, and two recently refurbished historic hotels, the **Hotel De Anza** and the **Hotel Sainte Claire**—help make the area attractive to conventioneers. But for families and other travelers, a variety of new or expanded museums—including the **Tech Museum of Innovation,** the **Children's Museum of San Jose,** and the **San Jose Museum of Art**—make downtown. Still under development these days is the **Guadalupe River Park,** a three-mile stretch of parks, gardens, jogging trails, and recreational facilities that will one day connect directly to San Jose International Airport. Another new downtown feature is the new **San Jose Arena,** a major sports facility, home to the National Hockey League expansion team, the San Jose Sharks. And to make it easy to get around once you've arrived in central San Jose, a **downtown transit mall** serves the light rail system, which runs all the way to Great America, and is also the place to catch public transit buses, even **vintage trolleys** for their around-downtown route.

San Jose Museum Of Art
Tucked in next to the newly restored **St. Joseph Cathedral** right downtown on the plaza, the San Jose Museum of Art is a sparkling touch of tradition hitched to the avant-garde art world. The striking dark Romanesque main building, built in 1892 as a post office, later became the San Jose City Library. Since 1971 it has been San Jose's public home for the arts. In 1991, with the addition of an ultramodern, 45,000-square-foot, $14 million annex, the museum took a giant step into the big-time art world. Able now to attract major traveling exhibits, concentrating on contemporary and culturally diverse regional, national, and international visual arts, San Jose also hosts most of the the Stanford University Art Museum's Rodin sculpture collection, at least until 1993 or 1994. The downtown museum also displays more of its own permanent collection, which emphasizes modern and American paintings, sculpture, drawings, and photographs. Works by David Best, Richard Diebenkorn, Sam Francis, Rupert Garcia, Robert Hudson, Nathan Oliveira, and many others are included. The San Jose Museum of Art also sponsors a very active public education program, from art classes, lectures, and symposia to art and art history instruction in the public schools.

Admission to the museum is always free on Thursdays. Otherwise: $4 adults, $2 seniors and students, free for children under age 12. The San Jose Museum of Art, 110 S. Market St., San Jose 95113, tel. (408) 294-2787, which also features a fine book and gift shop, is regularly open Wed.-Sun. 10-5, and until 8 p.m. on Thursdays. It may be open at other times as well, for special events. The museum book/gift shop is open the same hours, as well as Tues. 10-5. Free guided docent tours are offered daily at 12:15 p.m., and also scheduled at other times. Spanish- and Vietnamese-speaking docents are available, as are free audiotaped tours in English, Spanish, and Vietnamese.

The Tech Museum Of Innovation

People visiting San Jose often ask how to find Silicon Valley, that mythic destination where California has worked its high-tech, silicon-chip magic since the 1960s. The exact directions are difficult to give. Like so many wonders, once one gets close to the center of something, it—the thing itself—has all but disappeared. Silicon Valley is a phenomenon, more than any precise place—though that "place," to the extent it can be located on a map, is indeed here, in the general vicinity of the Santa Clara Valley. If one really wants to see the result of computer-related creativity, entrepreneurial drive, innovation, unrelenting competitiveness, and massive amounts of venture capital, one can easily find Silicon Valley. The facile facelessness of the area's contemporary industrial parks is as much a part of the San Jose's integrated circuitry as its freeway system.

A better place to "see" Silicon Valley, in the end, is at the community's new technology museum.

Everyone knows a purported "children's museum" is a smashing success when grown-ups practically knock each other over trying to get their hands on the exhibits. And San Jose's exciting **Tech Museum of Innovation,** temporarily housed inside the former convention center at 145 W. San Carlos St., tel. (408) 279-7150, is just that kind of place. Formerly known as the Technology Center of Silicon Valley and The Garage, after it opened to the public in November 1990, the Tech was instantly one of the

country's top 10 new attractions. Even a quick visit suggests why.

Outside is the fascinating 16-foot-tall *Imaginative Chip,* an audiokinetic sculpture by George Rhoads, a very large-scale kinetic maze that features billiard balls on the move—all to suggest, albeit imaginatively, how information moves through an integrated circuit chip. Even the conceptually disadvantaged will appreciate the serendipity and joy of this very entertaining art. Get up to speed, technologically speaking, by spending a few moments inside with "The Big Chip," a nine-foot-square version of a microchip that allows you to ask a question—then watch, as different sections light up, as it processes and computes the answer.

That's the magic of the Tech Museum. Everything is hands-on, just about as up close and personal as science can get. Interactive exhibits cover biotechnology, high-tech bikes (design your own with the help of a computer), materials—like fabric that can stop a speeding bullet, and ceramic knives stronger than steel—plus microelectronics, robotics, and space exploration. Several hands-on labs, available for workshops and special classroom use, encourage still more technological exploration. And some things here just *are*—like the 23-foot DNA molecule chain built from 500 telephone books. The gift shop is also entertaining, stocking an impressive selection of educational toys and oddities, like jewelry made with real chips and light-emitting diodes. The Tech Museum is open

Historic trolleys are a convenience for downtown visitors.

SAN JOSE CONVENTION & VISITORS BUREAU

KIM WEIR

There are no rules at the Children's Discovery Museum in San Jose.

Tues.-Sun. 10-5 (from 9:30 a.m. mid-June through Labor Day), closed also on Thanksgiving, Christmas, and New Year's Day. Admission is $6 adults, $4 for seniors and children ages 6-18, free for members and for children age five and younger. Discounts available for groups of 12 or more.

All you big spenders: fundraising is still underway to finance the Tech Museum's permanent, expanded facility, to be constructed in the mid-1990s in Guadalupe River Park. Contributions, corporate and private, would be greatly appreciated. To "help fight scientific illiteracy," which is the purpose of the Tech Museum, at the very least become a member. For membership information, call (408) 279-7165.

Children's Discovery Museum

The concept is enough to terrorize parents and babysitters, but the fact is, *there are no rules* at the Children's Discovery Museum of San Jose, a shocking purple presence in the southern section of Guadalupe River Park. Open since 1990, this is a learning and discovery center for children, families, and schools, based on the premise that children need a place where they can *be* children without undue interference. Three particular themes—connections, community, and creativity—drive the action here. Children can run the lights and sirens on police cars, for example, and clamber all over firetrucks, or slide down a culvert to "Underground," to explore sewers and termite colonies. They can write letters and send them anywhere in the museum via the U.S. Post Office, even experiment with pneumatic tubes, telecommunications, and ham radio. They can try their hand at banking, playing doctor or dentist, even moving water with pumps and valves. Always popular are Apple Computer's "Around the World, Around the Corner" multicultural exhibit, and Steve Wozniak's "Jesse's Clubhouse." In good weather, there are often adventures and games outside, too. Year-round, the museum offers a full calendar of special events.

The Children's Discovery Museum is close to downtown at 180 Woz Way—or, if you're coming from elsewhere, reached via the Guadalupe Parkway (Hwy. 87) between I-280 and Hwy. 101, then Auzerais Street. Call (408) 298-5495 for current hours and special activities. The museum's regular hours: Tues.-Sat. 10-5, Sun. noon-5. Admission: $6 adults, $3 seniors and children ages 4-18 (age three and younger are free).

MORE SAN JOSE SIGHTS

Quite unusual downtown is San Jose's **American Museum of Quilts and Textiles,** 766 S. 2nd St., tel. (408) 971-0323, which features galleries of historic and contemporary samples of the fabric arts in addition to special rotating shows by individual artists. The quilt museum is open Tues.-Sat. 10-4.

Also well worth a look-see in the San Jose area, in Milpitas, is the unique, free **Wall of Garbage Recycling Museum** at the Browning-Ferris **Recyclery,** 1601 Dixon Landing Rd., tel. (408) 262-1401. (Take the Dixon Landing Rd. West exit from I-880 and follow the garbage trucks.) The 100-foot-long, 20-foot high "wall" represents the amount of trash discarded by the entire United States every second, by Santa Clara County in three minutes, and by one person in

the Winchester
Mystery House

SAN JOSE CONVENTION & VISITORS BUREAU

about six years—empty beer cans, half-eaten food, disposable diapers, plastic foam cups and containers, egg cartons, plastic bags, paint thinner cans, old shoes, and broken toys and appliances. This museum is about as real as they get. (Despite the overwhelming odds, the garbage on display is not odiferous, since it's all been sterilized or preserved.) Other museum displays show how metals can be separated for recycling by an electromagnet; how garbage dumps can produce methane gas; and other aspects of refuse recycling. Children, and sometimes adults, especially appreciate the recycling trivia shared by the museum—including the fact that every recycled can saves enough energy to power a TV set for three years, and that the average car interior contains 60 pounds of recycled paper. The Recyclery is open Mon.-Sat. 7:30 a.m.-3:30 p.m. Free.

And if the kids are overly distressed by life in the real world, perhaps they can be distracted for a time by the waterslides and pools at **Raging Waters** just north of Hwy. 101 and east of I-680. Call (408) 270-8000 for the season operating schedule, admission price, and more exact directions.

Winchester Mystery House

Though somewhat expensive for voyeuristic time travel, at least once in a lifetime everyone should visit the beautifully bizarre Winchester Mystery House west of downtown (at I-80 and I-280), 525 S. Winchester Blvd., tel. (408) 247-2101, open daily, 9 a.m.-5:30 p.m. in summer, 9-4 or 9-5 in other seasons. Admission $12.50 adults, $9.50 seniors, $6.50 for children ages 12 and under. A six-acre monument to one woman's obsession, built up from eight rooms by Sarah L. Winchester and now a state historic monument, this labyrinth of crooked corridors, doors opening into space, and stairs leading nowhere includes 40 stairways, some 2,000 doors and trapdoors in strange places, and 10,000 or so windows. (Though only 160 rooms survive, 750 interconnecting chambers once testified to Winchester's industriousness.)

A sudden widow and heir to the Winchester firearms fortune, the lady of the house was convinced by a medium that she was cursed by her "blood money" and the spirits of all those shot by Winchester rifles, but that she would never die as long as she kept up her construction work. So Sarah Winchester spent $5.5 million of the family fortune to create and re-create her Gothic Victorian, working feverishly for 38 years straight. But death eventually came knocking on her door anyway and the around-the-clock racket of workers' hammers and saws finally ceased.

At least, that's the official version of the story, the one that draws the crowds to this amazing mansion. But others, including her personal attorney, recall Sarah Winchester as quite sane, a clearheaded businesswoman who actively managed her vast holdings and estate. According to a 1923 *San Jose Mercury* interview with Roy F. Leib, Winchester reconstructed the house "due to her desire to provide accommodations for her many relatives who she thought would come to California to visit her." And she stopped work on the house long before her death; according to Leib's records, she hired no more carpenters after the 1906 earthquake. The wild stories about Winchester's eccentricities, Leib suggested, grew out of her extreme reclusiveness, which may have been related to severe arthritis and limb deformities.

In any event, the lady of the house was quite a woman. People tend to focus on Sarah Winchester's craziness, but—once here—it's hard not to be impressed by her creativity and craft as an impromptu architect.

Rosicrucian Museum And Planetarium

A worthwhile destination and San Jose's most popular tourist attraction is the **Rosicrucian Egyptian Museum** and **Rosicrucian Planetarium and Science Center** complex, 1342 Naglee Ave. at Park Ave., tel. (408) 947-3635 and 947-3638, respectively, temples of possibilities (in the California tradition) set up in a park-like setting open to all. Most riveting is the Egyptian Museum, which includes outdoor statuary and the largest collection of Assyrian, Babylonian, and Egyptian artifacts in the western U.S.: amulets and charms, mummies, musical instruments, a life-sized walk-through replica of a pyramid tomb (guided tours every half hour), and other artifacts in the mystical mode. The planetarium is also a trip. One of the first stargazing structures of its kind, built in 1936, here you can see the night skies as the ancients saw them.

The Rosicrucian's Science Center, currently under development, will focus on earth and space themes—such as "Geological Gems," produced in collaboration with the California Academy of Science, emphasizing rock types, mineral properties, gemstones, quartz, and crystals. Parts of the "Earth's Geophysical Weather Report," including a seismograph and a satellite data station, are currently on display. Also worth looking in on are rotating exhibits in the art museum.

The main museum, tel. (408) 947-3636 for information, is open daily 9-5, with last admission at 4:35 p.m. Museum admission: $4 adults, $3.50 for seniors and students (with ID), $2 children ages 7-15, free for children under age seven. On Saturdays and Sundays, admission is free for everyone. The planetarium and science center is also open daily, 9-4:15, and admission is free—except to the planetarium shows. Call 947-3638 for show times and subjects. Planetarium admission: $3 adults, $2.50 for seniors and students, $1.50 for children ages 7-15, free for children five and six. (Children under five are not usually admitted.)

San Jose Historical Museum And Kelley Park

One of a string of parks developed (and being developed) along San Jose's past-trashed Guadalupe River is **Kelley Park** at 635 Phelan Ave., which offers some special pleasures. Among them: the **Japanese Friendship Garden,** six acres of serenity created around small lakes complete with *koi,* strong-swimming ornamental carp representing the male principle.

Also well worth some time is the small **San Jose Historical Museum,** tel. (408) 287-2290, a full-scale village of historic buildings moved here from downtown and mixed with replicas. Next to A.P. Giannini's first Bank of Italy (now Bank of America) branch office and looming above all else is a half-scale reconstruction of one of old San Jose's "Eiffel Towers." After a priest at St. Ignatius College invented arc lighting in 1881, San Jose latched onto the idea and constructed four 327-foot-tall light towers to illuminate the entire downtown district. The system worked—so well, in fact, that the entire sky was lit up at night and surrounding farmers complained that their livestock couldn't sleep and became confused and crotchety. But, way off in Paris, Alexander Eiffel heard about the towers' design and found his way to San Jose to study them.

In addition to historic homes, hotels, businesses—and de facto businesses, such as the volunteer-run O'Brien's Ice Cream and Candy Store, the Vintage Reflections costume shop, and Victorian-era gift shop, all fundraising concessions—the 16-acre outdoor museum also includes a **Trolley Barn,** where in-progress restoration of the city's trolleys can be observed, also the starting point for short trolley rides around "downtown." Inside the elegant **Pacific Hotel,** displays document the history and culture of the area's native Ohlone people. Fascinating, too, is the new replica of the 1888 *Ng Shing Gung* **Chinese Temple,** or the "Temple of Five Sages," once located at Taylor and 6th streets (the site of today's Fairmont Hotel) and central to San Jose's Chinatown. Original temple furnishings and other displays tell the story of the Chinese in Santa Clara Valley.

Another immensely popular area attraction is the Rosicrucian Egyptian Museum.

SAN JOSE CONVENTION & VISITORS BUREAU

Representing a more recent historical era, the 1927 **Associated Gasoline Station** is a classic. For a deeper sense of life in the Santa Clara Valley prior to freeways and suburban development, stop by the **Stevens Ranch Fruit Barn** and take in the "Passing Farms: Enduring Values" exhibit.

Located near the I-280/I-680 and Hwy. 101 interchanges, at Keyes/Story Road and Senter Road, 156-acre Kelley Park and all of its attractions are managed and maintained by the San Jose Parks and Recreation Department. New streets and other "infrastructure" were added in 1992 improvement projects. **Educational tours** are available daily, on a drop-in basis, and for large groups by prior arrangement. The historical museum and grounds are available for rent for outside programs and events; call (408) 287-2290 or 277-4017 for more information. The Leninger Center and a shaded Greek-style amphitheater are also available. For public parking, there are two nominal-cost public lots, both off Senter Rd. between Phelan and Keyes/Story roads.

Membership in the nonprofit San Jose Historical Museum Association, as low as $30 per year, supports the preservation of Santa Clara Valley's heritage. To contribute, as an individual or corporate sponsor, write: **San Jose Historical Museum Association**, 1650 Senter Rd., San Jose 95112, or call the museum at (408) 287-2290. The museum association also offers **free historical lunchtime walking tours,** no reservations required; call 277-4017

for information, or to arrange prescheduled group tours.

Special annual museum events include **Living History Days,** usually scheduled on a weekend in June, when turn-of-the-century San Jose springs to life, tel. (408) 277-4017 for information; and **A Victorian Christmas,** a two-day event in early December complete with period costumes and decorations, children's crafts activities and story hour, hot apple cider and roasted chestnuts, even surprise visits from Father Christmas. Special weekend events run 10-5, with slightly higher admission. Otherwise, the museum is open weekdays 10 a.m.-4:30 p.m., weekends just noon-4:30. Admission $2, $1.50 for seniors, and $1 for children.

At the opposite end of Kelly Park at 1300 Senter Rd., is the **Happy Hollow Park and Zoo,** tel. (408) 292-8188, great fun for the kiddos. Small admission fee.

NEAR SAN JOSE

Alviso Environmental Education Center

Just north of San Jose proper is tiny **Alviso,** an officially nonexistent city of 1,600 or so (plus chickens and stray dogs) technically incorporated into San Jose but actually at home on 11 square miles of bayside swampland. New here is the Environmental Education Center of the San Francisco Bay National Wildlife Refuge (at the southern tip of the bay and reached via Hwy. 237 then Taylor St. and Grand Blvd.), a solar-powered building plus trail complex dedicated to educating the public about the bay environment. The building itself is designed for classroom use, but the self-guided Alviso Slough Trail is available for marsh exploration and birdwatching. For more information, contact the **San Francisco Bay National Wildlife Refuge,** P.O. Box 524, Newark 94560, tel. (408) 262-5513.

Ames Research Center And Paramount's Great America

Two miles and a time warp away is NASA's space-age **Ames Research Center** at Mountain View's Moffett Field, tel. (415) 604-6497, reservations necessary; facilities include the world's largest wind tunnel and—more modern and certainly appropriate to Silicon Valley—computer-simulated aircraft-safety test facilities. (Tours are free, call for current information.) Several miles north of San Jose via Hwy. 101 is **Paramount's Great America** in Santa Clara, tel. (408) 988-1776 or 988-1800 for recorded information, one of the nation's largest family-style amusement parks, with more than 100 rides—some considerably more thrilling than the traditional roller coaster—plus kiddie diversions of all types, live entertainment, shops, and restaurants. Fairly new attractions at this 100-acre complex include the **Vortex,** a stand-up roller coaster, and **Whitewater Falls,** not to mention **Skyhawk** and **Berserker.** Group rates and season passes are available. Open daily from Memorial Day to Labor Day, otherwise weekends only from late March through May and early September to mid-October. At last report general admission was $21.95, $14.95 seniors, $10.95 for children ages three to six. (Santa Clara is also home to well-respected Santa Clara University, on the site of the original but long-gone Mission Santa Clara.)

Los Gatos And Saratoga Sights

Nearby Los Gatos and Saratoga are picturesque upscale communities tucked into the forested hills west of San Jose. Both of these one-time logging towns are noted now for their turn-of-the-century architecture and sophisticated downtown shopping districts. In **Los Gatos,** particularly worthwhile is the **Forbes Mill History Museum** at the end of Church (off Main) and, for movie buffs, the **Los Gatos Cinema** on Santa Cruz Avenue. Stop for some good joe and

baked goods at the **Los Gatos Coffee Roasting Company** at 101 W. Main, to fortify yourself before heading on to Saratoga—because if you go to Saratoga, you might as well go hiking in the redwoods. Unusual gardens seem to be the signature of **Saratoga,** an affluent foothill town southwest of San Jose and the starting point for the very scenic Hwy. 9 route up to Saratoga Gap and Skyline Blvd. then on past undeveloped Castle Rock State Park and the backdoor entrance to Big Basin Redwoods.

In Saratoga proper, near city hall, is world-class **Saso Herb Gardens,** 14625 Fruitvale Ave., tel. (408) 867-0307, possibly the most complete herb collection in the country, a stunning display of some 1,000 living herbs complete with educational displays. The herbally correct astrological garden is also a fascination. In April and August an open house is held, though organized tours can be arranged. Visitors are otherwise welcome to wander around on their own. Call for current hours. Free.

Saratoga's **Hakone Gardens** city park nearby, at 21000 Big Basin Way, tel. (408) 867-3438, is considered the finest of its type outside Japan, a 17th-century-style Zen garden: monochromatic, simple, and symbolically powerful. Open weekdays 10-5, weekends 11-5, closed holidays. Small donation requested.

Still in Saratoga, **Villa Montalvo** at 15400 Montalvo Rd., tel. (408) 741-3421, is a monument to wealth, one of California's last ostentatious country estates. Built for one-time U.S. senator and three-time San Francisco mayor James Phelan, patron of artists and writers, the villa is now an artists-in-residence hall plus gallery, book shop, and gift shop surrounded by terraced gardens with nearby arboretum and bird sanctuary. A variety of cultural events is offered regularly at the villa gallery and in the one-time carriage house (now a theater). Call for current information and hours. Small admission. The 170-acre arboretum is open weekdays 8-5 and 9-5 on weekends. Free.

Also in Saratoga: the **Paul Masson Mountain Winery** at 13150 Saratoga Ave., tel. (408) 257-7800, generally more famous for its performing arts programs than for its wines. The first California winery to offer entertainment as a draw (though the trend is now well-established elsewhere), the biggest "do" of the year at Paul Masson is its long-running **Summer in the Vineyards** series. Divided into three parts—"Music at the Vineyards," classical music; "Vintage Sounds," folk, jazz, and pop music by folks like Joan Baez, the Count Basie Band, Ray Charles, Ella Fitzgerald, and Mel Tormé; and the three-week "Valley Shakespeare Festival"—the schedule of performances runs from June through September. For a current brochure and ticket order forms, write: Paul Masson Summer Series, P.O. Box 2279, Saratoga 95070.

Lick Observatory

On the western peak of Mount Hamilton to the east of San Jose and reached from downtown via Hwy. 130 (the Alum Rock Ave. extension of E. Santa Clara St. which connects with adventurous Mt. Hamilton Rd.) is the Lick Observatory, which has been casting its 36-inch telescopic eye skyward since 1888. Named for its eccentric gold-rush millionaire benefactor James Lick, who was convinced there was life on the moon, at the time that it was dedicated as part of UC Berkeley's research facilities the Lick telescope was the world's most powerful and the only one on the planet staffed permanently. Nowadays, the Lick Observatory is administered by UC Santa Cruz, and four new telescopes (including the 120-inch Shane Telescope, built in the 1950s and one of the world's most productive) have been added to this mountaintop astronomy enclave. Excepting major holidays, the observatory is open to the public daily 10-5 with special Friday night programs conducted from April to October. Call (408) 274-5061 for current schedule or more information.

South Of San Jose

Consider a stop at **The Flying Lady** in Morgan Hill, 15060 Foothill Ave., tel. (408) 779-4136, an amazing airport-cum-museum-restaurant-saloon with collections of planes, cars, license plates, jukeboxes, Western memorabilia, and just about anything imaginable. To find the place, from Hwy. 101 take Tennent Ave. east to Foothill then head south.

Considerably farther away, at **Fremont Peak State Park** south of San Juan Bautista, the 30-inch homemade **Kevin Medlock telescope** is available to the public for the actual eyes-on experience of stargazing, on most new-moon or quarter-moon weekend nights—weather permitting; no reservations required, call (408) 623-

4255 for info. Medlock, a mechanical engineer at the Lawrence Berkeley Laboratory, scrounged up the necessary materials ($2,000 worth) for this project, an amazing accomplishment in itself. He's currently working on a 72-inch telescope, also for eventual installation here.

Mission San Jose

Well north of San Jose via I-680 then Mission Blvd. (Hwy. 238) is beautiful Mission San Jose at Mission and Washington boulevards in Fremont, tel. (510) 657-1797, open daily 10-5 for self-guided tours (slide shows on the hour, in the museum). Painstakingly restored at a cost of $5 million then reopened to the public in 1985, Mission San Jose was once the center of a great cattle-ranching enterprise—a successful Spanish outpost noted also for its Ohlone Indian orchestra. Very evocative, worth a stop. Wheelchair-accessible and free, though donations appreciated. Group tours available by advance reservation.

Hikes Near San Jose

South of downtown via Almaden Rd. is **Almaden Quicksilver County Park.** The old New Almaden mine here was once the largest U.S. mercury mine. These days, there's a small museum open Thurs.-Sun. as well as 23 miles of old mining roads now converted to trails. No dogs allowed. For more information on Almaden and other county parks, call (408) 358-3741. Off Alum Rock Ave. (Hwy. 130) is **Joseph D. Grant County Park,** a former cattle ranch now offering camping and hiking heaven, with 40 miles of trails—especially enjoyable in spring when wildflowers are in bloom.

Southeast of San Jose and reached via Hwy. 101 and E. Dunne Ave. is undeveloped **Henry W. Coe State Park,** California's second largest, with 67,000 acres of oak woodlands and pines, wildflowers, spectacular views, and the best spring and fall backpacking in the Bay Area. The Pine Ridge Museum here is also worthwhile. Family campsites and backpacking campsites are available—reserve the latter by calling (408) 779-2728. Day-use fee. For more information, contact Henry W. Coe State Park, P.O. Box 846, Morgan Hill 95038.

Stevens Creek County Park west of Saratoga includes a popular recreation lake and picnicking and hiking trails which interconnect with the **Fremont Older Open Space Preserve** to the east and adjacent **Pichetti Ranch** to the west. The **Sanborn-Skyline County Park** southwest of Saratoga and Los Gatos along Skyline Blvd. offers some walk-in camping, hikes, and a tie-in (at the park's north end) to the **Skyline-to-the-Sea Trail** which slips down through Castle Rock State Park then follows Hwy. 9 into Big Basin Redwoods State Park before reaching the Pacific Ocean. Also here: the AYH Sanborn Park Hostel (see below).

SAN JOSE AREA PRACTICALITIES

For more information about food and lodgings in the San Jose area, as well as area wineries and other diversions, contact the excellent **San Jose Convention & Visitors Bureau,** downtown at 333 W. San Carlos St., Suite 1000, San Jose 95110, tel. (408) 295-9600 or toll-free (800) SAN-JOSE. The visitors bureau also sponsors three **Visitor Information Centers,** one in the lobby of the San Jose McEnery Convention Center, the others inside Terminal C and the new Terminal A at the San Jose International Airport. (For more information about nearby communities, contact the **Santa Clara Chamber of Commerce and Convention and Visitors Bureau,** 1515 El Camino Real, P.O. Box 387, Santa Clara 95052, tel. 296-7111; the **Saratoga Chamber of Commerce,** 20460 Saratoga-Los Gatos Rd., P.O. Box 161, Saratoga 95071, tel. 867-0733; or the **Los Gatos Chamber of Commerce,** P.O. Box 1820, Los Gatos, 95030 tel. 354-9300.)

In addition to brochures and listings of major area attractions, the visitors bureau also offers a useful annual *Travel & Meeting Planner* and a *Visitors Guide to Greater San Jose* (both free). Also useful and available here: the "San Jose History Walk" brochure, the "Historic Trolley Rider's Guide," the "Downtown Public Art and Gallery Guide," and the "Santa Clara Valley Wine Growers Association" brochure.

Also request a current calendar of events, to get a sense of the depth and breadth of the local multicultural arts, entertainment, and community celebration scene. There's *always* something going on. For current San Jose events, call (408) 295-2265.

As befitting the megalopolis it has become, San Jose is equally serious about its public transportation. In addition to the **downtown historic trolleys** and the **light rail transit system,** which runs from South San Jose/Almaden to North San Jose and Santa Clara (slated for expansion into Milpitas and Sunnyvale by 1997), the local **Transportation Agency** also operates a fleet of mass transit buses that travel all over San Jose and also connect to other public transportation. The trolleys are primarily a downtown district convenience and entertainment, running along light rail tracks in the immediate vicinity of downtown attractions. Visitors can get farther on the commuter-oriented light rail—to Great America, and even to the **San Jose International Airport** from downtown. And buses and/or *CalTrain* and **Amtrak** connections can get you almost anywhere.

Get oriented to local public transit with a system map and a variety of other easily available publications, including the "Bus and Light Rail Rider's Guide," the "Light Rail Schedule," and the "Guide to Park and Ride." Try the visitors bureau, which usually carries most of them, or stop by the **Transportation Information Center** downtown along the trolley route at 4 N. 2nd St., open 9-5:30 Mon.-Fri. and on Saturday 10-2. Otherwise, for information on bus and light rail operations, including fares and schedules, call (408) 321-2300 5:30 a.m.-10 p.m. weekdays, 7:30 a.m.-6 p.m. weekends. (From San Francisco, Palo Alto, or elsewhere within the 415 area code, call toll-free tel. 800-894-9908.) To request public transit information in advance, write: Transportation Agency, Customer Services, P.O. Box 611900, 3331 N. 1st St., San Jose, CA 95161-1900. For information on **AC Transit** bus connections to Fremont, call (510) 839-2882; call 793-2278 for information on **BART** mass transit service connections in Fremont. For **SamTrans** bus service information, in San Mateo County up the peninsula, call toll-free (800) 660-4287.

Train transportation to and from the area, already a very viable option due to Amtrak's new routes through San Jose, will be even better once the historic **Cahill Street Station,** an Italian Renaissance Revival building circa 1935, is restored and refurbished as a full-fledged transit center—an event expected to occur by 1994. The station is currently used by both Amtrak and the 47-mile *CalTrain,* a freeway-commuter train service between San Jose and San

Francisco. For information on *CalTrain* service, call toll-free (800) 558-8661. For Amtrak route and schedule information, call toll-free (800) USA-RAIL, and see also the transportation information included in the "Sacramento and Vicinity" chapter.

Inexpensive And Moderate
San Jose Area Accommodations

Best bet on the low-cost end is out a ways: the AYH **Sanborn Park Hostel,** 15808 Sanborn Rd., Saratoga 95070, tel. (408) 741-0166, with the wonderful old redwood Welchhurst hunting lodge, listed on the National Register of Historic Places, and surrounding cabins. A plush place by hostel standards, Sanborn Park Hostel offers a fireplace-cozy lounge, dining room, and modern kitchen complete with three refrigerators, range, and microwave. Family room available. Rates: $7-10. Popular in summer, reservations advised.

Close to downtown San Jose, rooms at **San Jose State University** are available in summer, tel. (408) 924-6180. **Motel 6** is at 2560 Fontaine Rd. off Hwy. 101 (the Bayshore Freeway) and fairly close to everything, tel. 270-3131, rooms $31 s, $38 d. (There's another Motel 6 near the airport, reasonably accessible to downtown, on N. 1st St., tel. 436-8180, with rates $32 and up.) Also off the Bayshore is the **Best Western Gateway Inn** at 2585 Seaboard Ave., tel. 435-8800, rooms $70 and up. Downtown is the **Best Western Inn,** 455 S. 2nd St. (east off Hwy. 82), tel. 298-3500, with sauna, whirlpool, pool, rooms $48-68. The **Best Western San Jose Lodge** is at 1440 N. 1st St., tel. 453-7750, with rates $55-70. For more low and moderately priced accommodations choices, and/or suggestions on places to stay in a specific area of San Jose and vicinity, contact the very helpful visitors bureau (see above).

Fine Downtown Hotels

An immense presence towering over San Jose's newly redeveloped downtown plaza, the new **Fairmont Hotel** at 170 S. Market St., tel. (408) 998-1900 or toll-free in the U.S. (800) 527-4727, is a 541-room study in elegance and sophistication. San Jose's Fairmont, one of five in the world-class luxury chain, features comfortable rooms and every imaginable amenity, and is central to just about everything. There's a 58-foot rooftop pool on the Cabana Level, restaurant service too, and a complete fitness center below—exercise room with Nautilus, both men's and women's saunas, steam rooms, and massage. Restaurants here include the excellent continental **Les Saisons, The Pagoda** for Cantonese, and the more casual all-American **Fountain Restaurant.** Underground valet parking. Regular room rates run $135-195, with a bargain weekend rate of $89 s or d. (Inquire about specials and packages.) Suites run $400-1800.

The queen of San Jose's original hotels, the historic **Hotel Sainte Claire** downtown at the corner of San Carlos and Market streets, 302 S. Market St., tel. (408) 295-2000 or toll-free (800) 824-6835, is open again, after a major facelift by the same folks who made San Francisco's Sherman House world famous. The Sainte Claire is state-of-the-art, a small luxury hotel with every amenity and fine European-style service. The hotel has 170 rooms, including 17 suites, and offers services such as in-room safes and valet parking. Especially attractive is the newly restored interior courtyard, with exceptional Spanish tile work, circa 1927, by local artist Albert Solon. The Sainte Claire is also home to an outpost of **Il Fornaio** restaurant, noted for its Northern Italian specialties and wonderful bakery items. Rates: $80-800, with lowest regular rates on weekends. Another long-time local beauty, the 1931 art deco **Hotel De Anza,** 233 W. Santa Clara St., tel. 286-1000 or toll-free (800) 843-3700, is also newly redone, a national historic landmark and a 10-story study in elegance with a deco-esque bar, the **Hedley Club,** and a Northern Italian restaurant, **La Pastaia.** Rates: $120-150, with a special weekend rate of $89 including breakfast. Special packages are also offered, including "Remember the Romance."

The 17-story **San Jose Hilton and Towers** nearby at 300 Almaden Blvd., tel. (408) 287-2100 or toll-free (800) HILTONS, is brand new, right next to the convention center. Amenities here include health club, spa, private pool, restaurant, and bar. Regular room rates run $125-150 (corporate rate $115), tower rooms $145-165, suites $250-600, but do ask about midweek and off-season specials. Also in the neighborhood: the **Park Center Plaza Holiday Inn,** 282 Almaden Blvd., tel. 998-0400 or toll-free in the U.S. (800) HOLIDAY, with all the usual amenities and pool. Rates: $72-89.

Out near the airport are some other choices, including the French provincial **Radisson Plaza Hotel**, 1471 N. 4th St., tel. (408) 452-0200 or toll-free (800) 333-3333, with some great weekend bargain rates; the **Red Lion Hotel**, 2050 Gateway Place, tel. 453-4000 or toll-free (800) 547-5010; also the **Hyatt San Jose,** 1740 N. 1st St., tel. (408) 993-1234 or toll-free (800) 233-1234.

Area Inns, Bed And Breakfasts

One of Saratoga's hidden attractions is **The Inn at Saratoga**, 20645 4th St., Saratoga 95070, tel. (408) 867-5020 or toll-free (800) 338-5020 for reservations. This rather exclusive, romantic European-style retreat was named 1992's Best Little Hotel in Northern California in *San Francisco Focus* magazine's travel writers poll, a distinction easy for anyone to appreciate. The inn's 46 guest rooms and suites, some with double whirlpool baths, all overlook Saratoga Creek. Special retreat packages, all with a welcome gift, continental breakfast, afternoon refreshments, and access to the Los Gatos Athletic Club (exercise facilities, pool, spa, the works), include "Savor Saratoga," two nights double occupancy at $139 pp on a space available basis; the "Spa Retreat," two nights accommodations, a private catered lunch at Le Mouton Noir, and special spa treatments at the Spa at Preston Wynne for $499 single or $369 pp double occupancy; and the "Honeymoon Package," including champagne and the room of your choice for $145-440.

Back in San Jose, **The Hensley House** at 456 N. 3rd St. (at Hensley), tel. (408) 298-3537 or toll-free (800) 634-2567, is a statuesque Queen Anne Victorian with elegant dark wood decor, crystal chandeliers, and five comfortable guest rooms with queen-size beds and private bathrooms. Wonderful gourmet breakfast. Rates: $75-125. To commune with the memory of Maxfield Parrish, stroll through English gardens, and feast on real (and real good) food, plan on a stay at **The Briar Rose** at 897 E. Jackson St., tel. (408) 279-5999, an 1875 farmhouse-style Victorian with five rooms, full breakfast. Rates: $65-95.

Inexpensive San Jose Area Food

A shining star in San Jose's small downtown Japantown district, lively **Gombei** 193 E. Jackson St., (Jackson and 5th St.), tel. (408) 279-

4311, is well worth seeking out, for the specials and noodle dishes as much as the ambience. Open for lunch and dinner, closed Sundays. Also downtown and a bit more expensive is **Thepthai** at 23 N. Market (between Santa Clara and St. John), tel. 292-7515, open daily at lunch and dinner for Thai specialties, especially good for fried tofu dishes.

A place worth hunting for, if you've got the time, is unpretentious **Chez Sovan** next to a gas station at 923 Old Oakland Rd. (13th St. and Oakland), tel. (408) 287-7619, a decrepit diner-style joint serving exceptional Cambodian fare. All-American **Bini's Bar and Grill** at 337 E. Taylor St. (7th St. and Taylor), tel. 279-9996, is the place for burgers, fries, and homemade pies. Another find, if you're up for a drive and not looking for ambience, is **Sue's Kitchen** at 1061 E. El Camino Rd. in Sunnyvale, tel. 296-6522, noted for its home-style Indian selections.

Otherwise, back in central San Jose, there are plenty of inexpensive choices. (With a small appetite, some of the places listed below, under "Pricier Fare," may also fit into the budget category.) For the real McCoy in Mexican food, head for **Tacos Al Pastor**, 400 S. Bascom Ave., tel. 275-1619. **Original Joe's** at 301 S. 1st St., tel. 292-7030, is famous for its "Joe's Special" sandwich of scrambled eggs, spinach, and ground beef. The **Red Sea** at 684 N. 1st St., tel. 993-1990, serves Ethiopian food. Fairly reasonable, too, is **Sal and Luigi's**, 347 S. 1st St., tel. 297-1136, with its excellent homemade Italian food. **Quoc Te**, 155 E. San Fernando St. at 4th St., tel. 289-8323, offers authentic, very reasonable Chinese and Vietnamese fare, plus various seafood specialties.

Pricier Fare

Brewpub fans: **Gordon Biersch Brewery Restaurant** is an upscale place in an alley downtown between 1st and 2nd streets, 33 E. San Fernando St., tel. (408) 294-6784, where in good weather you can quaff a few of the namesake German-style brews out on the patio. The food's not bad, either. (Gordon Biersch also has outposts in Palo Alto and San Francisco.) Some people prefer the area's other notable brewpub, boisterous **San Jose Tied House Cafe and Brewery** at 65 N. San Pedro St., tel. 295-2739, with eight beers on tap and an American-style pubhouse menu. (Vegetarian dishes, too.) Chic for sushi and such is **California Sushi and Grill** at 1 E. San Fernando, tel. 297-1847.

The city's most genuine steak house and rib joint is **Henry's World Famous Hi-Life** at 301 W. St. John St. (at Almaden Blvd.), tel. (408) 295-5414, a no-frills thrill from the Formica tables and paper placemats to the classic rhythm and blues on the jukebox. Exotic in an entirely different dimension is **El Maghreb** at 145 W. Santa Clara (at San Pedro), tel. 294-2243, serving up unique Moroccan fare and belly dancers. The **Australian Restaurant** at 898 Lincoln Ave., tel. 293-1112, is also eclectic, a casual, Crocodile Dundee kind of place serving decent fare from down under. For German food, the people's choice is **Teske's Germania,** 255 N. 1st St., tel. 292-0291.

Eulipia at 374 S. 1st St. (between San Salvador and San Carlos), tel. (408) 280-6161, is chic yet casual, one of the South Bay's best for California cuisine at lunch and dinner. Longtime local legend **Paolo's** is now home downtown at at 333 W. San Carlos St., tel. 294-2558, across from the Center for Performing Arts, and noted for its contemporary turn on Italian classics. Open for lunch weekdays, for dinner nightly except Sunday. **La Foret,** inside an old hotel overlooking a creek, at 21747 Bertram Rd., tel. 997-3458, is an exceptional French restaurant specializing in seafood and wild game entrees. For other top-of-the-line choices, consider also the best hotels. But the general consensus is that the area's best restaurant is another local institution. In the four-star category, **Emile's,** 545 S. 2nd St., tel. 289-1960, is famous for its very expensive Swiss and French fare and classically romantic ambience. Surrounding communities, including Campbell, Santa Clara, and upscale Saratoga, also have their culinary claims to fame. (In Saratoga, for example, two top fine-dining selections include **The Plumed Horse** at 14555 Big Basin Way, tel. 867-4711, for French country, and the exceptional French **Le Mouton Noir,** housed in a classy Victorian at 14560 Big Basin Way, tel. 867-7017. Casual and contemporary in nearby Los Gatos: **Cats Restaurant** at 17533 Santa Cruz Hwy., tel. 354-4020, a roadhouse with good food and live music on weekends.) For current regional restaurant reviews, pick up a Friday edition of the *San Jose Mercury News.*

OAKLAND

Since the job description requires them to say what needs to be said, writers tend to offend. Gertrude Stein, for example, apparently insulted her hometown until the end of time when she described Oakland this way in *Everybody's Autobiography:* "There is no there there," most likely a lament for the city she no longer recognized. But, forever offended, Oakland proved Stein was wrong—by erecting a sculpture to "There," right downtown on City Square at 13th and Broadway where everyone can see it.

Long bad-rapped as crime-riddled and somehow inherently less deserving than adjacent Berkeley or San Francisco across the bay, Oakland has come a long way, with a booming economy, downtown redevelopment, and neighborhood gentrification, and both a thriving port industry and waterfront district to prove it. In many ways, Oakland has become one with Berkeley, with some neighborhoods defined most strongly by shared cultural associations. And the city has become a respectable neighbor to San Francisco, that relationship integrated by accessibility. But Oakland still struggles with its own contradictions. Genesis of the Black Power movement but also home base for the Hell's Angels, home of the World Series-winning Oakland A's

but also home of one of the most troubled public school systems in the nation, Oakland houses its immigrants and low-income residents in the flatlands while those with money and some semblance of power live up in the hills.

Shaken to its roots by the October 1989 Bay Area earthquake which collapsed a section of the Bay Bridge and flattened a double-decker section of the Nimitz Freeway (I-880) in the flatlands. No sooner had the city made peace with that disaster than another struck—in October, 1991, when instantaneous wildfires raged through the Oakland hills, killing 22 people, torching entire neighborhoods at a cost of some $2 billion, and stripping hills of the luxuriant growth so typical of the area. Though wildflowers and other sturdy survivors sprang back to life with the next spring's rains, these naked neighborhoods have been slow to rebuild. Times have been tough in many areas of Oakland.

And yet, Oakland abides. There's a *there* here, despite troubled times. Blessed with fair weather year-round, good health care services, a generally robust economy, and a decent public transportation system, Oakland ranked 20th in *Money* magazine's 1990 survey of the best U.S. places to live.

There is a there in Oakland.

OAKLAND CONVENTION & VISITORS BUREAU

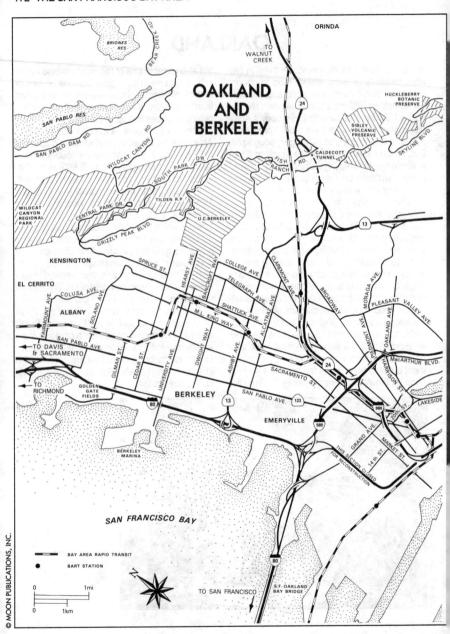

OAKLAND AND BERKELEY

ORINDA

TO WALNUT CREEK

BRIONES RES.

HUCKLEBERRY BOTANIC PRESERVE

SIBLEY VOLCANIC PRESERVE

SKYLINE BLVD.

SAN PABLO RES.

BEAR CREEK RD.

SAN PABLO DAM RD.

WILDCAT CANYON RD.

SOUTH PARK DR.

CALDECOTT TUNNEL

FISH RANCH

FISH RANCH RD.

24

13

WILDCAT CANYON REGIONAL PARK

CENTRAL PARK DR.

TILDEN R.P.

U.C. BERKELEY

GRIZZLY PEAK BLVD.

KENSINGTON

SPRUCE ST.

COLLEGE AVE.

CLAREMONT AVE.

BROADWAY

MORAGA AVE.

PLEASANT VALLEY AVE.

EL CERRITO

COLUSA AVE.

SOLANO AVE.

HEARST AVE.

BANCROFT WAY

TELEGRAPH AVE.

FAIRMOUNT AVE.

ALBANY

M.L. KING WAY

SHATTUCK AVE.

ALCATRAZ AVE.

PIEDMONT AVE.

OAKLAND AVE.

MacARTHUR BLVD.

SAN PABLO AVE.

TO DAVIS & SACRAMENTO

GILMAN ST.

CEDAR ST.

UNIVERSITY AVE.

DWIGHT WAY

ASHBY AVE.

SACRAMENTO ST.

24

HARRISON ST.

LAKESIDE

TO RICHMOND

GOLDEN GATE FIELDS

80

BERKELEY

13

SAN PABLO AVE.

123

EMERYVILLE

980

580

14th ST.

BERKELEY MARINA

GRAND AVE.

THIS SECTION CLOSED FOR RECONSTRUCTION

MARKET ST.

SAN FRANCISCO BAY

BAY AREA RAPID TRANSIT

BART STATION

0   1mi

0   1km

N

80

TO SAN FRANCISCO

S.F. OAKLAND BAY BRIDGE

© MOON PUBLICATIONS, INC.

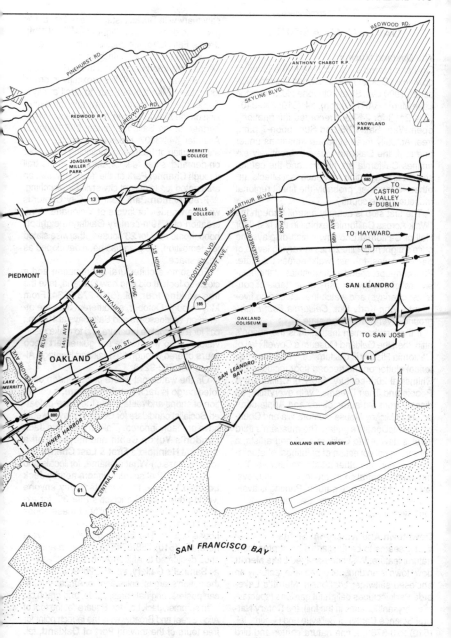

OAKLAND AREA SIGHTS

The Oakland Museum

On Lake Merritt's harbor side is the jewel of downtown Oakland, the renowned Oakland Museum, 1000 Oak St. at 10th (one block from the Lake Merritt BART Station), tel. (510) 273-3401 (834-2413 for 24-hour recorded information), open Wed.-Sat. 10-5 and Sun. noon-7 p.m., free. Actually three separate museums under one roof, the Oakland Museum creatively examines California art, history, and the natural sciences, suggesting how each fact affects another—altogether, probably the finest regional museum in the country.

The first stop is actually a stroll through the "Walk Across California" exhibit in the first-floor Hall of California Ecology, which displays the state's eight major life zones in varying levels of detail in a west-to-east "walk" across the state. For warm-ups, spend a few minutes at the massive relief map (with push-button "table of contents" overlays) and watch the astounding five-minute John Korty film, *California Fast Flight,* ground-level views of the state.

If the Smithsonian Institution is the nation's attic, then the Oakland Museum's Cowell Hall of California History is California's. The happy historical clutter on the second floor includes the whimsical 20th-century "Story of California: A People and Their Dreams," with everything on display from old automobiles and Apple computers to Mickey Mouse memorabilia and Country Joe McDonald's guitar. The museum's third level is devoted to California art and artists, a chronological collection of paintings, photography, pottery, and other artistic endeavors. The museum's central courtyard includes multilevel lawns and a sculpture garden. Parking is available beneath the museum. Call for current information on special exhibits.

Downtown And Waterfront Sights

Water seems to be Oakland's most prominent natural feature. Wishbone-shaped **Lake Merritt** downtown is an unusual urban lake, actually an enclosed saltwater tidal basin. Merritt's **Lakeside Park** includes delightful gardens (spectacular chrysanthemums in the fall), the **Rotary Natural Science Center** at Bellevue and Perkins, tel. (510) 273-3739, a fine nature center and bird sanctuary with Buckminster Fuller's first public geodesic dome (now a flight cage), and **Children's Fairyland,** the original inspiration for all the world's theme parks (including Disneyland). Despite the beads remaining in its 1925 necklace of lights and its relative proximity to downtown, Lake Merritt is not safe to stroll at night. To get the lake's point of view, take an excursion on the *Merritt Queen,* a riverboat sans river berthed at the Sailboat House, 568 Bellevue Ave., tel. 444-3807. Rides are available weekends starting at 1 p.m. and continuing every hour on demand, small fee. Or, stroll down the trail through **Channel Park** on the lake's bayside, an area noted for its decent city-style birdwatching.

Preservation Park near the City Center is worth a wander for lovers of Victoriana. A recreation of a 19th-century Oakland neighborhood, home now for 23 houses otherwise slated for demolition, the area has been developed as office space.

For some architectural appreciation and a close-up look at old and new Oakland, take the free **walking tour,** tel. (510) 273-3234. From May through October, six different trips are offered on Wednesdays and Saturdays at 10 a.m.; call for a descriptive brochure and to make reservations. Also worthwhile are guided **art deco tours** offered through the Oakland Heritage Alliance, tel. 763-9218.

On the waterfront where Jack London once toted cargo is **Jack London Square,** a collection of shops and restaurants the twice-defeated Socialist candidate for Oakland mayor would have probably ignored. (Take a peek into **Jack London's Yukon Cabin** and maybe quaff a couple at **Heinhold's First & Last Chance Saloon,** a classic.) What a shame, for locals and visitors alike, that so many ignore nearby **Jack London Village.** It's a mystery why anyone would prefer San Francisco's Pier 39, for example, considering the quality of these shops and businesses, all housed in a former warehouse district. The **Ebony Museum of Art** is here, tel. (510) 763-0745, a museum and gift shop dedicated to African-American art, as well as **Samuel's Gallery,** tel. 452-2059, with one of the nation's largest collections of African-American posters, original prints, cards, and graphics.

In summer, Jack London Square (at the foot of Alice Street and Broadway) is the launch point for free tours of the thriving **Port of Oakland,** tel.

OAKLAND CONVENTION & VISITORS BUREAU

Lake Merritt

(510) 839-7488. (Other good port-activity vantage points include Portview Park at the end of 7th St. and the view from the foot of Clay.) Or head seaward by car over the Bay Bridge to **Treasure Island,** created to accommodate the 1939 Golden Gate International Exposition and now a naval base. The **Treasure Island Museum,** tel. 765-6182, is housed in the old fair administration building and includes a great collection of end-of-the-Depression memorabilia. Free. Open daily except federal holidays 10 a.m.-3:30 p.m.

Other Oakland Sights

A walk up 10th St. from the Oakland Museum leads straight into thriving **Chinatown** (though "Asiatown" is actually more accurate) east of Broadway, its wide streets packed with authentic restaurants and shops but surprisingly few tourist traps. Also worthwhile is the **East Bay Negro Historical Society** at 5606 San Pablo Ave., tel. (510) 658-3158, its library and displays focusing on black history, particularly in California. Aside from regional parks offering hiking and recreation (see below), *the* park in Oakland is **Knowland Park and Zoo** on Golf Links Rd. off I-580, at 98th St., tel. 632-5923, admission $3 per auto. With more time to nose around, visit the campuses of **California College of Arts and Crafts,** one of the oldest art colleges in the nation at College Ave. and Broadway, tel. 653-8118, and well-respected **Mills College** at 5000 MacArthur Blvd., tel. 430-2255, the only independent all-women's college west of the Mississippi. Many of the buildings at Mills were designed by San Simeon architect Julia Morgan.

Oakland Outdoors

In the hills behind Oakland is large **Anthony Chabot Regional Park,** adjacent to Redwood Regional Park and smaller Joaquin Miller Park. Chabot is most noted for its large lake, peaceful and popular for fishing and boating (rentals only) but no swimming, since it's classified as an emergency local water supply. On weekends from April through September take the *Lake Chabot Queen* ferry (small fee) to points around the lake. Other attractions include picnic areas, archery and rifle ranges, and a golf course.

But the vast backyard of this 4,700-acre park has some hidden attractions, including a blue heron rookery and remnants of an old Chinese village. You can also camp here: 73 eucalyptus-shaded sites above Lake Chabot (including 35 walk-in sites), hot showers, flush toilets, group camping also available. To get here: take Castro Valley Blvd. east off I-580, then turn north onto Lake Chabot Boulevard. For more information about regional parks here and in nearby Berkeley, call the East Bay Regional Park District office at (510) 531-9300. To reserve camping and picnic sites here, call 531-9043.

Mushroom-shaped **Redwood Regional Park** is 1,800 acres of redwood serenity and forest meadows and creeks, right *there* in Oakland—wonderful hiking. To get here, take Hwy. 13 to the Redwood Rd. exit, then take Redwood uphill beyond Skyline for two miles to reach the main entrance.

Joaquin Miller Park was named for the irascible writer who once lived on 80 acres here and hoped to establish an artists' colony. (On the corner of Sanborn Drive and Joaquin Miller Road, at the park's entrance, you can see Miller's small home, The Abbey, where he wrote his masterwork, "Columbus"—equated with the Gettysburg Address before the poet's literary reputation was eclipsed by the passage of time. You can tip your hat to the house, but you can't go in.) Farther up Sanborn is a ranger's station, where you can appreciate the small display about Joaquin Miller and pick up a park brochure and map. The most lasting homage to the poet are the redwood trees here, planted by him and now integral to the park, said to be the world's only urban redwood forest. (Along with whiskey, women, and poetry, trees were a passion of Joaquin Miller's.) Facilities include picnic grounds and amphitheater. To get here from Hwy. 13, take the Joaquin Miller Rd. exit.

Surrounded on three sides by Redwood Park and by Joaquin Miller Park on the other is lush **Roberts Regional Recreation Area** off Skyline Blvd., which offers more hiking among the redwoods, picnicking, baseball and volleyball, an outdoor dance floor, and a heated swimming pool equipped with a hoist to assist the disabled in and out of the water.

Just north of this multi-park complex, in the hills behind Piedmont, are the wild surprises of **Huckleberry Regional Preserve**. Though the eucalyptus and logged-over redwoods here testify to the area's disturbance over time, most of the shrubs in this rare-plant community are natives— thriving in the park's unusually protective microclimate. Spring comes early every year, attracting hummingbirds, and autumn comes early too, with still more birds attracted by the harvest of berries and nuts. The narrow path can be almost invisible amid the thickets yet offers some scenic overviews in spots, an experience extended by looping back on the Skyline Trail.

Farther north is the **Robert Sibley Volcanic Regional Preserve**, actually the remnants of what was once the East Bay's dominant volcano. Exploring otherwise unimpressive Round Top Peak here is a favorite pastime for amateur and professional geologists alike. To find out why, follow the self-guided trail.

Bayshore Parks Near Oakland

A few areas along San Francisco and San Pablo bays offer some respite from modern reality. The **San Francisco Bay National Wildlife Refuge,** tel. (510) 792-0222, open for day use only (free), usually yields good birdwatching throughout the protected marshes and mudflats along the eastern edge of the South Bay. Trailheads are located at Alviso (see "San Jose and Vicinity"), at nearby Coyote Hills Regional Park, and at the visitor center at the end of the Newark Slough (reached via Thornton Rd.) parallel to the Dumbarton Bridge toll plaza.

An intriguing if downcast monument to the past is the 1876 ghost town of **Drawbridge** near the modern bridge, once a popular hunting resort area where rotating bridges across Coyote Creek and Warm Springs Slough permitted Southern Pacific trains to pass. Drawbridge died a slow death as marshland and birds disappeared—the latter partly due to "market hunting," which involved loading and firing cannons with nails and shot to kill 1,000 birds or more with one attack. (Drawbridge is accessible only on guided tours.) For current information (recorded) on refuge interpretive programs and other activities, call (510) 792-3178. To reserve space on a free docent-led Drawbridge tour, usually offered on Saturdays at 10 a.m. from May through October, call 792-0222.

In the midst of semi-industrial Fremont is an unusual Victorian-era farm park, the only one of its kind in the northstate. **Ardenwood Regional Preserve** is a 20-acre remnant of a major mid-1800s ranch that once included nearby **Coyote Hills Regional Park,** noted for its own living history program—one that re-creates the daily life of the Ohlone people who lived in these salt-marsh grasslands ("Old Ways" workshops are also offered). For more information on ranger-led tours to area shell mounds and other archaeological sights, including a reconstructed Ohlone village, stop by the Coyote Hills Visitor Center at 8000 Patterson Rd. in Fremont, open daily 10-5, or call (510) 663-1092. Coyote Hills Regional Park is also a good place to start a creekside trek along the Alameda Creek Bicycle Path, the longest (12-mile) paved bike trail in the East Bay. Pick up trail and park maps at the visitor center.

Restored by the East Bay Regional Park District to its upper-class 1880s ranch ambience, and including the historic Patterson

Oakland's Tribune Tower is a standout on the modern skyline.

ED AUST

House mansion with picket fences, period furnishings, and period-clothed character actors, Ardenwood offers a very different backward glance. Small admission fee. To get here: from I-880 take the Hwy. 84 (Decoto Rd./Dumbarton Bridge) exit, then exit at Newark Blvd. and follow Ardenwood/Newark north to the park's entrance. For more information, call (510) 796-0663.

Farther north, undeveloped **Hayward Regional Shoreline** (in two separate sections along the bay just north of Hwy. 92) is not particularly appealing—but will be one day, because this is the largest salt-marsh restoration project underway on the West Coast. Though it's much more difficult to reestablish what was so easily destroyed through diking and other diversions of nature, the birds are already coming back.

North of San Pablo and jutting into San Pablo Bay is 2,000-acre **Point Pinole Regional Shoreline,** an area once dedicated to manufacturing dynamite—which explains why there has been no development here—and now an amazement: several miles of pristine bay frontage and salt marshes sheltering rare birds, meadows, and peace.

OAKLAND PRACTICALITIES

Accommodations

In general, San Francisco offers a much wider range of accommodations options, from youth hostels to chic little downtown and neighborhood hotels. For a complete listing of recom-

mended places to stay in Oakland, contact the Oakland Convention and Visitors Bureau, tel. (510) 839-9000. Camping at Lake Chabot is always an option (see above), and with more money comes greater choice. The **Best Western Thunderbird Inn** near the entrance to Jack London Square, 233 Broadway, tel. 452-4565, offers cheaper rates on weekends than during the week plus pool, sauna, and parking garage: $75 and up. Just north of Jack London Square is the **Waterfront Plaza Hotel,** 10 Washington St., tel. 836-3800, with rates from $140.

The **Hampton Inn,** a few miles south of downtown off I-880 at 8465 Enterprise Way off Hegenberger Rd., tel. (510) 632-8900, offers the usual amenities plus whirlpool and airport transportation, rooms from $65. The big deal downtown these days is the **Parc Oakland Hotel** near the Convention Center, 1001 Broadway, tel. 451-4000 or (800) 338-1338, rooms with a view and substantially cheaper weekend rates.

Special Accommodations

The **Washington Inn** just across from the Oakland Convention Center at 495 10th St. (between Broadway and Washington), tel. (510) 452-1776 or toll-free (800) 464-1776 in California, (800) 477-1775 from elsewhere in the U.S., is an intimate 1913 hotel restored to its turn-of-the-century self yet with all the modern amenities, including a business center for corporate roadies and a great little bar and restaurant downstairs. Rates: $89-129, a true value. Also appealing in downtown Oakland is the art deco

Lake Merritt Hotel, 1800 Madison (19th and Madison), tel. 832-2300 or toll-free (800) 933-HOTEL, recently restored to its original elegance with deluxe and apartment-style suites with modern amenities like in-room coffeemakers, microwaves, and dataport phone connections, not to mention the plush appointments. Aside from basic business services, the Lake Merritt offers complimentary limo service to the downtown financial district in the morning, after continental breakfast downstairs. If at all possible, get a room facing the lake. Regular room rates: $89. Parlor suites: $119. Deluxe suites (with separate living room): $159. Another great bayside bargain.

Special in Oakland is the fabled **Claremont Resort and Tennis Club** in the hills at Ashby and Domingo avenues, tel. (510) 843-3000 or toll-free (800) 323-7500, an elegant white-as-a-handkerchief grande dame built in the 1915 chateau style, offering well-manicured grounds and luxury accommodations with all the frills: heated pools, saunas, whirlpools, 10 tennis courts, and—for a fee—health club, massage, steam room, restaurant. Weekly rates and suites are available, but a daily stay runs $185-270, with packages and specials sometimes available. People often come just for the self-pampering offered by the Claremont's exceptional spa.

Also unique in the Oakland neighborhood is the **East Brother Light Station Bed and Breakfast** on a tiny island just north of the I-580 Richmond-San Rafael Bridge, accessible only by boat, tel. (510) 233-2385, which offers accommodations plus dinner and breakfast Thursdays through Sundays, $300 per couple per night. Definitely different, reservations necessary well in advance.

In Alameda there are at least two bed and breakfast choices: **Garratt Mansion** at 900 Union St., tel. (510) 521-4779, with rates $70-120, and the **Webster House** at 1238 Versailles, $75-105 for a stay in the oldest house on the island, an 1854 Gothic revival. And if you're heading south anyway, **Lord Bradley's Inn,** an Early California-style inn adjacent to Mission San Jose in Fremont at 43344 Mission Blvd., tel. 490-0520, is another East Bay bed and breakfast option, with rooms $65-75. Good value. (Also in Fremont is one of the West's best burger joints, **Val's** at 2115 Kelly St., most famous for its one-

pound Papa Burger, though there's an entire family of excess to choose from at this old-fashioned fountain.)

Chinatown-Area Fare

For exotic food supplies and good restaurants head to Oakland's Chinatown, some 28 city blocks with most of the action centered between Clay and Webster and 7th and 9th streets; everything here is generally cheaper than in San Francisco. Come on Friday mornings, 8 a.m.-2 p.m., for the **Old Oakland Certified Farmers Market,** tel. (510) 452-FARM, Alameda County's largest. Otherwise, **G.B. Ratto & Company International Grocers** at 9th and Washington, tel. 832-6503, features an appetizing and eclectic collection of predominantly Italian wines and foods, from barrels of smoked fish to exotic cheeses and salamis and open crates of imported pastas, as well as an unpretentious cafeteria-style restaurant for lunch (sandwiches, salads, daily specials). Similar in some respects is the **Housewives Market** at 9th and Clay, tel. 444-4766, an indoor country market with separate specialized grocers selling everything from eggs and sausages to Asian vegetables and fish.

Some of the most reasonable restaurants around are either here in Chinatown or nearby. Among these, **Jade Villa** at 800 Broadway (on the corner of 8th St.), tel. (510) 839-1688, serves varied and very good dim sum during the day, Cantonese fare at night. **Nan Yang,** 301 8th St. at Harrison, tel. 465-6924, serves good Burmese food as well as Chinese selections. (There's another one in the Rockridge area, at 6048 College Ave., tel. 655-3298.) **Pho 84** at 354 17th st,, tel. 832-1429, is an Asian-style stop serving rich beef broth with noodles (and just about anything else you choose to add) or chicken or crab combination soups, also daily specials. The tidy **Gulf Coast Grill & Bar** at 8th and Washington, tel. 836-3663, serves wonderful Southern-style specialties and oysters on the half shell, fabulous but pricey.

But the oldest restaurant in Chinatown is still one of the best: the **Lantern** at 814 Webster, tel. (510) 451-0627, most tempting for its dim sum, served upstairs on the third floor. **Oakland Seafood Cuisine** at 307 10th St., tel. 893-3388, serves very inexpensive yet refined seafood specialties, attracting a largely Chinese clientele.

Inexpensive Food
Here And There

Bright blue **Mama's Royal Cafe** at 4012 Broadway, tel. (510) 457-7600, is a true neighborhood restaurant with an astounding breakfast menu. **Ann's Cafe** in a grim setting under the I-580 freeway at 3401 Fruitvale Ave., tel. 531-9861, is a simple lunch counter setup serving exceptional omelettes (but be prepared to stand in line), closed weekends. Delightful too, but in a dreary neighborhood is long-running **La Mexicana**, 3930 E. 14th St. north of the Oakland Coliseum, tel. 533-8818 (no reservations taken), which serves fabulous, inexpensive made-from-scratch Tex-Mex enchiladas, tacos, and tostadas (with cheese, chicken, or chorizo fillings), wonderful chiles rellenos—real food on Formica tables under fluorescent lighting. **Taqueria Morelia: Talk of the Town** at 4481 E. 14th St., tel. 535-6030, is a good choice for burritos and quesadillas.

Mikado at 6228 Telegraph Ave., tel. (510) 654-1000, features excellent sushi, though the combination dinners are definitely a bargain. **Flint's Barbecue** just over the line from Berkeley at 6609 Shattuck Ave., tel. 653-0953, serves the real thing. (There is another at 6672 E. 14th, tel. 569-1312.) Also on the border is **Fenton's Creamery**, 4226 Piedmont, tel. 658-7000, usually mobbed by the UC Berkeley crowd. For award-winning Chicago-style pizza, try **Zachary's** at 5801 College Ave., tel. 655-6385. Reservations or a wait in line usually necessary.

Fairly reasonable is **Pookie's Creole Kitchen,** 3010 Foothill Blvd., tel. (510) 436-6852, a nondescript storefront in a dismal neighborhood but famous for its fabulous food—from jambalaya and gumbo to crab, oyster-clam bisque, and honey glazed fried chicken.

Zza's Trattoria at 552 Grand Ave., tel. (510) 839-9124, is always packed, always cheerful, with a daunting line streaming down the sidewalk—testimony to the popularity of the pizzas and exceptional yet inexpensive entrees here. Another pizza hot spot is **Pizza Rustica** at 5422 College Ave., tel. 654-1601, serving traditional pizzas as well as California-style with cornbread crusts, and specializing in the exotic—like Cuban and Thai pizzas. The **Rockridge Cafe,** 5492 College Ave., tel. 653-1567, is an all-American hip diner beset by fans at breakfast, lunch, and dinner, great for burgers (on whole-wheat buns) and real food of all persuasions. **Asmara** at 5020 Telegraph, tel. 547-5100, is the place to go for East African fare. For Northern Indian specialties, try **Sabina Indian Cuisine,** 1628 Webster (at 17th, west of Broadway), tel. 268-0170.

But don't miss Australian-style **Noble Pies,** 5421 College Ave., tel. (510) 653-2790, open daily 11 a.m.-9 p.m. You can try pie for dinner: African Babootie Pie (beef and minced lamb with almonds, fruits, and curry), Quebec Tourtiere Pie (beef, pork, potatoes, spinach, and onions), Caribbean Pie (Jamaican beef pasty), the Oh! Calcutta meatless pasty, even vegetarian Thistle Pie (artichoke hearts, garbanzo beans,

Chinatown in Oakland is nontouristy—and offers unusual produce as well as good inexpensive restaurants.

black olives, and Swiss cheese). There are other menu entrees, too—plus pie for dessert, from fresh fruit to chocolate mousse and pecan.

And out there in Emeryville, bohemian **Carrara's Cafe and Gallery,** in a one-time warehouse at 1290 Powell St. (between Doyle and Beaudry, tel. (510) 547-6763, is the place for vegetarian soups (like black bean) and Italian sandwiches while listening to new music and watching the rotating art shows roll by.

More Expensive Oakland Fare
For "Louisiana Fancyfine" food, the place to go is visually astounding and somehow spiritually supercharged **The Gingerbread House** at 741 5th St., tel. (510) 444-7373, a chocolate-brown building dressed up like a fairy tale from the bayou and serving up Cajun/Creole specialties like iron pot jambalaya, cherry duck, sautéed quail, and catfish étouffée. Reservations essential.

Oliveto at 5655 College Ave., tel. (510) 547-5356, specializes in creative, very good Mediterranean fare, especially Northern Italian. Noted for its country French and Italian menu is **La Crème de la Crème** at 5362 College Ave., tel. 420-8822. The **Bay Wolf Cafe & Restaurant** resembles Berkeley's Chez Panisse in its homey setting at 3853 Piedmont, tel. 655-6004, and is known for its fine Mediterranean-style dishes and California cuisine, served here long before anyone thought to call it that. Reservations wise. One of the Bay Area's best French restaurants is **La Brasserie** near Lake Merritt at 542 Grand Ave., tel. 893-6206.

Chez Goldberg at 3719 MacArthur Blvd. (between 35th and High), tel. (510) 530-5332, at first glance looks like some desolate diner, but the artistic interior touches give the place away—a great gourmet eatery, with pastas, fresh fish, garlic roasted chicken, some exceptional homemade sausages. Open for dinner only.

Hong Kong East Ocean Seafood Restaurant in Emeryville at 3199 Powell St., at the end of the Emeryville Marina, tel. (510) 655-3388, serves views of the Bay Bridge, exceptional seafood and vegetable dishes, and dim sum. Also well worth seeking out in Emeryville: **Bucci's** at 6121 Hollis (between 59th and 61st), tel. 547-4725, with an upscale warehouse ambience of brick and glass and very good Italian-style California fare.

Events
In February, during Black History Month, Oakland hosts the annual **Black Filmmakers Hall of Fame** at the Paramount Theatre of the Arts downtown. The **St. Patrick's Day Unity Parade** takes place downtown in March, while April brings the **Asian/Pacific Performing Arts Festival.** In May various **Cinco de Mayo** celebrations are featured, and in June Oakland hosts its **Festival of the Lake,** good food and carnival-style fun along the shores of Lake Merritt. Also in June: the **Festival of American Music** and the start of the **Woodminster Amphitheatre Summer Theater and Musical Performances** at Joaquin Miller Park. From July through September, the Oakland Municipal Band's **free summer concerts** are held at the bandstand at Lake Merritt on Fri. and Saturday.

A special event at the Oakland Museum in August is the **Tasting of Summer Produce,** a quasi-professional food fest with 100 or so Northern California growers and produce vendors offering their wares to grocers and restaurant owners—the ultimate in-crowd foodie fest (admission charged). Also in August: the **Oakland Chinatown Streetfest,** celebrating a variety of Asian heritages. In September, come to the **Jazz and Blues Festival,** held at Dunsmuir House, and the **Oakland Blues Heritage Festival** at Estuary Park. In October, come to Oakland for the **Oakland Jazz Festival** and the **Black Cowboys' Parade** downtown. In December, check out the downtown **Santa Parade** and the Oakland Ballet's performances of *The Nutcracker.* Contact the visitor center (see below) for a current quarterly calendar of events. For a fairly inexpensive thrill anytime, have a drink atop Oakland's world at the **Hyatt Regency Oakland** downtown at 1001 Broadway, just to drink in the nighttime views of San Francisco.

Entertainment
If you're around during baseball season (June through September), do head south to the Oakland Coliseum to take in an **Oakland A's** baseball game, tel. (510) 638-0500 for information and tickets. Or, from October to April, take in **Golden State Warriors Basketball,** tel. 638-6300 for information, tel. 762-BASS for tickets. Another possibility, with the season ending in late June, is heading out to the **Golden Gate Field thoroughbred races** in Albany, tel. 526-3020.

For a complete round-up of sports, dance, music, theater, and special events, call the 24-hour **Arts & Entertainment Hotline,** tel. 835-ARTS. For other happenings and events, pick up local newspapers—including the *East Bay Guardian* and the *Express,* which both feature comprehensive calendar listings and worthwhile arts and entertainment coverage.

Oakland is famous for its nightclubs; jazz and blues are the town's mainstays but also popular are the reggae and the salsa scenes. **Eli's Mile High Club** at 3629 Martin Luther King, tel. (510) 655-6661, is the well-advertised historic heart of Oakland's homestyle blues but also honors the Mississippi blues tradition. (Since Eli's is not exactly in a tourist-oriented part of town, with no valet parking, one local wag observed that if you come sporting a shiny set of wheels, you can be sure someone else will park it somewhere else in Oakland and dismantle it for you.) **Keystone Korner** at 6030 Claremont Ave., tel. 652-9200, combines a Japanese restaurant with eclectic jazz. For information on other blues venues and special events, contact the **Bay Area Blues Society,** tel. 836-2227.

Then there's Emeryville, if Oakland proper is having a sleepy night. The old Other Cafe in San Francisco's Haight-Ashbury was a beloved local institution, a casual, classic comedic venue that closed in 1988—then was transplanted across the bay in Emeryville, incarnated here as the other **Other Cafe,** a stylish 250-seat, two-tiered venue, along with the California-Mediterranean **Club Politics** restaurant and nightclub. The new entertainment complex is at the Emery Bay Public Market at 5800 Shellmound St., tel. (510) 601-4888. (Come for the Gospel Brunch on Sunday.) Also at the market is **Kimball's East,** the most audience-friendly and fashionable jazz club in the area, tel. 658-2555. Other neighborhood diversions include **Chalkers Billiard Club** inside an old Emeryville tractor factory at 5900 Hollis St. (59th at Hollis), tel. 658-5821, an upscale pool hall with cafe and dart boards, open daily at noon. Or head to the **Oaks Card Club,** 4097 San Pablo Ave., tel. 653-4456, a 24-hour card club (Pai Gow, Hold-Em, Pan, Low-Ball) with hofbrau and grill.

Most publicized, though, are traditional mainstream entertainment arts, including one of the gems of the American dance scene, the **Oakland Ballet,** which usually performs in the equal-ly astounding art deco **Paramount Theatre of the Arts.** For more information about the ballet and its current performance schedule, call (510) 465-6400. Also well worth it while in town: the **Oakland Opera,** tel. 832-0559, and the **Oakland Symphony,** tel. 446-1992.

Movie buffs, head to the restored Egyptian-style art deco **Grand Lake Theatre,** 3200 Grand Ave., tel. (510) 452-3556. On weekends, enjoy the live organ music. Or come on Friday nights for the Paramount's $5 "Hollywood Classics" shows to appreciate this movie palace's spectacular interior as well as vintage cinema. For information on other events, call the theater at 893-2300 or 465-6400. (The city's Fox Theater, on Telegraph, may soon be fully restored to its Moorish grandeur and open again for business.)

Information And Transport

The **Oakland Convention and Visitors Bureau** in the Trans Pacific Centre, 1000 Broadway, Suite 200, Oakland 94607-4020, tel. (510) 839-9000 or toll-free (800) 2-OAKLAND, publishes a slick *The Oakland Book* each year, a fairly comprehensive listing of where to go, eat, and sleep, and is quite helpful with other information. The visitors bureau also publishes two newsletter-like tabloids, *Oakland Travel Monthly* (most useful for travelers) and *Oakland Monthly.* Worth the $2 price wherever you find it: "Oakland—A Guide to the Cultural, Architectural, Environmental, and Historic Assets of the City," a detailed map-style guide to the city's major (and minor) attractions. At 1001 Broadway, at street level, there's a walk-in **Visitors Center** for travel and tourism information, tel. 987-8200. The **Oakland Black Chamber Convention & Visitor Center** is at 654 13th St., tel. 451-9231.

The main traffic artery from San Francisco to Oakland is I-80 over the San Francisco-Oakland Bay Bridge (nightmarishly crowded most of the time), which funnels traffic toward downtown Oakland and beyond via I-580 or along the harbor route via the Nimitz Freeway (I-880). To avoid the traffic altogether, rely on public transit. Oakland is well-served by Bay Area Rapid Transit (BART), tel. (510) 465-BART, the high-speed intercity train system, which runs 4 a.m.-midnight, fare depending upon destination. Call for connecting bus service information or see fare charts at each BART station.

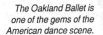

The Oakland Ballet is one of the gems of the American dance scene.

If BART doesn't do it, try **AC Transit** buses, tel. (510) 839-2882, which operate in and around Oakland daily—routes covered every six to eight minutes during peak hours (6-9 a.m. and 4-6 p.m.), every 15 minutes between "peaks," and every 30-40 minutes after 6 p.m. The #57 bus connects at major intersections with intercity express buses. Bus #61, which links downtown Oakland, Alameda, and San Leandro with the Oakland International Airport, runs weekdays 6 a.m.-8 p.m.

Travelers can also get to and from Oakland via **Greyhound,** though the depot north of downtown is in a questionably safe neighborhood at 2103 San Pablo Ave. at 21st St., tel. (510) 834-3070, doors open 5:30 a.m.-midnight. **Amtrak** is at 16th and Wood, tel. 654-4613 or toll-free (800) USA-RAIL for general information and reservations; but if you're coming into Oakland via Amtrak and aiming for Oak-

land International Airport, get off at the Richmond train station (which is adjacent to BART) then take BART to the Coliseum Station and catch the airport shuttle. BART buses, tel. 444-4200, leave the Fremont Line's Coliseum BART Station for the airport south of town every 10 minutes. To get to San Francisco from Oakland International, take AC Transit No. 57 to the Coliseum Station then switch to the Daly City line, or take the BART bus directly from the airport to San Francisco.

Oakland International Airport at Doolittle and Airport Dr. on the bay south of Oakland, tel. (510) 577-4000, is efficient, well-run, and preferred by many over San Francisco International due to its usually on-time flights. To reach downtown San Francisco or North Bay counties from the Oakland airport, take the **Oakland Airport Express,** tel. 499-9141. (See also the "San Francisco" chapter.)

BERKELEY

Berkeley is too casually dismissed as Berserkley or the People's Republic of Berkeley, epithets deriding fairly recent historical trends. Berkeley, after all, was named for evangelist Bishop Berkeley of Ireland who crossed the great waters to save wild America from itself with the cry: "Westward, the course of empire takes its way." But the course of empire in Berkeley has veered off to the left. The trend began in the 1930s, heated up in the '60s with Mario Savio and the Free Speech Movement, and continued on through years of anti-Vietnam War protests and activism on behalf of minorities, women, the politically downtrodden worldwide, and the beleaguered environment. Still the star at the city's center, the prestigious University of California at Berkeley has become the somewhat reluctant mother ship in the ever-expanding universe of ideas swirling around it.

The UC Berkeley campus, viewed
from the hills above

ED AUST

SIGHTS

The University Of California
Despite town-gown tensions, most everything in Berkeley radiates out from the campus here designed by Frederick Law Olmsted. **Sproul Plaza** behind Sather Gate, where Mario Savio and others dressed in suits and ties spoke out against university policies in the 1964 genesis of the Free Speech Movement, is still considered *the* University of California—despite the existence of other campuses, other plazas, other bell towers. The 61 fully chromatic carillon bells of **Sather Tower,** still known as the Campanile and usually played weekdays just before 8 a.m., at noon, and at 6 p.m., can be heard from almost anywhere on campus. (To watch the bell players at work, take a ride to the top.) Before wandering around this sprawling 1,232-acre institution, get oriented at the visitor information center at the Student Union, tel. (510) 642-4636, which offers maps and pamphlets for self-guided tours in addition to other information. Or take a guided tour, offered through the campus visitors center, tel. 642-5215.

To soak up some of the university's powerfully impersonal seriousness, spend time in any of its 25 libraries, a total information collection second only to Harvard's in size and prestige. The **Bancroft Library** is the most immediately impressive, its stacks open to the public, its excellent exhibits changing frequently. Also worth a stop: the **Phoebe Apperson Hearst Museum of Anthropology,** until recently known as the Lowie Museum of Anthropology, including many of A.L. Kroeber's contributions on display in Kroeber Hall, and the UC Earth Sciences Building, home of the **Berkeley Seismographic Station,** the **Museum of Paleontology,** and the **Museum of Geology.**

Modest **Le Conte Hall** on campus represents—in addition to Berkeley's less tangible world-changing creation, the Free Speech/political equality movement—a powerful symbol of the university's most striking achievements: physical and nuclear science breakthroughs that have changed the course of history. The

ED AUST

In addition to the people's art on Emeryville's mudflats, varieties of freeway art also thrive in the Berkeley-Oakland area.

university was already internationally renowned as a leader in the field of physics by 1939, when Ernest Lawrence won the Nobel Prize for inventing the cyclotron. By 1941, as a result of cyclotron experiments by Glenn Seaborg and others, plutonium had been discovered. And in that same year, Lawrence, Edward Teller, and J. Robert Oppenheimer began planning the development of the atomic bomb, at the behest of the U.S. government. For development and testing, that project was transferred from Berkeley to New Mexico—and the world saw the result in 1945, when the first A-bombs were dropped on Nagasaki and Hiroshima, the swan song of World War II, the birth of our brave new world.

One of two other on-campus monuments to the memory of William Randolph Hearst and clan is the **Hearst Memorial Mining Building.** Also donated by Hearst: UC's gorgeous outdoor **Greek Theatre.** The **University Art Museum** at 2626 Bancroft Way, tel. (510) 642-1207, also includes the **Pacific Film Archives** at 2621 Du-

rant, tel. 642-1124 or 642-1412, a cinema collection with screenings of oldies but goodies.

On UC's eastern fringe is the Strawberry Canyon **UC Botanical Garden** above Memorial Stadium along Centennial Dr., tel. (510) 642-3343, with 30 acres of native plants and exotics, one of the world's biggest and best botanic collections. Free guided tours are offered on weekends, though the garden is open daily 9-5. Pleasant picnicking. Across the way is the university's **Mather Redwood Grove,** open daily. Also in the neighborhood and exceptional is the **Lawrence Hall of Science** nearby on Centennial Dr., tel. 642-5132 or 642-5133, a top contender for the title of Northern California's best science museum, with hands-on exhibits (and the opportunity to try some freestyle physics experiments in the Wizard's Lab) and Holt Planetarium. Outside are fabulous giant wind chimes and a "solar observatory," Stonehenge style.

Other Sights

If you plan to be here awhile, an invaluable resource is a current copy of *Berkeley Inside/Out* by Don Pitcher and Malcolm Margolin, the definitive guidebook, published by Heyday Books and easily available in the Bay Area. Berkeley's northside, with its burgeoning bookstores and high-tech trendiness, attracts mostly the university crowd these days. More famous during its Free Speech heyday and later anti-war riots is the **Telegraph Avenue** and Durant area south of the university. From Dwight Way to Bancroft it's one busy blur of bookstores, boutiques, cheap clothing shops, record shops, ethnic restaurants, and fast-food stops—plus street people and street vendors, Berkeley's version of a year-round carnival. One wag has called Telegraph Avenue "a theme park with no theme"—an astute observation about much of California.

Since the area has also been inundated on weekends by bored teenagers and the drug dealers and other unsavories who prey upon them, cleaning up the area has become a new community rallying cry. The infamous **People's Park** on Haste just off Telegraph is owned by the university but hasn't yet been repossessed from the homeless, though UC plans to build dormitories here. Or maybe volleyball courts. A rallying point for community self-determination since the 1960s and '70s, though today the area is primarily a refuge for dealers and lost souls,

People's Park seems destined to have no genuine purpose in the community—which may, after all, be its purpose. Among the incredible numbers of bookstores in the area, **Cody's,** 2454 Telegraph at Haste, tel. (510) 845-7852, has been a haven for poetry (readings once a week) and prose since the days of the Beats.

But bookstores are almost as necessary to maintaining community consciousness as coffee. Older hipsters may remember **Moe's** just down the way, 2476 Telegraph, tel. (510) 849-2087, from *The Graduate*—four floors of used books, featuring also an antiquarian and art section. Literature and art lovers should also meander through **Shakespeare and Company,** 2499 Telegraph, tel. 841-8916, and, if you're in the Gourmet Ghetto, **Black Oak Books** at 1491 Shattuck, tel. 486-0698 or 486-0699, where they actually *hope* you'll sit down and start reading. Popular contemporary authors, from Ursula K. Le Guin and Toni Morrison to Salman Rushdie, are often on the guest lecture circuit here. **University Press Books** at 2430 Bancroft Way, tel. 548-0585, carries the largest selection of university press regional titles in the West.

Berkeley Outdoors
Tilden Regional Park and adjacent **Wildcat Canyon Regional Park** back up in the Berkeley Hills are the area's major parks. The trend at Tilden over the years has been toward recreational development, so this is the place for getting away from it all city-style: swimming in **Lake Anza** and sunning on the artificial beach; picnicking with family and friends; stopping off at **Little Farm** and riding the miniature train, merry-go-round, and ponies with the kiddies; and playing tennis or 18 holes at the golf course.

Tilden Park's popular **Native Plant Botanic Garden** (not to be confused with the university's), tel. (510) 841-8732, shelters 1,500 varieties of native California plants and wildflowers. Open 10-5 daily, with free tours offered on weekends from June through August. The park's **Environmental Education Center** is a good stop for trail brochures and other park information, also the starting point for the self-guided nature walk around little **Jewel Lake** on the Wildcat border. Though Tilden has its trails, for full-tilt hiking Wildcat Canyon is preferable—no paved roads and not many hikers or runners on the fire roads, which contour through grazing lands and foothill forests.

Right in town on the southeast side of the university is **Claremont Canyon Regional Preserve,** 200 steep, secluded acres suitable for deer-path wandering. **Indian Rock Park** on Indian Rock Avenue at Shattuck is popular with practicing mountain climbers. But for just smelling the roses, stop by the **Berkeley Rose Garden** on Euclid Avenue at Eunice, tel. (510) 644-6530, open May to September.

BERKELEY PRACTICALITIES

Accommodations
Since Berkeley residents have a hard time both finding a place to live in then affording it once they do, visitors shouldn't complain. A good deal on the cheap end for men only (age 18 and older) is the **YMCA,** 2001 Allston Way at Milvia, tel. (510) 848-6800. The **Golden Bear Motel** at 1620 San Pablo Ave., tel. 525-6770, is reasonable, with rooms $41-45. The **Best Western Berkeley House Motor Hotel** at 920 University Ave., tel. 849-1121, offers lodgings from $55. The **Hotel Durant,** 2600 Durant Ave., tel. 845-8981, is just a block from the university, with rooms at $80 s, $90 d, pay parking, airport transportation provided. Close to campus, too, is the stunning pink **Flamingo Motel,** 1761 University Ave., tel. 841-4242, a 1950s-style wonder with the basics plus in-room coffee, rates $40 and up. But if you want to get away from it all, or be near the water, consider the **Berkeley Marina Marriott** at 200 Marina Blvd. (take the College Avenue exit and head west), tel. 548-7920, where some rooms come with a view. Rates: $99-155, usually with lower weekend tariffs, and weekend getaway packages from $89.

The visitor bureau (information below) will happily provide a complete list of member accommodations.

The **French Hotel,** 1538 Shattuck Ave., tel. (510) 548-9930, is right across the street from Chez Panisse, smack dab in the center of Berkeley's food lover's zone, a consideration if you become too satiated to move. This small European-style hotel is right above its own cafe, a popular coffee-and-pastries hangout, so the wonderful aroma of freshly ground wafts right up the stairs. (Room service is available, but you can also go downstairs for some latte and join the Berkeleyites out on the sidewalk.) Rooms are airy and contemporary, and complimentary continental breakfast is a genuine pleasure. But once you park your stuff, parking your car can be a problem; ask the concierge for suggestions. Rates: $70-125.

For help in locating and reserving a bed and breakfast stay, contact either **Bed & Breakfast Accommodation in Berkeley,** tel. (510) 548-7556, or **Bed & Breakfast International/Berkeley,** tel. 525-4569. On your own, one possibility is the **Elmwood House Bed and Breakfast** at 2609 College Ave., tel. 540-5123, offering just four rooms. For a comfortable stay in Berkeley's brown-shingled, residential style, just two blocks from Telegraph Avenue yet quite quiet is the **Hillegass House** at 2834 Hillegass Ave., tel. 548-5517, close to campus but only four rooms, continental breakfast served, featuring specialties from nearby Nabalom Bakery. Rates are quite reasonable: $60-95, local tax included. An expanding local institution is **Gramma's Rose Garden Inn,** 2740 Telegraph Ave., tel. 549-2145, now offering (at last count) a total of 40 rooms in two huge old homes—originally a turn-of-the-century Tudor-style mansion, now the Victorian next door, too, plus a cottage, a carriage house, and garden house. English gardens in back. Rooms in the Fay House have striking stained glass windows and pristine hardwood floors; those in the carriage and garden houses have fireplaces. Guests can expect a basket of apples in their room. Coffee and cookies are available all day; complimentary wine and cheese are served in the evening. Rates, including breakfast and local bed tax: $85-175.

Student-style Food

For truly inexpensive food, head south toward Telegraph Avenue, though bargains can be found in and around the fringes of Berkeley's Gourmet Ghetto (see below). **The Blue Nile** at 2525 Telegraph, tel. (510) 540-6777, offers an upstairs view of the street scene below along with good Ethiopian food, both vegetarian and meat entrees. **Blondie's Pizza** at 2340 Telegraph, tel. 548-1129, is a local institution, quite good, pizza available by the slice. **Mario's La Fiesta,** 2444 Telegraph, tel. 540-9123, has excellent, inexpensive Mexican food (and lines inside and out at rush hours). The area's popular coffeehouses, including **La Bottega** at 2309 Telegraph, tel. 849-4099, and **Sufficient Grounds**

just off Telegraph at 2431 Durant, tel. 841-3969, offer good coffees, croissants and such, and Berkeley atmosphere. The neighborhood classic, though, where everybody goes, is **Caffe Mediterraneum** at 2475 Telegraph, tel. 841-5634. Among Berkeley's other coffeehouse hangouts: very hip **Cafe Milano** at 2522 Bancroft, tel. 644-3100, and **Espresso Strada** at 2300 College Ave. (at Bancroft), tel. 843-5282, a see-and-be-seen stop for the intelligentsia. That's not, of course, counting **Peet's**—see below—which is *the* Berkeley coffee label.

For authentic Chicago-style pizza, head to **Zachary's Chicago Pizza,** at 1853 Solano, tel. (510) 525-5950 (there's another on College Avenue in Oakland). Great for inexpensive real food in West Berkeley, from apple-cornmeal pancakes to hearty sandwiches, is the **Westside Bakery Cafe,** 2570 9th St., tel. 845-4852, open daily for breakfast and lunch. Good for lunch anytime is **Panini** in Trumpet Vine Court at Shattuck and Allston, tel. 849-0405, fresh gourmet everything in sometimes exotic combinations.

The **Berkeley Thai House** at 2511 Channing Way near Telegraph, tel. (510) 843-7352, has quite reasonable choices at lunch and dinner. Good for inexpensive pancake breakfasts and other basics is **Edy's** diner at 2201 Shattuck, tel. 843-3096. **Long Life Vegi House,** 2129 University Ave. at Shattuck, tel. 845-6072, serves vegetarian Chinese food (even potstickers) and brown rice. **Pasand Madras,** 2286 Shattuck at Bancroft, tel. 549-2559, serves very good Indian food, with dinners as cheap as $5.

The "Gourmet Ghetto," Other Fine Dining

The Shattuck Ave. and Walnut St. area between Rose and Virginia streets is known as Berkeley's Gourmet Ghetto (sometimes Gourmet Gulch) in wry recognition of the fine delis, food shops, gelato stops, and upscale restaurants so prominent here—a phenomenon started by the internationally renowned Chez Panisse. The entire neighborhood offers poor parking possibilities but wonderful opportunities for trend-watching. And the trend has spread far beyond its original geographical limits—onto University and San Pablo avenues, along 4th St., even onto Telegraph—hence the far-flung listings below.

Along Shattuck, people become drunk with pleasure on the liqueur-filled truffles at **Cocolat,** 1481 Shattuck, tel. (510) 843-3265. But the true heart of Berkeley's upscale ghetto is **Peet's,** a block off Shattuck at 2124 Vine St. at Walnut, tel. 841-0564, a much-loved local institution, with caffeine addicts buzzing like bees outside on the sidewalk. (Peet's has several other locations around town, on Domingo Ave., on Piedmont, and on Solano, and is even expanding into surrounding cities. But Peet's coffee fans will be happy to know they can order fresh coffee direct, from anywhere in California at least, by calling toll-free 800-999-2132.) **Poulet** on Shattuck, tel. 845-5932, is famous for its chicken specialties and organic and low-cholesterol chicken choices.

Gourmet grazing is also available along Hopkins Street, between Monterey and McGee, where you'll find **Made To Order,** 1576 Hopkins, tel. (510) 524-7552, a neighborhood deli with handmade sausages and at least 30 kinds of olive oil, and **Magnani Poultry,** 1586 Hopkins, tel. 528-6370, where you'll find those famous free-range chickens and even more unusual fowl, even rabbits. For very fresh fish, almost next door is the **Monterey Fish Co.,** tel. 525-5600. The **Monterey Market** at 1550 Hopkins, tel. 526-6042, specializes in organically grown local and exotic produce. But don't even walk down this street unless you stop at the **Hopkins Street Bakery,** 1584 Hopkins, tel. 526-8188, noted for its widely varied and unusual breads as well as decadent sweet treats. Chocolate cookie lovers, pick up a dozen Freak Outs.

Chez Panisse, 1517 Shattuck, tel. (510) 548-5525 for dinner reservations, tel. 548-5049 for cafe information, is the unassuming epicenter of California's culinary earthquake, Alice Waters's excellent and expensive but relaxed restaurant in a wood frame house. Dinners are fixed-price, with a daily changing menu, reservations a must. Cafe fare is served upstairs from the central open kitchen with brick ovens—little pizzas and other simple fare in a very amiable atmosphere. (No reservations.)

Locally mythic, too, and less expensive, is **O Chamé,** 1830 4th St., tel. (510) 841-8783, a Japanese-style wayside inn where people dress California casual to match the rustic interior, is an outgrowth of David Vardy's Daruma Teashop. The fare here reflects his Taiwanese Buddhist-Taoist culinary training, as well as Japan's Kansei and Kaiseki cuisine. The fixed-price menu at dinner allows patrons to choose delicacies from

S.F. CONVENTION & VISITORS BUREAU, PHIL COBLENTZ

The main transport link between Berkeley-Oakland and San Francisco is the Bay Bridge (viewed from Yerba Buena Island).

various categories. For lunch, select an entree—or buy a *bento* box lunch from the cart outside. Microbrews, both Japanese and American, are also served.

Lalime's at 1329 Gilman St., tel. (510) 527-9838, is another Berkeley fine dining delight, this one for California see-and-be-seen cuisine. The nightly changing menu may include chicken, beef, pork, and fresh fish, but people have been known to make a meal of the appetizer selections alone.

Cafe Fanny at 1603 San Pablo Ave., tel. (510) 524-5447, is another of Alice Waters's progeny, wonderful for breakfast and simple lunches, quite casual—just a counter and a bench or two. (Next door, at 1601 San Pablo, is another Alice Waters enterprise, the **Acme Bread Company,** for the best around.) The **Fourth Street Grill** at 1820 4th St., tel. 849-0526, serves hearty California-style fare: bacon and tomato sandwiches, homemade sausage, garlic-and-grits soufflés, excellent Caesar salad. For that red-vinyl-and-white-Formica ambience, complete with jukebox, **Bette's Ocean View Diner** at 1807-A 4th St., tel. 644-3230, serves thick milkshakes and other all-American standards. Popular for its burgers and simple suppers is **Christopher's Cafe,** 1897 Solano, tel. 526-9444.

Also in the general neighborhood is **Plearn Thai Cuisine,** 2050 University Ave., tel. (510) 841-2148, with good fiery Thai food—some say the Bay Area's best—though others swear by **Siam** at 1181 University, tel. 548-3278. For Northern Indian cuisine, the place is **New Delhi Junction** upstairs at The Village, 2556 Telegraph Ave., tel. 486-0477.

Outside the ghetto is **Narsai's Restaurant** in Kensington, 385 Colusa, tel. (510) 527-7900, with a classical French menu and impressive wine list. Tiny **À La Carte** in west Berkeley at 1453 Dwight Way, tel. 548-2322, serves superb traditional French fare as well. Psychologically far beyond the ghetto is **Augusta's Cafe** at 2955 Telegraph, tel. 548-3140, almost as famous for its fresh seafood specials as its annual May **Unmentionable Cuisine** dinner, with unforgettable taste treats like fried crickets and turkey testicles, sheep's eyes, grilled pigs ears, guinea pigs in peanut sauce, and jellyfish salad.

Arts And Entertainment

Count on the **The University Art Museum** on campus, 2626 Bancroft, tel. (510) 642-1207, for some unusual, and unusually brave, special exhibits. Also noteworthy in Berkeley is the **Judah L. Magnes Museum,** 2911 Russell St., tel. 849-2710, the West's largest Jewish cultural museum, with a Holocaust exhibit in addition to modern Jewish art and special exhibits. The lovely redwood and fir **Julia Morgan Theater** at 2640 College Ave., tel. 845-8542, considered its namesake's masterpiece, is a prime venue for local productions, including jazz, kids' shows, and chamber music. Best known for non-university theater, one of the state's finest repertory companies is the **Berkeley Repertory Theater,** tel. 845-4700, but the modern repertory of the **Theatre of the Blue Rose,** tel. 540-5037, is fun too. For the latest in dance, plays, and performance art by black artists, find out what's playing with the **Black Repertory Group,** 3201 Adeline, tel. 652-2120. The **UC Theater** at 2036 University, tel. 843-6267, shows nightly changing revival films, and count on the **Pacific Film Archives** at 2625 Durant, tel. 642-1412, for classics as well

as avant-garde and underground movies. For foreign films, try the **Northside Theatre** at 1828 Euclid Ave. (at Hearst), tel. 841-6000.

Call (510) 676-2222 for a recorded update on current activities and events. For information about local galleries and current arts and entertainment events on campus and off, pick up the UC Berkeley *Daily Californian* student paper, the free weekly *Express* (usually available in book and record shops), and the slick *Berkeley Monthly* magazine (quite reliable).

Definitely different is sake tasting at **Takara Sake USA,** 708 Addison, tel. (510) 540-8250, which brews exceptional sake from Sacramento Valley rice and Sierra Nevada water, open to visitors noon-6 p.m. daily. During the afternoon at least, before the place becomes standing-room-only, the **Triple Rock Brewery and Alehouse** brewpub at 1920 Shattuck, tel. 843-2739, is a hotspot for beer lovers after a taste of local brew, pale ales, and porter. Shuffleboard out back, roof garden. Less fratty, though, is **Bison Brewery** at 2598 Telegraph, tel. 841-7734, which experiments with the genre. Try some sagebrush ale.

Ashkenaz at 1317 San Pablo, tel. (510) 525-5054, is a folk-dance cooperative with folk, reggae, and world beat, though **Freight and Salvage** at 1111 Addison St., tel. 548-7603, is the Euro-style folkie hangout. For rhythm and/or blues, head to **Larry Blake's Downstairs** at 2367 Telegraph, tel. 848-0888, or the **Pasand Lounge** on Shattuck, tel. 848-0260. The **Starry Plough** is an Irish-style pub at 3101 Shattuck Ave., tel. 841-2082, with darts, a good selection of beers, and live music most nights.

Since every day in Berkeley is an *event,* organized activities per se aren't really the point here. One significant Berkeley event, though, is the **California Shakespeare Festival,** formerly the Berkeley Shakespeare Festival, usually held outdoors in Orinda from mid-June through mid-October (dress warmly). For information call the festival at (510) 548-3422, or, from January through October, the festival box office, tel. 525-8844.

Information And Transport
For basic Berkeley information, contact the **Berkeley Convention and Visitors Bureau** at 1834 University Ave., tel. (510) 549-7040 or toll-free (800) 847-4823, though budget travelers will find the **Council on International Education Exhange,** 2486 Channing Way at Tele-graph, tel. 848-8604, much more helpful. The ***Express,*** tel. 540-7400, is the most reliable and widely available publication that concentrates on East Bay events and community news. **AC Transit** buses and **BART** serve the community, though Oakland is closest and most convenient for **Amtrak** and **Greyhound** travelers. For more transit information, see "Oakland." For other information and options on public transport, cycling, and otherwise just getting around, contact **Berkeley TRIP,** tel. 644-7665. There are **ride boards** in the Student Union building on the UC Berkeley campus.

EAST BAY OUTBACK

The eastern expanse of the Bay Area is best known for its Berkeley-Oakland metropolis and surrounding suburban communities. But natural areas in the East Bay's outback offer snippets of silence and serenity in the midst of suburban sprawl, and an occasional glimpse of life as it once was in these hilly former farmlands. Many of the East Bay's treasures are collected into the **East Bay Regional Park District,** which includes some 60,000 acres of parklands.

A beautifully written "personal guide" to the East Bay's regional parks, the perfect hiking companion, is *The East Bay Out* by Malcolm Margolin, available in a recently updated edition published by Heyday Books. For brochures, maps, and other information about the major East Bay parks—including current information on the system's ever-expanding interconnecting trail system—call the district office, tel. (510) 531-9300; for picnicking and camping reservations, call 531-9043. For help in figuring out public transit routes to parks, call Bay Area Rapid Transit (BART), tel. 465-2278 (465-BART), and AC Transit, tel. 839-2882.

PARKS

Briones Regional Park
Over 5,000 semi-wilderness acres between Lafayette and Martinez, Briones Regional Park offers wonderful hiking up hillsides, down valleys, across meadows, with everything from wild-flowers and waterfalls to valley oaks and vistas of the bay and Mount Diablo. When tempera-tures and leaves fall and autumn winds whisk away the haze, you can even see the Sierra Nevada from the Briones Crest Trail. Grazing cattle and deer are fairly abundant year-round, but in the spring newts are more noticeable. Included in the park are the John Muir Nature Area, small lakes, self-guided nature trails, and an archery range.

Las Trampas Regional Wilderness
Over 3,000 acres of wilderness just west of Danville—home to mountain lions, wildcats, skunks, foxes, weasels, and golden eagles—Las Trampas Regional Wilderness offers heavenly hikes and great views, particularly from Las Trampas Ridge. Developed facilities include the Little Hills Ranch area near the park's entrance, with picnicking, swimming pool, playground, even a stocked fishing hole. To get here: from I-680 south of Danville, take Crow Canyon Rd. then Bollinger Canyon Rd. into the park.

Mount Diablo State Park
When early explorers and settlers first started groping toward California's great bay, they set their course by Mount Diablo's conical presence, and the peak itself was the base point for the U.S. government's first territorial surveys in 1851. Then—and on a clear day now, usually after a winter storm—views from Mount Diablo (elevation 3,849 feet) are spectacular: the Farallon Islands to the west, Lassen Peak to the north, even (with binoculars) Half Dome in Yosemite to the southeast. Mythic home of Eagle and Coyote to the Miwok, the rugged ter-

Mount Diablo's stone Summit Building, now a visitor center, under a rare blanket of snow

CALIFORNIA DEPARTMENT OF PARKS AND RECREATION

rain and wicked winds led settlers to believe the mountain was haunted. And, from a tale told to the state Legislature by Mariano Vallejo in 1850, linguistic confusion arose out of the native people's belief that their victory over Spanish troops in an early 1800s skirmish was due to assistance from the mountain's "spirit," which translated into Spanish as "devil"; thus the name Mount Diablo.

Mount Diablo State Park is a wonder, one which some half-million people enjoy each year. Peak experiences here include the view from the summit, the Mitchell Canyon hike to the summit (the park has a total of 50 miles of trails), rock climbing, fabulous spring wildflower displays, and Fossil Ridge (don't touch). Mountain bikers may ride unpaved roads to the west of North Gate and South Gate roads. There's a wonderful visitor center, open since 1984, in the beautiful 1939 stone Summit Building built by the WPA.

Diablo is open daily 8 a.m.-sunset, when both gates close. The day-use fee is $5, but when area fire danger is extremely high, the park may be closed for all uses. Three year-round campgrounds with water and flush toilets but no showers are often available on a first-come basis, but can be reserved in advance through Mistix, tel. (800) 444-7275. Remote walk-in environmental campgrounds are available only from October through May due to high fire danger; bring your own water. No alcohol is permitted in Mount Diablo State Park, the first in the state to ban it outright due to drunk driving incidents and other disasters. For more information, con-

tact: Mount Diablo State Park, P.O. Box 250, Diablo 94528, tel. (510) 837-2525.

Black Diamond Mines Regional Preserve

One way to beat the heat in summer is by heading underground for a stroll through the cool sandstone caverns deep within the six-level Hazel-Atlas Mine—part of the former Mount Diablo coal-mining district (the state's largest) and later, prime underground fields for harvesting high-grade silica sand. Included as part of the Black Diamond Mines Regional Preserve, the mine is open for two-hour tours by advance reservations only. For safety reasons, children under age seven are not allowed. For more information and reservations, call (510) 757-2620. To contemplate the generally short life spans of miners—too often killed in cave-ins, explosions, or by silicosis—wander through the nearby Rose Hill Cemetery. To get here: from Hwy. 4 in Antioch, head six miles south via Somersville Road.

Morgan Territory Regional Preserve

A fascinating feature on these remote eastern ridgetops beyond Mount Diablo as elsewhere throughout the East Bay (on Mission Peak in Fremont, near Vollmer Peak in Tilden Park, and on Round Top Peak in the Oakland Hills) are squat stone walls with no traceable history. Someone obviously went to considerable trouble to build them, hauling large stones up the mountainside, but the walls have no apparent practical value and follow no known property lines. Rumor has it that they predate the Spanish and even native populations, and were possibly built by early Chinese explorers as astronomical markers.

Even today this region is mysterious, remote, quiet, and almost inaccessible due to the wild one-lane road winding up the mountain. For those looking for solitude, here it is. Also here: a few picnic tables (pack out your trash), rusting farm equipment, and fruit trees from the land's one-time ranch status. To get here: from I-580 north of Livermore, head north on N. Livermore Ave. to the end, turn left onto Manning Rd., then turn right at Morgan Territory Road.

Sunol And Ohlone Regional Wildernesses

The **Ohlone Regional Wilderness** is some 7,000 acres of wild high ridges on the south end of Alameda County, accessible only via the Sunol Regional Wilderness to the west or the Del Valle Regional Recreation Area to the north (popular for swimming, windsurfing, picnicking, camping). Backpackers generally have the place to themselves, following old roads over ridges and through meadowlands then camping at one of several backcountry sites. The peak experience here is a day-hike (starting 10 miles in from either entrance) to the top of Rose Peak—brutal for heavily laden backpackers—which offers top-of-the-world views of the Santa Clara Valley, the bay, and Mount Diablo.

Sunol Wilderness also features oak woods and remoteness as well as developed family picnic facilities and backpack and walk-in camping, tel. (510) 862-2244. To get here: from the I-680/Hwy. 84 interchange take Calaveras Rd. to Geary Rd. and continue to the end.

OUTBACK COMMUNITIES

Benicia

The one-time capital of California just north of the Benicia-Martinez Bridge via I-780, Benicia is proud of its "firsts," though some seem stretched in significance. The town had the state's first chamber of commerce, law school, and public school—but also the first steamboat built by Americans in California, the first railroad ferry west of the Mississippi, and the first recorded marriage in Solano County.

Take a quick tour of the town's historic architecture (most buildings not open to the public) and stop at the restored **Benicia State Capitol Historic Park,** tel. (707) 745-3385, an 1852 brick building at 1st and G streets, which housed the Senate, the Assembly, and the state Treasury for 13 months in 1853-54. (Admission free, which also gets you into the Fischer-Hanlon House next door.) Benicia's **Camel Barn Museum** in the industrial park, the town's one-time military complex, is named for a short-lived 1860s experiment: using camels to transport military supplies across the Southwest. The cranky creatures were stabled here, now home to local memorabilia. Open 1-4 p.m. weekends only, small fee.

Benicia proper is experiencing an art-community boom and overall revitalization, with cafes and shops worth peeking into. Try breakfast, lunch, or dinner at Benicia's **Union Hotel,** noted for its creative (and fairly reasonable) California-style cuisine and nice hotel rooms, 401 1st St., tel. (707) 746-0100, or stop off at surprisingly good **Mabel's Cafe** also on 1st, tel. 746-7068, serving very nouveau diner fare. Just northwest of town along the strait is **Benicia State Recreation Area,** popular for fishing, hiking, picnicking. Day-use fee is $3, but be prepared for the automatic gates, which take only dollar bills or quarters.

Martinez

Martinez, on the other end of the bridge, settled by Italian fishing families, is historic home to both the martini and New York Yankee baseball great Joe DiMaggio. A modern-day attraction is the **John Muir House,** the naturalist's 1882 Victorian home and grounds, now a national historic site maintained by the U.S. Park Service at 4202 Alhambra Ave., tel. (510) 228-8860. Home to Muir and his wife during the last 24 years of his life, this is where he did most of his conservation writing. In addition to becoming an astute businessman, orchardist, inventor, pioneer of factory automation, patron of the arts, and magazine editor, the indefatigable Scot explored California and Alaska, established the U.S. Forest Service and five national parks, and co-founded the Sierra Club.

The house holds many of Muir's books and writings, also exhibits chronicling his amazing influence. In mid-December, come for Christmas carols and Victorian tea. Also on the grounds:

the **Martinez Adobe,** the 1844 home of Don Vincente Martinez, part of the old Rancho Las Juntas. Muir House is open Wed.-Sun. (except major holidays) 10 a.m.-4:30 p.m., small fee.

Also in the area is the new **Carquinez Shoreline Regional Park,** 969 acres for birdwatching, biking, and hiking, reached via Hwy. 4 (from I-80) then McEwen Rd. and Carquinez Scenic Drive. After a short hike down to Port Costa, backtrack to 343-acre **Martinez Regional Shoreline Park** and more views and usually fresh air (and wind).

Crockett
Crockett is most famous for the C & H sugar refinery here but is on its way to becoming an artsy-industrial enclave, like a smokestack-style Sausalito. Under the Carquinez Bridge, on the pilings, is the **Nantucket Fish Company,** tel. (415) 787-2233. One of many best bets: a platter of New England steamed clams, enough for two, under $10. (The view of the bridge's underbelly and the nearby sugar refinery is free.)

Danville
Worthwhile in Danville is a stop at Eugene O'Neill's **Tao House,** a two-story Spanish-style home and national historic landmark where O'Neill wrote some of his last plays, including *The Iceman Cometh, Long Day's Journey Into Night,* and *A Moon for the Misbegotten.* One day, the property may actually be opened to the public as a park for the performing arts, as has been the intention for decades, but neighbors still don't cotton to the idea. In the meantime, only two tours per day are offered, with buses leaving from downtown Danville. Call (510) 838-0249 for more information and advance reservations.

New in Danville is the opulent **Behring Auto Museum,** showcase for a $100-million collection of classic cars—including the 1924 torpedo-shaped Tulipwood Hispano Suiza built for Andre Dubonnet of French aperitif fame, Clark Gable's 1935 Duesenberg convertible, and Rudolph Valentino's 1926 Isotta Fraschini. Open Tues.-Sun. 10-5, until 9 p.m. on Wed. and Fri. nights. The Behring's former (and steep) $20 admission has been lowered substantially: $5 adults, $3 for seniors and students, free for children under age six. For more information, or to arrange a guided tour (reservations required, $10), call

the Martinez Adobe, part of the John Muir House historic complex in Martinez

(510) 736-2278. To get here: from I-680, exit at Crow Canyon Rd. 10 miles south of Walnut Creek, head east to Camino Tassajara, then turn right and look for the sign—and the mall.

Another local museum, right next door—and something of a surprise out here in the suburbs, especially in an upscale and exclusive shopping mall like Blackhawk Plaza—is the new **UC Berkeley Museum,** tel. (510) 736-2280, an extension of the Berkeley campus Phoebe Hearst Museum of Anthropology (formerly the Lowie Museum). Exhibits here represent everything but culture as defined by cars: the permanent exhibits include rare and unique objects from ancient and modern cultures around the world, organized into categories such as Power, Images of Childhood, The Domain of Women, and The Domain of Men. Elsewhere in the museum, the interactive displays are popular. Special changing exhibits explore topics like "In Pursuit of Ancient Life." The Berkeley Museum is open the same hours as the Behring Museum, admission $3 adults, $2 for seniors and students, free for children under age six.

If you get hungry out here in the hinterlands, the expensive, shiny, and automobile-oriented **Blackhawk Grill** at the other end of the mall, tel. (510) 736-4295, serves exceptional and eclectic food. Other good choices in the area, generally less pricey: **Bridges** at 44 Church St., tel. 820-7200, with an impressive East-West menu, and inexpensive **La Ultima** in downtown Danville, 455 Hartz Ave., tel. 838-9705, serving genuine New Mexican specialties quite rare in California. Also in the area: the Franciscan **San Damiano Retreat Center** on a hill overlooking the San Ramon Valley, P.O. Box 767, Danville 94526, which offers inexpensive psyche-saving retreats for people of any (or no) faith.

Livermore Valley

Pleasanton seems to be the face of California's future: more corporate business parks mixed with backyard barbecues. **Livermore** is home of the **Lawrence Livermore National Laboratory** on N. Greenville Rd. (follow the signs), tel. (510) 422-9797, which developed the X-ray laser for the U.S. Star Wars defense system, before the world changed. The visitor center here is open to the public daily, with scientific displays and videos of atomic test sites and the lab's underground linear accelerator (tours of top-secret research and development facilities are not available). One thing no one here will probably discuss is the fact that this is a Superfund toxic waste site (with a 50-year cleanup time frame) and that lab employees have a melanoma cancer rate about five times the national average. Visitors can stop to pray, though, at the town's lovingly handcrafted Hindu **Shiva-Vishnu Temple**, along with Lord Vishnu, the Goddess of Love, and Mother Earth. Unique because it combines the stylistic traditions of both northern and southern India, the temple is an architectural anachronism here in any event, amid Livermore's tract homes on Arrowhead Ave.; call 449-6255 for more information.

The surrounding Livermore Valley, home of the **Livermore Rodeo** every June, is noted for its wineries—some of the oldest in the state. The historic Cresta Blanca vineyard has been resurrected as the **Wente Brothers Sparkling Wine Cellars**, 5050 Arroyo Rd., tel. (510) 447-3023, picnicking available, also special events

---

AT JOHN MUIR'S GRAVE

I want to remember stumbling
across fresh–turned clods in the peach orchard
he would have planted a few years later . . .
but that's memory; these are words.

I walked to the isolated plot
where John Muir is buried
with the rest of his family.
An ornate fence kept me out.

His stone is simple,
factual with dates and place.
A bit of laurel,
alive and carved, befits the man

All beneath his loved and noted
incense cedar, a scraggly tree
often milled to pencils
for making words, for making words.

—Gary Thompson

---

like summer performances by the Oakland Symphony. Also in the neighborhood: **Concannon**, 4590 Tesla Rd., tel. 447-3760; award-winning **Fenestra Winery**, 83 E. Vallecitos Rd., tel. 447-5246, which offers limited winetasting in summer, otherwise only quarterly by invitation (call for info); and the traditional **Wente Brothers** at 5565 Tesla Rd., tel. 447-3603.

Beyond Livermore on the way to Tracy via I-580 is the **Altamont Pass** area, open foothill grazing land best known for the thousands of wind turbines in the power-generating "wind farms" here—an alternative energy source with the nasty negative side effect of chopping airborne birds into bits.

POINT REYES NATIONAL SEASHORE

Some 65,000 acres of fog-shrouded lagoons, lowland marshes, sandy beaches, coastal dunes, and ridgetop forests, Point Reyes National Seashore also features windy headlands and steep, unstable, colorful cliffs, populations of tule elk and grazing cattle, and a wonderful lighthouse all too popular for winter whalewatching. A dramatically dislocated triangular wedge of land with its apex jutting out into the Pacific Ocean, Point Reyes is also land in motion: this is earthquake country. Separated from mainland Marin County by slit-like Tomales Bay, the Point Reyes Peninsula is also sliced off at about the same spot by the San Andreas Fault. When that fault shook loose in 1906—instantly thrusting the peninsula 16 feet farther north—the city of San Francisco came tumbling down.

Geologists were long baffled by the fact that the craggy granite outcroppings of Point Reyes were identical to rock formations in the Tehachapi Mountains some 310 miles south. But the theory of plate tectonics and continental drift provided the answer. The Point Reyes Peninsula rides high on the eastern edge of the Pacific Plate, which moves about three inches to the northwest each year, grinding against the slower-moving North American Plate. The two meet in the high-stress, many-faulted rift zone of the Olema Valley, an undefined line "visible" in landforms and weather patterns. In summer, for example, fog may chill the coastal headlands and beaches while the sun shines east of Inverness Ridge.

To be fully informed about what's going on in and around Point Reyes while visiting, a good free companion is the quarterly tabloid *Coastal Traveler,* published by the area's Pulitzer Prize-winning *Point Reyes Light* newspaper and available at area shops and businesses. For advance or additional information, contact the **Western Marin Chamber of Commerce,** P.O. Box 1045, Point Reyes Station 94956, tel. (415) 663-9232.

POINT REYES SIGHTS AND HIKES

Get oriented at the park's barn-like **Bear Valley Visitor Center** just off Hwy. 1 near Olema, which, in addition to natural history and fine arts

exhibits, includes a seismograph for monitoring the earth's movements. Near the picnic tables at the visitor center is the short **Earthquake Trail** loop (wheelchair-accessible), which demonstrates the San Andreas seismic drama, from sag ponds and shifts in natural boundary lines to the old Shafter Ranch barn, a corner of which slid off its foundations during the 1906 San Francisco earthquake. Also near the Bear Valley Visitor Center are the short self-guided **Woodpecker Nature Trail,** the **Morgan Horse Ranch** where the Park Service breeds and trains its mounts, and **Kule Loklo,** an architectural re-creation of a Coast Miwok community. (When Sir Francis Drake purportedly arrived at Point Reyes in the late 1500s he found at least 113 such villages on the peninsula.) The best time to see Kule Loklo is during July's **Annual Native American Celebration,** when this outdoor exhibit, complete with sweathouse, thatched and redwood bark dwellings, and dancing lodge, comes to life with Miwok basketmakers, wood- and stonecarvers, and native singing and dancing.

The **Limantour Estero** near Drakes Estero and Drakes Beach is great for birdwatching; **McClures Beach** is best for tidepooling, and both **North Beach** and **South Beach** north of Point Reyes proper offer good beachcombing but treacherous swimming. However, protected **Drakes Beach** and **Limantour Beach** along the crescent of Drakes Bay are safe for swimming.

For astounding views when the fog lifts above the ship graveyard offshore, head out to Point Reyes proper and the **Point Reyes Lighthouse and Visitor Center** (at last report open daily 10-5 during whalewatching season, more limited hours at other times). The **Chimney Rock Trail** is wonderful for spring and summer wildflowers and, if you head west, is also a roundabout way to reach the lighthouse. On all Point Reyes hikes, carry water, wear proper walking shoes, and dress for sudden, unpredictable weather changes.

To experience the sound and fury of Coast Creek hurling itself into the Pacific via the "sea tunnel" at the **Arch Rock Overlook,** dress warmly, wear raingear and slip-proof shoes, and come (via the very popular Bear Valley Trail) during

THE MYSTERY OF SIR FRANCIS DRAKE

Though named by Vizcaino in 1603 while he was passing the rocky headlands on the 12th day of Christmas, or the Feast of the Three Kings, Point Reyes was actually explored earlier by the privateer Sir Francis Drake. Tired of pursuing Spanish ships around the world, he beached the *Pelican* (later known as the *Golden Hinde)* and came ashore at "a fit and convenient harbour" somewhere in California in June of 1579. Naming the land Nova Albion, here he made repairs, rested his tired crew, and claimed the area for Queen Elizabeth I with "a plate of brasse, fast nailed to a great and firme post." This much most historians agree on. The rest of the story is contentious at best.

Where exactly did Drake land? Since the main estuary at Point Reyes is named after Drake, as is the bay, the simple answer is that he came ashore here, some 20 nautical miles north of San Francisco. But some contend that Drake actually landed at Bolinas Lagoon or explored San Francisco Bay and landed near Point San Quentin or Novato, near an old Olompali village site where a 1567 English silver sixpence was discovered in 1974. Others say he stumbled ashore on Goleta Beach near Santa Barbara, where five cast-iron British cannons similar to those missing from the *Golden Hinde* were unearthed in the 1980s. But 70 pieces of antique Ming porcelain have been found near Point Reyes—proof enough, say true believers of the Point Reyes theo-

ry, since four chests of Chinese porcelain, which Drake stole from the Spanish, never arrived in England. (Unbelievers counter that the porcelain washed ashore instead from the wreckage of the *San Agustin* off Drakes Bay.)

Other related questions remain unanswered. Is the infamous brass plate found on a beach near Point San Quentin in 1936 genuine or a clever forgery? After years of controversy, in the 1970s the British Museum declared the corroded placard an "undoubted fake" despite the olde English ring of its language, and metallurgists say the plate is no more than 100 years old. (To judge for yourself, the brass plate is on permanent display at UC Berkeley's Bancroft Library.)

What became of Drake's journal, which supposedly documented this journey as well as Drake's discovery of the Northwest Passage? And what happened to the gold, gems, and silver Drake stole from the Spanish ship *Cacafuego* and others, estimated in today's currency values as worth $50 million? Some say no treasure was buried along the California coast, that Drake would have jettisoned cannons and china and other goods instead to lighten his ship's load. Drake, they say, took all his loot back to England where he and his crew became millionaires, and the queen retired some of the national debt and started the East India Company. Others, however, are still looking.

a storm. (For safety's sake, stay well back from the spectacle, and don't attempt to walk through the tunnel under any circumstances—though people often do in calm weather.)

To make the most of a full moon at Point Reyes, head to the **Wildcat Beach Overlook** via the Bear Valley Trail from the visitor center, then south via the Coast Trail to the area overlooking the beach, Alamere Falls, and the southern stretch of Drakes Bay. An alternate route to **Alamere Falls** about one mile south of Wildcat Camp (most spectacular after heavy rains) is via the Palomarin Trail from Bolinas or the Five Brooks Trail. For the best panoramic vista of Drakes Bay, take the Bear Valley, Sky, then Woodward Valley trails to the bay (alternatively, take the Coast Trail from Coast Camp to the Woodward Valley Trail) then climb up the small hill overlooking the bay, just northwest of the trail.

The new **Randall Spur Trail** created by the Civilian Conservation Corps now connects the Bolinas Ridge Trail with the various Inverness Ridge and Olema Valley trails—making Point Reyes's southern stretches more accessible for day hikers. Worth a stop on the way to the Palomarin trailhead in south Point Reyes is the **Point Reyes Bird Observatory**, tel. (415) 868-0655, established in 1965 as the first bird observatory in the U.S. (mailing address: 4990 Shoreline Hwy., Stinson Beach 94970). Though it's a full-fledged research facility, the Palomarin observatory is open to the public, with educational classes (call ahead for information), interpretive exhibits, and nature trail. To get here by car, take the unmarked turnoff to Bolinas (near highway marker 17.00 at the north end of Bolinas Lagoon), continue two miles or so to Mesa Rd., then turn right and continue four miles to the observatory's bird-banding station.

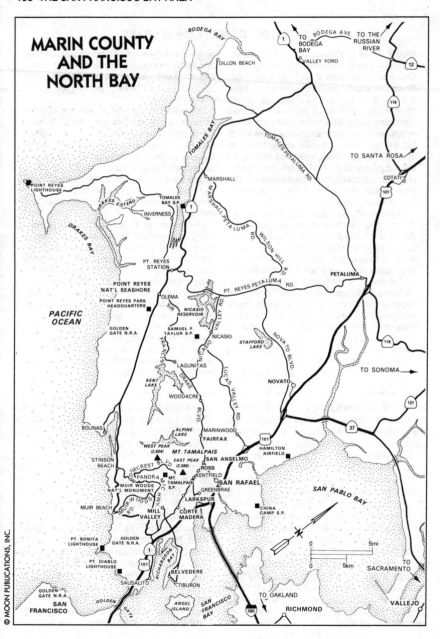

MARIN COUNTY
AND THE
NORTH BAY

© MOON PUBLICATIONS, INC.

Whalewatching

Whalewatching, particularly fine from the lighthouse, is immensely popular at Point Reyes and best from about Christmas through January, when whales pass from one to five miles offshore. (Come on a weekday to avoid the crowds.) A hundred or more whale sightings per day is fairly typical here, though a 307-step descent to the lighthouse must be negotiated first. There are good views also from the platform at the top of the stairs. The parking lot at the **Point Reyes Lighthouse** is fairly small, so most peak-season whalewatchers park at Drakes Beach near the park entrance and take the free shuttle bus to the lighthouse on January weekends. National Park Service naturalists are also available in January 10-4 daily, both at the lighthouse and at the small information center near the viewing platform, to provide whale facts and whale-watching tips. For more information about Point Reyes whalewatching, including the shuttle schedule for the rest of winter and special naturalist programs, call (415) 663-1092 or 669-1534. (For more information on the migration of the gray whales, see "The North Coast" chapter.) The lighthouse is now open to the public for self-guided and ranger-led tours, Thursday through Monday. Otherwise, the Point Reyes Lighthouse Visitor Center is open 10-5, and the steps down to the lighthouse open 10-4:30 (closed in the event of high winds). Since hours may change, call to verify before setting out.

Not far from the lighthouse is the **Point Reyes Historic Lifeboat Station,** established in 1889 with a "surfcar" (like a tiny submarine) pulled through the surf on a cable, hand-pulled surfboats, and a Lyle gun and breeches buoy. The facility is open infrequently, available for educational programs on marine biology and maritime history. For more information, call (415) 663-1092.

Information

For information about Point Reyes, including current trail maps, and to obtain permits for camping and backpacking, stop by any of the park's three visitor centers: the Bear Valley Visitor Center at the park's Bear Valley entrance, the Kenneth C. Patrick Visitor Center at Drakes Beach, or the Point Reyes Lighthouse Visitor Center. Or contact: **Point Reyes National Seashore,** Point Reyes 94956, tel. (415) 663-1092. Ask, too, about the annual **Coastwalk,** usually held in August, a nine-day two-county hike officially limited to only 40 people (though anyone can join the group to walk during the day).

For information about the year-round schedule of excellent classes and field seminars held at Point Reyes (most offered for credit through Dominican College, some offered cooperatively through the Elderhostel program), contact: **Point Reyes Field Seminars,** Point Reyes 94956, tel. (415) 663-1200, and ask for the current seminar catalog.

The headlands of beautiful Point Reyes: even on a foggy day you can see part of Drakes Bay.

WES DEMPSEY

A useful guidebook to the area is *Point Reyes—Secret Places & Magic Moments* by Phil Arnot.

For information about what's going on in Point Reyes and surrounding communities, pick up a copy of the Pulitzer Prize-winning *Point Reyes Light,* which made a name for itself with investigative reporting on the area's former Synanon cult. For information about area practicalities, see "Western Marin Accommodations" and "Good Food in Western Marin" below.

THE FARALLON ISLANDS

Visible from Point Reyes on a clear day are the Farallon Islands to the southwest. Protected as the Farallon National Wildlife Refuge, the largest seabird rookery south of Alaska, these islands are one of the five most ecologically productive marine environments on earth and now part of an international UNESCO Biosphere Reserve. Some 948 square nautical miles of ocean from Bodega Head to Rocky Point are included in the **Point Reyes-Farallon Islands National Marine Sanctuary.** These rugged granite islands 27 miles west of San Francisco are actually the above-sea-level presence of the Farallones Escarpment, which parallels the coast from the tip of Point Reyes to south of the Golden Gate. The natural but rare phenomenon of upwelling around the islands, with warm offshore winds drawing cold, nutrient-rich ocean water to the surface in spring, creates the phenomenal algae and plankton populations that support the feeding frenzies and breeding successes of animals farther up the food chain.

But during recent centuries, life has been almost undone at the Farallones. In the 1800s, "eggers" exploited the rookeries here to provide miners and San Franciscans with fresh eggs at breakfast. The islands have also survived assaults from sealers, whalers, gill netters, bombers, ocean oil slicks, and radioactive waste dumping.

In the summer, more than 250,000 breeding birds—from tufted puffins and petrels to auklets and murres—consider the Farallones home. Seals (including the almost extinct northern elephant seal) and sea lions also breed here, and gray and humpback whales as well as northern fur seals are often spotted in the area. The

nonprofit, member-supported **Point Reyes Bird Observatory,** 4990 Shoreline Hwy., Stinson Beach 94970, tel. (415) 868-0655, staffs a scientific study center at the Farallones (in addition to its center at Point Reyes), but otherwise people are not allowed on the islands—though the **Oceanic Society** (see "North Bay Diversions" under "East Marin and Vicinity" below) sponsors educational expeditions around the Farallon Islands from June through October and during the winter whalewatching season. (Bring binoculars.) The public is welcome, however, at the Point Reyes Bird Observatory's **Palomarin Field Station,** tel. 868-0655, at the end of Mesa Road near Bolinas, to observe **bird banding,** every day from May through November and on Wed., Sat., and Sun.; call for exact times and to make reservations for groups of five or more people.

For more information about the Farallon Islands, contact: **San Francisco Bay Wildlife Refuge,** P.O. Box 524, Newark 94560, tel. (415) 792-0222. For more information about the surrounding marine sanctuary, contact: Point Reyes-Farallon Islands National Marine Sanctuary, Building 201, Fort Mason, San Francisco 94123, tel. 556-3509.

GOLDEN GATE NATIONAL RECREATION AREA AND VICINITY

Immediately adjacent to Point Reyes near Olema is the Golden Gate National Recreation Area (GGNRA), which wraps itself around various state and local parks inland then extends southeast to include the Golden Gate Bridge and a thin coastal strip south to Fort Funston. Most notable is the dramatic natural beauty of the Marin Headlands—sea-chiseled chilly cliffs, protected valleys, and grassy wind-combed hills rich with wildlife and wildflowers, all opening out to the bay and the Pacific Ocean. Protected at first by the Nature Conservancy until coming under national management in 1972, the vast GGNRA features trails for days of good hiking and backpacking (stop by headquarters for a current trail map), also backcountry and group camps.

Best of all for views of the San Francisco Bay—not to mention the exceptional birding opportunities—is **Hawk Hill** (abandoned Battery 129, reached via Conzelman Rd.) above the Golden Gate Bridge. Come in the fall (with binoculars and fog-worthy clothing) to appreciate the incredible numbers of birds of prey congregating here, 100 or more each day representing 20 or so species. For more information, call (415) 331-0730.

Aside from the GGNRA's natural beauty, here also is historic scenery, from the 1877 Point Bonita Lighthouse to four military installations that protected the San Francisco Bay Area from the 1870s through World War II: Fort Barry, Fort Cronkhite, and Fort Baker. (Fort Funston, the fourth, is near San Francisco's Lake Merced.) **Fort Barry,** near the AYH youth hostel, includes an intact 1950s missile launch site and underground bunkers (not usually open to the public), one still home to a Nike Hercules missile. "Guardians of the Gate" military history tours offered twice-monthly by park personnel, tel. (415) 331-1540, include the various batteries just north of Point Bonita and end at the Nike site.

The **Point Bonita Lighthouse,** call (415) 331-1540 for hours and tour information, was one of the first lighthouses ever built on the West Coast and is still going strong. Technically, though, this isn't really a lighthouse—there's no house, just the French-import 1855 Fresnel lens with protective glass, walls, and roof, with gargoyle-like American eagles guarding the light. Getting here is as thrilling as being here—meandering along the half-mile footpath to the rocky point through hand-dug tunnels and across the swaying footbridge, in the middle of nowhere yet in full view of San Francisco. Especially enjoyable are the sunset and full-moon tours conducted by GGNRA rangers. Admission to the lighthouse and tours is free. (For seaside barbecues, head to the picnic area at

Battery Wallace near Point Bonita.) To get to the lighthouse, follow the signs to Fort Baker/Fort Cronkhite/Fort Barry from Alexander Ave. just off the Golden Gate Bridge, then turn left at Field Rd. and continue, following the signs. For more information about American lighthouses, contact the **U.S. Lighthouse Society,** 130 St. Elmo Way, San Francisco 94127, tel. 584-9748.

Also at Fort Barry: the **Headlands Center for the Arts,** tel. (415) 331-2787, which explores the relationship of art and the environment. Studio space for artists is provided, and public programs include lectures, installations, exhibits, and performances.

Fairly new GGNRA features include the **Slide Ranch** demonstration farm and family-oriented environmental education center two miles north of Muir Beach, tel. (415) 381-6155, reservations required for all events, and the hands-on **Bay Area Discovery Museum** at East Fort Baker, tel. 332-7674, designed for children ages 2-12 and their families, open Wed.-Sun. 10-5. Both offer a great variety of special programs year-round, for example "In the Dream Time" children's art workshops at the museum and "Family Farm Day" at the ranch.

Also included within the GGNRA is the **California Marine Mammal Center** (just above Cronkhite Beach), 1044 Fort Cronkhite, Sausalito 94965-2610, tel. (415) 331-SEAL (tel. 331-0161 to schedule a tour), since 1975 a hospital for wild animals, which returns its "patients," once fit, to their native marine environments. The Marine Mammal Center, with more than 400 active volunteers—a 1989 recipient of the presidential Volunteer Action Award—also sponsors hands-on environmental education programs for children and is open daily to the general public, 10 a.m.-4 p.m. Wheelchair-accessible. (New members and financial contributions always welcome.) Also at Fort Cronkhite: the **Pacific Energy and Resources Center,** which offers teacher training, special elementary and secondary school programs, and exhibits on local and global environmental issues.

The GGNRA also includes the headlands campus and headquarters of the **Headlands Institute,** at Fort Barry, Sausalito 94965, tel. (415) 332-5771, open for school tours only. However, the adjacent **Marin Headlands Visitor Center** is open to the public 8:30 a.m.-4:30 p.m. daily and offers hands-on natural science exhibits and educational and historical displays. Call for directions.

For more details, including information about the GGNRA's **Alcatraz Island** and other tours, contact: Golden Gate National Recreation Area, Building 201, Fort Mason, San Francisco 94123, tel. (415) 556-0560, or stop for maps and other information at the **Marin Headlands GGNRA visitor center** at Fort Cronkhite near Rodeo Lagoon, tel. 331-1540, open daily 8:30 a.m.-4:30 p.m. Or stop by the **Muir Woods Visitor Center** at Muir Woods on Mount Tamalpais, tel. 388-2596, another GGNRA information outpost. Pick up trail maps and events calendars, and ask about backcountry camping at the visitor centers. A variety of guidebooks published by the nonprofit Golden Gate National Park Association are well worth buying—including the 96-page *Park Guide,* which covers every feature of the recreation area.

To find out about how to become a GGNRA volunteer, call (415) 556-3535.

Alcatraz

Part of the GGNRA is infamous Alcatraz, one-time military outpost then island prison and federal hellhole for hard-core criminals (including mobsters Al Capone, "Machine Gun" Kelley, and Mickey Cohen, as well as Robert Stroud, the "Birdman of Alcatraz"—who, despite the romance of his popular myth, never kept birds on The Rock). Closed in the 1960s then occupied for two years by Native Americans who hoped to reacquire the property for a cultural heritage center, Alcatraz Island and its prison facilities are now managed as part of the Golden Gate National Recreation Area. For general information, call the GGNRA office in San Francisco, tel. (415) 556-0560; for Alcatraz tour reservations, call 546-BOAT for information, tel. 546-2700 for charge-by-mail tickets.

Tomales Bay State Park

Among the half-moon beaches and secret coves along the steep cliffs and shores of Tomales Bay are those protected within fragments of Tomales Bay State Park, with one section just north of Inverness, via Pierce Point Rd. off Sir Francis Drake Blvd., and others scattered along Hwy. 1 north of Point Reyes Station across the bay. One of the prime picnic spots at Tomales Bay is **Heart's Desire Beach,** popular for fam-

ily picnicking and swimming, usually private on weekdays. The warm, usually sunny, and surf-free inland beaches here are the main attraction, but hiking the forested eastern slope of Inverness Ridge is also worth it—especially in early spring, when trees, young ferns, and wildflowers burst forth from their winter dormancy. Unique is the park's fine virgin forest of Bishop pines. Walk-in campsites are available. For views and a great hiking trail, get directions to **Inverness Ridge** from the Tomales Bay State Park personnel. The southern grasslands section of Tomales Bay, now included in the GGNRA after the federal purchase of the 250-acre **Martinelli Ranch,** is prime turf for hiking (best in March for wildflowers) and birdwatching. The trailhead and parking area is just off Hwy. 1, about 1½ miles north of Point Reyes Station.

A new addition to the park is the **Marconi Conference Center** along the eastern edge of Tomales Bay, the 1914 Marconi Hotel once owned by Guglielmo Marconi, inventor of the wireless. This one-time communications center facility—taken over by the U.S. Navy during World War I, later operated by RCA, and most recently home to the much-praised then pilloried Synanon alcohol and drug abuse program—is now a state-owned conference center operated on the model of Asilomar on the Monterey Peninsula. For more information about the park, contact: Tomales Bay State Park, Star Rt., Inverness 94937, tel. (415) 669-1140. For information about the conference center, contact: Marconi Conference Center, P.O. Box 789, Marshall 94940, tel. 663-9020.

Samuel P. Taylor State Park

East of Point Reyes National Seashore and hemmed in by the Golden Gate National Recreation Area is Samuel P. Taylor State Park, 2,600 acres of redwoods, mixed forests, and upcountry chaparral reached via Sir Francis Drake Boulevard. The park offers an extensive hiking and horseback trail system, a paved bicycle path running east-west, and no-frills camping (including hiker/biker camps), picnicking, and swimming. For more information, contact: Samuel P. Taylor State Park, P.O. Box 251, Lagunitas 94952, tel. (415) 488-9897.

East of Samuel Taylor near Nicasio is the vast **Skywalker Ranch** owned by Lucasfilms and George Lucas, film- and mythmaker in the tradition of mythologist Joseph Campbell and his *Hero With a Thousand Faces*. The public is not welcome. (And for the record, Lucas Valley Rd., connecting Nicasio and Marinwood, was named long before Lucas bought property here.)

Bolinas Lagoon, Audubon Canyon Ranch

Well worth a visit is the **Bolinas Lagoon**, as serene as a Japanese nature print, especially in spring, when only the breeze or an occasional waterfowl fracas ruffles the glassy blue smoothness of this long mirror of water surrounded by a crescent-moon sandspit. Reflected above is wooded Bolinas Ridge, the northwestern extension of Mount Tamalpais. In autumn, the lagoon is much busier, temporary home to thousands of waterfowl migrating south along the Pacific Flyway as well as the salmon offshore waiting for a ferocious winter storm to break open a pathway through the sandbars blocking their migratory path. At minus tide any time of year, the surf side of the sandspit offers good beachcombing.

Facing out into the Bolinas Lagoon several miles north of Stinson Beach is the **Audubon Canyon Ranch**, a protected canyon offering a safe haven and rookery for great blue herons and common egrets in particular, though more than 50 other species of water birds arrive here each year. By quietly climbing up the canyon slopes during the March-through-July nesting season, visitors can look down into egret and heron nests high atop the redwoods in Schwartz Grove and observe the day-to-day life of parent birds and their young. Other hiking trails lead to other discoveries; picnic facilities also available.

The white Victorian farmhouse here serves as ranch headquarters and bookstore/visitor center, and participants in weekend seminar programs bed down in the bunkhouse, which features wind-powered toilets (God's truth) and solar-heated water. (Bring your own bedding, food, and other necessities.) The ranch is wheelchair-accessible and generally open to the public mid-March through mid-July only on weekends and holidays, 10 a.m.-4 p.m., admission free, though donations are always appreciated. Large groups can make tour arrangements for weekdays, though the ranch is always closed Mondays. For more information, contact: Audubon Canyon Ranch, 4900 Shoreline Hwy. (Hwy. 1), Stinson Beach 94970, tel. (415) 868-9244.

Mount Tamalpais State Park

Though the park also stretches downslope to the sea, take in the views of Marin County, San Francisco Bay, and the Pacific Ocean from the highest points of Mount Tamalpais. This long-loved mountain isn't particularly tall (elevation 2,600 feet) but even when foggy mists swirl everywhere below, the sun usually shines atop Mount Tam. And the state park here has it all: redwoods and ferns, hillsides thick with wildflowers, 200 miles of hiking trails with spectacular views (plus access to Muir Woods), beaches and headlands, also camping and picnicking.

Hiking on Mount Tam is best in spring, when the grassy hills are carpeted with wildflowers.

WES DEMPSEY

along the trail
in Inverness

WES DEMPSEY

The best way to get here is via Hwy. 1, then via the Panoramic Hwy., winding up past Pan Toll Ranger Station and park headquarters (stop for information and a map) to near the summit. From the parking lot, it's a quarter-mile hike up a steep dirt road to the fire lookout on top of Mount Tam.

The best way to explore Mount Tamalpais is on foot. Take the loop trail around the top. For the more ambitious, head downslope to the sea and the busy public beaches at **Stinson Beach,** still noted for its annual **Dipsea Race** held on the last Sunday in August, a tradition since 1904. Rugged cross-country runners cross the still more rugged terrain from Mill Valley to the sea at Stinson Beach; the last stretch down the footpath is known as the Dipsea Trail. Or hike into the park from Marin Municipal Water District lands on the east, tel. (415) 924-4600 for info, and head upslope, via the Cataract Trail from just off Bolinas Rd. outside of Fairfax and past Alpine Lake—something of a steep climb but worth it for the waterfalls, most dramatic in winter and early spring but sublime for pool-sitting in summer.

Via the Matt Davis Trail, or the Bootjack Camp or Pan Toll Ranger Station routes, hike to the charming old (1904) **West Point Inn** for a glass of lemonade and a rest in the porch shade. Four miles away is the **Tourist Club,** for overnight stays limited to members and their families only. This 1912 chalet at 30 Ridge Ave., tel. (415) 388-9987, serves snacks, cold imported beer, sodas, and juices to hikers arriving via the Sun, Redwood, or Panoramic trails. (To cheat for the beer, park at the end of Ridge Ave., which in-

tersects the Panoramic Hwy., and hike the quarter-mile down the driveway.) Open daily, great views of Muir Woods from the deck. More accessible for a picnic or snack stop (bring your own) is Mount Tam's Greek-style **Mountain Theater,** a 5,000-seat outdoor amphitheater on Ridgecrest Blvd., the site each spring of a major musical stage production.

Mount Tamalpais State Park (admission free, though parking may cost you) is open daily 7 a.m.-sunset. Limited primitive camping and other accommodations are available (see "Western Marin Accommodations" below). For more information, contact park headquarters at 801 Panoramic Hwy., Mill Valley 94941, tel. (415) 388-2070. For current information on Mount Tam's Mountain Theater productions, call 383-0155.

Muir Woods National Monument

Muir Woods is peaceful and serene but quite a popular place—not necessarily the best destination for getting away from them all. Lush redwood canyon country surrounds Redwood Creek within the boundaries of Mount Tamalpais State Park, with a short trail system meandering alongside the stream, up to the ridgetops, and into the monument's main **Cathedral** and **Bohemian redwood groves.** For an easy, introductory stroll, the **Muir Woods Nature Trail** wanders through the flatlands, identifying the characteristic trees and shrubs. Fascinating at Muir Woods, the first national monument in the U.S., are the **dawn redwood** from China and the park's **albino redwood,** the shoots from this freak of nature completely chlorophyll-free. But to avoid the crowds imported in all those tour buses clogging the parking lot, get away from the visitor center and the trails near the parking lot. Muir Woods is open daily 8 a.m.-sunset, admission free, no picnicking, camping, or dogs. For more information, contact: Muir Woods National Monument, Mill Valley 94941, tel. (415) 388-2595 or 388-2596.

WESTERN MARIN ACCOMMODATIONS

The Point Reyes Hostel

Best bet for non-camping budget travelers is the AYH Point Reyes Hostel on Limantour Rd., P.O. Box 247, Point Reyes Station 94956, tel. (415) 663-8811, with a well-equipped kitchen

POINT REYES HOSTEL
in the Pt. Reyes National Seashore

(get food on the way), reservations wise on weekends. To get here: from Point Reyes Station, take Seashore west from Hwy. 1 then follow Bear Valley Rd. to Limantour Rd. and continue on Limantour for six miles. Rates: $9 per person per night, AYH members and nonmembers alike. For information on getting to Point Reyes on public transit, call the hostel or **Golden Gate Transit,** tel. 332-6600. The hostel's office hours are 7:30-9:30 a.m. and 4:30-9-30 p.m. daily. Advance reservations advisable, by mail only. (Considerably closer to urban Marin but also an excellent choice is the AYH hostel within the Golden Gate National Recreation Area. See "Eastern Marin Accommodations" below.)

Camping

So popular that each has a one-day limit, the four primitive walk-in campgrounds at **Point Reyes National Seashore** are perfect for back-

packers since each is within an easy day's hike of the main trailhead and each other. Call (415) 663-1092 for information; permits required (available at park headquarters on Bear Valley Rd. just west of Olema). Stop, too, for maps and wilderness permits. The office is open weekdays 9-5, weekends 8-5.

Popular **Coast Camp** is most easily accessible from the parking lot at the end of Limantour Rd. and makes a good base for exploring the Limantour Estero and Sculptured Beach. **Wildcat Camp** is a group camp popular with Boy Scouts and others in Point Reyes's lake district (best swimming in Bass and Crystal lakes). **Glen Camp** is tucked into the hills between Wildcat Camp and Bear Valley, and **Sky Camp,** perched on the western slopes of Mount Wittenberg, looks down over Drakes Bay and Point Reyes.

Other area camping options include the backpack and group camps of GGNRA, tel. (415) 456-1286 or 331-1540; the state campground at **Samuel P. Taylor State Park,** tel. 488-9897; and the 18 primitive campsites plus backpack camps and group camp at **Mount Tamalpais State Park,** tel. 388-2070. All state campsites are available on a first-come, first-served basis.

Rustic And Inexpensive Stays

The state's quite reasonable **Steep Ravine Environmental Cabins** on Rocky Point in Mount Tamalpais State Park, looking out to sea from near Stinson Beach, are small redwood-rustic homes-away-from-home with just the basics: platform beds (bring your own sleeping bag and pad), woodstoves, separate restrooms with pit toilets. But such a deal: $30 per cabin per night (each sleeps five) and an almost-private beach below in a spectacularly romantic setting. Before the state wrested custody of these marvelous cabins from the powerful Bay Area politicians and other clout-encumbered citizens who held long-term leases, photographer Dorothea Lange wrote about staying here in *To A Cabin,* coauthored by Margaretta K. Mitchell. Even the walk down to the bottom of Steep Ravine Canyon is inspiring, Lange noted, with "room for only those in need of sea and sky and infinity." One cabin (there are only 10) is wheelchair-accessible; none have electricity but they do have outside running water. Bring your own provisions. To reserve (up to eight weeks in advance), contact Mistix, tel. (800) 444-7275, and request an application form.

West Marin Inns

Even those without wheels can explore the seaward coast of Marin County in comfort and fine style—by hiking or walking the whole way from the Golden Gate Bridge with little more than a day-pack and staying along the bay at a combination of hostels, campgrounds, hotels and motels, and the area's very nice bed and breakfast inns. (How far to go each day and where to stay depends upon time and money available.) Classic **Ten Inverness Way** on the town's block-long main street, P.O. Box 63, Inverness 94937, tel. (415) 669-1648, is comfortable and cozy. Rooms feature excellent beds, handmade quilts, and private baths; there's a stone fireplace in the living room, wonderful full breakfast, private hot tub, rates $90-140.

The **Blackthorne Inn** in a woodsy canyon just outside town at 266 Vallejo Ave. in Inverness Park, P.O. Box 712, tel. (415) 663-8621, offers simple Japanese-style furnishings in four-level "treehouse" accommodations with decks, all splitting off the vertically spiraling staircase. Good buffet breakfast, hot tub available. The peak experience here is a stay in the Eagle's Nest, the aptly named octagonal, glass-walled room at the top of the stairs. Rates: $105-185.

Also worthwhile near Inverness—a variety of bed and breakast-style cottages. Up on Inverness Ridge is **The Ark**, tel. (415) 663-9338, a rustic cabin with bedroom, sleeping loft, woodstove, and kitchen. Rates: $130-140. **Fairwinds Farm** at 82 Drakes Summit, tel. 663-9454, is a fairly modern Early American cottage on five acres with forest, garden, and pond, a good family setup with two beds in the bedroom, a double bed in the loft, and queen sofa bed in the living room. Full kitchen (breakfast fixings supplied, plus snacks, even a popcorn popper), fireplace, hot tub, deck. Playhouse for children, barnyard animals, too. Rates: $125-175. **Marsh Cottage** near Tomales Bay at 12642 Sir Francis Drake Blvd., tel. 669-7168, features a fireplace and a fine view, plus kitchen with breakfast supplies. Rates $95-110. Other good choices: **Rosemary Cottage** in the woods at 75 Balboa Ave., tel. 663-9338, and **Sea Star Cottage,** on the highway near Tomales Bay, tel. 663-1554.

The **Roundstone Farm,** farther south at 9940 Sir Francis Drake Blvd., P.O. Box 217, Olema 94950, tel. (415) 663-1020, is an American country-style cedar farmhouse on a 10-acre horse ranch, rooms with private baths, fireplaces, European armoires, down comforters. Rates: $115. Also quite nice is the **Bear Valley Inn,** a restored two-story Victorian ranch house with three country-style guest rooms upstairs, woodstove and oak flooring in the parlor, and full breakfast. Rates: $70-105. For a free brochure listing these and other fine area lodgings, write **Inns of Point Reyes,** P.O. Box 145, Inverness 94937, or call the referral number, tel. (415) 485-2649 or, from Point Reyes, tel. 663-1420.

For nostalgia with all the modern amenities (try to get a room away from the highway), the 1988 **Point Reyes Seashore Lodge** in Olema at 10021 Hwy. 1, tel. (415) 663-9000, is an elegant re-creation of a turn-of-the-century country lodge, a three-story cedar with three two-story suites and 18 rooms, all with down comforters, telephones, and private baths, many with whirlpool tubs and fireplaces, most with a private deck or patio. Continental breakfast. Rates: $85-175.

The place for a genuine West Marin-style stay is the eccentric **Tomales Country Inn** near Dillon Beach in Tomales, tel. (707) 878-9992, a comfortably casual and colorful old Victorian overgrown with vegetation and stuffed with artwork and antiques. Rates: $70-80. To get here, turn west from Hwy. 1 onto Dillon Beach Rd., then left again on Valley. The famous Victorian is at the end of the cul-de-sac. Also in the area: another very modern facsimile historic hotel, a superb 1989 replica of the original **U.S. Hotel,** at 26985 Hwy. 1, tel. 878-2742, a bed and breakfast with a hands-off hotel style, just eight rooms with private baths, continental breakfast served in the second-floor lobby. Rate: $85 s or d.

The top bed and breakfast choice in Bolinas is the **White House Inn** at 118 Kale Rd., tel. (415) 868-0279, a New England-style inn with two guest rooms sharing two bathrooms in the hall, continental breakfast, rates: $85-95. Or try a private cottage. The **Rose Garden Cottage** at 59 Alturas Ave., tel. 868-2209, features a fireplace, full kitchen, private patio, and amenities like TV and radio/cassette player. Rate $100. The two-room **One Fifty-Five Pine,** at that address, tel. 868-0263, is a cottage above Agate Beach with an ocean view, knotty-pine interiors, stone fireplace, and all the fixings for breakfast provided in the full kitchen. Rates: $100-125.

The original 1912 **Mountain Home Inn** restaurant on Mount Tamalpais, 810 Panoramic Hwy., Mill Valley 94941, tel. (415) 381-9000, has been transformed into an elegant three-story woodsy hotel with upstairs restaurant and bar. Fabulous views. Some of the rooms have fireplaces or Jacuzzis. Rates (including breakfast in bed): $121-178.

When Sir Francis Drake steered the *Pelican* to shore near here in 1579, he claimed everything in sight on behalf of Elizabeth I, Queen of England. For a taste of more modern true Brit, stop at **The Pelican Inn** on your way down from Mount Tam on Hwy. 1 (at Muir Beach Rd.), Muir Beach 94965, tel. (415) 383-6000 or 383-6005. A very British Tudor-style country inn, a replica of a 16th-century farmhouse, where guests sit out on the lawn with pint of bitter in hand on sunny days or, when the fog rolls in, warm up around the bar's fireplace with some afternoon tea or mulled cider or wine. Hearty pub fare includes meat pies, stews, burgers, homemade breads, various dinner entrees. Restaurant and pub open 11 a.m.-11 p.m. daily except Mondays. Not authentically old (built in 1979), the Pelican is still authentic: the leaded glass windows and brass trinkets, even the oak bar and refectory tables come from England. There's usually a six-month waiting list for the six rooms here; rates from $110 including breakfast.

GOOD FOOD IN WESTERN MARIN

Inverness And Vicinity
After a relaxed afternoon spent reading in the **Jack Mason Museum and Inverness Public Library** on Park Ave. (open limited hours, tel. 415-669-1288), head out Sir Francis Drake Blvd. from Inverness to **Johnson's Oyster Company,** tel. 669-1149, for a tour and some farm-fresh oysters. Open Tues.-Sat. 8 a.m.-4 p.m., free admission. **Barnaby's by the Bay** at the Golden Hinde Inn just north of Inverness, tel. 669-1114, open for lunch and dinner (closed Wednesdays), has daily pasta and fresh fish specials, barbecued oysters, clam chowder, and crab cioppino. Between Point Reyes Station and Inverness, in Inverness Park, stop at the **Knave of Hearts** bakery, tel. 663-1236, open 8-5 (closed Mondays), to pick up fresh bread and other baked goods or for espresso.

Back in Inverness, **The Gray Whale** pizzeria and bakery downtown, tel. (415) 669-1244, is the place for pizza, also salads and good desserts and espresso in a pub atmosphere. Open 9 a.m.-9 p.m. daily. Or, try one of the town's two popular restaurants: **Manka's** at the Inverness Lodge, tel. 669-1034, which serves rustic American-style fare (marvelous rooms upstairs, two cabins also available), or **Vladimir's Czechoslovak Restaurant & Bar** on Sir Francis Drake Blvd., tel. 669-1021, which serves good Eastern European food in an authentically boisterous atmosphere. (Yell across the room if you want dessert; that's what everyone else does.)

Marshall, Point Reyes Station, Olema
Popular in Marshall, along the east side of Tomales Bay north of Point Reyes Station via Hwy. 1, is **Tony's Seafood,** tel. (415) 663-1107. The food's quite fresh: they clean the crabs and oysters right out front.

Famous for its newspaper, the not-yet-too-yuppie cow town of Point Reyes Station is also noted for the mooing clock atop the sheriff's substation at 4th and C, though the bovine bellow, a technical creation of Lucasfilm staff, actually emanates—like clockwork, at noon and

6 p.m.—from loudspeakers atop the Old Western Saloon at 2nd and Main streets. For "udderly divine" bakery items, from French pastries, bran muffins, and scones to cookies, stop by the **Bovine Bakery** in town, tel. (415) 663-9420. The **Station House Cafe** at Main and 3rd streets in Point Reyes Station, tel. (415) 663-1515, is the local hotspot, a cheerful country cafe serving breakfast, lunch, and dinner daily but particularly wonderful for breakfast, especially on foggy or rainy days. **Chez Madeleine** on Hwy. 1 at the Inverness junction, tel. 663-9177, is popular for intimate French dinners and is moderately expensive.

Both a good restaurant and lodging stop, the **Olema Inn** at Hwy. 1 and Sir Francis Drake Blvd. in Olema, tel. (415) 663-9559, is a grandmotherly kind of place serving basic good food and soups as well as California-style cuisine. Open for dinner Fri. and Sat. at 6 p.m. and for lunch and dinner during the summer. For plain ol' American food, head for **Jerry's Farmhouse** on Hwy. 1 in Olema, tel. 663-1264: good burgers and hefty sandwiches, daily fresh fish specials.

Bolinas

Bolinas is noted for the locals' Bolinas Border Patrol, an unofficial group dedicated to keeping outsiders out by taking down road signs. Once in Bolinas, the gravel beach here is clean and usually uncrowded, and the colorfully painted **Bolinas General Store** is a good stop for snacks and picnic fixings. (Note the "Shrine to the Unknown Tourist," a hole in the wooden sidewalk across from locally popular Smiley's bar. Ask only if you really want an answer.) The **Bolinas People's Store,** tel. (415) 868-1433, is the place for organic produce. The **Bolinas Bay Bakery & Cafe,** tel. 868-0211, is a popular breakfast and lunch stop famous for its cinnamon rolls, croissants, breads, and other fresh bakery items. The **Shop** restaurant, tel. 868-9984, next to the general store, is comfortable and cozy on a foggy or rainy day. (At lunch, try the black bean soup.)

EASTERN MARIN AND VICINITY

Though the marshlands and open areas fringing the northern and eastern portions of San Pablo Bay could almost be included, the San Francisco Bay's northernmost boundary is actually Marin County. More than just the structural anchor for the other side of San Francisco's Golden Gate Bridge, eastern Marin has somehow become the psychological center for "the good life" Californians pursue with such trendsetting abandon. This pursuit costs money, of course, but there's plenty of that in Marin County, which boasts one of the highest per-capita income levels in the nation. Jaguars, Porsches, and more exotic automobiles are among Marin folks' favored means of transport, and BMWs are so common here that *San Francisco Chronicle* columnist Herb Caen has long referred to them as Boring Marin Wagons.

Jokes about Marin County change but other things stay the same. The weather here is unusually pleasant, mild in both summer and winter. Also, Marin *au naturel* is incredibly diverse. From Mill Valley west to the Bolinas Lagoon near Point Reyes, seven different ecological communities are typical: chaparral, grassland, coastal scrub, broadleaf forest, redwood and mixed evergreen forest, salt marsh, and beach strand. And almost one-third of the county is public parkland—national, state, and local.

CITIES AND SIGHTS

Sausalito

Sausalito is a community by land and by sea, a hillside hamlet far surpassed in eccentricity by the highly creative hodgepodge of houseboaters also anchored here. Though for a time mysterious midnight throbbings from the deep kept Sausalito's houseboat community awake night after summer night—with some locals even speculating that these nocturnal noises came from a top-secret CIA weapon being tested underwater in Richardson Bay—it eventually turned out that the racket was simply due to romance. Singing toadfish have become to Sausalito what swallows are to Capistrano, migrating into Richardson Bay from the shallows each summer for their annual mating song—comparable, collectively, to the sound of a squadron of low-flying B-17 bombers. People here have adapted to this almost indescribable language of love, and now welcome these bulging-eyed, bubble-lipped lovers back to the bay every year with their **Humming Toadfish Festival,** a celebration conducted by residents dressed up as sea monsters and clowns, playing kazoos.

Aside from the pleasures of just being here, stop in Sausalito at the U.S. Army Corps of Engineers' **San Francisco Bay Delta Model,** 2100 Bridgeway, tel. (415) 332-3871, a working 1½-acre facsimile built by the Corps to study currents, tides, salinity, and other natural features. We should all be grateful that the ever-industrious Corps realized it couldn't build a better bay even with access to all the bulldozers, landfill, and riprap in the world and settled, instead, for just making a toy version. Interpretive audio tours are available in English, Russian, German, Japanese, French, and Spanish. Guided group tours (10 or more people) can be arranged by calling at least four weeks in advance. Open Tues.-Sat. 9 a.m.-4 p.m., summer weekends and holidays 10 a.m.-6 p.m., free.

Also in Sausalito: the **Institute of Noetic Sciences,** an organization of mostly mainstream scientists dedicated to exploring the more mysterious machinations of the human mind—that foggy frontier at the edge of the California cosmos concerned with biofeedback, mental telepathy, telekinesis, altered states of consciousness, and mental imagery in physical healing. And among Sausalito's armada of houseboat residents and bayside shops is the **Heathware Ceramics Outlet,** at 400 Gate 5 Rd., tel. (415) 332-3732, open daily 10-5, a wonderful array of seconds and overstocks for fine dishware fans.

And Sausalito (or San Francisco, from Crissy Field via the Golden Gate Bridge) is a perfect place to start a serious **Bay Area bike tour.** For a 20-mile trip, head north along the paved bike path (Bay Trail), following the green "bike route" signs along the left arm of Richardson Bay to fairly new **Bayfront Park** in Mill Valley.

Continue north to (busy and narrow) E. Blithedale Avenue, and follow it east two miles or so to less-busy Tiburon Boulevard. From that thoroughfare, jog south along the bay on Greenwood Cove Road, picking up the two-mile Tiburon Bike Path at its end. To make it a complete circle, take a ferry from Tiburon (see "North Bay Diversions" below) past Angel Island and Alcatraz to Fisherman's Wharf in San Francisco. From here, head back via the Bay Trail, up the grade (fairly steep) to the Golden Gate Bridge and over the bay, then back into Sausalito via the Bridgeway Bike Path.

Easier bike trips from Sausalito include the several-mile trip into Mill Valley, via the bike path past the houseboats and mudflats and marshes to Bayfront Park (picnic tables and benches available). Then backtrack to Miller Avenue and roll into town, right into the midst of a pleasant plaza-style shopping district. To get to Tiburon, from Bayfront Park follow the route described above.

For more information about Sausalito attractions and practicalities, contact: **Sausalito Chamber of Commerce,** 333 Caledonia St., Sausalito 94965, tel. (415) 332-0505, open weekdays 9-5.

Tiburon

Tiburon ("shark" in Spanish), once a ramshackle railroad town, is an affluent bayside community most noted for the Audubon Society's 900-acre **Richardson Bay Audubon Center and Sanctuary** in the Belvedere Cove tidal baylands, 376 Greenwood Beach Rd., tel. (415) 388-2524. Wonderful for birdwatching and nature walks, also picnicking (pack out your trash), $2. Tiburon is also home to Dr. Gerald Jampolsky's **The Center for Attitudinal Healing,** a well-respected organization that emphasizes the emotional and spiritual aspects of healing in the face of catastrophic illness and events. The wooded 24-acre **Tiburon Uplands Nature Preserve,** south of Paradise Beach Park on Paradise Drive, tel. 499-6387, includes a natural history loop trail and great bay views from higher ground. Absolutely spectacular for spring wildflowers, though, are the few acres surrounding the gothic church at **Old St. Hilary's Historic Preserve** at Esperanza and Mar West, tel. 435-1853, open to the public Wed. and Sun. 1-4

from April through October, otherwise by appointment only. Nearby **Belvedere** is one of the nation's 10 most expensive outposts of suburbia.

For more information about Tiburon attractions and practicalities, contact: **Tiburon Chamber of Commerce,** P.O. Box 563, Tiburon 94920, tel. (415) 435-5633.

Mill Valley

Mill Valley is another affluent North Bay bedroom community, this one rooted on the eastern slope of Mount Tamalpais. Weird and well worth a stop here is the **Unknown Museum,** P.O. Box 1551, tel. (415) 383-2726 for current location and hours, Mickey McGowan's contemporary and ever-growing collection of American artifacts, a "visual newscast" of TV sets, car parts, Mr. Potato Heads (and anything else plastic), romance comics, and kitchen kitsch—all rolling by to the sounds of the 1950s.

The big event here every autumn is the **Mill Valley Film Festival,** the biggest little film festival outside Telluride, Colorado, with screenings of local, American independent, international, avant-garde, and various premiere films. For more information about the festival and other Marin art events—including a current schedule of Mimi Fariña's **Bread and Roses** performance art volunteers—contact the **Marin Arts Council,** 251 N. San Pedro Rd. Building O, San Rafael 94903, tel. (415) 499-8350, which publishes a free monthly *Marin ArtsGuide* and the quarterly *Marin Review* (available free to council members but also often available at local chambers of commerce).

Ring Mountain Preserve

Inland on the Tiburon Peninsula near Corte Madera is the Nature Conservancy's Ring Mountain Preserve, a protected tract of native California grasslands around a 600-foot-tall hill known for its unusual serpentine soils and rare endemic plants, geological peculiarities, and Native American petroglyphs. To get here, take the Paradise Dr. exit from Hwy. 101 then continue to the preserve's entrance, 1¾ miles down the road. For more information, contact: Ring Mountain Preserve, 3152 Paradise Dr. #101, Tiburon 94920, tel. (415) 435-6465. For information about visiting the Nature Conservancy's **Spindrift Point Preserve** near Sausalito, call 388-7399.

CALIFORNIA DEPARTMENT OF PARKS & RECREATION

Once-bustling China Camp now survives as a state park.

San Rafael

San Rafael is Marin's biggest little city and the county seat, a Modesto-like community where scenes from George Lucas's *American Graffiti* were shot (on 4th Street, restaurant row). San Rafael is known for its downtown mansion district, for the 1947 replica of the **Mission San Rafael** (second to last in California's mission chain, located at 1104 5th Ave., open daily 11-4), but most noted for the **Marin Civic Center** just off Hwy. 101, Frank Lloyd Wright's last major architectural accomplishment. The center, home to the county's administrative complex and quite the tour de force, exemplifies Wright's obsession with the idea that all things are (or should become) circular. Surrounded by 140 acres of lovingly groomed grounds, the county fair is held here every July. Docent-led tours available, but call at least several days in advance, (415) 499-7407. Wheelchair-accessible, open weekdays 8-5 (excepting legal holidays). And to find out what major events and entertainment programs are scheduled, request a current copy of the quarterly Civic Center arts magazine *Marin Center*.

Another San Rafael attraction is the 11-acre **Guide Dogs for the Blind** campus, where German shepherds, labradors, and golden retrievers are trained to "see" for their human companions. Monthly "graduations," which include tours and demonstrations of guide dog selective obedience work, are open to the public. Altogether it's a moving experience, especially when the 4-H children who raised these dogs to their pre-

training age of 15 or 16 months show up to say goodbye, as the graduates depart with their new owners. Guide Dogs for the Blind is located on Los Ranchitos Road, off N. San Pedro Road. For more information, call (415) 499-4000.

For more information about the area, contact the **San Rafael Chamber of Commerce,** 818 5th Ave., San Rafael 94901, tel. (415) 454-4163, open weekdays 8:30 a.m.-4:30 p.m.

Nearby **Greenbrae** is neighbor to **San Quentin State Prison**, home since the mid-1800s to sociopaths and other criminals, though more than 100 union members and organizers of the Industrial Workers of the World were also imprisoned here after World War I. San Quentin's disciplinary dungeons were closed in 1935. The new museum here and the Boot Hill prison cemetery—posthumous home now to a veritable Who's Who of Very Bad Guys—are open for (very popular) public visits.

Stop by the **prison gift shop** at San Quentin's entrance, tel. (415) 454-1460 for days and times, for inmate-made arts and crafts—from San Quentin T-shirts and hats to belt buckles, rings and other jewelry, artwork, and novelties. Head on through the entrance to visit the **California State Prison Museum,** artifacts, memorabilia, historical photographs, and records documenting the prison's history. Museum hours at last report (call ahead to verify): Mon. 1-4 p.m., Tues.-Thurs. 8:30 a.m.-4:30 p.m., Friday until 3:30 p.m., and Sat. and Sun. 8:30 a.m.-3 p.m.

China Camp State Park

After the gold rush, many of California's Chinese turned to fishing as a way to make ends meet. Chinese fishing camps were common all along the northstate's coast, and 30 or more flourished on the more remote edges of San Francisco Bay. The Chinese were quite successful at plying their trade in the state's waters—so successful that by the 1900s enforcement of anti-Chinese, anti-bag netting fishing laws essentially killed these Asian communities. Partially restored China Camp, once the Bay Area's largest Chinese shrimp center, is the last of these old fishing villages. The community, where John Wayne's *Blood Alley* was filmed, survives now as a memory complete with history museum, renovated buildings, and rebuilt rickety piers. The only actual survivor is Frank Quan's bait and sandwich shop, which serves up fresh bay shrimp when available (put in your order early, especially on weekends). The park's 1,600 acres of oak forest, grasslands, and salt marshes also offer hiking, picnicking, and walk-in primitive campsites, $9 per night. Reserve through Mistix, tel. toll-free (800) 444-7275.

New hiking trails at China Camp make it even more accessible. The **Shoreline Trail** starts near the historic district and heads across Point San Pedro Rd., then forks—the left path leading to a view, the right path onward to the northwest, through the grasslands and chaparral. Good views all the way. Backtrack and you've walked an easy four miles. Or, from the entrance to Back Ranch Meadows Campground outside the park, take the new **Bayview Trail** and climb up a ravine to an access road, returning by the **Back Ranch Meadows Trail**, over three miles altogether.

China Camp State Park is open daily, sunrise to sunset, day use $5; the museum is open daily in summers, weekends during the rest of the year. To get here, take the San Pedro Rd. exit from Hwy. 101 and continue for several miles past the Marin Civic Center. For more information, contact: China Camp State Park, Rt. 1 Box 244, San Rafael 94901, tel. (415) 456-0766.

Novato

To experience the Middle Ages modern style, head north from San Rafael to Novato and the long-running **Renaissance Pleasure Faire**, sponsored by the Living History Center, P.O. Box B, Novato 94948, tel. (415) 892-0937, or toll-free (800) 52-FAIRE, 9-5, and held on September and early October weekends in Black Point Forest off Hwy. 37. During the faire, life in the shire of Black Point Forest is an authentic return trip to 16th-century England, on the world's largest stage, a mile-long Elizabethan village with 16 separate neighborhood villages inhabited by thousands of corporate executives, computer programmers, housewives, and other amateur medievalists (including paying guests) dressed and acting in historical character and speaking only "Basic Faire Accent." Sir Francis Drake himself presides over each day's opening ceremonies; the queen leaves the shire by late afternoon. But in between, the activity never ends. There are madrigal groups and musical processions; games, juggling, singing, and dancing; full-contact fighting and jousting; feasts of broiled beef and fresh-baked bread with other aromas—incense and herbs and flower essence—in the air. Admission $16.50 adults; $13.50 seniors, students with current ID, and active military personnel; and $7.50 children.

The center usually sponsors a weekend **Dickens Christmas Fair** as well, on late November and December weekends prior to the holiday. Call or write for current information.

Also worthwhile: the Living History Center's July **Gold Rush Jubilee and Fiesta**, two weekends of the Wild West re-created (at last report) near mellow Santa Cruz, at Roaring Camp—from phrenologists and palm readers to banjo and fiddle contests, from gold panning and Mexican folk dancing at the Fiesta de San Juan to pioneer arts and crafts and Pawnee Bill's Wild West exhibit.

Two museums in Novato are worth a stop: the **Novato History Museum** at 815 De Long Ave., tel. (415) 897-4320, a monument to the town's pioneer past, open Thurs. and Sat. 10 a.m.-4 p.m. (free), and the **Marin Museum of the American Indian** and park at 2200 Novato Blvd., tel. 897-4064, a small but fascinating place with friendly staff and hands-on exhibits and other displays about Coast Miwok and Pomo cultures. Open Tues.-Sat. 10 a.m.-4 p.m., Sun. noon-4. Closed in December. Free.

New in the area is **Olompali State Historic Park**, a 700-acre ranch north of Novato with broad historic significance. At one time it was a major Miwok trading village, a fact archaeological

CALIFORNIA DEPARTMENT OF PARKS & RECREATION

Angel Island State Park, once the Ellis Island of the West

finds have verified. Sir Francis Drake and his men may have passed through, since a silver sixpence circa 1567 was discovered here. And a Bear Flag Revolt skirmish occurred at the Olompali Adobe in the mid-1800s. Olompali's tenure as a ranch is obvious, given the weathered barns and the Victorian home of the one-time ranch manager. Restoration and park development are still under way, but the public is welcome to stop for a picnic and a hike to the top of Burdell Mountain, for some good views of San Pablo Bay. Day-use fee: $5.

At last report, Olompali was open Fri.-Mon. only, 8-5. For more information, contact: Olompali State Historic Park, P.O. Box 1400, Novato 94948, tel. (415) 898-9963, or contact China Camp State Historic Park (above). Getting here is easy from the north; from Hwy. 101, just take the marked exit (north of Novato proper). From the south via Hwy. 101, exit at San Antonio Rd. and head west, then backtrack to the park on Hwy. 101.

Angel Island State Park

Still sometimes called the "Ellis Island of the West," at the turn of the century Angel Island was the door through which Asian immigrants passed on their way to America. Japanese and other "enemy aliens" were imprisoned here during World War II, when the island's facilities served as a detention center. Explore the West Garrison **Civil War barracks and buildings** at the 1863 site of Camp Reynolds—built and occupied by Union troops determined to foil

the Confederacy's plans to invade the bay and then the gold country. Among the buildings, the largest surviving collection of Civil War structures in the nation, note the cannons still aimed to sea (but never used in the war because Confederate troops never showed up). On weekends, volunteers in the park's living history program—with the help of apparently willing visitors—fire off the cannons, just in case the South rises again.

Though most visitors never get past the sun and sand at Ayala Cove, also worth a stop are the 1899 **Chinese Immigration Center,** quarantine central for new Asian arrivals, and World War II-era **Fort McDowell** on the island's east side near the Civil War battlements. Often sunny in summer when the rest of the Bay Area is shivering in the fog, outdoorsy types consider Angel Island's hiking trails its chief attraction. (The eucalyptus trees being felled on Angel Island are nonnatives first planted in the 1860s and now being removed so natural vegetation can be reintroduced.) On a clear day, the view from the top of Angel Island's Mount Livermore is spectacular—with three bridges and almost the entire Bay Area seemingly within reach—and both the **North Ridge Trail** and the **Sunset Trail** have been rebuilt, to make the grade less daunting and the ascent easier.

For unbeatable scenery (and sometimes brisk winds), **picnic** atop Mount Livermore. The intrepid can even camp on Angel Island, which features nine hike-in **environmental campsites.** Call park headquarters for information and reservations. (Campstove or char-coal cooking only—no fires.) If you're coming, come light, since you'll have to manage it on the ferry and pack it all into camp, at least a mile hike. The **Tiburon-Angel Island State Park Ferry,** berthed at the pier on Main St. in Tiburon, tel. (415) 435-2131, is available to is-land-bound hikers, bikers, backpackers, daily during summer (and often into autumn, weath-er permitting), but only on weekends during the rest of the year. The **Red & White Fleet,** tel. (415) 546-BOAT or 546-2700 to charge tickets by phone (small service fee), also offers Angel Island runs, from Tiburon, Vallejo, and San Francisco.

For more information about island hikes and docent-led tours of historic sites, also current ferry schedules, contact: Angel Island State Park headquarters at 1455 East Francis Blvd., San Rafael 94501, or P.O. Box 318, Tiburon 94920, tel. (415) 435-1915. For information about island tours for the disabled and about fundraising and other volunteer work to contin-ue the island's restoration, contact: Angel Is-land Association, P.O. Box 866, Tiburon 94920, tel. (415) 435-3522.

NORTH BAY DIVERSIONS

Bay Tours
In addition to the North Bay's astounding coastal access opportunities, particularly in western Marin County, there are also many ways to enjoy San Francisco Bay. In San Fran-cisco both the **Blue & Gold Fleet,** tel. (415) 781-7877, and the **Red & White Fleet,** tel. 546-2896 or 546-BOAT in San Francisco, offer bay ferry tours (including R & W's "Round the Rock" tour of Alcatraz conducted by one of the prison's former guards). Or design your own tours using the bay's ferry system. Red & White's San Francisco-based ferries offer reg-ular commuter service connecting Fisherman's Wharf to Sausalito, Tiburon, Vallejo, Angel Is-land, and Alcatraz; Tiburon and Vallejo ser-vice to and from San Francisco; and ferry ser-vice between Vallejo and Angel Island. New for Red & White is its Tiburon-Muir Woods tour, which includes ferry service to Tiburon from San Francisco then bus transportation to and

from Muir Woods. (For more information about ferry transport, see "Transportation: Getting to and from Town" under "Just the Facts" in the San Francisco chapter.) The Golden Gate Bridge District's fun triple-decker **Golden Gate Ferries** (tel. 415-332-6600 from San Francisco, tel. 453-2100 from Marin County) come com-plete with indoor and outdoor seating and full bars and connect the City's historic Ferry Build-ing with both Larkspur and Sausalito, with de-partures about once each hour on weekdays (early morning through evening), less frequently on weekends. And Golden Gate ferries fea-ture special roundtrip "Lunch for the Office Bunch" midday runs from San Francisco to Sausalito and back with live lunchtime jazz or rhythm and blues, every Friday from May through September, plus the "Jazz on the Ferry" run to and from Larkspur on the last Fri-day of the month, April through October.

For very special sightseeing beyond San Francisco Bay, a responsible nonprofit organi-zation offering guided **whalewatching boat tours** and other nautical expeditions is the **Oceanic Society** based in San Francisco, tel. (415) 474-3385, with local whalewatching trips and Farallone Islands tours. Advance reserva-tions required. The organization considers these tours part of their public education work on be-half of whales and some trips support ongoing whale research. Whalewatching boats leave from either Half Moon Bay (three-hour trip) or San Francisco (six hours) and head out to the migration paths near the Farallon Islands.

Bay Recreation
Weather and wave conditions permitting, dedi-cated kayakers, rowers, sailors, whaleboaters, and windsurfers are as at home on the bay as the ferries and big ships. Though San Francisco and other cities also offer good bay access and recreational opportunities, **Bluewaters Ocean Kayak Tours,** P.O. Box 1003, Fairfax 94930, tel. (415) 456-8956, specializes in weekend bird-watching and natural history sea kayak trips ori-ented to beginners in areas including Point Reyes, China Camp, San Francisco Bay, and the Petaluma River estuary. **Sea Trek** in Sausal-ito at Schoonmaker Point Marina, 85 Liberty Ship Way, tel. 488-1000, is a big-league kayak-ing center offering something for everyone:

(previous page) redwoods in spring fog, Del Norte Coast Redwoods State Park (Philip Wright);
(this page, top left) wine grapes (San Jose Convention and Visitors Bureau); (top, right) Yosemite in autumn (Keith S.
Walklet); (above) Yosemite in autumn: Half Dome (John Poimiroo)

THE BAY BEYOND MARIN

San Pablo Bay National Wildlife Refuge

Also along the shores of San Pablo Bay—to the northeast, between the Petaluma and Napa rivers south of Hwy. 37—are the salt marshes, mudflats, and open waters of the San Pablo Bay National Wildlife Refuge, a winter refueling stop for winter-migrating shorebirds and waterfowl, also permanent home to two endangered species: the California clapper rail and the salt marsh harvest mouse. Largely undeveloped but accessible—under certain strict conditions—for boaters and hunters, the only easy access for the general public is at **Tubbs Island,** originally acquired by the Nature Conservancy. To get here, park (well off the road) along Hwy. 37 just east of its intersection with Hwy. 121 (and just east of Tolay Creek) and walk. It's almost three miles (one-way) to these marsh ponds and nature trails on the northern edge of San Pablo Bay. Open during daylight hours only, no restrooms available, bring your own drinking water. For more information, call (707) 792-0222.

Marine World/Africa USA

Vallejo sprawls across the point where the Napa River flows into San Pablo Bay, near the Mare Island Naval Shipyard. Since 1986, Vallejo has also been home to Marine World/Africa USA, a big-time theme park next to the Solano County Fairgrounds. A popular venue for family-style fun, Marine World features trained-animal performances by sea lions and dolphins, while Africa USA has lions, trained tigers, elephants, and orangutans. The park features many other attractions as well, including exotic birds, a walk-through greenhouse full of flashy tropical butterflies, an ecology theater with live animals, outdoor entertainment, games, gift shops, restaurants.

Admission: $21.95 adults, $18.95 seniors, $16.95 children ages 4-12, toddlers three and under free. Parking fee, too. For more information, contact: Marine World/Africa USA, Marine World Foundation, Marine World Parkway, Vallejo 94589, tel. (707) 644-4000. For more information about Vallejo and vicinity, contact: **Vallejo Chamber of Commerce,** 2 Florida St., Vallejo 94590, tel. 644-5551.

Northeast of Vallejo and north of Suisun Bay is Fairfield and adjacent Travis Air Force Base with its **Travis Air Force Base Historical Society Museum,** tel. (707) 424-5605, open 9-5 weekends and 9-4 weekdays, a new collection of old aircraft—including a handmade 1912 wooden biplane, cargo planes, jet fighters, and bombers.

---

classes for all skill levels (beginners' classes, two-hour classes to improve basic skills, day-long "Open Bay" classes and family instruction also available), kayak rentals, guided day-trips, and overnight camping excursions. **Open Water Rowing** in Sausalito near Sea Trek, tel. 332-1091, requires equipment renters to have previous experience or certification, or to take their two-hour beginners' class or intermediate class before setting out for serious adventures to Tiburon, Angel Island, Alcatraz, or out through the Golden Gate.

Quite special is **Environmental Traveling Companions** in San Francisco, tel. (415) 474-7662, with its kayaking program (and other outings) for the physically disabled, including overnight kayak-camping on Angel Island.

To rent sailboards for windsurfing, head for Sausalito. A variety of companies rent sailboards and offer lessons.

For a complete and current listing of salmon and other oceangoing fishing charters in the Bay Area, contact: **Golden Gate Fisherman's Association,** P.O. Box 40, Sausalito 94966.

EASTERN MARIN ACCOMMODATIONS

For a fairly complete listing of Marin County accommodations and other North Bay information, contact the **Marin County Chamber of Commerce and Visitors Bureau,** 30 N. San Pedro Rd., Suite 150, San Rafael 94903, tel. (415) 472-7470. Best bet for budget travelers in eastern Marin County is the AYH **Golden Gate Hostel** in Building 941 at Fort Barry in Sausalito, tel. 331-2777, urban enough—just five minutes from the Golden Gate Bridge—but also rural, 60 rooms in a 1907 building in an otherwise abandoned fort in the midst of Golden Gate National Recreation Area. Basic dorm-style accommodations with hot showers (family

room available by advance reservation), but facilities also include a great kitchen, dining room, common room with fireplace, even laundry facilities, game room, tennis court, and bike storage. Quite popular in summer and on good-weather weekends, so reservations advised (by mail only). Rates: $9 per night for both AYH members and nonmembers, extra for linen rental (or bring sleeping bag). To get here: if coming from San Francisco take the Alexander Ave. exit just north of the Golden Gate Bridge (if southbound toward the bridge, take the second Sausalito exit), then follow the signs into GGNRA and on to the hostel.

To spend considerably more for a nice stay in the same general neighborhood, the Spanish-style **Sausalito Hotel** at 16 El Portal, tel. (415) 332-4155, offers 15 Victorian-style rooms and continental breakfast, $75-175. Another possibility in Sausalito is the **Casa Madrona Hotel,** 801 Bridgeway Blvd., tel. 332-0502, a cozy 1885-vintage inn with fireplaces in some rooms, continental breakfast, $95-200. The Casa Madrona is Sausalito's most mythic hotel, both its historic and modern sections built into the hillside and connecting by quaint pathways. Newer rooms are plusher, generally speaking, but all are unique and inviting; some have spectacular views of the bay. The cottages are the epitome

of privacy. The **Alta Mira Hotel** perched on the hillside above town, 125 Bulkley Ave., tel. 332-1350, offers rooms with a view in a magnificent Spanish-Colonial inn, also separate cottages, rates $70-155.

Ambassador Charters, 1505 Bridgeway, Suite 114, tel. (415) 331-5541 or toll-free from Northern California (800) 833-2406, offers varied yacht lodging possibilities in Sausalito as well as at the Berkeley Marina and at Pier 39 in San Francisco, $200 and up for 24 hours of floating affluence.

Other more urban North Bay accommodations include the eclectic 1910 Victorian **Panama Hotel** in San Rafael, 4 Bayview St., tel. (415) 457-3993, with bed and breakfast-style rooms with or without private baths, continental breakfast, $40-105. Also in San Rafael: the **San Rafael Inn** motel at 865 Francisco Blvd. E., tel. 454-9470, with rooms cheaper in the off-season, $40-65; and the **Holiday Inn,** 1010 Northgate Dr., tel. 479-8800, rooms $85-125.

GOOD FOOD IN EASTERN MARIN

At the Civic Center in San Rafael is the **Marin County Farmers Market,** P.O. Box 12682, San Rafael 94913, tel. (415) 492-0122, held year-round on Thursdays 8 a.m.-1 p.m., and on Sundays 9 a.m.-2 p.m. from May through October. **The Rice Table,** 1617 4th St., tel. (415) 456-1808, serves a 14-dish traditional Indonesian *risttafel*—appetizers, main dishes, and *pisang goreng* (banana fritters) for dessert—for about $15 per person (two-person minimum), also a smaller five-course feast and separate entrees available. Vegetarian fare served on Thursdays (but call ahead). Open Thurs.-Sun. for dinners. The longtime local standard for Thai food is **Anita's Kitchen** at 534 4th St., tel. 454-2626, open Mon.-Sat. for lunch and dinner, though **Royal Thai** at 610 3rd St., tel. 485-1074, is getting the raves these days. For Chinese, the place is **Chrysanthemum,** almost in San Anselmo at 2214 4th St., tel. 456-6926.

For very good Afghani fare, try **Bamyan Afghan Cuisine** in San Rafael's Montecito Plaza, 235 3rd St., tel. (415) 453-8809, open for lunch weekdays, for dinner nightly. New Mexico-style **Milly's Healthful Gourmet Dining** at 1613

4th St., tel. 459-1601, is known for its hard-core vegetarian fare (no butter, cream, or eggs), especially their enchiladas and salads. For the real thing, Mexican style, head to **Las Camelias,** 912 Lincoln Ave. (between 3rd and 4th streets), tel. 453-5850, or the taco cafe-style **Taqueria La Fiesta** nearby at 927 Lincoln, tel. 456-9730.

Other notable restaurants include the superb, somewhat pricey **Ma' Shauns** at 857 4th St., tel. (415) 453-9481, for California-style French.

Also in San Rafael, locals swear by **Adriana's** at 999 Andersen Dr., tel. 454-8000, which serves exceptional pasta and heart-healthy chicken, fish, seafood, and veal dishes at lunch and dinner.

Popular in Corte Madera south of San Rafael is **Il Fornaio,** a restaurant and bakery at 223 Corte Madera Town Center, tel. (415) 927-4400, an elegant Italian-style cafe with wonderful pastas, rabbit, chicken, and fish cooked in terracotta, other specialties. Another upscale Corte Madera contender, this one in a slightly Southern style, is the **Savannah Grill,** 55 Tamal Vista off Hwy. 101 at the Market Place Shopping Center, tel. 924-6774, with everything from hardwood-grilled chicken breasts to barbecued baby back ribs, plus unforgettable grilled corn with chili butter. Nearby is the **Island Cafe,** 59 Tamal Vista, tel. 924-6666, a great stop for exquisite vegetarian fare and health-conscious meat selections, like fajitas made with naturally raised Marin County beef. Well-prepared salads, even homemade pies.

The **Lark Creek Inn,** in a beautiful Victorian at 234 Magnolia Ave. north of Corte Madera in Larkspur, tel. (415) 924-7766, is considered one of the best restaurants in the state, with hearty Americana like Yankee pot roast as well as California continental-style mixed grill, seafood, and other specialties. For more casual fare, consider the **Coyote Grill** at 531 Magnolia Ave., tel. 924-7232, serving Mexican food in southwestern style, or the very popular **Marin Brewing Company** at 1809 Larkspur Landing Circle, tel. 461-4677, beloved for its microbrewery ales as much as its pizzas, calzones, and salads. Live music on weekends. Farther north, in Kentfield, the place for breakfast or lunch is the **Half Day Cafe** across from the college at 848 College Ave., tel. 459-0291, serving omelettes, good sandwiches, and just about everything else. The Half

Day goes the whole distance, these days, so you can do dinner, too.

In Mill Valley, the **Cactus Cafe** at 393 Miller Ave., tel. (415) 388-8226, is a locally loved hole-in-the-wall serving inexpensive Mexican food—the real thing, quite good. Almost invisible **Cafe Renoir** (there's no sign) at 100 Shoreline Hwy., tel. 332-8668, has more of that Marin ambience but is fairly inexpensive, even entertaining, with breakfast choices like Egg McRenoir (ham, poached eggs, and mozzarella and cheddar cheeses on an English muffin), sumptuous salads at lunch and dinner. **Jennie Low's Chinese Cuisine,** 38 Miller, tel. 388-8868, serves a decent lunch beginning at 11:30 a.m., also open for dinner. For great inexpensive vegetarian food, try **Lucille's** just upstairs, named for B.B. King's guitar, tel. 381-4613. The sautés and salads are exceptional, the vegetarian dolmas unforgettable. California-style cuisine served too, with meat, chicken, or fish.

The big news in Mill Valley these days, though, is the refurbished and revitalized **Buckeye Roadhouse,** on Shoreline Hwy. (at the Stinson Beach-Mill Valley exit from Hwy. 101), tel. (415) 331-2600, brought to you by the folks behind the Fog City Diner and Mustard's. The roadhouse is part of a very hip social scene (especially in the bar), with contemporary and quite good American fare served up in the cavernous dining room of this hybrid diner/hunting lodge. Try Sunday brunch, lunch Mon.-Sat., or dinner any night.

The **Avenue Grill** in Mill Valley at 44 E. Blithedale Ave., tel. (415) 388-6003, is hip and happening, along the lines of San Francisco's Fog City Diner, good for pastas and hearty American-style specialties. The **Da Angelo Restaurant** at 22 Miller Ave., tel. 388-2000, is up there among the Bay Area's best authentic Italian restaurants, serving excellent food—like linguine with fresh mussels in marinara sauce, homemade tortellini in chicken broth, and meat specialties including carpaccio—for reasonable prices. Pricey but well worth it to its fans is **Butler's** at 625 Redwood Hwy., tel. 383-1900, noted for its excellent and imaginative dinners: corn and red pepper fritters, empanaditas, and oysters Rockefeller for appetizers, entrees including rabbit pot pie, roasted chicken, steaks, pork, and lamb chops. These days, though, Butler's is available for large groups only. More informal **Perry's** downstairs, tel. 383-9300, draws its own crowd, a friendly relation with its own, and similar, charms.

Fred's Place on Bridgeway in Sausalito is a surprising local institution, a no-frills coffee shop where 500 or more people compete all day for Fred's 30 seats. Unpretentious food à la American grill, with an excellent Monterey Jack omelette and other standards plus Polish sausage and bratwurst, fresh-squeezed orange juice. Fred's is *the* place, for millionaires and houseboaters alike; people even wait outside in the rain to get in. Open only for breakfast and lunch, weekdays 6:30 a.m.-2:30 p.m., weekends 7 a.m.-3 p.m., no checks or credit cards.

But the **Casa Madrona Hotel restaurant,** tel. (415) 332-0502, offers the best food around, at breakfast, lunch (weekdays only), and dinner, Marin-style California cuisine using only the freshest available ingredients. For some fine food away from the tourist throngs, try tiny **Sushi Ran** at 107 Caledonia St., tel. 332-3620.

In Tiburon, **Sam's Anchor Cafe** at 27 Main St., tel. (415) 435-4527, is *the* traditional bayside eatery and bar scene for yachting types, open daily for breakfast, lunch, and dinner. Tiburon has an almost endless string of moderate to expensive bayside restaurants stretched out along Main. Nothing beats **Guayamas** at 5 Main St., tel. 435-6300, with upscale and imaginative Mexican food, but you can try at **Tiburon Tommie's** at 41 Main St., tel. 435-1229, noted for its Polynesian decor and food, and **Servino Ristorante Italiano,** 114 Main, tel. 435-2676, serving decent pastas and fresh fish specials.

BOB RACE

THE WINE COUNTRY

INTRODUCTION

The inland valleys of Napa, Sonoma, Mendocino, and Lake counties have become known as California's wine country—this despite the fact that only about 20% of California wines (an annual $2.5 billion business) are produced in this region. Quality, not quantity, is the point here; the area is home to some of the state's (and the world's) finest small wineries.

California's wine country "secret" has definitely been shared. An estimated three million visitors each year squeeze through the Napa Valley alone. On summer weekends (and on weekends generally), winetasting tourist traffic is bumper-to-bumper. The foothills and valleys, cooled by north coastal weather patterns yet usually fog-free, snap to life with lush greenery in spring when the vines and foothill trees leaf out. By late September and early October most of the summer's tourists have evaporated, though the sweet harvest heat still hangs in the air and the vineyards flame with autumn colors. This is the best time to

come. But whenever you come, stick to backroad routes (and destinations) whenever possible to avoid the worst of the wine-country crush.

FIRST AND LASTING IMPRESSIONS

For many, a first-time trip to the wine country is overwhelming. Particularly in the Napa Valley, the first impression is one of pleasure-seeking pretension: too few people have too much money and all arrive at the same place (at almost the same time) to spend it on themselves. Others just come to watch, satisfied to partake vicariously of the region's various indulgences.

Yet these first impressions aren't lasting. California's wine country is actually dedicated, consciously and otherwise, to an appreciation of the appetites—and to an understanding of how we human beings go about satisfying them.

vineyard sunset

SONOMA VALLEY VISITORS BUREAU

"Bottled Poetry" And Other Appreciations

Writer Robert Louis Stevenson hinted at modern wine-country trends in his *Silverado Squatters* when he described the 19th-century Schramsberg wines as "bottled poetry." Closer to the modern-day mark, though, is Sonoma Valley resident M.F.K. Fisher, food writer extraordinaire, who died in June, 1992. Fisher was America's finest prose writer according to W.H. Auden, and "poet of the appetites" to John Updike. More than anyone else, Mary Frances Kennedy Fisher is responsible (in America) for newly nonpuritanical and unaffected attitudes about the pure pleasures of good regional foods and wines. That she settled in California's wine country is no accident.

Indulgence And Overindulgence

Notably, but not exclusively American, is the blurred line between indulgence and overindulgence, particularly as applied to alcohol and other mood-altering drugs. When the appearance of pleasure is actually a self-administered remedy of "spirits" to alleviate personal spiritual pain, addiction shows up, the shadow side of the pleasure principle. Alcohol abuse and alcoholism aren't more prevalent in the wine country than elsewhere in California, but the opportunities for their more open expression are almost endless.

Perhaps it's also no coincidence that the phenomenally successful adventure novelist Jack London, whose alcohol-related death at age 40

shocked the world, lived here with his second wife, Charmian, for many otherwise charmed (if compulsive) years on their Glen Ellen ranch north of Sonoma. He lived by following the boldly defiant creed:

> I would rather be ashes than dust! I would rather that my spark should burn out in a brilliant blaze than it should be stifled by dry rot. I would rather be a superb meteor, every atom of me in magnificent glow, than a sleepy and permanent planet. The proper function of man is to live, not to exist. I shall not waste my days trying to prolong them. I shall use my time.

London also died by his personal creed. A noted barroom orator and people's philosopher who wrote of his struggles with alcohol, he died officially of gastrointestinal uremic poisoning in 1916. Whether his death was actually due to a morphine overdose is still disputed by his biographers.

A BRIEF REGIONAL WINE HISTORY

Winemaking got its local start in Sonoma, where Franciscan fathers planted the first grapes (though their bottled efforts were fairly foul, by most accounts). The locally recognized Hungarian "father of the wine industry," Agoston Haraszthy, soon followed suit, planting European varieties at his Buena Vista Winery. Samuele

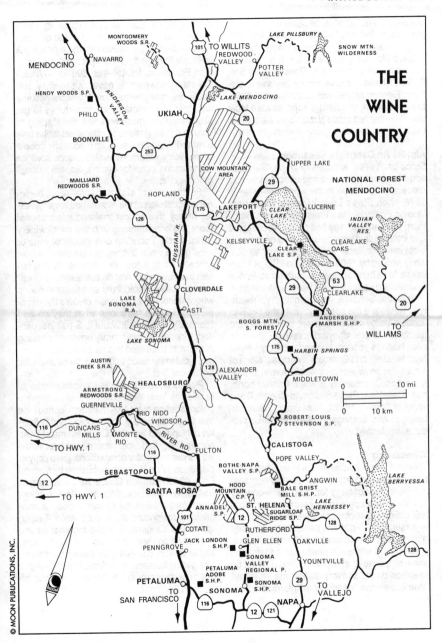

THE WINE COUNTRY

© MOON PUBLICATIONS, INC.

Sebastiani started what became a family empire nearby. In Napa Valley, one of the first California areas settled by American farmers, early settlers planted grapevines taken as cuttings from mission vineyards at Sonoma and San Rafael. Charles Krug was the valley's wine pioneer: Riesling grapes were introduced in 1861, the start of the flourishing, sophisticated local viticulture that has made Napa Valley the spiritual center of the country's growing wine industry.

Almost An Overnight Sensation

Since the 1970s, wineries in Napa, Sonoma, and Mendocino have gained almost overnight renown—largely due to the world's surprise in 1976 when Stag's Leap Winery's finest beat Mouton Rothschild in a Paris competition. Since then, vineyard acreage has more than doubled and international wine awards have become almost commonplace. California wines had definitely arrived by 1985, when Quail Ridge Vineyard's '81 Chardonnay was served to Prince Charles and Lady Di at a White House banquet.

In Napa, Sonoma, and vicinity, dry French-type wines are the specialty, while the hot San Joaquin Valley produces sweet, bulk wines from the state's largest vineyard acreages. The area near Napa is coolest, known for delicate Pinot Noir, Riesling, and Chardonnay grapes. North of Yountville grow world-class Cabernet Sauvignon and Chardonnay grapes. Farther north, near Calistoga, Petite Sirah and Chenin Blanc varieties flourish. Merlot, Pinot Blanc, White Zinfandels, and Sauvignon Blanc are also produced regionally.

Winetasting

Though there *are* other things to do, tasting superior wines (and finding out how they're made) is where the action is for most wine-country travelers. In preparation for winetasting, *don't* feel obliged to memorize lines like "rich, bold, unassuming," "light but perspicacious," and "flushed with heroic tonalities." Despite first impressions, pretense is passé; an honest personal response is all that's required. (To get up to speed on the sensory awareness skills and wine knowledge necessary for informed appre-

ciation, buy a copy of *The University Wine Course,* an excellent self tutorial and comprehensive text by Dr. Marian Baldy, a new book available through the Wine Appreciation Guild in San Francisco, tel. toll-free 800-231-WINE.) Courtesy, however, is never out of style. Because too many wine-country visitors assume winetasting is primarily an opportunity to get drunk for free, more wineries are starting to charge a tasting fee or to offer winetasting only after tours. And because still too many people come, some wineries now also require advance reservations even for tasting. So, always call before going.

For the sake of wine art appreciation, beginners should start at the established larger wineries (many give educational and informational tours) before venturing into the small winery avant-garde. Focus on one variety of wine or wine grape while tasting, or start with a white, proceed on to a rosé or red wine, then finish with a dessert wine. And do ask questions whenever possible (particularly at smaller wineries where hands-on experience *creates* the experience). People here love what they do and (generally) like to talk about it. Small independent wineries are often family operations: tasting rooms and tours tend to shut down when everyone's out in the fields or busy in the wineries. So again, call first.

Pick up current winery lists and informational brochures from local chambers of commerce before starting out. (AAA members, consult the free *California Winery Tours* booklet and "Wineries of Napa and Sonoma Counties" map.) For a current listing and more information about wineries honored in quality competitions, get a copy of *California Wine Winners,* published by Varietal Fair, 4022 Harrison Grade Rd., Sebastopol 95472. While winetasting, be selective about stops and if traveling by car choose a non-drinking designated driver in advance. Tasting rooms are dangerously close together as you head north on Hwy. 29 through the Napa Valley, so the unwary can easily be seeing double before getting as far as St. Helena. Drunk driving is not only dangerous, it's illegal—a serious offense in California.

NAPA AND VICINITY

A cozy 35 miles long and framed by rounded rolling hills, the Napa Valley is the nation's most famous vineyard and winery region. Though the town of Napa is more prosaic than Sonoma, the valley itself has seasonally changing charm, hill-hugging vineyards, world-renowned wineries, and famous spas—experiences available, for the most part, even to budget travelers. Disappointed refugees from the gold fields helped build the city of Napa, working in lumber mills, orchards, and on cattle ranches. Napa in the 1850s was already a rowdy town of hotels, saloons, and money. But the "silver rush" of the late 1870s brought more of all these, plus mine shafts throughout the county. The hottest currency nowadays: wine and rumors of wine, tourists and rumors of tourists.

For information on the entire Napa Valley, in addition to what's available from individual community chambers of commerce, contact the **Napa Valley Conference and Visitors Bureau,** 1310 Napa Town Center, Napa 94559, tel. (707) 226-7459.

NAPA VALLEY DIVERSIONS

Hot Air Balloons

Locals complain about the noise, but balloonists no doubt enjoy the finest of all possible wine-country views. An 18th-century diversion of the French aristocracy, ballooning somehow seems appropriate here (though for most people, an outrageously expensive airborne experience at $125 an hour and up). **Napa Valley Balloons Inc.,** P.O. Box 2860, Yountville 94599, tel. (707) 253-2224 or toll-free in Northern California (800) 253-2224, has been around the longest, with dawn balloon trips launched from Domaine Chandon, followed by brunch and sparkling wines. Also well known among local high-but-slow floaters is **Balloon Aviation of Napa Valley,** 6525 Washington (P.O. Box 2500), Yountville 94599, tel. 252-7067 or toll-free (800) FOR-NAPA. Other Yountville ballooning companies include **Adventures Aloft,** tel. (707) 255-8688, and **Napa Valley Balloon Flights,** tel. toll-free (800) NAPA-SKY.

For most trips (any company) advance reservations are required.

Winery Entertainment

Something is always happening on the winery scene. The Napa Valley's very big big-band, folk, classical, and jazz concerts at the **Robert Mondavi Winery** in Oakville are among the hot acts. Mondavi also sponsors other events throughout the year and fine art shows (the likes of Benjamin Buffano) at its Vineyard Room Gallery. For advance reservations for the Mondavi Sunday-evening **Winery Jazz Festival** concerts in July and early August, contact: Robert Mondavi Summer Festival, Box 106, Oakville 94562, tel. (707) 963-9611.

Domaine Chandon in Yountville, tel. (707) 944-2280, sponsors **The Great Cabaret Performers Series,** also jazz and various Monday-night concerts and endless other events, from benefit fashion shows to Bastille Day celebrations. Various performances are also hosted at the **Charles Krug Winery** in St. Helena, tel. 963-5057, and elsewhere.

Other Entertainment

Entertaining are May through December plays put on by the **Napa Valley Stage Company,** tel. (707) 257-6872. The **Napa Valley Symphony,** tel. 226-6872, performs year-round at the Lincoln Theatre in Yountville and elsewhere throughout the valley. The Seventh-day Adventist **Pacific Union College** in Angwin, tel. 965-7362, sponsors a year-round schedule of nonalcohol-oriented cultural events, from organ concerts and piano recitals to vocalists. Chamber music concerts, cellists, and other musical events are also regularly scheduled at Napa's Methodist Church, tel. 252-7122. In addition, particularly on summer weekends, bars and restaurants throughout the valley offer live entertainment.

Winery Events

The Robert Mondavi Winery's various **Great Chefs of France and America** weekend series of culinary education and indulgence are quite the event; call (707) 944-2866 for current information and reservations. Almost all the valley's wineries get into the act for the **Napa Valley Wine Auction** and related events, usually held in St. Helena in late June—the party of the year and a rich people's wine-bidding bash on behalf of charity. In 1985, for example, DuPont heirs paid $21,000 for the first case of "California Cognac," double-distilled Remy-Martin/Schramsberg Vineyards brandy. Offbeat and unhyped sweetheart wines can be reasonable, though bidding paddles (necessary to get in the door) cost plenty. For info contact: **Napa Valley Wine Auction,** P.O. Box 141, St. Helena 94574, tel. 963-5246.

Sonoma County has a similar soiree every August.

The **Napa Valley Grape Growers Association,** 4075 Solano Ave., Napa 94558, tel. (707) 944-8311, sponsors an annual **Chili Ball and Cook-off** and raffle, usually in July, to support agricultural land preservation (and to help prevent overly touristic trends that undermine agriculture in the area).

To find out what's going on throughout the entire wine country region, from special events to regular tastings and tours, call the 24-hour **Winery Hotline,** tel. (707) 427-5500 (touch-tone phones only). In addition to basic information, the hotline transfers calls, offers directions to specific wineries, and suggests other nearby destinations.

Other Events

In June, antique cars are the central attraction at the **Concours d'Elegance** (a benefit for the Children's Hospital in Oakland) at Napa's Silverado Country Club. The **Napa County Fair** at the county fairgrounds in Calistoga, tel. (707) 942-5111, usually takes place over the July 4th weekend, with main events including the sheepdog trials, livestock exhibits, a pulling contest for horses, sprint-car racing, and amusement rides. Other annual activities throughout the valley range from cat, dog, and horse shows to cribbage tournaments, spaghetti and crab feeds, and crafts fairs.

TRANSPORT

Touring By Bicycle

Napa County's back roads are paved and rural, among the best in the nation for bicycling. If it weren't for the treacherous traffic, cycling through the Napa Valley would be the only way

to go. Bicyclists brave enough to pedal into the wine country, avoid hair-raising Hwy. 29 (Napa Valley's wine spine) and opt instead for the generally safer **Silverado Trail** up the east side of the valley from Napa to Calistoga. (In peak season, though, even this route can be frightening.) Other good rides include the back roads threading through the Pope Valley/Lake Berryessa area (avoid on weekends, when Bay Area boaters take over the roads) and the killer hills into Sonoma County from the valley's west side. A good guide for route planning is *Cyclists' Route Atlas: A Guide to Yolo, Solano, Napa and Lake Counties* by Randall Gray Braun.

Rent bikes at **Napa Valley Cyclery** north of Napa proper (right next to the looming visitor info center), 4080 Byway East, tel. (707) 255-3377, at the **Village Peddler** in Yountville, at **St. Helena Cyclery,** 1156 Main St., tel. 963-7736, or—if you end up in Sonoma County—at **Spoke Folk** at 249 Center St. in Healdsburg, tel. 433-7171. Contact the visitor bureau and local chambers of commerce for suggested bike tour companies.

Travel By *Wine Train*

Popular with tourists but the root of intense local political ferment is the new *Napa Valley Wine Train,* which rolls along 18 miles of railroad from Napa to St. Helena, paralleling Hwy. 29, then loads passengers aboard buses for some winery cruising before the trip back to Napa. The $10 million *Wine Train* project is eventually expected to transport almost a half-million visitors annually. (Opponents fear that the train itself, theoretically a traffic alternative, will invite yet more tourists and further snarl valley traffic, since the tracks cross the main highway in two places and makes 90 public road crossings. Local drivers now play chicken with the train—a dangerous game.) The basic *Wine Train* tour includes food (brunch, lunch, or dinner) and costs $55-79, everything included. For more information, contact: Napa Valley Wine Train, 1275 McKinstry St., Napa 94559, tel. (707) 253-2111 or toll-free in California (800) 427-4124. Closed Monday.

Travel By Bus, Rental Car, Limo

In town, Napa has its own **V.I.N.E.** city bus system, 1151 Pearl St., tel. (707) 255-7631, which runs weekdays, with shorter hours on Saturday. The **Tri-City Bus,** operated by The Volunteer

Center of Napa County, Inc. in conjunction with Calistoga, St. Helena, and the county (call 963-4222 for trip reservations at least two days in advance), serves Calistoga, Deer Park, St. Helena, Angwin, and points in between.

Greyhound, 1620 Main St. in Napa, tel. (707) 226-1856, and on California Dr. in Yountville, tel. 944-8377, connects all Napa Valley towns, with buses each day between Napa and Calistoga (stops include Yountville, Oakville, Rutherford, St. Helena). Since Greyhound connects with Calistoga from Santa Rosa, the valley is a fairly easy destination from San Francisco (or from anywhere flanking Hwy. 101).

Evans Airport Service, 1825 Lincoln Ave., Napa 94558, tel. (707) 255-1559, offers daily executive-type service from San Francisco International Airport, as well as charters and limousine service, tel. 255-2577, and bus tours, tel. 252-6333. **Limousine d'Elegance,** 1825 Lincoln Ave., tel. 255-1557, has limos, but **Budget Rent-A-Car,** 407 Soscol Ave. in Napa, tel. 224-7845, has reasonable rental cars.

NAPA

Most Napa wineries aren't *in* Napa but are farther north, scattered among the more picturesque Napa Valley towns. Napa itself is a blue-collar town (where most of the farm workers live) on the way to becoming a permanent upscale bedroom community for San Francisco and the Bay Area—and an unabashed anchor for the fleets of winetasters sloshing northward. Over half the valley's 100,000-plus population is concentrated here. Despite the grape-stained march of progress, Napa's small town-ness lives on in older, shady neighborhoods (there are some dignified and stately Victorians on Division, Randolph, and 5th streets).

Napa has quite a few antique shops and galleries, including the **Napa County Historical Society Museum and Gallery** in the library building downtown at 1219 1st St., Napa 94559, tel. (707) 224-1739, open only Tues. and Thurs. 12-4 p.m. A new tourist diversion (daytime, brunch, and dinner cruises) is the recently refurbished **Napa Valley Riverboat** *City of Napa* (known as the *Bold Duck* before it made its new nest at the Napa Valley Marina, 1200 Milton Rd.), weekend cruises only, May through Oct.,

but boat can be chartered anytime. For schedules, prices, and information, contact: Napa Riverboat Co., 1400 Duhig Rd., tel. 226-2628.

For horseback riding here consider the **Wild Horse Valley Ranch** on Wild Horse Valley Rd., tel. (707) 224-0727. Or hike in **Skyline Wilderness Park** at 4th and Imola, tel. 252-0481, also nice for picnics. Or, plan a hike to the large, rare Sargent cypress grove in the obscure **Cedar Roughs** area west of Rancho Monticello on Lake Berryessa. There's no public trail or road; call the BLM office in Ukiah, tel. 462-3873, to find it.

Lake Berryessa

One of the state's big reservoirs and the county's eastern "escape" route since 1957 when the Monticello Dam was completed, Lake Berryessa, tel. (707) 966-2111 for info, is one place to avoid the wine-country crunch—arid oak foothills in summer, gorgeous greenery in spring—though it, too, is also popular on weekends. Berryessa has the usual lake action—good trout fishing, swimming, sailing, water-skiing, even houseboats—plus private campgrounds. Camp at **Spanish Flat,** tel. 966-2101, or **Putah Creek, tel. 966-0656. Lake Solano** below the dam is a Solano County park with 50 campsites—quiet (no motorboats); call 447-0707 for info.

Some Napa Area Wineries

Escape the crush by avoiding Hwy. 29 as much as possible. Instead, head up the **Silverado Trail** from Napa to Calistoga on the valley's east side. (Cut across the valley to Hwy. 29 and westside wineries via several main crossroads.) About six miles north of Napa is modern **Stag's Leap Wine Cellars,** 5766 Silverado Trail, tel. (707) 944-2020, its sudden fame helping to fuel wine-country crowds. Stag's Leap is noted for its Chardonnay, Cabernet Sauvignon, Sauvignon Blanc, and Merlot, but especially Cabernet Sauvignon. Open for tasting (fee) daily 10 a.m.-4 p.m., tours by appointment only. New at Stag's Leap is the decision to withhold sulphur from the crushed Chardonnay grapes and allow oxidation to occur. (The result of this German technique: the brown wine is "healed" to the classic pale gold color of straw during fermentation.) Old at Stag's Leap is an active ecological consciousness. Concern about crop diversification has led to plantings of kiwifruit and mandarin oranges, and, in Lake County, some wild rice.

Nearby, at 6154 Silverado Trail, is **Shafer Vineyards,** tel. (707) 944-2877, noted for its Cabernet Sauvignon, open for tasting and tours by appointment only. Also worth a stop in the hilly Stag's Leap area is tiny **Pine Ridge Winery,** 5901 Silverado Trail, tel. 253-7500, which produces 25,000 cases of its four premium wines annually, open daily 11 a.m.-4 p.m. for tasting and picnicking, tours by appointment. **Clos du Val Wine Co. Ltd.,** at 5330 Silverado Trail, tel. 252-6711, is open daily 10 a.m.-4 p.m. for tasting (European-style wines) plus shady picnics, tours by appointment only. The immense three-story redwood winery at **Trefethen Vineyards,** three miles north of Napa and just off Hwy. 29 at 1160 Oak Knoll Ave., tel. 255-7700, produces four premium varietals, open for tasting daily 10 a.m.-4:30 p.m., for tours by appointment.

Also well worth exploring near Napa: **Silverado Hill Cellars** at 3105 Silverado Trail, tel. (707) 253-9306 (tasting hours Weds.-Sun. 11 a.m.-5:30 p.m.); **Chimney Rock Winery,** 5350 Silverado Trail, tel. 257-2541 (tasting daily 10-4, tours by appointment only); and **Silverado Vine-**

yards, 6121 Silverado Trail, tel. 257-1770, known for its Chardonnays, Cabernets, and herb-scented Sauvignon Blancs (tasting daily 10 a.m.-4:30 p.m., tours by appointment). A good choice too on the valley's quieter side is **Monticello Cellars,** off Oak Knoll at 4242 Big Ranch Rd., tel. 253-2802, tasting and picnicking daily 10 a.m.-4:30 p.m., tours three times daily.

Saintsbury Vineyards is four miles southwest of Napa off Hwy. 12/Hwy. 121 at 1500 Los Carneros Ave., tel. (707) 252-0592, and emphasizes Pinot Noir and Chardonnay. Open Mon.-Fri. 9:30 a.m.-4:30 p.m. by appointment only. Exclusive is the word for **Acacia Winery** at 2750 Las Amigas Rd., tel. 226-9991, which took almost immediate bows for its Pinot Noir and Chardonnay. Open weekdays by appointment. As striking as the wine is the avant-garde architecture of **Codorniu Napa,** a sparkling wine venture by Spain's Codorniu clan rooted in the Carneros district at 1345 Henry Rd., tel. 224-1668. Tasting hours Mon.-Thurs. 10-5, Fri.-Sun. 10-3. **Domaine Carneros,** also in the heart of the Carneros region, four miles southwest of town just off Hwy. 121/12 at 1240 Duhig Rd., tel. 257-0101, produces *methode-champenoise* sparkling wine from Carneros grapes. Established in 1987 and already considered a regional landmark, Domaine Carneros is architecturally inspired by the historic 18th-century Champagne residence of the Taittinger family, as in Champagne Taittinger of Reims, France. Visiting hours: daily 10 a.m.-5:30 p.m. from June through October.

Definitely different in the Napa Valley: **Hakusan Fine Sake,** One Executive Way, south of Napa proper at the intersection of Hwy. 12 and Hwy. 29 (enter from N. Kelly Rd.), tel. (707) 258-6160, open for sake tasting and sales daily 9-6.

NAPA PRACTICALITIES

Accommodations:
Camping, Motels, Hotels

Camping is the cheapest and also the best way to take full advantage of the wonderful climate. **Lake Berryessa** to the east and **Bothe-Napa Valley State Park** north between Calistoga and St. Helena offer the campsites. But, in a pinch, camp at the far-from-elegant **Napa Town & Country Fairgrounds,** 575 3rd St., tel. (707)

226-2164, $15 for hot showers and tent sites in a field. There's a **Motel 6** at 3380 Solano Ave. (north of Napa proper via the Redwood Rd. exit off Hwy. 29), tel. 257-6111, a small motel with a/c, pool, TV, movies, from $36. (Fills up fast, so reserve in advance.) The **Silverado Motor Court,** at 500 Silverado Trail near Soscol Avenue, tel. 253-0892, has 15 clean units with small kitchens and TV, $40 and up, registration noon-6 p.m. The **Napa Valley Travelodge** is at 2nd and Coombs streets across from the courthouse (limited parking), tel. 226-1871; $60-85 from May through Oct. on weekend nights, cheaper on weekdays, cheaper still Nov. through April.

The **John Muir Inn** at 1998 Trower Ave., Napa 94558, tel. (707) 257-7220 or toll-free (800) 522-8999, has room rates from $75; suites are $105 and include a king-sized bed, double sleeper sofa, in-room spa, and wet bar/refrigerator. General amenities include in-room coffee, cable TV, continental breakfast, and access to the mineral pool and spa. The **Best Western Inn, Napa** at 100 Soscol at Aimola, tel. 257-1930 or (800) 528-1234, offers everything from single rooms to loft suites with living rooms. Amenities here include heated pool and spa, TV, and fresh-ground in-room coffee. Rates: $70-99, with midweek and off-season discounts.

The **Clarion Inn,** 3425 Solano Ave., tel. (707) 253-7433 or (800) 333-7533, is a full-service hotel with some country-inn charms, from lovely rooms to scenic courtyard with heated pool and Jacuzzi, and lighted tennis courts. Also restaurant and lounge. Rates: $95-105, substantially less on weekdays and in winter. The **Inn at Napa Valley** (formerly Embassy Suites) at 1075 California Blvd., tel. 253-9540 or (800) 433-4600, offers two-room suites overlooking a courtyard or atrium, each with vanity and sofa sleeper, wet bar, refrigerator, microwave, coffeemaker, and two multi-line phones. Heated indoor pools with private sundeck, sauna, and outdoor swan pool, too. Free cooked-to-order breakfast, complimentary beverages each evening. Rates: $119-154, $10 less in the off-season.

Napa Bed And Breakfasts
Characteristic of the region, Napa has many bed and breakfasts, none particularly inexpensive, one fairly reasonable: **Arbor Guest House** at 1436 G St., tel. (707) 252-8144, has a two-

night minimum on weekends; continental breakfast, and antique rooms (two have fireplaces) $60-135, $20 each additional person. An excellent choice is the Victorian stucco **Napa Inn,** 1137 Warren St., tel. 257-1444, with five rooms, full breakfast, $95-145. The wheelchair-accessible **Candlelight Inn** located west of Hwy. 29 off 1st St. at 1045 Easum Dr., tel. 257-3717, is a 1929 English Tudor offering two rooms and one suite, continental breakfast. Rates: $125-140.

Napa's historic homes have become the belles of the bed and breakfast ball. **La Belle Epoque,** 1386 Calistoga Ave., tel. (707) 257-2161, is an 1893 Queen Anne Victorian with many-gabled dormers and period antiques, vintage and contemporary stained glass, wine-tasting room/cellar. Six rooms with private baths, one with fireplace, full breakfast, winetasting and appetizers. Like most Victorian inns, from here it's a short walk to the *Wine Train* and local opera house. Rates: $105-140. The historic **Churchill Manor** at 485 Brown St., tel. 253-7733, is a three-story Second Empire mansion built in 1889 offering 10 rooms (three with fireplaces, one with spa) and full breakfast, on an acre of gardens. Rates: $90-160. Down the street at 443 Brown is **The Blue Violet Mansion,** tel. 253-2583, a striking 1886 Queen Anne Victorian with antiques and vintage Napa atmosphere, six rooms with private baths, two with balcony, two with spas, four with gas-burning fireplaces. Rates: $115-195. Full breakfast and refreshments, picnic baskets and dinner available. Another Napa landmark is **The Beazeley House** at 1910 1st St., tel. 257-1649, with 11 rooms (five with fireplace and whirlpool) plus carriage house, full breakfast and complimentary tea and cookies. Rates: $110-180.

More Napa Bed And Breakfasts
For non-Victorian ambience, consider a stay at the **Tall Timbers Chalets** off Hwy. 29 at 1012 Darms Ln., tel. (707) 252-7810, country-style cottages (breakfast is continental), some with decks or porches. Rates: $75-125. A pleasant change-up, too, is **La Residence Country Inn** two miles north of Napa at 4066 St. Helena Hwy., tel. 253-0337, 20 rooms in an 1870 Gothic Revival farmhouse and French-style barn, most with private baths. Full breakfast, pool and hot tub too. Rates: $75-160. Also outside town is the 1984 **Oak Knoll Inn** at 2200 E. Oak Knoll

Ave., tel. 255-2200, a French country-style inn built of stone with just three rooms, all with king-sized beds and fireplaces. Hot tub, heated pool, croquet, generous continental breakfast served on the deck or in rooms. Rates: $150-225.

For other bed and breakfast choices, contact **Bed and Breakfast Exchange,** 1458 Lincoln Ave., in Calistoga, tel. (707) 942-2924 from 9-5; **Sonoma County B&B Reservations,** tel. 433-4667; **Napa Valley Reservations Unlimited,** 1819 Tanen in Napa, tel. 252-1985; or the **Napa Valley Tourist Bureau,** tel. 258-1957.

Good Food

As in Sonoma County, doing the farm trails is a good way to gather up the freshest, best food available (the inexpensive prices are only incidental). In Napa stop off at **Lawler's Liquors,** 2232 Jefferson, tel. (707) 226-9311, for picnic supplies. The **Curb Side Cafe** at 1245 1st St., tel. 253-2307, has good sandwiches, decent breakfasts. For burgers, though, **Nation's Giant Hamburgers** at 1441 3rd St., tel. 252-8500, can't be beat—huge made-to-order burgers, very reasonable. **Jonesy's Famous Steak House** at the county airport, 2044 Airport Rd., tel. 255-2003, also serves almost-famous chicken, children's menu too. The talk of the town for food lovers, though, is the decidedly under-stated and unfussy **Table 29,** just north of Napa at 4110 St. Helena Hwy., tel. 224-3300. Lunch and dinner daily, quite reasonable. **Caffe 1991** at The Inn at Napa Valley, 1075 California Blvd., tel. 253-9540, serves pasta, seafood, and mesquite-grilled specialties.

Also popular is **Ruffino's** Italian restaurant in downtown Napa at 645 1st St., tel. (707) 255-4455, open for lunch and dinner, Thurs. through Tues. (but just for dinner on Sat.), closed major holidays. Reservations are wise. **La Boucane** French restaurant, 1778 2nd St., tel. 253-1177, offers fine dinners in an old Victorian. (In pricier Napa Valley restaurants, call first for reservations and to ask about corkage fee policies. It may not be worth it to bring your own bottle of local wine to dinner.)

Information And Services

The 100-year-old **Napa Chamber of Commerce,** P.O. Box 636, Napa 94559, is in new quarters downtown at 1556 1st St., tel. (707) 226-7455, open 9-5 for free maps, winery info,

suggested bike routes and picnic stops, also current brochures on lodging, restaurants, recreation, and places of interest. Ask for the "Farm Trails" brochure to find local produce. The free *Redwood Empire Visitors Guide,* usually available here, also has good regional information. An alternative is the **Tourist Information Office** at 4076 Byway E., tel. 253-2929, open daily 10 a.m.-3 p.m., with free brochures, also maps, accommodations listings, etc., for sale. Whenever you find it, the free *California Visitors Review* is a great winery information source.

Napa's **post office** is at 1625 Trancas (the eastward extension of Redwood Rd. from the freeway). **Bookends Book Store** downtown at 1014 Coombs St. near 1st, tel. (707) 224-1077, has books, magazines, and U.S. Geological Survey topo maps. Open Mon.-Wed. and Fri.-Sat. 9:30 a.m.-6 p.m., Thurs. until 9, Sun. 10-5. The **Hollow Reed** at 1741 Trancas, tel. 226-9230, has New Age, holistic, and metaphysical books. Stop by the **Salvation Army** thrift shop at 1234 3rd St. for good secondhand clothes (bargain hunting in rich people's backyards is almost always rewarding).

YOUNTVILLE

Yountville's humble beginnings—George Yount built the first house in the valley, a fortified log cabin, and planted the valley's first vineyard in the 1830s—are none too apparent these days. Yountville has gone yupscale. The **Veterans Home of California** here, now run by the state, first opened its doors in 1884, started by veterans of the Mexican War and members of the Grand Army of the Republic. And the doors are still open—a huge, somehow disturbing human warehouse. If you have time, spend some here. The attached **Armistice Chapel Museum,** tel. (707) 944-4000, is stuffed with military memorabilia, some items on loan from San Francisco's Presidio Army Museum. **Vintage 1870** at 6525 Washington St., tel. 944-2451, is an old winery now chock-full of specialty shops and restaurants. The town's main event, actually, is browsing through the tony clothing, jewelry, and art and antique shops. Particularly worthwhile are the artist-owned **Depot Gallery Inc.,** 6526 Washington, tel. 944-2044, open daily 10 a.m.-5:30 p.m., and the **Lawrence Gallery** at 6795

Washington, tel. 944-1800, open 10:30-5:30. Afterward, try a simple picnic in **Yountville City Park** at Washington and Lincoln. There's a fascinating cemetery nearby, where George Yount and other valley pioneers are buried.

Domaine Chandon

Fairly new but already famous is the modern $42 million Domaine Chandon facility, a subsidiary of France's Moet-Hennessey cognac and champagne producers (the Dom Perignon people), already renowned for its sparkling wines. (Never say "champagne" in public in the wine country. It's so déclassé, since traditional vintners—following the French—reserve the term only for bubbly produced in the Champagne region of France.)

Just west of Hwy. 29 and off California Dr. near the Armistice Chapel Museum, P.O. Box 2470, Yountville 94599, tel. (707) 944-2280, Domaine Chandon is striking architecturally, fieldstone walls with barrel-arched vaulted roofs over terraced stair steps—and just as famous for its champagne museum and fine, fairly expensive, fairly formal California-style French restaurant (call 944-2892 at least two weeks in advance for reservations). Among the decadent desserts here: blueberry ice-cream soup. At lunch, a continental buffet is served. Tasting fee charged at the winery. Regular tours (full "operations" tours only on weekdays) are among the best in the valley and can be given in several languages with advance notice. A wide variety of cultural events are also scheduled year-round. From May through October, the winery's open 11 a.m.-6 p.m. daily, otherwise just Wed.-Sunday.

Other Yountville Area Wineries

Cosentino Winery next to Mustard's Grill at 7415 St. Helena Hwy., tel. (707) 944-1220, is a local innovator, known for its pioneering Merlot and its sparkling Blanc de Noir. Just north at 7481 St. Helena Hwy. and technically in Oakville is **DeMoor Winery & Vineyards,** tel. 944-2565 or toll-free (800) 535-6400, popular for its tastings and picnics in the Wine Garden.

The **S. Anderson Winery** across the valley (near the Silverado Trail) at 1473 Yountville Cross Rd., tel. (707) 944-8642, is a small family-owned producer of sparkling wines. The facility itself is a fascination: 18-foot-high wine-aging caves tunnelled into a rhyolite hillside

(with peaked ceilings, cobblestone floors, even a stage). They host special winetastings, even concerts, but tours are by appointment only. Liquid fruit of the vines from **Chateau Potelle Winery** up the mountain at 3875 Mt. Veeder Rd., tel. 255-9440, open Thurs.-Mon., noon-5 p.m., were served at George Bush's inaugural dinner. **Chateau Chevre,** 2030 Hoffman Ln. (one mile south of Yountville off Hwy. 29), tel. 944-2184, is another small appointment-only place. The winery building was once a goat-milking barn, hence the name, "Goat Castle."

Yountville Eateries

Good restaurants cluster along Washington Street. **The Diner,** 6476 Washington, tel. (707) 944-2626, is just what it's advertised as: a wonderful roadside diner *very* popular (even with locals) for its inexpensive food. At lunch and dinner, choose from American and Mexican standards, everything from burgers to burritos washed down with Dos Equis, but breakfast is the meal of the day here (come very early or very late). Stick with the simple (perfect scrambled eggs with bacon or ham, good huevos rancheros) or go wild with banana-walnut waffles. Great place. Open Tues.-Sun. 8 a.m.-3 p.m. for breakfast and lunch, 5:30-9:30 p.m. for dinner. **Piatti,** 6480 Washington, tel. 944-2070, is very good, an offbeat pasta place also specializing in grilled chicken, even rabbit, with daily risotto specials. (There's another one in Sonoma.) For homemade pastas and Northern Italian specialties, head for **Mama Nina's,** 6772 Washington, tel. 944-2112, where the fettucine Alfredo is particularly good. Open for lunch and dinner daily (except major holidays).

Also rated high on the local restaurant scale is **Compadres,** 6539 Washington, tel. (707) 944-2406 in an old brick building (a vintner's mansion built in 1872) known as Vintage Estates. A Mexican bar and grill, festive and friendly.

Down the road a piece is **Mustards Grill,** 7399 St. Helena Hwy., tel. (707) 944-2424, an unassuming upscale place with good food right out of the wood-burning oven—the kind of place where you could easily dawdle the day away ordering one tasty tidbit after another. Appetizers, grilled vegetables and meats, good desserts, extensive wine list. The **California Cafe Bar & Grill** between Madison and the highway at 6795 Washington St., tel. 944-2330, is part of a chain popping up all over the north-state, offering California-style fare in a casual setting, expansive menu. Still hot is the **French Laundry,** 6640 Washington, tel. 944-2380, relaxed and leisurely; call ahead for each night's menu offering.

Yountville Accommodations

Lodging in Yountville is usually expensive. Fairly reasonable is the **El Bonita Motel** at 195 Main St., tel. (707) 963-3216, farther north near St. Helena. **The Magnolia Hotel,** actually a fine bed and breakfast (once a bordello) at 6529 Yount St., P.O. Box M, Yountville 94599, tel. 944-2056—12 rooms in 1873 brick-and-fieldstone lodges (plus cottage) furnished with Victoriana (five rooms with fireplaces) plus pool and whirlpool, full breakfast.

The **Burgundy House Inn,** 6711 Washington (P.O. Box 3156), tel. (707) 944-0889, is a French country-style stone house built in 1893, featuring five rooms with private baths, one with a fireplace and separate entrance. Full breakfast. Rates: $95-110. A more contemporary take on the French country theme, à la Laura Ashley, is two-story **Oleander House** at 7433 St. Helena Way (P.O. Box 2937), tel. 944-8315, all rooms with queen beds, private baths, balconies, fireplaces. Full breakfast. Rates: $105-160. **The Webber Place** in Old Town at 6610 Webber St. (P.O. Box 2873), tel. 944-8384, is an 1850 Greek Revival with four guest rooms (two share

a bath), full breakfast. Rates: $69-119. Unusual: the **Napa Valley Railway Inn** at 6503 Washington, tel. 944-2000, nine separate railroad cars converted into suites with bay windows, tiled baths, and queen-sized brass beds.

The Best Western **Napa Valley Lodge,** 2230 Madison at Hwy. 29, P.O. Box L, tel. (707) 944-2468, has very nice rooms, $115-165. The **Vintage Inn** in Yountville is a first-rate place at 6541 Washington St., tel. 944-1112, and perfect for a great grape escape. Built in the mid-'80s, all the rooms have wood-burning fireplaces, whirlpool baths, and wine bars. Most also have either a balcony or patio, not to mention other cushy wine-country comforts. There's a heated pool, and a canal that runs through the grounds, with spas situated here and there. Champagne and pastry breakfast, afternoon tea. There are a number of octagonal pitched roofs, so many of the upstairs rooms have very high ceilings. The hotel has a private limo you can hire, and a honeymoon package is available. Regular rates are $129-169 weeknights, and $139-179 Fri. and Sat. nights. Inquire about specials.

Information, Bike Rentals

Contact the **Yountville Chamber of Commerce,** P.O. Box 2064, tel. (707) 944-2929. Rent bikes or mopeds at the **Village Peddler,** tel. 944-8426, or at **Adventures Aloft,** tel. 255-8688, which also sponsors balloon flights.

ST. HELENA AND VICINITY

The next town to speak of "up valley," small St. Helena is surrounded by historic vineyards and wineries. Increasingly, the town seems to be an elite enclave catering to the monied minions from the city, though the area was originally settled by German, Italian, and Swiss farm families. If possible, park on the east side of the highway (so you don't have to try to cross it) then stop off at the **St. Helena Chamber of Commerce** office on the main drag, 1508 Main St., St. Helena 94574, tel. (707) 963-4456, to get oriented. Ideally, *leave* your car parked and rent mountain or touring bikes at **St. Helena Cyclery,** 1156 Main St., tel. 963-7736. Bikes rent for $5 an hour or $20 per day; the folks here will recommend local tour routes.

ST. HELENA SIGHTS

Area Diversions

Like Yountville, St. Helena is becoming something of a hoity-toity shopping mecca, though there are some still-surviving utilitarian farm-town businesses. Of all the upscale up-valley shops hereabouts, **Dansk Designs** in Dansk Square on Hwy. 29 (known near town also as St. Helena Hwy.), tel. (707) 963-4273, is a fascination, offering great deals (seconds, discontinued patterns, limited editions) on Danish glassware, ceramics, and other housewares. Also interesting is **Hurd Beeswax Candles,** where visitors can watch the process of handmade candlemaking, 3020 St. Helena Hwy. N., tel. 963-7211. The **Napa Valley Grapevine Wreath Company,** tel. 963-0379, specializes in handwoven wreaths and baskets. **Main Street Books** at 1371 Main, tel. 963-1338, carries both fiction and nonfiction, plus provides a children's book corner. A further stroll down Main St. in either direction leads visitors through St. Helena's heart of high-priced, tasteful consumerism. If nothing else is going on come nightfall (and, due to local preference, nightlife here is quiet), take in a movie at the local **Liberty Theatre,** which sometimes shows foreign films.

Robert Louis Stevenson Museum

Well worth a visit is the world-renowned **Silverado Museum** collection of Robert Louis Stevenson memorabilia in its own wing at the St. Helena Public Library Center, 1490 Library Ln., P.O. Box 409, St. Helena 94574, tel. (707) 963-3757 or 963-3002; open daily (except Mondays and holidays) noon-4 p.m. Stevenson's honeymoon story is the stuff of true romance. He met his bride-to-be (Fanny Osbourne, a married American woman) at an artists' colony in France, fell in love with her, then left his Scotland home for California in hot pursuit. Critically ill and poverty-stricken (living briefly in Monterey, San Francisco, and Oakland while awaiting her divorce), Stevenson managed to survive until his marriage to Fanny in May 1880. Too poor to afford the $10 a week for room and board in Calistoga, the two honeymooned in an abandoned bunkhouse at the Old Silverado Mine on Mt. St. Helena above the Napa Valley. Almost overnight, Robert Louis Stevenson regained his health, won his parents' approval of his new marriage, and returned to Scotland with his beloved Fanny to write his masterworks *(Treasure Island* and *The Strange Case of Dr. Jekyll and Mr. Hyde* among them).

CALIFORNIA DEPARTMENT OF PARKS & RECREATION

Robert Louis Stevenson

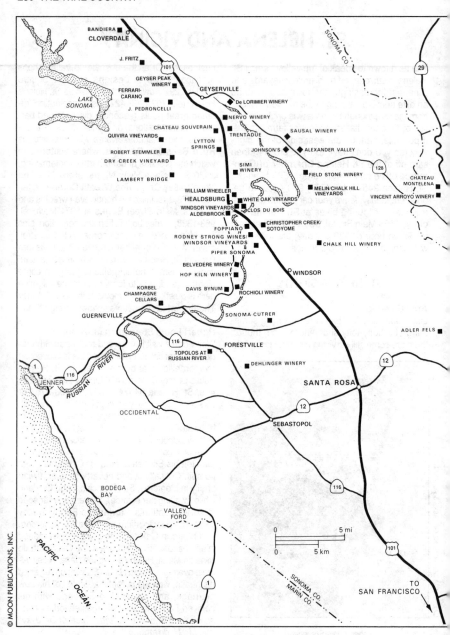

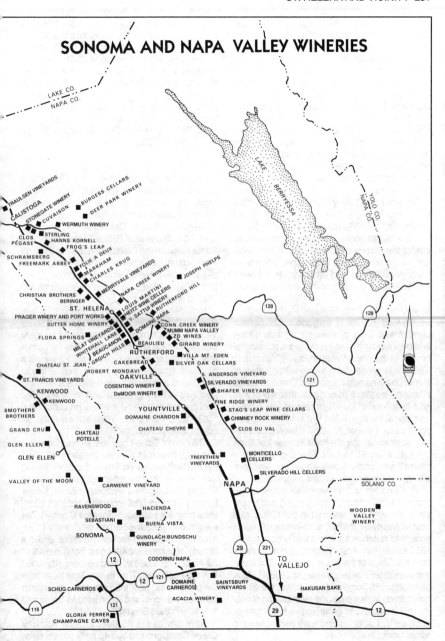

SONOMA AND NAPA VALLEY WINERIES

LAKE CO.
NAPA CO.

YOLO CO.
NAPA CO.

LAKE BERRYESSA

TRAULSEN VINEYARDS
CALISTOGA
STONEGATE WINERY
CUVAISON
BURGESS CELLARS
DEER PARK WINERY
WERMUTH WINERY
CLOS PEGASE
STERLING
HANNS KORNELL
FROG'S LEAP
SCHRAMSBERG
FREEMARK ABBEY
FOLIE A DEUX
MARKHAM
CHARLES KRUG
MERRYVALE VINEYARDS
NAPA CREEK WINERY
JOSEPH PHELPS
CHRISTIAN BROTHERS
BERINGER
ST. HELENA
LOUIS MARTINI
HEITZ WINE CELLARS
RUTHERFORD HILL
PRAGER WINERY AND PORT WORKS
V. SATTUI WINERY
SUTTER HOME WINERY
DOMAINE NAPA
CONN CREEK WINERY
MUMM NAPA VALLEY
FLORA SPRINGS
MILAT VINEYARDS
ZD WINES
WHITEHALL LANE
GIRARD WINERY
BEAUCANON
BEAULIEU
GRGICH HILLS
RUTHERFORD
VILLA MT. EDEN
CHATEAU ST. JEAN
CAKEBREAD
SILVER OAK CELLARS
ST. FRANCIS VINEYARDS
ROBERT MONDAVI
OAKVILLE
S. ANDERSON VINEYARD
KENWOOD
COSENTINO WINERY
SILVERADO VINEYARDS
KENWOOD
DeMOOR WINERY
SHAFER VINEYARDS
SMOTHERS BROTHERS
PINE RIDGE WINERY
YOUNTVILLE
STAG'S LEAP WINE CELLARS
GRAND CRU
DOMAINE CHANDON
CHIMNEY ROCK WINERY
CHATEAU POTELLE
CHATEAU CHEVRE
CLOS DU VAL
GLEN ELLEN
GLEN ELLEN
MONTICELLO CELLARS
TREFETHEN VINEYARDS
VALLEY OF THE MOON
SILVERADO HILL CELLARS
CARMENET VINEYARD
NAPA
SOLANO CO.
RAVENSWOOD
HACIENDA
WOODEN VALLEY WINERY
SEBASTIANI
BUENA VISTA
SONOMA
GUNDLACH BUNDSCHU WINERY
CODORNIU NAPA
TO VALLEJO
SCHUG CARNEROS
DOMAINE CARNEROS
SAINTSBURY VINEYARDS
HAKUSAN SAKE
ACACIA WINERY
GLORIA FERRER CHAMPAGNE CAVES

128
121
128
121
29
221
12
121
12
121
116
29
12

On display at this red-carpeted "jewel box" museum (which offers something for everyone) are over 8,000 items related to Stevenson's life and literary career: first editions and variant editions of almost all his works, over 100 books from his library in Samoa, original manuscripts and letters, paintings, photographs, sculptures, drawings. The collection here includes some of the first words he ever wrote, in the form of childhood letters, as well as his last written words. Also here: his wedding ring, his work desk, and the lead soldiers he played with as a boy. The Silverado Library is free, though voluntary contributions to the library's Vailima Foundation are always welcome.

The fine **Napa Valley Wine Library** next door in the new public library, 1492 Library Ln. (at Adams St.), tel. (707) 963-5244, has 3,000 or so wine-related books, journals, and magazines, one of the largest collections of libation literature on the West Coast. Wine appreciation seminars, winetastings, and other events are regularly scheduled, primarily during summer months.

Bale Grist Mill State Historic Park

Dr. Edward T. Bale (a surgeon originally from London and General Vallejo's medical officer and nephew by marriage) owned a substantial portion of the Napa Valley in the 1830s, due to Vallejo's largesse. A physician with a sense of humor, Bale named his spread Carne Humana Rancho—perhaps to suggest that we are all grist for the mill of life. (Bale himself was ground up early, at the age of 38.) But in 1846, he built a small state-of-the-art flour mill powered by a 20-foot waterwheel, the site on Mill Creek just north of modern-day St. Helena. The original grist for this mill was locally grown wheat, but later corn was ground into highly prized cornmeal.

The wooden waterwheel (this massive 36-footer a 19th-century improvement) and three-story mill were first restored in the 1920s, at a cost of nearly $1 million; a 10-year restoration project to reachieve the mill's fully operational 1850 status was recently completed by workers from the Office of the State Architect. The massive millstones inside are impressive just to look at, and though flume water to power the wheel now comes from a pipe and recirculating pump, the mill is capable of grinding five to six tons of grain daily. Lucky visitors may get to see the whole works in operation.

The park is a few miles north of St. Helena on Hwy. 29. To get to the waterwheel and millworks, follow the shaded, paved path downhill from the parking lot—a good stretch for car-cramped legs, and ramps make the area wheelchair accessible. Better yet, hike in on the mile-long History Trail from Bothe-Napa Valley Park just to the north; $1 admission. For more information, contact: Bale Grist Mill State Historic Park, 3801 St. Helena Hwy., Calistoga 94515, tel. (707) 963-2236.

Bothe-Napa Valley State Park

This is not exactly wilderness, but it's the only place to really camp in the valley. Its 100 acres of pleasant wooded valley and Coast Ranges ridges stretch four miles north of St. Helena, three miles south of Calistoga. You can hike here from **Sugarloaf Ridge State Park** near Santa Rosa on the California Riding and Hiking Trail (sometimes a hot trek in summer but usually tolerable). Here, hiking is a major attraction. Guided hikes and campfire programs are offered only in summer.

Included within the park's boundaries are Ritchey Creek, the foundation ruins of Napa Valley's first church, and a pioneer cemetery with Donner Party gravestones. Near the cemetery (and the speeding highway traffic) there's a pleasant maple-shaded picnic area, a group camp, and a rarity in state parks: a swimming pool (with dressing rooms and showers). The pool is open only mid-June through Labor Day, 10:30 a.m.-7:30 p.m., lifeguard on duty, $3 adults, $1 children.

The longest Bothe-Napa hike (almost four miles one-way) combines an easy lowland stroll along the **Ritchie Canyon Trail** (an old roadbed fringed with ferns, shaded by redwoods, and paralleling Ritchey Creek) with a moderate hike up **Upper Ritchey Canyon Trail** and past a waterfall. (Continue from here to reach Sonoma County.) The easy mile-long **Redwood Trail** offers early-spring access to blooming redwood orchids under a canopy of second-growth trees. For glimpses of the Napa Valley below, head up more strenuous **Coyote Peak Trail.** The **History Trail** leads from the picnic area, past the cemetery and church ruins, up the ridge, and down into Mill Creek and the historic **Bale Grist Mill.**

Park day use is $5 per car. The **Ritchey Creek Campground** has 40 fairly private fami-

the Bale Grist Mill, now centerpiece of a state historic park, before restoration

CALIFORNIA DEPARTMENT OF PARKS & RECREATION

ly campsites tucked into wooded thickets, each equipped with table, food locker, and barbecue stove, $14 per site. Restrooms have laundry tubs, flush toilets, drinking fountains, and hot showers. No RV hookups (though a dump station is available). The park also has 10 walk-in (tents only) campsites, one reserved for hikers and bikers. Camping reservations are wise in spring, summer, and fall; Memorial Day to Labor Day is prime time. For reservations, call Mistix at (800) 444-7275, from two days to eight weeks in advance. For more information, contact: Bothe-Napa Valley State Park, 3801 St. Helena Hwy. N., Calistoga 94515, tel. (707) 942-4575.

Other Sights Near St. Helena

Angwin, to the east of St. Helena (up into the hills via Deer Park and Howell Mountain roads), is home to the 1,500-student Seventh-day Adventist **Pacific Union College**, nestled into the crater of an extinct volcano. (On a clear day, folks here say, you can see both San Francisco and the Sierra Nevada from the top of Howell Mountain.) Most of the people in Angwin belong to the teetotaling church (you won't find coffee, tea, alcohol, meat, or cigarettes in the modern college-owned downtown grocery) and are less than thrilled at the prospect of more wineries clustered on nearby hills or imbibing tourists disturbing the peace.

Near here: the **Newton Observatory** and **Las Posadas State Forest**. To the north is **Pope Valley**, with its comfortably ramshackle 1913 Pope Valley Store. A few miles past the

Pope Valley Winery is the home of folk artist **Litto Damonte**, a visual ode to the functional beauty of car hubcaps, painted tires, and toilet-bowl planter boxes. South of Angwin (but more accessible via Hwy. 128 from the Rutherford area) is **Lake Hennessey**, a local recreation area (free picnicking, fishing, boating) created by the construction of Conn Dam.

WINERIES NEAR ST. HELENA

Oakville Area Wineries

Most famous of all is the **Robert Mondavi Winery**, 7801 St. Helena Hwy. in Oakville, tel. (707) 963-9611, with decent wines, a never-ending schedule of Napa Valley entertainment, and the best free tour available for the untutored. Drop by early or call first for reservations; tours are limited and fill up fast, especially in summer. The modernesque mission-style buildings here were designed by Cliff May, spiritual father of the Western ranch-style house. Open from May through October daily 9-5, otherwise 10 a.m.-4:30 p.m. Robert Mondavi co-owns the nearby **Opus One** winery with the Baroness Philippine de Rothschild, a Franco-American partnership that has produced expensive progeny.

Cakebread Cellars north of Mondavi, 8300 St. Helena Hwy., tel. (707) 963-5221, is a fine small family winery in an abstract-style barn, open daily for tastings (Chardonnay, Cabernet Sauvignon, Sauvignon Blanc), open daily 10-4, tours only by appointment. **Silver Oak Cellars**

is eastward at 915 Oakville Crossing Rd., tel. 944-8808, and produces only Cabernet Sauvignon, which it ages for five years before release. Open for wine sales Mon.-Fri. 9 a.m.-4:30 p.m. and Sat. 10 a.m.-4:30 p.m., tours by advance appointment only at 1:30 p.m. weekdays (visitors on tours can taste).

The **Girard Winery,** 7717 Silverado Trail on the valley's east side, tel. (707) 944-8577, is quite small but plays in the big leagues: Girard wines found an appreciative place on the White House dinner table during the Reagan years. Tours by advance appointment only, open weekdays 1-4, Sat. 2-4. Try the Chardonnay. **ZD Wines,** closer to Rutherford at 8383 Silverado Trail, tel. 963-5188, has a fine Pinot Noir (open daily). **Mumm Napa Valley** 8445 Silverado Trail, tel. 942-3434, open daily 10-5 for tasting and tours (last tour at 3:30 p.m.), is also worth a stop.

The Mediterranean-style **Villa Mt. Eden** halfway along the north side of Oakville Cross Rd. near the Silverado Trail, P.O. Box 147, tel. (707) 944-2414, is owned by the McWilliams family and is low-key and lovely, with winetasting in a little house (also an office) where rumor has it Clark Gable and Carole Lombard passed some time while filming a movie here. Open for tours by appointment only, for tasting (award-winning wines) and picnicking daily 10 a.m-4 p.m. (closed on major holidays). Try the Cabernet Sauvignon.

Rutherford Area Wineries

The well-known **Rutherford Hill Winery,** 200 Rutherford Hill Rd. on the east side of the valley, tel. (707) 963-7194, looks like an old-fashioned hay barn perched on the hill—but there's nothing really "country" here except the straw-colored white wines and flowery picnic grounds. Noted for its award-winning Merlot, Sauvignon Blanc, and several other varietals, Rutherford Hill's wine-aging caves are the largest in the world, the tunnels and cross-tunnels capable of storing 6,500 small oak barrels. (These caves, like most throughout the region, were dug by Alf Burtleson using a Welsh coal-mining machine with carbide teeth.) Open daily for tastings and public picnicking 10:30 a.m.-4:30 p.m. (until 5 p.m. Fri.-Sun.), tours on the hour starting at 11:30 a.m. Nearby **Conn Creek Winery,** 8711 Silverado Trail near Rutherford Crossing Rd., tel. 963-9100, is worth a stop (by appointment only) just to appreciate the energy-efficient modern building: steel, Styrofoam, and gu-

nite galore. (The Cabernet Sauvignon is state of the art too.) Open daily 10-4.

Vine-covered **Beaulieu** at 1960 St. Helena Hwy., tel. (707) 967-5200, is an old family winery (founded by Georges de Latour in 1900) which survived Prohibition by producing altar wines. BV (as it's often called) is known for its vintage-dated sparkling wines and table wines. Beaulieu is also credited with making Cabernet Sauvignon "king of the California wines." Open daily 10 a.m.-4 p.m., excellent guided tour and tasting.

Offering some of the finest Chardonnay and Zinfandels, tiny **Grgich Hills** at 1829 St. Helena Hwy., tel. (707) 963-2784, is open daily for tastings, 9:30-4:30, tours by appointment only. **Beaucanon** at 1695 St. Helena Hwy. S., tel. 963-1886, is also exceptional, open daily 10-5. **Domaine Napa** nearby at 1155 Mee Ln., tel. 963-1666, is noted for the Sauvignon Blanc, Chardonnay, Merlot, and Cabernet Sauvignon produced from its 200 acre vineyard. Family-operated **Whitehall Lane Winery,** 1563 St. Helena Hwy. just north, tel. 963-9454, is a modern redwood winery that produces both varietals and dinner wines and welcomes visitors in a friendly tasting room. Open daily 11 a.m.-5 p.m., but tours by appointment only.

St. Helena Wineries

Just south of St. Helena at 277 St. Helena Hwy. S. is **Sutter Home Winery,** tel. (707) 963-3104, famous for its Amador Zinfandel and, more recently, its Chardonnay. The tasting room is open daily 10 a.m.-4:30 p.m., no tours. Next door, off the highway at 1281 Lewelling, is **Prager Winery and Port Works,** tel. 963-PORT, open daily 10:30 a.m.-4:30 p.m., tours only by appointment. Nearby is the **Louis Martini Winery,** 254 St. Helena Hwy. S., tel. 963-2736, open the same hours daily, with group tours by appointment. Sunny St. Helena Winery (once a Mondavi enterprise) is now home to **Merryvale Vineyards** at 1000 Main St. (next to Tra Vigne), tel. 963-7777, noted for its award-winning wines, antique cask collection, and new bocce ball court. Merryvale offers a free and very worthwhile wine seminar every morning (call ahead for reservations). Open daily 10-5:30.

The small family-owned **V. Sattui Winery** south of St. Helena on the corner of White Ln. and Hwy. 29, tel. (707) 963-7774, is as much known for its fabulous 1885 stone-and-beam construction as it is for its award-winning wines, Euro-style deli, and pleasant picnic grounds. Open daily 9-5, tours by appointment. Another family enterprise well worth a stop is **Milat Vineyards** just south at 1091 St. Helena Hwy. S., tel. 963-0758, open daily 11-6.

Noted for its Martha's Vineyard Cabernet Sauvignon is the family-owned **Heitz Wine Cellars**, 500 Taplin Rd., tel. (707) 963-3542, open daily 11-4, tours by appointment only. Also popular is the **Freemark Abbey Winery** two miles north of St. Helena on the highway (3022 St. Helena Hwy.), tel. 963-9694, an 1895 building with new winery technology, specializing in Chardonnay, Riesling, and Cabernet Sauvignon, open daily 10 a.m.-4:30 p.m., tours at 2 p.m. only. The **Flora Springs Wine Company**, on W. Zinfandel Ln., tel. 963-5711, specializes in estate-grown Chardonnay, Sauvignon Blanc, Cabernet Sauvignon, and Merlot. Open Mon.-Sat. 10 a.m.-3 p.m., with tours by appointment.

Small, too, is **Markham Vineyards** in the 1876 St. Helena Cooperative Winery building at 2812 St. Helena Hwy. N., tel. (707) 963-5292, which emphasizes six premium varietals. Open daily 11 a.m.-4 p.m., with "sensory evaluation" and tours by appointment only. A favorite for those with a similarly peculiar sense of humor is **Folie A Deux**, 3070 St. Helena Hwy., tel. 963-1160, open daily 11 a.m.-5 p.m., with public picnicking, group tours by advance arrangement only. Two psychiatrists started this "shared fantasy or delusion," believing that people are crazy to go into the wine business but also believing that wine and life go together. Share their fantasy and taste the award-winning Chardonnay and Dry Chenin Blanc.

Across the valley, **Joseph Phelps Vineyards**, 200 Taplin Rd., tel. (707) 963-2745, requires appointments for tours, tasting, and picnicking. Nearby **Napa Creek Winery** in the old Sunshine Meat Packing plant at 1001 Silverado Trail, tel. 963-9456, is small but hospitable, specializing in white varietals plus two reds. Open for sales daily, 9-5, tastings following tours (call first).

FAMOUS WINERIES

In the tourist sweeps, the biggest and best St. Helena wineries are Christian Brothers, Beringer, and Charles Krug. The **Christian Brothers**' his-

toric 1888 three-story stone **Greystone Winery**, 2555 Main St., St. Helena 94574, tel. (707) 963-0765, was closed due to seismic safety concerns, then reopened to visitors in 1987 after extensive renovation. Owned by the Mont La Salle Vineyards (the corporate arm of the Catholic teaching order founded in 1879, which got its start in the California alcohol business making altar and "medicinal" wines in Martinez), Christian Brothers began shedding its stodgy image in the late 1980s—spurred on by sagging brandy sales and newly aggressive competition. Then the order sold its winery to Hublein, Inc., but the Christian Brothers order is still the Napa Valley's largest landholder, with all profits from its wine grape sales supporting its schools and colleges. Intriguing at Christian Brothers is the museum-quality winemaking memorabilia, including the unique collection of corkscrews. Open Sat. and Sun. for self-guided tours, sales, and tasting 10 a.m.-4 p.m.

The famous wine-aging caves at the 1876 **Beringer Vineyards** at 2000 Main St. (Hwy. 29), tel. (707) 963-7115 or 963-4812, were hand-dug by Chinese laborers hired by Frederick and Jacob Beringer. Open for business ever since, Beringer is the oldest Napa Valley winery in continuous operation. The strikingly ornate 17-room Victorian **Rhine House** (on the National Register of Historic Places), a study in stained glass and oak paneling surrounded by lovely gardens, dominates the domain. Thirty-minute Beringer tours (which include a peek at the wine caves) end at Rhine House, where a good time is had by all tasting award-winning wines. (It's a mob scene here in summer; to avoid the crowds, head up to Beringer's Reserve Room on the second floor of Rhine House, where generous samples of better wines are poured.) Open 10 a.m.-6 p.m. May through September, 10-5 otherwise. Closed on major holidays. Group tours by appointment only.

The **Charles Krug Winery** at the Charles Krug Home Ranch, 2800 St. Helena Hwy. (Main St.), tel. (707) 963-5057, was founded in 1861, making this the valley's oldest working winery. Now another Mondavi enterprise noted for its consistently good California Cabernets (among the best anywhere), Krug also offers very fine (and very popular) tours. Most basic (and free) is Krug's regular "tour and tasting," a 45-minute facility tour, from the ancient 30,000-

gallon redwood aging tanks to a review of new computer-assisted winemaking technology, followed by a 15-minute tasting session (no charge, no reservations required). The "select tasting" option (possibly in addition to the tour) offers visitors eight premium wines (including vintage reserve Cabernets) for leisurely tasting, no reservations needed. Call for other tour information. Complimentary tasting on Wednesday. Sales shop open daily 10-4.

Wineries North Toward Calistoga

Frog's Leap, 3358 St. Helena Hwy., tel. (707) 963-4704, seemingly an amphibious takeoff on Stag's Leap Winery, was actually once a frog farm at the turn of the century. Now the farm's one-time livery stable serves as a winery for premium Chardonnay, Cabernet Sauvignon, Sauvignon Blanc, and Zinfandel varietals. There's an annual open house for patrons on Frog's Leap mailing list. No tasting (a very small winery), but open for tours and sales Mon.-Fri. mornings by appointment only.

Across the valley, **Deer Park Winery,** 1000 Deer Park Rd., in Deer Park, tel. (707) 963-5411, doesn't have any deer (despite the antlers on the winery label) but does have a tiny vineyard and century-old "gravity flow" stone wine cellar plus antique winemaking machinery. Also, Deer Park has a guest cottage for bed and breakfasters. Open only by appointment (10 a.m.-4 p.m. daily) for tastings, tours, picnics, sales. **Burgess Cellars** nearby, 1108 Deer Park Rd. (P.O. Box 282, St. Helena 94574), tel. 963-4766, is another rare old stone and woodframe winery, this one also producing premium varietals (Cabernet Franc, Cabernet Sauvignon, Zinfandel, and Chardonnay), open for tasting and tours by appointment.

Kornell And Schramsberg

Two noted champagneries, Schramsberg Vineyards and Cellars and Hanns Kornell Champagne Cellars, are midway between Calistoga and St. Helena. The historic family-owned weathered-wood-and-old-stone **Hanns Kornell Champagne Cellars,** east of Hwy. 29 at 1091 Larkmead Ln., tel. (707) 963-1237, makes very fine sparkling wines (and brazenly calls them champagnes) in the *methode champenoise.* Tours here are a treat, since visitors walk through the winery itself rather than peeking

into the action from a visitors' gallery. Open daily 10-4 for tasting, tours, and sales.

Schramsberg, established in 1862 by Jacob Schram four miles south of Calistoga and five miles north of Hwy. 29, tel. (707) 942-4558, was the first hillside winery in Napa Valley, immortalized by Robert Louis Stevenson in his *Silverado Squatters* (". . . and the wine is bottled poetry"). Schramsberg produced the "California champagne" President Nixon took along on his first trip to China in 1971. And how appropriate: part of Schramsberg's secret of success is its collection of underground wine caves, dug by Chinese workers out of volcanic tufa deposits. The original Victorian home and old underground cellars, tucked into oaks and madrones, have been carefully preserved, but most visitors pay more attention to the wines. A beautiful peach-colored Cuvée de Gamay and a Cuvée de Pinot are among Schramsberg's prestigious specialties, though many other winemakers now make better sparkling wines (more like champagne). No tasting. Tours and sales by appointment only (closed Sundays and holidays).

ST. HELENA PRACTICALITIES

Accommodations:
Motels, Hotels, A Retreat

In general, there's not much room at the inn in St. Helena for people without *money.* Predictably, bed and breakfast establishments are the rule. A surprise, though, is the simple and sanely priced art deco **El Bonita Motel** just south of town at 195 Main St., tel. (707) 963-3216 or toll-free (800) 541-3284. Once a darker (and cheaper) 1950s motel, now the El Bonita is pure 1930s down to the last detail—the kidney-shaped swimming pool. Some rooms are smallish (and the walls thinnish) but come with TV, phone, alarm clock, wall heaters, window air-conditioners. Rates: $53-84, lower in the off-season.

The **Rancho Caymus Inn** at 1140 Rutherford Rd. in Rutherford, tel. (707) 963-1777, is a fine Old California-style inn, its 26 suites a marvel of craftsmanship, from stone fireplaces and hand-hewn beams and furnishings to stained glass. The **Bonadventure Balloon Company** is headquartered here too, part of the Rancho Caymus "Stay and Fly" package. Basic room rates (check for specials at slow times) run $95-150. Exceptional, too, is the English Tudor-style **Harvest Inn** at 1 Main St. in downtown St. Helena, tel. 963-9463, high season rates run $105-300.

Secluded is the word for **Willow Retreat** up the mountain from Oakville—there's not even a sign out front, just "Willow" on the mailbox—at 6517 Dry Creek Rd., tel. (707) 944-8173, a low-key and serene retreat popular with women yet "everybody-friendly." Quite popular with groups, but for an independent escape, rooms run $80-110 (double occupancy), including continental breakfast on weekdays. (Weekends there's an impressive brunch, extra.) Most rooms do not have kitchens, but there's hiking, tennis, sauna, solar-heated pool, hot-tub, usually a masseuse.

Area Bed And Breakfasts
Bed and breakfasters could stay for months in St. Helena alone, just keeping up with the new inns. Most have lower off-season rates. An updated version of 19th-century St. Helena is the **Hotel St. Helena,** 1309 Main St., St. Helena 94574, tel. 963-4388, most rooms with private baths, $100-190, continental breakfast in the lobby. The cedar-shingled **Deer Run Inn** outside town at 3995 Spring Mountain Rd., tel. 963-3794, has just three rooms (one with fireplace), $95-125 with continental breakfast, also swimming pool, hiking trails nearby.

The **Ambrose Bierce House** at 1515 Main St., St. Helena 94574, tel. (707) 963-3003, is the crotchety cynic's former residence, an 1870 Victorian with just two rooms available, $79-149. The **Cinnamon Bear Bed and Breakfast,** 1407 Kearney St., tel. 963-4653, the first in the Napa Valley, has four rooms in a 1904 Craftsman home, hearty breakfasts, wine or coffee and cookies in the afternoon, rooms $75-140. The **Wine Country Inn** just north of town at 1152 Lodi Ln., tel. 963-7077, is a large New England-style inn with swimming pool and whirlpool, many rooms with fireplaces, three suites, rates $125-161. The **Shady Oaks Country Inn** at 399 Zinfandel Ln., tel. (707) 963-1190, features four rooms in a 1920s country house and converted winery, full breakfast. Rates: $55-170. **Vigne del Uomo Felice,** 1871 Cabernet Ln., tel. 963-2376, is a stone French country cottage circa 1968, three rooms, continental breakfast, fresh fruit (in season) from the orchard. Rates: $100. **Bartels Ranch and Coun-**

try Inn at 1200 Con Valley Rd., tel. 963-4001, offers a secluded 60 acres and three "California country" rooms, expanded continental breakfast. Rates: $125-275.

The **Oliver House Bed and Breakfast Inn** at 2970 Silverado Trail, tel. (707) 963-4089, offers four antique-furnished rooms in a 1920s Swiss-style chalet overlooking valley vineyards. Rates: $55-135. Near the Silverado Trail on 600 acres in the Chiles Valley hills is the **Rustridge Ranch,** 2910 Chiles Valley, tel. 965-9353, three rooms in a 1940s Southwestern ranch-style house, expanded continental breakfast. Rates: $90-140.

For more bed and breakfasts in the area, contact the local chamber of commerce or the various regional inn referral services (see "Napa Practicalities" above).

St. Helena Food: The Basics
The **Oakville Grocery Co.** south of St. Helena and Rutherford in Oakville, 7856 St. Helena Hwy., tel. (707) 944-8802, is actually an up-scale deli featuring items like country hams, salmon jerky, pâtés, truffles, imported caviar and cheeses (and an endless array of imported curds, butters, chutneys, and marmalades), decadent desserts, pastries, premium wines

and beers. **Guigni's Grocery,** a local institution at 1227 Main St., tel. 963-3421, makes a hefty sandwich for about $3 (including salad) and is an unpretentious place for putting picnic fixings together. In bad picnic weather, you can even eat in the back. There's a 24-hour **Safeway** market at 1026 Hunt Ave., tel. 963-3833. Or get picnic supplies at the **Napa Valley Olive Oil Manufacturing Company** hidden away at 835 McCorkle Ave. south of town (call 963-4173 for hours and directions). Wonderful sausage, cheeses, other reasonably priced deli fare, even picnic tables.

Basic but a possibility for breakfast, lunch, and late lunch is the **St. Helena Coffee Shop,** 61 Main St., tel. (707) 963-3235. Modest, too, by St. Helena standards is **Teng's** just off Main at 1113 Hunt Ave., tel. 963-1161, for good Mandarin meals, open for lunch and dinner daily.

International and California Cuisine

Finding fine food (to accompany the area's fine wines) seems to be a favorite pastime in and around St. Helena. Reservations at the region's best restaurants are almost mandatory. Fresh and homey is the **Spring Street Restaurant,** 1245 Spring St., tel. (707) 963-5578, in the modest former home of opera singer Walter Martini. Quiche or sandwiches and salads at lunch, hearty homestyle dinners. Weekend brunch includes omelettes with fresh homemade muffins, sweet rolls, or biscuits with homemade preserves. Exceptional and simple (and very popular) **Tra Vigne** is in a stunningly serene setting at 1050 Charter Oak Ave., tel. 963-4444. And what you get is fine Italian fare in the Napa Valley style (but in the Tuscany tradition): simple sauces, fresh and hearty food. All this in a refurbished old stone setting, a relaxed, breezy atmosphere, refreshingly unaffected. Great desserts.

Taking the place of Knickerbockers and routinely raved about is the **Brava Terrace** French-American bistro at 3010 St. Helena Hwy. N., tel. (707) 963-9300, with exceptional food, friendly atmosphere. **Vines** across the way and down at 3111 St. Helena Hwy., tel. 963-8991, serves California fare in the wine country style, usually good for lunch. **Starmont** at the Meadowood Resort, 900 Meadowood Ln. (off the Silverado Trail), tel. toll-free (800) 458-8080, is beloved for its views and serves creative California cui-

sine. **Trilogy** at 1234 Main, tel. 963-5507, is a tiny restaurant with a heavy-hitting following, French-California fare considered among the valley's best. Excellent wine list.

More Fine Fare

At home in its earthy (and historic) stone surroundings is **Terra Trilogy** at 1345 Railroad Ave., tel. (707) 963-8931, some say the Napa Valley's best restaurant. The fare here is East-West, regionalized with local produce, meats, and fish—and of course wines. Sitting pretty in its French Provincial hotel setting down the block is **Showley's Miramonte,** 1327 Railroad Ave., tel. 963-1200, which serves California cuisine with a French and Italian accent, everything made fresh with local ingredients. Internationally acclaimed (and very expensive also) is **Auberge du Soleil** above the valley at 180 Rutherford Hill Rd. in Rutherford, tel. 963-1211. Fixed-price French dinners with creative California touches, a French country ambience, and the finest of all-American views. (A 36-room inn goes with the program, so stay overnight if it's at all feasible.)

CALISTOGA

Despite the Napa Valley's hectic hubbub, there's something fun and funky about Calistoga. The town is *hot,* built atop a boiling underground river. Industrious Sam Brannan officially laid out the town in 1859 on the site of the natives' Colaynomo or "oven place." Brannan's dream was to make the area the "Saratoga of California." So his original hotel and 20 cottages were christened "Calistoga"—an awkward combination of the state's name and the well-known resort spa in New York. The main stop nowadays (besides the spas and nearby wineries) is the **Sharpsteen Museum** and **Sam Brannan Cottage** next door, at 1311 Washington St., tel. (707) 942-5911. The modern brick museum, next to public restrooms and the senior center, features a well-designed diorama of 1865 Calistoga plus antique dolls, clothing, quilts. The cottage itself is furnished in wealthy San Franciscan, circa late 1800s.

Downtown on Lincoln, California's oldest surviving railroad depot has been converted into **The Calistoga Depot,** with shops, a simple restaurant and the chamber of commerce office. Some good galleries and shops are scat-

Sam Brannon's cottage

tered elsewhere throughout Calistoga. Also here: production facilities for well-known mineral waters, including Calistoga, À Santé, Crystal Geyser, and Napa Valley Spring Water.

The Spas

Bathe in a volcano—or at least the bubbling springs and murky mud generated by one. The combinations available for curing yourself are almost endless, but the basic routine is this: a soak in a mud bath usually followed by a mineral bath and whirlpool (with or without steam bath and blanket sweat) and finished with a massage. Some new twists: herbal facials, herbal wraps, eucalyptus steams, and Japanese-style enzyme baths (heat-generating tubs full of cedar, bran, and fiber). Depending upon the resort and available options, spa packages run $40-50 and up.

Nance's Hot Springs (also a clean and fresh downtown motel with nice mountain views), 1614 Lincoln, tel. (707) 942-6211, is a good place to take the mud cure. The basic program includes hot springs mineral bath, steam bath, black volcanic mud bath, and blanket sweat, extra for massage. Sam Brannan's original resort site is now completely renovated at nearby **Indian Springs Spa and Hot Springs Resort,** 1712 Lincoln, tel. 942-4913, with a huge 1914 geyser-heated mineral swimming pool. Mud baths (100% volcanic ash) with mineral bath, eucalyptus steam, and blanket wrap (all about one hour), with half-hour massage extra. Reservations are necessary for **Dr. Wilkinson's Hot**

Springs, 1507 Lincoln, tel. 942-4102: complete physical therapy package. The **Calistoga Spa Hot Springs,** 1066 Washingnon, tel. 942-6269, is family oriented, with use of outdoor mineral pools for a small fee, mud baths and massage extra.

The **Lincoln Avenue Spa,** housed in an old bank building at 1339 Lincoln, tel. (707) 942-5296, has the usual plus mineral Jacuzzi, acupressure face lifts, herbal facials, manicures and pedicures, mud wrap and massage, or one-hour massage. New and New Age-ish is the **International Spa,** 1300 Washington, tel. 942-6122—enzyme baths and flannel-sheet wraps (accompanied by music and environmental art), the usual mud and mineral baths and wraps plus herbal facials, herbal blanket wraps, acupressure, reflexology. The **Golden Haven Spa** at 1713 Lake, tel. 942-6793, has a complete exercise room you can use for the price of the baths.

Some Calistoga Area Wineries

Stop at Coca Cola's **Sterling Vineyards,** 1111 Dunaweal Ln. just south of Calistoga, tel. (707) 942-5151, for a $5 ($7 on weekends) gondola-car ride up to this majestic and modern monastic-style Martin Waterfield palace (the ticket price redeemable in wine). Great valley views. Open daily for tasting and tours (self-guided with visual aids) 10:30 a.m.-4:30 p.m. The **Stonegate Winery** nearby at 1183 Dunaweal, tel. 942-6500, is a small winery with a big reputation for its premium Cabernet Sauvignon, Sauvignon Blanc, and Chardonnay. Stonegate wines are now served in Paris and to first-class overseas fliers on both Lufthansa and American airlines. Open daily 10:30 a.m.-4:30 p.m. for tasting and sales, tours by appointment only. The postmodern terra-cotta **Clos Pégase** at 1060 Dunaweal, tel. 942-4981, conceived as a tribute to mythology, art, and wine, produces Cabernet Sauvignon, Sauvignon Blanc, Chardonnay, and Merlot. Open daily 10:30 a.m.-4:30 p.m., self-guided tours.

Cuvaison, 4550 Silverado Trail, tel. (707) 942-6266, is another elite small winery. Here wine lovers find some of the best Cabernet, Chardonnay, Merlot, and Zinfandel produced anywhere. Open daily for tastings and sales as well as public picnicking, 10 a.m.-5 p.m., tours by appointment. **Chateau Montelena,** 1429 Tubbs Ln., tel. 942-5105, is noted for its Cabernet Sauvignon (which has appeared on White House menus) *and* its intriguing medieval French chateau surrounded by Chinese gardens. (Somehow it's all very American.) Open daily 10 a.m.-4 p.m., tours by appointment only. Also well worth a visit: **Traulsen Vineyards,** 2250 Lake County Hwy., tel. (707) 942-0283, open Fri.-Sun. 11-4 and by appointment (tours by appointment only); **Vincent Arroyo Winery,** 2361 Greenwood Ave., tel. 942-6995, open weekdays 9-4:30, weekends 10-4:30 (tours by appointment); and **Wermuth Winery,** 3942 Silverado Trail, tel. 942-5924, open Wed.-Sun. 10-5.

Then, if Napa Valley's wineries still haven't quenched that vineyard thirst, head northwest on Hwy. 128 through the mountains above Calistoga into the Alexander Valley area near Healdsburg—such a pleasant, peaceful contrast that you'll wonder why you spent so much time in Napa Valley. The **Field Stone Winery, Alexander Valley Vineyards,** and **Johnson's Alexander Valley** all produce fine wines.

Sights Near Calistoga

On Tubbs Ln. to the northwest (the first leg of the scenic back-roads route to Santa Rosa and the Russian River) is California's **Old Faithful Geyser,** tel. (707) 942-6463, one of just three in the world that erupt on schedule. But lately Old Faithful has been acting up, erupting at the wrong times or erupting in brief "splits." The owners, and geologists throughout the state, believe that these irregularities predict seismic changes within the earth—like earthquakes. Small fee (children under 6 free) to see Old

Faithful blow for four minutes—a 60-foot blast of hot water, steam, even rainbows if the sun is right. Open daily 9 a.m.-dusk. About five miles farther west toward Santa Rosa is the **Petrified Forest,** 4100 Petrified Forest Rd., tel. 942-6667, a California historic landmark of volcano-flattened, fossilized remains of ancient redwoods along a quarter-mile, wheelchair-accessible trail, with fossils in the small museum. Picnicking. Open daily 10-6, winter 10-5, small fee.

Robert Louis Stevenson State Park

Twisting north up Mt. St. Helena like a corkscrew, Hwy. 29 out of Calistoga leads to an easy-to-miss sign at the pass marking essentially undeveloped 3,200-acre Robert Louis Stevenson State Park (about 10 miles out of Calistoga, with parking pullouts on both sides of the road). Particularly pleasant in spring and fall, the open mixed woodland offers good hiking and freestyle picnicking (no camping, no fires) and blissful quiet. Stevenson honeymooned on the cheap in the old bunkhouse here in 1880 with his American bride. There's a monument on the site of the old Silverado Mine, already abandoned when the couple spent two happy months here. Stevenson wrote parts of *Silverado Squatters* while here and generated notes for some of his later, greater works. He called Mt. St. Helena (the 4,500-foot peak named after a visiting Russian princess) "the Mont Blanc of the Coast Ranges," and, some say, modeled *Treasure Island* scenes from his impressions. Most of the trail to the summit follows an abandoned roadbed, but it's well worth the five-mile effort for panoramic views of Sonoma Valley, the Napa Valley, and San Francisco to the south, even (on rare, clear and cool smogless days) mighty Mt. Shasta far to the northeast.

Calistoga Area Accommodations

It's first-come, first-camped at the **Napa County Fairgrounds** here, 1435 Oak St., Calistoga 94515, tel. (707) 942-5111, fairly cool campsites with electricity and hot showers, $12. Otherwise, the cheapest lodging choices are out of town. A great deal is the **Triple S Ranch,** 4600 Mountain Home Ranch Rd., tel. 942-6730, tiny, rustic redwood cabins $35-45, $7 each additional person, children under age 5 free. Second night discount. Open April through December, registration 9 a.m.-6 p.m. The restaurant here is popular with locals, good food for a good price. (To get there from Calistoga, head west on Petrified Forest Rd. then north on Mountain Home Ranch.)

The **Mountain Home Ranch,** 3400 Mountain Home Ranch Rd., tel. (707) 942-6616, has a lake, creek, pools, cabins and rooms for rent. Reasonable. Another rarefied rustic possibility is the **Rainbow Ranch Group Retreat,** tel. 942-5127, atop the Mayacamas Mountains on 80 acres of foothill woodlands, with a huge redwood lodge, swimming pool, spring-fed lake, and hot tub. Guests can choose A-frame sleeping cabins, cottages, or high-beamed motel rooms. Group rates only.

In town is the friendly landmark **Calistoga Inn,** 1250 Lincoln Ave., tel. (707) 942-4101, a clean and cozy old hotel with genuine nicks in the down-home furniture, rooms $49.50 Sun.-Thurs., $60.50 Fri. and Sat., with all taxes, including continental breakfast (fresh flowers and wine or home brew in the room upon arrival); bathrooms down the hall. Good deal. Even if you're not doing the spa scene, rooms at **Nance's Hot Springs** at 1614 Lincoln, tel. 942-6211, are reasonable (some with kitchens), use of the hot mineral spa included.

Very special is a stay at the elegant art deco **Mount View Hotel,** now a beautifully restored 1917 bed and breakfast (with fine restaurant) at 1457 Lincoln Ave., Calistoga 94515, tel. (707) 942-6877. Rooms $90-165, with Jacuzzi and pool, fabulous full breakfast served in the dining room. Ask about special weekday and off-season weekend packages. In addition to its resorts and motel/hotels, including the fairly reasonable **Roman Spa** at 1300 Washington, tel. 942-4441 (rates $58-95) and the **Calistoga Village Inn & Spa,** 1800 Lincoln, tel. 942-0991 or toll-free (800) 543-1094 (rates $65-125, substantially less on weekdays), Calistoga boasts a dozen or more bed and breakfasts. Among the area's historic offerings, the restored Greek Revival **Brannan Cottage Inn** near downtown at 109 Wapoo Ave., tel. 942-4200, is one of the original Sam Brannan guesthouses, featuring two suites and six rooms, all with private entrances, private baths, and queen beds. Full breakfast. Rates: $95-140. Also included on the National Register of Historic Places is **The Elms,** 1300 Cedar St., tel. 942-9476, an 1871 home in the French Second Empire style, with five rooms

(carriage house available) and full breakfast. Rates: $95-180. Across the street is **La Chaumiere,** tel. 942-5139, a 1932 Cotswald cottage with just two guest rooms ($125), hot tub, full breakfast plus dessert and liqueurs. Also close to town: the **Pine Street Inn And Spa,** 1202 Pine St., tel. 942-6829, a 1930s-vintage Cape Cod ranch house and full-service spa with 15 rooms and one suite, buffet-style continental breakfast, pool and whirlpool. Rates: $65-95.

Many Calistoga-area bed and breakfast inns are clustered on Foothill Blvd. or tucked into more secluded rural settings. One welcoming possibility is the **Silver Rose Inn** at 351 Rosedale Rd., tel. (707) 942-9581, a contemporary and comfortable wine-country estate with individualized room decor, private baths, spectacular pool and setting. Complimentary bottle of house wine. Rates: $125-140 (two-night minimum stay on weekends), $110-125 weekdays, group rates available. Inquire at the local chamber of commerce for a more complete listing of accommodation options.

Calistoga Dining

Almost everything is on Lincoln Ave., Calistoga's main drag. **Fellion's Delicatessen,** 1359 Lincoln, tel. (707) 942-6144, is open daily 7 a.m.-5 p.m., a good inexpensive breakfast and basic sandwich stop as well as picnic headquarters. The **All Seasons Market and Cafe** down the street at 1400 Lincoln, tel. 942-9111, is another good bet for picnic fixings. For any meal, the uncutesy **Village Green** at 1413 Lincoln, tel. 942-0330, offers comfy booths and counter stools, good basic American food. The **Cafe Pacifico** at 1237 Lincoln, tel. 942-4400, has reasonable Mexican food. Another Mexican possibility is **Las Brazas** at 1350 Lincoln, tel. 942-4056. For Mandarin and Szechuan, **Soo Yuan** at 1354 Lincoln, tel. 942-9404, is open daily for lunch and dinner.

Edging into the moderate price range is casual **Bosko's Ristorante,** 1403 Lincoln, tel. (707) 942-9088, noted for its fresh pasta dishes and authentic Italian desserts. Open daily for lunch and dinner. Hipper by far than other local restaurants is the **Calistoga Inn** at 1250 Lincoln Ave., tel. 942-4101, a brewery/pub serving its own pale lager and a spicy contemporary menu—like grilled gulf prawns with red-curry Thai sauce, or a home-smoked turkey sandwich with double-cream jack cheese on rye. Meals are served outside (in season) on a relaxed backyard patio.

Better yet, though, is **Valeriano's** at the Mount View Hotel, 1457 Lincoln Ave., tel. (707) 942-0606, recently declared Calistoga's best restaurant by *San Francisco Focus* magazine. Open daily for lunch and dinner, Valeriano's serves "Italian peasant" cuisine, so expect hearty fare and plenty of it. Very popular, reservations are recommended (especially at dinner).

Information, Transport
Get oriented at the **Calistoga Chamber of Commerce** office in the back of the Depot building, 1458 Lincoln, Calistoga 94525, tel. (707) 942-6333. Calistoga is easy to see on foot, but you can rent bikes at **Jules Culver Bicycles**, 1227 Lincoln, tel. 942-0421. Get to Calistoga on **Greyhound,** 1408 Grant Ave., tel. 942-6021, from San Francisco via Santa Rosa, from points north, and also from Napa and other "down-valley" towns.

LAKE COUNTY

Suffocated by the sophisticated air of the wine country? Too mellowed by Mendocino? Lake County has the cure. The area supported various world-class health spas from the late 1800s through the early 1900s, but now it's a friendly, frumpy, working people's resort and retirement area, as familiar as an old sneaker. Things are inexpensive in the tiny towns around Clear Lake, there are no parking meters, and nobody seems to mind the noise that comes packaged as children. People have been coming here for a long, *long* time. The Clear Lake Basin is one of California's oldest known areas of human habitation: petroglyphs and artifacts found here in recent years date back 10,000 years or more.

Besides the area's hot springs and mineral springs, Lake County is famous for its Bartlett pears. The county's first pear tree was planted in 1854 near Upper Lake; today there are 1,350 pear orchards in Lake County, number two in the nation for total pear production.

History
Pomo peoples lived throughout the Clear Lake Basin, an area naturally rich with game, fish, nuts, and berries. The medicinal value of the hot springs and mineral baths along with abundant hunting spawned a Native American type of tourism: others paid with shells, woodpecker scalps, and fur pelts for the privilege of bathing at Clear Lake. Russian fur-trappers entered the region in 1811, but no real conflict occurred until Spanish-American rule. Salvador Vallejo's troops made "pacification raids" near Clear Lake in 1836, killing many Pomos. Children and young men and women were sold as slaves. Surviving

natives escaped smallpox, but many were felled by respiratory diseases. Vallejo cattle were driven into the valley to graze, but continuing Indian conflict provoked the land's sale to Americans. Small-scale war with natives came after still crueler treatment at the hands of the whites, that uprising crushed by U.S. troops from Benicia who slaughtered hundreds of Pomos in the Bloody Island Massacre. But the gold rush and the rapid arrival of settlers led to the final decimation of native peoples.

Today there are about 90 Elem people, part of the larger Pomo clan, living in Lake County near Clearlake Oaks on the Elem Reservation or Robinson Rancheria, most noted today for its 1,200-seat bingo emporium.

TO CLEAR LAKE

The trip from the Napa Valley to Clear Lake via narrow Hwy. 29 (the old Calistoga-Lakeport stage route) is slow but beautiful: thickly forested hillsides hug the old road, soft green in spring, hazy with blazing color in fall. The only settlement of any size in Loconomi Valley along the way to Clear Lake, Middletown isn't particularly exciting but *is* aptly named: it's exactly halfway between Calistoga and Lower Lake.

Harbin Hot Springs
Close to Middletown is historic Harbin Hot Springs New Age Center, P.O. Box 92, Middletown 95461, tel. (707) 987-2477 or toll-free (800) 622-2477. Clothing is optional at the springs, and most people exercise that option. Anyone

not drunk or "terribly psychotic" is welcome at the hot springs, a former place of worship for local Pomo people. Camp here and do the baths for a very reasonable fee plus yearly membership. Or stay in lodge or dormitory rooms, or try a tepee for two. To get there from Middletown, take Barnes St. to Big Canyon Rd. (turn right), then turn left outside town onto Harbin Springs Rd. and drive to the end.

Wineries

In the early 1900s there were almost 40 noted wineries in Lake County. Among the area's wine pioneers was Seranus C. Hastings, founder of the Hastings School of Law. More famous, though, was the notoriously beautiful and independent British actress Lillie Langtry, who left her husband and came here to raise thoroughbred horses and make Bordeaux wines on her 4,200-acre ranch. **Guenoc Winery and Vineyards** at 21000 Butts Canyon Rd. just east of town, P.O. Box 1146, Middletown 95461, tel. (707) 987-2385, was once owned by Langtry—friend of Oscar Wilde, mistress of the Prince of Wales (later King Edward VII), and the state's first celebrity winemaker. The winery, now back in business, welcomes visitors Thurs.-Sun. 11 a.m.-5 p.m. On special occasions, Langtry's house is open to the public for group tours (call in advance to arrange a visit) but her likeness is included on every Guenoc wine label. Also in the area is the small **Channing Rudd** winery, 15919 Butts Canyon Rd., tel. 987-2209, open for tasting and tours by appointment only.

Boggs Mountain State Forest

Northwest on Hwy. 175 from Middletown proper, Boggs Mountain is an experimental forest once logged, since regenerated. Most hiking is on secondary roads, but there's plenty of privacy, primitive camping (bring water: none available except at Houghton Spring and Big Springs). The park entrance is a mile north of Cobb. Spring hiking is better than fall, since the area's popular for deer hunting. Visitors need a map, and even then the poorly marked roads can get confusing. For more information and a map, contact: California Dept. of Forestry/Boggs Mountain, 135 Ridgeway Ave., P.O. Box 670, Santa Rosa 95402, tel. (707) 542-1331. A camp-fire permit (free) is required for camping. Pick one up in Santa Rosa or at the state forest heliport/office on Hwy. 175.

Boggs Lake Preserve

A 100-acre Nature Conservancy preserve at the base of Mt. Hannah, the "lake," home for frogs, newts, and migratory birds, is fed by annual snow melt and runoff and fringed by very rare plants and abundant wildflowers. (Best flowers in late spring and early summer, especially the stunning blue *Downingia.*) Boggs Lake was deeded to the Conservancy in 1956 by Fibreboard Products, Inc. The usual firm Nature Conservancy restrictions apply to visitors: no camping, no motorized vehicles, no pets, no radios, no collecting. Get permission and directions on how to get there from John Walters, 1630 E. Lake Dr., Kelseyville 95451, tel. (707) 279-1537.

AT CLEAR LAKE

Clear Lake

The volcanic lake itself is spring-fed and natural, one of the state's largest. (It takes about three hours to drive around its 70-mile shoreline.) Every so often huge dead carp line the lakeshore—not a pretty sight, and a powerful stench—but, Fish and Game folks say, this is a natural phenomenon attributed to "pre-spawning stress syndrome" and unseasonable heat. "Clear" Lake sometimes turns pea-soup green and smelly in late summer and fall, due to algae bloom. But the county has an "algae buster" squad that rounds up the errant floating plant colonies in bad years, using an algae skimmer designed by Ed Headrick (Frisbee inventor and local resident). Not so natural, though, are high levels of mercury in the lake's fish.

Mt. Konocti
And Soda Springs

The guardian of Clear Lake, Mt. Konocti is a prominent volcanic peak (technically "active") connected to the lake via an underground passage. The lake's giant Soda Springs bubble up from the reefs below. The waters of Clear Lake once flowed west to the Pacific, but the earth's upheavals redirected the outflow east from the

Cache Creek gap into the Sacramento River. Near Kelseyville, on a rock outcrop jutting from the water, is the **Devil's Gasometer,** where sulphurous hydrogen escapes from fissures and burns with a bluish flame. Only accessible by boat or by swimming.

Anderson Marsh State Historic Park

Lower Lake is little more than a seedy stretch of commercial zoning—unless you stop here for a better look. Just north of the Hwy. 29/Hwy. 53 junction is Anderson Marsh State Historic Park, an at-first nondescript 900 acres of tules, rare birds, and the rich remains of ancient villages. The area was inhabited at least 10,000 years ago by gatherers and hunters, then by various Pomo peoples and their descendants during the past 5,000 years. The marsh areas here and at nearby Borax Lake (considered one of the most important archaeological sites on the Pacific coast) suggest a very different ancient California near the end of the Ice Age: cooler, wetter, a land of endless lakes inhabited by fierce predators—the agile short-faced bear, saber-toothed cats, the dire wolf—and their prey. Abundant obsidian from Mt. Konocti's occasional eruptions made toolmaking (and hunting) here easy.

The historic and restored **John Still Anderson Ranch House** on the highway serves as a small discovery museum, the world's smallest jail, and headquarters for the park (and for archaeology field schools at work here on projects). Beyond the house are the marshes, in summer more like a prairie—dried mud, dry grasses, willows, and rattlesnakes, all overshadowed in places by gnarled but graceful valley oaks—and the 35-acre dig site known as Lake-589. At the other end of the ridge is a reconstructed model Pomo village, including a ceremonial roundhouse where the Elem people celebrate the Big Head Dance. Hiking trails follow Cache Creek and thread elsewhere throughout the area. For more information, contact: Anderson Marsh State Historic Park, 8825 Hwy. 53, Lower Lake 95457, tel. (707) 279-4293. Call ahead to make sure they're open.

Clear Lake State Park

Clear Lake State Park lies at the foot of Mt. Konocti, 500 acres of oaks, cottonwoods, and lakeshore. Primarily a camping park, hiking, picnicking, swimming, sunbathing, and boating are popular here. The **Indian Nature Trail** is an easy walk starting near the park's entrance, offering a brief appreciation of the medicinal plants central to Pomo and Lile'ek cultures. (To learn more, visit the museum in Lakeport.) The longer **Dorn Nature Trail** near the lake climbs up through chaparral and oak scrub for a lake view. Rent a boat and putt out to the **Soda Baths** from Soda Bay—no facilities, no restrictions, no fees, no address, no phone, just private, natural mineral baths on the island beyond the soda springs themselves. The park's year-round campsites (four campgrounds) include hot showers; camping is $14, with a 15-day summer limit, reservations necessary April through October. To reserve campsites, contact Mistix, tel. (800) 444-7275. For more information, contact: Clear Lake State Park, 5300 Soda Bay Rd., Kelseyville 95451, tel. (707) 279-4293. A park brochure is available. To get here, follow convoluted Soda Bay Rd. east four miles from Kelseyville.

The Museum, Local Wineries

The 1871 **County Courthouse** in Lakeport (on Main St. between 2nd and 3rd) is a state historic landmark, museum, *and* superior court. The surprisingly fine but small **Lake County Museum** includes a display of Pomo basketry, elegant ceremonial clothing, fish and bird traps, grinding stones, and more. Call (707) 263-4555 for hours.

Kendall-Jackson Winery, 700 Matthews Rd. south of Lakeport, tel. (707) 263-5299, is open Tues.-Sun. 11-5. Lake County's largest winery, known for its white wines, Kendall-Jackson has a rustic winetasting room, deck, and picnicking in the walnut orchard. To get there, take Highway Springs Rd. west from Hwy. 29 then turn right onto Matthews. **Konocti Winery,** halfway between Lakeport and Kelseyville (Hwy. 29 at Thomas Dr.), tel. 279-8861, offers good Cabernet Sauvignon, picnic sites, Sunday afternoon bluegrass in summer, and a fall harvest festival (second weekend in October). Konocti is open daily 11 a.m.-5 p.m. South of Lower Lake and acclaimed for its Fumé Blanc table wines and premium Cabernets is the family-run **Stuemer Winery,** tel. 994-4069, open Thurs.-Sun. 10-5 p.m.

City Life (detail) c. 1934 by Victor Arnautoff, from his fresco at Coit Tower, San Francisco. (Collection City and County San Francisco Courtesy San Francisco Art Commission)

(top, left) the Kelp Forest exhibit at Monterey Bay Aquarium (Monterey Bay Aquarium); (top, right) San Francisco: Chinatown lantern and the Transamerica Pyramid (Kerrick James, San Francisco Convention and Visitors Bureau); (above) the Oakland Museum (Oakland Convention and Visitors Bureau)

Practicalities

The **Lake County Visitor Information Center** is in Lakeport (875 Lakeport Blvd., Lakeport 95453), tel. (707) 263-9544 or toll-free (800) 525-3743, or contact the **Lakeport Chamber of Commerce,** tel. 263-5092, or the **Clearlake Chamber of Commerce,** tel. 994-3600. For local art events and exhibits, contact the **Lake County Arts Council,** tel. 263-6659. Camp at **Clear Lake State Park** on the lake near Kelseyville (bring mosquito repellent), at various public campgrounds in Mendocino National Forest, or—if heading westward—at pretty **Lake Mendocino** near Redwood Valley on Hwy. 20. The Best Western **El Grande Inn** at 15135 Lakeshore Dr. in Clearlake, tel. 994-2000 or toll-free (800) 528-1234, features 48 luxury rooms plus 24 suites overlooking its four-story atrium, with indoor heated pool and hot tub, $67-73.

Roadside cafes and fast-food eateries abound. Popular for steak-and-potato fare is **The Grotto** restaurant in Clearlake, 14732 Lakeshore Dr., tel. (707) 995-9800. **Anthony's** in Lakeport at 1509 Lakeshore Blvd., tel. 263-4905, is noted for its Italian and American specialties, good early-bird specials. Open for lunch and dinner weekdays (closed Wed.), for dinner only Sat. and Sun. nights. Reservations suggested. Very good, too, for dinner is the **Loon's Nest Restaurant** at 5685 Main St. in Kelseyville, tel. 279-1812—daily changing menu, mostly seafood and steak selections, plus interesting chicken choices, excellent desserts. Lake County wines served.

Events

There's a **Pear Blossom Square Dance Festival** in April at the county fairgrounds in Lakeport, and a **Spring Wine Adventure** open house at area wineries. Lucerne has a **Diamond and Mineral Show** in June. In August, there's a **Blackberry Festival** at Lower Lake's Anderson Marsh State Park plus the **U.S. Bass Fishing Tournament** and **National Boat and Ski Races** at Lakeport.

EAST AND NORTH OF CLEAR LAKE

Indian Valley Reservoir

Twenty-two miles east of Clearlake Oaks on Hwy. 20 is the Walker Ridge Rd. turnoff to Indian Valley Reservoir, a quiet place for fishing, warm-water swimming, camping in the foothills. Bush monkeyflowers, western wallflowers, and hound's tongue bloom along the road in spring. (You can also reach the reservoir via northward-winding Bartlett Springs Rd. between Lucerne and Nice.) For information, contact Yolo County Flood Control, P.O. Box 1940, Woodland 95695, tel. (916) 662-0265.

Lake Pillsbury, Snow Mountain Wilderness

Good for camping and recreation is the Lake Pillsbury reservoir in the Mendocino National Forest, with plenty of room for boating, fishing, swimming; 115 campsites. Head up Elk Mountain Rd. from Upper Lake, or Potter Valley Rd. if you're coming from the west. Pitch your tent at **Oak Flat, Pogie Point,** or **Sunset campgrounds,** or picnic at **Squaw Creek.** The **Mendocino National Forest** includes almost 900,000 acres of forest land, extending north of Clear Lake to boundaries with the Six Rivers and Trinity national forests. You'll need a forest map to get around ($3), and second sight to anticipate logging trucks and such on narrow, unpaved, sometimes dusty and steep roads (many closed by mud or snow in winter: check with rangers on road conditions).

The 37,000-acre Snow Mountain Wilderness is just east of Lake Pillsbury (wilderness permit required). Twin-peaked Snow Mountain itself is the southernmost peak in the northern Coast Ranges, the last outpost for a wide variety of mountainous plants—but far from the last time you'll see poison oak. Great backpacking, 52 miles of ridge trails. Best time: late spring, early summer. For current info, maps, and conditions, contact: U.S. Forest Service, P.O. Box 96, Upper Lake 95485, tel. (707) 275-2361, or drop by headquarters on Middle Creek Rd. in Lakeport.

THE VALLEY OF THE MOON: SONOMA VALLEY

Dubbed the "Valley of the Moon" by Jack London (a romantic but incorrect translation of the native name for the place), the narrow 17-mile-long Sonoma Valley is as rich in history as it is in natural beauty and agricultural wealth. Often called "the cradle of California history," surprisingly serene Sonoma County has been ruled by many flags—English, Russian, Spanish, Mexican, and of course, the U.S. Stars and Stripes—and much colonial fervor. But no other ruling power was quite as colorful as the Bear Flaggers, a seedy band of several dozen American freelance landgrabbers.

From modern-day Sonoma, fine varietal vineyards and wineries, fruit and nut orchards, and livestock and poultry farms radiate out in all directions.

SONOMA

Picturesque Sonoma, protected from progress today only by strict zoning laws, has survived the troops of tourists massing in the plaza for their wine country assault in spring, summer, and fall. A California-style Spanish town built around an eight-acre central plaza, Sonoma's center is surrounded by carefully preserved old adobes and historic buildings, friendly trees, rose gardens, and picnic tables. Many of the superb stone buildings here were crafted by Italian masons.

Sonoma State Historic Park

This spread-out collection of historic buildings includes the Sonoma Mission itself, the Sonoma Barracks, the remnants of Vallejo's La Casa Grande, the Blue Wing and Toscano hotels, and Lachryma Montis ("Mountain Tears"), Vallejo's adobe-insulated Gothic retirement home just outside town. Pick up basic information and a walking tour guide at park headquarters on the plaza, 20 Spain St. E., Sonoma 95476, tel. (707) 938-1578. A small fee covers admission to all historic attractions open to the public (10-5 daily, except major holidays but check before setting out due to the possibility of state budget cuts). The fee here also covers admittance to

uncrowded **Petaluma Adobe State Historic Park** west of town, where Vallejo's ranch headquarters still stands.

The Sonoma Mission, on the corner of Spain and 1st St. E., was an upstart enterprise founded in 1823 by Father Jose Altimira, who didn't bother to ask his superiors for permission. Now a museum with a restored chapel (Vallejo built the church for the pueblo in 1840) and adjacent padres' quarters (constructed in 1825, the oldest building in town), the mission also houses historic exhibits, displays on adobe-building techniques and restoration, and mission art. (The Russians at Fort Ross on the coast apparently weren't threatened by the mission's presence: they sent bells and other gifts in honor of its dedication.) The impressive and unrestored **Blue Wing Inn** across the street at 217 Spain

Sonoma Valley Vineyards

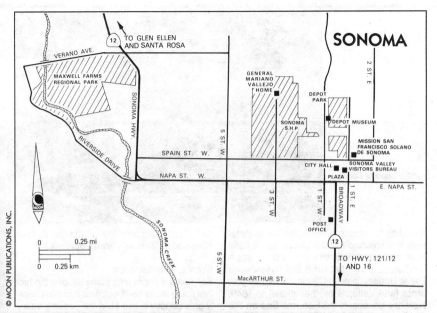

St. E., built in the 1840s, was the first hotel north of San Francisco.

The two-story adobe and redwood **Sonoma Barracks** building dates from the mid-1830s, when it provided troop housing and headquarters for Mexico's far northern frontier and later headquarters for the boisterous Bear Flaggers. In 1860, Vallejo started his winery here, next door to his home. Now a state-run history museum with exhibits on Sonoma-area Native Americans, Sonoma's rancho era, and the early U.S. years, the dusty courtyard and corral (complete with fowl underfoot) add even more historic authenticity. **La Casa Grande**, Mariano Vallejo's first home in Sonoma, stood near the barracks. The main house was destroyed by fire in 1867, but the servants' wing still stands in the dooryard of the **Toscano Hotel**, which offers free tours.

Just as California moved from a Mexican to an American national identity, Vallejo modified his house style in later years. Named "Mountain Tears" by Vallejo (after nearby natural hot and cold springs), this seemingly un-Spanish two-story New England mansion at the end of the tree-lined lane was built in 1851—the wooden walls wisely layered over adobe brick, tradi-

tionally appreciated for its insulating qualities. **Lachryma Montis** at Spain St. W. and 3rd St. W. is finely furnished with many of the general's family belongings, as if waiting for Vallejo himself to return. The grounds, too, are unusual, planted with prickly pear cacti, magnolia trees, even some of Vallejo's original grape vines. The white cast-iron fountains in front and back are part of the original garden decor of Vallejo's 17-acre homesite.

Other Sonoma Sights

Start at the plaza—the largest in California, intended as the center of community life—for a downtown walking tour. Shady green and inviting today, the plaza was a dusty, barren piece of ground in Sonoma's early years, trampled by Vallejo's marching troops and littered with animal skeletons left over from communal feasts. (The town still burns the bull here during the annual Ox Roast.) The small duck pond adds noise and feathers to the spacious gardens and picnic grounds, and the bronze **Bear Flag Republic sculpture** to the northeast is a reminder of the region's short-lived political independence. The impressive stone **Sonoma City Hall** and courthouse in the center of the plaza is post-Spanish,

the Sonoma Mission

SONOMA VALLEY VISITORS BUREAU

added by Americans in 1906. The **Swiss Hotel** near the Toscano Hotel was built by Mariano Vallejo's brother Salvador and now houses a restaurant. Down 1st St. is the 1846 **Jacob Leese House,** home of California's military governor (and Vallejo's brother-in-law) in 1849. New and unusual is the **Sonoma Spa on the Plaza,** 457 1st St. W., tel. (707) 939-8770, walk-in appointments okay, open daily 9-9. While wandering through downtown Sonoma, stop by the **Depot Park Historical Museum** for a look at annually changing local heritage exhibits. Operated by the local historical society in the small building between the free parking lots and the bike path at 285 1st St. W., tel. (707) 938-9765, open Wed.-Sun. 1-4:30 p.m.; donations are always appreciated. Ask here, or at the visitors bureau about historical walking tours.

A mile south of the plaza on Broadway, the miniature **Sonoma Gaslight and Western Railroad,** 20264 Broadway, tel. (707) 938-3912, is a quarter-scale model of the 1875 diamond-stack locomotive—the same size as everything else here. You can take the 15-minute ride through the Lilliputian landscape every day from mid-June through Labor Day, 10:30 a.m.-5:50 p.m., otherwise just Fri.-Sun. and holidays; small fee, babes-in-arms free.

A great spot for a picnic, **Agua Caliente Mineral Springs** is a summertime family spa just outside Sonoma at 17350 Vailetti Dr., tel. (707) 996-6822. Hot mineral pools and a cold pool, open April 15-Sept. 30, weekends and holidays 10 a.m.-7 p.m., Mon., Thurs., and Fri. 10:30

a.m.-6 p.m. Admission fee. (Farther north, near Kenwood, is **Morton's Warm Springs**.)

Events, Entertainment

Sonoma's a happening place despite the fact that some locals don't welcome tourists. Usually on a Sunday in mid-May, the Sonoma Valley Vintners sponsor an afternoon **Picnic in the Park** at Jack London State Historic Park in Glen Ellen, a food and entertainment fest featuring local foods and award-winning regional wines. (No parking available, but shuttle buses leave continuously from Glen Ellen proper down the hill.) This popular new event, which benefits restoration projects at the park, is often sold out, so advance tickets (pricey) are recommended. For more information and tickets contact: **Sonoma Valley Vintners Association,** 453 1st St. E., Sonoma 95476, tel. (707) 935-0803.

Also in May is the free **Sonoma Jazz Concert** at the Plaza Amphitheatre, and Sonoma's **Valley of the Moon Chili Cook-off** in the Sonoma Plaza. At **Sonoma Mission State Park** and nearby **Petaluma Adobe State Historic Park,** there are two "living history" weekends each year (in May and October), when park employees (practically the whole town) dress in period costumes to re-create the 1840s spirit of Spanish ranchos.

In June, Sonoma hosts its annual **Bear Flag Day** celebration and the **Annual Ox Roast** old-fashioned picnic and barbecue. At the late June **Red & White Ball** dinner and dance on the Plaza, people dress up in the colors of the wine

THE GROWLING OF THE BEAR FLAG REPUBLIC

Mexican fears of Russian territorial incursions weren't put to rest by the 1823 establishment of California's last missionary outpost, Mission San Francisco Solano de Sonoma, in what was then Mexico's far northern territory. So General Mariano Vallejo was sent to Sonoma to found a frontier pueblo for Alta California. Due to hostilities with Native American populations, Vallejo failed to establish colonies at both Santa Rosa and Petaluma. His third try, the town of Sonoma, was laid out near the mission in 1835. Troops rode out to subdue northern natives on many occasions, but General Vallejo further secured the town through his alliance and friendship with the chief of the Suisun, baptized "Solano."

Peace reigned until June 14, 1846, when a scruffy band of armed gringos rode into town and took over. Taking orders from Captain (later General) John C. Frémont, these Yankee trappers had camped out near Marysville on a "scientific expedition" while awaiting the opportunity to conquer California (or at least acquire some large tracts of land). Fearing expulsion by Mexican authorities, the ragtag revolutionaries decided to launch their own war for acquisition and independence, unaware that the U.S. had already declared war against Mexico in May.

There was no battle. Frémont and his freedom fighters met with Vallejo, who peacefully surrendered after offering the Americans some wine. The whole town surrendered, seemingly amused. To justify their theft of the township with a greater purpose, the Americans declared California a new republic, and quickly fashioned an appropriate banner and ran it up the flagpole in the plaza. (Almost no one saluted.) The banner of the Bear Flag Republic flew over Sonoma for just a few weeks, though, before U.S. Navy Commodore John Sloat sailed into Monterey Bay and on July 9 raised the American flag over the Alta California capital, ending Frémont's dream of an independent western republic.

As for Vallejo, after two months' imprisonment at Sutter's Fort he went on to become the district's first state senator, and later Sonoma's mayor. Though Vallejo owned over 175,000 acres of California lands at one time, his holdings shrank to a mere five acres by the time he died in 1890. But he wasn't bitter, despite the wild swings in his fate and fortune. "I had my day," he said, "and it was a proud one."

---

and party hearty. The annual **Sonoma Salute to the Arts,** sponsored by the Sonoma Valley Arts Alliance, is a multi-weekend art celebration—recognizing everything from the vintners' and culinary arts to visual and performing arts—held in the plaza and other locales. The **Sonoma Valley Shakespeare Festival** is held outdoors at the Gundlach-Bundschu Winery, weekends from mid-July through September, quite wonderful. For info and tickets, contact: Odyssey Theatre, P.O. Box 727, Sonoma 95476, tel. (707) 996-2145. Throughout the summer, various local wineries sponsor special events, including the **Catalan Food and Cultural Festival** at Gloria Ferrer in mid-July and the annual **Shakespeare at Buena Vista** theater festival (with the Sonoma Vintage Theatre troupe) on weekends from mid-August through mid-September. Buena Vista also sponsors classical and popular music events, including free **Jazz in June** on Sunday afternoons, noon-3 p.m. The **Annual Hooker Party** at Valley of the Moon Winery on Madrone Rd. actually honors General Hooker, the winery's founder. In September, Sonoma's **Valley of the Moon Vintage Festival,** the oldest winefest in the state, celebrates the harvest. (For more information on these and other area events, contact the local visitors bureau.)

But the *big* event, the **Sonoma County Wine Showcase and Auction,** comes in August, held at the Sonoma Mission Inn and Spa in Boyes Hot Springs. The benefit auction (like Napa Valley's similar scene, which attracts primarily trade people and also costs a fortune for a bidder's paddle) offers players an entrée into the best parties and an informal industry hotline into the hot local wine gossip. But other events (barbecue and dance, dinner gala, and seminars) are more accessible to the pedestrian public. For more information: Sonoma County Wine Showcase and Auction, tel. (707) 586-3795.

Sonoma Thunder, tel. (707) 996-3665, launches wine country balloon flights from El Verano. (Ask about other companies at the visitor bureau.) And if that doesn't do it, the **Sears Point International Raceway** at the junction of Highways 37 and 121 south of

Sonoma definitely offers life in the fast lane: Ford's California Grand Prix, Trans-Am, and professional stock car, drag, and motorcycle racing take place spring through fall.

Accommodations

Forget about camping in Sonoma, but **Sugarloaf Ridge State Park** isn't far north (for RVs and tent camping, also good hiking). If headed toward the Napa Valley, consider camping at **Lake Berryessa** and **Bothe-Napa Valley State Park.** Otherwise, budget accommodations are hard to find. **El Pueblo** motel, 896 W. Napa St., tel. (707) 996-3651, runs $55 and up. There's a **Motel 6** in Petaluma to the west and two more near Santa Rosa to the north.

The contemporary **Best Western Sonoma Valley Inn**, 550 2nd St. W., tel. (707) 938-9200 or toll-free (800) 334-KRUG, has all the amenities—from pool and whirlpool to fireplaces and complimentary continental breakfast—for high-season weekend rates in the $120-135 range, with substantial savings weekdays and in the off-season.

Bed And Breakfasts

The restored 1872 **Sonoma Hotel** on the main plaza, 110 Spain St. W., Sonoma 95476, tel. (707) 996-2996, isn't too steep as wine-country bed and breakfasts go ($62-115), with the third-floor rooms—very nice shared bathrooms down the hall—the cheapest. (Maya Angelou wrote *Gather Together In My Name* while staying in room 21.) The **El Dorado Hotel**, recently restored, is another gem, located at 405 1st St. W., tel. 996-3030, with 27 rooms (private baths) $80-140. Also convenient and reasonable is the turn-of-the-century Victorian **Thistle Dew Inn,** 171 Spain St. W., tel. 938-2909, $80-105, cheaper rates off-season, full breakfast, complimentary hors d'oeuvres, spa, bicycles. The 1870 **Victorian Garden Inn** farmhouse near the plaza at 316 E. Napa St., tel. 996-5339, has just four rooms, most with private entrances, and offers continental breakfast, swimming pool, even massage (extra). Rates: $79-135. The **Chalet** at 18935 5th St. W., tel. 938-3129, features four rooms in its chalet-style farmhouse (two shared baths), hot tub, expanded continental breakfast. Rates: $75-125. **The Hidden Oak** at 214 Napa St. E., tel. 996-9863, is a 1913 Craftsman with three rooms, private baths, full

---

CALIFORNIA'S FIRST AND FINAL FLAG

William Todd, a nephew of Mary Todd Lincoln, designed the flag that flew over Sonoma for less than a month in 1846. The grizzly bear became the primary symbol—reverse psychological warfare, since the rowdy Americans were nicknamed *osos* (bears) by the Mexicans. Like the republic's one star, the grizzly was drawn with blackberry juice; so clumsy was the original artwork that the Sonorans called the flat-faced bear a pig. A strip of red flannel was stiched along the bottom, below the words "California Republic." The same basic (but artistically improved) design, with a red star in the upper corner, was officially adopted as the state's flag in 1911. Charred fragments of the original flag (destroyed by fire in San Francisco's 1906 earthquake) are still on display in the Sonoma Mission museum.

---

breakfast. Rates: $95-130. The California Mission-style **Vineyard Inn** at 2300 Arnold Dr., tel. 938-2350 or toll-free (800) 359-INNS, has 12 rooms with private baths and entrances, expanded continental breakfast and English tea. Rates: $55-135.

There are at least two dozen bed and breakfast inns scattered throughout the Sonoma Valley, some in Kenwood, Glen Ellen, and Santa Rosa. Contact the visitor bureau for a current listing.

The Sonoma Mission Inn and Spa

The hot springs are long gone at **Boyes Hot Springs,** but the old hotel still stands. The peachy-pink **Sonoma Mission Inn and Spa,** 18140 Sonoma Hwy., P.O. Box 1447, Sonoma 95476, tel. (707) 938-9000, toll-free (800) 862-4945 in California, (800) 358-9022 outside the state, is elegant and old-fashioned. The facilities on these "eight acres of pure indulgence" include a Mobil four-star-rated hotel, restaurants, and an incredible health spa offering everything from aromatherapy and shiatsu massage to seaweed or herbal body wraps, from hydrating manicures to exercise classes and tennis. Rooms in the inn itself run $165-295 from late March through Oct. (sometimes good deals in the off-season), higher rates for the new "Wine Country" rooms.

the Sonoma Mission Inn

Picnic Supplies

The best food is the simplest. With a current "Sonoma County Farm Trails" brochure and map in hand (available here at local shops and at the visitors bureau), hunting down local produce in season is easy as pie. In Sonoma proper, combine a walking tour with the pleasure of putting together a homegrown picnic. An excellent cheese stop on the way up the hill and off the usual tourist track is the **Vella Cheese Company** at 315 2nd St. E., tel. (707) 938-3232. Vella has been in the cheese business since 1931, much of that time in this same sturdy stone building. Famous for its sweet, nutty-tasting "dry" Monterey cheeses, Vella also makes garlic, onion, and jalapeño jack varieties, tasty raw milk cheddar, and an Oregon bleu cheese.

The **Sonoma Cheese Factory,** 2 Spain St., Sonoma 95476, tel. (707) 996-1931, is known for its famous Sonoma Jack cheeses. Take a peek at the cheese makers, try some homemade salads or good basic sandwiches, and browse through the awesome array of deli and gourmet items while you wait.

Next stop: the **Sonoma French Bakery,** 468 1st St. E., tel. (707) 996-2691, for good Basque yeastless sourdough bread. (People line up for it.) The **Home Grown Baking Co.,** 122 W. Napa St., tel. 996-0166, has fresh bagels, salads, soups. The **Cherry Tree** at 150 Kentucky Rd., tel. 762-9096, is a combination fruit stand/deli with wonderful black cherry cider. Other delis abound.

Inexpensive Restaurants

Ma Stokeld's British Meat Pie Shop at 464 1st St. E., in Suite F of Place de Pyrenees Alley, tel. (707) 935-0660, has homemade bangers and pasties. For inexpensive and very good Mexican (Yucatecan) food, try the **Ranch House Cafe,** 20872 Hwy. 12, tel. 938-0454. Open Tues.-Sun. 11 a.m.-10 p.m. The long-running La Casa restaurant and bar is right across from the mission, 121 Spain St. E., tel. 996-3406, a good mid-priced choice for dinners, specializing in traditional Mexican food (very good enchiladas suizas). Sonoma also has a **Chevy's Fresh Mex,** at 136 W. Napa. Also interesting in the neighborhood: **Peterberry's Espresso Cafe** at 140 W. Napa. New on the Plaza: **Blum's Java Cafe** and a very good oyster bar, **Bonito's.** Different is the wild and wacky **Little Switzerland** family-style cabaret (once a house of ill repute) just west of town in El Verano at the corner of Grove St. and Riverside Dr., tel. 938-9990, which offers ballroom dancing (usually backed by accordion, tenor sax, and drums, but country and western on Friday nights) and goulash and sauerbraten dinners, also full bar. Friday, dinner starts at 5 p.m., with dancing at 8:30 p.m.; Saturday, dancing starts at 7:30 p.m.; and Sunday is like a matinee: dinner starts at 2 p.m., with dancing 3-10 p.m.

Fine Dining

Good for dinner is the small, locally popular **Sonoma Hotel** restaurant at 110 W. Spain St.; call (707) 996-2996 for reservations. The lunch menu is seasonal, the dinner menu changes twice each month, and the Sunday brunch is worth getting up for. Always featured: fresh local produce and fine local products, including area wines. **Ristorante Piatti** at the El Dorado Hotel, tel. 996-2351, is absolutely wonderful but far from stuffy, great for handmade pastas, pizzas, and calzones. **The Grille** at the Sonoma Mission Inn, 18140 Hwy. 12, tel. 938-9000, is renowned, a wine country institution, with exceptional (and expensive) cuisine and award-winning wine list. Fabulous Sunday brunch. Some say even better, though, is the Inn's **Big Three Cafe** next door, some unusual items (like apple oatcakes) for breakfast, also lunch and dinners in the Northern Italian regional cuisine tradition.

Information

The **Sonoma Valley Visitors Bureau** in the old library building on the plaza (public restrooms out back) at 453 1st St. E., Sonoma 95476, tel. (707) 996-1090, offers the free monthly *Valley of the Moon Visitor News* and the quarterly *Vintners Voice,* in addition to its official *Visitors Guide to Sonoma Valley* (a complete listing of sights, galleries, wineries, events, accommodations, and restaurants; available here and elsewhere) and abundant free brochures and fliers. Accommodations assistance also offered. Very helpful, worth a stop.

Bicycling

Though Napa Valley is touted as the area's bicycling mecca, Sonoma County is better in many respects—not nearly as trammeled with treacherous traffic and offering many more back-country routes. (Far better for cyclists than Hwy. 12, for example, is the parallel Arnold Dr.-Bennett Valley Rd. route through the Sonoma Valley toward Santa Rosa.) An excellent casual cyclist's guide to the region (including Sonoma and the Sonoma Valley) is *Sonoma County Bike Trails* by Phyllis L. Neumann, available in many local shops and bookstores. In Sonoma, rent bikes at **Sonoma Wheels,** 523 Broadway, tel. (707) 935-1366.

SONOMA AREA WINERIES

Near Sonoma

Sonoma is the birthplace of California's wine industry, the state's first vineyards planted at the local mission in 1824. Part of the Sonoma Mission's original vineyards are living history at **Sebastiani Vineyards,** headquartered at 389 4th St. E., P.O. Box AA, Sonoma 95476, tel. (707) 938-5532, or toll-free (800) 888-5532, and open daily 10-5 for tours, tasting, and sales. The winery was one of the few open during Prohibition, producing altar wine and a potent "wine tonic" patent medicine. In addition to the wines, there's an **Indian Artifacts Museum** established by August Sebastiani, and a large collection of oak barrel carvings.

Green Hungarian is bottled here (as elsewhere) in honor of "Count" Agoston Haraszthy, the aristocratic Austrian-Hungarian immigrant who convinced California's governor to send him to Europe in 1861 to collect vinifera vines. He returned with 100,000 or so, which he distributed throughout the area.

The striking stone **Buena Vista Winery,** a mile east of town at 18000 Old Winery Rd., tel. (707) 938-1266, or toll-free (800) 926-1266, open daily 10-5, is the Hungarian's original winery

Sonoma's historic Buena Vista Winery

and a state historic landmark. The stone cellars here (some tunnels collapsed during the 1906 earthquake) are the oldest in California, also headquarters for the only wine brotherhood in the U.S., the Knights of the Vine. Take the self-guided tour, which emphasizes the life and times of Haraszthy, then head to the original tile-floored press house for a taste. (Lift a glass of Green Hungarian in a toast to the count, then hike up to the art gallery on the second floor.) Buena Vista's picnic grounds are quite inviting.

Hacienda Wine Cellars, the former Sonoma Valley Hospital at 1000 Vineyard Ln., tel. (707) 938-3220, shares remnants of Haraszthy's old vineyards with Buena Vista, welcomes visitors for daily winetasting 10-5 (try the "Clair de Lune" Chardonnay), and is popular for picnicking. Tours by appointment only.

Noted for its Merlot is the prestigious but small **Gundlach-Bundschu Winery,** 2000 Denmark St., tel. (707) 938-5277, a family-run operation since the mid-1800s. Tasting daily 11 a.m.-4:30 p.m.; tours, picnicking outside.

The Spanish have returned to Sonoma County. The **Gloria Ferrer Champagne Caves,** about six miles north of Sears Point Raceway (in the valley's Carneros region) at 23555 Hwy. 121, tel. (707) 996-7256, is the American winemaking debut of Barcelona's 600-year-old Ferrer family enterprise, Freixnet S.A.—the world's largest producer of *methode champenoise* sparkling wines (called *cava* in Spain, after the aging caves). The "caves" here at Gloria Ferrer are not much to explore but the champagnery itself is as elegant in its understated way as the Napa Valley's Domaine Chandon is opulent—a Mediterranean-style villa with a terrace and "Hall of Tasters" for winetasting (fee for the wines, snacks provided free). Tours offered daily on the hour, from 11 a.m.-4 p.m., tasting room open 10:30 a.m.-5:30 p.m.

Carmenet Vineyard, 1700 Moon Mountain Dr., tel. (707) 996-5870, has better caves but no bubbly. The specialties here are Cabernet Sauvignon and Sauvignon Blanc, wines made using traditional French techniques, including barrel fermentation. The aging caves are large, with room for stacking wine barrels as well as daily hand-racking and washing. Tours by appointment only.

Also worth visiting in the Sonoma area are the **Schug Carneros Estate Winery** at 602 Bonneau Rd., tel. (707) 939-9363, to appreciate the German winemaking style transplanted to American soil, open daily 10-5, and rock-solid **Ravenswood,** 18701 Gehricke Rd., tel. (707) 938-1960, for award-winning wines, tasting, tours, and picnicking, open daily 10-4:30.

Glen Ellen Area Wineries

The popular **Glen Ellen Winery** at 1883 Jack London Ranch Rd., Glen Ellen 95442, tel. (707) 996-1066, produces good everyday Chardonnay and Cabernet Sauvignon marketed as its "proprietor's reserve" line for about $5 a bottle. Glen Ellen is on the way to Jack London State Park, and open daily 10 a.m.-4:30 p.m. for tasting (try the Sauvignon Blanc), tours, picnicking. Two miles north of Glen Ellen is **Grand Cru Vineyards,** 1 Vintage Ln., P.O. Box 789, tel. 996-8100, the winery itself built by a French winemaker in 1886. (Tasting room in Kenwood, see below.) Or try the White Zinfandel at the **Valley of the Moon Winery,** 777 Madrone Rd. (four miles west of Hwy. 12, near Arnold Dr.), tel. 996-6941. Founded by General "Fighting Joe" Hooker and including part of Senator George Hearst's 19th-century vineyards, Valley of the Moon is open 10-5 daily but tours are offered only during harvest season.

Kenwood Area Wineries

Taste buds still willing, visit the newly medieval **Chateau St. Jean,** 8555 Sonoma Hwy. (Hwy. 12), Kenwood 95452, tel. (707) 833-4134, tastings daily 10 a.m.-4:30 p.m. in the 1920s chateau (self-guided tours). The excellent **Kenwood Vineyards** nearby, 9592 Sonoma Hwy., tel. 833-5891, has exclusive rights to Jack London's vineyards and bottles a special wine in his honor each year. (According to *The Wine Journal,* Kenwood consistently produces one of California's best Sauvignon Blancs.) Open daily 10-4:30. In the celebrity winemaking category is the **Smothers Brothers Wine Store** tasting room at the intersection of Hwy. 12 and Warm Springs Rd. in Kenwood, tel. 833-1010, open (for tasting and sales only) 10 a.m.-4:30 p.m. daily. Stop, too, at **Grand Cru Vineyards Tasting Room** at 8860 Sonoma Hwy., tel. (707) 996-8100, open daily 10-4:30 for tasting and sales. Well worth some time and in the neighborhood is **St. Francis Vineyards** at 8450 Sonoma Hwy., tel. 833-4666, open weekends only, 11-5, tours and tasting by appointment.

Technically in Santa Rosa but overlooking the Sonoma Valley from its perch in the Mayacamas Mountains is the excellent but very small **Adler Fels Winery,** 5325 Corrick Ln., tel. (707) 539-3123, known for its Chardonnay, Sauvignon Blanc, and Melange à Deux sparkling wine. Open for tours, tasting, and sales daily but only by appointment.

JACK LONDON STATE HISTORIC PARK

When Jack London first saw the soft primeval forests sprawling up the sides of Sonoma Mountain in 1905, he knew this was his new home. The canyons and grassy hills separated by streams and natural springs, the mixture of redwoods, firs, live oaks, and madrones all spoke to him. This was his escape from city life, which he called "the man-trap." So here, at his beloved Beauty Ranch, Jack London lived with his second wife Charmian for 11 years, "anchoring good and solid, and anchoring for keeps" (except for a two-year sail through the South Seas). The Londons' former ranch, now an 800-acre state historic park near Glen Ellen, is a must-do destination, a strangely silent monument to one person's grand spirit.

Once out of the city, London became a hardworking, forward-looking farmer—eventually expanding his holdings from 130 to 1,400 acres, raising horses, cattle, and pigs, and growing innovative and unusual crops, a passion shared by his Santa Rosa contemporary and friend, "Mr. Arbor Day," horticulturist Luther Burbank. London also wrote here, voluminously—he sometimes scrawled away for 19 hours straight.

To get to the park, take London Ranch Rd. (up the hill from Arnold Dr. at the curve in "downtown" Glen Ellen) then follow the signs. The park is open from 8 a.m. until sundown (precise closing time posted at the entrance), no camping, day-use fee $5 per car. For more information, contact: Jack London State Historic Park, 2400 London Ranch Rd., Glen Ellen 95442, tel. (707) 938-5216. Fortunately for future visitors, restoration of Beauty Ranch is still underway. Contributions can be sent to Jack London Restoration Committee, California State Parks Foundation, 1212 Broadway, Rm. 436, Oakland 94216.

The House Of Happy Walls

The park's once-overflowing museum collection has been slimmed down substantially. At home in the two-story stone House of Happy Walls, which Charmian London built from 1919-22, the museum is still well worth the short hike uphill from the main parking lot. The impressive collection of rejection slips should comfort any writer (as will the meticulously worked page proofs), and much of London's correspondence is hilarious. In addition to the Londons' array of South Pacific paraphernalia, Jack London's study—too neat for a working writer—is quite evocative. A well-done display on his social life and socialist political adventures and polemics (London ran twice, on the Socialist ticket, for mayor of Oakland) is upstairs.

Wolf House

It's an easy half-mile downhill walk to the still-standing rock ruins of the Londons' dream home, Wolf House, a magnificent 15,000-square-foot mansion of carefully carved maroon lava and natural unpeeled redwood logs on an earthquake-proof concrete slab. Built with double-thick concrete walls to make it fireproof, Wolf House was nonetheless burned to the ground by unknown arsonists in 1913, just before the Londons planned to move in.

"Beauty Ranch" Trail

Take the Beauty Ranch Trail through the other side of the park to see what remains of London's experimental farm, which specialized in Shire draft horses (also friend Luther Burbank's spineless cacti, grown for feed). The circular, stone **Pig Palace** (still in need of restoration) is London's original design. Tucked among vineyards on the rolling gold and green hills, also begging for restoration, is the simple white woodframe **London Cottage** where Jack and Charmian lived and worked, and where Jack London died. Adjacent are the ruins of the old winery (severely damaged by the 1906 earthquake) where the Londons' many guests usually stayed.

London Ranch Horseback Rides

"I am a sailor on horseback!" Jack London once proclaimed. "Watch my dust!" Though elsewhere horseback rides seem like a mere tourist diversion, at Jack London State Park the trip is a real treat—and an opportunity to see parts of

JACK LONDON

A phenomenally successful and prolific author (the first writer ever to earn $1 million with his pen), Jack London (1876-1916) completed over 50 books and hundreds of short stories and articles between 1900 and 1916.

Colorful and controversial, Jack London was just as celebrated for his other activities: socialist lecturer, political activist, barroom orator, war correspondent, world traveler, sailor, and outdoorsman. Part of London's public appeal was the essential contradiction he represented: the rugged individualist in search of universal justice. The illegitimate Irish son of an astrologer, primarily self educated through public libraries (his formal schooling ended at age 14 when he went to work in the factories of West Oakland), Jack London became one of the founding members of the original Bay Area Bohemian Club (then an artists' club, now an elite social clique).

CALIFORNIA DEPT. OF PARKS AND RECREATION

London's ranch just as he and Charmian did (though hikers can cover the same terrain for free, of course). The **Sonoma Cattle Company,** P.O. Box 877, Glen Ellen 95442, tel. (707) 996-8566, offers small group rides (for either novice or experienced riders) through the park's hinterlands, past vineyards and London's one-time irrigation lake and bathhouse, abandoned ranch buildings, disappointing experimental forest of eucalyptus, even up the steep slopes of Sonoma Mountain. One- to four-hour rides available, plus box lunch, moonlight, and other specialty trips. Reservations wise. (The same company also offers rides in nearby Sugarloaf Ridge State Park.)

NEAR JACK LONDON PARK

Glen Ellen
The **Jack London Bookstore** on Arnold Dr. (toward Sonoma) has new and used copies of his works, including first editions. **The World of Jack London Museum** nearby features posters, paintings, and an eclectic mix of memorabilia. But not everything in and around tiny Glen Ellen revolves around memories of Jack London. The equally adventurous octogenarian,

globetrotting gourmet, and prolific prose writer M.F.K. Fisher, considered by most to be the ultimate food writer in the English language, lived (and wrote) just outside town. The author of *Serve It Forth* and *How to Cook a Wolf,* among many other books, Fisher believed that writers are born, not created. Once, when asked by a young girl why "so-and-so's" books were bestsellers but she was barely known, Fisher reportedly replied: "Because he is an author, and I am a writer." A cultural celebration of another sort is the annual **Art Farm Festival** of classical music held in late summer, tel. (707) 935-1563 for information and reservations.

Area Practicalities
Though Jack London's spread can't be beat for picnics, the large oak-forested **Sonoma Valley Regional Park** off the highway next to the forestry station is pleasant too. Adjacent is the **Bouverie Audubon Preserve,** with the best wildflowers in April (guided hikes only, tel. 707-938-4554). Stop off at the **Glen Ellen Square Deli** in Glen Ellen for sandwiches and picnic supplies, or linger for a breakfast or lunch at the **Garden Court Cafe,** 13875 Sonoma Hwy. (Hwy. 12), tel. 935-1565, open 7 a.m.-3 p.m., closed Mondays and Tuesdays.

Jack London's redwood
and stone Wolf House,
which burned to the
ground before the
Londons could move in

A real treat is a stay at the **Stone Tree Ranch** near Jack London State Park, P.O. Box 173, Glen Ellen 95442, tel. (707) 996-8173—just one cabin with sleeping loft (and sofabed in the living room), woodstove, fully stocked kitchen (including coffee beans and coffee grinder), even a hot tub (with valley view) available. Call for current rates. The **Beltane Ranch,** 11775 Sonoma Hwy., P.O. Box 395, tel. 996-6501, is a bed and breakfast once owned by Mammy Pleasant, a former slave who shook up some in San Francisco in the 1800s with her anti-racist voodoo. Four rooms with private baths, outside entrances, $95-120. The **Glenelly Inn** just outside town at 5131 Warm Springs Rd., tel. 996-6720, is peaceful, private, relaxed, with hearty country breakfasts, wine and cheese in the afternoon, $85-130.

Kenwood and Vicinity
The **World Championship Pillow Fights** take place here in July. **Morton's Warm Springs,** tel. (707) 833-5511, a family-style place, has two large pools and a wading pool for toddlers. Good for picnics. Closed in winter. Once a funky roadside diner, the **Kenwood Restaurant & Bar** at 9900 Hwy. 12, tel. 833-6326, is now a city-style surprise for lunch and dinner: good food (gazpacho and salads to roast duck and pork tenderloin), good country views. Also in the well-worth-the-drive category is **Oreste's Golden Bear** on the way to Sugarloaf State Park, 1717 Adobe Canyon Rd., tel. 833-2327. Serving authentic Northern Italian food, Oreste's is as warm as its surroundings are cool (a large shaded patio along Sonoma Creek under a

canopy of lush greenery). Call for current hours. **Caffe Citti** at 9049 Sonoma Hwy., tel. 833-2690, is an Italian-style trattoria (very popular) open Mon.-Sat. for breakfast, lunch, early dinner. Back down the road toward Santa Rosa, **The Melita Station Inn** bed and breakfast at 5850 Melita Rd., Santa Rosa 95404, tel. 538-7712, is comfortable and cozy, country-style lodgings in an old redwood barn once used as railroad depot, boardinghouse, feed and general store. Rooms $65-95.

The **Kenwood Inn,** 10400 Sonoma Hwy., tel. 833-1293, once a landmark antique store, is now a romantic Italian-style villa. Four elegant suites sporting tapestries and velvets, all with fireplaces and private baths, full breakast in dining room. Rates from $125.

Sugarloaf Ridge State Park
It's several steep and narrow miles via Adobe Canyon Rd. (mud or rockslides may close the road in winter) up to Sugarloaf Ridge State Park, a fine 2,700-acre wine-country park in the Mayacamas Mountains—hiking, horseback riding, fishing, rock climbing—with camping available. Summer days are hot, the vegetation is tinder dry, and Sonoma Creek dribbles into dust. But in spring the air is cool, the hillsides green and thick with wildflowers, and trout swim up Sonoma Creek's seasonal waterfall below the campground. On any clear day, the views from the park's ridgetops are worth the hike. (The **Sonoma Cattle Company,** tel. 707-996-8566, offers ridgetop rides for small groups.) There are 25 miles of trails throughout the park, which is connected to **Hood Mountain**

CALIFORNIA DEPT. OF PARKS AND RECREATION

Regional Park (tel. 527-2041, open for day use only on weekends and holidays, closed during the fire season) via the **Goodspeed Trail.** The **Creekside Nature Trail** introduces native vegetation and area landforms and starts from the campground on the meadow.

The turnoff to Sugarloaf Ridge is about seven miles east of Santa Rosa via Hwy. 12, or (winter or spring weekends and holidays only) hike in from Hood Mountain. The campground has flush toilets but no showers, reservations usually required from late March through Oct., $14, hiker and biker campsites also available. Day-use fee: $5 per car. Trail map available at the entrance or at the visitors' center near the campground. For more information, contact: Sugarloaf Ridge State Park, 2605 Adobe Canyon Rd., Kenwood 95452-9004, tel. (707) 833-5712. For Mistix camping reservations, up to eight weeks in advance, call (800) 444-7275.

PETALUMA

You can't always tell a town by its freeway. Petaluma, for example, is hometown America. Though inspired by the mores of Modesto, *American Graffiti* was filmed here, as were *Peggy Sue Got Married* and the forgettable *Howard the Duck.* Petaluma means "beautiful view" (or by some accounts "flat back," a reference to local Miwok people). Once promoted as the World's Egg Basket, the area still has plenty of chicken ranches and once even had a Chicken Pharmacy downtown, which dispensed poultry medicines. Dairy farming is another major area industry. So are antique shops, along with unusual stores like—for used items—Dead People's Things.

The **World Wristwrestling Championships** are held here in October, the **Butter and Egg Days Parade** (including "Cutest Chick In Town" contest) comes in late April or May followed in summer by the **Sonoma-Marin Fair** at the Petaluma Fairgrounds and its fun (especially for people who believe that pets resemble their people) **Ugly Dog Contest.** In August comes the **Petaluma River Festival,** and in September the **Petaluma Air Fair.** For mundane fun, two flea markets get hopping here every weekend.

Worth a quick stop in Petaluma is the free **Petaluma Historical Library and Museum,** 20 4th St., Petaluma 94952, tel. (707) 778-4398, open Thurs.-Mon. 1-4 p.m. Also downtown, along the Petaluma River, is a redeveloped historic district—shops, restaurants, yacht harbor—described by the good walking tour brochure available at the **Petaluma Chamber of Commerce,** 215 Howard St., Petaluma 94952, tel. 762-2785. (Free parking downtown in the city garage at Keller and Western.)

Head east via Hwy. 116 to Petaluma Adobe State Historic Park, or drive to the Sonoma coast via Petaluma-Valley Ford Rd. along eucalyptus-lined country lanes through coastal farmlands.

Petaluma Adobe State Historic Park
Due east of town on the way to Sonoma is Petaluma Adobe State Historic Park. The park's centerpiece is Vallejo's Casa Grande, a huge two-story adobe hacienda on a low hill, one-time headquarters for the old Rancho Petaluma.

The Cutest Chick in Town contest, part of Petaluma's spring Butter and Egg Days festivities

PETALUMA CHAMBER OF COMMERCE

the Old Adobe Fiesta at Petaluma Adobe State Historic Park

MERT DOSS

The area is almost as stark today as it was in its prime (intentionally barren, the better to spy potential interlopers). Vallejo's "big house" was originally a quadrangle, with a traditional interior courtyard and massive front gates. Only a U-shaped section remains, protected then as now by a wide redwood veranda and overhanging roof. The park's special events include weekend **Living History Days** in mid-May and October—with an 1840s atmosphere, authentic period costumes, and demonstrations of blacksmithing, breadbaking, and candlemaking—and the similar **Old Adobe Fiesta** in August, which includes adobe-brick making. Petaluma Adobe State Historic Park is at 3325 Adobe Rd. off Hwy. 116, tel. (707) 762-4871, and is open daily (except major holidays and barring state budget cuts) 10-5.

Petaluma Food And Accommodations

The Creamery Store, 711 Western Ave., tel. (707) 778-1234, sells local dairy cooperative products: "Petaluma Gold" butter, cheeses, ice creams, other goodies. Open daily 10:30-4. (Tour the art deco plant and historical display.) A fairly complete listing of area restaurants is included in the free tabloid *Petaluma Visitors Guide.* A great choice downtown is **Dempsey's Alehouse** in the Golden Eagle Center at 50 E. Washington, tel. 765-9694. This new microbrewery features both very good beer and food, everything homemade, down to bar snacks like spicy nuts and jerky. Grab a table outside, overlooking the Petaluma River. The **Washoe House** at the corner of Roblar and Stony Point Rd., tel. 795-4544, is California's oldest roadhouse and open for lunch and dinner daily, the place to pull over for steaks, prime rib, chicken in a basket, even buffalo burgers. For art deco atmosphere and Italian food, try **Fino Cucina Italiana** at 208 Petaluma Blvd. N. (at E. Washington), tel. 762-5966. A long-running local favorite for country French is bustling **De Schmire** at 304 Bodega Ave., tel. 762-1901, serving dinner nightly (no credit cards). If heading toward the Bay Area, stop at the **Marin French Cheese Co.** at 7500 Red Hill Rd., tel. 762-6001, for wonderful local Camembert. **Sonoma Joe's** just north of Petaluma at 5151 Montero Way (off Old Redwood Hwy.), tel. 795-5800, is popular for lunch and dinner (American fare).

There's a **Motel 6** nearby, 5135 Montero Way, tel. (707) 664-9090, $28 s, $34 d. The **Best Western Petaluma Inn,** 200 S. McDowell Blvd. (exit at Washington), tel. 763-0994, has rooms $49 and up. The **Cavanagh Inn,** a bed and breakfast at 10 Keller St., tel. 765-4657, offers rooms in both a 1912 Craftsman cottage and 1903 Neo-classic Georgian Revival, seven altogether (two rooms share a bath, one includes a private spa). Pool table, VCR and classic movies, full breakfast, cookies and lemonade. Rates are a real deal: $45-95. **The 7th Street Inn** at 525 7th St., tel. 769-0480, features two bed and breakfast suites and three rooms in an 1892 Victorian, full breakfast, tea, soft drinks, cookies, and fruit. Rates: $75-120.

SANTA ROSA AND VICINITY

A sprawling Bay Area bedroom community and one of the fastest-growing towns in Northern California, Santa Rosa with its suburban malls and housing developments is fast spreading into rich Sonoma County farmlands. The most prominent citizen historically was horticulturalist Luther Burbank (California celebrates Arbor Day on his birthday, March 7). But Robert "Believe It Or Not!" Ripley was a local boy who also made good, and *Peanuts'* cartoonist Charles Schulz (who owns the local ice-skating rink) is among the city's current leading citizens.

SIGHTS

Downtown

Santa Rosa looks so thoroughly modern—i.e., ordinary—to the casual observer that it's tempting to assume there's nothing much worth seeing. Not so. Though Santa Rosa lost most of its would-have-been historic heart to the 1906 earthquake, head downtown to experience Santa Rosa's true character—much disguised but definitely *there* (at least where the renovation wrecking balls were held back). **Railroad Square** west of Hwy. 101 along 3rd, 4th, and 5th streets downtown is now part of a restored 1920s shopping district with gift and antique shops, cafes, restaurants, and concentrated nightlife.

Santa Rosa's downtown oasis **Railroad Park**, with its trees planted by Luther Burbank, is bordered by the train tracks and 4th, 5th, and Wilson streets. The depot here, built of locally quarried stone, was among the few local buildings still standing in 1906 when aftershocks from the big quake subsided. (Alfred Hitchcock fans will recognize it as the train station in *Shadow of a Doubt.*) Other nearby quake survivors are the **Hotel La Rose**, the **Western Hotel** (Santa Rosa's first luxury hotel, now the visitors center, at 10 4th St., tel. 575-1191), and the **Railroad Express** building.

Luther Burbank Home And Memorial Gardens

Visit the Luther Burbank Home and Memorial Gardens on Santa Rosa Ave. at Sonoma Ave.,

tel. (707) 576-5115, where the gardens (free) are open year-round during daylight hours. Also take a trip through the Burbank Home adjacent (now a museum with original furnishings and Burbank memorabilia, open Wed.-Sun. 10 a.m.-3:30 p.m. from April through early Oct.), small fee. In his dining room, the 1946 edition of the Webster's dictionary is opened to the word burbank, a verb meaning: "to modify and improve plant life." Outside is Luther Burbank's greenhouse—his beloved tools still inside—where he burbanked his way to fame if not fortune. The "plant wizard" is buried just a few steps away beneath a large cedar of Lebanon. Guided tours include the house, carriage house, gardens, and greenhouse. In May, Santa Rosa hosts its **Rose Festival** here.

And for gardeners and plant lovers inspired by the fertility of Luther Burbank's life, another Santa Rosa stop might be the **Smith and Hawken** outlet at 360 Sutton Place, tel. 585-9481, for a wonderful array of top-of-the-line garden tools (overstocks and seconds—some great deals).

The Church Of One Tree And Ripley Museum

Originally built in downtown Santa Rosa and now at home in **Julliard Park** on Sonoma Ave. across from the Burbank Gardens is **The Church of One Tree**, an unusual Gothic church (70-foot spire and all) built entirely from 78,000 board feet of lumber from a single coast redwood felled near Guerneville in 1875. Robert L. Ripley made the one-time First Baptist Church famous in his syndicated "Believe It Or Not!" cartoon strip.

Now a state historic landmark, the Church of One Tree is also the city-run **Ripley Memorial Museum** at 492 Sonoma Ave., tel. (707) 528-5233. Included among the tremendous collection of Ripley's international memorabilia is a life-size wax facsimile of Ripley himself, in his Chinese robe and slippers, holding a battered suitcase held together by travel stickers. The museum is closed in winter, open March through late Oct., Wed.-Sun. 11 a.m.-4 p.m. Small fee. After seeing the world with Robert Ripley, Julliard Park is a good spot for a picnic.

LUTHER BURBANK

An astoundingly successful, self-taught horticulturalist, Luther Burbank (1849-1926) was also quite pragmatic. His primary aim in 50 years of work here was producing improved varieties of cultivated plants. Joaquin Miller wrote that Burbank was "the man who helped God make the earth more beautiful." And he did, with the help of Santa Rosa Valley's rich soils and mild climate. More modest, Burbank himself said: "I firmly believe, from what I have seen, that this is the chosen place of the earth, as far as nature is concerned."

Have you ever admired a showy bank of Shasta daisies or giant calla lillies? Ever bitten into a Santa Rosa plum, tried plumcots, or been grateful for stoneless prunes? These are just a few of the 800 or so "new creations" spawned at the Burbank Experimental Gardens here and in Sebastopol, whose alumni also include the Burbank cherry, gold plums, Burbank potatoes, asparagus, edible and thornless cacti, paradox walnuts, and countless other fruits, nuts, vegetables, trees, flowers, and grasses.

A calm and colorful but controversial figure and a student of Charles Darwin, Burbank openly advocated eugenics and outraged the general population with his heterodox religious views. Luther Burbank's long work days were often interrupted by visitors: his good friend Jack London, William Jennings Bryan, Thomas Edison, Henry Ford, Helen Keller, John Muir, and King Albert and Queen Elizabeth of Belgium. Others (via some 10,000 personal visits per year plus 2,000 letters each week) sought his advice on everthing from marigolds and mulch to mysticism.

Other Museums

The building that houses the **Sonoma County Museum,** 425 7th St., tel. (707) 579-1500, was once Santa Rosa's post office. This 1,700-ton Renaissance Revival building was moved to its present site, from deeper downtown, in 1979 (a slow trip, just 25 feet per day on railroad ties and rollers). The museum features changing exhibits on local history, culture, and the arts. Open limited hours, small fee. The free **Codding Museum of Natural History,** 557 Summerfield Rd., tel. 539-0556, includes a fine exhibit of worldwide wildlife habitats plus natural history displays. **The Jesse Peter Memorial**

Museum at Santa Rosa Junior College, 1501 Mendocino Ave., tel. 527-4479, features rotating exhibits of local interest, particularly Native American art and artifacts.

Spring Lake, Lake Ralphine

Spring Lake is a 320-acre county park at 5585 Newanga Ave. just east of Santa Rosa proper, with picnic sites, a 75-acre swimming and sailing lagoon, fishing, walking trails, and bike paths. One of the best things about Spring Lake, though, is camping, practically right in town: 31 campsites plus group camp, hot showers, $11, seven-day summer limit. (Small fee for five walk-in sites.) No reservations. To get there from Santa Rosa, head east on Hwy. 12 to Hoen Ave., turn left on Summerfield Rd. then right onto Newanga. For more information, contact: Spring Lake, 5390 Montgomery Dr., Santa Rosa 94505, tel. (707) 539-8092. From Spring Lake, hike into adjacent Annadel State Park via the Spring Creek Trail, or trek still further up into Sugarloaf Ridge State Park and—in season—next-door Hood Mountain Regional Park. (For more information on Sugarloaf and Hood, see "The Valley of the Moon: Sonoma Valley.")

Lake Ralphine is a small sailing pond in **Howarth Park** on Montgomery Dr., an area connected by bike path to adjacent Spring Lake. You can stop here for a picnic and swim, or go rowing on the lake in summer (no camping). Diversions for the young and young-at-heart include a mini steam train, pony rides, animal farm, merry-go-round, roller coaster, even a frontier village. Rent paddleboats, rowboats, and sailboats. For info, call the Santa Rosa Parks and Recreation Department, tel. (707) 528-5115.

ACCOMMODATIONS

Fairly Inexpensive Lodging

Camp at **Spring Lake** (see above) or farther east at **Sugarloaf Ridge State Park.** On motel row along Hwy. 101 north of town is **Motel 6,** 2760 Cleveland Ave. (take the Steele Lane exit west from 101, then turn north), tel. (707) 546-1500, $29 s, $35 d, $6 per room for each additional adult. Pool, a/c, TV, and movies. Popular, so reserve on weekends and in summer. (There's another Motel 6 just south in Rohnert

Park, tel. 585-8888.) Reservations are also a good idea at the **Sandman Motel,** 3421 Cleveland, tel. 544-8570, $36 and up (rates slightly lower from mid-Sept. to mid-May). The **Super 8,** 3421 Cleveland, tel. 544-8570, is also reasonable. Look for other relatively inexpensive motels downtown along Santa Rosa Ave. or north along Mendocino Ave. (actually an extension of Santa Rosa Ave., north of Sonoma Avenue).

Pricier Places

Quite nice in the expensive motel department is the **Fountain Grove Inn,** two miles north of Santa Rosa at 101 Fountain Grove Parkway (take the Mendocino Ave./Old Redwood Hwy. exit from Hwy. 101), Santa Rosa 95403, tel. (707) 578-6101, rooms from $75 plus packages. Adjacent to Coddington Center, **Los Robles Lodge,** 925 Edwards Ave., tel. (707) 545-6330 or toll-free (800) 255-6330, was completely redecorated in 1991. Rooms feature refrigerators and balconies or patios, free HBO, complimentary coffee. Swimming and wading pools, Jacuzzi, outdoor fitness center. Rates from $65, with great bargains sometimes available. The **Flamingo Resort Hotel and Fitness Center** at 2777 4th St., tel. 545-8530 or (800) 848-8300, has a heated Olympic-size pool, whirlpool, tennis courts, a full-service health club, and rooms complete with the usual amenities plus hair driers and refrigerators, complimentary newspaper, and complimentary breakfast. Some suites with in-room spas. Rates run $65-100 (suites from $120), with good golf and wine country "escape" packages often available.

Historically classy, though, is **Hotel La Rose** on Railroad Square at 308 Wilson St., tel. (707) 579-3200, with English country-house atmosphere in a 1907 cobblestone hotel, decent restaurant too. Rates: $80-110.

Bed And Breakfasts

One of the area's first bed and breakfasts is **Pygmalion House** downtown at 331 Orange St. (near Railroad Square), Santa Rosa 94501, tel. (707) 526-3407, an 1880s Victorian with Queen Anne tower, full breakfast. Rates: $45-70. **The Gables** at 4257 Petaluma Hill Rd., tel. 585-7777, features six rooms in the main house, an 1877 Victorian country mansion filled with antiques, plus a charming two-story honeymoon

---

ANNADEL STATE PARK

A good cure for the Santa Rosa shopping mall syndrome is a day hike through Annadel State Park, 5,000 acres of steep canyons, rolling foothills, woodlands, grassland meadows, and marshland (also poison oak) on the city's eastern edge. No camping, but good hiking. Most of the trail ascents here (except **Steve's S Trail**) are gradual. To beat the heat, come in spring or fall. Small **Lake Ilsanjo,** less than a half mile from the parking lot, is popular with fisherpeople (black bass, bluegill). Over 130 bird species have been spotted, primarily near **Ledson Marsh** along Bennet Ridge. In spring, appreciate the wildflowers: wild iris, lupine, shooting stars, poppies, buttercups, goldfields. *Don't* pick the delicate white fritillaria—it's endangered.

Annadel State Park is open daily from an hour before sunrise to an hour after sunset. To get to Annadel from Santa Rosa or from the Sonoma Valley area, head south on Los Alamos Rd., turn right on Melita Rd., then take a quick left onto Montgomery Dr. and left again on Channel Dr., which leads to the park office and the parking lot beyond. From Spring Lake, take Montgomery Dr. east. For more information, contact: Annadel State Park c/o Sonoma District Parks, 20 Spain St. E., Sonoma 95476-5729, tel. (707) 938-1519. Trail map available.

---

cottage in a rural setting. Three rooms have fireplaces; the cottage features a woodstove and kitchenette. Full gourmet country breakfast, refreshments in the afternoon. Rates: $95-155. **Gee-Gee's** at 7810 Sonoma Hwy. (Hwy. 12 on the way to Sonoma amid area wineries), tel. 833-6667, is a turn-of-the-century farmhouse with four rooms, shared baths, full breakfast, pool, free bikes to borrow. French and German spoken. Rates: $70-95.

More rural, contemporary-style bed and breakfasts include the **Sunrise Bed and Breakfast Inn** on Olivet Rd., tel. 542-5781, and **Hilltop House** on St. Helena Rd., tel. 944-0880. Nearby (same freeway exit) is the quite luxurious **Doubletree Hotel—Santa Rosa,** on top of the hill at 3555 Round Barn Rd., tel. 523-7555, rooms from $70 but a bit cheaper in the off-season (roughly Nov. to mid-May). Facilities include jogging track, whirlpool, pool, also (for a fee) tennis courts, 18-

hole golf course. Also popular in the higher price range is the **Vintners Inn,** 4350 Barnes Rd., tel. 575-7350, country French antique-decorated rooms (most with fireplaces) $118-195.

GOOD FOOD

Eating Well But Cheaply

Best and cheapest is stocking up on the basics —locally baked bread, cheese from Sonoma, Santa Rosa Valley fruits and veggies—then picnicking around. To find fresh local produce, pick up a current copy of the "Sonoma County Farm Trails" map and brochure at the visitor center downtown or at chamber offices. (Most Farm Trails stops are near Sebastopol and Forestville.) Or send a legal-size SASE to: Sonoma County Farm Trails, P.O. Box 6674, Santa Rosa 95406.

Vegetarian purists can stock up at **Organic Groceries** on the way to Sebastopol at 2841 Guerneville Rd., tel. (707) 528-3663, one of the largest natural food stores in the northstate, offering organic *everything* in bulk. Otherwise, garden-variety grocery stores are everywhere.

Inexpensive Eateries

For very good natural food, head downtown to **The Good Earth Restaurant and Bakery,** 610 3rd St., tel. (707) 523-3060, especially reasonable if you stick to the salads and sandwiches. Find some burger love atop the pink formica at **The Santa Rosa Grill,** 450 Mendocino Ave., tel. 578-4024, an art deco hamburger joint locally famous for its fries.

Good for breakfast and lunch is the cozy brick **Omelette Express,** 112 4th St., tel. (707) 525-1690, where making omelettes has become an art. Choose from 30 or so fillings and either whole wheat or white sourdough bread or toast. Also sandwiches, salads. Another locally popular choice is **Arrigoni's Deli,** 701 4th St. at D St., tel. 545-1297, cheerful, clean, great sandwiches.

Fourth Street seems to be Santa Rosa's restaurant hotspot. The only drawback to this phenomenon is the simple fact that new haute spots come and go at the speed of light. At last report, **Prospect Park** at 515 4th St., tel. (707) 526-2662, was *the* dinner place, although **The Cantina** across the way, 500 4th St., tel. 523-3663, was acknowledged as the see-and-be-

seen restaurant scene. (After dinner, stop by the eclectic and outlandish **Sonoma Coffee Company** at 521 4th St., tel. 573-8022, where you'll find some of the best coffee in town along with the best coffeehouse atmosphere. One good blend: nose-pierced skateboarders and tweedy professorial types.)

Ting Hau at 717 4th St., tel. (707) 545-5204, has inexpensive and good Chinese food, excellent lunch specials. For Mexican, try **Fonseca's** at 117 4th St., tel. 576-0131, noted for its authentic regional foods: shredded beef and cabbage in taquitos, black beans, chiles rellenos, seafood dishes, even cactus salad. Very good, very reasonable.

Some Moderately Priced Selections

Near the **Marquee Theatre,** an active vaudeville house in a renovated warehouse, is **Chevy's,** tel. (707) 571-1082, for reliable Mexican fare. Another local favorite is **Mixx,** at 135 4th St., tel. 573-1344, serving dinner daily and lunch Mon.-Friday. Their inventive and constantly changing menu includes sandwiches, fresh seafood, venison, fresh pasta, and in-house desserts. Box lunches are also available.

Popular too is **Caffe Portofino Ristorante and Bar,** downtown at 535 4th St., tel. (707) 523-1171, with sidewalk cafe tables under all those red umbrellas, brick and beam interior. Very fresh food, very reasonable. Modern, authentic Italian selections, including rigatoni with artichoke sauce and an unforgettable calamari salad. Even most meat entrees are under $10. Open for lunch and dinner (call for hours). Full bar, also espresso bar.

Across the tracks just off 6th is a homey Italian restaurant that has been around since the early 1900s: **Lena's,** 509 Adams St., tel. (707) 542-5532, featuring authentic linguini and clam sauce. **Ristorante Siena** at Parkpoint, 1229 N. Dutton, tel. 578-4511, offers reasonably priced Sonoma County fare with an Italian accent. Pasta entrees under $10. Very good wine list, emphasizing local fruit of the vine. Excellent Sunday brunch.

Folks from far and near brave the miles from Santa Rosa on the narrow road to the **Mark West Lodge,** 2520 Mark West Springs Rd., tel. (707) 546-2592, partly for its special locale. The American fare here is good and the place is popular (reservations advised), as much for the setting as the food. The original lodge burned to the ground not many years ago, so the building nowadays is nouveau rustic. But at least the grapes were saved. The ancient gnarled vines (purported to be the state's oldest and largest) add leafy green color to the latticework arbor stretched across the road. To get there take the Russian River exit (about four miles north of Santa Rosa) from Hwy. 101 then head another six miles east on Mark West Springs Road. **The Highland House** at 600 Los Alamos Rd., tel. 538-7800, is popular for prime rib, steaks, seafood, and Sunday brunch.

More Expensive Fare
Excellent and not really *that* expensive is **Restaurant Matisse**, 620 5th St., Santa Rosa 95404, tel. (707) 527-9797, reservations recommended. Wonderfully creative food, French country fare with American touches, a warm, informal atmosphere in a tastefully decorated hole-in-the-wall. Changing daily menu. Good local wines, fantastic desserts.

The acclaimed **John Ash & Company,** now at home amid the vineyards near the Vintners Inn, 4330 Barnes Rd., tel. (707) 527-7687, was once a contemporary cog in the grand local wheel of shopping malls. The romantic new setting seems to stimulate the appetites appropriate to the very local California cuisine (seafood cake with sole, shrimp, and crab, or Sonoma chicken breasts with corn and chives) served with imaginative French flair, Oriental overtones. Reservations. **La Gare,** in Railroad Square, 208 Wilson St., tel. 528-4355, is a legend in Santa Rosa (and beyond), known for its French-Swiss cuisine, decadent desserts, elegant white-linen atmosphere.

ENTERTAINMENT

Santa Rosa has a diverse arts scene: drama groups, prose and poetry readings, galleries galore, ballet, symphony, rock 'n' roll, even a local folk music society. Many special events are held at the **Sonoma County Museum** downtown (see above), the newish **Luther Burbank Arts Center** north of town on Mark West Springs Rd., and various area wineries. There's usually some kind of drama onstage at the **Lincoln Arts Center,** 709 Davis St., tel. (707) 523-4185, and other venues. Pick up a free "Calendar of Cultural Arts Events" at the visitors' bureau, or request one directly from: **Cultural Arts Council of Sonoma County,** P.O. Box 7400, Santa Rosa 95407-0400, tel. 579-ARTS. Ask about arts, entertainment, and events at the visitors bureau, or peruse local newspapers.

If your footwork is pretty sharp, take a few spins on the ice at Charles Schulz's **Redwood Empire Ice Arena** on Steele Ln., tel. (707) 546-7147, an impressive local showplace with the **Snoopy Museum** adjacent, tel. 546-3385.

INFORMATION AND SERVICES

The **Sonoma County Convention and Visitors Bureau,** 5000 Roberts Lake Rd., Suite A, Rohnert Park 94928, now shares quarters with the winery association visitor center in Cotati, south of Santa Rosa; to get there, take the Country Club Drive exit from Hwy. 101. For more information, call (707) 996-1090 or toll-free (800) 326-7666. The visitors bureau is open 8-5 daily. In addition to a free Sonoma County map, arts calendar, Farm Trails information, local public transit schedules, and a current listing of Santa Rosa's 20-plus shopping centers, pick up a free tourist guide and ask about local wineries. Better yet, though, for vineyard vignettes is the **Sonoma County Wineries Association** and its new **Sonoma County Wine and Visitors Center,** tel. 586-3795 (see below). If you're planning to do Sonoma County bed-and-breakfast style, get a copy of the "Wine County Inns of Sonoma County" brochure, P.O. Box 51, Geyserville 95441, tel. 433-4231, $1. The main Santa Rosa **post office** is at 730 2nd St. between D and E. For emergency medical care contact **Memorial Hospital** on Montgomery Street.

Public Transit
Sonoma County Transit, headquartered in the administration building at 2555 Mendocino, tel. (707) 576-7433, or toll-free (800) 345-RIDE, goes just about everywhere—to Sebastopol, Guerneville and the lower Russian River, even Jenner and Gualala. Best for getting around this spread-out town, though, is **Santa Rosa Transit,** tel. 524-5306 or 524-5238. For other public transit options, call **Ridefinder** toll-free at (800) 528-3433.

SANTA ROSA EVENTS

Santa Rosa hosts the **Miss California Junior Miss** pageant every January at the Veterans Memorial Hall; call (707) 527-2088 for info. Both the **Luther Burbank Rose Festival and Parade** celebration and **Old Time Fiddlers' Contest** are held in May. Other major events arrive in late summer and autumn: the **Sonoma County Fair,** the **Sonoma County Wine Showcase and Auction** (a benefit at various vineyards for enology and viticulture scholarships, also to support the wine library), and the **Sonoma County Harvest Fair.** The **Scottish Gathering and Games** takes place over Labor Day weekend. Thousands of kilted New World highlanders arrive at the fairgrounds to strut their stuff. Events include putting and throwing the stone, caber-tossing, soccer matches, bagpipe bands, dancers, plus plenty of ale.

Conveniently straddling Hwy. 101, Santa Rosa is well served by buses. From the **Greyhound** depot at 503 5th St., tel. (707) 542-6400, daily buses run north and south to major urban destinations and also connect to Calistoga, Sonoma, and Sebastopol. Call **Golden Gate Transit,** tel. 544-1323, for current schedule and stops. This bus line runs to Sebastopol and also to Rohnert Park/Cotati, but its mainline local links are to and from Petaluma, to and from the Bay Area's Transbay Terminal, and a one-way connection to the Civic Center in San Francisco.

The **Santa Rosa Airport** is seven miles north of town, 2200 Airport Blvd., tel. (707) 542-3139, served primarily by commuter services and "hops" by United and American. The **Santa Rosa Airporter,** tel. 545-8015, and the **Airport Express,** tel. 584-4400, are the main shuttle services to SFO.

COTATI/ROHNERT PARK

Once part of Sheriff Thomas Page's 1847 Rancho Cotate land grant (named after local Miwok chief Kotate, whose clan greeted the area's first Spanish settlers), more recently a quiet town catering to poultry ranchers and farmers, casual Cotati now is a haven for university students and campus hangers-on. The town square, Cotati Plaza (a state historic landmark), and its outer hub are laid out hexagonally. The six streets on the outer hexagon were named for Page's six sons. Old Redwood Hwy. south of the hub has a good selection of inexpensive and ethnic restaurants. The **Cotati Chamber of Commerce** is at 8000 Old Redwood Hwy., tel. (707) 795-5008.

Rohnert Park is primarily a residential/industrial suburb of Santa Rosa. New here, though, and well worth a stop, is the **Sonoma County Wine and Visitors Center** just off Hwy. 101 (take the Country Club Drive exit); open 10-5 daily. Sponsored by the Sonoma County Wineries Association, tel. (707) 586-3795, the new center is designed to orient and inform visitors about the diverse and far-flung winery industry in Sonoma County, "the Provence of California." Inside, a floor-to-ceiling topographical map locates winery regions. The center also features a demonstration winery with an audiovisual education on the art of winemaking. Outside, local varietals grow in the demonstration vineyard. Also here: a winetasting room featuring some of Sonoma County's finest, gift shop, plus maps and other current information on area accommodations, restaurants, special events, wineries, and wine tours. The Sonoma County Wineries Association also sponsors the annual **Sonoma County Wine Showcase and Auction,** usually held in August at the Sonoma Mission Inn.

Even newer, at the same location, is the **Sonoma County Convention and Visitors Bureau,** 5000 Roberts Lake Rd., suite A, Rohnert Park 94928, tel. (707) 586-8100. Stop by for whatever other information you may need, after roaming the wine center.

Fairfield Osborn Reserve

Near Cotati is a unique Nature Conservancy preserve open to visitors only with advance permission and only on weekends. This isolated foothill area on volcanic Sonoma Mountain (the rocks 300 feet below the surface are still warm, they say) is a fascinating oak woodland ecological patchwork of vernal pools, ponds, streamside riparian habitat, mixed evergreens, chaparral, freshwater marshes and seeps. Incredible spring wildflowers; California fuchsias bloom here in autumn. To get there, take E. Cotati Ave. to Petaluma Hill Rd. and turn right, then left at Roberts Road. From Roberts, Lichau Rd. leads to the preserve. Get more specific instructions when you call or write for permission to visit: Fairfield Osborn Preserve, 6543 Lichau Rd., Penngrove 94951, tel. (707) 795-5069.

SEBASTOPOL

Perched on Sonoma County's "Gold Ridge" and famous for its early-ripening, reddish-yellow Gravensteins, Sebastopol was once part of the original Analy Township. An early Irish settler, inspired by the British and French siege of the Russian seaport of Sebastopol, named the California town when one of two feuding local residents barricaded himself inside a store.

Stop off at **Ives Memorial Park** (duck pond, playground, picnic areas, public swimming pool nearby) next to the Veterans' Memorial Building on High St., the center of Sebastopol's April **Apple Blossom Festival,** which includes the crowning of the Apple Blossom Queen, an Apple Juice Run, parade, apple-pie-baking contests, good homemade foods, country music, arts and crafts. Or head west to the Ragle Ranch Park, where the Sonoma County Farm Trails' **Gravenstein Apple Fair** is held every August at the beginning of harvest season.

Just south of town at 1200 Hwy. 116 is the **Enmanji Buddhist Temple,** originally brought over from Japan for the Chicago World's Fair in 1933. Show up in July for the Teriyaki Chicken Barbecue and Japanese Bon Dancing Festival. For current information about these and other events, contact the **Sebastopol Chamber of Commerce,** P.O. Box 178, Sebastopol 95472, tel. (707) 823-3032, or stop by the office at 265 S. Main on weekdays during business hours, also open on Saturdays in summer.

Traffic congestion is a growing problem for fast-growing Sebastopol. Highway 116 heads northwest from here through Forestville and Guerneville—a scenic drive, especially beyond Forestville—and also southeast to Cotati, a good route for avoiding Santa Rosa's own traffic problems. The Luther Burbank Memorial Hwy. (Hwy. 12) connects Sebastopol to Santa Rosa but becomes the Bodega Hwy. as you head west to

Freestone, Bodega, and Bodega Bay—more traffic trouble in both directions.

But if you head out that way, **Freestone** is a peach of a place. Unusual is a Japanese-style spa called **Osmosis,** 209 Bohemian Hwy., tel. (707) 823-8231, where you can relax in an enzyme bath.

Sebastopol Area Apple Farms
A rare treat is a trip to Sebastopol during apple harvest in early August. Gravensteins, the best all-purpose apples anywhere, don't keep, which explains all the apple-processing plants in the area. (In the U.S., you can't get these red or green beauties beyond the Bay Area.) **Twin Hill Ranch,** 1689 Pleasant Hill Rd., tel. (707) 823-2815, has a playground and some tolerant animals to amuse the children while adults load up on fresh apples (40 varieties are grown here, but the Gravensteins ripen first) and apple cider, apple pie, and homemade apple bread. **Stipinovich Ranch Apples,** 9950 O'Connell Rd., tel. 823-2442, has both the garden-variety green and rarer red Gravensteins in addition to other popular apples later in the season. Pick your own if you wish. Another place you can pick your own is **Hallberg's Apple Farm,** 2500 Gravenstein Hwy. N., tel. 829-0187, with 36 apple varieties. For a complete listing and map of the area's fruit, nut, and vegetable (even fresh goat cheese) vendors, pick up the current farm trails brochure at the chamber office.

Wineries Near Sebastopol
The grape-growing area in the Russian River Valley near Forestville and Sebastopol is noted for its fine Pinot Noir, especially rich and balanced because of the cool and steady climate. The **Dehlinger Winery** at 6300 Guerneville Rd., tel. (707) 823-2378, a small vineyard and winery specializing in dry wines like Cabernet Sauvignon and Pinot Noir, welcomes visitors daily 10-5. Another good stop is **Topolos Russian River Vineyards and Restaurant,** 5700 Gravenstein Hwy. N., tel. 887-1562, noted for its fine varietals and very good Greek continental restaurant.

If you can find it (try Speer's Market on Mirabel Rd. in Forestville), pick up a bottle of Gary Farrell's Pinot Noir. Farrell, who emigrated from Australia's Yarra Valley region, has been dubbed "the crown prince of Pinot Noir" by California wine critics.

Sebastopol Practicalities

If you'd like to stay put in Sebastopol, there are several nice bed and breakfasts in the area; ask at the chamber, 265 S. Main, tel. (707) 823-3032. For cheap lodgings, travel 10 miles farther to the lower Russian River or head toward the coast to camp.

For continental cuisine at lunch and dinner, from tasty pastas to seafood, chicken, and beef, try **Côte d'Azur** at 1015 Gravenstein Hwy. S., tel. (707) 823-2433, open Tues.-Fri. for lunch, Tues.-Sun. for dinner. **Truffles** at 234 S. Main, tel. 823-8448, is another good choice (also serving Cajun specialties). Cafes and coffee shops abound, though the only true coffeehouse

around is **Coffee Catz** two blocks east of downtown on Hwy. 12 in the Gravenstein Station building, 6761 Sebastopol Ave., tel. 829-6600. This is *the* hangout for artists, writers, and other creative types—so enjoy the poetry readings, live entertainment, and original art along with your java. Light meals served, too. Well worth a stop for sandwiches and salads is **The Garden Cafe** at 305 N. Main, tel. 823-4458. A big hit with the natural foods crowd is the vegetarian **East West Cafe** on Main St., tel. 829-2822. Wonderful pancakes at breakfast, excellent fresh salads, well-prepared dinners for under $10. **Chez Peyo** at 2295 Gravestein Hwy. S. (Hwy. 116), tel. 823-1223, has French country fare (crepes, quiches, seafood) at lunch and dinner, and a good champagne Sunday brunch.

THE RUSSIAN RIVER

Most people think of the Russian River as the cluster of rustic redwood-cloistered resort villages stretching from Guerneville west along Hwy. 116 to Jenner-by-the-Sea, about an hour-and-a-half drive north from San Francisco. Once a popular resort area for well-to-do City folk, the Russian River's recreational appeal dried up as faster transportation and better roads took people elsewhere.

Lured by low rents and the area's strange spiritual aura, back-to-the-landers started arriving in the late 1960s. Some long-time locals still sniff at the hippies. But the newest wave of Russian River immigrants are the relatively affluent, bringing more urbane ways and much-needed money to renovate and revitalize the area.

Today's colorful cultural mix, including loggers, gays, sheep ranchers, farmers, and retirees, is surprisingly simpatico despite occasional outbreaks of intolerance. For all their apparent differences, people who manage to survive here share some common traits: they're good-humored, self-sufficient, and stubborn. After devastating winter floods occasionally inundate the area, for example, locals accept the raging river's most recent rampage and set out, as a community, to make things right.

It's a mistake, though, to view the Russian River as strictly a Guerneville-to-Jenner phenomenon. The river's headwaters are far to the

north, just southeast of Willits, though it's not much of a river until it reaches Cloverdale. Roughly paralleling Hwy. 101 inland, this slow, sidewinding waterway—called Shabaikai or Misallaako ("Long Snake") by Native Americans, and Slavianka ("Charming One") by early Russian fur traders—slithered into San Francisco Bay long before there were people around to notice. The river changed to its modern course over the eons and now flows west to Jenner. The Russian uncoils slowly through Sonoma County's northern wine country, and more than 40 small wineries cluster like grapes along its northern stretch. To find them, pick up a free map and brochure at local chamber of commerce offices.

Strictly as a matter of survival, people here tolerate tourists and tourist-related traffic tedium. To get off the road for a while, very fun is a spring or early summer canoe trip down the river with **Burke's Canoe Trips,** 8600 River Rd. (at Mirabel Rd.), P.O. Box 602, Forestville 95436, tel. (707) 887-1222, advance reservations advised. One-day canoe trips, including courtesy shuttle service back to Burke's, are $25. Longer trips (up to five days) are also offered. But the Pacific Ocean is so close—and the rolling coastal hills both north and south of Jenner so wide open and wonderful—that once here in summer it's hard to resist heading west for a negative ion recharge. In winter, Guerneville

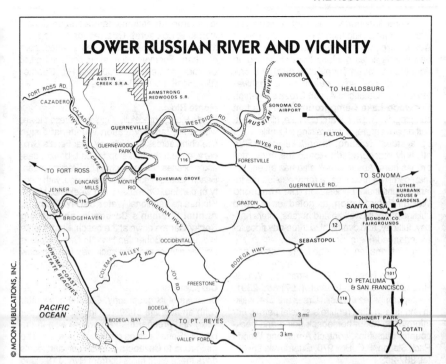

LOWER RUSSIAN RIVER AND VICINITY

© MOON PUBLICATIONS, INC.

and other lower river towns are often shrouded in ghostly white and bone-chilling fog for days, sometimes weeks at a time, and a special quiet—one transcending the mere absence of tourists—descends.

RUSSIAN RIVER RESORT AREA

Guerneville
Don't say "Gurneyville." The name's GURNville—and any other pronunciation pegs people straight away as tourists. George Guerne (his name's pronounced "gurney," so it's okay to be confused) founded the town after building the first sawmill here in 1865. Gregarious Guerneville is the big city in these parts, home to most of the area's resorts, restaurants, and bars, plus recreation central in summer for swimming, tubing, canoeing, river rafting. It's easy to walk the entire town.

Guerneville's annual **Slug Fest** the second week in March isn't an organized barroom brawl but a local celebration of "the noble banana slug," the slimy, six-inch native of redwood forests. (For the culinarily courageous, free recipes are available as part of the festivities. Bring your own toothpicks.) The **Russian River Rodeo** is held in June. The biggest deal of all, though, is the **Russian River Jazz Festival** in September—quite the event, featuring big-name talent from everywhere. For current information and advance tickets, contact the local chamber office.

Armstrong Redwoods
A small, 750-acre redwood reserve with first- and second-growth *Sequoia sempervirens*, Armstrong Redwoods State Reserve is a study of nature's moods in various shades of green, a peaceful place for picnics and hikes right outside Guerneville. (Day-use is free for those who walk or bike in, otherwise $5 per car.) The reserve itself includes a self-guided nature trail and the 2,000-seat outdoor Redwood Forest Theatre, site of various summer events.

Beyond Armstrong to the north, reaching up into the surrounding mountains, is the adjacent **Austin Creek State Recreation Area,** 4,200 backwoods acres of steep trails shinnying up ridgetops through sunny chaparral and oak woodlands, past small streams and freshwater springs. Getting to Austin Creek's sky-high **Redwood Lake Campground** (primitive tent camping, fishing in the artificial lake, hiking) is itself an adventure, a hair-raising 2½-mile climb up a steep, twisting, threadlike road (RVs strongly discouraged). Notice the huge madrones here. Austin Creek also has an equestrian camping area plus (a rarity outside the inland mountains) a pack station. The **Armstrong Woods Pack Station,** as noted for its camp cuisine as for its well-trained horses, offers half-day, full-day, and overnight to three-day rides for experienced riders.

For information about both the reserve and the recreation area, contact: Armstrong Redwoods State Reserve, 17000 Armstrong Woods Rd., Guerneville 95446, tel. (707) 865-2391. Family campsites at Austin Creek are $14; walk-in and hike-in sites require a special permit. For information about horseback riding and back-country pack trips, contact: Armstrong Woods Pack Station, P.O. Box 970, Guerneville 95446, tel. 887-2939.

Korbel Champagne Cellars

Dominating the big vineyard-hugging curve on River Rd. a few miles east of Rio Nido near Guerneville is the vine-covered red brick 1886 Korbel Champagne Cellars, well worth a stop for tastes of Korbel champagne and wines or a snifter of brandy—even for those not "doing" the wine country. Bohemian immigrants, the three brothers Korbel started out in the 1860s as loggers. Soon Anton and Joseph Korbel began planting vines between the massive redwood stumps on the rich bottomland along the river. And the rest, as the winery here still testifies, is history.

The Korbels sold the operation in 1954, but the old family estate still stands, as attractive as ever: the winery and tasting room, restored brandy tower, and hillside garden with 200 time-honored rose varieties, coral bells, and violets. Peaceful picnicking. Open 9-5 May through Sept. (shorter hours in the off-season). As America's largest premium champagne producer, Korbel is no secret. One reason to stop by, though, is to taste Korbel's table wines, sold only here. For more information, contact: Korbel Champagne Cellars, 13250 River Rd., Guerneville 95446, tel. (707) 887-2294.

Monte Rio

Monte Rio is a gracefully sagging old resort town, with a big faded Vacation Wonderland sign stretching across the highway near **Fern's Grocery,** almost the last stop for bait, booze, gas, and groceries before reaching the Pacific Ocean. Beach access is good near the bridge, with plenty of parking. On the July 4th weekend, Monte Rio has its traditional **Water Carnival Parade, Annual Fireman's Barbecue,** and the **Big Rocky Games** down at the beach. From Monte Rio, take the Bohemian Hwy. to Camp Meeker and vicinity, or take the back way (via Moscow Rd.) to Duncans Mills a few miles farther west.

Cazadero

Because of its geography, Cazadero is wetter (with an average of 80-100 inches of rain per year) and greener than anywhere else in the county. Banana slugs grow well here too. The main road to Cazadero is excellent, and locals drive these eight miles up from Hwy. 116 along Austin Creek *fast.* The town itself has a loud, real-life lumber mill, a general store, sometimes a cafe, even a post office. But the real fun starts outside town. Beyond Cazadero, the road becomes a twisting one-lane backcountry route (via Fort Ross Rd.) to historic Fort Ross farther north along the Sonoma County coast. Even more challenging is the backdoor trip from here through Kruse Rhododendron State Reserve. To get there, take King Ridge Rd., then the even more obscure (unmarked, dirt) Hauser Bridge Rd., then turn right at Seaview. (Talk to locals about road conditions before setting out, and gas up before going.)

Duncans Mills

Most of the redwood used to build San Francisco was shipped south from Duncans Mills and Duncan Landing. A lumber-loading depot during the region's redwood-harvesting heyday (the original mills were constructed in 1860), Duncans Mills is now a newly built old-looking collection of crafts and gift shops, deli, private campgrounds, a very good vegetarian restaurant, and a summer riding stable. The barn-red **DeCarly's General Store** has been in business forever and is one of this spot-in-the-road's only original buildings, though no longer the quirky *real* place it was. There's a small railroad museum at the reconstructed **Depot** south of the highway (open daily). This stretch of the Russian River is good for steelhead in winter. The bridge on Moscow Rd. marks the inland limits of tidewater flow. Definitely different for a thrill in late summer (and at other times by arrangement) are **Black Bart Stagecoach Tours** exploring some of Bart's favorite Sonoma County haunts, hold-up and bad poetry included, tel. (707) 887-7589.

PRACTICALITIES

Camping

For public camping, stay at **Austin Creek State Recreation Area** near Armstrong Redwoods, a few miles outside Guerneville, $14 per night, or either **Bodega Dunes** or **Wrights Beach campgrounds** south among the Sonoma Coast State Beaches (advance summer reservations through Mistix, tel. 800-444-7275) or **Fort Ross** or **Salt Point state parks** north along the coast. (For more information on nearby coastal camping, see "The Sonoma Coast.") The private **Ring Canyon Campgrounds**, tel. (707) 869-2746, are right outside the Armstrong Redwoods State Reserve. Open year-round. Also private, the

THE BOHEMIAN GROVE

Monte Rio's real claim to fame is the infamous Bohemian Grove on the south side of the river, the all-male elite enclave where the rich and powerful come to play. These 2,500 acres of virgin redwoods (the largest remaining stand in the Russian River region) are enjoyed exclusively by members and guests of San Francisco's Bohemian Club, founded (an irony only in retrospect) by anarchist-socialist types like Ambrose Bierce and Jack London.

Once each year, 1,500 or so Bohemians and guests—including U.S. presidents and cabinet members, members of Congress, captains of industry and finance, plus diplomats and foreign dignitaries—get together in this luxurious grown-up summer camp, according to local lore, to get drunk, urinate on trees, and put on silly skits and plays. And, according to the rules, they *never* discuss business or politics, and *never* make deals. It's difficult to verify these official facts, however. Double chain-link fences, guardposts, and highly sensitive security systems provide ample protection from riffraff. Unless invited, no one—and never a woman—gets inside the compound. But judging from the very visible, very professional imported prostitutes doing a brief, brisk local business during the week, each year at least some men manage to "jump the river" and get out.

At the right time in July, during the Bohemian Grove encampment, it's an astoundingly absurd sight: caravans of Rolls-Royces and black stretch limos jockeying for highway position among the ranks of one-eyed VWs and battered Ramblers. Most Bohos (a favorite local epithet) step down from their private Lear jets at the airport in Santa Rosa then travel to the Grove under the cover of darkness, to avoid unnecessary visibility. But the real bigwigs usually arrive by helicopter.

Among Russian River residents, there's at least begrudging acceptance of these ruling-class Bohemians, since locals do work at the Grove as waiters, carpenters, and repairmen. But there is also resentment, if rarely expressed openly. On the Russian River, for example, there are no hospitals or emergency health-care facilities, but the Bohemian Grove has a fully staffed emergency hospital and cardiac care unit—open year-round but rarely used—completely off-limits to the community. In the event of a heart attack or drowning accident, for residents it's a half-hour ambulance ride to Santa Rosa.

In the recent past, outside-the-gates "people's encampments" like the Bohemian Grove Action Network kept 24-hour vigils when the Bohos came to town, with banners ("See You In Hell!"), placards, and arrests for civil disobedience in protest of the incestuous relationship of business and government. But some years, it's all quiet on the Bohemian front. Except for the limos and the highly visible high-priced hookers, it's hard to know when the party's going on.

Schoolhouse Canyon Campground is four miles east of Guerneville at 12600 River Rd., Guerneville 95446, tel. 869-2311.

Farther west, **Rien's Sandy Beach,** just west of town at 22900 Sylvan Way, Monte Rio 95462, tel. (707) 865-2102, offers RV and tent camping, picnicking, swimming, and laundromat. Just east of Duncans Mills (turn south on Moscow Rd. then head east over the bridge) is the large **Casini Ranch Family Campground,** 22855 Moscow Rd., P.O. Box 22, Duncans Mills 95430, tel. 865-2255—a pasture-style camping area along the river with hookups and tent sites, plus a laundromat, general store, rec hall, private beach, and access to very good fishing.

Area Cabins And Inns
Some Guerneville lodgings are inexpensive. **Johnson's Resort** at 16241 1st St., P.O. Box 386, Guerneville 95446, tel. (707) 869-2022, has riverfront cabins for $22-25 per night (some with kitchens), $120-125 by the week, reservations only with weekly rates, closed Oct.-May. Well-equipped beach, waterslide, picnic tables, boat rentals. The **Fern Grove,** now a bed and breakfast close to downtown at 16650 River Rd. in Guerneville, tel. 869-9992, has newly remodeled cabins with kitchens, fireplaces, color TV, also swimming pool, $75-200.

The Village Inn (where *Holiday Inn* was filmed) at 20822 River Blvd., P.O. Box 850, Monte Rio 95462, tel. (707) 865-2304, has comfortably funky old hotel rooms (small, some with bathrooms down the hall) for $35 ($55-80 for small suites in the lodge next door). Rates drop $10 in winter. Unbeatably hip atmosphere. Pretty cool, too, is the **Highland Dell Inn** nearby at 21050 River Blvd., tel. 865-1759, rustic but renovated, whimsical style, rates $70-195. The **Cazanoma Lodge** at 1000 Kidd Creek Rd. (just off Cazadero Hwy.), P.O. Box 37, Cazadero 95421, tel. 632-5255, has five private housekeeping cabins, also rooms in the lodge, all including continental breakfast, open March-Nov. only.

Gay Resorts
The adults-only **Highlands Resort** at 14000 Woodland Dr. in Guerneville, P.O. Box 346, Guerneville 95446, tel. (707) 869-0333, caters primarily to gays and bisexuals, with cabins, pool, Jacuzzi, lounge, nude sunbathing. **Fife's Lodge** at 16467 River Rd. (also in Guerneville,

just west of Safeway), tel. 869-0659, is a large, completely private gay resort. Very nice in the cabin category is the recently remodeled **Camelot Resort** at 4th and Mill, P.O. Box 467, tel. 869-2538—well-insulated cabins with fireplaces and clean new kitchens, comfortable beds, also motel rooms, "solar-heated" pool, Ping-Pong, barbecues, and picnic area.

Bed And Breakfasts
A real bargain and pleasure is a stay at the **Creekside Inn Resort,** 16180 Neeley Rd., P.O. Box 2185, Guerneville 95446, tel. (707) 869-3623, which offers housekeeping cabins (and very nice rooms at the inn itself) for $30-60, including continental breakfast. Several redwoody acres, also pool, picnic area, RV sites. The 1906 redwood **Ridenhour Ranch House Inn** is down the road from Korbel at 12850 River Rd. in Guerneville, tel. 887-1033, antique furnishings, hot tub, croquet, gracious hosts, $65-115. Particularly nice, too, is **Santa Nella House** in Pocket Canyon (12130 Hwy. 116, between Guerneville and Forestville), tel. 869-9488, antique lodgings in the old Santa Nella Winery building, hot tub, champagne brunch, rooms $80-95. The quiet and secluded **House of a Thousand Flowers** between Duncans Mills and Monte Rio on Hwy. 116, P.O. Box 369, Monte Rio 95462, tel. 632-5571, has just two rooms, hot tub, full breakfast, $80.

Elegant in the country manor mode is **The Estate,** 13555 Hwy. 116 in Guerneville, tel. (707) 869-3313; 10 rooms (private baths, Jacuzzi, heated pool, TV, phones) for "the discerning few," fresh flowers and turn-down chocolates, wonderful breakfasts, wine and hors d'oeuvres in the afternoon, dinners available; $115-185. Top of the scale, though, is the very private ridgetop **Timberhill Ranch,** actually adjacent to Salt Point State Park at 35755 Hauser Bridge Rd., Cazadero 95421, tel. 847-3258—15 cottages with homemade quilts and fireplaces, also lodge and small conference center, $205-300 per night (meals included).

River Food
For groceries and the basics, there's a 24-hour **Safeway** on the south side of Hwy. 116 west of Guerneville. If coast-bound, stop for bait, groceries, and gas at tiny **Fern's Grocery** on the highway in Monte Rio; at the **deli** in Duncans

Mills for sandwiches and salads or cheeses, meats, wines, and picnic supplies; or for very basic basics at the **general store** in Jenner.

The simple **River Inn** right next to the theater in downtown Guerneville, tel. (707) 869-0481, is a lively homey-looking cafe with cheery yellow Formica tables and well-stuffed naugahyde seating in the booths, also a cafe counter with spin-around stools. Surprisingly good basic American food (an incredible number of choices on the menu). Down-home, too, is the **Breeze Inn Bar-B-Q** at 15640 River Rd., tel. 869-9208 or 869-9209, for take-out and delivery, too, picnic table out front. Just east of town in Rio Nido is the **Rio Nido Lodge,** 14580 River Rd., tel. 869-0821, serving healthier, heart-smart American fare. Pretty smart, too, back in Guerneville is tiny **Jerk's Pizza** next to the chamber office along the river at 16205 1st St., with homemade sauces made fresh daily and an outdoor deck. Another local favorite for casual outdoor dining is **Sweets Cafe** at 16251 Main, tel. 869-3383, a popular stop for cappuccino, vegetarian pizza, and other fairly sophisticated fare.

For California contemporary, **Burdon's** at 15405 River Rd., tel. (707) 869-2615, is always excellent. (People rave about the spinach salad.) A hotspot, too, for lighter fare, is **Friar Tuck's** at 14480 River Rd., tel. 869-1411, which serves a special fresh seafood entree every night. West of town in Monte Rio is the very popular 1908-vintage **Village Inn** hotel restaurant, tel. 865-2304, *the* breakfast spot. Pastas, steaks, chicken, fish at lunch and dinner. The excellent and relaxed **Blue Heron Inn** near the post office in Duncans Mills, tel. 865-2269, is noted for its innovative, very good vegetarian food, sometimes also chicken and seafood dishes. Serene Sunday brunch on the banks of the Russian River. Worth a stop just for a look at the striking rosewood bar in the tiny lounge, pleasant for a drink while waiting for a table.

Also popular, and "special" with Russian River residents, is the old **Cazanoma Lodge** at 1000 Kidd Creek Rd. off Cazadero Hwy. (a left turn on a curve, about halfway to Cazadero from Hwy. 116), tel. (707) 632-5255. Very good German and American food plus a working waterwheel, streams, waterfall, outdoor trout ponds. Open March through Nov. for dinner most nights, Sunday brunch, Sunday dinner. Full bar.

In the "close but worth the drive" category are various area restaurants, including the locally popular **River's End** in Jenner. Farther south at Valley Ford is **Dinucci's,** tel. (707) 876-3260, as famous for its cheery Italian atmosphere as for the historic memorabilia plastered on the walls and the abalone shells on the bar's ceiling. (For more on Dinucci's, see "The Sonoma Coast.") From Monte Rio, it's a 20-minute drive south via the Bohemian Hwy. to Occidental and its noted Italian restaurants: **Fiori's Pub and Cafe** and the **Union Hotel.** In Forestville, try the **Topolos Russian River Vineyards Restaurant** at the winery.

Information And Services

Contact the **Russian River Chamber of Commerce** at 16200 1st St., P.O. Box 331, Guerneville 95446, tel. (707) 869-9009, for a complete listing of river-area lodgings, restaurants, and upcoming events. The chamber has a complete business directory of gay-oriented establishments, available for reference. The area's main **post office** is in downtown Guerneville on Hwy. 116 (there are others in Monte Rio and Duncans Mills), tel. 869-2167. Stop off at **King's Tackle** on the highway downtown, tel. 869-2156, for current fishing info and supplies.

HEALDSBURG

Though most people head to Napa or Sonoma for wine-country tours, an increasingly popular destination in Sonoma County is Healdsburg, the urban convergence of three well-known wine regions: the Alexander, Dry Creek, and Russian River valleys. A one-time trading post founded by Harmon Heald, downtown Healdsburg is built around a Spanish-style plaza. Shaded by citrus trees, palms, and redwoods, **Healdsburg Plaza** is "community central," home to summer concerts and celebrations, pleasant for picnics, surrounded by shops and shoppers. The city-run **Healdsburg Veterans Memorial Beach** along the Russian River south of town (lifeguards in summer), offers a small solution to the persistent problem of public access along this stretch.

New in Healdsburg is the **Sonoma County Wine Library** in the new Healdsburg Regional Library at Center and Piper streets, tel. (707) 433-3772. This collection of wine and winery

The Hop Kiln Winery near Healdsburg is at home in stone hop-drying barns.

WES DEMPSEY

information includes the thousand-volume Vintner's Club Library of San Francisco. For information on the **Wine Country Film Festival,** an annual event usually centered in Healdsburg, call 935-FILM. Also here: **The Healdsburg Museum,** 221 Matheson, tel. 431-3325, with its north-county history displays. Also well worth a stop in Healdsburg is **Evans Ceramics, Inc.,** 55 W. Grant St., tel. 433-9392, the world's leading producer of raku pottery, with overruns, seconds, prototypes, and unique pieces for sale. (Time it right and watch the crew at work.) Stop by the **Sonoma Antique Apple Nursery** on Westside Rd., tel. 433-6420, for flavorful apples from yesteryear, even bareroot trees to grow your own.

The backroad routes connecting Healdsburg to the lower Russian River area are worthy detours. Both Eastside and Westside roads twist through rolling Russian River vineyard country (watch for slow tractors and trucks, especially during harvest season) then turn into River Rd., which leads west to Forestville then Guerneville. Even more thrilling is narrow Sweetwater Springs Rd., which shoots up over the ridge from Westside Rd. then drops down to Armstrong Woods Rd. just north of Guerneville near the park.

Wineries Near Healdsburg

Visiting the 50-plus wineries near Healdsburg is challenge enough for any wine lover. **Clos du Bois** downtown in its "utilitarian" building at 5 Fitch St., P.O. Box 339, Healdsburg 95448, tel. (707) 433-5576, has won so many awards since its inception in 1974 for its various fine varietal

and vineyard-designated wines that even most of the winery's fans have stopped counting. Open daily for tasting, tours by appointment only. Also downtown and within easy reach: the **William Wheeler Winery** just north of the plaza (130 Plaza St.), tel. 433-8786, open daily 11-5; **White Oak Vineyards** at 208 Haydon St., tel. 433-8429, open Fri.-Sun. 10-4; and **Windsor Vineyards,** 239-A Center St., tel. 433-2822, open weekdays 10-5, weekends 10-6. Just west of town at 2306 Magnolia Dr., tel. 433-9154, is **Alderbrook Winery,** open daily 10-5 for tasting and sales, for tours only by appointment. The **Hop Kiln Winery** at 6050 Westside Rd., tel. 433-6491, is an award-winning, well-respected winery. Hop Kiln's meticulously restored old stone hop-drying "barns" house the working winery, with winetasting (try the Zinfandel) in the more typical rustic barn adjacent. Nice views of the vineyards, pond, and picnic area. Open for tasting and sales 11-5 daily, tours by appointment only. The **Davis Bynum Winery** at 8075 Westside Rd., tel. 433-5852, produces small quantities of some winning wines, including Gewürztraminer. Open daily 10-5.

Also in the same general neighborhood and well worth a visit: **Rochioli Vineyards and Winery,** 6192 Westside Rd., tel. (707) 433-2305, open daily 10-5, and **Belvedere Winery,** 4035 Westside Rd., tel. 433-8237, open daily 10-4:30.

The 1896 **Foppiano Vineyards,** 12707 Old Redwood Hwy., tel. (707) 433-7272, is one of California's oldest family-owned wineries, open for tasting and picnicking daily 10 a.m.-4:30 p.m.

The 1876 handhewn stone and modernized **Simi Winery** just north of town at 16275 Healdsburg Ave., tel. 433-6981, is now owned by Moet-Hennessy/Louis Vuitton, of France. Simi once specialized in bulk wines, and now—like most Napa-Sonoma establishments—produces premium wines, available for sampling in the redwood-and-stone tasting room. Open daily 10 a.m.-4:30 p.m., with half-hour guided tours at 11 a.m., 1 p.m., and 3 p.m. Wonderful spot for picnics.

Wineries North Of Healdsburg

The small **Christopher Creek/Sotoyome Winery,** part of the original Rancho Sotoyome, is two miles south of Healdsburg just off Old Redwood Hwy. at 641 Limerick Ln., tel. (707) 433-2001, and produces only premium Chardonnay. Open daily 10-5 for tasting and tours. The ivy-covered stone winery at **Dry Creek Vineyards** four miles north of Healdsburg at 3770 Lambert Bridge Rd. (just off Dry Creek Rd.), tel. 433-1000, is known for its Cabernet Sauvignon, Sauvignon Blanc, Fumé Blanc, Dry Chenin Blanc, and other fine wines produced in very limited quantities. Pleasant picnic grounds. Open daily 10:30 a.m.-4:30 p.m. for tasting, tours. Wine critics can't stop raving about **Quivira Vineyards** at 4900 W. Dry Creek Rd., tel. 431-8333 or toll-free (800) 292-8339, noted in particular for its Cabernet Sauvignon, Sauvignon Blanc, and Zinfandel. Open daily 10-4:30 for tasting, tours only by appointment. The **Robert Stemmler Winery,** 3805 Lambert Bridge Rd., tel. 433-6334, specializes in gold-medal Pinot Noir. Open daily 10:30 a.m.-4:30 p.m., tours by advance arrangement.

The **Lambert Bridge** winery at 4085 W. Dry Creek Rd., tel. (707) 433-5855, resembles an old barn but is actually quite contemporary in all respects, including the view of the winemaking process from the tasting room. Open for tasting (Chardonnay, Merlot, Cabernet Sauvignon) daily 10-4. **Lytton Springs Winery,** 650 Lytton Springs Rd. (three miles north of Healdsburg off Hwy. 101), tel. 433-7721, produces a very traditional Zinfandel from the well-seasoned vines of the old Valley Vista Vineyards. Open 10 a.m.-4 p.m. daily.

Wineries East Of Healdsburg

Johnson's Alexander Valley Vineyards, a small premium winery at 8333 Hwy. 128 (seven miles southeast of Geyserville), tel. (707) 433-2319, hosts a Sunday open house once each month, inviting guests for picnicking and an afternoon theater pipe organ concert. (Write to receive the winery's regular newsletter.) Otherwise, open daily 11-5 for tasting and tours. In conjunction with **Five Oak Farm,** 15851 Chalk Hill Rd., tel. 433-2422, the Johnsons also offer horse-drawn surrey wine tours through the Alexander Valley, each excursion ending with lunch or dinner. The small **Alexander Valley Vineyards** at 8644 Hwy. 128, tel. 433-7209, the old Alexander homestead, is known for its estate-bottled varietal wines (including a very good Chardonnay, though "Sin Zin" is a popular choice). Open 10-5 daily, very complete guided tours by appointment only.

Sausal Winery at 7370 Hwy. 128 east of Healdsburg, tel. (707) 433-2285, produces Zinfandel, White Zinfandel, Chardonnay, and Cabernet Sauvignon. The small winery is owned and operated by Sonoma County's longest-running winemaking family. Open for tasting and picnicking daily 10 a.m.-4 p.m., tours by appointment only.

The earthy simplicity of the aptly named **Field Stone Winery** at 10075 Hwy. 128 (near the Chalk Hill Rd. intersection), tel. 433-7266, is striking yet deceptive. Literally a back-to-the-land bunker of concrete faced with fieldstone and sliced into this Anderson Valley hillside, Field Stone as a winery is actually quite contemporary. Noted for its Spring Cabernet, Petite Sirah, Rose of Petite Sirah, and other fine wines, Field Stone Winery also sponsors a 10-km run in the spring and a summer concert series. Winetasting daily 10-4:30, tours by appointment only. The **Chalk Hill Winery,** 10300 Chalk Hill Rd., tel. 838-4306, sponsors a summer music and wine festival and is noted for its Chardonnay. Open by appointment only. **Melim/Chalk Hill Vineyards** at 15001 Chalk Hill Rd., tel. 431-7479, is also quite highly regarded and open only by appointment.

Wineries South Toward Windsor

South of Healdsburg near Windsor (something of a poor relation to Healdsburg) is **Piper Sonoma Cellars,** 11447 Old Redwood Hwy., Healdsburg, tel. (707) 433-8843, a subsidiary of France's Piper-Heidsieck and a California-style champagnery. Open 10-5 daily for tastes of its Sonoma County sparkling wines; tours of the

vineyards in the
Alexander Valley
north of Santa Rosa

KIM WEIR

ultramodern facilities here offered hourly 10:30 a.m.-3:30 p.m. Also here is a cafe for lunch. Nearby is **Sonoma-Cutrer Vineyards,** toward Santa Rosa at 4401 Slusser Rd., tel. 528-1181, which produces only premium Chardonnay, open Tues.- Sat. by advance appointment only for tasting and tours.

Rodney Strong of **Rodney Strong Wines/ Windsor Vineyards,** 11455 Old Redwood Hwy., tel. (707) 433-6511, was recognized by the *L.A. Times* as Winemaker of the Year in 1983. Open for tasting, tours, and picnicking 10-5 daily.

Area Information

The **Healdsburg Chamber of Commerce,** 217 Healdsburg Ave., Healdsburg 95448, tel. (707) 433-6935, offers free winery and "Farm Trails" produce maps plus current information about accommodations and food.

For more information about the Windsor area, contact the **Windsor Chamber of Commerce,** P.O. Box 367, Windsor 95492, tel. (707) 838-7285.

Area Accommodations

To camp, head to **Lake Sonoma** (see below). Just a few blocks from the Russian River beach and quite reasonable is the **L & M Motel,** 70 Healdsburg Ave., Healdsburg 95448, tel. (707) 433-6528, with indoor pool, whirlpool, sauna, kitchens, cable TV, and phones. The **Fairview** next door at 74 Healdsburg Ave., tel. 433-5548, has jacuzzi, pool, color TV, phones, rates $38-

50. The Spanish-style **Dry Creek Inn** Best Western Motel, 198 Dry Creek Rd., tel. 433-0300, is $60-75, less on weekdays and in the off-season.

Downtown is the Victorian **Healdsburg Inn on the Plaza,** 116 Matheson St., P.O. Box 1196, Healdsburg 95448, tel. (707) 433-6991, a bed and breakfast with nine rooms (several with fireplace) furnished in antiques; $75-155 ($35 each additional person), cheaper on weekdays, full breakfast buffet served in the rooftop solarium. Champagne brunch on weekends. Other Healdsburg bed and breakfast choices include the French country-style cottages at **Belle,** 16276 Healdsburg Ave., tel. 433-7892, $115-185; and the **Camellia Inn,** an elegant 1869 Victorian with marble fireplaces at 211 North St., tel. 433-8182, $70-115; and the **Frampton House** at 489 Powell Ave., tel. 433-5084, $70-100. A good choice too is **The Raford House Bed and Breakfast Inn** at 10630 Wohler Rd., tel. 887-9573, with seven rooms in an 1889 Victorian farmhouse, surrounded by vineyards and orchards, $85-130.

At these and other bed and breakfast inns, midweek and off-season rates may be substantially lower.

The Madrona Manor
Hotel And Restaurant

A wine-country institution, this impressive country inn combines its venerable three-story 1881 Victorian mansion with renovated outbuildings to create the kind of place many people just can't stay away from. Nonetheless, some people come here just to eat. The restaurant at Madrona Manor has an international following.

Accommodations are luxurious in the European style, a total of 18 rooms and three suites, many with fireplaces, all with full private baths and every amenity. The newest addition is the French contemporary "Suite 400" in the Carriage House, with private deck, sitting room, and a Jacuzzi tub within romance range of the fireplace. Beyond the guest rooms are the inn's five common rooms, each with handmade Persian rugs, and outside, impressive gardens and pool.

The restaurant features three dining rooms complete with crystal and gilt chandeliers. In the slower winter months, Executive Chef Todd Muir hosts international chefs affiliated with Romantik Hotels and Restaurants, expanding the restaurant's culinary reach.

Madrona Manor rates vary with the seasons and with the days of the week: $200-290 for two people for rooms on the modified American Plan (breakfast and dinner) on Fri., Sat., and holidays; $120-210 for bed and breakfast only (available Sun.-Thurs.); $30 for each additional person per room. Dinner is also expensive.

For more information or to make reservations, contact: Madrona Manor, 1001 Westside Rd., P.O. Box 818, Healdsburg 95448, tel. (707) 433-4231 or toll-free (800) 258-4003 (fax: 433-0703).

Regional Food
For simple bakery specialties and snacks approaching perfection, try the **Downtown Bakery and Creamery** on the plaza at 308-A Center St., tel. (707) 431-2719. Nothing fancy but everything is excellent, from the fresh-baked breads and pastry items to the real ice cream milkshakes and sundaes—an enterprise launched by pastry chef Lindsey Shere of Berkeley's Chez Panisse and her daughters. (At last report, another alumnus of Chez Panisse, Todd Muir, was chef at the **Madrona Manor** restaurant; see above.) The **Plaza Grille** at 109-A Plaza St. (on the plaza), tel. 431-8305, serves good American food at lunch and dinner, beer and wine, reservations usually necessary. Newcomers (quite popular at lunch and dinner) include **Jacob Horner** at 106 Matheson St., tel. 433-3939, noted for its California and American specialties, and **Matuszeks**, 345 Healdsburg Ave., tel. 433-3427, serving continental/California cuisine.

GEYSERVILLE AND VICINITY

The tiny town of Geyserville is at the heart of the Alexander Valley at the foot of Geyser Peak. Geyserville hosts a **Fall Color Tour** on the last Sunday in October—a good time to enjoy the autumn blaze of red, gold, and russet grape leaves. Among the best wineries in the area is **Chateau Souverain**, with its kiln-like modern architecture, 400 Souverain Rd., P.O. Box 528, Geyserville 95441, tel. (707) 433-8281. In addition to its fine wines (Chardonnay, Cabernet Sauvignon, Sauvignon Blanc, Merlot), Souverain offers chamber music and jazz concerts during the summer months, other special events, and one of the better restaurants in Sonoma County (see below). Open for tasting and sales Wed.-Sun. 10:30-5. The family-owned **J. Pedroncelli Winery,** a mile north of town at 1220 Canyon Rd., tel. 857-3531, sold grapes to home winemakers during Prohibition, then specialized in producing bulk wines. The winery now offers award-winning Alexander Valley and Dry Creek Valley premium varietal wines, tasting and sales daily 10-5. A one-time bulk winery, the 1888 **Nervo Winery** at 19950 Geyserville Ave., tel. 857-3417, now sells young age-them-yourself wines directly to consumers. Open for tasting and sales only, 10-5 daily.

Other worthwhile Geyserville-area stops include **Geyser Peak Winery** on Chianti Rd. (Canyon Rd. exit from Hwy. 101), tel. (707) 857-9463 or toll-free (800) 255-WINE, open for tasting daily 10-5; **Trentadue Winery** at 19170 Old Redwood Hwy., tel. 433-3104, also featuring a gourmet food and gift shop, open daily 10-5; **De Lorimier Vineyards and Winery,** 2001 Hwy. 128, tel. 433-7718, open Fri.-Mon. 10-4; and **Ferrari-Carano Vineyards and Winery,** 8761 Dry Creek Rd., tel. 433-6700, open daily 10-5, tours by appointment only Tues.-Sat. at 10 a.m. and 2 p.m.

For more information about Geyserville and vicinity, contact the **Geyserville Chamber of Commerce,** 21035 Geyserville Ave., Geyserville 95441, tel. (707) 857-3745.

Geyserville Practicalities
Catelli's the Rex at 21047 Geyserville Ave., Geyserville 95441, tel. (707) 857-9904, is noted for its old-style Italian meals. The restaurant

has been in business here since 1938 and serves homemade ravioli, cannelloni, scampi, and more (zuccotto for dessert); lunch and dinner daily. Nearby, the **Hoffman House Restaurant** serves California country cuisine, tel. 857-3264. Truly superb for dining is **Chateau Souverain,** visible from just a few miles north of Healdsburg—twin buildings designed to resemble Sonoma County's traditional hop-drying kilns, on a knoll overlooking the Alexander Valley—actually in Geyserville at 400 Souverain Rd. (west from Hwy. 101 via Independence Ln. and Souverain Rd.), tel. 433-3141. Chateau Souverain serves up vineyard views at lunch and dinner, continental and California cuisine, fine Souverain wines. Dress code, though the cafe is casual. Reservations.

Definitely different for accommodations is the **Isis Oasis Lodge and Cultural Center** at 20889 Geyserville Ave., tel. (707) 857-3524. The Isis Oasis is a 12-room rustic lodge and honeymoon cottage, with pool, spa, and sauna, dinner theater most weekends, plus acres of grounds, exotic animals, even a "magic meditation tree." Bed and breakfasters, the **Campbell Ranch Inn,** 1475 Canyon Rd., tel. 857-3476, has just five rooms on a 35-acre spread, hot tub, pool, tennis court, bikes, complete breakfast, also coffee and dessert every evening, $90-145. The **Hope-Merrill House** and the **Hope-Bosworth House,** both on Geyserville Ave. (and both at P.O. Box 42, tel. 857-3356), are exceptional Victorians, with heated pool, full breakfast included, optional vineyard tours and picnics via horse-drawn stagecoach. Rooms $65-125.

Lake Sonoma

New, courtesy of the U.S. Army Corps of Engineers, Lake Sonoma is a mammoth recreation area—swimming, fishing, boating, camping, 40 miles of hiking and horseback trails over the tinder-dry wooded grasslands—in the making, despite long local wrangling over the environmental costs of dam construction. The flooding of popular hot springs, sacred Native American sites, and rugged scenic valleys led to court battles and public protests in the 1970s. But Sonoma County voters really wanted a lake and approved the construction of Warm Springs Dam in two separate elections. There's a fish hatchery near the dam, also a visitor center/mu-

seum emphasizing Native American culture, the area's early history, and natural history.

For secluded camping, hike, ride, or boat in to primitive lakeside campgrounds: tables, portable restrooms, no fee. Or car camp at first-come, first-camped **Liberty Glen** developed campsites (both individual and group), flush toilets and hot showers. October-March camping is free on weekends. Various other "primitive" campgrounds are near the lake. For more information, contact: Lake Sonoma Recreation Area, 3333 Skaggs Springs Rd., Geyserville 95441, tel. (707) 433-9483. For boating conditions and information: Lake Sonoma Resort and Marina, P.O. Box 1345, Healdsburg 95448, tel. 433-2200.

CLOVERDALE

Cloverdale, surrounded by foothills dotted with oaks, is usually free of summer's chilly coastal fog—but *hot* for getting speeding tickets. The fact that Hwy. 101 funnels down into Cloverdale Blvd., the town's main street, also means local police make a killing on speeders trying to quickly slip through this infamous traffic bottleneck. Watch it (particularly on the south side of town).

Cloverdale's name fit better a century ago, when the landscape was still thick with redwood forests and carpeted with clover-like trillium. The area then became orange-growing country, but vineyards are fast becoming the rage. The town's older residential streets are wide, shaded by maples and fragrant eucalyptus. The **Cloverdale Historical Museum,** 215 N. Cloverdale Blvd., tel. (707) 894-2067, is a worthy stop. Housed in the old brick Isaac E. Shaw home, the museum is loaded with local historical bric-a-brac, with one room displayed as an old California general store. (Free, donations appreciated.) Cloverdale has a foot-stompin' **Fiddle Contest** in January and hosts its annual

Citrus Fair in February. The **Russian River Wine Fest** in May is a big to-do, but nothing beats the **Sheepdog Trials.** The town's summer concert series begins the same month. In August comes the **Wine Country Fly-In,** then the annual **Grape Festival** in September.

Winter whitewater rafting (also summer canoeing and kayaking) is particularly good on the Russian River north of Cloverdale. Near the convergence of Pieta Creek, **Squaw Rock** looms overhead, old bedrock from the sea and now a historic landmark. (As the story goes, a jilted Native American woman grabbed a large rock and jumped from here onto her lover with his new woman below, crushing them like grapes.) Backroads Hwy. 128 from Cloverdale eventually twists and turns down into Mendocino County's inland Anderson Valley and Boonville.

Cloverdale Wineries

The vineyards and wineries thin out considerably near Cloverdale, though several local wineries have tasting rooms here. **Bandiera Winery** has a tasting room for its wildflower-labeled premium wines next to the chamber office on the highway, 115 Cherry Creek Rd., tel. (707) 894-4295, open 8:30-5:30 daily. **J. Fritz Winery** at 24691 Dutcher Creek Rd., tel. 894-3389, features a picnic area and patio with vineyard views, winetasting daily, tours by appointment only.

Cloverdale Practicalities

For information on the area and upcoming events, contact the **Cloverdale Chamber of Commerce,** 132 S. Cloverdale Blvd., Cloverdale 95425, tel. (707) 894-4470. City buses run weekdays (within city limits only), tel. 894-2521. Camp at **Lake Sonoma** to the west or at the **Cloverdale KOA,** 26460 River Rd., tel. 894-3337, with both tent and RV sites, hot showers, pool, rec hall, fishing ponds, miniature golf. Or try one of the basic local motels. The **Garden Motel** at 611 N. Cloverdale Blvd., tel. 894-2594, has reasonable rooms. The bright blue **Vintage Towers Inn,** a national historic landmark and bed and breakfast at 302 N. Main St., tel. 894-4535, is $80-110 with full breakfast (some suites with "towers," all rooms with private baths), Sonoma airport pickup available.

Other Cloverdale bed and breakfasts: **Abrams House Inn** at 314 N. Main St., tel. 894-2412, an 1870 brick Victorian with four rooms (one with private bath), full breakfast, gardens with gazebo and hot tub, $60-115, dinner and picnic baskets available; and **Ye Old Shelford House** at 29955 River Rd., tel. 894-5956, a country Victorian circa 1885 with six rooms (two share a bath), full breakfast, hot tub, deck, pool, free bikes. Rates: $85-115. (Closed in January.) "Surrey 'n' Sip" and antique-car vineyard tours available.

Lots of fast-food choices in Cloverdale, but the Greek-Italian fare at **Dann's Owl Cafe,** 485 S. Cloverdale Blvd., tel. (707) 894-3369, is a longstanding local tradition. Breakfast standards, homemade soup, good bread, chicken and steak. Open 6 a.m.-11 p.m. daily. **Zola's,** 102 S. Cloverdale Blvd., tel. 894-4443, features fine local wines, fresh ingredients, continental and California cuisine. (Another claim to fame for Zola's: it's located at the first stoplight north of San Francisco on Hwy. 101.)

INLAND MENDOCINO COUNTY

UKIAH

A sprawling old lumber town in the center of the inland Yokayo Valley, Ukiah is rowdy and rough-edged and populated by just plain folks: rednecks, redwood loggers, even redwood-loving tree huggers. The most interesting thing about Ukiah is its name: "haiku" spelled backward, but derived from the Pomo word Yu Haia, meaning either "south" or "deep." But the town itself isn't necessarily backward. The **Mendocino County Wine Auction and Barbecue** is held in June, tel. (707) 462-6613 for information, and later in summer comes the **Fourth of July** fireworks and other festivities. Truly unusual is the yule-season **Truckers Light Parade** in December, when big rigs all decked out with Christmas lights parade through town after dark.

Ukiah Sights

Downtown at 272 N. State St., the 1891 **Palace Hotel,** where the bandit Black Bart allegedly stayed, is both a state and national historic landmark. But hard times have come to the Palace, recently a residential hotel for the destitute. (Its historically popular downstairs restaurant is now closed, but the bar is still open.) The Palace has recently changed hands and may soon be back to its grand old self. **Moore's Flour Mill** on S. State still uses century-old waterwheel-powered grindstones (tours available). For tours of some of the town's historic buildings, contact the **Mendocino County Historical Society** at 603 W. Perkins, tel. (707) 462-6969.

Different in Ukiah is the **frisbee course** (played much like golf) at Ukiah's 80-acre **Low Gap Regional Park,** which also includes a playground, tennis courts, picnic facilities, and an amphitheater where local groups perform during summer.

Fourteen miles northwest of Ukiah on Orr Springs Rd. is **Montgomery Woods,** over 1,100 acres of undeveloped redwoods on Big River, a walk-in park with trails, trees, and marvelous seven-foot-tall woodwardia ferns. There's also privacy: a long, winding road keeps people away.

Hot Springs And Mineral Baths

Secluded **Orr Hot Springs,** 13201 Orr Springs Rd., Ukiah 95482, tel. (707) 462-6277, historically accessible only by stagecoach, is still remote. It's well worth staying once you arrive. Orr's is a "clothing optional" hot springs resort—but almost no one opts for clothes here. Facilities include a large redwood hot tub, four private hot tubs (Victorian porcelain), plus a tile-inlaid natural rock mineral pool (cool) and a healing and massage room. Next to the gas-fired sauna is the large mineral water swimming pool. Overnight rates include use of the springs and accommodations—campsites, the communal sleeping loft, or private cottages or cabins—plus use of the common kitchen, dining room, and lounge. Rates may increase in 1993, but overnight fees for cabins is $61 Mon.-Wed., $83 Thurs.-Sun.; for cottages or "vistas," $94 Mon.-Wed., $116 Thurs.-Sun.; for dormitory space,

---

TALMAGE AND THE "CITY OF TEN THOUSAND BUDDHAS"

The tiny Mendocino County town of Talmage has become a world center for Buddhist study. The City of Ten Thousand Buddhas put up its shingle at the one-time site of Mendocino State Hospital in the mid-1970s. The Tudor-style complex and well-landscaped grounds became seminary, monastary, and home for 250-500 Buddhist monks and nuns. Days spent in prayer, meditation, and low-key study—including the grade school and high school here—are now becoming more academic. Visitors are welcome to stop by and wander the grounds if they first check-in at the administration building. New is the **Dharma Realm Buddhist University,** a fully accredited four-year liberal arts college dedicated to Buddhist behavior standards and practices. With its purpose of offering Buddhist education in the West, the school is sponsored by the largely Asian, million-member Dharma Realm Buddhist Association. For more information, contact City of Ten Thousand Buddhas, P.O. Box 217, Talmage, CA 95481, tel. (707) 462-0939.

GRACE HUDSON MUSEUM AND SUN HOUSE

Sometimes the most amazing people and things turn up in the most unlikely places. Unconventional Grace Carpenter Hudson and her physician-turned-ethnologist husband John lived in Ukiah in a modest custom-created redwood home they affectionately called "Sun House." She was nationally recognized for her striking, sensitive paintings of Pomo Indians; he was a scholar and collector of Native Americana. Their former home is now part of the city of Ukiah's extraordinary museum complex honoring the contributions of both. Opened in 1986, the large new Grace Hudson Museum and gallery at 431 S. Main St., tel. (707) 462-3370, displays at least some of Grace Hudson's paintings (most of her work is in private and public collections elsewhere). Also here is an impressive array of John Hudson's artifacts collection, including some fine and rare examples of intricate and delicate Pomo basketry, essentially a lost art.

It is astounding that Ukiah (Lumbertown U.S.A.) hosts such a rare and valuable collection of lost Americana. But the *quality* of the museum itself is even more astounding. Comparable to New York's Natural History Museum, most of the credit goes to two women—museum director Suzanne Abel-Vidor, and curator Sandy Metzler—and their unfailing dedication to detail. The building's interior is laid out in a Pomo basketry pattern, bring together Pomo artifacts and examples of Grace Hudson's artwork, creating a powerful yet unconscious awareness of the cycle of birth and rebirth tht speaks of the *truth* at the heart of this place. An impressive accomplishment. Brava.

Adjacent Sun House (note the Hopi sun symbol over the entrance) and the museum are open Wed.-Sat. 10 a.m.-4:30 p.m. and Sun. noon-4:30 p.m. (closed on major holidays). In summer open also Tuesday. In addition to the museum's permanent displays, special exhibits of local artists are also featured. Docent-led tours of Sun House are also available.

$25.50 pp; and for camping, $20 pp. Fees for use of the springs only: $12 pp, $7 on Monday.

Now a state historical landmark, once host to last century's literary lions and U.S. presidents, the recently restored **Vichy Springs** mineral baths are at 2605 Vichy Springs Rd., tel. (707) 462-9515, $25 for day use. Also here: lodging, hiking trails. A wonderful low-key retreat, $80-150 to stay.

Ukiah Area Wineries
Near Ukiah are some fairly well-known Mendocino County wineries, among them Parducci and Weibel Champagne Cellars, plus some up-and-comers: Jepson Vineyards, Hidden Cellars, Olson Vineyards, and Parson's Creek Winery. Most of them are small family operations, and even the bigger places have grown slowly with the generations.

Parducci Wine Cellars, a few miles north of town at 501 Parducci Rd., tel. (707) 462-3828, or 462-WINE, has been in business since 1931, its modern-day emphasis on producing premium varietals from Mendocino County grapes. Open 9 a.m.-6 p.m. in summer, otherwise daily 9-5. Thirty-minute tours on the hour, winetasting. **Weibel Champagne Cellars,** noted for its Green Hungarian and brut champagne, is about five miles north of Ukiah at 7051 N. State St., technically in Redwood Valley, tel. 485-

0321. Open daily (no tours) 10-6.

Parsons Creek Winery, 3001 S. State St., tel. (707) 462-8900, welcomes visitors on weekends by appointment only. Family-run **Jepson Vineyards,** 10400 S. Hwy. 101, tel. 468-8936, offers tasting daily 10-5. **Hidden Cellars,** 1500 Cunningham Rd., P.O. Box 448, Talmage 95481, tel. 462-0301, is open for tasting and sales (but no tours), May-Oct. daily 10-4. Overlooking Lake Mendocino, very small **Olson Vineyards,** 3620 Rd. B, Redwood Valley 95470, tel. 485-7523, specializes in Chardonnay and Zinfandel, though the Fumé Blanc is fine too. Tasting room in the family home, with adjacent bed and breakfast lodging.

Some say the handmade brandy produced by the Franco-American partnership of Ansley Coale and Hubert **Germain-Robin** is the country's best, and a challenge to the finest French cognacs. To get more information: **Alambic Inc.,** P.O. Box 175, Ukiah 95482, tel. (707) 462-3221.

For more information about these and other area wineries, contact: **Mendocino County Vintners Association,** P.O. Box 1409, Ukiah 95482, tel. (707) 463-1704.

Area Accommodations
Camp at nearby **Lake Mendocino,** created in 1958 when construction of Coyote Dam blocked

HOPLAND: NO MORE HOPS, PLENTY OF VINEYARDS

Hopland is little more than a wide spot in the road but a perfect place to pull over. There's something *live* about Hopland, a tiny town reclaiming its own existence, even if that existence is primarily tourist-oriented these days. Named for the brewery hops once raised throughout the area, Hopland's returning to tradition—at least in a small way. The **Hopland Brewery** in the town's old brick general store/post office, tel. (707) 744-1361, is California's first brewpub since Prohibition. The tavern cum restaurant serves its own unpasteurized, unfiltered traditional Mendocino Brewing Company beers, ales, porters, stouts (the likes of Peregrine Pale Ale, Red Tail Ale, and Black Hawk Stout). The "brewery" also features a very relaxed beer garden, good food, good folks, entertainment. Wednesday, for example, is darts night. On Thursday, come for classical music, on Friday and Saturday nights for blues, jazz, reggae, or rock.

Wineries near Hopland include: **McDowell Valley Vineyards** at 3811 Hwy. 175, tel. (707) 744-1053 or 744-1516, open daily 10-5 in Hopland, winery tours only by appointment, a "solar-integrated" space-age setup. **Milano Winery**, at home in an old hop kiln at 14594 Hwy. 101, tel. 744-1396, specializes in Chardonnay, Cabernet Sauvignon, and dessert wines. Open daily 10-5, tours offered by appointment. **Fetzer Vineyards,** 13500 S. Hwy. 101, tel. 744-1737, is a pioneer of the organic wine trend. Fetzer also offers a cooking school. These and other wineries have tasting rooms in town.

Also in Hopland: a growing number of shops to peek into (like **The Hopland Willow Factory**) and some good places to eat (including **The Cheesecake Lady** and the **Fetzer Wine Tasting Room and Deli,** just one of the many Fetzer clan enterprises in the area). For grubby travelers, Hopland even has a laundromat (at the gas station). More attention grabbing, though, is the colorfully restored **Thatcher Inn** at 13401 S. Hwy. 101, tel. 744-1890, now a bed-and-breakfast-style stopover, $85-95. For some unusual entertainment, there's a new high-stakes bingo parlor at the nearby **Hopland Indian Rancheria**, with jackpots of $500-1,500.

the Russian River's east fork. The lake has 300-plus family campsites, four group camps, plenty of picnicking. The lake's popular for swimming, fishing, and water-skiing. Also here is a Pomo cultural center with an impressive basketry display. For info, contact: Lake Mendocino/Park Manager, 1160 Lake Mendocino Dr., Ukiah 95482, tel. (707) 462-7581.

In **Potter Valley** there's a small PG&E campground on Trout Creek near the Eel River. From Hwy. 20, head north on Potter Valley Rd., turn onto Eel River Rd., then continue to the bridge over the Eel. The campground is about two miles east of the Van Arsdale Reservoir, run by the Army Corps of Engineers.

Another place to camp is **Cow Mountain,** some 60,000 acres of BLM land east of Ukiah, most easily reached by the north fork of Mill Creek Rd. off Hwy. 20 on the way to Lakeport. Chaparral at lower elevations gives way to oaks, pines, and firs. Cow Mountain roads are narrow and steep, so trailers or RVs are a no-go. But the camping is easy: four campgrounds with water and pit toilets, plus unimproved camping areas and free trailside camping. (The area is popular with hunters, so either stay away during deer season or wear day-glo orange.) Pick up a map-leaflet at the Ukiah BLM headquarters, 555 Leslie St., P.O. Box 940, Ukiah 95482, tel. (707) 462-3873.

Motel 6 is at 1208 S. State St. (located almost south of town near the freeway: take Talmage Rd. exit west, then left at State), tel. (707) 468-5404, pool, a/c, TV and movies, rooms $26 s, $32 d. Also quite reasonable is the **Cottage Inn** at 755 S. State St., tel. 462-8509, 30 rooms (12 with kitchens), TV, and pool, rates from $35. The **Best Western Inn** at 601 Talmage Rd., tel. 462-8868, is quite comfortable and attractive, with the usual amenities and pool, rooms $44-68 during the high season (lower otherwise), and a special family rate. The **Discovery Inn** at 1340 N. State St., tel. 462-8873, is also quite nice, rates $40 and up. Downtown is the **Best Western Willow Tree Inn,** 406 S. State St., tel. 462-8611, with pool, whirlpool, sauna, tennis court, coin laundry; rooms vary seasonally, $40-52.

Ukiah Area Bed And Breakfasts

The contemporary redwood **Oak Knoll Bed and Breakfast** at 858 Sanel Dr. (P.O. Box 412), Ukiah

95482, tel. (707) 468-5646, offers just two rooms (shared bath) and full breakfast plus a great view for $65-70. The **Sanford House** at 306 S. Pine, tel. 462-1653, offers five rooms in a 1904 Victorian, expanded continental breakfast, $80-85.

Unbeatable for a relaxing getaway, of course, is **Vichy Springs Resort and Inn** outside town at 2605 Vichy Springs Rd., tel. (707) 462-9515, with three cottage rooms and 12 rooms in the main 1854 early California house. Expanded continental breakfast, hiking and mountain biking. Rates: $105-150.

Ukiah Food

Now that the restaurant in Ukiah's Palace Hotel has closed, the town isn't particularly known for its eateries. Get natural foods for the road at **The Ukiah Co-op**, 308 E. Perkins, tel. (707) 462-4778. **Main Street Wine and Cheese** at Main and Perkins, tel. 462-0417, is a decent deli with good sandwiches, fine wines. Other decent eateries include the **Sunset Grill** at 228 E. Perkins St., tel. 463-0740, the **El Sombrero Restaurant** at 131 E. Mill St., tel. 463-1818, and the elegant **Thatcher Inn** south of town in Hopland, tel. 744-1890 (also a striking and fully restored bed and breakfast). The **North State Cafe** inside an exquisite restored Victorian at 801 N. State St., tel. 462-3726, serves very good California cuisine. For more traditional selections, try the very varied menu at the **Ukiah Garden Cafe**, 1090-A S. State St., tel. 462-1221.

In summer, a side trip to the farm country of **Potter Valley** (where the headwaters of the Eel River's middle fork and the Russian's east fork trickle forth) is worth it, as much for the fresh produce as the pastoral scenery. Head up East Side Rd. toward "downtown" Potter Valley and stop at roadside produce stands for fresh corn, berries, melons, and other fruits and vegetables. (There's a heck of a farm-town **Spring Festival** here over Memorial Day weekend, with even more good food.) Head on (or backtrack) to the **Hopland Brew Pub** for a livelier atmosphere.

Wherever you eat, try some local wines or a bottle of locally famous Mendocino Mineral Water (the "living waters" popular with Pomo natives) bottled in Comptche. Mendocino Mineral Water is said to be salt-free but four times richer in dis-

solved minerals than other well-known waters (including Calistoga and Perrier). Another local choice: Vichy Springs Mineral Water.

Transportation, Information

Greyhound, on N. State St., tel. (707) 462-3682, runs north to Eureka and south to San Francisco daily. Get around town (and to Willits, Fort Bragg, and Mendocino) on **Mendocino Transit** buses, tel. 462-1422, 462-1462. The **Ukiah Chamber of Commerce** is at 495 E. Perkins, Ukiah 95482, tel. 462-4705.

The **Mendocino County Convention and Visitors Bureau** is at 33 N. School St., P.O. Box 244, Ukiah 95482, tel. 462-3091. For stamps and such, Ukiah's **post office** is at N. Oak and W. Standley, tel. 462-8814. For fun, the **Ukiah Redwood Theatre** is at 612 S. State, tel. 462-6788. For emergencies, the **Ukiah Valley Medical Center** at 275 Hospital Dr., tel. 462-3111, can handle them, as can the **Mendocino Community Hospital** at 860 N. Bush, tel. 463-4010.

THE ANDERSON VALLEY

Boonville

Some places have deep-down *personality* yet go to great lengths to disguise that fact from passersby. The Anderson Valley area between Ukiah and Mendocino is one of these places. Among other things, this insular but culturally *engaged* community created its own language. But people in this individualistic coastal valley also have a tendency to choose up sides and turn against each other—a trend established during the Civil War when the northern part of the valley allied itself with the Union cause and the south went Confederate.

Fascinating, almost frightening, in the tiny Anderson Valley is the opportunity to see what outside capital and the winemaking boom can do (and have done elsewhere, perhaps less noticeably) to undermine what can be loosely termed "community." Though change is constant—especially in California—the valley here is a domestic study in the relationship between colonizers and the colonized.

But some traditions are holding on. Among the best here is the annual **Mendocino County Fair and Apple Show** held in mid-September, one of the last completely noncommercial county fairs in America, and an incredibly good time. On a Sunday in mid-July, there's an equally traditional **Woolgrower's Barbecue and Sheep Dog Trials** at the fairgrounds. For a look at even more tangible artifacts of the Anderson Valley's fast-fading traditions, stop by the **Anderson Valley Historical Museum** in the one-room schoolhouse just northwest of Boonville. Open Fri.-Sun. only, or when the American flags are flying. Free.

For more information on the Anderson Valley area, contact the **Anderson Valley Chamber of Commerce,** P.O. Box 275, Boonville 95414 (no phone), or the **Mendocino County Convention and Visitors Bureau,** P.O. Box 244, Ukiah 95482, tel. (707) 462-3091.

Traveling northward into the Anderson Valley from Cloverdale via Hwy. 128, an enjoyable if slow and snaking roadtrip, **Mailliard Redwoods** is a serene spot for a picnic and a hike. Here are 200 acres of redwoods and the headwaters of the Garcia River (no fishing), the area named for conservationist John Ward Mailliard. To get here, head west on Fish Rock Rd. from Hwy. 128.

The *Anderson Valley Advertiser*

One of the most fascinating things about the area is its newspaper, the *Anderson Valley Advertiser*. Despite the tame name, it's not at all what people expect in such a place. Instead of one of those smarmy small-town shoppers filled with good news and happy talk, this paper is well-written and wild, dedicated to "fanning the flames of discontent." Notorious *AVA* editor and publisher Bruce Anderson is California's chief outlaw journalist, in the tradition of Mark Twain and Ambrose Bierce, raging without restraint

P.O. Box 332, Philo, CA 95466

at the world within his vision. To subscribe, contact: *Anderson Valley Advertiser*, 12451 Anderson Valley Way, Boonville 95415, tel. (707) 895-3016.

Wellspring Renewal Center

Even if the name sounds like it, this isn't one of those touchy-feely kind of places California is so famous for. Wellspring near Philo is, instead, a very caring, globally concerned, and (in the truest sense of the word) *Christian* place in the redwoods and oak woodlands along the Navarro River, with a central farmhouse lodge and dining hall, organic gardens for the basic ingredients of carefully prepared community meals, and lodgings: a camping area, tepees and tent cabins, very rustic 1920s cabins, and larger group cabins with bathrooms and kitchens.

Not really in the business of providing shelter for road-weary travelers, visitors are nonetheless welcome to stay here (but only by prior arrangement) anytime there's still room during one of the center's retreats, or when no other activities are scheduled. Excellent meals—primarily vegetarian fare and natural foods—also available when retreats are in session, quite reasonable. "Energy gifts"—help with kitchen clean-up, cutting firewood—are always appreciated from guests. Accommodations prices: $6 per person to camp, $12 for a tepee or tent cabin, lodge rooms or cabins $18-25 per person double occupancy.

Consider attending one of Wellspring's retreats on topics like "Creative Non-violence and Community Organization," "Renewal for Social Activists," "Ride the Redwoods" bicycling tours, "Healing Into Wholeness" and "Native American Spirituality," and the center's annual Storytelling Conference and "Exploring the Power of

BOONTLING: A SLIB OF LOREY

Until recently, the friendly people here in Boonville regularly spoke Boontling, a creative local dialect combining English, Scottish-Irish, Spanish, French, Pomo, and spontaneous, often hilarious words with strictly local significance. This private community language, locals say, was originally created by people now in their "codgiehood" (old-timers) to "shark the bright lighters" (confuse outsiders) and befuddle

children—a word game started by men toiling for endless hours in the hop fields. Outsiders still get confused, but local kids learn the lingo in school.

Bright lighters, by the way, are people from the city. A *walter levy* is a telephone, because Walter was the first person in town to have one. A more modern variation, *buckey walter* (pay phone), refers to the old-time nickel phone call and the Indian head or "buck" on the nickel's face. There's a buckey walter, so labeled, right outside the Horn of Zeese (coffee) cafe in town. Another sign in downtown Boonville—and a sign of the times, over a realtor's office—is a facsimile of a clock with the phrase *A teem ta hig, a teem ta shay,* meaning: "A time to buy, a time to sell."

A *featherleg*, in Boontling, is a cocky, arrogant person (because everyone knows banty roosters have feathers down their legs). *Shovel tooth* means "doctor," because the valley's physician had buck teeth. A *jeffer* is a big fire, since old Jeff built a huge fireplace into his house. A *madge* is a house of ill repute (in honor of Madge, who ran one of the best in Ukiah).

Burlappin' is a very active sexual verb (there are others in Boontling) referring to the time a shop clerk was caught in the act atop a pile of burlap sacks in the storeroom. *Skrage* means "to make love." *Charlie-ball* is a verb meaning "to embarrass," a direct reference to a local Pomo who was easily embarrassed.

But the ongoing creativity behind Boontling's evolution (and the community's insularity) started to get confused after World War I, with the coming of roads, telephones, and other inroads of civilization. To pick up whatever is left of the language, tutor yourself with the animated, sometimes outrageous, and impeccably written *Anderson Valley Advertiser* or the local language dictionary, *A Slib of Lorey.*

Myth." Usually in September, a week-long Elderhostel session is scheduled here as well.

For more information, contact: Wellspring Renewal Center, P.O. Box 332, Philo 95466, tel. (707) 895-3893 or 895-2953.

Hendy Woods State Park, Other Parks

A state park on the north slope of Greenwood Ridge just outside Philo looking back on An-

derson Valley, Hendy Woods includes two virgin groves of enormous redwoods: 80-acre Big Hendy Grove, with nature trail, and smaller Little Hendy Grove. Besides redwoods, you'll find Douglas fir, California bay, wildflowers. The Navarro River is a peaceful stream in summer (poor for swimming, though wading is a possibility) and a raging torrent in winter. Most of the park is on the valley floor. Good camping is

the Boonville Hotel

KIM WEIR

available at either the **Azalea** or **Wildcat camp-grounds.** Reserve one of the 92 campsites ($10) from May 1 through September through Mistix, tel. (800) 444-7275. Day-use fee: $3. To get here, take the Greenwood Rd. turnoff from Hwy. 128 northwest of Philo. For more information about Hendy Woods, contact: Mendocino Area Parks, P.O. Box 440, Mendocino 95460, tel. (707) 937-5804.

In addition, there are two county parks in the valley. **Indian Creek County Park** is four miles northwest of Boonville on the highway, pleasant for picnicking and a short walk (the entrance is obscure, just south of Indian Creek Bridge). Even more remote is **Faulkner County Park,** three miles west of Boonville via snake-like Mountain View Road.

Anderson Valley Wineries

Partly the result of the winds of change churning through the Anderson Valley, there are some fine small wineries in the area. Many of these enterprises have been around for quite some time. Remote **Greenwood Ridge Vineyards and Winery,** on the ridge between Philo and Elk, tel. (707) 877-3262 (tasting room: 895-2002), is home to the annual California Wine Tasting Championships. Tasting room (next to Navarro's, on Hwy. 128) open 10 a.m.-6 p.m. daily, but tours only by appointment.

Navarro Vineyards, 5601 Hwy. 128 near Philo, tel. (707) 895-3686, started by Pacific Stereo's founder, is open daily 10-5, until 6 p.m. in summer. Navarro produces an excellent estate-bottled Gerwürztraminer, also Chardonnay and Pinot Noir, even an Edelwicker table wine. Striking redwood tasting room, picnic facilities.

The oldest winemaking establishment in the area (here since 1971) and probably most famous is **Husch Vineyards** and bonded winery, 4400 Hwy. 128 in Philo, tel. (707) 895-3216, open daily 10-5. From its "unadorned rustic" wood-frame winery, Husch produces fine varietal wines from its estate-grown grapes. Husch Vineyards's 1983 estate-bottled Gerwürztraminer was one of several California wines taken to China in 1984 by President Reagan and served in Beijing at a state dinner honoring Zhao Ziyang. Just down the road a piece, at 4610 Hwy. 128, is **Lazy Creek Vineyard,** recognized for its Chardonnay, Pinot Noir, and Gewürztraminer. Open only by appointment, tel. 895-3623.

Roederer U.S. Inc., owned by one of the top champagne producers in France, is home here at 4501 Hwy. 128, tel. 895-2288, open for tasting and sales Fri.-Mon. 11-4, for tours by appointment only at 10 a.m. and 4:30 p.m. **Scharffenberger Cellars** down the highway at 7000, tel. 895-2065, also produces sparkling wines in the *methode champenoise,* open daily 11-5.

Kendall-Jackson has taken over the former Edmeades. Vineyards at 5500 Hwy. 128,

TOLL HOUSE
RESTAURANT & INN

tel. 895-3009, and is a very worthwhile stop, Fri.-Sun. 10-5. But don't miss **Handley Cellars** at 3151 Hwy. 128, tel. 895-2190, open daily 11-6—wonderfully eclectic artifacts and folk art on display—but tours are only by appointment. Winemaker Milla Handley is the great-great granddaughter of Henry Weinhard, mythic American beer meister. While you're in the neighborhood, stop at small **Christine Woods** next door, tel. 895-2115, also open daily 11-6. **Obester Winery** at 9200 Hwy. 128, tel. 895-3814, is open daily 10-6, a sunshine yellow farm bungalow surrounded with gardens, and the farm's original produce stands are now back in business.

Anderson Valley Accommodations

If there's space available, stay at the rustic and reasonable **Wellspring Renewal Center** just across the Navarro River from Hendy Woods (see above). Or camp at **Hendy Woods** just outside Philo; at the **Paul M. Dimmick Wayside Campground** beyond Navarro on the way to the coast, a 12-acre redwood-forested hideaway with damp, primitive camping and picnicking (flooded in winter, so open only May to October); or **Manchester State Beach** (see "The North Coast").

Head west via Mountain View Rd. to reach the **Colfax Guest House**, tel. (707) 895-3241, a modern cottage in a redwood grove, $75 d including breakfast. Two other possibilities: the **Philo Pottery Inn**, 8550 Hwy. 128, tel. 895-3069, with rooms $70-92, and the **Toll House Inn** near Boonville at 15301 Hwy. 253, tel. 895-

3630, a vintage-1912 Victorian farmhouse on 350 acres, five large rooms with shaded terraces (private baths), lavish full breakfast, hot tub, good hiking and swimming close at hand. Rates: $115-190. (Good restaurant here, too.) The contemporary ranch-style **Anderson Creek Inn** at 12050 Anderson Valley Way, tel. 895-3091, features four rooms, full breakfast, and swimming pool at a creekside site near area wineries. Rates: $95-125. Or consider a stay at the **Boonville Hotel** (see below).

Anderson Valley Food

For apples and local produce in season, stop at the Gowan family's roadside stand along the highway, 2½ miles north of Philo, or at other fruit and juice vendors. Even if the local pickin's are abundant, don't miss the **Boont Berry Farm** market in Boonville, 13987 Hwy. 128, tel. (707) 895-3576, an amazing, sophisticated store. The casual, crowded-aisle general store atmosphere can't disguise the thoughtful choices behind the selections of local and organic produce and other products, including an excellent variety of regional wines. Full deli here, too, with learn-to-speak-Boontling coffee mugs on the counter. In the same Boonville building as the **Cream Pump** ice-cream parlor is the very good **Upper Crust Bakery**, 14111 Hwy. 128, tel. 895-2512, for everything from fresh cinnamon rolls to picnic supplies. The bakery also serves excellent burritos (dinner time only).

The **Boonville Hotel**, tel. (707) 895-2210, serves simple, superb, and reasonably priced fare. Dinners, including roast pork loin with red chile sauce and chicken breast with salsa fresca, run to $15, dessert and wines extra. (Restaurant usually open Wed.-Sun., call ahead for other times.) The Boonville Hotel, also provides lodgings in its upstairs rooms from $70 for a small room to suites for $150 or more. Reservations advisable. For a casual meal, stop in at the bar where food is served 11 a.m.-11 p.m.

Across the street is Boonville's much more casual **Buckhorn Saloon**, tel. (707) 895-2337, open daily for lunch and dinner, popular with locals. One of the reasons: the Buckhorn is a brewpub. The **Anderson Valley Brewing Company** in the basement produces four different types of local brew, very good.

Red-meat eaters, locals claim there is no better place in the *world* to get a good steak than **Janie's Place** at 8651 Hwy. 128 in Philo, tel. (707) 895-2128, a local legend. Valley folk also highly recommend the *new* **Floodgate Store and Grill** near Navarro, tel. 895-2422, for its down-home and varied menu of *bahl gorms*

(good food). New and also raved about: the **Toll House Restaurant and Inn** at 15301 Hwy. 253, tel. 895-3630, open for lunch and dinner, with meals created around the produce of a five-acre showcase organic garden. Or, for some coastal views and equally enticing food, head toward Mendocino (see "The North Coast").

BOB RACE

THE NORTH COAST
INTRODUCTION

Fog created California's north coast, and still defines it. Fog is everywhere, endless, eternal, *there*. Even on blazing, almost blinding days of sunshine when the veil lifts, the fog is still present somehow, because life here has been made by it. The stranded stands of sky-scraping coast redwoods, for example, need fog to live. So do many other native north coast plants, uniquely adapted to uniformly damp conditions. The visual obscurity characteristic of the coast also benefits animals, providing a consistent, year-round supply of drinking water and, for creatures vulnerable to predators, additional protective cover.

Fog even seems to have political consequences. As elsewhere in the northstate, the secessionist spirit is alive and well on the north coast, but the fog makes it seem fuzzy and the urge is taken even less seriously here than it is elsewhere. When, in the mid-1970s, for example, some Mendocino County citizens banded together to form their own state (they called it Northern California), the response from Sacramento was off-the-cuff and casual: "The county's departure, if it ever goes, would scarcely be noticed, at least not until the fog lifted."

People often find fog disquieting, depressing. Some almost fear it. ("Fear death?" said Elizabeth Barrett Browning. "To feel the fog in my throat, the mist in my face . . . .") If only momentarily, in fog we become spatially and spiritually bewildered. Our vision becomes vague; we hear things. We fall prey to illusions; we hallucinate: trees walk, rocks smile, birds talk, rivers laugh, the ocean sings, someone unseen brushes our cheek. All of a sudden, we don't know where we are and haven't the foggiest notion where we're going. Life as we know it has changed. We have changed.

Dense coastal fog occurs along this cool-weather coast, according to meteorologists, as a result of shoreward breezes carrying warm, moist oceanic air over colder offshore waters. The air's moisture condenses into fog, which rolls in over the coastal mountains in cloud-like waves. As the marine air moves inland and is warmed by the sun, it reabsorbs its own moisture and the fog dissipates.

But science doesn't really explain fog at all—not fog as change, as creator, as fashioner of fantastic forms, as shape-shifting summoner of strange sounds, or protector of the primeval purpose. Fog, in the mythic sense, is magic.

THE LAND

California's northern coastline has few sandy beaches, even fewer natural harbors. Land's end is rugged and inhospitable, with surging surf and treacherous undertows. Because of this—and because of zero-visibility coastal fog—shipwrecks are part of the region's lore. Bits and pieces of hundreds of ships have washed up on these unsympathetic shores.

The region's major land feature is the Coast Ranges, consecutive ridges angling north to Eureka where they meet up with the westward edge of the Klamath Mountains. Geologically, the Coast Ranges (with few peaks higher than 8,000 feet) are composed of once-oceanic, uplifted, and relatively "soft" Franciscan Complex sedimentary rock. The deep soils covering the bedrock were produced over eons by humidity (gentle but constant enough to crumble rock) and, augmented by forest humus, are generally protected from erosion by the ancient forests themselves. The thick coastal soil gives these mountains their gently rounded shape. When saturated with water, and especially when atop typically weathered bedrock, coastal hillsides have a tendency to slide. Landslides are even more common in areas where extensive logging or other removal of natural vegetation occurs, since intact native plant communities make good use of soil moisture.

Federal Wild and Scenic River status has finally been extended to the north coast's Eel, Klamath, Smith, and Trinity rivers, protecting them from dam projects, other water-diversion schemes, and logging within their immediate watersheds. The Smith, the state's last undammed river, is now protected as a national recreation area. Other major north coast rivers include the Garcia, Mad, Navarro, Noyo, and Russian.

Climate

The north coast has a Mediterranean climate cooled in summer by the arctic California Current. Heavy rainfall, 80-160 inches per year, and winter's endless overcast days compete with thick fog the rest of the year for the annual let's-make-a-gray-day award. The sun is most likely to make its chilly appearance during early spring, but Sep-

STANDING ON SHAKY GROUND

Because of the gale-force winds driving storms against the western edge of California for half the year, most north coast settlements are in more protected inland valleys. But some of these areas, including those near the Eel, Garcia, and Mad rivers, parallel major northwesterly earthquake fault zones. As it turns out, even the redwoods, those gentle giants of the north coast, are standing on shaky ground. The seismically active San Andreas Fault (responsible for San Francisco's devastating earthquake and fire in 1906 and again in 1989) runs north from the Bay Area on the seaward side of the mountains before veering back out to sea at Point Arena. Other faults related to the 1992 Eureka-area quake, cluster farther north.

According to recent geologic speculations, a massive earthquake is likely somewhere along the Pacific Northwest's offshore Cascadia "subduction zone" within the next 50-150 years. Such a quake, expected to register as high as 9.5 on the "energy magnitude" scale (considered more accurate than the Richter scale for major quakes), could occur anywhere from Vancouver Island in British Columbia to Mendocino in California. Such an event would be more powerful than any earthquake the San Andreas Fault could generate, much more powerful than any quake ever measured in the mainland U.S., and roughly equal in destructive force to Chile's 1960 earthquake (so far, the century's most devastating).

Before arriving at this ominous conclusion, Humboldt State University geologists studied the Little Salmon Fault near Eureka. Their preliminary findings, announced in 1987 at the annual meeting of the Geological Society of America, suggest that the fault slipped 30-33 feet in separate earthquakes occurring roughly every 500 years during the past half-million years—suggesting quakes of "awesome, incomprehensible" power.

But even more incomprehensible, even more ominous, is the fact that PG&E's Humboldt Bay Nuclear Power Plant—now closed and slated for decommissioning, though the facility still contains high-level radioactive wastes—sits right on top of the Little Salmon Fault.

tember usually brings balmy weather. Often at the end of February, "false spring" comes and stays for a week or more. North coastal temperatures are moderate year-round, but can *feel* quite cold anytime, due to bone-chilling fog and moist air whisked ashore by steady ocean breezes.

A rarity along the southern Sonoma County coast but nonetheless widely observed is an offshore floating mirage resembling Oz's Emerald City, with towers, minarets, the whole show. This strange-but-true phenomenon is vaguely attributed to "climatic conditions." Also rare is the earthquake-related weather phenomenon of tsunamis, or giant coast-crushing waves. Radiocarbon dating of Native American cultural remains (which happen to coincide with dates of major Cascadia earthquakes) suggest that ancient tsunamis were so powerful they tossed canoes into the tops of trees. The most recent tsunami came in 1964, when a 13-foot wave generated by the 8.5-magnitude earthquake in Alaska smashed ashore in Crescent City on the Northern California coast, killing 11 people and destroying much of the town.

NORTH COAST FLORA

In one of his more famous gaffes as governor of California, Ronald Reagan once cut redwood trees with the old saw, "If you've seen one, you've seen 'em all." Despite Reagan's opinion on the subject, the north coast is noted for its deep, dark, and devastatingly beautiful forests of tall coastal redwoods or *Sequoia sempervirens* (sadly, a tree most often appreciated as construction timber for suburban sun decks). Another regional tree with commercial value is the Douglas fir, *Pseudotsuga Menziesii,* faster growing than redwoods so often replanted by foresters on clear-cut lands. Still another: the yew, the components of its bark now regarded as a primary treatment for breast cancer patients.

Yews, Sitka spruce, cedars, and lowland firs reach to the coast. Maples, sycamores, and alders add contrast and color in mixed streamside forests. Foothill woodlands—scattered oaks and conifers in a sea of grasses and spring wildflowers—are common north of San Francisco. Introduced groves of Australian eucalyptus trees—planted now primarily as windbreaks though at one time intended as timber trees— are common along the Sonoma County coast, inland, and up into Mendocino County.

Coastal shrublands have no true chaparral but share some of the same species: fragrant

WES DEMPSEY

coast redwoods

California laurel (bay) trees, scrub oak, dogwood, ceanothus, and purple sage. The least favorite shrub here, as elsewhere in California, is poison oak, usually found in shaded areas. Among the most beautiful coastal "shrubs" (sometimes growing to tree size) are the native rhododendron species, both the western azalea and the California rose bay.

Red elderberries, blackberries, salmonberries, raspberries, huckleberries, and gooseberries all grow wild along the north coast. Wildflowers are abundant, primarily in spring. Unusual are the creeping beach primroses, beach peas, and sea rockets on beaches and sandy dunes. Beneath redwoods grow delicate fairy lanterns, oxalis, and trillium.

NORTH COAST FAUNA

Landlubbing Animals
Deer are common all along the north coast. Protected colonies of Roosevelt elk can be seen far to the north in Redwood National Park.

Smaller north coast mammals include dusky-footed woodrats and nocturnal "pack rats," which nest in trees and rarely travel more than 50 feet in any direction; but more common are those gregarious California gray squirrels, which feast on patches of ice plant, wild strawberries, other fruit seeds, nuts, grasses. When surprised, black-tailed jack rabbits scurry frantically through foothill brush, areas brush rabbits or cottontail "bunnies" also inhabit. Raccoons and skunks are common. So are long-tailed weasels, though people rarely see them. Aquatic land mammals include muskrats or "marsh rabbits" and the vegetarian beaver.

Here, as elsewhere in California, gray foxes are common; those characteristically clever red foxes are less so. From more remote areas, particularly at dusk or dawn, comes the lonely howl of coyotes. Bobcats (truly "wildcats" when cornered) are fairly abundant but rarely seen, though mating squalls can be heard in midwinter. Very rare are mountain lions, who usually discover people before anyone discovers them. Black bears, found even at sea level though they range up into higher elevations, usually won't attack humans unless frightened or protecting their cubs.

A common nonnative Californian along the coast is the nocturnal opossum, the only native U.S. marsupial. Also nonnative, and preferring the cover of night for their ferocious forays through the world, are wild pigs—an aggressive cross between domesticated and imported wild European hogs. But the wildest (and largest) north coast land mammal is Bigfoot or Sasquatch, that half-man, half-beast of lore, first reported by native peoples but rarely seen. If you spot one (male or female), contact: **Bigfoot Information Center**, P.O. Box 632, The Dalles, Oregon, tel. (503) 298-5877.

Birds

A surprising variety of birds can be spotted along the shore: gulls, terns, cormorants, egrets, godwits, and the endangered brown pelican. Mallards, pintails, widgeons, shovelers, and coots are common waterfowl, though Canada geese, snow geese, sandhill cranes, and other species fly by during fall and winter migrations. Great blue herons are nearly as common along inland rivers as they are near the sea. If unseen, mourning doves can still be heard (a soft cooing), usually near water or in farm country. Families of California quail scurry across paths and quiet roadways, sadly oblivious to the dangers of traffic.

Great horned owls, keen-eyed nocturnal hunters with characteristic tufted "ears," usually live in wooded, hilly, or mountainous countryside. Their evening cries are eerie. The magnificent ravens, which seem to dominate the terrain as well as the native mythology of the Pacific Northwest, are quite territorial, preferring to live inland at higher foothill and mountain elevations. The American kestrel or sparrow hawk can often be spotted in open woodlands and meadows or near grazing lands. More common is the red-tailed hawk, usually seen perched on telephone poles, power lines, or fences along the road—getting a good view of the countryside before snaring rabbits, ground squirrels, or field mice (though they're not above picking up an occasional roadkill).

Least appreciated among the birds of prey are the common redheaded turkey vultures. Most often spotted in spring and summer, alone or in groups, they circle above dead or dying animals until dinner's ripe. (Strictly carrion eaters, they prefer putrid flesh.) Though grotesque to humans, their featherless heads are a fine ecological adaptation: bacteria and parasites that might attach themselves as the birds feast are quickly killed by constant exposure to sunlight. And, should any toxic bacteria be swallowed, the vulture's digestive tract kills them off.

In rugged coastal canyons are some (but not many) golden eagles, a threatened species wrongly accused by ranchers and tale-spinners of attacking deer and livestock. Even rarer are endangered bald eagles, usually found near water—remote lakes, marshes, large rivers—primarily in inaccessible river canyons.

California Gray Whales

A close-up view of the California gray whale, the state's official (and largest) mammal, is a life-changing experience. As those dark, massive, white-barnacled heads shoot up out of the ocean to suck air, spray with the force of a fire-hose blasts skyward from blowholes. Watch the annual migration of the gray whale all along the California coast—from "whale vistas" on land or by boat.

COASTAL REDWOODS

Though they once numbered an estimated two million, the native population of coastal redwood trees has been reduced through logging and agriculture to isolated groves of virgin trees. The tallest trees in the state but only the fourth oldest, *Sequoia sempervirens* are nonetheless ancient. Well established here when dinosaurs roamed the earth, redwood predecessors flourished throughout the Northern Hemisphere 60 million years ago. Isolated from the rest of their kind by thick ice sheets a million years ago, the redwoods made their last stand in California.

The elders among today's surviving coastal redwoods are at least 2,200 years old; the tallest stands 368 feet tall, the biggest 12 feet in diameter. These trees thrive in low, foggy areas protected from fierce offshore winds. Vulnerable to both wind and soil erosion, shallow-rooted redwoods tend to topple over during severe storms. Redwoods have no need for deep taproots since fog collects on their needlelike leaves then drips down the trunk or directly onto the ground, where the equivalent of up to 50 inches of rainfall annually is absorbed by hundreds of square feet of surface roots.

Unlike the stately, individualistic Sierra big trees or *Sequoiadendron giganteum,* the comparatively scrawny coastal redwoods reach up to the sky in dense, dark-green clusters—creating living, breathing cathedrals lit by filtered flames of sun or shrouded in foggy silence. The north coast's native peoples religiously avoided inner forest areas, the abode of spirits (some ancestral). But in the modern world, the sacred has become profane. A single coast redwood provides enough lumber for hundreds of hot tubs, patio decks, and wine vats, or a couple of dozen family cabins, or a hefty school complex. Aside from its attractive reddish color, pungent fragrance, and water- and fire-resistance, redwood is also decay-, insect-, and fungus-resistant—and all the more attractive for construction.

Despite the fact that downed trees are being floated overseas to Japan and Korea for processing as fast as the ships can load up, coast redwoods never really die. Left to their own devices, redwoods are capable of regenerating themselves without seeds. New young trees shoot up from stumps or from roots around the base of the old tree, forming gigantic woodland fairy rings in second- or third-growth forests. And each of these trees, when mature, can generate its own genetically identical offspring. Sometimes a large, straight limb from a fallen tree will sprout, sending up a straight line of trees. In heavily logged or otherwise traumatized forest areas, tiny winged redwood seeds find room to take root, sprout, and eventually flourish, blending into a forest with stump-regenerated trees.

CALIFORNIA DEPARTMENT OF PARKS AND RECREATION

Coast redwoods never really die, but regenerate in a variety of ways.

THE POLITICS OF HARVESTING REDWOODS:
TALL TREES, TIMBER, AND BIRDS

North coast timber politics are almost as universally explosive as the issue of offshore drilling. The battle to preserve redwoods, especially the remaining first-growth stands, has been going on for decades. So strong are the economic forces in support of logging and related industry that without the untiring efforts of the private Save-the-Redwoods League, Sierra Club, and other environmental organizations, most of the coast redwood groves now protected from commercial "harvesting" would be long gone. The fact that Redwood National Park north of Eureka was established at all, even if late, is something of a miracle.

Environmentalists adamantly oppose the accelerating practice of clearcutting, the wholesale denuding of hillsides and entire watersheds in the name of efficiency and quick profits. "Tree huggers" have argued for years that anything other than sustained yield timber harvesting (cutting no more timber than is grown each year) not only destroys the environment by eliminating forests, wildlife habitat, and fisheries but ultimately destroys the industry itself. Someday, they've been saying for several decades, the forests will be gone and so will logging and lumbermill jobs. "Someday" has arrived.

The failure of both the 1990 "Green" and Forests Forever initiatives, statewide ballot propositions in favor of forest protection, has only served to increase local furor. Earth First! and other activist groups have taken on Pacific Lumber Company and other timber firms—taking the battle into the forests and surrounding communities, as in 1990's "Redwood Summer." And timbermen and truckers have themselves taken to the streets defending their traditional livelihoods with community parades and other events accented by yellow solidarity ribbons. The fight has become so intense, philosophically, that the Laytonville school board was publicly pressured to ban *The Lorax* by Dr. Seuss because of the book's anti-clearcutting sentiments. (The book banning failed, ultimately.)

A further blow to business as usual came with the recent admission by the California Board of Forestry that the state has allowed timber companies to cut down so many mature trees—old growth and otherwise—that there now looms a serious "timber gap," a substantial reduction in future forest harvests. The "statewide emergency" is due to "past failure" to regulate industrial timberlands and "has resulted in long-term overharvesting, drastically reducing both the productive capability of the land and maintenance of adequate wildlife habitat." This new crisis has further shocked the California timber industry, long accustomed to the board's regulatory sympathies.

Federal and state restrictions related to preserving old growth forest habitats of the endangered spotted owl and the marbled murrelet—two bird species that live or successfully nest only in old growth or redwood forests—have become mired in bureaucratic procedure at all levels of governmental, legislative, and judicial review. But even this apparent victory will be short-lived, judging from current mill closures and logging company layoffs. The timber business has harvested its own industry into oblivion.

Despite the fascination they hold for Californians, little is yet known about the gray whale. Once endangered by whaling—like so many whale species still are—the grays are now swimming steadily along the comeback trail. Categorized as baleen whales (which dine on plankton and other small aquatic animals sifted through hundreds of fringed, horn-like baleen plates), gray whales were once land mammals that went back to sea. In the process of evolution, they traded their fore and hind legs for fins and tail flukes. Despite their fishlike appearance, these are true mammals: warm-blooded, air-breathing creatures who nourish their young with milk.

Adult gray whales weigh 20-40 tons, not counting a few hundred pounds of parasitic barnacles. Calves weigh in at a hefty 1,500 pounds at birth and can expect to live for 30 to 60 years. They feed almost endlessly from April to October in the arctic seas between Alaska and Siberia, sucking up sediment and edible creatures on the bottom of shallow seas then squeezing the excess water and silt out their baleen filters. Fat and sassy with an extra 6-12 inches of blubber on board, early in October they head south on their 6,000-mile journey to the warmer waters of Baja in Mexico.

Pregnant females leave first, traveling alone or in small groups. Larger groups make up the rear guard, with the older males and non-pregnant females engaging in highly competitive courtship and mating rituals along the way (quite a show for human voyeurs). The rear guard becomes the frontline on the way home: males, newly pregnant females, and young gray whales head north from February to June. Cows and calves migrate later, between March and July. (For information about whalewatching, see "North Coast Recreation" below.)

Other Sea Life

Among ocean animals fairly common along the coast are sea otters or "sea beavers" (see "Monterey Bay Area" for more information), fun to watch as they go about their business in offshore forests of seaweed. The large (1,200-2,000 pounds) northern sea lion can be spotted along rugged far northern shores, but more common is the barking California sea lion.

Coastal tidepools harbor clams, crabs, mussels, starfish, sand dollars, jellyfish, sponges, squids, sea anemones, and small octopi. (Look but don't touch: eager collectors and the just plain curious have almost wiped out tidepool communities.)

For those who enjoy eating mussels—steamed in butter, herbs, white wine, or even fried—find them on rocky sea coasts. People pry them off underwater rocks with tire irons, pickaxes, even screwdrivers. Keep these bivalves alive in buckets of cool, fresh seawater until you're ready to eat 'em. But *no* mussel collecting is allowed during the annual "red tide" (roughly May to October, but variable from year to year), when tiny red plankton proliferate. These plankton are fine food for mussels and other bivalves but are toxic to humans. (The red tide is less of a problem for clams, but to be on the safe side, just eat the white meat during the annual mussel quarantine.)

Anadromous Fish

North coast salmon, steelhead, and American shad are all anadromous, living in the sea but returning to freshwater streams to reproduce. Salmon and steelhead generally start their spawning runs up north coastal rivers between mid-November and late February (often earlier and later for steelhead), with distinct migration times between watersheds. There are five separate species of Pacific salmon along the coast, but nearly all are of the king and silver varieties. Unlike salmon, steelhead (large, ocean-going rainbow trout) don't die after reproducing and can spawn up to six times in a lifetime.

NORTH COAST HISTORY

A Portuguese sailor first sighted Cape Mendocino in 1543, but explorers avoided setting foot on the foreboding, darkly forested coastline due to the lack of natural harbors. According to some historians, Sir Francis Drake dropped anchor at Point Reyes in 1579, that landing most likely

a deer in wild parsnip

WES DEMPSEY

pivotal in convincing the Spanish to extend their mission chain from Mexico up the California coast to Sonoma.

But after Drake's "discovery" of the north coast, it took nearly three centuries for substantial settlement to occur. Misery was the common experience of early explorers. The intrepid Jedediah Smith nearly starved while trailblazing through the redwoods, called "a miserable forest prison" by other unlucky adventurers. The Russians arrived on California's north coast in the early 1800s to slaughter sea otters for fashionable fur coats and hats. Their Fort Ross complex on the coast north of the Russian River (now a fine state historic park) was built entirely of redwood. After the otters were all but obliterated, the Russians departed. So desperate for building materials and furniture was Sacramento's founder John Sutter that he traveled all the way up the coast to Fort Ross, purchasing (and dismantling) entire buildings for the lumber, also carting off rooms full of Fort Ross furnishings and tools.

With the gold rush and sudden onslaught of prospectors throughout the territory came new exploratory determination. The first settlements in California's far north, including the coastal towns of Eureka and Trinidad, started out as mining pack stations for inland gold mines. Then came redwood logging, a particularly hazardous undertaking in the early days, from felling to loading finished lumber onto schooners anchored off the rocky shoreline. (Most of the original logging towns and lumber "ports" have long since vanished.)

Now that the "harvesting" of the region's vast virgin redwood forests is all but complete, isolated protected groves, a few redwood state parks, and Redwood National Park offer at least an opportunity for increased tourism.

NORTH COAST ECONOMY

Depending upon the year, who's running for office, and whom you talk to, illicit marijuana growing pumps somewhere between $110 and $600 million into the north coast's economy each year. According to NORML, the National Organization for the Reform of Marijuana Laws, California leads the nation in pot production with an annual crop estimated at $2.55 billion. Tradi-

tionally, though, the lumber business has been the reigning industry, booming and busting along with construction and the dollar. Fluctuations in demand mean frequent unemployment and localized economic depressions.

Agriculture—sheep and cattle ranching, dairy farming, and commercial fishing—are less important overall, but dominant in certain areas. Recreation and tourism, along with related small businesses and service industries, are of growing importance, inviting incursions of "outsiders," which locals see as both a blessing and curse. There's begrudging gratitude for the money they spend and sometimes thinly disguised disgust for the foreign manners and mores that come with it.

NORTH COAST RECREATION

Despite predominantly private ownership and limited public access to the coast and forest lands, there's always something to do along California's north coast—walking, hiking, backpacking, beachcombing, biking, canoeing and kayaking, fishing, scuba diving (many of the

YUROK TIME

I like time before Darwin
and von Humboldt. I like Yurok
time, for example, when Umai
(a lonely girl) could sing herself
across the ocean into the world–
beyond–the–world

to visit the sunset and find
Laksis (Shining One), her nightly friend.
I like names without Latin:
seagull rather than Larinae,
stories without explanations,
a song for no reason,

a journey through the horizon
to unknowns without fear or shadow.
I like the sun going down
just now, a moment of gold
spraying out, a stunned instant when words
go back before books.

—Gary Thompson

THE POLITICS OF OFFSHORE OIL DRILLING: WHAT FUTURE THE NORTH COAST?

Along with other coastal areas, the unspoiled Northern California coast is destined for heavy industrialization—offshore oil drilling platforms, pipelines, oil tankers, processing plants, equipment-choked roads, and boom-bust economic turmoil—if the federal government leases massive offshore tracts to eager oil companies. Though an oil lease moratorium is in effect until the year 2000 unless there is an oil "supply disruption," the future of the north coast has yet to be decided, at least officially.

Original federal proposals to open up the Northern California coast for offshore oil drilling called for three-acre-sized offshore oil platforms. Not only has the idea not gone away during the past decade despite fairly consistent opposition up and down the coast, it has become more ambitious. The Department of the Interior's new national energy plan calls for 22-24 north coast oil platforms (more than California's current offshore total) and the leasing of an initial 1.1 million acres of ocean floor for oil exploration. The proposal will first affect the Eel River basin near Eureka and the Mendocino-Fort Bragg coastline between Point Delgada and Point Arena. Within five years of those developments, a total of 6.5 million acres of coastal territory, including Bodega Bay and San Francisco Bay, would be on the oil development auction block.

Despite former Governor George Deukmejian's earlier objections, the California Lands Commission recently declared the Mendocino-Humboldt seacoast part of the California marine sanctuary, which already protects most coastal areas from San Luis Obispo to Oregon. But since the state only has jurisdiction over waters within three miles of shore, that protection isn't enough; the federal government's territorial claim extends 20 miles out to sea. To circumvent the Interior Department's plans, environmentalists, other north coast community activists, and most California politicians support the establishment of a federal marine sanctuary.

As presented by the government and the oil companies, the benefits of mining the sea for oil include more jobs for economically depressed communities and at least a small step toward national energy self-sufficiency. Such arguments don't sway environmentalists and the majority of Californians, however. For one thing, they say, even the energy experts concede that the initial 1.1 million-acre offshore territory will yield at most 800 million gallons of oil—roughly equal to two months of the U.S. energy demand. The potential damages include the disruption of local fisheries, oil spills, and visual pollution. As one Eureka woman put it, drilling for oil off the north coast is like "rolling up a Rembrandt and selling it like a Presto Log."

state's coastal parks are also considered "underwater parks"), tidepooling, whitewater rafting, whalewatching. The region's rivers have good swimming holes, but ocean swimming isn't recommended (the water is cold, the coast rugged and ruthless, currents and undertows often treacherous) but determined surfers in wetsuits aren't uncommon.

Backpacking And Biking

Much of the north coast is privately owned and signed with gems like: No Trespassing: Violators Will Be Persecuted. Coupled with the fact that public lands can become pot war battlefields in spring, summer, and fall, choices for hikers are limited. But peaceful overnight trips are possible in **Redwood National Park,** and the nearby **Smith River National Recreation Area,** in the fantastically rugged **Sinkyone Wilderness** in the coastal **King Range,** also in larger state

parks like **Del Norte, Salt Point,** and **Humboldt Redwoods.** There's a thick finger of hikable national forest land stretching south through **Six Rivers National Forest.**

Bicyclists have problems here too, especially traveling along the coast. In most places Hwy. 1 is treacherously narrow, a paved rollercoaster ride advisable only for experienced cyclists. A good guide is *Bicycling the Pacific Coast* by Tom Kirkendall and Vicky Spring. For more southerly coast rides, consider some of the backcountry routes included in Phyllis Neumann's *Sonoma County Biketrails.* Inquire locally about mountain biking opportunities, usually abundant in national forests with old logging roads.

Beachcombing

Perfect for the less ambitious outdoorsperson is a casual stroll down the beach with an eye out for gifts from the sea. There are relatively few public beaches, as elsewhere in California, though public access is guaranteed even on private lands where the tradition of public use has been established. On the beach, find fishing floats, old bottles, an occasional old coin, polished agates, carnelian, jadeite, and jasper. The best places to troll for treasures are isolated beaches far from towns—eagle-eyed locals get out and about regularly, especially after storms.

Fishing, Clamming

Fish for something, somehow, year-round. Ocean anglers troll for silver and king salmon June through September (best in autumn when fish swarm in bays and lagoons near river-mouths). "Flatfish" including flounder, halibut, sole, turbot, and sand dabs are other popular ocean fish. North coast fishing enthusiasts also fish off the rocks for cabezon, greenling, ling cod, striped sea perch, and rockfish.

In spring, wading out for some "dip netting," trapping smelt with traditional native north coast A-frame nets, is challenging and tricky for beginners. (Spot a smelt school by the unusually tight cluster of fish-loving birds overhead.) The steelhead fishery is river-based. Serious river anglers: pick up Chronicle Books' *California Steelhead Fishing* and *California Trout Fishing* by Jim Freeman—detailed, firsthand guides to the best steelhead and trout fishing in California rivers, streams, and lakes.

For a slightly drier sport try clamming at low tide. The best clamming grounds north of Tomales and Drake's bays in Marin County are at Bodega Harbor and "the flats" of Humboldt Bay near Eureka and Arcata. But know your clams: limits and size restrictions vary from species to species. Find "little neck" clams and Japanese little necks a few inches below the surface in coarse gravel, using a trowel, rake, or garden hoe to dig for them. On sand bars are "big necks" or gapers, much larger and burrowed deep in the sand. (Spurts of water, little "clam geysers," show where to start digging—sometimes to depths of three feet or more. Serious sand clammers use metal tubes, more than a foot across, to prevent cave-ins while they're fast at work.) Under telltale siphon holes in soft mud are Washington clams, accessible with hooked rods. Also on beaches and along bayshores are bent-nose clams and basket cockles.

As noted elsewhere, public health warnings have been issued against consuming fish and seafood from the Eureka area, due to dioxin contamination.

River Trips

Also on the north coast are almost endless possibilities for whitewater rafting adventures. Kayaking, canoeing, even tubing are also possible in some areas. Without a doubt the best guide on the subject is *California White Water* by Jim Cassady and Fryar Calhoun, a very detailed and helpful introduction to remote back-country watersheds. But whitewater beginners should not go it alone on unfamiliar waters. For information about guided trips and licensed river guide companies, contact national forest offices and chambers of commerce. See also "The Northern Mountains" chapter.

Whalewatching

The California gray whale's travel habits mean the whalewatching season along the north coast is about six months long, from early December to early June. In December and January, you'll see the southward winter migration and from February until late spring the return trip—in straggly "pulses" of single adults and cow/calf pairs (new families traveling farther from shore). The best times to watch are mid-December through January, and all of March.

While whalewatching crowds at Point Reyes in Marin County create incredible traffic jams, the problem diminishes as you head farther north along the coast. Popular areas to whalewatch include **Bodega Head, Jenner, Fort Ross,** and **Salt Point State Park** in Sonoma County; **Gualala, Point Arena,** several vistas near **Mendocino,** and **Westport Union Landing State Beach** in Mendocino County; and **Shelter Cove, McKinleyville, Patrick's Point, Prairie Creek Redwoods,** and **Point St. George** farther north.

For an up-close look, contact the international **Oceanic Society,** Fort Mason Center, Building E, San Francisco 94123, tel. (415) 474-3385, an organization dedicated to protecting oceans and sealife, as well as to conducting maritime education and research and offering whalewatching boat trips.

Events And Festivals

The north coast has everything country folk could possibly have an interest in: county fairs, art festivals, harvest festivals, flea markets, wine tastings, ice-cream socials, marathon runs and bike races, backwoods hoedowns. Notably, some of the weirdest, most animistic goings-on you'll find anywhere in California happen here—everything from Mendocino's and Fort Bragg's **Whale Festival** in March to Klamath's traditional **Salmon Festival** in June. **Paul Bunyan Days** in Fort Bragg are *the* big deal. Along with the annual **Rhododendron Festival,** Eureka has its **Steam Donkey Days** (a logging festival) in April, the same month as Bodega Bay's **Fisherman's Festival and Blessing of the Fleet.** Quite out of the ordinary is the annual **Great Cross Country Kinetic Sculpture Race** from Arcata to Ferndale, featuring the most bizarre collection of homemade amphibious vehicles imaginable. Strictly aquatic, though, are the **Milk Carton Boat Races** each summer at Lake Benbow. Also every summer at Lake Benbow are performances of **Shakespeare,** and the **College of the Redwoods Star Show,** an all-night astronomy vigil. Check with state and national parks plus local chambers of commerce for comprehensive and current information.

THE SONOMA COAST

Northern California beaches are different from the gentler, kinder sandy beaches of the southstate. The coast here is wild. In stark contrast to the softly rounded hillsides landward, the Sonoma County coast presents a dramatically rugged face and an aggressive personality: undertows, swirling offshore eddies, riptides, and deadly "sleeper" or "rogue" waves. It pays to pay attention along the Sonoma coast. Since 1950, over 70 people have been killed here by sleepers, waves that come out of nowhere to wallop the unaware then drag them into the surf and out to sea. October is generally the worst month of the year.

But it is also one of the best months: in September and October the summertime shroud of fog usually lifts and the sea sparkles. Except on weekends, by autumn most Bay Area and tourist traffic has dried up like the area's seasonal streams, and it's possible to be alone with the wild things.

BODEGA BAY

Alfred Hitchcock considered this quaint coastal fishing village and the inland town of Bodega perfect for filming *The Birds,* with its rather ominous suggestion that one day nature will avenge itself. But people come to Bodega Bay and vicinity to avoid thinking about such things. They come to explore the headlands, to whalewatch, to beachcomb and tidepool, to catch and eat seafood (including local Dungeness crab), to peek into the increasing numbers of galleries and gift shops that keep locals alive, to *relax.* Bodega Bay's **Fisherman's Festival and Blessing of the Fleet** in April attracts upward of 25,000 people for the Mardi Gras-style boat parade, also kite-flying championships, bathtub and foot races, art shows, and barbecue. Ochlophobes, steer clear.

Just wandering through town and along the harbor is fascinating. Here and in the town of Bodega, look for Hitchcock settings: the cinematically foreboding schoolhouse (now a bed and breakfast), the coffee shop near the phone booth where Tippi Hedren was assaulted by feathered terrorists. Or watch the fishing fleet and chartered "party boats" at the harbor.

Near Bodega Bay and stretching north to Jenner are the slivers of collectively managed **Sonoma Coast State Beaches,** which include **Bodega Head** and **Bodega Dunes** near the bay itself. Inland are a variety of small spots-in-the-road, some little more than a restaurant or boarded-up gas station at a crossroads, all connected to Bodega Bay by scenic rollercoaster roads. Not far south of town in Marin County is **Dillon Beach,** known for its tidepools. Keep going south via Hwy. 1 to the sensational **Point Reyes National Seashore.**

History

Though Cabrillo and his crew were probably the first Europeans to spot the area, the Spanish lieutenant Don Juan Francisco de la Bodega y Cuadra anchored the *Sonora* off Bodega Head

THE SONOMA - MENDOCINO COAST

PACIFIC OCEAN

© MOON PUBLICATIONS, INC.

in October 1775 and named it after himself (breaking with the more modest tradition of using saints' names corresponding to the day of discovery). Ivan Kuskov, an agent of the powerful Russian-American Fur Company, arrived in Bodega Bay from Sitka, Alaska, in 1809. He and his company grew wheat inland, hunted sea otters, then returned to Alaska with full cargo holds. Two years later they built three settlements—Port Rumianstov on the bay, and the towns of Bodega and Kuskov inland—before the construction of Fort Ross began farther north. American settlers first arrived in 1835, increasing after the Russians left in the 1840s. Bodega Harbor was a bustling seaport by the 1860s, though large oceangoing vessels haven't anchored here for over a century.

Bodega Area Recreation

All popular along the Sonoma County coast: birdwatching, collecting driftwood, tidepooling, surf and rock fishing, hiking, bicycling the area's strikingly scenic backroads, whalewatching. Best yet, though—all these activities are free.

For good swimmers, "free-diving" for abalone (scuba gear is considered unsporting) is a special treat. Diving season is April 1 through the end of June, then August 1 through November, assuming the abalone population is adequate for harvest. Abalone divers are required to get a California fishing license, carry a shell gauge (minimum size is seven inches across at the shell's broadest point) and a legal abalone iron, and can take no more than four abalone. According to new information about these creatures' lifestyles, abalone move toward the shore in winter, farther out to sea in summer. So it's no wonder that "shore picking" at low tide is dismal.

Near Jenner at the mouth of the Russian River, a large population of harbor seals has established itself, attracting considerable human attention. Unlike sea lions, which amble along on flippers, harbor seals wriggle like inchworms until in the water, where their mobility instantly improves. On weekends, volunteer naturalists wearing orange vests (members of Stewards of Slavianka) are here to answer questions, lend binoculars for a close-up look, and protect the seals from unleashed dogs and too-curious tourists. When panicked, harbor seals will protect themselves by biting. Some carry diseases difficult to treat in humans (which is why sailors of old used to cut off a limb if it was seal-bitten).

"Pupping season" starts in March and continues into June. During these months, harbor seals and their young become vulnerable to more predators, since they give birth on land. Some worry that Jenner's large seal colony will attract other enthusiastic observers too, like sharks and killer whales. Not known to attack humans (though no one will guarantee that), killers also consider harbor seals a delicacy. To avoid predators, harbor seals swim upriver as far as Monte Rio while fishing for their own prey, salmon and steelhead.

Another fairly recent tradition has become an annual event: the **Sonoma Coastwalk,** a one-week summer walking and camping trip from Gualala south to the Bodega Bay area, organized to promote environmental awareness and the one-day dream of a continuous coastal trail from San Francisco to the Oregon border. There's a **Marin Coastwalk** too, usually held in conjunction with Sonoma's.

For more information on the area contact the **Bodega Bay Chamber of Commerce,** 555 Hwy. 1, Bodega Bay 94923, tel. (707) 875-3422.

Bodega Area Accommodations

Camp at **Bodega Dunes** just north of the harbor, at smaller **Wrights Beach** on the way to Jenner, or at primitive **Willow Creek Campground** near Goat Rock. (For more information on these state park campgrounds, see "Sonoma Coast State Beaches" below). **Doran Beach County Park** to the south has first-come, first-camped primitive outdoor accommodations. For information, contact the park, P.O. Box 372, Bodega Bay 94923, tel. (707) 875-3540. For camping reservations at Doran (also for Sonoma County campgrounds at Stillwater Cove and Gualala Point farther north), call toll-free in California (800) 822-CAMP, outside California call (800) 824-CAMP. Another possibility is the private **Porto Bodega Fisherman's Marina and RV Park,** 1500 Bay Flat Rd., tel. (707) 875-2354.

In town, the hotspot is the **Inn at the Tides** at 800 Hwy. 1, P.O. Box 640, Bodega Bay 94923, tel. (707) 875-2751 or toll-free (800) 541-7788; rooms $130-175, including amenities, views, and continental breakfast. Another fairly expensive choice is the **Bodega Bay Lodge,** off the highway on Doran Beach Rd., P.O. Box 357, tel. 875-3525 or toll-free (800) 528-1234; rates $118-198, continental breakfast included. Both places offer pool, sauna, whirlpool, TV and movies, phones, many rooms with fireplaces. Also quite nice is the **Bodega Coast Inn** at 521 Hwy. 1, P.O. Box 55, tel. (707) 875-2217 or toll-free (800) 346-6999, with high-season weekend rates of $130-180. In the Bodega Bay area as elsewhere, inquire about winter and weekday specials.

The **Sea Horse Ranch,** a few miles north of Bodega Bay on Hwy. 1, tel. (707) 875-3386, is a working horse and sheep spread that also boards people ($65-125), wonderful food and horseback riding extra. The **Inn at Valley Ford,** south of Bodega Bay, tel. 876-3182, is a cozy coast bed and breakfast with old-fashioned garden, fireplace, antique-stuffed rooms, $50-75 with breakfast (homemade breads). **The School House Inn,** 17110 Bodega Lane, Bodega 94922, tel. 876-3257, is one of the area's bed and breakfasts. A stay here includes continental breakfast, $70-80. Quite different in the bed and breakfast category is the **Bodega Vista Inn,** 17699 Hwy. 1, Bodega 94922, tel. 876-3300, a modern geodesic dome with hot tub, private baths, continental breakfast; rooms from $75, weekday specials.

Very new is the **Bay Hill Mansion** at 3919 Bay Hill Rd., tel. (707) 875-3577, a Queen Anne Victorian-style inn circa 1989 with five rooms (two share a bath) deck, hot tub, panoramic views, full breakfast. Rates: $80-150. Another possibility, inland, is the **Green Apple Inn** at 520 Bohemian Hwy. in Freestone, tel. 874-2526, an 1862 New England-style farmhouse featuring four rooms with private baths, full breakfast, rates $82-88.

Bodega Area Food

Get fresh fish and chips, even hot seafood to go, at popular **Lucas Wharf Deli and Fish Market** on the pier at the harbor, tel. (707) 875-3562. The adjacent sit-down **Lucas Wharf Restaurant,** tel. 875-3522, is open for lunch and dinner and is known for its pastas and steaks as well as seafood. Great clam chowder, fisherman's stew, sourdough bread. A bit more spiffy and adjacent is **The Tides Wharf Restaurant,** tel. 875-3652, which overlooks the bay near the wharf (and has its own dock and video arcade). It's quite popular for breakfast, and you can count on fresh seafood at lunch and dinner. Open daily; there's a fresh fish market and bait shop here too. The **Whaler's Inn** at 1805 Hwy. 1, tel. 875-2829, is the town's "country kitchen," open daily for breakfast, lunch, and dinner and serving fresh American-style specialties, from seafood and chicken-fried steak to barbecued ribs. (No checks or credit cards.) If out and about anyway, the hamburgers ("giant hamburgers") are great at **Rocco's Cafe,** a one-time gas station in Freestone.

But to drive somewhere in order to totally enjoy sitting down again, head out Hwy. 1 to Valley Ford, the town made famous by Christo's Running Fence. The frumpy white frame building is **Dinucci's,** tel. (707) 876-3260, a fantastically fun watering hole and dinner house. Study the massive rosewood bar inside, shipped around Cape Horn, while waiting for a table (folks are allowed to linger over meals). The walls in the bar are almost papered in decades-old political posters, old newspaper clippings, and an eclectic collection of lighthearted local memorabilia. The dim barroom lighting reflects off the hundreds of abalone shells decorating the ceiling. Dinucci's boisterous family-style dining room has close-together, sometimes shared (it's either that or keep waiting) checkerboard-clothed tables and a very friendly serving staff. Dinner starts with antipasto, a vat of very good homemade minestrone, fresh bread, salad, followed by seafood or pasta entrees and desserts. For $10 or so, after eating here people can barely walk to their cars.

SONOMA COAST STATE BEACHES

Most of the spectacular 13 miles of coastline between Bodega Bay and Jenner is owned by the state. The collective **Sonoma Coast State Beaches** are composed of pointy-headed offshore rock formations or "sea stacks," natural arches, and a series of secluded beaches and small coves with terrific tidepools. Don't even think about swimming here (though diving is a possibility in certain areas), since the cold water, heavy surf, undertows, and sleeper waves all add up to danger. But for beachcombing, ocean fishing, a stroll or a jog—perfect. Here and farther north at **Patrick's Point State Park,** rangers offer weekend whalewatching programs from mid-December through mid-April.

Bodega Head And Vicinity

Hulking **Bodega Head** to the north, protecting Bodega Bay from the heavy seas, is the bulwark for the state's area beaches. Good whalewatching from here. Nearby is the University of California's **Bodega Bay Marine Station,** a marine biology research center, open to the public every Friday. Hike on and around the head on well-worn footpaths, or head out for an invigorating walk via hiking trails to **Bodega Dunes.** Five miles of hiking and horseback riding trails twist through the dunes themselves (access at the north end of the bay, via W. Bay Road). To get to Bodega Head, take Westshore Rd. and follow the signs past **Westside Park.**

Doran County Park on the south side of the bay (day-use fee) looks bleak, but these windswept beaches and dunes provide safe harbor for diverse wildlife and hardy plants. Swim at these protected beaches; also good clamming. Or visit the water-filled sump once destined for the nuclear age (called "hole in the head" and "the world's most expensive duck-pond" by bemused locals). With Hitchcock's nature-vengeance theme in mind, we can only shudder at what might have been if PG&E had built its proposed nuclear power plant here, just four miles from the San Andreas Fault.

Other Sonoma Coast Beach Areas

Sprinkled like garnish between the various state beaches from Bodega Bay north to Jenner are a variety of **public beaches,** including **Miwok, Coleman, Arched Rock, Carmet, Schoolhouse, Marshall Gulch, Goat Rock, Shell,** and **Blind beaches.** First north of Bodega Bay among the state beaches is **Salmon Creek Beach,** part of which becomes a lagoon when sand shuts the creek's mouth. **Portuguese Beach,** best for rock fishing and surf fishing, is a sandy beach surrounded by rocky headlands. Plan a picture-perfect picnic near **Rock Point** on the headland (tables available). **Duncans Landing** midway to Jenner is also referred to as **Death Rock,** a former offshore lumber-loading spot during the redwood harvesting heyday and today one of the most dangerous spots along the Sonoma coast. Farther north is **Shell Beach,** best for beachcombing and seaside strolls, with

some tremendous tidepools and good fishing.

It's a spectacularly snaky road from Hwy. 1 down to dramatic Goat Rock, popular **Goat Rock Beach,** and the dunes just east. The craggy goat itself is an impressive promontory but illegal to climb around on: more than a dozen people have drowned in recent years, swept off the rocks by surging surf. In the **Willow Creek** area near the mouth of the Russian River are hiking trails and simple campground facilities.

Beach Practicalities

Along this stretch there are plentiful pulloffs for parking cars, with access to beach trails and spectacular views. Day use for the Sonoma Coast Beaches is $5. Camp at **Wright's Beach,** with 30 developed campsites (but no showers) just back from the beach. **Bodega Dunes,** a half mile south of Salmon Creek, has 98 developed sites secluded among the cypress-dotted dunes, with hot showers plus an RV sanitation station and a campfire center. Developed Sonoma Coast campsites are reservable in advance through Mistix, tel. (800) 444-7275. New is primitive walk-in camping at **Willow Creek** (no dogs). Reserve through Mistix, or register at the **Salmon Creek Ranger Station** just north of Bodega Bay.

For current conditions and other information, contact: **Sonoma Coast State Beaches,** Salmon Creek Ranger Station, Bodega Bay 94923, tel. (707) 875-3483.

FORT ROSS STATE HISTORIC PARK

A large village of the Kashia Pomo people once stood here. After the Russian-American Fur Company (Czar Alexander I and President James Madison were both company officers) established its fur-trapping settlements at Bodega Bay, the firm turned its attention northward to what, in the spring of 1812, became **Fort Ross,** imperial Russia's farthest outpost. Here the Russians grew grains and vegetables to supply Alaskan colonists as well as Californios, manufactured a wide variety of products, and trapped sea otters to satisfy the voracious demand for fine furs. With pelts priced at $700 each, no trapping technique went untried. One of the most effective: grabbing a sea otter pup and using its distress calls to lure otherwise wary adults into range.

The Russians' success here and elsewhere in California, which led to the virtual extinction of the sea otter, combined with devastating agricultural losses (due to greedy gophers) to bring serious economic problems. These worsened when attempts at commercial shipbuilding also failed. The Russians got out from under only by leaving, after selling Fort Ross and all its contents to John Sutter. Sutter (who agreed to the $30,000 price but never made a payment) carried off most of the equipment, furnishings, tools, and whatever else he could use to improve his own fort. Sutter's empire building eventually required James Marshall to head up the American River to build a sawmill. Marshall's discovery of gold led to Sutter's instant ruin but also to the almost overnight Americanization of California.

The First Fort

The weathered redwood fortress perched on these lonely headlands, surrounded by gloomy cypress groves, was home to Russian traders and trappers for 40 years. The original 14-foot-high stockade featured corner lookouts and 40 cannon. Inside the compound were barracks, a jail, the commandant's house, warehouses, and workshops. At the fort and just outside its walls, the industrious Russians and their work crews produced household goods plus saddles, bridles, even 200-ton ships and prefabricated houses.

Perhaps due to the Russian Orthodox belief that only God is perfect, there were—and are—no right angles anywhere. The fort's Greek Orthodox chapel was the only building here destroyed by the 1906 San Francisco earthquake. It was rebuilt, then lost again to arson in 1970, though it's since been reconstructed from the original blueprints fetched from Moscow. Outside the stockade was a bustling town of Aleut hunters' redwood huts, with a windmill and various outbuildings and shops. When the Russians at Fort Ross finally prepared to leave their failed American empire, the Pomo held a mourning ceremony to mark their departure—a testament to the visitors' amicable long-term relations with the native peoples.

The Reconstructed Fort, Other Facilities

A good place to start exploring Fort Ross is at its new million-dollar **visitor center** and museum,

Greek Orthodox Church at Fort Ross

CALIFORNIA DEPARTMENT OF PARKS AND RECREATION

which includes a good introductory slide program (shown throughout the day in the auditorium), Pomo artifacts and basketry, other historic displays, period furnishings, gift shop. The free **audio tour** of the fort is itself entertaining (balalaika music, hymns, and Princess Helena Rotchev—namesake of Mt. St. Helena near Calistoga—playing Mozart on the piano).

The fort's only remaining original building (now restored) is the commandant's quarters. Other reconstructed buildings include the barracks furnished as if Russians would sail up and bed down any minute, and the artisans' center and armory.

Practicalities

Just 12 miles north of Jenner along Hwy. 1, Fort Ross is open to the public 10 a.m.-4:30 p.m. daily (except major holidays), $5 per car. (Autophobes, get here via **Mendocino Transit** buses daily from the north, tel. 707-964-1800, or **Sonoma County Transit** from Jenner, tel. 707-585-7516 or toll-free 800-345-7433.) With fewer people around, it's easier to imagine the overwhelming feeling of isolation once surrounding Fort Ross. On **Living History Day** in July or August, the colony here suddenly comes back to life circa 1836. History buffs, have fun questioning repertory company volunteers to see if they know their stuff. The park's size has tripled recently with the addition of ridgetop redwoods behind the fort and a beach, along with other lands to the north and east. And thanks to the Sonoma County Coastwalk organization, new hiking access (including a handicapped-accessible trail) is also being added to the Black Ranch Park area south of the fort. Ask at the visitor center for current hiking information.

New at Fort Ross is the first-come, first-camped primitive **Fort Ross Reef State Campground** tucked into a ravine just south of the fort, once a private camp for abalone divers; 20 campsites, no dogs.

For more information, contact: **Fort Ross State Historic Park,** 19005 Hwy. 1, Jenner 95450, tel. (707) 847-3286.

Timber Cove

Hard to miss even in the fog, the landmark eight-story **Benjamin Bufano** *Peace* **sculpture** looms over Timber Cove Inn and surrounding countryside. Once a "doghole port" for lumber schooners, like most craggy north coast indentations, Timber Cove is now a haven for the affluent. But ordinary people can stop for a look at Bufano's last, unfinished work. From the hotel parking lot, walk seaward and look up into the the face of Peace, reigning over land and sea.

If camping's too primitive, try the unusually fine outback accommodations available at the **Timberhill Ranch** on the former site of an alternative school about four miles inland from the highway near Salt Point and the Kruse Reserve, 35755 Hauser Bridge Rd., Cazadero 95421, tel. (707) 847-3258. Lodge and cabins, fine food, total rest and relaxation. Rates on the modified American plan, run $205-300, lower weekdays. Dinner is a six-course feast, exceptional. Swimming pool whirlpool, tennis courts, birdwatching, hiking, fishing. Cabins with queen beds, fireplaces, wet bars. Advance reservations (at least a month ahead) wise on weekends.

SALT POINT STATE PARK AND KRUSE RHODODENDRON PRESERVE

This 3,500-acre park adjoining the seasonally astounding Kruse Rhododendron Preserve is most often compared to Point Lobos on the Monterey Peninsula. Among Salt Point's natural attributes are dramatic outcroppings, tidepools and coves (this is one of the state's first official underwater preserves), wave-sculpted sandstone, lonely wind-whipped headlands, and highlands including a pygmy forest of stunted cypress, pines, and redwoods.

Though most people visit only the seaward side of the park—to dive or to examine the park's honeycombed *tafoni* rock—the best real hiking is across the road within the park's inland extension (pick up a map to the park when you enter).

Among Salt Point's other attractions are the dunes and several old Pomo village sites. In season, berrying, fishing, and mushrooming are favorite activities. Park rangers lead hikes and sponsor other occasional programs on weekends and are also available to answer questions during the seasonal migration of the gray whales. The platform at Sentinel Rock is a great perch for whalewatching.

Kruse Rhododendron Preserve

This is an almost-natural wonder. Nowhere else on earth does *Rhododendron californicum* grow to such heights and in such profusion, in such perfect harmony—under a canopy of redwoods. Here at the 317-acre preserve, an unplanted and uncultivated native garden of rhododendrons up to 30 feet tall thrive in well-lit yet cool second-growth groves of coast redwoods, Douglas fir, tan oak, and madrone. (Lumbermen downed the virgin forest, unintentionally benefitting the rhododendrons, which need cool moist conditions but more sunshine than denser stands of redwoods offer.) The dominant shrub is the *Rhododendron macrophyllum* or California rosebay, actually quite common throughout the Pacific Northwest. Also here is the *Rhododendron occidentale* or western azalea, with its cream-colored flowers.

Most people say the best time to cruise into Kruse is in April or May when the rhododendrons' spectacular pink bloom is at its finest. (Peak blooming time varies from year to year, so call ahead for current guestimates.) Sublime too is a bit earlier in spring between sweetsmelling rainstorms, when the rhododendron buds just start to show color and the tiny woods orchids, violets, and trillium still bloom among the Irish-green ferns and mossy redwood stumps. But come anytime; the song of each season has its own magic note.

To get here from Hwy. 1, head east a short distance via Kruse Ranch Road. Coming in via the backwoods route from Cazadero is an adventure in itself, especially if the necessary signs have been taken down (again) by locals. To try it, better call ahead first for precise directions. Facilities at the preserve are appropriately minimal but include picnic tables and outhouses. For bloom predictions and preserve conditions, call (707) 865-2391.

Practicalities

Among its other superlatives, Salt Point is also prime for camping. The park has tent and RV campsites with hot showers, $14, as well as walk-in, bike-in, and environmental campsites. Make reservations, at least during the summer high season, through Mistix, tel. (800) 444-7275. Very pleasant picnicking here, too. Day-use fee: $5 per carload (dogs $1 extra). For more information about the park and the Kruse Rhodo-

dendron Preserve, contact: Salt Point State Park, 25050 Hwy. 1, Jenner 95450, tel. (707) 847-3221 or 865-2391.

Stewarts Point

Heading north from Salt Point, stop at the weatherbeaten **Stewarts Point Store,** just to appreciate the 120-plus years of tradition the Richardson family has stuffed into every nook and cranny. You can buy almost anything, from canned goods and fresh vegetables to rubber boots and camp lanterns (and if they don't have it, they'll order it). Not for sale are items creating the store's ambience: the abalone shells and stuffed fish hanging from the ceiling, horse collars, oxen yoke, turn-of-the-century fish traps, and an 1888 Studebaker baby buggy.

SEA RANCH

Almost since its inception, controversy has been the middle name of this 5,200-acre sheep ranch-cum-exclusive vacation home subdivision. No one could have imagined the ranch's significance in finally resolving long-fought battles over California coastal access and coastal protection. It was here in the 1970s that much of the war over beach access took place, ending with the establishment of the California Coastal Commission.

Sea Ranch architects get rave reviews for their simple, box-like, high-priced condominiums and homes, which emulate weatherbeaten local barns. The much-applauded cluster development design allowed "open space" for the aesthetic well-being of residents and passersby alike but no way to get to the 10 miles of state-owned coastline without trespassing.

In 1972 Proposition 20 theoretically opened access, but the *reality* of beach access through Sea Ranch was achieved only in late 1985, when four of the six public trails across the property were ceremoniously, officially dedicated.

Sights, Practicalities

On the northern edge of the spread is the new and gnomish stone and stained-glass **Sea Ranch Chapel,** designed by James Hubbell. Inside it's serene as a redwood forest. From the outside, the cedar-roofed chapel looks like an abstract artist's interpretation of a mushroom, perhaps a wave, maybe even a UFO from the Ice Age. What is it? Nice for meditation or prayer, if the door's unlocked.

For those who salivate over Sea Ranch and can afford the rates, consider an overnight stay (or maybe just a meal) at the **Sea Ranch Lodge,** 60 Seawalk Dr., Sea Ranch 95497, tel. (707) 785-2371; pretty and plush accommodations looking out over the Pacific, some rooms with fireplaces and private hot tubs, plus golf course, pools, saunas. Rates are in the $100 range (lower in winter).

UP THE MENDOCINO COAST

Gualala

Though people in the area generally say whatever they please, Gualala is supposedly pronounced Wah-LA-la, the word itself Spanish for the Pomos' *wala'li* or "meeting place of the waters." Crossing the Gualala River means crossing into Mendocino County. On the way to Gualala from Sea Ranch is **Del Mar Landing,** an ecological reserve of virgin coastline with rugged offshore rocks, tidepools, and harbor seals. Get here on the trail running south from Gualala Point Regional Park, a "gift" from Sea Ranch developers, or via Sea Ranch trails.

Life in this old lumber town still centers on the 1903 **Gualala Hotel,** tel. (707) 884-3441, a loud and lively bar and restaurant where haute cuisine is hearty food: chicken, fried shrimp, spaghetti. Open for dinner 6-9 p.m., weekends 5-10 p.m. (For fine dining, head to St. Orres—see below.) The hotel also offers 19 newly renovated rooms. For simpler accommodations camp at **Gualala Point Regional Park,** two miles beyond Gualala, with coastal access and two separate campgrounds (no RVs), or at **Gualala River Park** south of town, tel. 884-3533, with 142 RV and tent sites.

Saint Orres

Some rock 'n' roll-literate wits refer to a sit-down dinner at **St. Orres** north of Gualala, with its ornate onion-domed architecture, as "sitting in the dacha of the bay." Dazzling in all its Russian-style redwood and stained-glass glory, St. Orres, 36601 S. Hwy. 1, Gualala 95445, tel. (707) 884-3303 or 884-3335 (restaurant), is also a great place to stay. For peace, quiet, and total relaxation, nothing beats an overnight in one of the 11 handcrafted redwood cabins scattered through the forest, or in one of the eight lodge rooms (shared bathrooms). Rates $50-200. Come morning, breakfast is delivered to the door in a basket.

Even if they don't stay here, people come from miles around to eat at St. Orres, known for its creative French-style fare. The fixed-price dinners feature such things as a salad of greens and edible flowers from the garden, cold strawberry soup, puff pastry with goat cheese and prosciutto, venison with blackberries, salmon and very fresh seafood in season, wonderful desserts, good wines. Before dinner, sit outside and watch the sun set. Reservations a must, a month or more in advance.

Other Gualala Area Luxury Stays

For those who can afford it, a stay at the **Whale Watch Inn By The Sea,** perched on the cliffs overlooking Anchor Bay north of Gualala, is just this side of coastal condo heaven. The Whale Watch, 35100 Hwy. 1, Gualala 95445, tel. (707) 884-3667, is the kind of place where decadence and decency both reign and Debussy pours out over the intercom. Contemporary and elegant rooms with fireplaces and fresh flowers, decks, whirlpool tubs, some with kitchens, $160-250. Attendants bring breakfast to the door. Reservations a good idea.

Nearby is the **North Coast Country Inn** at 34591 S. Hwy. 1, tel. (707) 884-4537, redwood in the rustic mood with antiques and ocean views, library, fireplaces, kitchens, private decks. Antique store, too, not to mention gazebo, hot tub, full breakfast. Four rooms with private baths go for $115 per night. The **Gualala Country Inn,** tel. 884-4343, and the **Seacliff,** tel. 884-1213, offer in-room spas, fireplaces, ocean views, and more contemporary pleasures.

The **Old Milano Hotel,** listed on the National Register of Historic Places, 38300 Hwy. 1, Gualala 95445, tel. (707) 884-3256, is a fine bed and breakfast, Victorian style. Six rooms share two baths, but three have private baths. One room features the canopied bed where Cathy (Merle Oberon) lay before Heathcliff (Lawrence Olivier) carried her to the window for one last look at the moors. There's a "caboose" room not far from the main house, with wood stove, terrace, and observation cupola. Hot tub, full breakfast. Rooms $75-160.

POINT ARENA AND VICINITY

Farther north is remote Point Arena, "discovered" by Captain George Vancouver in 1792. Point Arena, another good spot for whalewatching, was the busiest port between San Francisco and Eureka in the 1870s. When a local pier was wiped out by rogue waves in 1983, the already depressed local fishing and logging economy took yet another dive. Now Point Arena has a new pier—folks can fish here, no license required—and a new economic boon: the sea urchin harvest, to satisfy the Japanese taste for *uni*. "New" too is **The Arena,** a 1927-vintage vaudeville theater, fully refurbished and open for concerts and stage productions as well as foreign, "art," and mainstream films.

Point Arena Lighthouse
A monument to the area's historically impressive ship graveyard, the Coast Guard's six-story, automated 380,000-candlepower lighthouse is open to visitors (limited hours) small donation requested. This lighthouse was the first in the U.S. built of steel-reinforced concrete, a 1908 construction that replaced the original brick tower that came tumbling down two years earlier. The adjacent **museum** tells tales of the hapless ships that floated their last here.

Point Arena Practicalities
Eat at the **Arena Cove Bar & Grill,** tel. (707) 882-2189, a safe bet for breakfast, lunch, or dinner (closed Mondays, bar open until midnight). **La Boube's Sea Shell Motel** at 135 Main, tel. 882-2068, has decent rooms with cable TV, phones, morning coffee, reasonable rates. The **Coast Guard House** bed and breakfast at 695 Arena Cove, tel. 882-2442, is a 1901 Cape Cod with six guest rooms (two share a bath), queen or double beds, expanded continental breakfast. Rates: $75-135. **Wagner's Windhaven** at 46760 Iversen Ln., tel. 884-4617, is a contemporary Cape Cod with two rooms and a cottage with whirlpool and fireplace, all with ocean views, full breakfast. Rates: $100-115.

Near Point Arena are some unusual accommodation options. To help protect the lighthouse and preserve public access (no government support has been available), local volunteer lighthouse keepers maintain and rent out "vacation rental homes" (actually somewhat bleak U.S. government-issue houses abandoned by the Coast Guard), a good deal for families. For more information and reservations, contact: **Point Arena Lighthouse Keepers,** Inc., P.O. Box 11, Point Arena 95468, tel. (707) 882-2777.

Manchester State Beach
A 760-acre park just north of Point Arena, foggy in summer and cold in winter, with a long stretch of sandy beach and dunes dotted with driftwood. Good birding at the lagoon. Also interesting here is the opportunity for some walk-in environmental camping, about a mile past the parking area. For more information about Manchester and a camping map, contact the **Mendocino State Parks** office, tel. (707) 937-5804. Once here, it's first-come, first-camped, with an opportunity to personally experience those predictable summer northeasterlies as they whistle through your tent. (For wimps, there's a private, more protected **KOA** campground adjacent to the park office.)

Elk
The tiny town of Elk perches on the coastal bluffs farther north. Elk was once a lumber-loading port known as Greenwood, hence **Greenwood Creek Beach State Park** across from the store, with good picnicking among the bluff pines, also a popular push-off point for sea kayakers. Elk is also home to the all-redwood **Harbor House** bed and breakfast, noted for its fine dining, at 5600 S. Hwy. 1, P.O. Box 369, Elk 95432, tel. (707) 877-3203; rates $121-230. Included in a stay here are full breakfast and dinners plus access to a private strip of beach. Also here is the **Elk Cove Inn,** 6300 S. Hwy. 1, P.O. Box 367, tel. 877-3321, offering seven rooms in the 1883 Victorian (upper level parlor and deck) plus four ocean-view cabins, full breakfast. Rates: $108-148. The **Griffin House at Greenwood Cove,** 5910 S. Hwy. 1, tel. 877-3422, is actually flower gardens and cozy cottages, three with sun decks and ocean views, all with private baths and woodstoves, full breakfast served in your room. Rates: $95-135. Other bed and breakfasts include the **Sandpiper House Inn,** 5520 S. Hwy. 1, P.O. Box 49, tel. 877-3587, a 1916 Victorian Craftsman with four rooms (two with fireplaces), full breakfast, rates $80-160; and the **Green Dolphin Inn** at 6145 S. Hwy. 1, P.O. Box 132, tel. 877-3342, a 1979 saltbox with three rooms, hot tub, full breakfast, rates $85-125.

MENDOCINO

People just love Mendocino. As a matter of fact, people are loving Mendocino to death. Not even 1,000 people live here, yet the community is usually clogged with people, pets, and parked cars. Mendocino-area rental homes are inhabited in summer and at other "peak" times, but in the dead of winter locals can barely find a neighbor to talk to. Almost no one who *lives* here can afford to now, but when it was exactly that things started to change for the worse—well, that depends on who you talk to.

The Arts And "Culture Vultures"

In the 1950s, when nearby forests had been logged over and the lumbermill was gone and the once bad and bawdy doghole port of Mendocino City was fading fast, the artists arrived. Living out the idea of making this coastal backwater home were prominent San Francisco painters like Dorr Bothwell, Emmy Lou Packard, and Bill Zacha, who founded the still-strong Mendocino Art Center in 1959. Soon all the arts were in full bloom on these blustery bluffs and the town had come alive. But even back then, as *Johnny Belinda* film crews rolled through Mendocino streets and James Dean showed up for the filming of *East of Eden,* old-timers and retirees could see what was coming. The town's possibilities could very well destroy it.

In the decades since, the costs of living and doing business in Mendocino have gotten so high that most of Mendocino's artists' community have long since crawled out of town with their creative tails between their legs—pushed out, locals say, by the more affluent "culture vultures" who consume other people's creativity. Though there are many fine artists, craftspeople, performers, and writers (including Alice Walker) working throughout Mendocino County, most art, crafts, and consumables sold in Mendocino shops are imported from elsewhere. Even finding a local place to park is nearly impossible in Mendocino, a town too beautiful for its own good, parked at the edge of one of the most sublime coastlines in California.

MENDOCINO SIGHTS

To stroll the streets of Mendocino or explore the headlands at the moodiest, most renewing time, come in November or January. This is the only time of year when Mendocino is still itself and can slip back to a time before this wood-frame New Englandesque village was even an idea. A sense of that self blasts in from the bleak headlands in winter, blowing rural reality back into town. In winter meet the community, the

CALIFORNIA DEPARTMENT OF PARKS & RECREATION

Mendocino

fishermen, fourth-generation loggers, first-generation marijuana farmers, apple and sheep ranchers, artists and craftspeople, even city-fleeing innkeepers and shopkeepers as they too come out of hiding and take off their masks.

A good first stop is the nonprofit **Mendocino Art Center**, 45200 Little Lake St. (between Williams and Kasten), P.O. Box 765, Mendocino 95460, tel. (707) 937-5818. Though not without its occasional political problems, like most community-involved organizations worth their salt, this place is a wonder, a genuine *center* for county-wide arts awareness and artistic expression, sponsoring ceramics, textiles, and weaving apprenticeships, fine arts programs, an art library, a separate center in Fort Bragg, also its own free *Arts and Entertainment* magazine, which lists almost every upcoming event in the county. Whatever is going on here, in Fort Bragg, and in clubs and galleries throughout Mendocino County, someone at the center knows about it. In **The Gallery** and **The Showcase** here are exhibits of member artists plus special outside shows of fine arts and crafts. The center also features three large studios, with the emphasis on textiles and fiber arts, ceramics, and fine arts, respectively. Since the belief here is that art should be accessible to everyone, the art center sponsors weekend art classes from Sept. to June, and in summer offers three-week workshops. Very reasonable (shared) accommodations are available in center-sponsored apartments with kitchenettes; if that's not feasible, the art center staff will help with other arrangements.

The number of art galleries in and around Mendocino is staggering. Some seem strictly oriented to the tourist trade while others are serious, sophisticated. South of town in Little River is the **Gallery Glendeven,** tel. (707) 937-0083, with quilted paper and other textile works, abstract art, and handcrafted furniture. A veritable fine furniture and woodworking emporium in town is the three-story **Highlight Gallery** at 45052 Main, tel. 937-3132, which also displays handwoven textiles. For fine jewelry in addition to handcrafted furniture, peek into **Gallery Fair** at Ukiah and Kasten, tel. 937-5121. **Gallery Mendocino** at 45062 Ukiah, tel. 937-0214, primarily features work by local artists, including block prints by Emmy Lou Packard, a protégé of Diego Rivera. For original wildlife, marine, and seacape paintings and sculpture, stop by the **Mayhew Wildlife Gallery** at 400 Kasten, tel. 937-3132, and the **Ruth Carlson Gallery** at Hwy. 1 and Main, tel. 937-5154.

Despite its small size, Mendocino is stuffed with shops and stores, enough to keep shopping addicts happy for an entire weekend. Particularly unusual, though, is **Alphonso's Mercantile** on Main between Kasten and Osborne, a classical music store and smokeshop (even though Alphonso doesn't smoke anymore) with a million-dollar view of the coast. Also fascinating and very Mendocino is **Mendosa's Merchandise and Market** at Lansing and Little Lake, tel. (707) 937-5879, one of those rare *real* hardware stores long gone from most California communities. Quite the contrast but equally wonderful (with its "food for people, not for profit" slogan) is the collectively run **Corners of the Mouth** natural food store on Ukiah between Ford and Lansing, tel. 937-5345. **Dick's Place,** 45070 Main St., tel. 937-5643, with few concessions to the changing times, is still Mendocino's real bar.

But Mendocino is at its best outdoors, seen from the seat of a bike or on foot. Get oriented at the state park's **Ford House** interpretive center near the public restrooms on the seaward side of Main, open daily 10-5, tel. (707) 937-5804 or 937-5397. The town—included in its entirety on the National Register of Historic Places—is noted for its Cape Cod architecture, a bit odd on the California side of the continent. The seaside saltbox look is not really so unusual, however, since the original settlers were predominantly lumbermen from Maine. Across the street, sedately settled into its old-fashioned gardens, is **Kelley House,** the Mendocino region's historical society museum and library, tel. 937-5791. (Take a guided walking tour of Mendocino, for a nominal fee, with **Mendocino Historical Research, Inc.,** which maintains and operates Kelley House as a historical research facility.) But one of Mendocino's earliest buildings is its joss house, the **Temple of Kwan Ti** on Albion between Kasten and Osborne, open to the public by appointment only, tel. 937-4506 or 937-5123. Also impressive is the elegant old **Mendocino Hotel** on Main, a full-service hostelry with restaurant.

If the weather's not brutal, stroll the **Mendocino Headlands** (pick up the path at the end of Main), with seaside meadows, sandstone cliffs whittled away by waves, and stony sea stacks just offshore.

MENDOCINO AREA STATE PARKS

Mendocino Headlands State Park

About the only reason there aren't shopping malls or condos and resort hotels between the town of Mendocino and its sea-stacked sandstone coast was the political creativity of William Penn Mott, the state's former director of Parks and Recreation. Mott quietly acquired the land for what is now Mendocino Headlands State Park by trading Boise Cascade some equally valuable timberlands in nearby Jackson State Forest.

The headlands and beach are subtle, more a monument to sand sculpture than an all-out ode to hard rock. The impressive stacks here and elsewhere are all that remain of sandstone headlands after eons of ocean erosion. Curving seaward around the town from Big River to the northern end of Heeser Dr., the park includes a three-mile hiking trail, a small beach along the mouth of Big River (trailheads and parking on Hwy. 1, just north of the bridge), sandstone bluffs, the area's notorious wave tunnels, offshore islands and narrows, and good tidepools. *The* peak experience from the headlands is whalewatching. (Whether watching the waves or whales, stand back from the bluff's edge. Sandstone is notoriously unstable, and the ragged rocks and wicked waves below are at best indifferent to human welfare.) For a map and more information, get oriented at Ford House or contact: Mendocino State Parks, P.O. Box 440, Mendocino 95460, tel. (707) 937-5804.

Van Damme State Park

This small state park is not famous but, despite the considerable competition, it's one of the finer things about this stretch of the coast. The excellent and convenient camping here midway between Mendocino and Albion is secondary. Van Damme State Park is an 1,800-acre, five-mile-long preserve around Little River's watershed, pointing out to sea. Squeezed into a lush ravine of second-growth mixed redwood forest, Van Damme's pride is its **Fern Canyon Trail,** a 2½-mile hiking and bicycling trail weaving across Little River through red alders, red-

woods, ferns—western sword ferns, deer ferns, bird's foot ferns, and five-finger ferns, among others—and past mossy rocks, pools, and streamside herds of horsetails.

Though the Fern Canyon Trail is easy, the going gets tougher at the east end as the path climbs the canyon and connects with the loop trail to Van Damme's **Pygmy Forest,** a gnarly thicket bonsaied by nature. (The forest is also wheelchair accessible. It is possible to drive most of the way to this green grove of miniatures via Airport Rd. just south of the park.) The short self-guided discovery trail here loops through dwarfed Bolander pine (a coastal relative of the Sierra Nevada's looming lodgepole), Bishop pine, Mendocino pygmy cypress (found only between Anchor Bay and Fort Bragg), and dwarf manzanita.

Beneath the thin layer of darker topsoil underfoot is the answer to the question "why?": podzol, or albino-gray soils as acidic as vinegar, leached of iron and other elements, which collect below in a reddish hardpan layer impossible for tree roots (even moisture, for that matter) to penetrate. Particularly noteworthy are the spring-blooming rhododendrons, which love acidic soils and here dwarf the trees. Similar fairy forests are common throughout coastal shelf plant communities between Salt Point State Park and Fort Bragg, an area sometimes referred to as the Mendocino White Plains.

Van Damme's tiny beach is usually safe for swimming though no lifeguards are on duty. The redwood-sheltered campground area is protected from winds but not its own popularity. Plan on making reservations (Mistix) from May 1 to October (small group camp also available).

After breakfast, stop by the visitor center and **museum** in the impressive Depression-era Civilian Conservation Corps rec hall built from handsplit timbers for an overview of the area's cultural, economic, and natural history. Or take the short **Bog Trail** loop from the visitor center to see (and smell) the skunk cabbage and other marsh-loving life. For more information, contact the regional state parks office (see above) or: Van Damme State Park, Little River 95456, tel. (707) 937-5855. Reserve campsites ($14) in advance through Mistix, tel. (800) 444-7275. Day use fee: $5.

Russian Gulch State Park

Just north of Mendocino on the site of another days-past doghole port, Russian Gulch State

Jug Handle
State Reserve

KIM WEIR

Park is 1,200 acres of diverse redwood forests in a canyon thick with rhododendrons, azaleas, berry bushes, and ferns; coastal headlands painted in spring with wildflowers; and a broad bay with tidepools and sandy beach, perfect for scuba diving. Especially fabulous during a strong spring storm is the flower-lined cauldron of **Devil's Punch Bowl** in the middle of a meadow on the northern headlands. A portion of this 200-foot wave tunnel collapsed, forming an inland blowhole, but the devil's brew won't blast through unless the sea bubbles and boils.

Russian Gulch is a peaceable kingdom, though, perfect for birdwatching (osprey, red-tailed hawks, ravens, seabirds, shorebirds, and songbirds), whalewatching, even watching steelhead in their spawning waters. Rock fishing is popular around the bay, also ocean salmon fishing and angling for rainbows in the creek (no fishing for spawning steelhead in fall or winter).

After a picnic on the headlands, take a half-day hike upcanyon. Make it a nine-mile loop by combining the southern trails to reach 36-foot **Russian Gulch Falls** (best in spring), then loop back to camp on the North Trail. (One of these trail links, the five-mile **Canyon Trail,** is also designated as a biking trail.) The far northern **Boundary Trail** is for hikers and horsebackers and runs from the horse camp on the eastern edge of the park to the campground.

Camping at Russian Gulch is itself an attraction, with 30 family campsites tucked into the forested canyon, amenities including stove, table, food lockers, hot showers, restrooms with laundry tubs, $14. The separate group camp accommodates about 40 people. (This close to the coast campers often sleep under a blanket of fog, so come prepared for wet conditions.) Reserve campsites in advance through Mistix, tel. (800) 444-7275. For more information, contact the Mendocino State Parks headquarters, tel. (707) 937-5804. Day use fee: $5.

Jug Handle State Reserve

For serious naturalists, the "ecological staircase" hike at this reserve just north of the Caspar Headlands is well worth a few hours of wandering. The staircase itself is a series of uplifted marine terraces, each 100 feet higher than the last, crafted by nature. The fascination here is the *change* associated with each step up the earth ladder, expressed by distinctive plants which also slowly change the environment.

The first terrace was a sand and gravel beach in its infancy, some 100,000 years ago, and is now home to salt-tolerant and wind-resistant wildflowers. (Underwater just offshore is an embryonic new terrace in the very slow process of being born from the sea.) A conifer forest of Sitka spruce, Bishop pine, fir, and hemlock dominates the second terrace, redwoods and Douglas fir the third. Jug Handle is an example of Mendocino's amazing ecological place in the scheme of things, since the area is essentially a biological borderline for many tree species. Metaphorically speaking, Alaska meets Mexico when Sitka spruce and Bishop pine grow side by side. The phenomenon of the hardpan-hampered Mendocino pygmy forest starts on the third step, transitioning back into old-dune pine forests, then more pygmy forest on the fourth step. At the top of the stairs on the final half-million-year-old step, are more pygmy trees, these giving ground to redwoods.

See-by-number brochures for the self-guided hike are available in a vending machine (quarters) in front of the small office off the parking lot just west of Hwy. 1. The only way to get to the staircase trail is by heading west from the parking lot to Jug Handle Bay then east again on the trails as marked, hiking under the highway.

Just south of Jug Handle Preserve is **Caspar State Beach** and headlands, reached via Pt. Cabrillo Drive (limited parking). Bordering the preserve on the east is **Jackson State Forest,** a 46,000-acre demonstration forest named after Jacob Green Jackson, founder of the Caspar Lumber Company. Extending east along the South Fork of the Noyo River and Hwy. 20, the Jackson Forest (logged since the 1850s) has almost unlimited trails (bike, hike, horseback), picnicking, camping. A forest map is necessary to get around. For more information (and a map), contact: **Dept. of Forestry,** 802 N. Main St., P.O. Box 1185, Fort Bragg 95437, tel. (707) 964-5674. For more information about Jug Handle State Preserve, contact the Mendocino State Parks office, tel. 937-5804.

MacKerricher State Park

This seven-mile stretch of ocean and forested coastal prairie is three miles north of Fort Bragg. MacKerricher State Park summarized: black-sand beaches, sand dunes, sheer cliffs and headlands, offshore islands, pounding surf, rocky outcroppings, abundant tidepools. Delicate spring wildflowers include baby blue eyes, sea pinks, buttercups, wild iris. Little **Lake Cleone** is near the campground and picnic area, a fishable freshwater lagoon. Waterfowl from Mono Lake often winter here. Harbor seals usually attract more attention, though, at the **Seal Rocks** watching station at **Laguna Point** (wheelchair accessible), also a popular place for whalewatching.

The eight-mile-long **Coast Trail** (easy but sandy, threading its way on the beach and headlands) runs north from popular **Pudding Creek Beach** to **Ten Mile River.** Only a short stretch of the parallel **Old Haul Road** is open to vehicles,

so this route is better for bicyclists. (For travelers heading north who crave more coast, **Westport Union Landing** is an unmarked state beach about 20 miles north of Fort Bragg between Westport and Rockport.)

The fine campgrounds at MacKerricher are woven into open woods of beach, Monterey and Bishop pines, abundant campsites but unsafe drinking water, $14. Camping amenities include picnic tables, food lockers, and fire rings, also full bathrooms and hot showers. Popular place, reservations wise: Mistix, tel. (800) 444-7275. Day use fee: $5.

NEAR MENDOCINO

Nestled among the headlands, inlets, and river ravines near Mendocino are other towns. The **Albion/Little River** area just south of Mendocino, famous for its salmon and crab fishing, is mostly a coastal citadel of bed and breakfasts and eateries. Most of the nightlife in town centers around the **Caspar Inn.** The tiny fishing port of **Noyo,** almost in Fort Bragg at the mouth of the Noyo River, is a safe harbor during stormy seas and also *the* place for fresh-off-the-boat fish and locally popular seafood restaurants. Delicious is the word for Noyo's **Salmon Barbecue** festivities every July.

Fort Bragg

Not counting Garberville, Fort Bragg is the last community of any size before Eureka. Mendocino's seemingly redneck sister city to the north was named after a fort built here in 1855 for protection against hostile natives. Unpretentious home now to working (and unemployed) lumbermen and millworkers, an active fishing fleet, and many of Mendocino's working artists and much of their work, Fort Bragg is friendly in that standoffish backwoods way. Fort Bragg is also home to the *Skunk Train* railroad ride to Willits inland, where true train buffs can connect with the *Northcoast Daylight's* run to Eureka, once it's back on track. The town's **Whale Festival** comes in March. To participate in Fort Bragg's biggest party, come for **Paul Bunyan Days** over the Labor Day weekend.

Fun and free is beachcombing along **Glass Beach** just north of town, sometimes littered at low tide with glass pebbles, good junk from the dump, even an occasional something from a shipwreck. Or whalewatch from **Todd's Point** near town, south of the Noyo Bridge then west on Ocean View.

Well worth the small admission fee is a tour of the nonprofit 17-acre **Mendocino Coast Botanical Gardens** two miles south of Fort Bragg, 18220 N. Hwy. 1, P.O. Box 1143, tel. (707) 964-4352, open 9-5 daily. The self-guided tour through native plant communities also features formal plantings of rhododendrons, azaleas, fuchsias, and other regional favorites. Also here (in addition to some smashing views of the crashing coast): a fine native plant nursery, picnic tables, a restaurant, and summertime music concerts. Wheelchair access is available.

For the local version of redwood logging history, as told through photos, artifacts, and tree-mining memorabilia, stop by the **Guest House Museum and Fort Building,** in a redwood mansion on Fort Bragg's Main St., tel. (707) 961-2825, and the only remaining fort building, both owned and operated by the city. Small fee. (For industry-filtered information, tour Georgia Pacific's **Union Lumber Company** mill; watching redwood logs shed their skins by sheer water force is something to see.) More life-affirming is the free tour of the **Georgia Pacific Tree Nursery,** 90 W. Redwood Ave., tel. 964-5651, open weekdays from April through October, an opportunity to commune with four million seedlings, take a stroll along the nature trail, and picnic. After November 1, the young-

sters here take root in nearby forests and a new nursery population takes their place.

The *Skunk Trains*

Assuming that brutal winter storms and landslides haven't obliterated the tracks or trestles recently, a ride on the California and Western Railroad offers some cliff-hanging non-oceanic scenery and on-board camaraderie. The railroad's steam, *Super Skunk* and diesel or electric *Skunks* chug out from the station at Laurel Street in Fort Bragg to Willits about 40 miles inland over snaking high-wire trestles above the redwood-thick and rugged Noyo River Gulch (with unscheduled stops along the way to drop off mail, medicine, and supplies). Also visible along the way: recent examples of redwood clear-cutting practices. You can also do the trip in reverse.

For the most part, in summer the steam-powered Baldwin steam engine ("Ol' Number 45") is available, rolling out daily on the 9:20 a.m. departure from Fort Bragg. In April, May, and October, the steam-powered *Super Skunk* also rolls on the second and fourth Saturdays (on the fourth Saturday only in September). Depending on number of passengers and other scheduling factors, diesel-powered or motorcar (electric) *Skunk* engines predominate on other summer and most off-season runs, including those departing midday from Fort Bragg and all departures from Willits. Half-day trips either start in Fort Bragg, with a turnaround at Northspur, or

The rhododendrons at the Mendocino Coast Botanical Gardens are spectacular in spring.

MENDOCINO COAST BOTANICAL GARDENS

A TRIP ON THE *NORTHCOAST DAYLIGHT*

Who says the good old days of train travel are gone for good in America? Certainly no one who's taken a ride on the *Northcoast Daylight* from Willits to Eureka, the most spectacular rail route in California, perhaps in the western U.S. Trouble seemed to be the railway's unofficial middle name after the resurrection of this 145-mile stretch in 1985 (following everything from passenger-stranding landslides in the Eel River Canyon to temporary cancellation of its liability insurance, then subsequent bankruptcy), but things have been rolling along better since. Though major track repair and passenger car renovations are well under way, the full route won't be open until 1994. Short Eureka-Arcata runs will have to suffice until then.

When the train is really rolling, the reincarnated old *Shasta Daylight* is part of the seven-hour journey's pure pleasure: plushly padded lounge cars, colorful window coaches from the old *Daylight,* a classic Frisco Line parlor car, even a rare "vista dome" club car from the *Santa Fe Chief.*

From Willits the *Northcoast Daylight* slithers through most of the wild Eel River Canyon at 10 mph, slow enough for passengers to observe the wildlife: bears, deer, river otters, birds of prey, even sunbathing skinny-dippers. On the way to Eureka, the train threads its way through 29 mountain tunnels and across almost endless bridges and trestles strung across river gorges. Slipping into Humboldt County through the back door (top train speed on straightaways: 30 mph), the *Northcoast Daylight* slides through Scotia with its Pacific Lumber Company, across the Scotia Bluffs, then through the coastal farmlands of the Eel River Valley to Humboldt Bay and Eureka. After an overnight in Old Town (a two-night stay on holiday weekends), roundtrip passengers board the train for the return trip.

Weekend excursions on the *Northcoast Daylight* will probably be scheduled from late May through October, with fares $100 or so roundtrip. For information and reservations, contact: **Coast Railroad,** 4 W. 2nd St. (at the depot), Eureka 95501, tel. (707) 444-8055.

---

start and end at the historic Willits railroad station, a marvel of redwood craftsmanship.

Scheduling can get confusing, but full-day trips depart from Fort Bragg every day of the year. To get a lift from steam-powered Ol' Number 45 or to otherwise ride the train you want to ride—barring last-minute breakdowns and other unavoidable mishaps—contact the railroad well in advance and make reservations. Rates: $23 roundtrip and $18.50 half-day or one-way for adults; $11 and $9, respectively, for children (under age five free if they sit on your lap). For current schedule information and advance reservations (a must in summer), contact: **California Western Railroad,** P.O. Box 907, Fort Bragg 95437, tel. (707) 964-6371.

Willits

Winsome little Willits is a friendly frontier town among the ranches and railroads of Little Lake Valley north of Ukiah, a slice of life whittled from the Old West: Black Bart used to love it here. Besides the horse shows, rodeos, and other regular town hoedowns, the best thing about this place is the **Willits Station** train depot on E. Commercial Street. Coming together here are the eastern terminus of the old

Union Lumber Company logging line (now the California Western Railroad's *Skunk Train* route), the southern terminus of the Eureka Southern Railroad and its current *Northcoast Daylight* line, and the northern terminus of the old Northwestern Pacific Railroad link to San Francisco and vicinity (a run which may again be resurrected one day). More amazing than this rail convergence, though, is the station itself, a little dowdy these days but an astounding architectural achievement carefully crafted from clear heart redwood.

Also worthwhile in Willits is the **Mendocino County Museum,** 400 East Commercial St., tel. (707) 459-2736, with its collection of Pomo artifacts, handmade quilts, and hop industry and pioneer chronicles. More quilts are on parade in summer during the impressive **Quilt Show** here. But Willits really becomes itself during its popular **Frontier Days** celebration for July 4th, a week filled with a rodeo (the oldest continuous rodeo in California, they say here), horse show, parade, carnival, barbecue, breakfasts, dances, and whatever else people can think of.

For more information about what's in and around Willits, contact the **Willits Chamber of Commerce,** 15 S. Main St., tel. (707) 459-4113.

MENDOCINO AREA ACCOMMODATIONS

The battle of the bed and breakfasts in and around Mendocino is just one aspect of the continuing local war over commercial and residential development. The conversion of homes to bed and breakfast establishments means fewer housing options for people who live here, but a moratorium on B&Bs means still higher prices for visitor accommodations. Most people here agree on one thing: only developers want to see large-scale housing or recreation developments in the area.

Avoid contributing to the problem altogether by camping. There are almost endless choices among the state parks nearby (see "Mendocino Area State Parks" above), and some very enjoyable, very reasonable alternatives inland along Hwy. 128 toward Ukiah (see "Boonville" under "Inland Mendocino Country" in "The Wine Country" chapter). There are over 2,000 commercial guest rooms available in and around Mendocino but that doesn't mean there's room at the inn (or motel) for spontaneous travelers. Usually people can find last-minute lodgings of some sort in Fort Bragg, though the general rule here is plan ahead or risk sleeping in your car or nestled up against your bicycle in the cold fog.

To stay in style in Mendocino, there are some great places to choose from. Advance reservations are absolutely necessary at most places on most weekends and during summer, preferably a month in advance. Most bed and breakfasts require a two-day minimum stay on weekends and an advance deposit.

A number of the inns listed below, in both Mendocino and Fort Bragg, are members of the **Mendocino Coast Innkeepers Association,** P.O. Box 1141, Mendocino 95460, and if one inn is full, it's possible that another can be accommodating. (Request a current brochure for full information.) **Mendocino Coast Reservations,** 1001 Main St., P.O. Box 1143, Mendocino 95460, tel. (707) 937-5033, offers over 100 fully furnished rentals by the weekend, week, or month, from cottages and cabins to homes and family reunion-sized retreats. **Mendocino Coast Accommodations,** tel. 937-1913, offers central reservations services for everything from motels and hotels to B&Bs and vacation homes (no fee to consumer).

The Mendocino Hotel

The grand 1858-vintage **Mendocino Hotel,** 45080 Main St., P.O. Box 587, Mendocino 95460, tel. (707) 937-0511, is one of those Mendocino experiences everyone should try at least once. All 51 of these meticulously restored rooms and suites are furnished in American and European antiques; many have fireplaces or woodburning stoves and views of Mendocino Bay or the one-acre gardens, plus such not-like-home little luxuries as heated towel racks, fresh flowers from someone else's garden, and chocolate truffles on the pillow at bedtime. The

Riding the Skunk is a popular diversion for train enthusiasts.

hotel's parlor (note the 18th-century sculpted steel fireplace) is infused with informal Victorian coziness, more casual than the crystal-studded dining room. Most rooms are expensive, but rates range $65-275, lower in the off-season.

Mendocino Bed And Breakfasts

Selecting "the best" bed and breakfasts in an area like Mendocino is like asking parents which of their children they love best. But the **MacCallum House,** 45020 Albion St., Mendocino 95460, tel. (707) 937-0289, is the town's oldest bed and breakfast, a restored 1882 Victorian and garden cottages with a friendly quilts-and-steamer-trunk feel like a fantasy weekend visit to grandma's. Rates (some rooms have shared baths) range $65-160 per night, creative continental breakfast included. For a little distance from the rest of the clan, consider a stay in the inn's water tower suite, complete with Franklin wood stove and ocean views. Or sleep over in the barn, with an apartment-style family suite. Other rooms in the barn have stone fireplaces and good views. There's a good restaurant on the premises plus the fine **Grey Whale Bar,** perfect for comfort-oriented whalewatchers.

Also in town is the **Seagull Inn,** 44960 Albion St., P.O. Box 501, Mendocino 95460, tel. (707) 937-5204, where an overnight can be quite reasonable, with rates $35-95. The **Joshua Grindle Inn,** 44800 Little Lake Rd., P.O. Box 647, tel. 937-4143, is a New England country-style inn with 10 rooms, most with fireplaces, full breakfast, rates $80-130.

The **Agate Cove Inn** at 11201 Lansing St., P.O. Box 1150, tel. 937-0551 or toll-free from Northern California (800) 527-3111, is an 1860s farmhouse (built by Mathias Brinzing, founder of Mendocino's first brewery) with a cluster of 10 bed-and-breakfast cottages, most with fireplaces and ocean views, all with private baths, country decor, and handmade quilts on the bed. Full breakfast (cooked on an antique woodstove) of omelettes or other entree with country sausage or ham, homebaked breads, jams and jellies, coffee and teas. Rates: $75-175. The **Sea Rock Bed and Breakfast Inn** at 11101 N. Lansing St., P.O. Box 286, tel. 937-5517, is also a collection of country cottages, these with Franklin stoves and TV, a few with kitchens. Breakfast buffet served in the lobby. Rates: $65-145, lower in the off-season. **Headlands Inn** at

the corner of Albion and Howard, P.O. Box 132, is a fully restored 1868 Victorian with five rooms, all with antiques, private baths, fireplace, fresh flowers and fruit, and city newspaper and full breakfast served in each room. Two parlors, English-style garden, afternoon tea and refreshments. Rates: $98-150.

The **John Dougherty House Bed & Breakfast** in town at 571 Ukiah St., P.O. Box 817, Mendocino 95460, tel. (707) 937-5266, is a Mendocino classic, an 1867 saltbox surrounded by English gardens and filled with antiques, included on the town's historic house tour. Two suites and six rooms, all with private baths, some with woodstoves. Expanded continental breakfast. Rates: $95-140. The **Sears House Inn** is an 1870 Victorian with four bed and breakfast cottages in Mendocino at 44840 Main St., P.O. Box 844, Mendocino 95460, tel. 937-4076. Six rooms have private baths, two share, and five rooms feature woodstoves or fireplaces. Continental breakfast delivered every morning. Rates: $60-110. Also in the neighborhood: **Mendocino Village Inn Bed and Breakfast,** 44860 Main, P.O. Box 626, tel. 937-0246, a New England-style Victorian circa 1882, with 12 rooms (two share a bath), many with fireplace or woodstove, full breakfast. Rates: $59-130.

The **Blue Heron Inn** is a charmer in the European country tradition, just two rooms (share a bath) and a garden cottage (private entrance, private bath) with deck and ocean views a half-block from the ocean, P.O. 1142, Mendocino 95460, tel. (707) 937-4323, room rates $58-68, cottage $90.

Mendocino Area Bed And Breakfasts

Cypress House on Chapman Point, 45250 Chapman Dr., P.O. Box 303, Mendocino 95460, tel. (707) 937-1456, is quite the place to get away from it all. This small redwood-and-glass home is itself a one-bedrooom suite looking out on Mendocino and the bay, with queen bed, fireplace, private hot tub, continental breakfast in garden kitchen nook. Rate: $140 per night. **B.G. Ranch Bed and Breakfast Inn** is outside Mendocino proper at 9601 Hwy. 1, tel. 937-5322, 14 acres with an 1880 Victorian farmhouse, four rooms share two baths. Full breakfast. Rates: $65-75.

The **Brewery Gulch Inn** just south of town near the beach at 9350 Hwy. 1, Mendocino 95460, tel. (707) 937-4752, is a pre-Victorian farmhouse in a farmlike setting: gardens, orchards, open pasture land, coastal forests, the 10-acre spread sheltered from harsh winds and sometimes even sidestepping the fog. Small and intimate (just five rooms, two with shared bath), stone fireplace, and outdoor deck beyond the French doors, plus hearty breakfasts: eggs or omelettes with homemade biscuits and gravy and fresh fruit, possibly cheese blintzes, sausage, toast and homemade jam served every morning. From the hollow here, it's a 10-minute walk to Mendocino along the bluffs. Rates: $75-115.

Rachel Binah is a very creative cook, the country caterer in these parts, but she's now noted for her **Rachel's Inn** adjacent to an undeveloped strip of Van Damme State Park two miles south of Mendocino at 8200 N. Hwy. 1 in Little River, P.O. Box 134, Mendocino 95460, tel. (707) 937-0088. Each room has its own bathroom, a big bed, fresh flowers and personal amenities, plus individual charm: a view of the ocean or gardens, a balcony, or a fireplace. Rates for rooms in the main house (single or double occupancy) range $96-125. Rates for rooms across the patio in The Barn (central sitting room with fireplace): $125-165. If you rent all or a combination of rooms for a casual conference or family gathering, special dinners can be arranged. Any day of the week a good full breakfast is served in the dining room.

The unusually charismatic **Fensalden Inn,** seven miles south of Mendocino at 33810 Navarro Ridge Rd., P.O. Box 99, Albion 95410, tel. (707) 937-4042, is a restored two-story stage station circa 1860 still straddling the ridgetop among open fields and forests. Seven rooms (five with fireplaces), hors d'oeuvres, full breakfast. Rates: $85-135.

Fort Bragg Bed And Breakfasts

The boxy, weathered clear heart redwood **Grey Whale Inn,** once the community hospital at 615 Main St., Fort Bragg 95437, tel. (707) 964-0640 or toll-free (800) 382-7244, could be just the thing for what ails you. This two-story whale of an inn offers peace and privacy, large yet reasonably priced rooms with private baths, two penthouse suites, pool table, fireplace, and a breakfast buffet of coffeecakes, fresh fruits and juices, yogurt or cheese, even good coffee. Rooms $60-160.

It's also an easy walk from the **Pudding Creek Inn Bed and Breakfast** down the street at 700 N. Main St., Fort Bragg 95437, tel. 964-9529, to the *Skunk Train* depot and other local hotspots. But just staying put is pleasant, in these two 1884 Victorians connected by a garden court. There are ten rooms altogether, all with private baths, two with fireplaces. Full breakfast buffet. Rates: $65-115, lower midweek and off-season. Closed most of January. Near everything, too, is the **Glass Beach Bed and Breakfast Inn,** 726 N. Main, tel. 964-6774, with nine rooms (four have fireplaces), hot tub, full breakfast in the dining room, rooms $59-92.

Other possibilities: the two-story **Noyo River Lodge** at 500 Casa del Noyo Dr., Fort Bragg 95437, tel. (707) 964-8045, a redwood Craftsman-style place (circa 1868) on the hill with both harbor and ocean views, rooms and suites with private baths, some with fireplaces (restaurant and lounge here, too) and big soaking tubs, skylights, gardens, rates $75-135. The **Avalon House** at 561 Stewart St., tel. 964-5555, is a 1905 Craftsman with six rooms (three with in-room spas, three with fireplaces), rates $70-125, lower midweek and in the off-season.

The **Jug Handle Beach Country Inn** just north of Caspar and across from the state park at 32980 Gibney Ln., Fort Bragg 95437, tel. (707) 964-1415, has just four rooms with private baths, $75-95, excellent breakfasts. Also in Fort Bragg is the newly restored **Coast Hotel,** 101 Franklin St., Fort Bragg 95437, tel. 964-6443. Rooms are $50-70; adjoining cafe serves dinner.

Motels And Lodges

Fort Bragg has the motels, in general the most reasonable accommodations option around besides camping. Most places have cheaper off-season rates, from November through March or April. Pick up a current listing of area motels at the chamber office (see "Information and Services" below).

The **Anchor Lodge** in Noyo (office in The Wharf Restaurant), 780 N. Harbor Dr., P.O. Box 1429, Fort Bragg 95437, tel. (707) 964-4283, has 19 rooms: $45-135. Also fairly reasonable: the **Fort Bragg Motel,** 763 N. Main St., tel. 964-4787, with rooms $38-70. Among more expensive motel accommodations: the **Surf Motel** just south of the Noyo River Bridge in Fort Bragg, P.O. Box 488, tel. 964-5361, rates $67-

92 (much less in winter), as well as the **Surrey Inn** just north of the bridge at 888 S. Main, tel. 964-4003, rooms $50-57 (also much less in winter), and the **Harbor Lite Lodge** just off the highway in Noyo, 120 N. Harbor Dr., tel. 964-0221, rooms $54-94.

Other Inns And Fine Lodgings

The epitome of accommodations elegance these days is **Reed Manor** on Little Lake St. just four blocks from Main St. in Mendocino, P.O. Box 127, Mendocino 95460, tel. (707) 937-5446, a very new New England-style inn up on a hill. Just four rooms and one suite, each with balcony or deck, king-sized bed, in-room whirlpool spa, fireplace, refrigerator, TV and VCR, phone, and many other amenities. Continental breakfast served in rooms. Rates: $175-375.

Back in Mendocino, among the priciest is **Dennen's Heritage House,** Little River 95456, tel. (707) 937-5885, once a safe harbor for that notorious gangster Baby Face Nelson (though things are quite civilized and serene these days). Heritage House itself is an old Maine-style farmhouse (now the inn's dining room, kitchen, and office) and the center of a large complex of antique-laden luxury cottages (with locally significant names like "Bonnet Shop" and "Country Store" and "Ice Cream Parlor") spread out among the grasslands and bull pines. Rates (which include dinner and breakfast) are $125-335. No TV, no phones.

Most fans of the "Murder, She Wrote" TV series (filmed largely in Mendocino) will recognize the fairly expensive **Hill House Inn** on the hill, 10701 Pallette Dr. off Little Lake, P.O. Box 625, Mendocino 95460, tel. (707) 937-0554, with restaurant and rooms in the $100-175 range. Comfortably luxurious is the **Stanford Inn By the Sea** (also known as the Big River Lodge) on Comptche-Ukiah Rd. and the south bank of Big River, P.O. Box 487 in Mendocino, tel. 937-5615, an elegant but friendly lodge in the country tradition, with big gardens, even llamas. Indoor pool. Rooms here have decks, big beds, fireplaces, decent reading lights and good books, writing desks, even little extras like coffeemakers, chocolate truffles, fresh flowers, and a selection of special soaps and lotions. Rates: $135-250.

At least locally famous is the **Little River Inn** on Hwy. 1 in Little River 95456, tel. (707) 937-

LITTLE RIVER INN

5942, originally just one rambling old mansion built by lumberman Silas Coombs in the area's characteristic Maine style, now part of a golf and tennis resort complex with fireplace cottages and modern lodging annex. But the old inn itself is a slice of Victorian gingerbread, with the cheapest rooms really the best: quilt-padded attic accommodations illuminated by seaward-spying dome windows. Wonderful place, all the way around. The Little River also serves simple and excellent white-tablecloth breakfasts including Swedish pancakes, absolutely perfect eggs, and fresh-squeezed orange juice. Room rates: $75-275.

GOOD FOOD

Good Basic Mendocino Food

Stock up on natural foods, for here or to go, at **Corners of the Mouth,** or get regular groceries at **Mendosa's.** Nibbling through all the delis and bakeries in town could satisfy anyone for a week. The **Main Street Deli and Cafe** at 45040 Main, tel. (707) 937-5031, is popular for people-watching, also sandwiches (on good sourdough or whole wheat) and cappuccino. Great breakfast special. Open 7 a.m.-9 p.m. daily. **Mendo Burgers** at 10483 Lansing, open 11-7, tel. 937-1111, has all kinds: beef, turkey, fish, and veggie varieties. For a hefty slice of pizza, quiche, homemade soups, and/or good pastries, head for **The Mendocino Bakery and Cafe** on Lansing, tel. 937-0836, open 8 a.m.-6 p.m. weekdays, weekends 8:30-6. For that sweet tooth, try the homemade pies at **Mendocino Goodies** at Albion and Lansing, tel. 937-4300; the famous ice cream (including quarter-pounder cones) at the **Mendocino Ice Cream Company** on Main, tel. 937-5884; and the definitely decadent chocolates at **Mendocino Chocolate Company,** tel. 937-1107.

Cafe Beaujolais

No one should come anywhere near Mendocino without planning to eat at least one meal at the noted **Cafe Beaujolais,** 961 Ukiah St., Mendocino 95460, tel. (707) 937-5614. The fresh-flower decor inside and on the deck of this old house is as refreshingly simple and fine as the food itself. People like Johnny Carson, Julia Child, the English food writer Elizabeth David, Robert Redford, and food critics from the *New York Times* eat here when they're in town. But since Margaret Fox, once a baker in the back room of the Mendocino Hotel, first opened the cafe's doors over a decade ago it's been a people's place. Despite its fame, it still is.

Breakfast at Beaujolais is an *event,* an always-intriguing array of things like buttermilk-cornmeal waffles, French toast with genuine maple syrup, omelettes with linguica or smoked pork and chilies, unusual sausages (like chicken-apple), homemade cashew granola, and the coffeecakes, muffins, and other baked goods the cafe is noted for.

Lunch is both straightforward (homemade soups, sandwiches, and salads created from the proprietors' garden, over 30 varieties of lettuce, plus herbs, nasturtiums, and other edible flowers) and eclectic: Thai-style short ribs, Cajun red beans and rice, surprising specials, and the cafe's famous panforte for dessert. (New here is **The Brickery,** a bakery producing breads and pizzas from the wood-fired oven.)

Dinner is a fixed-price French-and-California-cuisine affair featuring such things as local smoked salmon and roast duck with a purée of apples and turnips, still more decadent desserts, and an almost endless and excellent California wine list. Cafe Beaujolais is open for breakfast and lunch daily 8:30 a.m.-2:30 p.m., for dinner Thurs.-Sun. 6:15-9:30 p.m. The Brickery is open Mon.-Wed. 11:30 a.m.-3:30 p.m., Thurs.-Sun. 11:30 a.m.-7:30 p.m. Reservations necessary for dinner. Bring cash or personal checks; no credit cards accepted.

More Good Mendocino Restaurants

Neighbor to the much-more-famous Cafe Beaujolais is **955 Ukiah St.,** tel. (707) 937-1955, difficult to find in the fog despite its numerically straightforward attitude. (The entrance is 100 feet off the street around a few corners.) The dining room itself is a former art studio, and dinners feature excellent fresh seafood, unforgettable bread sticks, and Navarro and Husch wines from the Anderson Valley. No credit cards. Also quite good in town is the **MacCallum House Restaurant** at 45020 Albion, tel. 937-5763, open for dinner.

For prime rib, steaks, and seafood in a semiformal Victorian setting, consider the crystal-and-Oriental-carpet ambience of the **Mendocino Hotel,** 45080 Main St., tel. (707) 937-0511. The hotel's Garden Court restaurant and bar (the ceiling almost one immense skylight to keep the garden going) serves more casual lunch fare, good salads, sandwiches, specials. Open daily for breakfast, lunch, and dinner.

Moving away from Mendocino proper, there's at least one good restaurant in every tiny town. Though the **Little River Inn** across the way is noted for its breakfasts, for dinner the inauspicious, unaffiliated, and elegantly simple **Little River Restaurant** tucked away behind the post office, P.O. Box 396, Little River 95456, tel. (707) 937-4945, is not to be missed. Only 14 people can squeeze in here at any one time but what they sit down to is a perfect meal, soup through excellent dessert, with entrees like roast lamb in mustard sauce. Reservations essential, especially on weekends.

At the intimately elegant **Ledford House** in Little River at 7051 N. Hwy. 1, tel. (707) 937-0282, even vegetarians can try the excellent soups, since none are made with meat bases. Entrees include pasta picks like ravioli stuffed with ricotta cheese in sorrel cream sauce, and some definitely nonstandard seafood and meat specialties.

Good Food Fort Bragg Style

Finding a meal in Fort Bragg is more relaxed than in Mendocino, with less confusion from the madding crowds. Most places are quite casual. Noyo Harbor is *the* place for fish. Most noted among the "school" of inexpensive seafood eateries here is **The Wharf,** 780 N. Harbor Dr., tel. (707) 964-4283, famous for its creamy clam chowder and crispy-outside-tender-inside fried clams, though the prime rib sandwich here is nothing to throw a crabpot at. For dinner, specialties include seafood and steak. The specialty at the good and plastic-tableclothed **Cap'n Flint's,** 32250 N. Harbor, tel. 964-9447, open 11 a.m.-8:30 p.m., is shrimp won tons with cream cheese filling. **The Dock** is a favorite fisherman's cafe. Also excellent, the **Thanksgiving Coffee Company,** at 19100 S. Harbor, tel. 964-4711, serves and sells coffee daily 8 a.m.-5 p.m. **Restaurant El Mexican** at 701 N. Harbor Dr., tel. 964-7164, serves up authentic Mexican food, down to the fresh-daily tortillas. Open daily 10 a.m.-8:30 p.m.

In town, **Egghead Omelettes of Oz,** at 326 N. Main St., tel. (707) 964-5005, is a cheerful diner with booths, featuring unforgettable fried potatoes and omelettes with endless combinations for fillings, including avocado and crab. Good sandwiches at lunch. Worth writing home about. Open 7 a.m.-2 p.m. daily.

While you're in the neighborhood, head down the street to **Carol Hall's Hot Pepper Jelly Company,** 330 N. Main, tel. 961-1422, for some intriguing jams and jellies, fruit syrups, mustards, herb vinegars, unusual gift items. In the other direction, inside a one-time mortuary, is the **North Coast Brewing Co. Taproom and Restaurant,** 444 N. Main, tel. 964-BREW, a brewpub and grill featuring award-winning handmade ales and surprisingly good food. Open from 4 p.m. on weekdays, from 2 p.m. on Saturday. Ask Jim, the quintessential bartender, for his latest selection of jokes.

Very good, very natural, quite simple, and quite reasonable for lunch is **Lu's Kitchen,** once a bayside stand in Mendocino and now a cafe at 131 E. Laurel in Fort Bragg, tel. (707) 961-0627, with Mexican specialties like burritos and guacamole, good combinations. Open for lunch and dinner Thurs.-Sat. 11:30 a.m.-8 p.m. Sandwiches at the **Red Caboose** (yes, actually a red caboose) near the carwash by Payless at S. Main St. and Chestnut, tel. 964-9006, include almost a day's worth of food. For no-nonsense pizza, stop by the quite casual **Bernillo's,** 220 E. Redwood Ave., tel. 964-9314.

Fancy for Fort Bragg is the newly restored **Coast Hotel,** with its **Coast Hotel Cafe,** tel. (707) 964-6443, 101 N. Franklin, dinner served 5-10 p.m. The **Espresso Express** next door serves breakfast and lunch, everything homemade, from muffins and Belgian waffles to quiches and soups. Quite haute here, in the California-cuisine tradition, is **The Restaurant,** 418 N. Main St., tel. 964-9800, with dinner entrees including poached halibut, calimari, scallops, shrimp, steak, and quail. Open for lunch and

dinner (call for current schedule) and Sunday brunch. Children's menu. Reservations wise.

Mendocino doesn't have a corner on the sweets-to-slobber-over market, either. **Mendocino Popcorn** at 356 Main in Fort Bragg, tel. (707) 964-5671, has incredibly good candies, homemade ice cream, and flavored popcorn, **Goody's** at 144 N. Franklin St., tel. 964-7800, is the town's old-time malt shop and soda fountain, complete with checkerboard counter and other surprises. Open weekdays and Saturdays.

ENTERTAINMENT

According to the keepers of the statistical grail, Mendocino County has more performing artists per capita than almost anyplace else in California, second only to neighboring Humboldt County to the north. And where do these performers perform? Anywhere there's an audience and room enough to stand up. If it's music, someone around here plays it. The **Caspar Inn** in Caspar, tel. (707) 964-5565, is the noted rock 'n' roll hotspot and dance club. Fort Bragg is the center of the country-western scene. Jazz, though, is Mendocino County's music of choice.

Second-most popular music here is classical. Every July, in a 600-seat tent next to the Ford House, Mendocino hosts its new but already noted two-week music festivities, in the spirit of Mozart, Janacek, Delius, Tchaikovsky, Copland. Baroque and chamber music, opera, and less highbrow fare are also on the program. For information, tickets, even gift certificates: **Mendocino Music Festival,** P.O. Box 1808, Mendocino 95460, tel. (707) 937-2044. Also at home in Mendocino are the **Gloriana Opera Company,** the **Mendocino Theatre** and the very fine **Symphony of the Redwoods.** The **Footlighter's Little Theatre** in Fort Bragg, tel. 964-3806, features Gay '90s melodrama, performances on Wed. and Saturday. For the latest entertainment scuttlebutt, stop by the Mendocino Art Center or chamber of commerce.

Mendocino Area Events
Major area events include the **Mendocino Whale Festival,** with wine and clam chowder tasting, usually held the first weekend in March. Just so Mendocino doesn't have all the fun, the **Fort Bragg Whale Festival** is also scheduled in

March (third weekend), with beer and chowder tasting. Also in March: the performance season begins for the **Mendocino Theatre Company.**

Mendocino Heritage Days arrive in May, a ten-day downhome celebration of the city's pioneer past, with everything from quilt and heritage craft shows to a film festival (movies filmed in Mendocino), not to mention the Heritage Days parade and picnic, the Knights of Columbus pancake breakfast, and the Oldtimers Baseball Game. On July 4th, Fort Bragg hosts the **World's Largest Salmon Barbecue** at Noyo Mooring Basin. The **Mendocino Music Festival** (see above) usually starts in mid-July, as does the Gloriana Opera Company's six-week summer run.

Paul Bunyan Days in Fort Bragg are usually scheduled for Labor Day weekend. Come mid-September, the **Winesong!** winetasting and auction is on tap at the Mendocino Coast Botanical Gardens. Then there's Christmas. In Mendocino, the **Mendocino Christmas Festival** includes tree lighting, inn tours, and other uptown festivities. In Fort Bragg, it's a **Hometown Christmas,** with music, tree lighting—and truck lighting, a yuletide parade of logging trucks and big rigs all lit up for the holidays.

INFORMATION AND SERVICES

The **Fort Bragg-Mendocino Coast Chamber of Commerce** is an incredible resource for whatever you want to know or do, 332 N. Main St., P.O. Box 1141, Fort Bragg 95437, tel. (707) 961-6300 or toll-free (800) 726-2780, open most weekdays 9-5, Sat. 11-4, closed Wed. and Sunday. Among the free literature published by the chamber is the regularly updated *Mendocino* brochure and map (mostly a shop listing) and the *Walking Tour of Historic Fort Bragg* guide. Also available here and elsewhere is the free annual *Mendocino Visitor* tabloid, the coast guide to state parks, the *Guide to the Recreational Trails of Mendocino County,* and the Mendocino Art Center's publications. For an "advance packet" of information, send a self-addressed, stamped, legal-size envelope. New in Mendocino proper is the **North Coast Visitor Center**, 991 Main, tel. 937-1913.

Beachcombers and hikers: to get oriented along the Mendocino coast, a travel essential is Bob Lorentzen's *The Hiker's Hip Pocket Guide to the Mendocino Coast,* which keys off those otherwise mysterious white milepost markers along Hwy. 1, from the Gualala River north. Information about undeveloped public-held lands, such as the state's Schooner Gulch and Whiskey Shoals Beach along the southern Mendocino coast, is generously shared. Also worthwhile to carry anywhere along the coast is the *California Coastal Resource Guide* by the California Coastal Commission, published by the University of California Press.

The **post office** in Mendocino is at 10500 Ford St., tel. (707) 937-5282, open weekdays 8:30 a.m.-4:30 p.m., the one in Fort Bragg at 203 N. Franklin, tel. 964-2302, open weekdays 8:30-5. Both towns also have coin-operated **laundromats** (check the phone book for locations). For medical care, the **Mendocino Coast Hospital** at 700 River Dr. in Fort Bragg, tel. 961-1234, offers 24-hour emergency room services.

Transport

Mendocino Transit Authority headquarters at 241 Plant Rd. in Ukiah, tel. (707) 462-1422, is top rung of a multi-tiered bus system. Smaller **Mendocino Stage** buses, tel. 964-0167, run daily between Fort Bragg and Navarro via Mendocino, to connect with the MTA to Ukiah or Gualala. Climb onto the MTA's **Coast Van** for the weekday run between Ukiah and Gualala (also makes roundtrips between Point Arena and Santa Rosa). Connect with **Greyhound** in Ukiah. In Fort Bragg, rent mountain bikes, 10-speeds, and two-seaters at **Fort Bragg Cyclery,** 579 S. Franklin St., tel. 964-3509. **Mendocino Cyclery,** behind the deli on Main St., tel. 937-4744, rents out mountain bikes and 10-speeds (when they run out of rentals, the folks here even offer their own bikes), also bike packs. Prices from $5 per hour, $28 per day, including free tour maps and suggestions for appropriate day-trips nearby.

For sightseeing afloat, catch a canoe from among the **Catch A Canoe and Bikes Too!** fleet, tel. (707) 937-0273. For birders especially, try the very serene estuarine tour of the Big River. Or be (like Jack London) "a sailor on horseback" on a ride organized by the **Ricochet Ridge Ranch,** 24201 N. Hwy. 1, Fort Bragg 95437, tel. 964-7669, which offers a beach cruise daily at MacKerricher State Park and other rides (English/Western) with some advance arrangements.

THE LOST AND FOUND COAST

Dust off the backpack, get new laces for those hiking boots: this is the place. California's "Lost Coast," isolated, virtually uninhabited, remoter than any other stretch of coastline in the Lower 48, has been found. Here steep mountains soar like bald eagles—their domes tufted with chaparral, a few redwoods tucked behind the ears—and sink their grassy, rock-knuckled talons into the surf raging on black-sand beaches. Local people, of course, snort over the very idea that this splendid stretch of unfriendly coast was ever lost in the first place (even if area highways were intentionally routed away from it). *They* knew it was here. And others have known, too, for at least 3,000 years.

Finding A Lost Culture

The Lost Coast includes both the federal **King Range National Conservation Area** in Humboldt County as well as Mendocino County's newly expanded **Sinkyone Wilderness State Park.** Central to the decade-long battle over expanding the Sinkyone Wilderness, which since 1987 has doubled to include 17 more miles of Mendocino coast, was the fate of 75-acre Sally Bell Grove along Little Jackass Creek. The prolonged political skirmish between former property owner Georgia-Pacific (which planned to clearcut the area) and various private and public agencies focused first on the value of these thousand-year-old trees to posterity. But the war was also over preserving reminders of a lost culture.

Archaeologists believe that a site in the middle of Sally Bell was occupied by proto-Yukian people 3,000 to 8,000 years ago. Chipped-stone tools, stonecutting implements, milling tools, the remains of two houses, and charcoal from long-ago campfires have been discovered at the site. Since those ancient days, for at least 2,500 years up until a century ago, the Sinkyone and Mattole peoples lived permanently along this vast seaside stretch, though other groups came here seasonally when the valleys inland roasted in 100-degree heat. The living was easy, with abundant seafood a dietary staple.

The beaches fringing the King Range were sacred to the Mattole. Descendants talk about the legendary wreck of a Spanish ship along the coast from which the Mattole retrieved triangular gold coins for their children to play with. The coins were lost, however, when their caves along the coast collapsed after the 1906 earthquake. Archaeologists are now working at a site near Shelter Cove, known to the Sinkyone people for almost one thousand years as Thang-I-Keah. Up until 150 years ago, the Sinkyone gathered here regularly to fish and hunt. Ancient shell mounds or middens (protected by the Archaeological Resources Protection Act) still dot the seashore.

GETTING FOUND

King Range Conservation Area

The northern reaches of the Lost Coast stretch 35 miles from south of the Mattole River to Whale Gulch. Much of the BLM's King Range Conservation Area, a total of about 60,000 acres of rugged coastal mountains jutting up at 45-degree angles from rocky headlands, is now being considered for federal wilderness protection, the decision due in the early 1990s. Despite the fact that most beaches are already closed to motorized vehicles, rebel offroaders are becoming a problem.

Most people come here to "beach backpack," hiking north to south in deference to prevailing winds. The trailhead begins near the mouth of the Mattole River. Get there from Mattole Rd. near Petrolia via Lighthouse Rd. then head south on foot (it's about three miles from the dunes to the old lighthouse). On the rocks near the red-nippled relic of the Punta Gorda light station is a seabird colony and rookery for Steller's sea lions. Walk all the way south to Shelter Cove, a two- or three-day trip one-way (five days roundtrip), longer for those heading on to Sinkyone.

The trail saunters along miles of sandy beaches, around some tremendous tidepools, and up onto headlands to bypass craggy coves where streams flow to the sea. Quite the wild walk in wintry weather (check conditions before setting out); in any season watch for rattlesnakes

BROOKINGS
TO GOLD BEACH,
COOS BAY
TO
GRANTS
PASS
OREGON
101
CALIFORNIA
PELICAN
STATE BEACH
SMITH
RIVER
199
ST. GEORGE
PT.
CRESCENT CITY
JEDEDIAH SMITH
REDWOODS S.P.
SIX
RIVERS
N.F.
DEL NORTE
COAST
REDWOODS S.P.
KLAMATH
PRAIRIE CREEK
REDWOODS S.P.
KLAMATH RIVER
96
HUMBOLDT LAGOONS
ORICK
REDWOOD
N.P.
PATRICK'S POINT S.P.
TRINIDAD
HOOPA
LITTLE RIVER
STATE BEACH
AZALEA
S.R.
WILLOW
CREEK
299
ARCATA
BLUE
LAKE
TO
WEAVERVILLE
EUREKA
HUMBOLDT BAY
FIELDS LANDING
FERNDALE
FORTUNA
ROHNERVILLE
GRIZZLY CREEK
REDWOODS
SCOTIA
36
VAN DUZEN RIVER
HUMBOLDT
REDWOOD
S.P.
DYERVILLE
PETROLIA
HUMBOLDT
REDWOOD
S.P.
BULL CREEK
FLATS RD.
HONEYDEW
KING RANGE
REDWAY
GARBERVILLE
SHELTER COVE
BENBOW
LAKE S.R.A.
RICHARDSON
GROVE S.P.
0   10 mi
0   10 km
SINKYONE
WILDERNESS
S.P.
LEGGETT
TO
UKIAH
1

THE HUMBOLDT-DEL NORTE COAST

PACIFIC OCEAN

CAPE MENDOCINO

MATTOLE RD.

PUNTA GORDA

BRICELAND THORNE RD.

© MOON PUBLICATIONS, INC.

on rocks or draped over driftwood. Between self-protective downward glances, look around to appreciate some of the impressive shipwrecks scattered along the way. Also just offshore (in proper season) are gray whales, killer whales, porpoises, and harbor seals. Inland, forming an almost animate wall of resistance, are the mountains, their severity thinly disguised by redwoods and Douglas fir, forest meadows, chaparral scrub, and spring wildflowers. Make camp on high ground well back from the restless ocean, and always adhere to the backpacker's credo: if you pack it in, pack it out.

The 16-mile **King's Crest Trail** starts near Horse Mountain Camp and offers spectacular ocean views on rare sunny days, as does the **Chemise Mountain Trail.** Another fine inland hike is the **Buck Creek Trail** from Saddle Mountain, a challenging near-vertical descent through the fog to the beach. (Before taking the challenge, consider the comments scratched by survivors into the government's signs: "It's a real mother both ways" and "This hill will kill you.") There are four primitive BLM campgrounds in the King Range along both main access roads. It's five miles from Four Corners via Chemise Mountain Rd. to **Wailaki Camp,** picnic tables and 16 campsites on Bear Creek's south fork. (From Wailaki Camp, it's a steep 3½-mile scramble down to the wooden bench below, another half mile to the mouth of Chemise Creek and the beach.) A bit farther is **Nadelos Camp,** with 14 sites. The smaller **Tolkan** and the very pretty, very private **Horse Mountain Camp** are on King Ranch Road.

Sinkyone Wilderness State Park

Sinking into Sinkyone is like blinking away all known life in order to finally see. Named for the Sinkyone people who refused to abandon their traditional culture and hire on elsewhere as day laborers, this place somehow still honors that indomitable spirit.

More remote and rugged than even the King Range, at Sinkyone Wilderness State Park jagged peaks plunge into untouched tidepools where sea lions and seals play. Unafraid here, wildlife sputters, flutters, or leaps forth at every opportunity. The land seems lusher, greener, with dark virgin forests of redwoods and mixed conifers, rich grassland meadows, waterfalls, fern grottos.

The one thing trekkers won't find (yet) among these 6,400 wild acres is an intricate trail system. About seven miles of the coast are now accessible to hikers; the main trail system includes a north/south trail and some logging roads. Though it's now impossible to hike south from Shelter Cove, eventually Sinkyone's trail system will connect with King Range coastal trails.

Sinkyone Wilderness State Park is always open for day use. The park also offers limited camping at over 22 scattered and primitive environmental campsites, rarely full. To get oriented, stop by the park's **visitor center** at **Needle Rock House,** named for an impressive sea stack offshore just beyond the black-sand beach. (Take shelter in the cottage in bad weather, otherwise camp under alders and firs nearby.) **Jones Beach** features a secluded cove and an acre of eucalyptus trees at an abandoned homestead (steep trail). Easier to get to is **Stream Side Camp,** two campsites in a wooded creekside glen, with a third perched atop a nearby knoll (with great ocean views, fog permitting). Farther inland is **Low Bridge Camp,** by a stream 1½ miles from the visitor center.

Beautifully rugged **Bear Harbor** in the Orchard Creek meadow was once a lumber port serving northern Mendocino and southern Humboldt counties. All that's left of the nine-milelong railroad spur that served the area from the mid-1880s until 1906 is a short rusted section of narrow-gauge track. Fuchsias cascade over the small stone dam. (In late summer, harvest a few apples from the homestead's abandoned orchard before the deer do.)

Energized after the beach trails with no place else to go, hike unpaved Usal Rd., which runs north to south and passes through Bear Harbor. Most cars can't make it past the gully in the road just over a mile south of Bear Harbor, but it's an easy walk from there to Bear Harbor campsites (excellent beach also). There's also a secluded seaside campground at Usal Creek, and two new backpackers' camps at Jackass and Little Jackass creeks.

Some Lost And Found Towns

People in **Briceland** once made a living as bark peelers. There was a plant here for extracting tannic acid from the bark of the tan oak. The spot called **Whitethorn** near the headwaters of the Mattole River was once a

---

ALMOST LOST LAND

A side note to the recent expansion of **Sinkyone Wilderness State Park** is how it got expanded, an intriguing tale of life in the modern world. At the end of a complex series of events beginning in the mid-1970s—which included at times almost violent confrontations between logging company employees and protestors—the San Francisco-based Trust for Public Land in 1986 successfully negotiated with Georgia-Pacific to buy 7,100 acres of land appraised at $10.2 million. Seventeen miles of coastline (and 2,900 acres) were deeded by the Trust to the state park system. The state contributed $2.8 million to the pot but the public received land valued at $5.5 million. Another player in the game, the Save-the-Redwoods League, contributed $1 million and received protective custody of 400 acres of virgin redwoods, including the 75-acre Sally Bell Grove. In addition, the California Coastal Conservancy lent $1.1 million to the Trust for Public Land to help develop a land-management and marketing plan for timber harvesting and other activities on the remaining 3,800 acres — that plan to be jointly developed by the Coastal Conservancy, interested environmental groups, the Mendocino County Board of Supervisors, and the International Woodworkers Union. Native Americans will also participate, working with the Trust for Public Land to establish an **Intertribal Wilderness Park** (the first in the United States), to be managed "in traditional ways," adjacent to the Sinkyone Wilderness.

---

busy stage station, then a loud lumber camp with five working sawmills. East of Honeydew is old **Ettersburg,** now posted as **Divorce Flat** and first homesteaded in 1894 by apple grower Alfter Etter.

Honeydew (population two after 5 p.m.) was named for the sweet-tasting aphid dew beneath cottonwoods down by the river. There's a gas station/general store/post office in Honeydew, tel. (707) 629-3310, usually but not necessarily open Mon.-Sat. 9 a.m.-6 p.m. Head-turning from here, though, are the roadside views of Kings Peak and its rugged range. Perfect for picnicking is the **A.W. Way County Park** in the Mattole River Valley, loveliest in spring when the wild irises bloom.

There's good fishing on the Mattole River between Honeydew and eucalyptus-sheltered **Petrolia,** named for California's first commercial oil well, drilled three miles east of here in the 1860s. Also between Honeydew and Petrolia is a great place to eat, the **Hideaway** bar and grill near the Lindley Bridge, tel. (707) 629-3330, which has incredible cinnamon rolls and other baked goods, real American hamburgers, even good Mexican food (full dinners served only on Sunday nights); open daily 11:30 a.m.-2 a.m. Petrolia also has a well-stocked general store and gas station, and the **"Lost Coast" Mattole River Resort** close to Honeydew at 42354 Mattole Rd., tel. 629-3445, has housekeeping cottages.

Deluxe in the area and quite charming is the **Lost Inn** in "downtown" Petrolia (Box 161, Petrolia 95558), tel. (707) 629-3394. Actually a huge two-room suite in the front section of the family home (private entrance through the trellised opening in the hedges and flower gardens), the Lost Inn offers a double bed and separate sitting area, kitchenette, woodstove, and large glassed-in front porch perfect for capturing winter sun. In summer, the porch windows open wide, letting in sublime sea air. Rates: $60 per night for two, $10 extra person.

Farther north, past the Mattole River lagoon and the road leading to the abandoned Punta Gorda Lighthouse, past the automated light tower atop Cape Ridge (built to replace the 16-sided pyramid tower built there in 1868), and past Cape Mendocino and Scottish-looking farm country is the very Victorian town of **Ferndale** just south of Eureka. Get a great aerial view of the Eel River Delta as you come down to town.

The big city on this lost side of the world, though, is **Shelter Cove,** a privately owned enclave within the King Range Conservation Area once home to the Sinkyone and a major collecting point for the Pomos' clamshell money.

Today, this is the place for soaking up some wilderness within range of humanity, for whale-watching, beachcombing, skin diving, and sport fishing. Though no place serves breakfast, there are two restaurants in Shelter Cove (**Mario's,** tel. 707-986-7432, and **Pelican's Landing,** tel. 986-7793), and a general store, tel. 986-7733, connected to the **Shelter Cove Beachcomber Inn,** 7272 Shelter Cove Rd., Whitethorn 95989, tel. 986-7733 (call between 9 a.m. and 7 p.m. or write), which offers secluded rooms with brass beds, private baths, kitchens. The **Shelter Cove Campground** at 492 Machi Rd., tel. 986-7474, offers 100 RV sites (tent campers welcome) plus boat launch services and rentals. Most urbane, though, is the cozy **Howard Creek Ranch Inn** bed and breakfast near the south end of Usal Rd. north of Westport, P.O. Box 121, Westport 95488, tel. 964-6725, a New England-style farmhouse with newer outlying cabins (including one in a boat hull), gorgeous gardens, pool, sauna, wood-heated hot tub; $50-90.

Other area bed and breakfasts located near the Lost Coast's southern edge include **Bowen's Pelican Inn** at 321 N. Hwy. 1 in Westport (P.O. Box 358), tel. 964-5588, Western hotel and 1890 Victorian with eight rooms (three share two baths), continental breakfast, restaurant and bar on premises, room rates $45-75. The **DeHaven Valley Farm** at 39247 N. Hwy. 1, tel. 961-1660, is a large 1885-vintage Victorian farmhouse with a total of eight "view" rooms (two share a bath, four have fireplaces), full breakfast (dinner available in restaurant), rates $85-125.

GETTING LOST

Preparing To Get Lost

It's rainy and very wet here—100 to 200 inches of rain annually—from October to April and foggy during much of the rest of the year. In any season, come prepared to get wet. The land itself is unstable, with landslides common during the rainy season. Unpaved roads are rough and rugged even under the best weather conditions (some wags refer to driving the area as "car hiking"). Come with a full tank of gas and bring adequate emergency supplies, food, and drinking water.

To hike or backpack here, bring proper shoes. For coastwalking (often through sand but also over rocks), lightweight but sturdy shoes with good ankle support and nonslip tread are best. For hiking the inland backcountry—more grassland than forest due to the thin mountain soil, but there's also chaparral, mixed stands of conifers and oaks, and omnipresent poison oak—heavy-duty hiking boots are wise. Also bring current maps of the area since hikers here are on their own, sometimes (though not always) trekking for days without meeting another human soul.

For serious cyclists, consider signing on with the Chico Velo Cycling Club's annual two-day, 100-mile **Tour of the Unknown Coast,** usually rolling through the area on the mid-September weekend coinciding with Mattole Valley Grange's ham-and-eggs-and-pancakes Saturday morning breakfast. Though Chico-area cyclists travel quite some distance to get here, anyone from anywhere can come along with advance arrangements. For information, contact: Chico Velo Cycling Club, tel. (916) 343-8356. (See also "Eureka" below.)

Whalewatching charters along the Lost Coast are available through **King Salmon Charters,** 3458 Utah St., Eureka 95501, tel. (707) 442-3474.

Not Getting Lost

Visiting California's Lost Coast requires first getting there, something of a challenge. For current conditions, information, and maps, contact: **King Range,** U.S. Bureau of Land Management, 1585 J St., Arcata 95521, tel. (707) 822-7648, or the **BLM Ukiah District Office,** 555 Leslie St., Ukiah 95482, tel. (707) 462-3873. Alternatively, for state lands information, stop by **Humboldt Redwood State Park** north of Garberville (or send $2.65 and a self-addressed stamped legal-size envelope to **Eel River District,** Box 100, Weott 95571) or contact: **Sinkyone Wilderness,** P.O. Box 245, Whitethorn 95989, tel. 986-7711.

Roads here are not for the faint of heart and not for those with unreliable vehicles. For the fit and foolhardy, mountain biking down then back out just adds to the thrill. Though Lost Coast road signs usually disappear as fast as they go up (the locals' way of sending a message), existing signs that state Steep Grade—Narrow Road: Campers and Trailers Not Advised roughly translate as "Prepare to drive off the end of the earth then dive blindly into a fogbank."

From Humboldt Redwood State Park, take Bull Creek Flats Rd. west through the park to rugged, mountainous Mattole Rd. and continue north toward Petrolia. Lost Coast hikers "going the distance" south along the King Range beaches to Shelter Cove often start here near the squat old lighthouse (reached via Lighthouse Road). Arrange a shuttle system at Shelter Cove to keep it a one-way trip.

The only paved road challenging the steep grades to the sea is Shelter Cove Road. Stay on Briceland/Shelter Cove Rd. and follow the King Range signs to the cove. The wild Wilder Ridge Rd. connects with Mattole Rd. near Honeydew and meets with the Smith-Etter jeep trail (leaping straight downhill to the sea) one mile south of Honeydew.

To get into the King Range from Garberville, take Frontage Rd. one mile to Redway, and go west 16 miles on Briceland/Shelter Cove Rd. or—to head north—take Wilder Ridge Road.

From Garberville, get into the Sinkyone Wilderness via Briceland-Thorn Rd., the last nine miles unpaved, suitable in winter only for four-wheel-drive vehicles (and never suitable for RVs or trailers). At Four Corners, the road to the east snakes back toward Garberville; Usal Rd. straight ahead follows Jackass Ridge and eventually reaches Hwy. 1; and the road to the southwest, toward the ocean, leads to Needle Rock and Bear Harbor.

HUMBOLDT REDWOOD STATE PARK

This is the redwood heart of Humboldt County, where over 40 percent of the world's redwoods remain. The Save-the-Redwoods League and the state have added to the park's holdings grove by grove. Most of these "dedicated groves," named in honor of those who gave to save the trees, and many of the park's developed campgrounds are along the state-park section of the Avenue of the Giants parkway.

Humboldt Redwood State Park is the largest state park in Northern California, with over 50,000 acres of almost unfrequented redwood groves, mixed conifers, and oaks. Down on the flats are the deepest and darkest stands of virgin redwoods, including Rockefeller Forest, the world's largest stand of stately survivors. The rolling uplands include grass-brushed hills with mixed forest. Calypso orchids and lilies are plentiful in spring, and wild blackberries and huckleberries ripen from July to September.

As is typical of the north coast, heavy rainfall and sometimes dangerously high river conditions are predictable from November through April. But the rampaging **Eel River** shrinks to garter snake size by May or June, its emerald water fringed by white sand beaches good for swimming, tubing, fishing, and for watching the annual lamprey migration. The wild and scenic stretches of the Eel are also known for early-in-the-year whitewater rafting and kayaking. The **Avenue of the Giants Marathon** run through the redwoods is in early May.

Sights

Rockefeller Forest includes almost 13,000 acres, the main grove among the most valuable virgin stands remaining on the north coast (and yes, donated to the world by the John D. Rockefeller family). In **Founder's Grove,** the Founder's Tree was once known as the World's Tallest Tree, but the Dyerville Giant is—or was—actually the park's tallest at 362 feet, when last measured in 1972. (The Giant toppled over in a 1991 storm, and now lies on the forest floor.) For those unduly impressed by the power of comparative measurement, there are taller trees in Redwood National Park north of Orick, but these two are mindful monuments to the grandeur of the natural world. And if you didn't notice the one at Richardson Grove (see below), in Weott there's another *Metasequoia,* a dawn redwood native to China, kissing cousin of both species of California redwoods.

The park offers 35 miles of hiking and backpacking trails, plus 30 miles of old logging roads and surprising solitude so close to a freeway. Unusual at Humboldt Redwood State Park are five backcountry backpackers' camps, reservable in advance (first-come) at park headquarters. These camps each have piped spring water (but no fires allowed, so bring a campstove). Only one of the five is easily reached by non-hikers, **Bull Creek Trail Camp.** Closest to the road but an uphill climb are **Johnson Trail Camp,** a collection of four backwoods cabins used from the 1920s to 1950s by "tie hacks" (railroad tie makers), and the **Whiskey Flat Trail Camp,** a tent camp named for the Prohibition moonshine still once tucked among these massive old-growth

redwoods. **Grasshopper Trail Camp** is among the grasshoppers and deer on the meadow's edge below Grasshopper Peak (great view from the fire lookout at the top), and **Hanson Ridge Trail Camp** is tucked among firs and ferns.

Avenue Of The Giants

This scenic 33-mile drive on the old highway, a narrow asphalt ribbon braiding together the eastern edge of Humboldt Redwoods, the Eel River, and Hwy. 101, weaves past and through some of the largest groves of the largest remaining redwoods in Humboldt and Del Norte counties. Get off the bike (the avenue's very nice for cycling, but wear bright clothing) or out of the car and picnic, take a short walk, and just *appreciate* these grand old giants. People stop too at the least-inspiring attractions along the part-private, part-public avenue: the tourist traps offering redwood knickknacks and trinkets manufactured overseas and trees transformed into walk-in or drive-through freaks of nature. But the curio shops and commercial trappings barely distract from the fragrant grandeur of the dim, dignified forest itself, sunlit in faint slivers and carpeted with oxalis and ferns.

Among the tiny towns dwarfed still more by the giants along the avenue is **Phillipsville,** home to the Tolkienesque **Hobbitown U.S.A.** and the **Chimney Tree,** tel. (707) 923-2265, open 8 a.m.-8 p.m. from May to mid-October. The **One-Log House** (actually a mobile home) also in Phillipsville, tel. 943-3258, is a hollowed-out 32-foot section of redwood on wheels, with a seven-foot "ceiling." In **Meyers Flat** is the **Shrine Drive-Thru-Tree,** one of the state's oldest tourist attractions, tel. 943-3154. Wagon-train travelers heading up and down the Pacific coast once pulled *their* vehicles through it. The tree stands 275 feet tall, measures 21 feet in diameter, and people can see the sky if standing inside the eight-foot-wide tree tunnel. (Sandwiches available at the **Drive-Thru-Tree Deli.**) Other monuments include **The Eternal Tree House** in Redcrest, a 20-foot room inside a living tree, and **The Immortal Tree** near Founder's Grove, which has withstood almost every onslaught conceivable by both nature and humanity.

Park Practicalities

Camping is easy at Humboldt Redwoods, which offers hundreds of campsites and four picnic areas. **Burlington Campground** near Weott is fully developed (hot showers, restrooms, tables —the works for outdoor living), $14. Ditto for the **Albee Creek Campground** not far to the south, and **Hidden Springs Campground** near Miranda. In addition to the outback pleasures of the park's backcountry camps (see above), there are two walk-in environmental campgrounds here, **Baxter** and **Hamilton Barn** (pick apples in the old orchard), both with convenient yet secluded campsites, (sign up at park headquarters and get the particulars), also hiking and biking campsites, group camps, and horse camps. Or head south to **Richardson Grove** (popular, often crowded in summer, reservations usually necessary). There are 600 or so campsites in private campgrounds and RV parks nearby if the state facilities are full. For camping reservations at popular Albee Creek, Burlington, Hidden Springs, and Richardson Grove, call Mistix, tel. (800) 444-7275.

Day-use fee at Humboldt Redwoods is $5 per car. For maps and more information about the park, stop by or contact: Humboldt Redwood State Park headquarters at the Burlington Campground, P.O. Box 100, Weott 95571, tel. (707) 946-2409. The **visitor center** between headquarters and Burlington Campground, tel. 946-2263, is open 10 a.m.-5 p.m. (on weekends March-Oct. until 8 p.m., pending a new round of state budget cuts) and has excellent natural history exhibits. In summer park rangers offer guided nature walks, campfire programs, and Junior Ranger activities for kids.

Get a good sandwich at **The Peg House Deli** across from the park (also ice and basic groceries) or try the **Englewood Avenue of the Giants Restaurant** just south of Redcrest, tel. (707) 722-4210, for homestyle American cooking at breakfast, lunch, and dinner. For American and international cuisine and fine wines, head toward Myers Flat and **Knight's Restaurant,** tel. 943-3411. Two worthwhile dinner houses within driving distance: the **Scotia Inn** to the north in Scotia, owned (like the rest of the town) by the Pacific Lumber Company, and the very English **Benbow Inn** south along the freeway.

For determined noncampers, the **Madrona Motel,** P.O. Box 124, Phillipsville 95559, tel. (707) 943-3108, is a clean and pleasant fifties-feeling place, some units with kitchens, from $35. The **Whispering Pines** motel next to the

Eel River, P.O. Box 246, Miranda 95553, tel. 943-3182, offers a rec room with fireplace and pool table, heated pool, lawn games, rooms from $35. The **Miranda Gardens Resort** at 6766 Avenue of the Giants (P.O. Box 186), Miranda 95553, tel. 943-3011, is tops in the motel department: single or duplex cabins (some with two bedrooms, some with kitchens), rustic yet quite comfortable, several with fireplaces, one with spa. Rates: $35-145.

Very pleasant is a stay at the **Myers Flat Country Inn** at 12903 Old Redwood Hwy. in Myers Flat, tel. (707) 943-3259, a 1915-vintage two-story California-style hotel now functioning as a bed and breakfast—private baths, separate entrances, balcony, fireplace in lobby, continental breakfast. Rates: $55-65.

GARBERVILLE

A former sheep ranching town, Garberville is *not* an outlaw enclave paved in $100 bills by pot-growing Mercedes Benz owners, as media

the Humboldt Redwoods

mythology would have it. The town was once considered the sinsemilla cultivation capital of the world, an honor most locals are fed up with: the general belief is that the big-time Rambo-style growers have already gone elsewhere. But don't expect people here to share their knowledge *or* opinions on the subject, pro or con. With the annual CAMP invasions throughout the surrounding countryside, discretion is the rule of tongue when outsiders show up.

Not far north of Garberville is the **M. Lockwood Memorial Park,** a popular rafting departure point, also good fishing. Two small southerly outposts of Humboldt Redwood State Park are just north of Redway: **Whittemore Grove** and **Holbrook Grove,** both dark, cool glens perfect for picnicking and short hikes.

In June, the annual **Garberville Rodeo** is the big to-do in these parts, followed in July or early August by the West Coast's largest and usually most impressive reggae festival, the **Reggae on the River** concert, which attracts top talent from Jamaica and America. Call the **Mateel Community Center** in Redway at (707) 923-3368 for information.

Area Accommodations

Cheapest accommodations are found at the area's numerous developed and primitive campgrounds on the coast or in the forest (see above and below). Quite special, though, is the AYH-affiliated **Eel River Redwoods Hostel** 25 miles south of town and just north of Leggett. These inexpensive lodgings on the edge of the redwoods, close to the Mendocino coast and on the main bicycle route from Oregon to the Bay Area, attract visitors from around the globe and offer exceptional facilities, resort-type bungalows with bunk beds (couples' and family rooms available), laundry, sauna, swimming hole, saloon, good restaurant, also free loaner bikes and inner tubes for floating the Eel. Open all year. Rates: $10 AYH members, $11 nonmembers. For more information, contact: Eel River Redwoods Hostel, 70400 Hwy. 101, Leggett 95455, tel. (707) 925-6469. For advance reservations (optional but prudent, especially during summer) call ahead (credit card) or send a stamped, self-addressed legal-sized envelope.

In the same general area but definitely in a different price range is **Sky Canyon Ranch** P.O. Box 356, Leggett 95455, tel. (707) 925-6415,

a 250-acre wooded forest nature reserve bisected by the Eel River and Cedar Creek. Fully equipped guesthouses, even a stable, arena, and other facilities for horse owners. Rates: $110-195 per night. Massage available, also hiking (two meditation *skandas* nearby, overlooking the Eel River Canyon).

Just about everything in Garberville is on Business 101, called Redwood Drive. The 56-room **Best Western Humboldt House Inn,** 701 Redwood Dr., Garberville 95440, tel. (707) 923-2771 or toll-free (800) 528-1234, has rooms $55-70 (slightly less in the off-season), the extras here including coin-op laundry, pool and whirlpool, air-conditioning, color TV, movies, phones. The **Sherwood Forest Motel,** 814 Redwood Dr., tel. 923-2721, is quite a find, with all the amenities found at the more expensive Humboldt House (plus radios), with rooms $46-54. The **Hartsook Country Inn,** about eight miles south of town at 900 Hwy. 101, tel. 247-3305, has an impressive selection of cabins.

Good Area Food

Just north of Garberville in Redway is the **Mateel Cafe,** 478 Redwood Dr., tel. (707) 923-2030, a fine-food mecca that lures folks even from San Francisco. The fare here is delicious, health-conscious, and reasonably priced, from the exotic pizzas, soups, and salads to dinner entrees such as free-range chicken with leeks and Herb Linguini Papillon. Open for lunch, late lunch, and dinner most weekdays (call for current schedule), for dinner on Sat. nights. For fine omelettes, good vegetarian sandwiches, and like fare, everything locally and/or organically grown, locally famous is the **Woodrose Cafe** down the street at 911 Redwood, tel. 923-3191. Open daily for breakfast, for lunch only on weekdays. A good choice for wheat-bread-and-sprouts-style Sunday champagne brunch. For straight-ahead Italian food and pizza, not to mention the impressive amounts of Mexican and American fare, try **Sicilito's** behind the Humboldt House, 445 Conger Ln., tel. 923-2814, open daily. For fresh fish in season and good family-style Italian and American fare, the place is the **Waterwheel Restaurant,** 924 Redwood Dr., tel. 923-2031.

About seven miles south of Garberville is the excellent **Mad Creek Inn,** tel. (707) 984-6206, specializing in what the owners refer to as "gourmet home cooking." And what you get here is honest good food, American and continental, seafood specialties, steaks, pastas (like cannelloni stuffed with chicken or shrimp), stuffed mushrooms, hot crab meat sandwiches, burgers, fresh baked bread. Reasonable. Look for the windmill on the west side of the highway. Also very special for dinner is the rustic-looking **Bell Glen Restaurant** near the hostel in Leggett, tel. 925-6425, actually a fine seafood house set with linen on redwood burl tables but casual dress okay. Continental menu with limited daily selections, a good Sunday brunch, excellent overall and reasonable.

Information, Transport, Services
The **Garberville-Redway Chamber of Commerce,** Redwood Dr., P.O. Box 445, Garberville 95440, tel. (707) 923-2613, is open 9 a.m.-5 p.m. daily in summer, and Mon.-Fri. 9-5 only in winter. Nearby is the **Greyhound** station, inside **Calico's** cafe at 808 Redwood Dr., tel. 923-3259, open daily 8 a.m.-6 p.m., with departures north and south daily. The **post office** is at 368 Sprowel Creek Rd., off Redwood Dr., tel. 923-2652, and there's a coin-op **laundromat** at 649 Redwood, open daily 8 a.m.-9 p.m.

SOUTH OF GARBERVILLE

Benbow Lake State Recreation Area
This state recreation area in the midst of open woodlands just south of Garberville is aptly named only in the summer, when a temporary dam goes up on the Eel River's south fork to create Benbow Lake. The lake itself is great for swimming, sailing, canoeing, and windsurfing, with pleasant picnicking and hiking in the hills nearby. No fishing. It's also the scene of the summer's annual **Jazz on the Lake** festival, **Shakespeare at Benbow Lake,** the **Summer Arts Fair,** and the very fun **Benbow Lake Milk Carton Boat Races.** There's also a par course. In addition to state facilities, Benbow Valley has a private **RV resort** at 7000 Benbow Dr., Garberville 95440, tel. (707) 923-2777, with 100 sites, full hookups, and a golf course. For more information, contact: Benbow Lake State Recreation Area, Garberville 95440, tel. 923-3238. The lake may disappear but the campground is open all year. Quite popular in sum-

SHAKESPEARE AT BENBOW LAKE

mer, so reserve campsites ($14) in advance through Mistix, tel. (800) 444-7275.

The Benbow Inn
Also open year-round is the elegant four-story Tudor-style **Benbow Inn,** 445 Lake Benbow Dr., Garberville 95440, tel. (707) 923-2124. Designed by architect Albert Farr, the Benbow Inn first opened its doors in 1926 and over the years has welcomed travelers including Herbert Hoover, Charles Laughton, and Eleanor Roosevelt. A National Historic Landmark, the inn has been recently restored to a very English attitude. Complimentary scones and tea are served in the lobby every afternoon at 3 p.m., mulled wine at 4 p.m. when the weather is cold, and hors d'oeuvres in the common rooms between 5 and 7 p.m. The inn's dining room serves a good breakfast, lunch during the summer only, staples like steak-and-kidney pie for dinner. Full bar.

In addition to the summertime activities staged at Lake Benbow, the Benbow Inn hosts an annual Halloween Masquerade Party and Dance, special Thanksgiving festivities, a theme Christmas party, and a New Year's Eve Champagne Dinner Dance to the big-band tunes of Tommy Dorsey and Glenn Miller. Rooms run $88-275, the latter rate for the inn's Garden Cottage. Ask about the off-season special.

Richardson Grove State Park

Richardson Grove, south of Lake Benbow, with over 800 acres of fine redwoods, was named for 1920s California Governor Friend W. Richardson, a noted conservationist of the day. Popular and crowded in summer, though few people hike the backcountry trails. Picnic near the river or camp at any of three developed campgrounds (one open all year), also hike-and-bike campsites. Mistix reservations advisable. The **Seven Parks Natural History Association,** 1600 Hwy. 101, located in the visitor center at Richardson Grove Lodge, has a variety of redwood-country publications. For more information, contact: Richardson Grove State Park, P.O. Box E, Garberville 95440, tel. (707) 247-3318.

More Redwoods

Smithe Redwoods State Reserve, six miles south of Piercy on Hwy. 101, is a lovely redwood grove reachable only from the west side of the highway, though most of the protected trees are to the east (not open to visitors). It's a quarter-mile hike to the 60-foot waterfalls. Nearby is **Confusion Hill,** tel. (707) 925-6456, one of those places where gravity is defied and water runs uphill, etc., though you can also take the kids on a train ride through the redwoods.

Standish-Hickey State Recreation Area, one mile north of Leggett, is 1,000 acres forested with second-growth coast redwoods, firs, bigleaf maples, oaks, and alders, also thick with ferns and water-loving wildflowers in spring. Camp at any of the three campgrounds here (reservations through Mistix necessary in summer), also hike-and-bike campsites, fishing, swimming. Hike to the 225-foot-tall **Miles Standish Tree,** a massive mature redwood that

somehow escaped the loggers, on a trail heading on to a waterfall. The **Mill Creek** trail is a steeper, rugged five-mile loop. For more information, contact Standish-Hickey State Recreation Area, tel. (707) 925-6482, or address letters to the district office, Box 100, Weott 95571.

The **Drive-Thru-Tree Park** in Leggett is as schlocky as it sounds, but for some reason humans just love driving through trees. They carved this car-sized hole in the tree in the 1930s, and for a small fee people can "drive thru" it (RVs won't make it). About eight miles north of here is 400-acre **Reynolds Wayside Camp** along the Eel River, with 50 unimproved campsites, picnicking. The **Admiral William Standley State Recreation Area** halfway to the coast on Branscombe Rd. is a small, 45-acre park along the south fork of the Eel, with an impressive stand of coastal redwoods. Undeveloped (the road's only partially paved), perfect for picnicking and hiking.

Northern California Coast Range Preserve

The Nature Conservancy's 8,000-acre North Coast Range Preserve is that agency's first project, established in 1956 on the south fork of the Eel and now co-managed by the BLM. The hilly and mountainous preserve includes pristine Douglas fir forests on the Elder Creek watershed, some California bay, oaks, knobcone pines, redwoods, and meadows with incredibly diverse wildflowers. River otters are plentiful. For permission to visit, directions, and maps, contact: Northern California Coast Range Preserve headquarters, 42101 Wilderness Rd., Branscomb 95417, tel. (707) 984-6653. Reservations are required to enter, but once here, just park and walk into the real world.

EUREKA

When James T. Ryan slogged ashore here from his whaling ship in May of 1850, shouting (so the story goes) *Eureka!* ("I have found it"), what he found was California's largest natural bay north of San Francisco. Russian-American Fur Company hunters actually entered Humboldt Bay first in 1806, but the area's official discovery came in 1849 when a party led by Josiah Gregg came overland that winter seeking the mouth of the Trinity River (once thought to empty into the ocean). Gregg died in the unfriendly forests on the return trip to San Francisco, but the reports of his half-starved companions led to Eureka's establishment on "Trinity Bay" as a trading post and port serving the far northern inland gold camps.

While better than other north coast harbors, Humboldt Bay was still less than ideal. The approach across the sand bar was treacherous and dozens of ships foundered in heavy storms or fog—a trend that continued well into this century. In 1917 the cruiser USS *Milwaukee,* flagship of the Pacific fleet, arrived to rescue a grounded submarine and ended up winching itself onto the beach, where it sat until World War II (when it was scrapped and recycled). But ever-imaginative Eureka has managed to turn even abandoned boats into a community resource. Before the Humboldt Bay Nuclear Power Plant was built here in 1963, the city got most of its energy from the generators of the salvaged Russian tanker *Donbass III,* towed into the bay and beached in 1946.

Oddly expansive and naked today, huge Humboldt Bay was once a piddling puddle at the edge of the endless redwood forest. Early loggers stripped the land closest to town first, but the bare Eureka hills were soon dotted with reincarnated redwoods, buildings of pioneer industry and the stately Victorians which are still the community's cultural roots.

No matter how vibrant the colors of the old homes here, nothing can dispel the fog. Elsewhere along the coast, the fog burns off for at least a few hours during the day. But the sun rarely shines from Eureka north to Crescent City. And when the fog does finally lift, the rains come, washing away hillsides and closing the roads, trapping people here behind what they refer to as the Redwood Curtain. This sense of being isolated from the rest of the human world, and the need to transform life into something other than *gray,* may be why there are more artists and performers per capita in Humboldt County than anywhere else in the state.

SIGHTS

Humboldt Bay

Eureka's 10-mile-long Humboldt Bay was named for the German naturalist Baron Alexander von Humboldt, so it's fitting that the extensive (if almost unknown and largely neglected) **Humboldt Bay National Wildlife Refuge** was established on the edge of the bay's South Jetty to protect small migrating geese called brands (36,000 showed up in 1951; less than 200 come now) and more than 200 other bird species. With the recent inclusion of an adjacent 1,500-acre cattle ranch on South Humboldt Bay, the refuge has begun the habitat restoration necessary for protecting wild birds. The new refuge headquarters is on Beatrice Flat 10 miles south of Eureka off Hwy. 101, between Lolita and Fields Landing. Plans are in the works for developing an interpretive center, hiking trails, and birdwatching blinds, and for obtaining an additional 6,000 acres of area wetlands, including portions of Indian Island (an egret rookery surrounded now by commercial and industrial development), Sand Islands, Jacoby Creek, and Eureka Slough on North Humboldt Bay.

Other harbor life includes sea lions, harbor seals, porpoises, and gray whales offshore in winter and early spring. To get a look from the bay, take the **Humboldt Bay Harbor Cruise** (see "Transport and Tours" below). Human wildlife includes fishing crews, sailors, and the California State University Humboldt crew teams out rowing at dusk (best bird's-eye view from the Cafe Marina on Woodley Island). Another way to tour the area is by train whenever the **Northcoast Daylight** is offering runs between Fort Seward near Arcata and Eureka.

Fields Landing, where the last Northern California whaling station operated until 1951, is the

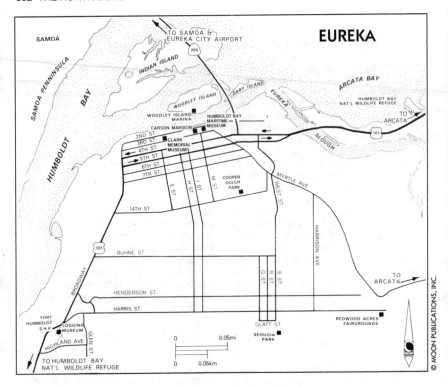

EUREKA

(map labels)
TO SAMOA & EUREKA CITY AIRPORT
255
SAMOA
INDIAN ISLAND
SAMOA PENINSULA
DABY ISLAND
ARCATA BAY
WOODLEY ISLAND
BAY
HUMBOLDT BAY NAT'L WILDLIFE REFUGE
TO ARCATA
WOODLEY ISLAND MARINA
HUMBOLDT BAY MARITIME MUSEUM
CARSON MANSION
2ND ST
3RD ST
CLARK MEMORIAL MUSEUM
4TH ST
5TH ST
6TH ST
7TH ST
E ST
H ST
I ST
M ST
COOPER GULCH PARK
SLOUGH
101
MYRTLE AVE
WEST ST
HUMBOLDT BAY
14TH ST
HARRISON AVE
101
BUHNE ST
BROADWAY
Q ST
R ST
S ST
TO ARCATA
HENDERSON ST
HARRIS ST
FORT HUMBOLDT S.H.P.
LOGGING MUSEUM
GLEN ST
HIGHLAND AVE
GLATT ST
SEQUOIA PARK
REDWOOD ACRES FAIRGROUNDS
TO HUMBOLDT BAY NAT'L WILDLIFE REFUGE
0   0.05mi
0   0.05km
© MOON PUBLICATIONS, INC.

bay's deep-water port, the place to watch large fishing boats unload their daily catch (the rest of the fleet docks at the end of Commercial St. in downtown Eureka). This is also the place to pick up fresh Dungeness crab, usually available from Christmas to February or March. Stop when the flag's flying at **Botchie's Crab Stand** on Field's Landing Dr. just off Hwy. 101, where *only* the hand-picked best of the day's catch are for sale.

The **Samoa Bridge** connects the city of Eureka with the narrow peninsula extending south from Arcata (almost across Humboldt Bay) and the old company town of **Samoa,** the name inspired by the bay's resemblance to the harbor at Pago Pago. The **Samoa Cookhouse,** noted rustic restaurant and the last logging camp cookhouse in the West, also is a fascinating museum. The **Eureka City Airport** and **U.S. Coast Guard** facilities occupy the fingertip of Samoa Peninsula, near county-owned fishing access (very basic camping, restrooms, boat ramps).

Old Town Eureka

Part of Eureka's one-time skid row (the term itself of north coast origin, referring to the shantytowns and shacks lining the loggers' "skid roads" near ports) has been shoved aside to make room for Old Town. Most of the fleabag flophouses, sleazy sailors' bars, and pool halls along 1st, 2nd, and 3rd between C and G streets were razed and others renovated to create this bayside concentration of new cafes, art galleries, and trendy shops. The big event every summer is the **Old Town Fourth of July Celebration.**

Most people stop first for a look at the gaudy, geegawed Gothic **Carson Mansion** at the foot of 2nd St. (locals say "Two Street") at M, once the home of lumber baron William Carson. Those in the know say this is the state's—perhaps the nation's—finest surviving example of Victoriana. Now home to the exclusive all-male (how Victorian) Ingomar Club, even unescorted

THE HUMBOLDT BAY BLUES

These are not easy times along the state's far northern coast, particularly in and around Eureka. The economy has been nightmarish for decades now, at least for many, what with the decline of the timber industry and equally rough sailing for fishing companies.

Then there was all that federal fuss over PG&E's Humboldt Bay Nuclear Power Plant at Buhne Point, decommissioned and mothballed after a 1976 leak (though its radioactive contents remain) primarily due to the fact that the reactor sits atop an active earthquake fault.

Then there was an impressive earthquake in April of 1992, centered just south of town near Petrolia, which shook everyone—and everything, especially outlying towns like Ferndale, Fortuna, and Scotia—but good.

Now, concerns about water pollution have intruded on local life and livelihoods, leading to a public health warning about eating local seafood. Even normally apolitical surfers have gotten into the act, doing "the green thing" and demanding relief through the courts from poisonous pulp-mill pollution.

Until recently, 40 million gallons of toxic waste were dumped into the bay each year by Simpson Paper Company and Louisiana-Pacific, both located on the Samoa Peninsula. (Simpson has since closed, and business has been slow at L-P.) The dumping is permissible under a special exemption to the federal Clean Water Act. According to the state Department of Health Services, this problem has led to unsafe levels of dioxin—a very potent carcinogen and the most powerful toxin known on earth—in area fish and shellfish.

Though both paper manufacturers are now substituting oxygen for chlorine in their papermaking processes to reduce discharge levels of dioxin, health officials strongly advise consumers to avoid eating fish and shellfish from the area. Even if one were to eat contaminated seafood no more than once a month, the dioxin levels are at least ten times the acceptable risk levels—a situation likely to continue for some time, since there is long-term contamination of the ocean's food chain.

Migratory fish species, such as salmon and steelhead trout, are exempted from the health warning.

men are not welcome inside or in the club's palatial gardens. So be happy with a look at the incredibly ornate turrets and trim of this three-story money-green mansion built of redwood. Inside are superb stained-glass work, hand-worked interiors of hardwoods imported from around the world, and fireplaces crafted from Mexican onyx.

Better, though, and much more accessible despite the protective plate glass, is the fabulous folk art at the **Romano Gabriel Wooden Sculpture Garden** just down the street at 325 2nd St., a blooming, blazing, full-color world of delightful plants, people, and social commentary, crafted from packing crates with the help of a hand-saw. This is "primitive art" (snobs say "poor taste") on a massive scale, one of two pieces of California folk art recognized internationally (the other is Watts Towers in Los Angeles). Gabriel, a gardener who died in 1977, said of his work: "Eureka is bad place for flowers—the salty air and no sun. So I just make this garden." He worked on this garden, which includes likenesses of Mussolini, the Pope, nosy neighbors, and tourists amid the fantastic flowers and trees, for 30 years. After Gabriel's death, it was restored, then transplanted downtown from his front yard.

Well worth it, too, is a stop at the fine and friendly **Clarke Memorial Museum** at 240 E St. at the corner of 3rd, tel. (707) 443-1947, like stepping into a 19th-century parlor. The museum was founded in 1960 by Cecile Clarke (a history teacher at Eureka High 1914-1950), who personally gathered most of the collection. This is the place for a look at various Victoriana including toys and dolls, glassware, and jewelry; pioneer relics, including antique guns and frontier weaponry and a signed first edition of *The Personal Memoirs of General Grant;* and the incredible, nationally noted Nealis Hall collection of Native American artifacts and basketry, including ceremonial dance regalia. The museum building, the Italian Renaissance one-time **Bank of Eureka** with stained-glass skylight and glazed terra-cotta exterior, is itself a collector's item, now listed on the National Register of Historic Places.

The fairly new **Humboldt Bay Maritime Museum** is a block east of the Carson Mansion at 1410 Two St., tel. (707) 444-9440, and housed in a replica of the George McFarlan home originally built here in 1852. The museum, opened in 1984, chronicles the area's contributions to Pacific seafaring heritage with original photographs, ship models, maritime artifacts and library, even an old Fresnel lens from the Table Bluff lighthouse and a refurbished Coast Guard lifeboat. Humboldt Bay Harbor Cruises on the *Madaket* are launched from here.

Located in the old E. Janssen and Company mercantile building at 422 1st St., the Humboldt Arts Council's **Cultural Center,** tel. (707) 442-2611, hosts concerts and performances during much of the year as well as major art exhibits, and offers the work of local artists for sale. Or drop by just to see the building, the exterior of iron, wood, and glass painted in unforgettable "gold rush" mustard with black and white trim, the interior noted for its "steamboat Gothic" mezzanine. The **ArtCenter** on G St. between 2nd and 3rd, also features an impressive gallery.

Fort Humboldt
And Sequoia Park

Not necessarily worth writing home about is Eureka's **Fort Humboldt State Historic Park,** at 3431 Fort Ave., Eureka 95501, tel. (707) 443-7952, free, the essentially unrestored site of the U.S. military's 1850s Indian Wars outpost, one-time stomping grounds of the young U.S. Grant. As depressed in Eureka as elsewhere in California, Grant reportedly spent much of his six months here in saloons then resigned his commission to go home and farm in Missouri. The fort does have an excellent (and wheelchair-accessible) indoor/outdoor museum display of early logging technology, also picnic tables with a good view of Humboldt Bay, and restrooms. Get here via Highland Ave. off Broadway (call for actual directions—it's tricky to find).

There's something sad, too, about **Sequoia Park,** the last significant vestige of the virgin redwood forest which once fringed Humboldt Bay, situated southeast of downtown at Glatt and W streets, tel. (707) 443-7331, open from May through October Tues.-Sun. 10 a.m.-8 p.m., until 5 p.m. otherwise. It's melancholy here, despite the peace of these dark woods laced with walking paths, the rhododendron dell, the duck pond, and the children's petting zoo (open only in summer, located near the playground and picnic area). The recent improvements at the Sequoia Park Zoo (with an-

imals from six continents though the native river otters are best) do not disguise the fact that it's just another animal jail.

ACCOMMODATIONS

Inexpensive And Medium-priced Motels
Camping throughout Humboldt County is best in the wilds, but in a pinch campers can call the **Redwood Acres Fairgrounds** home, south off Myrtle at 3750 Harn's St., tel. (707) 445-3037, full hookups, or try the **KOA** a few miles north of town at 4050 N. Hwy. 101, tel. 822-4243, with facilities including "kamping kabins," tent and trailer spaces, laundry room, rec room, playground. Some lodging is cheaper in Arcata just to the north, which has a **Motel 6** and a **Super 8,** but Eureka has most of the inexpensive and expensive choices. Broadway is "motel row," with reasonable motels also on 4th Street. Most Eureka motels offer substantially cheaper rates from October through April, and even the cheapest places usually have color TV and cable and/or free HBO. (Television is important in Eureka.)

The **Town House Motel** at 933 4th St. (corner of 4th and K), tel. (707) 443-4536, is $48-52 in summer, substantially cheaper off-season. Other good bets include the **Econo-Lodge** at 1630 4th St., tel. 443-8041, some rooms with kitchens, from $36; and the **Fireside Inn** at 5th and R Streets, tel. 443-6312, $35-55. The **Best Western Thunderbird Lodge** at 232 W. 5th St. (at Broadway), tel. 443-2234, features many large rooms and the usual amenities plus pool and whirlpool, $74-88, substantially less in the off-season. The **Travelodge** at 4 4th St., tel. 443-6345, runs $59-71. The **Red Lion Inn** at 1929 4th St. (between T and V Streets), tel. 445-0844, is quite large, attractive, with rates $71-130. Still fashionable for a Eureka stay, though, is at the exceptional **Carson House Inn** at 1209 4th St. (between M and N streets), tel. 443-1601, rooms $60-135.

Fine Hotels
The excellent **Eureka Inn** at 7th and F streets, Eureka 95501, tel. (707) 442-6441, is a 1920s Tudor-style hotel and a National Historic Landmark, with luxuries like sauna, whirlpool, pool, the locals' favorite seafood-and-steak restaurant, also free transportation to and from the airport.

Rates: $70-135, two-bedroom suites $175. The 1986 **Hotel Carter** (not to be confused with the also-new Carter House, see below), is a Victorian facsimile at 301 L St., tel. 444-8062 or 445-1390, with 20 rooms, some with whirlpools, three with fireplaces, complimentary hors d'oeuvres, and a fine full or continental breakfast served downstairs in the dining room every morning at 8:30 a.m. Room rates: $70-180.

The Carter House Inn

Most recently famous among Eureka's fine lodging establishments is the four-story Carter House Bed and Breakfast Inn in Old Town at 1033 3rd St., Eureka 95501, tel. (707) 445-1390 or toll-free (800) 235-1552, an "old" place built of fine rustic redwood following the very authentic (and very exacting) specifications for a stately 1884 "stick" Victorian designed by Carson Mansion architects Samuel and Joseph Newsom. The 1981 Carter House Inn is otherwise quite modern, with very un-Victorian sunny rooms (one with fireplace and whirlpool) and an uncluttered, almost contemporary inner dignity. Mark Carter's 1958 Bentley is available for limo service to and from the airport. Breakfast here is breath-taking. Room rates: $59-299.

Other Good Bed And Breakfasts

The **Camellia Cottage** near Old Town at 1314 I St., Eureka 95501, tel. (707) 445-1089, is a 1928 Craftsman cottage with country French decor, three rooms (one share a bath) and one suite, classical music library and CD player, TV and phones available, full breakfast, bedside cookies or mints every evening. Rates: $60-70. Quite lovely, too, is **The Daly Inn** at 1125 H St., tel. 445-3638, three rooms (two share a bath) and two suites in a 1905 Colonial Revival, full breakfast, afternoon tea, phones, TV, library, gardens with a fish pond. Rates: $65-120.

A **Weaver's Inn**, 1440 B St., tel. (707) 443-8119, is an impressive 1883 Queen Anne Victorian with three rooms (two share a bath) and one suite, antiques and a weaving/fiber art studio, Japanese gardens, full breakfast, afternoon tea. Two rooms have fireplaces, one has a Japanese soaking tub. Rates: $45-85. Other Victorian bed and breakfast inns in Eureka include the landmark **Hollander House**, 2436 E St., tel. 443-2419, with just two rooms, rates from $80; **Huerr's Victorian Inn** at 1302 E St.,

tel. 442-7334, with three rooms (two share a bath), $65; and **Old Town Bed and Breakfast Inn,** 1521 3rd St., tel. 445-3951, rates $65-180.

FINE FOOD EUREKA STYLE

Seafood

Eureka's fishermen's wharf is the real thing, not a tourist trap like San Francisco's. The **Eureka Seafood Grotto** at 6th and Broadway, tel. (707) 443-2075, is the locals' choice for seafood. Eureka's fisheries' retail outlet as well, the Grotto is a tremendous place to slide into seafood stupor, with immense quantities of everything, all quite reasonable. The "Eureka-style" clam chowder is justifiably famous (get a quart to go), though the seafood chef sandwiches (grilled oyster, shrimp, or crab meat) and lunch and dinner specials are also excellent. Order up a plate of clams and cutlets. The **Cafe Marina** on Woodley Island, tel. 443-2233, is another popular fish house, as are the **Waterfront Oyster Bar and Grill** at 102 F St., tel. 443-9190, and **The Sea Grill,** 316 E St., tel. 443-7187. World famous for its seafood, of course, is **Lazio's** at 327 2nd St., tel. 443-9717.

The only place to buy fresh crab is **Botchie's Crab Stand** at Field's Landing off Hwy. 101, open for business when the white flag (with orange crab) is flying. Crab season usually runs from December to May, weather permitting.

The Samoa Cookhouse

At least once in a lifetime, everyone should eat at **The Samoa Cookhouse** on the Samoa Peninsula, tel. (707) 442-1659 ("open after 0600" but no reservations taken). All major credit cards accepted, gift shop next door. The Samoa is a bona fide loggers' cookhouse oozing redwood-rugged ambience. The phrase "all you can eat" takes on new meaning here: portions are gargantuan. Good ol' American food—platters of thickly sliced ham, beef, turkey, and spare ribs (choices change daily), plus potatoes, vegetables, fresh-baked bread—is passed around among the checkered oilcloth-covered tables. Soup and salad are included in the fixed-price meal (about $9.95), not to mention homemade apple pie for dessert. Hearty breakfasts and lunch too. Come early on weekends, particularly in summer, and be prepared to wait an hour or so. To get here, head west from Eureka over the Samoa Bridge, turn left, then left again at the town of Samoa (follow the signs).

Quite Casual Fare

The **Eureka Baking Company,** 3562 Broadway (Hwy. 101), tel. (707) 445-8997, is wonderful for croissants, muffins, sourdough bagettes, and other fresh-baked fare. **Ramone's Bakery** at 209 E St., tel. 445-2923, is excellent for pastries and fresh breads, not to mention espresso and other good coffees. A great choice, too, for pastries and coffee is **Janie's Gourmet Gallery** Coffee Roasting Company and Cafe at 211 F St., tel. 444-3969, also noted for good breakfasts and homemade soups at lunch. Another good stop for soup and sandwiches—and quite possibly the best ice cream anywhere on the north coast—is **Bon Boniere Ice Cream Parlor** at 215 F St. in Old Town, tel. 444-8075.

The **Sweetriver Saloon** at the Bayshore Mall, tel. (707) 444-0444, serves everything from omelettes and decent appetizers to sandwiches, burgers, and cowboy-size dinners, but the Sunday brunch is perhaps most impressive. Friday and Saturday. stand-up comedy night.

Not Quite As Casual

The best around for Chinese is **Shanghai Low** at 1835 4th St., tel. (707) 443-8191. **Sergio's** in Old Town at 201 D St., tel. 443-8187, is quite popular for lunch (weekdays and Sat.), dinners nightly after 5 p.m. Justifiably famous for its tomato and spinach pies and other straightforward selections—one slice of the Sicilian pizza makes a meal—**Tomaso's** at 216 E St., tel. 445-0100, is open for lunch and dinner weekdays and Saturday, also a worthy choice for dinner. Best bet for steaks: **O.H.'s Town House** at 6th and Summer, tel. 443-4652. For decent pasta and quiet atmosphere, try **Mazzotti's Ristorante Italiano,** 305 F St., tel. 445-1912. The elegant and small **Hotel Carter** restaurant, 301 L St., tel. (707) 444-8062, is open for candlelight and classical music dinners with seafood specialties like Eureka's famous Kumamoto oysters (in season), on select nights only, 6:30-9 p.m. The Hotel Carter also offers a famous four-course breakfast. Reservations a must.

But the locals' long-time choice for fine dining is the **Prime Rib Room** at the Eureka Inn, 7th and F streets, tel. (707) 442-6441, noted for its seafood specialties and steaks. If the more formal dining room is too much, try breakfast or lunch at the **Eureka Inn Coffee Shop.**

Events And Entertainment

Fog or no fog, almost everybody crawls out in April for the annual **Rhododendron Festival,** and in May comes the infamous **Kinetic Sculpture Race,** starting in nearby Arcata. In July and August, the **Humboldt Arts Festival** keeps the area jumping with concerts, plays, exhibits, even special museum displays. From June to August, count on **Summer Concerts in the Park.** In August comes the **Tour of the Unknown Coast Bicycle Race.** In December, the **Eureka Inn Christmas Celebration** is quite the shindig. But so is the **Trucker's Christmas Convoy Parade.**

For information about what's happening at the Humboldt Arts Council's **Cultural Center,** call (707) 442-2611. For local arts information, call the local **ArtsTIP Hotline** at 442-1824. The bar scene in Eureka is fairly confused, typical of rowdy redneck towns trying to change their ways. Arcata offers the main entertainment alternatives. Good bets, though, for live music: **The Ritz Club** in Old Town, **Club West** on 5th at G St., and **The Rathskeller** at the Eureka Inn. Non-art lovers and people who tire of Eureka's usual benefits (flea markets and singles' dances) sometimes head north in July to the annual **Orick Rodeo** or east to the **Fortuna Rodeo.**

OTHER PRACTICALITIES

Information And Services

The **Eureka Chamber of Commerce,** 2112 Broadway, Eureka 95501, tel. (707) 442-3738, is the best stop for visitor information. Pick up Old Town information (including a listing of local antique shops) and the free Victorian walking tour guide. (*Really* taking the Victorian tour, though, means getting some exercise, since Eureka boasts well over 100 well-preserved Victorian buildings and homes, and more than 1,000 "architecturally significant" structures.) The **Eureka-Humboldt County Convention and Visitors Bureau** at 1034 2nd St., tel. 443-5097 or toll-free (800) 338-7352, offers an ample supply of countywide information.

For local events and insights into the community's personality and political scene, pick up local newspapers.

The **post office** in Eureka is at the corner of 5th and H streets. **Eureka General Hospital,** 2200 Harrison Ave., tel 443-1627, offers 24-hour emergency medical care, tel. 442-4545. The local **California Dept. of Fish and Game** office is at 619 2nd St., tel. 445-6493, and offers regulations and licenses. Main headquarters for **Six Rivers National Forest** is at 507 F St., tel. 442-1721, a good place to stop for camping info and forest maps ($2). The regional **California Dept. of Parks and Recreation** office is at 600A W. Clark, tel. 445-6547.

Transport And Tours

Get around town on **Eureka Transit,** 133 V St. (catch most buses at 5th and D streets), tel. (707) 443-0826, which runs Mon.-Saturday. The V St. station is actually headquarters for **Humboldt Transit,** same phone, which serves the area from Scotia north to Trinidad (including bicycle transport, call for details), weekdays only. Catch it along Hwy. 101.

The **Greyhound** depot, 1603 4th St. at P, tel. (707) 442-0370, offers runs north to Crescent City and beyond, also south on Hwy. 101 to San Francisco. **Redwood Empire Transit** buses also depart from the Greyhound depot, connecting Eureka and Arcata to Willow Creek near Hoopa Valley before continuing east via Hwy. 299 to Redding.

Cyclists, **Beats Walkin'** is at 4th and B streets, tel. 443-2070, for bike rentals. Tour the bay on **Humboldt Bay Harbor Cruises'** MV *Madaket* (once the Eureka-Samoa ferry) from the Maritime Museum; call 445-3471 for information. The **Eureka Chamber of Commerce,** tel. 442-3738, offers a five-hour history and sightseeing tour (Victorians, Fort Humboldt, the park and zoo, Clarke Museum, Samoa Cookhouse, the bay cruise, and more) on Tues. and Thurs. from mid-June to mid-September. **North Coast Redwood Tours,** 124 Himalay Dr., P.O. Box 177, Trinidad 95570, tel. 677-0334, has tours north to Redwood National Park from Eureka, Arcata, Trinidad, or Orick. Call for current information and prices. Or tour by train, via the *Northcoast Daylight,* headquartered at the depot downtown, 4 W. 2nd St., Eureka 95501, tel. 444-8055.

VICINITY OF EUREKA

ARCATA

Arcata is Eureka's alter-ego, no more resigned to the status quo than the sky here is blue. Far-from-the-mainstream publications are available even at the visitor center. A relaxed and liberal town, Arcata is determined to make a difference.

It would be easy to assume that the genesis of this backwoods grass-roots activism is the presence of academia, namely Humboldt State University, the only university on the north coast. But the Arcata *attitude* goes back much further. When Arcata was still a frontier trading post known as Union Town, the 24-year-old writer Bret Harte set the tone. An unknown underling on Arcata's *The Northern Californian* between 1858 and 1860, an outraged Harte—temporarily in charge while his editor was out of town—wrote a scathing editorial about the notorious Indian Island massacre of Wiyot villagers by settlers and was summarily run out of town, shoved along on his way to fame and fortune.

Besides activism, general community creativity, and education, farming and fishing are growing concerns. (Appropriately enough, the popular semipro baseball team here is called the Humboldt Crabs.)

Almost an industry and wildly popular is the exuberant 38-mile, three-day trans-bay **World Championship Great Arcata to Ferndale Cross-Country Kinetic Sculpture Race** founded by Hobart Brown and Jack Mays and held in May. A moving display of "form over substance," this almost-anything-goes tribute to unbridled imagination does have a few rules. The mobile "sculptures" must be people-powered (though it is legal to get an assist from water, wind, or gravity), amphibious, and inspired by the event's high moral and ethical standards—"cheating is a privilege, not a right." (Kinetic cops patrol the course and interpret the rules.) Otherwise, anything goes (and rolls, floats, flounders through sand, salt water, and swamp slime) in this ultimate endurance contest. Some historical favorites include Brown's own floating bus-boat,

The action at the annual
Kinetic Sculpture Race
is always—well, kinetic.

KINETIC SCULPTURE MUSEUM

the ever-popular **Pencilhead Express,** the man-eating and mobile **Hammerhead Cadillac,** and the **Chicken-and-Egg Mobile,** some race survivors on display at the sculpture museum in Ferndale. Coming in first, even dragging in last, is not the point of this race. The contest's most coveted award is the Aurea Mediocritas, for the entry finishing closest to dead center—because, as the founders explain, winning and losing are both extremes, therefore "perfection lies somewhere in the middle." Pre-race festivities include the **Kinetic Kickoff Party** and **crowning of the Rutabaga Queen** at Eureka's Ritz Club.

For information about the race, contact **Kinetic Sculpture Race, Inc.,** P.O. Box 916, Ferndale 95536, tel. (707) 725-3851. "The Glory" newsletter offers information about kinetic sculpturing internationally—just ask to be added to the mailing list—and the annual official rule book, for racers and spectators alike, is available for $2.

Arcata Area Sights

The presence of the university keeps things in Arcata quite lively. Humboldt State, east of town on Fickle Hill near 14th St. and Grant Ave., quite naturally emphasizes the study of forestry practices, fisheries and wildlife management, and oceanography, with a worthwhile campus **arboretum,** a **fish hatchery,** as well as an **art gallery.** Arcata's downtown **plaza,** with its memorial statue of President McKinley and out-of-place palm trees, is custom-made for watching people come and go from surrounding cafes and shops, or for resting up after a tour of local Vic-

torian homes. Several of the historic buildings framing the plaza are worth a look, including the **Jacoby Storehouse** on the south side, a stone-and-brick beauty with iron shutters (now housing woodwork, glass, and other fine local crafts) and the **Hotel Arcata.** The **Humboldt State Natural History Museum** at 13th and G, open 10-4 Tues.-Sat., features local natural history displays in addition to its impressive fossil collection.

The town's pretty 20-acre **Redwood Park** is off Park (head east on 11th Street). Just beyond is the 600-acre **Arcata Community Forest,** with its educational **Historic Logging Trail,** nature trails, and picnicking. For more information and maps, contact or stop by the city manager's office at 736 F St., Arcata 95521, tel. (707) 822-5953.

The **Azalea State Reserve,** tel. (707) 677-3570, is a 30-acre preserve just north of Arcata on North Bank Rd. (Hwy. 200), famous for its cascading fragrant pinkish-white western azalea blooms (usually best around Memorial Day) and other wildflowers, all in the company of competing rhododendrons. Good steelhead fishing nearby along North Bank Rd. near Hwy. 299's Mad River bridge. To get to **Mad River County Park,** with its good ocean fishing and beach, take Alliance Rd. from K St. to Spear Ave., turn left onto Upper Bay Rd., then left again.

Arcata Marsh

Walk along Arcata Bay to appreciate the impromptu scrap wood sculptures sometimes in bloom. The most fascinating bayside sights, though, are at the town's Arcata Marsh and Wildlife Preserve at the foot of I St., one of the first in the U.S. developed from an old landfill dump and "enhanced" by treated sewage water. These very aesthetic settling ponds offer excellent birdwatching. The Audubon Society offers guided walks at 8:30 a.m. on Saturday mornings. For more information, stop by or call the **North Coast Environmental Center**, 879 9th St., Arcata 95521, tel. (707) 822-6918.

The Lanphere-Christensen Dunes Preserve
Just east of Arcata is the Nature Conservancy's 213-acre Lanphere-Christensen Dunes Preserve on the Samoa Peninsula near the Mad River Slough, open to the public for tours every Saturday morning at 10 a.m. (except during July and August). The Wiyot people once camped in summer on the pristine dunes and beach here, gathering berries in the coastal pine and spruce forest and clamming, fishing, and hunting. Settlers later grazed cattle in this fragile ecosystem, which today is noted for its many well-preserved plant communities, from vernal pools to salt marsh to forest.

First purchased and protected in the 1940s by the Lanpheres, biologists at the university, the area is unique for another reason. At this latitude, the northern and southern dune floras overlap, meaning rare and typical plantlife from both are present as well as over 200 species of birds and other animals. The best dune wildflowers come in June, but every season has its attractions. From April to September, bring mosquito repellent. Rain gear is wise during the rest of the year, and always wear soft-soled shoes. For more information, contact the Lanphere-Christensen Dunes Preserve, 6800 Lanphere Rd., Arcata 95521, tel. (707) 822-6378. Supporters receive the quarterly *Dunesberry* newsletter.

Accommodations
There's a fairly inconvenient **Motel 6** along Hwy. 101 north of town (take the Guintoli Ln./Janes Rd. exit), 4755 Valley West Blvd., tel. (707) 822-7061; $27 s, $33 d, TV and movies, pool, even usually unnecessary air-conditioning. Nearby at 4887 Valley West is the **Arcata Super 8**, tel. 822-8888. Other area motels, with amenities from pool, spa, and gym or tennis facilities to HBO, videos, and room service, include the **Quality Inn** at 3525 Janes Rd., tel. 822-0409,

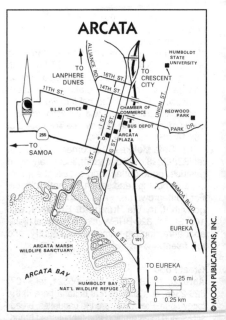

summer rates $69-76, winter rates $38-42 (fall and spring rates somewhere in between). Or try the new **Best Western Arcata Inn** at 4827 Valley West Blvd., tel. 826-0313, and the nearby **North Coast Inn** at 4975 Valley West, tel. 822-4861 or toll-free (800) 233-0903.

The **Lady Anne** bed and breakfast inn at 902 14th St., Arcata 95521, (707) 822-2797, features five rooms (some with fireplaces, all with antiques and robes) in an 1988 Queen Anne Victorian, plus full breakfast and bicycles to borrow. Rates: $70-100. Another possibility is the **Plough and Stars Country Inn** at 1800 27th St., tel. 822-8236, a rural farmhouse offering five rooms (two share bathroom), one with fireplace, refreshments served in the evening, full breakfast in the morning. Rates: $75-105.

Good Food
What Arcata lacks in accommodations it more than makes up for in good restaurants—even very inexpensive ones. First stop for those heading on, though, should be **The Co-op** natural foods store at 8th and I streets, tel. (707) 822-5947, open 9 a.m.-9 p.m. (until 8 on Sunday). Ask here too about the local farmers' market.

Los Bageles at 1061 I, tel. 822-3150, is a popular student hangout offering mostly coffee and bagels and bread items served up with a Nicaraguan flair. The **Wildflower Cafe and Bakery** at 1604 G St., tel. 822-0360, has fresh bakery items, veggie food, homemade soups and salads, and "macrobiotic night" every Wednesday. For groceries, deli fare, fresh-baked breads, also tofu burgers and spinach turnovers, even organic coffees, stop by **The Tofu Shop** at 768 18th St., tel. 822-7409.

The **Cafe Mokka** at the corner of 5th and J, tel. 822-2228, has decadent, incredibly good pastries, good coffee, and excellent espresso, also hot tubs and sauna for rent out back. For homegrown brew and good basic food to go with it, try the **Humboldt Brewery,** 856 10th St., tel. 826-BREW, also a hot local nightspot attracting big-name blues, country, and folk talent.

Great Food

Abruzzi, 791 8th St., Arcata 95521, tel. (707) 826-2345, is a slice of real Italiana here in the foggy north. Fresh daily are the baguettes, breadsticks, and tomato-onion-and-fennel-seed bread, also the Humboldt-grown veggies and seafood specialties. Good calzone, wonderful for pastas. And do try the 14-layer torte. Though it was a barely kept secret even when hidden away in Westhaven, the fairly new **Larrupin' Cafe** at 1658 Patrick's Point Dr. to the north near Trinidad, tel. 677-0230, is friendly and fine, noted for things like barbecued cracked crab, barbecued oysters, steamed mussels, and chicken breast wrapped up with artichokes and cream cheese in phyllo dough. Excellent desserts too. Worth the drive (but no credit cards).

Excellent back in Arcata is **Casa de Que Pasa,** 854 9th St., tel. (707) 822-3441, which also spurns credit cards but definitely dishes up your money's worth in the healthy Mexican food category. The "House of What's Happening" mixes sunflower seeds, tofu, and walnuts together in burritos (you can get meat), sticks sprouts in the tacos, and offers live entertainment some nights.

Ottavio's at 686 F St., tel. (707) 822-4021, is noted for its saki cooler but more famous for its organic gourmet vegetarian fare in the Chinese, Thai, Greek, Hungarian, Italian, and French style. Primo prime rib available, too, for meat

and potatoes fans. Open for lunch, dinner, and Sunday brunch (call for hours).

Information, Services, And Transport

The very helpful **Arcata Chamber of Commerce** visitor information center is at 1062 G St., Arcata 95521, tel. (707) 822-3619, open weekdays 10-5 in tourist season, just 10-3 in winter. Among the free publications available here are the "Tour Arcata's Architectural Past" brochure, "Arcata Outdoors," and the free "Welcome to Arcata" map, in addition to a tidal wave of free local newsletters and newspapers. The very good annual *Humboldt Visitor* and the monthly *North Coast View* are particularly worthwhile for travelers. The Arcata **BLM office** is at 1125 16th St., tel. 822-7648, a worthwhile stop for obscure backcountry information on camping in the King Range.

Both the **Arcata** (tel. 707-823-5951, ext. 31) and **Arcata Mad River Transit** (tel. 822-3775) buses are headquartered at 735 F Street. The **Greyhound** depot is at 645 10th St. at G, tel. 822-0521, with service to and from Eureka as well as points north.

FERNDALE

Ferndale is a perfect rendition of a Victorian village, the kind of place Disneyland architects would create if they needed a new movie set. Ferndale, however, is the real thing, a thriving small town where people take turns shuttling the kids to Future Farmers of America and 4-H meetings, argue about education at the PTA or ice-cream socials, and gossip on street corners. Nowadays, people are probably still talking about what was—and wasn't—left standing after the 6.9 Richter scale earthquake, which hit the area in April, 1992. Construction, deconstruction, and reconstruction continue. First settled in 1864 by Danish immigrants, when the delta plain was heavily forested, followed by Portuguese and Italians, Ferndale is quaint and quiet, a sophisticated if separate Eureka suburb, a village of 1,400, which values its streets of colorfully restored Victorians. The May **Kinetic Sculpture Race** from Arcata ends near here at Centerville County Beach, the surviving sculptures proudly paraded through town. Some also take up residence at the Kinetic Sculpture Museum here

KIM WEIR

Ferndale's Gingerbread Mansion

(for more information about the race, see "Arcata" above). The Portuguese **Holy Ghost Festival** is also in May, with a parade, dancing, feasts. The annual **Scandinavian Festival** is in June, the **Preview of Arts and Flowers** in August. But come in December for the town's month-long **Victorian Christmas** celebrations, which include lighting up the world's tallest living Christmas tree (the 125-foot Sitka spruce on Main), the arrival of Saint Nicholas on a white horse, and the arrival of Santa Claus in a fire truck.

Ferndale Sights

Lovers of Victoriana, take the walking tour. Pick up a free guide to historic buildings (almost everything here qualifies) at the **Ferndale Chamber of Commerce**, 248 Francis (an extension of Main), P.O. Box 325, Ferndale 95536, tel. (707) 786-4477. Most of the historic commercial buildings are concentrated on three-block-long Main St., including the Roman-Renaissance **Bank of America** building at 394 Main, originally the Ferndale Bank. Worth a stop, too, is the 1892-vintage **Golden Gait Mercantile** on Main, a squeaky-floored emporium of oddities and useful daily items, from sassafras tea and traditional patent medicines to butter churns, bushel (and peck) baskets, and treadle sewing machines. There's a museum on the second floor. Also on Main: the **Kinetic Sculpture Museum,** with a decidedly eclectic collection of survivors of the annual kinetic sculpture race, as well as works in progress.

While touring the town—probably the best-preserved Victorian village in the state—travelers will be relieved to find that Ferndale has public restrooms (next to the post office on Main). Once off Main, most people head first to the famous **Gingerbread Mansion** tucked into its formal English gardens at 400 Berding, a Queen Anne with "Eastlake stick," a Victorian virtually dripping with its own frosting, one of the most photographed and painted buildings in Northern California.

Worth it to fully appreciate the town is a quick visit to the **Ferndale Museum** just off Main at the corner of Shaw and Third, tel. (707) 786-4466. This small museum also includes an Oral History Library, written histories, and newspaper archives on microfilm of the old *Ferndale Enterprise*.

Centerville County Park at the end of Ocean is small (pass **Portuguese Hall** on the way) but provides access to the 10 miles of beaches between False Cape and the Eel River lagoon: good beachcombing, driftwood picking, and smelt fishing in summer. On the way to **Russ Park** in the opposite direction, pass **Danish Hall** (built in the late 1800s, still used for community events), Ferndale's **pioneer cemetery,** and the former **Old Methodist Church**, built in 1871, at the corner of Berding.

Ferndale Practicalities

Camp at the handsome **Humboldt County Fairgrounds** off Van Ness at 5th, tel. (707) 786-9511, available for tent camping and RVs.

(There's a **rodeo** here followed by thorough-bred racing at the track, and the **Humboldt County Fair** is held in August.) Bed and breakfast possibilities include **Grandmother's House** at 861 Howard St., tel. 786-9704, and the **Francis Creek Inn** at 577 Main St., tel. 786-9611. The most notable local star, though, is the **Gingerbread Mansion,** 400 Berding St., P.O. Box 40, tel. 786-4000, which offers eight antiqued rooms, unabashed luxury, afternoon tea or coffee and cake, full breakfast. Rates: $90-175.

Picnickers: plan to stop off in Loleta and Fernbridge for meat-and-cheese supplies, or stop here at the **Ferndale Meat Company,** 376 Main, tel. 786-4501, for handmade smoked sausages and other meats from the two-story stone smokehouse. Good cheeses and other surprises. Good for breakfast, lunch, or dinner is the **Fern Cafe** at 606 Main, tel. 786-4795, fine food in a casual atmosphere. Ice-cream fountain, too. Quite popular in these parts for both lunch and dinner is the **Victorian Village Inn** at 400 Ocean Ave., tel. 786-7400, notable too for the Henry Ford memorabilia parked just about everywhere. About 15 minutes south of Eureka, on Hwy. 101 at Fernbridge, is the **Angelina Inn,** tel. 725-3153, locally loved for its Italian dinners and prime rib, steaks, seafood. Open daily for dinner, full bar open later, live music on weekends. In Carlotta, well east of Ferndale, the restored **Carlotta Hotel,** tel. 768-3101, once that town's stage stop, is located on Hwy. 36, next to the mill. Open 5-9 p.m. for dinner, Sunday noon-9 p.m.

NEAR FERNDALE

Fernbridge

Between Eureka and Ferndale is **Fernbridge,** a stately seven-arch Romanesque structure called "the queen of bridges" up here in the north and the center of a war between local folks and Cal-Trans' plans to tear it down. The area's new **Humboldt Creamery** plant is to the west, and to the east (turn in between the rows of John Deere equipment at the Barnes Tractor Company to get there) is the **Fernbridge Meat and Cold Storage Company,** 52 Depot Rd., Fernbridge 95540, tel. (707) 725-2134, a must-stop for meat eaters. Here purchase award-winning, specially cured Swiss sausage and salami, incredible jerky, smoked salmon, turkey, ham. You can tour this four-generation Giacomini family operation, too. Open Mon.-Fri. 9-5, 9 a.m.-noon Saturday.

Loleta

Dairies account for nearly half of Humboldt County's agricultural income, much of the milk processed into butter, cheese, and dried-milk products because of shipping logistics. The pasturelands near Loleta are among the richest in the world, so it's only natural that the area's first creamery was established here in 1888. Even today this is a bucolic village of woodframes and old brick buildings—stop by the **Gilded Rose** for a meal—and most of the action in town

the Fernbridge
Meat and Cold
Storage Company

KIM WEIR

is at the award-winning **Loleta Cheese Factory,** 252 Loleta Dr., Loleta 95551, tel. (707) 733-5470, with its famed natural Jersey milk cheeses, tasting room, and retail sales of cheese and wine. Step inside to sample and buy cheese right out of the display case: the company's famous creamy jack (plus garlic, green chili, caraway, jalapeno, even smoked salmon variations) and cheddar cheeses, flavors including salami and smoked salmon. Watch the cheese-making, too. Call for current hours (seasonal) or contact the company for its mail-order catalog.

Big doin's here is the **Loleta Antique Show** in October, not to mention **Swauger Station Days** in July. For more information about these and other events, contact the **Loleta Chamber of Commerce,** P.O. Box 327, tel. (707) 733-5430.

SCOTIA AND VICINITY

Scotia is a neat-as-a-pin town perfumed by the scents of apple pie, family barbecues, and redwood sawdust. A company town built (to last) from redwood and founded on solid economic ground created by sustained-yield logging, picture-perfect Scotia is one of California's last wholly owned company towns. Generations of children of Pacific Lumber Company (PALCO) loggers happily grew up in Scotia, then went to work in the mills—or went away to college on PALCO-paid scholarships before returning to work as middle managers in the mill offices. The company was the epitome of all things American, yet run "progressively" long before the Japanese management model became the rage and William Ouchi wrote about M-forms and Z-forms.

But Scotia's peace has been obliterated, to a large degree, by major economic and political events. One round of trouble started in 1985, when Pacific Lumber Company was taken over in a Michael Milken-related stock raid by the Maxxam Group. Though environmentalists have loudly mourned the passing of the old PALCO—friend of Save-the-Redwoods League and sympathetic to conservationist thought, opposed to clear-cutting as a forestry practice—at least company employees seem satisfied that their jobs are secure. For now. The long-term fate of the new PALCO, seriously accelerating the

clearcutting of its last privately owned reserves of old growth redwoods, is unclear.

As if such stresses weren't enough, the town's entire business district was lost in April, 1992, when fires started by a massive north coast earthquake destroyed the entire business district. (The mill, however, was saved.) Much damage was done, too, to area homes. The quake's total regional price tag: somewhere in the neighborhood of $61 million.

Scotia Sights And Practicalities

The big event in Scotia is taking a tour of the Pacific Lumber Company redwood sawmill, the largest in the world. Visitors are welcome to observe the operation on the company's self-guided Mill B tour (free). Also stop by the **Scotia Museum** and visitor center, tel. (707) 764-2222, ext. 247, housed in a stylized Greek temple built of redwood, with logs taking the place of fluted columns. (Formerly a bank, the building's sprouting redwood burl once had to be pruned regularly.) Open summers only.

About five miles south of town is the company's **demonstration forest,** open daily in summer (also free), and a picnic area with restrooms. **Rio Dell** across the Eel River is a residential community, its main claim to fame good fossil-hunting on the shale-and-sandstone Scotia Bluffs on the banks of the Eel.

Scotia has a **Wildwood Days** festival in August. The **Rio Dell/Scotia Chamber of Commerce** is at 715 Wildwood Ave., Rio Dell 95562, tel. (707) 764-3436. While in Scotia, consider a stop or a stay at the spruced-up **Scotia Inn,** a classic 1888 redwood bed and breakfast, very good restaurant, and bar at the corner of Mill and Main streets, P.O. Box 248, Scotia 95565, tel. 764-5683, with eight rooms and two suites (one with hot tub and whirlpool), continental breakfast; rates $55-150. For a simpler meal, the **Wildwood Cafe** at 203 Wildwood Ave. in Rio Dell, tel. 764-2284, is a good bet for breakfast and lunch. **Cinnamon Jacks** nearby at 341 Wildwood, tel. 764-5858, is a coffee shop locally famous for its cinnamon rolls and muffins.

Van Duzen County Park

Humboldt's largest county park, Van Duzen harbors four groves of nearly undisturbed redwoods along the Van Duzen River east from Hwy. 101

via Hwy. 36. Georgia-Pacific donated these groves, as well as Cheatham Grove farther west, to the Nature Conservancy in 1969, one of the largest corporate conservation gifts to date, land subsequently deeded to the county and the Save-the-Redwoods League. You can hike, swim, fish, picnic, and camp at both **Pamplin** and **Swimmer's Delight** groves. **Humboldt Grove** is pristine old-growth forest open only for hiking. **Redwood Grove** was severely damaged by windstorms in 1978, but hikers can still walk the old roads. Day-use fee. For more information, contact: Humboldt County Dept. of Public Works, Parks and Recreation Division, 1106 2nd St., Eureka 95501, tel. (707) 445-7491.

Grizzly Creek Redwoods State Park And Vicinity

Gone but not forgotten is the now-extinct California grizzly bear, exterminated here by the late 1860s. The smallest of all the redwood parks, Grizzly Creek Redwoods State Park 35 miles southeast of Eureka was once a stage-coach stop, surrounded by mostly undeveloped forests along the Van Duzen River (visited now by an occasional black bear) among which are a few redwood groves. The main things to do: hike the short trails, swim, and fish for salmon, steelhead, and trout in winter when the river's raging. Grizzly Creek also has a natural history museum inside the restored stage stop.

The campground here (30 campsites, 30 picnic sites) is open year-round. Mistix reservations are a good idea from late April through August, tel. (800) 444-7275. For more information, contact: Grizzly Creek Redwoods State Park, 16949 Hwy. 36, Carlotta 95528, tel. (707) 946-2311. Get very basic supplies at **Hydesville, Carlotta,** or **Bridgeville,** former Mail Ridge stage stops along the highway, though **Fortuna** closer to Eureka is cheaper and has a bit more to offer, such as **Clendenen's Cider Works** on 12th St. next to the freeway, tel. 725-2123, open daily August through February and *the* place for half-gallons of homemade apple cider and fresh local produce. **The Hungry Hutch** at 12th and Main, tel. 725-5620, serves breakfast, lunch, and dinner. The **Fortuna Motor Lodge** at 275 12th, tel. 725-6993, is the best bet in the motel department, though there's also a **KOA** RV campground in town.

Worth going a bit out of the way for is the **Carlotta Hotel** at 138 Central Ave., Carlotta 95528, tel. (707) 768-3101, about five miles from Hwy. 101 via Hwy. 36. This historic one-time stage stop has been completely refurbished and remodeled, with rooms from about $50. (A suite is $70.) Complimentary breakfast is included—and guests may be back for dinner since the restaurant downstairs is locally famous for its generous cuts of prime rib. Most entrees (chicken, pasta, etc.) are under $10, with relish tray, pasta, soup, salad, baked potato, bread, and apple rings included.

For more information about Fortuna and vicinity, contact: **Fortuna Chamber of Commerce,** 735 14th St., Fortuna 95540, tel. (707) 725-3959.

NORTH FROM ARCATA

Blue Lake

In the Mad River Valley just northeast of Arcata on Hwy. 299 is Blue Lake, a tiny town in farm, dairy, and timber country with weatherbeaten barns and silos as picturesque backdrops to the steam-spewing ultramodern **Ultrapower** plant generating electricity from sawmill waste. One thing *not* in Blue Lake is a lake, due to the Mad River changing its course some time ago—the original lake is now a marsh.

Among things that are here: the **Mad River Fish Hatchery,** where a million or more salmon eggs (not to mention steelhead and rainbow trout) become fish each year, and the **Blue Lake Museum** in the old Arcata and Mad River Railroad Depot on Railroad Ave., stuffed with historic memorabilia, limited hours or by appointment, tel. (707) 668-5655. The old railroad itself—known locally as the Annie and Mary Railroad, after two company bookkeepers—was originally called the Union Wharf and Plank Walk Company and boasted $7\frac{1}{2}$ total miles of track. But Plank Walk employees proudly declared: "We're not as long as other lines, but we're just as wide." Come on the first or second Sunday in August for **Annie & Mary Day,** with parade, barbecue, music, theater.

East And Northeast From Blue Lake

Willow Creek east from Blue Lake on Hwy. 299 is perhaps most noted as the high-country hamlet coast folks escape to when the summer fog finally becomes unbearable. It can get hot here in the heart of Bigfoot country. The town has basic accommodations and eateries—such as **Cinnabar Sam's** on the east side of town, tel. (916) 629-3437—plus summer repertory theater and the **Big Foot Golf Course**, tel. 629-2977. Continue east on Hwy. 299 to follow the Trinity River back to its source near Weaverville and the Trinity Alps.

Alternatively, from Hwy. 299 head north along Hwy. 96, passing through the Hoopa Valley and the **Hoopa Valley Reservation** (now partially subdivided into the **Yurok Reservation,** which takes in much of the lower Klamath River). Originally more of a refugee camp for regional peoples than a reservation—since it was established and expanded by orders of presidents Pierce, Grant, and Harrison rather than by treaty between sovereign nations as was more typical elsewhere in the United States—the Hoopa Valley Reservation was nonetheless the first California land granted to Native Americans by post-gold-rush civilization, set aside in 1864. These days, Hoopa boasts **high-stakes bingo** and the very attractive, very comfortable **Best Western Tsewenaldin Inn** overlooking the Trinity River at the Hoopa Shopping Center, tel. (916) 625-4294, with rooms $50 and up (lower rates in the off-season). Nearby is the **Hoopa Indian Museum**, tel. 625-4110, with exhibits on the cultural traditions of the Hupa people, from basketry and feather arts to weaponry. For a hands-on outdoor introduction to Hupa cultural history, sign on with **Kimtu Outdoor Adventures**, P.O. Box 938, Willow Creek 95573, tel. (916) 629-3843 or toll-free (800) 562-8475, for easy family float trips and regional whitewater adventures.

Up The Coast

Heading north from Arcata on Hwy. 101 the first wide-spot-in-the-road is **McKinleyville**, actually an Arcata suburb "where horses still have the right of way," adjacent to the **Azalea State Reserve.** Worth stopping for is whalewatching from **McKinleyville Vista Point.** Farther north off Hwy. 101 via Clam Beach Dr. is **Clam Beach County Park**, a good place for collecting agates and moonstones, also camping for $5 a night. Adjacent is **Little River State Beach,** where

Josiah Gregg and company arrived from Weaverville in December 1849, exhausted and near starvation. Little River has broad sandy beaches backed by dunes, clamming in season, good surf fishing, picnicking. For more information, call (707) 677-3570.

Trinidad

A booming supply town of 3,000 in the early 1850s and later a whaling port, Trinidad is now a tiny coastal village recognized as the oldest incorporated town on California's north coast. Impressive **Trinidad Head** looms over the small bay, with a white granite cross at the summit replacing the first monument placed there by Bodega y Cuadra for Spain's Charles III. The **Trinidad Memorial Lighthouse** on Main St. (the original light tower relocated to town as a fishermen's memorial) features a giant two-ton fog bell. Humboldt State's **Marine Biology Laboratory** here has an aquarium open to the public. Besides solitary beachcombing on **Trinidad State Beach** (day-use only, good for moonstones and driftwood), surfing at rugged **Luffenholtz Beach** two miles south of town, and breathtaking scenery, the area's claim to fame is salmon fishing: commercial and sport-fishing boats, skiffs, and tackle shops line Trinidad Bay.

In April or May each year, the town hosts a massive **crab feed** at Town Hall. Otherwise, *the* place to eat in Trinidad is the very relaxed and rustic **Seascape Restaurant** (once the Dock Cafe) at the harbor, tel. (707) 677-3762, with hearty breakfasts, excellent omelettes, and seafood specialties (good early bird specials). Reservations a good idea at dinner. Open 7 a.m.-9 p.m. daily. Also here, just outside town, is the excellent **Larrupin' Cafe** (see "Arcata" above). Other choices include the **Trinidad Bay Eatery & Gallery** (breakfast and lunch) at Trinity and Parker, closed Mon. and Tues., and **Merryman's Dinner House** at 100 Moonstone Beach Rd., tel. 677-3111, noted for its sunsets as well as its food.

For the most reasonable accommodations, head north on Patrick's Point Dr. to the state park and its excellent camping. Nice for cabins is the **Bishop Pine Lodge**, 1481 Patrick's Point Dr., tel. (707) 677-3314, $55-65 (cheaper in the off-season), also featuring two-bedroom units and cottages with hot tubs, from $90.

Another possibility is the **Shadow Lodge** at 687 Patrick's Point Dr., tel. 677-0532. The **Trinidad Bed and Breakfast** in town at at 560 Edwards St., P.O. Box 849, tel. 677-0840, is a Cape Cod-style home circa 1950, offering four rooms with king or queen beds (private baths, one room with fireplace). Rates: $90-145. About five miles north of Trinidad proper and adjacent to the state park is **The Lost Whale Bed and Breakfast Inn,** 3452 Patrick's Point Dr., tel. 677-3425, a contemporary Cape Cod with six guest rooms (two share a bath), full breakfast, tea and scones in the afternoon. Rates: $75-120. Trinidad's **Chamber of Commerce** is at Scenic and Main streets, P.O. Box 356, Trinidad 95570, tel. 677-3448.

Patrick's Point State Park

The Yuroks who for centuries seasonally inhabited this area believed that the spirit of the porpoises came to live at modern-day Patrick's Point State Park just before people populated the world, and that the seven sea stacks that stretch northwest to southwest like a spine were the last earthly abode of the immortals. Most impressive of these rugged monuments is **Ceremonial Rock,** nicknamed "stairway to the stars" by fond rock climbers. Fine forests grew here until the area was logged and cleared for farming and grazing; the surrounding meadows are spectacular with wildflowers every spring, forest succession held temporarily at bay by the parks people.

Elsewhere, though, the Port Orford cedars, Sitka spruce, shore pines, azaleas, and abundant berry bushes are returning. Here too and just north at Big Lagoon is the place for those "fungus among us" jokes. During the rainy season duff from spruce trees produces delicious mushrooms—also fantastically fatal ones, so be sure you're an expert (or in the company of one) before you go rooting through forest detritus for dinner. Take the easy, self-guided **Octopus Grove** nature trail near Agate Beach Campground for an introduction to life's hardships from a spruce tree's viewpoint.

Old trails once walked by native peoples lead to and beyond rocky **Patrick's Point,** one of the finest whalewatching sites along the coast. "Patrick" was Patrick Beegan, the area's first white settler and a warrior after Indian scalps. Stroll the two-mile **Rim Trail** for the views, but stay back from the hazardous cliff edge. Sea lions are common on the park's southern offshore rocks near **Palmer's Point.** The short trail scrambling north from near the campground (steep going) leads to long, sandy, and aptly named **Agate Beach,** noted for its many-colored, glass-like stones.

For all its natural wonders, Patrick's Point is also fine for people (good picnicking). Except for mushroomers and whalewatchers, best visiting weather is late spring, early summer, and fall. **Whalewatching** from Ceremonial Rock or Patrick's Point (weekend ranger programs Jan. and Feb.) is best from November to January but also good on the whales' return trip, February to May. Dress warmly and bring binoculars. For current whalewatching info, call (707) 445-6547. The **museum** here has natural history and native cultural exhibits. Day use fee: $5.

Patrick's Point has three developed campgrounds: **Agate Beach, Abalone,** and **Penn Creek** west of the meadows, with 123 naturally sheltered tent or trailer sites, hot showers, $14 per night. In addition, there are two group camps and 20 hike-and-bike campsites. Mistix reservations, tel. (800) 444-7275, are mandatory during the summer. For more information, contact: Patrick's Point State Park, Trinidad 95570, tel. (707) 677-3570.

Humboldt Lagoons State Park

The community of **Big Lagoon** just off the highway north of Patrick's Point is also the site of Big Lagoon County Park with its dirty sand beaches and camping. Humboldt Lagoons State Park includes Big Lagoon itself (and the miles-long barrier beach separating it from the sea) and three others, a total of 1,500 beachfront acres best for beachcombing, boating, fishing, surfing, and windsurfing (swimming only for the hardy or foolhardy).

Next north is freshwater **Dry Lagoon,** five miles of sandy beach and heavy surf particularly popular with agate fanciers and black jade hunters. Camp beside this marshy lagoon, at one of six environmental campsites: outhouse, no water, no dogs. Ocean fishing in winter only, but no fishing at Dry Lagoon, which lives up to its name most of the year. **Stone Lagoon** two miles north is prettier but smaller, with boat-in primitive campsites. A half mile farther north is part-private, part-public **Freshwater Lagoon**, planted with trout for seasonal fishing, with no official camping though RVs are a permanent fixture along the highway here. The **Harry A.**

Merlo State Recreation Area, 800-plus acres named for a noted Louisiana-Pacific executive, entwines throughout the lagoon area.

The small **Humboldt Lagoons Visitors Center** is at Stone Lagoon, open summers only. For more information and to reserve campsites, contact Prairie Creek Redwoods State Park, tel. (707) 488-2171.

REDWOOD NATIONAL PARK AND VICINITY

Pointing north to Oregon like a broken finger is Redwood National Park, California's finest temple to tree hugging. Remote and often empty of worshippers—and many visitors are just passing through to the Trees of Mystery, barely aware they're witnessing a miracle, forests being raised (albeit slowly) from the dead—Redwood National Park is complete yet unfinished. Standing in the shadow and sunlight of an old-growth redwood grove is like stepping up to an altar mindful only of the fullness of life. But out back toward the alley and looking like remnants of some satanic rite is a shameful (and still growing) scar of scabbed-over sticks and earth. Yet here at least, the healing has finally begun. Three of the world's six tallest trees (including numero uno) grow in the park. UNESCO declared the park a World Heritage site in 1982, the 113th such site in the world, ninth in the U.S., and first on the Pacific coast.

But other people call it other things. When the sawdust finally settled after the struggle to establish this national park (the costliest of them all, with a total nonadministrative price tag of $1.4 billion), no one was happy. Despite the park's acquisitions to date, purists protest that not enough additional acres of old-growth redwoods have been preserved. Philistines are dismayed that there is so little commercial development here, so few gift shops and souvenir stands. And locals are still unhappy that prime timber stands are now out of the loggers' reach, and that the prosperity promised somewhere just down the skid roads of Redwood National Park never arrived—or, more accurately, never matched expectations.

Flora And Fauna

Some of the terrain included within the borders of Redwood National Park is so strange that filmmaker George Lucas managed to convince much of the world it was extraterrestrial in his *Return of the Jedi.* But this strangeness was appreciated as the essence of life to the Yurok, Tolowa, and Chilula peoples who traditionally lived throughout the area, thriving on occasional beached whales, deer, salmon, shellfish, berries, and seaweed as supplements to an acorn-based diet.

The park's dominant redwoods host over 1,000 species of plants and animals. Sitka spruce, firs, and pines grow on the coast. Leather-leaved salal bushes, salmonberries, and huckleberries control the forest's understory. Rhododendrons and azaleas bloom in May and June, followed by flowering carpets of oxalis or redwood sorrel, their tiny leaves folding up like umbrellas when sunlight filters down to the forest floor. Mushrooms, various ferns, lacy bleeding hearts, and other delicate wildflowers also flourish here. In the meadows and along coastal prairies are alders, bigleaf maples, hazels, and blackberries.

Roosevelt elk or wapiti survive only here and in Washington's Olympic National Park, though they once roamed from the San Joaquin Valley north to Mt. Shasta. Black bears, mountain lions, bobcats, deer, beavers, raccoons, and porcupines are fairly common. Offshore are gray whales, seals, sea lions, porpoises, sea otters, and creatures large and small in the tidepools. Trout and salmon are abundant in all three of the park's rivers.

Lady Bird Johnson Grove

KIM WEIR

The park is also home to 300 species of birds, including Pacific Flyway migrants, gulls, cormorants, rare brown pelicans, raptors, and songbirds. Redwood-loving birders listen for the mysterious marbled murrelet, a rare black-and-white seabird often seen but seldom heard and believed to nest in the treetops. If it can be established unequivocally that murrelets nest in old-growth forests (like the now-infamous spotted owl), then their habitat will have to be protected from logging.

THE POLITICS OF PARK PRESERVATION

Logging in areas now included within Redwood National Park began in the 1850s, but peaked after World War II, when annual harvests of more than one million board feet were the rule. By the early 1960s, the redwoods' days were clearly numbered. Lumber mills were closing and only 300,000 of the state's original two million acres of pristine coast redwood forest remained. Just one-sixth of that total was protected, with persistent urging and financial contributions from the Save-the-Redwoods League, the Sierra Club, and other environmental organizations. As demands for redwood lumber increased, it was also increasingly clear that the time to save remaining old-growth redwoods and their watersheds was now—or never.

One Park, Two Compromises
The establishment of Redwood National Park by Congress in 1968 consolidated various federal, state, and private holdings along the coastline from Crescent City south to the Redwood Creek watershed parallel to Trinidad. The park totalled only 58,000 acres, half of which was already protected within the Prairie Creek, Del Norte, and Jedediah Smith state parks. Included were only a small portion of the Mill Creek (Del Norte Redwoods) area and less than half of the important Redwood Creek watershed (including the Tall Trees Grove). And this unsatisfactory settlement cost almost $200 million, more than the U.S. government had ever spent on land acquisition in one place.

Even as the bigwigs (including then-President Richard Nixon, former President Lyndon B. and Lady Bird Johnson, and Governor Ronald Reagan) bunched together in August of 1969 for dignified dedication ceremonies in the Lady Bird Johnson Grove, the shortsightedness of the compromise was all too obvious: bulldozers and logging trucks were making clearcut hay on the ridgetops and unprotected watersheds beyond. Despite adequate bureaucratic procedures, Governor Reagan's administration didn't believe in regulating the timber companies.

With devastation of even the protected groves imminent due to the law of gravity—the onrushing impact of rain-driven erosion from clearcut sites on areas downhill and downstream—environmentalists initiated another long round of legal-and-otherwise challenges. "Think big" U.S. Congressmember Phil Burton of San Francisco proposed an additional acquisition of 74,000 acres, countered by the National Park Service's think-small suggestion of just 21,500 acres. A final compromise, this one engineered by President Carter's administration in 1978, added a total of 48,000 acres of new parklands (much of it already clearcut and in desperate need of rehabilitation) at a cost of $300 million more, not to mention $33 million for resurrecting the destroyed slopes of Redwood Creek or the millions set aside to compensate out-of-work lumber-industry workers. In addition, the compromise included a political coup of sorts, giving the National Park Service regulatory authority in a 30,000-acre Park Protection Zone upstream from the Redwood National Park proper.

Some Healing,
Slowly But Surely

The rehabilitation of clearcut lands remains a top park priority—more important than recreational development. Because of the immensity of the task and the slow healing process, Redwood National Park will probably not be "finished" for decades.

For good war stories from the environmentalists' camp, the Sierra Club's *The Last Redwoods and the Parkland of Prairie Creek* by Edgar and Peggy Wayburn and the definitive *The Fight to Save the Redwoods* by historian Susan Schrepfer are among the best books out. The logging industry position can be read any day of the week on the devastated slopes around the park, especially in Six Rivers National Forest.

SIGHTS AND RECREATION

The main thing to do in Redwood National Park is simply *be* here. Sadly, "being here" to many area visitors means little more than pulling into the parking lot near the 49-foot-tall Paul Bunyan and Babe the Blue Ox at Klamath's Trees of Mystery, buying big trees trinkets, or stopping for a slab or two at roadside redwood burl stands in Orick. Though fishing, kayaking, surfing, and rafting are increasingly popular, nature study and hiking are the park's main recreational offerings. For those seeking views with the least amount of effort, take a drive (one-lane dirt road) along Howland Hill Rd. through some of the finest trees in Jedediah Smith Redwoods State Park. (Howland Hill Rd. transects the park and can be reached via South Fork Rd. off Hwy. 199 just east of the park or via Elk Valley Rd. south of Crescent City.) Or try a sunny picnic on the upland prairie overlooking the redwoods and ocean, reached via one-lane Bald Hills Rd., eight miles or more inland from Hwy. 101.

Hiking Trails

The together-but-separate nature of the park's interwoven state and federal jurisdictions makes everything confusing, including figuring out the park's trail system (such as it is). Pick up a copy of the joint "Trails" brochure published by the Redwood Natural History Association available at any of the state or national park information centers and offices in the area. "Trails" divides the collective system north and south and includes corresponding regional trail maps, describes the general sights along each trail, and classifies each by length and degree of difficulty. Fifty cents well spent.

Among the must-do walks is the easy and short self-guided nature trail on the old logging road to the **Lady Bird Johnson Grove.** Near the grove at the overlook is an educational logging rehabilitation display comprised of acres of visual aids—devastated redwood land clearcut in 1965 and 1970 next to a forest selectively logged at the end of World War II. At the parking lot two miles up steep Bald Hills Rd. (watch for logging trucks) is a picnic area and restrooms.

It's just over a mile down into the famous **Tall Trees Grove.** The easy way there involves taking a shuttle from the information center near Orick (buses leave four times a day in summer, otherwise thrice-daily, small fee). For those shuttled in, the guided tour includes a ranger-led discussion of logging damage and reforestation techniques. The 368-foot tallest tree of all, the **Howard Libby Redwood,** is much like the tallest peaks in the Sierra Nevada—hard to appreciate apart from the surrounding majesty. The traditional route for true tree huggers, though, is the long (but also easy) 1½-mile roundtrip hike (at least five hours one-way, overnight camping possible with permit) along **Redwood Creek Trail.** Another possibility: coming in via the shuttle then walking back out on the longer trail.

The longest and most memorable trek in Redwood National Park, the 30-mile-long **Coastal Trail,** runs almost the park's entire length (hikable also in sections), from near Endert's Beach south of Crescent City through Del Norte Redwoods State Park (and past the AYH hostel there), inland around the mouth of the Klamath River, then south along Flint Ridge, Gold Bluffs Beach, and Fern Canyon in Prairie Creek Redwoods State Park. A summers-only spur continues south along the beach to the information center.

If the entire coast route is too much, the **Flint Ridge Trail** section from the east end of Alder Camp Rd. to the ocean (primitive camping) is wild and wonderful, passing beavers and beaver dams at Marshall Pond. Quite easy and exquisite is the short **Fern Canyon Trail** just off the Coastal Trail in Prairie Creek Redwoods State Park, less than a mile roundtrip through a 60-foot-high "canyon" of ferns laced up the sides of Home Creek's narrow ravine. To get there by car, take Davison Rd. from near Rolf's west over the one-lane bridge—watch for cattle being herded home—for six miles to the Gold Bluffs Beach Campground then continue for another 1½ miles to the parking lot. Even better is the four-mile hike west on the **James Irvine Trail** from the visitor center (or via the **Miners Ridge Trail**, which connects to Irvine by means of the **Clintonia Trail**). However you get there, the trip is worth it for the jeweled greenery—sword, deer, five-fingered, chain, bracken, lady, and licorice ferns—clinging to the canyon's ribs along the chuckling stream.

The **Revelation Trail** just south of the visitor center in Prairie Creek Redwoods State Park is a short self-guided nature trail for blind and sighted people, with rope and wood handrails the entire length, "touchable" sights, and trailside features described on signs, in brochures also printed in Braille, and on cassette tapes available at the visitor center. Also special, rarely visited, and especially rich in rhododendrons is the short **Brown Creek Trail** east of Hwy. 101 and north of the Prairie Creek visitor center.

Orick And Vicinity

The privately owned wide-spot-in-the-road of Orick, mostly a strip of souvenir stands and supply stops (good little grocery), is the first outpost of civilization north of the park's excellent **Orick Redwood Visitor Center** at the mouth of Redwood Creek. The center features a massive relief map of the park, wildlife and cultural displays, an excellent bookstore, and complete information about the national park (including the three state parks). Wheelchair-accessible, open daily mid-June to Labor Day 8 a.m.-7 p.m., otherwise 9-5 daily.

Visit the **Prairie Creek Fish Hatchery**, 3½ miles north of Orick on Hwy. 101, where each year one to two million salmon eggs are "stripped" from dying females, fertilized by hand,

Paul Bunyan and Babe the Blue Ox at Trees of Mystery in Klamath

then incubated, hatched, and raised to fingerling size each year. (Look for the **Indomitable Salmon** redwood sculpture.)

Prairie Creek Redwoods State Park

An almost dangerous feature at Prairie Creek is the permanent and photogenic herd of Roosevelt elk usually grazing in the meadow area right along Hwy. 101. Whether or not a loaded logging truck is tailgating, drivers tend to screech to a halt at the mere sight of these magnificent creatures (which, despite their technically wild status and correspondingly unpredictable behavior, have that bemused and bored look of animals all too familiar with humankind). A separate herd of elk grazes in the coastal meadows along 11-mile **Gold Bluffs Beach,** also noted for its excellent whalewatching, sand dunes carpeted in wild strawberries, and primitive campground with solar showers.

Elsewhere in Prairie Creek Redwoods State Park heavy winter rainfall and thick summer fog produce rainforest lushness. Redwoods rub elbows with 200-foot-tall Sitka spruce, Douglas fir, and Western hemlock above an amazing array of shrubs, ferns, and groundcover, not to mention 800 varieties of flowers and 500 different kinds of mushrooms. **Fern Canyon** (see "Hiking Trails" above) is unforgettable. Also particularly worthwhile at Prairie Creek: beach-combing, surf fishing, nature walks and photography, picnicking, camping. There are some fine family campsites near the visitor center, with flush toilets and hot showers, as well as a small museum. The more primitive beach camp-sites are first-come, first-camped, as are the adjacent hike-and-bike sites. Register first with the office at Prairie Creek; for more information call (707) 488-2171.

Klamath And The Klamath River

Traditionally fishing and hunting territory of the Yuroks, the native people here were hunted by miners for sport, their villages burned, their fish-eries ruined. In 1964 when 40 inches of rain fell within 24 hours in the Eel and Klamath river basins, the entire town of Klamath was washed away—and not as easily replaced as the gilt grizzlies on the remnants of the Douglas Memorial Bridge outside town. Their gold cement den mates, frequently defaced by graffiti artists, decorate the new Klamath River Bridge. Klamath's **Salmon Festival** in late June attracts mostly locals for the unforgettable salmon bar-becue, traditional Yurok dances, singing, bas-ketry displays (not for sale), stick games, and logging skills contests.

And at least in some years, fishing is making a comeback. The Klamath River itself is the major attraction—one of the finest fishing streams in the world and California's second-largest river, a 263-mile-long waterway drain-ing 8,000 square miles, fed by over 300 tribu-taries, including the Salmon, Scott, and Trinity rivers. Most anglers line the Klamath and the lagoon from late fall through winter for the salmon run, though fishing for cutthroat trout downstream from town is good year-round.

The site of old Klamath is now overgrown with blackberries. New Klamath is dominated by the **Trees of Mystery**, P.O. Box 96, Klamath 95548, tel. (707) 482-5613, made famous by Robert Ripley's "Believe It Or Not!" Like it or not, visitors become unwitting promoters just by parking in the lot (where employees attach

those gawdawful bumper stickers). Chainsawed redwood characters are the featured attraction along Mystery's Trail of Tall Tales. The free End of the Trail Indian Museum is worth some time, though, with its end-of-the-line artifacts from everywhere in the U.S. and Canada. Basic restaurant and Motel Trees are just across the highway. Just south of Klamath is the **Tour-Thru-Tree,** this one chainsawed in 1976.

Requa is a tiny settlement on the Klamath's north bank, once an important Yurok village, later a booming mining supply camp then a mill town and lumber port. Aside from the wonderful four-mile walk north from the end of the road along the Coastal Trail (to the accompaniment of barking sea lions on the rocks below), most no-table in Requa is the restored **Requa Inn,** a bed and breakfast and good restaurant. Among sights along the primarily unpaved **Coastal Drive**, which starts on the south side of the Kla-math River (great views on sunny days), is a World War II-vintage early-warning radar sta-tion cleverly disguised as a farmhouse (with false windows and dormers) and nearby barn.

Del Norte Coast Redwoods State Park

Del Norte is a dense and foggy coastal rainfor-est comprised of 6,400 acres of redwoods, meadows, beaches, and tidepools. It's so wet here in winter that the developed campgrounds close. The **Damnation Creek Trail,** crossing Hwy. 1 en route, leads through magnificent old-growth *Sequoias,* spruce, Oregon grape, and seasonal wildflowers to a tiny beach with off-shore sea stacks and tidepools. Or, take the **Coastal Trail** from Wilson Creek to the bluffs. Easier is the short walk to the north coast's finest tidepools (and the Nickel Creek Primitive Camp) at the end of **Enderts Beach Trail,** ac-cessible from Enderts Beach Rd. south of Cres-cent City. To see the park's second-growth red-woods, and for exceptional birdwatching, take the almost four-mile **Hobbs Wall Trail.** Beyond Del Norte Coast Redwoods as the highway de-scends to Crescent City is the **Rellim Demon-stration Forest** with its well-maintained self-guided nature trail—and comfortable lodge for fireplace-warming afterward.

Jedediah Smith Redwoods State Park

Though the competition is certainly stiff even close by, this is one of the most beautiful places on earth—and almost unvisited. Few people come inland even a few miles from Hwy. 101 near Crescent City. Once Tolowa tribal territory, the Smith River, which flows through the park, was crossed by mountain man Jedediah Smith on June 20, 1828, after his grueling cross-country effort to reach the Pacific. Despite the realities of the mid-1800s gold rush, which brought first trappers, miners, and loggers—and the rapid destruction of the native populations—then fishermen and farmers into the extreme northwestern corner of California, this 9,200-acre stand of old-growth redwoods, Douglas fir, pines, maples, and meadows seems almost unscathed.

Historic **Howland Hill Rd.,** once a redwood-paved thoroughfare, is now graveled and meanders like the summer river through the quiet groves. The **National Tribute Grove,** a 5,000-acre memorial to veterans of world wars I and II, is the park's largest. Tiny **Stout Grove** includes the area's largest measured redwoods. For an easy two-mile loop, walk both the **Simpson** and **Peterson trails** through primeval redwoods and ferns. Even shorter is the combined walk along the **Leiffer** and **Ellsworth trails,** something of a Jedediah Smith sampler. The 30-minute **Stout Grove Trail** offers trees and access to some of the Smith River's excellent summer swimming holes (complete with sandy beaches). Take the **Hiouchi Trail** for rhododendrons and huckleberries. More ambitious are hikes along both forks of the **Boy Scout Tree** and **Little Bald Hills trails.** Also among the Smith River redwoods are excellent developed campsites.

Smith River National Recreation Area

California's only completely undammed river system, the Smith River, is now a focal point of the new Smith River National Recreation Area, a 305,337-acre preserve (including 118,000 acres of old-growth forest) that protects the North, Middle, and South forks of the Smith River. Though the environmental protections aren't as strict as they would be under national park status, establishment of this new national recreational area means that the Smith River will remain undammed, that no new mining claims will be allowed, and that logging will be strictly limited. Fishing, hiking, camping (some campgrounds are open year-round, $6 per site) are the primary pleasures here.

Since the Smith River National Recreation Area abuts the western edge of Jedediah Smith Redwoods State Park/Redwood National Park, another possibility is setting up camp at Jed Smith. Basic supplies and reasonable motels (some motor-court style) are available in Crescent City, but Gasquet and Hiouchi may be closer. The **Hiouchi Cafe** serves up hearty breakfasts and lunch. The **Gasquet Steak House** is famous for its Wed.-Sun. prime rib dinners.

For maps and other information, contact the **Gasquet Ranger District Office** for Six Rivers National Forest, P.O. Box 228, Gasquet 95543, tel. (707) 457-3131, open daily 8-5 in travel season, weekdays only mid-October to April, or stop at the **Hiouchi Visitor Center** just a few miles west (picnic area and bookstore), open daily 9-5.

Six Rivers National Forest

Almost one million acres of public forest lands, extending in a long, fairly narrow block from the Oregon border to southeast of Garberville, are included within Six Rivers National Forest just west of the Klamath and Trinity forests. Six Rivers' six rivers are the Smith, Klamath, Trinity, Mad, Van Duzen, and Eel. Fall colors are outstanding, with alders, maples, oaks, Oregon grape, even poison oak splashing the dark pine, fir, and cedar forests. Hawks and hummingbirds, ravens and robins, woodpeckers and warblers are among the birds here. Official camping throughout the forest is plentiful—there are 15 major campgrounds, at least one in each area open year-round on a first-come basis—plus campers can pitch a tent almost anywhere, trailside or roadside, with a permit. There are also free "rustic camps" and seasonal hunting camps throughout; ask at area ranger stations.

Backpackers have privacy and a long season since winters in many areas are fairly mild. The **South Kelsey Trail** and **Horse Ridge Trail** are good backpacking routes. The **North Fork Wilderness,** most accessible from Alderpoint or Covelo near Garberville, has poor trails and is best suited for experienced woodspeople. River fishing, whitewater rafting, and hunting are the other main recreational activities here.

For a $3 forest map—definitely advisable—and current river, trail, and camping information, contact **Six Rivers National Forest Headquarters,** 507 F St., Eureka 95501, tel. (707)

442-1721, or any of the **ranger district offices:** P.O. Box 228, Gasquet 95543, tel. (707) 457-3131; P.O. Drawer B, Orleans 95556, tel. (916) 627-3291; P.O. Box 668, Willow Creek 95573, tel. (916) 629-2118; or Star Rt. Box 300, Bridgeville 95526, tel. (707) 574-6233.

PARK PRACTICALITIES

Camping
Four developed family-type campgrounds, with hot showers and such, are in the state parks: **Prairie Creek Redwoods** and its Gold Bluffs Beach area (with solar-heated showers), **Del Norte Redwoods,** and **Jedediah Smith Redwoods.** Disposal stations for RVs are available but no hookups. Popular in summer, $14 basic fee; advance reservations through Mistix, tel. (800) 444-7275, advisable. Though the Del Norte Campground is closed off-season due to very wet conditions (sometimes washouts), winter drop-in camping at the other campgrounds is usually no problem. Primitive sites are at **Nickel Creek** at Endert's Beach, at **Flint Ridge** west of Klamath, **DeMartin** between Damnation and Wilson creeks along the Coastal Trail, and along the Redwood Creek Trail (necessary permits available at information centers or at park headquarters in Crescent City). Prairie Creek Redwoods State Park also offers walk-in campsites at **Butler Creek Primitive Camp.**

In Crescent City, there's the **Harbor Anchorage RV Park** right on the beach at the north end of town, 159 Starfish Way, tel. (707) 464-1724. Other private regional campgrounds include **Riverwoods Campgrounds** 12 miles north of Prairie Creek (Klamath Beach Rd. exit from Hwy. 101), tel. 482-5591, shaded grassy sites with full hook-ups, hot showers, beer and tackle shop, river access. At the north end of the Klamath River Bridge is the **Camper Corral,** tel. 482-5741. **Chinook RV Resort,** also in Klamath, tel. 482-3511, is another fisherpeople's favorite, as is **Terwer Park** at 614 Terwer Riffle in Klamath, tel. 482-3855, full hook-ups, pool and spa, baths and laundromat, cottages.

Food And Accommodations Near Orick
Prices in and around Orick are quite reasonable, partly because Redwood National Park is too far north for most travelers but also because

it's foggy here during peak tourist season. Most people follow the sun. Best bet for a fascinating meal, not to mention friendly people, is **Rolf's Park Cafe** on the highway north of Orick proper (take the Fern Canyon exit), 123749 Hwy. 101, Orick 95555, tel. (707) 488-3841. Tables are set in the solarium and (weather permitting) outside on the deck. Rolf Rheinschmidt is known for his exotic dinner specialties, like wild turkey, elk and buffalo steaks, wild boar and bear roasts, even antelope sausage, plus chicken and pasta dishes, vegetarian dishes, and forest fare like fiddlehead ferns and wild mushrooms. Rolf also cooks up some great breakfasts, including the house specialty, German Farmers Omelette, a creation of eggs with ham, bacon, sausages, cheese, mushrooms, potatoes, and pasta topped with salsa and sour cream for under $5, also fine and filling pancakes. Lunch served too, featuring Rolf's special clam chowder, a grilled German sausage sandwich, smoked salmon and sweet onions on rye, hot chicken and mushrooms, burgers, and salads. Beer and wine, linzertorte for dessert. Great place. Other possibilities: basic diner fare and good cream pies at the **Palm Cafe** in Orick, tel. 488-3381, or a quick grocery stop at the **Orick Market.**

Choice in area motels is meager, but the **Prairie Creek Motel** next to Rolf's, tel. (707) 488-3841, is certainly convenient, rooms from $30 or so. A better bet and just a bit higher is the refurbished **Park Woods Motel** in Orick at 121440 Hwy. 101, tel. 488-5175. The **Orick Motel and RV Park,** tel. 488-3501, has rooms, tent spaces, and RV hookups.

Accommodations
And Food Near Klamath
Farther north, right on the coast and in the park (about 12 miles south of Crescent City at the Hwy. 101 junction with Wilson Creek Rd.), is the fairly new and fabulous AYH **Redwood Hostel,** known locally as the DeMartin House. A 30-bed hostel perfect even for small group retreats, with small dorm rooms, a common room cozied up with a woodstove, dining room, outdoor redwood decks with fine views, even good kitchen facilities. The hostel is wheelchair-accessible. Couple and family rooms available with adequate advance notice. Rates $9 per night, AYH members and nonmembers alike. For information and advance reservations (definitely advisable in

summer) contact: AYH Redwood Hostel, 14480 Hwy. 101, Klamath 95548, tel. (707) 482-8265.

Motel Trees on Hwy. 101 across from Trees of Mystery, P.O. Box 309, Klamath 95548, tel. (707) 482-3152, has rooms from $40, including color TV and movies, even a tennis court. For those not traveling totally on the cheap, stay at the historic **Requa Inn,** 451 Requa Rd., Klamath 95548, tel. 482-8205, an English-style country inn opened in 1885 and serving steak-and-kidney pie in the **hotel dining room** at dinner, good breakfasts. Open 5-9 p.m. nightly, reservations advised. Lodgings, even view rooms with clawfoot bathtubs, run $50-75.

Information And Transport

In general the visiting weather is best in late spring and early autumn. August and September are the busiest times here (the salmon fishing rush), but September after Labor Day offers fewer crowds and usually less fog.

Redwood National Park Field Seminars are sponsored by the College of the Redwoods, 883 W. Washington Blvd., Crescent City 95531, tel. (707) 464-7457, including studies of local Native American culture, birdlife, freshwater stream ecology, the ecology of the north coast black bear, and basic outdoor photography.

The new **Orick Redwood National Park Information Center** at the old lumber mill site at the mouth of Redwood Creek is an imposing, excellent new interpretive museum near Orick (north of Freshwater Lagoon and west of the highway), P.O. Box 234, Orick 95555, tel. (707) 488-2171. Enthusiastically staffed, very helpful. Open mid-June to Labor Day 8 a.m.-7 p.m. daily, otherwise 9-5 daily. Pick up a map for the total 150-mile trail system. The **Orick Chamber of Commerce** is here, too (or to contact in advance: P.O. Box 234, Orick 95555, tel. 488-2525). Another good visitor center is **Hiouchi** on Hwy. 199 at Jedediah Smith Redwoods State Park, tel. 458-3134, which features among other exhibits a handmade traditional canoe, constructed on-site. Ask, too, about the new Smith River National Recreation Area, as well as new park-sponsored activities and events. Open the same longer hours as the Redwood Center through summer, otherwise daily 8-5.

Least helpful to visitors is the **Redwood National Park Headquarters and Information Center** at 1111 2nd St., Crescent City 95531, tel. (707) 464-6101. (Headquarters' phone number functions as a 24-hour information line, however.) For more information about the individual state parks within Redwood National Park, contact: **Prairie Creek Redwoods State Park,** Orick 95555, tel. 488-2171, and **Del Norte and Jedediah Smith Redwoods State Parks,** P.O. Drawer J, Crescent City 95531, tel. 458-3115 for Del Norte, tel. 464-9533 for Jedediah Smith. Day-use fee for the state parks is $5.

Greyhound in Crescent City, tel. (707) 464-2807, stops on its way south to Eureka or north from there at the AYH hostel north of Klamath, at Paul's Cannery in Klamath, and at the Shoreline Deli just south of Orick.

CRESCENT CITY

Most of the world's Easter lilies, that ultimate modern-day symbol of resurrection, are grown north of Crescent City, the only incorporated city in Del Norte County, a proud if historically downtrodden town laid out in 1853 along the crescent moon harbor. Crescent City is a grim weatherbeaten gray, pounded so long by storms it has become one with the fog. Grim, too, is life for prisoners at the state's largest maximum-security prison, the new **Pelican Bay State Prison,** locked up just outside town because they blew it badly somewhere else. The probable new site of California's Death Row, the prison primes the community's economic pump with some $40 million per year, and was the focus of California Senator Barry Keene's Name That Prison contest. Among the unselected but otherwise superior suggestions from clever north coast minds: The Big Trees Big House, Camp Runamok, Dungeness Dungeon, Saint Dismos State (a reference to the patron saint of prisoners), and Slammer-by-the-Sea.

Crescent City still suffers from the 1964 tsunami that tore the town off its moorings after the big Alaska earthquake, as well as a freak typhoon with 80-mile-an-hour winds in 1972. Life goes on, however; the once devastated and denuded waterfront is now an attractive local park and convention center. Crabbing from the public **Citizens' Wharf,** built at Crescent Harbor with entirely local resources and volunteer labor when government rebuilding assistance fell through, is

KIM WEIR

coastal scene near Crescent City

especially good. (The harbor breakwater is unique, of French design, a system of interlocking, 25-ton concrete "tetrapods.")

In February the town hosts its annual **Crab Races** and community dinner. Crescent City's **July 4th** festivities include everything from cribbage and kite flying to sandcastle sculpting. At Smith River just north, the local **Easter in July Lily Festival** celebrates the lily bloom, the festivities including sunrise church services, a lily float contest, and food and crafts booths decked out with you-know-what. Also fun the last weekend in July is the two-mile **Gasquet Raft Race** on the Smith River, with contestants limited to rafts and other crafts paddled only by hand. (The local pronunciation is "GAS-key," in the same vein as "Del Nort" County.)

Crescent City Sights

See the **Battery Point Lighthouse** near town (weather and tides permitting, walk out to it on a path over 100 years old), an island museum open Wednesday through Sunday 10 a.m.-4 p.m., small donation. Decommissioned in 1953

though it was 12 more years before they turned the light out, the Battery Point Lighthouse was restored in 1981 by Craig Miller with local donations of materials and has been operated as a private navigational aid since 1982 by the Del Norte Historical Society. Spend some time in the **Del Norte Historical Society Museum** at 577 H St., (707) tel. 464-3922, a collection including Native American artifacts, quilts and kitchenware, logging and mining paraphernalia, open Mon. through Sat. 10 a.m.-4 p.m., donation. Also there is the first-order lens taken from the lighthouse on St. George reef, over 18 feet tall. Stop by the historic **McNulty House** nearby, 710 H St., tel. 464-5186, to take in exhibits of antiques, old clocks, and works of area artists.

Accommodations

Nothing in Crescent City beats camping at Jedediah Smith Redwoods State Park, though there are also four national park or forest campgrounds northeast of town near Gasquet, others to the southeast via Southfork Rd., and still more scattered through the Smith River/Six Rivers region.

Motel rates in Crescent City are fairly inexpensive and markedly less in winter. Among nicer lodgings is the **Pacific Motor Hotel** north of town at 440 Hwy. 101 North, tel. (707) 464-4141, with summer rates from $44-60. Nearby is Crescent City's **Travelodge,** 725 Hwy. 101 North, tel. 464-6106, rooms $57-67. Farther north, in Smith River, is the **Best Western Ship Ashore Motel,** 12370 Hwy. 101, tel. 487-3141, $54-64 in summer. The **Curly Redwood Lodge** a half mile south of town on the highway (701 Redwood Hwy. South), tel. 464-2137, has large rooms, $50-54 (winter rates: $30-37). Top of the line, motel-wise, is the **Best Western Northwoods Inn** just south of town at 655 Hwy. 101 South, tel. 464-9771, rates $69-79 (less in winter).

The **Pebble Beach Bed and Breakfast,** 1650 W. Macken Ave., Crescent City 95531, tel. (707) 464-9086, offers rooms in a 1957 home, full breakfast, even a tandem bike to borrow. Rates: $65-75. The **Fairwinds Inn Bed and Breakfast** at 484 Pebble Beach Dr., P.O. Box 333, tel. 532-1479, is a shipshape contemporary on a bluff above the ocean, just one guest room occupying the entire third floor. Full breakfast. Rate: $100.

the Ship Ashore
north of Crescent City

KIM WEIR

Food

Standard grocery chains, like Safeway, exist in Crescent City. Better though is a stop (and plant tour) at the north coast's noted **Rumiano Cheese Company** at 9th and E streets, tel. (707) 465-1535, open 8:30 a.m.-3:30 p.m. Mon.-Friday. The **Crescent Meat Company** at 1298 Elk Valley Rd., tel. 464-6767, smokes its own bacon, ham, sausages, jerky, and turkey.

Many restaurants here don't take credit cards, so bring cash. Basic for breakfast is **Glen's Bakery,** 722 3rd St., tel. 464-2914, a coffee shop and adjacent bakery. **The Loft,** 3030 Lesina Rd., tel. 464-2886, offers American, Mexican, and Indonesian fare. The **China Hut Restaurant,** 928 9th St., tel. 464-4921, serves Cantonese, Mandarin, and Szechuan.

The best dinner restaurant around, though, is **Jim's Bistro** across from the fairgrounds at 200 Hwy. 101 North, Suite A, tel. (707) 464-4878, open nightly 5-9. The emphasis here is on lighter fare, though mesquite-grilled specialties and fresh seafood entrees abound. Children's menu, too.

Quite popular locally for seafood is the **Ship Ashore** restaurant at 12370 Hwy. 101 north of town in Smith River, tel. (707) 487-3141. (The very bizarre Ship Ashore Museum and Gift Shop by the highway—a boat beached in the parking lot—clues diners in to the turnoff.) Also good choices for seafood are the **Harbor View Grotto** at 155 Citizen's Dock Rd., tel. 464-3815, open noon-10 p.m.; the continental **House of Rowlands,** north of town at 400 Hwy. 101 North, tel. 464-4727, also a coffee shop, open 6 a.m.-9 p.m.; and **Northwoods Restaurant** at the motel.

Transport, Information, Services

The Crescent City **Chamber of Commerce** and cultural center is on Front St., tel. (707) 464-3174. **Greyhound** at 1125 Northcrest Dr., tel. 464-2807, has two buses heading north and two heading south daily. The **post office** is at 2nd and H, tel. 464-2151, the **public library** at 190 Price Mall, tel. 464-9793. For medical care and emergencies, contact **Sutter Coast Hospital** tel. 464-8511. For current road conditions, call 445-3125.

BOB RACE

THE NORTHERN MOUNTAINS

The northern mountains are too far north for most travelers, and despite the economic benefits of tourism, most people living here prefer it that way. Here in the Klamaths and Cascades, mountains tower like monuments to the gods and lava badlands pocked with mudpots and fumaroles create nightmare scenes from hell. Here is "the heart of the great black forests" described by badman poet Joaquin Miller, remnants of the virgin old-growth forests that once defined the land from here to Canada. Here also are craggy mountain peaks under cobalt blue skies, rushing rivers, crystal-clear lakes, and delicate meadows where dainty wildflowers bloom during the very short summers. The glacial high-country terrain is as spectacular as the Sierra Nevada. Attention hikers and backpackers: Bigfoot (or Sasquatch), that legendary hairy but harmless 600-pound man-ape of Northwest lore, is spotted here from time to time.

Almost as wild as the land is the area's history, a stream of rebellions, secessions, and regional wars. Trappers first came to the northern

mountains in the late 1820s, traversing the territory from Oregon to San Francisco via the Siskiyou Trail until the 1840s. In 1842, English pirates discovered gold at Sailors Bar on the Trinity River, and in 1849 one of Frémont's men, Major Pierson Barton Reading, likewise found nuggets at Big Bar near his namesake, modern-day Redding. New gold dreams brought a new gold rush, and the fever soon spread north: nuggets were found at Scott Bar near the mouth of the Scott River and farther north in the Siskiyous and Rogue River country. But if gold brought white people to these mountains, the lure of lumber kept them here.

States Of Rebellion
In 1852 a bill to form the separate State of Shasta was introduced in the California Legislature, then headquartered in Vallejo, with the intent of providing more military protection, better roads and mail service, and lower taxes for northstate territory. That bill died in committee, but it was hardly the end of the idea. In 1853 came the

THE NORTHERN MOUNTAINS

© MOON PUBLICATIONS, INC.

call for the formation of the State of Klamath, an area running roughly from Cape Mendocino to the Umpqua River. The following year, a meeting in Jacksonville, Oregon, was convened to plan the statehood convention for Jackson; in 1855 the issue came up again.

Those who sought separate statehood during the mid-1800s were quite serious, feeling isolated and victimized, complaining about the area's inadequate roads and lack of protection against angry, militant native peoples. The widespread support among settlers toward secession was also reflected locally, resulting in the creation of Modoc County (once part of Siskiyou County) and, after the Sagebrush War in what came to be known as Nevada Territory, Lassen County.

Organized acts of rebellion weren't confined to settlers. Attacks by native warriors were expressions of their rage over decimation due to disease and violence. Most famous of these "unwritten histories," as Joaquin Miller would call them, was one actually written—the long-running Modoc War of "Captain Jack" and his band, among the last major Indian Wars fought by U.S. troops.

The State Of Jefferson
Possibly only half seriously during this century the issue of secession came up again. On November 27, 1941, the State of Jefferson officially seceded from Oregon and California. Citizens of the new "state" put up roadblocks on Hwy. 99 and stated their intent "to secede each

Thursday until further notice"—or until they got good roads into the copper belt between the highway and the sea. The short-lived state of Jefferson ran from the Pacific over to the high plateau in Nevada, north to Roseburg, Oregon, and south to Redding, California. The new state's capital was Yreka, and its symbol was a gold pan. In the center of the state seal was "XX," indicating just how the people here felt about California and Oregon: doublecrossed.

On December 4, Judge John L. Childs of Crescent City was selected as acting governor of the new U.S. state, and his inauguration ceremony took place on the lawn of the courthouse in Yreka. "Our roads are not passable, barely jackassable; if our roads you would travel, bring your own gravel" read signs posted for the benefit of *Time, Life,* and film crews. Plans to release film footage of that event, the formation of what was to be America's 49th state, were foiled on December 8 by the greater news of Japan's attack on Pearl Harbor the day before. If it weren't for World War II, California travelers today would cross Jefferson on the way to Oregon. But the rebellion wasn't ineffective. Roads *were* finally paved in the far north, the construction of a major interstate freeway was inspired, and Stanton Delaplane of the *San Francisco Chronicle* won a Pulitzer Prize for his news coverage.

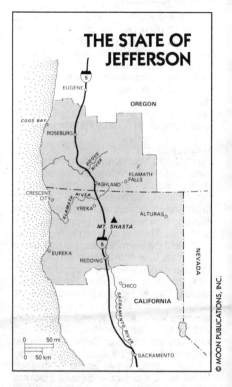

© MOON PUBLICATIONS, INC.

THE KLAMATHS

"Klamath Mountains" is the collective name for several separate ranges in northwestern California 6,000-9,000 feet in elevation and oriented in all different directions. Close to Oregon, the **Siskiyou Mountains** are one of several California coastal ranges milking moisture from storms headed inland. The Siskiyous, averaging 5,000-6,000 feet in elevation, run mostly east-west along the Oregon border from the Pacific Ocean to the Rogue River Valley. But the western end runs north-south, forming the divide between the Smith and Klamath rivers.

South of the Siskiyous are the towering peaks, meadowlands, and glacial lakes of the rugged **Marble Mountains,** laced by interconnecting trails, and the nearby **Russian Mountains.** The **Salmon** and **Scott** mountains (to the south and southeast, respectively) form the

northerly fringe of the **Trinity Alps,** which include the Trinity Wilderness and the easterly Trinity Mountains. Most notable in the Trinities is evidence of ancient glacial activity: scoured mountain lakes, serrated ridges, high, sloping meadows. One glacier remains on Thompson Peak, the highest point in northwestern California. The **Yolla Bolly Mountains** (named from the Wintu Yo-la Bo-li, meaning "high, snow-covered peak") include the **Yolla Bolly-Middle Eel Wilderness** and are the most southerly of the Klamaths. Near Mt. Shasta, **Castle Crags** (now a state park) are technically part of the Klamath range, forming its eastern boundary (see "Shasta").

The Klamaths include the wildest and least-known wilderness areas in California, also among the most fragile. The fresh, clear streams are still important for salmon and steelhead spawning because there are few roads into these areas. The timber industry hasn't yet cut out all the heart of the wilds here, though under current "timber harvesting" timetables, it's predicted that *that* operation will be completed by the turn of the century, on land primarily owned by the federal government. Except for token remnants of old-growth forest, the last of the great trees will be gone by the year 2000.

Geology

The Klamath Mountains, a northwestern extension of the Sierra Nevada, are older and more geologically complex than the surrounding northern California terrain—an "upwarp" or arc of ancient igneous and metamorphic rock plunging downward under younger adjacent land forms. The area once connecting the Klamaths and the Sierra Nevada was buried long ago by lava flows from the southern Cascades. Pleistocene glaciers slowly sculpted the granite and other resistant ridges into the jagged peaks of Castle Crags, the Marble and Salmon mountains, and the Trinity Alps. U-shaped valleys were formed where advancing alpine glaciers encountered serpentine and other soft rock. Concave cirques and lakes were scoured out by glaciers and are most noticeable today on north-facing slopes above 5,500 feet. Moraines, piles of sand and gravel deposited along the sides of glacial troughs, are evident in the Klamaths.

In the past 10,000 years, some of the glacial landforms here have been modified by stream erosion, forest succession, and rock weathering. Hundreds of tributaries from three major rivers, the Klamath, the Trinity, and the Scott, make this the most naturally divided landscape of its size in the state.

Well-written and worthwhile for regional natural history is *The Klamath Knot* by David Rains Wallace (Sierra Club Books).

Climate

The area is cold and snowy in the winter with cool summers (sometimes hot days at lower elevations). Rainfall averages 50-70 inches per year, with about 35 inches in Weaverville and 100-125 inches in the western Siskiyous and some parts of the Trinities. Summer thunderstorms are fairly common.

Flora And Fauna

There are many rare and endemic plants in the Klamaths, an open-air botanical museum with about 1,300 species. Lush growth is the rule for forests nearer the Pacific: mosses, fungi, and thick mantles of wildflowers. Big-leaf maple, dogwood, other deciduous trees, and vine maple add brilliant fall colors to the pines, Douglas firs, incense cedars, and the occasional Pacific yew and Port Orford cedar. Higher up, mixed evergreens blend with white fir and chinquapin; Shasta fir, lodgepole pine, western white pine and mountain hemlock are common only at highest elevations. Rare here is the weeping or Brewer's spruce. This gnarly veteran grows on north slopes at 7,500-7,600 feet and is found only in the Siskiyous and Trinities. Also here is the Alaska yellow cedar. On dry slopes are vast expanses of almost impassable mountain chaparral: oaks, manzanita, snowbrush.

Klamath vegetation is quite different on serpentine soils, which is toxic to many plant species. Scattered Jeffrey pines, lodgepoles, and western whites can be seen in these areas. On those rare serpentine spots where water seeps to the surface, the insectivorous cobra lily may be found.

Rare and endangered animals live here largely undisturbed, among them wolverines, martens, fishers, and mountain lions, bald eagles, peregrine falcons, spotted owls, and pileated woodpeckers. Deer abound. Bears are present but rarely seen; nonetheless, poaching has been on the increase recently, fueled by the demand for dried bear gallbladders used in exotic health remedies. Bald eagles are still occasionally shot by mountain men unable to read well enough to look up "endangered" in the dictionary.

THE TRINITY MOUNTAINS

There's not a single parking meter or traffic signal in Trinity County. *Wild* is the word here—rugged, glacier-carved peaks and rounded, scoured-out valleys, steep canyons, dramatic waterfalls. Whitewater rafting is good on the Trinity River, as are salmon and trout fishing along quieter stretches. Early in summer, before hot days take their toll, mountain wildflowers are everywhere. In the Trinities, the ultimate destination is the Trinity Alps Wilderness to the north, though there's plenty to see and do else-where. There are few people here but cattle (open rangeland) and deer are many, so watch for them while driving on narrow backcountry highways. Also watch for logging trucks.

The Trinity Alps Wilderness

Revel in these glacier-gouged goliaths looming over sapphire lakes. Though not as tall as major Cascade or Sierra Nevada peaks, these moun-tains, likened to the Swiss Alps, are snow-cov-ered even in summer and thickly forested on lower slopes. The Trinity Alps are rocky and rugged, intimate and close. Moist meadows hug crystal-clear streams that offer great fishing. Depending upon snowpack and trail conditions, late June to late July is generally the ideal hiking time here. Wildflowers are best in July and early August, but the Trinity Alps are especially nice for fall hiking: no crowds.

With passage of the Wilderness Act of 1984, the old Salmon-Trinity Alps Primitive Area be-came California's Trinity Alps Wilderness, sec-ond in size only to the John Muir Wilderness in the Sierra Nevada. The area takes in more than a half-million acres, the headwaters of both the Salmon and Trinity rivers, and more than 400 miles of trails, including a stretch of the Pacific Coast Trail and the New River area to the west. Once ruled by occasionally armed pot growers, New River has since been declared "safe for public use"—but don't count on that; the New River town of **Denny** has been called the most lawless place in the state. Also, about 15 percent of the wilderness burned in 1987 fires. To avoid those areas, pick up a free burn map from Shas-ta-Trinity National Forest headquarters in Red-ding or at the Weaverville district office. A good overall guide to the area is Wilderness Press's *The Trinity Alps: A Hiking and Backpacking Guide* by Luther Linkhart. Before planning even a day trip into the wilds here, however, check lo-cally on current conditions.

Some Trinity Hikes

Current information about area hiking and back-packing is available through the county chamber of commerce and regional Forest Service of-fices. But there's something here for everyone. Short treks include the 10-minute hike to **Lake Eleanor** near Trinity Center (from the Swift Creek Road trailhead), and the three-mile hikes to **Stoddard Lake** (from the Eagle Creek Loop off Hwy. 3), to **Tangle Blue** at the base of Scott Mountain, and to **Deadfall Lakes** (from Parks Creek Road). For more ambitious backcountry journeys, Deadfall Lakes is one access point to this region's stretch of the 2,600-mile **Pacific Crest Trail,** which intersects Parks Creek Road and Hwy. 3 at the crest of Trinity Drive.

Trinity Cycling And Mountain Biking

Trinity County's rollicking backcountry roads make for great cycling. Popular routes include the 30-mile **Trinity-Lake Lewiston Loop** out of Lewiston, the fun 45-mile **Hayfork-Peanut-Wildwood** loop starting in Hayfork (park at the county fairgrounds), and the very challenging 100-mile **Mad River-Wildwood** route starting at Ruth and skirting the Yolla Bolly-Middle Wilderness. Annual organized rides include the **Terror of the Trinities** century on Hwy. 3, usu-ally held in April.

Mountain bikers have their day too, of course, especially in October during the annual **metric century tour of the Trinity Alps.** Otherwise, popular treks are plentiful and various, due to the area's many abandoned logging roads. Espe-cially challenging is the 22-mile **South Fork Trail** along the South Fork of the Trinity River from Wildwood Road to Scotts Flat Campground (saner with a car shuttle).

Trinity Lake

Officially known as **Clair Engle Lake** in honor of the senator behind the damming of the Trinity here, locals refuse to recognize that name. The hard feelings of those whose land was taken for this reservoir at the foot of the Trinity Alps have only solidified with time. People here call the lake "Trinity," after the river which once roared through the valley past the gold rush towns of Minersville and Stringtown (now under water). With 150 miles of forested shoreline, the lake is warm enough for swimming in sum-mer. Fishing for catfish, bass, trout, and salmon is popular, as are all types of boating.

Trinity Center, the main town near the lake, was founded in the 1850s and named for its original location at the center of the Shasta-Yreka Trail (but relocated to its present site due to dam construction). Visit the **Scott Mu-seum** here for its outstanding collection of his-torical material, including 500 types of barbed

a gold rush-era
Chinese family
in Weaverville

CALIFORNIA DEPARTMENT OF PARKS & RECREATION

wire. Other area diversions include the **Coffee Creek Trout Farm** on Coffee Creek Road, tel. (916) 926-8293, and **Aspen Cellars Winery** on East Fork Road, tel. 226-3363. **Treasure Creek** near Trinity Center was named for a stray Wells Fargo strongbox rumored to still sleep with the fishes.

Lewiston Lake

Just south of Trinity Lake, Lewiston Lake is a cold lake just below the dam. The cooler water means excellent fishing for rainbows and browns in the upper channels. Good picnicking here and, because boat speeds are restricted to 10 mph, no roaring engines. Camping is also good, with some sites free—try Cooper Gulch, good swimming—and often less crowded than Trinity. The most automated salmon and steelhead hatchery anywhere, worth seeing (to believe), is the **Trinity River Fish Hatchery** just south of the Lewiston Dam. Good steelhead fishing along this stretch of the Trinity River.

The town of **Lewiston,** south of the lake and about five miles from Hwy. 299 via Rd. 105, is just three miles upriver from where the first gold dredger was built. Among other shops, a real find for antique lovers is **The Country Peddler,** tel. (916) 778-3876, along Deadwood Road in historic downtown. The town's **Sons of Temperance** meeting hall was erected in 1862 and still stands. Near Lewiston there's a newly restored cabin at **Limekiln Gulch** (once an active gold-mining area, now mostly visited by river-runners, hunters, hikers), its architecture

reminiscent of the French Colonial style common in the Mississippi River delta.

And if the attractions of these two lakes don't suffice, head to **Whiskeytown Lake** (see "Redding and Vicinity").

WEAVERVILLE

This is the place for people contact, a friendly little city of 3,500 at the base of the Trinity Alps and also the county seat. In Weaverville, cottages and old brick or woodframe homes are corralled by picket fences and covered with creeping vines. Notable here are the gold rushera buildings with exterior spiral staircases. The **Weaverville Drugstore** at 219 Main St. is the oldest drugstore in California, a veritable pharmacological museum inside (extraction percolators, druggists' mortars and pestles, pill-rolling machines) in addition to being a 1950s-feeling Rexall. Antique dolls are on display at **Big Ben's Doll Museum** at The Laag's place on Main, open April through mid-December or by special arrangement: tel. (916) 623-6383. Also along restored Main Street is the old *Trinity Journal* newspaper office, home of one of the state's oldest newspapers. Definitely worth a stop is **The Bookseller** at 220 Main, tel. 623-2232, a tiny bookshop with a huge selection of good taste. An inventory of local historic buildings and sights is included in the free "Walking Tour of Historic Weaverville" brochure and map. In the 1850s, half the town's population was Chinese, so it's not surprising that the old firehouse is a Chinese rammed-earth adobe. A marvelous monument to the Chinese presence in Weaverville, the **Joss House** here is the oldest Chinese temple in continuous use in California.

On the south side of Trinity Lakes Blvd. between Washington and Main (near the school) is **Five-Cent-Gulch**, site of the local Chinese Tong War of 1852. Cheering miners watched from the sidelines as 800 members of two rival tongs (gangs) met in battle. The Ah Yous were outnumbered and soon badly defeated by the Young Wos; the last two opposing warriors calmly stabbed each other with crude iron pitchforks for 15 minutes until one finally fell dead. (The victor died two weeks later.) There were no other casualties—perhaps only because whites didn't allow the Chinese to have firearms.

The Joss House Temple

A fine old Taoist temple is the focal point of the Weaverville Joss House State Historic Park ("joss" is a corruption of the Spanish word *dios,* "god"). Originally built in 1853 then torched 20 years later, the temple was rebuilt in 1874 and has since been in continuous use. Inside the brightly painted woodframe (the red interior beyond the "spirit screens" symbolizes happiness) are three ornately carved wooden canopies. The ancient altar, over 3,000 years old, holds candles, incense, an oracle book and fortune sticks, and glass-painted pictures of Immortals. In front are a table and urn for food and alcohol (usually whiskey) offerings to the gods. Adjacent to the temple is an unpainted lean-to, once a conference room and temple attendant's quarters. Mysteriously returned in 1989 was one of the temple's guardian "devil dogs," one of four missing since World War II (replica only on display).

Closed to the public when Taoists come to worship at "The Temple of the Forest Beneath the Clouds," Joss House tours (small fee) are scheduled on the hour whenever the park is open—increasingly hard to predict due to state budget cutbacks. For more information, contact: Weaverville Joss House State Historic Park, P.O. Drawer W, Weaverville 96093, tel. (916) 623-5284.

J.J. Jackson Museum

Across the parking lot from the Joss House is the county historical society's excellent local J.J. "Jake" Jackson Memorial Museum, a handsome brick building with an extensive collection of firearms, mining equipment, Native American basketry, Chinese artifacts, and other documentation of California's development. Also on the grounds of this "historical park" are an original miner's cabin from La Grange; a working two-stamp mill (once used by miners to crush rock and extract gold) housed in a replica of the original building; and a facsimile blacksmith and tin shop. Open daily May 1-Oct. 31, 10-5, noon-4 p.m. April and Nov., free but donations much

CALIFORNIA DEPARTMENT OF PARKS & RECREATION

Weaverville Joss House

appreciated. For more information, contact: **Trinity County Historical Society,** P.O. Box 333, Weaverville 96093, tel. (916) 623-5211.

PRACTICALITIES

Camping

In summer camping is the first choice, and there's lots of choice here (424 Forest Service campsites alone, some free, most $5-9, $15.50 for multiple family units). Popular (reserve campsites in summer through Mistix) is the large **Tannery Gulch Campground** on the west side of Trinity Lake. The **Alpine View Campground** under the Trinity Alps at the north end of the lake has 66 campsites and a nature trail. Large **Hayward Flat Campground** also up north has a nice swimming beach. Public campgrounds with no safe drinking water (or no water, period) are always free. Of these, especially nice (and private) are **Eagle Lake Campground,** about 12 miles north on Hwy. 3 then five miles on a dirt road (sign), and **Horseflat Campground,** 1½ miles after the Eagle Creek turnoff (same road). Both have pit toilets, good swimming, but no drinking water, open mid-May through October. **Jackass Springs** on the east side of the lake is the most isolated. The **Ackerman Campground** at Lewiston Lake is open year-round, as is **Cooper Gulch.** For private camping options, get information in Weaverville at the chamber office.

Weaverville City-style Stays

With any luck at all, by the turn of the millenium the proprietors of the **New York Saloon and Hotel** downtown will complete the building's historic renovation and open again as a hostelry. In the meantime, a good choice is cozy **Granny's House Bed and Breakfast** at 313 Taylor, P.O. Box 31, Weaverville 96093, tel. (916) 623-2756. An 1897 Queen Anne Victorian, Granny's features three rooms (which share two baths) with old-fashioned feather beds, luscious breakfasts. Rates from $65 (ask about off-season specials). The very large **Weaverville Victorian Inn** on Hwy. 299 at 1709 Main St. (P.O. Box 2400), tel. 623-4432, is actually a motel, quite new, quite contemporary, with modern conveniences ranging from satellite TV to in-room spas. Rates from $49, AAA and AARP discounts. And you can't go too far wrong at ei-

ther the **49er Motel** at 718 Main, tel. 623-4937, or the **Motel Trinity** at 1112 Main, tel. 623-2129, both with rates in the $30 range. **The Weaverville Hotel** at 201 Main St., tel. 623-3121, features old-fashioned rooms (no phones) with private baths (either tubs or showers), very clean and pleasant, morning coffee, rates from $35. Quite a find.

Bed And Breakfasts Near Weaverville

The casually elegant **Carrville Inn Bed & Breakfast** on Carrville Loop Rd. just off Hwy. 3 north of Trinity Lake, Star Rte. 2, Box 3536, Trinity Center 96091, tel. (916) 266-3511, is just about the area's most popular phenomenon since the arrival of paved roads. Once a stage stop, this refurbished historic hostelry features five upstairs guest rooms (two share a bath), a lacy two-tiered front veranda that serves as unofficial social hall, an eclectic game room, and den with fireplace. This pastoral place presides over a vast mountain meadow and includes roses, fruit trees, a full-sized swimming pool, and a small barnyard animal family. Full country-style breakfast, very genial hosts. Advance reservations strongly advised (the inn is open only mid-March through October). Rates from $95.

In the historic sector of Lewiston—and complete with prime fishing frontage along the Trinity River near the old bridge—is **The Old Lewiston Inn,** P.O. Box 688, Lewiston 96052, tel. (916) 778-3385, a completely refurbished tin-roofed gold rush-era building "as romantic as all get out," the innkeepers say. Four very comfortable motel-style rooms (private baths) with separate entrances and individual decks, plus an adjacent house-style annex. Rates from $60, including full breakfast.

About 50 miles west of Weaverville via Hwy. 299 is the **Madrone Manor Inn,** HCR #34, Burnt Ranch 95527, tel. (916) 629-3642, a luxurious home-stay bed and breakfast with two available suites (one a separate guesthouse) and almost every imaginable amenity, including a party-size outdoor sauna. Though there's a dearth of urban entertainments, birdwatching along the Trinity River and hiking in nearby state parks are definitely worthwhile. In Willow Creek, there are a few eateries, a nine-hole golf course, and summer concerts and repertory theater. (And from Burnt Ranch, it's about an hour to the coast.) Rates: $65-75 per couple.

Unique Cabins And Retreats

New among the Weaverville area's more out-doorsy lodging options and quite unique: **Ripple Creek Cabins,** Star Rte. 2, Box 3899 (on the Eagle Creek loop off Hwy. 3), Trinity Center 96091, tel. (916) 266-3505 or 266-3608—seven beautifully restored cabins (with both wood-stoves and electric heat) casually scattered through the woods near a meadow. Cabins vary in size and capacity—one is wheelchair-accessible and can also accommodate group meetings and seminars—but each features "basics" like garlic presses, collanders, cork-screws, and wineglasses, not to mention out-door Weber barbecues and picnic tables. There's even a playground. Children and pets welcome. Rates start at $70 per couple per day, $435 per week, substantially less from Oct.-May (holidays excepted).

Fully furnished private vacation homes offer even more seclusion, including the **Coffee Creek Chalet,** Star Rte. 2, Box 3969, Trinity Center 96091, tel. (916) 266-3235, and **The Cedars Lodge,** Star Rte. 2, Box 3899, Trinity Center 96091, tel. 266-3505 or (805) 595-7756.

Traditional Rustic Resorts

Most of the area's truly rustic accommodations are veritable family-vacation traditions, usually booked at least a year in advance with one-week minimum stays during the peak summer season. (Call for the possibility of cancellations.) Weekly cabin rates average $500-650 in summer (lower in spring and fall), though full-service resorts, which provide all meals and dude ranch-style amenities, may run that much per person per week. Depending upon the facility, substantially less expensive family accommo-dations are available.

The 1920s-style **Trinity Alps Resort,** is the oldest resort around, with rustic cabins along Stuarts Fork River (good fishing and river rafting), horseback riding, pool hall and game room, bingo and Ping-Pong at the resort's General Store.

The **Bonanza King,** Rt. 2 Box 4790, Trinity Center 96091, tel. (916) 266-3305, is three miles from upper Trinity Lake on Coffee Creek (near a pack station if you're literally hoofing it into the Alps), fully furnished, comfortable, porched log cabins (some with fireplaces or woodstoves) with kitchens, plus laundromat with solar drier, sandy beach and swimming hole, good fishing.

The **Coffee Creek Ranch,** HC 2 Box 4940, Trinity Center 96091, tel. (916) 266-3343 or toll-free (800) 624-4480, is also on Coffee Creek Rd. (and right on the creek), another good choice—especially if you liked the movie *City Slickers.* Heated pool, private pond, plus square dancing, evening bonfire, horseback riding, a steak feast on weekends, stream fishing, and every imaginable dude ranch amenity.

The **Josephine Creek Lodge** is within the Trinity Alps Wilderness area, with rustic lodge rooms and cabins, also a restaurant and laundry. Sister facility **Mountain Meadow Resort** is also open only during the summer season, and offers lodge rooms and cabins, organized activities such as gold-mine exploration, horseback riding, and volleyball—even childcare. (Tots must be supervised at the wading pool.) Pack trips into the wilderness can also be arranged. For infor-mation or to make reservations year-round, con-tact: **Josephine Creek Lodge/Mountain Meadow Resort,** 24225 Summit Woods Dr., Los Gatos 95030, tel. (408) 353-1663. During summer, call (916) 462-4677.

Weaverville Eateries

Quite good downtown is **The Mustard Seed,** 252 S. Main, tel. (916) 623-2922, open daily for breakfast and lunch. Vegetarian selections avail-able. (Absolutely organic eaters don't need to starve in Trinity County. The Trinity Organic Growers Association, P.O. Box 314, Douglas City 96024, sponsors weekly farmers markets in Weaverville and Hayfork.) Also popular: the deli fare at the **New York Saloon,** burgers at the **La Grange Cafe** near downtown on the high-way. But don't turn your nose up at the **A&W** stand here which—in authentic shades of the '50s—features carhop tray service. The **Brew-ery** in the 1855 Pacific Brewery building at 401 S. Main, tel. 623-3000, is locally loved for its food—everything from chicken fajitas to lasagna, seafood, and steaks—as well as eclectic decor. An old horse buggy hangs from the ceiling, a mannequin masquerades as a dancehall girl, and the old stove shares space with beer kegs and whiskey jugs.

Restaurants Near Weaverville

Way out there—north of Trinity Center at the intersection of Hwy. 3 and Coffee Creek Rd.—and quite popular is the year-round **Forest Deli,** tel. (916) 266-3575, known for its great breakfasts, burgers, and home-style dinner specials.

The **Bear's Breath Bar & Grill** at the Trinity Alps Resort on Trinity Alps Rd. (off Hwy. 3), tel. (916) 286-2205, is justly proud of its riverside deck dining, American standards plus pastas, and almost adventurous items like "Joss House chicken" marinated in soy sauce and honey then stir-fried with vegetables. The name and atmosphere both may be less evocative but the food (European and American fare, primarily fish and meat selections) is more enticing at the **Airporter Inn** on Airport Rd. (at the airport), tel. 266-3223.

Home to the only traffic signal in Trinity County—and this one is in the bar, to control wait staff traffic between the dining room and kitchen—is **The Lewiston Hotel** in Lewiston, tel. 778-3823, another local favorite, this one famous for homemade soups and daily specials as well as additive-free steaks and other cuts of beef. And do spend some time appreciating the decor here, perhaps best described as country eclectic with accents of urban humor. Also quite popular is **Mama's Place,** a country cafe on Lewiston's main drag, tel. 778-3177.

Serious food lovers drive north to Etna and **Seng Thong's,** tel. (916) 467-5668, a regionally popular Vietnamese-Thai restaurant written up in *Bon Appetit,* or head west on Hwy. 299 to sample coastal culinary pleasures (see "The North Coast").

Wilderness Information

For general information (prerecorded) about Trinity area camping and recreation, call (916) 246-5338. For information and campfire permits for the Trinity, Lewiston, and Whiskeytown lakes areas (all part of the Whiskeytown-Shasta-Trinity National Recreation Area), contact the Forest Service **Weaverville Ranger District** office on Hwy. 299 in Weaverville, P.O. Box 1190, Weaverville 96093, tel. 623-2121, open weekdays 8-5 (daily in summer), or the **Coffee Creek Ranger Station** at the north end of Trinity Lake on Hwy. 3, Coffee Creek 96091, tel. 266-3211. (Highway 3 past this point, eventually leading to Yreka, is twisting and treacherously narrow, not recommended for trailers or the fainthearted.)

Wilderness permits for the **Trinity Alps Wilderness Area,** national forest maps ($3), Marble Mountains and Yolla Bolly wilderness maps ($3), and other regional camping and recreation information are available at both places, as well as at **Big Bar Ranger Station,** Star Rt. 1 Box 10, Big Bar 96010, tel. (916) 623-6106. (With some advance notice these places, open weekdays 8-5, will leave a permit outside for campers arriving after 5 p.m. Outside the Weaverville office, Trinity wilderness and national forest maps are available via vending machine, quarters only.) Other area Forest Service offices: **Hayfork Ranger Station,** P.O. Box 159, Hayfork 96041, tel. 628-5227, and **Yolla Bolla Ranger Station,** Platina 96076, tel. 352-4211.

General And Recreational Information

For more information about the Trinity Alps area and its attractions, including community events and lake recreation, contact the **Trinity County Chamber of Commerce,** 317 Main St., P.O. Box 517, Weaverville 96093, tel. (916) 623-6101 or toll-free (800) 421-7259. In addition to the downtown walking tour brochure, ask for the "Trinity Heritage Scenic Byway" auto tour and map of the Hwy. 299 corridor, jam-packed with useful details.

This is fishing country. Trout season opens in late April. California fishing permits are available are local sporting goods stores and bait shops. In fall and spring, Gerry Gray's **God's Country Guide Service,** tel. (916) 266-3297, offers guided fishing at Lewiston Lake and on the Trinity, Klamath, Smith, and other northstate rivers.

This is also whitewater country. For an unusual educational twist on the rafting theme, contact **Kimtu Outdoors Adventures** P.O. Box 938, Willow Creek 95573, tel. (916) 629-3843 or toll-free (800) 562-8475. Kimtu offers unique one- or two-day Native American river tours of the Trinity River's historically rich Tish Tang Gorge, with firsthand introductions to ancient Hupa cultural practices and visits to the Hoopa Museum, an ancient village, and local sweat lodges. The company also offers everything from easy float trips to Class V whitewater thrill rides on the Trinity, Klamath, and Smith Rivers, plus a kayaking school, kids' camp, and special trips for teenagers. Overnight retreat accommodations (rustic) available.

Turtle River Rafting Company, P.O. Box 313, Mt. Shasta 96067, tel. (916) 926-3223, offers Salmon, Klamath, Upper Sacramento, Eel, and Rogue river trips (hot-springs soaks and saunas at Stewart Mineral Springs after the Klamath and Rogue trips), plus kayaking, a whitewater rafting school, and guided climbs of Mt. Shasta. Discounts available.

Other good raft and river trip options include **Wilderness Adventures,** P.O. Box 938, Redding 96099, tel. (916) 238-8121, with summertime runs on the Trinity and Upper Klamath rivers, and **Klamath River Outfitters** in Somes Bar (see "Young's Ranch Resort" below).

Shasta Llamas, P.O. Box 1137, Mt. Shasta 96067, tel. (916) 926-3959, offers a variety of guided pack trips, including adventures in the Trinity Alps and Marble Mountain wildernesses. Plenty of fun, with excellent food and other niceties, plus recommendations for overnights at the Carrville Inn, Stewart Springs, and other unusually good area accommodations. New are the company's three-day family trips with an emphasis on children ages 5-12, complete with storyteller. For more traditional pack trip options, inquire at the county chamber office.

OTHER SIGHTS

West On Highway 299

Junction City, known as Milltown, was once a booming trade center for ranchers and miners. North of Junction City along Canyon Creek was the town of **Canyon City,** a.k.a. Raggedy Ass. Just one mile farther north, where the Little East Fork branches from Canyon Creek, is **Dedrick.** Here were the Bailey, Silver Gray, and Globe mines—the territory's major gold producers. Settled in 1849 by French Canadian prospectors, **Helena** once had a hotel and boardinghouse. The economy here peaked in 1855 when there were over 200 acres of fruit orchards. Some old fruit trees and a few brick buildings are all that remain now, though the area was once wild enough for the nickname "Baghdad of the Frontier." **Big Bar** was one of about nine gold rush-era spots of the same name in California. The most notorious local resident was "Commodore Ligne," who sold mining claims to the Chinese then shooed them off the land with a shotgun and sold the sites again. (Justice was eventually served when the commodore was shipped out to San Quentin.) The name **Burnt Ranch** comes from the torching of farmhouses here in 1853 during an Indian raid.

South Of Trinity: Ghost Towns, Dead Dreams

Old **Douglas City** was once a big placer and hydraulic mining area, still scarred. All that remains is the water tower just above Reading's gold site on the Trinity River near the mouth of Reading's creek. (Reading was responsible for naming the region "Trinity," mistakenly believing that the river led into Trinidad Bay on the coast.)

From Hwy. 3, the 22-mile road to **Deer Lick Springs** follows Brown's Creek to the mineral springs and store (also campground), eventually leading into the Chanchelulla Wilderness (see below).

Head out of Douglas City on Steiner Flat Rd. (or take Wildwood Rd. off Hwy. 3), then turn onto Bridge Gulch Rd. to the 200-foot limestone **Kok-Chee-Shup-Chee Natural Bridge,** site of the Bridge Gulch Massacre of March 1852. The ultimate in vengeance, 150 Wintu men, women, and children were knifed and shot to death here by a sheriff's posse of miners in revenge for the killing of one of their own. (There's a half-mile self-guided trail through the area.)

Hayfork was once called Kingsberry Hay Town, a farming and ranching community "attacked" during World War II by the Japanese. The attack was impersonal, consisting of one of 6,000 or so 70-foot-tall balloons with bombs attached for the purpose of setting American forests afire and diverting resources from the war effort. (At least one flaw in the plan was the fact that all 300 bombs known to have reached the U.S. got here in the middle of a cold, wet winter.)

Ruth, once known as White Stump, was built where old-timers say a bolt of lightning struck a pine tree. **Ruth Reservoir,** Trinity County's second-largest lake in lush, remote countryside, has campgrounds and other lodging (basic services available in town). From Ruth Lake, it's a thrilling trip over to the coast. For information contact: Ruth Lake Community Services, P.O. Box 31, Mad River 95552, tel. (707) 574-6332.

Yolla Bolly Wilderness

Bigfoot was last spotted here in 1970, so watch for hairy hikers. The Yolla Bolly-Middle Eel Wilderness Area is lush and green early in the season, otherwise hot, dry, and steep, also heavily forested and lonely. Less rugged than the Trinity Alps, Yolla Bolly is open for hiking by late May. To get here from Weaverville, head east on Hwy. 36 (look for the shadows of logging trucks before blind curves) then south. You can also come in from Red Bluff. Call or obtain a wilderness map in advance for more specific directions, since they differ from trailhead to trailhead. Also new in the area since 1984: the **North Fork Wilderness** (taking in most of the Middle Eel River's headwaters) and **Chanchelulla Wilderness.** This area includes Chanchelulla Peak (6,399 feet), trails up through thickly forested hillsides, meadows sweet with wildflowers.

For information about the Yolla Bolly-Middle Eel Wilderness, contact Mendocino National Forest, tel. (916) 934-3316, or Six Rivers National Forest (North Fork), tel. (707) 442-1721, or Shasta-Trinity National Forest, tel. (916) 628-5227. For info on Chanchelulla Wilderness, contact Shasta-Trinity or the Hayfork Ranger District office, tel. (916) 628-5227. For info on the **North Fork Wilderness,** contact Mendocino National Forest.

If finished off by the wilderness, plan a stay at **Henthorne Lake Wilderness Camp,** P.O. Box 67, Covelo 95428, a 3,000-acre rustic retreat with access to Yolla Bolly.

THE SALMON RIVER

The Salmon And Scott Mountains
The Salmon Mountains snaggle toward the southeast from the Siskiyous; part of the range is included in both the Trinity Alps and Marble Mountain wildernesses. The Scott Mountains snake down from the north, the two ranges never quite intersecting but coming close just south of the Marble Mountains. The north and south forks of the wild, undammed Salmon River flow west to their confluence at Forks of Salmon, then northwest to Somes Bar, where they flow into the Lower Klamath River. The headwaters of the Scott River start just miles from the Salmon's, joining the North Fork near Callahan before flowing north then northwest to join the Upper Klamath River just east of Hamburg. The two rivers, separated only by a finger of mountains, create a wide mountain valley like a sliver of moon arching south from the lower Klamath then northwest to its headwaters.

There aren't many people in these parts, but there is plenty to see and do: fishing, whitewater rafting, kayaking and canoeing, short hikes, week-long backpack trips, historical reconnaissance. Travel along the Salmon River is via a one-lane gravel road etched into steep granite.

Somes Bar To Forks Of Salmon
There's a sign where the town of Somes Bar once stood, now a popular year-round fishing and camping spot (king salmon and steelhead are the prized catches here) and starting point for western trails to the Marble Mountains Wilderness. Also here: a Forest Service district ranger's office. The general store at Forks of Salmon was built in the early 1800s. Secluded camping nearby includes **Hotelling Gulch,** a small campground (four sites) three miles southeast of here on Cecilville Road. (Boil your water.) Seven miles farther, on the Salmon River's south fork, is **Matthews Creek Campground** (14 sites, piped water).

Otter Bar Lodge:
Kayaking And Mountain Biking
Not for budget travelers, except those willing to save up for a supreme whitewater experience, Otter Bar Lodge is a world-class kayaking school, mountain-biking mecca, and wilderness resort near Forks of Salmon on the banks of the river: $1,050 per person per week with everything. New at Otter Bar are the seven-day mountain bike trips, also optional three-day guided pack trips into the Trinity Alps. Fall fishing is another popular excuse for coming here. The facilities are also available for groups of up to 10 people interested mostly in fishing, rafting, hiking, even seminars. Corporate think-tank retreaters welcome.

To describe Otter Bar as "rustic" is to suggest that Hearst Castle is a tract home. But it is 100 miles from any place you've ever heard of, and over two hours from the nearest store. The four-bedroom lodge has down comforters, antiques, and good books in every room. Also at Otter Bar, great food (raved about in *Bon Appetit)* and an outdoor sauna and hot tub. For info or reservations: Otter Bar Lodge, Forks of Salmon 96031, tel. (916) 462-4772.

Young's Ranch Resort
And Klamath River Outfitters

A family-oriented resort, Young's Ranch, Somes Bar 95568, tel. (916) 469-3322 or toll-free (800) KLAMATH, is a very fine yet rustic vacation spot, the kind of place where children have the chance to *act* like children without getting into too much trouble. Because of the resort's remoteness—just off Hwy. 96 about halfway between Happy Camp and Willow Creek, a site near the Klamath River surrounded by a million acres of national forest—electrical power here is generated by a gold rush-style Pelton water wheel. The flume which supplies the ranch's running water was built by Chinese laborers in the 1800s. Completely stocked housekeeping cabins come in various sizes, one to three bedrooms. If you plan to cook, bring your own food,

Marble Mountains

but guests can opt for family-style meals in the lodge. Cabin rates run $40 per night and up, from $230 per week. A stay at the luxurious two-bedroom Quail Woods cabin/home atop the ridge is substantially more.

Young's Ranch has some of the finest swimming holes anywhere, access to great hiking, plus basketball and volleyball. Fishing expeditions are offered from spring through fall, as well as guided family raft trips and horse pack trips into the wilderness *(you* walk, the horses carry the load).

THE MARBLE MOUNTAIN
WILDERNESS

With the best hiking and backpacking north of the Trinity Alps, the Marble Mountain Wilderness Area is a quarter-million acres of thick forests teeming with wild things: bears and mountain lions (though you'll rarely spot either), ever-abundant deer, grouse, quail, and chipmunks. Alpine wildflowers cascade from rocks and meadows and peek out from beneath the forest canopy. Snow-covered peaks tower above. Fishing is excellent in hundreds of miles of streams. Visit about 50 crystal lakes, most to the north in the Marble Mountains proper (two-thirds of the wilderness, named after Marble Mountain peak, is actually part of the Salmon range).

Marble Mountain, 8,925 feet tall, is the highest point and something of a natural monument, limestone and marble streaked with white. Camp at **Marble Valley, Paradise Lake, Sky High Valley, Spirit Lake,** and **Upper Cabin,** but better are makeshift campsites near (but not very near) lakes and streams. A wilderness permit (free) is required for backcountry travel, available from any Klamath National Forest ranger district office (see "Yreka" below). A worthwhile and well-written book about the region's natural history is *The Klamath Knot* by David Rains Wallace (Sierra Club Books).

Also within Klamath National Forest is the tiny (12,000-acre) **Russian Wilderness,** a few miles southeast of the Marble Mountain Wilderness. The Russian takes in the Klamath's Russian Mountains, a tall granitic ridge with prominent peaks and U-shaped valleys, an area ranging in elevation from 5,000 to more than 8,000 (atop Russian Peak).

Hikes, Llamas, Whitewater Rafting

The epitome of Marble Mountain hikes is a **Sky High Lakes** trek, a possible loop trip with outstanding views and lovely lakes, trailside snow in June. Not to be forgotten is **Paradise Lake**, an alpine jewel on a grassy ledge next to Kings Castle and above a narrow emerald valley. Come in late June for the best wildflowers. Enjoy great fishing (and usually plenty of privacy) at **Wright Lakes.**

Hiking and backpacking is the way most people get around in the Marble Mountain Wilderness, but you can do the trip with llamas carrying the load (not cheap but fun, catered meals, wine): **Shasta Llamas,** P.O. Box 1137, Mt. Shasta 96067, tel. (916) 926-3959. This outfit also leads outings into the Trinity Alps and other northstate areas. For other more traditional pack outfits (using horses and mules, either on guided trips or to pack in supplies) contact area chambers of commerce. For a rare springtime thrill, Dean Munroe of **Wilderness Adventures,** 19504 Statton Acres Rd., Lakehead 96051, tel. (916) 238-8121 or 8131 or toll-free (800) 323-

RAFT sometimes offers whitewater runs on Wooley Creek as it careens and crashes out of the wilderness, Class III to Class V water. Munroe and company, pioneers of the "Hell's Corner" run on the Klamath, were also the first down this one (for experts only).

Getting There

There are many routes, many trailheads. Come in from the southwest via Camp Three Rd. or Wooley Creek Trail; from the southeast, up from Mule Bridge Camp on the North Fork of the Salmon. From the northeast, hike in on the Boulder Creek, Canyon Creek, or Kelsey Creek trails. (Just outside the northeastern wilderness boundary in the Klamath River valley is a cluster of public campgrounds, most along Scott River Road.) From the northwest, come in from Happy Camp via Elk Creek Road. It's possible to walk on unimproved roads to the edge of the Marble Mountain Wilderness (though it'll take a while): start from Greenview, Etna, or Happy Camp. The **Pacific Crest Trail** eventually enters the wilderness south of Seiad Valley.

YREKA

Yreka is the only city to speak of in the central far north. People here (all 6,500 of them) are proud of their pioneer history (there's a good museum, gold nugget display in the courthouse, well-preserved old Victorians, and brick gold-rush buildings) but equally proud of their historic, steam excursion train.

Local History

The gold rush gave birth to Yreka. Nuggets found at Scott Bar in 1851 brought 2,000 miners within six weeks. The local legend goes like this: Abraham Thompson stopped to spend the night here and was astonished when grazing pack mules pulled up flecks of gold, tangled in grass roots. Named variously Thompson's Dry Diggings, Shasta Butte City, Wyeka, Wyreka, then Yreka, the town gradually grew, boasting 27 saloons before churches began to gain ground. A big fire on July 4, 1871, demolished one-third of the town in an hour. "Indian Peggy," a Modoc woman, is credited with saving the townspeople from slaughter by warning of an impending Klamath raid in the 1850s; the town eventually gave her a pension.

KIM WEIR

If Yreka seems too tame, try downtown Fort Jones

Yreka Sights

Most of the town's gold rush-vintage buildings, included in the National Register of Historic Places, are concentrated between Oregon and Main, and W. Lennox and Miner streets. Many of the buildings on Miner Street were built up from the walls left standing after the 1871 fire. Below street level are the remains of tunnels and mine shafts honeycombing the area. (Pick up a free "A Door to the Past" walking guide to Yreka's historic district at the chamber of commerce.) Above ground, horsehead hitching posts rear up out of modern-day sidewalks. The **Siskiyou County Museum,** at 910 S. Main St., tel. (916) 842-3836, is an indoor-outdoor collection of historical relics, Native American and gold mining exhibits, firearms, and paraphernalia left behind by trappers and pioneers. (Ask for admittance to outdoor area.) Historical publications are available during normal museum hours, Mon.-Fri. 9-5 (plus evenings and Sun. 1-5 in summer), closed Sun. and Mon. in winter. Free.

Eye-opening are the gold displays in the foyer of the **Siskiyou County Courthouse,** 311 4th St., tel. (916) 842-4531, a fortune in natural gold nuggets taken from local mines and placers (including one of the largest nuggets ever found south of Alaska). Open Mon.-Fri. 8-5, also free. Worth a stop too, is the **Klamath National Forest Interpretive Museum,** part of the headquarters complex at 1312 Fairlane Rd., tel. 842-6131, with an extensive collection of historical and natural history exhibits, one of the most impressive offered at any U.S. National Forest outpost. Step into the lookout and check out the "firefinder." Free.

Ride The *Blue Goose*

Yreka's pride and joy is the Yreka Western Railroad and its *Blue Goose* steam excursion train. The 1915 black Baldwin locomotive pulls the art deco-vintage cars and a open-air passenger flatcar through the Shasta Valley to Montague then back again, about 15 miles roundtrip. All in all the ride is quite peaceful and uneventful—unless bandits should happen to hold up the train. Even more exciting is the summertime "Murder on the Blue Goose Express" social adventure, a scripted day-long melodrama of mayhem and mystery (period costumes mandatory). Other special events include occasional Saturday night "steak and steam" dinner runs and the annual "Great Wild Goose Chase" fun run. During its regular summer schedule, the *Blue Goose* departs at 10 a.m. Weds.-Sun., with weekend-only runs in fall and very limited winter holiday runs (wear your goose downs!). The train schedule is subject to change, so call ahead. Advance reservations advisable. For current information, just stop by the depot (jog east from I-5's Central Yreka exit) or contact: **Yreka Western Railroad,** 300 E. Miner St., P.O. Box 660, Yreka 96097, tel. (916) 842-4146.

Area Camping

No camping in town, but Klamath National Forest has 26 campgrounds with more than 350 campsites. Get information at headquarters here, tel. (916) 842-6131. **Humbug Creek Campground** is about 12 miles west of Yreka via Yreka-Walker and Humbug roads, five canyon campsites near the site of old **Humbug,** a wild mining town Joaquin Miller described as having "neither the laws of God nor man" in a setting "out of sight of everything—even the sun." (The saloon in Humbug was called the Howlin' Wilderness.) Nearby, where McAdams and Cherry creeks converge, was the mining town of **Deadwood,** second only to Yreka among mid-1850s boom towns. Miller wrote his first poem here, an epitaph commemorating the marriage of a local cook. He then recited it at the couple's wedding reception and a literary career was launched. **Iron Gate** and **Copco lakes** are administered by Pacific Power & Light and fed by the Klamath River. Camping is possible here, though some sites have no water; there are cabins at Lake Copco. No motor boats allowed at Iron Gate, but great fishing in the river, also swimming, hiking. For info: **Pacific Power & Light,** 300 S. Main, Yreka 96097, tel. 842-3521. Free.

Yreka Accommodations

Yreka has a number of fairly inexpensive motels, most of these clustered along "motel row" on Main. The **Wayside Inn** about a mile south of town at 1235 S. Main St., tel. (916) 842-4412, is quite attractive, a few units with kitchens, one deluxe suite with amenities such as whirlpool bath and fireplace. General rates are in the $30-40 range, in line with both the **Thunderbird Lodge** at 526 S. Main, tel. 842-4404, and the

Motel Orleans on Fort Jones Rd., tel. 842-1642. Quite nice in the same price category is the **Klamath Motor Lodge** 1111 S. Main, tel. 842-2751. Top of the mark for Yreka-area motels is the **Best Western Miner's Inn** near the I-5 freeway at 122 E. Miner, tel. 842-4355, with rates from $45.

For a B&B stay, **McFadden's Inn**, 418 3rd St., Yreka 96097, tel. (916) 842-7712, offers three rooms in an 1890 Victorian, continental breakfast, sauna and hot tub, rates from $100.

Good Food, Local Color

The **Yreka Bakery** (note the palindrome) on W. Miner, tel. (916) 842-7440, is great for breakfast, not to mention lunch and dinner. Across the way and housed in the city's old meat market is the **Miner Street Deli,** with original mining-era art on the walls. **Grandma's House** at 123 E. Center, tel. 842-5300, has good breakfasts, lunch specials. Try **Ming's** at 210 W. Miner, tel. 842-1286, for Cantonese, Mandarin, Szechuan, or the **Wah Lee Chinese Restaurant,** 520 S. Main, tel. 842-3444, also good. **Lalo's,** at 219 W. Miner, is popular at lunch and dinner for its Mexican fare. **Tim Burke's Restaurant,** 1601 S. Oregon, tel. 842-5444, has good lunch specials and an early-bird dinner special every night, 4-7 p.m. Excellent is the continental-American **Old Boston Shaft Restaurant** and bar, 1801 S. Main, tel. 842-5768, seafood and beef, wonderful Old World desserts. Reservations a good idea.

Those in the know say the **Rex Club** downtown is the best local bar.

Information And Services

Pick up the *Siskiyou Daily News* for local news and events. Tourist info, maps, and walking tour brochures are available at the **Yreka Chamber of Commerce** office, 117 W. Miner St., Yreka 96097, tel. (916) 842-1649 or toll-free (800) ON-YREKA (recorded message). For more information about the area's historic buildings, contact the **Yreka Historic Preservation Corporation,** 115 S. Oregon St., tel. 842-3232. Rent sailplanes at **Montague Aviation** at Rohrer Field in Montague, tel. 459-3456.

At **Klamath National Forest** headquarters, 1312 Fairlane Rd., Yreka 96097, tel. (916) 842-6131, pick up camping, recreation, and wilderness information plus topo maps and wilderness and campfire permits. Klamath Forest Ranger District offices are: **Oak Knoll,** 22541 Hwy. 96, Klamath River 96050, tel. 465-2241; **Happy Camp,** P.O. Box 377, Happy Camp 96039, tel. 493-2243; **Salmon River** in Sawyers Bar, P.O. Box 280, Etna 96027, tel. 467-5757; **Scott River,** 11263 S. Hwy. 3, Fort Jones 96032, tel. 468-5351; **Goosenest,** 37805 Hwy. 97, Macdoel 96058, tel. 398-4391; and **Ukonom,** Somes Bar 95568, tel. 469-3331.

For information on camping and recreation along and beyond the Oregon border, contact **Rogue River National Forest,** P.O. Box 250, Medford, OR 97501, tel. (503) 776-3579.

And if you'll be in the neighborhood, from here it's a short trip north to Ashland and its famed theater program. For information: **Oregon Shakespearean Festival,** Box 158, Ashland, OR 97501, tel. (503) 482-4331.

MOUNT SHASTA AND VICINITY

"Lonely as God and white as a winter moon"—so Joaquin Miller described California's most majestic mountain in the 1800s. And so it still is. Mount Shasta is California's sixth-highest peak but more awesome than any other—perpetually snow-covered, glowing orange, pink, and purple at sunset, casting shadows on the lava lands below. Area Indians revered Shasta as the abode of the Great Spirit. Others, too, attribute special influences to this peak. French mountaineer Rene Daumal, author of the unfinished cult classic *Mount Analogue: a Novel of Symbolically Authentic Non-Euclidian Adventures in Mountain Climbing*, which chronicles the great mountain climb to God, somehow also describes Shasta:

> *In the mythic tradition the Mountain is the bond between Earth and Sky. Its solitary summit reaches the sphere of eternity, and its base spreads out in manifold foothills into the world of mortals. It is the way by which man can raise himself to the divine and by which the divine can reveal itself to man.*

Visible sometimes from as far away as 150 miles, close up Shasta is more obscure. Officially unknown until 1827, the origin of the name Shasta is unclear though it's shared by a vanished Indian tribe, a dam, a lake, some fascinating caverns, a national forest, and (in slightly modified form) Shastina, Shasta's sister peak. The newest Shastas—Shasta Dam and Lake Shasta, both about an hour south of the mountain—are main features of California's Central Valley Project, a massive feat of water engineering.

First And Sudden Impressions

Mount Shasta is the highest point in California's Cascades. Though Mt. Whitney is taller by 332 feet and other mountains are bigger by different degrees of measurement, their grandeur is lost among ranks of lofty peaks. Not so Shasta, which stands alone at 14,162 feet and towers 10,000 feet above the surrounding countryside. But height isn't everything. Shasta is the largest volcano in the contiguous 48 states, and with a diameter of over 20 miles, it is perhaps in sheer volume the largest mountain as well. There is always snow on Shasta. Hikers and backpackers walk up into it via forest trails from June or July to early September, but only fit and fairly serious hikers get to the top. Nonclimbers, take the highway up the mountainside to where the road ends. From there, 8,000 feet up, enjoy the view of the entire north end of the Sacramento Valley, Burney Falls, Lassen Park, the Trinity Alps, Castle Crags, the Sacramento River canyon, and Lake Siskiyou below.

THE LAND

The Formation Of The Cascades

Every rock in California's northeastern volcanic wonderland was once part of a river of molten lava sometime within the past 30 million years. Once an ocean, then a flat plateau, finally a faulted mountain range roped in on the west by a string of volcanoes, the Cascades and Modoc Plateau are the southernmost tip of landforms that dominate the entire Pacific Northwest. Volcanically the Cascades form part of the Pacific Ring of Fire, the eastern half of which burns from Alaska's Aleutian Islands to South America.

The Sierra Nevada and Klamath Mountains separated some 140 million years ago, creating a 60-mile-wide alley for the Cascades. Andesite volcanoes, like all those in the Cascades, typically develop into long chains parallel to the coast in areas also characterized by active earthquakes. Geologists believe these strings of volcanoes are pushed upward when the sea floor collides with the North American continental plate and plunges deep into the earth's molten lava. Cascade lavas, then, were once part of the Pacific Ocean floor before being transformed some three million years ago.

Shasta Geology

Shasta is classified as extinct, though the term "dormant" is probably more prudent. Those boiling sulphur springs near Shasta's summit (among other indicators) mean there's still volcanic life below. Despite the fact that Shasta looks like a single volcanic mountain, it's actually a volcanic system, one that has become increasingly complex over time. The main cone, once 200-300 feet higher than it is today but ground down by glaciation, is actually the result of three separate vents. The tallest, Steep Rock or "Hotlum" in the native vernacular, appears to be Shasta's peak. The geologically recent "parasitic" cone, Shastina, is 12,433 feet tall and forms a vent on Shasta's west flank. Shastina has an obvious volcanic crater, while Shasta's is buried in ice and snow. Seven glaciers cluster on the mountain's north and east sides.

Despite substantial snow melt and constant glacial shrinkage, little water pours off Shasta in summer. Instead, most runoff percolates through the porous surface rock and soil then gushes forth near the base of the mountain, most notably north of Dunsmuir at Shasta Springs (where bubbly Shasta mineral water was once bottled and marketed worldwide). Invisible runoff from Mt. Shasta flows into the Sacramento River and, eventually, Shasta Lake.

When Will Shasta Erupt Again?
Locals blew their stacks when a recent booklet, published by the U.S. Geological Survey, predicted that Shasta will erupt every 250-300 years. Though people aren't overly concerned about the volcano (the last eruption, a minor event, was in 1786, though sister peak Mt. Lassen erupted in a big way in 1915), many *are* worried about scaring away retirees and new businesses; the government has since added an insert stating that there are no indications that Mt. Shasta is about to blow.

However, based on knowledge of the area's geological past, it's likely that some time this century or next a flutter of earthquakes will sound some advance warning. Then an explosion of ash, rock, and gases will announce Shasta's awakening, or—if the eruption is non-explosive—a lava dome will form inside the crater and searing rivers of hot lava will flow down the mountainside.

Shasta Climate
It's frigid here in winter, always cool but sometimes cold in summer. The weather at the summit is quite changeable, often severe. Even in summer, sudden storms—wicked icy winds, thunderstorms, sometimes snow or hail—are possible, so always be prepared. Shasta, in a sense, creates its own weather and affects the

---

OCCULT VISITORS

In 1987, spiritualists of all stripes converged on Mt. Shasta for the excessively media-hyped Harmonic Convergence of international meditators dedicated to a new era of worldwide peace. Of the seven "power centers" in the world due to harmonically converge that August weekend, Shasta was the only peak chosen in the continental U.S.

Local native people, as well as those farther afield, respect the mountain's spiritual presence. An old Hopi legend says that ancient lizard people once built 13 underground cities, one beneath Mt. Shasta, to escape a major Pacific coast meteor shower. (As recently as 1972, a visitor to Shasta reported seeing a reptile person clad in pants, trousers and—presumably—good boots, hiking near here.) Bigfoot has been spotted on Shasta too, of course, but rangers maintain that plaster casts of oversized footprints are actually smaller critter prints naturally enlarged as the snow melts.

Some students of the occult believe that descendants of the once-great continent of Lemuria live within Mt. Shasta, a Rosicrucian theory widely circulated during the 1930s. As the story goes Lemuria (continent of Mu, the world's oldest civilization, preceding even Atlantis) was once to the west of California. Because of great geological changes, Lemuria began listing into the Pacific. That continent's eastern shore became the modern-day Cascade Range (then separated from the North American continent by an inland sea) where the white-robed Lemurians, both physically and psychically gifted, live secretly to this day. In 1930 Guy Ballard, a paperhanger-cum-government surveyor from Chicago, met up with "a majestic figure, God-like in appearance, clad in jeweled robes, eyes sparkling with light and love," none other than St. Germain. Inspired, Ballard wrote *Unveiled Mysteries* and spawned the I AM group of believers who still have a retreat in the mountain's shadows. The Old Ones, Space Brothers, or Ascended Masters, ageless astral vegetarians, contact only those with synchronistic spiritual vibrations. (To improve your vibrations, there is an I AM Reading Room in Mt. Shasta City, open whenever it's open.)

Sacramento Valley as well, blocking the wet Canadian north winds in winter and turning the north valley into a summertime oven, the primary reason Redding is often among the hottest spots in the nation.

Nothing about Mt. Shasta weather is stranger, though, than the sudden flying saucer-shaped cloud formations generating intense greenish-blue beams of light—evidence of UFOs to many, or celestial spirit-beings of one sort or another. Scientists, however, explain it like this: cold, fast-moving northerly winds push cold dry air over the top of Shasta and also around the mountain's sides and up. Wind shear is created where these winds meet and, between 6,500 and 10,000 feet, icy, almond-shaped lenticular clouds form. The sun's reflection off the miniscule ice particles creates the mountain light show.

HISTORY

Native peoples believed Mt. Shasta to be the abode of the Great Spirit and out of respect never ascended past the timberline. Fur trader Peter Ogden passed through Shasta Valley in 1827 and noticed Mt. Shasta, which he dubbed "Sastise" after the local Indians. But some believe Father Narciso Duran noted the mountain on a Spanish expedition 10 years earlier and called it "Jesus Maria"—one holy name for each peak. The Russians settled along the Northern California coast could see Shasta clearly, and some say they named it Tshastal, "White and Pure Mountain."

But Shasta's history is primarily one of mountaineering conquests. A Yreka merchant, E.D. Pearce, is credited with first ascending Shasta, in August 1854. Scientists first braved the mountain in 1862, when Josiah Whitney led a Geological Survey party to the summit. When they got to the top they found tin cans, broken bottles, a Methodist hymn book, a newspaper, a pack of cards, "and other evidences of bygone civilization."

John Muir

Founder of the Sierra Club and its president until his death in 1914, John Muir first climbed Shasta on November 1, 1874 and was enchanted. Waking up the next day he saw:

. . . a boundless wilderness of storm clouds of different degrees of ripeness . . . congregated over all the lower landscapes for thousands of square miles, colored gray, and purple, and pearl, and deep-glowing white, amid which I seemed to be floating, while the great white cone of the mountain above was all aglow in the free, blazing sunshine.

The storm Muir watched forming soon hit, forcing him to shelter in a spruce grove for five days.

The following year Muir made two trips up Shasta, the first (uneventful) on April 28, and the second (nearly fatal) just two days later. Caught in a savage snowstorm, he and his guide kept from freezing by burrowing into the hot mud of the sulphur springs at the summit—each alternately scalding one side of his body and losing all sensation in the other. Black Butte, near I-5, was once called Muir Peak in the mountain man's honor.

RECREATION

Popular Hikes

Get current hiking information at the ranger district office in town. Among Shasta sights are virgin stands of rare Shasta red firs—some 300 years old, untouched by loggers—mountain hemlocks, secluded lakes in alpine meadows, clear streams, open valleys. There are few hiking trails on Mt. Shasta, and the popular mountain trails within the **Mt. Shasta Wilderness Area,** particularly near Avalanche Gulch, Horse Camp, and Lake Helen, are overused. To get up the mountain to these areas from Mt. Shasta City, head east on Alma St. to the flashing red light and turn left onto Everitt Memorial. The road continues on to the old Ski Bowl area, which may one day soon become the **Mt. Shasta Ski Area.**

From the Bunny Flat or Sand Flat areas, it's a short hike from red fir forests and ferns to **Avalanche Gulch** and **Horse Camp,** where the Sierra Club's historic 1922 lodge stands, a traditional starting point for hikes to Mt. Shasta's summit. Visitors from around the world have stayed here and recorded their impressions in the logbook. (Nowadays too many people make

MOUNT SHASTA AND VICINITY

© MOON PUBLICATIONS, INC.

*Sierra Club founder John Muir first climbed
Mount Shasta in 1874.*

CALIFORNIA DEPARTMENT OF PARKS & RECREATION

the trip, so Horse Campers camp outside.) From the Panther Meadows Trailhead at the campground, the **Grey Butte Trail** starts at the sign in the meadow then heads uphill along the stream. The **Squaw Valley Creek** stroll passes red fir forests, mountain hemlock, meadows, and summer pools on its way through "The Gate" to the Ski Bowl.

The short 1½-mile **Clear Creek/Mud Creek Trail** (access via McCloud) is good for a whole day's exploration: mysterious Sphinx Rock, views of small Konwakiton and Wintun glaciers, plus a miniature Grand Canyon and waterfalls along the way. Hike to Ash Creek Falls and get a good look at Wintun and Hotlum glaciers via the nearby (and higher) **Brewer Creek Trail.** Several other Shasta trails are accessible only from Weed and Hwy. 97. The **Black Lava Trail** is a six-mile roundtrip through some of Shasta's thickest forests. The higher **Bolam Trail** (very rough access road) crosses Bolam Creek, climbs 1½ miles to Whitney Falls, five miles to Coquette Falls, and offers views of Bolam and Whitney glaciers.

To The Summit

In summer, as many as 100 hikers ascending Mt. Shasta pass each other daily. (Wilderness permits—free—are now required.) Thousands try to get to Shasta's summit each year, but only half make it. Except for those who purposely make it harder on themselves (choosing more difficult routes up or racing against the clock), reaching the summit is possible for most people who are reasonably fit and sensible. But despite this fact, an average of two people each year die climbing Mt. Shasta, for different reasons: avalanches, falling rocks, hypothermia, or falls (caused by wearing unsafe shoes, being unprepared for ice and snow, or climbing recklessly). Many more have been hurt.

Experienced mountaineers ascend Shasta from all directions, but these hikes are technical climbs requiring expertise and special equipment (inquire at local sports shops). Mountain hikers, however, can scale Shasta from any of three primary routes. June and July is prime time.

The popular and traditional trip up via **Horse Camp/Avalanche Gulch** takes an average of eight hours from the Sierra Club lodge, five hours from Lake Helen. Because Horse Camp is a popular starting point, the lodge itself is open for day use and emergencies only, though climbers and hikers sometimes stay the night outside to acclimate and get an early start. Fill canteens at the natural springs here.

In June, snow is common above 8,000 feet; by September, it's loose rock almost the whole route. Also from Horse Camp, climb due north and up **Shastina.**

Or from the Mt. Shasta Ski Bowl, hike to Green Butte, contour over to Lake Helen, then head up Shasta via one of the two main **Avalanche Gulch** routes. Set out at daybreak on any ascent to improve your odds of getting off the mountain before dark (and bring a flashlight just in case).

Someday Soon: A New Trail

Discussed for more than 60 years, work is now underway on a new trail on Mt. Shasta—one that goes *around* the mountain instead of straight up. As planned, this 40-mile, four-day trail will range between 6,000 and 8,000 feet in elevation, circling Shastina and passing near

Bunny Flat, Horse Camp, the old Ski Bowl, and Panther Meadows. Since less than one-third of trail construction costs will be financed by the federal government, donations of money and time (including fundraising, publicity, and trail-building labor) are welcome. Contact the Mt. Shasta Ranger District office for more information and volunteer applications (see "Information and Services" below).

Shasta Hiking Safety

Climbers need to register with the Forest Service office in Mt. Shasta City both before going up *and* after coming down; the sign-in trail register is outside. Never hike or climb alone, and check the weather before heading out. Know the symptoms of altitude sickness and hypothermia. Get started early, go slowly, watch your footing (especially on the mountain's east side where crevasses may be covered with snow), and be alert for falling rocks. Rest frequently. Bring crampons and ice axes for climbing hard snow and ice fields.

Necessary basic equipment for summer climbs includes good hiking boots or shoes, extra wool socks, high-energy food, adequate water for the day (at least one quart per person), a flashlight, and first-aid supplies including sunscreen and bandaids or moleskin for blisters. In addition, since weather can change, bring layerable clothing and a lightweight waterproof poncho. Sunglasses are also a good idea. Dispose of human wastes properly (wilderness shovels available at the Forest Service office in Mt. Shasta City), and remember: whatever else you pack in, pack it out. For even slightly off-season climbs, more preparation is prudent (contact the Forest Service office for guidance).

Shasta Adventuring

The Mount Shasta Book (by Andy Selters and Michael Zanger, Wilderness Press) is a valuable resource. **The Fifth Season Sports** at 426 N. Mt. Shasta Blvd., tel. (916) 926-2776, and **House of Ski** at 1208 Everitt Memorial Hwy., tel. 926-2359, both rent ice axes and crampons. For Fifth Season's **24-hour climbing report,** call 926-5555.

Shasta Mountain Guides, 1938 Hill Rd., Mt. Shasta 96067, tel. (916) 926-3117, offers mountaineering, ice and rock climbing, glacier travel instruction, and leads guided Shasta and Castle Crags climbs. Among popular nontechnical climbs is the two-day "Traditional John Muir Route." Custom climbs are easily arranged. Unusual, too, is Shasta Mountain's wilderness program for the physically disabled.

Mount Shasta

KIM WEIR

Turtle River Rafting Company, P.O. Box 313, Mt. Shasta 96067, tel. (916) 926-3223, offers a tremendous selection of fun runs (kayaks and rafts) of northstate rivers, spring through fall, from the Upper Sacramento, Scott, Salmon, and Smith to the Middle Eel, Owyhee, Rogue, Klamath, and Trinity. Turtle River has an exceptional safety record, is fully insured, leaves its schedule "open" to a remarkable degree (to accommodate traveler's particular needs), and happily works with schools, churches, and other groups. Many raft trips are appropriate for children; families are welcome. Unusual "custom workshops" for river lovers approach true myth, somehow appropriate for a Shasta-based company: "Medicine Way" and "Alchemical Hypnotherapy," for example, in addition to "Dancing with the Goddess," "Healing with the Harp," and "Men in the Flow: Discovering the Mythology that Moves You Onward." Contact the company for current rates, reservations, and further information.

Great fun, too, is a guided pack trip with **Shasta Llamas,** P.O. Box 1137, Mt. Shasta 96067, tel. (916) 926-3959, with three-day leisurely strolls on Mt. Eddy (for some great Shasta scenery) and treks into the Trinity Alps and Marble Mountain wildernesses. The company's three-day family trips emphasize all things of interest to children ages 5-12, complete with storyteller. (And as just one measure of how good the food is, people often gain weight after just a few days of "roughing it" with Shasta Llamas.)

Another style of Shasta thrill is **bungee jumping**—from a specially constructed bridge in a canyon above Lake Siskiyou. Approved by the county in 1993, the venture was still under construction at last report. Contact the visitor bureau for current informtation.

Cross-country Skiing

In addition to the beginners' **Bunny Flat** and **Sand Flat** cross-country ski trails and the intermediate **Overlook Loop Trail,** experienced Nordic skiers often chart their own course on (and up) Shasta for some of the finest cross-country skiing in the state.

For more information and suggested routes, contact **The Fifth Season Sports** in Mt. Shasta City, tel. (916) 926-2776, which also offers seminars on avalanches, ski-touring clinics, races.

Mount Shasta Ski Park

Opened in 1985, Shasta's Mt. Shasta Ski Park downhill ski facility has two triple-chair lifts for novice to advanced skiers, a poma lift for beginners, and almost 1,500 acres (15 groomed runs) of excellent skiing in the same league as Tahoe's Alpine Meadows. New here is snowmaking, a protection against drought years. Snug in a valley at lower elevations and protected from wicked winter winds, the Ski Park is family oriented and friendly, reached via Hwy. 89 near McCloud. Lift tickets run $25 for adults, $16 for "juniors" (children under age eight free) or seniors, with night skiing Wed.-Sat. 4-10 p.m. at the half-day rate. Disabled skiers welcome, snowboarders too. The adult all-day "learn to ski" package at the ski school includes equipment and lesson. Lifts run daily 9 a.m.-4 p.m., half-day starts at 12:30 p.m. Lodge, cafeteria, rental shop.

Part of the new "summer too" trend for winter resorts, in the off-season visitors can take snowless rides on the ski lift for hiking access, or partake in nature hikes and mountain-bike tours. For more information: **Mt. Shasta Ski Park,** 104 Siskiyou Ave., Mt. Shasta 96067, tel. (916) 926-8610 (lodge), 926-8600 (business office), 926-8686 (snow and weather conditions).

MOUNT SHASTA CITY

Perpetually in the mountain's shadow, this tiny town popped up in the 1850s and was first called Sisson after J.H. Sisson, John Muir's friend and guide (also the local postmaster and innkeeper). With the growth of tourism here in the 1920s came the more marketable moniker.

Taste the mountain's (and the town's) pure sweet water at the public water fountain downtown. Just outside town is the **Sisson Fish Hatchery Museum** at 1 Old Stage Rd., tel. (916) 926-5508, the state's first successful hatchery, located here because of the pure water and the railroad (for fish transport). Though "Hatchery A" has become a museum, the century-old hatchery itself still thrives, birthing new generations of rainbow trout for planting as far afield as New Zealand. In a well-manicured park with oaks, cedars, and 50 ponds for the small fry, the hatchery is capable of producing millions of fish per year. The museum covers all aspects of

Mount Shasta rises 10,000 feet above the surrounding landscape, a permanent presence in Mount Shasta City.

KIM WEIR

local history and includes a new major exhibit each year. Open daily in summer 10-5, in winter 12-4 daily.

Area Camping

On Shasta, summertime camping is available at both **McBride Springs** and **Panther Meadows campgrounds,** Mistix reservations necessary. The **Mt. Shasta KOA** (trailers and tent camping) at 900 Mt. Shasta Blvd., tel. (916) 926-4029, with hot showers, rec room, laundry facilities, small pool, and bike rentals, is $15, extra for RV hookups, cabins $25 and $35. Camping at **Lake Siskiyou,** just five miles south of town via Old Stage and W.A. Barr roads, includes hot showers, coin-operated laundry, and recreational diversions galore, $13-17. For more information: Lake Siskiyou, P O. Box 276, Mt. Shasta 96067, tel. 926-2618. In addition, there are more than 100 public campgrounds throughout Shasta-Trinity National Forest, most open from May to mid-September. Particularly nice is camping at nearby **Castle Lake** (primitive, free). For other suggestions, ask at the ranger station.

For travelers heading north, private **Lake Shastina** on Hwy. 97 is a locally popular recreation lake (swimming, sailing, boating, water-skiing, and fishing). There's plenty of camping (also townhouse apartments from $98, a restaurant, and the Robert Trent Jones Jr. golf course). For information: Lake Shastina, 5925 Country Club Dr., Weed 96094, tel. (916) 938-3201. Or try the Forest Service **Shafter Campground** just down the road. For info: **Goosenest Ranger**

District office, 37805 Hwy. 97, Macdoel 96058, tel. 926-7426. On winter Sundays in Macdoel proper are the **Cal-Ore Chariot and Cutter Racing Association** chariot "drag races" across the ice. Ask about it in town.

The Alpenrose Hostel

The best choice for an amicable and inexpensive Shasta stay is the independent Alpenrose Hostel next to the KOA just north of town, 204 E. Hinckley St., Mt. Shasta 96067, tel. (916) 926-6724, a brand new two-story place surrounded with flowers, with magnificent views of the mountain. There are separate dorm-style rooms for men and women (three bunkbeds in each) plus a couples room. Everything is clean and homey, with communal kitchen and living area with woodstove. In summer, guests sometimes haul their mattresses out to the deck to sleep under the stars. Since it's just over an hour from here to Ashland in Oregon, some folks opt to stay here and commute to and from the theater scene. (The hostel there is often full—or too full of activity.) Rates: $10 per person per night.

Motel Accommodations

Among the cheaper motels: **Das Alpenhaus,** 504 S. Mt. Shasta Blvd. at High St., tel. (916) 926-4617; the **Evergreen Lodge** at 1312 S. Mt. Shasta Blvd., tel. 926-2143; and the **Pine Needles,** 1340 S. Mt. Shasta Blvd., tel. 926-4811. Off the main drag and usually available is the **Mountain View Motel,** 305 Old McCloud Rd., tel. 926-4704.

The **Mountain Air Lodge** at 1121 S. Mt. Shasta Blvd., tel. (916) 926-3411, has rooms (some with kitchens). Very popular, if farther away, is the **Swiss Holiday Lodge** at 2400 S. Mt. Shasta Blvd. near the junction of I-5 and Hwy. 89 heading toward McCloud, P.O. Box 335, Mt. Shasta 96067, tel. 926-3446, with rooms from $35, plus community kitchen, lounge with fireplace, heated pool, covered Jacuzzi. One apartment has a kitchen and a fireplace. Top of the line in the motel department is **The Tree House Best Western**, next to I-5 (Central Mt. Shasta exit), tel. (916) 926-3101 or toll-free (800) 528-1234 for reservations, rooms $60 and up.

Mount Shasta Ranch

The **Mt. Shasta Ranch Bed and Breakfast** at 1008 W.A. Barr Rd., Mt. Shasta 96067, tel. (916) 926-3870, is truly something special—a classic in the Dutch Gambrel tradition. Some people would say it's a barn, albeit a barn with covered veranda and unobstructed views of Mt. Shasta. But the atmosphere here is actually like a 1920s lodge, tasteful, almost formal, from the 1,500-square-foot living room with original oak floors and huge stone fireplace to the huge upstairs suites. Five rooms in the separate Carriage House share two bathrooms, and the "cottage" here is a completely equipped two-bedroom home with woodstove and electric heat. Unusual for B&Bs these days, children are genuinely welcome. Rates run from $45 for the Carriage House and from $75 for the lodge suites or the cottage.

More B&Bs
And Unusual Accommodations

Other worthwhile lodgings include the **Mt. Shasta House Bed and Breakfast,** 113 South A St., Mt. Shasta 96067, tel. (916) 926-5089, a one-time loggers' boardinghouse with one family suite and four rooms (three share one bath). Rates from $60. The **Sisson House 1904 Bed and Breakfast** at 326 Chestnut St. in Mt. Shasta, tel. 926-6949, offers four rooms with shared baths from $55. For an exceptional overnight and wonderful food, consider a stay at the recently refurbished **McCloud Guest House** on the other side of the mountain (see "McCloud").

Train fanatics, head south to Castle Crags and the **Railroad Park Resort** just off I-5 at 100 Railroad Park Rd., Dunsmuir 96025, tel. (916) 235-4440 or toll-free (800) 974-RAIL (motel, main office). In keeping with area history, this unique establishment is a modern motel composed almost entirely of refurbished railroad cars (there are also a few cabins). The good American-style dinner house and bar here, tel. 235-4611, is a successful meshing of nine separate railroad cars; there's also an RV park and tent campground, tel. 235-9983. Room rates from $65.

Mount Shasta Eateries

The **Mt. Eddy Bagel Bakery and Cafe** on the corner at 105 E. Alma St., tel. 926-2800, is something of a local countercultural mecca: witness the bulletin board just outside or drop by weekend nights for good coffee and live entertainment. (The food is okay too.)

Lalo's at 520 N. Mt. Shasta Blvd., tel. (916) 926-5123, serves decent Mexican food and in summer has outdoor dining. Very good and reasonable is **Michael's,** 313 N. Mt. Shasta Blvd., tel. 926-1835, locally famous for its homemade pastas (including *pelemy,* or Russian ravioli) and sauces and soups. A big hit at lunch is Michael's "rancho burger," a half-pound slab of fresh hamburger cooked to order and served on french bread with good fries on the side.

The Avalanche at 412 S. Mt. Shasta Blvd., tel. (916) 926-5496, is a fresh fish market plus very good restaurant specializing in (naturally enough) fresh seafood and steaks. Tucked into a hole in the wall at 204A W. Lake St. is **Bellisimo,** tel. 926-4461, unusual cuisine its claim to fame. Hours can be erratic, so call ahead.

But the talk of the town these days is **Lilys,** 1013 S. Mt. Shasta Blvd., tel. (916) 926-3372, fabulously popular for its California cuisine at breakfast, lunch, and dinner. There are at least four Mexican entrees at every meal, plus abundant vegetarian choices. Morning fare includes unusual omelettes, huevos ranchereos, machaca, a very good breakfast burrito, plus eggs Benedict (the eggs Arnold subsitutes avocado for the ham, the eggs Benedict Arnold combines the two). Other breakfast fare: malted waffles, French batter pancakes, and Danish pancakes. At lunch, expect fascinating salads, the Quesadilla Pacifica (with several cheeses and shrimp), and sandwiches such as the exceptional eggplant hoagie. Dinner selections include fresh seafood (like scallops in Thai sauce), pastas (jalapeño pasta is a house specialty, served with various sauces), chicken Debra, roasted pork loin, and standards such as prime rib.

Another fine choice for fine dining (dinners only) is the **McCloud Guest House** (see "McCloud" below).

Information And Services

Very helpful for visitor information is the **Mt. Shasta Convention and Visitors Bureau** at the local chamber office, 300 Pine St., Mt. Shasta 96067, tel. (916) 926-4865 or toll-free (800) 926-4865, open weekdays 9-6, weekends 10-4. The bureau provides brochures and other information about local services, and also offers guided bus tours. At the Shasta-Trinity National Forest's **Mt. Shasta Ranger District office** at 204 W. Alma (1½ blocks across the railroad tracks from Mt. Shasta Blvd.), tel. (916) 926-4511, stop for camping and climbing information, fire permits, forest maps ($3), the Mt. Shasta-Castle Crags Wilderness Map ($4), topo maps, wilderness permits—free, now required for all climbs—and friendly advice. A climber's guide to Mt. Shasta is available for $3. Open 8-4:30 p.m. weekdays and 8-8 weekends in summer, Mon.-Fri. in winter. Outside there's water to fill canteens, the trail register for Shasta climbers and hikers, and other posted information. Alternatively, for Mt. Shasta information contact the **McCloud Ranger District** office, P.O. Box 1620, McCloud 96057, tel. 964-2184.

The **Sisson Fish Hatchery Museum** on Old Stage Rd. (follow W. Jessie west from town) has a decent selection of books on the Mt. Shasta region. The **Golden Bough Bookstore** downtown is the place to go, though, for tales of Lemuria and general Shasta strangeness, as well as an eclectic selection of used books. (For non-print entertainment, the nearest movie theater is in Weed.)

Vicinity Of Mt. Shasta City

The trouble with climbing Mt. Shasta is that you can't see it if you're on it. So hike up nearby **Mt. Eddy** (9,025 feet elevation) and along adjacent stretches of the **Pacific Crest Trail** for majestic Mt. Shasta views. Remote is the **Grayrock Lakes** area (excellent primitive campsites and fair fishing for brook trout) about 11 miles west of town via a logging road paralleling the South Fork of the Sacramento River. The trout fishing along the Sacramento River is generally excellent from Mt. Shasta City south to Lake Shasta, with favorite spots for anglers at **Ney Springs Creek** and lush **Mossbrae Falls** north of Dunsmuir (also nice for picnicking); inquire about after effects of a recent toxic waste spill. **Castle Lake** is so named because it's tucked away behind Castle Crags, accessible only from the north, about eight miles out of Mt. Shasta City via Ream Avenue. Crystal water, swimming, fishing, picnicking, a few campsites. **Lake Siskiyou** is a reservoir in Mt. Shasta's morning shadows, an easy 4½ miles from Mt. Shasta City, with sandy swimming beaches, fishing, boating, paddleboat and canoe rentals.

Stewart Springs And Vicinity

The scenic, **Stewart Mineral Springs Therapeutic Mountain Retreat** seven miles north of Weed was founded in 1875 by the near-dead Henry Stewart, brought here by local Indians and healed by the waters. Facilities include a bathhouse with 12 individual mineral baths, a communal tub, Jacuzzi, massage rooms, sauna (separate fees for the use of each) plus a sun deck and herb shop. On most Saturday nights you can join a ceremonial Karok Indian purification sweat. Stewart Springs also offers accommodations, and special packages in conjunction with **Turtle River Rafting Company** and **Shasta Llamas.** Hiking access is nearby, to the **Deadfall Lakes,** some of the prettiest on the Trinity Divide.

Accommodations (which include cabins, motel rooms, tepees, campsites, and a three-level A-frame for large groups) are quite reasonable, from $30. The resort's **Serge's Restaurant** is excellent: vegetarian, fish, and meat selections with a French accent. For more information: Stewart Mineral Springs Mountain Retreat, 2222 Stewart Springs Rd., Weed 96094, tel. (916) 938-2222 or toll-free (800) 322-9223. To get there from I-5 north of Weed, take the Edgewood Exit and head west four miles on Stewart Springs Road.

McCLOUD

Just north of Dunsmuir, head east on Hwy. 89 into McCloud country. The McCloud River is an excellent trout fishing stream, but only short stretches are open to the public (lots of lumbering,

KIM WEIR

Castle Crags State Park offers good hiking and camping right next to I-5.

difficult access). The carnivorous Dolly Varden char, a relict species no doubt more at home during the Pleistocene, survived in California only here—until recently, when the local population was declared extinct.

Good fishing areas for Shasta rainbows include **Fowlers Camp, Lakin Lake, Big Springs,** and **McCloud Reservoir.** Nice camping at Fowlers Camp, a Forest Service campground about six miles east of town. The upper, middle, and lower falls of the McCloud River are all spectacular; there's a picnic area at Lower Falls. For more info about camping and area recreation, stop by the **McCloud Ranger District** office here, tel. (916) 964-2184.

Aside from fishing, McCloud is most famous for the 60,000-acre Wyntoon estate (still standing, in a way, burned in the 1992 fire), a private retreat closed to the public designed by architect Julia Morgan for mythic American media magnate William Randolph Hearst. Otherwise, even today the town reflects its more humble milltown history, from the general store to the variations on camptown architecture.

The exceptional **McCloud Guest House** at 606 W. Colombero, P.O. Box 1510, McCloud 96057, tel. (916) 964-3160, is an elegantly refurbished 1907 mansion near the foot of Mt. Shasta, once home to J.H. Queal, president of the McCloud River Lumber Company. When it later became the company's guest house, celebrities from the Hearsts to Jean Harlowe and President Herbert Hoover hung their hats here. This is a classy and classic country inn, a pastel jewel on velvet lawns under stately oaks and conifers. Upstairs are five romantic guest rooms, plus a large parlor complete with a pool table once part of the Hearst collection. Downstairs is a very fine restaurant: pasta dinners to chicken, veal, and seafood; prime rib on weekends; reservations strongly suggested. The dining room showcases the inn's fine woodwork, from carved ceiling beams to the built-in sideboard with leaded glass accents. Room rates from $75, dinners from $10. Closed Mon. and Tues. during the May.-Sept. high-season, more frequently during the off-season (call for Oct.-April days and hours).

McCloud Reservoir

Take Squaw Valley Rd. south to McCloud Reservoir and its pine trees and rocky shores. About nine miles east of McCloud, with everpresent Mt. Shasta looming over your shoulder, the lake belongs to PG&E (which built the dam in 1965) but the surrounding land is owned by the Hearst Corporation (the family retreat, designed by architect Julia Morgan, is nearby at the mouth of Mud Creek) and the Nature Conservancy. There's a Forest Service campground at **Ah-Di-Na,** unimproved campsites (with toilets) at **Star City Creek.**

McCloud River Preserve

The private, nonprofit Nature Conservancy operates this preserve along seven miles of the McCloud River. Though the Conservancy's single mission is preserving species diversity, visitors are welcome to hike here without reservations (no camping) from sunrise to sunset any day of the week: a three-mile trail passes a good swimming hole and a one-mile self-guided nature trail. Volunteers can stay in the several cabins free while helping out. An autumn hike is a stroll into timelessness, the last colored leaves frosted by the first snows along the sleepy river. In winter, visitors have to ski in. By spring, the runoff-rejuvenated river is a rushing torrent again. Fishing is strictly controlled.

For information, contact McCloud River Preserve, P.O. Box 409, McCloud 96057, tel. (916) 926-4366. To get there, from McCloud Reservoir turn right on the dirt road and continue for 10½ miles (veering always to the right) until the road dead-ends at the preserve.

CASTLE CRAGS

A prominent presence 40 miles north of Redding above I-5, Castle Crags is the southeastern edge of the Klamath Mountains, a foreboding granite formation created by volcanic forces some 170-225 million years ago. The Crags offer challenging rock climbing, easy and difficult hikes, good camping (but within earshot of the freeway), and picnicking. The first settler here was "Mountain Joe" Doblondy, one of Frémont's guides, who had troubles with angry gold miners (the rush here was short-lived) and native peoples disturbed by the encroaching chaos of civilization. Joaquin Miller chronicled several versions of the 1855 Indian slaughter here.

Hikes, Sights

Castle Crags State Park is 6,000 acres of dogwoods, oaks, cedars, pines, and firs plus rare Brewer's spruce. In summer, tiger lilies, orchids, azaleas, and columbine brighten the granite trailsides. Rarely seen but also here: mountain lions and bobcats. The **Pacific Crest Trail** swings through the park, a good spot for trekkers to arrange a supply drop and to pick up mail.

The impressive silver-gray crags snaggle upward at an elevation of 6,000 feet. Rock climbing here is only for the experienced. The strenuous **Crags/Indian Springs Trail** to Castle Dome (which resembles Yosemite's Half Dome) is worthwhile for hikers, especially with the side trip to the springs. Easier is the one-mile **Root Creek Trail,** which offers views of the crags and picnicking at Root Creek (soak your feet). High-country hikers, don't wander off the trail: cliffs have sudden 2,000-foot drop-offs, no warning signs. The pleasant, one-mile **Indian Creek Nature Trail** loops over the creek and passes old mining paraphernalia. Near Castle Crags is the **Seven Lakes Basin** area of the Trinity Divide, with lakes from two to 13½ acres in size, good trout fishing. To get there: take the Castella exit from I-5 (at Castle Crags State Park), follow Whalen Station Rd. 10 miles to the trailhead, then hike in 3½ miles.

Due to the Sacramento River's need for ecological recovery after a recent pesticide spill, no fishing is allowed.

Practicalities

Park headquarters is at the park's entrance in Castella (follow the signs from I-5). **Dunsmuir,** six miles to the north, is a good supply stop. In summer, reserve attractive campsites (64 total, some large enough for 21-foot trailers, with table, stove, food lockers, hot showers, and flush toilets) through Mistix, tel. (800) 444-7275. In the off-season, campsites are first-come, first-camped. Contact the park office to reserve **environmental campsites.** Trailside camping is okay in surrounding Shasta National Forest (campfire permit required), but not in the park. Fees: $14 to camp, $7 for environmental sites, $5 for day use. For information: **Castle Crags State Park,** P.O. Box 80, Castella 96017-0080, tel. (916) 235-2684.

SHASTA DAM

The Sacramento River is one of the most channelized, diverted, and dammed rivers in the world and Shasta Dam is its ultimate diversion. The mainstay of the federally funded Central Valley Project (CVP), Shasta Dam was constructed between 1938 and 1945. Flooding the canyons and holding back the waters of the Sacramento, Pit, and McCloud rivers in addition to Squaw Creek, Shasta Dam is the second-largest concrete dam in the U.S. Enough concrete to build a three-foot-wide sidewalk around the world created this backwater behemoth: 602 feet high, 3,460 feet long, and 883 feet across at its base. The cost of construction:

$182 million, 14 workers' lives, and the taming of the northstate's most impressive river.

Sights, Tours

Walk or drive across the top of the dam for an above-water-level view of this technological tour de force. The **Pit River Bridge** spanning the lake is the world's tallest double-decker, a north-south aerial artery carrying both I-5 and Southern Pacific Railroad's main line. To the east is an endless five-armed expanse of blue-green water, that sight accompanied by the roar of water crashing down the spillway. From here and from the vista point, see "the three Shastas" at once: dam, lake, and mountain. Tours are available only during occasional open houses. But the **visitor center** tells at least some of the story, with exhibits and a short film. Open 7:30 a.m.-4 p.m. daily in summer, closed weekends in winter.

For more information about Shasta Dam, contact: **U.S. Bureau of Reclamation,** Shasta Office, Shasta Dam, Redding 96003, tel. (916) 275-1554. To reach the dam, from I-5 take the Shasta Dam Blvd. exit (about 10 miles north of Redding). To get to Keswick Dam and power plant, head north on Iron Mountain Rd. from Hwy. 299 just west of Redding (or take Oasis Rd. from I-5 farther north).

SHASTA LAKE

Super-sized Shasta Lake (when full) has 365-370 miles of shoreline—one-third more than San Francisco Bay—and a surface area of 30,000 acres, more than enough space for the two million or so people who come here each year to camp, picnic, fish, swim, sail, and water-ski. Shasta is not always the best place for those seeking complete solitude or serene natural beauty—despite its gigantic girth, the lake is often ugly, an impression mostly due to the swath of bare-naked red dirt above the water line, like a giant-sized bathtub ring. The lake's popularity hasn't been helped by years of drought—or by the unfortunate accidental dumping in 1991 of 14,000 gallons of pesticides into the Sacramento River above the lake.

Shasta is dazzling these days, revivified by twice-normal rainfall. And people love being at Shasta Lake, which by virtue of its sheer size is water-skiing heaven. Houseboating is particularly

THE CENTRAL VALLEY PROJECT

One of the largest water-resource developments in the world, the Central Valley Project is a labyrinth of interconnecting reservoirs, canals, and causeways (total estimated cost when completed: $3.7 billion). The Shasta Unit of the Central Valley Project includes Shasta Dam, Lake Shasta, and the Shasta power plant, Shasta is the state's largest hydroelectric plant, generating upward of two billion kilowatt-hours per year—enough to support a city the size of Sacramento. Shasta's smaller cement sibling, Keswick Dam and power plant, created the nine-mile long Keswick Reservoir, a recreation lake (no camping), which runs like a ribbon toward Redding.

Sacramento dam's water storage capacity, a maximum of $4\frac{1}{2}$ million acre-feet, has been important in California's post-World War II agricultural development. Controlling river runoff form a 6,666-square-mile drainage area, Shasta provides flood protection and irrigation, industrial, and municipal water for the Sacramento Valley—plus water for export to the formerly arid areas of the San Joaquin Valley. As Los Angeles and the Bay Area rushed to gobble up their farmlands and spit them back out as suburbs, the Central Valley Project opened up new agricultural possibilities in the Central Valley, boosting agricultural productivity but virtually destroying the native riparian forests in the process. The end of the valley's annual flooding also meant an end to the rich river-borne sediment deposits which, over the eons, created California's richest loam.

popular here: with so much lake (and so many coves and inlets to tie up in) houseboaters either party Shasta-style or drift off alone for some peace and quiet. Shasta's rental houseboat fleet is probably the state's finest, some units featuring every amenity imaginable. Warm-water fishing is another big draw (spring is best) with anglers going after crappie, brown and rainbow trout, but primarily small and largemouth bass.

All this recreational opportunity has had its price, however, including the flooding of several small towns upstream from the dam site. The old copper mining town of Kennett is gone for good, along with an Indian burial site and miles of salmon spawning grounds—a loss requiring the construction of special fish hatcheries below the dam.

Lake Shasta Caverns

If you've got the time, tour these ancient caves. Only the out-and-out adventurous had access to the caverns until 1964, when a tunnel was driven into the mountain below the original entrance. Now, even armchair adventurers visit these beautiful wonders where California's Coast and Cascade ranges, Sierra Nevada, and Klamath Mountains come together. The 60-foot wide, 20-foot tall drapolite "draperies" of the Cathedral Room were formed from calcium carbonate crystals in a stalactite waterfall. Elsewhere, stalagmites reach up from the cave floor and, fusing with stalactites, create multicolored fluted columns. In the **Spaghetti Patch,** gravity-defying masses of straw-thin helictites seem to swirl and swarm. Though the tour route itself is well lighted, with concrete steps and guard rails, fit purists can still go spelunking through the dank darkness and primal ooze (by reservation only).

Two-hour tours of Lake Shasta Caverns start at **O'Brien** across the lake and cost $12 for adults, $6 for children (under age three free). Spelunking tours are four hours long. Either way, it's a 15-minute ferry trip by catamaran then a thrilling bus ride up an 800-foot hill to the lower cave entrance. Bring a sweater or sweatshirt even in summer: the temperature inside is a constant cool 58 degrees. Open year-round, with hourly tours May-Sept. from 9 a.m. on, Oct. through April at 10 a.m., noon, and 2 p.m. only. Special group and spelunking tours by advance reservation only. For more information, contact: Lake Shasta Caverns, P.O. Box 801, O'Brien 96070, tel. (916) 238-2341.

Trails

Most trails around and near Shasta Lake provide fishing access, including **Sugarloaf Creek Trail** from the Sugarloaf Creek crossing on Lakeshore Dr. and the **Dry Fork Trail** north from Shasta Dam. **Packers Overlook Trail** offers a view of the lake's Sacramento arm. There are two interpretive trails, the half-mile **Hirtz Bay Trail,** which explores the territory of the long-gone McCloud River Wintu (starts at the Hirtz Bay Amphitheater) and the slightly longer **Samwel Cave Trail** from Point McCloud Campground, which leads to the cave and explains its relationship with both the Wintu and regional prehistoric animals.

Camping

Shasta Lake has five recreation areas connected to its arms: **Jones Valley** (near the Pit and Squaw arms), **Gilman Rd.** (upper McCloud River arm), **O'Brien** (lower McCloud River arm), **Salt Creek** (Salt Creek inlet off the Sacramento arm), and **Lakehead** (upper Sacramento River arm). Dozens of public campgrounds are scattered throughout. Popular at Shasta are the boat-in campgrounds as well as walk-in campsites. Campgrounds along Gilman Rd. to the north and at backcountry sites near the Squaw and Pit arms near Jones Valley on the southeast are quietest. These areas have more campsites (and more bears too: keep food well out of reach) and are popular with fishing enthusiasts. Jones Valley and Lakehead are particularly popular with water-skiers; worth visiting is Jones Valley, tel. (916) 275-7950, which offers the easiest access from the lake's south side, along with a well-run marina and spanking new house boats. O'Brien is the major marina-resort center, the hub of hubbub. In addition to public camping, most resorts offer tent and RV campsites with amenities like hot showers.

Lake Shasta Information

For more information about Shasta Lake, from restaurants and accommodations to houseboat rentals, contact the excellent **Shasta-Cascade Wonderland Association,** 1250 Parkview Ave., Redding 96099, tel. (800) 326-6944 or (916) 243-2643, or the **Redding Convention and Visitors Bureau.**

REDDING AND VICINITY

REDDING

A boom town that never busted, this is The City of the northern mountains, with a total urban population of over 115,000. Redding perches just beyond the northern edge of the Sacramento Valley on the banks of the Sacramento River, which is joined here by 14 tributaries. Early explorer John C. Frémont described the Redding area as "fertile bottom lands watered by many small streams." Still watered by streams, the fertile bottom lands have become lucrative subdivisions and malls. Intersected by I-5 and Highways 44 and 299, well served by bus and even by Amtrak, Redding is the northern getaway gateway. The Shasta County seat was established here in 1888, one year after the torching of Chinatown City and the forced exodus of its residents. Evidence of the once prominent Chinese is still preserved in nearby Old Shasta, however.

Redding isn't known for its cultural attractions —with the possible exception of April's **Shasta Dixieland Jazz Festival, Redding Rodeo Week** in May, and other community events— and it's easy to understand why. The breathtaking landscape surrounding the town tends to draw people away, into nearby mountains and beyond. Entering or leaving the wilderness, stop here for supplies and almost-urban sustenance.

How Reading Became Redding

Major Pierson Barton Reading, paymaster for Frémont's California Batallion, was Shasta County's first white settler. His home, the county seat when Shasta became one of California's original 27 counties in 1850, was built on the site of an old native village, part of his 26,633-acre Mexican land grant. The arrival of the first Central Pacific Railroad line in 1872 signaled the end for the booming town of Shasta a few miles west but the beginning for Redding. The new town became a flourishing trade center, outfitting ranchers, miners, timber companies, even U.S. Army troops during the Modoc Wars. But Reading was somehow christened "Redding," after a land agent for the Central Pacific Railroad. Though state legislation changed Redding back to "Reading" in 1874, the railroad prevailed again in 1880, making it Redding once and for all.

Shasta State Historic Park

About three miles west of Redding is the town of Shasta, in its heyday the leading gold mining center of the northstate. Originally known as Reading Springs (named for Redding's Reading, who found gold here in 1848), in the early 1850s Shasta was a lively little city by all accounts— with up to 100 freight wagons, 2,000 pack mules, and countless drunken miners in the streets on any day of the week. Old Shasta became an overnight ghost town when area mines played out but was remembered again in 1950 with its designation as a state historic monument.

A fine museum is located in the **Old Courthouse of Shasta**, the "Queen City" of the Northern Mines. The building's interior has been beautifully restored, the collections continually expanded. Downstairs is the jail, with representative Shasta law-breakers. Early California writer Joaquin Miller, who'd been living among Indians noted for horse theft and was considered guilty himself, had the good fortune to escape from the original log jail. (Miller "smoked three cigars at once and bit the ankles of English debutantes" while on tour of London's literary salons, according to *Benet's Reader's Encyclopedia*.) Out back, to remind visitors to behave themselves, is a reconstructed double gallows, complete with gallows poetry. Farther back behind the public restrooms in the park area is a **Pioneer Barn,** reassembled here to display old farm implements and technologies. The brick **Masonic Hall** just down the highway (Main St.) from the museum is the state's oldest, built in 1853 and still in use; Peter Lassen brought the charter here from Missouri by ox train.

The **Litsch General Store,** another brick building across the highway, has also been restored. Explore Shasta's iron-doored crumbling brick ruins along the highway here, or between the old Trinity and Boell alleys via the short **Ruins Trail.** The park is open Thurs.-Mon. 10-5 (due to possible budget cuts, call ahead to make sure it's open at all), admission to the museum $2. Come to town in May for the **Shasta Arts and Crafts Faire** and **Oldtime Fiddlers' Jamboree.** In December, Shasta hosts an old-fashioned **Christmas Celebration.** For more information, contact: Shasta State Historic Park, P.O. Box 2430, Shasta 96087, tel. (916) 243-8194.

Whiskeytown

The original Whiskeytown was settled by miners on the trail to Oregon, near Whiskey Creek (so christened when a mule fell off a cliff and spilled its precious cargo). That town is now under water, but its spirit lives on in the brick store north of Hwy. 299 in the new Whiskeytown. The **Whiskeytown Dam,** connecting the waters of the Trinity River with the Sacramento, is another link in the Central Valley Water Project's chain of reservoirs. John F. Kennedy dedicated the dam in 1963. A monument (turn at the information center) marks the spot with a tape recording of his speech. A little farther down the road are the **Whiskeytown Cemetery** and old **Mount Shasta Mine** (an easy hike). On the north side of the lake is the **Judge Francis Carr Powerhouse** (good fishing, picnic area).

Whiskeytown Lake is pretty but packed in summer, subject to water levels. Recreation is the big attraction: boating, water-skiing, swimming, scuba diving, horseback riding, hiking, gold panning, fishing, deer and duck hunting in season. Camp free in backcountry areas (get wilderness permits at the information center). **Oak Bottom Campground,** 14 miles west of Redding on Hwy. 299, has abundant campsites, cold showers, more tents than RVs, (14-day limit), reserve May-Sept. through Mistix, tel. toll-free (800) 365-CAMP. Get incidentals at the marina, but bring supplies from Redding. For more information, contact: **Whiskeytown National Recreation Area,** P.O. Box 188, Whiskeytown 96095-0188, tel. (916) 241-6584, or stop off at the lake's visitor information center, 246-1255, just off Hwy. 299 at Kennedy Drive.

Shingletown Wild Horse Sanctuary

Western culture fans, come rendezvous with mustangs. At this preserve near Manton (southeast of Redding, northeast of Red Bluff), get up close and personal with the wildest of free-ranging horses. Dianne and Jim Clapp started adopting "unadoptable" mustangs over a decade ago, the only private effort in America to protect them from domestication or destruction, and the herds here now number over 300 (not counting the dozens of wild burros). The sanctuary office is open to the public 10-3 Thurs.-Sat.; visitors are welcome to hike the horse trails. More exciting, though, are the guided horseback trips and two- or three-day overnight rides, complete with hearty campfire fare and a sleeping-bag stay in rustic kerosene-lit cabins. Mustang lovers: you can even "adopt" a wild horse, through regular financial contributions. For more information, contact: Wild Horse Sanctuary, P.O. Drawer B, Shingletown 96088, tel. (916) 474-5770.

REDDING AREA PRACTICALITIES

Camping, Motels, And Hotels

Closest is Whiskeytown Lake (see above), but many campgrounds are also available near **Shasta Lake** and **Weaverville.** Seven miles north of Redding proper is the shady **Shasta Dam El Rancho Motel,** 1529 Cascade Blvd. (take the Shasta Dam-Central Valley exit from I-5), P.O. Box 1033, Project City 96079, tel. (916) 275-1065, with a/c, TV, rooms from $24.

Most motels in Redding are clustered along Hwy. 299 or Hilltop Dr., but there are cheaper places (mostly south of town on Market St., a.k.a. Hwy. 273).

Redding has two **Motel 6** complexes to choose from. The original is at 1640 Hilltop Dr. (Hwy. 44 exit from I-5), tel. (916) 221-6530, and the second is north of town off I-5 at 1250 Twin View Blvd. (take exit of the same name), tel. 221-1800. Rates: $30-32 s, $36-38 d. Redding's **Super 8 Motel** is at 5175 Churn Creek Rd., tel. 221-8881, and there's a **Motel Orleans** (formerly the Monterio Inn) at 2059 Hilltop, tel. 221-6530. Redding, a northstate convention center, also has a number of higher-priced large motels, most of these along Hilltop Drive and including the **Best Western Hilltop Inn,** tel. (916) 221-6100, the **Grand Manor Inn** (just off Hilltop on Mistletoe Ln.), tel. 221-4472, **Holiday Inn of Redding,** tel. 221-7500, and the **Red Lion Inn,** tel. 221-8700.

Redding Bed And Breakfasts

Quite nice for a home stay is **Palisades Paradise**, 1200 Palisades Ave. (just off Hilltop near I-5), Redding 96003, tel. (916) 223-5305. The aptly named Sunset Suite opens onto the back patio/spa area and features two sliding-glass doors set in a wall of glass plus a cheerful collection of contemporary furnishings and antiques. The smaller Cozy Retreat is adjacent, and both rooms share a full bath and half-bath (it's simple to schedule showers). Rates from $50.

The gabled **Tiffany House Bed & Breakfast Inn** atop a hill at 1510 Barbara Rd., Redding 96003, tel. (916) 244-3225, is the town's first showplace inn, with enticing views of the area, spacious living areas and deck, and three appealing rooms complete with namesake Tiffany-style lamps and private baths. Rates $75-95.

Also new, also a showplace, and quite close to downtown is the **Cabral House Bed and Breakfast**, 1752 Chestnut St., Redding 96003, tel. (916) 244-3766, a fascinating ode to America's "golden years." Marlene Dietrich would have loved it here, since the elegant art deco ambience pays homage to women of the 1920s through '40s. Unusual details abound, from lead-bordered glass windows and wood floors with unique rugs to old photographs and heavy chenille bedspreads. All three main-floor guest rooms have private baths (with old Pomona color tile and authentic fixtures of the era). In the evening, listen to big band tunes and enjoy hot hors d'oeuvres. Come morning, it's a fabulous homemade breakfast, from the fresh bread to entree, served on very individual, period place settings. Rates from $100, business rate from $90.

Inexpensive Eateries

Get good fresh seafood at funky **Buz's Crab**, 2159 East St. behind Safeway, tel. (916) 243-2120, everything from snapper and swordfish to Dungeness crab in season. Buz's is also a good cheap eatery: fish and chip selections plus charbroiled swordfish or snapper and much more. For a hearty inexpensive breakfast and a hefty helping of local color, try **The Shack**, 1235 Eureka Way, tel. 241-5126, open daily. For a few dollars, stuff yourself on eggs, bacon, and pancakes. At lunch and dinner, mostly burgers and chicken on the menu.

For unusual ambience, though, no place beats **Andy's Cow Patty Palace** at 2105 Hilltop Dr., tel. 221-7422, open just for breakfast and lunch, Mon.-Sat. So nondescript it's almost invisible (parking out back), Andy's has good breakfasts, burgers at lunch, and a Middle American cow cafe atmosphere—enlivened still more by Andy (a former Hollywood entertainer) behind the grill, gabbing with locals, telling jokes, even singing show tunes.

Started as a home-based wholesale cheesecake enterprise, **Cheesecakes Unlimited & Cafe** next to Maxwell's just north of the Downtown Redding Mall at 1334 Market St., tel. (916) 244-6670, is now also a cozy cafe serving breakfasts and lunch Mon.-Sat., everything simple and fresh. And don't miss the cheesecake, everything from lemon or lime to Dutch cholcolate almond and mocha Baileys.

Quite wonderful but a bit hard to find is **Le Chamois**, 630 N. Market, tel. (916) 241-7720, which combines an Old World cafe atmosphere with down-to-earth food for breakfast and lunch Mon.-Saturday. To get here: head north on Market from downtown Redding toward the Miracle Mile, a bustling commercial strip; Le Chamois is in the North Market Square mini-mall on the west side of the highway, just south of Lim's.

A good all around choice for breakfast, lunch, or dinner is **The Italian Cottage** at 1630 Hilltop Dr., right in front of Motel 6, tel. (916) 225-4062, open 6 a.m.-11 p.m. At dinner, try the tasty calzone or pasta dishes, pizzas, decent chef salad, or vegetarian choices.

Fine Dining

For the best steaks in town, **Jack's Bar & Grill** is the place, downtown at 1743 California St., tel. (916) 241-9705, a funky 1930s tavern where people start lining up outside at 4 p.m. in order to get a table. (Closed Sunday.) Upscale and unusual in these parts is the **River City Bar and Grill**, 2151 Market St., tel. 243-9003, noted for its Cajun food. For French food, try **Maxwell's** downtown at 1344 Market St., tel. 246-4373.

A true local legend is **Nello's Place** in a nondescript setting at 3055 Bechelli Ln. (at Hartnell), tel. (916) 223-1636, a very fine Italian restaurant that probably really belongs in San Francisco. The food here is superb and, like the wine list, the selection impressive. Though Nello's is pricey, by local standards, the early-bird dinner special is a remarkable bargain. But be sure to leave room for dessert, since this place is famous for its crepes Suzettes, cherries jubilee, and bananas à la crema. After dinner, women receive a fresh carnation as a parting pleasure.

Redding Area Information

For information, contact the **Redding Convention and Visitors Bureau** a half mile from town at 777 Auditorium Dr. (take Park Marina Dr. east then turn north on Auditorium or, from I-5, follow the signs), tel. (916) 225-4100 or toll-free (800) 874-7562, open Mon.-Fri. 8 a.m.-5:30 p.m., Sat. and Sun. 9-5, or the **Greater Redding Chamber of Commerce**, 747 Auditorium Dr., tel. 243-2541. An unbeatable info source, though, is the **Shasta-Cascade Wonderland**

Association a block south of Safeway at Pine St. and Parkview (1250 Parkview), tel. (916) 243-2643 or toll-free (800) 326-6944, open Mon.-Fri. 8-5.

Headquarters for **Shasta-Trinity National Forest** is at 1400 Washington, call (916) 246-5222 for information about regional recreation areas (from Whiskeytown and Trinity lakes to the Trinity Alp Wilderness Area and the Mt. Shasta Wilderness), also necessary permits. The **Shasta Lake Ranger District** office, 6543 Holiday Dr., tel. 275-1587, is best for local (and lake-oriented) camping and regional recreation information. The **BLM Redding Resource Area** office, for information about recreation on BLM lands, is at 355 Hemsted Dr., tel. 246-5325.

LASSEN PARK

Visitors to **Lassen Volcanic National Park** and its backcountry wilderness should cultivate a better sense of direction than the park's namesake, Danish immigrant and intrepid traveler Peter Lassen. According to a journal entry by his friend, General John Bidwell, Lassen "was a singular man, very industrious, very ingenious, and very fond of pioneering—in fact, of the latter, very stubbornly so. He had great confidence in his own power as a woodsman, but, strangely enough, he always got lost." This almost led to his lynching on at least one occasion, when he confused Lassen and Shasta peaks while guiding a party of immigrants westward, inadvertently taking them more than 200 miles out of their way. More recently, one of the best-known seasonal residents of the Lassen area was Ishi, "the last wild man in North America." In 1916, the year Ishi died and a year after Lassen Peak finished blasting its way into the 20th century, Lassen was designated a national park.

THE LAND

Native peoples knew Lassen Peak by several names: Little Shasta, Water Mountain, Broken Mountain, Fire Mountain, and Mountain-Ripped-Apart. The Atsugewi people tell the story of a warrior chief who burrowed into Lassen Peak to rescue his abducted lover. The mountain spir-

its, impressed by his audacity, invited him to marry his beloved and live with them inside the peak; storm clouds above the volcano are explained as smoke from the warrior's peace pipe. The Atsugewi also have an earthquake story, possibly connected to the great avalanche that formed the area's Chaos Jumbles about 300 years ago. The Maidu explained earthquakes mythically and quite simply: the earth is anchored in a great sea by five ropes. When the gods get angry, they give these ropes a good tug.

Geology: Remnants Of Glaciers And Old Volcanoes

Lassen is the southernmost outpost of the Cascade Range, which runs almost due north from here to British Columbia. Much of Lassen Peak is cradled within a huge caldera formed by the volcano's collapse 300,000 years ago. Of the four types of volcanoes found in the world, Lassen Park has three: cinder cones, shield volcanos, and dome volcanos. (An example of the fourth type of volcanic mountain, a composite or stratovolcano and a classic Cascades version, is Mt. Shasta.)

Lassen's unimaginatively named Cinder Cone is a classic one, composed entirely of pyroclastic or "fire-broken" rock, molten fragments that solidify before they hit the ground. Prospect Peak is a shield volcano, formed from lava flows. Lassen Peak itself is a dome volcano formed by a single, solid mass of rock squeezed up

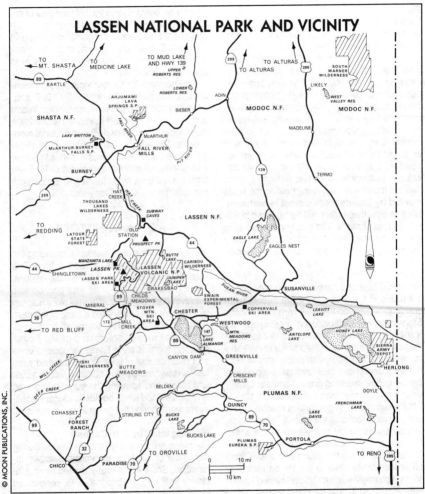

LASSEN NATIONAL PARK AND VICINITY

© MOON PUBLICATIONS, INC.

through the vent of a previous volcano, referred to as a "plug." Relatively recent volcanism here—pumice showers, lava flows, and mudflows—has buried most evidence of earlier glacial action, but the scouring of the Warner, Blue Lake, and Mill Creek valleys suggests ancient ice sheets more than 1,000 feet thick.

Climate
The short summer is "spring" in Lassen: sunny cool days, cold nights. Pacific storms are usually blocked by high-pressure areas off the coast, so summer weather is generally dry except for occasional surprise thunderstorms (and very rare snowstorms). The rest of the year, late Sept. to May, is winter. About 400-700 inches of snow falls each year (an average 30-foot snowpack), and Lassen's winter temperatures are extremely invigorating. Gale winds, sub-zero temperatures, and blinding snow flurries are expected in winter and unpredictable during most of the year.

Flora

Lassen Volcanic National Park is alive with alpine wildflowers during summer—balsam root, monkey flowers, blue stickweed, corn and fawn lilies, larkspur, lupine, monkshood, mountain heath, pennyroyal, pussypaws, shooting stars, skyrocket gilia, snow plant, wallflowers, and white rain orchids. Trees here as well as other plants are separated into fairly distinct vegetation zones influenced by elevation, exposure, soil types, and moisture. Common Lassen trees include incense cedar, white fir, and ponderosa as well as sugar pines on southwestern (warmer) exposures, a species usually found at lower elevations. Lodgepole pines and quaking aspens thrive in the Devastated Area, healing the scars created by Lassen Peak's most recent eruptions. In time these trees will be replaced by climax forests of red fir. The gnarly whitebark pine grows only at higher elevations and is usually found near droopy-topped mountain hemlocks.

Fauna

Both mule deer and the black-tailed subspecies are found in the park though the mules (with only a tip of black on their tails) are the minority. Signs everywhere declare that feeding animals is *not* in their survival interests. Some insensitive visitors disregard these pleas since remarkably tame deer often approach picnickers to beg. But the rodents have their revenge: people feeding the golden-mantled ground squirrel usually get bitten. Also common throughout the park is Clark's nutcracker. A gregarious relative of jays and crows, it looks like a stubby-tailed mockingbird and is partial to the nuts of the whitebark pine. Large numbers of waterfowl, including Canada geese and the exotic wood duck, stop off at Manzanita Lake in the fall on their way south. You might also see sharp-shinned hawks, peregrine falcons, and rare bald eagles gliding low over mountains, lakes, and streams in search of dinner.

History

Don Luis Arguello, one of the early governors of Spanish California, called Lassen "San Jose." Jedediah Smith anglicized this to "St. Joseph," which was altered to "Mt. St. Joseph" by Charles Wilkes on his 1841 map. Then Peter Lassen, a Danish blacksmith lured to the area by immigrant fever, appeared on the scene. Mexican officials gave him a large tract of land east of the Sacramento River where he established a ranch and put out his "immigrant guide" shingle. (His "Lassen's Cutoff," running south of Lassen Peak and treacherous for laden wagon trains, was used only a short while.)

The demand for lumber increased as more settlers moved into the region. By 1907, lumberjacks threatened Lassen's magnificent forests and in an effort to protect the area, Lassen Peak and Cinder Cone were declared national monuments. Lassen's volcanic eruptions of 1914-15 created such a national stir that the area was granted full national park status in 1916—at first in name only, since funding for actual park protection was delayed for years.

VOLCANIC HISTORY

In the early 1900s area residents, including the "experts," believed Lassen was extinct. The naked 10,457-foot peak had stood mute for eons. Though the immediate area was pocked with volcanic scars and various thermal sinks, Lassen as an *event* was considered a thing of the past.

But in late May 1914, preceded by a small quake, columns of steam and gases began spewing forth, littering Lassen's upper slopes with small chunks of lava. During the next year, Lassen blew more than 150 times, spitting dust and steam and spraying the surrounding area with cinders and small boulders. Curious spectators were thrilled but generally unconcerned.

Blasting Into The 20th Century

Following an unusually heavy snowfall during the winter of 1914-15, the volcanic activity intensified. Snow in the crater melted almost instantly and, seeping into the earth, contributed large volumes of liquid to the volcanic brew. Then, on May 19, 1915, molten lava bubbled up to the rim of the crater, spilled over on the southwestern side, and flowed 1,000 feet down the mountain slope before cooling into a solid mass. On the peak's north side, lava poured over the rim, steam shot from a vent near the peak, and chunks of lava fell like hard spring rain. Boiling mud flows peeled off tree bark 18 feet above ground and submerged meadows with six feet of debris as the ooze flowed into the valleys of Hat and Lost creeks.

Lassen Peak erupting on June 14, 1914 (as seen from Viola)

U.S. PARK SERVICE

But the Big One came three days later: billowing smoke shot five miles into the air, catapulting five-ton boulders skyward. Steam blasted out again, this time horizontally, flattening trees and anything else in its path. After a few more minor eruptions in following years, Lassen was officially declared asleep (again) in 1921, after seven years of volcanic activity.

The Sisters Sleep

Lassen, the largest "plug" volcano in the world, today offers relatively subtle reminders of its fiery nature. Hot springs, hot lakes, fumaroles or steam vents, and boiling mudpots are found in seven thermal areas within Lassen Volcanic National Park. Though no one is comfortable predicting when, or even if, Lassen will wake up again, another volcanic eruption—perhaps from an entirely new volcano created from the churning magma below—will probably occur in the general vicinity and in the fairly near geological future (measured in hundreds of years).

THE NATIVE PEOPLES

Four groups of Indians inhabited the area, their respective summer territories radiating outward from the peak like spokes. The permanent villages of the Atsugewi to the north, the mountain Maidu to the south and southeast, and the westerly Yana and Yahi were at lower elevations, but as deer migrated annually to higher elevations, so did the Indians. They lived in temporary summer camps and hunted, fished, and gathered wild foods.

Life was fairly harmonious, despite occasional intertribal conflicts. Their various cultures were surprisingly similar, considering these four groups sprang from two different tribal families and three language groups. Basketweaving was the outstanding art; women of the Maidu and Atsugewi tribes specialized in intricate, coiled willow baskets of all shapes and sizes, the Yana and Yahi making mostly twine types. Acorns, leached of bitter tannic acid then pounded into flour for cakes, were the dietary mainstay. Roots, bulbs, and bugs were dug from the ground (hence the derogatory term "digger Indians"). Hunters wore or carried deer head decoys and sometimes bushes as camouflage. They hunted California grizzlies (now extinct) by building simple stick traps outside dens, then cautiously enticing the bears out.

According to guesstimates, the four Lassen peoples together numbered 4,025 total in 1777, 1,080 in 1910, and just 385 by 1950. Here as elsewhere in California, native peoples were virtually wiped out by waves of settlers, introduced diseases, and starvation.

In Search Of Ishi

For years it was believed that the last of the Yahi people were wiped out in a massacre by settlers at Kingsley Cave in Tehama County. But in 1908, power-company surveyors in the Deer Creek foothills south of Lassen came across a naked Indian man standing near the

ISHI COUNTRY

The best way to get into Ishi country from the Lassen area is near the headwaters of Mill and Deer creeks (ask at park headquarters). But another way is via unpaved Ponderosa Way off Hwy. 36 at Paynes Creek—a good side trip through the foothills if you're heading down to the valley. Once you get here, you'll understand how Ishi and his family could so successfully shun "civilization": steep ravines separated by sharp ridges, dense brush, scattered digger pine and black oaks, small plateaus with stands of ponderosa pine. Lots of jeep and foot trails. You can take Ponderosa all the way through Ishi country to Cohasset then down into Chico (but don't try it in winter). Or, turn left onto the old Lassen Trail and cut over to Hwy. 32 above Butte Meadows then drive back to Lassen along Deer Creek. Before setting out, get good maps (especially the Panther Springs and Butte Meadows topo quadrangles).

and several local Native American dialects, to no avail. Finally, for lack of a better place to put him, the sheriff locked him in a cell usually reserved for mental cases.

The "Wild Man of Oroville" made good newspaper copy, but news of his appearance caused even more excitement in the anthropology department at the University of California. Befriended by Alfred Kroeber and others, Ishi (as he was called, though he never revealed his true Yahi name) soon moved to San Francisco, where he lived for almost five years in the old UC Museum of Anthropology. On trips through his people's lands with Kroeber and others, Ishi shared his knowledge of his own and other tribes' beliefs, customs, crafts, and technology. *Ishi in Two Worlds: A Biography of the Last Wild Man in North America* by Theodora Kroeber tells this fascinating story. Ishi died of tuberculosis in 1916 but not before sharing with a friend his observation that whites were "smart but not wise, knowing many things including much that is false."

stream, poised with a double-pronged fishing spear. The next day a stone-tipped arrow whistled through the underbrush past other members in the same party. The surveyors pushed on and stumbled onto the camp of a middle-aged Yahi woman and two elders, a man and a woman. To prove their find, the interlopers carried off blankets, bows, arrows, and food supplies. They returned the next day (reputedly to make reparations), but the camp and the Yahi were gone. Anthropologists searched the area to no avail.

Ishi's Journey:
From Chapparal To City Life
But in August of 1911, butchers at a slaughterhouse in Oroville were awakened by barking dogs at the livestock corral. There they found a near-naked man crouched in the mud, surrounded by snarling dogs. The man's only clothing was a piece of dirty, torn canvas hanging from his shoulders. He was emaciated and suffering from severe malnutrition. His skin was sunburned a copper brown, his hair burnt close to his skull (a Yahi sign of mourning). But the oddest thing was the man's speech, a language no one in the area had ever heard. People tried to communicate with him in English, Spanish,

LASSEN SIGHTS

The most hospitable season is summer, roughly mid-June to October. In years with unusually heavy snowfall, the road through the park may open in July and close in Sept., however, so call ahead if planning to visit either early or late in the season. Those serious about getting to know Lassen might also make a winter visit—for skiing, snowshoe hiking, or simply appreciating winter vistas. Many Lassen sights, including major volcanic peaks and glacial lakes like **Emerald** and **Helen,** are visible from the road. See examples of Lassen's explosive personality at **The Sulphur Works, Little Hot Springs Valley, Bumpass Hell** (where the unfortunate Mr. Bumpass lost a leg to a mudpot), **Devil's Kitchen, Boiling Springs Lake, Terminal Geyser,** and **Drakesbad.**

The Road Tour
Unlike other wilderness areas, many of Lassen's more notable features are easily visible and/or accessible from the one paved road that traverses the park—making a tour of Lassen enjoyable for families with small children as well as for anyone with physical limitations. The *Road*

WORDS STAY

Ishi country. Cold. Our lungs make the words stay in air long enough for us to watch them drift off. We're eyeing each other as if we were strangers, as if we came from different cultures. The striations in the granite become a game we must play, not to break our mothers' backs. Deer Creek could do this to any being, but it does it best to those who love.

You can't be more alone, and not crazy, than Ishi. I couldn't dream up a game that would come close. And when the crazy came too near, he walked out, away from his women's deaths, into the Oroville streets. And into the California he went to his grave knowing was not Deer Creek, and therefore, was not the world. There were two Yana languages: a man's and a woman's. Ishi's had the flavor of the woman's, his new friend said. Two worlds. Two stubborn hearts.

Our shoes drag over Ishi land, and we don't bother about cracks. Words float. It is sacred, right now, this not–touching. It is enough to get ourselves lost, as Ishi would want, to give our trust over to this place—Deer Creek—that will be its own story for longer than even Ishi can tell it.

—Gary Thompson

Ishi in his world

Ishi in another world

PHOEBE HEARST MUSEUM OF ANTHROPOLOGY

PHOEBE HEARST MUSEUM OF ANTHROPOLOGY

Guide to Lassen Park (available for at park headquarters and visitor centers) gives a useful overview of what you'll see along the park road, whether walking, biking, or driving.

Easy Hikes

Two new trails offer public access to remnants of Lassen's disruptive past: the quarter-mile **Devastated Area Interpretive Trail** (wheelchair accessible) and the mile-long **Lily Pond Nature Trail** into the Chaos Jumbles area.

Lassen's 150 miles of interconnecting hiking trails (including 19 miles of the Pacific Coast Trail) offer both short easy strolls and rigorous backcountry treks. Bring water on all walks, and

pack a lunch or high-energy snacks on longer hikes. (Mountain bikes not allowed on any trails.) Among the less strenuous Lassen hikes are those to the volcanic "hot spot" **Bumpass Hell** and the best-for-midsummer-wildflowers **Paradise Meadows.** The mostly downhill hike to impressive **Kings Creek Falls** from Kings Creek Meadows is not difficult (though what goes down does have to come back up). Extend the hike by continuing to Cold Boiling Lake and eventually Bumpass Hell, or to Crumbaugh Lake and the Sulphur Works.

Or try the three-mile **Devil's Kitchen Trail**, which begins and ends at the Warner Valley Picnic Area and explores thermal features. (Hikers can get closer to the volcanic action here than at Bumpass Hell.) The trail to **Boiling Springs Lake** starts from the same spot and offers contrasts of forest, meadow, and a lake fringed with mudpots and steam plumes. Special guided hikes (including wildflower and nature walks, and trips to **Forest Lake** and **Mill Creek Falls** in Ishi country) led by park rangers and naturalists are scheduled at regular intervals.

Tougher Treks

More challenging trips include the steep switchback climb up **Lassen Peak** on the wide and well-graded trail. Bring water and a jacket or sweater. From the summit, see majestic **Mt. Shasta** to the north, **Brokeoff Mountain** to the southwest, and **Lake Almanor** ("Little Tahoe") just south. On a clear day (most likely in spring or fall), the broad Sacramento Valley and the Sutter Buttes are also visible. A hike up Brokeoff, the park's second-highest peak, is also outstanding: good views of Lassen plus strolls through thick woods and blooming meadows. In ancient times, Brokeoff was the southwestern peak of mighty Mt. Tehama before most of that ancient mountain collapsed into a caldera.

To hike the Lassen stretch of the **Pacific Crest Trail,** which traverses Drakesbad and Twin Lakes, start at Little Willow Lake at the park's far southern border. Less challenging is the 1½-mile loop from Summit Lake east to the Bear and Twin lakes areas. Less difficult (but a trudge through loose volcanic cinders then a corkscrew climb) is the five-mile roundtrip from Butte Lake via the **Cinder Cone Nature Trail.** After skirting the **Fantastic Lava Beds,** the panoramic views and close glimpses of the **Painted Dunes** lava flow make the unsteady going worthwhile.

Lassen Area Backpacking

Three-fourths of the park is designated wilderness. Instead of hiking in from the main park road, enter the park's wilderness areas from the southeast or northeast and backpack. Reach the **Juniper Lake** area and adjacent **Caribou Wilderness** via Chester-Juniper Lake Rd. and the **Warner Valley** via Chester-Warner Valley Rd.; both roads originate near the town of Chester south of the park. To get to **Butte Lake** area wilderness, there's a well-marked turnoff from Hwy. 44.

Overnight outings within the park's 106,000 acres can be a chilling experience early in the season, especially before July 1 or in early fall. Unmelted snow is common through June, and the first snowstorms of winter usually arrive by the end of September. "Winter" can occur anytime in the high country, however, so never hike alone and always bring equipment and apparel suitable for abrupt weather changes. Wilderness permits are required for backcountry camping, and no campfires are allowed in wilderness areas, so pack a campstove and fuel. Remember also that backcountry camping is a privilege; leave the area as clean as you found it (if not cleaner).

WINTER RECREATION

Lassen Ski Area: Skiing

In summer "Go Climb a Volcano" T-shirts abound at Lassen, in winter, "Go Ski a Volcano" sweatshirts. The downhill runs of the Lassen Park Ski Area above the "chalet" near the park's southwest entrance were far from famous and, as of press time, had closed. So it's rarely crowded here, instead friendly and unpretentious, and Lassen has something for everyone—beginners, families, occasional skiers, snowboarders, hotdogs recovering from last season's major injuries, even experts and teams. The chairlift to the upper slopes, novice poma lift, and two rope tows are no longer in service.

Snow permitting, the park was open for skiing mid-Nov. to April, Wed.-Sun., lifts opened at 9 a.m. Downhill and Nordic ski lessons were also offered in addition to the children's instructional package.

Burgers, and drinks were available in the chalet, but brownbaggers had to eat elsewhere. Rental skis, boots, and poles, formerly available at the chalet, are cheaper in Mineral, Red Bluff, or Chico. For information about new hours contact: **Lassen Park Ski Area,** Adobe Plaza, 2150 Main St., Suite 5, Red Bluff 96080, tel. (916) 595-3376. Call the "Snowfone" for ski reports, tel. 595-4464; for weather, tel. 246-1311; for road conditions, tel. 244-1500.

Nordic Skiing, Snowshoeing, Snow Camping

Only the southwestern part of the road into

Lassen is snowplowed in winter and only as far as the chalet. (The highway *to* the park at Manzanita Lake is also plowed, allowing access for Nordic skiers and snowshoe hikers.) Most of the park's main snowshoe and ski-touring routes start from the unplowed road and are well marked during the season. **Lassen Peak, Brokeoff,** and **Bumpass Hell** are difficult treks, but trips from the chalet to **Lake Helen, Kings Creek Meadows,** and **Summit Lake** are possible even for beginners. The entire main road through Lassen Park is available in winter for cross-country ski touring (stunning views). In addition, winter camping is allowed at the **Southwest Campground** near the chalet. For safety reasons, registration is necessary for both day

and overnight trips. Day-trippers can sign in at the First Aid Room at the chalet or at the Manzanita Lake office, as can overnighters. Overnight campers can also register at park headquarters in Mineral (see "Lassen Area Information" below).

Park naturalists lead snowshoe hikes, emphasizing snow ecology, to various areas in winter. On most hikes, meet the ranger Wed.-Sun. outside the chalet and wear boots or heavy shoes (snowshoes provided free). Winter wilderness survival programs are offered by reservation only (call headquarters for info). Snowmobiles, once allowed in the park experimentally, are now banned.

Sierra Wilderness Seminars, P.O. Box 707, Arcata 95521, tel. (707) 822-8066, offers winter courses at Lassen in cross-country skiing, telemarking, and winter mountaineering.

LOOMIS MUSEUM, OTHER MANZANITA LAKE FACILITIES REOPEN

Due to official concerns that Lassen Park's Castle Crags might be unusually vulnerable to devastating avalanches, since the early 1970s most visitor facilities in the northern Manzanita Lake area have been closed. But circumstances have changed again, and most Manzanita Lake services have been reinstated.

Thanks to a $40,000 grant from Redding's McConnell Foundation, the venerable Loomis Museum has been fully renovated and refurbished and is scheduled to reopen as soon as August of 1993—which means the museum's impressive collection of archaeological and cultural artifacts will be available for public viewing. In addition, the comprehensive B.F. Loomis photographic record of Lassen Peak's 1914-1921 eruptions will again be on display. New educational exhibits include the particularly impressive interactive volcano exhibit designed and produced by the Carter House Museum in Redding—featuring four model volcanos that actually erupt and that are controlled by child-size handles.

To support private efforts to restore and expand Lassen Park's educational facilities and visitor services, and for more information about park conservation, contact the private, nonprofit **Lassen Volcanic National Park Foundation,** P.O. Box 8, Mineral 96063, tel. (916) 896-8960. New members are always welcome.

LASSEN AREA PRACTICALITIES

Camping

Campsites are abundant both in the park and surrounding national forest areas, with fees $6-8. Because Lassen is the most "unvisited" national park, there is no campground reservation system but there *is* a 14-day limit (seven days only at popular **Lost Creek Group Campground,** reservations required, and both **Summit Lake** campgrounds: no showers but swimming okay). The spacious and more private campground at **Manzanita Lake** (facilities including hot showers, even electric outlets) is considered "out of the line of fire" should Castle Crags ever shake loose in an earthquake or volcanic explosion. The park's overflow, **Crags Campground** five miles from Manzanita Lake near Lost Creek, is quite basic, and open only after Manzanita Lake is full.

Southwest Campground is an easily walked-into area adjacent to the Lassen Chalet parking lot at the park's southwestern entrance. Of more remote campgrounds, only **Butte Lake** charges a fee (flush toilets, no showers, swimming). Neither **Juniper Lake** (13 miles from Chester, primitive, no fee, treat lake water before drinking) nor **Warner Valley** (17 miles from Chester, pit toilets, piped water) are recommended for trailers since access is via rough dirt roads. The best way to land a campsite within Lassen Park is to arrive early in the day, preferably mid-week but otherwise early Fri. for weekend camping, and Sun. for the following week.

If the park's campgrounds are full, many fine campgrounds throughout Lassen National Forest often have room for one more. There are 43 public campgrounds alone totaling about 1,000 campsites, most open May 1-Nov. 1, (free if no safe water source is available). Most are fairly primitive, none have showers, but many are near streams and lakes fine for fishing, swimming, boating. Nearest Lassen to the south, popular and easily accessible are **Battle Creek** on Hwy. 36 just west of Mineral (flush toilets); **Gurnsey Creek** on Hwy. 36 near Fire Mountain, north of Hwy. 32; and **Almanor Campground** near Chester on the lake's west side: spacious, private, close to the beaches and hiking trails.

North of Lassen and easy to get to are **Big Pine** a half mile off Hwy. 44/89 and five miles south of Old Station; **Hat Creek** just south of Old Station; **Cave Campground** just north; and **Rocky, Bridge,** and **Honn** campgrounds along Hat Creek and Hwy. 89 farther north. A non-public alternative is the **Shingletown KOA** 14 miles outside the park's northern entrance at Hwy. 44 and KOA Rd., Rt. 1 Box 400, Shingletown 96088, tel. (916) 474-3133 (tent campers also welcome).

Along Deer Creek and Hwy. 32 toward the valley are the **Elam, Alder Creek,** and verdant **Potato Patch** campgrounds. Farther west, **Soda Springs,** accessible via two miles of dusty roads, and **Butte Meadows** are best reached on the way to or from the valley. In the beautiful Feather River Canyon along Hwy. 70 west from Greenville or Quincy are various Plumas National Forest campgrounds.

Cabins, Lodges, Motels

There are numerous reasonable "resorts" with cabins at Lake Almanor and motels in Chester. Popular near Lassen is **Lassen Mineral Lodge,** Mineral 96063, tel. (916) 595-4422, motel rooms from $42 plus one cabin, pool and tennis court, restaurant, gift shop, ski shop with rentals, even a gas station with AAA tow service. The 10 cabins at **Mill Creek Resort** in the woods on Hwy. 172 just a few miles off Hwy. 36/89, tel. 595-4449, are rustic but comfortable, and prices are consistent year-round. Cabins have one or two

bedrooms with kitchens, some with sitting rooms, $38-60; one cabin sleeps six, has a cozy fireplace. (Small grocery and restaurant with breakfast and sandwich menu.) The **Fire Mountain Lodge** on the west side of Hwy. 36/89, just north of the Hwy. 32 junction, tel. 258-2938, has 10 housekeeping cabins (one, two, or three bedrooms) for $33-53. A big draw here is the main lodge and its huge stone fireplace, a bar, and restaurant.

The **Black Forest Lodge,** Rt. 5 Box 5000, Mill Creek 96061, tel. (916) 258-2941, about 10 miles west of Chester on Hwy. 36/89, is most noted for its restaurant and bar (see "Lassen Area Food" below), six units here from $45. Motel open year-round, reservations rarely needed. The **Deer Creek Lodge,** a mile farther west, tel. 258-2939, has cabins (one to three bedrooms), $25 and up, plus lodge with restaurant and bar.

The Bidwell House Bed And Breakfast

Close to Lake Almanor and Lassen, the historic Bidwell House country inn at 1 Main St., Chester 96020, tel. (916) 258-3338, was once the summer home of noted California pioneers John and Annie E.K. Bidwell. When the Bidwells first started retreating in summer to the cool mountain meadow below Mt. Lassen, the trip took three days (one-way) by wagon caravan and "home," once they arrived, was a massive circus tent. But after 30 years of this summertime tradition, Annie apparently tired of the tent and insisted upon a cabin. John built this lovely two-story home instead. First located in a meadow along the Feather River, the house was rolled into town on logs in 1919.

As perfect now as ever for summer retreats—and a great choice in winter, too, given the area's exceptional cross-country skiing and other attractions—the impressive, completely renovated Bidwell House offers a total of 14 guest rooms, most with private baths, some with in-room Jacuzzis, two with woodstoves. Full breakfast is included. Rates: $60-90 per couple, $110 for the separate cottage (perfect for two couples or families). A variety of business, group travel, length-of-stay, and other discounts are available.

Drakesbad: A True Mountain High

Comfortably rustic simplicity at its finest, but only for those with the urge (and resources) to splurge, this unusual complex sprouts up seemingly out of nowhere in the Warner Valley, actually part of Lassen National Park. **Drakesbad,** named for trapper and guide Edward Drake (who claimed to be a descendant of Sir Francis), is an *experience.* Soak in the ancient hot springs, now a crystal clear 116-degree swimming pool, and snuggle under quilts in kerosene-lit rooms in the simple pine lodge or cabins (no electricity though a generator runs the kitchen). Meals are generous, announced with a clang of the chow bell: big ranch breakfasts, hot lunches (or, sack lunches for hikers if requested in advance), and full dinners with fine wines and beers (alcohol extra). Vegetarian meals available too by request. Rates are on the American plan, starting from $81 per person per night (double occupancy) or $550 per week. In addition to "country basic" lodge rooms, bungalows and other units with private baths are available. Per-day rates increase about $5 per person annually. Open mid-June to late September, reservations often booked a year in advance.

An eccentric who valued his privacy, Drake and his sheep lived alone here for 15 years. From the early 1900s, Drake's Hot Springs and Ranch (shortened to "Drake's baths" or Drakesbad, *bad* being German for "spa") was a family resort noted for the health-giving properties of the springs, catering mostly to San Franciscans. E.R. Drake sold the land to Alex Sifford in 1900, and the Sifford Family owned and operated Drakesbad. Then, in the 1950s, the U.S. government bought the place as an addition to Lassen Park. Sifford Mountain, south of Drakesbad, is named in the family's honor, since much of their land was given to the park.

Drakesbad is accessible by car only via the Chester-Warner Valley Rd. from Chester (heading east on Hwy. 36, turn left at the firehouse then left again when the road forks), about 17 miles. For a special treat, hike in—from the Pacific Coast Trail, from Bumpass Hell, Kings Creek Meadows, or from the Summit Lake area—all routes basically downhill.

Even if you don't stay at Drakesbad, hike through the area. (Call ahead to arrange a meal or two, a guided horseback tour, or "hot dog ride"—an afternoon outing by horseback followed by a wiener roast at Willow Lake—nonguest space permitting.) The spa is open only to Drakesbad guests. For more information and to make reservations, contact: **California Parks Co.,** 2150 N. Main St. #5, Red Bluff 96080, tel. (916) 529-3376 or (off-season) 529-1512.

Lassen Area Food

There's a limited restaurant at the **Lassen Chalet,** open during business hours, and a grocery store at **Manzanita Lake.** A fairly complete listing of area eateries (and available lodgings) is included in the newspaper handed out to park visitors. Fabulous north of the park is the **Mt. Lassen Inn** in Old Station, tel. (916) 335-7006, reservations essential. (See "North and West of Lassen" below.)

People go well out of their way, too, to eat at the **Black Forest Lodge** 10 miles west of Chester on Hwy. 36/89, tel. (916) 258-2941, an unassuming, simple place noted for its excellent German food and select American entrees, *fresh* trout from the pond out back (catch your own if you wish), friendly service, full bar. Also breakfast till noon—try the trout and eggs—and lunch fare (homemade soups are the best bet, but bratwurst and hot or cold frikadellen are also worthwhile). Open daily except Mon., May-Nov., usually open weekends the rest of the year (but call ahead to check).

Next door is the **St. Bernard Lodge,** tel. (916) 258-3382. In addition to substantial lunches, the St. Bernard serves up breakfasts of blueberry pancakes, eggs, hash browns, sausage, and sirloin steak. Dinners include fried chicken, steak, and seafood with fresh bread, homemade soup, and salad. (Unlike the Black Forest, no fishing for trout in the pond here: they're pets.) The bar is a 1929 vision of stained glass and antiques. Open Thurs.-Mon. during late spring through summer, Fri.-Sun. other times. Closed November.

In Chester, **La Comida,** tel. (916) 258-2124, has inexpensive Mexican food, from nachos to chimichangas. The interconnected **Village Market Deli,** tel. 258-2125, has good sandwiches, pasta dishes, even some vegetarian selections. Near Lake Almanor, the **Chester Saloon** at 159 Main in Chester, tel. (916) 258-2887, has amazingly good Italian food, including exceptional calamari. Quite good for a lighter meal—salads and such, burgers, deli fare—is the **Knotbumper Restaurant** at 274 Main, tel. 258-2301. (Enjoy the patio in milder weather.) Best for Chinese is **Ming's Dynasty** at 453 Peninsula in Lake Almanor's Hamilton Branch area, tel. 596-4253.

Infamous in Chester, though, is the **Timber House Lodge** restaurant on the highway at 1st St., tel. (916) 258-2729. The Timber House is an anomaly built into an enigma—Sam Harreld's creation of huge quarried stone and "forest duff and storm fall," massive timbers hauled into town in the back of an old Studebaker. Inside, tree trunks (cut into sections then reassembled with cement), carved wooden bars, barstools, tables, even light fixtures suggest a cave-dweller ambience. Check it out.

Bucks Lake Lodge at Bucks Lake, tel. (916) 283-2262, has crepes and buttermilk pancakes for breakfast, burgers and sandwiches at lunch, seafood and steaks at dinner. Wednesday is barbecue ribs night.

Lassen Area Information

Pick up a free *Lassen Park Guide* (with complete calendar of seasonal park activities, maps, and other pertinent information) upon arrival at the north or south park entrance (admission pass $5 for cars, $2 hikers or bikers, good for one week), or at **Lassen Park Headquarters** on the main drag, P.O. Box 100, Mineral 96063, tel. (916) 595-4444, open 8 a.m.-6 p.m. in summer, 8-4:30 Sept.-May. Excellent Loomis Museum Association books and other publications are available at park headquarters and the **Lassen Park Visitor Center** at Manzanita Lake, tel. 335-7575. Free wilderness permits, required for backcountry trekking in Lassen, can be obtained at park headquarters in Mineral, at the park entrance stations and visitor center, or by mail (contact park officials at least 14 days before you plan to arrive).

For information about camping and recreation in surrounding 1,060,588-acre **Lassen National Forest,** contact headquarters at 707 Nevada St., Susanville 96130, tel. (916) 257-2151, or any of the individual ranger districts: **Almanor,** P.O. Box 767, Chester 96029, tel. 258-2141; **Eagle Lake,** Johnstonville Rd., Susanville 96100, tel. 257-2595; **Hat Creek,** P.O. Box 220, Fall River Mills 96028, tel. 336-5521. A

forest map ($3), visitor's guide, campground information, and leaflets about both Thousand Lakes and Caribou wildernesses are available. To find out about **PG&E** camping and picnicking facilities in the Lassen-Almanor area, call toll-free (800) 624-8087.

For local tourist info, contact: **Chester/Lake Almanor Chamber of Commerce,** P.O. Box 1198, Chester 96020, tel. (916) 258-2426, and the **Plumas County Chamber of Commerce,** P.O. Box 11018, 500 Jackson St. (in the museum), Quincy 95971, tel. 283-6345 or toll-free (800) 326-2247.

Getting There

If Peter Lassen got disoriented in his time, contemporary travelers could easily do the same if they fall prey to the common-sense notion that Lassen Peak should be located within Lassen County. It's not. When plotting your journey, look for Lassen Peak, and much of Lassen Volcanic National Park, in Shasta County. The usual routes to Lassen are east on Hwy. 44 out of Redding (to the park's north entrance) or east from Red Bluff on Hwy. 36 or from Chico on Hwy. 32 to enter the park from the south side. (If the weather is bad in winter, Hwy. 36 is safer than Hwy. 32.) Westbound travelers can get to Lassen only via Highways 89 and 44 from the north, or Highways 44 or 36 out of Susanville.

Like most worthwhile backwaters in California, there are limited transportation options for those without wheels. A combined mail and passenger service runs near the park daily (except Sundays and holidays) from Red Bluff to Mineral (hitch into the park from here), Mill Creek, and Susanville then back again. For info, contact: **Mt. Lassen Motor Transit,** 22503 Sunbright Ave., Red Bluff 96080, tel. (916) 529-2722. Buses leave the Greyhound Station in Red Bluff for Mineral Mon.-Sat. at 8 a.m.; consult with the driver about the return schedule. Fare: $7 one-way. Bicyclists with a sturdy 10-speed or mountain bike and all necessary gear for emergencies will find the trip up any of these highways invigorating and breathtaking (in more ways than one).

VICINITY OF LASSEN PARK

EAGLE LAKE

Bordering Lassen National Forest, Eagle Lake is the largest natural lake entirely within Northern California. Five miles wide and 14 miles long, its deep waters are fed from below by hundreds of springs. At first glance, Eagle is no jewel. A basin lake on the southern tip of the Modoc Plateau, the lake is fringed by large and small rocks and—at least in some places—ponderosa, Jeffrey, and sugar pines as well as incense cedar, junipers, and white fir.

Fishing

As an evolutionary testament to the area's isolation over the eons, Eagle Lake is most noted for its excellent fishing—especially for the unique Eagle Lake trout, capable of surviving in highly alkaline waters. Very good eating. Another special thrill: watching the birds of prey fishing. Bald eagles (most numerous in winter) remain remote even while fishing and hunting, but the awesome osprey also fish here and in greater numbers. It's humbling to watch one work the waters, scooping prey from the lake and winging homeward, trout writhing in its talons.

There's an **osprey nesting area** on the lake's west shore. These magnificent (and, up close, menacing) birds rear their young high atop huge platform nests built on old telephone poles. Don't bother the osprey—they are protected here, which is why they still come—but observe them from a distance with binoculars. Brown pelicans and other waterfowl are also abundant here. For another sight, try **Antelope Mountain Lookout,** 15 miles west of the lake via gravel road (Rd. A-1), open 8-5 daily during the fire season —great views.

Camping, Information

There are plentiful campsites at Eagle Lake, those at the **Christie** and **Merrill** areas the quietest. Reservations through Mistix, tel. (800) 283-CAMP, are required only for the **Eagle Campground,** which is most forested, prettier, and very popular with fishing fans. Food and gas are available at Spaulding Tract nearby, but it's cheaper to stock up in Susanville. Eagle Lake has a new boat launch at **Gallatin,** suitable even for low lake levels, and an associated breakwater with fishing access for the disabled. Also here in the old Gallatin House at Gallatin Beach is the new **Camp Ronald McDonald,** a summer camp for seriously ill, disabled, and disadvantaged children. For information about Eagle Lake, contact the Forest Service office in Susanville, tel. (916) 257-2595. To get to

*summer sunset
on Eagle Lake*

KIM WEIR

Eagle Lake, turn north on Rd. A-1 just two miles west of Susanville (the turnoff is marked by a sign and by a long-destroyed gas station on the south side of the highway).

SUSANVILLE AND VICINITY

Susanville is at the heart of a new secessionist movement, the idea this time to sever Lassen County ties with California and hitch the area's hopes to neighboring Nevada. A rough 'n' tumble lumber town full of history, lumber mills, loggers, and cowboys on the dry eastern slope of the Sierra, pioneer Isaac Roop built the first home here in 1854, naming the town and the river after his daughter Susan. Roop's cabin became **Fort Defiance,** capital of Nataqua ("woman") Territory and headquarters for the Sagebrush War of the early 1860s. Peter Lassen struck gold here though area mining quickly petered out. Cattle and timber have dominated the local economy for years; there are still two lumber mills and a door factory in operation, survivors of recent hard times. But the biggest employer in Susanville is the California Department of Corrections, providing over 1,000 jobs at the minimum-security prison just outside town.

Stop off at **Roop's Fort and the William H. Pratt Museum** at 75 N. Weatherlow, tel. (916) 257-3850, for a look at Fort Defiance, historical photographs, plus Native American and lumbering artifacts.

The tiny but steep **Coppervale Ski Area** between Susanville and Chester is used primarily by Lassen College ski classes, but the public is welcome. Worth it if you're in the area. For information, contact: Coppervale, c/o Lassen College, P.O. Box 3000, Susanville 96130, tel. (916) 257-6181. For a slower trip west to Westwood, take the 25-mile-long **Bizz Johnson Trail** along the Susan River and the old Fernley & Lassen Railroad route from Susanville to Duck Lake four miles north of Westwood—open to hikers, mountain bikers, horseback riders, and cross-country skiers.

Susanville Practicalities

Stop for groceries in Susanville at **Safeway,** 2970 Main St., open 24 hours. For Italian, try the **River Inn Restaurant** downtown, tel. 257-

The rare carnivorous pitcher plant, which eats insects, is native to some northern mountain areas.

3600; for steaks and seafood **Hotel Mt. Lassen,** tel. 257-6161.

New and quite pleasant is **The Roseberry House** bed and breakfast, 609 North St., Susanville 96130, tel. (916) 257-5675, a 1902 country Victorian with four rooms (private baths), rates from $50. Inexpensive for accommodations is the **Cozy Motel,** 2829 Main, tel. 257-2319, clean modern rooms. Or try the **River Inn Motel** just east of town on Hwy. 36, tel. 257-6051, rooms from $32, or the **Trailside Inn Best Western** motel at 2785 Main., tel. 257-4123, rooms $42 and higher. Camping of course is cheapest, with many campsites available at Eagle Lake. For area recreation and camping information, stop off at the **Eagle Lake Ranger District** office of Lassen National Forest Johnstonville Rd., Susanville 96100, tel. 257-2595. At the **BLM Office** here, 2545 Riverside Dr., tel. 257-0456, ask about petroglyph sites in Rice Valley. For other local information, contact the **Lassen County Chamber of Commerce and Tourism Council** at 36 S. Lassen St., P.O. Box 338, Susanville 96130, tel. 257-4323.

Spanish Springs Ranch

Okay, all you urban cowboys and cowgirls. Been hankerin' after the chance to ride the range like an Old West drover? Headquartered on the sagebrush plateau near Ravendale some 60 miles from Susanville, Spanish Springs Ranch is a 70,000-acre working cattle ranch which rolls out the red carpet for paying guests. Cattle drives, horse round-ups, and trail rides are just part of the action. Family-oriented activities also include barbecues, hayrides, rodeos, and fishing excursions during balmy weather, horse-drawn sleigh rides and cross-country skiing in winter. Guests can also opt for city slicker-style diversions, from swimming, tennis, and volleyball to archery and skeet shooting. For younger children, there's a playground and petting zoo.

The vacation options here (American Plan) are almost staggering, from camping out on the open range to staying in the comfortable log cabin-style lodge or cabins, duplexes, deluxe suites, and far-flung ranch houses. At ranch headquarters, there's even a bunkhouse with separate dormitories for girls and boys (private rooms for parents). Rates cover most activities, including horseback riding, and start at $100 per person per night for adults, $50 for children. And if you're just passing through, stop by for dinner and a peek into the saloon.

Lake Almanor

Lovely Lake Almanor is a manmade reservoir but otherwise like a tiny Tahoe, a very pretty deep blue. Almanor is incredibly lonely despite being so close to major valley cities. Its attractions include clean cool air, clear water at a near-perfect 65-70 degrees, good fishing, swimming, sailing, water-skiing. Even in summer there are days when not a single outboard motor disturbs the silent waters (though sailboats appear quickly whenever the wind's up). The lake's west side is more rustic and relaxed; the east side is newer, mostly private subdivisions and upscale resorts.

In April, there's a popular **Bass Fishing Tournament** here (the lake is home also to trout and salmon). In July are the **High Water Regatta Boat and Yacht Races,** also the **Miniature Aerobatic Plane Fly-In,** featuring remote-control planes. Also in summer: the 106-mile **Mile High One Hundred** bike race. For more information about Lake Almanor, contact the local chamber office, P.O. Box 1198, Chester 96020, tel. (916) 258-2426. Most people get here via Hwy. 32 from Chico then Hwy. 89 (good road), though a trip on the Old Red Bluff Rd. (Hwy. 36) to Chester is quite scenic—squeezing

through steep-walled Deer Creek Canyon, where dogwood and redbud bloom in early summer (nice campgrounds along the way, too). Another way to go is up Hwy. 70 from Oroville through Feather River Canyon.

Chester/Westwood

A rustic logging town in the shadow of Lassen Peak on Almanor's north shore, Chester is less redneck than Susanville. Peter Lassen led immigrants through this little valley on his infamous Oregon Trail shortcut. There are reasonable motels here, fast-food joints and restaurants, gas stations, a small **museum** in the local library, and various places to pick up sporting goods and outdoor equipment. But the best place to get outdoor supplies and sundries is fascinating **Ayoob's Department Store,** a great general store with a quirky array of merchandise.

In **Westwood,** the museum (tel. 916-256-3709) tells the story of the old Red River Lumber Company, which created the story of **Paul Bunyan and Babe the Blue Ox** as a promotional gimmick. So it's only appropriate that a carved statue of both stands near the western end of the nearby **Bizz Johnson Trail.** (See "Susanville and Vicinity.")

Stover Mountain Ski Area

With just a short rope tow and 300-yard poma lift, the small **Stover Mountain Ski Area** overlooking Lake Almanor is strictly local, open weekends and holidays only. No facilities here aside from the tiny warming hut, but much of the downhill terrain is "advanced" and challenging. The county road turnoff to Stover Mountain is five miles north of Hwy. 36 where it joins Hwy. 89. For information, contact: Ted Pilgrim, ski club president, tel. (916) 258-2193. Due to lack of snow in recent years, Stover Mountain isn't always open.

The Feather River Canyon

For a pleasant side trip or alternate route to the Sacramento Valley from Chester or Almanor, head west on Hwy. 89 then Hwy. 70 down the rugged, steep canyon of the north fork of the Feather River: autumn colors through here can rival Vermont. The Southern Pacific "Y" railroad trestle over the Feather River at **Keddie** is the only one of its kind in the world. Farther west, cross the narrow bridge and stop in **Belden**

Town for a snack and a look around, admiring the old stamp mill here (across the highway, near public restrooms). For a dose of riverside relaxation, stop off at **Woody's** farther down the canyon, tel. (916) 283-4115: hot springs-fed hot tubs.

NORTH AND WEST OF LASSEN

Latour State Forest
These 9,000 acres on the west side of Lassen National Forest, part of the Cascade Range and not far from Thousand Lakes Wilderness, are frequented mostly by hunters. Three primitive campgrounds (free), no hiking trails but miles of forest roads. Mammals include black bears, mountain lions, bobcats, pika, and mountain beaver. Birds include the sharp-shinned hawk and goshawk, blue grouse, mountain quail, screech owls, woodpeckers. Pines, firs, mountain shrubs, and delicate water-loving wildflowers abound.

High winds, extreme cold, and wet snow are the norm here in winter and spring, so come from early July to late October. For information, write Latour State Forest, P.O. Box 2238, Redding 96099, or stop by at 1000 W. Cypress St., tel. (916) 243-1436 or (Latour Station) 474-3197. To get here, at Millville take Whitmore Rd. northeast to Bateman.

Old Station
The closest thing to a town you'll find immediately north of Lassen (gas available). Most of the "town" is **Uncle Runt's**

Place, tel. (916) 335-7177, a cheap, cozy burger palace, restaurant, and bar, good dinner specials, open Tues.-Sun. noon-8 p.m. (no credit cards). Across Hwy. 44/89 from the Hat Creek Campground a half mile west of Old Station is the **Spattercone Crest Trail,** a free two-mile self-guided trail through lava tubes and domes, volcanic blowholes and spattercones. (It can get hot here in summer, so hike in the early morning.)

One mile north of Old Station is the **Subway Cave,** a 2,000-year-old lava tube you can walk through for one-third mile. Self-guided brochure available at National Forest offices; for more about the lava flows in Hat Creek Valley, stop off at the **information center** a half mile south of the cave on Hwy. 89. (The cave is dark as doom inside and always cool, so bring a powerful flashlight, sweater, sturdy shoes.)

Ashpan Park, Prospect Peak
Nine miles south of Old Station (and 4½ miles north of the **Eskimo Hill Snowplay Area)** is Ashpan Snowmobile Park, miles of marked snowmobile trails, a cooperative recreational venture sponsored by Shasta County, the state of California, and Lassen National Forest.

Also in the general area: Prospect Peak, an ancient volcano just northeast of Lassen Park. From the Forest Service fire lookout on the summit, you can see for miles and miles. The turnoff to **West Prospect Fire Lookout** is a mile south of Big Pine Campground on Hwy. 89; the lookout itself is another 12 miles on a fairly decent road.

Hat Creek
Considered one of the best trout-fishing streams in the U.S., Hat Creek is a destination in its own right. The season opens May 1 usually, but the two-trout 18-inch-length limit is meaningless to many fishing enthusiasts here, as most throw their catch back. At Cassel, a general store and PG&E campground, Hat Creek is joined by Rising River. A mile downstream is the **Crystal Lake Fish Hatchery,** then Crystal Lake and

Baum Lake. Farther on, below the Hat Creek II Powerhouse and before the creek empties into Lake Britton, are the Lower Hat Creek waters of the **Hat Creek Wild Trout Project,** with big wily fish (catch-and-release only). From Hat Creek proper, take Doty Rd. for four miles to the **Radio Astronomy Observatory,** a computer-controlled 85-foot-diameter radiotelescope designed to track objects in space.

Clearwater House

A very comfortable bed and breakfast in the style of an English angling lodge, Clearwater House is especially appropriate for fly-fishing aficionados. Relaxed yet tasteful, from the fish and game prints on the walls to the oriental rugs over hardwood floors, this inn is the only Orvis-approved fishing lodge in California—a natural outgrowth of proprietor Dick Galland's experience as a wilderness and fishing guide. Tucked into the town of Cassel, between Burney and Fall River Mills on the banks of Hat Creek, a premier wild trout stream, Clearwater offers an

extensive array of fishing programs, from weekend instruction to five-day "Mastering the Art of Fly Fishing" and "Big Trout Tactics." Some of the organization's fishing guides also provide fishing experiences near Mammoth, Truckee, and on the Trinity River, but the emphasis here is Hat Creek, a waterway internationally renowned for its stream-bred and wily wild trout but surrounded mostly by private property (difficult access).

Clearwater attracts a largely male clientele, but family members and older children are also welcome, especially if they're interested in fishing. The area offers other attractions, after all, from mountain biking and wilderness exploration to excellent golfing at Fall River. Rates, which include all meals, start at $105 per person per night. Reservations almost mandatory. Clearwater House is closed mid-Nov. through April. For information and reservations, contact: **Clearwater Trout Tours,** 274 Star Rt., Muir Beach, CA 94965, tel. (415) 381-1173.

BURNEY FALLS AND VICINITY

Halfway between Lassen Peak and Mt. Shasta, 15 miles northeast of Burney, is one of the state's oldest parks, **McArthur-Burney Falls Memorial State Park.** This is heavily forested northern lava country at about 3,000 feet. Birdlife is abundant, including great blue herons, Canada geese, a variety of ducks and grebes, owls, evening grosbeaks, and sometimes bald eagles. The park is especially popular in summer but open year-round; $5 per car for day use.

Sights, Hikes

Called "The Eighth Wonder of the World" by Teddy Roosevelt, Burney Falls is fed by spring flows of 200 million gallons daily and thunders down a moss-covered 129-foot cliff into emerald-green water before flowing into Lake Britton. The porous volcanic basalt makes for some fascinating water action. Delicate plants thrive here in the cool moisture. Rare black swifts (normally seabirds) build nests of lichens on cliffs near the falls from spring until the first frosts and dart erratically through the mists after insects. Another fascinating bird near Burney Falls is the wren-like water ouzel, which dives into the creek and walks along the streambed

Burney Falls, Teddy Roosevelt's Eighth Wonder of the World

looking for larvae and other delicacies, then shoots up out of the water like a space shuttle launch.

There are two easy walks, the half-mile **Headwaters Trail** to Burney Creek above the falls (for the best view), and the one-mile self-guided **Nature Trail** circuit into the gorge. For a longer trip, follow the **Burney Creek Trail** all the way down to Burney Creek Cove (and beach) at Lake Britton, then climb back up on the **Rim Trail**.

Park Practicalities,
Plus Burney And Fall River Mills

California's financial hard times have hit the hardest in the state's outlying areas—particularly those tiny towns once almost completely dependent on the timber industry. Rather than just give up and give in to destitution, highway-straddling Burney is making a comeback. Local businesses have spruced up and expanded; downtown has sprouted wall murals, planter boxes, and a flower garden, everything a labor of love and community pride. So slow down a bit and be neighborly. For more information, contact the **Burney Chamber of Commerce,** P.O. Box 36, Burney 96013, tel. (916) 335-2111. If you're in town and in the mood for intelligent conversation and useful suggestions, stop by the **Burney Bookworm** at Caldwell's Corner on the highway, 37371 Main St., tel. 335-4994. Nearby is Fall River, most noted for its outcroppings of white diatomaceous rock, the **Fort Crook Museum,** and the noted **Fall River Valley Golf Course.** There are motels in both towns, but unusual here is the **Fall River Hotel,** tel. 336-5550, a local variation on the bed and breakfast theme with Victorian-style rooms, some newly refurbished.

Or camp at Burney Falls year-round (118 sites in two campgrounds, hot showers, $14, reservations in summer through Mistix), at **Ahjumawi Lava Springs State Park** (accessible only by boat), or at PG&E's **Lake Britton Campground:** good swimming (but steep drop-offs from shore), bass and trout fishing, a natural stopover for hikers passing through on the nearby Pacific Crest Trail (facilities usually open May 1-Oct. 31). Also, six national forest campgrounds are within easy driving distance. For more information about Burney Falls, contact: **McArthur-Burney Falls Memorial State Park,** Rt. 1, Box 1260, Burney 96013, tel. (916) 335-2777.

Ahjumawi Lava Springs State Park

A lovely lava springs area of pine, juniper, and chaparral, Ahjumawi ("Where the rivers meet") is a good place to get away from it all (especially since you can only get there by boat). This remote state park is 6,000 acres of wilderness fringing the lakes at the north end of Fall River Valley: fascinating basalt formations, many freshwater springs, incredible views, tent camping, tables, outhouse, 30-day maximum stay. Waterfowl and bald eagles nest here.

To get there, from McArthur head north on Main St. past the Intermountain Fairgrounds and turn onto Rat Ranch Rd. (dirt road, unlocked gate—please close) and continue four miles through PG&E's McArthur Swamp (known locally as "the Rat Farm") to the boat launch area. For more info, including suggestions about where to rent boats and where to camp, contact the rangers at McArthur-Burney Falls State Park.

Big Bend Hot Springs And Iron Canyon

To get far from the madding crowds, head out Big Bend Rd. (past the town of Montgomery Creek) and continue past Wengler, through Big Bend, then over the Pit River to little Iron Canyon Reservoir in the Shasta-Trinity National Forest. Free Forest Service camping is at Deadlun Creek; 10 PG&E campsites at Hawkins Landing. Near Big Bend on the Pit is Big Bend Hot Springs, 196 Hot Springs Row, tel. (916) 337-6680, a run-down resort with natural stone pools. Back on Hwy. 299, stop where the bridge crosses Hatchet Creek, a half mile from Big Bend Road. Hike upstream a quarter mile through thick brush to **Hatchet Falls** and an isolated pool ideal for swimming.

BOB RACE

MODOC COUNTRY

Native peoples called the high Modoc Plateau area "the smiles of God," a strangely fitting name for this rugged remnant of the Old West. One of those rare places in California where local folks still wave to strangers passing on back roads, Modoc is dramatic in its desolation. Even in the thick of winter's tule fog, accompanied by the lonely musings of migrating waterfowl, cowboys still ride the range here (and belly up to the bar in local saloons on Saturday nights). And here in Modoc country, California's outback and site of one of the last major Indian wars in the United States, there is still distrust between native peoples and settlers. The hundreds of lava caves and craggy outcroppings at what is now Lava Beds National Monument enabled charismatic "Captain Jack" and his Modoc warriors to hold out against hundreds of troops (and superior arms) for more than three months before being starved into defeat by the U.S. Army in 1873. A 19th-century domestic Vietnam, the Modoc War cost U.S. taxpayers $40,000 for every Native American killed. The other costs cannot be counted.

Despite the deep sadness that seems to seep up from the lava caves and obsidian cliffs, there is great beauty here. On a clear day from the flat-topped, blue, and brooding Warner Mountains, majestic Mt. Shasta to the west seems so close one can imagine reaching out for a handful of snow. And the view east to the alkaline lakes of Surprise Valley and across the Great Basin is nothing short of spectacular.

THE LAND

To the west, mysterious Mt. Shasta presides over the lava-topped tableland of the Modoc Plateau. Sister volcano Lassen Peak, the southernmost sentry of the Cascade Range, looms up from the south. By virtue of their *presence* Shasta and Lassen stand out visually, but the dividing line between the Cascades and the Modoc Plateau is obscure. Defining the area's plateau-ness is also difficult: this high country is both the southern tip of the vast Columbia Plateau and part of the Great Basin, which extends from the Sierra Nevada through Nevada and into Utah, Idaho, Oregon, and Washington.

Remnants Of Ancient Seas And Glaciers

Compared to the Klamaths and the Cascades, this region has few rivers, lakes, or forests. The Pit River, the only major Modoc waterway, originates in the Warners and cuts diagonally through the lava plateau and mountains before entering the Sacramento River via Shasta Lake. Modoc lakes are landlocked remnants of ancient glacial runoff. Lower Klamath Lake, Tule Lake, Clear Lake Reservoir, and Goose Lake are all major migratory refuges for geese, ducks, and swans. During the past two million years, immense seas covered much of the area. Along the remote far-north section of Hwy. 395 ancient sand dunes, layered sedimentary rocks, and beach terraces suggest a very different long-ago landscape. During the Pleistocene era, the plateau's lava formations trapped water runoff from the Cascades to create Tule Lake. Now little more than an impressive pond among radish and potato fields, the lake was once 185,000 acres of water, marshes, and wildlife until post-World War II reclamation turned three-quarters of it into farmland.

Violence And Volcanoes

Violent volcanism was the great creator of regional landforms. The Cascades and the Modoc Plateau are the only places in California almost completely created from young basaltic lavas and extrusive igneous rocks like those seen at Lava Beds National Monument. Belying the "softness" of its name, the black moonscape of Lava Beds offers harsh but impressive examples

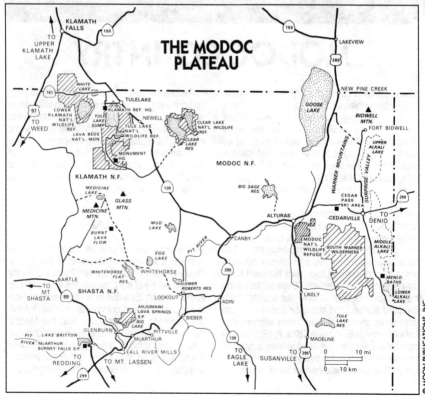

THE MODOC PLATEAU

© MOON PUBLICATIONS, INC.

APOLOGIES TO WATER BIRDS

Industry in Modoc County is agriculture: cattle, sheep, horses, and crops including barley, clover, oats, wheat, potatoes, apples, apricots, and plums plus the finest alfalfa hay and seed. Recreation (primarily hunting) is a seasonal economic boon. Beyond the grain and hayfields, endless shades of gray-green and yellow are the subtle colors of these rolling sagebrush grasslands. Higher, from the plateau to the mountains, chaparral and junipers blend into pine forests and glacial meadows abloom with wildflowers.

But what *is* nature is not necessarily natural. The Modoc Plateau is a heavily "managed" environment. Most modern-day wetlands are artificial, timber is second-growth, and the endless expanses of sage and bitterbrush have taken the place of native perennial grasses. In the Devil's Garden area of Modoc National Forest grows the most generous jumble of juniper in any U.S. national forest—but juniper would not thrive in this plant world without the competitive edge provided by cattle grazing. As the writer William Kittredge (who grew up a rancher in the shadow of the Warner Mountains) observed in his 1988 *Harper's* article, "Who Won the West? Apologies to the Water Birds and Ranch Hands":

Maybe we should have known the world wasn't made for our purposes, to be remodeled into our idea of an agricultural paradise, and that Warner Valley wasn't there to have us come along and drain the swamps, and level the peat ground into alfalfa land. No doubt we should have known the water birds would quit coming. But we had been given to understand that places we owned were to be used as we saw fit. The birds were part of that.

So, where did otherwise good people go wrong, Kittredge asks, using other people (as well as the land and its natural inhabitants) as tools to build our version of a greater destiny? Was it coldheartedness, crass commerce, and/or stupidity in the face of the sacred? Imagining a world where "in the end all of us would be able to forgive ourselves and care for ourselves," he answers: "We would have learned to mostly let the birds fly away, because it is not necessarily meat we are hunting."

of basalt pahoehoe (smooth) lava formations. Throughout the plateau, mineral springs and hot springs abound (most of the latter, unfortunately for travelers, on private property). The geology of the Warner Mountains and adjacent Surprise Valley to the east—visible from the road on the way to Cedarville from Alturas—is the result of the interaction of a double fault through the area.

Climate
Relatively dry, with an average precipitation of 12.6 inches annually, Modoc County experiences cold winters, hot summers. Snow is erratic but never extremely heavy, usually four to six inches. Tule fog creates the more common type of white Christmas in these parts.

Fauna
The region's national wildlife refuges are home to a million shorebirds and waterfowl migrating each year along the Pacific Flyway in fall and spring, still outstanding though much diminished by extensive "reclamation" of wetlands for agricultural uses. Snow geese, Canada geese, mal-

lards and other ducks, cormorants, and snowy egrets touch down for the annual interspecies flutter, along with pheasants, great blue herons, marsh hawks, meadowlarks, and other songbirds. Many species nest and raise their young here and are present until summer. In winter, most amazing are the large numbers of bald eagles; 500 to 600 bald eagles winter in the great Klamath Basin, where they feed on carcasses of the less fortunate waterfowl. Local birds are typical of Northern California: quail, pheasants, hawks, golden eagles, woodpeckers, jays, various songbirds. Not so typical: the spectacular strutting sage grouse.

Mule deer are common, as are coyotes, smaller mammals and rodents, and rattlesnakes. Mountain lions, bobcats, and pronghorn are rarer. But the small and sleek, tan, white-rumped pronghorn are making a comeback here. They run in the largest numbers among the juniper and sage of remote Devil's Garden between the Warners and Tule Lake, in the company of browsing mustangs. When Europeans first reached California, a half million or more pronghorn roamed throughout the state. Now about

7,000 remain, most of these in Modoc County. Also here, primarily in the South Warner Wilderness, are California bighorn sheep, though this introduced population has recently been decimated by pneumonia.

Getting There

Arriving in middle-of-nowhere Modoc is rarely accidental. (Without a car—better yet, a pickup truck—forget it.) Highway 139 from Klamath Falls in Oregon provides the most direct access, cutting through the plateau between the Lava Beds/Klamath wildlife area and Clear Lake. Also get here from the south via Hwy. 299 from Red Bluff, Hwy. 139 from Eagle Lake (then Hwy. 299), or via Hwy. 395 as it winds north from Susanville and the farthest reaches of the Sierra Nevada.

LAVA BEDS AND VICINITY

Technically part of Siskiyou County, the 72 square miles of **Lava Beds National Monument** is dry, inhospitable, and rugged, a tumble of lava caves, craggy volcanic chimneys, and cinder cones dusted by sagebrush and tumbleweed. Fog is common, especially in winter, adding to the landscape's eeriness. Somehow this desolate patch of plateau became the perfect staging ground for the most expensive war ever launched against native peoples by the U.S. government, and the only full-blown Indian war ever waged in California. During the presidency of U.S. Grant, the U.S. government, spent over a half-million dollars in the relentless six-month war against Chief Kentipoos (or Kentapoos or Keintpoos) and his mixed band of freedom fighters. Known also as "Captain Jack," Kentipoos gained notoriety both for his strategic shrewdness and his habit of wearing brass buttons and military insignia. The Modoc Indian War was costly not only in money and human lives, but also cultural disintegration when the surviving Modocs were shipped off to a reservation in the Midwest.

Fascinating background reading is *Life Amongst the Modocs: Unwritten History* by Joaquin Miller, written at the time of the Modoc War. This visionary 1873 based-on-fact fiction is drawn from Miller's personal experiences in Shasta and Siskiyou counties during the gold rush, among settlers and native peoples alike. His protagonist eventually learns that at the edge of the frontier, that all-American symbol of democratic hope and justice, treachery and self-betrayal are just as likely.

The Modocs

Though they were enemies, Oregon's Klamath tribe named the Modocs *moa,* meaning "southerner," and *docks,* "near." A small group of people even before its systematic destruction during California's settlement, little is now known about the Modocs and their culture. The Klamath and Tule lake basins were first inhabited 7,500-9,000 years ago; unusual petroglyphs carved in sandstone cliffs near Tule Lake feature characters never painted or carved by any other western people. Remains of ancient dwelling sites have been discovered near Lower Klamath Lake though anthropologists suspect that volcanic activity made the area largely unsuitable for human habitation until the 1400s, when ancestors of the closely related Klamath and Modoc clans first arrived.

Fragile, incredibly intricate pottery has been unearthed in Klamath-Modoc territory in recent years, but the Modocs were primarily basketweavers who dressed in buckskin, furs, bark, and tule cloth. They also used tule reeds from the lakes to build boats and homes. The Modoc people subsisted primarily on game—the deer, pronghorn, and mountain sheep once so plentiful in the Lava Beds area—and stalked furbearing animals, including the now-extinct pine marten. With more tribal solidarity than most California native peoples, the Modocs were considered "the model tribe" by early northern Californian settlers, since they were peaceable and helpful. The characterization of the Modocs as inherently warlike was (and is) unfortunate and untrue but a common belief based on later history.

Aside from the Modocs (and occasional marauding Klamaths), northern Paiutes or Toloma (a Shoshone people) lived to the east in and around Surprise Valley. Virtually nothing is known about the native people of Surprise Valley, though a Nevada Paiute inspired the great but doomed Ghost Dance movement of the late 1800s—a spiritual doctrine passed on first to Modoc and Achomawi tribes then to the Shasta, Karok, Yurok, and others in Northern California. Ritual remnants of this yearning for the Old Ways remain in modern-day Native American ceremonies. The Achomawi lived throughout Pit River country, their villages usually on streambanks (except near Burney and Hat creeks, where the Atsugewi lived). Deer weren't overly abundant, so they developed a unique trapping system—concealing pits two or three yards deep in the middle of deer paths so their prey would just fall in. (This practice, considered a nuisance by settlers who later banned it, gave the Pit River its name.)

THE MODOC INDIAN WAR AND "THE DARK AND BLOODY GROUND"

Early Skirmishes

Not until the mass migrations of whites during the California gold rush (and the rush to settle fertile Oregon Territory) did local native peoples begin attacking whites in warfare—except in north-

"Captain Jack," Chief Kentipoos

eastern California, where the Modocs and Paiutes lived. The Modoc Plateau was known as "the dark and bloody ground of the Pacific" and became center stage for the 30-year regional struggle between whites and Native Americans throughout California's Lassen, Siskiyou, and Modoc counties, Klamath and Lake counties in Oregon, and western Nevada. From the start, wagon trains of settlers frightened away the game so necessary to survival, and a smallpox epidemic in 1847 wiped out infants and tribal elders. Young warriors raided settling parties for survival and in retaliation. The "facts" are unreliable, but an estimated 300 whites were killed by 1852 and another 112 by 1858.

Captain Jack And His "Hothead" Warriors

Pressure to solve "the Indian problem"—by relocating the Modocs—intensified, and in 1864 the U.S. Bureau of Indian Affairs negotiated a peace treaty with the Modocs. They agreed to leave their ancestral homeland and settle at the Klamath Reservation in Oregon in exchange for money and supplies. But animosity between the Modocs and the Klamaths was great and the threat of starvation real. Because the Klamaths considered the reservation and its resources theirs alone, the Modocs were forced to slaughter their horses for food. When there were no more horses they began drifting back to their Lost River fishing grounds. Kentipoos gradually emerged as leader of the young Modocs characterized as "hotheads." Angered over being forced off their ancestral lands, he and his band left the reservation at will to raid and steal. Eventually, Captain Jack openly asserted that his people were back on their tribal lands to stay, and that he could lead his band into the lava beds south of Tule Lake and never be dislodged —an almost prophetic statement.

The War Begins

The war, variously considered "farce tragedy" and "a comedy of errors" by observers, began in late November 1872, three years before Custer fell at the Little Bighorn. United States soldiers dispatched to herd the Modocs back to the reservation ended up on the run, carrying off 13 dead or wounded. Then the Modocs, who had vowed to kill off every man in Tule Lake Valley if attacked by soldiers, did so. (Captain

Jack, not in favor of all-out war or the valley murders, was outvoted by a more militant Modoc faction.) The band retreated to the crumpled lava plateau south of Tule Lake and climbed into its subterranean trenches to await the inevitable Army pursuit.

On January 12, 1873, 175 regular soldiers, 20 Klamath Indian scouts, and 104 volunteers headed by Lt. Col. Frank Wheaton, the Army's district commander (in all, about 300 rifles and two howitzers), moved into position outside what came to be known as "Captain Jack's Stronghold."

The Modocs were excellent marksmen and good strategists. The battle at dawn the next morning was disastrous for the U.S. Army. Fog blanketed the battlefield. Wheaton's cold, confused troops fired at phantoms all day—dodging bullets from nowhere, unnerved still more by the Modocs' derisive comments—and retreated all night, leaving behind enough rifles and ammunition to fight another war. They carried off nine dead and 28 wounded; there were no Indian casualties. As the siege wore on, media-conscious Captain Jack gave interviews to various newspaper reporters, a shrewd move that won broad public support for his band, 52 Modocs holding a thousand soldiers at bay.

The War Ends
Then, suddenly, whatever sympathy the Modocs had won through the media was lost. On April 11, militant Modocs killed two members of the Army's Peace Commission negotiating team and half scalped a third. Furious soldiers forgot their fear and renewed their attack on the stronghold. Army mortars rained missiles for two nights. When soldiers finally reached the Indian command post, it was deserted. The retreating band, on foot and short of water, finally surrendered on May 27. All except Kentipoos. But in a cruel irony, the very warriors who against their leader's wishes had incited the group to murder, helped the government track down Captain Jack. He was captured on June 1, tried, and hung, at Fort Klamath. Afterward, his head was hacked off and shipped to the Army Medical Museum in Washington, D.C.

"This is vengeance, indeed," wrote an appalled *San Francisco Chronicle* correspondent. "Captain Jack said that he would like to meet the Great White Chief in Washington face to face.

The government evidently intends that his dying wish shall be respected." Captain Jack's skull eventually arrived at the Smithsonian but was later returned to tribal members.

LAVA BEDS NATIONAL MONUMENT AND VICINITY

This is where it all happened, the bleak scene of Captain Jack's last stand. Especially when the black lava and death-gray sagebrush are shrouded in drifts of tule fog, unquiet ghosts seem to dwell here. Scrambling into lava caves and up cinder cones, it's apparent how clever the Modocs were. Captain Jack's battlements were perfect: a lava fortress surrounded by deceptively "easy" terrain almost impossible to cross without being vulnerable to sniper fire.

Even those uninterested in the bloody march of history will enjoy Lava Beds National Monument, however. Two separate, high-desert wilderness areas (no fires, bring water, camping by permit only) offer hiking and some arid vistas. Outside the park to the northeast is an area rich in ancient petroglyphs. (Vandalism has been a problem, so ask for directions and more information at park headquarters.) Also near Lava Beds, in forest clearings along the highway between the towns of Alturas and Tulelake, are three huge, recently installed U.S. Air Force "backscatter" radar antennae linked to military installations in Mountain Home, Idaho, and NORAD.

Volcanoes And Lava Tubes
At Lava Beds, the area's volcanic history (and the area is still considered volcanically active) is everywhere apparent. Cinder cones, spatter cones, stratovolcanoes, shield volcanoes, chimneys, flows of both smooth pahoehoe and rough and chunky aa lava, and lava tubes abound. Lava tubes formed by streams of superheated magma as it cools are not unusual in volcanic areas, but the sheer quantity (almost 200) found at Lava Beds is.

The Indian Well Caves
Mushpot Cave, in the Indian Well parking lot, is the only lighted cave at Lava Beds, complete with good interpretive displays and a film. A loop road from Indian Well toward the south offers

access to most of the other park caves that can be visited without passes. (People are allowed to explore these and other caves alone, but despite the fact that there are few side caves and it's difficult to get lost, this is not wise.) To a large extent, the names of loop caves describe what visitors see: Blue Grotto, Sunshine, Natural Bridge, and Catacombs (where spelunkers have to crawl to get through). **Crystal Cave** across from the Catacombs' entrance has red lava wells and frost crystals that flash like jewels. Best of all, though, are the **Labyrinth** and **Golden Dome.** Not far south of the loop group, near Caldwell Butte, is **Valentine Cave,** a locals' favorite.

Skull Cave And Others

Not a human graveyard, **Skull Ice Cave** was named for the many pronghorn and bighorn sheep skulls found here. The cavern itself is enormous—the domed roof in the main chamber 75 feet high—and the floor below is a solid sheet of ice. (When you think you've come to the end, you haven't: get down on your knees and keep crawling into the next black-walled chamber.) **Big Painted Cave** has fascinating Indian pictographs, some also faintly visible on the bridge at **Symbol Bridge Cave** nearby.

Schonchin Butte above, named for a Modoc chief, is the largest of the area's 11 scoriaceous cinder cones. (A three-quarter-mile trail climbs to the summit, where there's a fire tower and great views of the monument.) Others are across the road in the wilderness area: Mammoth, Hippo, Bearpaw, Modoc, and Whitney. **The Castles** are two large groups of fumaroles or chimneys of gas-inflated lava, similar to the fire fountains on Kilauea in Hawaii. Off on a side road farther north are **Boulevard** and **Balcony** caves. (To visit more remote caves, ask at park headquarters, then sign in—required, just in case you don't come back.)

Modoc War Sites

About a mile past Boulevard and Balcony caves, between Black Crater and Hardin Butte, is the **Thomas Wright Battlefield.** Here, on April 26, 1873, two-thirds of Capt. Thomas's troops met their maker during the Modoc War. The park road crosses over it then continues past Gillem's Bluff for four miles to **Gillem's Camp,** Army headquarters during the six-month Modoc War. **Canby's Cross,** a white wooden marker erected by U.S. troops, marks the spot where he was gunned down during the last session of the Peace Commission negotiations. At the park's northeast corner near Tule Lake Sump is the complex maze of caves, lava trenches, and natural rock battlements of **Captain Jack's Stronghold,** the center of the war zone. Wounded Army soldiers were sheltered at **Hospital Rock,** another natural fortification nearby where the cavalry camped in 1873.

Lava Beds Practicalities

Come with a full tank of gas and bring food as well as hard-soled shoes and warm- and cool-weather clothes. It can snow here any season though it can also get quite hot in summer. (But even in summer heat, it stays cool in the lava caves.) If you plan to explore the caves, bring two flashlights (in case one dies in the darkness), or get flashlights (free, but they must be returned) and buy protective hardhats ($2-3) at headquarters. Forty campsites, 30 of them closed Sept. 15-May 15, are at **Indian Well** near park headquarters, $6. (After mid-September, when

Captain Jack's Stronghold

the park service turns off campground water to prevent frozen pipes, camping here is free—and campers can carry water from headquarters.) Plague warnings are sometimes posted, so think twice before bringing pets and stay away from rodents and other wild animals. Day-use fee for Lava Beds is $3.

Freestyle camping in nearby national forest areas is free (permit necessary for motorized vehicles). A quiet meadow campground is at **Howard's Gulch,** 30 miles south on Hwy. 39 (free). Or camp at the **Medicine Lake Highlands** area to the south, reached via 20 miles of gravel road. The town of Tulelake is not much of a destination—boarded-up storefronts in a summertime dustbowl and cold as frozen tule lakes in winter. But if you're bone-tired or just sick of the great outdoors, here are motels. For special fun, come to Tulelake's big fair in September.

Information, Getting There

For basic information and a map, contact **Lava Beds National Monument** headquarters, P.O. Box 867, Tulelake 96134, tel. (916) 667-2283. Free publications include plant and animal species checklists, a pamphlet about Captain Jack's Stronghold, and leaflets on rock art and local geology. At park headquarters at Indian Well (reached most easily via the southeast entrance) there is a good selection of books on the area and its history plus cultural and historical exhibits. Pick up a copy of *Lava Beds Underground,* which has detailed diagrams of all caves open to the public.

During summer (mid-June to Labor Day), campfire programs are offered in the evenings. During the day, an orientation program and film are offered at the visitor center, and a ranger-led cave trip is scheduled daily. From Tulelake, the park's northeast entrance is about eight miles away. The Lava Beds' southeast entrance is 30 miles south of Tulelake (or 58 miles from Klamath Falls) on Hwy. 139 then Tionesta Rd. (follow the signs from the highway). From Canby via 139, the park's southern entrance is 47 miles. Major airlines serve Medford and Klamath Falls, where rental cars are available.

Medicine Lake Highlands

About 14 miles south of the monument by gravel road, the Medicine Lake region truly qualifies for the "lunar landscape" label so often used to describe volcanic areas. In 1965, astronauts from the Manned Spacecraft Center in Texas came here to study the highlands in preparation for the first moon landing. The rumble of earthquakes beneath Medicine Lake in late 1988 has also attracted the attention of geologists, who believe an eruption from one of the state's most powerful volcanoes is due. Snows close this national forest area for general use from November to mid-June (though the popular "trail" from Mammoth Crater provides 26-mile roundtrip off-season access for cross-country skiers and snowmobilers). **Medicine Lake,** deep crystal-blue water fringed with lodgepole pines in an old volcanic crater, has sandy beaches, good swimming, picnicking, and camping. The area also offers good birding opportunities, good fishing, and water-skiing. "Big medicine" rites were held here, by various Native American peoples.

Above the lake is the black jumble of **Burnt Lava Flow,** a "virgin area" because virgin forests form islands within these 14 square miles of very young (300-500 years old) lava. Five miles northeast just off Medicine Lake Rd. is **Medicine Lake Glass Flow,** a square mile of stone-gray dacite formations from 50-150 feet tall. **Glass Mountain** is a 1,400-year-old flow of black obsidian and glassy dacite, ending suddenly in a stark contrast of white pumice. Pumice rock is so light an average person could toss huge boulders with ease. (But don't: all of the area's natural features and any artifacts or archaeological sites within the area are protected.)

Wear proper shoes and be careful here. Native peoples used these flint-edged obsidian stones for making arrowheads, and a fall can cause puncture wounds and lacerations. If all this close-up volcanism isn't enough, the panoramic view of the Cascades and the Modoc Plateau from the seldom-used lookout tower on Mt. Hoffman is worth a little huffing and puffing.

There are three developed camping areas at Medicine Lake (elev. 6,700 feet) with a total of 72 sites: **Hemlock, Medicine Camp** and **Headquarters.** All campgrounds close by Oct. 15. (To get away from it all, head to **Bullseye Lake, Blanche Lake,** or **Paynes Springs,** campfire permits required.) For Medicine Lake information and permits, contact the **Doublehead Ranger District Office** of Modoc National Forest, P.O. Box 818, Tulelake 96134, tel. (916) 667-2246, or

Modoc National Forest headquarters in Alturas. The **McCloud Ranger District Office,** tel. 964-2184, handles all camping inquiries.

THE KLAMATH BASIN WILDLIFE REFUGES

The Klamath Basin was once an almost endless expanse of shallow lakes and marshes. But things have changed: reclamation has vastly diminished the region's wetlands, and the onetime autumn bird population of six million or more has been reduced to one million. But the area is still one of the top 12 birding spots in the nation.

Birdwatching

Since hunting is as close to big business as Tulelake and like towns ever get, birdwatchers aren't as popular as hunters in these parts. Be that as it may, come here to birdwatch. Spring (early March through early May) is good for birders, but fall is the best—phenomenal, in fact; this is when the largest concentration of migrating waterfowl in North America can be seen. At both Lower Klamath and Tule lakes, most famous for bird populations, the best observation blind is your car (while traveling the dike-road tour routes), but canoe routes at Upper Klamath and Tule lakes offer the chance (best from spring to fall) to get up-close and personal.

The Klamath Basin National Wildlife Refuges include six separate refuge areas. Farthest north is the **Klamath Forest** area; also in Oregon, just south of Crater Lake and north of Klamath Falls, is the **Upper Klamath.** Newest, established in 1978, is the **Bear Valley** refuge between the Oregon towns of Keno and Worden, winter nighttime roosting area for bald eagles. Straddling the California-Oregon border is the large **Lower Klamath** refuge, the first U.S. waterfowl refuge, created by President Teddy Roosevelt in 1908. Just east are the **Tule Lake** and **Clear Lake** refuge areas.

Between 70-80% of the birds on the Pacific Flyway come together here, more than 250 species. Among them: snow, white-fronted, cackling, Canada, and Ross geese; avocets and egrets, swans and sandhill cranes; grebes and herons; pelicans, ospreys, and eagles. In addition, ducks abound. Redhead, gadwall, cinnamon teal and canvasback, shoveler, mallard, and pintail ducks nest near the lakes, with tens of thousands of ducklings hatched each year. (The duck population usually peaks in late October, geese two to three weeks later.) Besides wintering bald eagles and hawks, many shorebirds, songbirds, falcons, and owls can also be spotted here.

The cold dead of winter, when the lakes freeze over and ice forms on the tules, is the peak time for observing hundreds of migrating American bald eagles, the largest population on the North American continent outside Alaska. Though bald eagles are present year-round, in winter hundreds may be spotted in one place, usually congregating around unfrozen patches of ice on the lakes. Access restrictions to protect bird populations (Upper Klamath, for example, is closed from spring through fall) vary from refuge to refuge.

Another spot with sometimes excellent, easy opportunities for observing migrants, especially geese, is the state's **Ash Creek Wildlife Area** in Big Valley Marsh near Bieber, east of town then north three miles on the Bieber-Lookout Highway. For information on the Big Valley area, contact the **Adin Chamber of Commerce,** P.O. Box 327, Adin 96006, and the **Bieber Chamber of Commerce,** P.O. Box 452, Bieber 96009.

Information

The Klamath Basin refuges are open to the public during daylight hours only. Birders, bring warm (and water-resistant) clothing, comfortable walking shoes, extra wool socks, binoculars. For current information about refuge access and the natural rhythms of bird migration, contact: **Klamath Basin National Wildlife Refuges,** Route 1, Box 74, Tulelake 96134, tel. (916) 667-2231. The **visitor center** at refuge headquarters (at the Tule Lake reserve, reached via Hill Rd. from Hwy. 61 or from Lava Beds National Monument) has excellent wildlife exhibits and a museum, also information on birding, hunting, upcoming events, and road and weather conditions. Ask for information on the annual **Bald Eagle Conference,** a three-day celebration (usually in mid-February) of field trips, photography workshops, and speakers sponsored by the Audubon Society at the Oregon Institute of Technology in Klamath Falls.

THE WARNER MOUNTAINS

The Warner Mountains were named for William H. Warner, who was killed here by Paiutes while mapping the upper reaches of the Pit River. Widespread lava flows containing quartz crystals (now called Warner basalt) oozed up from the earth several million years ago and covered much of the Modoc Plateau. The later Warner Mountains, a remote spur of the Cascades but technically part of the plateau, are typical of ranges in the Great Basin that are "fault-bounded." As a result of double faulting, the mountains rose and Surprise Valley dropped. Pine forests, clear blue glacial lakes, and good fishing streams are characteristic of the Warners at higher elevations, with chaparral and juniper below. Most of the Warner Range is included in Modoc National Forest, which also contains the South Warner Wilderness Area. Eagle Peak is almost 10,000 feet tall, but most of the range stands at half that height—a green, gently rolling highland area wonderful for walking.

THE SOUTH WARNER WILDERNESS

The South Warner Wilderness Area is possibly the finest summer hiking spot in the state: 70,000 acres of streams, natural springs, some small lakes, and very few people. On the flat-topped ridge, there are relatively few trails. The trail along the narrow crest offers awesome views of sunken Surprise Valley and Nevada to the east, the entire Modoc Plateau to the west, and Mt. Shasta beyond. In the Warners are exotic Cascade wildflowers plus more typical summer blooms: buttercups, monkeyflowers, paintbrush, shooting stars. Bighorn sheep are making a comeback here after being hunted nearly to extinction during the last century, and pronghorn, coyote, raccoons, beavers, even wide-ranging mustangs are fairly common. Bald and golden eagles, ospreys, and hawks soar overhead; seabirds including gulls and terns are common.

The Summit Trail

The Summit Trail is 26 miles long, easy walking along the mountains' crest and especially scenic along the trailhead to the cirque lake. The trail is an ideal introduction to the Warners and perfect for a weekend backpack. (A longer loop around to the east, coming or going via North Owl Creek and other trails, is also possible for a longer backpack.) Hiking from the south, the trail (sometimes vague and marked by cairns) winds up to the summit through white fir then levels off, with splendid views on both sides. As you walk, avoid disturbing the vegetation and

Modoc country, looking east to the South Warner Wilderness

KIM WEIR

other features of this delicate tundra area. Dark basalt flows, tilting westward, created the immense cliffs along the way.

Within the state game refuge are lovely campsites down below, along a spring-fed creek near the trail. Or, continue to the Patterson Lake area: fishing here is usually excellent, particularly for brook, brown, and rainbow trout. (The first reliable water source, a tasty spring, is at Pepperdine near Porter Reservoir, about 4½ miles past this point.) From here, you can veer to the west and follow the official trail or descend via switchbacks on the Squaw Peak connector trail, crossing the lake's outlet a few times and also Cottonwood Creek below the spectacular falls. Then, heading north, skirt the east side of 8,646-foot Squaw Peak before reconnecting with the Summit Trail at Pepperdine.

To reach the north end of the Summit Trail from Alturas, head east on Road 56. Then, a half mile after it becomes good dirt road, turn left at the Pepperdine-Parker Creek sign onto Parker Creek Rd., continuing another seven miles to the trailhead sign. Turn right and go another two miles. You can park your car here or (if you can make it up the rocky, steep road) car-camp farther up before heading out the next morning. The trailhead in the clearing is just past the campground. Reach the southern end of Summit Trail from Likely in the south: turn right on Jess Valley Rd., travel past Jess Valley on West Warner Rd. to Mill Creek Springs then follow the trails from here to Summit.

Other Sights, Trails, Trailheads, Camping

From **Blue Lake Campground** in the southwest (the only wilderness campground with paved road access and the only one with a camping fee), the **Blue Lake National Recreation Trail** circles west and around the lake's perimeter. Farther north are beautiful **Mill Creek Falls** and **Clear Lake** above the **Mill Creek Campground**, also the **Poison Flat/Mill Creek Trailhead** and the **Soup Spring Campground** at the **Slide Creek** trailhead. From the north, **Summit Trail** is reached from the **Pepperdine Pack Station** and **Porter Reservoir Area.** Tiny **Emerson** and **Patterson campgrounds,** reached via dirt or gravel roads from south of Eagleville, offer steeper access to South Warner Wilderness trails.

Warner Practicalities

Hiking and backpacking is best from late June to Labor Day, with peak wildflowers in late July and August. When exploring the remote Warners, bring water or water-purification tablets and a backpacking stove and fuel, since firewood is in short supply. Also bring a topo map and good compass; trails sometimes seem to disappear. Otherwise, come prepared for anything.

Predictable for the South Warner Wilderness is its unpredictable weather, with freezing temperatures, thunderstorms, and brutal winds possible anytime, though less likely in July and August. Wilderness permits are necessary for backcountry camping. Camp away from moist meadow areas and well away from streams and lakes and, as always, if you pack it in, pack it out. Summer lightning storms are possible; if lightning bolts strike, seek shelter in low forested areas or between rocks in boulder jumbles, *never* in open areas near an isolated boulder or tree.

For wilderness permits and more information, including forest, wilderness, and trail maps, contact **Modoc National Forest** headquarters, 441 N. Main St., P.O. Box 661, Alturas 96101, tel. (916) 233-5811, or Modoc's **Warner Mountain Ranger District** just one block north and west of the main intersection in Cedarville, the eastern slope's main town, P.O. Box 220, Cedarville 96104, tel. 279-6116. Wilderness maps and Modoc National Forest maps are $3 each. Winter activities in the South Warners are limited, but snowshoeing, cross-country skiing, and ice fishing at Clear Lake are becoming popular.

ALTURAS

With several thousand people, a few restaurants and motels, and the county's only two traffic lights, Alturas is the biggest city around. Part of the dry, sparsely vegetated landscape in the western shadow of the Warners, Alturas is predictably hot in summer and cold in winter. The roads in town weren't even paved until 1931, about the same time talking pictures came. There are some crotchety old buildings—the **Elks Hall** at 619 N. Main, one-time headquarters of the old Narrow, Cantankerous, and Ornery Railroad, is now on the National Register of Historic Places—and a fine new museum, but the center of social life is the wild and woolly Old

West **Niles Hotel** and saloon on Main St., a museum in its own right and the most popular restaurant in Alturas.

Area Sights

Pick up a free Alturas **historic tour** guide and Modoc County historic homes brochure at the local chamber office. (Striking at first glance is the archaic **Sears Roebuck and Co.** mail-order storefront at Main and Carlos near the Niles Hotel.) Next door to the chamber is the **Modoc County Museum** in a new building at 600 S. Main St., tel. (916) 233-2944, housing 400 firearms and other antiquities; a collection of arrowheads, knives, spears; 500 woven baskets and other Native American artifacts; photo and oral history archives. Open May through October (and two weeks at Christmas).

The **Modoc National Wildlife Refuge** extends for miles along Hwy. 395 south of Alturas, with access via county roads 56 then 115. Part and parcel of the semiarid landscape surrounding Dorris Reservoir and open during daylight hours March-Sept., the refuge hosts migrating waterfowl in fall and spring and is a major summer nesting area. Birdwatching is especially good near headquarters, where a general map/guide, bird list, and hunting brochures are available. For more information, contact: Modoc National Wildlife Refuge, P.O. Box 1610, Alturas 96101, tel. (916) 233-3572.

Area Accommodations

No nearby public campgrounds, but there is a **KOA** in town on Hwy. 395 North, tel. (916) 233-4185, complete with laundromat, hot showers, pool, handball court. **Cedar Pass Campground** at Cedar Pass (12 miles northeast of Alturas) is free, as is **Stough Reservoir Campground** a few miles farther east. There are inexpensive motels in Alturas, among them, the **Drifter's Inn** on Hwy. 395, tel. 233-2428. The **Dunes Motel,** 511 N. Main, tel. 233-3545, has rooms from $35. The **Best Western Trailside Inn,** 343 N. Main, tel. 233-4111, has similar prices, a few units with kitchens. The **Dorris House** bed and breakfast on Parker Creek Rd., P.O. Box 1655, Alturas 96101, tel. 233-3786, borders the Modoc wildlife refuge on the shores of Dorris Reservoir (and even offers accommodations for horses), rooms $45. Inexpensive rooms are available about 15 miles west of Alturas at the

Canby Hotel and Trading Co., Canby 96015, tel. 233-4841, also a restaurant ("home of the world famous Modoc Burger") and antique store.

Alturas Eateries

Alturas has fast food restaurants and coffee shops, but good for Basque food is the **Brass Rail** restaurant on Lakeview Hwy. (Hwy. 299 a few blocks east of the intersection with Hwy. 395), tel. (916) 233-2906. Locals highly recommend the **Niles Hotel and Saloon,** 304 S. Main, tel. 233-3411, for American fare, open for lunch Wed.-Fri. only but dinners served nightly. Good meat-and-potatoes meals; the window displays and posters plastered on the streetside, whitewashed walls invite people to a veritable Buffalo Bill Cody Wild West Show—hardly false advertising, in this case. *Don't* miss the saloon. (Rooms are also available at the Niles.) For special lunches and dinners, also breakfast on weekends, head to the northern end of Surprise Valley and the surprisingly good **Fort Bidwell Hotel and Restaurant** (a bed and breakfast and cozy eatery).

Information

For information about accommodations and sights, the **Modoc County Chamber of Commerce** is at 522 S. Main St. next to the historical society museum, tel. (916) 233-2819. Open 9-5 weekdays. The **Modoc National Forest,** almost two million acres of volcanic plateaus, lakes, and mountains, offers recreational opportunities for hikers, backpackers, hunters, photographers, and rockhounds. Most campgrounds are free, as are picnic areas. Headquarters are at 441 N. Main St., P.O. Box 611, Alturas 96101, tel. 233-3521 and 233-5811. (Modoc ranger district offices are also in Adin, tel. 299-3215; Canby, tel. 233-4611; Tulelake, tel. 667-2246; and Cedarville, tel. 279-6116.) Available publications include forest and off-road vehicle maps, camping and recreation listings, and brochures/maps for Modoc National Forest, the South Warner Wilderness, and the Medicine Lake Highlands areas. Very helpful and friendly staff.

Events

This is cowboy country, and most of what goes on is predictably *country*. The annual summer **Modoc Trail Ride,** for example, is one of the state's biggest and best. The **Warner Mountain Roundup,** a professional rodeo in June at the county fairgrounds in Cedarville, is a good opportunity to taste good barbecue and the dust of ranch life. Other events include summer-long open roping competitions, **Fandango Days** celebrated on July 4, and the **Modoc District Fair** during the last week in August.

VICINITY OF ALTURAS

Goose Lake is the biggest among several clustered on both sides of Hwy. 395 north of Alturas near Oregon: high mountain conifers, abundant game and fish, few people. **Cave** and **Lily lakes** are pristine, reached via the **Highgrade National Recreation Trail** (rough road), with good rainbow and eastern brook-trout fishing.

Cedar Pass Ski Area
Friendly and fun for Alpine and Nordic skiers, this small day-use ski area 20 miles northeast of Alturas near Cedar Pass has a bunny hill for beginners, T-bar lifts to more challenging downhill runs, and cross-country skiing (one-way) on groomed tracks or through uncharted areas. Snowboarding is okay. For more information, contact: Cedar Pass, Box 162, Alturas 96101, tel. (916) 233-2723.

Surprise Valley
The farthest reaches of outback California. It's a surprise this place is even here, a rich little valley on the parched eastern side of the Warners, with Nevada's Hayes Canyon to the east. Surprise Valley is about 70 miles long and 10 miles wide with an average elevation of 4,700 feet. The valley is an agricultural area, producing mostly cattle and alfalfa; the alfalfa seed grown here produces hay exceptionally high in protein. The entire area was once submerged under a small sea now reduced to three alkaline lakes. From the valley, don't plan on zipping into Nevada via Hwy. 299: the businesslike paved road dries up in the desert just across the border.

Cedarville And Vicinity
Except for pickup trucks, the gas station, and the one pay phone, Cedarville could inhabit the 19th century: Rangeland, USA. The town's sleepy facade is shattered only on Saturday nights,

when ranch hands come from miles around to quench their thirst at local watering holes. Tiny **Sunrise Motel** three miles east of the Cedar Pass ski hill on the highway, tel. (916) 279-2161, is just about the only place to stay; rooms $25 d and up. **Don's Valley Burger** across Hwy. 20 from the gas station, tel. 279-6301, is open seven days a week, but most locals eat at **Ila's Kitchen** on Main St., tel. 279-2157. **Eagleville,** 15 miles south of Cedarville, was named for the Warners' Eagle Peak soaring above. It's a sleepy collection of aging farm-country wood frames, a handful of homes, general store, and livestock loading chutes. Just a few miles south, across the road from the turnoff to Middle Fork Spring and Patterson, is **Menlo Baths,** a hot springs area on private land (often used by locals).

Fort Bidwell
The farthest northeast town in the far northeastern corner of California, Fort Bidwell was named after Chico's General John Bidwell, who never saw or visited the area but was the territory's most prominent citizen in the mid-1800s. Get here from Cedarville via Hwy. 20, or drive east over the Fandango Pass Rd. (dirt) to Surprise Valley then head north. Built in 1865, Fort Bidwell was first an important military post protecting settlers from Indian attacks and later converted into an Indian school. The fort's only original building still standing is the hospital, but fascinating is the 100-year-old **Fort Bidwell General Store** just a block off Main, something of a museum and the town's unofficial information center. Also off the beaten track is the small wood frame **Fort Bidwell Hotel and Restaurant,** actually a bed and breakfast on Main and Garrison streets, Fort Bidwell 96112, tel. (916) 279-6199. Rooms run $33-50, including breakfast, but meals alone (seafood and American food) are worth stopping for. Dinners are served Thurs.-Sun. nights, breakfast and lunch on Sat. and Sun. only. (Ask about the Overnight Special.) After eating, consider a soak in the **Fort Bidwell Hot Springs** just outside of town. **Fee Reservoir,** just to the east of Fort Bidwell, is noted for its large rainbow trout.

Hot Springs
There are several private hot springs in this area. Heading seven miles east of Cedarville, take the dirt road north; four miles ahead is the

remnant of **Leonard Hot Springs,** once a resort known as Kelley Hot Springs, with primitive pools and a natural underground spring. Just two miles farther is **Glen Hot Springs,** shallow pools on the east side of Upper Alkali Lake. No facilities, no address, no phone, no fax machines, no restrictions, no worries. For more information about regional and area hot springs, stop by or call the Cedarville ranger station, tel. (916) 279-6116.

BOB RACE

THE SIERRA NEVADA

INTRODUCTION

Though the many ancient peoples who once shared California's vast Sierra Nevada territory would surely be puzzled by his comparative historical prominence, John Muir has become California's preeminent mountain man. Long before his fame as freedom fighter for the wilderness and Great White Father of the modern American conservationist ethic, Muir began to act on his then-heretical belief that the orderly beauty of nature was the highest revelation of the One Mind. Unyoked from his heavy sense of social duty by an industrial accident that temporarily blinded him, Muir finally set out to see God. His decade-long, 19th-century wanderings led him to the Sierra Nevada's "sunbursts of morning among the icy peaks," to its "noonday radiance on the trees and rocks and snow," and to its "thousand dancing waterfalls." But the solitary naturalist (also a Civil War draft dodger) renamed the mountains even before personally meeting them, looking upwards from Pacheco Pass. "Then it seemed to me the Sierra should be called not the Nevada, or Snowy Range, but the Range of Light. . . . the most divinely beautiful of all the mountain chains I have ever seen."

The young run-amok Mark Twain, too, was smitten with these mountains and their magic: "Three months of camp life on Lake Tahoe would restore an Egyptian mummy to his pristine vigor, and give him an appetite like an alligator," he wrote. "The air up there in the clouds is very pure and fine, bracing and delicious . . . the same the angels breathe."

Yet something about his experience in this near-vertical expanse of the Old West upset Twain's sense of common humanity. Covering his contempt for Indians with the acceptable sanctimony of the day—"If we cannot find it in our hearts to give these poor naked creatures our Christian sympathy and compassion, in God's name let us at least not throw mud at them"—he himself flung invective with both hands. In *Roughing It,* Twain rejected the "mellow moonshine of romance" about noble red men, whom he found "treacherous, filthy, and repulsive." And though he derided one tribe in particular in his racist tirade, he managed, by inference, to include all Native Americans. His views reflect perfectly the prejudices of his time—precursors to the cultural cataclysm that occurred when gold seekers and settlers swept into California:

> [They are] a silent, sneaking, treacherous look-ing race; taking note of everything, covertly . . . and betraying no sign in their countenances; indolent, everlastingly patient and tireless. . . . prideless beggars—for if the beggar instinct were left out of an Indian he would not "go," any more than a clock without a pendulum; hungry, always hungry, and yet never refusing anything that a hog would eat, though often eating what a hog would decline; hunters, but having no higher ambition than to kill and eat jackass rabbits, crickets and grasshop-pers, and embezzle carrion from the buzzards and cayotes [sic]; savages who, when asked if they have a common Indian belief in a Great Spirit, show a something which almost amounts to emotion, thinking whiskey is re-ferred to. . . .

Cataclysm or no, the Old Spirits, some of the Old Ways, even some of the Old Ones survive still in the secrecy of lost and lonely places. And among the survivors, there are now new tradi-tions. Followers of the Tipi Way, scattered mem-bers of the Washoe Nation from the eastern slopes of the Sierra Nevada, worship the Great Spirit and seek collective salvation with the rel-atively new sacrament of the Medicine (hallu-cinogenic peyote buttons), a religious practice first borrowed from the Paiute people in the 1920s and '30s. Warren L. Azevedo's *Straight with the Medicine: Narratives of Washoe Fol-lowers of the Tipi Way* shares the truth about these survivors' spiritual depth:

> How can an Indian pray like a white man? The white man gets his prayers out of books . . . old books about things maybe thousands of years ago. He don't even have to think about it. He just says it and it is supposed to do him some good. He can be a drunk bum for a long

time, do all kinds of no good thing, think all kinds of bad thoughts about people. But then he can walk right into that Church and pray one of them prayers and he gets away with it. Anybody can go into them Churches anytime and walk out without anything happening to him. . . .

> The way a man sing shows you what kind of person he is. If he sings good, he can help people. His song goes through them and the Medicine is working. Singing is like praying . . . it's the same thing. When we sing here it is for a reason. . . . So when I sing, it ain't like on the radio or to pass the time. I'm trying to get myself up good as I can. I don't just sing a song . . . I'm taking a trip. When I'm singing I'm praying in the Tipi and going on that trip over that Road.

Many who visit California's astounding Sierra Nevada come for essentially the same purpose: to take a dose of the mountains' Medicine, to sing praises to the spirits, to get "up good as I can," to embark on a seriously joyous trip.

THE LAND: CARVED BY FIRE AND ICE

A massive block of granite some 450 miles long and 60 to 80 miles wide, the Sierra Nevada range starts in the north, just south of Lassen Peak, shimmies down to the southeast toward Walker Pass east of Bakersfield, then dribbles off into the desert where it meets the Tehachapis. Tilting gracefully to the west, the range's under-lying rock foundation gives the broad western side its very gradual slope. Most of the moun-tains' drama is reserved for the eastern ascent—where spectacular peaks rise in dizzying de-grees from the flat high-desert plateaus—and for the range's craggy high country, natural an-archistic architecture of the highest order.

From average elevations of 6,000-8,000 feet near the Feather River in the north, Sierra Neva-da summits increase in altitude toward Yosemite, Sequoia, and Kings Canyon national parks. Mount Whitney, the tallest mountain in the continental U.S. (excluding Alaska) and the

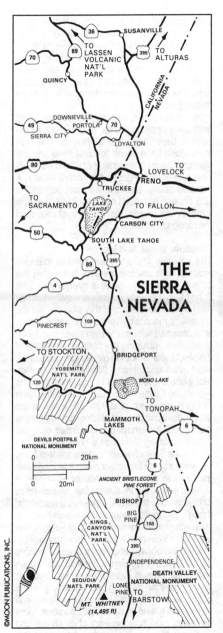

THE SIERRA NEVADA

©MOON PUBLICATIONS, INC.

range's triumph, pierces the sky at 14,495 feet. Near Mt. Whitney almost a dozen other peaks stand taller than 14,000 feet, and more than 500 throughout the Sierra Nevada exceed 12,000 feet. But the High Sierra, technically speaking, refers to the 150-mile-long, 20-mile-wide stretch of near-naked glaciated granite peaks, icy blue alpine lakes, and relatively level highlands above treeline from just north of Yosemite south to Cottonwood Pass.

Creation: Fire And Earth

The calm, cool facade of the Sierra Nevada range almost succeeds in hiding the region's deep fiery nature—almost, but not quite. Ancient calderas, old volcanic rock formations (basalt and andesite), young volcanoes, and quite contemporary earthquakes and hot springs—all common throughout the eastern Sierra—verify the fire below. Some say the region's abundant hot springs are evidence of decreasing volcanic vigor along the eastern Sierra Nevada; others suggest that the earth's fire is merely sleeping.

Though the greenstone, marble, and slate common to westerly foothills are some 200 million years old, these early, well-eroded formations sank and were submerged by the sea during the late Paleozoic era. After eons of Mesozoic underwater sedimentation and sporadic volanic activity (creating marine sediment layers interspersed with solidified lava flows), pressure from the superheated magma swirling below pushed these heat-hardened rocks upwards in folds, creating the general outlines of today's mountain ridges and valleys.

Not yet finished with the Sierra Nevada, the earth's volcanic violence surged forth again starting 100 million years ago during the Cretaceous period and "injected" molten granite under, into, and around the undulating rock formations on the surface. These massive granite intrusions were gradually exposed and "peeled" by the erosive forces of nature, creating the granitic domes characteristic of the High Sierra. Found few other places in the world, the best examples of these rounded and unjointed rock formations crop up in the Yosemite region—among them, awesome and enormous Half Dome, which dominates Yosemite Valley's eastern end.

WES DEMPSEY

Like other Sierra Nevada regions, Yosemite Valley was carved and polished by glaciers.

Granite intrusion is also responsible for the Sierra Nevada's mineral wealth. As the hot rock boiled and bubbled up through the earth's crust, it became "contaminated" and transformed by liquified concentrations of surrounding minerals. Mountain and foothill deposits of gold, copper, tungsten, aluminum, and other valued minerals have all caused some excitement during the course of California history. But in 1986, the discovery of a previously uncharted, 150-mile-long band of tungsten-rich "true granite" on the western slopes of the Sierra Nevada created a stir among geologists, challenging earlier assumptions about granite formation as well as the accepted simplicity of the Sierra Nevada's creation.

The embryonic mountains were still gently rolling and covered in deep clays when erosion began to expose the range's underlying rock formations. But during the Eocene Epoch some 60-70 million years ago, California's coast ranges "folded up" into existence and the Sierra Nevada tilted to the west. Another long period of mountain uplift followed until, about 12 million years ago, the eastern mountains had reached a height of 3,000 feet above sea level. Toward the end of the Pliocene Epoch the Sierra Nevada's most dramatic and final upward surge took place. Most of the glacial scouring and earthquake faulting responsible for the range's spectacular scenery occurred during the past one million years.

In modern times, a very active 400-mile-long fault zone shakes, rattles, and rolls along the eastern base of the Sierra Nevada. The area from Mono Lake south to Lone Pine and the now dry Owens Lake area (parallel to Mt. Whitney) has been hardest hit in recent history. A massive quake, perhaps the most powerful in U.S. history, flattened Lone Pine in 1872 and, in a matter of seconds, elevated a vast section of the range by 13 feet.

Creation: Water And Ice

The creative fire underlying these massive mountains is usually unseen, but water, the other great shaping force, is everywhere. Like John Muir, everyday mortals are overwhelmed here by the aesthetics of this elixer of life the crystalline mountain rivers and streams, waterfalls crowned with misty rainbows, and 1,500 or so lakes (including the breathtaking "lake of the sky," Lake Tahoe) in glacier-ground basins. Most rivers and streams flow to the southwest. Many of the west side's 11 major river systems —from the Feather and Yuba rivers in the north to the Kings, Kern, and Kaweah rivers in the south—flow first through glacier-scoured gorges then through V-shaped unglaciated canyons before reaching California's great central valley. On the Sierra Nevada's steep eastern flank, the waters of the few major rivers—among them the Truckee, Carson, and Walker—fly downhill in liquid freefall before settling into alkaline lakes or drying up in the desert. Dramatic waterfalls, though, are more common in western river valleys with glacier-created "hanging valleys," especially in Yosemite National Park and vicinity.

Over the eons, water has played its erosive part in shaping the Sierra Nevada, but frozen water has exerted even more power. Seeping into cracks then freezing and expanding, veins of ice eventually break boulders down into stones and gravel- or sand-sized particles. More dramatic, though, is the work of ice sheets and glaciers, which—as they accumulate rock debris on their downslope route—slowly gouge and scour the landscape. During three separate periods of the ice age or Pleistocene Epoch until about 10,000 years ago, glaciers and ice fields worked hardest, particularly in the area from Lake Tahoe to Yosemite. The magnificent U-shaped Yosemite Valley is perhaps the most dramatic example of nature's persistent, always-unfinished sculpture.

Climate

Sierra Nevada weather patterns are dictated by the land; the region's wide latitude and altitude shifts, in addition to local landforms, create innumerable distinct microclimates. To *really* find out about local weather, ask locals.

The range's usually impressive snowpack starts to melt during April and May, and in general, summer is springtime in the Sierra Nevada—those few short months when snow flows as water and snow melt turns mountain meadows into marshy bogs thick with wildflowers. Summer temperatures are relatively cool (often cold at night), especially at higher elevations, but locally variable. Though little rain falls during the summer, sudden thunderstorms and occasional freak snow flurries aren't that unusual, especially at higher elevations. Be prepared for anything.

Following the frosty temperatures and flaming colors of fall, winter settles in to stay, often into May. Most precipitation (rain and snow) falls from January through March, though early and late major storms can close many Sierra Neva-da passes from Labor Day through Memorial Day. Especially in low precipitation years, cloud-seeding is a fairly common practice in various Sierra Nevada watersheds, to increase the annual snowpack and to fatten up downslope reservoirs. Naturally or otherwise, most rain and snow falls on the range's western slopes—the amount increasing with altitude until about 6,500 feet, then decreasing dramatically on eastern slopes, the Sierra Nevada "rainshadow." Latitude also influences precipitation patterns, with substantially more rain and snow falling in northern and central regions than in the south.

SIERRA FLORA

Late spring and summer is wildflower season, when unusual and unusually delicate plants peek up from forest duff and marshy meadows. Though visitor centers in the national parks and elsewhere offer various good localized natural history guides, one of the better books for Sierra Nevada wildflower identification is *California Mountain Wildflowers* by Philip A. Munz, coauthor of *A California Flora,* the botanists' bible and ultimate key to all California plantlife.

Like wildflowers, Sierra Nevada trees and shrubs thrive in fairly specific environments. Though regional plant distribution depends on altitude and latitude, other local environmental factors (such as availability of water and sunlight, soil type, and whether or not a particular place is

Tree sniffers along the trail: one way to distinguish among types of pines in the Sierra Nevada boreal belt is by smelling the aromatic tree bark.

KIM WEIR

on a north- or south-facing slope) also influence the development of plant communities. In general, though, chaparral and drought-adapted digger pines and oaks dominate the vegetation of the Sierra Nevada's lower western slopes, from elevations of 500 to 5,000 feet (the range generally lower in the north, higher in the south). Next in the vertical progression of plant life comes the transition zone (and predominant timber region) of yellow and sugar pines, Douglas and white firs, incense cedar, and various broadleaf trees such as cottonwoods, oaks and maples—a broad botanical band ranging from 1,200 feet in the north to nearly 9,000 feet in the southern Sierra Nevada.

Still higher is the lower boreal belt so popular with winter sports fans, characterized by lodgepole pines and red firs but also home to Jeffrey and silver pines, Sierra junipers, aspens, and various mountain chaparral shrubs. (On the range's drier eastern slopes, this zone may consist primarily of Jeffrey pines with scattered drought- and snow-adapted species typical of the higher "sagebrush belt": Utah juniper and mountain mahogany.)

Higher still comes the Sierra Nevada's subalpine belt, an area with heavy snow and long, severe winters "above timberline," where some lodgepole, whitebark, and foxtail pines grow (often in beautifully contorted and weather-twisted forms) in the company of mountain hemlock and heathers. In alpine areas, where slopes and summits are typically bare of vegetation, one dwarfed but sturdy survivor is the alpine willow, which branches out along the ground. Unique in the White Mountains southeast of Mono Lake are specimens of the world's oldest living things —the Great Basin's ragged and rugged bristlecone pines—including the Methuselah Tree, estimated to be over 4,600 years old.

Sierra Big Trees

Also ancient and unique is the Sierra Nevada's "big tree" or *Sequoiadendron giganteum*, a species of redwood quite distinct from California's coastal redwoods and surviving in substantial numbers only in Yosemite and neighboring national parks and at Calaveras Big Trees State Park. Also called giant sequoias, these massive forest monarchs are botanical dinosaurs, living relics that first evolved some 160 million years ago—15,000 times older than

A THREATENED NATURAL COMMUNITY

Though plant and animal life is, to some extent, naturally adapted to forest fires, they are nonetheless a hazard to mountain ecosystems. California's success in controlling all types of forest fires to protect lumber, residential, and recreational lands has allowed unnatural quantities of tinder-dry forest duff and deadwood to accumulate throughout the Sierra Nevada. As a result, when fires do occur, they're devastating—burning too high and too hot for most fire-adapted trees to survive. And in the wake of major mountain fires, no to mention clearcutting and other controversial forestry practices, soil erosion and downslope flooding become serious problems as well.

But it would be naive to assume that the wild granite-and-tree spirit of the Sierra Nevada, otherwise so far removed from city life, is unaffected by faraway humanity. Ozone pollution, a byproduct of automobiles and fossil fuel-burning industries, is a clear and present danger. More than half the trees in Yosemite National Park and more than 90% of those in nearby Sequoia and Kings Canyon national parks have been damaged by high concentrations of ozone in the air. Acid rain and acid snow are other human-caused plant predators, and these are now affecting the Sierra Nevada's delicate lake ecosystems as well. And due to increasing evidence that salt sprinkled on Sierra highways is at least partially responsible for killing miles of roadside trees, Caltrans has rescinded its "bare pavement policy" in most areas; mountain travelers on winter roads must now stop and put chains on their vehicles much more frequently.

Not all damage to Sierra Nevada forests is directly due to human influence, however. Nearly all pines and cedars in and around Yosemite Valley will eventually die from root rot, while tussock moths (now being fought with bacterial sprays) and voracious beetles have taken their toll elsewhere, successfully attacking forests of trees weakened by drought and pollutants.

Yosemite Valley.

Sierra Nevada big trees are indeed big—so gigantic that few people can escape an overwhelming feeling of awe when looking (up) at them. The everyday, garden-variety giant sequoia measures 10 to 15 feet in diameter at maturity and stands some 250 feet tall. The true giants, including the most massive trio, the General Sherman, General Grant, and Boole trees in or near Sequoia and Kings Canyon national parks, are almost 30 feet across well above ground level. The lowest limb branching off from General Sherman is seven feet thick and would create a canopy for a 12-story office building. During California's pioneer past, people hollowed out big trees for cabins or barns. And though they live to a ripe old age (the oldest verified mature tree is about 3,200 years old), they also grow vigorously and rapidly throughout their life spans. Theoretically, Sierra big trees could live forever, but sooner or later, too-heavy winter snow and brutal winds topple otherwise healthy elders.

Adapted to fire, insect pests, and just about every other natural scourge, the Sierra Nevada big trees were not at first able to escape the saws of loggers. Not counting John Muir's advocacy on their behalf and the accompanying public out-

cry, one major difference between coast and mountain redwoods eventually saved the big trees' skins: the wood of the giant sequoia is brittle and weak. After a big tree is toppled—a task that once took four men sawing by hand up to a month to achieve—it tends to shatter. Though industrious lumber crews still managed to market giant sequoias as shingles, fenceposts, and such, the difficulty of felling big trees and hauling them off to lumbermills slowed the destruction of old-growth groves. Unfortunately, government protection of today's 70 surviving groves of Sierra Nevada sequoias still came too late to save most of California's ancient big trees.

SIERRA FAUNA

Since animals also require specific conditions in order to survive and thrive, the range of many species coincides with particular climates and types of vegetation. A wide variety of small mammals and birds thrives year-round throughout Sierra Nevada foothill areas, but seasonal migrants—including mule deer and black bears—are more common at lower elevations in winter; in summer, when the living is easier, they mosey back up into the wooded mountains. A fairly common predator, but nocturnal and rarely seen, is the ringtail or big-eyed civet cat, actually a small, sleek cousin of both raccoons and bears. Common, too, are raccoons and spotted and striped skunks, which also range at much higher elevations.

The Sierra Nevada's major timber zones provide food and shelter for larger mammals, including cougars, bobcats, foxes, coyotes, and the ever-busy beaver, whose handiwork can be found along mountain waterways. Native to the foothills, beavers are now considered "exotic" where found. Among other rodents common throughout the range's mid-elevations are the porcupine or "quill pig," northern flying squirrel, western gray squirrel, golden-mantled ground squirrel, chipmunk, woodrat, and various mice species. Rare is the nocturnal mountain beaver, which looks like a muskrat but has no tail.

Among birds common to Sierra Nevada mixed yellow pine forests are pygmy owls and rare spotted owls. (The latter have become targets for the wrath of lumber companies, since old-growth forests and the potential board-feet of

---

SIERRA BIGHORN SHEEP

The ragged beauty and rugged agility of Sierra bighorn sheep, John Muir's "animal mountaineers" and Native Americans' "white buffaloes," can still sometimes be appreciated firsthand by mountain visitors. Though bighorn hunting was banned in California in 1878, the law provided little real protection, and the state's native sheep population dropped off steadily until the 1970's, when High Sierra bighorn reserves were established and relocation efforts (so far only moderately successful) began in earnest. Now numbering in the hundreds, it seems possible that the Sierra bighorn sheep will be spared the fate of California's wolves and grizzly bears.

As alive, alert, and independently ingenious as domestic sheep are stupid and herd-bound, these magnificent creatures somehow take in stride whatever tough territory the Sierra Nevada offers. Bands of bachelor rams or small family groups of ewes and lambs, watched over by a wary old ram with massive curved horns, can be spotted in spring and summer, usually in remote and desolate terrain, scrambling up impossibly steep and unstable inclines or leaping across ravines.

GOING THE EASY WAY: GUIDED PACK TRIPS

For first-timers to the Sierra Nevada outback, or for those who will never warm up to the physical exertion necessary for backpacking and bicycling, a guided pack trip—far from cheap but very enjoyable—is the easy way to go. To cover the same territory backpackers do but without carrying the necessities of life oneself, **Mama's Llamas,** P.O. Box 655, El Dorado 95623, tel. (916) 622-2566, offers a variety of excellent Sierra Nevada pack trips, usually guided by experienced naturalists (including college professors). Some High Sierra packers offer similar burro trips and/or the option of packing in supplies at pre-arranged destinations and times, so backpackers can travel farther with a lighter load.

Most Sierra Nevada packers and guides operate (summer only) from major trailheads along the range's east side—the closest access to the highest high country. For a complete and current listing of reputable firms, contact: **Eastern High Sierra Packers Association,** c/o the Bishop Chamber of Commerce, 690 N. Main St., Bishop 93514, tel. (619) 873-8405, or contact the **Mammoth Lakes Visitors Bureau,** tel. (619) 934-2712 or toll-free (800) 367-6572. For a list of packers on the western slope, write Box 1362, Clovis 93613.

Some recommended packers: **Frontier Pack Train,** Box 18, Star Rt. 33, June Lakes 93529, tel. (619) 648-7701 (summer), 872-1301 (winter); **High Sierra Pack Station,** P.O. Box 1166, Clovis 93613,

tel. (209) 299-8297 (winter address and phone), Mono Hot Springs 93642 (summer address); **Kennedy Meadows Resort,** P.O. Box 4010, Sonora 95370, tel. (209) 532-9096; **Kennedy Meadows Pack Trains,** P.O. Box 61, Three Rivers 93271, tel. (209) 561-3404 in summer, 561-4142 in winter, under new management and offering short trips to the Kern Plateau, longer trips into Sequoia National Park and to Jordan Hot Springs; **Leavitt Meadows Pack Station,** P.O. Box 1244, Bridgeport 93517, tel. (702) 495-2257; and the **Little Antelope Pack Station,** P.O. Box 179, Coleville 96107, tel. (702) 782-4528 or 782-4960.

Other reputable Sierra Nevada packing companies include: **Mammoth Lakes Pack Outfit,** P.O. Box 61, Mammoth Lakes 93546, tel. (619) 934-2434; **McGee Creek Pack Station,** Rt. 1, Box 1622, Mammoth Lakes 93546, tel. (619) 935-4324 in summer, 878-2207 in winter; **Mt. Whitney Pack Trains,** P.O. Box 1514, Bishop 93515 (no phone); **Rainbow Creek Pack Outfit,** P.O. Box 1791, Bishop 93515, tel. (619) 873-8877; **Red's Meadow Pack Station,** P.O.Box 395, Mammoth Lakes 93546, tel. (619) 934-2345; **Rock Creek Pack Station,** P.O. Box 248, Bishop 93514, tel. (619) 872-8331 in winter, 935-4493 in summer; and the **Virginia Lakes Pack Outfit,** HC Route 1, P.O. Box 1076, Bridgeport 93517, tel. (702) 867-2591 in winter, (619) 932-7767 or 872-0271 in summer.

the easy way to see the Sierra Nevada on foot or horseback: letting the pack animals carry life's necessities

WES DEMPSEY

EDUCATIONAL ADVENTURES IN THE SIERRA NEVADA

Among the many groups in California offering educational experiences and seminars in the Sierra Nevada (primarily in summer), the University of California's **California Adventures,** 2301 Bancroft Ave., Berkeley 95724, tel. (415) 642-4000, specializes in backpacking and family-oriented natural history trips, also photography workshops in Yosemite. **Field Studies in Natural History,** San Jose State University, San Jose 95192, tel. (408) 277-3736, features natural history seminars in Sequoia National Park. **Natural Discoveries,** P.O. Box 2022, Mill Valley 94942, tel. (415) 331-3322, offers beginning and intermediate naturalist-led backpack trips into the central Sierra Nevada (spring and fall) and in the eastern Sierra (fall only).

Mama's Llamas (see "Going the Easy Way: Guided Pack Trips") also offers excursions with an environmental education emphasis.

The **Mono Lake Committee,** P.O. Box 29, Lee Vining 93541, tel. (619) 647-6386, sponsors summer naturalist-led tours (biology, birds, pioneer history), courses in photography and Paiute basket making, also weekend study excursions that leave from San Francisco and include overnights at Yosemite and Lee Vining. Especially fun, if currently offered, is the "Native American Survival Skills for Kids" weekend workshop. The **Sacramento Science Center,** 3615 Auburn Blvd., Sacramento 95821, tel. (916) 485-8836, offers a history and ecology trip through the eastern Sierra Nevada.

At the group, chapter, and national level, the **Sierra Club** and the **Audobon Society** also offer hikes and treks, some free, some almost free (like working wilderness outings), some guided trips with fees. For information, inquire regionally for club contacts. **The Nature Conservancy,** 785 Market St., San Francisco 94103, offers no-cost or low-cost natural history expeditions and restoration work parties throughout the state. Inquire for current schedules—and also ask about major trips and tours including expeditions tracing the footsteps of John Muir and Ishi.

The UC Davis University Extension **Wilderness Venture** program sponsors natural history studies of California raptors and Sierra Nevada wildflowers, stream ecology for fly fishers, and hands-on-reins mountain horsemanship workshops (including safe off-trail travel) in the Sierra Nevada, as well as camping trips on horseback and up-close seminars on wild mustangs. For a current schedule and more information, contact: University Extension, UC Davis, Davis 95616, tel. (916) 752-3098.

The **Yosemite Association,** P.O. Box 545, Yosemite National Park 95389, tel. (209) 372-4714, sponsors a variety of excellent field seminars, from bird studies and botany weekends to "saunters for seniors" and spring ski tours, plus courses in Yosemite region basketry, glaciology, history, and photography. The unaffiliated **Yosemite Institute** campus at Yosemite National Park, P.O. Box 487, tel. 372-4441, offers camping and ecology programs for school children and families.

Mama's Llamas offers Sierra Nevada excursions with an emphasis on environmental education.

WES DEMPSEY

these areas are theoretically protected as the owl's habitat.) Also teetering on the edge of extinction in California is the mysterious and reclusive great gray owl, sometimes called "the phantom of the northern forest," an impressive predator with night vision one million times keener than human sight.

Few birds are common to the Sierra Nevada's sparse subalpine forests but the rosy finch, pine grosbeak, and three-toed woodpecker fly through it; very few mammals make their home near timberline. Aside from fair-weather migrants from lower elevations, including marmots and ground squirrels, jack rabbits and pika live in the high country year-round.

Less common but quite impressive are High Sierra predators. Sworn enemy of self-respecting squirrels and songbirds is the pine marten, an agile and top-notch treetop hunter with a savage temperament. The ferocious wolverine or "skunk bear" (elusive and now endangered) shares this disposition problem. Territorial loners known for their diabolical cunning, apparent maliciousness, and brute strength, wolverines will attack anything they can overpower—even bears or cougars—in the serious high-country competition for food. Also aggressive and good hunters are weasels and the very rare mink. Rarer still is the elusive fisher or "fisher cat," a non-fishing fox-sized hunter and member of the weasel family found in treetops in thick, damp forests. But most impressive of all, to visitors fortunate enough to spot them in the near-perfect camouflage of their pale rocky climbing grounds, are rare Sierra bighorn sheep—found only in remote areas in and around Yosemite and Sequoia national parks.

SEEING AND DOING THE SIERRA NEVADA

Following The Paths Of The Pioneers

Those who truly fear and loathe the great outdoors can still appreciate the Sierra Nevada by car. Even the highest mountain passes are usually snow-free and open all summer and often into autumn, when colorful quaking aspens light up the summits (the most spectacular show occurs along snake-like Sonora Pass and the canyons and high roads to the south).

Among the historic thoroughfares challenging the Sierra Nevada's heights is the I-80 freeway. Descendant of the old Lincoln Highway—the first transcontinental highway in the U.S., a 1912 string of mostly unpaved cowpaths promoted by auto companies to help sell their rolling stock—modern I-80 follows much of the original route but the exciting hairpin-turn and mud-rut thrill is gone.

Before the Lincoln Highway was built, a section of the the **Emigrant Trail** threaded over difficult Donner Pass. At the summit (just off the old Hwy. 40), park at the Mary Lake trailhead for the Pacific Crest Trail and hike a couple of miles to the Roller Pass alternate route, where emigrant wagons were hauled up over the crest between 1846 and 1852. (A third route was Coldstream or Middle Pass.) For help tracing these paths of early California settlers, stop for information at **Donner Memorial State Park** adjacent to Donner Lake (ranger-guided walks sometimes offered).

The **Pacific Crest Trail,** which weaves north-south through the Sierra Nevada, is itself something of a historical accomplishment: it's the longest trail in America, 2,600-plus miles of footpath climbing mountains and crossing deserts between Canada and Mexico, completed after more than 60 years of labor.

But all passes over the Sierra Nevada are "historic," since all routes were once commonly used by bighorn sheep, deer, native peoples, and finally California pioneers. Fredonyer Pass on Hwy. 36 west of Susanville marks the range's far northern reach. Beckwourth Pass on Hwy. 70, northwest of Hallelujah Junction, was named for black mountaineer and trail blazer Jim Beckwourth. Next south are Yuba Pass on Hwy. 49 east of Bassetts, Donner Summit west of Truckee on I-80, Echo Summit on Hwy. 50, then Luther Pass northwest of Picketts Junction on Hwy. 89, Carson Pass on Hwy. 88 east of Kirkwood, and Monitor Pass southeast of Markleeville on the way to Nevada. Ebbetts Pass slinks over the summit on Hwy. 4 between Bear Valley and the Hwy. 89/Monitor Pass junction. Very narrow Sonora Pass on Hwy. 108 (trailers and RVs definitely inadvisable) is next south, then Tioga Pass just outside the eastern border of Yosemite National Park on Hwy. 120, which looms up over the vast basin near Mono Lake.

The High Sierra passes south of Tioga cut through the tallest, most rugged terrain in the state and still defy the road builders—even now these routes are open only in summer, and used only by hikers, backpackers, and horseback adventurers. Walker Pass east of Bakersfield and Lake Isabella on Hwy. 178, where the Sierra Nevada starts drifting off into the desert as low, rolling mountains and plateaus, is open to travelers year-round.

Hiking, Backpacking, Biking

To personally experience the breathtaking beauty of the Sierra Nevada, get out of that car. Throughout its vast range, the Sierra Nevada offers outdoor opportunities for people of all ages and inclinations—from short, easy self-guided nature trails and day-hikes along sections of major trails to challenging climbs over peaks and summits. For those who are physically able, backpacking through remote areas of the range is truly a "peak" experience. Maniacal mountain climbers often breeze into the high country, set up base camp, then *really* set out to see (and cling to and clamber over) the Sierra Nevada. Bicycling—again, only for the fit and fatalistic—is another great way to experience California's snowy mountains (see "The Gold Country" for more information on regional cycling guidebooks).

Fishing And Water Recreation

From about May until whenever the lakes freeze over, the fishin' is easy in the Sierra Nevada. For premier trout fishing, head north of I-80 and on into the Feather and Yuba rivers' watersheds. Stampede and Prosser reservoirs are quiet and quite popular fishing lakes, though others are also excellent. Stream and river fishing can be good too, but the persistent construction of dams in Northern California means good trout streams are harder to find. Most major reservoirs offer some type of water recreation, from sailing or water-skiing to swimming, but even in summer Lake Tahoe and most High Sierra lakes are too cold for swimming by most people's standards (though a quick dip *is* invigorating and washes away that trail dust). For various reasons but primarily because near their sources even the wildest rivers are small and shallow, whitewater-rafting on the Sierra Nevada's western slope is better a ways downstream. (See "The Gold Country" for more rafting information.)

Winter Sports And Recreation

Downhill skiing is big-time fun in these parts and a major economic boon for the Sierra Nevada. Many world-class ski resorts are within easy reach of I-80 and the Lake Tahoe area, from Sugar Bowl and Squaw Valley (host of the 1960 Winter Olympics) to Alpine Meadows and Kirkwood, but keep sledding south to other worthwhile ski spots: Dodge Ridge, June Mountain, and Mammoth Mountain.

The peak experience for some downhillers is heli-skiing—catching a lift by helicopter to high, otherwise inaccessible powder—but more accessible for most is Nordic or cross-country skiing. Backcountry skiing is increasingly popular, with more private and public tracks and marked trails available every year. Ski mountaineering (using shorter, wider skis than Nordic varieties) combines cross-country and downhill skiing for wide-ranging backcountry adventure and exploration. Snow camping may or may not be included. Snowshoe hiking, sledding, tobogganing, "tubing," ice fishing, ice-skating, and just plain snow play are other enjoyable winter pastimes.

State of California **Sno-Park** sites are legal, snow-cleared parking areas scattered throughout the Sierra Nevada that provide easy access to major winter recreation areas without risking

---

SKI TOURING AND WINTER MOUNTAINEERING

Among instructors and guides offering backcountry ski trips in the Sierra Nevada are: **Alpine Skills** near Truckee and Lake Tahoe, P.O. Box 8, Norden 95724, tel. (916) 426-9108; **High & Wild Mountain Guides**, P.O. Box 11905, Tahoe Paradise 95708, tel. (916) 577-2370; the **Palisades School of Mountaineering**, P.O. Box 694, Bishop 93546, tel. (619) 935-4464; **Sierra Ski Touring**, Box 176, Gardenville, NV 89410, tel. (702) 782-3047 or (415) 849-9292; **Sierra Wilderness Seminars**, P.O. Box 707, Arcata 95521, tel. (707) 822-8066; and the **Yosemite Mountaineering School**, Yosemite National Park, Yosemite 95389, tel. (209) 372-1244. Some of these companies (including the Palisades and Yosemite mountaineering schools) also offer mountain-climbing, rock-climbing, ice-climbing, and other special outdoor skills instruction.

a parking ticket or burial by a passing snow-plow. Sno-park permits ($3 for a one-day parking pass, $20 for a season ticket at last report) are available at winter sports equipment outlets, at Donner Memorial and Calaveras Big Trees state parks, and at California State Automobile Association (AAA) offices. Or order a Sno-Park permit by mail; include your name, address, and a check payable to Department of Parks and Recreation Sno-Parks and send to: **California Dept. of Parks and Recreation,** Attn.: Reservations Unit, P.O. Box 942896, Sacramento 94296-0001. Everyone who buys a season Sno-Park pass (good from whenever the snow first flies until May 30) might also request a current copy of the "Recreation Guide to California Sno-Park Sites," $3, which includes basic information about all Sno-Park areas plus topo maps marked with cross-country skiing and snowmobile trails.

HEALTH AND SAFETY

All Sierra Nevada travelers—backpackers, cyclists, day-hikers, even car campers and those who plan no outdoor trips—should be reasonably prepared for anything, for despite the Sierra Nevada's recreational popularity, there may be no one around to help if something goes wrong. Though snow storms are common in winter, these and other freak storms also come in summer. Drivers should always carry tire chains, blankets, and some water and food in case they become stranded. To help avoid that possibility, have some sort of itinerary and get current destination and road information before setting out.

Even casual hikers need to remember that the air is thin at high elevations and it takes a day or two to adjust. Plan outdoor excursions and exertions accordingly; altitude sickness and hyperventilation are not fun.

Even in the most pristine backcountry areas, drinking water also poses a problem. Sadly, because of the widespread presence of a single-celled intestinal parasite called *Giardia lamblia,* it's no longer safe to dip that tin Sierra Club cup into marshy mountain meadows for a drink of the world's best-tasting water. Backpackers and hikers far from water faucets should boil all drinking water (for at least five minutes), carry water purification tablets (available at sporting

Cross-country skiing is increasingly popular.

goods stores and elsewhere in the region), or invest in a more expensive, portable purification pump. Whatever your choice, also bring a container or containers adequate to the task and a couple of good-sized canteens to help avoid the temptation of drinking unpurified water when suddenly thirsty.

Symptoms of giardiasis include the sudden onset of nausea, stomach cramps, and debilitating diarrhea. Though rarely life-threatening even without treatment, becoming weak or sick from giardia contamination in the Sierra Nevada is no joke, since any physical ailment also increases the possibility of falls and serious injury. Sometimes, too, the malady's symptoms are delayed (average incubation period: one to three weeks) and people fail to connect the sickness with its original cause, suffering unnecessarily for months. To prevent further giardia contamination in the Sierra Nevada, camp well back from lakes and streams and—with the help of one of those cute little plastic shovels—always bury fecal and other wastes at least six to eight inches deep and at least 100 feet from water.

LAKE TAHOE VISITORS AUTHORITY, JOHN KELLY

Adequate food is the next most important necessity. Always bring more than you think you'll need (avoid canned or bottled items if backpacking), including high-energy trail snacks, but not so much you can't carry the load comfortably. Hikers and backpackers need good, broken-in and waterproofed hiking boots, plenty of cotton and wool socks (packed accessibly), long pants, cold-weather clothing, and at least minimal rain gear—including a tarp or small waterproof tent, a poncho large enough to keep most of one's body and pack dry, and waterproof matches. (Even for day-hikes, a handy item is an inexpensive and lightweight mylar "space blanket," to help stay dry and warm if lost or unexpectedly stranded. A big plastic garbage bag is less effective but even cheaper.) A whistle, good compass, and topographic maps are also wise; it's not uncommon for even experienced woodspeople to accidentally stray from established trails. Insect repellent is another essential (voracious mosquitos are usually worse in marshy meadow or lake areas) as is sunscreen and sunglasses.

Necessities for backcountry camping include a good, well-insulated sleeping bag and pad as well as cooking utensils, cookstove, and fuel. Campfires are not allowed in many wilderness areas—and even if they are, downed and dry firewood is not always available. Also bring sturdy nylon cord and extra stuff sacks to stow food (and any garbage or clothes smelling like food) high in the trees and well away from sleeping areas—to help prevent midnight encounters with bears. A good flashlight, pocketknife, and first-aid and snakebite kits are essential on longer treks, and not a bad idea even on short hikes.

Snow Safety

Special precautions are prudent in winter. If driving, always carry tire chains, blankets, even extra food if storms are possible. Check weather forecasts and snow conditions before setting out. On snowshoes or skis, allow extra travel time if snow is soft. Always take along at least one extra day's food, extra clothing, shelter, and a portable stove—whatever's necessary for an unplanned overnighter—plus extra bindings, ski tips, and other emergency repair supplies. If caught in a storm, wait it out in an avalanche-safe area.

Snow Avalanches

About 80% of avalanches occur during or after storms. Even a tiny avalanche is no joke if one becomes "one" with it, so pay attention to weather changes. Lightning may never strike the same place twice, but avalanches often do. Avoid open slopes. Evidence of recent avalanches, or snowballs rolling downslope, means the area's probably unstable. If crossing a bad spot is unavoidable, go one at a time and stay near the top, avoiding fracture lines. If going up or down, go *straight* up or down—no traversing.

OTHER PRACTICALITIES

Camping, Accommodations, Food

Public and private campgrounds abound throughout the Sierra Nevada. Most national forest service campgrounds are strictly first-come, first-camped, rarely feature hot showers, and may or may not have flush toilets and other amenities. Running water, fire rings, and picnic tables are the norm, however. Most mountain campgrounds are available in summer only, open as soon as snows melt enough to allow access but closed (and the water turned off) before the first fall frosts. Sometimes, early and late high-country bivouacs are possible—campgrounds may be open, and free (though drinking water would be unavailable). Contact regional forest service offices for current camping, picnicking, and outdoor recreation information.

State-run campgrounds like those at Tahoe's Sugar Pine Point State Park (open year-round, snow or no snow) and Grover Hot Springs State Park farther south (also open all year but especially nice in early spring) are quite popular, with Mistix reservations necessary in summer, tel. (800) 444-7275. Almost too popular are Yosemite National Park campgrounds; in general, camping is less crowded at redwood-rich Sequoia and Kings Canyon national parks farther south. Campsites at reservable national park campgrounds—not all are—can be secured in advance by calling Mistix toll-free at (800) 365-CAMP; for reservable national forest campgrounds, (800) 283-CAMP. To really get away from it all, try snow camping. Summer or winter, free permits are necessary for backcountry camping on public lands.

For those who never pine for nights spent sleeping under dazzling Sierra Nevada stars, a variety of more civilized accommodations—from motels to hotels and bed and breakfasts—is available year-round in "urban" mountain areas like Lake Tahoe and Yosemite Valley and in more remote areas near downhill ski facilities. Rustic accommodations, from knotty pine-paneled cabins to old stage-stop hotels and hunting lodges, are scattered throughout the mountains. Sit-down dining comes close to city standards only in and around Tahoe and Yosemite, though most tiny towns have some sort of grocery store and/or cafe. But if traveling long distances in remote areas of the Sierra Nevada, always carry some groceries—just in case you discover, when hungry for a hot meal, that the town you roll into after dark rolls up its sidewalks at 5 or 6 p.m.

Sierra Nevada Entertainment

It's hard to imagine anything more rewarding after a day of sweat and trail dust than slipping into a High Sierra hot spring or plunging hot, swollen feet into an icy stream. But, even in God's country, some people prefer casinos and nightlife, apres-ski lodges, and the bar scene. The best Sierra Nevada bars, though, are those that spring up like mushrooms in the middle of nowhere—hometown bars in small mountain communities. Once astride a bar stool, and after the shock of being a stranger wears off, the experience can be unforgettable. If you're lucky, you just might strike up a friendly conversation with some of the old-timers, the craggy people who have lived the hard life of the mountains so long they now resemble them.

Sierra Nevada Events

Events in the Sierra Nevada run the gamut from transplanted urban entertainment to dog sled races and hoedowns. In January comes June Lake's **Winterfest,** ski, snowmobile, and other freezing fun centered around June Lake village. Pinecrest's **Mother Lode Classic** ski race is also scheduled in January, followed in February by the **Sonora Pass Classic.** More out of the ordinary are the **Sierra Sweepstakes Dog Sled Races** in Truckee, where they harness the hounds and go for the gold ($5,000 purse) with distance and sprint races, and Markleeville's annual **Canine Connection** sanctioned dog sled races.

At the end of February and into March, at both Truckee and North Lake Tahoe, is **Snofest,** one of the country's most ambitious winter carnivals, complete with parades, ski races, dances, and fireworks. March is usually prime-time for Sierra Nevada ski races, including the **Great Ski Race** from Tahoe to Truckee, California's largest cross-country skiing competition benefiting the Tahoe Nordic Search and Rescue Team; the **Rossignol 5-K Night Race** at Tahoe Donner; and the annual **Echo-to-Kirkwood Race.** In April, try the **Sierra Mountain Race and Relay,** a winter triathlon.

Different in early March is the **Owens River Trout Derby** at Bishop, a "blind bogey" tournament on the open waters of Pleasant Valley Reservoir and along 25 miles of the Owens River; Lone Pine's **Early Trout Opener** usually takes place simultaneously. Also in March comes the **Wagon Wheel Race Days,** a 68-mile cycling road race and 24-mile criterium. In April is Bishop's **Rainbow Day,** with awards for best opening-day trout catches, and the **Wild West Marathon** run at Lone Pine.

In May, the **World Championship Cribbage Tournament** in Quincy is quite the showdown, with 400 or more participants and $10,000 in prize money. Or hang around Lone Pine to see what's left of the **Death Valley to Mount Whitney Bike Race** contestants when they roll into town. But don't miss **Mule Days** in Bishop, when the self-proclaimed Mule Capitol of the World honors the heroic hybrid by holding its World Championship Packing Team contest, also a barbecue, parade, and dance.

June's the month for the **Truckee-Tahoe Air Show,** complete with aerobatics, fly-bys, hot air balloon rallies, and parachute drops. Also in June is the three-day **Bear Valley Bike Trek** that starts in the Sierra Nevada above Calaveras Big Trees, rolls through the gold country, and ends in Oakdale. In July come plenty of Fourth of July fireworks—at Donner Lake, Mono Lake, and Lake Almanor far to the north near Chester —plus festivities at Mammoth Lakes, including dancing in the streets, good barbecue, and a chili cook-off. At Graeagle, the holiday is celebrated with swimming in the Old Mill Pond, a parade, barbecue, and more. Also in July: toe-tapping, hand-clapping, thigh-slapping fun at Quincy's **Old Time Fiddling Championships,** a hoedown with square dancing and barbecue, and a 50-K endurance run during **Trailblazer Days** at Walker and Coleville.

Serious cyclists shouldn't miss Markleeville's **Death Ride Tour of the California Alps,** a very fast almost vertical tour of Sierra Nevada mountain passes, usually held in July. Another species of fun is the **Western States 100/Tevis Cup** cross-country horse race, covering the 100 miles between Squaw Valley and Auburn. Then comes the **Tri-County Fair** in Bishop, the annual family fun fest for Alpine, Inyo, and Mono counties. The **Truckee Rodeo** is held in August, as is Bishop's **Huck Finn River Festival,** with canoeing, kayaking, and rubber rafting on the Owens River. The town's **Homecoming and Labor Day Rodeo** means cowboys converge for two rodeos, and old-timers return for the parade and western dance. In September, the **Tahoe Fat Tire Festival** offers an orgy of events for mountain bikers, from bicycle polo and rodeo to backroads tours and downhill races.

Information And Transport

At least one good regional visitor bureau or chamber of commerce exists in each of the Sierra Nevada's major travel regions. Also helpful are the visitor centers at state and national parks. Usually best for current backcountry conditions and other information (including topographic maps) are national forest headquarters or ranger district offices. The topo maps "of record" are those put out by the U.S. Geological Survey, but many are more more than 20 years old and don't necessarily reflect accurate trail routes, though they do show elevations and essential features of the terrain. Serious hikers and backpakers should also invest in the various relevant maps and/or trail guides published by Wilderness Press.

Sierra Club Books also publishes some helpful titles, but the best all-around companion volume to tote is *Sierra Nevada Natural History: An Illustrated Handbook* by Tracey I. Storer and Robert L. Usinger, a classic, easy-to-carry guide to plants and animals published by the University of California Press.

Because distances are long, populations sparse, and terrain treacherous in the Sierra Nevada, few public transport options exist (except in urbanized Tahoe and Yosemite Valley). Greyhound buses provide limited but regular service along both the eastern and western sides of the Sierra Nevada Crest, but buses transect the mountains only via I-80 and Hwy. 50. Though some hardy souls explore the range on foot, by bicycle, on horseback, on skis, or take their chances hitchhiking (best in and around Yosemite and the Tahoe area), most people drive. Of the Sierra Nevada pioneer trails that have since become highways, many are as impassable in winter as they ever were; only sometimes are snow-snarled I-80 and highways 70 and 50 kept open year-round. Hwy. 395 along the eastern side of the range is usually open in winter. For regional road conditions, call the California Highway Patrol at (916) 445-7623.

LAKE TAHOE AND VICINITY

Like a vast oval mirror laid across the California-Nevada border reflecting both states back on themselves, sapphire-blue Lake Tahoe is North America's largest alpine lake. Mark Twain described Lake Tahoe as "a noble sheet of blue water . . . walled in by a rim of snow-clad mountain peaks. . . . As it lay there with the shadows of the mountains brilliantly photographed upon its still surface I thought it must surely be the fairest picture the whole earth affords." If you ignore modern-day condo-to-condo encroachments and the area's unsightly strip development, the lake itself is still some picture.

Lake Tahoe exists by the grace of geologic accident. Despite the area's later glacial scouring, the Tahoe Basin was created by the earth's faulting; as the land sank, the Sierra Nevada rose on the west and the Carson Range on the east. Over the eons, snow melt and rain filled this great basin, and kept on filling it: volcanic lava flows then glacial debris plugged the lake's original outlets. (Today, Tahoe's only outlet is the Truckee River, which begins at Tahoe City and flows north and east to Reno and Nevada's Pyramid Lake.) Surface measurements alone—Tahoe is 22 miles long, 12 miles wide, and has a 72-mile shoreline—still don't do the great lake justice. Tahoe's depth averages 989 feet (it plunges down 1,645 feet at its deepest point) and the lake usually contains 122 million acre-feet of water, enough to cover the entire state of California to a depth of about 14 inches.

But more important than quantity is the *quality* of the lake's waters. Even today, though there are water quality problems, Lake Tahoe water is some of the purest in the world, with dissolved gases, salts, minerals, and organic matter rivaling the ratios found in distilled water. Tahoe water is so clear that, despite measurable increases in algae growth and sedimentation during the past 20 years, objects can be spotted to depths of 75 feet or so. One of the lake's stranger characteristics is that, because of its great depth, it never freezes. As surface water gets colder it sinks, forcing warmer, lighter water upwards. Though Emerald Bay (a natural beauty created by glacial moraine) and other shallow inlets may occasionally freeze over, the lake itself is ice free because of its own gentle temperature-controlled dance.

TAHOE PAST TO PRESENT

Tahoe History

The area's first recorded residents were the Da-ow people or Washoes, peaceable regional nomads who gathered each spring at Tahoe's Taylor Creek to fish, hunt, and conduct tribal rituals. Some speculate that the Da-ow word *tahoe,* which means "big water" or "high water," may have come via the Spanish *tajo,* "steep cliff area" or "chasm." Though others disagree, George Wharton James, who wrote the definitive guide to Tahoe in 1915, contended that the correct pronunciation is similar to the one-syllable *tao,* "like a Chinese name."

Life as native people had known it changed drastically after explorer John C. Frémont and his guide Kit Carson first spied the great lake in 1844. The wave of westward migration that washed over the Sierra Nevada passed near Tahoe. But even during the gold rush, the difficult Tahoe-area terrain was avoided by most migrants—a tide that turned after the Comstock Lode silver discovery in Nevada. Johnson's Cutoff, the old "Bonanza Road" and now the Hwy. 50 route up from Placerville, swung up and over the Sierra Nevada and through the Tahoe Basin, a treacherous mountain-clutching route for people and products on the move from California's gold fields to the new diggin's near Virginia City. Subsequent chiseling of the Central Pacific Railroad route over the Sierra Nevada by California's hardworking Chinese made access even easier.

The timber demand created by the silver rush led to large-scale logging of Tahoe forests between 1860 and 1890, but once the Comstock Lode petered out by the turn of the century, Lake Tahoe slowly became a resort area for the rich, who were transported from one gala party to another via the lake's steamship fleet. During the 1930s, when roads throughout the Tahoe Basin were finally paved, the middle class began to arrive in California's sky-high vacation land. But modern times have taken their toll on Tahoe. In the 1950s, only 2,500 people lived in the Tahoe Basin year-round, though the area was becoming increasingly popular. Then, when the 1960 Winter Olympics were held at Tahoe's Squaw Valley ski resort, Lake Tahoe became part of the world's vocabulary, setting off an avalanche of commercial and residential development. More than 60,000 permanent residents now call the area home, not to mention the millions of summer and winter part-timers and passersby.

Lured by the climate (brisk invigorating winter temperatures, pleasant days and cool nights in summer), the area's natural beauty, and man-made attractions, everyone loves Tahoe. To avoid all this affection, come in late spring when the snowpack is waning or during fall—usually quite nice, depending upon the weather, from mid-September into November.

The Fate Of The Donner Party

The Tahoe region's most chilling and most familiar California-bound migration story is that of the Donner Party, an ill-fated group of wagon train travelers who split off from the main train in Utah in the spring of 1846 to try the more southerly, supposedly easier and shorter Hastings Cutoff to California. But the shortcut, which passed through the alkaline deserts of Utah and Nevada and over difficult mountain ranges, was much too long. Nevertheless, led by George and Jacob Donner, the group decided to cross the rugged Sierra Nevada in late October. And despite some early snows, the Donner Party almost made it up and over the California Emigrant Trail pass—almost, but not quite. Having found the pass and prepared for the passage, the group decided to sleep then set out at sunup, and this delay of one day sealed their fate. New snowfall during the night obliterated the trail, and a decision to wait for a break in the weather meant still more snow.

Most of the group's oxen were lost in the ensuing storms, due to carelessness and panic, and the Donner Party—without adequate provisions and huddled in flimsy tents, makeshift cabins, and snow caves along Alder Creek—settled in for a horrible winter. As the elderly and babies started to sicken and die, the Donner Party's "forlorn hope" group of men and women set out on foot toward the Sacramento Valley to get help. Thirty-two days later, after great pri-

vation and misery, the survivors (who cannibalized their fallen travel companions) finally reached Wheatland, and a rescue party of expert mountaineers immediately set out to save the others. Several successive rescue parties carted out those most capable of making the trip, but only about half of those who set out from the eastern side of the Sierra Nevada—reduced to eating mice, sticks, shoes, and even their own dead just to survive—ever made it to the west side. An 1840s medallion found recently on the archaeological excavation site of Murphy's Cabin contained the inscription: "Blessed Virgin Mary Pray For Us." Even more recent excavations suggest that the actual "last camps" of both George and Jacob Donner have finally been found.

Modern Times: More Troubles

Lake Tahoe's tremendous popularity with summer vacationers and winter sports fans has brought increasing problems—traffic congestion, air pollution, construction-related erosion,

monument to the ill-fated Donner Party, at Donner Memorial State Park near Truckee

CALIFORNIA DEPARTMENT OF PARKS & RECREATION

LAKE TAHOE
AND VICINITY

© MOON PUBLICATIONS, INC.

pollution of the lake's pristine waters, and ever-more-limited public access to the lake. For more than 20 years, development interests, environmentalists, and hot-under-the-collar citizens (on both the California and Nevada sides of the lake) have been at war over what to do to save Lake Tahoe. Skirmishes are usually waged over various decisions of the two-state Tahoe Regional Planning Agency (TRPA), which has had ultimate control over most Tahoe planning issues since its establishment in 1969.

But the decades-long battle over how to save the lake from its own loveliness has finally simmered down some, with the final acceptance, in the late 1980s, of a new 20-year master plan restricting additional home construction to just 300 per year and controlling commercial development even more tightly. No construction of any kind is now permitted on the lake's more environmentally sensitive areas, including remaining marshlands (which naturally filter the water flowing into Lake Tahoe). In addition, various public and private agencies—the U.S. Forest Service, the California Tahoe Conservancy, the Nature Conservancy, and the Trust for Public Lands—have been buying up much of Tahoe's undeveloped land, to guarantee its permanent protection. But despite all these efforts, Lake Tahoe's water quality is still declining, and researchers suggest that changes for the better, when things do start to turn around, will be quite slow.

Redevelopment: Back To The Future

Determined to upgrade visitor facilities while improving environmental protections, the city of South Lake Tahoe has launched a $236 million redevelopment project. The first phase (completed) created park-like areas where older motels once stood, the reclaimed open land near the lake now serving as filtration basins to purify water runoff. And new construction projects, such as the Embassy Suites Resort, reflect a contemporary variation of the "Old Tahoe Style" combination of Tudor and Alpine architecture favored here in the early 1900s. (For every new hotel room added as part of South Lake Tahoe's redevelopment, 1.31 old rooms are being "retired.")

New and renovated commercial development along the state line, an improved "linear park" along Hwy. 50 for hiking and biking (between

Stateline and the new Ski Run Marina Hotel), more hotels (including a 54-room adult-themed Fantasy Inn), and the new "loop road" that will reroute Hwy. 50 around the casino area are also included in the city's redevelopment plans.

TAHOE AREA SIGHTS

Lake Tahoe has a monster, people say. This is a modern phenomenon, swimming along with Tahoe's trend toward cable TV, condos, and casinos. But so many people claim to have seen the Unidentified Swimming Object now casually referred to as Tahoe Tessie, that in 1984 a USO Hotline was set up to take the flood of calls. The more scientifically oriented suggest that those who spot Tahoe's monster are actually seeing a "standing wave," a phenomenon which occurs when separate boat wakes traveling miles and miles across the lake's still surface finally cross each other and collide. Tessie is described as a 10-foot-long (or longer) dark humpbacked creature, undulating along the water's surface fast enough to leave a wake of its own. Old-timers hope the monster is at least some sort of mutant sturgeon (though no one's ever seen one here) or giant trout.

One definite place to *see* gigantic trout, though—except in drought years when the river has died—is at Fanny Bridge on the Truckee River in Tahoe City, named for the fascinating collection of derrieres on display as fish fans lean over to get a good look. (No fishing allowed.)

Most sights on Lake Tahoe proper are easily accessible, even for bicyclists enjoying the bike lanes that help keep cyclists off the highway (50 miles paved). Along Hwy. 28 just north of Tahoe City is **Burton Creek State Park,** near (but not on) the lake, which offers forested hikes (and short cross-country ski trails in winter), tel. (916) 587-3789, and tiny **Tahoe State Recreation Area** on the lake, popular for summer camping and beach fun.

In Tahoe City is the **Gatekeeper's Log Cabin Museum,** 130 W. Lake Blvd., tel. (916) 583-1762, a several-acre park (picnic area, restrooms) at the Truckee River's outlet, with museum displays of local geology and fossils, also Washoe and Paiute artifacts and other relics of Lake Tahoe history. A real hit with most folks is the dachshund-sized dogsled. Also popular:

Monday evening film and lecture programs. (Open from mid-May through mid-October.)

North from Tahoe City via Hwy. 89 (or via Hwy. 237) is the down-home community of **Truckee,** a relaxed old railroading town. South from Tahoe City are houses and condominiums and a string of fine state parks: Sugar Pine Point between Tahoma and Meeks Bay, and the run-together D.L. Bliss and Emerald Bay farther south—all filled to the gills in summer (see below for more information). Still farther south is the Pope-Baldwin Recreation Area and Tallac Historic Site near Camp Richardson and Fallen Leaf Lake. Worth a stop in South Lake Tahoe is the **Lake Tahoe Historical Society Museum,** 3058 Hwy. 50, tel. (916) 541-5458, containing the area's best collection of native cultural artifacts and Tahoe area pioneer relics. (Call for current days and hours.)

Truckee And Vicinity

The once wicked tin-roofed town of Truckee, which grew up here during construction of the transcontinental railroad, also once had a thriving Chinatown. The Wild West ambience, still intact today despite gentrification, inspired Charlie Chaplin to film *The Gold Rush* here. Even during Prohibition, Truckee's saloons did a blatantly brisk business, and Truckee's red-light district lasted well into this century—not cleaned up, locals say, until the 1960 Olympics in Squaw Valley. Commercial Row off I-80 is where most of Truckee's action is these days: the 1896 railroad depot (an Amtrak and Greyhound stop, also the local information center), shops and restaurants—and bars. These days Truckee is boasting shopping centers and astounding levels of new development, an attempt perhaps to become a Reno suburb. The combination of tourists rolling down off I-80 with its freight and passenger traffic, not to mention Truckee's famous southern-right-of-way four-way stop, makes for some exciting traffic jams. Truckee's first motel, the old Gateway, is now a museum sponsored by the local historical society. (For more information on Truckee, see "Tahoe Area Information" below.)

Donner Memorial State Park at Donner Lake south of Truckee, just two miles off I-80 via old Hwy. 40, P.O. Box 549, Truckee 96160, tel. (916) 587-3841, is a choice summertime spot for picnicking, camping, short hikes, and water recreation. Most notable here, though, is the park's **Emigrant Trail Museum,** which tells the stories of the Donner Party's winter of 1846-47, the construction of the Central Pacific Railroad, and the Sierra Nevada's natural history. Open daily 10 a.m.-noon and 1-4 p.m., small admission fee (but free to campers and picnickers who show their receipts). Rangers often offer free guided hikes to interpret the Donner story; call for current information. Day-use fee for the park: $5. The campground is open from late May to October (10-day camping limit), $14 for the works, and quite popular—Mistix reservations necessary, tel. (800) 444-7275.

Worthwhile is the **Western America SkiSport Museum** a few miles west off I-80 at Boreal, tel. (916) 426-3313, operated by the Auburn Ski Club and open summers Wed.-Sun., winters Tues.-Sun., from 11 a.m.-5 p.m. Also worthwhile in the vicinity: the hike to **Loch Leven Lakes** (trailhead at the Big Bend exit off I-80 across from the Big Bend ranger station west of the Rainbow Tavern), about a six-mile roundtrip to see all three glacial lakes.

Sugar Pine Point State Park

A main attraction at Tahoe's Sugar Pine Point State Park is the baronial **Ehrmann Mansion,** probably Tahoe's finest example of a rich person's summer home, built here in 1903 by San Francisco banker Isaias W. Hellman. An amazing shoreline fortress of all-native stone and fine woods (Hellman called the place Pine Lodge), the mansion-cum-interpretive center is open only in summer for tours, but poke around the estate's spacious grounds anytime. Also worth a look: the old ice house and the Phipps cabin. Down by the lake, at one of the estate's boathouses, peek through the window for a bit of local boat racing history. (Boathouses are usually open to the public over the July 4th weekend.)

Also at Sugar Pine Point: almost two miles of mostly rocky lake frontage for sunbathing and swimming, plus hiking and biking trails, picnicking, good year-round camping at the **General Creek Campground,** and the **Edwin L. Z'Berg Natural Preserve** (walk to the point here to see Tahoe's only operating lighthouse). Park day-use fee: $5. For more information, stop by the area's state park headquarters at D.L. Bliss or call (916) 525-7982.

Emerald Bay

D.L. Bliss And Emerald Bay State Parks

Managed as one unit, these two contiguous state parks on Lake Tahoe's southwest shoreline offer camping—268 family campsites, 20 accessible only on foot or by boat—swimming, fishing, boating, and hiking. Day use: $5. Sandy **Lester Beach** at Bliss is packed by noon on summer weekends. Even if you're not up for the longer haul south to Emerald Bay, hike to **Rubicon Point** to get a good, deep look into Tahoe's clear waters. Or take the short **Balancing Rock Nature Trail.**

Emerald Bay offers one of Tahoe's best brief hikes—a very scenic one-mile downhill scramble (people say it's two or three miles climbing back out) to **Vikingsholm,** a Scandinavian-style summer mansion on the bay's fjord-like shore. The trail heads downhill from the Emerald Bay overlook (fairly small parking lot, so arrive early), though you can also get here the long way, via the easy 4½-mile Rubicon Trail from D.L. Bliss State Park just north. Considered the Western Hemisphere's finest example of Scandinavian

architecture, Vikingsholm seems inspired by all things Norwegian and Swedish—11th-century castles, churches, forts, even sod-roofed homes —and was built in 1928-29; its half-million-dollar price tag included the now ruined stone teahouse on tiny Fannette Island. Tours of Vikingsholm are scheduled from mid-June through Labor Day.

Worthwhile, too, is the short hike up to **Eagle Falls** overlooking the bay (picnicking, also the trailhead to Eagle Lake and the Desolation Wilderness). Even from this far away, you can hear the blaring loudspeakers of tourist-loaded paddlewheelers heading in and out of Emerald Bay.

For more information about these two parks, contact: Sierra State Parks, P.O. Drawer D, Tahoma 96142, tel. (916) 525-7232. Or stop by the central state parks headquarters off the highway at D.L. Bliss. For information about the state parks' excellent year-round schedule of guided hikes, send a self-addressed, stamped business envelope to the address above.

The Tallac Historic Site

An enclave of peace preserving the past, the Tallac Historic Site is a 74-acre monument to Tahoe's social heyday, when Lake Tahoe was the elite retreat for California's rich and powerful. Though the Tallac Hotel Casino is long gone, undergoing gradual restoration here under Forest Service supervision are several impressive summer estates featuring distinct architectural affectations, including "Mr. Santa Anita" Lucky Baldwin's **Baldwin Estate** (now a summers-only museum) and the lavish **Pope-Tevis** and pine-pillared **Valhalla** mansions. Thursday night jazz at Valhalla takes full advantage of the great hall downstairs, most notable for its massive stone fireplace. A project awaiting only ample private donations—through the nonprofit Tahoe Tallac Association, a cultural arts organization that also raises funds for restoration—is the transformation of the estate boathouse into the **Valhalla Boathouse Theatre.**

And that's the point about Tallac. Though it is indeed a monument to Tahoe's past, the complex is fast becoming a cultural and fine arts center. The Tallac Association's "Artists in Action" program, for example, showcases local artists and their talents in various on-site open studio settings, including various guest cottages and the **Dextra Baldwin Cabin,** the **Anita Gib-**

son Cabin, and the Honeymoon Cabin. The twin cabins near Valhalla house the Cultural Arts Store, featuring (for sale) arts and fine crafts created by Tallac artists. Almost all summer long, Tallac hosts a refreshingly uncommercial arts and music festival (see "Tahoe Area Events"), well worth several trips, and other creative cultural experiences.

The Tallac Historic Site is part and parcel of the Pope-Baldwin Recreation Area near Camp Richardson and popular southwestern Tahoe beaches. Just north of Tallac is a picnic area, a multi-agency visitors center open only in summer, tel. (916) 544-5050, and some self-guided nature trails. Particularly worthwhile is the Rainbow Trail, which dips down below Taylor Creek into a glass-walled "stream profile chamber" for observing creek life, particularly the October run of Kokanee salmon. For a longer walk, take the trail to Fallen Leaf Lake.

Tours of Tallac are conducted by the Forest Service. If you come here just to wander—and the dock at the boathouse is often empty, a great spot for sunbathing—there is no on-site parking, though visitors can park just north at the Kiva Picnic Area or south at Camp Richardson. For more information about the area, contact: Tahoe Tallac Association, P.O. Box 1595, South Lake Tahoe 96156, tel. (916) 542-ARTS (summer only) or 541-4975 (year-round).

Nevada Side Sights

Across the state line on the lake's northern end is Incline Village, for Nevada-style diversions and Ben Cartwright's tourist-trampled Ponderosa Ranch movie set, tel. (702) 831-0691, open Memorial Day to October. More worthwhile but some 25 miles northeast is the entire town of Virginia City, tel. 847-0311, "capital" of the historic Comstock Lode itself with museums, tours of old silver mines and hard-luck cemeteries, and endless eateries, saloons, and shops. Also interesting, and closer, is Carson City, Nevada's capital.

There are a number of worthwhile outdoor destinations on the Nevada side of the lake. One is Lake Tahoe Nevada State Park, tel. (702) 831-0494, which includes popular Cave Rock (shore fishing and boating), very popular Sand Harbor (sandy beaches and boating, plus an excellent summer drama and music festival), and Spooner Lake (good backcountry access).

Straddling the border on the lake's south side is the flushed flash and flutter of Stateline, with slot machines and more sophisticated gaming as well as top popular entertainment acts year-round at Caesars Tahoe, Harrah's Tahoe, Harvey's, and Del Webb's High Sierra casino hotels.

For more suggestions about what to see and do in Nevada, the best guide available is Nevada Handbook by Deke Castleman, published by Moon Publications. Or, contact the region's Nevada visitors bureaus listed under "Tahoe Area Information" below.

TAHOE AREA HIKING AND BACKPACKING

Local state parks offer nature trails and longer hikes, plus they sponsor a full schedule of guided hikes (including winter snowshoe and Nordic ski treks) throughout the Tahoe area. Popular short hikes include the trip to seasonally swimmable Five Lakes (the trailhead is two miles off Hwy. 89 on Alpine Meadows Rd.), a steep six-mile roundtrip with great scenery. Or take the Shirley Lake hike from the Squaw Valley tram building, a five-mile roundtrip of granite and waterfalls.

The Donner Summit area offers exceptional hiking, some routes quite challenging (and therefore least traveled). A complete listing of longer trails in the Tahoe National Forest, including lonely routes like the Hawley Grade trek from near Meyers, and the Tucker Flat and Duck Lake-Lost Lake hikes, are available locally from national forest headquarters. Ask, too, about progress on the Tahoe Rim Trail, a volunteer-powered effort to complete a 150-mile-long trail around the lake through two states, six counties, and three national forests. Planned for completion in the 1990s, the trail will feature near-constant lake views plus sights such as Basque tree carvings, the Sierra Nevada's largest bog, and the botanical wonder of Hellhole. For more information, and to volunteer some trail construction time, contact: Tahoe Rim Trail, P.O. Box 10156, South Lake Tahoe 96158, tel. (916) 577-0676.

For more information about long hikes and Tahoe area backpacking, contact Forest Service headquarters for the Lake Tahoe Basin

Management Unit (open year-round; see "Tahoe Area Information" below) or, in summer, stop by the visitors center on the highway near Camp Richardson.

The best available guidebook to Tahoe area hiking and backpacking is *The Tahoe Sierra* by Jeffrey P. Schaffer, published by Wilderness Press, though Schaffer's *Desolation Wilderness and the South Lake Tahoe Basin* and Thomas and Jason Winnett's *Sierra North: 100 Back-Country Trips* (also published by Wilderness Press) are also good.

With its glaciated High Sierra scenery, the **Desolation Wilderness** straddling the Sierra Nevada divide on Tahoe's southwestern side is far from desolate. In fact, this rugged 63,475-acre wonderland is so popular that the wilderness permit system is actually a quota system to minimize human impact in the wild. Half of all wilderness permits for the backpacking season (mid-June through early September) are issued up to 90 days in advance of planned trips, the other half reserved for entrance dates. To obtain free advance permits to enter from the east, contact the U.S. Forest Service office in South Lake Tahoe (see "Tahoe Area Information" below). To enter from the west, contact the U.S. Forest Service, 3070 Camino Heights Dr., Camino 95709. (Hikers not planning an overnight can get tips from rangers on avoiding the crowds.)

Usually better for privacy on backpacks and longer hikes is the **Granite Chief Wilderness** to the west of Tahoe City, established in 1984 to protect the headwaters of the American River. Also not yet subject to visitor rationing and within easy reach of Tahoe is the 105,165-acre **Mokelumne Wilderness** between Hwy. 88 and Hwy. 4—meadows, lakes, and mountains dominated by Mokelumne Peak and the canyon of the Mokelumne River. Farther south still but almost adjacent to Mokelumne is the **Carson-Iceberg Wilderness** between Hwy. 4 and Hwy. 108 and—south of Hwy. 108—the 112,000-acre **Emigrant Wilderness** on the edge of Yosemite, another glaciated lakes-and-meadows volcanic landscape, quite accessible. The Sierra Nevada stretch of the Pacific Crest Trail either skirts (on other national forest lands) or climbs through all of these wilderness areas.

TAHOE AREA SKI RESORTS

See all the latest in Alpine ski wear on Tahoe's flashier fashion slopes, and maybe overhear conversations about investments and stock market risks and whether or not this is the year to get a new cover for the hot tub. For most, making the Tahoe ski scene is a fairly expensive escape from city life—bringing most of that urban baggage along for the ride. But purists are here just *for* the ride—straight down some of the finest downhill slopes in North America. Most Tahoe-area resorts have ski schools and ski shops, equipment rentals, day lodges, and some

downhill skiing at Tahoe

LAKE TAHOE VISITORS AUTHORITY, KEN MIRELL

sort of accommodations and food. Many also have good programs for disabled skiers. New, here and elsewhere, are private Nordic ski resorts (sometimes affiliated with downhill facilities) offering great cross-country ski access and/or groomed trails, and low-key but much-appreciated amenities like trailside warming huts.

Due to so many years of drought in California, most resorts have also invested in snowmaking equipment, so skiing is possible even when the weather refuses to cooperate.

Donner Summit And North Tahoe Resorts

Closest and most accessible to San Francisco and the Bay Area are the four major ski resorts along Donner Summit and two others near Truckee. Farthest west and just off I-80 is small, family-oriented **Soda Springs**, open to the public weekends and holidays but otherwise rentable by groups on an advanced-reservation-only basis. Often uncrowded and oriented to beginners and intermediates, advanced skiers still get a good workout on the upper slopes. Snowboarding allowed. Located on old Hwy. 40, one mile off I-80 via the Norden/Soda Springs exit. For more information, contact: **Boreal/Soda Springs Ski Area,** P.O. Box 39, Truckee 96160, tel. (916) 426-3666. Next east and affiliated with Soda Springs is **Boreal** (named for Boreas, Greek god of the north wind), another beginner-intermediate resort noted for its night skiing with a new triple chairlift. They also make snow at Boreal, when nature won't cooperate. Located just off I-80 via the Castle exit.

Three miles off I-80 via the Norden/Soda Springs exit is **Donner Ski Ranch,** an unpretentious place by Tahoe standards, with cozy down-home lodge, inexpensive dormitory-style accommodations, and impressive terrain most suited to advanced and intermediate Alpine skiers (beginners' slopes too). For more information, contact: Donner Ski Ranch, P.O. Box 66, Norden 95724, tel. (916) 426-3635. Nearby 1,000-acre **Sugar Bowl** offers some of California's best Alpine skiing, emphasizing advanced slopes more than any other resort along I-80 (though intermediates and beginners also have plenty to do here). Snowmaking on at least three main runs. To get to the lifts and lodge (with accommodations and restaurant), skiers ride the gondola up from the parking lot. For more in-

formation, contact: Sugar Bowl Ski Resort, P.O. Box 5, Norden 95724, tel. 426-3651.

Small **Tahoe Donner** northwest of Truckee on Northwoods Blvd. off Donner Pass Rd. (take Donner State Park exit from I-80) is primarily for beginners and intermediates, excellent for first-timers and children, with a special Snowflakes Ski School for children ages three to six. For more information, contact: Tahoe Donner, P.O. Box 11049, Truckee 96162, tel. (916) 587-9444. A definite change-up is **Northstar-at-Tahoe** between Truckee and Lake Tahoe on Hwy. 267, a noted make-the-scene ski scene. Ranked among the nation's best in 1991 by *Snow Country,* Northstar features a cluster of condominiums and creature comforts, with some excellent advanced and intermediate Alpine as well as Nordic ski opportunities included. For more information, contact: Northstar-at-Tahoe, P.O. Box 129, Truckee 96160, tel. 562-1010 or toll-free (800) 533-6787. Not far across the Nevada border are **Diamond Peak at Ski Incline,** tel. (702) 832-1177, noted for its cross country skiing, moonlight tours, and sleigh rides, and **Mount Rose** northeast of Incline Village, tel. 894-0704.

Right across the highway from Mt. Rose is the site of the new **Galena** ski resort. At last report open for cross-country skiing, the huge lodge/casino/resort and downhill facilities were not yet developed. For current information, contact Alpine Meadows (below).

More North Shore Resorts

The most famous of all Tahoe ski resorts, offering some of the world's finest Alpine skiing, is 8,300-acre **Squaw Valley USA,** on Squaw Valley Rd. off Hwy. 89 northwest of Tahoe City. This is heaven to truly adventurous skiers, but also one of the most popular and crowded resorts around—a ski-oriented city in its own right. Squaw Valley offers slopes for advanced, intermediate, and beginning skiers, night skiing, snowboarding, and restricted access for disabled skiers. Even non-skiers show up just to ride the tram up the mountain for the views (a year-round pleasure). New at Squaw Valley is the **climbing wall** in the tram building—have fun and get some exercise while you wait—and an increasing array of summer recreational opportunities. Astounding is the **Bath and Tennis Club** atop the mountain at High Camp, which includes the Olympic Ice Pavilion, spas, a swimming lagoon, and tennis courts (heated for winter play). Also new: the valley's deluxe **Resort at Squaw Creek,** urban luxury in the middle of the wilderness, primarily a conference and convention center with three restaurants, fitness center, shopping, and a winter-only outdoor ice rink. For more information, contact: Squaw Valley USA, P.O. Box 2007, Olympic Valley 96146, tel. (916) 583-6985 or (800) 545-4350 (reservations).

Closer to the lake is the **Alpine Meadows** ski area off Hwy. 89 (via Alpine Meadows Rd.), one of the West's best ski resorts. With six bowls and exceptional views and runs, Alpine is expansive yet low-key, a fine family-oriented alternative to Squaw Valley. (And this is where locals ski.) Busy on weekends, Alpine Meadows also offers one of the state's superior disabled ski programs and is excellent for spring skiing. No snowboarding allowed. For more information, contact: Alpine Meadows, P.O. Box 5279, Tahoe City 96145, tel. (916) 583-4232.

West Shore Resorts

More resort than ski area is **Granlibakken** just south of Tahoe City (off Hwy. 89 via Tonopah Rd., at the end of Granlibakken Rd.), mostly a beginners' hill perfect for families. For more information, contact: Granlibakken Ski and Racquet Resort, P.O. Box 6329, Tahoe City 96145, tel. (916) 583-4242 or toll-free (800) 543-3221. **Ski Homewood** six miles south of Tahoe City is unassuming and small, with stunning Tahoe views, perfect slopes for intermediate skiers (but also some good advanced runs, beginner and family ski possibilities, even a child care center), good spring skiing. For more information, contact: Ski Homewood, P.O. Box 165, Homewood 96141, tel. 525-7256. The **Tahoe Ski Bowl** next door (watch your turns or you'll accidentally end up there) was a private, members-only resort, now incorporated into Homewood.

"Interchangeable Tickets" And Ski Packages

New are the north shore's "interchangeable ticket" program and ticket/ski packages. For Alpine skiers, the three nights lodging/three days ski option starts at $173 per person (double occupancy) and includes a ski-'til-you-drop pass valid at Squaw Valley USA, Alpine Meadows, Diamond Peak, Ski Homewood, Mount Rose, Northstar-at-Tahoe, and Sugar Bowl. The four nights lodging/four days ski option applies to downhill but also extends to Nordic ski resorts (from $119 per person, double occupancy), and the cross-country trail pass is valid at Diamond Peak, Northstar-at-Tahoe, Royal Gorge, Spooner Lake, Squaw Creek, Tahoe Donner, and the Tahoe Nordic Center. Downhill and cross-country multi-resort ski passes are also available *without* accommodations: for downhill skiing from $113 per adult or $36 per child (three days), for cross-country skiing from $40 per adult (four days). For more information or to make reservations, call the Tahoe North Visitors and Convention Bureau: toll-free (800) TAHOE-4-U (824-6348).

South Shore Resorts

Heavenly Valley, "America's Largest Ski Resort" on the California-Nevada border near South Lake Tahoe, is geared toward advanced and high-intermediate skiers. However, there are many trails and runs for beginners. Heavenly Valley has expanded ambitiously, with a new chairlift into "expert" terrain in Mott Canyon, snowmaking on 60 percent of the mountain, and a newly enlarged children's ski center. Get here via Ski Run Blvd. from Hwy. 50 in South Lake Tahoe. For more information, contact: Heavenly Valley, P.O. Box 2180, Stateline, NV 89449, tel. (916) 541-1330.

A few miles west of Echo Summit off Hwy. 50 is impressive **Sierra Ski Ranch,** with something for everyone: open bowls and tree runs for experts and intermediates, also plenty of fun for beginners and families. The emphasis here on better access and options for beginning skiers continues. The Ranchhouse restaurant up top is a worthy destination anyway, just for the views. For more information, contact: Sierra Ski Ranch, P.O. Box 3501, Twin Bridges 95735, tel. (916) 659-7453. South of Tahoe via Hwy. 89 then Hwy. 88, but close enough for Tahoe skiers, are **Iron Mountain** and **Kirkwood.** (See "South of Tahoe" below.)

Nordic Skiing: Public Trails

Fun is the three-mile **Castle Peak Trail,** a Sno-Park site near Boreal (exit I-80 at Castle Peak/Boreal) which also offers unmarked backcountry cross-country access and a nearby ski hut. (There are other backcountry huts in the area as well.) A variety of other marked and unmarked Nordic ski trails are maintained by the Forest Service in and around Tahoe in winter, including **Donner Memorial State Park** (easy), **Martis Lookout** (moderate), **Tahoe Meadows** (easy), and **Spooner Lake** (easy) in the north and east. Cross-country ski trails along the lake's west shore include **Five Lakes** (strenuous), **Paige Meadows** and **Blackwood Canyon** (both moderate), **Sugar Pine Point State Park** and Meeks Creek (both easy), and **McKinney/Rubicon** (moderate).

The most strenuous Nordic trails near the south shore are at **Angora Lookout** and **Trout Creek/ Fountain Place**. The **Taylor Creek/Fallen Leaf** trail is moderately difficult (but good for beginners). There are moderate trails at the **Echo Lakes** area (which also offers good ski camping access into Desolation Wilderness), **Benwood Meadows,** and **Big Meadow/Round Lake**. The easiest trails are at the **Lake Tahoe Visitor Center** and at **Grass Lake** and **Hope Valley**.

For more information about the area's national forest ski trails, and to find out about ranger-led interpretive ski tours (usually scheduled January through mid-March), contact the Forest Service (see "Tahoe Area Information" below).

South and southwest from Tahoe are other good public Nordic ski areas, including the **Loon Lake** area north of Hwy. 50 (reached via Ice House Rd.) and **Strawberry Canyon** near Strawberry and Twin Bridges; the invigorating **Leek Springs Loop** and **Winnemucca Lake Loop** off Hwy. 88; at various sites along **Hwy. 4** (including—a good workout—skiing the highway beyond Bear Valley's Hwy. 4 closure gate to Ebbetts Pass); and at **Pinecrest** (24 miles of trails) above Sonora on Hwy. 108.

Nordic Skiing: Private Resorts
Closest to Sacramento (off I-80 at Yuba Gap) is **Eagle Mountain,** with groomed trails, lessons, day lodge, special events. For more info, tel. (916) 389-2254. Nordic skiing is big news at Tahoe ski resorts. Among the best in the country (and largest in North America) is **Royal Gorge** in Soda Springs, with 77 trails and 175 miles of track, warming huts and Eurostyle wilderness lodge, also day lodge, cafe, and rental-retail ski shop. New are Royal Gorge's lifts, for easier access to upper slopes and for practicing downhill cross-country on steeper slopes. For more information, contact: Royal Gorge Cross-Country Ski Resort, P.O. Box 1100, Soda Springs 95728, tel. (916) 426-3871. The Sierra Club's **Clair Tappaan Lodge** nearby in Norden, one of the best inexpensive places to stay near Tahoe, offers lessons, rentals, and a few miles of track, tel. 426-3632. **Tahoe Donner,** tel. 587-9484, has 31 trails and 42 miles of track (with some night Nordic skiing), and **Northstar-at-Tahoe,** tel. 562-1010, has 45 miles of cross-country track. **Squaw Valley** also offers Nordic skiing.

The **Tahoe Nordic Ski Center** near Tahoe City offers 36 miles of track and 36 miles of trails, moonlight ski tours, daytime tours, and

different in winter: a sleigh ride

LAKE TAHOE VISITORS AUTHORITY, JOHN KELLY

clinics. For more information, contact: Tahoe Nordic, P.O. Box 1632, Tahoe City 96145, tel. (916) 583-0484 or 583-9858. Resort areas south of Tahoe also offer good cross-country skiing opportunities (see "South of Tahoe"). Just south of the airport is the **Lake Tahoe Winter Sports Center** with many miles of groomed trails, tel. 577-2940. Quite close to Tahoe: the **Cody Hut Ski Treks** from the Strawberry Lodge on Hwy. 50 to the dormitory-style hut halfway to Hwy. 88; guided and self-guided trips (for intermediates and above), also guided "hot springs" treks for beginners and intermediates. Call 626-5097 for information and reservations. Also here: 11 miles of marked national forest ski trails.

Other Winter Diversions

Depending upon the weather and other circumstances, some "summer" activities (below) are also feasible in other seasons. Strictly winter diversions offered by **Sierra Ski Touring**, Box 176, Gardnerville, NV 89410, tel. (702) 782-3047, include "Husky Express" dog sled rides and expeditions (advance reservations required). Sleigh rides and other unusual cold-weather activities are offered by other companies. Not nearly as mellow: the **Lake Tahoe Winter Sports Center** at the intersection of Hwy. 50 and Country Club Dr., tel. (916) 577-2940, which offers snowmobiling on groomed tracks adjacent to its cross-country ski trails.

MORE TAHOE RECREATION

The Summer Resort Trend

As elsewhere in the state, transforming ski resorts into year-round vacation destinations is the coming recreational trend in and around the Tahoe area. Formerly winter-only resorts now offer everything from guided hikes (sometimes with llamas), mountain biking, and horseback riding to tennis and fly fishing.

During summer months, for example, **Northstar-at-Tahoe** near Truckee, tel. (916) 587-0248 or toll-free (800) 533-6787, offers hiking and mountain biking (rentals available) on 1,700 acres of diverse trails, not to mention full use of its recreation center with swimming pool, tennis courts, exercise room, and hot tubs. Golfing (including golf school) and horseback riding available, too, as well as organized programs for children. Special events in summer are almost endless. Vacation packages, featuring rodeos to romance, can be very good deals. Nearby **Squaw Valley** also dedicates itself to endless summers, offering everything from Alpine mountain biking, ice skating, tennis, horseback riding, and swimming at its **High Camp Bath & Tennis Club** (elev. 8,200 feet) to a full roster of special events.

Near Tahoe, **Sorenson's Resort** (see "Hope Valley and Sorenson's" under "Southeast from Picketts Junction" below) is perhaps the epitome of resort creativity any time of year, with special activities like summer historical hikes, spring stargazing, and other educational adventures. In the off-season, **Kirkwood** on Hwy. 88, tel. (209) 258-6000, provides private tennis courts, mountain bike trails, guided llama hikes, a historical hike along the old Emigrant Trail, horseback riding (and pony rides for children), fly-fishing in Kirkwood Creek, and a week-long July watercolor workshop with artist Robert Reynolds.

Mountain Biking

The Tahoe area, particularly the west shore, is perfect for fat-tired bike enthusiasts. (Mountain bikes aren't allowed in wilderness areas, though other national forest areas are accessible.) Come in September for Tahoe's annual **Fat Tire Festival,** a mountain biking blowout. If you don't tote your own, rent bikes at **Porter's Ski and Sport** in Tahoe City, tel. (916) 583-0293, or **CyclePaths** two miles south of town on Hwy. 89, tel. 581-1171, also a great stop for trail maps and suggestions, including guided half-day or full-day mountain bike tours of the area. Information about more ambitious mountain bike routes, including old area logging roads, is also available through national forest headquarters and local ranger district offices (see "Tahoe Area Information" below).

An unusually scenic and far from lonely bike route is the **Flume Trail** from the trailhead at Spooner Lake (a loop if you return, a fun one-way if you arrange a car shuttle from Incline Village). Fairly challenging is the 12-mile **Paige Meadows/Truckee River** loop, starting from Fanny Bridge in Tahoe City and heading south then west, ending up back in Tahoe City after cruising several miles along the Truckee River bike path. Much easier: the six-mile **Blackwood Canyon** loop or the six-mile loop through undeveloped sections of **Sugar Pine Point State Park.**

windsurfing regatta,
Lake Tahoe

Many major ski resorts offer mountain biking trails, rentals, and even tote-your-bike lift rides to quite challenging high altitude terrain and trails.

Other Summer Diversions

In spring, summer, and fall, **North Tahoe Cruises,** P.O. Box 7913, Tahoe City 96145, tel. (916) 583-0141, offers tours of Emerald Bay, cocktail and dinner dance cruises, and a west shore "Shoreline Treasure" tour of historical sites and astounding private estates (just about the only way most folks will ever see them). **Lake Tahoe Cruises,** P.O. Box 14292, South Lake Tahoe 96151, tel. (916) 541-3897 or toll-free (800) 238-2463, is noted for its endless variety of cruises (popular with tour groups) aboard the glass-bottomed sternwheeler *Tahoe Queen,* including runs to Emerald Bay. Also popular for similar tours is the M.S. *Dixie,* P.O. Box 1667, Zephyr Cove, NV 89448, tel. (702) 588-3508 or 882-0786, which schedules a breakfast cruise along the lake's eastern shore, served up with local history. For all three, call or write for current schedule and rates.

Kayakers with lake-sized appetites can shove off on a **Tahoe Paddle and Oar** kayak brunch tour, departing from the North Tahoe Beach Center with a mid-trip meal at the La Playa Restaurant in Tahoe Vista. For more information about the brunch bunch and other kayak tour options, call Paddle and Oar at (916) 581-3029. Quite popular, for rentals, tours, and instruction, is **Kayak Tahoe** at Camp Richardson's Anchorage Marina, tel. 544-2011. For another unique take on Tahoe water touring, try **Woodwind Sailing Cruises,** Box 1375, Zephyr Cove, NV 89448, tel. (702) 588-3000.

Aerial Perspective, tel. (916) 541-6262, is just what you get when you take an airplane tour of the Tahoe Basin. Seaplane tours are the specialty of **Cal-Vada Aircraft** near Homewood, tel. 525-7142. Near the north shore **Mountain High Enterprises,** tel. toll-free (800) 231-6922, gets you into the air with hot air balloons. For the same thrill near South Lake Tahoe, try **Alpine Adventures Aloft,** P.O. Box 151, Minden, NV 89423, tel. toll-free (800) 332-9997 or (702) 782-7239. Also silent and soaring is a glider ride over the Sierra Nevada; for information or reservations, contact **Soar Minden** at the Douglas County Airport in Nevada, tel. toll-free (800) 345-7627 or (702) 782-7627.

More down to earth: horseback riding. Many resorts offer guided rides and/or horse rentals. For other options, contact area visitors bureaus. Golfing is even more down to earth. There are eight courses in the North Lake Tahoe/Truckee area (two designed by Robert Trent Jones) and five courses in South Lake Tahoe, including nationally recognized **Tahoe Edgewood** and **Glenbrook.**

For other area recreation information—on everything from parasailing, sailboarding, jet-skiing, fishing charters, scuba diving, and boat rentals to the best places to go rollerblading or wildflower hiking—contact local visitors bureaus ("Tahoe Area Information" below).

LAKE OF THE SKY ACCOMMODATIONS: NORTH

Camping, The North Lake Tahoe Hostel

State park campgrounds at Lake Tahoe (see "Tahoe Area Sights" above) are popular, with reservations through Mistix (tel. 800-444-7275) necessary from May through early September—though all campgrounds may be open considerably longer, weather permitting, on a first-come, first-camped basis, and **Sugar Pine Point** is open to campers year-round. Nearby state parks with campgrounds include **Donner Memorial State Park** and **Grover Hot Springs State Park** (the latter also open year-round). Most national forest campgrounds—there are plenty near the lake, and dozens throughout the greater Tahoe area—are first-come, first-camped, but popular campgrounds like **Fallen Leaf** can be reserved in advance, for $10 per night, through Mistix, tel. (800) 283-2267. One of the area's best-kept camping secrets is near South Lake Tahoe across the Nevada border, at **Nevada State Beach,** with open, pine-shaded lake frontage camping ($14) just a stone's throw from the beach and an easy walk to Safeway and other signposts of civilization. Ask about other regional campground choices at ranger stations, chambers of commerce, or visitors centers.

The AYH-affiliated **North Lake Tahoe Hostel** at the **Star Hotel** in Truckee, 10015 W. River St., P.O. Box 1227, Truckee 96160, tel. (916) 587-3007, is both a hotel (rooms $35-60) and a dormitory-style hostel just a half-block from downtown. Hostel rates: $10 AYH members, $15 nonmembers. (Especially popular during the winter ski season, so reserve well in advance.)

Truckee Area Accommodations

Get complete accommodations listings from local visitors bureaus. Most ski resorts in and around the Tahoe-Truckee area (see above) and elsewhere offer restaurants and various accommodations options, but unusually interesting inns are also scattered throughout the greater Tahoe area. Downtown in Truckee is the **Truckee Hotel** at Commercial and Bridge streets, P.O. Box 884, Truckee 96160, tel. (916) 587-4444, an old 1868 lumberjack hotel spruced up to suit the modern world, with 37 rooms but

only eight with private baths, fairly reasonable for the Tahoe area. Rooms with private baths run $89-114; "European-style" rooms with shared baths are $74-106 during the winter high-season, lower in summer. Continental breakfast buffet included. Restaurant and bar downstairs.

Motels in the Truckee area include the **Donner Lake Village** "apartment motel" about six miles west of town on old Hwy. 40 at the west end of Donner Lake, tel. (916) 587-6081 or toll-free (800) 621-6664, with studios and one- and two-bedroom units, $65 and up. Just over a mile outside town at 11331 Hwy. 267, P.O. Box 34049, Truckee 96160, is the **Best Western Truckee Tahoe Inn,** tel. 587-4525, with weekend rates from $68 (less on weekdays).

Also near Truckee is the 1881 Victorian **Richardson House** bed and breakfast at Spring and High streets, P.O. Box 2011, Truckee 96160, tel. (916) 587-5388, with rooms $50-75, full breakfast included. (Lower midweek and spring/summer rates.) The small **Donner Country Inn** across from Donner Lake at 10070 Gregory Place, tel. 587-5574, has five rooms with fireplaces, $85-95.

The Sierra Club's **Clair Tappaan Lodge** at Norden (P.O. Box 36, Norden 95724, tel. 916-426-3632) is a time-honored skiers' tradition—inexpensive dormitory-style rooms, family rooms, and tiny two-person rooms in a rambling, cedar shake-sided lodge complete with hot tub, library, kitchen, and dining facilities. Three family-style meals per day are included in the rates: $27 and up per person per night during the week for Sierra Club members, $32 for nonmembers, and $62 members, $72 nonmembers for the two-day minimum on weekends. Extra fee for cross-country ski rentals, ski school, and hot tub. (Good weekend and summer programs.)

Also a pleasure and nearby is the **Rainbow Lodge** about six miles west of Soda Springs on old Hwy. 40 (take the Rainbow Rd. exit from I-80), P.O. Box 178, Soda Springs 95728, tel. (916) 426-3871 or 426-3661, now affiliated with the Royal Gorge Nordic ski resort. Built in 1925 of granite and hand-hewn timbers, with a log-beamed ceiling and knotty pine interiors, the one-time Rainbow Tavern and Trout Farm now features 32 homey rooms (20 with private baths) and one suite, rates (winter) $59-99, (summer) $49-75, breakfast included. The fine **Engadine**

Cafe is on the premises, as well as a tavern with live weekend entertainment. (Those in the know say the Rainbow Lodge also features a ghost named Mary, who lives on the third floor.)

The **Donner Summit Lodge**, P.O. Box 115, Soda Springs 95728, tel. (916) 426-3638, has modern, moderately priced motel rooms ($40-80) plus a restaurant and bar; it was built in 1914 as a fur-coat farm (silver fox). A stay here atop Donner Summit in snowy winter suggests why.

North And West Shore Accommodations

Overall best bets for travel bargains are seasonal vacation packages—suited to all interests and income levels—offered in the north shore area (including Truckee) through the Tahoe North Visitors and Convention Bureau, tel. toll-free (800) TAHOE 4 U. The visitors bureau will also recommend (and make) lodging reservations based on budgetary and other preferences.

The **Cedar Glen Lodge** on Hwy. 28 just a few miles west of the Nevada border, P.O. Box 188, Tahoe Vista 96148, tel. (916) 546-4281, has motel rooms from $55, also housekeeping cottages, sauna, whirlpool, pool, and playground. Farther from the madding crowds too is the **Charmey Chalet Resort** (pronounced shar-MAY) in Tahoe Vista at 6549 N. Lake Blvd., tel. 546-2529, where the highway widens into four lanes. A new hot tub at the pool and other recent renovations have jazzed up this hill-climbing motel with tall trees and outdoor patios, sliding glass doors, in-room refrigerators, TV, phones. Coffee and sweet rolls at breakfast. Rates (from $65) are higher on weekends and in summer, substantially lower at other times. Nearby are other decent mid-range motels.

In Tahoe City, the **Tahoe City Inn** at 790 N. Lake Blvd., tel. (800) 800-TAHO for reservations, has rooms with waterbeds and in-room spas, quite inexpensive at non-peak times. Also an off-season bargain, especially for AAA members, is the **Tahoe City Travelodge** at 455 N. Lake Blvd., P.O. Box 84, Tahoe City 96145, tel. (916) 583-3766, comfortable and attractive, near the lake, golfing adjacent. A popular après-ski spot, fun in summer for riverside dining, and decent year-round for lodgings is the **River Ranch** on the Truckee River just off Hwy. 89 at Alpine Meadows Rd., P.O. Box 197, Tahoe City 96145, tel. (916) 583-4264. Rooms with

antiques and modern amenities from $50.

For classic Old Tahoe ambience, consider the **Sunnyside Lodge and Restaurant** on the lake and south of town at 1850 W. Lake Blvd., P.O. Box 5969, Tahoe City 96145, tel. (916) 583-7200, rooms with private decks from $120. For cabins, those at the **Tahoma Lodge** at 7018 W. Lake Blvd., P.O. Box 62, Tahoma 96142, tel. 525-7721, are quiet, comfortable, and reasonably priced from $65.

For current information on Nevada-side accommodations, as well as suggestions on condominium and cabin rentals, contact the visitors bureau.

North Tahoe Bed And Breakfasts

The north shore boasts B&B accommodations in addition to those near Donner Pass and Truckee (see above).

The **Mayfield House** bed and breakfast inn at 236 Grove St., P.O. Box 5999, Tahoe City 96145, tel. (916) 583-1001, is the former cottage home of Norman Mayfield (a contractor who worked closely with architect Julia Morgan), a half mile north of the Hwy. 28/Hwy. 89 intersection and just blocks from the lake. Upstairs rooms share a bath (as do those downstairs), full breakfasts served. Room rates are $70-105. Another good choice and a Tahoe classic with its dark brown buildings and blue shutters: the **Cottage Inn** just south of town, 1690 W. Lake Blvd. (Hwy. 89), P.O. Box 66, Tahoe City 96145, tel. 581-4073, a cluster of cozy knotty-pine bed and breakfast cabins (full breakfast served in guest rooms or in dining room) with beach access and sauna, rates $75-135. Scandinavian decor. The lakefront **Chaney House** bed and breakfast, five miles south of Tahoe City proper at 4725 W. Lake Blvd., P.O. Box 7852, Tahoe City 96145, tel. 525-7333, is a 1920s-vintage stone house complete with Gothic arches and massive fireplace, four rooms or suites with private baths (two share a shower), private beach and pier, full breakfast. Rates from $85.

The **Rockwood Lodge** bed and breakfast at 5295 W. Lake Blvd., P.O. Box 544, Homewood 96141, tel. (916) 525-5273, offers antique furnishings in a plush, 1930s-vintage Tahoe rock-and-pine home, rates $100-150. Near Sugar Pine Point State Park is **The Captain's Alpenhaus**, 6941 W. Lake Blvd., P.O. Box 262, Tahoma 96142, tel. 525-5000, rooms and suites

$60-175, full breakfast, pool, and whirlpool. Cottages (two bedrooms) suitable for four start at $100. Wednesday night is Basque dinner night at the restaurant.

LAKE OF THE SKY ACCOMODATIONS: SOUTH

The **Lake Tahoe Visitors Bureau** (serving South Tahoe) has instituted a "pine tree" rating system for its member accommodations, with the number of pine trees (one to four) making it simple for visitors to compare the relative quality of similarly priced accommodations—a very useful (and successful) service. The system also applies to property management companies, so consumers can compare cabins, condos, and other rentals. To receive a current listing of South Lake Tahoe accommodations, call the visitors bureau, toll-free (800) AT-TAHOE.

Two good motels outside town are both great bargains. The **Lazy S Lodge,** 609 Emerald Bay Rd., South Lake Tahoe 96150, tel. (916) 541-0230, is a quiet find, quaint cottages with kitchens and Swedish wood-burning fireplaces or motel-style rooms, also barbecues, picnic tables, lots of lawn, pool and deck. Closer still to Sierra Ski Ranch and Kirkwood is the **Ridgewood Inn,** 1341 Emerald Bay Rd., tel. 541-8589, a small motel (12 units), some adjoining rooms perfect for families.

Motels clog the artery of Hwy. 50 toward South Lake Tahoe and Stateline. Inexpensive and predictable is **Motel 6,** on Hwy. 50 just east of the Hwy. 89 junction, 2375 Lake Tahoe Blvd., P.O. Box 7756, South Lake Tahoe 96158, tel. (916) 542-1400. The usual amenities are offered, with rates $30-36.

Swank Stays

The new **Embassy Suites Resort** hotel right on the California-Nevada border, 4130 Tahoe Blvd., South Lake Tahoe 96150, tel. (916) 544-5400 or toll-free (800) EMBASSY, is the best example to date of South Tahoe's new redevelopment style, a modern take on the traditional early-1900s architecture on display at Tallac and elsewhere. Suites start at $159 during summer and other peak periods, $119 at other times, though specials may be substantially less. Other nice accommodations close to the

casinos (which are housed in four-star hotels) include the **Best Western Station House Inn** at 901 Park Ave., P.O. Box 4009, South Lake Tahoe 96157, tel. 542-1101, rates starting at $98 (less in winter).

Top-flight farther up the hill: the **Tahoe Seasons Resort** at Heavenly Valley, Saddle Rd. at Keller, P.O. Box 5656, South Lake Tahoe 96157, tel. 541-6700, featuring comfortable suites with in-room spas, kitchenettes (refrigerators, sink, microwave), TVs and VCRs, and fold-out sofa bed in sitting room, all with adequate privacy for families or two couples traveling together. Valet parking. Room rates (for up to four people): $95-128, from $160 for larger suites. Exceptionally elegant and with every imaginable resort amenity is **The Ridge Tahoe,** P.O. Box 5790, Stateline, NV 89449, tel. (702) 588-3553, a resort complex at an elevation of 7,300 feet, just a gondola lift to the slopes. High season rates $155-400, lower in summer, even lower in spring/fall.

South Shore Inns, Rustic Resorts

South Lake Tahoe is short on bed and breakfasts. **The Christiana Inn** ("The Chris" to its fans), P.O. Box 18298, South Lake Tahoe 96151, tel. toll-free (800) 4-CAL-SKI or (916) 544-7337, has been around almost forever, an elegant European-style country inn on Saddle Rd. almost under Heavenly's main chairlift. Six unique suites, all with private baths, plus lounge and excellent restaurant. Also cozy and continental yet somehow simpler is **Les Geraniums,** P.O. Box 6319, South Lake Tahoe 96157, tel. (916) 544-6450, just two rooms.

A time-honored rustic retreat is the **Zephyr Cove Resort** on Forest Service land across the border at 760 Hwy. 50, P.O. Box 830, Zephyr Cove, NV 89448, tel. (702) 588-6644, with choices of lodge rooms, bungalows, cabins, and chalets. Reasonable rates, good restaurant.

The 83-acre **Camp Richardson Resort,** a lodge, cabin, and campground resort complex a few miles south of Emerald Bay on Hwy. 89, P.O. Box 10648, South Lake Tahoe 96158, tel. (916) 541-1801, is a wonderful 1930s-style rustic respite among the pines. The circa-1923 lodge includes a rugged stone fireplace, log rafters, and 30 rooms with private baths for $59-79. Out back are Camp Richardson's 42 cabins, complete with kitchens and bathrooms, available for

$469-910 per week (for up to eight people) in summer, $79-110 per night in winter. The resort's campground across the highway features 112 campsites with amenities like hot showers for $16-22 per night. Camp Richardson also offers a beach, marina, and other recreational attractions, including Nordic skiing in winter.

The granite-and-log **Echo Chalet** south on Hwy. 50, 9900 Echo Lakes Rd., Echo Lake 95721, tel. (916) 659-7207, is quiet and isolated, with 10 rustic woodsy cabins (which sleep two to four), $66-86 per night. (Take the chalet's water taxi service across the lake to Desolation Wilderness.) Also special, winter or summer, is the refurbished **Strawberry Lodge** roadhouse, tucked under the granite cliffs beyond Echo Summit about 20 miles west of South Lake Tahoe via Hwy. 50, P.O. Box 1076, South Lake Tahoe 96156, tel. 659-7200, the first genuine ski lodge in the Sierra Nevada, originally built in the 1850s. Smack dab in the middle of the popular Strawberry Canyon cross-country ski area, lodge rooms (either in the main lodge or the annex across the highway) run $55-100. Also here: dining hall with stone fireplace, hearty restaurant fare (open-air deck dining in summer), even an ice cream shop.

EATING WELL HIGH IN THE SKY: NORTH TAHOE

Truckee Area Eateries

Most everything is along Commercial St. or within a block or two. For cheap eats in Truckee, try the **Squeeze Inn** on Commercial Row, tel. (916) 587-9814, noted for its 22 kinds of sandwiches, 57 varieties of omelettes, and city-style pizzas (with toppings like artichoke hearts and prosciutto). Open for breakfast and lunch daily. After lunch, stop off at **Bud's Fountain** inside the sporting goods store for that old-fashioned ice cream soda.

More upscale in the California cuisine tradition is **The Passage** in the Truckee Hotel, tel. 587-7619, and **O.B.'s Pub and Restaurant,** tel. 587-4164 (fabulous Sunday brunch). For elegant French fare, the place in Truckee is the **Left Bank,** tel. 587-4694. Or, try dinner at the **Rainbow Lodge** (see "Truckee Area Accommodations" above).

North And West Shore Restaurants

Much-loved is **Rosie's Cafe** at 571 N. Lake Blvd. in Tahoe City, tel. (916) 583-8504, for reasonably priced and excellent American favorites like ham and eggs for breakfast, burgers at lunch. Very "Tahoe" and a genuine locals' hot spot is the **Fire Sign Cafe** two miles south of Tahoe City at 1785 W. Lake Blvd. in Tahoe Park (near the Cottage Inn), tel. 583-0871—wholesome homestyle cooking in a casually eclectic atmosphere, fabulous for a morning meal (fresh-squeezed juices, homemade muffins, omelettes and other hearty fare) and open seven days a week (until 3 p.m.) for both breakfast and lunch. In good weather, sun yourself out on the deck. **Hacienda del Lago,** referred to as "the Hac" by locals, 760 N. Lake Blvd., tel. 583-0358, is open daily for lunch and dinner—*the* place for Mexican food and great margaritas, a local hangout. Especially at lunch, another good spot to soak up local atmosphere, pool tables and all, is **The Bridgetender** near Fanny Bridge in Tahoe City, best for burgers (including veggie burgers).

Fun and quite good for hot and spicy Cajun food is **Colonel Claire's** on the highway in Tahoe Vista. A locals' favorite for breakfast and lunch in Carnelian Bay is the **Original Old Post Office Cafe,** 5245 N. Lake Tahoe Blvd., tel. (916) 546-3205.

Area resorts also serve some good food; ask at the visitors bureau for the newest offerings. At Squaw Valley alone: try a midday meal at top-of-the-tram **Alexander's,** tel. (916) 583-2555, or an exceptional contemporary French dinner at **Glissande** (brought to you by the former La Cheminée folks) at the valley's Resort at Squaw Creek, tel. 583-6300.

For more fine dining—reservations always recommended—North Tahoe choices include **Christy Hill** in the Lakehouse Mall, 115 Grove St. in Tahoe City, tel. (916) 583-8551, noted for its California cuisine, views, and fireplace, and **La Playa** at 7046 N. Lake Blvd., tel. 546-5903, popular for creative salads, seafood, and Sunday brunch. Considered one of the best French restaurants on the west coast is **Le Petit Pier** at 7252 N. Lake Blvd., tel. (916) 546-4464.

The **Tahoe House** restaurant and bakery, a half mile south of Tahoe City's "Y" on Hwy. 89, tel. (916) 583-1377, serves European fare (specializing in Swiss-German and Swiss-French entrees at dinner), also pastas and fresh seafood specials. Children's menu, takeout available.

Most famous of all in Tahoe City—and unforgettable for its excellent if high-priced vegetarian fare—is **Wolfdale's,** 640 N. Lake Blvd. in Tahoe City, tel. (916) 583-5700, noted for its Japanese-flavored California cuisine. Good wine list, full bar. Expensive. Also excellent in the high-priced dinner category is the **Swiss Lakewood Restaurant** at 5055 W. Lake Blvd., tel. 525-5211, unstuffy yet elegant fare, dining room dress code.

EATING WELL HIGH IN THE SKY: SOUTH TAHOE

South Shore Restaurants
The cheapest eats of all are available in the casinos in Nevada's Stateline; the big hotels are happy to serve breakfast for $1 or so just to get folks within reach of those one-armed bandits. In South Lake Tahoe, fast-food eateries, small cafes, and some very decent restaurants manage to coexist. For an incredibly generous breakfast, try **Red Hut Waffles** at 2723 Hwy. 50, tel. (916) 541-9024, noted for its huge waffles and good omelettes. (There's another Red Hut across the border in Nevada, on Kingsbury.) Another local favorite, quite casual in the lunch and dinner fast food tradition, is **Izzy's Burger Spa,** 2591 Hwy. 50, tel. 544-5030. For fabulous woodoven-baked pizzas and other delectables in a decidely more upscale setting, new here (but well established elsewhere) is **Zackary's Lake Tahoe** in the new Embassy Suites Resort, 4130 Lake Tahoe Blvd., tel. 544-5400, ext. 140.

For special dinners, **Nephele's** at 1169 Ski Run Blvd., tel. (916) 544-8130, has excellent daily specials, also pastas, baby back ribs, and scampi. Private hot tubs on the premises. **Scoozi!** nearby on Ski Run, tel. 542-0100, has imaginative pizzas and calzones, great pastas (try one of the specialties) and select chicken, fish, seafood, and steak entrees, all in a lively atmosphere. Also raved about: the exceptionally fine dining room at the **Christiana Inn** at 3819 Saddle Rd., tel. 544-7337.

Popular for European cuisine (mostly German and Swiss) and fairly casual is **The Swiss Chalet Restaurant,** four miles west of Stateline at 2540 Tahoe Blvd. (Hwy. 50 at Sierra Blvd.), tel. (916) 544-3304. For good Italian food (dinner only) **Petrello's Ristorante** is the place, 900 Emerald Bay Rd., tel. 541-7868. Probably the best for seafood is **The Dory's Oar,** 1041 Fremont, tel. 541-6603, a New England-style restaurant and lounge with fresh seafood from both coasts plus a selection of steaks.

The Edgewood Terrace at the Edgewood country club, tel. (702) 588-3566, has great food, good views. Sometimes a meal here is a real bargain, too, with two-for-one coupons available in winter and at other slower times. The **Zephyr Cove Lodge** is also quite good, the dining room cozied up in winter by wood heat. Also worth it, Nevada-side, is **Pisces,** the new seafood and fish restaurant at Caesar's Tahoe, 55 Hwy. 50, tel. 588-3515. Also exceptional is **Llewelyn's** on the 19th floor at Harvey's on Hwy. 50 at Stateline, tel. 588-2411. The wonderful view is unveiled, on sunny days, by light-sensitive electronic shades that raise automatically at sunset.

But for fine dining, *the* place to eat in South Lake Tahoe these days is **Evan's American Gourmet Cafe** at 536 Emerald Bay Rd., tel. (916) 542-1990, a tiny restaurant (just 12 tables) enthused over by none other than *Bon Appetit.* Reservations essential.

TAHOE AREA EVENTS

For both major and minor area events, contact local chambers and visitors bureaus for current information. (See "Tahoe Area Information" below.)

In winter, most of the action centers around the ski resorts and—Nevada-side—the casino scene. South Lake Tahoe's **Lake Tahoe Winter Festival** in January is some show, with Heavenly Valley ski events (some televised) combined with community events like the torchlight parade down the mountain and ice-carving contests. North Tahoe's **Snowfest** comes in late February and early March. This cold-weather fun fest is considered the largest in the western U.S., events and activities including ski racing and films and concerts but also offbeat antics like the Polar Bear Swim, Diaper Derby, Napkin Hat Contest, and the Dress Up Your Dog Contest.

Come summer, activities and events spin by. Fun for everyone in June: the **Truckee-Tahoe Air Show,** with hot air balloons, daredevil aerialists, and more. Fun for some: the **Western States 100 Mile Run** from Squaw Valley to Auburn. New for cyclists is **America's Most Beautiful Bike Ride,** a fully supported one-day tour around Tahoe's 72-mile shoreline (with shorter and longer mileage options) starting and ending at Zephyr Cove near South Lake Tahoe.

The don't-miss Tahoe event, though, is the **Valhalla Arts & Music Festival** at the Tallac Historic Site near South Lake Tahoe, a multi-faceted experience which runs from late June or early July into September. Galleries and working exhibits showcasing fine artists and their craft are open to the public Fri.-Wed., 11-3. Exhibits and events change weekly. Increasingly prominent is the annual **Wa She She E Deh** ("Washoe People's Hand") **Native American Fine Arts Festival & Celebration,** usually held late July/early August and featuring basketry and other cultural contributions from the Da-ow people. Other events are musical, ranging from bluegrass and mariachi performances to **Thursday Evening Jazz** in Valhalla—great music and a mellow crowd—and **Sunday Afternoon Chamber Music** at Tallac. The phenomenally popular **Starlight Jazz Series,** usually held on consecutive weekends in early September at the Lake of the Sky Amphitheatre (at the Forest Service visitor center adjacent to Tallac), presents major jazz artists like Johnny Otis, Queen Ida, Zachary Richard and the Bon Ton Boys, and the Dirty Dozen Brass Band. For more information about the Valhalla Arts & Music Festival, contact the Lake Tahoe Visitors Bureau or: **The Tahoe Tallac Assocoation,** P.O. Box 1595, South Lake Tahoe 95705, summer tel. (916) 542-ARTS or 541-4975, winter tel. 541-4975. Also held at Tallac: the **Great Gatsby Festival.**

Hot in July: the **Isuzu Celebrity Golf Championship** at South Lake Tahoe's Edgewood Tahoe Golf Course and the north shore's **Music at Sand Harbor** festival at the Nevada State Beach in Nevada. The **Lake Tahoe Summer Music Festival** runs from mid-July to mid-August, the north shore's answer to Valhalla, quite wonderful in its own right, with everything from pops and classical and children's music to jazz and highland bagpipes. Concerts are held at a wide variety of venues. In the same vein: **Tahoe Mountain Musicals,** usually held in August, as is the **Shakespeare at Sand Harbor** festival. Quite the draw for the cowboy set, urban and otherwise, is August's **Truckee Championship Rodeo.** But only the truly intrepid show up in late August to participate in Lake Tahoe's **World's Toughest Triathlon,** which those in the know say is indeed more difficult than Kona, Hawaii's legendary Ironman. One of four events now included in the Lake Tahoe Summer Sports Festival, the World's Toughest is now a qualifying event for the Ironman.

The **Great Reno Balloon Race,** with over 100 hot-air balloonists in hot competition, and the **Virginia City International Camel Races** offer some oddball fun on the Nevada side come September. In October comes the **Kokanee Salmon Festival** near South Lake Tahoe, as well as **Octoberfest** at Alpine Meadows. With or without nature's cooperation, ski season starts in November, kicking off an endless parade of **ski races** and other snow-related celebrations.

TAHOE AREA INFORMATION

General And Recreational Information

To get current information on the entire Tahoe area and its attractions, contact *all* area visitors bureaus, since each represents a limited geographical area.

The best source for South Lake Tahoe information is the **Lake Tahoe Visitors Authority** at the corner of Ski Run Blvd. and Tamarack, P.O. Box 16299, South Lake Tahoe 96151, tel. (916) 544-5050 or toll-free (800) AT TAHOE (for a copy of the annual *Lake Tahoe Travel Planner* or the seasonal *Package & Lodging Guide,* and to make accommodations reservations). If you stop by, be sure to pick up the "Tahoe Resource Brochure," an all-around Lake Tahoe-at-your-fingertips guide produced in conjunction with the Nevada Commission on Tourism and the Tahoe-Douglas Chamber of Commerce.

The **Tahoe North Visitors and Convention Bureau,** P.O. Box 5578, Tahoe City 96145, tel. toll-free (800) TAHOE-4-U (for accommodations, rates, special package information, and reservations) or tel. (916) 583-3494, shares space at 950 N. Lake Tahoe Blvd. in Tahoe City with the **Greater North Lake Tahoe Chamber** of Commerce, tel. 581-6900. Visitors arriving after business hours can use the light-up "locator map" and free reservations phone for lining up last-minute lodgings, plus rifle the racks for brochures and free local publications. To take advantage of Tahoe North's aggressive marketing of vacation packages, from ski weekends to honeymoon and wedding specials, advance planning is necessary—and usually well worth it.

For more regional information, contact the **Truckee-Donner Chamber of Commerce,** P.O. Box 2757, Truckee 96160, tel. (916) 587-2757 or toll-free (800) 548-8388, located inside the train station; the **Incline Village Chamber of Commerce,** 969 Tahoe Blvd., Incline Village, NV 89451, tel. (702) 831-4440 or toll-free (800) GO TAHOE. For Reno visitor information and assistance, call (800) FOR RENO.

Headquarters for the Forest Service's **Lake Tahoe Basin Management Unit,** P.O. Box 8465, South Lake Tahoe 96158, tel. (916) 573-2600, are at 870 Emerald Bay Rd., and open year-round. Regional ranger district offices are another good source for camping, hiking, recreation, and other national forest information. Local outdoors and recreation stores are always good sources for information, as well as rental equipment. Summers-only information centers, at the Pope-Baldwin visitor center and at the west shore's William Kent campground, can be useful. Stop by or contact the local state parks headquarters (see "D.L. Bliss And Emerald Bay State Parks" above) for current information about state parks camping, hiking, and other activities.

One of the most useful publications around is the *Lake of the Sky Journal* published jointly by the U.S. Forest Service and California and Nevada state parks offices. Another great free publication is *North Tahoe/Truckee Week,* available everywhere around the north shore. For very comprehensive and updated regional tourist information, everything from recreation and sightseeing to area accommodations and select restaurant menus in magazine style, buy *The Guide to Lake Tahoe,* available locally for $5.

Tahoe Area Transportation

At last report, the **South Lake Tahoe Airport** was served only by American Eagle, tel. toll-free (800) 433-7300, the commuter line of American Airlines. Many travelers prefer flying into the **Reno-Cannon International Airport,** served by a half-dozen major carriers (including American, Southwest, United), then renting a car or taking the local "luxury shuttle"—the latter quite a good deal. For $15 per person (one-way), the **Tahoe Casino Express,** tel. (702) 785-2424 or toll-free (800) 446-6128, offers nonstop transport to and from the Reno airport and south shore destinations (skiers and non-casino guests welcome, with room for ski gear and luggage).

TART (Tahoe Area Regional Transit) buses, tel. (916) 581-6365, run year-round, serving the northwest Placer County area and the Incline Village area, stopping only at TART signs. Exact fare only, $1 per ride, commuter passes available. **STAGE** (South Tahoe Area Ground Express) buses, tel. 573-2080, provide 24-hour service around South Lake Tahoe, more limited routes elsewhere, $1.25 fare (10-trip pass, $10).

To take a taxi ride anywhere around the lake, **Yellow Cab,** tel. (916) 544-5555, offers 24-hour service. An unusual Tahoe-style transport option is the stern-wheeler *Tahoe Queen,* which runs from South Lake Tahoe to the north shore regularly and—in combination with a bus shuttle system—even carries skiers to Northstar, Squaw Valley, and Alpine Meadows in winter. For more information (tours and dinner-dance cruises also offered), contact: **Lake Tahoe Cruises,** P.O. Box 14292, South Lake Tahoe 96151, tel. 541-3897 or (800) 238-2463. For other Tahoe tour information, contact local chambers of commerce and visitor bureaus.

If you're not cycling, driving, flying, or hitchhiking, **Greyhound** can get you to Lake Tahoe. Buses leave daily from South Lake Tahoe, 1099 Park Ave., tel. (916) 544-2241, to San Francisco and Los Angeles, also to Las Vegas, Reno, and other Nevada destinations. (Or connect with Greyhound in Truckee at the train station, tel. 587-3822.)

Best bet for sights and serenity, though, is riding the rails on **Amtrak,** which stops at Truckee's restored train depot (but no office here or ticket sales; tel. 800-872-7245 for fare and route information). Coming from Oakland, Amtrak's *California Zephyr* rolls through Berkeley backyards, over the Benicia-Martinez Bridge, through the Suisun Marsh (good bird views in winter and a look at the Mothball Fleet), then across farmland and fields to Sacramento—where docents from the state's Railroad Museum come aboard (Thurs.-Sun.) to share the lively history of the rail route to Reno. Once educated, riders are then treated to some fine, rare views: a cliff-hanging peek into the yawning canyon of the American River's north fork, the Yuba River, Sugar Bowl's slopes, then through the Judah Tunnel and Coldstream Valley to Truckee.

FROM TAHOE

NORTH FROM TAHOE-TRUCKEE

Quincy And Vicinity

The northernmost reaches of the Sierra Nevada are north of Lake Tahoe and I-80—scattered forested lakes, reservoirs, and rivers among still more scattered small towns. Quincy, on Hwy. 70/89 south of Lake Almanor and Indian Valley, is a picturesque mountain town with a long-time lumber history.

Any time, stop off at the **Morning Thunder Cafe** at 557 Lawrence, tel. (916) 283-1310, good for Mexican and American fare, fine desserts, espresso bar. Open for breakfast through dinner weekdays and Saturday, for brunch only on Sundays. **Moon's Restaurant** down the street, tel. 283-0765, serves Italian-American food, dinner only.

Very nice in town and reasonably priced is the **Ranchito Motel,** 2020 E. Main St., P.O. Box 956, Quincy 95971, tel. (916) 283-2265, with roomy rooms from $35. **The Feather Bed** bed and breakfast, 542 Jackson St. near the courthouse, P.O. Box 3200, tel. 283-0102, has cozy rooms with private baths, full breakfast, even bikes to borrow, rates $60-95.

A special stay nearby is the **Greenhorn Creek Guest Ranch** on Hwy. 70 in Spring Garden, P.O. Box 7010, Quincy 95971, tel. (916) 283-0930, a ranch-style resort with modern cabins and motel units, family-style meals, even daytime child care for toddlers. Weekly rates run from $450 per adult, from $350 per child, depending on the season. More rustic, a bit of a drive, but much cheaper even in summer are the housekeeping cabins and campgrounds at **Buck's Lake Lodge** at Buck's Lake west of town, P.O. Box 236, Quincy 95971, tel. 283-2262 or 283-4243 for lakefront cabin reservations, open May through October, $49-79 per day for cabins (one, two, or three bedroom), weekly rates available. Cheaper still: camping at **Antelope Lake** southeast of Greenville near Taylorsville, tel. 284-

7126, a beautiful recreation lake with very nice national forest campgrounds. The **Indian Valley Museum** east of Taylorsville, tel. 284-6600, chronicles regional history.

For more information about Quincy and vicinity, stop by Quincy's very nice **Plumas County Museum** at 500 Jackson St. (very helpful folks, and an excellent array of area information) or contact the **Plumas County Chamber of Commerce** at P.O. Box 11018, Quincy 95971, tel. (916) 283-6345 or (800) 326-2247, or the **Quincy Main Street Chamber,** tel. 283-0188. For information about the greater Lake Almanor area, contact the **Chester/Lake Almanor Chamber of Commerce,** P.O. Box 1198, Chester 96020, tel. 258-2426, and see also "Vicinity of Lassen." For more information on Plumas County destinations along the Hwy. 49 corridor which deadends at Loyalton.

Portola And Vicinity

Highway 70 east from the Blairsden-Graeagle area passes through Portola before lurching up over Beckwourth Pass then hooking up with Hwy. 395 at Hallelujah Junction in the high desert. Mount Ina Coolbrith south of the pass was named for California's first poet laureate, who met James Beckwourth while an 11-year-old girl traveling westward by wagon train over his same-named pass. A dark-skinned man usually riding bareback and dressed in moccasins and leather jacket, his two long braids tied up in colored cloth, the adventurer apparently made quite an impression. Jim Beckwourth's delapidated cabin, which still stands near the town of Beckwourth (though old maps carry the distorted "Beckwith"), may soon be restored thanks to the efforts of local volunteers.

In Portola, the most popular attraction is its **Portola Railroad Museum** (cross the river and follow the signs), an all-volunteer effort sponsored by the Feather River Rail Society, P.O. Box 1104, Portola 96122, tel. (916) 832-4131. The quantity and quality of in-process

KIM WEIR

The main attraction in Portola is the Portola Railroad Museum, staffed by volunteers.

and already-restored iron stock on display at the railway yard here is impressive (admission is free, but donations appreciated). A new twist: visitors can rent a diesel locomotive and drive it around the yard, rates from $60 per hour.

As good a place as any for a meal in Portola is the **Alpine Moon** coffee shop on the highway, open for lunch and dinner, tel. (916) 832-5360, though if you're headed east anyway, locals also recommend the **Beckwith Tavern** dinner house on Hwy. 70 at Clover Valley Rd. in Beckwith, tel. 832-5084, with good ol' American food, fireplace, bar, dance floor—and Friday night is Basque night. Reservations recommended, closed Wednesdays.

Reasonable and quite nice is the **Sierra Motel** at 380 E. Sierra, P.O. Box 1265, Portola 96122, tel. (916) 832-4223, with queen beds, TV and cable, radios, phones, rooms $30-50. Close to the railroad museum is the **Upper Feather Bed and Breakfast,** 256 Commercial St., P.O. Box 1528, tel. 832-0107, casual country rooms (all share baths) $40-60, in what was once a board-

ing house. For more information about Portola and vicinity, contact the **Eastern Plumas County Chamber of Commerce,** P.O. Box 1379, Portola 96122, tel. (916) 832-5444, or the **Plumas County Chamber of Commerce,** tel. toll-free (800) 326-2247.

Just north of Portola via Davis Rd. is **Davis Lake,** tel. 836-2575, noted for its very fine trout fishing, boating and swimming, fishing and camping. The shores of **Frenchman Lake** reservoir just north of Chilcoot, tel. 253-2223, are studded with sage and pine, and there's good fishing and camping April-Oct.; the water level takes quite a dive by late summer and fall, even in good years.

For other regional water recreation, just north of I-80 and the Tahoe-Truckee area are: **Prosser Creek Reservoir,** quiet and popular for canoeing, sailing, and fishing, with both primitive and developed Forest Service campsites; **Boca Reservoir,** a powerboat lake with excellent sailing, free campsites, and a more stable water level; and **Stampede Reservoir,** a very large lake with excellent westerly winds for sailors—though the water drops severely by the end of summer, mainly through diversions to Pyramid Lake to save two rare trout species—also hundreds of national forest campsites. For more information about these and other area lakes, call the Tahoe-Truckee Ranger District office at (916) 587-3558.

The Sierra Valley Lodge

Quite a treat just 15-20 minutes south of Graeagle is the Sierra Valley Lodge, P.O. Box 107, Calpine 96124, tel. (916) 994-3367, a log-cabin restaurant serving good seafood and great steaks and featuring a decent wine list. Sit out on the deck for a cocktail before dinner, or head to the bar—which has a great jukebox and a trophy case illustrating the illustrious history of the Calpine Marching Band (mostly members of the local volunteer fire brigade, including a saxophonist, kazoo players, and hummers). On summer weekends, plan on some square dancing in the back room.

The hotel rooms here are small and very down-home, as is the hallway with its three-dimensional western memorabilia (even a full-size saddle) coming out of the wall. The lodge is open year-round, but most of the rooms are closed in winter, due to lack of insulation. Pretty basic, but okay. Inexpensive.

SOUTH FROM TAHOE

Instead of heading east to the South Lake Tahoe strip and the Stateline casino wilderness, jog due south into the rock-hard heart of true wildness. Highway 50 veering west toward Placerville and Sacramento is a major mountain thoroughfare that shoots past pretty little **Echo Lake** (fishing, picnicking, and boating; no camping but good access to the Desolation Wilderness) and up and over Echo Summit for some fine high-mountain scenery. Way on down the road at Pollock Pines, on the movie-set stage of the **Ghost Mountain Resort**, 5560 Badger Hill Rd., tel. (916) 644-2415, stop on Sundays for the famous buffet-style Sunday jazz brunch—good food and excellent jazz year-round, also bigtime talent like Richie Cole, George Cables, Buddy Montgomery, Jessica Williams, even bands like Free Flight and the Manhattan Transfer on a special-event basis. (Brunch is served 11 a.m. and 1 p.m., but jazz entertainment usually lasts all weekend long.)

Off in the other direction from just south of Meyers, Hwy. 89 leads into big-sky country, including both the Mokelumne and Carson-Iceberg wilderness areas. Heading west on Hwy. 88 from Picketts Junction leads to Carson Pass and its gorgeous granite high lakes. South of fun and funky Markleeville and nearby Grover Hot Springs State Park, Hwy. 4 also cuts west, this time over Ebbetts Pass and the Pacific Grade Summit, dipping slightly into the Bear Valley-Lake Alpine high country before sliding down the Sierra Nevada's western slope to Calaveras Big Trees State Park then Angels Camp and vicinity. (Archaeologists working near Ebbetts Pass recently unearthed evidence of a Native American campsite some 10,000 years old—one of the oldest ever found in the Sierra Nevada—and the clay floor and hearth of an ancient hunting hut, the oldest prehistoric structure ever found in North America.)

Southeast from the Hwy. 4 junction, Hwy. 89 heads up and over Monitor Pass—special in autumn, with fiery fall-colored aspens and an unusual autumn fishing season at **Heenan Lake** for rare Lahontan cutthroat trout (strict limits, current fishing license necessary). At Hwy. 395, the eastern Sierra Nevada's only major roadway, head north to windy **Topaz Lake** straddling the California-Nevada border for trophy-sized trout, camping, and (once across the state line) that omnipresent casino scene. Or roll south past the lonely towns of Topaz, Coleville, and Walker to Sonora Junction then on into Bridgeport, the nearby Mono Lake Basin, and the breathtaking beauty of the Sierra Nevada as experienced from the backside (see "Mono Lake"). But heading west on Hwy. 108, past the U.S. Marine Corps' Mountain Warfare Training Center then up and over incredible **Sonora Pass** (closed in winter), is equally enticing.

NEAR CARSON PASS

Highway 88 from Picketts Junction—where a roadside monument marks the old Pony Express route—climbs to an elevation of 8,573 feet at Carson Pass. From the vista point downslope to the east, often muddy **Red Lake** below offers surprisingly good fishing for brook and rainbow trout. More aesthetic, some distance south of the pass, and accessible via Blue Lakes Rd., are the **Blue Lakes** (which include Granite, Meadow, Tamarack, and Twin lakes), for fishing, swimming, picnicking, and camping at PG&E campgrounds, also good access into the Mokelumne Wilderness via the Pacific Crest Trail which traverses the area.

The Caples Lake Area And Kirkwood

Also quite serene, with fine national forest campgrounds (some operated by concessionaires) open in summer, are the alpine lakes just off the highway west of Carson Pass. Small **Woods Lake** a couple of miles south of Hwy. 88 offers a quiet wooded campground (water, no showers), nice lakeside picnicking (wheelchair accessible), fishing, also a nice hike to the old Lost Cabin Mine. Large **Caples Lake** farther west and right on the highway, like tiny **Kirkwood Lake** nearby, also offers good camping, picnicking, swimming, fishing, and boating. No motorboats are allowed at Kirkwood; larger RVs also discouraged. From near the dam at Caples Lake, hike south into the Mokelumne Wilderness. Near the highway maintenance station near Caples Lake is the trailhead for Round Lake and relatively remote Meiss Lake. (For more information about these lakes, trails, and campgrounds, contact the **Amador Ranger**

District office in Pioneer, tel. 209-295-4251.)

Popular here in winter is the excellent **Kirkwood Ski and Summer Resort**, P.O. Box 1, Kirkwood 95646, tel. (209) 258-6000 (for ski conditions, tel. 258-3000; for resort lodgings, tel. 258-7000), a modern yet relaxed ski complex with a frontier feel, far removed from Tahoe's glitz and glitter. New here: sleigh rides and snowboarding, not to mention endless summer activities. The 1860s **Kirkwood Inn** and bar, 1½ miles down the road from the lifts, is now home base for popular **Kirkwood Cross Country** for Nordic skiers, 80 kilometers of track with warming huts, lessons and tours also offered, tel. 258-7248.

Silver Lake And Vicinity

About six miles west of the Caples Lake-Kirkwood area is **Silver Lake**, another popular granite-and-blue water recreation lake along Kit Carson's trail. Good camping at both national forest and PG&E campgrounds as well as **Plasse's Resort** at the lake's south end. Rent cabins at **Kay's Silver Lake Resort** on the highway, or motel rooms ($85-90) or cabins ($100-135) at the wonderful, knotty-pine-and-naugahyde **Kit Carson Lodge**, Kit Carson 95644, tel. (209) 258-8500, open from late May to early October. (For more information about Silver Lake and vicinity, contact **El Dorado National Forest headquarters** in Placerville, tel. 916-622-5061.)

About 10 miles west of Tragedy Springs just southwest of Silver Lake, where members of the Mormon Battalion were killed in 1848 (the original tree blaze is on display at Marshall Gold Discovery State Park in Coloma) is the Bear River Rd. turnoff to upper and lower **Bear River reservoirs.** Lower Bear River Reservoir often gets quite low in late summer and fall—the reason lazy fishing enthusiasts get such good catches here. Most of the year, though, there's plenty of water—enough for water-skiing and good swimming (especially south of the dam near the campgrounds) in summer, ice skating and snowmobiling across the frozen lake in winter. First-come, first-camped Forest Service campgrounds, $7 per night, have water, but camping (with hot showers and RV hookups) as well as lodging is also available at the **Bear River Lake Resort,** tel. (209) 295-4868, with rates $70 per night (for four people). Bear River becomes a Nordic ski center in winter. For more

information about the Bear River reservoir area, contact the **Lumberyard Ranger District office** in Pioneer, tel. (209) 223-1623.

Between Silver Lake and the Bear River reservoirs, at the junction of Hwy. 88 and the Mormon Emigrant Trail, is the relatively new **Iron Mountain Ski Resort,** oriented primarily to intermediate Alpine skiers, with a ski school, ski shop, rentals, lodging, and food. For more information, contact: Iron Mountain, P.O. Box 1500, Pioneer 95666, tel. (209) 258-8700. There's good national forest cross-country skiing in the area too.

SOUTHEAST FROM PICKETTS JUNCTION

Hope Valley And Sorensen's

Due to massive land purchases by the Trust for Public Lands, developers shoveled out of the Tahoe Basin have also been held at bay here. With any luck, Hope Valley will remain a peaceful mountain valley where camping, fishing, hiking, and Nordic skiing are the main attractions. **Sorensen's Resort** on Hwy. 88/89 south of Lake Tahoe (a half mile east of Picketts Junction) is *the* local institution, with cafe, cozy cabins, and roadside serenity far removed from the Stateline casino scene. Most cabins have kitchens and woodstoves; all have gas heaters and bathrooms. But otherwise each cabin is unique, with different features. Rates are complicated (two-night minimum on weekends), calculated on a per-cabin basis, starting at $75-80, some rates lower midweek, everything higher in winter. Two bed-and-breakfast rooms share a bath. (To make an enlightened choice, contact Sorensen's well in advance and request the current brochure/rate card.) New is Sierra House, which sleeps up to six people. Fairly new is the refurbished Norway House, a large cabin perfect for large families or small company conferences. Also fairly new is Sorensen's sauna (small fee) and wedding gazebo.

Besides good food (breakfast, lunch) and reasonably priced lodging, Sorensen's also offers a variety of special events, from historical tours of the Mormon Emigrant Trail over Carson Pass to river rafting on the East Fork of the Carson River, from watercolor painting and photography workshops to cross-country ski tours and sleigh rides. In the works: plans for a new bed and breakfast lodge and dozens more cabins. For more information and to get on the mailing list for Sorensen's seasonal newsletter, contact: Sorensen's Resort, 14255 Hwy. 88, Hope Valley 96120, tel. (916) 694-2203 or toll-free (800) 423-9949. The **Hope Valley Cross-Country Ski Center,** with 60 miles of trails, is also affiliated with Sorensen's.

The **Hope, Charity,** and **Faith valleys** near the Hwy. 88 and Hwy. 89 junction are great for picnics.

Markleeville And Vicinity

Except for a few memorable bar brawls and an occasional natural disaster here in Pleasant Valley, the biggest thing to happen for decades in the tiny one-time timber town of Markleeville was the news in 1988 that Bank of America was getting out of town. County seat and social center of rugged Alpine County (total population: 1,200), Markleeville residents were—and are—insulted. So when you come to Markleeville, bring cash.

The next biggest thing to happen in Markleeville: the annual **Death Ride Tour of the California Alps,** considered one of the top ten cycling challenges in America (and one of the top five toughest). This is a *tour,* not a race—a fact most participants are probably eternally grateful for, since just finishing is an accomplishment. Cyclists can pick their poison, climbing one high mountain pass (a distance of 48 miles) or up to five (about 130 miles). All tours start and end at Turtle Rock Park, halfway between Markleeville and Woodfords. This adventure is limited to the first 2500 prepaid applicants. For more information and applications, contact the Alpine County Chamber of Commerce (see below).

Up on the hill above town is the **Alpine County Historical Museum** complex, P.O. Box 24, Markleeville 96120, tel. (916) 694-2317, open Wed.-Mon. noon-5 p.m. from Memorial Day through October (free but donations greatly appreciated). Here stands the white clapboard **Old Webster School,** restored to its one-room 1882 ambience, and the county's unusual **Old Log Jail,** with hand-riveted iron jail cells imported north from the original Silver Mountain City building in 1875. Also here: miscellaneous farming, mining, and lumbering artifacts. The modern museum itself has an impressive display

of local historical memorabilia, including some beautiful Washoe basketry (used for gathering then winnowing pine nuts, a dietary staple).

On the west side of town in the new Webster School, is the **Alpine County Library and Archives,** tel. 694-2120, a collection of everything from mining and property records to voting registrations.

A fascinating feature in downtown Markleeville is the redneck **Cutthroat Bar** inside the Alpine Hotel and Cafe. Typical are the D.A.M.M. ("Drunks Against Mad Mothers") bumper sticker on the pool table, brand-name beer mirrors, and animal heads on the walls. Unusual, though, are the "trophies" hanging from the ceiling—an impressive but somehow empty collection of women's bras. The standing deal is that any "gal" can trade in her bra for a free Cutthroat Saloon T-shirt, as long as she makes the trade right then and there. (Despite the lingerie on display, there aren't that many takers.)

Markleeville Area Practicalities

To stay awhile, camp at Grover Hot Springs State Park (see below) four miles west of town. If there's no room at Grover, try the BLM's **Indian Creek Reservoir** campground for tents and RVs a few miles north of Markleeville off the highway—no swimming but fishing, picnicking, hikes with good views, also the Curtz Lake Environmental Study Area to explore. (Call the BLM office in Carson City, Nevada, at 702-882-1631 for information.) Or camp at the county's **Turtle Rock Park** midway between Markleeville and Woodfords, first-come, first-camped. National forest campgrounds are also good choices; inquire at regional ranger district offices or the Markleeville Guard Station (see below).

There are accommodations options aside from camping. The 1920s-vintage **Shady Lady Restaurant & Hotel,** on Main across from the chamber office, offers decent food and clean motel rooms. Also good for a meal—enter from the side door to avoid the bar scene up front—is the **Alpine Cafe** behind the Cutthroat Bar (in the same building). Other good possibilities for an area stay: the **East Fork Resort,** P.O. Box 457, Markleeville 96120, tel. (916) 694-2229; the **J. Marklee Toll Station,** P.O. Box 395, tel. 694-2507; and **Woodfords Inn,** P.O. Box 426, tel. 694-2410.

Quite unusual is **The House of York,** P.O. Box 123, Markleeville 96120, tel. (916) 694-2442, a very remote (no electricity) rentable house (sleeps six) on private land within the Mokelumne Wilderness, about a two-hour hike in from the trailhead. The experience is for wilderness lovers, not comfort enthusiasts, since there's no hot water (heat some on the woodstove or the propane-powered stove). Things to do include hiking, climbing, fishing, sunbathing on the one-time helicopter pad, lolling in the hammock by the creek, and reading (extensive library). The kitchen is fully equipped and linens and towels are supplied, but whatever you pack in—food and clothing and (biodegradable) soap and shampoo—you'll have to pack out. For a family or other group, rates are reasonable: $125 per night, $350 for three nights, $700 per week (50% advance deposit required—check or money order—refundable with more than two weeks' notice).

For more information about the area, contact: **Alpine County Chamber of Commerce,**

WOLF CREEK PACK STATION

at the corner of Main and Webster, P.O. Box 265, Markleeville 96120, tel. (916) 694-2475. For current area trail and recreation information, contact Grover Hot Springs (below) or the U.S. Forest Service **Markleeville Guard Station,** tel. 694-2911. The **Wolf Creek Pack Station,** tel. (702) 345-6104 or (916) 694-2562, offers fishing and pack trips.

Grover Hot Springs State Park

Just west of Markleeville via Hot Springs Rd. is Grover Hot Springs State Park, the perfect hot-soak antidote to weary high-country hikers. Tucked into a mountain meadow near the northeastern edge of the Mokelumne Wilderness, the hot and cool natural spring-fed pools at Grover Hot Springs aren't particularly aesthetic (caged with cement and nonclimbable fence like public swimming pools, but complete with changing rooms and pre-soak showers—bathing suits required). Yet who cares? The water feels so *good.* (Mineral purists, walk up the hill to the spring's source to find out the water's exact mineral content.)

Except for two weeks in September when the pools are closed for their annual cleaning, Grover Hot Springs is open all year (if you can get here), popular in winter for hardy souls hankering for a hot soak and a roll in the snow. The small pool-use fee is good all day, so you can leave and come back. During the high season, April through September, the pools are open daily 9 a.m.-9 p.m., but otherwise more limited hours (call for current schedule). The park, including campground, is open year-round.

Most developed campsites, just outside the valley, are in an open forested area, none too private—but tired muscles first tightened by the trail then suddenly soak-stretched into relaxation rarely complain. Campsites $14, Mistix reservations usually necessary in summer, tel. (800) 444-7275. Park day-use fee, $5. For more information, contact: Grover Hot Springs State Park, P.O. Box 188, Markleeville 96120, tel. (916) 964-2248.

EBBETTS PASS AND VICINITY

Near Ebbets Pass
Another impressive after-the-snows climb is up and over Ebbetts Pass via Hwy. 4 (toward the top, on very narrow roads with hairpin turns) and down the other side to Bear Valley, Calaveras Big Trees, Murphys, and ultimately Angels Camp in the Sierra Nevada foothill gold country. The **Highland Lakes** area off the highway just west of Ebbetts Pass offers good trout fishing and primitive camping (no drinking water), as do the tiny, very picturesque **Mosquito Lakes** beyond Hermit Valley on the Pacific Grade Summit.

Lake Alpine And Vicinity
The sky-high Lake Alpine area northeast of Bear Valley features backpacking trailheads into both Mokelumne and Carson-Iceberg wilderness areas, spring and early summer whitewater rafting on the North Fork of the Stanislaus River (usually from Sourgrass to Calaveras Big Trees downriver), and lake recreation: canoeing, kayaking, and sailing (motorboats: 15 mph speed limit) in addition to fishing for rainbows, swimming, picnicking, and casual hiking.

National forest campgrounds at Lake Alpine include **Lake Alpine, Pine-Marten, Silver Tip,** and **Silver Valley,** all "full-service" (but no hot showers), open only in summer. Nearby and free are other lake and riverside campgrounds, including **Boards Crossing, Highland Lakes, Sand Flat,** and **Sourgrass.**

The newly renovated, previously primitive **Spicer Reservoir** area at Spicer Meadows also offers lake recreation and campgrounds. For more information about Lake Alpine and vicinity, contact the **Calaveras Ranger District** at P.O. Box 500, Hathaway Pines 95233, tel. (209) 795-1381, or stop by the ranger station on the north side of the highway just west of the Silver Tip and Lodgepole (overflow) campgrounds.

Bear Valley Ski Resorts and More
Though Hwy. 4 is closed just east of Bear Valley by winter snows, the **Bear Valley Ski Area** is accessible from the gold country even in winter. (Even more accessible, though, is **Cottage Springs** just above Dorrington, a snow-play and learn-to-ski center; call 209-795-1209, or 795-1401 for snow conditions.)

Another medium-sized mellow alternative to the Tahoe ski scene, Bear Valley is an uncrowded but top-notch downhill ski slope (with views from the top into the Mokelumne Wilderness), including a comfortable lodge (with a wonderful fireplace) recently refurbished, and lifts halfway up the mountain, also a condominium city complete with mall. Bear Valley offers good beginning, intermediate, and advanced ski runs, an excellent restaurant, also a well-developed program for disabled skiers. Bargain prices on weekdays and for groups. As a matter of fact, even with renovations and improvements (including snowmaking) since 1991, all prices have dropped substantially. Good deal folks.

Accommodations at the **Lodge at Bear Valley,** can be steep, especially in the new fourth-floor luxury suites. Inquire about packages and specials. Food service at the Hungry Bear is unusually good, with an impressive menu and various homemade specialties. But if you bring your own food, anyone can brown-bag it in the lodge. The **Red Dog Lodge** in town, tel. 753-2344, has rooms with bathrooms down the hall (also a sauna), and the **Tamarack Pines Inn,** tel. 753-2080, has rooms with private or shared baths.

Weekend live entertainment in Bear Valley proper (shuttle service available from the slopes) often includes rock 'n' roll and other bands at the Red Dog and other saloons.

For more information, contact the **Bear Valley Ski Company,** P.O. Box 5038, Bear Valley 95223, tel. (209) 753-2301 (753-2308 for snow conditions). For lodging and visitor center information, call toll-free (800) 695-3737. For lodging referrals, contact **Mountain Guest Services,** tel. 753-6700.

What was once the Bear Valley Mountain Bike Center has expanded substantially—into **Bear Valley Cross Country,** just one aspect of the large resort facility right in town. You can

east of Ebbetts Pass

still rent mountain bikes, take a guided Sunday tour, even sign up for mountain bike weekends including lodging, some meals, a bike maintenance clinic, and more. To tour nearby alpine lakes, this is also the place to rent canoes and two-person kayaks. And the ski facilities, from trails to warming huts, are quite impressive.

For more information about any or all of these activities, contact: Bear Valley Cross Country at 1 Bear Valley Rd., P.O. Box 5207, Bear Valley 95223, tel. (209) 753-2834 or toll-free from Northern California (800) 232-7123; for lodging reservations, call (209) 753-2327 or toll-free from Northern California (800) 794-3866.

The **Bear Valley Bike Trek,** a three-day cycling trip for charity (usually scheduled in June), starts in Bear Valley, rolls past Mercer Caverns to Murphys and on to Columbia for the second night, then to Knights Ferry via Jamestown and Chinese Camp before ending at Oakdale. For more information, contact Bear Valley Cross Country or call toll-free (800) 827-2453.

Independent from other Bear Valley enterprises is the **Bear Valley Climbing School,** P.O. Box 5123, Bear Valley 95223, tel. (209) 753-6228, which offers basic, intermediate, and advanced rock-climbing instruction near Bear Valley as well as guided climbs near Ebbetts Pass.

Music From Bear Valley

For some musical Ebbetts Pass rambling in summertime, come to Bear Valley and the tent pavilion set up outside the Bear Valley Lodge for the annual **Music From Bear Valley** concert series—a long-standing tradition usually scheduled from late July through mid-August, featuring everything from classical music and opera to Rodgers and Hammerstein and pop groups like the Four Freshmen. For more information, contact: Music From Bear Valley, P.O. Box 5068, Bear Valley 95223, tel. (209) 753-2334. Season tickets and single-event tickets are available. You can also arrange accommodations with ticket purchase, but plan well ahead.

SONORA PASS AND VICINITY

Though the old Sonora & Mono Toll Road has been a state highway since 1901, the stomach-churning, switchback slither over shoulderless Sonora Pass, where the granite meets the clouds above timberline at an elevation of 9,626 feet, is unforgettable. Assuming he or she survives, anyone attempting the pass in an RV or pulling a trailer of any kind up this lonely string-like stretch of Hwy. 108, one-time film location for *For Whom the Bell Tolls,* should check into the nearest mental health clinic immediately. But otherwise, don't hesitate—especially if you're cycling. It's beautiful, and literally breathtaking. Stop near the top for a picnic or to camp.

Sliding down the western slope from Sonora Pass, just south of the Carson-Iceberg Wilderness and north of the 107,000-acre Emigrant Wilderness of alpine meadows, high lakes, and granite adjacent to Yosemite National Park, the road leads to **Kennedy Meadows** (trailhead and pack station) and **Dardanelle,** with a string of national forest campgrounds between the two. (For off-highway camping, head northeast on Clark Fork Rd. west of Dardanelle to the campgrounds on the way to **Iceberg Meadow** just outside the wilderness area.) The volcanic peaks known as the Dardanelles were named by the Whitney Survey Party in the 1860s, based on their resemblance to the mountains in Turkey overlooking the entrance to the Sea of Marmora.

Pinecrest Lake And Dodge Ridge

About 20 miles southwest beyond Dardanelle are the tiny towns of Strawberry and Pinecrest near **Pinecrest Lake,** quite popular in summer for lake recreation—from fishing and horseback riding to swimming, canoeing, and boating (no water-skiing)—and family camping. Some campsites are reservable, others are first-come, first-camped.

Also at Pinecrest is the casual, gold rush-flavored **Dodge Ridge** ski resort, with exceptional but underrated downhill skiing for beginner, intermediate, advanced, and disabled skiers, also a ski school. For more information, contact: Dodge Ridge, P.O. Box 1188, Pinecrest 95364, tel. (209) 965-3474.

Summer or winter the **Pinecrest Lake Resort,** P.O. Box 1216, Pinecrest 95364, tel. (209) 965-3411, has cabins and condos for rent, also a restaurant. Another possibility (for housekeeping cabins) is **Sparrow's Lodge** nearby, P.O. Box 1, Strawberry 95375, tel. 965-3278.

Get local hiking, horseback riding, and nature trail information, national forest and wilderness maps, as well as wilderness permits, topo maps, and updates on trail conditions for both Emigrant and Carson-Iceberg wilderness areas at the **Summit Ranger Station** at the "Y" on Hwy. 108 near Pinecrest, 1 Pinecrest Lake Rd., Pinecrest 95364, tel. (209) 965-3434. Various natural history and campfire programs and tours are offered by Pinecrest rangers in July and August. You can even check out free audio tour tapes for the Hwy. 108 route (from Pinecrest to Sonora Pass) at the ranger station.

MONO LAKE AND VICINITY

Calling it "one of the strangest freaks of Nature found in any land," Mark Twain was particularly impressed by his mid-1800s visits to Mono Lake, then commonly referred to as the Dead Sea of California:

Mono Lake lies in a lifeless, treeless, hideous desert. . . . This solemn, silent, sailless sea— this lonely tenant of the loneliest spot on earth—is little graced with the picturesque. It is an unpretending expanse of grayish water, about a hundred miles in circumference, with two islands in its centre, mere upheavals of rent and scorched and blistered lava, snowed over with gray banks and drifts of pumice-stone and ashes, the winding sheet of the dead volcano whose vast crater the lake has seized upon and occupied.

Mono Lake's water was so alkaline, Twain quipped, that "the most hopelessly soiled garment" could be cleaned simply by dipping it in the lake then wringing it out. He also noted the peculiarity of a sky full of seagulls so far from the sea, and the region's predictable two seasons:

"the breaking up of one winter and the beginning of the next."

While some characteristics of modern-day Mono Lake are still as Twain described them, the depth, size, and very nature of this high-desert sea have changed greatly. Mono Lake today is at the center of one of the hardest-fought environmental wars of the century, a pre-eminent political hot potato pitting Los Angeles water consumers against lovers of the land and landowners in the eastern Sierra Nevada.

MONO LAKE
NATURAL HISTORY AND SIGHTS

To understand what all the fuss is about, visit Mono Lake. For the best "big picture" view, head to the top of the **Black Point fissures** near the county park, reached via Cemetery Rd. northwest of the lake off Hwy 395. No trail—also no shade or water—so come prepared and pick your way carefully up the volcanic-cinder terraces to the top, defined by solid red rock, about a 45-minute meandering climb. Stop, afterward, at the park and **Mono Basin Historical Society Museum** in the restored 1922 schoolhouse, open in summer Tues.-Sat. noon-6 p.m.

Despite the craters-of-the-moon look, highly alkaline waters, and surrounding day-old stubble of sage, life abounds at million-year-old Mono Lake, now protected as both the **Mono Basin National Forest Scenic Area** and the **Mono Lake Tufa State Reserve.** Though early settlers considered the lake "dead," since it was too salty to support even fish life, native peoples knew better. They observed the huge seagull populations nesting here in spring—85% of the total California gull population—and some 300 other bird species, including migrants like phalaropes and eared grebes, and knew they depended on lake shrimp and brine flies for survival. (The word *mono* means "fly" in Yokut. The Kutsadika Paiutes who lived near Mono Lake harvested the brine fly grubs, a protein-rich delicacy, and traded them to the Yokuts for acorns.)

When spring winds stir the lake's waters, algae grows to support increased new populations of both brine flies and brine shrimp. The delicate cycle of life at Mono Lake is easily observable in spring and summer, anywhere around the lake's shoreline. By mid-summer it peaks, when some four-trillion brine shrimp reach maturity and become the birds' second major food source, about the time fledgling gulls and other birds first take flight and go foraging.

Still a vast gray-blue inland sea despite Los Angelenos' water predation, Mono Lake's saline waters make for fun, unusually buoyant swimming. Old-timers claim a good soak in Mono Lake's medicinal waters will cure just about anything. (One of the best beaches is **Navy Beach** along the south shore; avoid salt in the eyes or open wounds.) But Mono's most notable features are its surrounding salt flats and peculiar tufa formations—strangely beautiful salt-white pillars of calcium carbonate (limestone). Naturally created underwater when salty lake water combines with calcium-rich fresh spring water bubbling up from below, these 200- to 900-year-old "stone" spires are now more exposed due to receding water levels. (Since 1941, the first year that water from four of Mono Lake's feeder streams was shipped south to L.A., the lake's level has dropped an average of 18 inches per year, a total drop of about 45 feet.) The best place to see and wander through these fantastic tufa formations—no climbing or souvenir-taking allowed—is in the **South Tufa Area** off Hwy. 120. Here and elsewhere, due to deceptively soft pumice "sand," heed warnings about driving on less-traveled roads (particularly on the lake's east side) without a four-wheel-drive vehicle.

Mono Lake has two major islands: the yin-yang twins of white **Paoha** and black **Negit;** until recently the latter was the gulls' preferred nesting spot. (The islands, and the lake itself within one mile of them, are closed to the public from April through July to protect nesting birds.) Environmentalists fighting for Mono Lake's right to life point out that L.A.-bound water diversions, made worse by natural disasters like drought, created the land bridge that now connects the islands to the mainland and allows coyotes and other bird and egg predators to reach nesting seagull colonies on Negit Island. But lack of fresh water has also increased the lake's salt levels by two or three times, threatening both Mono Lake's brine shrimp and brine fly populations, a more subtle but long-term threat to gulls and other bird species dependent on these creatures for food.

Other problems as well may have affected area life. Long-term measurements of the levels of radioactive carbon in Mono Lake, for example, suggest that nuclear waste may have been dumped here in the 1950s (leading to an almost instantaneous 60% increase in carbon-14) and possibly again in the 1970s. But even with the lake's future—and future water levels—still clouded by politics, in some ways life has already "returned" to the Mono Lake Basin: bald eagles came back to the area's stream canyons in 1985.

Sights Near Mono Lake

Just south from Mono Lake's bitter waters are the **Mono Craters,** a dozen dove-colored volcanoes tinged with black. These explosion pits, domes, and lava flows with light-colored slopes of ash and pumice are volcanic infants just 60,000 years old. Despite Mt. St. Helens's recent performance, volcanologists still rate these hot-blooded babies at the top of the list of continental American volcanoes most likely to blow any day. Most accessible from Mono Lake is **Panum Crater** (trailhead reached via dirt road heading south from just west of the South Tufa Area turnoff), an easy climb for a great view. To get to **Devils Punchbowl** at the Mono Craters' southern end, head south on Hwy. 395

THE WAR WAGED FOR MONO LAKE

The war of politics and power waged on behalf of Mono Lake and its water is so contentious, convoluted, and long-running, and has involved so many public agencies and public hearings, so many lawsuits and compromises, that the simple facts are virtually impossible to separate from the details.

Central to the saga, though, is the Los Angeles Department of Water and Power. "If we don't get the water," said self-taught engineer and water czar William Mulholland in 1907, "we won't need it." And to get water to the L.A. desert—necessary to fulfill his vision of a lush southstate paradise, only incidentally profitable to real estate interests secretly connected to the plan—Mulholland and his DWP proposed an aqueduct that would carry the eastern Sierra Nevada's water south from the Owens Valley (and the towns of Bishop, Big Pine, Independence, and Lone Pine) to Los Angeles. To gain support (and municipal bond funding) for "Mulholland's ditch," even the *Los Angeles Times* helped fudge on the facts—convincing the public in the early 1900s that a drought existed, a deception unchallenged until the 1950s.

After buying up nearly all private land in the Owens Valley (usually dishonestly, by condemning the land and water rights by lawsuit to drive down the price), Mulholland and his water people had their finest day in November of 1913, when the first Owens Valley water flowed into the aqueduct: 30,000 people showed up for the event.

Commenting on the subsequent, permanent desolation of the once lush, quarter-million-acre Owens Valley, the cowboy comedian Will Rogers said soberly: "Los Angeles had to have more water for its Chamber of Commerce to drink more toasts to its growth."

As L.A.'s thirst grew ever more unquenchable—by 1930, its population had grown from 200,000 to 1,200,000—violence over eastern Sierra Nevada water rights became commonplace. Denied use of the land as abruptly as their forebears had denied the native Paiutes, outraged ranchers "captured" and controlled the aqueduct on many occasions, and dynamited it 17 times. But urban growth was seemingly unstoppable, and in 1930 L.A. voters approved another bond issue—to extend the aqueduct north into the Mono Lake Basin.

Following completion of this northern stretch in 1941, runoff from Rush, Lee Vining, Walker, and Parker creeks was diverted into the ditch-tunnel

drilled under the Mono Craters and into the Owens River and aqueduct. Even worse for Mono Lake—with its water level dropping and its delicate aquatic ecology suffering almost instantaneously—Los Angeles completed a second aqueduct in 1970, to "salvage" runoff otherwise lost to the lake. Mono Lake has been shrinking ever since. As of 1990, it's estimated that about 17% of Los Angeles water comes from Mono Lake. California's Dead Sea has nearly died as a direct result.

Central to the modern-day chapter of Mono Lake's story is David Gaines, long-time Lee Vining resident and founder of the Mono Lake Committee—killed, along with committee staffer Don Oberlin, in a January 1988 car accident near Mammoth Lakes. Starting in the 1970s, Gaines and his growing, loosely organized band of Mono Lake lovers starting taking on the Los Angeles Department of Water and Power—and anyone else involved, even through passive inaction. From guerrilla theater and educational "events" (such as public picketing,

tufa formation at Mono Lake

KIM WEIR

protests, and volunteer bucket brigades hand-carrying water from Lee Vining Creek to Mono Lake) to press conferences and political confrontations, the Mono Lake Committee was untiring in its war against water diversions.

As a result, the Interagency Mono Lake Task Force—including representatives from Mono County, the L.A. Department of Water and Power, the California departments of Water Resources and Fish and Game, the U.S. Forest Service, the U.S. Fish and Wildlife Service, and the federal Bureau of Land Management—was convened. The group agreed, by 1980, that the only way to protect the natural resources of the Mono Basin was by curtailing water diversions and raising the lake's level. An almost endless round of lawsuits against the DWP and state and federal regulatory agencies (along with countersuits) in both the state and federal court systems has subsequently helped implement the task force recommendations.

A state Supreme Court decision in 1983—specifically related to Mono Lake but setting the California legal precedent that now protects all state waters—declared that lakes, rivers, and other natural resources are owned by all the people and must be protected by the state for the public trust. Though competing needs are undeniable, the right to divert water from any ecosystem depends upon that system's continued health—and if harm occurs, water rights must be adjusted accordingly, throughout time.

But though the tide finally turned in Mono Lake's favor, at least legally, skirmishes continue over how much water must be released into the Mono Lake Basin to ensure the health of that ecosystem—how much water will protect island-nesting gulls from coyote predation, how much water will protect the lake's brine shrimp, how much water will protect the region's stream fisheries. Needless to say, the opinions of Mono Lake Committee members and other environmentalists differ from those of L.A.'s Department of Water and Power. Actual cutbacks in diversions—under court order—didn't begin until 1989.

Political pundits contend that recent state legislation to make peace at Mono Lake merely pays the city of Los Angeles, with public funds, to strike a rather vague deal with the Mono Lake Committee—and encourages L.A. to increase groundwater pumping from Inyo County's Owens Valley, all at California taxpayers' expense. "If this is what peace looks like for Mono Lake and the Owens Valley," comments the Sacramento Bee's Bill Kahrl, "it's hard to understand what anyone thought was worth fighting for in the first place."

Members of the Mono Lake Committee answer that even successful lawsuits have not yet protected Mono Lake, and that state legislative action at least opens the door for making a lasting peace.

The war over eastern Sierra Nevada water goes on.

from Lee Vining for 12 miles then east for 1¾ miles on unpaved Punchbowl Road. As elsewhere, avoid pumice soils and stay on the roads—if signs say travel is unsafe for ordinary vehicles, believe them.

NORTH FROM MONO LAKE: BODIE AND VICINITY

Evocative even these days is the published 19th-century response of a young girl when told her family was moving to this bad, brawling, desolate frontier town on the lonely, wind-sheared plateau: "Goodbye, God, we are going to Bodie." In defense of this godless Gomorrah, a gold mining town with a population of over 10,000 employed at 30 mines in its heyday, a Bodie newspaper editor claimed the child had been misquoted—that what she actually said was: "Good, by God, we are going to Bodie." But the town's own citizen-

ry boasted that Bodie had the widest streets, wickedest men, and worst climate and whiskey in the West. Fisticuffs and murders were daily events. (Another local newspaper editor observed: "There is some irresistable power that impels us to cut and shoot each other to pieces.") Virgin Alley and Maiden Lane in Bodie's redlight district boasted neither, and a local minister described the community as "a sea of sin lashed by tempests of lust and passion."

What remains of the busted boomtown of Bodie, California's largest ghost town, is now protected as part of **Bodie State Historic Park.** A strangely silent place still standing (more or less) in the shadow of the old Standard Mine, where the sage-whistling winds speak loudest of days gone by, Bodie still somehow evokes the spirit of the truly wild Wild West. Preserved in its entirety in a state of arrested decay, what's here is certainly worth at least a half-day's exploration, but only about five percent of Bodie's well-weathered 1860s and 1870s wood frames still stand, the rest destroyed over the decades by fire and the elements. Pick up a self-guided tour brochure at the small museum (in the old Miner's Union Hall) or at the ranger's office/residence on Green Street (one of the few occupied buildings in town).

Visitors are free to wander at will through godless, lawless, treeless Bodie. Peek through tattered lace curtains into general stores, restaurants, saloons, livery stables, and miners' shacks abandoned for over a century, and peer into dusty rooms furnished with cracked and peeling wallpapers and woodstoves, sprung bedframes, banged-up wash basins, even battered old shoes and clothing. Most poignant of all, though, is the time-twisted, rusted child's wagon abandoned in the middle of the street. Done with town, head for the hillside cemeteries for an introduction to some of Bodie's colorfully memorialized former residents. (The fenced-in cemetery was set aside for local decent folk; most bad Bodie boys were buried on Boot Hill.)

Ask rangers about the status of Gallactic Resources' plans to start a modern, noisy, open-pit gold mining operation on Bodie Bluff and Standard Hill above town. Though test drilling is underway, critics, including the independent California State Park Rangers Association, contend the project will destroy the Bodie experience.

Bodie Practicalities

For obvious reasons, beyond the parking lot no smoking is allowed in Bodie. Camping is also prohibited, but picnicking is okay (no shade, just tables and pit toilets). Pack a lunch and bring your own drinking water—Bodie is a ghost town, with no stores or services. The park is open daily 9 a.m.-7 p.m. in summer, just until 4 p.m. the rest of the year—hours strictly enforced (the rangers close and lock the road gates). Day-use fee: $5. For more information and to volunteer time and/or money to help The Friends of Bodie preserve the town, contact: Bodie State Historic Park, P.O. Box 515, Bridgeport 93517, tel. (619) 647-6445.

Most Bodie visitors come anytime but winter, via 13-mile Hwy. 270/Bodie Rd. (paved most of the way) from Hwy. 395, the turnoff about seven miles south of Bridgeport and 20 miles north of Lee Vining. Even when Bodie Rd. is closed by winter snows (usually November

Bodie was the wickedest Old West mine camp of them all, locals boasted, but there were a few churches in town.

through mid-April), the park is still open. The truly intrepid sometimes snowmobile or ski in, but this isn't advisable. If you insist, do call ahead and tell rangers you're coming—just in case you don't make it. (It's lonely out here, and winter storms can be brutal.) Alternate good-weather routes include (from Mono Lake) the washboard-style dirt and gravel Cottonwood Canyon Rd. from Hwy. 167 and (from Bridgeport) the narrow Aurora Canyon-Masonic back roads.

Bridgeport

A middle-of-nowhere supply stop and center of local social action (such as it is), Bridgeport is the place to get extra food, parts for emergency car repairs, and outdoor equipment—as well as to rest one's head in a real bed. Motels line the highway. The **Walker River Lodge,** P.O. Box 695, Bridgeport 93517, tel. (619) 932-7021, has the usual amenities plus heated pool, whirlpool, and fish cleaning and freezing facilities, rooms $65-100 from April through October, substantially less otherwise. The **Best Western Ruby Inn** north of downtown, P.O. Box 475, tel. 932-7241, offers the same basic features and even more comfort, rooms $60-85 (less in winter). Equally nice and quite unusual is **The Cain House** at 11 Main (P.O. Box 454), tel. 932-7040, a restored historical home with bed and breakfast, rates $80-130. Rustic lodges, cabins, and campgrounds abound at nearby lakes (see "From Bridgeport to Lee Vining" below).

Get basic food supplies at local groceries. Locals recommend the **Bridgeport Inn** on Main, tel. (619) 932-7380, for breakfast, lunch, and dinner (open March-November). A better choice for dinner, also an overnight, is **Virginia Creek Settlement** about five miles south of town (see below).

Bridgeport attracts an eclectic array of visitors, and events. On the last weekend in June, the entire western U.S. chapter of organized **Harley-Davidson motorcyclists** convenes here. The town's **July 4th celebration** is one of the nation's oldest Independence Day parties, locals say. And later in July comes the rodeo. But perhaps Bridgeport's most notable party is the fairly new **Big Mountain Man Rendezvous** in October, like stepping 150 years back into the past (no cars allowed). Participants dress in period frontier attire; competitions and friendly rivalries include everything from shooting contests to bake-offs. Fun, too, is "Trader's Row," a frontier-style marketplace where everything is historically authentic, from trading beads to children's toys.

For more information about the area, contact: **Bridgeport Chamber of Commerce** on Main St. (the highway), P.O. Box 541, Bridgeport 93517, tel. (619) 932-7500. Another good information source, especially for national forest maps, wilderness permits, and area campground and hiking information, is the **Bridgeport Ranger Station**, P.O. Box 595, tel. 932-7070.

From Bridgeport To Lee Vining

Ask in Bridgeport for directions to the primitive **Big Hot Warm Springs** just south of town and east one-half mile off the highway. Nearby **Bridgeport Reservoir** (sometimes little more than a massive mud puddle) and **Kirman Lake** are popular for trout fishing. Excellent for rainbow and brown trout fishing are the pretty, high-altitude **Twin Lakes** southwest of Bridgeport via

Twin Lakes Rd., which also offer trailhead access into the Hoover Wilderness.

In addition to eight national forest campgrounds along Robinson Creek, the area also offers picnicking, lake recreation, and several popular private resorts (closed in winter). The **Hunewill Guest Ranch** between Bridgeport and the lakes, tel. (619) 932-7710, is a working cattle ranch complete with comfortable accommodations, good food, and guided horseback trips into the wilderness. **Doc & Al's** resort on the way to Lower Twin Lake, tel. 932-7051, is a time-honored fishing retreat. And at the end of the road, at the far western edge of Upper Twin Lake, is the rustic **Mono Village** resort, tel. 932-7071, with cabins and private camping.

About halfway between Bridgeport and Lee Vining on the south side of Conway Summit is the turnoff to **Virginia Lakes,** a cluster of 10 small lakes (no swimming) in the high country (elevation 9,700 feet) just six miles west of Hwy. 395 and perfect for camping. There's a national forest campground at Trumbull Lake, also various undeveloped creekside campsites. Also here: the summers-only **Virginia Lakes Resort** (mailing address: Bridgeport 93517, no phone), with cabins, small grocery, restaurant, and public bathhouse.

Also close to both Bodie and Mono Lake is **Lundy Lake,** reached via Lundy Lake Rd., which heads west at the Hwy. 395/Hwy. 167 intersection. Trailhead into the Twenty Lakes Basin area, the aspen-and-pine fringed lake is also noted for its fishing, its beaver ponds, its out-of-the-way camping (there are 100 primitive county campsites along Mill Creek below the dam), and the relaxed rustic charms of the **Lundy Lake Resort,** P.O. Box 265, Lee Vining 93541, with housekeeping cabins, RV and tent camping, also grocery, laundromat, and hot showers.

Virginia Creek Settlement

The best little dinner house (and overnight stop) for miles around is the Virginia Creek Settlement on Hwy. 395 five miles south of Bridgeport, just a half-mile north of the turnoff to Bodie. A windmill out front marks the spot. The settlement was once part of Dogtown, the region's first gold-rush mining camp, though nearby Bodie surpassed it in reputation and longevity. These days, Virginia Creek Settlement (tel. 619-

932-7780) serves a variety of good American-style dinners and nightly specials, from steaks and chicken to pastas, but the real prize here is the pizza. Choose either whole wheat or white, then ponder the toppings—everything from Canadian bacon and garlic to artichoke hearts and jalapeño peppers. The family dinner special is a good deal: $25 (for four) will get you salad, garlic bread, spaghetti, and a medium-sized cheese pizza. The restaurant is open for dinner Wed.-Sat. 5-9 p.m., 5-8 on Sunday.

An equally great deal is a stay in the large suite directly above the restaurant, the only historically authentic rooms remaining from the building's past as a boarding house for Bodie miners. The two bedrooms have iron bed frames and country-style floral decor plus a shared sitting room. The entire suite runs $70, either for two couples or for a small family (with older children or infants only, since the staircase presents a possible hazard for toddlers). If the rooms are rented separately, as available, it's still a bargain: $34 per couple.

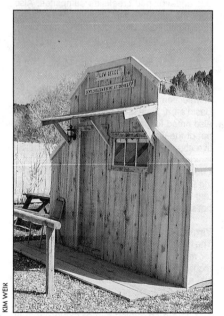

KIM WEIR

false-front tent cabins at Virginia Creek Settlement—"Dewey, Cheatam & Howe" law office

Behind the restaurant and well back from the highway are a few log cabin-style motel units with knotty-pine walls, iron bed frames, in-room brewed coffee. Clean and comfortable, with rates $35-58 for up to four people. Even more intriguing for a not-too-intrepid outdoors experience is an overnight in one of Virginia Creek's wood-fronted tent cabins, available during mild weather only. Each looks like an Old West storefront, complete with tongue-in-cheek business shingle (like "Dewey, Cheatam, & Howe" for the law office). Inside are a table and chair plus two double beds with bare mattresses (bring your own sleeping bags or rent linens and blankets, $3.50 per bed; $1.50 extra for towels, washcloths, and soap). Outside is a barbecue and picnic table. Rates: $16 per night for two people, $2 each additional person. You can also camp at Virginia Creek, right along the creek, $10 for two, $2 each additional person. Some sites have electricity, but no RV sewer hook-ups are available. (RVers might want to check in at Willow Springs Resort just up the highway toward Bridgeport, which has full facilities—and extra rooms, if Virginia Creek is full.) Though no rooms at Virginia Creek Settlement have telephones, there *is* a pay phone. Just step into the outhouse up by the highway and see for yourself.

MONO LAKE PRACTICALITIES

Mono Lake Area Camping And Accommodations

Lee Vining is "town" for Mono Lake, a pleasant roadside collection of motels, gas stations, and supply stops on Hwy. 395 just north of the junction with Tioga Rd./Hwy. 120. Before Hwy. 120 begins its straight-ahead descent through desert-dry rock to Mono Lake (look for Sierra bighorn on the unstable shale slopes above the road) and just two miles east of Yosemite is the rustic **Tioga Pass Resort,** P.O. Box 7, Lee Vining 93541, winter phone only, tel. (209) 372-4471 (Nov. 1-May 1). Lodge accommodations and cabins are available by advance reservation; open year-round.

No developed camping is available at Mono Lake, but sometimes unoffical campsites can be staked out above the 1941 waterline. For more information, ask at the Lee Vining Ranger Station on Hwy. 120 or at the new visitor center.

(See "Other Information and Practicalities" below.) In town, **Murphey's RV Park,** tel. (619) 647-6316, and the **Mono Vista Trailer Park,** tel. 647-6401, both offer RV and tent sites. But the best place around is back up Hwy. 120 at the Forest Service's **Big Bend Campground** along Lee Vining Creek—a beautiful but basic creekside setting (even a small waterfall) reached via a gravel and dirt road from the highway, with chemical-flush pit toilets, piped-in untreated creek water, no showers, 14-day limit. Usually open mid-April through October (weather permitting).

Farther east, and closer to the highway, are the county-run **Aspen Grove** and **Lee Vining campgrounds** in a creek meadow setting. Many other public campgrounds are within 15 miles of Lee Vining. Free and low-cost camping is available at **Saddlebag Lake** north of Hwy. 120 and just outside the Hoover Wilderness. Also here is a summers-only resort, at the highest California lake accessible by public road, reached via narrow, steep Saddleback Lake Road.

Almost as inexpensive as camping, and not too far away, are two area youth hostels. For more information, see "Mammoth Lakes and Vicinity."

For non-campers, usually the cheapest motel around (pets allowed) is the **King's Inn** two blocks off the highway on 2nd St., P.O. Box 160, Lee Vining 93541, tel. (619) 647-6300, with small, cozy rooms, kitchen units extra. Also reasonable and pet friendly is **Murphy's Motel** on the highway, P.O. Box 57, tel. 647-6316, rates $48-68 (lower in winter). The **Gateway Motel** in town on the highway, P.O. Box 250, tel. 647-6467, has comfortable rooms with queen beds, coffee, and TV for $55-70 (rates less from November through mid-May). Another good motel choice is the **Best Western Lake View Lodge,** P.O. Box 345, tel. 647-6543, complete with coin-op laundry and putting green, with rooms $65-75 in the mid-April through mid-October birdwatching-and-summer-travel high season, substantially less at other times.

Eating Out At Mono Lake

Folks here will tell you *the* place to eat in town is **Nicely's Restaurant** ("real nicely people") on Main, tel. (619) 647-6446, open daily for good cafe fare—breakfast, lunch, and dinner. North of town about four miles, in the otherwise long-gone town of Mono Lake, is the fancier **Mono Inn** dinner house, tel. 647-6581, open weekends only in winter and famous for its chocolate pecan pie, though **Virginia Creek Settlement** near the turn-off to Bodie (see above) is worth the longer drive. There's a deli inside the **Yosemite Trading Company,** tel. 647-6369. Also recommended is the **Yosemite Trails Inn** across the street, tel. 647-6369. Best bet for supplies is the **Lee Vining Market,** tel. 647-6301, open 8 a.m.-8 p.m. daily.

Mono Lake Committee Information And Events

Stop by the **Mono Lake Committee Information Center and Bookstore** (the funky building on the highway, once a dancehall, now undergoing renovation), P.O. Box 29, Lee Vining 93541, tel. (619) 647-6386. Headquarters also serves as an all-purpose visitor center (tel. 647-6595) providing the latest information on Mono Lake politics (including educational slide show), schedules of lake hikes, tours, and canoe trips, suggestions about what else to see and do in the area (including where some of the best hot springs are), and practical guidance on visiting the eastern Sierra Nevada.

The *Mono Lake Guidebook* by David Gaines and the Mono Lake Committee is updated and out in a new edition, still the best guidebook available. Even a small donation in support of the committee's work will yield a subscription to the group's quarterly *Mono Lake Newsletter,* the best information source for the ongoing politics of water and power in the eastern Sierra Nevada, also for keeping abreast of current ecological research. For a good solid background on relevant California water politics, read *Water and Power* by William Kahrl. Or watch the movie *Chinatown.*

Among the many fundraising/educational activities organized by the Mono Lake Committee is the annual mileage-sponsored **Bike-a-thon** from Los Angeles to Mono Lake (volunteer cyclists always welcome). The committee also sponsors a fundraising **Bird-a-thon** each autumn (in conjunction with the Point Reyes Bird Observatory), sponsors a wine drawing, and sells T-shirts, caps, calendars, books, and postcards year-round to raise money.

Many educational field seminars are held annually, primarily from late spring to early fall, by the Mono Lake Foundation (P.O. Box 153, Lee

Vining 93541), including: Birds of the Mono Basin; High Country Birds; High Country Wildflowers; Natural History Canoe Tours; Geology of the Mono Basin; Volcanoes of the East Side; Mono-Bodie Historical Tour; Writing of the Eastern Sierra. Most weekend workshops are $75 ($60 for members of the Mono Lake Committee), family and photography trips more.

Other Information And Practicalities

Easy **ranger-guided walks** of Mono Lake are offered year-round, daily in summer and every Saturday and Sunday from mid-September through mid-June (call for current times). For fall and winter hikes, meet at 1 p.m. in the South Tufa area, 10 miles southeast of Lee Vining via Highways 395 and 120.

For more Mono Lake information, stop by the impressive new **Mono Basin National Forest Scenic Area Visitor Center** just north of town off the highway, tel. (619) 647-3044, open daily 9-5 most of the year, until 8 p.m. from mid-June through Labor Day, open weekends only in winter. An impressive contemporary museum overlooking the lake, it features an information center (the introductory video "Of Ice And Fire" is shown every half-hour in summer), a good bookstore, and very well done natural history exhibits. Many are of the interactive "hands-on" educational variety, like the Guess Your Weight In Brine Shrimp display. (An average-sized adult weighs 450,000 shrimp, for example, roughly equivalent to 150 pounds.) Particularly amusing, though—since we humans consider ourselves the world's most discriminating cultural connoisseurs—is the display of "gull juju," odd treasures scavenged by seagulls and incorporated into their nests. Birds here have collected everything from Styrofoam cups and cocktail-sized American flags to decapitated toy soldiers, plastic cowboys, and a Daryl Strawberry baseball card—all in all, a fairly insightful representation of U.S. society.

Another good source for general information, including area day hikes, forest and wilderness maps ($3), topo maps, wilderness permits, and regional campground information is the **Lee Vining Ranger Station,** 1½ miles west of Hwy. 395 on Hwy. 120, P.O. Box 10, Lee Vining 93541, tel. (619) 647-3000. Open Mon.-Sat. 8-4:30 in summer, closed on off-season weekends. Ask too about surrounding national forest areas—including the eastern Sierra Neva-

da's Hoover Wilderness adjacent to Yosemite north of Hwy. 120 and the Ansel Adams Wilderness south of the highway.

Greyhound stops twice daily at the Lee Vining Market, tel. (619) 647-6301 or toll-free (800) 237-8211 for route and fare info, with one bus heading south toward Los Angeles, the other north toward Reno. While you wait, throw those dirt-burdened clothes into the **laundromat** machines next door. The local **post office,** tel. 627-6371, is behind the Yosemite Trading Post. For AAA emergency road service, call 647-6444. Hospital and **medical care** is available in Bridgeport, tel. 932-7011, or Mammoth Lakes, tel. 934-3311, but for medical emergencies contact the **Mono County sheriff's office** in Bridgeport, tel. 932-7451.

SOUTH FROM MONO LAKE: THE JUNE LAKE LOOP

About five miles south of Lee Vining off Hwy. 395 is Hwy. 158, the northern end of the June Lake Loop, leading to a high-country collection of lakes and summer cabins eerily shadowed in late afternoon by the saw-toothed snowy peaks looming up from the Ansel Adams Wilderness just to the west. Also worthwhile in the area: the short hike to **Obsidian Dome,** a poetically poised mountain mass of once-molten black- and color-streaked glass (trailhead reached via dirt road 1½ miles south of June Lake Junction), and the excellent, usually uncrowded **June Mountain ski resort** (now owned by the Mammoth Mountain folks), P.O. Box 146, June Lake 93529, tel. (619) 648-7733. In theory, you can buy lift tickets at one place and ski at both. Cross-country skiing also offered.

The stunning subalpine scenery here includes four lakes—Grant, Silver, Gull, and June—popular for fishing and water recreation (water-skiing at Grant Lake only) and a multitude of Forest Service campgrounds. Perhaps prettiest are the campgrounds near Silver Lake, but the **Oh! Ridge Campground** is accessible for the disabled, and **Hartley Springs,** not far south of June Lake Junction, is free. For non-camping accommodations, try **Silver Lake Resort,** P.O. Box 116, June Lake 93529, tel. (619) 648-7525, which offers housekeeping cabins, RV and tent camping, restaurant, store, gas station, and rental boats and launch ramp. Other possibilities include the **Fern Creek Lodge,** Rt. 3, Box 7, tel. 648-7722, motel units plus housekeeping cabins (some with fireplaces), and the **Boulder Lodge,** P.O. Box 68, tel. 648-7533, for cabins and motel units plus swimming pool and tennis courts.

A good place to eat is **Casey's** across the road from the Fern Creek Lodge, open for hefty breakfast, lunch, and dinner. Even if you're just on the roll through town, in June Lake proper stop by **Schat's Dutch Bakery** for some sweet rolls or fresh-baked bread. For more information about local accommodations and restaurants, contact the **June Lake Chamber of Commerce,** P.O. Box 2, tel. (619) 648-7584.

MAMMOTH LAKES AND VICINITY

The Mammoth Lakes area offers surprising contrast to the sagebrush scrub along the main highway—and good summer hiking among the geological wonders, mountain lakes, hot springs, and cool conifers of this otherwise hotshot winter ski area.

One thing not immediately apparent, however, is the fact that the Mammoth Lakes area is near the southwestern edge of the massive Long Valley Caldera, which stretches north to near Obsidian Dome and east to beyond Lake Crowley—one of the biggest, most powerful volcanoes in the West yet essentially invisible to the eye. Only its crater—and a new, emerging volcanic dome at its center—remain after the volcanic peak which once stood here was blasted to the four winds some 700,000 years ago during a monstrous eruption. Ash and pumice spewed for at least 50 miles in all directions; no other volcanic event in recorded history, volcanologists say, has approached that level of volcanic fury. Despite recent resurgence in area volcanic activity—an event occuring everywhere in California—scientists don't believe the Big One will hit, here at least, any time soon.

MAMMOTH LAKES AND THE MAMMOTH LAKES BASIN

Aside from the area's lovely lakes and streams, the star attraction of the Mammoth Lakes Basin is **Devil's Postpile National Monument,** a seemingly pile-driven vertical collection of three- to eight-sided basalt columns formed by slowly cooling lava flows (getting there involves an easy day hike, after a national forest shuttle ride). Nearby is colorful **Rainbow Falls,** complete with mountain pools for invigorating swimming. Near Devils Postpile is **Fish Creek Hot Springs,** with no facilities, no fees, no restrictions, reached from Reds Meadow by hiking south on the Fish Creek Trail past the Sharktooth Creek Trail (about 100 yards along the path beyond the campground).

But the area's all-time favorite hot soak is at **Hot Creek,** three miles east of Hwy. 395 via Long Valley Airport Road. Officially "not recommended" for swimming or soaking by the Forest Service, people hop in happily nonetheless. The steaming Hot Creek experience is created by a *very* hot spring bubbling into an ice-cold stream—so the trick is finding a spot that's not so hot you'll get scalded. (Most people manage.) Swimsuits required. Open daily from sunrise to sunset, free.

To get an eagle's-eye view of the area, in summer take a tram ride up **Mammoth Mountain** (open daily 11 a.m.-3 p.m., fee) and stop halfway for a snack or cup of coffee. Do explore some of the area's 100-plus lakes. The only one noted for swimming is **Horseshoe Lake,** which is also the trailhead for the Mammoth Pass Trail. For shorter hikes, there are many ways to get to **Lake George.** Picture-perfect for picnicking is **Lake Mamie.** Diehard trout fishing enthusiasts may want to visit **Lake Crowley,** some 15 miles south of Mammoth Lakes.

Almost a religious experience for adventure cyclists is flying down the Kamikaze Trail on Mammoth Mountain, just one of many mountain highs offered through the resort's summer **Mammoth Mountain Bike Park** (75 miles of trails) at Mammoth Mountain Inn. The inn is home base, too, for **Mammoth Adventure Connection,** which offers mountain-bike tours, mountain climbing, and a variety of other adventures year-round.

For more Mammoth-area recreation ideas, from hot-air ballooning and golfing in summer to sleigh rides and dogsledding in winter, contact the **Mammoth Lakes Visitors Center** in Village

Center Mall West (a mini-mall across from the post office), P.O. Box 48, Mammoth Lakes 93546, tel. (619) 934-8006 or toll-free (800) 367-6572. If you arrive after hours, there are useful publications available in the racks outside.

Winter Sports At Mammoth

At the center of the area's winter ski scene is the **Mammoth Mountain ski resort** just past town, P.O. Box 24, Mammoth Lakes 93546, tel. (619) 934-2571 or toll-free (800) 367-6572 for accommodations. The area's 2,500 acres of great skiing are far from everywhere but particularly popular with the L.A. crowd—the main reason the area has all the urban amenities, from good restaurants and mini-malls with clothing outlet stores and other shops to jet set-style nightlife. To cope with drought conditions, the resort now has 200-acre snowmaking capabilities. To avoid the parking crunch at the slopes, take the shuttle from the village. (And if the crowds seem unbearable, remember a lift ticket for Mammoth's slopes is also good, on the same day, at June Mountain.)

WES DEMPSEY

Devil's Postpile National Monument

Mammoth also offers good cross-country skiing. The **Tamarack Cross-Country Ski Center** at Tamarack Lodge, P.O. Box 69, tel. (619) 934-2442, offers extensive backcountry trails (children under age 12 free), telemarking, tours, rentals, and lessons. The **Sierra Meadows Ski Touring Center** at Sherwin Creek Rd. off Old Mammoth Rd., P.O. Box 2008, Mammoth Lakes 93546, tel. 934-6161, has groomed trails and set track plus lessons, rentals, and warming hut.

Forest Service cross-country ski trails include the **Obsidian Dome Trail**, which begins at the junction of Hwy. 395 and Glass Flow Rd. (south of June Lake Junction), as well as several near Mammoth Lakes, such as the **Earthquake Fault Trail** to Inyo Craters. Winter camping is available, too, at the national forest's Shady Rest campgrounds.

MAMMOTH PRACTICALITIES

Mammoth Area Camping

The best bet in summer is camping. There are numerous Inyo National Forest campgrounds in the Mammoth Lakes Basin, including sites at **Twin Lakes, Lake Mary,** and **Lake George,** as well as some near town—including **Pine City** (tents only), **Coldwater** (near the trailhead into the John Muir Wilderness), **Pine Glen** (wheelchair accessible), and **New Shady Rest** and **Old Shady Rest campgrounds.**

Forest Service campgrounds are also available at crystal-clear **Convict Lake** south of Mammoth Lakes and at **Rock Creek Lake** halfway between Mammoth Lakes and Bishop. Some of the national forest campsites can be reserved in advance through Mistix, toll-free tel. (800) 283-CAMP. For complete listings of regional camping choices, contact the Mammoth Ranger Station (see "Mammoth Events and Information" below).

Camp High Sierra just west of New Shady Rest, operated by the L.A. Department of Recreation, tel. (619) 934-2368, has nice tent sites, rustic cabins, hot showers, even a lodge.

Long Valley And Hilton Creek Hostels

Despite the area's overall upscale trend, Mammoth Lakes is almost becoming a mecca for budget travelers. Near enough to Mammoth sights, Mono Lake, and other eastern Sierra Nevada pleasures—about 15 minutes south of Mammoth proper and just west of Crowley Lake—are two decent AYH hostels, a great way for anyone to organize an inexpensive stay. (No credit cards.)

The **Long Valley AYH Hostel** just off Hwy. 395 at Crowley Lake Drive (Long Valley turnoff), R.R. 1, P.O. Box 189-B, Mammoth Lakes 93546, tel. (619) 935-4377, is a historic ranch with a pretty chalet, just 10 beds and the basics (kitchen, linen rentals, equipment storage, on-site parking), but who cares when there's so much to do? The friendly folks here can help you get oriented. Family rooms are available. Usually open only May through September, but check for the possibility of an extended fall season. Rates: $8.50 per person for AYH members, $11.50 for nonmembers. Reservations aren't usually necessary, but call ahead if it's a concern.

Open year-round and relaxed is the **Hilton Creek International AYH Hostel**, R.R. 1, P.O. Box 1128, Crowley Lake 93546, tel. (619) 935-4989. This renovated and refurbished "cowboy bunkhouse" sleeps up to 22, with two dorms and a family room. The kitchen is well-equipped, the living room and lounge spacious and cozy (complete with fireplace, Sierra Nevada natural history library, games, and a 500-gallon trout aquarium). And there's a great view from the dining room, though some swear it's even better from the redwood hot tub outside. Low-cost continental breakfast available on weekends and holidays. Other amenities include laundry facilities, lockers and baggage storage, linen rentals, and on-site parking.

Hilton Creek's winter "Intro to Ski Touring" program is a remarkable deal, with or without meals; you can even rent your equipment here. But worthwhile outdoor adventures are offered year-round, from hikes and backpacking trips to free guided mountain-bike tours of area mines.

Reservations for Hilton Creek are accepted by phone (advisable from mid-November through mid-May), 50% advance deposit required. Otherwise it's first-come, first-served. Rates per person: $10 winter, $8 summer, half-price for seniors and children under age 18 (with parents).

Other Inexpensive Mammoth Area Accommodations

Surprising for such an elite retreat, in winter and summer Mammoth does offer other reasonably priced accommodations, generally most appropriate for travelers on their own. Most inexpensive are lodges which provide dorm-style rooms for $15-25 per person in winter, $8-15 in summer. These include: **Asgard Chalet,** tel. (714) 962-6773; **Innsbruck Lodge,** tel. (619) 934-3035; the **Kitzbuhel Lodge,** tel. 934-2352; and **Ullr Lodge,** tel. 934-2454.

Relatively inexpensive motels—and do call around in summer, since there may be great deals available elsewhere—include the very popular **Motel 6** on Hwy. 203, 3372 Main, P.O. Box 1260, Mammoth Lakes 93546, tel. (619) 934-6660, with rooms $38-60 in winter, less in summer. In the same general category (prices sometimes less) is the **Econo Lodge** at Main and Sierra, tel. 934-8892. The **White Stag Inn** west of town on the highway (P.O. Box 45), tel. 934-7507, offers rooms for $45-85 in winter, $36-62 in summer. Other mid-range motels include the **Wildwood Inn,** tel. 934-6855, winter rates $54-89; the **Swiss Chalet Motel,** tel. 934-2403, $60-64 in winter; and the **North Village Inn** at 103 Lake Mary Rd., tel. 934-2525, rates $49-69 in winter.

Mammoth Area Bed And Breakfasts

The **Rainbow Tarns** bed and breakfast, tel. (619) 935-4556, south of Mammoth Lakes on Rainbow Tarns Rd. off Crowley Lake Dr., a mile north of Tom's Place, offers unusual serenity, access to cross-country skiing, hiking, and horseback trails, and a full country breakfast.

There are other good choices, though. Near town is the **White Horse Inn Bed & Breakfast** at 2180 Old Mammoth Rd., P.O. Box 2326, Mammoth Lakes 93546, tel. (619) 924-3656, which offers several theme rooms in a private home. The Emperor's Room, for example, paying homage to the area's mining-era Chinese influence, features as a centerpiece an heirloom antique Chinese bed. All rooms have private baths; a full country breakfast is served every morning, wine and cheese in the afternoon. Two-night minimum stay required. Rates: $125-200.

The **Nugget Lodge,** 75 Joaquin Rd., P.O. Box 3006, Mammoth Lakes 93546, tel. (619) 934-2710 or toll-free (800) 358-2710, has a ski rack and goose-down comforter in every room, a shared lounge with huge stone fireplace and indoor diversions, even an upstairs guest kitchen. Winter room rates run $65-85 midweek, $80-100 on weekends and holidays. Ask about

father and son fishing for dinner

WES DEMPSEY

midweek packages, summer rates, senior discounts. Other bed and breakfasts with reasonably low rates include the **White Feather Lodge,** tel. 934-4439, rooms $70-90 in winter, and **Wildasinn House,** tel. 934-3851, $75-95.

Another good choice—noted for the great breakfasts and casual yet cozy ambience—is the **Snow Goose Inn** lodge at 57 Forest Trail, P.O. Box 946, Mammoth Lakes 93546, tel. (619) 934-2660 or toll-free 800-874-7368, with rooms $78-168 in winter, $58-88 in summer.

Mammoth Hotels And Major Motels

People who plan to stay a while often opt for comfort on the group living plan—renting condominiums, cabins, or homes by the week and cooking most meals "at home." For information on reputable area rental agencies, contact the Mammoth Lakes Visitors Bureau (see "Mammoth Events And Information" below).

The **Sierra Lodge** is a completely nonsmoking luxury hotel at 3540 Main, tel. (619) 934-8881 or toll-free (800) 356-5711. Rooms include kitchens and microwaves, refrigerators, TV and cable, access to spa. Rates in winter are $85-95 on weekdays, $110-130 on weekends, with extended stay, group, and summer rates available—the latter about half the winter rate, a great deal. Children under age 12 stay free. Nice, too, is the **Alpenhof Lodge** a mile west of town on Hwy. 203, tel. 934-6330, mini-suites (some with fireplaces) close to the slopes, with spa, sauna, and pool in summer. Rates: $64-110 in winter. Ask about midweek ski pack-

ages, summer specials. Another good choice is the **Quality Inn** just west of town on the highway, tel. 934-5114, prime-time rates $94-99. The all-suites **Shilo Inn** on the highway east of Old Mammoth Rd. at 2963 Main, tel. 934-4500, rooms with kitchens, refrigerators and wet bars, continental breakfast, free access to complete fitness center and sauna, whirlpool, indoor pool, and steamroom. Rates: $125-150 on winter weekends.

Time-honored and very traditional for a stay almost right on the slopes is the very nice, bustling, and mammoth **Mammoth Mountain Inn,** P.O. Box 353, tel. (619) 934-2581 or toll-free (800) 228-4947 for reservations. Rooms during ski season run $80-170, studios and suites $115-350. All rooms are less expensive during midweek in winter, and substantially less in summer. Call or write for special packages and off-season deals.

Rustic Regional Resorts

The special **Tamarack Lodge** hotel a few miles beyond town on Lake Mary Rd. (the extension of Hwy. 203), P.O. Box 69, Mammoth Lakes 93546, tel. (916) 934-2442, is a 1920s mountain lodge on Twin Lakes at the foot of Mammoth Mountain with restaurant, fireplace-anchored lobby, and knotty pine-paneled lodge rooms (only four have private baths). Outlying housekeeping cabins have kitchens, bathrooms, some fireplaces. Fish for trout in summer, try Nordic skiing in winter—also ice skating, when the lakes freeze over.

Also recommended in the area: the summers-only **Red's Meadow Resort** near Devil's Postpile and Rainbow Falls, next door to a hot springs and practically in the middle of the Pacific Crest Trail. Trout fishing is popular here, but so is hiking: the Ansel Adams Wilderness is one mile away, and the John Muir Wilderness is two miles away. Facilities include cabins, cafe, and store, also a large string of horses and mules for wilderness rambling. For more information and reservations, contact: Red's Meadow Resort, P.O. Box 395, Mammoth Lakes 93546, tel. (619) 934-2345 in summer, tel. 873-3928 in winter.

The **Rock Creek Lodge** in Little Lakes Valley halfway between Mammoth Lakes and Bishop (take the Rock Creek Rd. turnoff at Tom's Place on Hwy. 395) is heaven for anglers and the outdoorsy, good fishing and access to excellent high country hiking. A home-style restaurant is close to the small rustic cabins; and two-bedroom cabins have completely equipped kitchens (but no bathrooms: showers and flush toilets a short walk away), or rent two-story A-frames with the works. In winter, cross-country skiing and guided tours are offered—with the extra added attraction of backcountry trailside huts for overnights. For more information and to make reservations, contact: Rock Creek Lodge, Rt. 1 Box 12, Mammoth Lakes 93546, tel. (619) 935-4452, or Rock Creek Winter Lodge, Rt. 1 Box 5, tel. 935-4464.

Another great choice, in lush meadows and Jeffrey pine forests along the Owens River, is the **Alper's Owens River Ranch**, Rt. 1, Box 232, Mammoth Lakes 93546, tel. (619) 648-7334 in summer, 647-6652 in winter, a collection of simple cabins on a one-time cattle ranch. Very reasonable.

Mammoth Area Food

Though fast-food stops have popped up in this forested town like mushrooms after the first fall rains (there's a Safeway here too), Mammoth Lake's attractions include its restaurants, a better selection of good eateries than anywhere else along the Sierra Nevada's eastern slope. Excellent and a bit off the beaten path is **Blondie's Kitchen** in the Sierra Centre Mall on Old Mammoth Rd., tel. (619) 934-4048, noted for its exceptional all-day breakfasts (including breakfast burritos) and daily specials. Also excellent for breakfast and lunch is the casual **O'Kelly & Dunn Co.** in Minaret Village Shopping Center on Old Mammoth Rd., tel. 934-9316, now also open for dinner. **Anything Goes** in Sherwin Plaza on Old Mammoth Rd. at Chateau Rd., tel. 934-2424, is another good bet for food-conscious and cost-conscious breakfast and lunch, though dinner is also enticing (California-style bistro fare, menu changes weekly).

For bakery goods, deli fare, and decent sandwiches (including some veggie choices), stop off at **The Gourmet Grocer & Co.** in the Village Center West mall off Main, tel. (619) 934-2997, open daily 8 a.m.-6 p.m. Fairly new and definitely different is the **Brewhouse Grill** behind Goodyear Tires at 170 Mountain Blvd., tel. 934-8134, noted for its chili (at lunch and dinner) and its trademark Bodie Bold, Dogtown Ale, and Lundy Light brews. Good views from the deck, if you dine outside. Folks show up on Sunday nights for folk music and bluegrass, but live music is the norm almost every night.

For lunch and dinner, **Grumpy's** on Old Mammoth Rd., tel. (619) 934-3587, is most famous for its bacon-avocado burger and other simple favorites, but **Berger's** on Minaret Rd. (at Canyon) on the way to the slopes, tel. 934-6622, also has good burgers and other American fare, excellent fries, and great homemade desserts. **Perry's Pizza and Italian Cafe** in the Village Center West on Main, tel. 934-3251, serves it Sicilian style, along with good all-you-can-eat specials on Tuesday and Wednesday nights.

The **Cask 'n' Cleaver** on Old Mammoth Rd., tel. (916) 934-4200, is a relaxed dinner house with chicken, steak, and seafood, though **Whiskey Creek** on Hwy. 203, tel. 934-2555, is the locals' choice for steaks, prime rib, and barbecued ribs. Just as good, others say, smaller and usually less crowded, is **Mogul** on Tavern, tel. 934-3039.

Petrello's Ristorante on Viewpoint Rd. off Hwy. 203, tel. 934-6767, is the place for imaginative pastas, while the **Ocean Harvest** restaurant just south of Hwy. 203 on Old Mammoth Rd., tel. 934-8539, is noted for its fresh mesquite-grilled seafood. **Natalie's** ("no charge for lousy sunsets") below the Cask 'n' Cleaver in Sherwin Plaza on Old Mammoth Rd., tel. 934-3902, serves California-style French country cuisine (specialty entrees every night), California and French wines, homemade desserts, cappuccino and espresso. Worthy, too, at dinner is **Anything Goes** (see above). Very small (ten tables) **The Lakefront Restaurant** at Tamarack Lodge Resort at Twin Lakes, tel. 934-2442 or 934-3534, serves salmon and other fresh fish plus such classics as rack of lamb and beef Wellington, "excellent meals that will satisfy both the heartiest of appetites and the most finicky," according to *Bon Appetit*. Also near the top of the local food chain in the continental style is **Nevados** on Minaret Rd. at Main St., tel. 934-4466. Reservations recommended.

Mammoth Events And Information
Local bars and lodges offer quite the social scene, at least in winter, and the year-round events calendar is usually full. One of the year's biggest big deals is the **Sierra Summer Festival of the Performing Arts,** an excellent music festival (from pops to classical) usually held mid-July into early August. New in early July is the **Mammoth Lakes Jazz Jubilee.** Cycling events, fishing derbies, even roller blade and tennis and volleyball tournaments round out summer events. Also worthwhile in summer are Palisade School of Mountaineering rock-climbing and mountaineering courses offered here through **Mammoth Adventure Connection,** P.O. Box 353, Mammoth Lakes 93546, tel. (619) 934-0606 or (800) 228-4947 at the Mammoth Mountain Inn. These folks also sponsor mountain biking tours and other outback fun.

For more information about Mammoth Lakes and vicinity, contact the **Mammoth Lakes Visitor Information Center** on Hwy. 203, located in a mini-mall (look for Perry's Pizza), P.O. Box 48, Mammoth Lakes 93546, tel. (619) 934-2712 or 934-8006 or toll-free (800) 367-6572. For Forest Service and wilderness maps ($3), wilderness permits, and current information on national forest hiking, backpacking, and camping, contact the **Mammoth Ranger Station,** at the **Mammoth National Forest Visitor Center** off the highway; P.O. Box 148, tel. 934-2505. (The "Mammoth Trails Hiking Guide" available for $1 is worth the investment if you're staying a while.)

Mammoth Transport
Greyhound stops twice daily at McDonald's on Main—at 1 a.m. for the bus to Reno, at 12:30 p.m. for the bus to L.A. (Buy your ticket elsewhere in advance, or pay onboard.) For AAA emergency road service, call (619) 934-3385. Those with private planes can fly in to the **Mammoth/June Lake Airport,** tel. 935-4442.

The Mammoth Lakes area is so popular in winter that public transit is almost mandatory. **Mammoth Area Shuttle (MAS)** buses, tel. (619) 934-2571, run only during the ski season; the "red line" connects the main lodge and the village, and other lines connect to base chairlifts. Another shuttle, tel. 934-2442, serves Tamarack in winter for cross-country skiing.

In summer, it's almost necessary to take the Forest Service shuttle to reach the Agnew Meadows, Red's Meadow, and Devil's Postpile areas beyond Mammoth Lakes. Backpackers *must* ride the shuttle, because wilderness permits prohibit driving into the valley or parking at trailheads. Car campers, however, *can* drive in—assuming they first get a camping permit—but during the summer high season, anyone opting to drive must do so either before 7:30 a.m. or after 5:30 p.m. Board shuttles at the Mammoth Mountain Inn near the ski slopes; buses leave every half hour between 8 and 10 a.m., between 3:30 and 5 p.m., and every 15 minutes from 10 a.m. to 3:30 p.m. (Returning to Mammoth Mountain, the last bus leaves Red's Meadow at 6:15 p.m.) Roundtrip fare: $6 adults, $3 children age 5-12, also family rates.

BISHOP AND VICINITY

Some 40,000 people descend on Bishop over the Memorial Day weekend for kick-over-the-traces celebrations of native mulishness—mule races, mule-drawn chariot races, and braying contests for people who (apparently) would rather be mules—during the town's annual **Mule Days Celebration.** The next biggest community party comes during the Labor Day weekend, during the **Homecoming Wild West Rodeo Weekend.** For the Lion's Club pancake breakfast, followed by rodeo, chili cookoffs, western-style dinner, and street dancing, come on home to Bishop. There are other events worth showing up for though, including April's **kick-off for the eastern Sierra fishing season** (trout) and the **Millpond Bluegrass Festival** in late September.

Bishop Area Sights

Bishop itself is pleasant in the neon-and-highway category, with a few parks and swimming pools scattered among the markets, motels, and cowboy cafes. Worth a stop just outside town on the reservation is the **Paiute-Shoshone Indian Cultural Center and museum,** where traditional gambling "stick games" are sometimes played at night.

About 25 miles north of Bishop and east of the highway is **Crowley Lake,** where thousands of anglers swarm on opening day of trout season (the last Saturday of April)—quite the human zoo. Some of the big German browns hooked here weigh in at 25 pounds or so (until recently, California's record for trophy trout). Nearby, to the west, is more serene **Convict Lake.** More beautiful still, and providing entry points for fine high-country hiking on the backside of the John Muir Wilderness and Kings Canyon National Park, are **Lake Sabrina, North Lake,** and **South Lake** in Bishop Creek Canyon. Locals can give directions to the area's wildest and woolliest out-there hot springs.

Laws Railroad Museum

About five miles outside town on Hwy. 6 is the Laws Railroad Museum, P.O. Box 363, Bishop 93514, tel. (619) 873-5050, the old Laws Station railroad depot complete with the Slim Princess narrow gauge train and a collection of historic buildings with indoor and outdoor museum displays. (Across the road is the newly old Drover's Cottage, built in 1966 for the Steve McQueen movie *Nevada Smith.)* Like the rest of the Owens Valley, death came to the Carson & Colorado Railroad by the 1930s, when Los Angeles' groundwater pumping decimated local ranching and farming and there was nothing left to ship. A new project here, sponsored by the Inyo County Arts Council, is the opera house now under construction. The Laws Station railroad-history complex is open daily 10 a.m.-4 p.m. during the summer high season, weekends only from mid-November to Easter.

Chalfant Valley Petroglyphs

From Laws, keep going northeast on the 50-mile **Petroglyph Loop Trip** through the sagebrush tableland of Chalfant Valley, earthquake country in the shadow of the stone-faced White Mountains. A total of six stops offer up-close looks at unusual (and unusually varied) ancient rock drawings which predate the Paiute people. Due to increasing problems with vandalism, the BLM office in Bishop now "screens" those interested in seeing local petroglyphs. If you pass muster and get directions, look but do not touch.

Bishop Area Accommodations

Camp almost in town (just south) at **Brown's Town** (complete with free museum), tel. (619) 873-8522, or outside town at **Mill Pond Recreation Area,** tel. 872-1301. You can also camp at the city of Los Angeles campgrounds at Crowley Lake, tel. (213) 485-4853, or (better yet in the same neighborhood) try the national forest campsites at Convict Lake. Other near-Bishop public camping (some sites free) is available at the sky-high-country lakes in Bishop Creek Canyon 20-some miles southwest of town via Hwy. 168, tel. (619) 873-4207, an area also rich in summer resorts and lodges.

Quite wonderful finds: both the **Hilton Creek International AYH Hostel** and the **Long Valley AYH Hostel** about 25 miles north of Bishop near Crowley Lake. For more information, see "Mammoth Lakes and Vicinity" above. Motels abound in Bishop, where most people are either going fishing or just passing through on the way to someplace else. Most accommodations are quite reasonable, often with cheaper off-season rates. Off the highway (one block east, near the Best Western Westerner) is the **Bishop Elms Motel,** 233 E. Elm St., Bishop 93514,

MULE DAYS
BISHOP, CALIF.
MEMORIAL DAY WEEKEND
MULE CAPITAL OF THE WORLD

tel. (619) 873-8118, with rooms $30-42. Amenities here include fish cleaning and freezing facilities. Actually, most motels have a similar fishing bent, including the **Bishop El Rancho Motel,** off the highway at 274 Lagoon St., tel. 872-9251, with rooms $30-41, and the very nice **Bishop Inn** at 805 N. Main St., tel. 873-4284, with rates $39-60. The **Best Western Holiday Spa Lodge** at 1025 N. Main, tel. 873-3543, has a coin laundry, pool, whirlpool—and fish cleaning and freezing facilities—with rooms $50-70. There's another Best Western south of town and just east of the highway, the **Westerner** at 150 E. Elm, tel. 873-3564 or toll-free in California (800) 356-3221, with the usual amenities and rates from $50, lower in the off-season. (The toll-free reservations number for all Best Western motels is 800-528-1234.)

The historic **Matlick House Bed and Breakfast** north of town at 1313 Rowan Ln., Bishop 93514, tel. (619) 873-3133, provides pleasant and peaceful rooms far removed from motel-style accommodations, rates from $65. (Weekly rates also available; lunch, too, by reservation only.) For a very special stay, try updated **Parcher's Resort** near South Lake, P.O. Box 1658, Bishop 93514, tel. (619) 873-4177 in summer, tel. (415) 472-6940 in winter, a time-honored trout lover's retreat of rustic cabins now also featuring a fine restaurant and weekend seminars on natural history, mountaineering skills, and photography. Open from the start of fishing season through summer only. Also unusual, and unusually inviting, is the **Rainbow Tarns** high-country bed and breakfast inn (7,000 feet in elevation), with waterfalls, solitude, and great hiking and ski access, even horseback riding (it's okay to bring your own). For information and reservations, call (619) 935-4556.

Bishop Chow

A good bet among possible chow stops in Bishop is **Whiskey Creek** at 524 N. Main, tel. (619) 873-7174, for hearty omelettes and other breakfast choices, a variety of sandwiches and salads at lunch, good ol' American fare at dinner. Locally popular is **Jack's Waffle Shop** at 437 N. Main, tel. 872-7971, open 24 hours. **Erick Schat's Bakery** ("Home of the World-Famous Sheepherder Bread") at 763 N. Main, tel. 873-7156, is also an unmissable local institution.

New and different is the **Inyo Country Store** at 177 Academy St., tel. (619) 872-2552, open for breakfast and lunch Mon.-Sat., for dinner Thurs.-Sat. nights. This is *the* place for fine coffee, cappuccino, and espresso, not to mention American bistro fare and gourmet picnic items. More traditional dinner houses—steaks and such—include the **Brass Bell** at 635 N. Main, tel. 872-1200, saloon open from 10 a.m., good "early chimes" 5-6 p.m. dinner specials, and the **Firehouse Grill** north on the highway, tel. 873-4888. For out-of-town dining—sometimes the best food around, depending on who's in the kitchen—head southwest some 20 miles via Hwy. 168 (then South Lake Rd.) to **Parcher's** (see "Bishop Area Accommodations" above) or the nearby **Bishop Creek Lodge,** tel. 873-4484. Or head to **Glacier Lodge** (see "Big Pine" under "From Bishop to Lone Pine" below).

Bishop Area Information

An excellent book to tote along is *Sierra South: 100 Back-Country Trips* by Thomas Winnett and Jason Winnett, published by Wilderness Press. Also worthwhile, especially if you'll be staying awhile (or returning often) are *John Muir Trail Country* and *Sequoia-Mt. Whitney Trails,* both by Lew and Ginny Clark and published by Western Trails Publications.

For more information about Bishop and vicinity, stop by the **Bishop Visitors Center** at City Park or contact: **Bishop Chamber of Commerce,** 690 N. Main St., Bishop 93514, tel. (619) 873-8405. Or visit the **Inyo National Forest headquarters** at 873 N. Main, tel. 873-5841 (also the Bishop area BLM office, tel. 872-4881), though the national forest's **White Mountains Ranger Station** nearby at 798 N. Main, tel. 873-4207, is actually better for national forest and wilderness maps ($3), wilderness permits, and information on area hikes, sights, and campgrounds.

Contact the **Palisade School of Mountaineering** (which is actually based during summer farther south at Big Pine Lakes), P.O. Box 694, Bishop 93514, tel. (619) 873-5037, for current information about its July-into-September mountaineering, rock-climbing, and ice-climbing courses (the latter offered also from January through March), its High Sierra summer treks, and its worldwide guided climbing expeditions. Private instruction also available.

FROM BISHOP TO LONE PINE

Heading south from Bishop, it's hard to notice anything except the awesome Sierra Nevada looming ever higher, but in this long, lonely country, watch out for gray dust devils rising up from long dead Owens Lake—stormy clouds of flour-like alkali dust creating driving and health hazards, some of the highest levels of dust ever recorded on the continent—and for elk, which may suddenly loom up near the highway from their sagebrush and charcoal-colored stone camouflage.

The White Mountains And
The Ancient Bristlecone Pine Forest

Anthropologists have recently retrieved some 24,000 artifacts from two peoples who lived, from 1300 B.C. to the 14th century, high in the White Mountains. But today's most notable old-timers are the gnarled and gristly *Pinus longaeva* trees which still thrive here in the Ancient

WES DEMPSEY

Bristlecone pines in the White Mountains are the oldest living things on earth.

Bristlecone Pine Forest, apparently unperturbed by summer drought and heat, severe winters, or the passage of time—though smog may now be doing them in.

Bristlecones growing in this stark, dry, and dramatic mountain range have been alive longer than anything else on earth, many for more than 4,000 years. And studies of these austere, graceless, scruffy ancients have revolutionized traditional understanding about the origins of human civilization.

Starting in the 1950s, Edmund Schulman of the University of Arizona began his tree-ring studies of the bristlecone pines here, discovering that the oldest among them are 4,600 years or older (nearly twice as old as any redwood). But conflicts between his dendrochronological data and that derived by the then unquestioned carbon-14 dating techniques of Willard F. Libby led to C-14 testing corrections. The corrections resulted in a shake-up of the accepted time frames of world history—eliminating the theory of Greek and Roman cultural diffusion to explain the astronomical accuracy of Stonehenge and other peculiarities of early European society, among other revelations.

Along the **Schulman Grove**'s short **Pine Alpha Trail** and 4½-mile **Methusaleh Trail,** home turf of the Methusaleh Tree, the planet's oldest living being (unidentified for its own protection), there's a strange sense of timelessness. Life and death, past and future, are almost indistinguishable.

These dwellers on the threshhold—storm-sculpted abstractions in wood—are dead and alive simultaneously, with naked trees sometimes bursting forth with just enough contorted, curved branchlets of pine needles to sustain life and to produce resin-covered red cones ripe with fertile seeds. Eleven miles and 40 minutes farther up the road, another 1,000 feet higher in elevation, the moonscape at the **Patriarch Grove** (home of the biggest known bristlecone) is even bleaker, with just scattered specimens of firm-rooted, living driftwood.

A visit to the White Mountains' Bristlecone Pine Forest is at least an all-day journey. Start out with a full tank of gas and bring food, water (none is available, even at campgrounds and picnic areas), good walking shoes, and sun protection as well as warm clothing, since even in summer it's cool at higher elevations and the weather is always changeable. To get here, head northeast on Hwy. 168 from Big Pine to near Westgard Pass, about 13 miles, then head north on White Mountain Road. Picnic near the fossil area beyond Cedar Flat; family campsites are available in summer at **Grandview Campground** on the way to Schulman Grove.

To get oriented to these trees and their significance, pick up a brochure/map at the Cedar Flat entrance station and study the interpretive displays at the Schulman Grove, starting point in summer for naturalist-led hikes.

For more information about the 100-million-year-old White Mountains—home also to ghosts of mining history, mustangs, and golden eagles —stop by or call the **White Mountains Ranger Station** in Bishop, tel. (619) 873-4207. There you can also find out about special summer events like mountain bike racing, and off-season possibilities including cross-country skiing and snow camping.

Big Pine

The Palisade Glaciers looming above Big Pine Canyon to the west and looking down on the town of Big Pine are small but distinguished, being the continent's southernmost "living" glaciers (which means they melt, break-off, and otherwise diminish at the low end while new snowpack-turned-to-ice replenishes them on the high side). Big Pine itself offers no comparable experiences or sights.

Camp in Big Pine Canyon or, for a real bed, try either the **Big Pine Motel**, tel. (619) 938-2282, or the **Starlight Motel**, tel. 938-2011. Eat at local cafes or—for a High Sierra dining experience—head out to **Glacier Lodge**, 11 miles west of town at Big Pine Creek, tel. 938-2837, usually open for breakfast 7:30-9 a.m., for dinner 6-10 p.m. (but call first). Gourmet grub, domestic and foreign wines, reservations preferred. Glacier Lodge, closed in winter, sometimes features monthly dinner concerts.

Independence

The next town south is Independence, the Inyo County seat, once a trading post called Putnam's (or Little Pine, after the creek) which grew in stature and significance when gold was discovered in the Inyo Mountains to the east. Worth a sidetrip just north of Independence is the **Mt.**

Whitney Fish Hatchery, possibly the most beautiful in the world—an Old World-style fish monastery with a Tudor tower, built in 1917 of native stone. (Pleasant pond, park, and picnic facilities.) Near the turn-off are the ruins of old **Fort Independence.** The World War II-vintage **Manzanar Relocation Center** stood southeast of Independence, one of California's internment camps, temporary "home" to 10,000 Japanese Americans. Stop for a look at the **Mary Austin Home** in town (follow the signs), designed and built under the supervision of the very independent author of *Land of Little Rain,* an ode to the once-beautiful Owens Valley.

Also worthwhile is time spent at the modern, wheelchair-accessible **Eastern California Museum,** with its excellent displays of Paiute and pioneer artifacts, including a yard full of old farming implements, photo archives, books, and publications. Open Sun.-Mon. and Thurs.-Fri. noon-4 p.m., Sat. 10 a.m.-4 p.m. (Free, but donations always appreciated.)

To see if current renovations are complete, stop by the 1926 **Winnedumah Country Inn** on the highway, 211 N. Edwards, Independence 93526, tel. (619) 878-2040. The Winnedumah features a fireplace in the lobby, casual, over-stuffed furniture, and an ambience attractive to outdoor adventurers. The cafe is just off the lobby. (The hotel also has its own history, since it was once a popular stay for movie stars and film crews during the region's Hollywood heyday and a favorite stopover for Death Valley Scotty.) Eat here or north and west of town at the **Aberdeen Resort,** tel. 938-2663, Mexican and American standards. Open Tues.-Sat. 10 a.m.-8 p.m.

Mount Whitney
And The Alabama Hills

A climb up Mt. Whitney, California's highest point, is not an experience for solitude seekers. It seems everyone wants to do it (though it's a strenuous vertical walk, most people can), and they all want to hike the 10-mile trail at the same time, during the snow-free period from mid-July (sometimes as early as mid-May) into early October. Mount Whitney is the most frequently climbed peak in the Sierra Nevada—and possibly the United States. For this simple reason, ascending Mt. Whitney requires a permit. (Contact the Forest Service office in Lone Pine;

RETURN TO MANZANAR

The land itself says little about the devastating experience of Japanese Americans imprisoned during World War II at Manzanar some six miles south of Independence. Now, as then, Manzanar is bleak and desolate, dust and sagebrush surrounded by barbed wire and remnants of chain-link fencing. Two pagoda-style stone guardhouses, sans doors and windows, stand near what was once the entrance to the internment camp; remnants of building foundations seem like skeletons exposed by shifting sands. A new monument, white and austere, honors those who lived here during the post-Pearl Harbor days of the war. The Eastern Sierra Nevada Museum in Independence, worth a stop despite its off-putting modern facade, tells some of the story. Collected photographs of both Ansel Adams and Dorothea Lange tell more.

Executive Order 9066, signed by President Franklin Roosevelt, created Manzanar and other isolated Pacific Coast internment camps. That decree meant that some 100,000 people of Japanese descent—men, women, and children—were immediately removed from their communities and imprisoned by the U.S. Army. Ten thousand people, most of these U.S. citizens, many with sons in the military, were herded into tarpaper shacks at Manzanar ("apple orchard" in Spanish). The name of the place seemed inappropriate, but not for long. Allowed irrigation water and the opportunity to work the land, internees soon transformed their arid section of valley into lush and productive farm acreage.

The U.S. Supreme Court struck down Roosevelt's executive order in 1944, ruling it unconstitutional, and Manzanar was closed. Its legacy lived on, however. Upon returning to their home towns, former internees often found themselves facing blatant racism and discrimination from former neighbors—and, this time, facing it largely alone.

Every year, camp survivors and their families and friends make the pilgrimage to Manzanar, to remember. In April of 1992, the Owens Valley pilgrimage attracted some 1,500 people, to formally celebrate the establishment of the Manzanar National Historic Site by the U.S. Congress. (In the hope that we'll all remember.) If funding is ever forthcoming, restoration will begin on this vast and empty monument to a nightmarish political past.

KIM WEIR

applications accepted only by mail.) No permit needed for day hikes. Savvy hikers can put quick distance between themselves and the crowds, however, by continuing on from the summit along the John Muir Trail. Because parking can be such a problem at the trailhead— and parking tickets are expensive—contact the chamber office in Lone Pine and ask if the shuttle system is up and running.

Among other thoughts to ponder while here in God's country: Mount Whitney is the highest point in the Lower 48, but quite nearby is the lowest. Southeast from Lone Pine via Hwy. 136 is **Death Valley National Monument,** dramatic, endless desert which boasts the lowest elevation in the continental U.S.—and often the highest summer temperatures.

For those cycling or driving up and back via 13-mile Whitney Portal Rd., take the dirt-road detour through the area's **Alabama Hills** (follow the signs), a sparse desert sage landscape most people have seen before as the jumbled, round-bouldered granite backdrop for countless movies *(High Sierra, Red River, Bad Day at Black Rock,* and *They Died With Their Boots On)* and TV westerns including "Bonanza," "Have Gun—Will Travel," and "Tales of Wells Fargo." (For more information, pick up "The Movies of Lone Pine" brochure at the chamber of commerce. And to really celebrate the local cinematic past, show up in October for the **Sierra Film Festival.**

Camping Near Mount Whitney

Camp at the scrub-shrouded national forest **Lone Pine Campground** on the way to Mt. Whitney, with water, picnic tables, stoves (but not showers), $6 per night, with the extra free thrill of waking up at dawn to see Mt. Whitney bathed in the orange glow of morning's first light. More probable for early arrivals (or in spring or fall), try the **Whitney Portal** or **Whitney Portal Trailhead campgrounds** (the latter with just 11 walk-in sites, one-night limit) near the trailhead to the top of California (trailers not recommended on the narrow, steep road). In addition to other nearby Forest Service campgrounds, other camping possibilities include the county's **Portagee Joe** campground just outside town (off Whitney Portal Rd.); the **Diaz Lake county campground** south of town, with 300 campsites; and the BLM's free **Tuttle Creek Campground.**

Lone Pine And Practicalities

Lone Pine below Mt. Whitney has abundant motels, restaurants, and other services. Stop by the **Indian Trading Post** to see "the wall": even movie stars have tried to buy it or steal it, for the priceless autographs. Another diversion is the nine-hole **Mt. Whitney Golf Course,** just south of town.

Rates for most local lodgings should range from $35 to $70—and if they're much higher than that, stop by the chamber office and let them know. Sometimes the best deal around is the **Mt. Whitney Motel,** 305 N. Main St., Lone Pine 93545, tel. (619) 876-4207, with pool, a/c, color TV (even a movie channel), also in-room coffee. Also open year-round, quite comfortable and reasonable, are the **National 9 Trails Motel** at 633 S. Main, tel. 876-5555, and the **Portal Motel** at 425 S. Main, tel. 876-5930, both with abundant amenities. The **Best Western Frontier Motel** at 1008 S. Main St., tel. 876-5571 (or toll-free 800-231-4071 in California), is another good choice.

But don't miss the **Dow Villa Hotel** and motel at 310 S. Main St., tel. (619) 876-5521 (or toll-free in California, tel. 800-824-9317), built in the 1920s to house the movie stars; the modern 42-unit motel was added later. Another in the "unusual" category is the **Little Lake Hotel** about 40 miles south of Lone Pine (and 70 miles north of Mojave), tel. 377-5973, a hotel and restaurant famous for its charbroiled steak and Basque dinners.

For groceries, a good stop is **Joseph's Bi-Rite Market** on Main at Mountain View, open daily 8:30 a.m.-9 p.m. A good deal for breakfast can be found at **Schat's** cafe and bakery at 335 S. Main, tel. 876-5912; try the egg specials and omelettes. The **Frosty Stop** at 701 S. Main, tel. (619) 876-5000, has the best cheeseburgers around.

Bo-Bo's Bonanza, also known as the Bonanza Restaurant, on the highway at the south end of town, tel. (619) 876-4768, is the town's most popular spot for pre- and post-backpack gluttony. For quite reasonable 24-hour homestyle cooking, including wonderful pies, try **P.J.'s** at 446 S. Main, tel. 876-5542. Also popular is the **Sportsman Cafe** at 206 S. Main, tel. 876-5454, with photos of an impressive array of film stars plastered on the walls. An excellent choice for dinner is small **Margie's Merry-Go-Round,** 212 S. Main, tel. 876-4115, specializing in barbecue and charbroiled steaks. (Reservations advised.)

For national forest and wilderness maps, wilderness permits, and regional recreation and camping information, contact the **Mount Whitney Ranger Station** office, 640 S. Main St., P.O. Box 8, Lone Pine 93545, tel. (619) 876-5542. For more information about Lone Pine proper, including events and activities sponsored by the Inyo County Arts Council, contact the **Lone Pine Chamber of Commerce** at 126 S. Main St., P.O. Box 749, tel. 876-4444. Especially fun, and free, is the chamber's "Southern Inyo Self-Guided Tours" brochure (with map). If available, also pick up the "Campground Guide" put out by the Inyo County Parks and Recreation office. Just south of Lone Pine, at the Hwy. 395/Hwy. 136 junction, is the excellent **Eastern Sierra Interagency Visitor Center,** tel. 876-4252, with in-depth information about hikes, sights, and practicalities, wonderful books, also public bathrooms and picnic area.

YOSEMITE AND VICINITY

Somewhere in Yosemite National Park there should be a placard which reads: "This is the spot where John Muir fell in love with life" because this *is* the spot. When Muir found Yosemite (from the native *uzumati* or "grizzly bear"), he found his spiritual home, a place where even this notable traveler was "willing to stay forever in one place like a tree." He also found himself. His passion for this high holy place became the impetus behind a life-long commitment to preserving this and other great works of wildness. Though even John Muir couldn't save Hetch Hetchy Valley (from the native *hatchhatchie* or "grass," since seeds were an important native food source) from the water engineers acting on behalf of urban thirst, he did manage to achieve U.S. National Park protection for most of his beloved Yosemite country.

Despite the chiselings of progress, Yosemite is still a wild wonder of granite, gorges, and silent God-like peaks with names that only hint at their true presence: El Capitan, Half Dome, Royal Arches, Cathedral Rock, Clouds Rest, Three Brothers. Even the trees, the ancient giant sequoias, are larger than life. The sky itself can barely keep the area's grandness down to earth. But the laws of gravity hold true even in Yosemite—witness the waterfalls. Cascading from a height of 2,425 feet, Yosemite Fall is the highest waterfall in North America and the fifth highest in the world. Other park waterfalls—which often seem to shoot out from nowhere, sometimes right off the edge of glacier-scoured hanging valleys—include Yosemite Valley's equally famous Bridalveil, Vernal, and Nevada falls plus many of the park's lesser-known liquid gems. The abundance of water in Yosemite also sustains the subtle, flower-rich summer lushness of its meadows, the mountain-fringed and massive Tuolumne Meadows still among the loveliest in the Sierra Nevada.

The pitfalls of John Muir's enthusiastic promotion of Yosemite Valley and vicinity are all too apparent these days. Once word of its wonders got out, people from around the world started coming to see Yosemite for themselves, and what was once a tourist trickle has now become a rampaging torrent. With its increasing all-season popularity, well over three million people visit the park each year. In summer, a virtual city—complete with rush-hour traffic, litter, overflowing garbage cans, smog, juvenile delinquency, and crime—sprawls out across the valley floor. Despite the Park Service's commitment to "de-develop" Yosemite for the sake of saving the place from its own overwhelming popularity, congestion is still the rule. Visitors who relish even some semblance of solitude in the wilds should plan a Yosemite visit in early spring or late fall—and anytime of year, come on weekdays if at all possible.

YOSEMITE HIKES AND BACKPACKS

Like its campgrounds, the overall level of activity on Yosemite trails is directly related to the distance traveled from Yosemite Valley. Some of the short, easily accessible trails to the valley's most famous sights can resemble pedestrian freeways in summer and on peak visitor weekends. The best way to avoid the crowds, on any hike, is to start out very early in the morning. Except on the park's shortest strolls, bring water on all excursions.

For casual short-distance hikers, the Park Service's trail map is adequate for getting oriented. For backcountry hiking and backpacking, more detailed maps (including topo maps), a compass, and a good guidebook are advisable. Wilderness permits are required for overnight camping in the Yosemite outback (see below). Those planning an extensive backpacking trip should inquire, too, about access into adjacent and nearby federal wilderness areas—including the Emigrant, Hoover, Ansel Adams, and John Muir wildernesses—which is also limited by national forest permit. There are many good books of use to Yosemite area hikers and backpackers. Among the best: the *Tuolumne Meadows* hiking guide by Jeffrey B. Schaffer and Thomas Winnett; Schaffer's *Yosemite National Park;* and *Sierra North: 100 Back-Country Trips* by Thomas Winnett and Jason Winnett, all published by Wilderness Press.

Shorter Hikes

Among Yosemite's most popular trails are the easy half-mile, half-hour hikes to **Lower Yosemite Fall** and to **Bridalveil Fall,** called Pohono or "puffing wind" by native people. Also fairly easy, and noted for its magnificent view of Half Dome, is the two-mile roundtrip to **Mirror Lake** (trailhead accessible only by shuttle), though you can make the walk longer by circling the lake. With some assistance, all the paved trails are wheelchair accessible. Along the Glacier Point Road is the one-mile trail to **Sentinel Dome,** a fairly easy hike, the last 200 yards strenuous. The nearby Taft Point Trail that offers great views of El Capitan and Yosemite Falls. Though often quite crowded, the stroll to the scenic splendor of **Glacier Point** should not be missed.

Longer Hikes

Strenuous but short is the Inspiration Point Trail which starts at the park's **Wawona Tunnel,** good views. For a panoramic view of Yosemite Valley, the seven-mile roundtrip hike to **Upper Yosemite Fall** starts from the Sunnyside Campground—a steep trail with many switchbacks, hot in summer; quite a vigorous workout, allow an entire day. The **Vernal Fall** hike from Happy Isles via the Vernal Fall Mist Trail (closed in winter) is less strenuous but a three-mile, half-day roundtrip nonetheless. It's a seven-mile hike up and back on the Nevada Fall Horse Trail to take in both **Vernal and Nevada falls,** a day's outing for most people.

But unforgettable (and only for the determined and fit) is the 10-12 hour "hike" from Happy Isles up the back side of **Half Dome,** a 17-mile roundtrip with hang-on-for-dear-life as-

Yosemite Falls in spring

JOHN POIMIROO

sistance at the end from steel cables anchored in granite (the cables are usually taken down in mid-October).

Also challenging: the five-mile Four Mile Trail from the valley up to **Glacier Point** (trail closed in winter), easily a full-day roundtrip. Easier but longer is the 8½-mile, half-day (one way) downhill route from **Glacier Point to Yosemite Valley** via the park's Panorama Trail. (A popular all-day excursion is hiking up via the Four Mile Trail then back down on the Panorama route.) Another option is starting from Glacier Point and taking the all-day, 13-mile (one way) Pohono Trail hike to **Wawona Tunnel**—well worth it for the rim-hugging views.

Backcountry Backpacking And Camping

The best way to get away from it all is to head into the Yosemite backcountry for camping, long-distance hiking, and backpacking. Because of the popularity of this option, to protect the park from overuse, access to each trailhead is by wilderness permit only. Permits are free, and

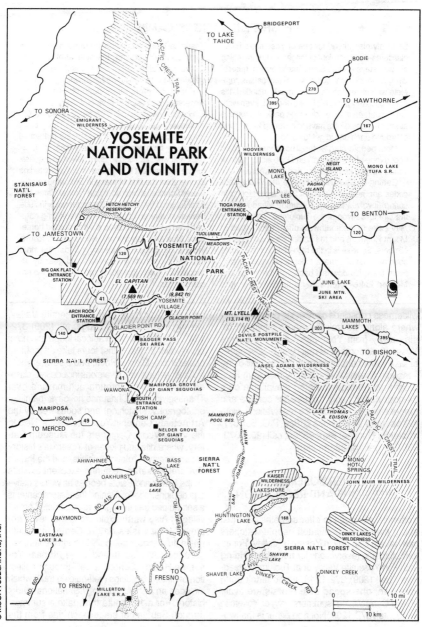

YOSEMITE NATIONAL PARK AND VICINITY

© MOON PUBLICATIONS, INC.

HIGH SIERRA HIKERS' CAMPS

Definitely plan ahead for one of Yosemite's finest pleasures—an overnight or longer "luxury" camping trip with stays at High Sierra **backcountry hikers' camps**—a trail-connected loop of tent cabins complete with clean sheets, some meals included. It's not necessarily a piece of cake, though, even without the burden of a heavily laden pack: the route is strenuous, and hikers have to cover up to 10 miles of ground each day to get to camp.

Most people start at the Tuolumne Meadows Lodge (one of the "camps") and loop either north or south, but you can start and end elsewhere.

Getting to **Glen Aulin** beside the White Cascades and near Waterwheel Falls (spectacular in spring) involves leaving Tuolumne Meadows into the Grand Canyon of the Tuolumne. The climb to **May Lake** to the southwest offers good views of Mount Hoffman, and the camp is a good base for climbers. **Sunrise** is in the high-lake Sunrise Lakes country south of Tenaya Lake, a splendid setting. From there it's downhill back into the forest and **Merced Lake**—then either a further descent to

Yosemite Valley alongside the Merced River or a climb up to **Vogelsang,** the highest of the high, rooted in an alpine meadow, the last stop before trekking back to Tuolumne Meadows.

For more information, contact: High Sierra Reservations, Yosemite Park and Curry Co., 5410 E. Home Ave., Fresno 93727, tel. (209) 454-2002. Yosemite's backcountry camps are usually open from late June through Labor Day, but the actual dates vary from year to year, depending on snowpack and weather conditions. Reservation requests for the subsequent hiking season are accepted no sooner than the first Monday in December and—though cancellations do occur—most dates are booked solid by January. Overnight rates include breakfast, dinner, and showers. Week-long naturalist-led hikes and four- to six-day guided horseback trips are also offered. Backpackers following the camp loop but sleeping under the stars can lug substantially less food and gear by arranging for meals (breakfast and dinner) at the encampments.

wilderness-conscious camping is permitted anywhere along the trail (beyond a minimum radius away from Yosemite Valley). Reserve Yosemite wilderness permits well in advance—or take your chances come summer. Half of the season's permits are issued by mail from February through May, the others available on a 24-hour-notice basis from visitor centers and ranger stations. For advance reservations, write to **Yosemite Wilderness Office,** P.O. Box 577, Yosemite National Park 95389; call (209) 372-0307 for general information.

OTHER YOSEMITE DIVERSIONS AND RECREATION

Yosemite manages to offer something for just about everyone. Dedicated people watchers can have a field day in Yosemite Valley. For information and reservations for **horseback riding** (either in Yosemite Valley or at Tuolumne Meadows), call (209) 372-1248. If you didn't bring your own, **one-speed bike rentals** are available at Curry Village (summers only) or Yosemite Lodge, tel. 372-1208. Not free either is the two-

hour open-air **tram tour** of Yosemite Valley, leaving from Yosemite Lodge, tel. (209) 372-1240, or get information at local lodge and hotel activity/tour desks. (Other tours take off for Mariposa Grove, Glacier Point, and elsewhere.)

Other entertaining diversions include free classes offered spring through autumn and over Thanksgiving and Christmas holidays (painting, photography, sketching) and sponsored by the **Art Activity Center** in Yosemite Village. Next to the Valley Visitor Center are the **Museum Gallery,** where bits and pieces of Yosemite's history are on display in rotating exhibits, and the **Indian Cultural Museum,** featuring excellent exhibits on the Miwok and Paiute peoples as well as native arts demonstrations. (Behind the visitors center is a self-guided trail through a reconstructed native village.) Also worth exploring is the newly improved **Happy Isles Nature Center,** complete with nature shop, open daily through September.

At the park's south end is the **Pioneer Yosemite History Center,** a walk-through collection of historic buildings (self-guiding trail), which includes an introduction to U.S. national parks history. For a 10-minute thrill, take a summer-through-September stagecoach ride from the

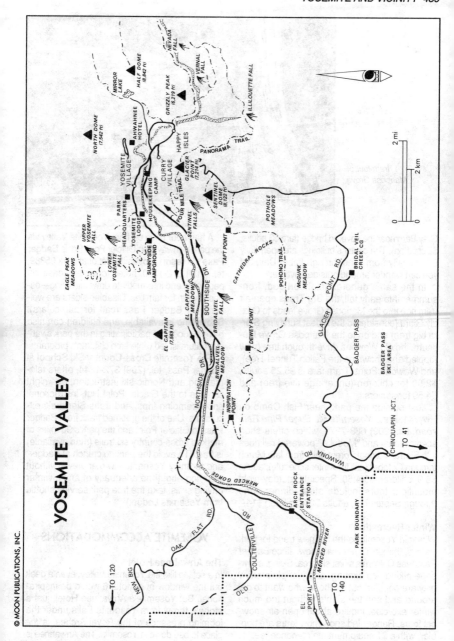

© MOON PUBLICATIONS, INC.

YOSEMITE VALLEY

tram tour of
Mariposa Grove

KEITH WALKLET

Gray Barn near the covered bridge (fare $3 adults, $2 children). The center's buildings are open daily 9-5, usually from June through Labor Day, but you can wander around outside anytime.

In the same general neighborhood, from summer into early fall, the **Big Trees** open-air tram ride into the Mariposa Grove leads to Grizzly Giant (considered the oldest surviving Sierra big tree) and on to the Mariposa Grove Museum, the old Wawona drive-through tree (now toppled and known as the Fallen Tunnel Tree), and Wawona Point. Tram fare is $5.25 adults, $2.50 for children (under age five free) and $4.50 for seniors.

Just outside the park, near Fish Camp on Hwy. 41, is the *Yosemite Mt. Sugar Pine Railroad,* tel. (209) 683-7273, which offers short scenic steam and "Model A"-powered rail rides into Sierra National Forest daily from late March through October (call for winter schedule), adults $6-9, children $3-4.50. Special Saturday-night moonlight tours include steak dinner June through September, adults $25, children $14.

Winter Recreation
Winter in Yosemite is the hot new trend for park visitors, though it's not *really* new, since Badger Pass was California's first ski area. Skiing, snowshoe hiking, ice skating, and just plain snow play are popular, but for those who want to get around and see the sights without too much winter exercise, inquire about open-air snowcat tours. Ranger-led snowshow tours are popular, with a $1 equipment maintenance fee.

A half-hour drive up from Yosemite Valley via the park highway then Glacier Point Rd. is **Badger Pass ski resort,** Yosemite National Park 95389, tel. (209) 372-1330, noted for its emphasis on beginning and intermediate downhill skiing—especially fun for families. Disabled skiers are welcome at Badger Pass (call for particulars). Babysitting is available, and children can also have a good time participating in the park's various naturalist-led wintertime children's programs.

The **Yosemite Cross-Country Ski School** at Badger Pass, tel. (209) 372-1244, offers telemarking and Nordic ski instruction, overnight ski trips to the Glacier Point Hut, instructional snow-camping trips, and trans-Sierra ski excursions. Use of the groomed track from Badger Pass to Glacier Point and the park's 90 miles of marked cross-country ski trails (map available) is free. (To avoid the parking crunch at Badger, and to enjoy Yosemite's winter views without worrying about the adequacy of one's winter driving skills, take the free park service shuttle from Yosemite Lodge.)

YOSEMITE ACCOMMODATIONS

The Ahwahnee Hotel
In a setting like the Yosemite Valley, even a peek out the window of a Motel 6 would be inspirational. But Yosemite's Ahwahnee Hotel, just a stone's throw from Yosemite Falls under the looming presence of the Royal Arches, is *the* place to bed down in Yosemite. The Ahwahnee is

as much a part of the changeless Yosemite landscape as the surrounding stone, sky, and water—and quite possibly the most idyllic (and most popular) hotel in all of California.

Open to the public since 1927 (except for a short two-year commission as a U.S. Navy hospital during World War II), this plush six-story hotel handcrafted of native stone combines art deco and Native American flourishes with that Yosemite sense of *vastness*. The impressive fireplace in the ruggedly comfortable Great Lounge, the downstairs floor-to-ceiling windows, and the 130-foot-long dining hall with open-raftered ceiling trussed with unpeeled sugar pine logs all reinforce the idea that at the Ahwahnee, the outdoors is welcome even indoors. For an extra taste of the hotel's native ambience, try the Indian Room bar. Other diversions include swimming, and tennis.

Stay either in the palatial stone lodge, with its large, comfortable public rooms and recently redecorated guestrooms, or in the cottages. Rates, for either option, run $182-202 for two persons. To stay at the Ahwahnee, make reservations early; unless there are cancellations, the hotel will be booked. (Reservations are accepted a year and a day in advance.)

Eat at least one meal at the Ahwahnee, tel. (209) 372-1489. The dining room looks out on one of the most spectacular settings imaginable, though the food is expensive and usually far from extraordinary. (Dress code at dinner, and during most of the year reservations are a must.) The Sunday buffet breakfast is a good bet. The hotel's "special event" meals, like the annual Bracebridge Dinner at Christmas, are also well worth it—if you can get tickets. (See "Events" below.)

For more information about the Ahwahnee Hotel (and all other concessionaire-operated accommodations at Yosemite) and to make reservations, contact: The Yosemite Park and Curry Co., Reservations, 5410 E. Home, Fresno 93727, tel. (209) 252-4848 (TTY: 209-255-8345). To contact the hotel directly, call 372-1407.

The Wawona Hotel

Set amid the lush summer meadowlands of one-time Clark Station near the park's southern entrance, the wood frame Wawona Hotel is the Ahwahnee's rustic kissing cousin. Here, at the main hotel and its adjacent wings (known as

---

YOSEMITE MOUNTAINEERING

Yosemite is a natural magnet for rock-climbers, ice-climbers, and mountaineers of every persuasion. The **Yosemite Mountaineering School,** Yosemite National Park 95389, tel. (209) 372-1244, is the place to leave behind one's fear and scale the heights.

Headquartered in Yosemite Valley with a summers-only outpost on the highway at Tuolumne Meadows, this mountaineers' mountaineering school offers exceptional training and outings for beginners, intermediates, and the expert let's-go-hang-off-the-edge-of-the-world granite-hugging Yosemite subculture.

Basic rock-climbing classes are offered daily in summer, with ground school then some hands-on experience in bouldering and rappeling. For children ages 10-13, private lessons are offered. Intermediate classes are scheduled on weekends and alternating weekdays; call for information on advanced classes. (Even amateur mountaineers must be "in reasonably good condition," and need to bring lunch and water.) Reservations are advisable, though drop-ins sometimes find space available. Yosemite Mountaineering also offers backpacking instruction and rents outdoor equipment—the obvious plus backpacks, sleeping bags, ski mountaineering necessities.

"cottages"), sit out on the veranda and imagine that the next stagecoach full of tourists will be arriving any minute. Time seems forgotten, judging from some interior touches, too. Rooms (half have private baths) feature brass doorknobs, push-button light switches, steam radiators, and clawfoot bathtubs.

Other pleasures here include the swimming pool, golf course, and tennis court, also a dining room and lounge. During summer and on weekends at other times, rent horses at the stables. Or wander through the **Pioneer Yosemite History Center,** explore the **Mariposa Grove** of big trees nearby, or hike to Chilnualna Falls. Open weekends year-round and from Easter week through Thanksgiving, rates $60 for rooms without bath, $80 otherwise.

Other Accommodations

For budget accommodations in Yosemite Valley, the place to stay is **Curry Village** two miles east

Wawona Hotel

JOHN POIMIROO

of park headquarters, where tent cabins (no food or cooking allowed) are $30 d, $5 for each extra person. Other basic back-to-back cabins without baths are $44 d, $6 each extra person (cheaper during the winter); cabins with baths are also available.

The facilities at the **Yosemite Lodge** near the foot of Yosemite Fall include cabins with and without baths and garden-variety motel rooms, with rates $43-85 (cheaper from November to early March).

The summers-only **White Wolf Lodge** on Tioga Rd. offers both tent cabins (without private bath) and regular cabins with bath. Lodgings at the **Tuolumne Meadows Lodge**, just a half-mile from the visitor center at Tuolumne Meadows, consist of tent cabins. Rates are $31-35 ($6 extra for each additional adult and $3 for each child). For cabins with bathroom, rates run $55 ($6 more for each additional adult and $3.50 per child).

Accommodations not affiliated with the Yosemite Park and Curry Co. include **Yosemite West Condominiums** six miles from Badger Pass, tel. (209) 372-4240. **The Redwoods,** P.O. Box 2085, Wawona 95389, tel. 375-6666, are very nice fully equipped one- to five-bedroom cabins (houses, actually) with picture windows, fireplaces, and cable TV. Quite comfy, laundry facilities available, close to the Merced River. Rates run $74-266.

Also private and just outside the park's southern entrance is the **Apple Tree Inn,** P.O. Box 41, Fish Camp 93623, tel. 683-5111, with rates $75-90. Also here is Marriott's **Tenaya Lodge,** tel. (209) 683-6555 or toll-free (800) 635-5807 or (800) 228-9290, four-star rusticity with all the amenities and rates $150-250 (more for suites), substantially lower in the off season. In El Portal, the **Cedar Lodge,** tel. 379-2612, offers rooms for $63-115, and five miles east is **Yosemite View Lodge,** tel. 379-2681, with rates from $65. Other good choices are available in Mariposa and vicinity—overflowing with bed and breakfasts these days, including (nearby) the very elegant **Chateau du Sureau** in Oakhurst—as well as in Groveland, Coulterville, Jamestown, Sonora, and Columbia. (See "The Gold Country" chapter.)

Campgrounds

Why come to God's country if you refuse to introduce yourself? Sleeping under the stars is one way to say hello. Camping possibilities abound in Yosemite—but to come even close to a spiritual rendezvous, it's necessary to get far from those we-brought-along-everything-but-the-kitchen-sink RV encampments that dominate Yosemite Valley. Except for backcountry tent pitching—see "Yosemite Hikes and Backpacks" above—camping outside designated campgrounds is not allowed.

Reservations for developed year-round valley campgrounds are advisable from April into November. Most Yosemite National Park campsites can be reserved up to eight weeks in advance through Mistix, P.O. Box 85705, San Diego 92138-5705, tel. toll-free (800) 365-

CAMP. From May through September, you can also try the park service's **Campground Reservation Office** at Curry Village (show up early for the possibility of a cancellation). In the mid-September through May off-season, the maximum campground stay is 30 days, but the summertime limit is seven days for Yosemite Valley campgrounds, 14 days for camping outside the valley. Yosemite also has five group campgrounds, reservable up to 12 weeks in advance through Mistix.

One problem with camping for any length of time at Yosemite is that campgrounds here have no showers. To get cleaned up, from spring into fall, buy yourself a shower at Curry Village in the valley, at Curry's housekeeping cabin complex, or at the lodges at White Wolf and Tuolumne Meadows in summer.

For those committed to a stay in the valley, the **Lower River** and **Upper River** campgrounds a mile east of Yosemite Village, open May through mid-October, are urban zoos in summer, with water and flush toilets, $12 per night. The same facilities and prices apply to the **Lower Pines, Upper Pines,** and **North Pines campgrounds** another half mile east. Lower Pines is open year-round, Upper Pines is open April through October, and North Pines is open May through October.

More peaceable in general is the very basic walk-in **Backpackers Camp** behind North Pines, open summer through mid-October, with running water and toilets, $2 per night, available without reservation but only to campers carrying wilderness permits, two-night limit. The year-round **Sunnyside** walk-in campground near Yosemite Lodge is also $2, no reservations, with a seven-day limit in summer; this is *the* rock climbers' camp, collecting climbers from around the globe in season.

In general, the quantity of peace available while camping out is directly proportional to distance removed from Yosemite Valley. One exception to this rule, though, is the **Tuolumne Meadows Campground** about 55 miles northeast on Tioga Rd., with 314 family campsites, $10 per night. The campground is usually open from early June to mid-October; half the campsites are reservable through Mistix, the others are first-come, first-camped. The walk-in campsites here are strictly for backpackers with wilderness permits, one-night limit, $2.

Both **Porcupine Flat** and **Yosemite Creek** campgrounds farther west are peaceful and primitive—no drinking water, pit toilets only, but cheap at just $4 per night. The **White Wolf campground** a few miles west of Yosemite Creek does have water, and thus a higher price: $7.

The year-round **Hodgdon Meadow Campground** is close to Yosemite's Big Oak Flat entrance on Big Oak Flat Rd., $10 per night for the usual amenities, limited facilities in winter, Mistix reservations required through October. The **Crane Flat Campground** is spread out and fairly serene, open from late May through September, and reservable through Mistix, $10 per night. More remote and more primitive in the same general vicinity is **Tamarack Flat Campground** reached via Old Big Oak Flat Rd. heading south from Tioga Rd., $4 per night.

Heading south from Yosemite Valley, very nice for a summer stay is the **Bridalveil Creek Campground** halfway to Glacier Point on Glacier Point Rd., the usual facilities, $7 per night. The **Wawona Campground** on Old Wawona Rd. north of the park's south entrance is open all year, $7.

YOSEMITE FOOD AND ENTERTAINMENT

Food

If you're backpacking, camping, staying in tent cabins, or otherwise trying to do Yosemite and vicinity on the cheap, bring your own food. Groceries are available in Yosemite Village at the **Village Store,** open daily 8 a.m.-10 p.m. in summer, just 9-7 otherwise, but it's more expensive to stock up at the park than in a major town en route. (Groceries are also available, summer into early fall, at White Wolf, Tuolumne Meadows, Crane Flat, and at the valley's Housekeeping Camp.)

The **Village Grill** next door is just a snack bar serving basic breakfasts and burgers, the most inexpensive place around. The village's **Degnans Deli** fast-food stand and ice cream parlor is another option, but upstairs is **The Loft,** which serves darn good hamburgers (on French rolls with the works). The **Yosemite Lodge** features a cafeteria open for breakfast, lunch, and dinner (they put together box lunches here for lazy picnickers if you remember to order the day before), the Four Seasons coffee shop, and the dinners-only Mountain Broiler Room restaurant.

Curry Village has a cafeteria (closed in winter) and a seasonal hamburger stand. The **Tuolumne Meadows Lodge** serves meals until the snow flies, and there's also a grill here. Sandwiches, salads, pizza, and such are available at the **Badger Pass Lodge** (open winters only).

For a good breakfast and decent lunch in Yosemite Valley's priciest price range, or for those who simply must dress for dinner, try the **Ahwahnee Hotel** restaurant, tel. (209) 372-1489, open 7-10:30 a.m. for breakfast, noon-2:30 p.m. for lunch, and 5:30-8:30 p.m. for dinner. (Hours may change slightly from season to season; a snack service is available in the afternoons between meal times.) Less expensive and more casual is the **Wawona Hotel** near the park's southern entrance, open 7:30-11 a.m. for continental and American breakfasts, noon-1:30 p.m. for lunch, and just 6-8 p.m. for dinner. Sunday brunch is a special treat here, 7:30 a.m.-1:30 p.m. (The hotel and restaurant are usually open only mid-March through October, but—depending on the weather—sometimes stay open on weekends into November.)

But for a truly fine meal, set out for **Erna's Elderberry House** in Oakhurst or other foothill destinations (see the "Gold Country" chapter for more information about Erna's and other restaurants).

Events

One of the biggest big deals in Yosemite Valley is the annual Christmas season **Bracebridge Dinner** in the Ahwahnee Hotel, a 1927 brainchild of photographer Ansel Adams and cohorts. Modeled after the Yorkshire feast of Squire Bracebridge as portrayed in *The Sketch Book of Geoffrey Crayon, Gent.* by Washington Irving, the three-hour medieval pageant includes a full-dress, seven-course processional English feast of fish, "peacock pie," boar's head, baron of beef, and more, accompanied by music, song, and great merriment. The Lord of Misrule and his pet bear provide still more entertainment. Because of the event's great popularity, there are five dinner seatings these days—but even so, it's almost impossible to get tickets.

The same is true of Yosemite's other great holiday tradition, the **New Year's Eve Dinner-Dance**. To attend either event, contact the Yosemite Park and Curry Co. (see "Information and Services" below) to request ticket-lottery applications—a separate application is necessary for each event—in November. Applications (for the *following* year's festivities) are accepted from December 15 to January 15.

Other Ahwahnee-centered events include the **Vintners' Holidays,** for wines-among-the-pines appreciation from November into December. Some 30 California winemakers are invited to bring their best to these special tastings, seminars, and dinners usually scheduled Sunday through Thursday. For more information about these events, contact the Yosemite Park and Curry Co. (see "Information and Services" below).

Not park-sponsored but a great party nonetheless is the **Strawberry Music Festival** held at Camp Mather, usually each spring and fall—a parking lot full of VWs with Grateful Dead bumper stickers along with BMWs, everyone assembled for a long weekend of folk music, bluegrass, and big-time good times. Plan ahead if you're going—the event often sells out well in advance due to headliners like Emmylou Harris, Vassar Clements, and the David Grisman Quartet.

Activities

Park rangers sponsor a wide variety of guided nature walks and campfire programs year-round (current schedule of events listed in *Yosemite Guide*). Come nightfall, the visitor center auditoriums become center stage for **Yosemite Theater** performing arts programs, including music, films, and live drama like "An Evening with John Muir: A Conversation with a Tramp"—an acclaimed one-man show starring Lee Stetson—and its sequel, "Another Evening with John Muir: Stickeen and Other Fellow Mortals." Nominal admission fees in the $3-5 range.

The stone-and-wood Tudor-style **LeConte Memorial Lodge,** built by the Sierra Club to honor geologist Joseph LeConte and staffed in summer by club members, also marks the northern terminus of the John Muir Trail. The lodge sponsors a variety of free summer programs on natural history, conservation issues, and outdoor adventure, three evenings each week starting at 8 p.m. Also at LeConte: a very good bookstore, including a wide range of Sierra Club titles, books by and about John Muir, and a children's nature literature section. Ask here and at the visitors center about park pro-

*touring Yosemite
on skis*

ROBERT HOLMES

grams sponsored by **The Yosemite Institute,** a nonprofit organization which offers environmental education programs and campouts for schoolchildren and families.

The **Yosemite Association** offers a year-round schedule of natural history and field seminars, everything from Native American basketry, botany, and birdwatching to photography and photo history courses, special hikes and backpacks, and winter ski tours. (For more information, contact the visitors center or write park headquarters.)

Near the visitor center in Yosemite Village is the **Ansel Adams Gallery,** with a breathtaking collection of prints, posters, postcards, and books commemorating the life's work of Yosemite's most renowned photographer. (John Muir may have described the Sierra Nevada as the "Range of Light," but Ansel Adams managed to capture the same truth without words—on film.) Special activities and events include photography workshops, camera walks, and free screenings of the one-hour documentary film *Ansel Adams: Photographer.* (Rent camera equipment here, too.)

YOSEMITE INFORMATION AND TRANSPORT

Information And Services

The $5-per-car park entry fee is good for one week, if you'll be coming and going, though it's only $2 for walk-in and bike-in visitors and those who arrive by bus. Except hiking, backpacking, and free park-sponsored activities, almost everything else in Yosemite—camping and other lodging, food, and park-related services of all kinds—is extra.

The all-purpose clearinghouse for information about the park itself and about current activities is the National Park Service. For general information, contact: **Yosemite National Park,** P.O. Box 577, Yosemite National Park 95389, tel. (209) 372-0265 or, for 24-hour recorded information, 372-0264 (TTY: 372-4726).

Though the current edition of the *Yosemite Guide* tabloid and a park map are included in the "package" passed out to visitors at all park entrances, the **Yosemite Valley Visitors Center** in Yosemite Village (at the west end of Yosemite Village Mall), tel. (209) 372-0299, open 9-5, is the place to get oriented. The displays here are excellent, also the various park-sponsored special programs, but the visitors center also offers maps, hiking and camping information, do-it-yourself trip planning assistance, and wilderness permits. Foreign-language pamphlets and maps are also available.

A good selection of books about Yosemite, including *Yosemite Wildflower Trails* by Dana C. Morgenson, plus *Birds of Yosemite, Yosemite Nature Notes,* and other titles published by the Yosemite Association, is available in the visitor center bookstore. Worth it, especially for first-time visitors, is the *Yosemite Road Guide,* a key to major sights throughout Yosemite. To get a publications list and/or to obtain books and pamphlets in advance, contact: **Yosemite Association,** P.O. Box 545, Yosemite National Park 95389.

Next door is the park's **Backcountry Office,** tel. (209) 372-0308 (or 372-0307 for 24-hour recorded trails and wilderness information), the place to stop for those seriously setting out to see Yosemite. Other visitor information stops include **Big Oak Flat** near Crane flat, tel. 379-2445, and **Wawona,** tel. 375-6391.

For information about non-camping accommodations and most other facilities and services available at Yosemite, contact the concessionaire's headquarters: **The Yosemite Park and Curry Co.,** 5410 E. Home Ave., Fresno 93727, tel. (209) 252-4848. Yosemite Park and Curry's general in-park phone number is 372-1000.

As an urban outpost in a wilderness setting, Yosemite National Park offers most of the comforts of home. The main **post office** (open even on Saturday mornings) is next to the visitors center in Yosemite Village. There's another at Yosemite Lodge, and a stamp vending machine at Curry Village. To contact the local **lost and found** bureau, call (209) 372-4720. For both regular appointments and 24-hour emergency care, the **Yosemite Medical Group,** tel. 372-4637, is located near the Ahwahnee Hotel in Yosemite Village. Other valley services include the **laundry facilities** at Housekeeping Camp, an **auto repair garage,** gas stations, 24-hour tow service, even warm-weather-only **dog kennels.**

Transport

Coming from most places in Northern California, Hwy. 140 through Merced and Mariposa is usually the best route into Yosemite (especially in winter), though Hwy. 41 from Fresno is more convenient when coming from the south. The only trans-Yosemite road, Hwy. 120 or Tioga Rd., is usually open between Groveland and Yosemite Valley (via New Big Oak Flat Rd.), but the high country stretch from beyond Crane Flat to Mono Lake and the eastern Sierra Nevada is closed in winter. When driving Yosemite roads in spring, fall, and winter, come prepared for frosty road conditions (snow tires or chains).

You can't get to Yosemite by train, but **Amtrak,** tel. (800) USA-RAIL, does come close. From the Amtrak stop in Merced, buses take you the rest of the way. Greyhound doesn't serve the park directly either, but **Yosemite Via,** 300 Grogan Ave. in Merced, tel. 722-0366, makes two daily bus trips between Merced's Greyhound station and Yosemite via Mariposa and Midpines, $17 one way ($15 fare plus $2 park admission) or $10 from Mariposa. From July into early September only (and only with advance reservations), the **Yosemite Transportation System,** tel. (209) 372-1240, connects with Greyhound in Lee Vining. And if you want to leave the driving and planning to someone else, **Gray Line of Merced,** tel. (209) 383-1563, offers one-day trips and overnight tours from $50.

Most people drive to Yosemite (gas stations available on the way, also in Yosemite Valley) ,but because of the park's immense popularity, getting around on the park's free **shuttle bus system** is the best option during summer and other "peak" popularity periods (this holds true, to avoid slick snowy and icy roads, for getting to Badger Pass and elsewhere in winter). The only way to get to Mirror Lakes Junction and Happy Isles is via shuttle. Though the shuttle schedule changes with the seasons, in summer buses run every five minutes from 9 a.m. until 10 p.m.

THE SOUTHERN SIERRA NEVADA

NEAR YOSEMITE: SIERRA NATIONAL FOREST AND VICINITY

To most California mountain lovers, the "Southern Sierra" means Mt. Whitney and other eastern slope destinations (see "Mammoth Lakes and Vicinity"). But the term technically refers to all the range south of Yosemite, including places most accessible from the western slope. Sierra National Forest fills in most of the gaps between Yosemite National Park and Sequoia and Kings Canyon national parks farther south. The national forest's **Bass Lake** area directly south of Yosemite is popular for lake and forest recreation (see "Gold Country"), as are both **Huntington** and **Shaver lakes.** Other popular recreation areas include **Dinkey Lakes** (named after a beloved dog killed by a bear) and **Pine Flat Reservoir** on the Kings River.

Truly worth it for back-roaders, though, is the hair-raising climb up from Huntington Lake and over Kaiser Pass via a one-lane paved cowpath—possible only in summer (honk your horn on the hairpin turns) and impossible anytime for trailers or RVs—to reach **Mono Hot Springs** between Lake Thomas A. Edison and Florence Lake in the morning shadows of the John Muir Wilderness. A summer stay here is almost as memorable as the trip in.

Another don't-miss pleasure is the new 90-mile **Sierra Vista Scenic Byway** route up the San Joaquin River Canyon from either Oakhurst or North Fork; some 16 miles of this backroads tour are on gravel roads. (Free pamphlet available from Sierra National Forest headquarters or ranger district offices; see below.) Especially worth the slight detours required: the short hike to **Fresno Dome** and a stroll through the 1,500-acre **Nelder Grove** of big trees, which includes the Bull Buck Tree. The true marvels of Sierra National Forest and vicinity, after all, are its wilderness areas.

Southern Sierra Nevada Wilderness Areas
The spectacular **Ansel Adams Wilderness** nearest to Yosemite (once known as the Minarets Wilderness, then doubled in size and renamed with the passage in 1984 of the California Wilderness Act), headwaters for San Joaquin River's middle and north forks, is known for its glaciers, gorges, and alpine granite. Adjacent just south, crossing the crest into Inyo National Forest and practically surrounding Kings Canyon National Park, is the **John Muir Wilderness,** a wild array of snow-crowned peaks, meadows, and hundreds of lakes.

Immediately north of Huntington Lake is the **Kaiser Wilderness**—red fir and Jeffrey pine forest, the alpine Kaiser Ridge area, and small mountain lakes. To the west of the John Muir Wilderness and just north of Courtright Reservoir is the **Dinkey Lakes Wilderness,** a 30,000-acre land of lodgepole pines, lakes, meadows, and rocky outcroppings.

Just west of Kings Canyon National Park and south of John Muir is the **Monarch Wilderness,** which stretches into Sequoia National Forest and straddles the Kings River Canyon, very rugged and difficult terrain but not completely unfriendly.

Also in Sequoia National Forest are the **Golden Trout** and **Jennie Lakes wildernesses,** the former named for the trout originally found only in the Kern River watershed—the official state fish since 1947—and the latter known for its lakes.

The **South Sierra Wilderness** bordering Golden Trout is shared by both Sequoia and Inyo national forests: meadows and meandering streams, rolling hills, forested ridges, and high country granite. The almost-unknown **Domeland Wilderness** just south reaches up to heights of 9,000 feet, though the predominant vegetation is sagebrush and piñon pine.

Real road access to most of these areas, especially the Kern River and Kern Plateau, is quite recent. Here there is little granite, so typical of the rest of the Sierra Nevada, but abundant timberland, even magnificent redwoods along the Tule River. **Camp Nelson** on Hwy. 190, tel. (209) 542-2461, is a small motel and restaurant.

For more information, including national forest and wilderness maps ($3 each), and to obtain backcountry wilderness permits, contact local ranger stations or Forest Service headquarters: **Sierra National Forest,** 1130 O St., Fresno

93721, tel. (209) 487-5155; **Sequoia National Forest,** 900 W. Grand Ave., Porterville 93257, tel. (209) 784-1500; **Inyo National Forest,** 873 N. Main St., Bishop 93514, tel. (619) 873-5841.

Winter Recreation

Just south of Yosmite off Hwy. 41 in Sierra National Forest (access road one mile north of Fish Camp) are the 18 miles of marked **Goat Camp** cross-country ski trails, including a three-mile trek into Yosemite's Mariposa Grove. Some trails are perfect for beginners, others adequate for advanced Nordic skiers. Trail map available; for more information, call (209) 683-4665.

The **Sierra Summit ski resort** on Hwy. 168 at Huntington Lake, P.O. Box 236, Lakeshore 93634, tel. (209) 893-3316, is designed for expert and advanced skiers, though there are beginner and intermediate runs here too. Sno-Park snowplay areas, including cross-country ski trails, are also nearby (see the Sierra Nevada "Introduction," above, for more information on the state's Sno-Park program). Other national forest Nordic trails include several at **Hume Lake** near Kings Canyon National Park. To obtain a free trail map, contact the Hume Lake Ranger Station, 35860 E. Kings Canyon Rd., Dunlap 93621, tel. 338-2251.

Huntington And Shaver Lakes

Both mountain recreation lakes are popular in summer. When the water level's up, Shaver Lake is a boater's paradise, with some 2,000 surface acres of clear blue water perfect for water-skiing, houseboating, and fishing. From Shaver, head south 12 miles on Rock Creek Road for hiking access into the Dinkey Lakes Wilderness. Huntington Lake (also actually a reservoir) is higher and prettier, particularly popular for sailing and windsurfing, surrounded by resorts, marinas, and summer cabins—also very nice campgrounds and picnic areas. It's a good hike (and five-mile climb) from the D & F Pack Station near here to College Rock. Then again, you can always pack it in—summers only, advance planning advisable—with the help of area pack outfits: **D & F Pack Station,** tel. (415) 946-1475 or (209) 893-3220; the **High Sierra Pack Station,** tel. (209) 299-8297; **Lost Valley Pack Station,** tel. 855-8261 or 855-6215; or the **Muir Trail Ranch,** tel. 966-3195.

National forest camping and picnicking are available at both Huntington and Shaver lakes—both are popular and crowded in summer—and elsewhere throughout Sierra National Forest and at nearby Bass Lake. For more information, contact Sierra National Forest Headquarters (see above) or stop by or call the local **Shaver Lake Ranger Station,** P.O. Box 300, Shaver Lake 93644, tel. (209) 841-3311. For advance reservations at popular regional national forest campgrounds—at Shaver, Huntington, and Bass Lake to the north—call Mistix toll-free at (800) 283-CAMP. Developed **Southern California**

After the exciting trip via paved cow path over Kaiser Pass, a summer stay at rustic Mono Hot Springs is quite refreshing.

KIM WEIR

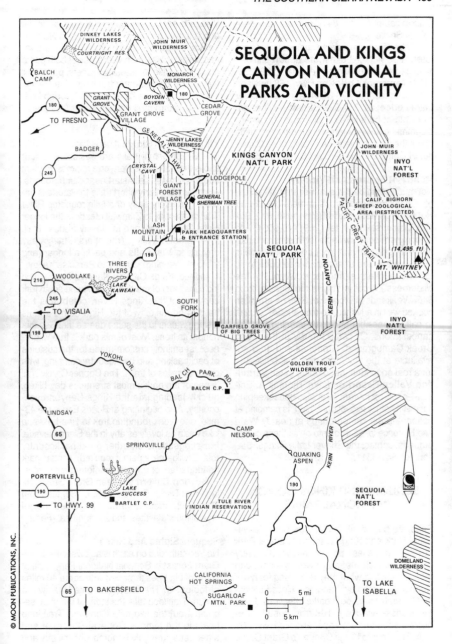

SEQUOIA AND KINGS CANYON NATIONAL PARKS AND VICINITY

Edison campsites, tel. 841-3444, are also available at Shaver Lake.

To stay city-style, lodging choices include the rustic 1922-vintage **Lakeshore Resort** and outlying cabins at Huntington Lake, tel. (209) 893-3191; **Tamarack Lodge** on Hwy. 168 between the two lakes, tel. 893-3244; and the **Shaver Lake Lodge**, tel. 841-3326. Basic services are available at both lakes; ask around for locally recommended restaurants. For more information about the area, contact the Shaver Lake Chamber of Commerce, P.O. Box 58, tel. 841-3350.

Mono Hot Springs And Vicinity

Not much could beat a summer stay at the rustic cobblestone cabins at summers-only **Mono Hot Springs Resort and Bathhouse,** P.O. Box 128, Oakhurst 93644, tel. (209) 449-9054, with a hot mineral soak available (swimsuits required) a few steps from your front door. (Massage is available too, the total experience quite tonic for backpackers stumbling down out of the wilderness.) A cabin stay is reasonable, from $45. Weekends at Mono Hot Springs are often booked well in advance, so plan ahead—or plan to call for possible midweek openings and/or cancellations. Or camp nearby at the Mono Creek Campground. Groceries and grub are available at the tiny store and post office, but for a real good time, head on up to the **Vermillion Valley Resort** on Lake Thomas A. Edison—good restaurant fare, also housekeeping cabins. Another exceptional "high" is camping at national forest campgrounds at nearby Ward and Florence lakes. (For info on all these campgrounds, contact the Shaver Lake Ranger Station, tel. 841-3311.)

SEQUOIA AND KINGS CANYON NATIONAL PARKS

Separate but equal, contiguous Sequoia National Park and Kings Canyon National Park are Yosemite's less-popular redwood country cousins—which means privacy seekers can more easily find what they're looking for here. Connected by the big tree-lined, closed-in-winter Generals Hwy., both parks offer limited winter access—via Hwy. 198 from Visalia, Sequoia's southern entrance, and via Hwy. 180 from Fresno into Kings Canyon's Grant Grove

Village area. But because of the ruggedness and haughty height of eastern Sierra Nevada peaks, including Mt. Whitney, no road connects west to east—so vast areas of both parks are inaccessible to casual sightseers, perfect for hiking and backcountry trekking. The Pacific Crest Trail threads its way north through both parks, and through adjacent wilderness areas, to Yosemite.

Kings Canyon Sights And Hikes

The **Grant Grove** trails are easiest, pleasant strolls through Kings Canyon's impressive giant sequoias; most trails start near campgrounds. Also easy are fairly short trails to waterfalls, including the very easy one-mile roundtrip River Trail on the way to Zumwalt Meadow, the longer Hotel Creek Trail, and the lovely Sunset Trail. The Paradise Valley Trail offers a fairly easy day trip to **Mist Falls** and back, a longer (and more challenging) journey to Paradise Valley.

Indeed, Kings Canyon National Park, which includes most of the deep middle and south fork canyons of the Kings River, celebrates the height and majesty of the High Sierra and its rushing waters to the same degree that Sequoia honors its trees. Most of this park is true wilderness, seemingly custom-made for the customs of backpacking and backcountry camping, with over 700 miles of trails. The Copper Creek Trail is one of the park's most strenuous day-hikes, quickly leading into the Kings Canyon backcountry. Also beginning at Roads End is the 43-mile, one-week roundtrip trek to Rae Lakes, a lake basin as lovely as any in the Sierra Nevada. For suggestions on other good backcountry routes (wilderness permit required), contact park headquarters or any visitor information center.

Boyden Cavern between Grant Grove Village and Cedar Grove on Hwy. 180, tel. (209) 736-2708, offers a 45-minute guided tour of crystalline stalactites and stalagmites. (Fee.)

Sequoia Sights And Hikes

No tree cathedral on earth is as awesome as the **Giant Forest** in Sequoia National Park, a silent stand of big trees threaded with some 40 miles of footpaths. The easy, one-mile Hazelwood Nature Trail loop tells the story of the giant sequoias, but the two-mile Congress Trail loop leads to the famous **General Sherman** and other trees strangely honored with military and

(top) the Vortex (Paramount's Great America);
(above) whitewater rafting (Whitewater Connection)

(top) looking west to the Sierra Nevada from near Lone Pine (Kim Weir);
(above) Lembert Dome in Yosemite's Tuolumne Meadows (Keith S. Walklet)

political titles (General Lee, Lincoln, McKinley, House, Senate, etc.).

Even better are some of the longer, more lyrical loops: the moderately challenging, six-mile Trail of the Sequoias and Circle Meadow trip through the eastern forest (some of the finest trees) and adjacent meadows; the five-mile Huckleberry Meadow journey into the heart of the redwoods; and the Crescent Meadow and Log Meadow walk around the forest's fringe—since sometimes a view of these giants from afar is the best way to really *see* them. Near Giant Forest Village is the Moro Rock and Soldier's Loop Trail to the impressive granite dome **Moro Rock**—famous for its views of the Kaweah River's grand middle fork canyon.

Hiking in the park's impressive **Mineral King** area (all trails start at an elevation of near 7,500 feet) is only for fit fans of fantastic scenery. Steep but very scenic is the White Chief Trail, a four-mile roundtrip through luscious summer meadow flowers to and from the old White Chief Mine. (Mineral King was named for the Nevada-generated silver mining mania which stormed through the area in the 1870s.) For unforgettable views of the southern Sierra Nevada, take the Monarch Lakes Trail to Sawtooth Pass, a challenging roundtrip of just over four miles. Other worthwhile trails lead through dense red fir forests to Timber Gap; to the alpine granite of Crystal Lake; to sky-high Franklin Lake; and to Eagle and Mosquito lakes.

Most spectacular, though, are Sequoia's high country trails, some of the finest in the nation and the only way to appreciate the land's grandeur once the park's big trees have been honored. Most popular is the High Sierra Trail, which connects with the John Muir (Pacific Crest) Trail and eventually arrives at hiker-congested Mt. Whitney.

Winter Recreation

Ranger-led snowshoe hikes (snowshoes provided) and cross-country ski trips are offered on winter weekends. Challenging downhill runs are available at **Sierra Summit** near Shaver Lake (see "Near Yosemite: Sierra National Forest and Vicinity" above). But you can ski here too. **Sequoia Ski Touring at Wolverton,** two miles north of Giant Forest Village off Hwy. 198, Sequoia National Park 93262, tel. (209) 565-3381, offers instruction, rentals, and free ac-

cess to 35 miles of beautiful backcountry Sequoia trails (trail map available). **Sequoia Ski Touring in Grant Grove,** tel. 335-2314, includes access to 75 miles of Kings Canyon trails (lessons, rentals, trail map also available). But marked ski trails are available throughout Sequoia and Kings Canyon national parks; pick up a map at any visitor center.

The private **Montecito-Sequoia Nordic Ski Center and Family Vacation Camp** between Sequoia and Kings Canyon on Hwy. 180, nine miles south of Grant Grove, offers convenient access to 52 miles of marked and groomed national forest ski trails (trail map available), also private and group lessons and equipment rentals. Nice here are the old-fashioned lodges, offering cozy accommodations (private baths) and good home-style food, reasonable rates, also holiday packages. Moonlight photo tours, ski football, igloo-building, and other activities are also sponsored. With summer comes a program of week-long summer camps for families (singles and couples welcome too). For more information, contact: Montecito-Sequoia Lodge, P.O. Box 858, Grant Grove, Kings Canyon National Park 93633, tel. (209) 565-3388. For reservations, call (415) 967-8612 or toll-free (800) 227-9900 in California, (800) 451-1505 from out of state.

Accommodations And Food

If you'll be camping or backpacking, the best bet is to bring your own food, though small grocery stores and restaurants are available. Campgrounds at Sequoia and Kings Canyon are reservable through Mistix, toll-free tel. (800) 365-CAMP. Both parks have a 14-day camping limit (in summer). Among the most popular in Sequoia is **Lodgepole Campground,** an enclave with its own visitor center and organized activities. In Kings Canyon, popular campgrounds cluster near Grant Grove: **Azalea, Sunset, Swale,** and **Crystal Springs.** For information and reservations for other lodging options in both national parks, contact: **Sequoia Guest Services,** Reservations, P.O. Box 789, Three Rivers 93271, tel. (209) 561-3314.

The **Cedar Grove Lodge,** about 30 miles north of Grant Grove at the end of Hwy. 180, open only from late May into September, has rooms in its small 18-room lodge for $75. Another possibility, and quite reasonable, is the

Grant Grove Lodge at Kings Canyon, which offers a variety of year-round cabins—from comfy cabins with two double beds and a tub bath to more rustic models without electricity and with or without baths—for $35-70. Between Giant Forest and Grant Grove villages is the national parks' **Stony Creek Lodge,** small and quiet lodge accommodations, open only late May into September.

In Sequoia, the **Giant Forest Lodge** in Giant Forest Village is open year-round, with average and above-average motel rooms with private baths for $60-85 d (cheaper in the off-season). Cabins with fireplaces run $110, while standard, deluxe, and family cabins are $80 in summer. Rustic semi-housekeeping cabins (with bath) are $40, while rustics for sleeping only run $30 per night. (These cabins, some with kerosene lanterns instead of electricity, are not available in winter.)

The **Bearpaw Meadow High Sierra Camp** offers tent cabins and clean sheets, showers, and home-style meals. Depending on weather and snowpack, Bearpaw is usually open from late June to early September. Call for current rates and information.

If entering the park via Hwy 198, **The Gateway Restaurant and Lodge** on the highway in Three Rivers, tel. (209) 561-4133, serves good cafe-style meals, champagne breakfasts on Saturday and Sunday, fine dinners. Motel, too—among others in the area. (While in Three Rivers do stop at **Reimer's Candies** on the highway—a fantasyland of sweets along the Kaweah River.) From Hwy. 180, a particularly cozy choice in winter is the **Montecito-Sequoia Lodge** and cross-country ski resort about nine miles south of Grant Grove Village; for more information, see "Winter Recreation" above.

Information

The $5-per-car entrance fee is good for one week, in either park. (If you walk, cycle, or arrive by motorcycle or bus, it's $2.) For more information, contact: **Kings Canyon National Park,** Box E, Kings Canyon National Park 93633, tel. (209) 335-2315, and/or **Sequoia National Park,** Ash Mountain, P.O. Box 10, Three Rivers 93271, tel. 565-3341. For road and weather information, call 565-3351 (message updated after 9 a.m. daily).

Bicycles aren't allowed on park trails. RVers should note that Hwy. 180 from Fresno is the best route in. Generals Highway from Hwy 198 to Giant Forest is narrow and steep; trailers and vehicles longer than 15 feet are advised not to travel beyond Potwisha Campground during business hours on summer weekends and holidays.

Stop by the parks' visitor centers for current information—especially regarding trail status, since major forest fires burned into the parks in 1988—and a good selection of trail maps, guidebooks, and natural history titles. (To obtain complete publications lists in advance, contact the parks directly.) The *Kings Canyon Country* hiking guide by Lew & Ginny Clark is worthwhile, and the Sierra Club and Wilderness Press publish various excellent, useful titles. The best overall guide for backpacking in and around the region is *Sierra South: 100 Back-Country Trips* by Thomas Winnett and Jason Winnett. Informational brochures, maps, and other information are available in foreign languages at the visitor centers. The park newspaper, *Sequoia Bark,* provides current information on activities, events, and services.

The **Grant Grove Visitor Center** is the main information stop in Kings Canyon, open daily 8-5; the **Cedar Grove Visitor Center** is open only May to October. In Sequoia National Park, the **Ash Mountain Visitor Center** near the park's southern entrance is the best stop for books, maps, wilderness permits, and information; the summer-season-only **Lodgepole Visitor Center** has good history and natural history exhibits.

BOB RACE

THE GOLD COUNTRY

INTRODUCTION

When James Marshall found flakes of gold in the tailrace of Sutter's sawmill on the American River, hundreds of thousands of fortune hunters —a phenomenal human migration—set sail for California via the brutal boat trip around South America, the treacherous overland crossing at the Isthmus of Panama, or landlubbing prairie schooners sailing the North American plains. The money-hungry hordes who soon arrived swept aside everything—the native populations, land, vegetation, animals—between them and the possibility of overnight wealth. The California gold rush was largely responsible for the Americanization of the West.

Though the region's native peoples were obliterated by the gold rush, the wildness of the life and land they loved lived on through the colorful cast of characters from around the world who came in search of adventure, freedom, and overnight wealth. They also (unwittingly) came to create a new collective cultural identity; without the old social restraints that once bound them, men and women in the gold camps made up new rules. From bandits like Black Bart and Joaquin Murrieta to literary scalawags like Mark Twain, from the gambling Madame Moustache to the railroad barons who controlled California politics, from scandalous Lola Montez and her "spider dancing" to her innocent young song-and-dance protégée, Lotta Crabtree, the first U.S. entertainer ever to become a millionaire— somehow these and other creative individualists combined into one great psychological spark that became the essence of the modern California character.

Mark Twain wryly observed that "a gold mine is a hole in the ground with a liar at the entrance." There were, and still are, many gold mines here, and some say there's at least as much gold remaining in the ground as has been taken out. Today, recreational goldpanners and more serious miners are increasingly common. And just as tourists flooded into the gold-laced Sierra Nevada foothills in the mid- to late 1800s (the literate ones lured in part by the tall tales of writers like Twain and Bret Harte), so they come today, inheritors of a landscape systematically scarred and transformed by greed. But while strolling through the relics of an era, gold country travelers can witness the evidence that some scars do heal, given a century or two.

THE LAND

The Mother Lode, or "la Veta Madre," is the name often given to California's gold country, though purists say this generality is incorrect. Only the Southern Mines, those from the Placerville area south, comprise the mythical Mother Lode—the never-found vein from which all foothill gold was thought to derive. The gold territories from Auburn and Grass Valley north to the Oroville area and northeast to Loyalton and Vinton make up the Northern Mines. But "Mother Lode" is still a convenient and poetic name for these rolling, rounded foothills on the western slope of the Sierra Nevada. Some 135 million years ago, these granite mountains pushed up from the sea, transforming sedimentary and volcanic rock into metamorphic rock. Rich veins of gold, silver, tungsten, and molybdenite formed at the places where ancient rock and the newer, upward-pushing granitic magma connected. Eons of erosion gradually exposed the gold-bearing quartz, freeing the nuggets and flakes later plucked from streams.

The Landscape
For the most part the gold country's foothill terrain is gently sloping, ranging in elevation from about 1,000 to 3,000 feet. These red-dirt hills and flat-topped rock ridges are defined by gullies and steep ravines carved by year-round rivers and countless seasonal streams. Flowing downslope to the west, the region's major rivers include the Feather, Yuba, American, Bear, Cosumnes, Mokelumne, Stanislaus, Tuolumne, and Merced. Soils are generally poor, volcanic, granitic, or serpentine. Iron, leached out of rock over the ages by rain, creates the soil's reddish color.

Climate
Hot, dry, 100-degree summers lasting well into October are typical for the lower foothill areas, with cooler temperatures at higher elevations. Rain, 20- to 40-plus inches annually, comes from late fall through spring, though Sierra summer storms occasionally bring surprise

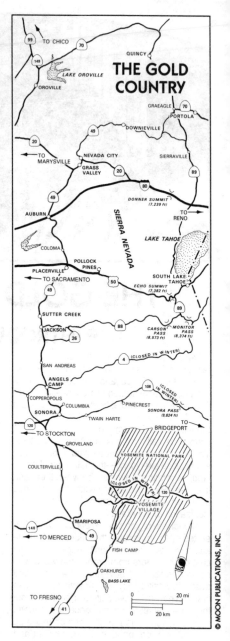

THE GOLD COUNTRY

© MOON PUBLICATIONS, INC.

BLACK BART

South across the Mokelumne River, the infamous Black Bart tossed and turned at least a little while in the San Andreas jail (now a museum). The "gentleman bandit" robbed 28 stagecoaches of their gold shipments, on foot and with the aid of an unloaded shotgun, before his capture in 1883. Black Bart (a.k.a. Charles Bolton or Charles Boles of San Francisco), a lover of the finer things in life, was characteristically polite, if commanding, and left quaint rhyming poetry with his unhappy victims. One of his finer efforts read: "I've labored hard and long for bread, for honor and for riches. But on my corns too long you've tred, you fine haired sons of bitches. Let come what will, I'll try it on, my condition can't be worse. And if there's money in that box, 'tis munney in my purse." Black Bart was something of a New World Robin Hood, since he stole nothing from the passengers—just money from Wells Fargo.

As successful as he was, the "PO8" of the placers violated the never-return-to-the-scene-of-the-crime rule of criminology and was finally undone. Wounded in a holdup at Funk Hill near Copperopolis, the scene of his first and last known robberies, Black Bart dropped a handkerchief before he fled. Wells Fargo detective Harry Worse traced the hankie's laundry mark to an apartment house on Bush Street in San Francisco, and Charles Bolton's days of highway robbery were over. Arrested and returned to San Andreas, the county seat, Black Bart confessed to only the Funk Hill holdup and was sentenced to six years in San Quentin. Freed for good behavior after four years, Bolton then disappeared. An old rumor has it that Wells Fargo pensioned him in exchange for his promise to cease his stage (robbing) career, a suggestion dismissed by historians.

---

thundershowers. In winter, snow isn't uncommon down to 2,500 feet, in cold years falling at elevations of 2,000 feet or lower. Fingers of valley fog can creep up through river canyons to the hills in winter, though most of the gold country soaks up the sun on winter days while flatlanders shiver in the bone-chilling mists below.

Foothill Flora

The best time to explore the hills of the gold country is March and April, when the wildflowers are (almost) the most colorful characters around. Wild mustard, a European import, grows everywhere, but natives like valley goldfields, yellow monkeyflowers, buttercups, and Mariposa lilies add ephemeral, natural gold to the hillsides. Lupine, Brodiaea, the poisonous nightshade and larkspur, baby blue-eyes, meadowfoam, shooting stars, pink bell-blossomed manzanita bushes, and the lovely redbud (a shrub related to the common garden pea) are also abundant. Fritillarias are rarer. The native California poppies—the state's flower and the "gold" which once carpeted miles and miles of the great central valley—are among the latest to bloom, popping up along roads and on hillsides in May and June. By the start of summer, once-green flowers usually become fields of gold-brown grass, little more than tinder for wild fires. In the autumn, the searing summer heat softens and the area's golden grasses and blazing fall foliage look like the backdrop of an impressionist painting.

Climbing in elevation—always watch for poison oak in shady areas below 5,000 feet—rangy gray-green digger pines and small oaks stand guard above fire-resistant chaparral scrub. Even in early summer, the peculiar habit of the California buckeye catches the eye: the round pear-shaped white "fruits" and desiccated orange-tan leaves announce early dormancy. Usually not far from the maples, oaks, and streamside cottonwood, alders, and sycamores is the flashy dogwood. Higher up, heat-seeking vegetation eventually bows to forests of pine, fir, and deciduous trees.

Foothill Fauna

Black bears (which are either black or cinnamon-colored) aren't unusual, especially near campgrounds, but bobcats and mountain lions are rare. Deer are most abundant in the foothills during winter and spring. Gray foxes slink through the underbrush, seeking cottontails, black-tailed jack rabbits, California gray and ground squirrels, and other smaller mammals for dinner. Skunks are plentiful, as are opossums and raccoons—both usually seen at night. Visitors may not see "packrats," but may find their caches of shiny trinkets stashed in logs or tree trunks.

One of the bold busybodies of the bird world, the California or scrub jay seems to enjoy snooping and yammering; the jays comment at length on current events (such as your flat tire or miserly lunch crumbs). Travelers might also spot gregarious yellow-billed magpies and, rarely, chaparral-loving California thrashers. Along steepwalled rock valleys in spring, listen for canyon wrens; to spot them, look for their striking red backs and white throats. They usually live in barren canyons, but can also be found near cabins. If you want to see wrentits (found only in California), crawl under chaparral brush and "screep" out loud; they (or curious locals) may come to investigate. Keep an eye out for the rare red-legged frogs near stream pools, lakes, and ponds. Most of the Mother Lode's rivers have abundant rainbow and brown trout, steelhead, and salmon.

HISTORY: GOLD IN THEM THAR HILLS

Gold And The Death Of An Empire

In the fall of 1847, Sacramento businessman John Sutter sent his carpenter James Marshall up the American River to build a sawmill for his expanding agricultural empire. The mill was all but complete by January 28, 1848, when Marshall strolled into Sutter's office with the news that there was gold in them thar hills—the beginning of the end for Sutter, who lost his work force, then his empire, to the ensuing gold rush. "What a great misfortune was this sudden gold discovery for me!" Sutter wrote in 1857 in *Hutchings' California Magazine*. "Had I succeeded with my mills and manufactories for a few years before the gold was discovered, I should have been the richest citizen on the Pacific shore." He died a poor, unhappy man.

Marshall fared no better, for all the excitement and glory of his discovery. He had little success himself as a miner and tried blacksmithing, growing grapes, lecturing, even selling autographed photos of himself. He died penniless in 1885 at Kelsey, but was buried in Coloma, overlooking the site of his momentous find.

If James Marshall and John Sutter died paupers, others did well. Levi Strauss started his blue jeans empire by manufacturing trousers for miners, Philip Armour by selling meats. And

---

THE NOTORIOUS LOLA MONTEZ AND LITTLE LOTTA CRABTREE

Most fascinating of all Grass Valley's characters were two women: Lola Montez and Lotta Crabtree. The infamous Lola Montez was a charming Irish actress from Galway who reinvented herself as a Spanish dancer. The mistress of pianist Franz Liszt, but pursued by Bazac, Dumas, and Hugo, Montez (Liza Gilbert) was eventually run out of Europe and came to California during the gold rush, where she singlehandedly created more excitement than the completion of the transcontinental railroad. Montez's notorious "spider-dance" (the arachnids may have been imaginary, but the kick-off-your-knickers dance routine was real) was too popular in sophisticated San Francisco. After about three days in any city venue, the fire department had to be called in to hose down the overheated all-male crowd.

Finally run out of the City, Lola moved to the gold fields, where her spider dance was jeered by miners. So Montez retired to Grass Valley with her husband, a bear, and a monkey. She stayed long enough to scandalize respectable women, to send her hubby packing after he shot her bear, and to encourage the career of schoolgirl Lotta Crabtree before setting sail for Australia, where she continued her career and lectured in theosophy.

Little Lotta Crabtree sang and danced her way into the hearts of California's miners and later the world. The darling of the gold camps, Lotta began her career at age six and was the first entertainer ever to become a millionaire. When she died in 1924 at age 77, she left $4 million to charity.

---

it was in the mines that Leland Stanford (of Stanford University fame) made his first fortune, the foundation for his railroad investments and other political exploits. John Studebaker started manufacturing wheelbarrows, and bandits like Joaquin Murrieta and Black Bart raked it in as highway robbers.

The Rush Rushes On

By July of 1848, 4,000 feverish miners worked the river above and below Sutter's Mill in Coloma. That winter, shiploads of would-be prospectors,

JOAQUIN MURRIETA: ROBIN HOOD OF THE PLACERS

The notorious bandit Joaquin Murrieta reportedly ranged from San Andreas to Murphys and beyond, but may have been more legend than reality, a composite of many "Joaquins" forced into crime by the racism of the day. There's hardly a town in the gold country without tunnels, cellars, or caves supposedly frequented by him, or nearby hills where he gunned someone down. According to some versions, Joaquin Murrieta was a bright, handsome young man who settled on the Stanislaus River with his bride and his brother. Primarily interested in farming, the Murrietas nonetheless took the liberty of panning for a little gold, ignoring the prohibition against Mexican miners until accosted by drunken whites. His brother was gunned down (or lynched), his wife assaulted or killed. Horsewhipped and left for dead, Murrieta survived and assembled a bandit band, and one by one, those who had murdered his wife and brother eventually met death at Joaquin's hands.

Settling just north of Marysville, Murrieta and his men became accomplished horse thieves and stagecoach robbers. According to legend, much of Joaquin's booty went to poor Mexican families, who considered him a modern-day Robin Hood. (Others claim that Joaquin Murrieta committed nearly 30 murders, usually victimizing unarmed men, including many Chinese.) Pursued by vigilantes, he moved farther north to Mt. Shasta (where writer "Joaquin" Miller borrowed the name for his nom de plume), then south to San Jose and various San Joaquin Valley towns. Turned in by a former lover, Joaquin Murrieta was eventually tracked down in the Tehachapis by bounty hunters and state rangers—or so at least one version of the story goes.

---

enthralled by the possibility of bringing home some of the "one thousand millions" in gold said to be waiting for them in the Mother Lode, set sail from the eastern U.S.; stories of disasters at sea, disease, Indian attacks, and starvation did nothing to slow the flow.

The '49ers

The main wave of miners, the '49ers, began to pour in the following year. Mostly the young sons of middle-class and well-to-do American families, they were well-educated, could pay the passage to the distant California frontier, and sought adventure as much as wealth. True adventure or not, life in the California gold fields was rough. Most of the year the '49ers labored 12 to 16 hours a day in icy water, though the century-mark summer heat was scorching. When clothing wore out it was seldom replaced, and these hardscrabblers paid little attention to their health. Meals consisted of beef jerky and stale bread, usually supplemented with copious amounts of hard liquor. Ironically, the miners knew nothing of the medicinal plants and natural tonics that kept

the native peoples healthy. Malnutrition, scurvy, cholera, and typhus were common ailments. While a few became millionaires, many returned to their family homes broken men.

A rougher breed, men determined to share the wealth by whatever means available and described by Scotsman Hugo Reid as "vagabonds from every quarter of the globe, scoundrels from nowhere ... assassins manufactured in Hell for the express purpose of converting highways and byways into theaters of blood," arrived in California's gold country by the early 1850s. Others in the new gold rush towns, once decent men, sunk to new lows, spurred on by poverty, bad company, and the devil's brew. The opening of the Concord Stage line, which connected the mines to San Francisco, Stockton, Marysville, and other valley cities, kept the hopeful coming.

Respectability, Then Decline

By the peak year of 1852, more than 100,000 miners were tromping through the Sierra Nevada foothills in search of fortune. Towns sprang up overnight near productive finds, each with an almost predictable life cycle: first as a supply town for serious miners, then a drunken boom town gradually giving way to respectability, then failure of the mines, overnight depopulation, community collapse and decay. But during the 10 major years of California's gold rush, over $600 million (in 1850 dollars) was carried off from the Mother Lode and the more far-flung Northern Mines—wealth accumulated more successfully by financiers and merchants than by the hardworking miners themselves, very few of whom ever realized their dreams of riches.

By the late 1850s, along with shipments of goods from the East came the influences of civilization and the possibility of "respectable" family life. That development, plus the emergence of hydraulic and hardrock mining, brought more stable wealth and "community" to the foothills. Fear of wildfires fostered the formation of volunteer fire brigades, local governments, and the solid construction of adobe, stone, and brick-and-iron buildings.

But by the time civilization arrived, the gold rush was all but over. The miners, young men still, began to migrate toward San Francisco, Sacramento, Stockton, and other new cities that had flourished on the profits from gold mining and related commerce. As gold mining declined, so did the foothill towns created by the gold rush. Some were all but abandoned when the last mines closed during World War II; the rest became backwater burgs with declining populations, crumbling old buildings, weed-grown ruins.

MINING HISTORY: SCRATCHING THE SURFACE

The first gold hunters merely scratched the surface of California's gold country, sloshing through foothill streams and rivers to pan for that telltale color. Later they created their own large-scale erosion. Placer miners scooped up dirt, gravel, and sand, and, using broad, finely woven Native American baskets or shallow metal pans like pie tins, swirled the watery slurry round and round, looking for the gold already mined by the forces of nature. ("Bars," on the convex side of bends in rivers and creeks, usually yielded rich finds and were the sites of the first mining camps and towns.)

In their search for wealth, the lustful legions

ELEANOR DUMONT, "MADAME MOUSTACHE"

Eleanor Dumont arrived in Nevada City in 1854, a 25-year-old woman with a vague past and a French accent. Within 10 days of her arrival, she held a gala opening for her new gambling house, the ultimate in respectability by gold camp standards. She was an overnight sensation and fabulously successful. Miners, all dusted off for the occasion, came from far and wide to bask in her genteel presence and lose their hard-earned gold dust.

But, almost as suddenly, her fortune faded. After a business partnership soured and before hardrock mining took hold, she grew restless and drifted out of Nevada City in 1856 into less amiable gold camps. Twenty-one years later she turned up in Eureka, Nevada—a harder, stouter, and older woman nicknamed "Madame Moustache" by a California wit. Dumont's new establishment in Eureka offered entertainments other than gambling, and though the Wild West was fast becoming tamed, mining camps had become Dumont's life.

In September 1879, in the desolate High Sierra town of Bodie, she committed suicide and was buried and forgotten. The last line of her obituary, printed in the 1880 History of Nevada County, California, read: "Let her many good qualities invoke leniency in criticising her failings."

whittled and blasted away entire hillsides, dug up and rerouted rivers, and dynamited their way into the earth. Miners quickly discovered they could hit pay dirt faster if they used larger rockers and cradles to process the murky gold-rich slurry. Another early innovation was the "long tom" or small version of the later sluice box, a shallow wooden trough 12 to 24 feet long connected at the lower end to a sieve-covered "ripple-box" where the gold collected. The long tom's upper end was usually inserted into a dam, ditch, or flume, to take advantage of gravity. At the end of the day, miners panned the contents of the ripple-box.

Sluicing meant greater productivity but also required steady supplies of water—not naturally available during summer or autumn. So massive wooden flumes—seen everywhere throughout the gold country today—were built to deliver water to dry areas from year-round mountain streams, construction projects that required considerable capital investment and encouraged the formation of mining companies, then corporations.

Hydraulic Mining

By the early 1850s, foothill rivers and streams had been picked clean. Hydraulic mining, using huge rawhide firehoses and one-ton iron nozzles called "monitors" to blast pressurized water against hillsides, exposed placer gravel and gold but destroyed the land and created muddy runoff that killed streamlife and ruined downstream farmland. (The technique created the weirdly beautiful landscape preserved today at Malakoff Diggins near Nevada City and the scoured rocks near Columbia.) The sediment or "slickens" from big-time gold mining made its way to the lower reaches of both the Sacramento and San Joaquin rivers and filled in about one-third of San Francisco Bay during a 10-year period. Outraged downstream landowners, including California's powerful railroad lobby, petitioned the courts for relief and won. Hydraulic mining was banned in 1883, the first major U.S. political victory on behalf of the environment.

Hardrock Mining

When the surface gold was gone, the search went deeper. Fortune hunters, like monstrous moles, burrowed into hillsides with machinery to bleed ancient veins of gold-bearing quartz. Hardrock mining, with shafts hammered into and under mountains, was another later development. One factor that delayed it was the assumption by early miners that all gold, like placer gold, came from rivers and streams. Also, the dynamite necessary for such massive earth-moving enterprises wasn't invented until 1860. As hardrock mining was only feasible with large infusions of capital, this method and big business arrived hand in hand.

Mining crews working down below with pick-axes and shovels separated the gold-bearing quartz ore from bedrock and hauled it to the surface in mule-driven carts. To crush the rock and free the gold, the mule-powered Mexican *arrastra*, a device similar to a giant mortar with a drag-stone pestle, was first used. More efficient, though, were the deafening stamp mills that loomed up like two-story hotels around gold rush towns. The piston-like stamps quickly pulverized the stone, then the gold was separated through amalgamation with mercury: at temperatures of 2,600 degrees Fahrenheit, the mercury vaporized and the molten gold was ready for pouring into 80- to 90-pound ingots.

Dredging For Dollars

The effects of later large-scale gold dredging, popular in the 1890s, are all too apparent a century later. Gasoline-powered dredges mounted on barges turned river and streambeds upside down and inside out, sucking up loads of river-bottom rock, gravel, and sand for sluicing, then dumping

---

MARK TWAIN

After staying for a time in Carson City, Nevada, with his brother Orion, the governor's secretary, Samuel Clemens wandered through western Nevada in the early 1860s, suffering from a severe case of gold fever. Deeply in debt after his prospecting attempts repeatedly failed, in 1862 he walked 130 miles from Aurora to Virginia City to accept a $25-a-week job as a reporter on the *Territorial Enterprise*. Later, in San Francisco, Twain became part of the city's original Bohemia, mixing with Prentice Mulford, Ina Coolbrith (California's first poet laureate), Cincinnatus Heine "Joaquin" Miller, and Bret Harte. He defamed the city police in print, then decided to leave town after another bad turn of affairs, escaping in 1865 to the Mother Lode and an isolated cabin on the Stanislaus River's Jackass Hill near Angels Camp.

Surrounded by a few remaining pocket miners, Twain was content with wandering through the abandoned town and nearby settlements, symbols of the vagaries of fate and fortune. Most of the locals bored him, but he enjoyed the company of his more well-read cabin mates. Twain's laziness was legendary—his unwillingness to draw one more bucket of water later meant his friend lost out on a $20,000 gold find—but the period here was productive nonetheless. Many of the stories shared by his imaginative friends ended up in Twain's later books, and it was here that he first heard the miner's tale of a local frog-jumping competition. "The Celebrated Jumping Frog of Calaveras County" was an overnight success with the Eastern literary establishment.

the tailings along creek banks and farther afield, burying entire areas with mounds of rock, choking off natural vegetation, and permanently changing the courses of rivers and creeks. Serious contemporary gold-seekers face restrictions unheard of in the past. Small-scale dredging, with portable pumps, is restricted to only a few months in summer, to avoid permanent damage to the fisheries and other creek life.

NATIVE PEOPLE

The Maidu, who did not value gold, had long used gold-laced quartz for ceremonial purposes and for spear tips, knives, and mortars. They inhabited the northern reaches of the gold country south to the Placerville and Coloma areas. Nearby, in the valley now cradling the Coloma Road, lived the Cullooma. The peaceable, quiet Miwok ranged throughout the broad central foothill area, roughly from El Dorado County south to Mariposa, and fringe groups of Yokut lived in the southern reaches of the Mother Lode near the valley.

Like Maidu and Yokut (and many other Native American "tribal" names), *miwok* means "people." The interior Miwok were true foothill people, rarely inhabiting the valley and moving into the mountains only to hunt or escape the summer heat. Untouched by early Spanish missionaries but brutally eliminated by gold rush immigrants, by 1910 the Miwok numbered only in the hundreds. Little is known about their civilization, but they were hunters and gatherers who shared the spiritual bent of the Maidu, dressing in unusual costumes for varied rituals and spirit impersonations enacted in half-underground ceremonial dance houses and sweat lodges.

MINING MODERN GOLD: TRAVEL AND RECREATION

No matter how you go, several separate trips to the gold country are advisable, since the abundance of museums, old hotels, and other attractions is almost overwhelming on one long trip. Towns along Hwy. 49, the much-ballyhooed "Golden Chain Mother Lode Highway," are the most touristy. If you're allergic to commercially

tainted quaint, keep in mind that there *is* historic, scenic, and actual gold to be mined here.

Travel off the beaten track is not easy without a car or bicycle. If you're planning to explore most of the gold country's major towns on wheels, take the interconnecting old highways and county roads roughly paralleling Hwy. 49 whenever possible.

Bicycle tours of the Mother Lode are great fun; towns and campgrounds aren't far apart and the area's many scenic back roads are too narrow and harrowing for most autophiles. The *Cyclist's Route Atlas: A Guide to the Gold Country & High Sierra/North* and *Cyclist's Route Atlas: A Guide to the Gold Country & High Sierra/South,* both by Randall Gray Braun (Heyday Books, each $8.95), map out some good rides.

Historical exploration, gold seeking, hiking, camping, fishing, swimming and tubing, boating, and water-skiing are other popular gold country pursuits. River-running offers even more thrills. April and May are usually the "high water" months, though in some years even June is wet and wild. Summer and fall offer a tamer experience. Pick up a copy of *California Whitewater* by Fryar Calhoun and Jim Cassady—a very worthwhile investment for fans of the inland wave.

Whitewater Rafting Companies

Get a listing of the many reputable local rafting companies from chambers of commerce or national forest offices. Of the commercial rafting guides operating throughout the area, some offer more adventurous and/or cheaper trips than others. Midweek rates are often cheaper, and a variety of group plans are available.

Many of the companies listed below also offer river trips in the state's far northern mountains, along the north coast, or elsewhere in California. Some even offer trips in other parts of the U.S. and the world. To gather complete and current information, with plenty of time to make an informed choice (and reservations), contact any of the companies listed below in early fall and request a current expeditions catalog for the following winter/spring season. Most trips include rafts, guides, and meals and beverages, and the rafting companies will state specifically what else to bring. Most companies accept credit cards.

For information on other worthwhile river trips and rafting companies, see "The Northern Mountains" above.

whitewater rafting in California's gold country

WHITEWATER CONNECTION

Whitewater Connection, with offices near Marshall Gold Discovery State Park on Hwy. 49 and a stone's throw from the American River, P.O. Box 270, Coloma 95613, tel. (916) 622-6446 or toll-free (800) 336-7238 in the U.S., is a very popular concern, offering everything from family float trips to whitewater adventures (Class VI) designed "for those with suicidal tendencies." Whitewater emphasizes runs on the American, naturally enough, including challenging Class III-IV Middle Fork and North/South Fork combination runs, as well as Class IV North Fork trips (experience and wetsuits required). Any of these trips are worth doing, as soon as possible, since the construction of the Auburn Dam, in some form, seems imminent despite the dedicated opposition of many environmental organizations. (For more information on this particular controversy, see "Auburn And Vicinity" following, and/or contact the American River Coalition in Sacramento, tel. 916-448-1045.) Like other companies, at least until California's long drought is over, Whitewater Connection also offers trips down the Stanislaus River, "reborn" for rafters and other canyon lovers with the receding waters of the very controversial New Melones Reservoir. Fun, too, if a bit hedonistic, is the company's Tahoe trip, "a three-day orgy of food, festivity, and frolic" combining horseback riding, parasailing, sailing, hot-air ballooning, and a raft trip down the American's South Fork. People rave about the food (lobster for dinner, along with Mother Lode wines) and other little extras on Whitewater Connection's longer trips. But this business is not all fun and games: all Whitewater Connection trip prices include a contribution to the American River Coalition, the American River Land Trust, and the Friends of the River.

Other firms offering American River raft and whitewater trips include **Adventure Connection,** P.O. Box 475, Coloma 95613, tel. (916) 626-7385 or toll-free (800) 556-6060; **Tributary Whitewater Tours,** 20480 Woodbury Dr., Grass Valley 95949, tel. (916) 346-6812, which also specializes in Yuba River runs; and **Mother Lode River Trips,** P.O. Box 456, Coloma 95613, tel. 626-4187 or toll-free (800) 427-2387. **O.A.R.S., Inc.,** P.O. Box 67, Angels Camp 95222, tel. (209) 736-4677 (toll-free 800-446-2411 for catalog), is noted for its Whitewater Guide School as well as its excellent trips, including the Jawbone Canyon run on the upper Tuolumne River.

Ahwahnee Whitewater Expeditions, P.O. Box 1161, Columbia 95310, tel. (209) 533-1401 or toll-free (800) 359-9790, is a fairly small firm offering some big rides within reach of both Tahoe and Yosemite. The one- to three-day trips include easy floats on the Carson River in the high Sierra or more challenging plunges down the Tuolumne (one of the state's best), Merced, and Stanislaus rivers as well as Cherry Creek near Yosemite. Different, too, are Ahwahnee's special adventures, from gourmet and trout-fishing trips to raft trips including a bed and breakfast overnight in the wilderness. **Zephyr River Expeditions, Inc.,** P.O. Box 3607, Sonora 95370, tel. 532-6249, offers reasonably priced runs on the American and wilder rivers, including the almost unrunnable Upper Tuolumne (experts only), the Kings River and Merced, and charter group "gourmet" trips. Zephyr also contributes a pass-through fee to river conservation and relevant environmental groups. **Sierra Mac River Trips, Inc.,** P.O. Box 366, Sonora 95370, tel. 532-1327, also comes highly recommended. They offer one- to three-day trips, meals and shuttle included, from the American River to the Stanislaus and Tuolumne, plus a five-day White Water School.

Mariah Wilderness Expeditions, P.O. Box 248, Point Richmond 94807, tel. (415) 233-2303, offers various reasonably priced California outdoor adventures, including mountain bike tours and sea kayaking, in addition to its

one- or two-day trips on the Merced River and the south, middle, and north forks of the American River (some for women only, some for fathers and sons, some even for single parents and children).

Sobek, originally at home in the gold country's Angels Camp area, has been among the world's most highly regarded adventure travel outfitters since its establishment in the mid-1970s by expert rafter and writer Richard Bangs. A 1991 business merger has combined Sobek with a major world trekker, creating **Mountain Travel-Sobek,** 6420 Fairmount Ave., El Cerrito 94530, tel. (415) 527-8100 or toll-free (800) 227-2384. The new combined list of treks and raft trips offered worldwide should keep adventure consumers busy for years to come.

NEVADA CITY

In this small sophisticated mountain town near the beloved San Juan Ridge of earth poet Gary Snyder, ghost-white Victorians cling to the hillsides, most streets are little more than paved crisscrossing cowpaths, and the creek running along the downtown area blazes with New England color in autumn. Officially populated by only a few thousand these days, Nevada City once competed with Sonora for recognition as California's third-largest city. First called Deer Creek Dry Diggins and Caldwell's Upper Store, the Spanish *nevada* ("snow covered") seemed more fitting after the particularly brutal winter of 1850. But the state of Nevada stole the name about 15 years later, so the town has referred to itself as Nevada City ever since.

History

Nevada City was first a placer mining camp but, due to only seasonal natural water supplies, soon evolved its own unique mining techniques. The long tom, the ground sluice, and hydraulic mining were all Nevada City "firsts." In this area, over $400 million in gold was violently unearthed. Bold and brazen women were and still are a fact of life in and around Nevada City. It's probably no coincidence that the lives of this town's infamous gambler, Eleanor "Madame Moustache" Dumont, as well as precocious Lotta Crabtree and outrageous Lola Montez of Grass Valley,

all intersected here. Appropriately enough, the U.S. senator who introduced legislation eventually leading to women's suffrage lived in Nevada City. Other local historical footnotes: world-class soprano Emma Nevada and cable car inventor Andrew Hallidie were both born here.

Nevada City's Baptist church stands on the site of the joint session of the Congregational Association of California and the San Francisco Presbytery, a meeting which eventually led to the establishment of the University of California. Water barons created by the conglomeration of capital necessary for mining-related water engineering also met here to create Pacific Gas and Electric Company (PG&E), the world's largest utility. Not so successful was the railway connecting Nevada City and Grass Valley, built in 1901: service stopped for good after a brutal 1926 snowstorm.

SIGHTS

Nevada City Walking Tour

Though the town nestles on steep hills, downtown Nevada City, primarily along Broad and Commercial streets, is fairly level. Start exploring at the **Chamber of Commerce** at 132 Main, the old office of the South Yuba Canal Company, where you can pick up free guides and maps

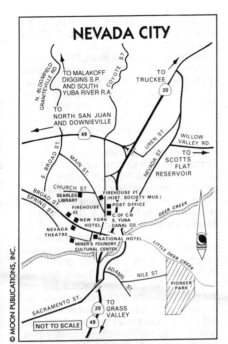

NEVADA CITY

TO MALAKOFF
DIGGINS S.P.
AND SOUTH
YUBA RIVER R.A.

TO
TRUCKEE

TO
NORTH SAN JUAN
AND DOWNIEVILLE

N. BLOOMFIELD
GRANITEVILLE RD.

COYOTE ST.

20

E. BROAD ST.

MAIN ST.

UREN ST.

NEVADA ST.

WILLOW
VALLEY RD.

TO
SCOTTS
FLAT
RESERVOIR

CHURCH ST.

BROAD ST.

SPRING ST.

SEARLES
LIBRARY

FIREHOUSE #1
(HIST. SOCIETY MUS.)

POST OFFICE

C. OF C.B

DEER CREEK

FIREHOUSE
#2

NEW YORK
HOTEL

S. YUBA
CANAL CO.

NEVADA
THEATRE

NATIONAL HOTEL

MINER'S FOUNDRY
CULTURAL CENTER

LITTLE DEER CREEK

MOON

ADAMS ST.

NILE ST.

PIONEER
PARK

SACRAMENTO ST.

TO
GRASS
VALLEY

20

49

NOT TO SCALE

© MOON PUBLICATIONS, INC.

to local sights, almost endless arts, entertainment, and New Age info, even copies of the exhaustive *Compleat Pedestrian's Partially Illustrated Guide to Greater Nevada City* ($4.50). **Ott's Assay Office,** now an antique store, is next door.

Stroll up the hill to **Firehouse Number 1,** now a small Nevada County Historical Society Museum, 214 Main, tel. (916) 265-5468, open 11 a.m.-4 p.m. daily, small fee. Housed in this tall, thin gingerbread is a dusty collection of Donner Party relics, fine Maidu basketry, and the original Joss House altar from Grass Valley's old Chinatown. On gaslamp-lit Broad Street is the handsome stone-and-brick **Nevada Theatre** (401 Broad), one of the oldest theaters in the state, built in 1865 and renovated a century later. Mark Twain launched his career as a lecturer here. You can stroll through the lobby of the green and white **National Hotel.** Open continuously since 1856, despite a few fires, the National is one of several gold rush hotels claiming to be the state's oldest hostelry; this one also claims to be the oldest hotel in

continuous operation west of the Rockies. The old **New York Hotel** at 408 Broad was built in 1853 then rebuilt four years later after burning to the ground. Right next door is the red brick **Firehouse Number 2.**

A quarter mile west on E. Broad lies the stone medicinal monolith, known locally as Nevada City's first hospital, an unintended gift from the Maidu. Native peoples, believing the sun healed all, climbed up on top of this impressive sunning rock and nestled into the hollow to take the cure.

Some Places To Linger

The **Miner's Foundry Cultural Center,** formerly the American Victorian Museum, and still the town's de facto arts center, is in the meandering old Miner's Foundry building at 325 Spring St., tel. (916) 265-5804. There's a large pipe organ and a stage for local drama companies, music, and other events in the huge freespan Old Stone Hall, a dining room for special occasions, even broadcasting booths for the excellent local radio station, KVMR.

The **Searles Library,** once a law office at 215 Church St., tel. (916) 265-5910, now houses a curious collection of historical Nevada County manuscripts, books, photographs, and genealogical materials, open Mon.-Sat. 1-4 p.m. The **Mount Wesley House,** 431 Broad St., tel. 265-5804, and the **Martin Luther Marsh House,** 254 Boulder St., tel. 265-6716, both offer tours by appointment only (donation). If you're here on a Friday, worth a stop is the **Nevada County Narrow Gauge Railroad** workshop at 774 Zion, open 2-4 p.m. The local historical society is reassembling the aged and unreliable "Never Come, Never Go" railroad which ran between Nevada City, Grass Valley, and Colfax until the Malakoff Mines closed. (Old Engine No. 5 was recently rescued from a back lot at Universal Studios.)

Fans of small independent breweries can stop Sat. noon-5 p.m. for a tour and a taste of local natural draft lager at the **Nevada City Brewery Company,** 75 Bost Ave., tel. (916) 265-2446 (special tours by arrangement). Or stop by around 2 p.m. for tasting at the **Nevada City Winery,** 321 Spring St., tel. 265-9463, open daily noon-dusk. Half a mile east of downtown up Boulder is **Pioneer Park,** good for Frisbee-tossing, picnics, or cooling your toes in the creek.

ACCOMMODATIONS

Camping

Camp at **Malakoff Diggins State Park** (open all year, $14/night, no showers; also cabins for rent) if you're heading that way. Closer is the public **White Cloud Campground,** 1½ miles east on Hwy. 20, and smaller **Skillman Campground** just a few miles beyond, both without showers, open late May through Sept., call (916) 273-1371 for info. Very basic but clean and pleasant camping is available in the South Yuba River Recreation Area (contact the BLM office in Folsom, tel. 985-4474, for info and map) and in nearby national forest areas; get current information at Forest Service offices in Nevada City or Grass Valley.

Among other tent-pitching possibilities is private **Scotts Flat Lake,** four miles east on Hwy. 20 then five miles south at 23333 Scotts Flat Rd. (second gate), tel. (916) 265-5302—year-round campsites in the pines near the lake, beach and swimming, fishing, playground, hot showers, coin laundry, reservations advisable in summer. Farther east off Hwy. 20 in Washington near the Yuba River is the private **River Rest Campground,** General Delivery, Washington 95896, tel. 265-4306; tent sites, also RV sites, amenities including hot showers. If you're heading toward Downieville and Sierra City, camp at **Bullards Bar Reservoir** in the foothills north of North San Juan, accessible via Marysville Rd. just south of Camptonville. For info: Yuba County Water Agency, tel. 692-2166, or Emerald Cove Resort and Marina, tel. 741-6278.

A Retreat,
Motels, And The Hotel

For a unique stay, try **The Expanding Light,** the nearby Ananda Village meditation retreat of Swami Sri Kriyananda and his followers, off Tyler Foote Crossing Rd. near North San Juan, tel. (916) 292-8958. Sign up for a retreat or call in advance to work out lodging and food arrangements, possible labor exchange. A good bet for a reasonably priced motel room is the **Airway Motel** at 575 E. Broad St., tel. 265-2233, not fancy but comfortable, with pool and TV, knotty pine walls, close to everything. The owners built each unit themselves in the 1950s. Prices at the **Northern Queen Motel** at 400 Railroad Ave., tel. 265-5824, are $50-62 for modern and clean motel rooms, $75-100 for cottage units.

Staying at the **National Hotel,** 211 Broad St., tel. (916) 265-4551, can be something of a disappointment, considering the hotel's illustrious past. But it's not so bad if you land in a spacious room with balcony. Complete with saloon, restaurant, pool, clean Victorian rooms with hand-painted if tired old wallpapers, soft beds.

Historic Bed And Breakfasts

Grandmere's Bed and Breakfast at 449 Broad St., Nevada City 95959, tel. (916) 265-4660, is generally considered Nevada City's downtown showplace inn. This grand dame Colonial Revival was built by former U.S. Senator Aaron Sargent and his wife Ellen. He was a political mover and shaker also involved in establishing the Transcontinental Railroad. She was a suffragette and an early champion of women's rights; Susan B. Anthony and other feminists were guests here. That her husband authored the U.S. legislation that eventually allowed women to vote seems no coincidence. Dignified still, the house today only hints at its past. Rooms are homey in an elegant country style, and some are quite spacious. All have private baths and unusual touches, from the original gas fireplace in the suite's sitting room to an upstairs sunporch and rough pine four-poster beds. Willa's Room, with kitchen and separate garden entrance, has a double-sized sleeper sofa in addition to the queen bed, most appropriate for families with children. Full breakfast served downstairs.

Just down the street, at 427 Broad St., tel. 265-9478, is **The Parsonage Bed & Breakfast Inn,** once the home provided for the local minister by the Nevada City Methodist Church. This historical emphasis just begins there, however, since Innkeeper Deborah Dane is the great-granddaughter of California pioneer (and Mark Twain's editor) Ezra Dane. The Parsonage is proper, like a living museum, from the tasteful selection of family antiques and other period pieces to the line-dried and handpressed linens. Though it's peaceful here, it's far from stuffy. All rooms have private baths; the two toward the back of the house also have an extra sofa bed or daybed. Continental breakfast is served in the formal dining room or, weather permitting, out front on the veranda. Rates: $65-90, lower off-season and midweek.

Architecturally and historically fascinating, in a more eclectic sense, is the wonderful **Red Castle Inn** across the highway and up the hill at 109 Prospect Street (call for directions), tel. 265-5135. This towering four-story brick home, painted barn red and dripping with white icicle trim, is one of only two genuine Gothic Revival mansions on the West Coast. And the Red Castle has been in business since 1963, well in advance of America's bed and breakfast trend, perhaps the oldest U.S. hostelry of its type. Despite apparent propriety and genuine antique treasures—a Bufano cat guards the Gold Room and its Renaissance Revival Victorian bed—this place is friendly and sometimes downright funny, from the antique mannequin arms doing duty as towel racks in the bathroom of the Garden Room to the fishing tackle baskets dispensing tissues in the child-scale suites on the former nursery floor. Though it's quite a climb up—the stairs are steep and narrow, and the shared bathroom is down one floor (bathrobes provided)—the fourth-floor garret suite offers the finest possible view of Nevada City, from the veranda. The Forest View Room, four floors down and very secluded, with a separate entrance and private garden, is perfect for honeymooners. All rooms, however, come with a private veranda or garden area. And all guests get to experience at least one Red Castle breakfast, a full meal and a feast, everything homemade. (Vegetarians are easily, and happily, accommodated, as is anyone with specific dietary needs.) Rates: $70-110.

Other Good Bed And Breakfasts

The **Palley Place** about a mile from downtown at 12766 Nevada City Hwy., Nevada City 95959, tel. (916) 265-5427, offers simple and unpretentious accommodations in a relaxed private home. Meg Palley, proprietor, doesn't discriminate against people traveling solo, either, a fact reflected in the rates: $30 per person. And if you're lucky, Meg will tell you all about local events (the real ones) and community fundraisers. She might even give you a lesson or two in the weaver's art. Her loom tends to dominate the living room, and handwoven blankets cover the beds.

Also surprisingly free of the typical bed and breakfast Victoriana is bright and airy **Downey House** atop Nabob Hill at 517 W. Broad St., tel. (916) 265-2815 or toll-free (800) 258-2815, a pale yellow Eastlake Victorian with a very contemporary inner attitude. Each of six large rooms features pastel contemporary decor, built-in bed, private modern bathroom, even an aquarium (fish provided). Coffee and homemade cookies are served at 3 p.m., wine at 5 p.m.; at bedtime, expect some fresh candy from Hooper's in Oakland. Full breakfast is served buffet style, everything from quiche or chiles rellenos to fresh homemade cinnamon rolls and platters of fresh fruit. Large back gardens, even private offstreet parking in the barn. Rates: $75-95.

The Kendall House: An Inn up the hill at 534 Spring St., tel. 265-0405, is also a light and cheerful place, graced by the gracious Southern hospitality of its hosts. Some rooms are spacious, others small and intimate, but all feature unique touches and private bathrooms. There's a gym room, too, with Soloflex. The Barn out back, once home to the Cicigoni family's cow, is essentially a separate country-style home with all the essential comforts and conveniences, including a completely equipped tiled kitchen and wood-burning stove. Just outside is a large private deck, which looks down on the swimming pool. Full and hearty Arkansas-style breakfast. Rates: $106-205, including local bed tax.

Unusual, too, is the **Piety Hill Inn**, 523 Sacramento St., tel. (916) 265-2245 or toll-free (800) 443-2245, motor court-style cottages converted into very nice bed and breakfast units decorated in Early American, Victorian, or 1920s furnishings. Some units are small, others are larger two-room suites, but all include kitchen or kitchenette, wet bar, refrigerator, and covered offstreet parking. Units in the back are quietest. Breakfast (in a basket) is delivered to your door in the morning. There's a spa in the gazebo out back, plus a small garden area for barbecuing, picnicking, lawn games, or just sitting around. Children are genuinely welcome here; there's room to play outdoors, plus a school playground adjacent. And a newly renovated house has become the bridal suite with complete caterer's kitchen and other features, making this a good choice for wedding parties and other large group events. Basic room rates: $75-120 double occupancy, $20 each additional person.

Under new ownership and newly refurbished is **Flume's End Bed & Breakfast Inn** on Gold

Run Creek across the one-car-at-a-time bridge at 317 Pine St., tel. (916) 265-9665. This eclectic, carefully tended inn was once a quartz mill, then, until the 1950s, a brothel. Terraced like the gardens and decks to fit to the hillside, Flume's End offers something for everyone. Down the steep spiral staircase are two rooms—the Garden Room and spectacular Creekside Room—which share a sitting/living room and refrigerator, wet bar, and TV, a good set-up for two couples traveling together. Among other rooms, the Master Bedroom has its own Jacuzzi; the Penthouse in the attic has a spacious sitting room and bedroom, and a wonderful clawfoot bathtub that soaks up morning sun. The Cottage, perched above the creek near the roadside parking area, comes complete with kitchenette and woodstove. Rates: $75-120.

GOOD FOOD

Hip Food, Just Plain Good Food

How can a town with barely 2,500 people have restaurants, most of them very good? **Cowboy Pizza** at 515 Spring St., tel. (916) 265-2334, is the locals' favorite for fast food, and quite a find. Cowboy's slogan—"Small children cry for it, mothers ask for it by name"—becomes believable once you pass the "Free Tibet" bumpersticker and open the door. The aroma of garlic is almost overwhelming—garlic blended with traditional gourmet pizza toppings and some very untraditional ones (like Danish feta cheese, spinach, pine nuts, and onions). Pizzas here take a while, so either call ahead or sit down and enjoy some of California's best handmade beers and ales (Red Tail, Sierra Nevada, St. Stan's) while studying the oddball collection of decorative cowboy kitsch, from the Gene Autrey: Singing Cowboy poster to the official emblem of Manure Movers of America. For very fine Japanese and macrobiotic meals, the tiny (seven tables) **Rainbow Mountain Inn** at 238 Commercial, tel. 265-9935, is the only place to go. Hard to find—not a tourist joint—but worth it for cafe fare is the **Northridge Inn,** a few minutes' drive away at 14773 Nevada St. Extension (ask locally for directions), tel. 265-2206. Fabulous burgers and home fries, cafe standards like BLT and grilled-cheese sandwiches, *real* milkshakes, and over 100 beers to choose from, including

the local Nevada City brew. For dinner, barbecued chicken or ribs, fresh trout, daily specials. Back in town and trendier is the **Posh Nosh** deli restaurant and wine bar at 318 Broad St., tel. 265-6064, fairly casual with an outdoor patio, homemade rolls, cured meats, huge sandwiches, and a lunch menu with good pasta dishes. Breakfast, though, is the point here—with 11 different omelettes, crepes, waffles, steak and eggs, even surprises like apple sausage. At dinner, Posh Nosh serves some of its most noteworthy sandwiches plus pastas, fresh fish (charbroiled or grilled), seafood, and entrees such as Apple Brandy Chicken. Everything is quite good, quite reasonable. Open for breakfast Wed.-Sat., for lunch daily, and for dinner Thurs.-Sat. only. **Cirino's** downtown at 309 Broad St., tel. 265-2246, is a local institution with gold brocade walls and garish red to liven up the dark wood decor, famous for its hearty Italian fare and open for lunch and dinner daily. For more down-home cooking, head two miles west on Hwy. 49 to **The Willo,** tel. 265-9902, an unpretentious restaurant and bar where you grill your thick steak yourself, baked potato and green salad included. Open for dinner only, 5-9:30 p.m. daily.

Fancier Fare

Friar Tuck's at 111 N. Pine St., tel. (916) 265-9093, is very cozy, specializing in creative seafood and steak variations, beloved for its fondue, with a full wine bar in a warm brick-and-beam setting. Reservations a good idea at dinner, but not usually necessary at lunch. Open daily for lunch, for dinner Wed.-Sat. only. Not far away—nothing's *that* far away in Nevada City—at the corner of Commercial and Pine streets, tel. 265-6248, is **The Country Rose Cafe,** a Country French-style bistro with wonderful lunch specials. (If the weather's nice, ask to sit outside in the garden patio.) The Country Rose features a daily-changing dinner menu with an emphasis on seasonal fresh fish and seafood plus standards like rack of lamb and filet mignon. Open for lunch Mon.-Sat., for dinner daily. Besides being a study in Victorian good taste, people say the homey **Michael's Garden Restaurant** at 216 Main, tel. 265-6660, is among the best. Continental selections served either in the house or out in the garden. **Peter Selaya's,** at 320 Broad St., tel. 265-5697, is usually considered Nevada City's answer to more citified connoisseurs. In an 1886 building once home to a bakery run by an Irish immigrant—the original wood-burning stove is a historic monument, walled off behind the kitchen—even today Selaya's has decidedly international airs. Appetizers include smoked salmon carpaccio and blue walnut mushrooms (large caps stuffed with bleu cheese and roasted walnuts). For pasta, choose Selaya's "market ravioli," usually exceptional, with different ingredients daily depending upon what's freshest and available. Also wonderful is the smoked trout salad. For dinner, plan on anything from scallops Rockefeller to tournedos béarnaise. But non-carnivores certainly won't starve: the Gourmet Vegetarian features seasonal vegetables with cheeses and garlic butter baked in pastry, served with cashew-stuffed mushrooms.

For those in the mood for lunch or takeout, visit Peter Selaya's new "Gourmet Food To Go" deli outlet around the corner, tel. 265-0558, everything house-made and delicious, from salads, sandwiches, and entrees *en croûte* to cookies and pastries.

ARTS AND ENTERTAINMENT

Nevada City is more *event* than destination, so some people tend to get bored if they arrive without the right attitude. To get with the program, you must participate. Nevada City's rich local cultural life—besides the rugged Yuba River backcountry, attractive town, and good restaurants—is the main reason for coming here and/or staying a while. For an overview, get a complete listing of current goings-on from the **Nevada City Arts Council,** 408 Broad St., tel. (916) 265-3178, and inquire at the chamber office.

Music, Theater, And Movies
For information about year-round local musical events, from pop music and cabaret to the classics—and especially the three-week summer festival here—contact **Music in the Mountains,** P.O. Box 1451, Nevada City 95959, tel. (916) 272-4725. The **Nevada County Dance Guild,** P.O. Box 1917, tel. 292-3844, sponsors two major events (and many smaller ones) each year.

Off Broadstreet is another option, very enjoyable theater at 305 Commercial, tel. 265-8686. First-rate plays are performed at the Miner's

Foundry or at the Nevada Theater by the award-winning **Foothill Theatre Company,** P.O. Box 1812, tel. 265-TKTS, on most Fri. and Sat. nights during the season. (Grass Valley's **Community Players** also grace the stage here as well as at the county fairgrounds. For info: P.O. Box 935, Grass Valley 95945, tel. 477-1107.) The long-running film series at the **Nevada Theatre,** 401 Broad St., tel. (916) 265-8587, offers foreign and offbeat movies on Sundays—high local turnout. Also popular for fine film buffs is **The Magic Theatre,** 107 Argall Way, tel. 265-8262.

Community Events
There's a **Robbie Burns celebration** every January at the Miner's Foundry, featuring Scotch whiskey, bagpipers and other traditional music, authentic food, and Romantic verse in honor of Scotland's famed poet (who never slept, slummed, or spoke here). Come in March for the annual **Psychic Expo.** About 10,000 people line the streets for the Father's Day **Nevada City Bicycle Race,** which draws some of America's best cyclists and Olympic hopefuls. There's a long-running **Victorian Christmas** celebration here in December, with expensive Christmas shopping, period costumes, caroling, sometimes even snow-frosted windows.

Information And Services
The **Nevada City Chamber of Commerce,** 132 Main St., Nevada City 95959, tel. (916) 265-2692, staffed by helpful and friendly folks, has dozens of pamphlets and promotions. Pick up free publications like the Nevada County Art Council's monthly *Art Matters,* KVMR radio's program guide, and North San Juan's *Local Endeavor: Planetary News Advocating Personal Involvement.* More useful, perhaps, for most people are the "Insiders Guide to Parking in Nevada City," the "Nevada City Walking Tour," and "Nevada County Calendar of Events." The **post office** is at 100 Coyote St., open Mon.-Fri. 8:30-5. **Tahoe National Forest headquarters** is on Coyote St. at Hwy. 49, tel. 265-4531; stop by for forest-wide recreation and camping info, or send $3 to request a forest map in advance.

Local Transport
Greyhound has abandoned the area, making public transport all but impossible—except for the Amtrak bus connecting to Sacramento's

Capitol trains. You can get to Grass Valley and back on the local **Gold Country Stage** bus, tel. (916) 265-1411, arrivals and departures at the National Hotel (and elsewhere). Rent bikes at **Sierra Adventure Company,** tel. (916) 265-

9240. Tours, too. To play tourist to the hilt, take a **horse-drawn carriage ride** (20 minutes for $10 for two people) with the **Nevada City Carriage Company,** tel. 265-5348, weekends only in the off-season.

VICINITY OF NEVADA CITY

Nearby Nature Trails

Six miles north of Nevada City, before the Hwy. 49 South Yuba River crossing and along Rush Creek, is the **Independence Trail,** constructed *in* a hill-hugging flume to provide wilderness access for people in wheelchairs: waterfalls, wildflowers, nice view of the canyon. There's even a ramp, with seven switchbacks, leading down to a fishing pool. Sequoya Challenge, the same local group which worked to preserve the covered Bridgeport Bridge, bought the land here and sold it back to the state, but continues to repair and maintain the trail. Donations and support always welcome: Sequoya Challenge, P.O. Box 1026, Nevada City 95959, tel. (916) 432-3183.

About 4½ miles east of Nevada City on Hwy. 20 then 1½ miles northeast on Rock Creek Rd. is the **Rock Creek Nature Study Area,** a small picnic area with pit toilets (no treated water) and a one-mile self-guided nature trail with an explanatory brochure.

THE SAN JUAN RIDGE

Yuba River

The Yuba, formerly called Rio de las Uvas ("River of Grapes") for the vines woven along its rocky banks, squeezes the rugged San Juan Ridge from both sides. During and since the gold rush, the Yuba and its tributaries have yielded more gold than any other U.S. river system. Miners blasted away at the San Juan hillsides during the peak years of greed, when the area's population boomed to 10,000. About $5 million was spent just on the 300 miles of elaborate, interconnecting flumes and canals necessary for hydraulic mining on the ridge. Some estimate that $200 million in gold remains in the earth, but ridge people arm themselves (at least verbally) and go after every new corporate mining proposal. Enough is enough, after all.

Despite the historically recent devastation here, there's a wild, untouched feeling about this stretch of northern mine country—steep, rocky ridges, dramatic gorges, dense pine and oak forests, thick underbrush. A strong spirit never dies. Gary Snyder, California's poet laureate under former Governor Jerry Brown, lives, chops wood, and writes here, and sometimes teaches courses concerning the fate of the earth at UC Davis.

And there is regeneration, culturally too. The **North Columbia Schoolhouse Cultural Center** on San Juan Ridge hosts plays, concerts, and storytelling and folk music festivals.

North San Juan

A spot in the road worth a wander, North San Juan mixes gold rush memorials with new accomplishments like the lovingly handcrafted **North San Juan School** built by local people and parents. The long-running Ananda commune near North San Juan, fairly well accepted even by redneck mountain folk, is a notable presence. To the southwest (via Pleasant Valley Rd.) is what's left of **French Corral,** the oldest town on San Juan Ridge, named after a mule pen. The 1878 long-distance telephone line from here to French Corral was the state's first, connecting hydraulic mining centers. That service saved lives in the 1880s, when the upstream English Dam broke after heavy rains and siltation: phone calls spread the warning. Other technological "firsts" here were electric arc lamps and the Burleigh drill.

To the north is **Bullards Bar Reservoir,** a steep-sided recreation lake with campsites reached from this area via either Moonshine or Marysville roads. Wandering the narrow back roads from here into the far northern gold camps is only for those with time to get thoroughly lost.

But if you have the time and inclination, head out in search of **Renaissance Winery,** P.O. Box

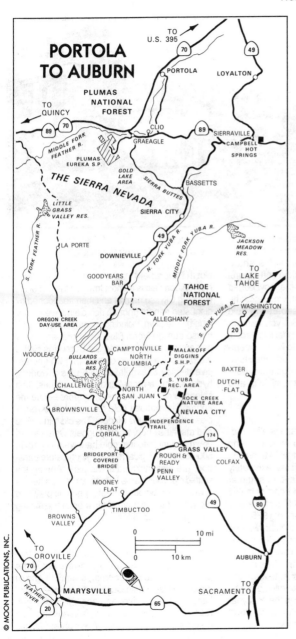

1000, Renaissance 95962, tel. (916) 692-2222, a legend almost before its first wines were sold, in part due to the exquisite Chinese antiques on display. Tours by appointment only.

Oregon Creek

Just north of the bridge over the Yuba River is the turnoff to the Oregon Creek Day Use Area, nice for picnicking and swimming, even some shallow wading. Popular with nude sunbathers. There's a wrong-way covered bridge here: when the English Dam upstream failed in the 1880s, the Oregon Creek Covered Bridge broke loose but didn't break up, whirling around instead in the backwater. When workers hitched it back up to the road, they got it backward.

MALAKOFF DIGGINS

North and then east of Nevada City is Malakoff Diggins State Historic Park, an unforgettable, ecologically horrifying, yet strangely seductive monument reminding one that positive thinking may move mountains, but greed can do it too. Here's the proof—a ghoulish moonscape created by 1870s "high-tech" hydraulic mining.

The Malakoff Mine

Hydraulic mining scoured the area into barren, colorful spires haunted by the lonely spirit of Utah's Bryce Canyon. You can wander below San Juan Ridge along 16 miles of trails cutting through otherworldly terrain. The mine pit itself, once an ancient riverbed, is about one

Modern–day travelers can visit what remains of North Bloomfield, now part of the historic legacy of hydraulic mining preserved at Malakoff Diggins.

square mile in size and 600 feet deep in places, and produced about $5 million in gold. The elements have weathered Malakoff's sharp edges, tinting the exposed rock in soft natural tones. A 1½-mile-long tunnel here, now buried by mud at the bottom of the pit, was once the world's longest "sluice box," separating gold from the gravel and sludge. But you can explore the much smaller Hiller Tunnel it replaced, off to the left near the entrance to North Bloomfield. Other trails in the area include the Humbug, Rock Creek, and South Yuba trails, generally easy walks through grassy hills and forests.

An Environmental Outrage

The North Bloomfield mining case finally eroded hydraulic mining. Outraged farmers in the valley below banded together in 1873 to protest the monumental quantities of silt that alternately clogged downstream waterways in summer and buried their croplands and communities after winter floods. The town of Marysville was flooded due to mining siltation in 1875, and even San Francisco Bay turned as brown and murky as a cup of coffee. Backed by the Southern Pacific Railroad, a powerful valley landowner, the farmers and flatlanders finally won their war. The Federal Anti-Debris Act—banning sediment dumping, not hydraulic mining per se—was passed in 1883, followed in the next year by a sympathetic California Supreme Court opinion which effectively ended water-nozzle land rape in California. After this, the first major legal victory on behalf of the environment in the U.S., the Malakoff Mine closed.

North Bloomfield

North Bloomfield is a ghost town on the site of old Humbug City, so named and then abandoned by disgusted miners (though rich claims were later found). The town, including its large 1872 schoolhouse outside North Bloomfield proper, is now part and parcel of the park. Old **Cummins Hall** is the park's interpretive center, with an impressive display of simulated gold plus a working hydraulic mine model and other exhibits. The saloon is right next to the drug store—note the appropriate popular gold rush-era home remedies on display in the window. The old mine office and machine shop, where nuggets were melted down and molded into gold bars weighing up to 500 pounds (a typical month's yield) before transport, are also included in the park. Among the spiffed-up wood frame homes and shops here is a weathered wooden meeting hall display and monument to the anarchistic men of the mining camps, E Clampus Vitus.

Practicalities

Camp at Malakoff Diggins (30 individual sites, $14, plus group camp, no showers but water and sinks in the bathrooms), or stay in one of three restored, original cabins "in town"—rustic, historically evocative, and only $20 per night, reservations required five days in advance. To reserve campsites in summer, contact Mistix, tel. (800) 444-7275; otherwise just show up.

To reserve a cabin call the park office at (916) 265-2740, at least two months in advance. The park's interpretive center and other exhibits are open daily 10-4:30 in summer, but in other seasons you may have to track down the ranger to get in. For info: Malakoff Diggins State Historic Park, 23579 North Bloomfield Rd., Nevada City 95959, tel. 265-2740. Ask, too, about planning progress for the new, narrow, 21-mile-long state park proposed for the South Yuba River between Malakoff Diggins and Englebright Lake.

INTO THE SIERRA NEVADA

Past North San Juan and the intriguing dance of light and shadow on the canyon walls, Hwy. 49 starts climbing to the northernmost reaches of the gold country, up past Loyalton. Camptonville, just off the highway, with its old-fashioned flower gardens, was once a booming way station. Lester Alan Pelton, the millwright who invented the tangential waterwheel, lived here before moving to Nevada City. Stop by the Tahoe National Forest office here, tel. (916) 288-3231, for camping and recreation information. Special in Camptonville is the cowboy continental **Mayo Restaurant** on Cleveland, the town's main street, tel. (916) 288-3237, with creatively prepared soups, salads, and entrees served in a vintage Western saloon. Open for lunch Mon.-Sat., for dinner Wed.-Sat., for brunch on Sunday.

A Backroads Route

From Camptonville, head into the mountains on Henness Pass Rd., once an immigrant trail connecting Marysville and Nevada's Comstock Lode. This paved road, though narrow, is much less frightening than the Foote Crossing route from Malakoff. Picnic by the river. Very scenic, several campgrounds, a few old gold towns to explore, and if you keep going you'll eventually connect up with Hwy. 89 north of Truckee and Lake Tahoe. Or, from Alleghany head back toward Downieville and Sierra City on Ridge, Pliocene Ridge, and Gallaway roads. Another possibility: take treacherous Mountain Ranch Rd. down into the ravine then snake up to Goodyear's Bar at the confluence of Goodyear's Creek and the north fork of the Yuba River. Today, just a handful of houses whisper the names of long-gone mining camps like Cutthroat Bar, Hoodoo, and Ranse Doddler.

Alleghany

Alleghany's original Sixteen-to-One Mine was the last old-time working gold mine in California.

It closed in the 1960s when a fire almost destroyed the town. But today the mine is again back in business on a small scale. The buildings (and collections of decrepit cars) are tucked into terraced hillsides with winding streets.

If you really want to get away from it all, consider a stay at the **Kenton Mine Lodge** at 3 Foote Crossing Rd., P.O. Box 942, tel. (916) 287-3212 or toll-free (800) 634-2002, an old miners' boarding house with bar, bunkhouse rooms or cabins, and meals served family style in the cookhouse. The Kenton Lodge has an old mine tunnel, ore cart tracks, and stamp mill to explore. Great skiing in winter. Kanaka Creek here (fish, swim, or pan for gold) was named for Hawaiian miners who settled the area. Rates are complex—options range from rooms or cabins without meals to packages including all meals—but everything is a bargain. No children under age 10. Rooms in the main house run $29.95 pp with breakfast ($40 with two meals); cabins with woodburning stoves, private baths, and kitchens are $27.50 pp, or $45 for two, no meals included.

DOWNIEVILLE

A tidy, tiny brick-and-tin-roof town is squeezed into the cool canyon at the confluence of the Yuba and Downie rivers. Locals sit on the storefront porches and watch the tourists go by. Downieville is sleepy these days (with about 500 souls of Sierra County's total 3,500), but was colorful and crazy during the placer boom days after William Downie and his multiracial mining crew panned upriver riches. Nuggets weighing up to 25 pounds were found here in Slug Canyon, so named because gold just waited atop the stream gravel to be found, like coins on a street. A bad, bustling city far from the mainstream, miners had to pay high prices in exchange for their seclusion: eggs were $3 each, whiskey $16 a bottle, and medicinal pills $10 each without advice ($100 with). Prices are a bit more reasonable nowadays. During the gold rush, Downieville was known for its spontaneous sense of justice. One collective citizen action earned national headlines. In 1851 a local dancehall girl fatally stabbed a Scottish miner—in self-defense, she said, since he "pressed his attentions" on her—and was summarily convicted of her crime and lynched from a bridge over the Yuba River, the first woman in California executed by hanging.

Sights

Downieville Heritage Park near the river forks downtown has picnic tables and a rusty outdoor collection of mining mementos (you can pan for gold here, right in town). In the trees near the jailyard of the **Sierra County Courthouse** is the state's only remaining original gallows, used for the first and last time in 1885 to hang convicted murderer James O'Neal. Recently rescued from oblivion with help from the state and the new county sheriff and his Friends of the Gallows (seriously), the **Downieville Gallows** is now refurbished and restored, a state historic monument.

The **Sierra County Museum** on Main St. is a homey hodgepodge of pioneer and mining memorabilia housed in a former Chinese store, gambling hall, and opium den. Open daily in summer, weekends only at the beginning and end of the travel season. (Free, but donations appreciated.) Newspaper hounds please note: the town's *Mountain Messenger* has been published since 1853.

Camping And Accommodations

Camp at the public **Union Flat Campground** about six miles east on Hwy. 49, no showers, tel. (916) 289-3216, or at any of the Forest Service campgrounds near Sierra City and the Gold Lakes area. Or backtrack to the campgrounds clustered near the highway midway between Camptonville and Downieville. The **Carlton Flat camping areas,** one just a mile north of the bridge at Indian Valley, the other on Cal Ida Rd., are undeveloped with untreated drinking water, as are the **Fiddle Creek** and **Rocky Rest** campgrounds—all free. The **Indian Valley** and **Ramshorn campgrounds** have piped water and

pit toilets, no showers. Also in the area are the tiny **Convict Flat** and **Indian Rock picnic areas** (purify water before drinking).

Downieville has a few motels. **Saundra Dyer's Resort and Bed & Breakfast** along the river at the end of River Street (cross the Nevada Street Bridge then turn right), P.O. Box 406, Downieville 95936, tel. (916) 289-3308, is the best bet. The main building is over a century old, and the rest stretch out in all directions. Accommodations include motel-style rooms, some housekeeping cottages, even a small travel trailer with front porch and snow roof. There's a pool here, available only in summer. (In winter, it's enough just to keep the pipes from freezing.) An unusual treat is the opportunity to witness Dyer's dog Baron, a serious-looking Rottweiler, croon a few choruses of "Happy Trails." People love to videotape the performance. ("And if you can't actually come," says the proprietor, "send money.") Rates: $55 and up for two, $70 and up for cottages, sometimes substantially less in the off-season and midweek. Weekly rates available. Top of the line in local cabin competition is secluded **Sierra Shangri-La,** P.O. Box 285, tel. 289-3455, a few miles north of town on a rugged rock ledge above the foaming North Yuba River in narrow, pine-forested Jim Crow Canyon. Potbellied woodstoves in the clean cabins with kitchenettes (some with decks jutting right out over the water), also bed and breakfast units in the pre-World War II fieldstone lodge, $55 and up, off-season rates even a better deal (weekends only, usually, Nov. 1 through Dec., plus March and April). The resort is closed completely in January and February. In the summer all cabins rent by the week, by the day only if space is available (unlikely). Regular visitors usually reserve cabins for summer a year in advance, but call for possible cancellations.

Downtown Dining In Downieville

For Downieville-style fine dining, **Cirino's At The Forks** on Main Street is the place, tel. (916) 289-3749 or toll-free (800) 540-2099, kissing cousin to Cirino's in Nevada City and serving essentially the same Italian menu. Open daily for lunch, for dinner Wed.-Sun. only. The **Downieville Diner**, tel. 289-3616, just down the street and also on the Downie River, is the best place around for breakfast, from omelettes to home-made muffins and Texas toast (French toast made with thick American-style white bread), and a darn good choice for American-style lunch and early dinner. Salads, homemade soups, and sandwiches share the bill of fare with a few dinner entrees: Southern fried chicken, chicken fried steak, New York steaks, roast beef. Open daily 7 a.m.-7 p.m. during much of the year, closed at 4 p.m. (no dinners) in winter. And if you can manage it, try a decadent Downieville dessert, like the Kahlua mocha mousse pie ("as if you've Died and Gone to Chocolate"). **The Downieville Bakery** in the old stone Craycroft building at the Hwy. 49 bridge is locally popular for baked goods, also homemade soups and very good sandwiches.

SIERRA CITY

Another tiny mountain town, the kind of place where fathers play football with their small sons right on the highway on a Saturday morning in autumn. Sierra City is the reputed birthplace of The Ancient and Honorable Order of E Clampus Vitus, hog Latin meaning "from the handshake comes life." In the 19th century, avalanches were the main hazard in Sierra City: crushing snow slides flattened the town in 1852, 1888, and 1889 and again in 1952. Otherwise, the steep rocky cliffs have been kind to the local economy. The Sierra Buttes Mine was richly veined with high-grade gold; one nugget found here weighed 141 pounds. There's an impressive collection of Sierra City gold at the U.S. Mint's museum in San Francisco.

The Old Kentucky Mine

Definitely stop by **Sierra County Historical Park** at the old Kentucky Mine just north of town. Thanks to the efforts of Sierra County citizenry, this old hardrock mine is now a beautifully restored historical park, its original machinery still intact. Note the intrusive modern amphitheater, then step into the excellent museum (small admission), a rebuilt version of Sierra City's old Bigelow House hotel. Best of all are the tours of the mine itself and the stamp mill. The system here included a Pelton wheel, an air compressor for dynamite drilling, and a mammoth mill operation with jaw-like ore crushers and stamps. New and well attended are summer concerts and performances, from cowboy poetry and

E CLAMPUS VITUS

Members of a gold rush fraternity established in 1857, the Clampers were and are a parody of brotherhoods like the Masons and Odd Fellows. The organization's stated purpose was assisting and comforting orphans and "widders"—especially the latter. In addition to this vital public service, and the many worthwhile community activities the group actually *did* support, Clampers spent most of their time holding drunken initiation ceremonies and thinking up overblown titles to recognize all members' equality. Throughout the gold country, E Clampus Vitus met in their "Halls of Comparative Ovations" (the Latin motto over the door meaning "I believe because it is absurd").

Revived in San Francisco in 1931 by historian Carl Wheat, E Clampus Vitus thrives today, its primary modern mission marking historical sites and otherwise bringing early California history to life. But the order's debauched traditions continue to this day, with drunken annual celebrations still sometimes causing consternation for Sierra City citizenry.

opera to jazz and swing. The park's open daily from Memorial Day through Sept., 10-5, and usually on weekends through October. For info, call (916) 862-1310.

Practicalities

Camp at public campgrounds near here or head toward Gold Lakes, most quite basic. Just two miles west of town is the free **Loganville Campground.** Just east and closest to town is the larger **Wild Plum Campground** off Hwy. 49 on Wild Plum Rd. along Haypress Creek; water but no showers, $6 per site. Past the Gold Lakes turnoff on the way to Sierraville are the **Sierra, Chapman Creek,** and **Yuba Pass** national forest campgrounds along the north fork of the Yuba River, open May until mid-Oct., no reservations, $4; call (916) 289-3216 for information.

The **Mountain Shadows** cafe serves breakfast and lunch. Try **Herrington's Sierra Pines Lodge,** P.O. Box 235, Sierra City 96125, tel. (916) 862-1151, for fresh trout, homemade bread and other baked goods. (The nice motel here has rooms and a few cabins.) Or stop for a meal at the **Sierra Buttes Inn** on the highway,

P.O. Box 320, tel. 862-1300, open for breakfast and lunch Fri.-Mon., dinner daily, American fare with an intriguing salad bar presentation. Rooms in this century-old tin-roofed clapboard hotel are $25 and up (shared bath) or $40 and up with private bath. Even better, if it's open, is pizza or Italian fare at Carlo's Ristorante inside the lovely **Busch & Heringlake Inn** (see "Area Bed and Breakfast Inns" below). The **Sardine Lakes Resort,** tel. 862-1196, and **Packer Lake Lodge,** tel. 862-1221, in the Lakes Basin area serve great dinners (by reservation, during summer only) if you're in the mood for a drive. An all-time favorite but even farther away is the **Gray Eagle Lodge** on Gold Lake Rd. in Blairsden, tel. 836-2511 or toll-free in Northern California (800) 635-8778, noted for its fresh fish and family-style table service (reservations necessary). Sardine Lakes and Gray Eagle also offer nice cabins, breakfast and dinner included at Gray Eagle.

This stretch of Hwy. 49 through the Lakes Basin area features a number of rustic and quasi-rustic resorts, though most are closed during winter. (For a fairly complete listing beyond Sierra County, contact the Plumas County chamber office, see "Area Information and Recreation" below.) An unusual delight and definitely secluded is the **Salmon Lake Lodge,** P.O. Box 121, tel. (415) 771-0150 (the reservations phone in San Francisco), a resort in Sierra County's high country that has been in continuous operation since the 1880s: rustic cabins and tent cabins, bring your own grub, kitchen supplies, bedding. Cabin rates include the use of resort boats. To get there, park at the east end of Salmon Lake (see "Lakes Basin" following); a barge takes you across. Write for current rates.

Area Bed And Breakfast Inns

A new choice for a pleasant stay in town is the **Busch & Heringlake Inn** on the highway, P.O. Box 68, Sierra City 96125, tel. (916) 862-1501, in a beautifully renovated brick and stone building once home to Wells Fargo, Western Union, and the local general store. (Appreciate the fabulous French doors facing the street and, inside, the huge woodburning heater and A.C. Busch safe.) Downstairs is the inn's restaurant, Carlo's Ristorante, sometimes in flux as far as hours but usually open for dinner Wed.-Sun. and serving wonderful pizza and simple but so-

phisticated meals with an Italian emphasis. The four bed and breakfast rooms are upstairs, cozy and contemporary with modern appointments and elegant country-style touches (all have private baths; two have Jacuzzis), along with a guest kitchen and a comfortable common sitting room. Rates: $75-110.

The **High Country Inn** some distance north of town at Bassetts and the junction with Gold Lakes Rd., HCR 2, Box 7, Sierra City 96125, tel. (916) 862-1530, is a modern mountain home smack dab in an astounding setting. From the deck and some of the rooms—particularly the second-story suite, which also features a woodstove and spacious vanity and bathroom with huge antique tub—the view of the Sierra Buttes is spectacular, and the sound of rushing river water and wind in the aspens is almost hypnotic. The folks here are well-informed about the area and happy to share their knowledge. The food is fabulous, gourmet fare in every respect. Rooms all feature private baths and cozy, homey features, and guests also enjoy lolling around in front of the downstairs family room fireplace. A great escape. The inn is open year-round, the area increasingly popular for mountain biking and winter cross-country skiing and usually accessible even in severe weather, since Hwy. 49 is open when I-80 is not. Rates: 70-110.

Wonderful, too, are the **White Sulphur Springs Ranch** near Clio and the **Clover Valley Millhouse** in Loyalton. See below for information on both.

LAKES BASIN

Beyond the Kentucky Mine, turn north at Bassetts onto Gold Lakes Highway. The Sierra Buttes area is a dramatic, seemingly unspoiled glacial landscape and a locally popular spot for fishing, swimming, hiking, and backpacking in summer, for cross-country skiing in winter. On the way to Gold Lake proper you'll pass Sand Pond (good swimming), Sardine Lake, and others. Gold Lake is a reminder of Donner Party guide Caleb Greenwood's tall tale of a lake in the Sierra with nuggets so large and plentiful that pioneer children played with them like marbles. Modern-day Gold Lake is easy to reach and a gem in its own right, with nearby waterfalls. From the Gold Lakes area head to Graeagle and nearby Johnsville (turn at Road A14), part of the **Plumas-Eureka State Park,** a ghost town mining camp in steep canyon country.

Plumas-Eureka State Park

One of those almost-undiscovered outdoor gems, Plumas-Eureka State Park amid the thick pines and firs offers good hiking, fine camping, a ski tour trail in winter, even limited, low-key downhill ski facilities. Formerly the territory of the Sierra Buttes Mining Co., one of the area's old mining trams served as the world's first ski lift when snowbound miners organized, promoted, and wagered on high-speed downhill ski competitions.

At Plumas-Eureka proper, the old Mohawk Mill and other mining outbuildings have been restored. Nearby is the park's excellent interpretive center and museum, a former two-story miner's bunkhouse with mining technology, natural history, and skiing history displays. Open daily in summer. On Saturdays, tour **Moriarty House,** restored and furnished to reflect 1890s mining camp domesticity.

The park features several short hiking trails (good views from the top of Eureka Peak) plus access to the remote northern section and backcountry. The campground is about a mile downhill from the interpretive center via a narrow, winding paved road. Open only seasonally, 67 family campsites, hot showers, tables, and fire rings, $16. Popular, so reserve in advance through Mistix, tel. (800) 444-7275. For more information, contact: Plumas-Eureka State Park, 310 Johnsville Rd., Blairsden 96103, tel. (916) 836-2380.

To La Porte

A worthwhile side adventure, at least when the roads are passable, is the backroads (dirt road) route from Plumas-Eureka to **Little Grass Valley Reservoir** and the one-time mining town of La Porte, the town with the distinction of inventing the sport of downhill ski racing. Not counting the campsites at the little lake, best bet is the historic old **Union Hotel** on Main, tel. (916) 675-2525, with rooms from $41, also restaurant and bar. Swimming, water-skiing, hiking, and fishing are popular in warm weather. In winter, the road around the reservoir is great for cross-country skiing; more challenging, though, is Lexington Hill a few miles south of town off Quincy/La Porte Road. Trails are unmarked and ungroomed, and snowmobilers like the area too.

Area Information And Recreation

For a map and guide to the Lakes Basin area, as well as recreation and other information, contact the **Plumas County Chamber of Commerce,** 500 Jackson St., P.O. Box 11018, Quincy 95971, tel. (916) 283-6345 or toll-free (800) 326-2247. Ask here, at the Sierra County Historical Park and Museum, and at area businesses for current information on upcoming concerts and unusual annual events such as the challenging **Downieville Downhill** mountain bike race and the **Tour de Portola** from Graeagle to Bassetts. Another good source for recreation information is the **Tahoe National Forest Ranger District office** in Sierraville, tel. 994-3401. For **guided llama backpack trips,** contact Rock and Cindy Wood at tel. 582-0743. The **Gold Lake Pack Station & Stables** at Lakes Basin, tel. 836-0940, offers guided horseback rides and pack trips in both the Gold Lake and Bucks Lake areas (tel. 283-2532 for Bucks Lake). For more detailed information and to make reservations well in advance, contact the sponsoring **Reid Horse & Cattle Co., Inc.** at 1540 Chandler Rd., Quincy 95971, tel. 283-1147.

Practicalities: Camping, Accommodations, And Food

You can't camp at most of the lakes, but there are campgrounds nearby. The public **Sardine Lake Campground** is 1½ miles north of Bassetts along Gold Lake Hwy., then a half mile southwest along Sardine Lake Rd., no showers. Some supplies are available at the **Sardine Lake Lodge** and marina.

Two miles north of Bassetts is **Salmon Creek Campground,** no showers. A few miles farther north is **Shag Lake Campground** (camp free, undesignated sites, purify your drinking water) then several other free campgrounds a short distance west along Packer Lake Rd. (all at about 6,000 feet): **Diablo Camping Area, Berger Campground,** and **Packsaddle Camping Area** (as the name suggests, pack and saddle animals permitted). For information (no reservations), call (916) 289-3216.

If you're just passing through and heading toward Graeagle or Plumas-Eureka State Park, consider staying at the **White Sulfur Springs Ranch** on Hwy. 89 just south of Clio proper, P.O. Box 136, Clio 96106, tel. (916) 836-2837. This is an old stage stop on the meadow edge of

Mohawk Valley, now a bed and breakfast with antiques in the attic, even a spring-fed swimming pool, $70-140. A very special place in an idyllic setting. For more nearby inns, see "Sierra City" above, and "North From Tahoe" in the preceding chapter.

EAST ON HIGHWAY 49

Sierraville
A tiny town beyond Yuba Pass in fertile Sierra Valley first "discovered" by the legendary black mountain man Jim Beckwourth, the Sierraville area was a breadbasket for the mines. There's a **Tahoe National Forest office** here; stop by or call (916) 994-3401 for camping and recreation information. Or camp about five miles southeast at either **Cottonwood Campground** or **Cold Creek Campground,** or head toward Truckee from Sierraville and the **Upper** and **Lower Little Truckee campgrounds.** From Sierraville, head northwest on Hwy. 89 to Graeagle, Quincy, and the volcanic wonders of Lassen National Park, or south to Truckee and Lake Tahoe.

Loyalton
Stop in this mountain ranching town for a picnic at the **Loyalton City Park,** complete with tennis courts, playgrounds, barbecues. Visit the **Sierra Valley Museum,** open from just before Memorial Day through mid-Oct., Wed.- Sun. noon-4:30 p.m., free but donations appreciated. The museum has an eclectic display of memorabilia from 19th-century farms, depression-era glassware, even Odd Fellows vestments from an early local temple. The **Country Cookin' Cafe** downtown on Hwy. 49, tel. (916) 993-1162, serves up just what the sign says— steak and eggs and omelettes for breakfast, good burgers, soups, and sandwiches for lunch, and the extra treat of local artwork (for sale) displayed on the walls. Reasonable for bed and breakfasts is the **Clover Valley Mill House** on Railroad at S. 1st St., P.O. Box 928, Loyalton 96118, tel. 993-4819, a surprising find in the midst of wilderness. This 1906 Colonial has three rooms sharing a bath-and-a-half, one suite with a private bath and sitting room and its own sundeck. Full breakfast served inside or out on the deck. Good advice, too, on what to do and see in the area. Rates: $45-105.

GRASS VALLEY

Some people, including many who live here, think of Grass Valley as a redneck alternative to the effete egghead ambience of neighboring Nevada City. It's hometown working-class America, complete with fast food, tire repair shops, and other ungainly development, but Grass Valley has a charm all its own, especially downtown, where a sidewalk stroll takes you straight into the '50s (of both this century and the last).

HISTORY

In 1850 George McKnight discovered gold-laced quartz here, and Grass Valley, a company town of former copper miners and their kin from England's Cornwall, quickly became a hardrock mining capital. It's estimated that nearly a billion dollars in gold was deep-mined in and around Grass Valley during the gold rush. The high cost of underground mining meant capital investment and consolidation: the Idaho-Maryland, North Star, and Empire mines soon became the area's main operations. The Empire Mine, now a state park but once the largest of these 19th-century mining conglomerates— some say the richest gold mine in the U.S.— operated profitably until the 1950s.

Some Colorful Characters

Among Grass Valley's famous and infamous was Amos Delano, a Wells Fargo agent and very funny writer better known as "Old Block," a descendant (he said) of the Block-Head family. Also creative: inventor and early amateur aeronautical engineer Lyman Gilmore, who locals say launched a successful airplane here over a year prior to the Wright brothers' first flights. Isaac Owen, the Methodist minister who preached Grass Valley's first sermon, later moved on to the Santa Clara Valley, where he founded the College of the Pacific. Josiah Royce was born in Grass Valley, attended Harvard University, studied philosophy with William James, and later became James's academic successor.

William Bourn of Empire Mine fame survived the boom and bust years to become one of the wealthiest men in California. He also owned the Spring Valley Water Company in San Francisco and the San Francisco Gas Company; besides his stone lodge and expansive estate in Grass Valley, he built beautiful homes in San Francisco's Pacific Heights district, the Filoli estate in Woodside, and the huge stone winery in Napa Valley now owned by the Christian Brothers.

SIGHTS

Grass Valley Walking Tour

None of the boom town's original buildings survived the hellish two-hour fire of 1855, one of the gold country's worst, but the surrounding hillsides were quickly clearcut for lumber to rebuild the town. Take a walk around town for a glimpse of the colorful past: brick buildings, wooden awnings, and old gas streetlamps. The **Lola Montez House** at 248 Mill St. (a replica of the original building condemned and demolished in 1975) now houses the chamber of commerce and a small one-room museum with some of Lola's belongings. The town's first election was held here in November of 1850. Two doors down at 238 Mill is **Lotta Crabtree's House** (now private apartments), where Lola Montez taught the six-year-old redhead to dance and sing.

The **Grass Valley Public Library** is down the street at 207 Mill, built in 1916 with Carnegie funds on the site of Josiah Royce's birthplace. Mark Twain slept at the impressive **Holbrooke Hotel** at 212 W. Main Street. Originally two separate buildings, later destroyed by fire, the saloon was rebuilt immediately (gold country priorities) and the later hotel incorporated it, so now the hotel has two separate bars. The **Purcell House** behind the Holbrooke at 119 N. Church St. was once living quarters for the adjacent livery stable. At the end of Main St. is Lyman Gilmore's airfield (now a school), where he reportedly flew his 20-horsepower steam-powered aircraft on or before May 15, 1901— more than 1½ years before the Wright brothers took off from Kitty Hawk.

The **Biblical Gardens** at 16343 Auburn Rd., tel. (916) 272-1363, offer picnic tables and steep hills (wear walking shoes) and a bit of botany with a biblical theme. Open May 1 to mid-October. Donation.

Empire Mine State Historic Park

English miners from Cornwall, called "cousin Jacks," worked this area on Gold Hill, one of the richest and oldest hardrock mines in the state. Closed in 1956 and now a 784-acre state park at 10791 E. Empire St., the Empire Mine is easy to find by following the signs around town. In business for over 100 years, the Empire's 367 miles of tunnels reluctantly yielded millions of ounces of gold; it's estimated that four times as much is still there, too expensive to dig out. Near the park's entrance is a model of the underground tunnel maze.

The **Bourn "cottage"** on the hill, an elegant epistle to wealth tucked into the estate's impressive gardens, was designed by San Francisco architect Willis Polk and built from mine tailings and stone, panelled inside with hand-rubbed heart redwood, and finished with leaded stained-glass windows. Take the tour and appreciate the original furnishings. The fragrant roses in the formal garden outside are pre-1929 varieties; there's also a gardener's cottage, carriage house, and shingled clubhouse for guests built in 1905.

See the mining and geology displays at the **visitors center** and museum, also a small book and gift shop. On your way in or out, stop for a look at the Rowe Mine headframe near the parking lot—a gallows-like contraption used as an elevator to ferry men and minerals up and down mine shafts. Down the hill are the well-preserved mine offices, machine shop, retort room and furnaces, and hoist house. Most of the mine shafts are now flooded, so forget about an underground hike. You can get a feeling for life in the tunnels by taking the stairs down into the one open shaft as far as it goes. The **Hardrock Trail,** a 2½-mile walk through the forest past mining relics and old shafts, loops up into the hills for a peek at the Betsy, Daisy Hill, and Prescott mine remains.

The park is open year-round, 10-5 daily. Films and slide shows are offered regularly, tours of the "cottage" and grounds at 1 p.m., of the mine at 2 p.m.. (Hours and schedules for all events vary considerably with the seasons, and the annual budget and staffing decisions made in Sacramento, so call ahead.) For information,

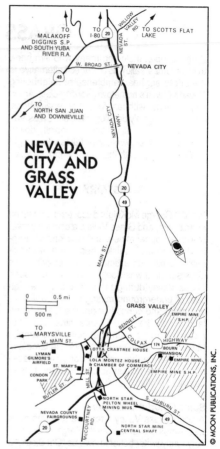

contact: Empire Mine State Historic Park, 10791 E. Empire St., Grass Valley 95945, tel. (916) 273-8522 or 273-7714. Small admission fee.

North Star Mining Museum

The mine's old power station on Allison Ranch Rd., near the intersection of Mill St. and McCourtney Rd, is now a local historical museum, unfortunately open only during the tourist season. On display here is a 30-foot-diameter, 10-ton Pelton wheel, the world's largest, used to harness water power and later to generate power for the mines with air compressors. Also here are displays of changing mine technology, mine models, old photos, dioramas. You can pick your way down to Wolf Creek for a picnic on the rocks, then take a look at the Cornish water pump, a device which made pit mining possible. The museum is open 11 a.m.-5 p.m. daily (except Mon.) during the travel season, tel. (916) 273-4255. Small fee. The docents do an exceptional job. Farther down Allison Ranch Rd. are the massive, eerie ruins of a 60-stamp mill, part of North Star Mine Number 2.

Grass Valley Museum

A restored 1865 school and orphanage behind imposing brick walls at the corner of Church and Chapel streets, the Old Mount St. Mary's Academy (and St. Joseph's Chapel) includes the Grass Valley Museum. The grounds themselves are inviting, and inside museum exhibits include period memorabilia, music room, parlor, doctor's office, even fine old lace and a collection of glass slippers, all on the convent's second floor. Downstairs is a thrift shop. Fairly new is the **Gold Country Fine Arts Center.** Also here is the **Pacific Library,** a collection of 10,000 old scientific and historical books dating from the 16th century. Call owner Peter Vander Pas for an escorted look-see; books can't be checked out. Museum open June 1 to Oct. 1, call for current hours: tel. (916) 272-8188 or 272-5154. Admission free, donations appreciated.

ACCOMMODATIONS

Camping

RVers can camp at the **Nevada County Fairgrounds** off McCourtney Rd., tel. (916) 273-6217, $12. Otherwise, the closest camping is at **Scotts Flat Lake** to the northeast (see "Nevada City" above). Very pretty area but crowded in summer, so call ahead. Another possibility is **Greenhorn Campground** at Rollins Lake about 11 miles south on Hwy. 174, tel. 272-6100; pit toilets, solar showers, picnic tables. Or camp free at **Englebright Reservoir** north of Smartville, off Hwy. 20 heading west. Mostly a lowland boating lake, you'll need to rent a skiff at Skippers Cove Marina to reach the campsites.

Area Motels

Grass Valley has most of the area's motels, though most cheaper ones have essentially become low-income public housing. **Holiday Lodge** at 1221 E. Main, tel. (916) 273-4406, has a spa, sauna, and swimming pool, rooms $38-50. A couple of miles south of town at 13363 Hwy. 49, the **Golden Chain Resort,** tel. 273-7279, has the usual amenities plus putting green. Fairly reasonable at $48-58, much less in winter. Or try the **Best Western Gold Country Inn,** 11972 Sutton Way, tel. 273-1393, with pool and spa, kitchens and kitchenettes, and close to the local bus stop, $49 and up.

A Fine Hotel: The Holbrooke

At the other extreme is the very fine **Holbrooke Hotel and Restaurant** downtown at 212 W. Main St., tel. (916) 273-1353 or toll-free (800) 933-7077—seasoned elegance, rich green colors and fine wood interior, bar, and a restaurant. Stay in most of these authentic gold rush rooms (named for luminaries and famous lunatics who once snored here, including roustabouts like Mark Twain and Ulysses S. Grant) for the price of a mid-range motel elsewhere. There are 17 units in the hotel itself, 11 more in the Purcell House annex, all recently refurbished as part of the hotel's complete restoration. Now this historic landmark is one of a few truly fine gold country hotels. Regular rates run $66-145 (veranda rooms and suites are highest, as are weekend rates), $50-115 from January through March. Because Main Street is Grass Valley's main drag, and because the Golden Gate Saloon downstairs is the best bar in town, light sleepers should request accommodations away from both.

Bed And Breakfasts

For casual artsy surroundings, try the **Swan-Levine House** at 328 S. Church, Grass Valley 94945, tel. (916) 272-1873, home away from home for the artistic soul. Rooms in this 1880 Queen Anne Victorian run $55-85. More elegant in the Victorian mode is the **Golden Ore House,** 448 S. Auburn, tel. 272-6870 or 272-6872, rooms $70-85. Finest of all, though, is the legendary **Murphy's Inn,** once the personal estate of North Star and Idaho mine owner Edward Coleman. Located just off S. Church at 318 Neal St., tel. 273-6873, the inn has large opulent rooms, many with subtle Victorian floral motifs. Outside are exquisite gardens, a sunporch topiary, and a towering 2,000-year-old Sierra big tree just above the large outdoor deck

the Bourn "cottage"
at Empire Mine
State Historic Park

KIM WEIR

and swimming spa. Breakfast is a feast, with fresh juices and fruits sharing center stage with egg dishes, Belgian waffles, and other house specialties. Rates: $75-125. Fun too, and also close to downtown, is **Annie Horan's,** 415 W. Main, tel. 272-2418, with antique furnishings from around the globe, rates $80 and up.

FOOD

Basic Good Food

A modest local landmark and legendary among Grass Valley's cheaper eateries is cozy brick-and-oak **Tofanelli's,** 302 W. Main St., tel. (916) 273-9927; breakfast and lunch every day, dinner Mon.-Friday. Every breakfast you can imagine is on the menu, or dream up your own egg specialty with their design-your-own omelettes. Sandwiches, salads, and lots of burger choices, including veggie burgers, also a nice selection of teas and desserts. Good dinner specials and even more reasonable "early-bird" dinners. Open Mon.-Fri. 7 a.m.-8:30 p.m, Sat. 8 a.m.-2 p.m., Sun. 9-2.

The hole-in-the-wall **Gold Star Cafe** across the way at 207 W. Main, tel. (916) 477-1523, is another great find for vegetarians and whole-food fans, open daily for breakfast and lunch. Formerly the Aldebaran Cafe, the Gold Star serves great fare every morning, from breakfast crepes and ollalaberry buttermilk pancakes to homemade sausage—even genuine maple syrup. Despite an extensive menu, there are numerous daily specials, perhaps fresh crab and artichoke baked eggs, or a mushroom-cheese omelette topped with scallions, or croissant French toast. Fascinating sandwiches and such at lunch, including the all-star tofu tempeh stir-fry. Desserts, too, are wonderful, from the chocolate walnut pie to cheesecake topped with ollalaberry sauce. A nice touch with the check: a star-shaped butter cookie.

Peppers nearby at 151 Mill St. (almost invisible inside a historic building and easy to miss), tel. 272-7780, is also a great gustatory hideaway—a soft, cool, and uncluttered restaurant dishing up a fresh approach to Southwest and Mexican fare. Lunch features homemade tamales, chiles rellenos, burritos, tacos and tostadas, even chimichangas, but everything authentically spiced, down to the brown mole sauce and both red and green El Yucatan salsa on every table. Look for more of the same at dinner (larger portions) plus surprises like Southwest calamari and the prawns Guillermo. Open for lunch Mon.-Sat., for dinner daily.

If you're heading that way anyway, stop off at the **Happy Apple Kitchen,** 10 miles south of town on Hwy. 174 in Chicago Park, tel. (916) 273-2822, for great salads, sandwiches, burgers, and other simple lunches. On a cold day, cozy up to the fireplace for some unforgettable desserts, or get a treat for takeout. Open 9:30 a.m.-4 p.m. Mon.-Sat., closed Sundays.

Pasties: Historical Fast Food

In Grass Valley, sample the local specialty: Cornish "pasties," hot turnover-like pies with various spicy meat and vegetable fillings favored by early miners. Stop by **Mrs. Dubblebee's** tidy white wood frame shop next to the Veteran's Memorial at 251-C S. Auburn St., tel. (916) 272-7700, for the best (also drinks and desserts and a front porch for passing the time). Another good choice is **King Richard's Pasties** near the freeway at 217 Colfax, tel. 273-0286, which also serves fruit turnovers and other picnic packings. **Marshall's** pasties at 203 Mill St., tel. 272-2844, are also good, less spicy, "like eating a piece of heaven," according to one fan.

Fine Dining And Fancier Places

The **Holbrooke Hotel Restaurant,** 212 W. Main St., tel. (916) 273-1353, is excellent for continental and American lunches and dinners (written up in *Bon Appetit,* no less), also a famous weekend brunch. Popular on weekends, reservations a must. Lunch features pasta, salads, some exceptional sandwiches, and unusual choices like chicken pesto and a spinach omelette. If you pass up the onion rings, you might have room for a piece of the Holbrooke's locally famous Chocolate Hazelnut Cake. Dinner entrees are dressed up with some unique sauces and garnishes and include salmon, prawns, rack of lamb, tenderloin of pork, steaks, chicken dishes, blackened prime rib, plus pastas for vegetarians. Weather permitting, dine out on the patio. Open for lunch weekdays, for dinner Mon.-Sat., and for brunch on Sunday.

Another contender in the fine food sweeps is the **Main Street Cafe & Bar** just across the street from the Holbrooke at 213 W. Main, tel. (916) 477-6000—contemporary and casual, with lunch selections from Warm Thai Peanut Salad and Madras Chicken to pastas, dinner choices from Main Street Mixed Grill to New Zealand Rack of Lamb and Ginger Prawns and Scallops. Unusual appetizers include wild boar sausage and tempura veggies. Good here, too, is the long list of coffee drinks. Open for lunch Mon.-Sat., for dinner daily. New too is **The Stewart House** on the corner of Bank and Stewart, 124 Bank St., tel. (916) 477-MENU or toll-free (800) 464-MENU, a gracious 1880s Queen Anne with good food in a casual yet dignified setting. Lunch choices include chicken or seafood salads, pasta, sandwiches, and burgers. Fresh fish and seafood star at dinner, sharing the bill of fare with pastas, steaks, and chick-

en entrees. Open for lunch and High Tea on weekdays, for dinner every night except Sunday.

EVENTS AND INFORMATION

Events

Show up in mid-April (and at other times) for **Living History Days** at Empire Mine State Park. In June, there's the **Cornish Miners' Picnic** at the Empire Mine. Another major June event, on Father's Day weekend, is the **Grass Valley Bluegrass Festival** at the Nevada County Fairgrounds here, tel. (916) 622-5691, three days of virtually nonstop music from the nation's bluegrass bluebloods. The California Bluegrass Association sponsors two other bluegrass festivals in the area, one in August and another over Labor Day weekend.

Incidentally, most of Nevada City's famous **Music in the Mountains** June tune festival (see "Nevada City" above) actually happens here in Grass Valley at the fairgrounds and at St. Joseph's Hall at Church and Chapel streets: orchestras, chamber music, and an outdoor "pops" concert. In September is the **Nevada County Fair,** with the Logger's Olympics, country-western music till your ears bleed, a rodeo, even a destruction derby. In December there's the **Cornish Christmas Street Faire,** fun, especially if it's been snowing.

Information And Services

The **Nevada County Chamber of Commerce** at the rebuilt Lola Montez home, 248 Mill St., Grass Valley 95945, local tel. (916) 273-4667, toll-free within California (800) 752-6222, or toll-free from elsewhere in the U.S. (800) 521-2075, is very helpful: maps, walking tour guide, current events, accommodations and eateries, other info. The **Tahoe National Forest** Nevada City Ranger District office, is at 12012 Sutton Way, tel. (916) 273-1371. **Mark Sports** across the street at 12105 Sutton, tel. 272-4498, is the place for camping, backpacking, and other outdoor supplies, including rentals.

For **Nevada County History Tours** of both Grass Valley and Nevada City, and for reasonably priced gold panning expeditions, stop by or call the Holiday Lodge at 1221 E. Main St., tel. (916) 273-4406, or contact guide Doss Thornton, tel. 272-4552 or (800) 445-GOLD.

NEAR GRASS VALLEY

Rough And Ready

Once a wild mining camp founded by Mexican War veterans remembering General Zachary "Rough and Ready" Taylor, this town seceded from the Union during the Civil War to protest a miners' tax. But the "Great Republic of Rough and Ready," population 3,000, lasted only from April 7, 1850, until the 4th of July—when latent patriotism erupted and Old Glory waved once again. The town is now bypassed by Hwy. 20, so head west on W. Main St., which becomes the Rough and Ready Highway.

Center of community activity is the Rough and Ready Grange Hall, built in 1854. The old school and blacksmith shop still stand, as does the Old Toll House, now an antique shop. The post office, once in the old Rough and Ready Hotel, now has its own building. On the last Sunday in June is the town's **Secession Day** revival. For info, contact the volunteer-staffed Rough and Ready Chamber of Commerce, P.O. Box 801, Rough and Ready 95975, tel. (916) 273-8897.

The Bridgeport Covered Bridge And Environs

North off Hwy. 20 via Pleasant Valley Rd. (or south from North San Juan) is the shingle-sided Bridgeport Covered Bridge stretching across the south fork of the Yuba. This is one of the longest single-span covered bridges in the U.S., a 233-foot length of timber, iron bolts, and braces. In regular use from 1862 to 1971, the bridge is now a state historic monument. (Good swimming below it, near the trail.)

Smartville, named not for the locals' collective intelligence but after the proprietor of the town's old hotel, was a vigorous burg during the days of hydraulic mining. Ruins of the old Wells Fargo building are just about all that remain of **Timbuctoo.** The **Penn Valley** area, once called the "pantry of the mines," is still primarily small farm and ranch land; there's a big rodeo here in April. For info, contact the Penn Valley Chamber of Commerce, P.O. Box 604, Penn Valley 95946, tel. (916) 432-1104.

THE MUSEUM OF ANCIENT AND MODERN ART (MAMA)

Worth looking into in Penn Valley is the Museum of Ancient and Modern Art, located in the Wildwood Business Center, one mile north of Hwy. 20 at 11392 Pleasant Valley Rd., P.O. Box 975, Penn Valley 95946, tel. (916) 432-3080. MAMA's mainstay is a collection of Western Asiatic artifacts excavated at Amarna in the 1920s and '30s under the auspices of the Egypt Exploration Society. Masks, pottery, and statues here also come from Greece, Rome, Alexandria, Carthage, Mesopotamia, Assyria, Sumer, and other significant sites of antiquity. Also here is an impressive collection of African masks and statues from 20 tribes and eight countries. Appropriate to its location in the gold country is the museum's collection of ancient gold jewelry, examples from Neolithic to historical times, many of the more spectacular pieces part of the Theodora Van Runkel Collection of Ancient Gold.

The art here includes works on paper spanning the 15th to 20th centuries, from an extensive and exquisite collection of Rembrandt etchings to works from many schools, including Manet, Renoir, Goya, Picasso, Chagall, Miro, and Matisse. Major exhibits change every few weeks. Also at home at MAMA: historical art books which document the history of printing as well as art.

The museum also supports research, cataloging, documentation, and conservation/preservation programs related to its collection. Donations of art and money are welcome. A tax-exempt nonprofit educational organization, MAMA raises funds primarily from its monthly Fine Art and Collectibles Benefit Auction and occasional Black Tie Auctions. The museum also sells books and educational toys through its gift shop, and offers art education classes, art collecting classes, and free Saturday morning art workshops for children.

The Museum of Ancient and Modern Art is open daily 10-5, until 7 p.m. on Saturdays. Docent-led tours are available for groups. Admission is free.

(top, left) evidence of glaciation in Yosemite National Park (Kim Weir); (top, right) Vernal Fall in Yosemite National Park (Keith S. Walklet); (above) Devil's Postpile National Monument (Kim Weir); (following page) the Palace of Fine Arts at night (Kerrick James, San Francisco Convention and Visitors Bureau)

AUBURN AND VICINITY

Hill-hugging Auburn, once a tent city called North Fork Dry Diggins, then Wood's Dry Diggins, was one of the first towns in the gold country. In the spring of 1848 Frenchman Claude Chana, a friend of James Marshall, found three gold nuggets here while panning in the north fork of the American River. Auburn today has a small Old Town, a homey downtown, shady old streets lined with Victorian homes, and some fine restaurants. The Auburn *Journal* has published regularly since 1852, its longevity (and the town's) assured by the construction of the transcontinental railroad through here.

One of the big construction issues these days is the controversial proposal to complete the long-stalled Auburn Dam on the American River. (We need the jobs, say some locals, and more water and down-river flood protection. It's a boondoggle and ecological travesty, say environmentalists.) Another issue is suburbia: Sacramento-style sprawl is fast approaching and the population mushrooming. The town has grown up around Hwy. 49 but is also bisected by I-80: friendly little Auburn seems doomed to become tract homes squished between a water-filled canyon and an ever-faster and -wider freeway.

Downtown
And Old Town

Downtown Auburn, the business district along Lincoln Way, is distinctly Midwestern; visitors feel more like neighbors than suckered tourists. Old Town, a national landmark, is nearby but separate, a five-square-block area at the intersection of Lincoln and Sacramento streets. The stately **Placer County Courthouse** on Lincoln, its impressive arcaded dome looming above Old Town, was built in 1849 entirely of local materials. The town's volunteer fire department was established in 1852, the state's oldest, but the odd four-story, red-and-white **Hook and Ladder Company Firehouse** in Old Town was built in 1893. Inside is California's first motorized fire engine. Antique hunters like the area for its antiquities and junk

shops. Take a peek inside the **Shanghai Bar** on Washington, Auburn's oldest and almost a museum.

Area Museums

The very fine **Gold Country Museum** is at the fairgrounds, 1273 High St., tel. (916) 889-4134, open Tues.-Sun. 10 a.m.-4 p.m., closed holidays, small fee. The log-and-stone building itself is a 1940s WPA project. Inside, there's an elaborate model of the old courthouse crafted from leaded and stained glass, plus an aged doll collection and artifacts from the town's former Maidu and Chinese communities. Among other gold rush memorabilia are a walk-through hardrock mining tunnel and a display of quartz crystals and gold. Nearby, on Auburn-Folsom Rd., is the **Bernhard Museum Complex,** tel. 889-4156, actually an annex of the main museum (same hours, one ticket admits you to both), an old Auburn family home furnished with Victorian antiques typical of the 1800s' middle class. And do stop by the grandly domed, meticulously restored **Placer County Courthouse** on a rise above Old Town at 101 Maple, tel. 889-6500, new home of the **Placer County Museum.** After taking in the exhibits on the ground floor, its displays and dioramas documenting the local march of history, appreciate the courthouse itself, its fine wood, marble stairways, and terrazzo floors. The prettiest picture of all, though, may be from outside at night.

Diehard museum fans may want to visit some smaller local samples of the species, including the **Griffith Quarry Museum and Park** at Taylor and Rocks Springs Rd. in Penryn, tel. (916) 663-1837 (park open daily during daylight hours, museum open only on weekends); the **Foresthill Divide Museum** on Harrison Street in Foresthill, tel. 367-3988, with exhibits on gold rush and area logging history, open weekends only; and the one-room miner's cabin **Dutch Flat Museum** on Main Street in Dutch Flat, tel. 389-2774, open in summer on Wed. and weekends, by appointment at other times. All of these museums are free.

AUBURN TO ANGELS CAMP

ACCOMMODATIONS AND FOOD

Area Camping

In town, a good deal for tent campers is **Bear River Park** on Plum Tree Road, tel. (916) 889-7750. Another choice is the **Auburn State Recreation Area** south on Hwy. 49 toward Placerville, P.O. Box 1680, Auburn 95603, tel. 885-8461. If you're aching for more hill country solitude, head out Foresthill Divide Rd. 13 miles past Foresthill to Tahoe National Forest's **Big Reservoir Campground,** elevation 4,000 feet; piped water, pit toilets, and beach, operated by DeAnza Placer Gold Mining Company, P.O. Box 119, Foresthill 95631. Six miles farther on a treacherous, unpaved road is the primitive **Secret House Campground** (free, just two sites, purify your water, pack garbage out), and after another eight miles, **Robinson Flat Campground,** also primitive, also free.

For real mountain camping, 35 miles beyond Foresthill via Mosquito Ridge Rd. is **French Meadows Reservoir** (no gas here). Abundant campsites at the **Ahart, French Meadows,** and **Lewis campgrounds,** but the lake level gets very low in late summer and fall. On the way you'll pass near the tiny **Placer Grove of Big Trees,** the northernmost grove of Sierra redwoods (picnic tables, flush toilets, nature trail).

Area Motels

The Old Auburn Hotel downtown on Lincoln Way is no more, alas, converted into a new shopping and office complex. Most of Auburn's motels line the freeway north of town near the Foresthill turnoff. Reasonably priced in the area is the **Country Squire Inn** at 13480 Lincoln Way, tel. (916) 885-7025, with pool, whirlpool, and on-site restaurant, rooms $37-52. There's a **Super 8 Motel** in the area, too, tel. 888-8808, but both of the area's luxury motels are really better bargains: the **Best Western Golden Key Motel** off I-80 at 13450 Lincoln Way, tel. 885-8611 or toll-free for reservations (800) 528-1234, with rooms $46-60, and the **Auburn Inn** at 1875 Auburn Ravine Rd., tel. 885-1800 or toll-free (800) 272-1444, with rates $52-66.

Area Bed And Breakfasts

Not far from Auburn proper is the **Victorian Manor Bed and Breakfast,** 482 Main St., P.O. Box 959, Newcastle 95658, tel. (916) 663-3009, an absolutely authentic example of both Victorian oddity and propriety, from the historically correct doll collection and fringed lampshades to the starched and ironed bed linens. Rates here are remarkably reasonable: $57-65. **The Victorian Hill House** on a hill above Old Town, 195 Park St., P.O. Box 9097, Auburn 95604, tel. 885-5879, is an 1860 Victorian tucked into trees, with flower gardens and a yard with a pool, hot tub, and covered patio. (To get here from I-80, exit at Maple St., turn right onto Lincoln Way, then immediately right again onto Park and continue up the hill.) All four rooms are colorful, their individual atmospheres cued from unique antiques. (In the front hallway is a fabulous Louis XVI writing desk and chair; there's a likeness of Lou himself on a porcelain plate displayed in the dining room.) Two of the best rooms, "Grandma's" (with a spectacular view of Old Town and the courthouse) and The Blue Willow, have half-baths; guests are welcome to use the outdoor showers. Full country breakfast served every morning. Rates: $65-85.

Guests walk over the small footbridge spanning the pond of koi and water hyacinths to enter the **Lincoln House Bed and Breakfast** at 191 Lincoln Way, Auburn 95603, tel. (916) 885-8880, a quiet, casual, and cozy place which actually welcomes families with children. All three rooms here have private baths and a country atmosphere. Common areas include the large living room with fireplace, and a den furnished with TV, VCR, and localized library. The inn's most fascinating history display, though, is in the kitchen, with its wall displays of antique cookware and a 1934 wood-burning stove (complete with trash burner). Rates: $55-80.

Auburn's showplace inn, **Powers Mansion Inn** downtown at 164 Cleveland Ave., tel. (916) 885-1166, is luxurious but less personal. This pastel pink Victorian beauty, built by gold rush millionaire Harold T. Powers at the turn of the century, offers 15 unique rooms—one has a sunken tub, and the suites are something special—with antique touches yet modern private baths. Breakfast is served in the dining room downstairs. Rates: $75-160.

Good Food In Auburn

Pursue the best local produce with the help of "The 49er Fruit Trail and Christmas Tree Lane" brochure; to request a current copy, send a self-addressed stamped legal-sized envelope to the organization at P.O. Box 317, Newcastle 95658. **Pasquale T's,** an all but unknown hole-in-the-wall at 22515 Grass Valley Hwy. (Hwy. 49), tel. 888-8440, serves great Italian food. (Businesses along this almost endless commercial stretch of Hwy. 49, which almost merges Auburn's newer business district with Grass Valley's, can be difficult to find amid the malls and mini-malls and car dealerships. So call ahead to make sure you know where you're going.) Old Town and downtown offer decent cafes and fine dining establishments:

Mary Belle's at 1590 Lincoln Way, tel. (916) 885-3598, serves American standards at breakfast and lunch. One of the better Asian eateries in the gold country is the **Shanghai Restaurant** in Old Town's former American Hotel, 289 Washington, tel. 823-2613. Open daily for lunch and dinner.

Legendary in these parts is **Butterworth's,** 1522 Lincoln Way at Court St., tel. (916) 885-0249, elegant English-American decor in a dignified Victorian mansion overlooking Old Town, best known for its intimate dinners of prime rib and Yorkshire pudding. Though the restaurant has changed hands (and chefs), Sunday brunch here is still unforgettable, with many entrees to choose from—everything from steak-and-kidney pie to excellent eggs California, from quiche to crepes Bengal stuffed with curried seafood. Reservations wise.

The new kid in town—and even better, in many people's opinion—is **Latitudes** nearby, across from the county courthouse at 130 Maple, tel. (916) 885-9535, serving exciting food in serene historic surroundings.

Good Food Near Auburn

Just north of Auburn proper (via I-80 then Bell and Musso roads) is the **Headquarter House,** 14500 Musso Rd., tel. (916) 878-1906, a carnivore's fantasy made manifest. This dark woods-and-glass restaurant, unofficial clubhouse for the surrounding golf course and putting greens, was once a working Angus cattle ranch, which perhaps explains why there's a deli outlet near the pro shop. But meat-eaters of all sporting persuasions herd themselves in here whenever it's open—for the huge sandwiches (try the Winner's Circle Club), salads, and other lunch or dinner delicacies, from Texas roast beef, chicken curry or blackberry chicken, and salmon saute to lemon basil fettucini and old-fashioned liver and onions. Dinner includes more of the same, plus chicken cordon bleu, filet mignon, blackened prime rib, and all manner of steaks, fish, and seafood. This place is so popular that aficionados make reservations for special meals —like Thanksgiving—up to a year in advance. Open for lunch Wed.-Sat., for dinner Wed.-Sun., and for brunch on Sunday.

Definitely a surprise is the friendly, intimate **Czechoslovakian Restaurant,** 16770 Placer Hills Rd., tel. (916) 878-9979, just off I-80 north of Auburn in "downtown" Meadow Vista. Operated by Czech immigrants, the menu is Central European, offering entrees from Bavaria, Czechoslovakia, Hungary, Serbia, and beyond. Dinner is served Wed.-Sun. nights. Call for directions and reservations. For very good German-American food, head south on Hwy. 49 about 10 miles to the **Nugget** in Cool, tel. 823-1294, open daily.

EVENTS AND INFORMATION

Auburn Events

E Clampus Vitus hosts a **bean cook-off** at the Gold Country Fairgrounds here in February. The **Auburn Professional Rodeo** comes in April. In June, stand downtown and watch people drop at the finish line of the **Western States Endurance Run,** a one-day, 100-mile run so popular that runners are selected by lottery for the privilege of brutalizing their bodies on the horse trail between here and Squaw Valley. Horses and riders undergo the same ordeal in August during the **Tevis Cup 100 Miles One Day** cross-country endurance race. In July, in conjunction with the Mother Lode Miners Association, Auburn hosts a **Gold Fair and Panning Championship.** Hilarious is the only word to describe Auburn's **Funk Soap Box Derby Nationals** in August when dozens of weird and wacky homemade vehicles, from mobile outhouses to UFOs, parade down Lincoln Way. The **Placer County Fair,** complete with demolition derby and stock dog trials, is also in August.

Area Information

The **Auburn Chamber of Commerce** is now housed in the attractive and restored railroad depot at 601 Lincoln Way, tel. (916) 885-5616, open weekdays 9-5. Stop by to request the local walking tour brochure and other visitor information. The very helpful **Placer County Visitors Center** at 661 Newcastle Rd., P.O. Box 746, Newcastle 95658, tel. (916) 663-2061, is open Wed.-Sun. 9-4—though you can peruse the racks outside at other times, or call or write for information in advance. To get current state camping and recreation information for the area, contact the **Auburn State Recreation Area,** P.O. Box 3266, Auburn 95604, tel. 885-4527 or 988-0205. For whitewater rafting, hiking, and other camping options, contact the U.S. Forest Service **Foresthill Ranger District office** at 22830 Foresthill Rd. in Foresthill, tel. 376-2224—or contact Tahoe National Forest headquarters in Nevada City, tel. 376-2224.

"AUBURN DAM" AND VICINITY

The Foresthill Bridge

East of Auburn near the confluence of the American River's north and middle forks, the half-mile-long Foresthill Bridge is hard to miss, pulled taut across the canyon like a giant concrete clothesline. Built to connect Foresthill to the outside world if and when the Auburn Dam ever inundates the canyon, the $1.5 million bridge is a solution without a problem, though it has created problems of its own. Looming almost 800 feet above the chasm, the span is a temptation for thrill-seeking (if stupid) parachutists, hang gliders, and (sadly) the suicidal. If you don't mind heights and speeding traffic, walk across for a spectacular vista. To get to the big bridge, head north from Old Town on Lincoln Way then turn south on Foresthill Road.

Damning The Dam

What outragged environmentalists couldn't stop—a massive dam construction project destined to create a two-fingered, 25-mile-long lake in these canyons of the American River—nature did. In 1975, an impressive earthquake with its epicenter at Oroville Dam 60 miles to the north revealed a major, previously unrecognized fault line directly beneath the Auburn Dam site.

But it looks like the dam may be back in business, one day soon, much to the chagrin of environmentalists and whitewater rafting enthusiasts. (For more information, see "Whitewater Rafting Companies" in this chapter's Introduction.)

The first calls in support of Auburn Dam construction came in response to potential downstream flooding problems—and also in response to the state's prolonged drought conditions and ever-increasing demand for energy. (A major dam, the argument went, would create some balance between the dangers of either too much or too little water, plus generate hydroelectricity.) But the costs of such a dam, and lack of unanimity about the genuine need for it, has led to great acrimony, and to a variety of scaled-down proposals. One possibility, proposed by the U.S. Army Corps of Engineers, called for a smaller yet expandable 498-foot-high dry dam for flood control—a project since scaled down to a height of 430 feet. That proposal was subsequently attacked by independent consultants because downstream levees along the American River may not withstand the calculated high-water river flows, and because the environmental consequences of a "dry" dam—which would create a substantial lake—were significantly underestimated.

Late in 1992, legislation authorizing construction funds for the Auburn Dam was killed in congressional committee. Pundits now say the issue is "dead" until 1994—perhaps forever, due to the moribund state of the U.S. economy.

The saga continues. Stay tuned.

Cool

The best thing about Cool is the sign announcing the town's existence and—if you're from around these parts—being able to say "I'm from Cool." How *cool.* Once a stage stop, Cool's now just a semi-commercial spot in the road where Hwy. 49 joins Hwy. 193. Limestone quarries operate north of here, and the area supports cattle ranching, pear orchards, even an experimental tea plantation.

Pilot Hill

"Pilot" fires were lit on the tallest hill near here to guide one of Frémont's parties into the Sierra, hence the name. Not much to see except a unique gold country phenomenon, the only Southern-style plantation around: "Bayley's

Folly," an 1862 red-brick railroad roadhouse doomed when the tracks were rerouted. Next to the old hotel is the first California grange hall; by 1860 wheat was a more valuable commodity than gold.

COLOMA

Coloma was the site of a former Cullooma Maidu village but is most notable for its historic role as birthplace of the California gold rush. Actually, by 1849, over 10,000 miners populated this tiny valley, but the town was "gold-dry" and dull (at least by miners' standards) just two years later. Most of Coloma is now part of the 240-acre **Marshall Gold Discovery State Historic Park.** You could spend a lazy day wandering through Coloma's scattered buildings and exhibits, especially pleasant in spring when sweet peas, poppies, and blackberry bushes bloom, or in fall when the leaves turn gold in honor of the town's historic beginnings. Pleasant picnicking by the river, good swimming and wading in the American River's south fork (look out for rampaging rafts), also foothill hiking trails.

Waves of river rafters (up to 1,800 people a day on summer weekends) have slowed somewhat, heading instead for the new **Lotus County Park** downstream. Expect bumper-to-bumper traffic complete with trash problems, quarrels over parking spaces, theft, and hearty partying. Serious rafters should leave Coloma, at least in summer, to the partiers. The park is open 10 a.m.-9 p.m. year-round. Day-use fee, $5. But the park's main attraction, with summer tourists buzzing around it like wasps, is the full-size replica of **Sutter's Mill** near the river. Demonstrations and lectures about how it works are held daily at 2 p.m. Adjacent is a restored miners' cabin. The stone-and-shuttered **Wah Hop Store and Bank** just aross the highway from the mill is a revivified Chinese general store; on display are herbs and animal parts for medicinal potions, an altar and ancestral portraits, business desk, tea cups, and rice bowls. Another store—and you can shop at this one—is the **Argonaut,** a soda fountain and candy shop with home-brewed root beer.

Farther south, note the freestanding steel jail cell and crumbling old stone jailhouse ruins. Nearby is the new **Papini House Museum,** a turn-of-the-century home complete with antique garden tools. There's plenty else to see: mining technique demonstrations, stagecoaches, the old "Mormon Cabin" (a reconstruction of Marshall's cabin, downhill from his final resting place near the Catholic church). Art lovers should peek into the 1855 **Friday House,** the gallery home of the late artist George Mathis. On the hill behind Coloma is a monumental statue of James Marshall, erected in belated gratitude by the state after his death.

New, on the American River across from Sutter's Mill, is the **Coloma Outdoor Discovery School,** P.O. Box 484, Coloma 95613, tel. (916) 621-2298, offering three-day, "experiential learning" natural history and environmental education programs for children, from October through May.

Other Sights

The park's **Gold Museum** and visitors' center across the highway from the mill is first-rate and a good place to start exploring. Here are a rare collection of Maidu artifacts, history exhibits, some of James Marshall's memorabilia, plus dioramas and films. Open daily 10-5, except on major holidays.

Gold Hill

A ghost town about a mile north of Vineyard House, with a lovely Japanese garden shrine at the school. Here in the 1860s a German immigrant who'd spent most of his life in Japan started the first Japanese settlement in California. The Wakamatsu Tea and Silk Colony brought bamboo, tea seeds, grape cuttings, and mulberry trees here from Japan in hopes of starting a major tea and silk plantation. Despite the favorable climate, unhealthy stock and damaging incursions by miners prevented the venture from becoming a success.

Area Accommodations

The **Sierra Nevada House** on Hwy. 49 at Lotus Rd., P.O. Box 496, Coloma 95613, tel. (916) 621-1649, is the latest incarnation of the 1850-vintage hotel (twice burned to the ground), crafted of wood and stone and back in business as a bed and breakfast. The six rooms here feature simple Early American furnishings and private baths; one room has its own ghost, Isabella, who reportedly caught her husband here in a compromising position. (No one knows whether

CALIFORNIA DEPARTMENT OF PARKS & RECREATION

Sutter's Mill
in Coloma,
circa 1849

or not Isabella is acquainted with the poor fellow at Vineyard House—see below.) There's a saloon adjacent, also an ice-cream parlor with a lunch menu. Rates: $75 and up in summer, from $60 in winter.

Home base for area **hot-air ballooning**—ask about combined balloon-and-bed packages—is the very fine and friendly **Coloma Country Inn** on High Street just a two-block stroll from Sutter's Mill, P.O. Box 502, Coloma 95613, tel. (916) 622-6919. This sunny yellow-and-white home with sitting porch and gardens has been painstakingly restored, with five quilt-cozied guest rooms (two with shared bath) and other homey touches. Rates: $79-89. More rustic is the **American River Resort,** P.O. Box 427, tel. 622-6700 or toll-free (800) 443-4773, on the banks of the American River near where James Marshall discovered gold. Cabins from $75, campsites $18-24, open year-round. The American River Resort has a swimming pool, fishing pond, even a miniature animal farm for the kiddies. **Camp Lotus,** P.O. Box 578, Lotus 95651, tel. (916) 622-8672, has hot showers, picnic tables, BBQs, volleyball, and horseshoes, $12 mid-week, $18 and up on weekends. Sometimes rowdy with river rafters, call ahead for weekend reservations. Another possibility is newly renovated **Coloma Resort** right on the river, offering fishing and gold panning, rates

$18-23. Contact the resort at P.O. Box 516, Coloma 95163, tel. 621-2267.

More Accommodations And Food
The **Vineyard House** on Cold Springs Rd., tel. (916) 622-2217, once an old stagecoach stop and now an inn rumored to be haunted, has rooms with a shared bath, $70 and up, plus one room with private bath. Lovely gardens. The gold rush-era winery once here was famous; U.S. Grant came by twice to verify the quality of the vintage. The restaurant here is great. But the saloon is the real reason to stop. It's down in the old brick wine cellar where "the ghost" lurks, just a wispy shadow of the crazy man once chained here by his wife (or so the story goes). There's a special party in the poor guy's honor every Halloween, including a midnight trip to the cemetery across the street. Otherwise, stop by any Friday or Saturday night for live music and general good times. An especially big hoedown happens in June, when coonskin-capped wagoneers on their Emigrant Trail trek show up here to party. The restaurant/bar at Vineyard House is open at least Fri.-Sun.; call for current hours.

Another good choice for meals is the **Coloma Club Cafe** on Hwy. 49 at Marshall Rd., tel. (916) 626-6390, open daily. Western humor and generous helpings. The lasagna is particularly good. Also, live C&W music here on weekend nights.

Simpler area eateries include **Joe's Taco Stand** a half mile north of the American River Bridge; the **Coloma Deli,** tel. 622-1122; and **Yossums Pizza,** tel. 622-9277.

Entertainment, Events, Information

In May, Coloma hosts its **Art in the Park** weekend arts and crafts festival in conjunction with El Dorado County's Celebrate the Arts week. For drama and melodrama on weekend nights (May-Sept.), try the Crescent Players' performances at the **Olde Coloma Theatre** just up the hill off Cold Springs Rd. (near Vineyard House); call (916) 626-5282 for reservations. Big doin's here on **Discovery Day,** January 24, but also during the **Christmas in Coloma** festivities each December. Tours of the town's **Pioneer Cemetery** are offered on weekends, subject to the availability of docents. And fund raising continues for various projects, including the restoration of the schoolhouse—a task completed in 1987 before the building was demolished by a logging truck. For info on the park or special events, contact: **Marshall Gold Discovery State Historic Park,** P.O. Box 265, Coloma 95613, tel. 622-3470. For current river rafting information, contact **Whitewater Connection** (See "Introduction," this chapter).

VICINITY OF COLOMA

Kelsey

"Mr. Gold Rush" James Marshall, reclusive blacksmith, lived here from 1848 until he died, penniless, in 1870 at age 73. His blacksmith shop still stands just outside town, though most of Marshall's memorabilia is in the museum at Coloma. Mining-camp names near here (except self-evident Fleatown) reflected miners' ethnic origins: Irish Creek, Louisville (French), Elizatown (English), American Flat, Spanish Flat. Take Rock Creek Rd., then Reservoir Rd. to pretty **Finnon Lake,** where you can camp, picnic, fish, hike. There's even a restaurant. Or, take Marshall Rd. back down toward the river and Coloma.

Quite pleasant for a stay is the **Mountainside Inn,** P.O. Box 165, Kelsey 95643, tel. (916) 626-0983 or (800) 237-0832, a 1920s-vintage country home featuring several bed and breakfast rooms (queen beds, private baths) and an

James Marshall

CALIFORNIA DEPARTMENT OF PARKS & RECREATION

attic dormitory that sleeps eight (king and queen beds plus four twins). The view from the deck, and the hot tub, is panoramic. Rates: $70-75.

Georgetown

Here in the far north of the mythic Mother Lode on the divide between the American River's north and south forks—once called Growlersburg (because the nuggets found here were so large they "growled" in the gold pans)—Georgetown is like a tiny New England hill town with pretty Victorians and fragrant rose gardens. The **Balzar House** was originally a three-story dance hall, built in 1859, later used as an opera house and now the Odd Fellows Hall. The **Shannon Knox House,** like a few other gold country structures, was constructed from lumber shipped around the Horn. Near Georgetown is the 3,000-acre **Blodgett Experimental Forest,** a UC Berkeley outdoor laboratory where computer models help create U.S. commercial forests of the future. From Georgetown, head west on Wentworth Springs Rd. to **Stumpy Meadows Reservoir,** a pretty 320-acre lake with clear, cold water, plentiful pines and firs. Good camping.

The balconied **Georgetown Hotel** on Main St., tel. (916) 333-2848, is a very reasonable place to hang your hat: rooms with shared baths $45 and up. Even if you're just passing through, stop by to eat here and to appreciate the rough stone bar and fireplace, the rich woodwork and eclectic furnishings: tractor seat barstools, decorative farm equipment, cowboy boots dangling from the ceiling. Live music, usually on weekends. The **American River Inn** at Main and Orleans, P.O. Box 43, Georgetown 95634, tel. 333-4499 or toll-free (800)

245-6566, once a Wells Fargo office and a mining camp boardinghouse, offers nothing but elegant country-style luxury now—pool, spa, lovely gardens, aviary, and yes, an antique shop, plus fabulous breakfasts, $74 and up.

For more information contact the **Georgetown Divide Business Association,** P.O. Box 1536, Georgetown 95634, tel. (916) 333-1569 or 888-7849.

PLACERVILLE AND VICINITY

A wild town in bygone days once known as Dry Diggins, Ravine City, and Hangtown (in honor of the locals' enthusiastic administration of oak tree justice), Placerville throbs as the historical heart of the gold country and nowadays is the seat of El Dorado County. Strategically located on the old Overland Trail (now Hwy. 50) and the road to Coloma, Hangtown eventually bowed to the pressures of respectability and settled on its new name. During the rush to Nevada's Comstock Lode, the town prospered as the chief way station, with telegraph, Pony Express, and Overland Mail service.

A few industrial kingpins got their start in Placerville. Railroad magnate Mark Hopkins set up shop on Main Street, peddling groceries from Sacramento. Canned meat king Philip Armour ran a small butcher shop here. John Studebaker built wheelbarrows for miners, one-wheeled predecessors of his later automobiles. And Leland Stanford, progenitor of Stanford University, ran a store in nearby Cold Springs.

These days, Placerville is losing much of its charm to progress, often crowded to overflowing with a fast-growing local population and Tahoe traffic.

HANGTOWN SIGHTS

The town's pride and joy is the 60-acre **Gold Bug Mine** in Bedford Park (about a mile north of town on Bedford Ave.), tel. (916) 622-5232, the only city-owned gold mine in the U.S. Take a guided tour of the well-lit Gold Bug, one of 250 gold mines once active within the park's perimeter; bring a sweater. Open daily 10-4, May to mid-Sept., weekends only otherwise. The **El Dorado County Historical Museum,** 100 Placerville Dr. at the

county fairgrounds two miles west of town, tel. 621-5865, is worth a stop. There's a yard full of aged vehicles and equipment here, including a restored Concord stagecoach, one of Studebaker's wheelbarrows, Pony Express paraphernalia, even a pair of Snowshoe Thompson's skis. Open Wed.-Sat. 10 a.m.-4 p.m., Sun. 1-4 p.m., free.

Downtown Hangtown

At 305 Main is the spot where Hangtown's old hangin' tree once grew; a doomed dummy strung up from the second story of the Hangman's Tree Bar offers graphic testimony to the reality of the bad ol' days. Hangtown's old fire bell, used to summon both vigilantes and volunteer firefighters, also hangs—from an 1898 steel tower up the street at Main and Center. The narrow, rugged old firehouse is now **Placerville City Hall** at Main and Bedford streets. The local **courthouse,** circa 1912, is flanked by two Civil War cannons. The classic brick **Cary House,** which replaced the old Raffles Hotel at 300 Main, is worth a look-see: an elegant hostelry also housing professional offices. Also peak into the **Placerville News Company** on Main, a genuine old general store-style newsstand.

Probably the ultimate local experience, though, is a visit to **Sam's Town** along Hwy. 50 in Cameron Park, overwhelming Western kitsch (30,000 square feet of it), from arcades and eateries to museum, open daily, tel. (916) 677-2273.

ACCOMMODATIONS

Camping

Restaurants galore, this town has, but choice in reasonable accommodations is harder to come by. For close-in camping, clean, with hot showers (RVs only, unfortunately), the **El Dorado County Fairgrounds** on Placerville Dr., tel. (916) 621-5820, is $10. There are primitive campgrounds throughout El Dorado National Forest but most are well into the Sierra Nevada. **Sly Park** at Jenkinson Lake, tel. 644-2545, is RV paradise; drive 17 miles east on Hwy. 50 at Pollock Pines then turn at Camp Rd. E16: swimming, fishing, no showers, $9 per night per vehicle.

Motels, A Fine Hotel

The **Gold Trail Motor Lodge** at 1970 Broadway, tel. (916) 622-2906, has a playground and pool, rooms $45 and up. Nearby, at 1940 Broadway, tel. 622-0895, is the **Mother Lode Motel,** rooms $34-51. Placerville also hosts a **Days Inn** on Broadway, tel. 622-3124, and the **Best Western Placerville Inn** on Green Leaf Dr., tel. 622-9100 or (800) 528-1234. But the best bet, really, is a stay at the **Cary House Hotel** downtown at 300 Main, tel. 622-4271, with refurbished and cheerful 19th-century country-style rooms, all with private baths. Rates from $45.

Bed And Breakfasts

The elegant **Chichester House** at 800 Spring St., tel. (916) 626-1882 or (800) 831-4006, has three guest rooms with half baths, parlor, library, conservatory, large porches, and breakfast served in the dining room. Rates: $75-80. The **Combellack Blair House** at 3059 Cedar Ravine, tel. 622-3764, is another lovely local Victorian, with three rooms. The porch swing just adds to the old-days ambience. Breakfast, though, is very much in the here-and-now. Rates: $89-110. The **River Rock Inn** north of town near Chili Bar, P.O. Box 827, Placerville 95667, tel. 622-7640, has four rooms all opening onto the deck (hot tub) above the American River, two with half baths. Children genuinely welcome, full breakfast served. Rates: $75-85. For a current bed and breakfast brochure, send a self-addressed stamped envelope to: **Historic Country Inns of El Dorado County,** P.O. Box 106, Placerville 95667.

GOOD FOOD

Hangtown Fry And Other Basics

Placerville is the hometown of "Hangtown Fry," a tasty creation of oysters and bacon wrapped up in an omelette. Try it downtown at the **Soup 'n' Such** diner at 423 Main, tel. (916) 626-3483. For American cafe fare, **Cafe Sarah's** across from the Cary House Hotel at 301 Main, tel. 621-4680, serves basic breakfasts and burgers and such at lunch. **La Casa Grande** at 251 Main, tel. 626-5454, is a good bet for Mexican standards. For genuinely good food, try **Lil' Mama D'Carlos** at 482 Main, tel. 626-1612, beloved for its Italian fare, or the **Carriage Room Restaurant at Smith Flat House,** 2021 Smith Flat Rd. in Smith Flat, tel. 621-0667, a fascinating old building and the place for American-style steaks, chicken, and other standards. Appreciate the saloon.

For barbecue lovers, **Poor Red's** bar and restaurant on Main St. in El Dorado, tel. (916) 622-2901, is material for myth. Somewhat unsavory looking, stark institutional-green stucco with metal door and neon on the blink, this is the town's 1858 Wells Fargo building and the perfect place to hide decent food: oakwood pit-broiled ribs, chicken, ham, and steak. People here and elsewhere swear Red's barbecue is the best in the West, but it's not good enough to justify a three-hour wait for a table on weekends. If you do wait, try Red's secret-recipe alcoholic concoction, the "golden cadillac." You can stuff yourself plus walk out with that unmistakable golden glow for just over $10. To beat the weekend wait for tables, try takeout (at least on the food).

ET CETERA

Entertainment And Events

For local theater, enjoy **Theatre El Dorado,** tel. (916) 626-5193. Most live music and dancing around town is on weekends. In March, pros and amateurs alike tear it up at the **Hangtown Motocross Classic** in Prairie City Park on White Rock Rd., the old Mormon Emigrant Trail. More wholesome, though, are the numerous art shows and other festivals sponsored by area wineries, starting in spring. From June-Sept. free **Jazz in the Plaza** concerts are offered in Fountain Plaza downtown from 3-6 p.m. Late in June, there's the **Pioneer Days Festival,** coincidentally the high point of the annual wagon train trip overland from Carson City, Nevada to Sacramento.

The **El Dorado County Fair** takes place in early August at the county fairgrounds. At month's end before Labor Day is the annual **Mother Lode Antique Show and Sale**, also at the fairgrounds. By mid-September, 45 area farms open their gates for apple picking. Downtown Placerville is the site of the **Hangtown Dixieland Jubilee Jazz Festival** on the third Sunday of October.

Information And Services

Hangtown has a huge, free parking garage downtown. Stop by the **El Dorado County Chamber of Commerce** at 524 Main, Placerville 95667, tel. (916) 621-5885, for information on what's going on plus free maps and guides, especially the "El Dorado County Ranch Marketing And Rural Recreation Guide" for finding farmer-to-you produce. Ask, too, about local events and entertainment. The local **parks and recreation office** is across the street at 549 Main, tel. 622-0832. There are about 35 wineries in the county, most near Placerville; get a complete listing of them at the chamber office, or contact: **El Dorado Wine Grape Growers Association**, P.O. Box 248, and the **El Dorado Winery Association**, P.O. Box 1614, tel. 622-8094. If you're heading east anyway, stop off at the newish **El Dorado National Forest Visitor Center** off Hwy. 50 in Camino to take in the exhibits and pick up current information on outdoor activities, open 7 a.m.-6 p.m. in summer, otherwise 8-5.

APPLE HILL

On the ridge east from Placerville to near Camino, the Apple Hill "tour" follows a path originally blazed by Pony Express riders—a great bike ride when the roads aren't choked with cars. It's hard to believe that half a million people visit this suburban ranch region each autumn, but they do. Nightmarish weekend traffic. In late summer and fall, various farms along the way sell tree-fresh apples and delectable, decadent homemade treats: apple pies and strudel, cheesecake, other fine baked goods, apple cider, spicy apple butter, even caramel and fudge apples. Earlier in the year you can get cherries, strawberries, plums, peaches, and pears; natural honey is available year-round.

The **Apple and Pear Blossom Festival** in spring and the **Harvest Festival** are the main hometown hoedowns. People come up to Apple Ridge in November and December to cut their own locally grown yule trees. For free Apple Hill maps and other info, get oriented at the **Apple Hill Visitor Center**, 4123 Carson Rd., P.O. Box 494, Camino 95709, tel. (916) 622-9595, or guide yourself with the county "Ranch Marketing Guide."

"New" and quite nice, just a half block from Apple Hill's new visitors center, is the **Camino Hotel Bed and Breakfast** downtown at 4103 Carson Rd., P.O. Box 1197, Camino 95709, tel. (916) 644-7740, a fully renovated historic hotel (The Seven Mile House) along the old Carson Trail. The ten guest rooms here—several have private baths—are intimate, and as cheery as the parlor. Enjoy breakfast (and dessert, in the evening) on the sun porch or inside by the wood-stove. Special events, such as the annual Camino Art Show, are sometimes scheduled here, too. Rates: $55-85.

Apple Hill Wineries

Fruit of the vine is also a hot item around Apple Hill. The biggest establishment is **Boeger Winery** on Carson at Schnell School, tel. (916) 622-8094, with a fine 1860s stone cellar and tasting room open daily and picnicking near a stream. Nearby are three smaller wineries, most with winetasting on weekends only, picnic facilities: **El Dorado**, tel. 676-0912; **Lava Cap**, tel. 621-1660; and **Madrona**, tel. 644-5948. There are some special wineries near Fair Play, southeast of Placerville via back roads, including **Gerwer** and **Granite Springs.**

TO JACKSON

Plymouth

Heading south from Placerville on Hwy. 49 toward Jackson, the rolling foothills become the steep canyon sides of the Cosumnes River. (This is where the "Visitors Guide to Amador County" starts becoming useful.) Plymouth, formerly Pokerville then Puckerville, was a late-in-the-game but lucrative mining center. A short walk along Main Street takes you by most of the tattered historic sites. In July or August, stop by for the **Amador County Fair and Rodeo** here. Other big parties at the fairgrounds include the **Sierra Showcase of Wines** in May, The **Wine Festival** in June, the **Bluegrass**

Festival in August, and the **Gold Country Jubilee** in September.

Plymouth Area Wineries

From Plymouth travel east into a cluster of old mining and lumber camps—River Pines, Mt. Aukum, Fair Play, Grizzly Flat, Cole's Station, Somerset—in the Shenandoah Valley, which now flourishes with foothill vineyards and winemakers. This is Zinfandel country, reached via Plymouth-Shenandoah Rd. (Rd. E-16). Pick up free wine tour pamphlets locally or send a stamped, self-address business-sized envelope to the **Sierra Foothill Winery Association,** P.O. Box 425, Somerset 95684, and request the current **Amador Vintners Association** brochure at the county chamber of commerce office in Jackson (see below).

Most famous for a taste and a tour is the **D'Agostini Winery,** the fourth-oldest winery in California and a state historic landmark. There's something very comfortable about D'Agostini, with its vintage stone cellar, handhewn beams, and ancient oak vats; it's just northeast of town on Shenandoah Rd., tel. (800) 722-4849, open daily 9 a.m.-4:30 p.m. except holidays. An excellent newcomer in the Zinfandel sweeps is the very modern **Amador Foothill Winery** at 12500 Steiner Rd., tel. (209) 245-6307, open weekends only, noon-5 p.m. Also worth a stop is the award-winning, family-run **Shenandoah Vineyards** nearby at 12300 Steiner Rd., tel. 245-3698, open daily all year 10-5. Pleasing to the eye as well as the palate is the Mediterranean **Montevina,** 20680 Shenandoah School Rd., tel. 245-6942, open daily 11 a.m.-4 p.m. The annual **Music at the Wineries** festival, a benefit for the **Amador County Arts Council,** is usually held in May. For info, contact the arts council at P.O. Box 217, Sutter Creek 95685, tel. 267-0211.

Plymouth Area Practicalities

For lunch or dinner barbecue (prime rib and fresh fish on weekends), hearty soups, and salad bar, try the **Bar-T-Bar** south of town on the highway, dinner served Wed.-Sat., tel. (209) 245-3729. Plymouth has a massive new luxury motel just south of town too, looming over the landscape next to the highway: **The Shenandoah Inn,** 17674 Village Dr., Plymouth 95669, tel. (209) 245-4491, with all the amenities (including conference room), rates $50 and up, higher on weekends.

Also new, and more remote, is the **Indian Creek Bed & Breakfast** several miles north of Plymouth proper at 21950 Hwy. 49, tel. (209) 245-4648 or toll-free (800) 24-CREEK. This 1932 stucco-sided lodge has hidden its log-cabin spirit inside, where the interior woodwork becomes just part of the intriguing decor. A grand design with cathedral ceilings and two-story fireplace, the house was built here in the woods by a Hollywood producer and was known locally as the John Wayne House, since America's mythic cowboy was a frequent guest. (The Duke spent time in Jackson, too, as the folks at the National Hotel will tell you.) The four rooms here are "dedicated to the ladies who inspired them," two with private baths, two with balconies (great garden views), one with a fireplace, and all with antiques and a slightly Southwestern attitude. Rates: $45-95, lower midweek and off-season.

Fiddletown

Bret Harte immortalized this rowdy placer mining town in "An Episode of Fiddletown," though today it's considerably calmer, a friendly, slightly down-at-the-heels spot in the road. Fiddletown was reportedly named by a Missourian who noted the townspeople's fondness for "fiddlin'" (though what he meant is still a matter of speculation, since he didn't mention violins). Center of social life here is the old **Fiddletown General Store,** where locals loiter on the front porch and gossip. Rest or play a while at the community's green and well-groomed **Ostrom-McLean Park,** with its picnic tables, playground, and basketball and tennis courts. Come in May for the town's annual celebration—more fiddlers are always welcome.

Walk down Oleta Rd. to see most of the town's older buildings. Rare in California is the 1850s Chinese rammed-earth adobe **Chew Kee Store** on Main Street. A medicinal herb shop run by the doctors Yee (father and son), it was in remarkably good shape even before its recent restoration. Now a museum, there are many rare items here, including a private altar and oddities like paper good luck charms, ginger jars, and rubber stamps with Chinese characters. Call the historical society for museum hours, (209) 296-4519. During the gold rush,

Fiddletown was home to the state's largest Chinese population outside San Francisco. The brick-and-stone Chinese "gambling hall" is nearby, next to the old blacksmith shop (complete with original forge).

Drytown

Once noted for its 27 saloons (they called it "dry" for the diggins here), you'll find mostly antique and other shops in Drytown today. Near Drytown were some colorfully named mining sites: Blood Gulch, Murderer's Gulch, Rattlesnake Gulch. The **Old Well Motel and Grill** on Hwy. 49, P.O. Box 187, Drytown 95699, tel. (209) 245-6467, is a good burger and sandwich stop, with rustic "cabin" rooms, swimming pool, picnic area, gold panning in the creek. The Claypipers offer old-time melodrama on Saturday nights at the **Piper Playhouse** here, tel. 245-3812 (reservations usually necessary).

Amador City

Amador City straddles the Mother Lode. Mines along the "Amador strip" between here and Plymouth produced half the $300 million in gold

the Imperial Hotel in Amador City

KIM WEIR

yielded by Southern Mines. The Keystone Mine was most famous, yielding about $40,000 the first month and $24 million or so between 1853 and the 1940s. Amador City today is tiny, just one block long and the state's smallest incorporated city, but as pretty as Sutter Creek. Strolling up and down the block, dodging cars while trying to cross the highway, and poking into shops are the town's main events. Sadly, businesses come and go almost as quickly as the traffic. But not so the **Buffalo Chips Emporium**, tel. (209) 267-0570, once the old Wells Fargo Bank. Offbeat ice cream parlor decor, juke box, good breakfast and lunch, and decadent ice cream and soda fountain treats. You can sit out front on the time-polished benches and watch the world buzz by.

Ballads on the other side of town and just up the hill, tel. (209) 267-5403, is a fine dining establishment serving a seasonally changing contemporary American menu. Open for dinner (after 5 p.m.) Thurs.-Tues., and for brunch on Sunday. **Rollie's Express Texas Bar-B-Q,** halfway between here and Drytown, is also **Rollie's Express Amador House,** tel. 267-0966 or toll-free (800) 821-2963, with three bed-and-breakfast rooms with private baths. New and right in town, just down the shady side street from the Imperial Hotel, is **The Culbert House Inn,** 18011 Water St., Amador City 95601, tel. 267-0750, a huge home with three guest suites decorated in French Country style, sometimes even a friendly dog on the lawn. Rates: $70-105. Once the office for the Keystone Mining Company, the **Mine House Inn** on the highway, P.O. Box 245, tel. 267-5900, is a fully restored bed and breakfast inn. The rooms are named after their original purpose—the Mill Grinding Room, the Retort Room, the Vault Room—and are quite comfortable, furnished in gold rush antiquities. All eight rooms have private baths. Rates: $50-65. Another possibility, of course, for dining and an overnight, is the lovingly restored Imperial Hotel.

The Imperial Hotel

This reincarnated red brick gold-rush hotel, the one boldly embracing the big curve as Hwy. 49 snakes through Amador City, is a delightful surprise upstairs and down. But take a few moments to appreciate the weight-bearing construction of the building itself, a thickness of twelve bricks at the base tapering to four at the roofline. Inside, the striking **Oasis Bar** and small lounge area adjoins the open dining area. At dinner (served seven days a week) the weekly-changing menu might feature entrees like poached salmon in mandarin orange dill sauce, cinnamon roasted pork loin, and grilled filet of beef with shallot tarragon sauce. And at least consider dessert—creations like chocolate orange torte and hazelnut praline cheesecake—everything house-made by the hotel's pastry chef. (Lunch is served only on a special-event basis.) Or come for Sunday brunch, served 10 a.m.-2 p.m., with choices from Kahlua French toast and fruit crepes to omelettes or quiche.

Upstairs, the six guest rooms are all artistically eclectic, some with a fun, almost folk-art feel. All feature very modern private bathrooms (with "extras" like hair dryers and heated towel racks); several have balconies or access to the back upstairs patio. Best of all, though, a stay here also includes a full breakfast. Room rates: $75-115, lower on weekdays. For more information and to make reservations, contact: Imperial Hotel, P.O. Box 195, Amador City 95601, tel. (209) 267-9172.

SUTTER CREEK

John Sutter passed up this area as a possible site for his lumber mill, but he did set up a lumber camp along the creek, hence the name. Never much of a placer mining town, though Leland Stanford started amassing his fortune by means of the hardrock Lincoln Mine here, Sutter Creek grew slowly as a supply center. The area's Central Eureka Mine became one of the state's richest, finally shutting down in 1958.

A tiny town of 1,500, Sutter Creek is among the most attractive and authentic gold rush towns, its cheerful, spiffed-up Main Street a blend of aged wood frames and solid brick-and-stone buildings. Take the walking tour (pick up a guide in the local civic auditorium or write: Sutter Creek Area Merchants Association, P.O. Box 600, Sutter Creek 95685).

The **Knights Foundry** on the creek east of Main, at 13 Eureka St., tel. (209) 267-5543, is the only water-powered foundry in the country and is still in business, taking orders for custom machine parts from around the world. Peek

in on Friday afternoons. A favorite pastime here is browsing through the excellent antique and other shops. May brings Sutter Creek's **Poppy Days,** and in June there's the **Italian Benevolent Society's annual picnic,** quite the bash, steeped in 100-plus years of tradition, with food, music, and dancing.

For more information, contact the **Sutter Creek Business and Professional Association,** P.O. Box 600, Sutter Creek 95685, or call the city at (209) 267-5647.

Accommodations

Motels are *out* in Sutter Creek, fine bed and breakfasts definitely in. The pick of the litter is probably **The Foxes** at 77 Main St., P.O. Box 159, Sutter Creek 95685, tel. (209) 267-5882; $90 and up for elegant surroundings and foxes everywhere, floor to ceiling. Full breakfasts are cooked to order and served in your room. Bears are the critters of choice at the country-style **Hanford House,** 3 Hanford St., P.O. Box 847, tel. 267-0747; $65-110, full wheelchair access, continental breakfast. New and quite fine is **The Gold Quartz Inn,** 15 Bryson Dr., tel. 267-9155 or toll-free (800) 752-8738, a huge contemporary inn with the look of a Victorian farmhouse—and 24 large guest rooms with modern private baths and all the amenities. Wheelchair-accessible, with elevator. Full breakfast plus afternoon tea, complimentary beverages. Rates: $75-125.

Very popular is the **Sutter Creek Inn,** 75 Main St., P.O. Box 385, tel. (209) 267-5606, $50-135. Proprietor Jane Way is a legend in her own time, especially among the bed and breakfast crowd: hers is one of the first established in California. Rooms at this "country estate" are romantic, with spacious gardens. Breakfast is lavish, served at oak tables in the sunny country kitchen. Sometimes there's even parlor entertainment: lectures, concerts, palm reading, handwriting analysis. Very California.

Food And Entertainment

The dress-up dining choice is the **Sutter Creek Palace** at 76 Main St., tel. (209) 267-9852, an elegant Victorian with fine food—seafood, chicken, and beef for the most part, with creative and contemporary preparation—and friendly service. On weekends especially, reservations are a good idea. Open for lunch Fri.-Wed., for dinner Fri.-Tuesday. **Pelargonium** on Hwy. 49

(1 Hanford St.), tel. 267-5008, is also in the Victorian mood, the food quite contemporary, almost as colorful as the wallpaper. Open for dinner only, closed Sundays.

You can get à la carte items or just a burger at the **Bellotti Inn** at 53 Main, tel. (209) 267-5211, but the main reason to come here is for the huge, family-style Italian meals (don't miss the minestrone); fairly reasonable prices (no credit cards). For some fun (and exercise) after stuffing yourself, go bowling at the **Gold Country Lanes** on Ridge Rd.; the setup here includes video games plus live music and dancing on weekends.

JACKSON

Jackson, far from being the wildest of the gold rush settlements, was nonetheless a rambunctious place on the Sacramento-Stockton branch of the old Carson Pass Emigrant Trail. Not a classic boomtown, Jackson has had a surprisingly stable population for over 100 years. The town has remained lively even in recent times, with local bordellos and gambling halls open until the 1950s. Even now, there are card parlors on Main Street. Plan on spending some time in and around Jackson if you're not already museumed, ghost-towned, Victorian gingerbreaded, and gift "shoppe"ed out.

History

In the political-karma-can-be-serious department: Jackson's citizens literally stole the county seat—archives, seals, assorted legalistic paraphernalia, and all—out from under Double Springs in 1851, the apparent final round in a dispute which included the judge gunning down the county clerk. But this battle for power and prestige wasn't over yet: when nearby Mokelumne Hill won the political prize (honorably, through the electoral process) and held it for two terms, stubborn Jacksonians, determined to maintain their collective clout, voted to create a new county—Amador County, one of the state's smallest. Despite the much-improved electoral odds, Jackson barely maintained its status as county seat when challenged by nearby Volcano.

Placer mining started it all, but Jackson's real wealth came from hardrock mines like the mile-deep Kennedy and Argonaut (at one time the world's deepest mines). Both these consolidated conglomerates closed briefly during World War I and again, finally, during World War II. One of the gold country's infamous disasters happened here in 1922, when 47 miners died in the Argonaut Mine fire.

SIGHTS

Amador County Museum

The best thing to see in town is the museum, 255 Church St., tel. (209) 223-6386, in an 1850s red-brick house at the top of the hill. Out back, for a clear explanation of what gold mining was and is, are the scale models of local mining history: the (working) North Star Stamp Mill, the Kennedy Mine headframe, a tailing wheel. Tours every hour if enough people show up, otherwise at 10 a.m. and 2 p.m. Also worth appreciation: the shiny black *Hooterville Cannonball* on display near the street and the cool shady garden full of mining paraphernalia and a few picnic tables. Open Wed.-Sun. 10 a.m.-4 p.m., small admission fee.

Jackson Walking Tour

Get a walking tour map from the **Amador County Chamber of Commerce** on Hwy. 49 (at the southern juncture of Highways 49 and 88) near the Chevron gas station, P.O. Box 596, Jackson 95642, tel. (209) 223-0350. Stone buildings with iron doors and shutters are the architectural rule in downtown Jackson. Main Street, with its high wooden sidewalks, is narrow and crooked and intersected by hillclimbing alley-like streets. Many intriguing old homes are around town, easily enjoyed on foot. (The entire town is better for walking than either biking or driving, and parking is just about impossible. To find out about area bike tours, contact the **Amador County Bike Club,** tel. 223-3890.)

The tiny white **St. Sava Serbian Orthodox Church** is unusual (note the stained-glass work), tucked in between trees and terraced tombstones at 724 N. Main St., tel. (209) 223-2700; it's the "mother church" of the Serbian Orthodox faith in the U.S. Peek into the sanctuary on

Sundays before services to appreciate the stars on the church's "sky dome."

The imposing **National Hotel** down at the end of Main at 2 Water St. is another California hostelry claiming the oldest-in-continuous-operation title. A peek into the National's saloon is almost like peering into a black hole—but one with brassy crystal light reflected from the bar mirror, absorbed by the honky-tonk piano and fake red velvet wallpaper. Lively place on weekend nights.

Kennedy Mine

Do see the Kennedy "tailing wheels." Built in 1912 to lift mine tailings into flumes, then over two hills to a holding dam, the system theoretically solved mining-related environmental problems—stream erosion, siltation, water pollution—caused by dumping tailings into streams and rivers. Only one of the original four is still standing though another lies just downhill in pieces. There's also a very modest city park here; stop for a picnic, pleasant in spring before the heat descends and hillside grasses turn to straw. Nearby is the gold rush-era **Chichizola Store.** (To get here, take Jackson Gate Rd. up the hill from Main Street.) Visit the above-ground remnants of both the Kennedy and Argonaut mines.

Kennedy tailing wheel in Jackson

PRACTICALITIES

Camping

Head toward **Chaw'se Indian Grinding Rocks** near Volcano or camp at one of three reservoirs just west of Jackson. Closest is tiny **Lake Amador,** where you can fish or sail. There's a separate one-acre swimming pond with sandy beaches, playground, about 150 campsites. For info: Lake Amador Resort, 7500 Amador Dr., Ione 95640, tel. (209) 274-2625. Or try either **Camanche** or **Pardee,** two reservoirs slaking the thirst of San Francisco's East Bay area. You can't swim in these waters, but you can boat, fish, or camp here (1,100 campsites altogether) or hike on trails through 15,000 acres. Cheapest is **Lake Pardee Resort,** 4900 Stony Creek Rd., tel. 772-1472; with hot showers, flush toilets, some RV hookups available. There are several campgrounds at Camanche, including the **Camanche Northshore Resort,** 2000 Jackson Valley-Camanche Rd. in Ione, tel. 763-5121, which has showers, flush toilets, tent and RV sites.

Also here: a laundromat, cabins, houseboats, coffee shop, market, gas station, and stables.

Area Motels

El Campo Casa Resort Motel, 12548 Kennedy Flat Rd., Jackson 95642, tel. (209) 223-0100, is a pleasant, middle-aged Spanish-style establishment northwest of town near the intersection of Highways 49 and 88, with pool and wonderful gardens, rooms $37-70. Down the highway toward Jackson proper is the **Jackson Holiday Lodge,** tel. 223-0486, with rooms $37-55. New and noticeable downtown, near the southern Hwy. 48/49 junction, is the **Best Western Amador Inn** at 200 S. Hwy. 49, tel. 223-0211, modern red brick with the usual motel amenities, pool, restaurant, $46-74.

Bed And Breakfasts

The **Broadway Hotel,** once an old miners' hotel at 225 Broadway, Jackson 95642, tel. (209) 223-3503, is a relaxed bed and breakfast now; redwood hot tub in the gazebo, rooms $50 and up. The **Court Street Inn,** 215 Court St., tel. 223-

0416, is an elegant state historic monument also on the National Register of Historic Places; with a cottage and five rooms (two share a bath), $75-125. **Ann Marie's Country Inn,** 410 Stasal St., tel. 223-1452, is $80 and up for two, for early American decor and breakfast, or choose the "garden cottage," heated by a potbellied woodstove, $100. Another choice and a noted hostelry here is the elegant, largely original Queen Anne **Gate House Inn** at 1330 Jackson Gate Rd., tel. 223-3500; four rooms in the main house plus a two-room summer house, full breakfasts, $70-105.

Fairly new Jackson bed and breakfasts include the **Windrose Inn** nearby at 1407 Jackson Gate Rd., tel. (209) 223-3650, an authentic Victorian farmhouse with three guest rooms and a cottage (private baths), fish pond, fruit trees, flowers, and full breakfast, rooms $85-110, and **The Wedgewood Inn** tucked into the woods at 11941 Narcissus Rd., tel. 296-4300 or (800) WEDGEWD, featuring six old-fashioned guest rooms (private baths, some rooms with woodstoves), terraced gardens, croquet, full breakfast. Rates: $70-110.

Food, Entertainment, And Events
A local hotspot is **Mel and Faye's Drive-in** at 205 N. Hwy. 49, tel. (209) 223-0853: chili, "moo-

burgers," daily specials, takeout. Not bad for Chinese food is the **Great Wall of China** at 12300 Martell Rd., tel. 223-3475 (takeout orders, too). **Rosebud's Classic Cafe** at 26 Main, tel. 223-2358, is a good American-style cafe open daily for breakfast, lunch, and dinner.

Out of town a bit, and across the street from each other in the 1200 block of Jackson Gate Rd., are two locally famous Italian-American restaurants: **Teresa's,** tel. (209) 223-1786, and **Buscaglia's,** tel. 223-9992—both OK. Back in town, the **Balcony** restaurant, 164 Main, tel. 223-2855, has continental dinners, sandwiches and salads at lunch. Justifiably popular with Elvis Presley fans.

For entertainment stroll over to the National Hotel for a hand of poker upstairs—at John Wayne's favorite table—or some honky-tonk piano (and musical washtubs) in the bar. Usually there's a singalong on Saturday nights, sometimes even a "saints go marching into the bridal suite" Dixieland procession complete with red-faced newlyweds. Or catch a movie at the **Jackson Cinemas** on the highway.

Events worth going out of your way for include the **Mother Lode Dixieland and Jazz Benefit** in late April.

VICINITY OF JACKSON

Ione

First called Bedbug then Freeze Out, the town's new name, honoring one of the characters in Edward Bulwer-Lytton's *The Last Days of Pompeii,* came with the arrival of the post office. The dark "castle" outside town was the state's first reform school, the **Preston School of Industry,** now a historic monument (condemned, no tours) surrounded by the modern-day Preston complex. Country-western singer Merle Haggard, tennis player Pancho Gonzales, movie star Rory Calhoun, and Eddie "Rochester" Anderson of the Jack Benny radio show all grew up at Preston. Sometimes bad boys do OK after all. And sometimes they don't: Ione is also home to the new **Mule Creek State Prison.** Downtown has some historic restoration, but mostly this is a reform school-and-prison company town.

At the intersection of Lancha Plana-Buena Vista and Jackson Valley roads south of Ione is the **Buena Vista Saloon and Store,** all that's left of the town of the same name. This old fieldstone store was originally in Lancha Plana, one of the historic sites now under water at Camanche Reservoir. Chinese laborers carried the building, stone by stone, seven miles uphill and rebuilt it. The buttes here were a protective citadel for the thousands of Miwok people who once lived throughout Jackson Valley. Take Jackson Valley Rd. then Camanche Rd. to get to the buttes.

Winetasting is a possible diversion in these parts. The **Greenstone Winery** at Hwy. 88 and Jackson Valley Rd., tel. (209) 274-2238, has a picnic area plus tasting and tours. **Winterbrook Vineyards,** 4851 Lancha Plana Rd., tel. 274-4627, welcomes tasters in an old barn.

To stay near here, cheapest is camping at nearby Lake Amador or either Camanche or Pardee reservoirs farther south (see "Jackson—Practicalities" above). A night at **The Heirloom** bed and breakfast at 214 Shakeley Ln., P.O. Box 322, Ione 95640, tel. (209) 274-4468, is like a trip to the antebellum South: sweet magnolias and wisteria, rambling verandas, croquet. Four restored rooms in the main house plus two rooms in a rammed-earth adobe, $50-85.

CHAW'SE INDIAN GRINDING ROCKS

A small state park in the foothill terrain east of Jackson and just north of Pine Grove on the road to Volcano, Chaw'se Indian Grinding Rocks is a grassy meadow with clusters of oaks and over 1,100 ancient mortar holes *(chaw'se)* and petroglyphs on a flat limestone plateau. Miwok women used the holes as mortars in which to grind acorns and other seeds. This is the largest grinding rock in the U.S.; a replica is on display at the Smithsonian Institution. Also here: a reconstructed native village, with roundhouse or *hun'ge,* bark tepees, a granary, a Miwok ball field (the traditional game was similar to soccer). The **Chaw'se Regional Indian Museum** features a good collection of artifacts from 10 area tribes plus other displays, open daily (except holidays).

On the last weekend in September, there's a traditional **Native American Big Time Celebration** acorn harvest ceremony and festival here sponsored by the Amador Tribal Council, also the annual **Chaw'se Association Art Show.** The park has two short hiking trails (watch out for poison oak and rattlers), also guided tours to a reconstructed Miwok village; $5 day-use fee, senior rates. For information, contact: Chaw'se Indian Grinding Rocks State Historic Park, 14881 Pine Grove-Volcano Rd., Pine Grove 95665, tel. (209) 296-7488.

Camping

There are about 20 year-round campsites here, $14, but no showers. Or you can live like the Miwok in one of five bark houses, an "environmental camping" experience with a seven-day limit. Each house, built of cedar poles interwoven with wild grape vines then covered with cedar bark, holds up to six people. Tables outside, fire rings, pit toilets, but bring your own water or tote it from the main campground. Also bring firewood. You can reserve a bark house separately (or all five together as a group camp), but plan ahead as prices and availability vary. To make a reservation, get an application and return it to: U'Macha'tam'ma' Environmental Campground in care of the park, or call (209) 296-7488. Reservations for standard camping (necessary during tourist season) can be made in advance through Mistix, tel. (800) 444-7275 in California.

VOLCANO AND VICINITY

Not a volcano in sight, but early settlers thought the landscape resembled a crater and abandoned the original name, Soldier's Gulch. Because the town sits in a little dale atop limestone caves, it's fairly green here year-round. Sleepy Volcano is a ghost town that wouldn't die, refreshingly free of tourist lures and alive with history, including a number of cultural "firsts." The **Miner's Library Association** here was the state's first lending library. California community theater was born here, too, with the formation of the 1845 **Volcano Thespian Society** and the subsequent construction of two local theaters. The state's first literary and debating society also thundered up from Volcano. On **Observatory Hill** two miles away was California's first observatory. Volcano also once had a law school. The trip from Volcano to Sutter Creek on the Sutter Creek-Volcano Rd. is lovely any time, but especially in spring and fall. There are no fences, a rarity in these parts, so you can stop along the way for an unimpeded picnic.

A Volcano Stroll

The Odd Fellows and Masonic halls here were the state's first (outside town is the Masonic Cave, where the brotherhood met before the lodge was built). On one side of Main Street near the park is a block of crumbling stone ruins, including the **Cobblestone Theatre,** once the old assay office. Note the "Old Abe" **Volcano Blues Cannon** in the middle of town. Without ever firing a shot, Abe helped the Yanks win the Civil War, then was smuggled from San Francisco to Volcano, where it was occasionally used for Saturday-night crowd control. **Sing Kee's Store,** built in 1857, is now a fine gift shop specializing in gems and minerals. And whether you stay there or not, the venerable old St. George Hotel is worth seeing.

The Saint George Hotel

Treat yourself to a stay at the St. George Hotel, P.O. Box 9, Volcano 95689, tel. (209) 296-4458. Included on the National Register of Historic Places, the St. George is a character—straight-laced exterior with vine maple twining down from the overhanging balconies, lace curtains and functional Victoriana inside—and even more characters in its tiny bar. Once the most elegant hotel in the gold country, now an architectural elder statesman, the St. George is also quite a good bargain. Rooms are $62-75 on weekdays, $110-113 on weekends, breakfast included. Quieter but less intriguing lodgings are available in the motel annex next door. The St. George's

Miwok hun'ge, a ceremonial roundhouse at Chaw'se Indian Grinding Rocks State Park

CALIFORNIA DEPARTMENT OF PARKS & RECREATION

modified American plan on Saturday nights includes dinner, lodgings, and breakfast.

If you're in no hurry, and if it's open, linger a while in the St. George's small saloon, its folk-artsy atmosphere best expressed by the three-dimensional completion of General George Custer's portrait: a suction-tipped arrow to the head. Just outside the bar is a public telephone booth with a message from Superman himself.

Other Practicalities

Campers, stay at **Chaw'se.** Brunch at the **Jug and Rose Confectionary** on Main St., tel. (209) 296-4696—all the sourdough pancakes you can eat plus ham, scrambled eggs, fresh fruit. Sandwiches here are also good, not to mention the homemade soups and pie. Try a blackberry milkshake or plain ol' vanilla ice cream with homemade rose petal syrup.

Children are welcome at Volcano Pioneers theater performances at the **Cobblestone Theatre,** April through October. Limited seating, so reservations are a must. Summer theater is roomier at the outdoor amphitheater, picknicking encouraged. For information and/or reservations, contact: **Volcano Theatre Company,** P.O. Box 88, Volcano 95689, tel. (209) 223-HOME or 295-5537.

Daffodil Hill

The McLaughlins started planting daffodils here in the 19th century when the area was a stage stop, a tradition continued to this day by their descendants. Daffodil Hill is a private four-acre farm with 300,000 daffodils (250 varieties), plus crocuses, tulips, hyacinths, lilacs, violets, a few almond trees—an entire blooming hillside, free for the looking. The daffodils are best from mid-March through April, but it's nice to come here any time to picnic (tables available) and to visit with the farm animals. To get here, take Ramshorn Grade north from Volcano. Ramshorn eventually intersects with Shake Ridge Rd.; you can shake on down to Sutter Creek, or head east, then turn west onto Fiddletown Rd. at Lockwood Junction.

JACKSON TO ANGELS CAMP

Mokelumne Hill

A block-long town perched on the divide between the Mokelumne and Calaveras rivers, known affectionately as Mok Hill. So rich were gold claims at Mokelumne Hill they were limited in size to 16 square feet. Destroyed by fires in 1854, 1864, and 1874, the town was best known for its gold rush wars. One was between miners and a Chilean doctor accused of using slaves to work his claims. Another involved sudden patriotic fervor: Yanks jumped some French miners' claim—a particularly rich find, incidentally—allegedly because they'd raised the French flag over it.

Poke around the saloon, eat in the restaurant, and perhaps stay at the bold gold **Hotel Leger** on Main St., tel. (209) 296-1401. Peek into the museum at Main and Center. There's a quiet small park, complete with drinking fountain, on the downhill end of Main. Just across the street is the dusty and seemingly decrepit **Adams and Co. Genuine Old West Saloon and Museum and Less** in the old I.O.O.F. hall, usually open only on Fri. and Sat. from 3:30 p.m. until whenever the bartender feels like going home.

SAN ANDREAS

Once a Mexican town with a few adobes, San Andreas is now the Calaveras County seat, a bustling metropolis with a touristy downtown. The block-long historically interesting part of town is perpendicular to the highway. Still standing: both the courthouse where Black Bart finally faced justice and the jailhouse cell he called home before doing time in San Quentin. A walk through the pioneer cemetery west of town is sobering, so many young men, such short lives. Since San Andreas has never had a daily newspaper, obituaries are posted on the traditional "death tree" outside the old post office, now office space for the weekly *Calaveras Enterprise.*

Calaveras County Museum

The brick county Hall of Records complex, beautifully restored, now houses the outstanding Calaveras County Museum and Archives, also a de facto visitors center, 30 N. Main St., tel. (209) 754-6513, open daily 10 a.m.-4 p.m., small admission fee. A Miwok bark tepee, artifacts, and basketry are on display; you can even try your skill at grinding acorns into meal. Study the legal papers, including a black-bordered public hanging invitation signed and sealed by the sheriff. The mining displays include a tip of the hat to early Spanish prospectors and Depression-era miners. Full-size room displays include a typical miner's cabin and a gold rush-era general store. The jail is downstairs in the courtyard, which is planted with native flora. This little stone-walled garden is a shady, pleasant respite from highway traffic and hot sun.

Accommodations

To camp, head west on Hwy. 12 to the **New Hogan Reservoir Recreation Area,** 1955 New Hogan Pkwy. in Valley Springs, tel. (209) 772-1343. Or try the **Black Bart Inn,** 55 St. Charles, P.O. Box 576, San Andreas 95249, tel. 754-3808; both the old-time brick hotel and modern motel rooms run $45 and up.

B&Bers have a few choices; cheapest is **Bonnie's Inn** at the junction of Highways 12 and 49, P.O. Box 356, tel. (209) 754-3212, large and simply furnished cottages with refrigerators and movies on TV, also a hot tub and barbecue area, $55 and up. **The Robin's Nest** downtown at 247 W. St. Charles, P.O. Box 1408, tel. 754-1076, is a cozy stop with 1900s travelers' decor, good continental breakfasts, and occasional "theme" weekends for mystery buffs, chocolate lovers, and wine enthusiasts, also chamber music concerts in the Victorian garden; rooms $65-110.

Food

The Early American-furnished coffee shop downstairs at the **Black Bart** serves tasty, large, inexpensive omelettes, other breakfast and lunch choices, and dinner. Also good and a bit more upscale is **Wendells** at the intersection of Hwy 49 and W. Center St., tel. (209) 286-1338, open for dinner Wed.-Sun., for breakfast

and lunch only on weekends. Or try **Nonno's Cucina Italiana** at the Hotel Leger in Mok Hill, tel. 286-1401, substantial pasta dishes and specials, open Thurs.-Sun for dinner only.

California Caverns

The one-time resort town of Cave City has long since bitten the dust, but the California Caverns on Mountain Ranch Rd., tel. (209) 736-2708, are still going strong. First opened in 1850 and now a state historic landmark, the caverns ain't what they used to be, due to visitor overload and vandalism. But they're still worth a peek. The easy "trail of lights" tour is $6 adults, $3 kids, but the more adventurous (and muddy) trips, which involve squeezing through fissures to get to caves and underground lakes, run about $60, including guide, rafts, hardhats, and coveralls. Open June to Oct. 10-5 daily, weekends only in November.

Near California Caverns

Near the caverns are some fascinating back roads and ghost towns to explore. **Sheep Ranch** was once a former quartz mining camp where William Randolph Hearst's dad started the family fortune. Beautiful San Antonio Falls is nearby. **Mountain Ranch,** an early tourist destination once called El Dorado, supported two separate mining camps: typical gold rush buildings, most still in use. The Domenghini Store was once a saloon, and has been a general store since 1901. The Mountain Ranch Hotel is a well-preserved Victorian closed to the public.

Calaveritas, closer to San Andreas, was another alleged outpost for Joaquin Murrieta. Not much to see here except a few old buildings, including the 1852 adobe store built by Luigi Costa. But the countryside whispers of bygone travelers, long-dead dreamers. If you're heading south from San Andreas, take Dogtown Rd. from Mountain Ranch Rd. to Calaveritas and across a few creeks to Angels Camp—the old miners' route.

ANGELS CAMP

Originally a simple trading post (and officially named City of Angels, though no one calls it that), Angels Camp became a jumping mining camp after Bennagar Rasberry accidentally shot the ground while cleaning his muzzle-loader—murdering a manzanita bush and revealing an impressive chunk of gold-seamed quartz dangling from its roots. Placer gold was found here by either Henry Angel or George Angell, depending on the story, but the pans soon came up empty. The town boomed again, though, with help from later hardrock mining companies.

Jumping Frogs
And Other Celebrations

Mark Twain once hung out in the Hotel Angels bar and pool hall here, where he first heard the miners' tall tale about the jumping frogs—inspiration for his first successful story, "The Celebrated Jumping Frogs of Calaveras County," published in 1864. When the roads in Angels Camp were finally paved in 1928, someone jokingly suggested holding a jumping frog contest to commemorate the fictional athletic humiliation of that now-famous toady, Dan'l Webster. And so the town's **Jumping Frog Jubilee** was hatched.

The event is now staged for tourists every May at Frogtown (the fairgrounds just south of Angels Camp) in conjunction with the county fair (rental frogs available). Considered quite serious sport by some, don't kiss or otherwise distract the frogs until after the $1500 prize has been awarded.

Another annual contest in Angels Camp involves hanging out the town's literal dirty laundry on clotheslines strung across Main St., with the most outlandish and/or unmentionable collection winning the prize. For current information about these and other local events, stop off at the Angels Camp Museum on Main. Or stop by the **Calaveras County Lodging & Visitors Association,** 1301 S. Main St., P.O. Box 637, Angels Camp 95222, tel. (800) CAL-FROG (225-3764), which publishes the very useful *Calaveras County Visitor's Guide* and also serves as a reservations and information service for lodg-

ing, skiing and other recreation, and area events. Or contact the **Calaveras County Fairgrounds,** P.O. Box 96, tel. 736-2561.

Sights

Though not exactly a vintage gold rush town these days, Angels Camp is also not yet overrun by corporate America. Main Street isn't too touristy, but it *is* an amphibian's paradise. Frogs leap from store windows, perch atop monuments, hang from balconies, swing from shop signs, and decorate sidewalks. The **Angels Camp Museum** at 753 Main, tel. (209) 736-2963, is open daily 10-3 from April to Thanksgiving, Wed.-Sun. otherwise, small fee. Stop by if you're especially interested in horse-drawn wagons, buggies, and rock collections. There were once many Chinese here but only two brick Chinatown buildings remain.

South of town just off Main between Angel and Altaville is **Utica Park,** with picnic tables and playground. The low spot here is a permanent reminder of the 1889 mine cave-in directly below, a disaster which killed 16 men. The model undershot water wheel resembles the one that once powered the Utica Mine's ore-crushing mill. The Mark Twain statue was a gift to the town in 1945 from a movie company doing the story of Mark Twain (played by Frederick March).

PRACTICALITIES

Area Accommodations

For camping, try **Frogtown** (the county fairgrounds) just south of town, P.O. Box 96, Angels Camp 95222, tel. (209) 736-2561, $10 for decent tent or RV sites, including hot showers. Also close is **New Melones Reservoir.** Up into the Sierra Nevada but worth the trip is **Calaveras Big Trees State Park.** The **Jumping Frog Motel,** 330 Murphys Grade Rd. in Altaville, tel. 736-2191, from $39, offers community kitchens, special rates for seniors. The town's first B&B is the **Cooper House Bed and Breakfast Inn** at 1184 Church St., P.O. Box 1388, tel. 736-2145, built in 1911 for a local doctor, now operated

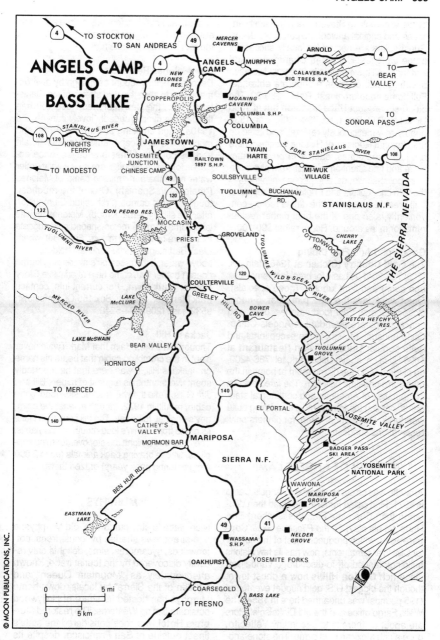

ANGELS CAMP TO BASS LAKE

TO STOCKTON
TO SAN ANDREAS

MERCER CAVERNS

ARNOLD

ANGELS CAMP   MURPHYS

CALAVERAS BIG TREES S.P.

TO BEAR VALLEY

NEW MELONES RES.

COPPEROPOLIS

MOANING CAVERN

COLUMBIA S.H.P.

TO SONORA PASS

STANISLAUS RIVER

KNIGHTS FERRY

JAMESTOWN

COLUMBIA

SONORA

S FORK STANISLAUS RIVER

TO MODESTO

YOSEMITE JUNCTION
CHINESE CAMP

RAILTOWN 1897 S.H.P.

TWAIN HARTE

SOULSBYVILLE

MI-WUK VILLAGE

TUOLUMNE

BUCHANAN RD.

STANISLAUS N.F.

THE SIERRA NEVADA

TUOLUMNE RIVER

DON PEDRO RES.

MOCCASIN

PRIEST

GROVELAND

COTTONWOOD RD.

CHERRY LAKE

TUOLUMNE WILD & SCENIC RIVER

COULTERVILLE

LAKE McCLURE

GREELEY HILL RD.

BOWER CAVE

HETCH HETCHY RES.

MERCED RIVER

LAKE McSWAIN

BEAR VALLEY

TUOLUMNE GROVE

HORNITOS

TO MERCED

EL PORTAL

YOSEMITE VALLEY

CATHEY'S VALLEY

MORMON BAR

MARIPOSA

SIERRA N.F.

BADGER PASS SKI AREA

YOSEMITE NATIONAL PARK

BEN HUR RD.

WAWONA

MARIPOSA GROVE

EASTMAN LAKE

WASSAMA S.H.P.

NELDER GROVE

OAKHURST

YOSEMITE FORKS

COARSEGOLD

BASS LAKE

TO FRESNO

0   5 mi
0   5 km

© MOON PUBLICATIONS, INC.

by the winemaking Stevenot family. Family antiques and original artwork are part of the decor. Guest suites are named for locally successful grape varieties: Cabernet, Chardonnay, and Zinfandel. All have private bathrooms, two have private decks, one has a separate entrance. Full homemade breakfast. Rates: $80-90. The 5,000-square-foot **Utica Mansion Inn** at 1090 Utica Ln., P.O. Box 1, tel. 736-4209, is an 1882 beauty now meticulously restored and listed on the National Register of Historic Places. There are just three suites, each with private bathroom and fine attention to detail, from plush carpets, polished woods, and period wallpapers to the tulip chandeliers and English-tiled fireplaces. Full breakfast served in the dining room—conveniently, also one of the best dinner restaurants for miles around. Room rates: $90-100.

Good Food And Fine Dining

The **Gold Country Kitchen** at 1246 Main, tel. (209) 736-2941, is basic for breakfast (omelettes and such) and light lunches (good specials). Open weekdays 5 a.m.-2 p.m., Sat. 5-noon, closed Sunday. Fast food eateries, delis, and snack shops are abundant in Angels Camp. Quite unusual, though, is the exceptional and quite popular **Utica Mansion Restaurant** at 1090 Utica Ln. above Utica Park, tel. 736-4209, an elegant Victorian dining room at home in the mansion's one-time ballroom. The fare here is a combination of American and continental standards, nothing too trendy, most everything quite wonderful. Open Thurs.-Mon. for dinners only, reservations suggested.

VICINITY OF ANGELS CAMP

Altaville was officially annexed to Angels Camp in 1971. First called Forks in the Road then Winterton then Cherokee Flat, this is where Bret Harte set his play, *To the Pliocene Skull.* **Copperopolis,** which produced most of the copper for Civil War armaments, now has its few historic buildings fenced off to discourage vandalism. Once-rich **Carson Hill** is now a ghost town, though the biggest U.S. gold nugget ever found (195 pounds) was unearthed here in 1854. The Wells Fargo office and the old Dinkelspiel Store are about all there is to see in tiny **Vallecito,** once a rich Mexican gold camp. The stone-and-

iron Gilleado building, formerly a store and bank, still stands in **Douglas Flat,** an old gold camp at the foot of Table Mountain.

New Melones Reservoir

Despite a bitterly fought campaign by environmentalists to save this wild stretch of the Stanislaus River, the New Melones Reservoir has flooded the river's ruggedly lovely canyon, the 1840s stage crossing at Parrott's Ferry, and much of the landscape familiar to Mark Twain and his cohorts. Limestone caves, once enclaves for native peoples, are now mostly under water as is the early mining camp of Melones ("melons" in Spanish). One of the roughest, toughest gold camps (first called Slumgullion after the slimy riverbank mud), Melones took its later name from the melon-shaped gold nuggets found here by Mexican miners. **Funk Hill,** where Black Bart staged his first and last holdup, is still above water. If the reservoir's river-killing karma doesn't bother you, camp here at primitive **Glory Hole** or **Tuttletown,.** For current info, contact: Park Manager, Star Rt., Box 155-C, Jamestown 95327, tel. (209) 984-5248.

Jackass Hill

Though old-timers claim that Mark Twain never slept in the crumbling cabin that bears his name on Jackass Hill, it was here that he reportedly spent five months as a guest of miners Bill and Jim Gillis. Take the well-marked side road to the cabin, rebuilt in 1922, though at least the chimney's original, folks say. The hill itself didn't take its name from Twain's loud mouth or lazy habits. The area was a nighttime stopover for mine suppliers, whose braying pack animals (up to 2,000 a night during peak years) grazed there.

MURPHYS

Nice place to stay put awhile, old Murphys: a one-street town shaded by locust trees, cottonwoods, sycamores, elms, delights only recently discovered by the tourist trade. Known affectionately as "Mountain Queen" and "Queen of the Sierra" by locals, down-home Murphys has hosted its share of Hollywood outsiders filming Westerns. The restored **Murphys Hotel** was once considered the state's finest outside of San Francisco, despite its

Wild West reputation (genuine bullet holes decorate the doorway). Across from the hotel is the **Oldtimers Museum,** tel. (209) 728-3679, a rock fortress with iron-shuttered front windows, musty memorabilia, books, and a period blacksmith shop out back. Best of all, though, is the E Clampus Vitus "Wall of Comparative Innovations," a peculiar collection of self-praise for this historically haughty bunch of good ol' boys. (Usually open Thurs.-Sun. 11-4, Mon. 9:30-3, weekends only in the off-season.) The 1860 **Murphys Elementary School** was once called Pine Grove College, so locals could claim they'd been to college.

Pick up a schedule for local performances, by the **Black Bart Players,,** tel. (209) 728-3956 or 728-3675—classics, comedy, mysteries, musicals, melodramas.

Accommodations

The **Murphys Hotel and Lodge,** 457 Main St., P.O. Box 329, Murphys 95247, tel. (209) 728-3444, is a national historic monument and a hot night spot to boot. Good literary and financial vibes: Black Bart, U.S. Grant, Will Rogers, Mark Twain, Daniel Webster, Horatio Alger, and J.P. Morgan have all slept here. Fairly reasonable at $45 d and up (special winter skiers' rates, too), reservations are always a good idea. The Murphys Hotel has a wonderful Western bar. To guarantee a good night's sleep, remember that hot air rises, in this case barroom noise, into the rooms overhead. Light sleepers might prefer the more mundane but quiet motel units next door. Nearby is the grand **Dunbar House** bed and breakfast inn, an Italianate Victorian at 271 Jones St., P.O. Box 1375, tel. 728-2897. Pleasant accommodations, including generous breakfasts, $95-105, midwinter and midweek rates often cheaper.

Quick Food And Fine Dining

Stop for a picnic or just a rest at **Murphys Town Park** just off Main near the creek. First pick up a sandwich and a sweet treat at the **Peppermint Stick Ice Cream Parlor,** 454 Main, tel. (209) 728-3570; try the miner's soup, served in its own French bread "bowl." Open midday daily. Another good choice for a quick, hearty meal is the **Nugget Restaurant** at 75 Big Trees Rd., tel. 728-2608, open for breakfast, lunch, and dinner (no dinner on Sunday nights). Wonderful fried chicken. More than a dinner house and surprisingly good is the **Murphys Hotel Restaurant** on Main, tel. 728-3444. American-continental fare at dinner, great breakfast and lunch.

Murphys Wineries

A few scenic miles north of town is the **Stevenot Winery,** 2690 San Domingo Rd., P.O. Box 548, tel. (209) 728-3436; good White Zinfandel and Fumé Blanc to taste in the inimitable ambience of a sod-roofed barn. Open daily 10-5. Or stop by **Milliaire** in town at 276 Main, tel. 728-1658. There are quite a few others. For a complete current listing, contact the **Calaveras Wine Association,** toll-free tel. (800) 999-9039.

Mercer Caverns And Moaning Cavern

About one mile north of Murphys via old Sheep Ranch Rd., Mercer Caverns were formed from an earthquake-caused fissure. Note the unusual aragonite crystals in these limestone formations. Nowadays, the experience is a bit flashy, with colored lights, but offers good examples of "flowstone," stalagmites, and stalactites. The Mercer caves were called Calaveras Caverns at one time *(calaveras* means skulls in Spanish) because human bones were found here: the Miwok lowered bodies into caves as part of their traditional burial rites. Open daily 9-4:30 Memorial day through Sept., just weekends and school holidays, otherwise, 11-3:30; $5 adults, $2.50 children. For info, contact: Mercer Caverns, P.O. Box 509, Murphys 95247, tel. (209) 728-2101.

More pristine is **Moaning Cavern** on Parrotts Ferry Rd. off Hwy. 4 between Vallecito and Douglas Flat, reportedly the largest hidden hole in the ground in California. Don't be put off by the hype. Local Native Americans were said to hold this spot in awe because of the voices calling out from the cave's mouth. Moaning Cavern is really a vertical cave with a main cavity large enough to hide the Statue of Liberty (if anyone could ever figure out how to get it down the staircase). Thrill-seekers (over age 12) can rappel down into darkness on a special tour. Admission for the regular tour is $6 for adults, $3 for children. Open daily 9 a.m.-6 p.m. (10-5 in winter). For more information contact: Moaning Cavern, P.O. Box 78, Vallecito 95251, tel. (209) 736-2708.

CALAVERAS BIG TREES

The first grove of *Sequoiadendron giganteum* or Sierra redwoods ever discovered by white explorers was noted by northstate pioneer John Bidwell in 1841. These trees grow only on the western slopes of the Sierra Nevada and are more plentiful in the Yosemite, Sequoia, and Kings Canyon areas to the south. Here, about four miles east of Arnold, there are relatively few "big trees," and these grow in isolated groves among mountain yew, sugar pine, white fir, and flowering dogwood. But Calaveras Big Trees are a good summer escape (it's cool up here), also nice for uncrowded autumn campouts and wintertime snowshoe hikes, cross-country skiing. For information, contact: Calaveras Big Trees State Park, P.O. Box 120, Arnold 95223, tel. (209) 795-2334.

Sights, Hikes

Start at the **Big Trees Visitor Center,** with a nod to the wooden grizzly outside, for a good orientation to the area's natural and cultural history. There's an easy one-mile **nature trail** through the park's North Grove. A brochure is available in Braille for the 600-foot **Three Sense Trail,** where you touch, smell, and hear the forest. The North Grove area near the highway is most accessible and therefore most visited, but the South Grove has about 1,300 big trees in a nearly primeval setting. It's only a mile to the southern group of trees from the parking lot, up the **Big Trees Creek Trail** to the self-guided loop. The longer **Lava Bluffs Trail** winds through ancient lava formations and natural springs. Great swimming in the Stanislaus River.

Camping

You can camp at the **North Grove Campground** or at **Squaw Hollow.** Very pleasant campsites with wonderful hot showers and handpumped water for the usual state rate of $14, reservations a must in summer. Contact Mistix, tel. (800) 444-7275. Or come for the day to picnic and hike on trails and fire roads, $5 per car day use. There are 10 primitive "environmental campsites" at Calaveras, all quite different and far from the madding crowds, but usually only available with separate reservations three to eight weeks in advance. Otherwise first-come, first-camped. There's a seven-day limit, and no more than eight people allowed per site. For a specific "environmental camping" sites map and reservation info, contact the park or call the California Dept. of Parks and Recreation toll-free, tel. (800) 952-5580 weekdays 8-5, or write: CDPR Reservations Office, P.O. Box 2390, Sacramento 95811.

Nearby Practicalities

Just west of Calaveras Big Trees, **Arnold** has a decent store and some fairly good restaurants and accommodations. If the campgrounds at Calaveras are full, take Boards Crossing Rd. to the primitive **Sourgrass Campground,** or take Hell's Half Acre Rd. four miles to free **Boards Crossing Campground.** For a pleasant bed and breakfast stay, the **Lodge at Manuel Mill** on White Pines Rd., P.O. Box 998, Arnold 95223, tel. (209) 795-2622, has five rooms with historic western decor, private baths, and woodstoves, $85-105.

COLUMBIA

There are no drunken bar brawls, shady ladies, or muddy, manure-filled streets in Columbia these days. The "Gem of the Southern Mines," Columbia served as capital city to an area population of over 15,000 in its prime. But in 1854, the town lost the sensitive scuffle for state capital to Sacramento by just two legislative votes, a devastating political loss for the biggest, richest, and wickedest gold town of them all. Much of the land near Columbia has been laid waste by hydraulic mining. When the mines declined in the 1870s, over $87 million in gold had been stripped from the earth.

Even before its painstaking restoration, the former American Camp was the most beautifully preserved of all gold country towns. Quite a few Westerns, including *High Noon,* have been filmed here. Now a state park, downtown Columbia is a fine outdoor "museum" with no cars allowed in the historic sector, only tourists—about a half million each year. Most of the town is "open" daily 9-5.

To get oriented, pick up a free guide at the visitors center, then wander through blocks of fire-resistant brick and iron buildings in the Greek-Revival style, built following devastating fires in 1854 and 1857. Main Street today is only half the length it once was, the northern arm never reattached to the town. Push the "talking buttons" outside various buildings; tape-recorded "guides" explain what you see as you peer into old windows and doors.

SEEING COLUMBIA

Museums, Banks, And Bars
The tiny **William Cavalier Museum** at Knapp's Corner, Main and State streets, is a good first stop. The museum's collection includes real gold, plentiful Western paraphernalia, displays chronicling the massive town-wide restoration, also slide shows and films. The **Museum of the Gold Rush Press** in the old *Columbia Gazette* building has a collection of old-time newspapers and a rogue's gallery of gold rush journalists. The two-story red brick **Columbia Grammar School** on Kennebec Hill was in use

from 1860 to 1937 and is in excellent condition —old desks with ink wells, dusty books, writing slates, tobacco-can lunchboxes, woodburning stoves.

The seedy **miner's cabin** at the end of Main is a bleak, definitely unromantic reminder of prospectors' real lives. About $55 million in gold bullion and nuggets passed through the authentically furnished **Wells Fargo office** here. Notice the beautiful scales. The **D.O. Mills** building next door was one of the first branches of the later Bank of California. Another authentic touch is the town's ample supply of saloons; before the first big fire, about one-fifth of Columbia's business establishments were bars.

Hotel Finery,
A Fine Haircut, And Papeete
The very fine **Fallon Hotel,** with its elegant theater and restaurant, has been righteously restored. No matter what else you do, stop here to appreciate the careful craftsmanship. The **City Hotel** is less ostentatious but still impressive. Also in Columbia is the state's oldest barbershop (need a haircut?), dentist's office, Chinese herb shop, smithy, carpenter shop, tintype photography studio, ice house, and livery stable. **Papeete,** Columbia's first and most extravagant fire pumper (originally destined for the Society Islands), is now just for show, used only during the annual Firemen's Muster festivities.

DOING COLUMBIA

Accommodations
Both tent campers and RVers are welcome at the **'49er Trailer Ranch** at 23223 Italian Bar Rd., P.O. Box 569, Columbia 95310, tel. (209) 532-9898; hot showers, picnic tables, barbecues, laundromat, nightly campfire, even a square-dance center, $17.50. Or try the **Marble Quarry Resort** nearby at 11551 Yankee Hill Rd., P.O. Box 850, tel. 532-9539; swimming pool, laundromat, picnic tables, barbecues, RV hookups, $17-22.

If you want a motel, the clean, old-fashioned **Columbia Gem Motel** at 22131 Parrotts Ferry

Rd., P.O. Box 874, Columbia 95310, tel. (209) 532-4508, is quite pleasant. The tiny barn-red-and-white 1940s-style cottages with mini sitting porches run $25-65, depending on the time of year, plus there are a few standard motel rooms. (This "gem" has just a handful of units, so be sure to reserve in advance.) New and just three blocks from downtown is **The Harlan House Bed and Breakfast** at 22890 School House, P.O. Box 686, tel. 533-4862.

Columbia has two wonderful and fairly reasonable hotels to choose from. The ornate lobby of the **Fallon Hotel** on Washington St. just off Broadway, with its almost too perfect vintage wallpapers, green velvet drapes, oak furnishings, and Oriental rugs, is probably an overstatement of Old West luxury; when this was a miners' lodging house, the accommodations were much more spartan. No wandering through the elegant hallways unless you're a paying customer. Exquisitely redone Victorian rooms, with chain-pull toilets and porcelain basins in the half-baths (showers shared), $60-85. For reservations, contact the Fallon Hotel, P.O. Box 1870, Columbia 95310, tel. (209) 532-1470.

The **City Hotel**, on Main St., P.O. Box 1870, Columbia 95310, tel. (209) 532-1479, has an authentic Victorian parlor, nine rooms with half-baths and shared showers, all less fancy than the Fallon yet probably more true to gold rush Columbia. Rooms start at $65-85, including continental breakfast. Before it became a hotel in the 1870s, the building was used as an assay office, opera house, stagecoach office, and newspaper headquarters. Hotel management students from the local junior college, dressed in 1850s attire, tend to your every need at both the City and Fallon hotels—the works, down to fluffing your pillows.

Good Food

Eat, at least once, at the **City Hotel** dining room, another community college "project." Very good and very reasonable: contemporary American regional cuisine with classic French touches, light sauces, intriguing appetizers (including that '49er favorite, oysters on the half shell), crisp linen and fresh flowers, fine service. Reservations necessary. The **Columbia House** on Main, tel. (209) 532-5134, is relaxed and reasonably priced. Besides its hale and hearty name, the adjacent **What Cheer Saloon** has a comfortable Western atmosphere. **El Sombrero** at 11256 State St., tel. 533-9123, serves very good house-made Mexican food.

For family-style Italian (stick to the pasta dishes), try the garishly wallpapered **Stagecoach Inn** on Parrotts Ferry Rd., tel. (209) 532-5816, open Mon.-Fri. for lunch and dinner.

Back in Columbia, the **St. Charles** is a beer and wine bar for adults (kids can order a sarsaparilla). More unnecessary calories are available at **Nelson's Columbia Candy Kitchen** on Main, a third-generation family operation featuring old-recipe specialties like rocky road, almond bark, peppermint or horehound candies, even genuine licorice whips, plus decadent hand-dipped truffles. Another treat: good ice cream in fresh-baked waffle cones at the **Fallon House Ice Cream Parlor.**

Activities And Entertainment

With the right attitude (nothing wrong with being one more tourist among the multitude) anyone can enjoy Columbia's family-focused entertainment. Taking a stagecoach ride through the woods on the **Columbia Stage Line,** P.O. Box 1777, Angels Camp 95222, tel. (209) 785-2244 or 785-2263 (in Columbia, tel. 532-0663), is worth the small fare. Stage trips (also horse and

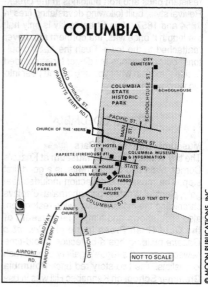

CALIFORNIA DEPARTMENT OF PARKS & RECREATION

the Columbia stage

pony rides) are offered daily from mid-June through Labor Day, weekends only otherwise. Or get a glimpse of gold-bearing quartz at home on the guided tour of a nearby working gold mine (daily in summer, otherwise usually on weekends only). For info: **Hidden Treasure Gold Mine,** P.O. Box 28, Columbia 95310, tel. 532-9693, or stop by the Matelot Gold Mine Supply Store at the Corner of Main and Washington. If you're going, bring a sweater.

The **Fallon Theatre** in the hotel has old-time melodramas during the high season, put on by University of the Pacific drama students (get reservations in advance), and the local **Columbia Actors Repertory** stages musicals and modern dramas. For community theater information, contact the Fallon Theatre, P.O. Box 1849, Columbia 95310, tel. (209) 532-4644.

About a mile southwest of the park is the **Springfield Trout Farm,** 21980 Springfield Rd., tel. (209) 532-4623, a fun place offering family fishing from the stocked pond. When you catch your rainbow trout—raised here just for that purpose, in spring water—the folks here even clean it for you and pack it on ice. Tackle and bait are part of the deal, but you can also buy fresh-dressed trout to go. Or you can just wander around a while and watch the fingerlings grow. Open daily 10-6 in summer, Thurs.-Mon. 10-5 otherwise.

For adults who've had enough of everything else, there's always winetasting—at attractive

Yankee Hill Winery just off Yankee Hill Rd. at 11755 Coarsegold Ln., tel. (209) 533-2417, where you can also picnic and at least peek into the production facility, and the **Gold Mine Winery** at 22265 Parrotts Ferry Rd., tel. 532-3089.

Events And Information

Show up on Easter Sunday for the town's **Victorian Easter Parade,** quite the mobile display of bonnie bonnets. The **Firemen's Muster** here in May is also a major event. Volunteer fire brigades from around the state, dressed in period costumes, haul their antique engines to Columbia to compete in pumping contests and otherwise join in the general jolliness. There's a **Columbia Diggins** living history weekend in early June, a gold rush tent-town reenactment. The inhabitants, dressed in period clothes, discuss only "current" events (go ahead, try to trip them up) and ply their trades: panning for gold, preaching to the heathen hordes, and running for political office. Also big in Columbia: an Americana-filled **Fourth of July Celebration.** Other events include the **Poison Oak Show** in late September, the **Fiddle and Banjo Contest** in early October, and the **Christmas Lamplight Tour** on the first Saturday in December—part of the two-weekend **Miner's Christmas,** with Santa driving the stagecoach. For info about events, contact: Columbia State Historic Park, P.O. Box 151, Columbia 95310, tel. (209) 532-4301.

SONORA

Sonora, the "Queen of the Southern Mines" and old-time Columbia rival, is today something of a suburban octopus, its tentacles of one-acre ranchettes flailing out in all directions. And no wonder people want to live here: this *is* a pretty town (downtown).

History
Mexican miners founded the town during a particularly nasty period of Yankee us-firstism. Greedy gringos eventually forced the first Sonorans off their claims, creating considerable outlaw backlash. The newish novel *The Last Californian* by modern-day Sonora resident and schoolteacher Feliz Guthrie spins the story of the infamous Rancheria Massacre, a telling tale about anti-Hispanic racism in the Mother Lode. After the Latino "lawbreakers" were eliminated, the rich placer fields near Sonora harvested, and the pocket mines turned inside out and emptied, lumber became the area's main industry, spurred by the arrival of the railroad in 1898. Orange crates for packaging California citrus were manufactured here by the millions.

SIGHTS

Washington is the town's main street, an identity shared with Hwy. 49 and Hwy. 108 as both squeeze through Sonora's central ravine. Travelers flow in fits and spurts through a mother lode of boutiques, specialty shops, and eateries, all tucked into and around some noteworthy architecture. Pick up a free "The Life And Times Of Sonora" tabloid at businesses around town, and the "Heritage Home Tour" guide at the county museum, then rest and read by Sonora Creek in **Coffill Park** downtown at S. Washington and Theall.

Strolling Sonora
The elegant and unusual red **Saint James Episcopal Church** at Washington and Snell is still a place of worship, but also a museum (in the rectory) open 9-5 weekdays. Next door is the **Bradford Building,** complete with copper doors

and an elaborate dome, constructed by local lumber baron S.S. Bradford. He also built the impressive, very San Francisco **Street-Morgan Mansion** across from the church at 23 W. Snell.

The original 1850 **Gunn Adobe** at 286 S. Washington later grew a balcony and new wings, becoming the Hotel Italia and today a motel. The main entrance to the **Tuolumne County Courthouse** is on W. Yaney; the building itself is bizarre yet stately, built from local materials: green sandstone, yellow pressed bricks, Columbia marble, and Copperopolis copper for the Byzantine clock tower and doors. In the **County Recorder's office** there's a predam photo of Hetch Hetchy Valley—second only to Yosemite Valley in natural beauty, according to John Muir—and also a good collection of old newspapers.

Tuolumne County Museum
Located in the former jailhouse at 158 W. Bradford, P.O. Box 299, Sonora 95370, tel. (209) 532-1317, the Tuolumne County Museum And History Center is worth some time for its paintings by William West and some fascinating Western photography. The jailhouse setting itself lends an intriguing atmosphere, with local gold rush relics and other historical items exhibited in a "cell by cell" arrangement. Picnic in the jailyard. Open daily 10-3:30 in summer, otherwise closed Sundays.

ACCOMMODATIONS

Camping
Far from wilderness but close to town are the **Mother Lode Fairgrounds,** off Hwy. 49 south of town at 220 Southgate Dr., Sonora 95370, tel. (209) 532-7428, $11. Nothing fancy, a basic RV setup with hot showers and picnic tables, but you can pitch tents on the lawn. Camp at **New Melones** (see "Angels Camp" above), or for a change of pace, head east up into the Sierra Nevada high country on Hwy. 108 and pitch your tent at **Fraser Flat Campground** past Long Barn (take the Spring Gap turnoff north),

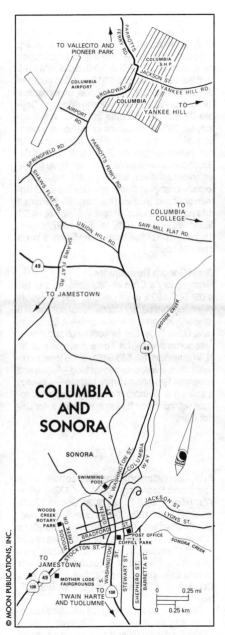

COLUMBIA
AND
SONORA

© MOON PUBLICATIONS, INC.

tel. 586-3234, $7. (Other possibilities near Pinecrest.) For seclusion and scenery, take Cottonwood Rd. from Tuolumne to **Cherry Valley Campground** at Cherry Lake just outside Yosemite. If you're heading into Yosemite via Hwy. 120 from the gold country, there are wonderful primitive campsites near the wild Tuolumne River (see "Groveland" following).

Motels And Hotels
Right downtown (and worth it for the "feel" of local history) is the **Sonora Inn,** a beige Spanish California beauty with tile roof, pool, hot tub, saloon, and restaurant, 160 S. Washington, Sonora 95370, tel. (209) 532-7468. Rooms here are fairly reasonable, $45-95 (less for adjoining motel units). **The Gunn House Motor Hotel,** 286 S. Washington, tel. 532-3421, incorporates the original two-story adobe house into a pleasant inn-like motel oozing local charm, with private baths, and rates $40-75. (Ask for a room in the back, off the street.)

The **Sierra Gold Lodge** across from the fairgrounds just southwest of town along Hwy. 49/108, 480 W. Stockton St., tel. (209) 532-3952, is a settled-in motel with big shade trees, rates $48-64. Right downtown and convenient is the **Sonora Towne House Motel** at 350 S. Washington, tel. 532-3633 or toll-free (800) 251-1538, a large, multistoried contemporary motel with the usual amenities, two pools, hot tub. Rooms run $55-65 during the high season; ask about off-season discounts. Several miles east of downtown via Hwy. 108 at 19551 Hess Ave., tel. 533-4400 or toll-free for reservations (800) 528-1234, is the deluxe **Best Western Sonora Oaks Motor Hotel,** rooms $60-115, lower rates in the off-season.

Area Bed And Breakfasts
Close to downtown but quiet is **The Ryan House,** 153 S. Shepherd St., P.O. Box 416, Sonora 95370, tel. (209) 533-3445 or toll-free (800) 831-4897, rooms with handmade quilts and private baths, $75-80. **Lulu Belles's** at 85 Gold St., tel. 533-3455, is sedate and serene but has rooms with private entrances so you can stay out all night, $60-95. The **Barretta Gardens Inn** overlooking the town at 700 S. Barretta St., tel. 532-6039, is $80 d and up, including a full breakfast.

Lavender Hill nearby at 683 S. Barretta St., Sonora 95370, tel. (209) 532-9024, has comfortable Victorian rooms, two share a large bath, $65-75 including breakfast. Different but quite exceptional for families is the **Llamahall Guest Ranch,** 18170 Wards Ferry Rd., tel. 532-7264; comfortable rooms in the midst of a llama farm, plus hot tub, sauna, full breakfast, $85-105.

Outside Sonora proper are some other fine inns, including **La Casa Inglesa** at 18047 Lime Kiln Rd., Sonora 95370, tel. (209) 532-5822, an elegant country home on a former gold-mining site, rooms with queen beds and private baths, full breakfast served, $75-100. **Via Serena Ranch** at 18007 Via Serena Dr., tel. 532-5307, is contemporary and quiet, with rooms $60. Also out a distance—do call for directions—is the aptly named **Serenity** at 15305 Bear Cub Dr., tel. 533-1441 or toll-free (800) 426-1441, a gorgeous two-story contemporary country inn with little touches like lace-trimmed (and ironed) linens, lovely quilts, covered veranda, and homemade cookies or brownies almost always available. Rates: $80. Out there, too, is the new **Hammons House Inn Bed and Breakfast,** 22963 Robertson Ranch Rd., tel. 532-7921, a custom two-story ranch house of cedar and redwood with guest rooms $70-80, the separate one-bedroom cottage (with complete kitchen, sleeps up to four) $110.

For a current bed and breakfast brochure, contact **Gold Country Inns of Tuolumne County,** P.O. Box 462, Sonora 95370 or call (209) 533-1845 for reservations and referrals.

GOOD FOOD

Good Sonora Restaurants

Wilma's Cafe downtown at 275 S. Washington, tel. (209) 532-9957, is locally famous for its hickory-smoked barbecue. Wilma The Flying Pig sits by the cash register; other pig statues and oddities are everywhere. But it's also one of those downhome American-style cafes—there's a genuine cafe counter—where everyone can find something good to eat. Great deals, too, like the early-morning "Weekday Worker's Special": two eggs, fruit or hash browns, either toast or biscuits, and coffee for $2.50. Great homemade pies. Open daily. **Sonoma Joe's** at 1183 Mono Way, tel. 532-9380, is the best local steakhouse. Open daily, dinners only.

More sophisticated, in the culinary sense, is **Good Heavens** in the Yo Semite Hotel at 49 N. Washington, tel. (209) 532-3663, specializing in gourmet California-style fare at lunch. Open daily, Mon.-Sat. 11-3, Sun. 10-2. **Bradley's** at 85 N. Washington, tel. 536-0916, is a fine gourmet deli and small cafe, popular, too, on weekdays for continental breakfast. Closed Sundays. **Coyote Creek Cafe & Grille** at 177 S. Washington, tel. 532-9115, serves contemporary samples of just about everything, from just about everywhere—from the Zuni black bean plate, Szechuan chicken salad, and The Bayou (chicken breast sandwich with Cajun spices) at lunch to daily-changing dinner specials like BBQ Korean pork and chicken Thai curry. **Stuft Pizza** a mile past the Junction Shopping Center at 14721 Mono Way (Hwy. 108), tel. 532-1097, serves the best. The coffee shop at the **Sonora Inn** is open 24 hours.

Great Sonora Restaurants

Hemingway's Cafe at 362 Steward St., tel. (209) 532-4900, is an unusual and enjoyable place, contemporary international cuisine in a ranch-style home dressed up like a European cafe. Open Tues.-Sat. for both lunch and dinner, reservations wise. **La Torre** downtown at 39 N. Washington, tel. 533-9181, is the town's current crown jewel, exceptional food—Italian and American fare with a continental flair—served in a striking and appropriately dignified second-floor setting. Open for lunch weekdays, for dinner nightly.

ET CETERA

Arts, Entertainment, And Recreation

The **Sierra Repertory Theatre** at 13891 Mono Way (Hwy. 108), P.O. Box 3030, Sonora 95370, tel. (209) 532-3120, offers a year-round schedule of comedies, dramas, musicals. There's no lack of other nightlife (the bar scene, live music, dancing) around town, either, especially on weekends. Pick up or request a current arts events calendar at the **Central Sierra Arts Council,** 48 S. Washington St., P.O. Box 335, tel. 532-2787.

Trout and salmon fishing are popular throughout nearby mountain areas. Whitewater rafting on the Tuolumne River is passionately pursued

Saint James Episcopal Church

and the **Annual Christmas Faire,** a commercial cornucopia of quality handicrafts.

Other local events—chili cook-offs, pancake breakfasts, charity brunches, fashion shows, rummage sales, square dances, musical extravaganzas—tend to stitch Columbia, Sonora, and even Dodge Ridge and other mountain areas together into a countywide patchwork of activity; get a current calendar at the chamber.

Information And Tours
Get public camping, trail, and outdoor recreation information and permits at the **Stanislaus National Forest headquarters** across from the fairgrounds at 19777 Greenley Rd., Sonora 95370, tel. (209) 532-3671. The **Tuolumne County Visitors Bureau,** downstairs at 55 W. Stockton St., P.O. Box 4020, tel. 533-4420 or 984-4636 or toll-free (800) 446-1333, is very helpful, dispensing information about just about everything. There's even a photograph flip-book on area bed and breakfasts, so you can see how they look. Upstairs at the same address is the **Sonora Chamber of Commerce**.

G.E.O. Expeditions, tel. (209) 532-0150 or (800) 351-5041, offers guided tours of the Sierra Nevada and foothill territory.

VICINITY OF SONORA

The trip south on Hwy. 49 toward Jamestown is hideous—unattractive helter-skelter construction, heavy traffic, cars wheeling onto the highway from every which way—so go on back roads if at all possible. A worthwhile excursion is up Hwy. 108 (nice autumn colors) to explore Standard, Soulsbyville, Tuolumne, and the area from Twain Harte to Long Barn. **Standard City** is a ghost town abandoned in the 1970s. Don't be fooled by **Twain Harte.** The town's name comes from a 1920s effort to promote Mother Lode tourism through its literary legacy. To find out what is and isn't happening in these parts, contact the Twain Harte Chamber of Commerce on Joaquin Gully Rd., P.O. Box 404, Twain Harte 95382, tel. (209) 586-4482. **Mi-Wuk Village** is a subdivision named after the Miwok people, though none live here. (For steaks, eat at **Diamond Jim's Feedlot.**) **Long Barn's** long barn burned to the ground but once was a way station for oxen teams and their drivers before they crossed the Sierra Nevada.

from spring to fall. (Get a list of commercial rafting companies at the visitors bureau, and see this chapter's "Introduction.") If you go on your own—no beginners—you'll need a permit, available at the Forest Service office here or in Groveland, where you can also pick up hiking and camping information.

Events
Still competing with Columbia after all these years: while Columbians are mustering firefighters in May, in April Sonorans have their annual **Sonora Smoke Polers** festival, an early Western shoot-'em-up, with flintlocks and muzzleloading rifles, even mountain men in animal skins living in tepees. In May is the sheriff posse's **Mother Lode Round-up Parade and Rodeo.** Show up in late September for **Wild West Days,** a big party featuring BBQ, benefit dinners, a film festival, movie stars, and movie memorabilia museum. Fun for fiddlin' types in November is the **Annual '49er Banjo Jam Session.** Also at the fairgrounds in November: the genealogical society's pre-Thanksgiving **Country Craft Faire**

a gold-prospecting
expedition

TUOLUMNE COUNTY VISITORS BUREAU

Soulsbyville

This old mining camp north of Tuolumne City was settled by Cornish miners and their families, and was noted for its tranquility even in the gold rush heyday. Ben Soulsby was a farmer and lumberman who became a hardrock miner (and mine owner) when his son, Little Ben, stumbled over a large gold nugget on a cowpath. You can stay here at Ben Senior's old Victorian ranchhouse, the **Willow Springs Inn,** a bed and breakfast complete with hot tub at 20599 Kings Court, Soulsbyville 95372, tel. (209) 533-2030.

Tuolumne City

"Tuolumne" comes from a Miwok word meaning "those who live in stone houses," a possible reference to native people who fled with the arrival of the Spanish and became Stanislaus Canyon cave dwellers. Tuolumne today is a pretty, crisp-aired mountain town with some charming homes, a playground, public swimming pool. In September the annual Indian **Acorn Festival** is held near here at the Sierra Miwok roundhouse on the **Tuolumne Rancheria** (one of the last remaining Miwok reserva-

tions) on Miwok Road. (The community's other major event, in Tuolumne City, is the annual **Lumber Jubilee,** celebrating another reality altogether.) From Tuolumne City you can drive east all the way to Hetch Hetchy Reservoir in Yosemite; Buchanan Rd. connects up with Cottonwood Rd., a winding but well-paved mountain path through magnificent countryside.

Camp here at the private **River Ranch Campground** off Buchanan Rd., Tuolumne 95379, tel. (209) 928-3708; open year-round, with hot showers and barbecues. For a more luxurious stay, try the **Oak Hill Ranch** at 18550 Conally Ln., P.O. Box 307, tel. 928-4717, country Victorian rooms and a cottage, $65-95. Turn off at the Westside RV Park just west of Tuolumne to find the **Westside Depot Kitchen,** tel. 928-4008; generous American fare for the most part, also good soups, cheesecake, all in a railroad depot atmosphere. **Sonka's Apple Ranch** on Cherokee Rd., tel. 928-4689, has delicious apples in season, also apple-nut bran muffins, "mile-high" pies, jams, and other goodies, open 8 a.m.-5:30 p.m. The **Tuolumne City Merchants Association,** P.O. Box 1291, tel. 928-4297, can supply local information.

JAMESTOWN

Once a supply station for area mines and now pretty as a tintype photograph, Jamestown (also known as Jimtown) gained attention as the site of the Crocker family's Sierra Railroad Company, the main line running from here through Sonora and on to the mill at Fasler—rails you can still ride today. Countless movies, including *High Noon, The Virginian, Dodge City,* and *My Little Chickadee,* not to mention TV westerns like "The Lone Ranger," "Tales of Wells Fargo," and "Lassie," have been filmed at least partially in Jamestown. There's a state historic park here, Railtown 1897. Worth exploring too, when it's open, is the movie set for *Back to the Future III.*

JIMTOWN SIGHTS

Downtown Jimtown

Main Street is a quarter-mile-long hustling cowboy alley lined with pickup trucks. Hold down a bench in Jamestown Park on Main and just watch the summer sideshow pass by, or brave the streets and explore the stores. Gold rush stores and jewelry shops abound. But if you're a serious gold-lover, try finding some of your own. **Gold Prospecting Expeditions** in the old livery stable at 18170 Main, tel. (209) 984-4653, can tell you how to go about it. Kids pan for free in the horse trough outside the stable, but basic placer mining, dredging, "rafting for riches," high-tech helicopter gold trips, and classes for grownups cost money. An hour of basic panning instruction costs $25, and you can "rent" a gold mining claim too. The possibilities are endless.

Railtown 1897 State Historic Park

Jamestown's Railtown 1897 State Historic Park, the old Sierra Railway depot on Fifth Ave. just above Main and off the highways, is worth at least a quick stop. With its expanse of cool green lawn, tables, barbecues, and running water, the park is pleasant for picnics; the 26-acre site includes a collection of venerable old railroad cars (be sure to see the parlor car from the *California Zephyr*) and the Sierra's old roundhouse (tours every half-hour, small fee).

You can take the one-hour, 12-mile trip on the steam-powered *Mother Lode Cannon Ball,* departure times 10:30 a.m., noon, 1:30 and 3 p.m., $9 adults, children 12 and under $4.50, babes in arms free; combination ticket discounts for the ride and the roundhouse tour available. On special weekends, the Keystone Special is a two-hour-plus trip through the foothills to Keystone and back beginning at 5 p.m., adults $17.50, children $11. Ask about the Saturday night Twilight Limited run to Hetch Hetchy Junction during the summer, including cocktails en route and barbecued steaks once back at the ranch, and other special runs. The park is open daily from mid-May to mid-Nov., 10-5, otherwise just on weekends. For information, contact: Railtown 1897, P.O. Box 1250, Jamestown 95327, tel. (209) 984-3953.

Accommodations

The closest campgrounds are at unattractive **Don Pedro Reservoir** (RVs and tents), P.O. Box 160, La Grange 95329, tel. (209) 852-2207. Considerably farther south are **Lake McClure** and **Lake McSwain,** reservoirs with ample campsites (see "Coulterville," following).

The **Jamestown-Railtown Motel** at 10301 Willow St. just up from Main, tel. (209) 984-3332, has rooms for $55-80. The very fine **Jamestown Hotel** on Main St., P.O. Box 539, tel. 984-3902, has eight modern Victorian-style rooms with brass beds, $55-110, including continental breakfast.

Most bed and breakfasts in Jimtown are called "hotels." The elaborate, eye-catching balcony and wooden boardwalk at the **National Hotel** on Main, P.O. Box 502, Jamestown 95327, tel. (209) 984-3446, mark this authentic gold rush relic, now a bed and breakfast with some original furnishings and pull-chain toilets; $65-80. The **Palm Hotel** at 10382 Willow, P.O. Box 515, tel. 984-3429, or 984-3429, runs $45-110, with full breakfast. This white-trimmed Victorian is a treasure trove of artifacts and antiques from around the world. Some shared baths.

The **Royal Hotel** on Main St., tel. (209) 984-5271, is one of those local institutions that attracts mostly regulars, at least in the hotel itself.

downtown Jimtown

(Great bookshop downstairs.) Best bet for travelers are the rooms and suites in the secluded cottages out back. Rates for the hotel, $50-70; for cottage suites, $75-80. New in Jamestown—and refreshingly straightforward in its marketing approach—is **Sheets and Eggs,** three guest rooms in a 1949 country cottage tucked into the foothills at 18665 Hwy. 108, P.O. Box 657, tel. 984-0915. Private baths. Your choice of continental or full breakfast. Rates: $75-80.

Food

At **Kamn's Chinese Restaurant,** 18208 Main, tel. (209) 984-3025, you can get a five-course Cantonese meal for next to nothing. Even better and still reasonable is **The Smoke Cafe** on Main, tel. 984-3733, good margaritas and decent Mexican dinners such as chile verde and pollo de poblano in a tin-walled Western atmosphere. The specials here are usually enticing. Quite good, too, is **Michelangelo** at 18228 Main St., tel. 984-4830, surprising contemporary black-and-white decor against pressed-tin Old West walls, everything accented by Michelangelo prints on the walls. Wide-ranging Italian menu, full bar, espresso bar. The overall ambience at the Jamestown is most appealing, and the food at the National is usually more exciting, but both the **Jamestown Hotel Restaurant,** tel. 984-3902, and the **National Hotel Restaurant,** tel. 984-3446, offer American continental cuisine at lunch and dinner, full bar. Perhaps even more popular with locals is **The Willow Restaurant** and saloon in the old hotel at Main and Willow,

tel. 984-3998, reservations usually necessary on weekends; also a good choice for a Sunday brunch, served 10:30 a.m.-4:30 p.m. There's a beautiful brass and oak bar at the **Jamestown Hotel,** which offers a continental dinner menu.

Entertainment And Events

For some legal high-stakes California gambling, check out the red-hot bingo games (and they *do* get hot when the purse reaches five figures) out at the **Chicken Ranch** on the Miwok reservation, 16929 Chicken Ranch Rd. (about one mile west of Jamestown), tel. (209) 984-3000 or toll-free (800) 752-4646. Different, for a thrill, is **Hill Valley** about eight miles west of town on Hwy. 108, the "old" movie set for the film *Back to the Future III,* just south of the highway. Ask locally about current tours.

Show up in April for the annual **Gunfighters Rendezvous** downtown. Ask around for saloons and restaurants with live music.

VICINITY OF JAMESTOWN

Take Rawhide Rd. north, the starting point for worthwhile hikes to 40-mile-long **Table Mountain** and colorful displays of spring wildflowers. The half-mile walk to **Peppermint Falls** starts at the end of Peppermint Falls Rd., or hike to volcanic **Pulpit Rock.** The main road continues on to Rawhide Flat, where you'll see remnants of the 1890s **Rawhide Mine** and the long-gone town of **Jefferson.** A jaunt up Jamestown Rd.

toward Shaw's Flat also leads to the gracefully decaying gold rush-era **Mississippi House** hotel. From Jamestown, Jacksonville Rd. runs toward Quartz Mountain, site of the once-prosperous Heslit-App Mine and the remains of old **Quartz.** Nearby **Stent** was called Poverty Hills during the gold rush because the pickin's were so poor.

Just 12 miles west of Jamestown toward the valley, **Knights Ferry,** with a historic district of old brick and pine-frame buildings along the banks of the Stanislaus River, is a haven for swimmers, picnickers, and campers in summer. Stop by the Knights Ferry Covered Bridge, reportedly the longest of its type in the U.S., designed by U.S. Grant; there's also a fine small museum and visitors' center.

Also here is the historic yet unpretentious **Knights Ferry Hotel,** 17713 Main St., P.O. Box 817, Knights Ferry 95361, tel. (209) 881-3418 or 881-3271, beautifully renovated and refurbished by its owners as a bed and breakfast inn—just in time for the hotel's 135th birthday in 1989. (Check out the in-house museum.) Four of the rooms have in-room wash basins and share a bath and "water closet," but one guest room, the suite, and the separate cottage all feature full private baths. Room rates run $45-110, but a good deal for a larger group is renting both The Suite and Elizabeth's Room—each has a private bath, and together can sleep four to seven —for a discounted price. Doc's Cottage features both a king-sized bed and sofa bed, woodstove, dry bar, a private bathroom with shower, and private patio. Good for a meal in town, almost as enjoyable for its riverside setting, is the **Knights Ferry Resort** restaurant just down the road, tel. 881-3349, open for breakfast, lunch, and dinner (full bar), and champagne brunch on both Saturday and Sunday.

Chinese Camp

Near the junction of Hwy. 49 and Hwy. 120 and east of Yosemite Junction is Chinese Camp—a post office, a combination store/bar/ restaurant/ gas station, aged adobes, creaky wood frames, and crumbling brick buildings hidden by trees of heaven along Main. There's obviously not much happening here today, but this was once one of the largest U.S. Asian settlements. In September 1856, 2,000 Chinese from rival tongs battled after one group was excoriated in print by the other as "perfect worms" who "ought to be exterminated." Onlookers were disappointed when only four warriors were dead and a few dozen wounded after it was all over several hours later.

Groveland

Past Moccasin Creek Fish Hatchery and the brutal climb up Hwy. 120 to Priest (locals say the old road was worse) is Groveland. Once called Garrote and founded by the gold rush, Groveland boomed again during the construction of Hetch Hetchy Reservoir. The town is now a pine-woodsy, pleasant resort community.

The 1920s **Hotel Charlotte** on Main St. (Hwy. 120), P.O. Box 787, Groveland 95321, tel. 962-6455, is now a bed and breakfast serving good prime rib, chops, chicken, and other American fare along with Early American decor. Rooms, nothing fancy but nice, start at $48.60 with shared bath, $59.40 with private bath.

A real '49er old-timer, the adobe and wood **Groveland Hotel** on the highway, tel. (209) 962-4000, offers refurbished rooms and suites for $80-155. Or get a rustic room at the 1860s **Sugar Pine Ranch** four miles east on Hwy. 120, P.O. Box 588, tel. 962-7823, $40 and up.

For information about nearby camping in Stanislaus National Forest, contact the **Groveland Ranger District** office on the highway, P.O. Box 709, tel. (209) 962-7825 ($3 for a forest camping and recreation map). From here to Yosemite are **The Pines, Lost Claim, Sweetwater,** and **Carlon** campgrounds. Also in the area but accessible by rugged dirt road are the **Lumsden, Lumsden Bridge,** and **South Fork** national forest campgrounds (turn north at Buck Meadows), all free. If you're traveling to or from Yosemite, a time-honored stop for a countrystyle breakfast is **Buck Meadows Lodge,** tel. 962-5281, with restaurant, saloon, and motel.

Or head north to **Cherry Lake** a few miles past Buck Meadows; there's camping along the creek outside Yosemite National Park. Take the Camp Mather turnoff from Hwy. 120 just outside Yosemite to get to the more accessible **Middle Fork Campground.** Take the turn even if you're not camping. It's a spectacular drive to Hetch Hetchy, a lovely vista even with the dam. To stay, take a cabin at **Evergreen Lodge** near Camp Mather, Star Rte. 160, Groveland 95321, tel. (209) 379-2606. Open summers only.

COULTERVILLE

Coulterville is unpocked by progress and is, in its entirety, a state historic landmark (Main Street is listed in the National Register of Historic Places). The second-largest town in Mariposa County, fringed by barren oak and chaparral slopes, Coulterville is safe (so far) from the stylized rusticity that's raking in the tourists elsewhere. From Coulterville, take Greeley Hill Rd. (J20) east, then follow Old Yosemite Rd.—the locals' route —into **Yosemite National Park.**

Along the way is **Bower Cave,** called *Oo-tin* or "Home of the Evening Star" by the Miwok people, a once-popular 1800s tourist destination with a down-deep dance floor. The cave was technically closed to the public in the 1950s, after an accidental death, and was acquired in 1990 by the Forest Service. Inquire about its current status. Or head west to the valley on Hwy. 132 to La Grange, south to Snelling, then east to **Hornitos, Mt. Bullion,** and John C. Frémont's **Mariposa.**

Stop by the **North County Office of the Mariposa County Chamber of Commerce,** 5007 Main St., P.O. Box 33, Coulterville 95311, tel. (209) 878-3074, for current visitor information.

History

Coulterville started as a Mexican village called Banderita, named, some say, after the miners' red bandanas. Others claim the name comes from the perennially tattered American flag which flew above founding merchant George Coulter's blue tent. Like clockwork, the new town of Coulterville burned to the ground at 20-year intervals during the booming 1800s. When gold fever finally broke, the Yosemite Turnpike toll road from here offered the only vehicle access to the park (and tourist-related business opportunities for local merchants) into the early 1900s.

Northern Mariposa County History Center

The Northern Mariposa County History Center, tel. (209) 878-3015, open Tues.-Sun. 10 a.m.-4 p.m. from April 1 to Sept. 1, just weekends and holidays the rest of the year, is definitely worth a stop. Enter this aged stone museum complex, the old Wells Fargo and McCarthy's Store buildings, through the roofless shell of an open-air "courtyard" with cascading vines and flowers. Inside are well-done displays of Victorian Americana, the apothecary's art, surface mining, Wells Fargo boxes and gold scales, also a well-preserved antique gun collection and the old Studebaker buckboard Grace Kelly graced in *High Noon.* Nice, too, is the attention paid to "women's work," the wicked wooden washboard, flat iron, and butter churn all telling the truth about hard work.

Whistling Billy is what locals call the small steam engine by the town's hangin' tree outside. Bill once pulled ore carts to the stamp mills from the nearby **Mary Harrison Mine** along a snaking, nearly vertical route.

Sights And Practicalities

Pick up a free map and guide to local sights and services on the counter just inside the door at the museum. Since most of the old saloons, cafes, storehouses, and homes have neither been restored nor vandalized, you can peer in windows and see original, faded wallpapers, heavy old doors with ancient handles, miscellaneous old-time oddities.

Intriguing is the **Coulterville General Store,** seemingly tossed into the middle of a six-way junction of highways and streets. (Note the tiny jail nearby, next to the volunteer fire department.) There are two original buildings still standing in Chinatown just off Main, one of them the old adobe **Sun Sun Wo Company Store**—not open to the public. Next door is the town's time-honored wood frame whorehouse, **Candy's Place.** The ancient rosebush out front was harvested by Candy, who handed out the blooms to "gentlemen callers."

Most imposing of all, though, is the tin-sided pine-green-and-tan **Hotel Jeffery** at 1 Main St., P.O. Box 440, Coulterville 95311, tel. (209) 878-3471 or (800) 464-3471, a natural summer hideout with thick original adobe walls built in 1851. (Legend has it that, among others, Ralph Waldo Emerson, Teddy Roosevelt, and Carrie Nation once slept here.) Restored rooms $55-68, lower in the off-season, continental breakfast included. There's a small restaurant downstairs, tel. 878-3473, open for breakfast, lunch, and dinner.

Swing open the batwing doors of the **Magnolia Saloon** right next door and step into another

weeds and weather-beaten wood near Coulterville

KIM WEIR

century: tintype photographs, mineral collections, dusty memorabilia, even a wooden Indian. There's one concession to life in the 20th century: a juke box. (Come by on Saturday nights for live music.) There's a cool and pleasant park right next to the Jeffery where local events like barbecues, bluegrass festivals, and the annual **Coyote Howl** and **Gunfighters Rendezvous** happen.

More Practicalities
Maxwell's Station at 5015 Main St., tel. (209) 878-3118, is a good choice for no-frills country-style American food—barbecue ribs, pork chops, fried chicken. Come hungry: it's all-you-can-eat at lunch and dinner. The **Yosemite American Inn** at 10407 Hwy. 49, tel. 878-3407, has rooms from $40.50 (cheaper from late fall through early spring), also some RV and tent camping sites. Or camp at McClure and McSwain lakes at the bottom of the long Hwy. 132 grade down from Coulterville. Most campsites are at **Lake McClure,** tel. (800) 468-8889 for reservations, which spreads out over old mines and the one-time town of Bagby; closest to town is **Horseshoe Bend. Lake McSwain** is McClure's forebay (cold water, good fishing, no powerboating). Rates $10-13 plus $4 registration fee.

To Bear Valley
The stretch of "highway" between Coulterville and Bear Valley is beautiful but brutal, with hairpin turns, steep ascents, and sudden descents, a reminder of the demanding terrain challenged daily by hardscrabblers forced to traverse Merced River Canyon (nicknamed "Hell's Hollow"). You'll notice many closed mines along the way, but resist the temptation to go exploring; abandoned mineshafts are dangerous, each for different reasons.

John C. Frémont, intrepid explorer, militarist, and California's first U.S. senator, established his empire's headquarters in Bear Valley. He once owned the entire area from Mariposa to Bagby (fudging on the eastern boundary by about 50 miles when gold was discovered outside his original holdings). Frémont's scout Kit Carson discovered the first gold at the main Mariposa Mine and made strikes at other Bear Valley sites. But high overhead, lawyers' fees, and claimjumpers (Frémont had the governor call in the state militia to forcibly oust them) gradually nibbled away at the mines' potential profits. In his later years, Fremont bragged ruefully that he came to California penniless, "but now I owe $2 million!"

Today, note the ruins of **Frémont's house,** poke into the **Oso House** museum (actually the old Odd Fellows Hall—the original Oso, Frémont's headquarters, was lost to fire), visit the jail, explore the graveyard. There's not much else here except the **Bon Ton Cafe** and bar, closed at last report. If you feel drawn to this place, to the dust of Frémont's dreams, stay at **Granny's Garden Bed and Breakfast,** a yellow-and-white Victorian at 7333 Hwy. 49, Bear Valley 95223, tel. (209) 377-8342, $75. Rooms with private baths, breakfast, afternoon wine, spa privileges.

Hornitos

Hornitos was once Mariposa County's only incorporated city until the state Legislature took even that status away—a wild place in its day, named after outdoor Mexican bread ovens or *hornos,* though some say the oddly shaped gravestones in the cemetery are the eponymous inspiration. Hornitos, right here and now, is becoming a ghost town; its central plaza is empty, its sad cemetery more populous than the town. There's an old fandango hall here, a two-story hotel, and the ruins of the red-brick **Ghirardelli Store** (the San Francisco chocolate king's humble beginnings, now a de facto garbage dump). From Hornitos, take the Hornitos-Old Toll Rd. east to **Mt. Bullion** (named after John Frémont's father-in-law, Thomas Hart "Old Bullion" Benton—a Republican senator adamantly opposed to paper money), the site of the Princeton Mine.

MARIPOSA TO BASS LAKE

MARIPOSA

Mariposa (Spanish for "butterfly"), a woodsy town of 1,500 with old homes and wide, peaceful streets, was named by General John C. Frémont during his sneaky land grab. Mariposa is the southernmost of the major gold camps and one of the southern gateways to Yosemite. (The highway from here into the park is almost always open, even in winter.) The hills near here—like half of California, if you believe all the stories—were once Joaquin Murrieta's stomping grounds. Also in these hills: muchos ghost towns, most not marked by so much as a stone. Good luck.

To get oriented, stop by the **Mariposa County Chamber of Commerce** office and visitors center at the juncture of Hwy. 140 and N. Hwy. 49, P.O. Box 425, Mariposa 95338, tel. (209) 966-2456.

Frémont's old **Mariposa Mine,** the first steam-powered quartz mining operation in California, is at the end of Bullion, though visitors aren't exactly encouraged. Nearby is the white-steepled landmark, **St. Joseph's Catholic Church.** The grizzled granite **Old Mariposa Jail** on Bullion between 4th and 5th has natural rock walls more than two feet thick and was used until 1960. The office building of the *Mariposa Gazette* has burned to the ground twice but the paper has never missed an issue since 1854.

Mariposa County Courthouse

Mariposa boasts California's oldest courthouse in continuous use, built in 1854 with local white pine. Since Mariposa County has no incorporated cities, this is where the governmental action—such as it is—is. The courthouse has original furnishings on the second floor, including a potbellied woodstove and simple wooden benches. As elsewhere in the gold country, mineral wealth seems to be the holy grail. There's a large rock collection here, too, and a mineral collage monument outside. The courthouse, open for business as usual weekdays 8-5 and for tours on weekends, is on Bullion between 9th and 10th streets.

Mariposa County History Center

Just one block off Hwy. 140 at Jessie and 12th streets, the Mariposa County History Center, tel. (209) 966-2924, is an excellent free museum sharing space with the local library. In the outdoor courtyard, note the mule-powered Mexican *arrastra* used to grind ore (as well as corn for tortillas), and the full-scale model of a five-stamp mill. Push the button on the miniature version inside and you'll see how gold-rich rocks were pulverized. Also here are displays of printing and mining equipment, an old-time apothecary, school rooms, Miwok dwellings and sauna, a lady's boudoir, a sheriff's office, a miner's cabin—altogether a thoughtfully tended historical record. The museum is open daily 10 a.m.-4:30 p.m. April-Oct., 10-4 weekends Oct.-March.

The California State Mining And Mineral Exhibit

Also in Mariposa is the excellent **California State Mining and Mineral Exhibit,** now installed as a permanent exhibit at the county fairgrounds. Some of the finer examples of the state's mineral riches are gathered here, and assay office and mine tunnel. For more info, contact the California Mineral Exhibit Association, P.O. Box 1192,

Mariposa 95338, tel. (209) 742-ROCK. Adults $3.50, Children $2.50.

Area Wineries

The Mariposa-Oakhurst area has its boutique wineries, like almost everywhere in California. Inquire at the chamber of commerce for information on new ones. You can taste **Radanovich Winery** wines at the tasting room in the Mariposa Hotel, and tour the winery by appointment (tel. 209-966-3187). **Butterfly Creek Winery** at 4063 Triangle Rd., tel. 966-2097, most accessible from just north of town, offers some award-winning chardonnay, cabernet sauvignon, White Riesling, Pinot Blanc, and merlot. Open Saturday 10-4 in summer or by appointment.

MARIPOSA PRACTICALITIES

Camping

In a pinch, pitch your tent at the **Mariposa County Fairgrounds** all year (except Labor Day weekend, when the fair is underway), just two miles south of town on Hwy. 49, tel. (209) 966-3686 or 966-2432; hot showers, picnic tables, barbecues $12-15. There are various private campgrounds in and around Mariposa, too; ask locals for suggestions. Or sleep under the stars (first-come, first-camped) at nearby national forest campgrounds: **Jerseydale Campground,** about five miles north on Hwy. 140 then another nine miles on county roads, open from about May 1 until Nov. 1; **Summit Campground,** about 12 miles east on Hwy. 49, then seven miles northeast on a county road, open June 1 to Nov. 1; or **Indian Flat,** 25 miles east on Hwy. 140 on the Merced River near Yosemite, open July 15-Sept. 15. None of these has showers, and some have no safe drinking water (bring your own). For current information about area camping, hiking trails, and other recreational possibilities, contact the **Mariposa Ranger District** office at Highways 140 and 49 S., P.O. Box 747, Mariposa 95338, tel. (209) 966-3638. Pick up a Forest Service recreation map/brochure there for $3.

Midpines Home Hostel

Near Mariposa—ask for directions when you make your reservations—is the AYH Midpines Home Hostel, P.O. Box 173, Midpines 95345, tel. (209) 742-6318, at $7.50 per night (per person) one of the least expensive lodging options around. Facilities here are somewhat spartan—unisex sleeping room with five beds, and there's no electricity, so arrive before dark—but all in all the simplicity just puts you in the mood for some genuine gold-panning, in Plumbar Creek out back. (The hostel provides the equipment.) Kitchen facilities (gas-powered stove and lights), off-street parking. Groups (and families) welcome.

Accommodations In Town

A wonderful find in these parts, an unlikely gem, is the tiny **Sierra View Motel** at 7th and Bullion just a half-block off the highway, 4993 7th St., P.O. Box 1467, Mariposa 95338, tel. (209) 966-5793 or toll-free for reservations only (800) 627-8439. Managers George and Betty Ragus have transformed this old-time motor court motel into a miniature mom-and-pop country inn (just seven units at last report, two of them suites) with simple but attractive rooms—light and airy and very clean, with fresh paint, wallpaper, and white bedspreads—and a small backyard garden and patio area swarming in summer with happy hummingbirds. Rooms have one, two, or three bed (queens, doubles, or twins) and clean but tiny bathrooms with showers, also color TV, air-conditioning, phones. Suites have a sitting area, wet bar and refrigerators, and bathrooms with showers and bathtubs. Continental breakfast served in the office. Rates: $35-55 for rooms, $60-110 for suites. A great deal.

The renovated and recently opened 1901-vintage **Mariposa Hotel** is a bed and break-fast-style inn right downtown at 5029 Hwy. 140, P.O. Box 745, tel. (209) 966-4676—generous rooms with exceptional Victorian detail, completely modern private baths, even in-room TV, tape player, radios, and coffee or tea. Plus, there's a wonderful "roof garden" area perfect for coffee or breakfast in the morning. Rates: $70-95. Discounted winter rates (Dec. 1 through March). Closed in January.

Most other lodgings in town provide the usual motel ambience at comparable prices. (Scout around on your own for bargain discoveries—almost a fruitless effort in areas so close to Yosemite.) Some of Mariposa's better choices: the **E.C. Yosemite Motel** near the junction of Hwy. 49 and N. Hwy. 140 at 5180 Jones St., tel. (209) 742-6800, rates $50-55 during the area's prime travel season (spring through fall); the imposing **Yosemite Miners Inn** across the highway, tel. 742-7777 or toll-free (800) 237-7277, $50-70 (sometimes even better prices); the **Best Western Yosemite Way Station** at the junction of Hwy. 140 and S. Hwy. 49, tel. 966-7545 or toll-free for reservations (800) 528-1234, rooms $70-76; and the nearby **Yosemite Gold Rush Inn** at 4994 Bullion, tel. 966-4344 or toll-free (800) 321-5261, $60-72.

A better bet, about ten miles east of town, is the **Muir Lodge Motel** on Hwy. 140, tel. (209) 966-2468, a rustic yet comfortable lodge, $50-80.

Bed And Breakfasts Close To Mariposa

Visitors could spend an entire vacation just trying to count all of the area's bed and breakfast inns, sprouting up in these parts like spring wildflowers. The following listings are admittedly incomplete. For more information, at least about member inns, stop by or call the Mariposa County Chamber of Commerce (see above) or request a current brochure from the **Yosemite-Mariposa Bed and Breakfast Association,** P.O. Box 1100, Mariposa 95338.

One block from Hwy. 140 (look for the American flag outside) is **Schlageter House,** 5038 Bullion St., P.O. Box 1202, Mariposa 95338, tel. (209) 966-2471, a lushly landscaped 1859 Victorian with three guest rooms, full breakfast. Rates: $70-80. **Villa Monti** in town at 4990 8th St., P.O. Box 1888, tel. 966-2439, is an elegant 1920s-vintage Spanish-style inn with two rooms (shared bath) and one suite, plus TV, pool, patio, hot tub, full breakfast. Rates: $55-75. In town, too, is **Oak Meadows Too** at 5263 N. Hwy. 140 (P.O. Box 619), tel. 742-6161, a contemporary Early American Colonial-style inn with six rooms, private baths, expanded continental breakfast. Rates: $64-79. **Boulder Creek Bed & Breakfast,** 4572 Ben Hur Rd., tel. 742-7729, is just outside town, a contemporary chalet with cheerful country-style rooms (two share a bath), full breakfast, therapeutic spa. German spoken. Rates: $65-75.

Bed And Breakfasts Farther Afield

The friendly **Meadow Creek Ranch** inn halfway to Oakhurst, 2669 Triangle Rd. at S. Hwy. 49, Mariposa 95338, tel. (209) 966-3843, was originally a stage stop and cattle ranch headquar-

ters. These days, Meadow Creek offers three guest rooms with antiques and continental country decor (all sharing one bath), a separate cottage, and an almost formal candlelight breakfast raved about by the *Los Angeles Times.* Rates: $65-95. **Canyon View Bed & Breakfast** at 7117 Snyder Ridge Rd., tel. 742-6268 or (800) 344-CNYN, offers three rooms in a chalet-style Justus Cedar home, all with separate baths, one with in-room spa and private deck exit. In winter, the proprietors will let you see their dogsled team. Rates: $75-105.

Shangri-La about seven miles out of town in the woods at 6316 Jerseydale Rd., tel. (209) 966-2653, is a very Japanese retreat in every respect, three rooms complete with Japanese-style beds (two share a bath, one has a sunken bathtub) and gardens with fish pond and waterfall. Gazebos and trails offer still more intimacy with the outdoors. Rates: $40-60.

Quite unusual in the genre, too, this time for the food, is **Chibcha's Inn** at 2747 Hwy. 140 in Cathey's Valley, tel. (209) 2940, a bed and breakfast inn serving steak and eggs for breakfast and authentic Colombian cuisine in the restaurant next door.

The **Yosemite Fish Camp Bed & Breakfast Inn** barely more than a mile from Yosemite and just off Hwy. 41 at 1164 Railroad Ave., P.O. Box 25, Fish Camp 93623, tel. (209) 683-7426, is a 1940s cabin-style mountain home with just three guest rooms (all share a bath), a shared sitting room with woodstove, hot tub in season, and full country breakfast. Rates: $55-70. Practically next door and cozy in a more contemporary sense is two-story **Karen's Bed and Breakfast Yosemite Inn,** 1144 Railroad Ave., P.O. Box 8, tel. 683-4550, all three rooms with private baths, full breakfast, afternoon tea or refreshments with homemade pastries and such. Rates: $80-85.

Good Food

A great find for Mexican food—everything quite tasty, served in humongous portions—is inexpensive **Castillo's** up the hill from the highway at 4995 5th St., tel. (209) 742-4413. Open daily after 10 a.m. for lunch and dinner. The best local choice for Chinese food is **China Station** on Bullion between 2nd and 3rd Streets. Quite good, too, for breakfast and lunch and steaks and seafood at dinner is **The Red Fox** on Hwy.

140 at 12th St., tel. 966-5707. Locally popular, for basic cafe standards at breakfast and lunch, is the **Country Pantry** at 5029 Charles St., tel. 966-4097.

Not counting Erna's Elderberry House in Oakhurst, the area's fine dining salon is the **Charles Street Dinner House** on Charles at 7th, tel. (209) 966-2366, American fare with the area's inimitable Old West flair.

For incredibly good coffee—the "handmade" gourmet roast variety—stop by the small **Mariposa Coffee Company** outlet downtown, or the **49er Trading Post** at 2945 S. Hwy. 49, tel. (209) 742-7339, to stock up for camping and backcountry treks—or for the trip home.

Vicinity Of Mariposa

Mormon Bar predates the gold rush. Its first residents were Mormons determined to establish the state of Deseret (capital: Salt Lake City)—an application denied by the federal government. The **Dexter Museum** here, once a newspaper office, is worth a peek. Andrew Cathey grew fruits and vegetables in **Cathey's Valley** and marketed them in the gold camps, with Chinese laborers clearing the land and building characteristic stone fences. (Locals pronounce the name Ca-THAY's, though that's not how Cathey said it.) The **Guadalupe Mountains** nearby are the first foothill "step" up into the Sierra.

OAKHURST AND VICINITY

Oakhurst, a scrubby little foothill town in Madera County, is the tail end of the southern Mother Lode and the southernmost official route into Yosemite. The talking grizzly statue downtown at the intersection of Hwy. 41 and Rd. 426 is an unusual monument to extinction. The historical society's **Fresno Flats Historical Park**, 49777 Road 477 (on School Rd., just off Crane Valley Rd.), Oakhurst 93644, tel. (209) 683-6570, is a park complex with a museum in the old schoolhouse displaying old lace, quilts, and "Yosemite Sam" guns and memorabilia. There's also a jail, blacksmith shop, double "dog-trot" log cabin, and several wagons and stagecoaches—everything here collected, restored, and maintained by local volunteers. Open Wed.-Sat. 1-3 p.m. and Sun. 1-4 p.m. through the summer, just weekends 1-4 during the rest of the year. Admission $2 adults,

$1 children. North of town, Oakhurst's **Golden Chain Theatre**, P.O. Box 604, tel. 683-7112, offers old-time melodramas in summer, reservations advised. For other local information, contact the **Eastern Madera County Chamber of Commerce** at 49074 Civic Circle, P.O. Box 369, tel. 683-7766, or the **Southern Yosemite Visitors Bureau,** P.O. Box 1404, tel. 683-INFO.

Practicalities

The hautest place to eat here is elegant **Erna's Elderberry House**—French-influenced country cuisine with a California sensibility served in a Mediterranean-style villa at Hwy. 41 and Victoria Ln., Oakhurst 93644, tel. (209) 683-6800. The fixed-price dinners change daily Wed.-Mon. 5:30-8:30 p.m.; prix fixe luncheon is served Wed.-Fri. 11 a.m.-1:30 p.m.; Sunday brunch, 11-1. Reservations wise. Eat outside on the terrace, or inside in one of three tapestry-rich dining rooms. Lodgings here match the meal, with a stay at **Chateau de Sureau,** another aspect of Erna's Estate by the Elderberries (same phone). Rooms are $250-350.

The **Old Barn** at 41486 Old Barn Way, off Hwy. 41 just north of town, tel. (209) 683-BARN, has chicken, chops, steaks, fish. Pick up wonderful fresh-baked cinnamon rolls at the **Pointe of View** restaurant at the **Best Western Yosemite Gateway Inn,** 40530 Hwy. 41, tel. 683-2378, which offers nice rooms for $68-78 in summer, much less in winter. For inexpensive accommodations, consider heading to Bass Lake—abundant campsites.

Vicinity Of Oakhurst

A valley excursion from Oakhurst: take Raymond Rd. west for about 10 miles, then veer left on Rd. 606 to **Knowles**, where most of the granite needed to rebuild San Francisco after the 1906 quake was quarried. Turn right on Rd. 600 and travel north to **Raymond,** the hillside farm country here stitched together with 100-year-old stone fences built by the Chinese. The **Sierra Mono Museum** is south between Oakhurst and North Fork via Rd. 247 (off Rd. 222), an eclectic collection of basketry, beadwork, and natural history organized by the local Mono people. Open Mon.-Sat. 9 a.m.-4 p.m., tel. (209) 877-2115, small fee.

The **Wassama** ("leaves falling") **Round House** northwest of Oakhurst, now a state historic park, was constructed in the mid-1970s though the original structure dated to the 1860s. Open daily 11 a.m.-4 p.m., tel. (209) 683-8867, small admission fee. To get to Wassama, head north from Oakhurst on Hwy. 49 for 5½ miles to Ahwahnee, then turn right on Round House Rd. (Rd. 628) and continue for a half mile. Special events sometimes scheduled.

Northeast of Oakhurst, heading toward Yosemite, a variety of nondescript Sierra National Forest roads eventually arrive at Yosemite's **Mariposa Grove** of Sierra big trees—very scenic and uncrowded, the locals' favorite route. Nearby is the **Nelder Grove** of *Sequoiadendron giganteum* (giant sequoias) near John Muir's Fresno Dome. To appreciate these and other area delights, take the spectacular 90-mile **Sierra Vista Scenic Byway** tour up into the San Joaquin River Canyon (16 miles on unpaved gravel) via Mammoth (sometimes called Minarets) and Beasore roads. A free descriptive pamphlet should be available from Sierra National Forest Headquarters (see "The Southern Sierra Nevada" above) or at the ranger stations at Oakhurst and Bass Lake. If coming from the south, stop off in North Fork at the Minarets Ranger District office, tel. (209) 877-2218.

Another late bloomer and more of a gold camp than Oakhurst (a $15,000 gold nugget was unearthed here in 1890), **Coarsegold** was mostly a farm and timber town when it went by the poetic name of Fresno Flats. There's a rodeo, the seventh largest in the state, held here on the first weekend in May.

BASS LAKE

Basic reservoir recreation amid evergreens and summer homes. Lots of other action: bike races, classic car shows, a Coors marathon (running, not drinking), etc. For current camping, picnicking, hiking, and other recreation info, contact the **Bass Lake Ranger District** office at 41969

Hwy. 41, Oakhurst 93644-9435, tel. (209) 683-4665. A forest recreation map is available for $3, by mail or stop en route. At the lake, get information and trail brochures at the Bass Lake Visitors Station on the west shore. For other information, contact the **Bass Lake Chamber of Commerce,** P.O. Box 126, Bass Lake 93604, tel. 642-3676, or the **North Fork Chamber of Commerce,** P.O. Box 426, North Fork 93643, tel. 877-2410.

Practicalities

Popular lakeside campsites in summer include **Wishon Point, Spring Cove, Lupine, Forks,** and **Denver Church;** call Mistix at (800) 283-CAMP for reservations. More remote campgrounds (tables, fire rings, no safe drinking water, no reservations) follow a mostly unpaved route east of Hwy. 41 between Bass Lake and Yosemite. (Only **Chilkoot** on Rd. 434 is accessible via paved road.) Among these, **Nelder Grove** campsites are unique—near an impressive, isolated grove of Sierra big trees. To the southwest there's a mile-long self-guided interpretive walk, "The Shadow of the Giants," along Nelder Creek on the National Recreation Trail. To get to Nelder Grove, take Sky Ranch Rd. (Rd. 632) from Hwy. 41, north of the turnoff to Bass Lake, then turn left on California Creek Road. See also "Vicinity of Oakhurst" above.

New and quite plush is **Ducey's on the Lake,** with rates from $140 per couple, built on the former site of Ducey's Bass Lake Lodge and sister resort to **The Pines Resort.** For reservations at either, call toll-free (800) 350-7463. Open all year. Best bet for dinner here is the **Pines Resort** restaurant, tel. (209) 642-3233, decent American fare, outdoor deck in summer. Eateries and weekend entertainment are nearby in **Old Town,** which is actually new and touristy. Among the few authentic historical features is the horse-drawn hearse advertising funerals for $5 (with discounts if the family helps dig).

BOB RACE

THE GREAT VALLEY
INTRODUCTION

When John Muir wandered west out of the Sierra Nevada in the late 1800s, he was overwhelmed by California's great central valley. "When California was wild," he wrote, "it was one sweet bee garden throughout its entire length . . . so marvelously rich that, in walking from one end of it to the other, a distance of more than four hundred miles, your foot would press about a hundred flowers at every step." As if in Kansas, early immigrants to California's great valley gazed out upon green waves of vegetation washed clean by April rains but burnished to a golden brown by August. The *tulares* or marshes and shallow lakes rippled with birdsong, and ancient rivers meandered through woodland jungles of deciduous trees, riverside thickets that were home to the valley's most complex web of wildlife. Grassland prairies, stretching to the distant foothills on every horizon, buzzed with life.

Millions of ducks, geese, swans, and other waterfowl once flocked here in feathery winter clouds so thick that amazed explorers claimed their flight blotted out the sun. Vast herds of tule elk, pronghorn, and deer browsed through woodlands and prairies. Even grizzly bears galloped across valley grasslands just over a century ago. Supported by the land's natural richness, California's great valley was also home to one of the continent's densest native populations, the Maidu, Miwok, Wintu, and Yokut peoples. To the native Maidu who populated much of the north, California's great valley was the source of life itself.

THE LAND

California's great central valley forms a 50-mile-wide, 400-mile-long plain between the rugged Sierra Nevada and the gentler Coast Ranges, stretching north to near Redding and south to the Tehachapis. There is no other flatland area of comparable size in the U.S. west of the Rocky Mountains. The great valley is the state's primary watershed basin, collecting almost half of California's precipitation.

MAIDU CREATION MYTH

There was no sun, no moon, no stars. All was dark, and everywhere only water. A raft floated down from the north, carrying Turtle and Father of the Secret Society. Then a rope of feathers was let down from the sky, and down came Earth Initiate. When he reached the end of the rope, he tied it to the bow of the raft and stepped in. His face was never seen, but his body shone like the sun.

Earth Initiate wanted to make land so there could be people. Turtle said he would dive for some, then was gone for six years. When he came back, Earth Initiate scraped out the dirt from under Turtle's fingernails, rolled it into a ball the size of a pebble, then looked at it until it was as big as the world and they had run aground on it. All around it were mountains. Father of the Secret Society shouted loudly and the sun came up. Then he called out the stars, each by name. Then he made a giant tree with 12 different types of acorns. Earth Initiate called the birds from the sky and made all the trees and animals. Later, Coyote and Earth Initiate were at E'stobusin Ya'mani (the Sutter Buttes). Earth Initiate decided to make people, mixing dark red earth with water to make two figures, the first man and woman, Ku'ksu and Morning-Star Woman.

Most of the valley today is slightly above sea level, excepting the delta area near San Francisco's Bay Area, which is *below* sea level and dry only due to an extensive system of levees and dikes. But more than 140 million years ago, the area was an inland sea complete with swimming dinosaurs. Geologists speculate that this great trough started to fill with sediments when it became an isolated oceanic arm; sedimentation accelerated when the newborn Sierra Nevada range was carved by glaciers. Though flecks of gold still wash down through the foothills to the valley, the region's real wealth is its rich loamy topsoil, up to thousands of feet deep. The only interruption of the steady soil-and valley-building process occurred about three million years ago, when a series of volcanic eruptions near what is now Yuba City and Marysville created a large volcano. Today its remains are the handsome and heavily erod-ed Sutter Buttes, the world's smallest mountain range and the only peaks on California's vast interior plain.

As recently as 200 years ago great shallow lakes covered the southern San Joaquin Valley, and when Sierra Nevada snow melt transformed creeks into raging rivers, the entire central valley became an inland sea once more, this time with fresh water lapping against the Sutter Buttes and the valley's encircling foothills.

Though the central valley has long been considered "stable ground," recent geological discoveries suggest that the western edge of at least the Sacramento Valley is webbed with numerous earthquake faults, capable of producing a tremor above magnitude 6 on the Richter scale. The 6.4 magnitude quake in Coalinga in 1982 suggests that this phenomenon is also applicable to the San Joaquin Valley farther south.

Taming the Watershed

Water is life in California's great valley, a fact reflected in the words on the sign arched across the old highway in Modesto: Water Wealth Contentment Health. But land is likewise necessary for economic wealth—for cities, local industries, and agriculture—and during the past 150 years the valley's marshes and lakes have been drained and "reclaimed" to obtain that land. Converting California's vast central valley to farmland has also meant taming the rivers within its watershed. All major rivers have been dammed, redirected, or "channelized." The Central Valley Project and other 20th-century feats of water engineering have made it possible to transport water from the rain-soaked north to the arid San Joaquin Valley in the south, transforming inland deserts into gardens—truck gardens.

Despite its almost complete remodeling by water engineers, the largest and longest California river is still the Sacramento, which flows south from near Mt. Shasta to its confluence with the Pit and McCloud rivers at Shasta Lake, then snakes south through the Sacramento Valley, where it is joined by the American, Feather, and Yuba. The San Joaquin River, which lends its name to the southern reaches of the great valley, once flowed westward until pushed north by the Coast Ranges, fed along the way by the Merced, Tuolumne, Stanislaus, Mokelumne, and Cosumnes rivers. Due to agricultural water

WATER ENGINEERING: TAMING A WILD RIVER

Illustrating the high price paid for California's water-engineering success, in the currency of environmental stability as well as taxpayer dollars, is the sad saga of the once-mighty Sacramento River—now mostly an irrigation ditch. Its banks originally a deciduous jungle of native trees and vines extending as far as 20 miles on each side, the Sacramento has been stripped bare by the purveyors of progress. Taking the place of the natural riverbank vegetation—which slowed the river's flow, held the riverbanks in place, and protected the fisheries—are some 980 miles of levees, 430 miles of channels, and 100,000 acres of bypasses. For decades, channelizing the north valley's namesake river with "riprap"—reinforcement of rocks, crushed autos, and other garbage—both to inhibit its natural meanderings and to efficiently deliver water to agricultural users, has been a priority of the U.S. Army Corps of Engineers. And where the Corps didn't strip away the native vegetation, farmers and ranchers did, to maximize their productive acreage.

But with the destruction of the Sacramento's rich riparian vegetation came serious erosion problems, increased siltation, and the additional loss of wildlife habitat. The river also flowed faster and with more force than ever before—making more channelization controls necessary to prevent still more erosion and flooding. With the painfully slow realization that the native vegetation contributed valuable stability to the ecosystem, the Corps is now experimenting with new riverbank protection techniques at Woodson Bridge State Park northwest of Chico. In the meantime, environmental groups are lobbying at the state level for "meanderbelts" (buffers of land which permit the river to follow its own shifting, natural channel) and other legislation to further protect what little remains of the river's natural state.

diversions, the San Joaquin River has been dry since the 1940s. What remains of the valley's two dominant river systems converge in the delta region, now a predominantly unnatural maze of canals, sloughs, islands, and levees, before flowing through the Carquinez Strait into San Pablo and San Francisco bays.

Climate: Summers Like A Bake Oven, Winters Of Fog And Ice

John Muir noted that in California's great valley "there are only two seasons—spring and summer." Summers are long and hot, and "winter" in the valley—though often foggy and cold—coincides with the state's rainy season, the only time of year this part of the Golden State is green without the assistance of irrigation. If less than hospitable for humans, the valley's climate is perfect for crops. In most areas, characteristic 100-degrees-plus summertime temperatures are unforgettable and virtually unlivable, but worse throughout the valley in summer is air pollution. (In fall, the valley's otherwise crisp, clear air is often colored by smoke and air borne detritus from field burning.)

The rainy season usually begins in November, with little or no precipitation after April or May. Though nothing is really typical due to the state's increasingly erratic weather patterns, 20-40 inches of rain falls in the north valley during the rainy season, and less than seven inches in the desert-like plains farther south near Bakersfield.

Thick ground-hugging tule fog is common between winter storms, insulating the valley from most winter freezes. (Sacramento is derisively known as the Tule Fog Capital of the World by its bone-chilled residents.) On clear nights after a good rain, blankets of mist form which the weakened winter sun can't burn through for days, sometimes weeks. When it settles in for a stay, California's valley fog creates one of the world's largest ground clouds, a moist, ghostly shroud often going the distance between Redding and Bakersfield and stretching across the farmland between the Coast Ranges and the Sierra Nevada foothills; fog ceilings usually reach 1,000 feet or more above the valley floor.

When driving in valley fog (don't, if it's possible to avoid), always use the car's low-beam headlights, don't panic, and never stop suddenly, even in surprise "zero-visibility" situations. Multiple-car accidents involving drivers who freeze up due to fog blindness are an all too common occurrence in the valley and delta areas. If the fog becomes so thick you can't see, pull off onto the road's shoulder, *then* stop. The same rules apply to dust storms, which can occur suddenly along I-5 and Hwy. 99 in the San Joaquin Valley.

The sun still shines in the foothills when thick tule fog blankets the valley below.

WES DEMPSEY

Without fog, valley winters become even colder, with subfreezing temperatures no surprise from December through February. A phenomenon colloquially known as "false spring" sometimes occurs in late January or February, unseasonably balmy weather which encourages people to believe, albeit briefly, in the promise of spring. To experience California's heartland at its best, try a sparkling day in early spring when snowcapped coastal mountains and Sierra Nevada peaks seem just within reach beyond the wildflower-thick foothills.

Native Flora

The tule marshes, the prairies of perennial grasses, and the riverside woodlands—each of these three ecosystems dependent on different soil types and moisture levels—once covered the land, forming a vast marshland prairie. Due to the demands of agriculture and the reclamation projects which have made possible California's phenomenal agricultural productivity, all of these natural environments are now rare. In modern times fields of cotton, alfalfa, and vegetables, vast expanses of watery rice acreage, and orchards and vineyards now take their place.

Unusual in the valley but typical of its bone-dry southern reaches are salt-tolerant desert plants and salt marsh species like pickleweed. Even in the desert areas spring carpets of wildflowers once stretched to every horizon: blooming fields of orange poppies, blue dicks and other *Brodaeia* species, lupines, native grasses, and cream cups, goldfields, and endless other tiny "vernal pool" plants. These slight depressions in valley hardpan areas—called vernal pools because they catch winter rainfall which slowly evaporates come spring—host a unique array of annual wildflowers where the pattern of bloom succession can be observed with the changing fairy rings of flowers. Rare now, threatened by overgrazing and encroaching development, vernal pools nonetheless remain in some grazing areas on the valley's fringe and in areas protected by the Nature Conservancy. (Tread lightly while visiting.)

The valley's hardy native bunchgrasses and many native wildflowers have been replaced by introduced pasture grasses and flowers that turn to straw by May. Agriculture and housing developments have replaced wild vegetation altogether in sprawling urban and suburban areas.

Ecologically rich riparian woodlands once covered vast areas of the great central valley: dense, tall forests of oaks, sycamores, willows, ash, alders, maples, and cottonwoods entwined with wild roses, berry vines, and wild grapes, and fringed with tules and cattails. The sheer volume of riparian loss is staggering: less than two percent of the valley's original riparian habitat remains. In the northern Sacramento Valley alone, an estimated 800,000 acres of riparian forest have dwindled to about 12,000. Surviving, scattered remnants of California's riparian vegetation still represent the state's most diverse ecosystem, home to 60-some species of birds (including the rare western yellow-billed cuckoo) and seasonal stopover for more than 200 others.

Of all the tree species native to the region, most impressive—for its sheer size and gnarled grace—is California's valley oak, *Quercus lobata*, now endangered partly because early farmers soon realized that the most fertile and deepest soils (along with high natural water tables) were found wherever it grew. The largest oaks in North America, these light-barked, gray-green giants can grow to over 100 feet in height, with a trunk diameter of up to eight feet. In addition to agriculture and the woodcutter's axe, encroaching development projects also threaten the valley oak. For reasons still incompletely understood (though livestock grazing, reduction of river flooding, and competition from introduced grasses are among the suspected problems), for decades valley oaks have not been successfully reproducing. This fact alone presents the most permanent threat to the species' survival, since many remaining trees are now dying of old age.

Native Fauna

Though many ducks and other species are year-round residents, 92% of the valley's four million acres of wetlands have disappeared forever. But to the federal and state wildlife refuges established on former marshes and lakes (now productive grain fields) come the migrating winter waterfowl common in the valley, including whistling swans and Canada, white-fronted, and snow geese. Visiting shorebirds include avocets, curlews, egrets, sandpipers, and stilts. In summer, blue-winged and cinnamon teals are fairly common. Black-crowned, night, green, and great blue herons also thrive in the valley. The region's rich native grasslands once supported vast herds of prairie grazers: deer, the exclusively Californian tule elk, and the now-rare pronghorn. The only remaining species of its family (related to neither deer nor European antelopes), the pronghorn has almost vanished in the state, surviving only in restricted ranges.

In rapidly vanishing native riverside forests is a wildlife wonderland: songbirds and waterfowl, cottontails and jack rabbits, beavers, raccoons, striped skunks, coyotes, and gray foxes. Turtles and salamanders thrive near the river rapids, but salmon and steelhead attract more human attention. Threatened by water diversion projects and river pollution are the spring-

---

THE LESSON OF BIRDS: SIX

Canada Geese
on the wing on the flyway
above our house
in Spring. V
after V stars the day sky
in a straight–line journey
home. The ah–honks
of their joy are like haunting
jazz solos—
"wings of meaning"
Stevens sort of said.
One blue afternoon
I watched a lead goose
lose its way (the wingless
can't say why), drop,
and circle—
its well–taught flock
strung behind.
Each new skein joined
the confusion, and soon
thousands of geese were swirling,
wildly honking.
I felt scared
hearing those birds. We know
so little about home,
let alone the world,
and there's so much wing
up there.

—Gary Thompson

---

and winter-run chinook salmon whose numbers once nearly choked the Sacramento River and its tributaries—particularly "wild-strain" fish not descended from fish hatchery stock.

Where there are valley oaks there are also acorn woodpeckers, mischievous red-capped birds which store acorns and seek insect larvae in carefully bored holes in trees and telephone poles. Bold scrub jays abound in bottomland forests—where they "plant" new oaks by burying their acorn booty in the ground—though they also thrive in cities and towns throughout the valley.

Though the valley's elderberry longhorn beetle, one of only 13 U.S. insects on the nation's endangered species list, is at home only in the valley's vanishing riparian forests, more noticeable in this environment is the complex relationship of oak and insect embodied in light-as-a-ping-pong-ball oak galls. Female wasps lay their eggs on oak stems, then the hatched-out larvae feed on plant tissue and secrete an irritant which stimulates the oak to produce the light-colored, apple-sized galls—actually benign "tumors" which protect and nourish the larvae.

THE LAND AS FARMLAND

Given the region's rich loam soils and abundant water, it's no surprise that immigrants came—and still come—to the valley primarily to farm or work in the fields. The valley's first landed gentry were recipients of Mexican land grants who transformed wildlands into ranchos dedicated first to livestock grazing, then to more diversified agricultural enterprises. Disillusioned fortune hunters from California's gold fields, attracted to the fertile heartland and its more predictable wealth, were followed by generations of farmers from around the country and the globe.

But almost from the beginning, helped along by the completion in 1869 of the transcontinental railroad, California agriculture developed to suit the interests of large landholders. Though foreign immigrants still find their way to the central valley—about one in every 10 new valley residents was born outside the U.S.—most are destined to become manual laborers on corporate farms. Modern-day farm communities include produce patches tended by Hispanics, Sikhs, and Hmong refugees, but in California, Thomas Jefferson's ideal of the yeoman democrat and the romance of the family farm have primarily been fiction.

Agriculture in California is agribusiness, and it's big business. The enormous holdings of corporate agriculture dominate both the landscape and local economies. Even the University of California has historically dedicated its agricultural research to the high-yield, chemically enhanced, and mechanically harvested farming styles typical of California agribusiness. The state's agricultural production, a $17 billion-a-year industry, includes one-fourth of all food consumed in the United States, most of the country's raisin and wine grape production, and massive cotton, rice, and orchard crops.

Trouble In Paradise

But if the world began here, as the Maidu believed, California at least may soon end here. Nothing fails like success, and hard times have come to the valley. Massive publicly funded water-engineering projects coupled with corporate agricultural expansion soon eliminated most of the valley's native beauty and wildlife and now directly threaten the region's economic and environmental health.

The valley is one of the richest, most productive agricultural areas on earth, but the price of that productivity climbs higher every year—a price paid in ongoing economic and social injustice, large-scale ecological disruptions, and escalating environmental contamination. California's great central valley is fast becoming the state's toxic waste sump—and since rivers draining the valley flow to sea via the delta and San Francisco Bay, these environments, too, are becoming increasingly polluted. Experts also predict that millions of acres of farmland, particularly in the naturally arid San Joaquin Valley, will soon be abandoned due to increasing costs of irrigation as well as accumulated salt deposits and other contamination, a side effect of irrigating poorly drained desert soils.

But urban and suburban growth also threaten agriculture. Thousands of acres of prime farm land are paved over each year for shopping malls, parking lots, and new subdivisions as the San Francisco Bay Area expands into the San Joaquin Valley and as farm towns create their own suburbs. With the region's four-million-plus population growing rapidly, about 2½ times faster than the rest of the state, California's country is quickly disappearing.

Can Paradise Lost Be Regained?

There is still hope that solutions can be found for most of the valley's serious environmental problems—problems only exacerbated by prolonged drought conditions in California, and by the resulting wars over possession of lake, river, and groundwater supplies. Small but dedicated armies of volunteer environmentalists are determined to save—and even expand, through habitat restoration—native plant communities

CALIFORNIA'S GRAPES OF WRATH

During the Great Depression of the 1930s California's fertile valley was flooded with the down-and-out from the Midwest's dust bowl. Almost overnight the valley, which historically relied on migrant farm labor, became center stage for a real-life drama of human abuse and exploitation in the fields and squalid migrant labor camps. The story was best told by John Steinbeck in his Pulitzer Prize-winning *The Grapes of Wrath;* Steinbeck researched the novel while working as a journalist for the *San Francisco News*. Befriended by government worker Tom Collins, the two wandered up and down the valley, tending to people living in unimaginable poverty and despair. Steinbeck's many articles, illustrated by the wrenching photographs of Dorothea Lange, are now collected in Heyday Books' *The Harvest Gypsies: On the Road to the Grapes of Wrath*.

Thus, in California we find a curious attitude toward a group that makes our agriculture successful. The migrants are needed, and they are hated . . . for the following reasons, that they are ignorant and dirty people, that they are carriers of disease, that they increase the necessity for police and the tax bill for schooling in a community, and that if they are allowed to organize they can, simply by refusing to work, wipe out the season's crops. . . . Wanderers in fact, they are never allowed to feel at home in the communities that demand their services.

Despite the surprising popularity of Steinbeck's work, salvation for the migrants came only with the arrival of World War II. Most moved into the cities, getting well-paying jobs in munitions factories and other war-related industry. Desperate for cheap labor once again, California farmers turned to Mexico with the aid of the federal government's "bracero" (laborer) program. With Anglo workers removed from the picture, most Americans remained unconcerned about worsening agricultural labor conditions until 1965, when the Delano Strike, Cesar Chavez and his fledgling United Farm Workers union, and long-running lettuce and table grape boycotts began to focus worldwide attention on the same story Steinbeck had told—illustrated now with different faces.

There have been some improvements in the lives, wages, and working conditions of at least some farm laborers since the 1960s, but abuses continue. In 1975 the California Legislature acted on one of Steinbeck's ideas and established its strife-torn Agricultural Labor Relations Board, though critics contend it's ineffective and politically stacked in favor of growers. But no matter what legal protections exist for farm workers, the continuing flood of illegal aliens into California's fields almost guarantees exploitation at the hands of the unscrupulous, since those avoiding deportation rarely speak out about even the most basic human rights (such as drinking water and sanitation facilities). Growers insist that workers' rights are being protected, but all evidence suggests that this is no truer now than it ever was.

Though few people even in California have been paying attention, at the time of his death in 1993, Cesar Chavez and his supporters were still boycotting table grapes, this time primarily over the issue of worker protection against pesticide poisoning. Some former supporters contend the union has become ineffective, beset by infighting and not seriously concerned about the welfare of farm workers, and embittered growers claim the UFW has become "a boycott looking for an issue."

and waterways essential to threatened and endangered wildlife. The disaster at Kesterson Wildlife Refuge has stimulated a new awareness of the price of agricultural productivity. Business as usual, it has become clear, won't last for long.

Though almost unimaginable even a decade ago, the serious study and promotion of agricultural practices emphasizing water conserva-

tion, including the fairly simple technology of drip irrigation, is now underway. Solar-powered desalination plants, designed on the Israeli model to clean up agricultural waste water *and* generate electricity, are one promising alternative. An experimental plant of this type is now operated by the state's Department of Water Resources near Los Banos.

THE NEW GRAPES OF WRATH: THE KESTERSON STORY

To some degree, pesticides and herbicides pollute most rivers draining valley agricultural land, and river-dumping of toxic wastes and sewage only compounds the problem. In the San Joaquin River, residues of DDT and other pesticides banned in the early 1970s are still present—at levels hundreds of times higher than those the federal government says are safe for fish and wildlife. In many agricultural communities nitrate contamination of groundwater has become an increasing problem, and pesticides and other environmental contaminants are the suspected culprits of unusual childhood cancers and cancer "clusters" in the farm towns of Rosamond, Fowler, McFarland, and Earlimart. Even air pollution has become a problem, particularly in the San Joaquin Valley, where it also damages field crops and trees in the adjacent Sierra Nevada.

But the most widely publicized disaster of them all is the story of Kesterson National Wildlife Refuge and reservoir near Los Banos, an area set aside to preserve and protect migrating waterfowl populations but offering instead silent and deadly testimony to the dark side of modern agriculture.

The first signs, in 1983, that something had gone wrong at Kesterson were hideous ones: dead and deformed wildlife, including the most severe examples of bird deformities ever recorded in the wild. Even cattle and other livestock in the vicinity were suffering horrible, slow deaths, and vegetation was dying for no apparent reason. The cause was toxic levels of selenium, a naturally occurring trace mineral so potent that levels over 10 parts per billion (ppb) in drinking water are considered unsafe. At Kesterson, selenium was measured at levels of 236 ppb and higher in the water alone; concentrations increased exponentially as the poison moved up the food chain.

How did the selenium get there? Tainted agricultural drainage water produced by heavy "soil washing," which involves adding gypsum to the soil, then irrigating to eliminate undesirable minerals and salts, flowed via the unfinished San Luis Drain into evap-

oration ponds at the refuge. The rest is history—the history of an ongoing environmental nightmare.

The first response to the problems at Kesterson was a program designed to "scare away" birds and other wildlife from the contaminated refuge—a solution that failed, as animals continued to arrive and rates of death and reproductive deformity climbed. After government cover-ups of the circumstances were revealed in a series of excellent *Sacramento Bee* articles published in 1985, earnest efforts to remedy the situation began.

Initial proposals to "clean up" Kesterson by dumping tainted refuge waters into the San Joaquin River (already a selenium "hotspot," especially the stretches alongside but parallel to Merced and Bakersfield) and repeatedly flushing the refuge with fresh water, created an uproar. Why, critics argued, spread the contamination still further? Following much government wrangling, a solution was finally arrived at: after the surface water evaporated, dig up all contaminated soil and mud at Kesterson and treat it like the toxic waste it was by reburying it in a sealed on-site dump. This plan was finally underway in 1988.

Estimates of what it will really cost to clean up the Kesterson Wildlife Refuge range from $25 million to $100 million or more. Because groundwater supplies beneath the refuge ponds are tainted with selenium, it was necessary to add topsoil to the refuge ponds to prevent upward seepage of selenium when groundwater levels rise in winter. In addition, no one has yet estimated the cost of new waterfowl and wildlife habitat. Critics of federal water-management practices argue that the economic costs are much higher than most people realize, since the public subsidizes the delivery of low-cost water to agricultural users growing federally subsidized crops, then ends up footing the bill for the resulting pollution.

But there are other more horrifying costs. Ducks with selenium levels higher than those at Kesterson have been found in adjacent wildlife marshes, and scientists are also concerned that migrating birds are carrying selenium north to contaminate nesting grounds. Even scientific detachment falters at the possibility that the dramatic decline in Pacific Flyway duck populations (a 20% decrease from 1984 to 1985 alone) has been caused by selenium toxicity and other environmental poisons created by agricultural practices and water-development policies.

Equally nightmarish are the recent discoveries of "mini-Kestersons" elsewhere throughout the San Joaquin Valley and toxic levels of selenium in groundwater supplies—raising fears that drinking water is affecting the health of humans and livestock as well as wildlife. Even eating produce (particularly green leafy vegetables) irrigated with selenium-contaminated groundwater, or meat from animals whose food and water supplies have been contaminated, may pose serious threats to human health.

The nightmare seems destined to continue. In 1991, toxic mushrooms—of the otherwise edible variety—were discovered in "clean" Kesterson soil used to fill drained ponds at the refuge. With selenium levels measured at 320-660 parts per million, eating just a few ounces could prove fatal.

SACRAMENTO AND VICINITY

People have long poked fun at Sacramento, California's capital city. Mark Twain himself was among the first. In Sacramento, he observed, "It is a fiery summer always, and you can gather roses, and eat strawberries and ice cream, and wear white linen clothes, and pant and perspire at eight or nine o'clock in the morning." Comparing it to New York, the Big Apple, people from Sacramento call their metropolis the Big Tomato—a reference to the area's agricultural heritage. San Franciscans, noted for their tendency toward snobbery, have been known to call the place Excremento. And though Sacramento has long been dismissed as an overgrown cowtown—an epithet more appropriate to Vacaville down the road—this rural hub of commerce and political wheeling and dealing is now a real city around which the county's one million-plus people revolve.

Sacramento has a professional basketball team and hopes to lure a pro football franchise (meanwhile dreaming still about major league baseball). It has one of the state's finest newspapers, as well as skyscrapers, air-conditioned offices clearly visible from surrounding rice fields, and reverberating rings of suburbs. It also has traffic congestion, air pollution, and the seemingly hopeless problem of human homelessness.

Lately Sacramento has set its more personal sights on bodily fitness, possessions, and "lifestyle." Writer Cob Goshen protests this new trend toward trendiness. "It's as if we've packed up and moved to the remotest suburbs of Eliot's Wasteland," he suggests, "[and] exchanged lives of quiet desperation for those of cheerful inconsequence. No more long hot days. No life and death struggle. It finally happened. We're in California now." Well, maybe not quite yet. Despite its big-city ways, Sacramento is still somehow uniquely lovable. The town is stuffed with good restaurants, sparkles with unpretentious arts and entertainment, and still offers some evidence of its friendlier but wilder past at the edge of the frontier.

Unique in Sacramento is the opportunity to observe the antics of the state Legislature up close and personal, as if at the zoo. There's nothing quite like sitting in on committee hearings or other wrangles to appreciate the absurd beauty of political fisticuffs, California style. Try exploring the Capitol building during the final days before legislative recess in summer, when hallways are crowded with arm-twisting lobbyists, and exhausted politicians are most likely to call each other names in public or slip up and tell the truth to the press. All in all it's great fun—but only for those with strong constitutions.

HISTORY

The Spanish claimed much of California's heartland from the 1540s until the early 1800s but never settled it. The first Europeans to see the Sacramento River were members of the Pedro Fages expedition of 1772, which discovered the confluence of the San Joaquin and Sacramento while exploring San Francisco Bay. Russian

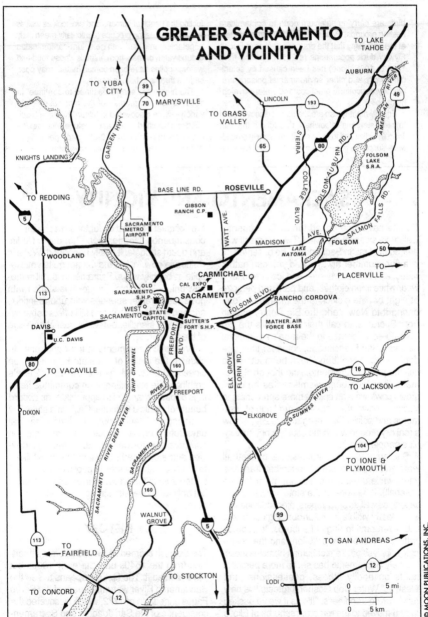

GREATER SACRAMENTO AND VICINITY

© MOON PUBLICATIONS, INC.

and Canadian fur trappers followed in the 1820s and '30s. First here, of course, were the Maidu and Miwok peoples. In 1839, when Johann August Suter (John Sutter) and his Hawaiian crew moored his ships near the future site of Sacramento's city dump on the American River, the native population had already been laid low by introduced diseases. Well before the end of the century, they were all but eradicated by cultural displacement and straight-ahead slaughter.

Though native peoples had long navigated the region's rivers in tule-reed boats, the valley's great waterways became commercial transportation arteries only with the arrival of the gold rush. The crush of gold-crazed forty-niners initiated the shipping and inland port industries which still thrive on the fringes of the Sacramento-San Joaquin Delta. New gold dreams, the area's water transport potential, the transcontinental railroad, and the valley's amazing agricultural productivity quickly created the city of Sacramento.

John Sutter: King Of Sacramento

John Sutter arrived at a fortunate time when he put down roots here in 1839. California's Mexican government was fretting over territorial invasions by trappers and mountain men, and Governor Alvarado happily granted the Swiss

CALIFORNIA DEPARTMENT OF PARKS & RECREATION

John Sutter, "King of Sacramento"

immigrant 50,000 acres—a move partially intended to thwart General Vallejo, his political rival. Sutter's fortunes increased again when the Russians abandoned Fort Ross and Alvarado's successor gave him still more land. Sutter's dream was to "civilize" the entire valley, and he set out to attract other European immigrants to Nueva Helvetia, his New Switzerland. Together with his small band of fellow travelers and native peoples he built his adobe outpost, the center of his short-lived agricultural empire. By 1845, with fur trapping all but exhausted by the near extinction of both beavers and otters, John Sutter had become the undisputed king of Sacramento.

But the official arrival of the United States presence the next year virtually ended his rule. Even then, John Sutter managed to land on his feet, and he became a delegate for the task of writing the new state's constitution. Though essentially a blundering businessman, Sutter's empire was nonetheless becoming so large his only limitation was lack of lumber. So, in 1848, he sent carpenter and wagon builder James Marshall to a site 40 miles east of Sacramento on the American River to build a lumber mill. With Marshall's discovery of gold, the end of Sutter's reign soon followed.

With the assistance of his son, Sutter became financially solvent for the first time in his life in 1849, but neither he nor his son could hold the empire together against the forces of Sutter's alcoholism or the dirty-dealing march of California history. Within five years, over a half-million people arrived in the Sacramento area to seek their fortunes. Asians, Pacific Islanders, Central and South Americans, Europeans, and migrants from all regions of the U.S. flooded into the eastern foothills. Gambling and gambolling thrived in Sacramento, the de facto capital of the new Wild West.

But gold seemed to line everybody's pockets except John Sutter's. Though he was actually the victim of his own excess, Sutter saw things differently. "I was the victim of every swindler that came along," he said. "These swindlers made the cornerstone of my ruin." In Washington, D.C., where he went to beg a pension for the services he rendered America prior to the gold rush, John Sutter died a bitter and broken man in 1880.

Sacramento's Railroad Ties

The valley's first railroad, completed in 1856, ran the 22 miles between Folsom and Sacramento. But the railroad's engineer, Theodore Judah, dreamed of a transcontinental railroad connecting California growers and merchants to the rest of the nation. Judah convinced four Sacramento business leaders that this east-west link over the treacherous Sierra Nevada could be built. With the help of California's "Big Four"—Charles Crocker, Mark Hopkins, Collis Huntington, and Leland Stanford—he founded the Central Pacific Railroad Company, which soon began lobbying the U.S. Congress for federal construction loans. And in 1862, legislation finally authorized loans to construct a railroad route over Donner Pass—but with the proviso that no money would be lent until 40 miles of track were laid.

Central Pacific's plans to sell stock in its speculative venture failed, so the company's founders financed much of the first-phase work with their own resources. But the Big Four made money even during this difficult construction phase by convincing Congress that the Sierra Nevada started 12 miles farther west than it actually did and pocketing the extra funding. For almost seven years, thousands of Chinese workers, seasoned in the California gold fields, picked tunnels through mountains of solid rock and hand-graded the railroad beds.

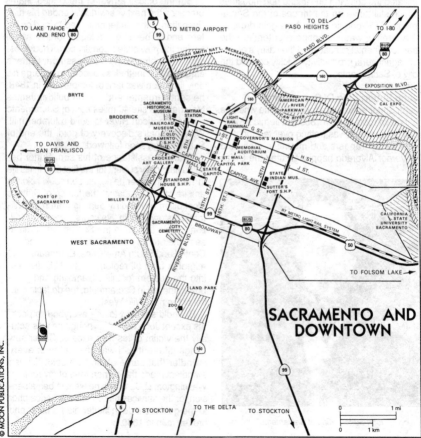

SACRAMENTO AND DOWNTOWN

© MOON PUBLICATIONS, INC.

In the spring of 1869, the Central Pacific and Union Pacific railroads were ceremoniously joined at Promontory Point, Utah. As Oscar Lewis noted in *The Big Four,* the slogan of the day was: "California Annexes the United States." Half in arrogance and half playfully, the wildest of the western colonies, he noted, "prepared to take its place (near the head of the table) with the family of states."

Soon after, railroad feeder lines connected Sacramento to Benicia and Oakland, and links were planned to Southern California and Oregon. As portrayed in the novel *The Octopus* by Frank Norris, Southern Pacific's tracks became tentacles reaching out in all directions to control the state's economy and political climate for more than 40 years, and Theodore Judah's financial backers became the richest, most politically powerful men in the state.

Becoming California's Official Capital

After Benicia, San Jose, and Vallejo had each taken their turn, by 1854 Sacramento was influential enough to become the state's official capital. During the late 1850s when California's gold fever had subsided, people still came to Sacramento, drawn by dreams of business success and landed wealth. Growth meant jobs and opportunities; the most important field of opportunity was agriculture.

By the 20th century, valley farming expanded far beyond rain-watered winter wheat fields to embrace big-time irrigation and an endless array of field and orchard crops, from beans and tomatoes to cotton and rice, from peaches and pears to almonds and walnuts. Institutions like the California Packing Corporation (later to become Del Monte) and the Libby Cannery became symbols of the community's economic backbone.

During and after World War II, people still came to Sacramento for the jobs at Mather and McClelland Air Force bases and the Sacramento Signal depot. In the 1950s with Aerojet's expansion into the space program, engineers and rocket scientists arrived—Sacramento's first big taste of high-tech economic development. Government bureaucracy and politics here are also growth industries. And in Sacramento as elsewhere in the state, orchards and productive farms have given way, and are still giving way, to business and industrial development and suburban housing projects.

OLD SACRAMENTO SIGHTS

The original gold rush boomtown of Sacramento boomed first as a tent city on the mudflats along the river near the old Tower Bridge, more or less defined these days by Front and J streets downtown. Mark Twain wrote here, Lola Montez danced here, and William Fuller painted here. These eight city blocks, appropriately called Old Sacramento and now both a state historic park and national landmark, almost capture the ambience of the Old West—especially on those

Old Sacramento

SACRAMENTO CONVENTION & VISITORS BUREAU

low-key days when tourists are scarce. But, despite the careful restoration of the area's old buildings, the freeway looming overhead and the all-too-modern commercialism of the hundreds of shops and restaurants detract from the illusion.

Most worthwhile in Old Sacramento are the excellent **historic museums** clustered in the northern sector. Plans are in the works for still more museums and an old-fashioned waterfront park. Another unusual attraction is the five-story *Delta King,* the last of California's original steam paddle-wheelers and a 1920s Prohibition-era pleasure palace. The *King,* now a floating luxury hotel and restaurant/saloon, faithfully delivered passengers between San Francisco and Sacramento until the 1940s and World War II, when he and sister ship *Delta Queen* turned battleship gray and became Navy troop transports. (To paddle-wheel up and down the river, other boats are available. See "Old Sacramento Tours" below.) While wandering through Old Sacramento, note the elevated boardwalks and original streetside curbing, reminders of the days when neighborhood rivers regularly rampaged through town in winter.

Less obvious, now that Old Sacramento is all spruced up and spit-shined, is the fact that it was until recently a fairly typical urban slum. When the unwanted old buildings once again became desirable, the addicts, homeless, and mentally ill were shoved aside. They now mix and mingle throughout downtown, rubbing elbows with politicians, lobbyists, state office workers, and tourists, most notably in the vicinity of the Greyhound bus station.

For more facts about Old Sacramento, pick up a current copy of the free "Sacramento State Historic Parks Guide" at any local historic park or contact the **Sacramento State Parks Docent Association** office at 111 I St., Sacramento 95814, tel. (916) 323-9278, or 445-7373, for general parks information. (The area's state park administrative office is upstairs in the Big Four Building.) There are two visitor information centers in Old Sacramento. One, run by the **Convention and Visitors Bureau,** 1104 Front St., tel. 442-7644, offers free maps and countless brochures. The other, sponsored by the **Old Sacramento Merchants Association** at 917 Front St., tel. 443-7815, also offers maps and brochures, plus up-to-date info about what's

going on in the neighborhood. For current events, call 443-8653.

Parking in Old Sacramento proper is usually impossible, but the large public lots just to the east (under the freeway) and south are usually ample, and from there it's an easy stroll straight into the olden days. Or get into or out of Old Sac on the city's light-rail system via the K Street route.

Also, if you're here to really "do" Sacramento, consider purchasing **discount joint tickets** to the area's major attractions. For a cost of $11 for adults and $5 for children, these multiple-use admission passes (available at any of the following) will get you into the Sacramento History Museum, the California State Railroad Museum, the Crocker Art Museum, Sutter's Fort, the State Indian Museum, and the Governor's Mansion. Another plus: discount tickets are valid for an entire year from the date of purchase.

Old Sacramento Tours

Free **Old Sacramento Walking Tours** leave from the train passenger station (Front and J streets) on weekends at 11:30 a.m. and 1:30 p.m., tel. (916) 322-3676. Rent bikes at **Surrey Cycle Rentals,** 916 2nd St., tel. 441-3836, especially fun for a day's outing along the American River Bike Trail accessible from Old Sac. Or take a **horse-drawn carriage ride.**

With time and a little cash to spare, consider a one-hour paddle-wheel tour (spring, summer, and fall only) or a lunch or dinner cruise. Channel Star Excursions offers two boats: the newly arrived (and very large) *Spirit of Sacramento,* once a star in the John Wayne movie *Blood Alley* but all cleaned up now, and the smaller *Matthew McKinley.* Sightseeing tours, happy hour, dinner, and dinner theater cruises, even champagne brunch, are offered. Private parties are also popular. The company's office is at 1207 Front St., but trips depart from the L Street Landing, tel. (916) 552-2933 or toll-free (800) 443-0263. Or take a classic rock (golden oldies) dance-and-booze cruise aboard Capital City Cruises's huge (158 feet long) *Elizabeth Louise* steamer, tel. 921-1111, which shoves off about twice monthly for 9 p.m.-to-midnight river adventures. (This boat, by the way, is the only operating steam-powered paddle wheeler west of the Mississippi.) Capital City, which ties up its boats north of town at the Riverbank Marina,

1401 Garden Hwy. No. 125, also offers guided cruises, dinner dances and dinner theater, and Sunday brunch; also Sacramento or American River trips aboard the double-decker *River City Queen* paddle wheeler. Call both companies for current events, schedules, prices, and departure points.

For full-steam-ahead train fans, take a ride on the railroad museum's fairly pedestrian **Sacramento Southern Railroad,** tel. (916) 445-7387, 40-minute steam-powered excursions to Hood and back which start from the park's newly reconstructed freight depot. Trips run summer weekends, on the hour from 10-5 and from Oct. through April, the first weekend of the month only, noon-3 p.m. Fare: $4 adults, $2 for ages 6-17, charters and group trips available. No trains are scheduled on the July 4th weekend.

The California State Railroad Museum

Situated at the old terminus of Southern Pacific, the huge California State Railroad Museum (at 111 I St. in Old Sacramento) warehouses an exceptional collection of locomotives and railway cars which once rode the rails "over the hump," connecting California with more civilized areas of the United States. It's worth a stop just to appreciate the painstaking restoration of these fine old machines, among them Central Pacific's first locomotive. Exceptional is the North Pacific Coast Railroad's *Sonoma,* the finest restored American Standard locomotive in the nation, all brass and elegant beauty. Also fine is *The Gold Coast* private car, an updated 1890s business suite. *Santa Fe Number 1010* was "Death Valley Scotty" Walter Scott's iron steed during his high-speed 1905 L.A.-to-Chicago run. And *Southern Pacific Number 4294* is the last of the behemoth cab-forwards that formerly scaled Sierra Nevada summits. Ever-popular is the *St. Hyacinth,* a restored 1929 sleeping car which rocks and rolls in simulated nighttime travel. The railroad history museum's walk-through introductory diorama is well done, as are the films and interpretive exhibits. Docent-led tours are available daily starting at 1 p.m. Next door, housed in a one-time coffee and spice mill, is a railroad bookshop.

Separate, too, but included as part of the state's railroad museum is the **Railroad Museum Library** on the second floor of Old Sacramento's Big Four Building, a research and reference library of books, blueprints, corporate

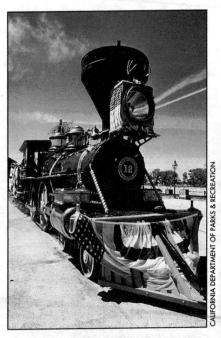

CALIFORNIA DEPARTMENT OF PARKS & RECREATION

Beautifully restored locomotives, the stars of the California State Railroad Museum, chronicle the state's railroad history.

records, and photographs. Open to the public Tues.-Sat. 1-5 p.m. Also part of the museum complex is the **Central Pacific Railroad Passenger Station** at 1st and J streets, restored to its 1870s appearance. The museum's newest addition is a reconstruction of the old **Central Pacific Freight Depot.**

A rollicking event rolling out each September from the railroad museum is the **U.S. National Handcar Races.** Up to 150 five-person teams compete in various divisions of this 300-meter, timed event—and some people are quite serious competitors. The record is 31.782 seconds, clocked by the Holy Rollers in 1984. Great fun, even for spectators.

Except for the library (hours as noted above), the railroad museum is open daily 10-5, admission $5 adults, $2 for ages 6-17. (The same all-day ticket is good for admission to the passenger station.) For more information, stop by the museum at 111 I St. or call (916) 448-4466.

The Sacramento History Museum

Also well worth a stop is the Sacramento History Museum near the waterfront at 101 I St., tel. (916) 264-7057, an impressive array of thematic local history lessons conveyed via artifacts, hands-on activities, and interactive video. The museum focuses on regional change created by humans interacting with their environment. The **California Gallery** has changing exhibits. The **Community Gallery** pays homage to the multicultural pioneers who have created Sacramento and environs. Particularly impressive are the re-created lobby of the old *Sacramento Bee* building and the agricultural display, with everything from antiquated tractors to stacks of period produce crates.

One of the newest features is the center's **Gold Rush Gallery,** which includes gold displays, a step-on scale to discover one's worth in gold, even a dismally authentic representation of a gold miner's cabin. The center's **Museum and History Division** features taped oral histories and vintage photos recounting how Sacramento came to be. The Sacramento History Museum is open Tues.-Sun. 10-4:30. Admission is $3 adults, $1.50 for children ages 7-17.

California Citizen-Soldier Museum

The newest historical attraction in Old Sacramento is the four-story California Citizen-Soldier Museum at 1119 2nd St., tel. (916) 442-2883. Exhibits chronicle the early days of the California Militia, and the long-running history of the state's National Guard—first headquartered in the Pacific Stables building across the street. At home here are thousands of military relics, many genuine blasts from the past, from rifles, World War I machine guns, and Civil War muskets and bayonets to uniforms predating the Civil War—and the sword that Major General Zachary Taylor carried into battle during the Mexican War. The museum and gift shop are on the ground floor; the remaining three floors house a library, conference rooms, and offices for the sponsoring National Guard Association. Open Tues.-Sun. 10-5. Admission $2.50 adults, $1.50 seniors, $1 children.

Other Old Sacramento Sights

The **B.F. Hastings Building** at 2nd and J streets was the old Wells Fargo office, rebuilt in 1852 after a fire destroyed most of the city. The small communications museum downstairs honors Sacramento's importance in Old West information flow. This was the end of the line for the original Alta Telegraph Company and the western end of the Pony Express, the place where trail-weary horses and dog-tired riders laid down their mailbag burdens after the last leg of the 10-day, 1,966-mile cross-country relay race against time. (From here, correspondence went on to San Francisco via steamboat.) Upstairs are the original chambers of the **California Supreme Court,** the quality of jurisprudence supposedly reflected in the dignified courtroom and dark justices' chambers now polished by the passage of time.

The **Big Four Building** on I St. between Front and 2nd, Central Pacific's original headquarters, actually stood on K St. when Theodore Judah made his bold pitch to the Big Four of California railroading fame; the building was moved to its present site to make way for the I-5 freeway. Downstairs these days is an open-for-business re-creation of the original 1880s **Huntington & Hopkins Hardware Store** (where visitors can gain recognition for themselves by correctly identifying samples of 19th-century hardware). Upstairs is the park's railroad museum and a replica of Central Pacific's board room.

The tiny **Old Eagle Theatre** at 925 Front St. across from the railroad depot is a careful canvas reconstruction of the 1849 original, open for a peek and a short slide show during the day, and for live theater productions on weekends; call (916) 446-6761 or 323-7234 for current performance schedule, prices, and reservations. Stop by the **Old Sacramento Schoolhouse** at Front and L Sts., tel. 483-8818, to reminisce on the romanticism of one-room schools. Museum open Mon.-Fri. 9:30-4, weekends noon-4.

OTHER SIGHTS

The State Capitol

Painstakingly restored to a 1900s ambience in the early 1980s, California's elegant state Capitol is hard to miss in its central Capitol Park location at 10th St. and the Capitol Mall (between L and N streets). Started in 1860 and completed by 1874, the magnificent gold-domed rotunda, bronze and crystal chandeliers, rich walnut

the original state Capitol, circa 1900s

woods, "Eureka tile," and marble mosaic floors speak of an era when buildings represented material yet high-flying ideals. The red-hued Senate and soft green Assembly chambers on the second floor hint at Greco-Roman governmental tradition. Official declarations of these respective political bodies—"It is the duty of a Senator to protect the liberty of the people" and "It is the duty of the Legislators to pass just laws" —are inscribed in gold leaf but in Latin, perhaps so most citizens (including politicians) can't decipher them. Worth seeing, too, are the individual county displays, which offer a view of various communities' official self perceptions. The **Capitol Museum** displays in Room 124 are historically authentic 1906 re-creations of Governor Pardee's anteroom and offices plus the offices of the secretary of state, treasurer, and attorney general. Open 9-5 daily except Thanksgiving, Christmas, and New Year's Day.

The Capitol also includes a fairly decent cafeteria serving short-order meals and snacks (in the basement, which also includes a gift shop and the museum headquarters) but more enjoyable is a picnic outside in **Capitol Park.** This elegantly landscaped 40-acre park of impressive and unusual trees—many planted in the 1870s, three the largest known specimens of their kind—includes a redwood grown from a seed that circled the moon aboard Apollo 13 in 1970. A new **Vietnam Veterans Memorial** hon-

oring California's war dead has been added near the rose garden at the east end of the park: 22 black granite panels with the final roll call, weeping cherry trees, and statue of a 19-year-old soldier reading a letter from home.

Guided tours focus separately on the Capitol building's restoration, its history, the legislative process, and Capitol Park (weather permitting). Sign-language and foreign-language tours available upon request. Get oriented in a more general way by watching the 10-minute film shown in the basement (Room B-27), where free tour tickets are available a half-hour or more in advance. In summer (Memorial Day through Labor Day) tours are offered hourly from 9 a.m.-4 p.m. (last tour leaves at 4 p.m.), otherwise 9-4 weekdays, 10-4 on weekends. Capitol Park tours are offered from spring through fall. For tour information, or to arrange group (10 or more) or school tours, call (916) 324-0333. To get tickets for the visitors galleries of the state Legislature (in session on Tuesdays and Thursdays when the political season is on), contact individual Assembly or Senate representatives or call 445-5200.

The California State Indian Museum
Not far from the Capitol and sharing the same city block with Sutter's Fort is the newly refurbished and updated California State Indian Museum at 2618 K St., tel. (916) 324-0539, open

California's state
Capitol, now restored

CALIFORNIA DEPARTMENT OF PARKS & RECREATION

10-5 daily except major holidays. With its fine collection of artifacts and exhibits, selected and approved by Native American elders, the museum chronicles the material, social, and spiritual development of California native culture. Particularly fascinating is the significance of basketry, a sacred survival art in which the basketmaker first offers thanks to the plant world for the materials gathered, then becomes part of that world and the basket itself, thereby guaranteeing abundant future harvests.

Development of a new exhibit room of native culture in the central valley and a demonstration area with everything from a native garden to a hand-game house is underway. In addition to puppet shows, slide shows, and films (including *Ishi in Two Worlds*) offered on weekends, **California Indian Days** in October attracts Native Americans from around the state for the festivities. Admission to the museum: $2 adults, $1 for children ages 6-17. Metered parking for both the museum and Sutter's Fort is available on K and L and 26th and 28th streets nearby.

Sutter's Fort

Sutter's Fort, around the corner at 2701 L St., tel. (916) 324-0539, was Sacramento's—and the valley's—first nonnative settlement, the center of John Sutter's attempted agrarian empire. Among other cross-country travelers who shared Sutter's hospitality were rescued survivors of the ill-fated Donner Party. Many of Sutter's original furnishings and implements actually came from Fort Ross, which Sutter bought from the Rus-

sians in 1841. During the gold rush, unruly, rampaging forty-niners plundered Sutter's storehouses, gardens, and fields, squatted on his territory, and even shot his cattle for food and sport; the "fort" was all but destroyed before restoration began in 1891, though the original adobe brick walls of the central building somehow survived.

Contemporary exhibits at the fort complex re-create the feel of daily life in 1846—quite popular with school and tour groups. Take a self-guided tour with "audio wand." Special events at Sutter's Fort include **Living History Days** (usually held in March, April, June, Sept., and Nov.), when docents and volunteers dressed in 1846 fashions reenact life at the fort and demonstrate the settlers' survival arts, everything from candlemaking and weaving to blacksmithing and musket drills. **Pioneer Demonstration Days** in spring and early fall focus even more specifically on survival skills. The very fun **Mobile Living History Program** is designed primarily for school children—volunteers reenact an 1840s fur-trapping expedition at various sites (usually including Red Bluff, Colusa, and Negro Bar at Folsom Lake). Even more fun for school children, parents, and teachers is the fort's day-long (24-hour) **Environmental Living Program,** which allows fourth-to-sixth graders the opportunity to live and work as early settlers did. Sutter's Fort is open daily 10-5 except on major holidays, (gift shop open till 4:30); admission $2 adults, $1 for children (higher on special-event days).

CALIFORNIA'S HOMELESS GOVERNORS

SACRAMENTO CONVENTION & VISITORS BUREAU

the Governor's Mansion

One of California's official peculiarities is the fact that the state has had no official governor's residence since 1967, when the old mansion was added to the state park system. It's a somewhat typical tale of California political throat-tearing. After Ron and Nancy Reagan moved out of the old place, a group of influential business people who the Reagans counted among their friends and political allies bought an 11-acre lot along the American River in Carmichael for a new Governor's Mansion and donated it to the state. After considerable partisan wrangling—since Democrats felt coerced by the Republican land contribution—the state eventually paid $1.3 million to build an ostentatious but otherwise fairly ordinary home on the site. The mansion was not completed in time for the Reagans' benefit, however. Ronald Reagan's successor, then-Governor Jerry Brown, pointedly called the place a "Taj Majal," partly to embarrass the Republicans, and refused to move into it. Even though Brown's successor, Republican Governor George Deukmejian, wanted to move in, the Democrat-dominated Legislature defied him and auctioned it off to the highest bidder in 1984.

The Governor's Mansion

Now part of the state park system, this 1877 Victorian home at 16th and H streets (public parking available in the lot at 14th and H if street parking is impossible), tel. (916) 324-0539, was one of the first houses in California to feature indoor plumbing, central heating, and other niceties of modern life. Other more elegant touches include seven unique marble fireplaces from Italy, gold-framed mirrors, and impeccably handcrafted doorknobs and hinges. Home to 13 California governors (including Ronald Reagan, but he and Nancy moved out in 1967), the Governor's Mansion is now furnished with an eclectic collection of items including a 1902 Steinway piano owned by Governor George Pardee's family, Hiram Johnson's 1911 plum-colored velvet sofa and chairs, the state's official 1950s china, and a clawfoot bathtub off the master bedroom with each toenail painted red by

Jerry Brown's younger sister Kathleen (now state treasurer) during their father's term in office. Special events held at the Governor's Mansion include **Living History Day** (usually in summer), depicting the life and times of particular gubernatorial families, and the two-day **Victorian Christmas Celebration** in early December. Admission is usually $2 for adults, $1 for children ages 6-17, though prices are double on special-event days. Tours start on the hour from 10 a.m.-4 p.m. at the two-story Carriage House (now a gift shop and visitors center). The mansion is open daily 10-5 for guided tours only.

The Crocker Art Museum

Among the oldest public art museums in the West, the very Victorian Crocker Art Museum at 216 O St. (on the corner of 3rd and O, a short walk from Old Sacramento), tel. (916) 264-5423, is one of Sacramento's finest features. Built in

1869 by banker B.F. Hastings and later sold to E.B. Crocker (Charles "Big Four" Crocker's brother), the museum is listed on the National Register of Historic Places and is itself a work of art— High Italianate art, with twin curving stairways, ornate painted plaster, elaborate woodwork, and inlaid polychromed tile floors. The interiors echo San Francisco's early Nob Hill nuance. The Crocker family's original collection of predominantly 19th-century European paintings and drawings has been supplemented by many new works over the years, including samples of Victorian decorative arts and Asian ceramics.

Among the most interesting works in the Crocker Museum collection, though, are the California landscapes and photography. Special exhibits are the rule at the adjoining **R.A. Herold Wing** (call for current schedule). With restoration of the original Crocker home completed, the museum's new **Mansion Wing** expands existing gallery space by 50% and includes a re-creation of the Crocker family parlor, a gallery of 19th-century German paintings, and a display of modern Northern Californian art upstairs. Community cultural events are almost the Crocker's main claim to fame, from lectures to musical programs. In addition to its special hours for special activities, the museum is open Wed.-Sun. 10-5, until 9 p.m. on Thursday, closed Mondays and Tuesdays and major holidays. Admission: $3 adults, $1.50 for children ages 7-17. Wheelchair-accessible. Parking is available at the nearby lot off 2nd Street. Tours available.

Miscellaneous Sights

Now undergoing restoration by the state parks department, the **Leland Stanford Mansion** at 8th and N Sts., tel. (916) 324-0575, is the mid-19th-century home of railroad baron and former California governor and senator Leland Stanford. Even before renovations are complete, you can take the tour—to learn about archaeological and other research involved in re-creating the building's historical authenticity. The **Towe Ford Museum** just a few blocks south of the Crocker Art Museum, 2200 Front St. at the corner of Front and V streets, tel. 442-6802, is a must-do for Ford fans. The most complete collection of antique Fords anywhere, Towe's beautifully restored stable of horseless carriages includes Henry Ford's first production model, a red 1903 Model A Runabout, also the

later Model A, flathead roadsters, classic Thunderbirds, even woodies and firetrucks. Special monthly car club exhibits. Open daily 10 a.m.-6 p.m., admission $5 adults, $2.50 children.

The modern brick **Blue Diamond Growers Visitors Center** of the California Almond Growers Exchange (whose nuts get around on Air Force One and the space shuttle), 1701 C St., tel. (916) 446-8409, offers free one-hour tours of the world's largest almond-processing plant, plus free almond tasting at the end of the line. Call before you go, since the Blue Diamond plant has considered leaving town.

The **Sacramento Science Center** at 3615 Auburn Blvd., tel. (916) 277-6180, is a great place for children, with nature trails, fine nature displays and hands-on exhibits, a walk-through aviary, and resident native Californians from snakes to small mammals. Open daily noon-5 p.m., from 10 a.m. on weekends. Adults $2.50, children ages 3-15 $1.50. The new **Sacramento Children's Museum** at 1322 O St., tel. 447-8017, features hands-on exhibits and sponsors various workshops appropriate for children ages 4 to 12. Open to the general public Tues.-Thurs. 10:30 a.m.-4:30 p.m. Admission $2. Also fun for children is **The Visionarium** on the second floor of the Sutter Square Galleria at 29th and K streets, tel. 443-7476, with a variety of experiential exhibits, from bubble-making to movie-making, and a gift shop emphasizing educational toys. Open Mon.-Sat 10-6, Sun. noon-5. Admission $4 children, $2.50 adults (children must be accompanied by at least one adult).

The new Wells Fargo Center downtown at 400 Capitol Mall includes a **Wells Fargo History Museum** in its five-story lobby, with exhibits ranging from an authentic Concord Stagecoach —exercise your imagination to comprehend how nine passengers actually managed to fit— to a facsimile of a 19th-century Wells Fargo agent's office to a collection of gold ore samples from the Grass Valley area, and a set of Howard & Davis gold balance scales. Well worth a stop if you're in the neighborhood. Free. Open during regular business hours, Mon.-Fri. 9-5; closed on bank holidays.

But for those with deep historical interests, the best museum in town could well be the immense **Sacramento Cemetery** founded by John Sutter in 1849 at Broadway and Riverside, where 20,000 pioneers from around the

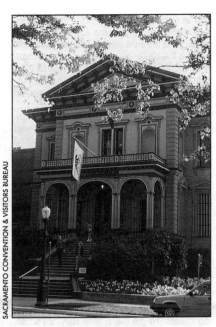

the Crocker Art Museum

globe take their final rest; these marble monuments make good reading.

American River Parkway

The American River Parkway is Sacramento's outdoor gem, a 23-mile-long riverside stretch of public parklands for river lovers, cyclists, runners, walkers, horseback riders, and just plain nature lovers. The river itself is popular for fishing, rafting, and swimming, but the parkway corridor is perfect for spring birdwatching (as are the oak woodlands surrounding Folsom Lake). The parkway goes the distance from the American's confluence with the Sacramento River to below Folsom Dam. Though it's sadly unsafe for women alone even during the daylight hours, the parkway's **Jedediah Smith Memorial Bicycle Trail** starts near Discovery Park (due to flooding, usually closed in winter), once a Depression-era shantytown. Passing restrooms and clusters of picnic tables along the way, the bike trail (equally popular with hikers and runners) heads east along the river's north bank, then crosses the river to Goethe Park and continues on to Hazel Ave. and Nimbus Dam at Lake Natoma.

Another public park in the area, across the river from Goethe, is **Ancil Hoffman Park** in Carmichael, noted for its self-guided nature trails along the American River and the educational exhibits and live animals at the **Effie Yeaw Nature Center,** tel. (916) 489-4918, open daily 10-5. Free, $3 parking fee. (For information about these and other area parks, contact **Sacramento County Parks and Recreation,** tel. 366-2061.) River rafting is popular along the parkway stretch of the American, with most trips shoving off from rental places near Sunrise Blvd. from April through September.

Folsom And Folsom Lake

At the edge of the gold country is the Folsom Lake State Recreation Area, the Sacramento area's biggest outdoor draw. It begins some 20 miles east of Sacramento where the American River Parkway ends near Folsom and its antique shops and old-brick downtown. Also in the neighborhood: the well-sung slammer immortalized by Johnny Cash in his "Folsom Prison Blues." The original dam at Folsom Lake housed the nation's first viable hydroelectric plant, which supplied power to Sacramento in 1895 via what were then the world's longest electrical lines. For another view of the Central Valley Water Project, take a tour of the dam (this one built in 1955) by contacting Folsom Dam Tours, 7794 Folsom Dam Rd., tel. (916) 988-1707. The oak woodlands surrounding Folsom Lake and its campgrounds and picnic areas are threaded with hiking and horseback-riding trails, but the area's main attraction is summertime water recreation, everything from sailboarding to jet-skiing. The 150 campsites ($14) are quite popular during the sizzling summer; Mistix reservations are necessary from Memorial Day to Labor Day, tel. (800) 444-7275.

Tiny **Lake Natoma** behind Nimbus Dam is Folsom's forebay—more idyllic for rowing and sailing because the speed limit prohibits speedboats and water-skiing. Just downriver from Nimbus Dam is the **Nimbus Fish Hatchery,** a salmon and steelhead farm adjacent to the **American River Trout Hatchery.** Both attempt to compensate for technologically blocked access to upriver spawning grounds, and both offer tours.

Annual organized activities at Folsom Lake Recreation Area include the **Pac Ten Rowing Championships** and the **National Canoe and Kayak Championships.** Folsom area activities (winetastings, rodeos, and craft fairs) are also fun; the **Folsom Prison Art Show** is in May.

For more information, contact **Folsom Lake State Recreation Area,** 7806 Folsom-Auburn Rd., Folsom 95630, tel. (916) 988-0205, and the **Folsom Chamber of Commerce,** 200 Wool St., tel. 985-2698.

Other Recreational Sites

William Land Park, a few miles south of the Capitol, is home to the 15-acre-plus **Sacramento Zoo,** 3930 W. Land Park Dr., tel. (916) 264-5885 or 449-5166, which is itself home to some 650 animals, including 23 endangered species. Open weekdays 9-5, weekends until 4 p.m. (closing times vary with the season). Admission $3.50 adults, $2 children ages 3-12. Among Land Park's other attractions are a nine-hole golf course, athletic fields, picnic areas, FairyTale Town kiddie playground across from the zoo (closed December and January), tel. 264-5223, and the Funderland Amusement Park and pony rides nearby, tel. 456-0115. (On the way to or from Land Park and in the mood for record shop nostalgia, stop at the humble beginnings of the now-national **Tower Records** chain at the corner of Land Park Dr. and Broadway, tel. 444-3000, open 9 a.m.-midnight. In keeping with the times, Tower now has an outlet store—in the Country Club Centre mall at 3422 El Camino Ave.)

The Sacramento area in general is a neighborhood recreation wonderland, with almost endless public parks, pools, tennis courts, and recreational programs, plus amusement centers, bowling alleys, and skating rinks. The **Gibson Ranch County Park** near Watt Ave. and Elverta Rd., tel. (916) 366-2066, is particularly fun for children, with its farm setting and petting zoo of domestic animals. Horseback riding, too. Strange as it seems, even Sacramento's notoriously troubled (and now, by a vote of the electorate, seemingly defunct) **Rancho Seco Nuclear Power Plant** south of town has its recreational aspect: hiking, horseback riding, plus swimming, boating, sailboarding, and water sports at Rancho Seco Park's fish-stocked lake—all in the long shadows of the plant's cooling towers. To get there, take Hwy. 99 south, then head east from the Twin Cities exit.

SACRAMENTO PRACTICALITIES

FOR A CAPITAL STAY

Smack dab in the center of California's great valley, Sacramento offers a good selection of accommodations in all price ranges. For a complete and current listing, contact the **Sacramento Convention and Visitors Bureau** (see "Information" below).

Camping is possible at various city-style RV campgrounds in the area, but the nearest public camping, at Folsom Lake, is almost too far away for convenience. Cheapest in Sacramento and friendly and quiet is the new AYH **Gold Rush Home Hostel** near I-5, 1421 Tiverton Ave., Sacramento 95822. Call (916) 421-5954 for advance reservations and directions. Rates are $8 for members and $10 nonmembers.

Finding suitable accommodations in and around Sacramento is usually no problem, except on certain holiday weekends and when a major convention or other event is underway. Sacramento motel and hotel prices listed below do not include the city's rather steep (over 10%) motel-hotel room tax. The newly incorporated warehouse district of West Sacramento has quite reasonable lodgings just across the Sacramento River from downtown and Old Sacramento.

Area Motels

Almost downtown at 1415 30th St., **Motel 6,** tel. (916) 457-0777, is just a mile away from both the Capitol and Sutter's Fort, rooms $29 s, $36 d. (There's another Motel 6 off Hwy. 50 at the Howe Ave. exit, 7850 College Town Dr., tel. 383-8110; a third in North Highlands at 4600 Watt Ave., tel. 973-8637; and a fourth in Rancho Cordova at 10271 Folsom Blvd., tel. 362-5800, with more on the way.) The **Mansion View Lodge** at 711 16th St. (Hwy. 160), tel. 443-6631 or (800) 446-6465, is comfortable and convenient with the usual amenities, rooms $34-36. Great deal. Nearby (next to the Governor's Mansion) and also fairly central is the **Central Motel,** 818 16th St., tel. 446-6006, rates $30-35. The **Canterbury Inn** a few miles east of the Capitol at 1900 Canterbury Rd., tel. 927-3492 or (800) 932-3492, is another good

choice, with rooms $55-65, plus the popular Shanley's Bar and Grill. (Ask about specials, especially in the off-season.) Farther out but cheap is **Motel Orleans,** 228 Jibboom St. (exit I-5 via Richards Blvd.), tel. 443-4811. Also quite reasonable is the nearby **Best Western Sandman Motel,** 236 Jibboom St., tel. 443-6515: $44-60. The **Holiday Inn Capitol Plaza** (there's another northeast of town), 300 J St., tel. 446-0100, has rooms for $80-90.

Area Hotels

Not far from downtown, just a few miles away, is the newly renovated **Radisson Hotel,** 500 Leisure Rd. off 16th St. (Hwy. 160), tel. (916) 922-6251, actually a motel with rooms for $84-124. The **Sterling Hotel,** is a small, contemporary luxury hotel designed for businesspeople and tucked into the time-honored Hale Mansion at 1300 H St. (13th and H), tel. 448-1300. The understated yet elegant rooms include bathrooms of Italian marble with whirlpools, $95-225. The Sterling also has excellent in-room food service, a fine restaurant, meeting rooms, good phone systems, and fax machine. The huge Mediterranean-style **Hyatt Regency** downtown at 1209 L. St. (12th and L), tel. 443-1234, is Sacramento's newest luxury hotel, complete with sauna, whirlpool, small heated pool, and valet parking, rooms $90-185. Very comfortable, very luxurious—and a good deal for pleasure travelers, since weekend rates are the lowest. Quite special, too—how many people actually sleep *on* (or in) the Sacramento River?—is a stay at the **Delta King River Boat Hotel** in Old Sacramento, tel. 444-KING.

Other higher quality motel/hotel stays in the Big Tomato include the newly renovated **Sierra Inn** at 2600 Auburn Blvd. (off I-80 Business at Fulton), tel. (916) 482-4770 or toll-free in California (800) 848-7744, rates $58-65; the **Sacramento Hilton** at 2200 Harvard St. (off I-80 Business at Arden Way), tel. 922-4700 or (800) 344-4321, rooms $69-124 (good off-season specials); and the nearby **Red Lion Hotel,** tel. 929-8855, and **Red Lion Sacramento Inn,** tel. 922-4700 (or toll-free 800-547-8010 for both). Convenient to downtown and the airport is the **Gov-**

ernors Inn off I-5 at 210 Richards Blvd., tel. 448-7224 or (800) 999-6689, with rates $60-65.

Bed And Breakfasts
The 1910 California bungalow **Bear Flag Inn** two blocks from Sutter's Fort at 2814 I St., tel. (916) 448-5417, has five tasteful Queen Anne-style rooms (one a former sunporch) and full breakfasts with specialties like sausage and leek quiche, $75-140. **Hartley House** at 700 22nd St., tel. 447-7829 or (800) 831-5806, once a boarding house, is now a homey small inn with rooms $75-125, full breakfast.

Amber House at 1315 22nd St., tel. (916) 444-8085 or (800) 755-6526, is a Craftsman under the elms, decorated with antiques and offering full breakfasts, eight rooms with private baths, some with in-room spas, $70-195. The **Driver Mansion Inn** at 2019 21st St., tel. 455-5243, is a study in luxurious Victorian propriety, catering to business execs during the week, romantics on weekends. Seven rooms, and two suites many with fireplaces and Jacuzzis, $75-225 per night.

Aunt Abigail's at 2120 G St., tel. (916) 441-5007, is formal and starched on the outside, relaxed and warm on the inside. Upstairs solarium, five rooms, fine breakfasts, garden and hot tub, $70-125.

FOR CAPITAL FOOD: INGREDIENTS

The greater Sacramento area is full of ethnic markets and specialized food shops. Among these: **Sakai G.T. and Company,** 1313 Broadway, tel. (916) 446-7968, known for its specialty ingredients for Asian, Indonesian, Lebanese, and Puerto Rican dishes, open daily 9 a.m.-6 p.m., Sun. 9-5. Cheapest and best for organic groceries is the **Sacramento Natural Foods Co-op,** 1900 Alhambra, tel. 445-2667, with an incredible selection of herbs and teas, natural foods in bulk. "Sac Natch" has a decent cafe, too, sometimes live music. Or check out the **Sacramento Central Market** held Sundays 8 a.m.-noon under Hwy. 80 at 8th and W streets: farm-fresh fruit, vegetables, baked goods, flowers. **DeFazio's Market** at Arden Way and Eastern, tel. 484-1116, is an upscale grocery with organic produce, fresh roasted coffees, seafood, winetasting, even cooking demonstrations. The

ultimate upscale shopping, though, is at the local **Corti Brothers** at 5810 Folsom Blvd., tel. 736-3800, and several other locations (call for addresses) which carry every gourmet menu item imaginable, excellent meats, fine produce, cheeses and deli items, and a wide selection of fine wines. Sacramento now has a **Trader Joe's,** 2601 Marroni in the Town and Country Village, tel. 481-8797, much cheaper for an eclectic gourmet selection.

INEXPENSIVE CAPITAL MEALS

Inexpensive And Exceptional
Best anywhere for garlic steak sandwiches is **Club Pheasant,** 1822 Jefferson Blvd., tel. (916) 371-9530, a folksy family-style Italian restaurant across the river in West Sacramento, two miles south of I-80 on Jefferson Boulevard. Also worth hunting for in West Sac is **The Russian Deli** at 2921 W. Capitol Ave., tel. 372-9775, with fresh-baked piroshkis (no preservatives).

Since this is America, hamburgers are available throughout the Sacramento area. The best burger stop around is **Ford's Real Hamburgers** at 1948 Sutterville Rd. on the south side of Land Park, tel. (916) 452-6979. Also good, almost downtown, and open for breakfast and lunch is the **Lucky Cafe,** 1111 21st St., tel. 442-9620; besides burgers, its blue plate specials and homemade pies are immensely popular. Great for breakfast (open only for breakfast and lunch on weekends, for dinner too on weekdays). **Greta's Cafe** 1831 Capitol Ave., tel. 442-7382, is also a find—and many people have found it. Bakery items alone, from scones to croissants and cinnamon rolls, make a morning meal. But the cheerful cafe really jumps at lunch; and you won't have to wait so long in warm weather, when there's outdoor dining. Menu favorites include the black bean chili, deep-dish quiches, pizzas, stews and soups, salads (like Greek pasta) and sandwiches, even nutburgers.

Good Gracious at 7213-B Florin Mall Dr., tel. (916) 395-3354, is a fine deli specializing in healthy foods. The **Good Earth Restaurant and Bakery,** 2024 Arden Way, tel. 920-5544, is noted for its natural foods (vegetarian and otherwise) and fresh, wholesome baked goods. **Food for Thought,** 2416 K St., tel. 441-3200, gives a new-wave twist to the valley's agricultural

INEXPENSIVE, EXCELLENT, AND EXOTIC

For fabulous, very reasonable Vietnamese-French food served on straightforward formica tables, **Andy Nguyen's** at 2007 Broadway, tel. (916) 736-1157, can't be beat. (There's another Andy Nguyen's at 10145 Folsom Blvd., tel. 362-2270.) Another local hot spot for Vietnamese is **Bo Bois Cafe** at 5412 Madison Ave., tel. 348-1750. **Siam** at 5100 Franklin Blvd., tel. 452-8382, warms the heart (and everything else) with its hot-and-sour soup. Other specialties include fresh prawns in chili paste and coconut sauce, various curries, and Thai squid salad.

Simon's at 1415 16th St., tel. (916) 442-9437, serves eclectic yet fairly inexpensive Chinese, from Cantonese to Mandarin beef stew and squid with hot garlic sauce, combination plates under $5, excellent pot stickers (takeout available). No lunch on Saturdays, closed Sundays. The original **Juliana's Kitchen** (now closed) was long noted for its quirky decor and inexpensive, excellent Middle Eastern fare. The new Juliana's is a cafeteria-style outpost at 14th and G, tel. 444-0966, open Mon.-Sat. 11 a.m.-4 p.m. Vegetarians are particularly happy here and can choose from falafel sandwiches, other pita bread selections (eggplant, zucchini, cauliflower, spinach), tabuleh salad, fresh juices, good desserts, everything under $5.

Unusual too, at breakfast and lunch, is Mediterranean **Pennisi's Cafe** at 11th and J streets, tel. (916) 446-6988, especially popular for its seafood and fish specials. Of the area's many noteworthy cheap Mexican eateries, consider **El Taquito Rice** at 6223 Franklin Blvd., tel. 392-5290, a great stop for a carne asada burrito. Other very inexpensive, exotic, and sometimes exceptional fare is available at the **Food Fair at the Arden Fair Mall** in the 1700 block of Arden Way.

heritage. Bold, too, are the hearty sandwiches, pastas, complex salads, and wonderful desserts. Great food, zero pretense.

Fairly new, too, is cheerful, contemporary **Alex Lichini II** (aka Alex) downtown at 1806 Capitol Ave., tel. (916) 446-1686 or 446-1430, a combination deli/market and cafe dominated by seafood and noted for its hot seafood sandwiches. Open for breakfast, lunch, dinner, and Sunday brunch; Alex's morning selections include seafood Benedict and various omelettes. Also good for a quick bite downtown is **La Boulangerie** at 901 K St., tel. 444-8902, the first in the chain.

About 15 miles north of downtown Sacramento (call for directions) is **Elkhorn Station** bar and restaurant ("Home of the Fish Fry"), tel. (916) 372-5086, which serves up a slightly weird and wild slice of Americana (Patsy Cline on the jukebox, 1950s repros of the Woodland High School *Orange Peal* newspaper as placemats) with its famous fried prawns and catfish. The all-you-can-eat famous fish fry (either cod or pollock) is about $6. The first Tuesday of the month is cioppino night, an event so memorable that just about everyone for miles around hops off the tractor and into the pickup for the drive over to this down-home dive on the Sacramento River. From northbound I-5 take the Elkhorn exit, turn right at the stop sign, and it's about one-half mile up on the other side of the freeway.

MORE EXPENSIVE CAPITAL MEALS

Things get a bit confusing in Sacramento once beyond the definitely dirt-cheap category of good restaurants. Breakfast and lunch can be quite reasonable, for example, in places that lean toward pricey at dinner. Also, depending upon what's ordered and how hungry one is, a fairly expensive place can seem almost inexpensive. Keep such qualifiers in mind while sorting through the following, somewhat arbitrary quality and price classifications.

Excellent With Apostrophes
A whole herd of good Sacramento restaurants is distinguished by names ending in apostrophe ess. For very good Italian and northern Italian specialties, **Americo's Trattoria Italiana** in a one-time brick machine shop at 2000 Capitol Ave., tel. (916) 442-8119, is the place. Wonderful fettucine al pesto, lasagna, other pasta dishes. No reservations taken, so come early (especially on weekends) or stand and wait around the wine bar. **Harlow's Bar & Cafe** at 2714 J St., tel. 441-4693, makes most of its pastas and serves excellent northstate variations of hearty northern Italian fare at lunch and dinner. **Celestin's**, 2516 J St., tel. 444-2423, features French Caribbean fare with some Thai

touches. **Paragary's Bar and Oven,** midtown at 1401 28th St. (there's another in the 'burbs near Fair Oaks and a third out in Folsom), tel. 457-5737, is a media-type hangout known for its unusually good Italian-style entrees, brick-oven pizzas, and San Francisco-style atmosphere.

Virga's Restaurant and Bar at 14th and O (1501 14th St.), tel. (916) 442-8516, is a small place serving big meals, California-style Italian cuisine from pasta selections and risotto to seafood, fish, and meat entrees. Full bar. Good food, great desserts, good value. Open for lunch weekdays, for dinner Mon.-Sat. nights (late-night cafe menu from 11 p.m. until midnight). **Ricci's,** 705 J St., tel. 442-6741, is also Italian, and excellent for seafood, shellfish, chicken, and steaks. A one-time downtown bar now transformed into a popular contemporary restaurant, **Shanley's Bar & Grill** at the Canterbury Inn, 1900 Canterbury Rd., tel. 925-3199, serves fine fare with Irish and French accents, from corned beef and cabbage to rack of lamb.

New in the Sacramento area (and like the ones in San Francisco and elsewhere) is **Max's Opera Cafe,** a New York deli-style bistro with the nerve to serve huge amounts of everything, from hickory pork ribs, Chinese chicken salad (with half a chicken), and corned beef to fresh seafood, pasta, and sandwiches so tall only a person double jointed at the jaw can do the job. Still not full? Try a slice of that five-layer chocolate cake, or an oversized serving of other temptations on display in the dessert case. The staff here sings for your supper every night, show tunes and opera. Max's is located in Market Square at Arden Fair, 1735 Arden Way, tel. (916) 553-2489, and open daily from lunch until late. Reservations wise at dinner.

If you happen to be downtown, though, don't overlook **Frank Fat's,** 806 L St., tel. (916) 442-7092, a success in Sacramento since 1939 and a local showplace almost as revered as the Capitol building itself. The fact that lawmakers almost live here doesn't detract at all from the ambience, from the fine regional Chinese fare, or from the very American New York steaks. Open for lunch on weekdays, for dinner every night. Reservations advisable. Not nearly as elegant but more popular with just plain folks is **King's** across the river in West Sacramento, 1500 W. Capitol Ave., tel. 371-8131, beloved for its dim sum and seafood dishes. Quite reasonable, no frills.

Strict vegetarians need not despair. **Mum's,** 2968 Freeport Blvd., tel. (916) 444-3015, is good for vegetarian fare, full-blown Sunday brunches. **Pava's** at 2330 K St., tel. 443-2397, with its excellent natural foods menu (both meat and vegetarian), good weekend brunches, and excellent coffees, is a downtown favorite.

Superb Without Apostrophes

The **Tower Cafe,** 1518 Broadway, tel. (916) 441-0222, next to the movie theater and otherwise a prominent part of the "trendy triangle" of Towers at Land Park and Broadway, isn't really known as a fine dining spot. It's a decent restaurant with coffeehouse style, evening dress and dreadlocks okay. People come here to people-watch, to grab a bite (pre- or post-movie), and to talk—about films, about ideas, about what's going on. That's the idea, anyway, and the staff, menu, and decor reflect a one world/global village attitude. Cultural artifacts and oddities are prominent. During decent weather, the patio outside is packed. Open for lunch and dinner daily, open until 1 a.m. Fri. and Sat. nights, for desserts, pastries, and beverages served after 11 p.m.

The **Capitol Grill** across from Paragary's at 28th and N, 2730 N St., tel. (916) 736-0744, is comfortable and unpretentious—nothing fancy, just good food and a fascinating collection of original political paraphernalia—and a great place for people-watching, for breakfast on weekend mornings, and for dinner or late-night supper. Just a few of the appetizers here can make a meal. Or try a bowl of white bean/applewood-smoked bacon soup, topped off with a tantalizing dessert. A la carte menu, great food, great value.

Caffe Donatello in the Town & Country Village, 2627 Town & Country Place, tel. (916) 973-1800, is another one of those great people-watching places. The walls, too, are worth watching—covered with Punchinello murals—but sooner or later the food gets center stage. An Italian trattoria, Donatello serves what it calls "rustic" cuisine from Northern Italy, from traditional antipasti and homemade pastas to spit-roasted meats. The **Fish Emporium** at 2310 Fair Oaks Blvd., tel. 923-5757, is wonderful for clam chowder and fresh seafood specials.

Best for tempura and sushi downtown is the stylish **Kyoto** in the old Ramona Hotel at 6th and J streets, tel. (916) 448-3570, noted especially for offbeat sushis including high-spiced "dynamite" and tiger-eye varieties. **Shige Sushi** at 1608 Howe Ave. (Arden Howe Plaza), tel. 929-1184, is excellent, featuring a robata bar for traditional fireside grilling. **Lemon Grass,** on the former site of Moveable Feast at 601 Munroe St., tel. 486-4891, is noted for its excellent exotic and sophisticated Vietnamese and Thai dishes. (Reservations taken at lunch, but not for dinner.)

For traditional Moroccan dinners (accompanied by belly dancing on Friday and Saturday nights), the place is **Marrakech Moroccan Restaurant** at 1833 Fulton Ave., tel. (916) 486-1944, reservations recommended. The **Star of India** at 1148 Fulton Ave., tel. 481-9970, features the refined cuisine of Northern India and serves excellent appetizers, eight types of bread, simple specials like its tandoori mixed grill, and traditional desserts. Related **Maharani Indian Restaurant** along Broadway's ethnic eatery strip, 1728 Broadway, tel. 441-2172, is exceptional—a good alternative to the Tower Cafe if you're going to the movies—with 10 quite distinct curries and tandoori meats drenched in classic marinade then cooked over a mesquite fire.

Fine Dining
Chinois East/West, along fine-restaurant row at 2232 Fair Oaks Blvd., tel. (916) 648-1961, serves up dim sum, pasta salads, and simpler meals along with more elaborate (and more expensive) French-Chinese cuisine. But a big night out for Big Tomato residents often includes dinner at **Biba,** 2801 Capitol Ave., tel. 455-2422, with specialties like tortelloni (giant tortellini) in cream tomato sauce, smoked-salmon fettucine, decadent desserts. **Chanterelle** in the Sterling Hotel, 1300 H St., tel. 442-0451, is very small (14 tables) and very good, fast becoming famous for its California-French cuisine. Reservations are a must for dinner (breakfast and lunch also served).

Mace's at 2319 Fair Oaks Blvd. (at the Pavillions shopping center), tel. (916) 922-0222, is very American, very "Western," the fare ranging from Northwestern to Southwestern with more than a trace of California. Lunch and dinner served daily. **Silva's Sheldon Inn,** south of Sacramento near Elk Grove at 9000 Grant Line Rd., tel. 686-8330, attracts local cowboy hats as well as more urban fine-food fanatics. Silva's specializes in American classics with hints of Asian and Italian influence—steaks and other red meat, predominantly, but also fresh fish and pastas. Open Tues.-Sun. for dinner. A full country-style breakfast is served Sunday 9 a.m.-12:30 p.m.; Sunday dinner is served family-style and early (4-8:30 p.m.).

Offering a slightly different twist on the West's outdoor heritage is **Mitchell's Terrace** at 544 Pavilions Ln. (near the rear of the shopping center), tel. (916) 488-7285, an exceptional restaurant where game and unusual seafood selections—buffalo, elk, moose, caribou, even parrotfish—served up continental style are one of the house trademarks. Fairly formal, expensive, but well worth it. Full bar, extensive wine list. The menu changes on the first Friday of every month, so call to hunt down current game. Open for dinner Mon.-Sat., for brunch on Sunday.

Eating Out In Old Sacramento
California Fats at 1015 Front St., tel. (916) 441-7966, makes a colorful splash with its bright neon, granite, and indoor-waterfall interior, also with its East-West cuisine like honey-glazed duck salad. The **Fat City Bar and Cafe** at 1001 Front, tel. 446-6768, is a more casual relative with a relaxed European/art deco sensibility.

For fine dining Old Sac-style, the place to go is **The Firehouse,** 1112 2nd St., tel. (916) 442-4772, reservations wise. Known for decades as the place to go for rococo atmosphere and heavy, rich French fare, The Firehouse is lightening up some all the way around. Most of its classics are still on the menu, but new selections (such as excellent pastas, sautéed scallops with pine nuts in a light cream sauce, braised chicken with wild mushrooms, and surprising daily specials) keep pace with California's changing tastes. Expensive. The **Pilothouse** restaurant on-board Old Sacramento's *Delta King,* 1000 Front St., tel. 444-5464, serves good (expensive) dinners and Sunday brunch, traditional French influenced by California's cuisine.

Coffee, Baked Goods, Sweets
One of the best stops for coffee and gelato in the downtown/midtown area is **Java City,** 1800 Capitol Ave., tel. (916) 444-5282, open 6:30 a.m. until 11 p.m., until midnight Friday and Saturday, a popular hangout. Among others is the time-honored and low-key **Weatherstone Coffee & Tea Company,** 812 21st St., tel. 443-6340, Java's sister company, open 7 a.m.-11 p.m. Gray-and-

pink **Terra Roxa** (pronounced "Rosa") at 3262 J St., tel. 448-8327, is a good retreat for pastries and coffee, with a slightly European attitude, newspapers everywhere, and books stuffed into its library shelves. The **Guild Coffeehouse** at 35th and Broadway, tel. 456-9932, offers audience-participation improvisational theater every Friday night (with the troupe RSVP). On Saturday nights, the Guild usually offers jazz, probably poetry readings on Tuesday nights. Call for current goings-on. **Gelati Robi** at 2317 J St., tel. 442-7624, is as much a neighborhood ice cream bar as a coffee shop. Classic for ice cream in Sacramento, *the* local tradition is **Gunther's,** 2801 Franklin Blvd., tel. 457-6646, famous for its 1940s neon and its unconcerned-about-cholesterol, 16% butterfat ice creams, shakes, sundaes, and banana splits.

Caffe Ettore at 2376 Fair Oaks Blvd., tel. (916) 482-0708, is a European-style cafe well worth it for soups, salads, and such. But the real claim to fame here is dessert—elaborate and exceptional cakes, fruit tarts, and other bakery items. **Rick's Dessert Diner,** 2322 K St. next to Pava's, tel. 444-0969, has decadent desserts and great coffees in a '50s-retro atmosphere. **Chocolate Ripple Desserts,** 1309 2nd St., tel. 446-3107, has truly sinful chocolate baked goods, like tricolor mousse and triple fudge cake (also some healthier simple lunches to dilute all that cholesterol).

Eating Out in Folsom
The **Lake Forest Cafe** at 13409 Folsom Blvd., tel. (916) 985-6780, is a great breakfast stop, for sweet rolls and omelettes, even lox and eggs. In addition to its own outpost of well-known **Paragary's,** Folsom's better dining choices include **Damiano's Ristorante Italiano** at 9580 Oak Avenue Parkway (at the rear of the Village Shopping Center), tel. 988-9757, a Sicilian-style Italian menu at lunch and dinner, great Sunday brunch. **C'est la Vie! Bistro & Grill** near Folsom Lake at 6949 Douglas Blvd. in Granite Bay, tel. 791-1500, is an informal, fun French bistro in an unlikely setting—a shopping center space transformed with both innovative and Old World design touches—and serving exceptional food with an emphasis on regional dishes. Open for lunch Tues.-Fri., for dinner Tues.-Sat., for brunch on Sunday. For French dining in classic style, **Christophe's** at 6608 Folsom-Auburn Rd., tel. 988-2208, is wide-

ly regarded as one of the very best restaurants in the Sacramento metropolitan area. Unusual for such an extraordinary restaurant, patrons can order early-dinner specials (between 5 and 6 p.m.) for under $15. Christophe's is a dinner-only restaurant, open Tues-Sun. nights 5-10 p.m. Reservations definitely advisable.

CAPITAL ENTERTAINMENT AND EVENTS

Things happen year-round in Sacramento. The withering summer heat does nothing to slow the pace of local activity, but winter is definitely sluggish. For current information about area events, contact the Convention and Visitors Bureau (see "Information" below).

Sacramento's long-running **Camellia Festival** in March (sometimes April) includes over 30 events, among them the Camellia Show, Camellia Parade, and Camellia Ball. In March or April comes the high-flying annual **Spring Kite Festival** sponsored by the American River Natural History Association and other organizations, usually held in Carmichael's Ancil Hoffman Park and attracting over 3,000 people and their kites. Great fun.

A bigger event by far is the **Festival de la Familia,** usually scheduled in late April, tel. (916) 321-1793 or (800) 846-0959, an ambitious culural festival celebrating Latin American heritage and featuring folk art, music, dancing, and storytelling, plus fabulous food from everywhere (homemade tamales, fish tacos, *carimanolas, hallacas, tequenos,* Spanish roasted corn on the cob, Mexican and Cuban desserts, Cuban-style coffee, and much more). Headliners have included major international entertainers such as Jose Feliciano and Sergio Mendes and Brasil '99.

In late April or early May look for the local **Highland Scottish Games and Gathering,** with most events open to the public. The gathering includes Scottish Clan and Family Society tents, native foods, bagpipes, and events such as "tossing" the caber, the hammer throw, and more sedate performances by Highland dancers.

Cinco de Mayo, celebrated throughout the city, is a major event on and around May 5. The entire month of May is **Asian Pacific-American Heritage Month,** with most events hosted at Sacramento City College. Also in May: the

the California State Fair

Sacramento County Fair at Cal Expo. Over the Memorial Day weekend in late May is the city's famous **Sacramento Jazz Jubilee** (for more information, see below). In June comes the annual **Pony Express Reride,** and the **Sacramento Renaissance Faire.**

Just to be weird, people in Old Sacramento celebrate **Independence Day** on July third instead (no fireworks, alas). But then on the fourth, Independence Day festivities get under way in Capitol Park with a parade, a classic car exhibition, bands, live entertainment, and good food —not to mention all the fireworks and fun at Cal Expo and Folsom Lake. The **Sacramento Water Festival** along the river in July—if there's water—features serious high-speed boat races, water- and jet-skiing shows, and the Anything That Floats Parade. Also in July, real aquatic athletes are among the throngs of ironpersons participating in **Eppie's Great Race,** a running, cycling, and kayaking competition billed as "the world's oldest triathlon."

For cycling fans, in August the **California Lottery Classic** bike race draws 10,000 or so spectators and an elite field of contestants (usually including the Sacramento area's own Tour de France winner Greg LeMond) to Old Sacramento. The **Japanese Cultural Festival** in August at the Sacramento Buddhist Church is a noncommercial, neighborhood-style celebration complete with kimono fashion show, dancing to koto music, and calligraphy and Kabuki makeup demonstrations.

The area's biggest commercial event is the

California State Fair at the California Exposition grounds (Cal Expo), a bigger-than-life bash starting in August and lasting through Labor Day. The fair offers bushels of aggie-style activities: top-name country-western, swing, and rock concerts, plus fiddling contests and other entertainment; grape-stomping, cow-milking, and pie-eating contests; winetasting, horse races, rodeos, and destruction derbies; quilt-making and bake-offs; livestock and produce on parade; sometimes even a dancing fruits and vegetables show. Complete schedule of events available; call (916) 924-2015.

In September and also at Cal Expo: the **Greek Food Festival.** Heating things up one September weekend or another is the annual **Sacramento Blues Festival** in Old Sacramento, with advance tickets available at Tower, BASS, and Ticketron outlets as well as the Howe Avenue and Community Center box offices. Also in September is the Easter Seal Society's **'49er Western Frontier Show** at Cal Expo, one of the largest country-western jamborees in the country. For information, call (602) 843-5303.

In October, of course, comes **Oktoberfest,** two days of beer, food, music, and traditional German and Swiss dancing sponsored by the local Turn Verein, the oldest western chapter of the venerable German Athletic Club. The **Sacramento Harvest Festival** takes place the same month, with folk arts and crafts, good food, jugglers, storytellers, and other entertainment. Also in October is Sacramento's **Constitution Day Celebration,** with the state's constitution on

the Sacramento
Jazz Jubilee

SACRAMENTO CONVENTION & VISITORS BUREAU

display in the Capitol Museum *and* the chance to buy votes and your own public office during **Old Sacramento Historic Area Elections.**

For those in town in December and just itching to put on that black tie, the **Baroque Ball** at the Crocker Art Museum is the museum's holiday fundraiser and incidental parade of formal fashion. Alternatively you can show up for the **California International Marathon** run from Folsom Dam to the state Capitol.

The Sacramento Jazz Jubilee

Sacramento's almost overwhelming Dixieland Jazz Jubilee is now the Sacramento Jazz Jubilee, held each year over the Memorial Day weekend and attracting 150,000 often outlandishly dressed but friendly fans and 100 or more bands from around the country and the world—groups like Australia's Corner House Jazz Band, the Benko Jazz Band from Hungary, the Leningrad Dixieland Ensemble, England's Merseysippi Band, and the Scottish Society Syncopators.

But with the new name comes a broader emphasis, and the Jazz Jubilee now includes groups like the Four Freshmen, the New York Society for the Preservation of Illegitimate Music, the Hot Tomatoes Dance Orchestra, Sons of Bixes, Paco Gatsby, and Igor's Jazz Cowboys. You name it, it'll probably be here. For more information, contact the Sacramento Jazz Jubilee headquarters at 2787 Del Monte St. in West Sacramento, tel. (916) 372-5277.

As the jubilee has grown, so has its need for space—so Cal Expo (site of the annual state fair) has become the event's secondary "hub." Most concert and cabaret sites are clustered in and around Old Sacramento (from I to L streets between the river and I-5) and at "satellite" concert centers linked to festival central by shuttle buses. Wear walking shoes and dress for comfort (and temperature extremes, from blistering outdoor heat to ice-like air conditioning), and consider a sun hat, sunscreen, and a flashlight if you plan to party till the cows come home. Ticket badges for the entire weekend are $70 each, one-day tickets $30 each for Friday, Saturday, or Sunday events. Half-day badges are $20. Admission to the Jubilee's kick-off ceremony, usually assembled at Plaza Mall across from Macy's and marching to the 4th and J streets concert site, is free. Also free: all that jazz at local clubs and theaters and watering holes over the weekend.

Unlimited transportation is available on concert shuttles, which run 10-15 minutes apart, as well as Regional Transit's light-rail system. Almost the only way to survive and/or know what's going on amid the merry madness is to buy a program ($5 or so), though the *Sacramento Bee* usually publishes a free and very useful jubilee guide on the Friday kicking off the party.

Bars And Nightclubs

Joe Marty's bar on Broadway is a veritable baseball shrine: the original home plate from Edmond's Field is nailed to the wall, and caps, pennants, and other memorabilia create the light in an otherwise dark dugout. For politician-watching, popular eat-and-drink places include **Frank Fat's,** also a restaurant at 806 L St., tel. (916) 442-7092, unofficially recognized as the state's unofficial Capitol; the **Metro Bar and Grill** at 1225 K St., tel. 447-3837; and meat-and-potatoes **Posey's Cottage** at 1100 O St., tel. 444-6300. The **Capitol Grill** at 28th and N, tel. 736-0744, has a bustling bar and is sometimes good for politician-watching, though those in the know say the *real* state schmooze center is **Brannan's Bar & Grill** at 1117 11th St., tel. 443-2004, a hiding place for office workers and others across from the Capitol's northern entrance. For more laughs: **Laughs Unlimited** in Old Sacramento at 1124 Firehouse Alley, tel. 446-5906, hosts good national acts. (There's another Laughs Unlimited at the Birdcage Walk Shopping Center.) Laid-back **Luna's Cafe** at 1414 16th St., tel. 441-3931, is a breakfast-lunch-dinner restaurant true to the concept of Mexican juice bars, with evening Hispanic culture and entertainment some nights.

The Fox and Goose, in a refurbished old brick warehouse at 10th and R streets, tel. (916) 443-8825, is comfortably dark and pub-like, with a bustling bar and live music nightly, everything from bluegrass, country-western, and folk to blues and jazz.

The Fox and Goose is noted for its impressive national and international beer selection. Local brewski fans and fanatics, Sacramento's **Rubicon Brewing Co.** at 2004 Capitol Ave., tel. (916) 448-7032, is probably the best brewpub choice around, with brews including Summer Wheat and Irish Red. The **Hogshead Brewpub** down in the basement at 114 J St. in Old Sac, tel. 443-2739, is Sacramento's oldest brewpub, a no-frills rock and blues bomb shelter with Old Sac's only pool table. And if the Sacramento selection isn't enough, head to Davis—a beer-loving university town with both impressive quantity and quality in brewpubs.

Making the scene—the dance scene, or the singles scene, or whatever—might require some effort. The "scene" here changes faster than the political roster down at the Capitol. Ask around for the type of entertainment you're looking for, and/or check local newspapers for ideas.

Melarkey's, at 1517 Broadway, tel. (916) 448-2797, with blues, jazz, and rock, is popular with the young singles set. Casual. Tuesday is hip-hop night. For some urban R&B, and for En Vogue stylin' it, head to **Club Mercedes** (inside Shangri La) at 6339 Mack Rd., tel. 533-2271. Alternative clubs are the trendiest of the trendy. **Cattle Club** at 7042 Folsom Blvd., tel. 386-0390, has DJ-ed music on Fridays, "older music" bands on Saturdays. **The Rage** next to Circuit City at 1890 Arden Way, tel. 929-3720, is *the* high-energy dance spot on Friday and Sunday, with techno-rave on Sundays. Sacramento's biggest club (with the smallest sign) is inside the Yucatan Drink Stand at 1696 Arden Way, tel. 922-6446, across from the Arden Fair Mall: the **Shark Club,** with predators and prey alike happily sharing the long wait outside on the sidewalk.

Aging hipsters head for places like **The Big Chill** downstairs at the Sheraton Sunrise in Rancho Cordova, 11211 Point East Dr., tel. (916) 638-1100, though the **Classic Juke Box** in Roseville, at 8200-D Sierra College Blvd., tel. 969-1165, is the real classic, especially in the bar. If you happen to be out near Folsom, stop by the **Sutter Street Saloon** at 614 Sutter St., tel. (916) 985-3280, an up-and-coming blues club with live music Thurs.-Sun. nights (cover varies), good beer any night. ("No trendoids.") **The Pink Panther** at 3121 26th Ave., tel. 451-9192, is a country-western bar with TV trivia questions on its bar napkins, but better for C&W dancing—real civilized, dude-ranch style—is **The Yellow Rose** at 5809 Auburn Blvd., tel. 332-7062, no rowdies allowed.

Crawdad's River Cantina, at 1375 Garden Hwy., tel. (916) 929-2268, is noted as the place where yuppies go fishin' (for whatever yuppies fish for when they're all dressed up), with live music on Friday and Saturday nights. **The Clubhouse** at 10089 Folsom Blvd. in Rancho Cordova, tel. 362-3367, is the ultimate contrast (dress code: "dirty Levi's and leathers mandatory"), a place for bikers and Vietnam vets and women wearing little more than tattoos, its walls decorated with Harley-Davidson drawings and love-it-or-leave-it Americana. Back in Sacramento, another contrast: **A Shot of Class** supper club, with big-band dancing on Fridays and Saturdays, 1020 11th St., tel. 447-5340. **Eddie's Brau-Hof** at 2428 Auburn Blvd. tel. 489-7668, a local institution and way station for bus tours to Tahoe and Reno, was where the 60-something crowd came to polka on a Saturday night, though everyone was welcome—until Eddie's closed in 1993. Some kind of Resurrection has been rumored.

Other Entertainment

Quite thorough is the *Sacramento Bee*'s "Ticket" section, included in the Friday edition. (For more information courtesy of the *Bee,* call the free 24-hour Beeline, tel. (916) 552-5252, and get current updates on local entertainment, music, movie times and locations, and area arts.) Check out the *Sacramento News & Review,* too, for its calendar section and current reviews, as well as *The Suttertown News.* Cultural events and entertainment scheduled at UC Davis and CSU Sacramento, as well as Sacramento City College, are usually included in all of these listings. For movies, find out what's playing at the elegant Crest Theater downtown at 1013 K Street Mall, tel. 442-7378: dramatic gold-leaf ceilings and such, described by one local writer as like being inside a Fabergé egg. And the neon tower and marquee now glow again. In addition to movies, the Crest sponsors concerts and other special events. Also unique is The Tower Theater at 16th and Broadway, tel. 443-1982, noted as much for its fabulous neon and good movie food as for its foreign, art, and cult film schedule. Newly renovated and reopened is the 90-seat Guild Theatre (close to the coffeehouse) at 2830 35th St., tel. 456-9932, one of the country's first "art theaters," originally a silent-movie palace and now a popular local venue for concerts, plays, and other performances as well as American independent and foreign films.

Among many local theatrical groups is the professional Sacramento Theatre Company, 1419 H St., tel. (916) 443-6722, which offers a five-show "mainstage season" from mid-September to mid-May, plus less expensive Stage Two and preview performances. The Music Circus, 1510 J St. suite 100, tel. 441-3163 or 446-5880 (information), takes over during Sacramento Theatre's off-season, its summer stock musicals staged under a circus tent. The Stagedoor Comedy Playhouse at the Sacramento Inn Plaza, tel. 927-0942, opens its doors on Friday and Saturday nights. For improvisa-

THE B STREET THEATER

Pretty big news in The Big Tomato is the arrival of serious (and seriously cheap) theater, thanks to Timothy Busfield—you remember, Elliot the red-headed ad agency guy from "Thirtysomething" and his brother Buck, founders of Sacramento's B Street Theater. At home in a midtown warehouse near the railroad tracks, the theater is strictly Manhattan basement, complete with subway-like rumble. Nothing posh; the emphasis here is on the plays and the performance. *Content.* The Busfields also run Sacramento's Fantasy Theater for children, performing professional plays in the public schools and sponsoring an annual playwriting contest, the eight winning plays becoming the Fantasy Festival. (If you're a celebrity hound—if you must have a taste of that glitz and glitter—plan to show up at the Fantasy Theater's annual black-tie fundraiser, which attracts some of the Hollywood crowd. Yup. Even to Sacramento.) The B Street Theater is located at 2711 B St., tel (916) 443-5300, with ticket prices usually in the $12-16 range. For information about the Fantasy Theater, which sometimes offers performances at B Street, call (916) 442-5635.

tional comedy, find out where the RSVP troupe is playing, tel. 442-7787. In addition to other venues, including Old Sacramento's Old Eagle Theatre, the Sacramento City College Actor's Theater (SCAT), tel. 449-7228, offers community performances throughout the year as well as its popular Shakespeare in the Park summer theater schedule. Suspects Dinner Theater at 1023 Front St. in Old Sacramento, tel. 443-3600 for information, offers a murder mystery with your meal, with actors "on stage" throughout the restaurant, interacting with the audience while enacting their current tale of murder and mayhem. Dinner and show on Fri. and Sat. nights, usually about $30. Monthly-changing menu and mystery.

The informal Camellia Symphony Orchestra, tel. (916) 344-5844, is a volunteer troupe performing traditional and more exotic works, including music by local composers. The Sacramento Opera Association, tel. 442-4224, performs professional and lunch-time "brown bag" operas throughout the year. The Sacramento Ballet, tel. 736-2860, has combined forces with the Capitol City Ballet, and presents several major traditional ballets each year, including *The Nutcracker* at Christmas, plus contemporary and original ballets.

INFORMATION

In addition to the okay but specialized visitor centers in Old Sacramento, the **Sacramento Convention and Visitors Bureau** at 1421 K St. between 14th and 15th streets, tel. (916) 264-7777 or (on weekends) 442-7644, is small but accommodating. Shopaholics, ask here about the area's major department stores, shopping centers, and smaller, more specialized shops. (Always entertaining outside Sacramento is **Denio's Roseville Farmers Markets & Auction, Inc.,** a lively flea market free-for-all on the wrong side of the Roseville Train Yard's tracks, held every Saturday and Sunday.) The visitors bureau is open Mon.-Fri. 8-5.

The best all-around source of information in Sacramento is the award-winning *Sacramento Bee,* main link in the valley's McClatchy chain, noted for its political coverage, enlightened editorials, and mainstream but informative features. The new kid in town, vying for community loyalty, is the free weekly *Sacramento News & Review* especially strong on news features and entertainment coverage and attracting the younger crowd. Another good freebie paper is *The Suttertown News.*

For information on foreign-currency exchange, call (916) 442-5542. The **post office** most convenient to downtown is at the Metro Station at 801 I St. at 8th, tel. 442-0764. Nearby is the **Sacramento Public Library,** 828 I St., tel. 449-5203. For information about Sacramento city parks, call 449-5200; for county parks, 366-2061. Though the best source for local **weather** facts and predictions is the excellent paperback *Climate of Sacramento, California* published by the local office of the National Weather Service (available free at the service's 16th St. office, as long as the annual print run lasts), prerecorded weather info is available by phone, tel. 923-3344.

Tower Books at the corner of 16th and Broadway, tel. (916) 444-6688, is the area's best general bookstore and newsstand; if they don't have it, they'll get it for you. And if you

"study" music, too, Tower Records next door is mighty convenient (for real bargains, head to Tower's outlet store in the Country Club Centre on El Camino). For used books, **Beers Book Center** at 1116 15th St., tel. 442-9475, is the place to go. **Lioness Books** at 2224 J St., tel. 442-4657, is Sacramento's feminist thought outlet—nonfiction and novels, you name it—and also serves as a community news and events clearinghouse.

Getting Oriented

Traditionally, Sacramento's "formal entrance" has been from the Bay Area: over the Tower Bridge and up Capitol Mall, passing blocky business buildings and federal then state office buildings. The valley's great transportation hub, Sacramento is now served by an impressive maze of freeways and major highways which converge in unusual and confusing ways. Downtown Sacramento is defined by two rivers—the American to the north, the Sacramento to the west—and some of these thoroughfares. To the west of downtown, fronting the Sacramento River, is I-5, in tandem with Hwy. 99 (the valley's other major north-south roadway). South of downtown, Hwy. 99 splits off, heads east, and comes together with Business I-80 and the beginning of Hwy. 50. (I-80 proper swings west about five miles north of the city, connecting traffic between San Francisco and Reno.) Business I-80 then jogs northward and rejoins I-80, creating the downtown area's eastern boundary. Highway 50 arrows eastward toward Placerville (Hwy. 16 is another route from Sacramento into the gold country), and Hwy. 99 continues south through the San Joaquin Valley. Highway 160 shoots out from downtown at both ends of 16th Street.

But however one arrives, central Sacramento itself is fairly easy to navigate. From west to east, streets are numbered one to 28. From north to south streets are "lettered" from A to W, with the Capitol Mall taking the place of M St. between 7th and 9th. With a street address, it's fairly simple to derive the exact location of anything downtown (400 3rd St., for example, would be at the intersection of D St., the fourth letter of the alphabet). Many of these streets are one-way—G and H Sts., between 16th and 29th were recently converted from one-way to two-way thoroughfares—so pay attention.

TRANSPORT

By Air

The **Sacramento Metro Airport,** 12 miles north-west of town via I-5, tel. (916) 929-5411, is served by major airlines plus a few connector services. Airport traffic has definitely picked up since no-frills Southwest Airlines has carved out a major section of Sacramento airspace. Metered parking space for short stops is available near the terminals. Long-term and short-term parking lots are available, serviced by a shuttle system. Better hotels offer airport transport. To get to and from the airport by other means, call **Skyline Airporter** service, tel. 444-6888 or (800) 464-0777.

By Train

The **Amtrak** depot at 4th and I streets, tel. (916) 485-8506 or (800) 872-7245, is a wonderful remnant of Sacramento's railroading heyday. The terminal is open daily 5:15 a.m.-10 p.m. (No snacks, not even vending-machine fare, so bring your own to munch while you wait.) Well worth it on Amtrak is the climb over the Sierra Nevada to Reno on board the Zephyr, an appropriate time to honor the efforts involved in building the nation's first transcontinental railroad.

But train service—especially connecting Sacramento to the Bay Area—is becoming a truly viable major transport option, thanks to Amtrak's new *Capitol* trains. Three trains daily connect San Jose and Oakland/Berkeley with the Sacramento/Roseville area (on the northeastern end, the *Capitol* route will one day extend to Colfax). Amtrak "feeder" bus links connect the *Capitol* trains with nearby destinations: Auburn, Grass Valley, and Nevada City or Reno-Truckee-Colfax (the latter also served by the Amtrak *Zephyr);* the far north Sacramento Valley (an area also served by separate Amtrak route); the Napa Valley; and Santa Cruz and Monterey. (A separate Amtrak route connects San Jose and Salinas/Monterey to the central coast, Santa Barbara, and L.A.) The *Capitol* trains also connect to Amtrak's *San Joaquin* trains, which run from Oakland to Stockton then south through the San Joaquin Valley to Bakersfield (with bus connections onward to just about everywhere). From Merced or Fresno, Amtrak buses connect to Yosemite National Park.

Trains depart from Sacramento for the Bay Area daily at 7:15 a.m., 12:30 p.m., and 5:55 p.m.; basic departure times from San Jose, for the reverse trip, are 6:35 a.m., 12:35 p.m., and 5:10 p.m. (departures 70 minutes later from Oakland, other time adjustments for Martinez, Fairfield, Davis, and other stops en route). Fares are remarkably reasonable: $30 roundtrip, for example, for the Sacramento-San Jose trip. Make advance reservations through any travel agent, or directly through Amtrak's toll-free reservation service (800-USA-RAIL). You can also take your chances on a space-available trip; Amtrak station agents accept cash and major credit cards (personal checks accepted only from passengers age 65 and older). There's no checked baggage service on either the *Capitols* or *San Joaquins,* but overhead baggage racks are available. Basic food service is also provided, or bring your own brown bag.

For more information on Amtrak's California train service, write **Caltrans Division of Rail,** P.O. Box 942874, Sacramento 94274-0001, or call the toll-free Amtrak information and reservation number (above).

By Delta Waterways

Equally quaint in these days of frenetic freeway travel is a delta cruise from San Francisco to Sacramento, an overnight weekend trip or a day trip (with the option of returning to S.F. by bus). For information, contact: **Delta Travel Agency,** 1540 W. Capitol Ave., P.O. Box 813, West Sacramento 95691, tel. (916) 372-3690. Depending upon the trip and other options, rates range from about $60 per person. More ambitious tours are also substantially more expensive. Four-day trips through **Lindblad's Special Expeditions,** 720 Fifth Ave., New York, NY 10019, tel. (212) 765-7740 or toll-free (800) 762-0003, include shore trips into the wine country and Old Sacramento, and meals and accommodations aboard the 70-passenger M.V. *Sea Lion* for $600-860. One-week delta trips with a similar itinerary (some side excursions extra) are offered by **Clipper Cruise Line,** 7711 Bonhomme Ave., St. Louis, MO 63105, tel. (314) 727-2929 or (800) 325-0010, and range from $1,400 per person to $2,300 (double occupancy) on the line's 138-passenger *Yorktown Clipper.* Both tours depart from San Francisco.

By Bus,

The **Greyhound** terminal in downtown Sacramento, 715 L St. between 7th and 8th streets, tel. (916) 444-6800, is open 24 hours and centrally located but in a derelict-strewn part of town. Buses from here go to Reno, L.A., San Francisco, Portland, and just about everywhere in between and beyond.

Getting Around
By Public Transit And Car

Local transit options include **Sacramento Regional Transit** buses, which provide service throughout downtown 5 a.m.-10 p.m. daily. For current fare and route information, call (916) 321-BUSS. The wonderful **Yolo Bus** commuter line connects downtown with Old Sacramento, West Sacramento, Davis, and Woodland; call 371-2877 (same as Sac Transit) for current fare and route information, and express bus information.

Most fun of all, though, especially to get out into the northeastern and eastern suburban sectors, is the city's new **RT Metro light-rail trolley** system. Two separate links (roughly paralleling I-80 and Hwy. 50) connect downtown with the suburbs, primarily to get people to work without their cars. The light-rail runs 4:30 a.m.—12:30 a.m. daily with trolleys every 15 minutes. The Art in Public Places program is behind the eclectic, often amusing artwork at each trolley station, where tickets are dispensed from vending machines (riders get 90 minutes per ticket, on the honor system). The best trolley deal is the midtown ride, which reaches to Old Town via the K Street Mall.

For a current map of light-rail stops and routes and for other public transit information, contact Regional Transit headquarters at 1400 29th St., P.O. Box 2110, Sacramento 95810, tel. (916) 321-2877.

But since this is California, most people drive. Though not that bad downtown, traffic elsewhere is hellish. To keep abreast of traffic snarls (usually worse during the morning commute), tune into local radio stations or watch morning TV news broadcasts. For general regional **road conditions**, call (916) 445-7623. To rent a car for delta or gold country day trips and other adventures afield, contact the visitors bureau for a listing of reputable local companies.

NEAR SACRAMENTO: DAVIS AND VICINITY

Northwest of Sacramento via I-80 but close enough to be socially connected is **Davis**, primarily home to the University of California, Davis, and its student body. People in self-consciously casual Davis, the self-proclaimed Bicycle Capital of the World and an intellectual oasis amid the fields of beans and tomatoes, are conscious about environmental and global responsibilities—despite the fact that some in California still dismiss the campus as an agricultural school. Among its many other distinctions, UC Davis has the largest enology department in the nation, with 200 or so students dedicated to studying winemaking, and a distinguished program in viticulture.

A community fueled these days by good food, good ideas, and a fairly creative cultural atmosphere, Davis's biggest event of all nonetheless dates back to the early 1900s. **Picnic Day** in April attracts up to 80,000 people each year for the academic open house plus parade, partying, picnicking, and participatory sports like Ozz Ball (volleyball played in ankle-deep mud). Earthy in a different way is the long-running **Whole Earth Festival** in early May, its focus on spirituality and environmental values enforced by the Karma Patrol. Also famous in Davis are the town's long-distance bicycle races, among them the semi-suicidal **Double Century Bike Tour** in May, a 200-mile roundtrip from Davis to Clear Lake, and the July 4th **Criterium Bicycle Races.**

In town the best way to appreciate Davis is to do like the students do—just hang out. A walking tour of public art is worth it (ask for guidance at the chamber office). And art galleries, like bookstores, abound.

For incredibly eclectic indoor entertainment, *the* place is **The Palms Public Playhouse,** a drafty 150-seat barn southeast of town on Drummond Ave. off Chiles Rd., tel. (916) 756-9901, its folk music ambience attracting homegrown regional talent as well as some of the top acts ever to make it to Northern California. **Mansion Cellars** at 132 E St., tel. 758-8881, is an interesting local bar, attracting college students, assistant professors, and hip locals with its 150 or so foreign beers. Notable, too, is **Sudwerk**

NEAR DAVIS

The Nature Conservancy's **Jepson Prairie Preserve** near Dixon includes over 1,500 acres of native grasslands. Spectacular on a small scale at Jepson is the concentric-ring bloom progression of vernal pool wildflowers that grow in rainwater-collecting "hog wallows." Starting in early spring, the subtle show changes almost weekly. Access by permission only. To get there, head south on Hwy. 113 from Dixon then dogleg left onto Cook Lane (dirt road). For permission and more specific instructions, contact the **Cosumnes River Preserve** manager, 6500 Desmond Rd., Galt 95632, tel. (916) 684-2816.

North from Davis via Hwy. 113 is **Woodland**, once a sleepy farm town but now a fast-growing commercial center with little of its hayseed history intact. So do stop by the **Hays Antique Truck Museum**, 2000 E. Main St., tel. (916) 666-1044, open daily 8-4, to appreciate its collection of all-American trucks from over 100 manufacturers (like Graham Brothers, Old Reliable, and Oshkosh), the world's largest truck museum. Admission $3. The Gibson House at 512 Gibson Rd., now the **Yolo County Museum**, is a restored 1872 farmhouse, prime for picnicking, open Mon. and Tues. 9-5, weekends noon-4 p.m. John Phillip Sousa and Sidney Greenstreet once performed at the **Woodland Opera House**, the only 19th-century theater in California to survive without being put to other uses; call 666-9617 for info.

Since *vaca* in Spanish means "cow," impolite passersby have attached the literal "cowtown" to **Vacaville** as a modern epithet, though the community is one of the valley's oldest and actually named for the area's original landowner, Don Manuel Vaca. Though the California Medical Facility at Vacaville is the place mass murderer Charles Manson now calls home, the town itself was most noted as that stretch of freeway perfumed by the overpowering aroma of onions. But even though the local dehydrating plant has closed its doors, Vacaville's annual Onion Festival lives on.

But **The Nut Tree**, tel. (916) 448-6411, is still here—a humble roadside fruit stand shaded by a pioneer-planted black walnut when it opened for business in the 1920s, now a sprawling commercial complex including a restaurant (usually a wait without reservations) famous for its small loaves of fresh-baked bread, gift shops, children's entertainment and miniature train rides, even an airport for the fly-in lunch bunch. Special Nut Tree events include the annual **Scarecrow Contest** in mid-October.

Winters, on Hwy. 128 near Lake Berryessa as you head north off the 505 cutoff, is a Western outpost with one of California's last working blacksmith shops (Anderson Iron Works), the elegant white terra-cotta First Northern Bank of Dixon with antique opaque glass and marble floors and counters, and a well-known trout stream (Putah Creek) running right through town. Otherwise, the biggest excitement in Winters is at the home video rental shops or the **Buckhorn** saloon and dinner house, tel. (916) 795-4503, decorated with a mountain lion pelt over the bar and omnipresent mounted heads hanging everywhere: bucks, rams, goats, antelopes, even a moose. (Without reservations, it's a long wait playing liar's dice at the mahogany bar or sitting on "the horny bench" built of bullhorns and cowhide.) The food is vegetarian nightmare fare: three kinds of prime rib, excellent steaks, or combos.

Privat braueri Hubsch on Poleline Rd. at 2nd, tel. 756-BREW, the first computerized U.S. microbrewery, with German-style brewskies.

The member-owned **Davis Food Co-op** at 620 G St., tel. (916) 758-2667, is a good stop for nonmembers too: organic produce, bulk foodstuffs, even more standard grocery items. Local coffeehouses and cafes serve inexpensive fare appropriate to student budgets. **Murder Burger** ("So Good They're To Die For") at 978 Olive Dr., tel. 756-2142, open 11 a.m.-8 p.m. daily, serves very good burgers (not necessarily worth dying for, even though the cattle did) and has the additional distinction of being listed in the *National Lampoon* review of perverted restaurants.

Davis also has less perverted eateries, including the vegetarian **Blue Mango** at 330 G St., tel. (916) 756-2616; the **Orange Court Cafe**, 129 E St., tel. 758-3770, great for breakfast; and over a dozen Asian eateries. **Dominic Cafe**, at 408 G St. serves Vietnamese food. Tiny **Colette**, 802 2nd St., tel. 758-3377, is one of several fine yet reasonably priced restaurants in the area—this one with a weekly changing menu and unpretentious atmosphere. (Very popular, reservations a must.) Also excellent in Davis is

Cafe California, 808 2nd St., tel. 757-2766, serving Chinese chicken salad and Cajun-style prime rib as well as tortellini alfredo and tarragon chicken fettuccine. Lunch served Mon.-Sat., dinner seven nights a week, Sunday brunch. Also popular, reservations essential.

Soga's at 222 D St., tel. (916) 757-1733, with a red British call box out front, serves contemporary American fare with some international accents. **Dos Coyotes Border Cafe** at the Mar-

ketplace, 1411 W. Covell Blvd., tel. 753-0922, serves a great Southwestern-style food. For Mexican food, head to Dixon just down the road. Mandatory is lunch or dinner at the fluorescent-lit **El Charro Cafe,** 116 N. 1st St., tel. (916) 678-5969, locally famous.

For more information about the area, contact the **Davis Chamber of Commerce Visitors Center,** 228 B St., Davis 95616, tel. (916) 756-5160.

THE SACRAMENTO VALLEY

THE SUTTER BUTTES

Heading north from Sacramento through the rice fields and orchards, up ahead near Yuba City loom the unusual mid-valley mountains known as the Sutter Buttes, the world's smallest mountain range. The sacred, spiritual center of the world to the Maidu, the place where woman and man were created, the buttes were included in John Sutter's original New Helvetia land grant and also provided safe haven for General John C. Frémont and his ragtag ruffians before they launched their Bear Flag Republic invasion of Sonoma to the southwest.

The Sutter Buttes were known by many names (including Ono Lai Tol, the Middle Mountain to the Wintu people; Los Tres Picos, or the Three Peaks to the Spanish; and both the Marysville and Sacramento Buttes to Americanized settlers) before the county's name was attached in 1949. The area was valued highly by early settlers who homesteaded here to avoid valley flooding. Small farms, cattle and sheep ranches, coal mines, rock quarries, natural gas wells, communications towers, even a 1950s Titan missile base have since changed the landscape. Yet despite the incursions of civilization, there is something about the land that refuses to be shaped by human hands.

Sutter Buttes Natural History
Rising like some natural fortress from the surrounding flatlands, the circular Sutter Buttes include 20 or so separate peaks anchored by deep volcanic roots to the bedrock below. In the 1920s, UC Berkeley geologist Howel Williams first likened the buttes to a castle, with the sur-

rounding low hills the ramparts, the small interior valleys the moat, and the cluster of peaks and rocky spires at the center the castle itself. Unconnected to both the Sierra Nevada and California's coastal ranges, some speculate (especially because there are similar but below-ground buttes near Colusa) that the Sutter Buttes are a volcanic extension of the Cascade Range.

True or not, about 2½ million years ago streamers of hot magma surged up through the soggy sediments to create a rounded rhyolite dome eight miles across and up to 2,500 feet tall. Cracks created during this process of volcanic uplift broke the tilted layers into blocks subsequently worn down into small mounds by the forces of nature. Some half-million years later another burst of volcanic violence disrupted the watery sediments with steam explosions and spewed rock. Molten magma again reached the surface, and this outer ring of domes created an inner lake basin which gradually filled with rock debris and mudflows. Andesite domes created by still hotter lava thrust up from the center and tumbled the lake's contents outward to the "ramparts" region. These brittle new mountains (including today's Twin Peaks and North, South, and West buttes) split into craggy spires and slabs, sometimes crashing down in avalanche trails of rough-hewn boulders.

The plant and animal life of the Sutter Buttes is almost typical of the valley's foothill oak woodland areas, with lizards and rattlesnakes sunning themselves on rocks while golden eagles and red-tailed hawks soar over grasses, chaparral, and gnarled oaks. And in the buttes' wetland fringes, red-winged blackbirds bob from their high-grass perches while nonnative ring-necked pheasants dart out from the brush.

Since genetic isolation here has never been complete (or, if it was, didn't last long), there are no native animals or plants which exist only in the Sutter Buttes. Unlike the surrounding valley, a dozen different types of ferns thrive here. Also among the region's unusual vegetation are the rock gooseberry, otherwise found in Alameda and Tuolumne counties and farther south; the narrowleaf goldenbush, a coastal shrub; and the Arizona three-awn, generally ranging east from southern California and south to Guatemala. Also fascinating is the fact that many plants common throughout the valley and its foothills *aren't* here, including the digger pine, three types of oak, California buckeye, and meadowfoam.

The best guide to the buttes' natural history is *The Sutter Butte: A Naturalist's View* by Walt Anderson, available through Sutter Buttes Naturalists (see "Hiking The Sutter Buttes: Practicalities" below).

Circling The Sutter Buttes By Bike Or Car

For a general orientation to the Sutter Buttes, not to mention a fabulous bike ride or leisurely car trip, circle these middle mountains via an interconnecting 39-mile loop of county roads. From Hwy. 99 just west of Yuba City, head west on Hwy. 20 then, after about six miles, turn right (toward the tiny town of Sutter) onto Acacia Ave. and head north just over a mile to Acacia's junction with Butte House Rd.—the journey's official starting point. (To get off the highways as soon as possible, an alternate approach to Sutter is taking Butte House Rd. all the

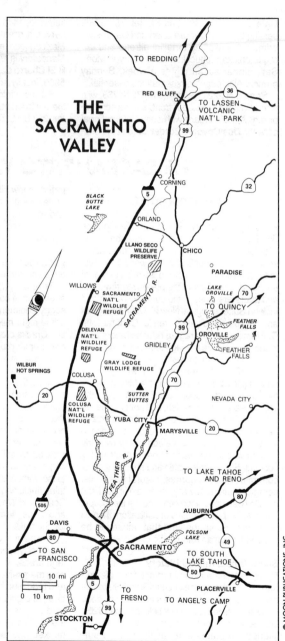

THE SACRAMENTO VALLEY

© MOON PUBLICATIONS, INC.

WES DEMPSEY

South Butte, part of the world's smallest mountain range at Sutter Buttes

way from just north of the Hwy. 20-Hwy. 99 intersection.) From the Acacia-Butte House junction, head west onto Pass Rd., which climbs past the **Frémont Monument** near where Frémont and company camped in 1846 (good views of the buttes' interior), past the Kellogg Rd. turnoff into Moore Canyon, then past Potato Hill and a good view of South Butte, the miniscule mountain range's tallest peak. At the crest, rows of large rocks mark the old wagon route through the Sutter Buttes.

At the intersection with West Butte Rd. turn right and continue northward, skirting the western flanks of the Sutter Buttes and the triangular **Goat Rocks** just south of jagged **West Butte.** To the west, almost as far as the eye can see, is the **Butte Sink** area, which hosts one of the north valley's largest populations of migrating waterfowl. Turn right again at the intersection with North Butte Rd. and continue on, past the well-paved road to the old Titan missile base (private property) and through the almond orchards. (Heading north at the intersection with Pennington Rd. leads you straight into the state's Gray Lodge waterfowl refuge.) Continue east to what's left of the town of Pennington; shortly thereafter, the road jogs sharply south (becoming Powell Rd.) then east again (as Pennington Rd.). Just west of Live Oak, turn south onto Township Rd., then west onto Clark Rd., which becomes East Butte Rd. when it turns south. East Butte Rd. eventually connects with Butte House Rd.—thus completing the circle.

Hiking The Sutter Buttes: Practicalities
Though it's possible to see the Sutter Buttes from near and far, the buttes themselves are privately owned and off-limits to the public. The only way to truly explore the area is on a guided tour conducted with the cooperation of landowners. **Sutter Buttes Naturalists** ("Interpretive Access to a Magical Place") offers tours throughout the Sutter Buttes. Wildflower fans flock to the area in early spring, when the green hillsides are dotted with the subtle colors of new bloom. But worthwhile year-round are organized weekend interpretive trips, including *The Heart of the People* (Indian Life in the Lands of Middle-Mountain); *A Flower of Stone* (The Geology of the Sutter Buttes); *An Inland Island* (Habitats of a Unique Ecosystem); and *The Center of the World* (The Sacred Mountain, its Myth and Meaning). Though every trip has a particular emphasis, each also shares the story of the Sutter Buttes' natural history, history, and cultural significance. For more information and for trip reservations, contact: **Middle Mountain Foundation,** Ira Heinrich, (916) 343-6614.

YUBA CITY AND MARYSVILLE

Yuba City
Yuba City, which sprawls like a fast-food jungle beyond the southeastern edge of the Sutter Buttes, has been the butt of north valley humor since 1985, when mapmaker Rand McNally, in

its *Places Rated Almanac,* listed the town as the worst place to live in the entire United States. Community leaders decided to sidestep the notoriety Yuba City had accidentally earned for all it doesn't have by focusing attention on one thing it *does* have—prunes, about two-thirds of the nation's $200 million crop. The new September **Prune Festival,** designed to celebrate Yuba City's uniqueness, at first only seemed to make things worse, since the idea of 20,000 people sampling pitted and whole prunes, prunes dipped in chocolate, prune-spiced chili and hamburgers, and chicken barbecued in prune sauce inevitably generated scatological jokes about the town. But at least the new public relations effort helped some. By 1988, according to a *Money* magazine survey, Yuba City was no longer the worst U.S. city. It had elevated its social standing to fourth from the bottom of the list.

There's more to Yuba City, of course, than ribald repartee at the town's expense. Fascinating, for example, is the large Sikh community living here, transplants from the Punjab region of India and Pakistan. Some have become successful rice farmers and ranchers since immigrating to the U.S. at the turn of the century, though most make a living working in someone else's fields. Though there are three Sikh temples in the area, all of which welcome respectful visitors for worship services, the **Tierra Buena Sikh Temple** at 2468 Tierra Buena Rd. west of Yuba City, (call 916-673-9918 or 673-8623 for permission to visit), is the largest and most architecturally authentic. Tour the grounds, discuss the Sikh religion, even share a meal. (Visitors are asked to wear a scarf or other appropriate head covering and to remove their shoes while touring the temple.) Stopping in at **The Punjab Bazaar** at 624 Plumas in Yuba City (closed Tuesdays), tel. 673-4503, is also like taking a side trip to India, with everything from incense, Indian silks, and perfumed hair oils to pickled mango slices and every imaginable herb and spice available for sale.

Considerably more mundane is the **Yuba-Sutter County Fair** held every July at the fairgrounds, 442 Franklin Ave., tel. (916) 674-1280. Among other community events held there is the **Combine Demolition Derby,** where "dinosaurs from down on the farm" roar and rip to prove that "combines aren't just for farming anymore." Indeed.

Marysville

Just across the Feather River from Yuba City is Marysville, a gold rush-era town founded by Chilean miners. If most people in Yuba City work in the prune orchards or at the Sunsweet processing plant, most people in Marysville are somehow affiliated with Beale Air Force Base, home of the now-doomed SR-71 spy plane. After a look-see at the two-story **Mary Aaron Museum** at 7th and D streets, open Tues.-Sat. 1:30-4:30 p.m., especially worthwhile is a visit to the **Bok Kai Temple** on the levee at the foot of D St. (call 916-742-5486 for permission to visit) built to honor the Chinese river god of good fortune—the only such temple in the U.S. In March, Marysville hosts its two-day **Bok Kai Festival and Parade. Beckwourth Western Days** in October honoring black pioneer Jim Beckwourth, who settled here, also add up to quite a party.

Also particularly pleasing is the town's tiny **Ellis Lake,** a piece of peace and quiet (picnic with the ducks and geese) amid the traffic threading through downtown via the confusing conjunctions of Highways 20 and 70. (Highway 20, heading east is a pretty route to Grass Valley and Nevada City.) Get picnic fixings locally or stop by the **Foster's Freeze** burger stand just to the north for takeout—then enjoy the park.

For more information about the area, contact the **Yuba-Sutter Chamber of Commerce,** 10th and E streets, P.O. Box 1429, Marysville 95901, tel. (916) 743-6501.

Marysville/Yuba City Accomodations

Marysville has motels, most of them clustered along the Hwy. 20 corridor. Best bet is the **Oxbow Motel** south of town off Hwy. 70 at 1078 N. Beale Rd., tel. (916) 742-8238, with rooms $31-38. (Different and worthwhile *near* Marysville, if you're heading that way anyway, is the small **Mountain Seasons Inn** in Brownsville. See "Marysville Restaurants" below.) Most of Yuba City's motels are also along main throughfares. **Motel 6** off Hwy. 99 at Bridge St., tel. 674-1710, has rooms for $28. Nearby is the **Motel Orleans,** tel. 674-1592, with slightly higher rates. New, just south of the Hwy. 99/Hwy. 20 intersection on the west side of the highway, is the comfortable **Yuba City Motor Inn,** tel. 674-4000, rooms $51-65. In the same league, a block north of Hwy. 20 at 1001 Clark Ave. (between Yuba City and Marysville), is the **Bonanza Inn Best**

Western, tel. 674-8824 or toll-free (800) 528-1234 for reservations, rates $65 and up.

Quite nice, though, are Yuba City's bed and breakfasts. **The Harkey House** downtown across from the courthouse, 312 C St., Yuba City 95991, tel. (916) 674-1942, is a lovely 1864 Victorian Gothic once home to the local sheriff, now noted for its antiques and eclectic yet tasteful decor. All four rooms feature queen beds and private baths. Particularly nice, upstairs, is the spacious Harkey Suite, with its paisley attitude, wood stove, and adjoining library/sitting room. Equally inviting, with more feminine sensibilities, is the Empress Room, a study in soft gray and green (and at least a distant reminder of the town's Chinese historical roots). Continental breakfast, basketball court, pool, spa. Advance reservations required. Rates: $65-100.

The **Moore Mansion Inn** at 560 Cooper Ave. (three stoplights east of Hwy. 99 at the corner of Bridge and Cooper), Yuba City 95991, tel. (916) 674-8559, is a 5,000-square-foot mansion in the Arts and Crafts bungalow style, built in 1920 by Charles Moore, one-time owner of the Omega Gold Mine. The fine woodwork, spacious design, and simple, colorful yet elegant decor add still more grace. Rooms and suites are all unique—some interconnect for more convenient family or group accommodations—with private baths. Not the grandest but perhaps loveliest is the Feather River Room: white walls and green ivy accents show off the step-up white pine bed. Full breakfast. Rates: $65-85, midweek business rates substantially lower.

Marysville Restaurants

Nostalgia fans, don't miss the 1940's-style 31-stool luncheonette counter at Marysville's **F.W. Woolworth** five-and-dime department store downtown at 420 D. Street. No gourmet fare here—just burgers and such, served up on plastic plates and placemats in an all-American environment of gleaming stainless steel and wood-grained formica. Considerably more sophisticated, for fresh-ground coffees and just-baked pastries at breakfast, or homemade soup at lunch, is the **K.C. Coffee & Trading Company** across from the courthouse on 5th St. between B and C, tel. (916) 749-1710. Open Mon.-Sat. for breakfast and lunch.

Particularly popular with the cowboy and cowgirl set is the **Silver Dollar Saloon** next door

to the Bok Kai Pavilion (on 1st St. between C and D), tel. (916) 743-0507. Contributing to its ambience are a genuine frontier relic wooden Indian just inside the door, country-western music on the jukebox, a massive Old West bar—and one wild time on Friday or Saturday night. The former brothel upstairs, rooms reservable for meetings, private dinners, or other special events, is a veritable museum of Western memorabilia, including "artifacts" from Nevada's Mustang Ranch. Downstairs, place your lunch or dinner order at the counter behind the indoor open-pit grill—strictly carnivore fare, steaks and steak sandwiches, or maybe a half-rack of barbecued ribs. Open daily for lunch and dinner.

More mainstream is **The Cannery Restaurant** at 606 J St., near the Twin Cities Memorial Bridge, tel. (916) 743-3005; spiffed-up brick warehouse ambience with a menu of steaks, chicken, seafood, plus a few pasta or non-meat selections. Open weekdays only for lunch, Mon.-Sat. for dinner.

East of Marysville, in the blink-and-you'll-miss-it mountain town of Brownsville is surprisingly good **Lottie Brennan's Bakery & Eating Establishment**, 9049 La Porte Rd., tel. (916) 675-1003, at home in the gold-rush-era building which once housed the Knoxdale Institute for Girls. Like the building, the menu here is uncluttered: thoughtful salads and sandwiches at lunch and seasonally changing dinners, from standards like garlic-grilled prawns and rib-eye steak to Austrian peasant casserole, scallops Provençal, and Alsatian chicken. But people drive the distance just for rich homemade cheesecakes and fruit pies to elaborate European creations like Swedish princess cake with marzipan, Austrian walnut cake, and Black Forest cake; goodies to go too. Usually open for lunch Wed.-Sat., dinner Fri. and Sat., and brunch on Sunday, but the hours do change. (Call ahead if your coming to Brownsville just for a meal.) Next door, if you decide to stay a while is the small **Mountain Seasons Inn,** tel. 675-2180, a mountain cottage surrounded by herb and flower gardens—there's a dried flower and gift shop downstairs—with three pleasant guest rooms (all share one bath). Rate: $50.

Yuba City Restaurants

Yuba City is much more than a fast-food jungle—though in that genre, get off the highway and try **Margie's Deli & Diner** at 728 Forbes Ave., tel. (916) 673-2203, with booths like the back of a customized '57 Chevy, golden oldies on the jukebox, and other fifties affectations. Open for breakfast and lunch Mon.-Sat., 6 a.m.-3 p.m.; kids can eat free (call for details).

Truly exceptional, though, is **Al's Cafe American** in the nondescript Civic Center Plaza mini-mall across from the Yuba City Police Department, 1538 Poole Blvd., Suite H, tel. (916) 674-3213. Known for its casual elegance and contemporary cuisine, Al's offers astounding specials at lunch—jambalaya, for example, or perhaps grilled pascilla pepper stuffed with feta and monterey jack cheese, rice, and beans—including at least two daily "recession specials" for under $5. (Though service is generally quite good, try to avoid the noon-to-one office workers' lunch hour, quite hectic. Lunch begins at 11:30 a.m. and ends at 2 p.m.) Dinner entrees include South American and European cuisine in addition to variations on American standards, from blackened red snapper to mesquite-grilled New York steak. Al's offers a decent selection of beers and ales in addition to its small wine list, which features some of California's finest. Open for lunch Mon.-Fri., for dinner daily. Call ahead for directions on how to get there. For simpler dinners and smaller portions, step into Al's alterego, the **Blue Parrot Coffee House,** open evenings only for pastas, pizzas, and late-evening dessert and coffee.

Not far away, just south of the Hwy. 99/Hwy. 20 intersection on the west side—*inside* Sperbeck's Nursery—is **Lusio's,** tel. (916) 671-2050. The one-time greenhouse is now a two-tiered casual dining room. Most of the lunches and dinners here—good specials—have a distinct south-of-the-border flair; try the vegetarian quesadillas, homemade chicken tamales, bay shrimp empanada, or broiled lime-garlic chicken. Full bar. Open for lunch and dinner Tues.-Sat., for brunch on Sunday. Even more delectable, though, is **Ruthy's Restaurant & Bakery** at 229 Clark Ave. (east of Hwy. 99, south of Franklin), tel. 674-2611, a contemporary bistro hiding inside the Hillcrest Plaza mini-mall. Ruthy's is beloved for breakfast, serving everything from homemade wholewheat and buttermilk pancakes to French toast (made with Ruthy's own cinnamon raisin bread) and scampi omelettes. (If

you're just passing through, stop for a bag of fresh-baked bagels, cinnamon rolls, and blueberry or English Tea muffins.) A good light lunch: homemade soup and a pass or two at the salad bar—quite exceptional, with at least a dozen prepared salads plus fresh ingredients for make-up-your own green salad. At dinner, appetizers include surprises like alderwood-smoked salmon mousse with garlic toast and chicken quesadillas. Entrees include stir-fry for vegetarians, smoked salmon fettucini Alfredo, Cancun chicken, and teriyaki beef brochettes. Friendly and attentive service. Open for breakfast and lunch daily, fabulous Sunday brunch. Call for current dinner schedule.

Another Yuba City eating alternative is **The Refuge** at 1501 Butte House Rd., tel. (916) 673-7620, where the Rotary Club meets every Friday. The most obvious draw here is the building itself, the outdoorsy aesthetic quite appropriate. For an American-style dinner house, the food is quite imaginative. Open for lunch Mon.-Fri., for dinner daily.

North of Yuba City—near the slow S-curve over the railroad tracks, about five miles south of the stoplight in Live Oak—is **Pasquini's,** tel. (916) 695-3384, a warm and sometimes raucous roadhouse restaurant and bar attracting "regulars" from surrounding farm towns and from as far away as San Francisco. The dinner menu here is as thick as a magazine, offering an endless selection of steaks, seafood, chicken, and veal, also Basque lamb and smoked lambchops, plus pastas and crepes and eggplant Parmesan. Come Monday or Wednesday for Pasquini's specials—selections like blackened prime rib, beef ribs, or lasagna on Monday, all kinds of pastas on Wednesday ("half and half" combinations, mixing pastas and/or sauces, are allowed). Pasquini's has a full bar—the best one for miles around, and quite the scene on weekend nights—and is open daily for dinner.

Also within reach of Yuba City—and currently culinary home to Pasquini's original dinner chef, Bene Pasquini—is the **El Rio Club** in Meridian, tel. (916) 696-0900, just off Hwy. 20 east of the Meridian Bridge, between Yuba City and Colusa. Good food, interesting ambience—especially in the bar with animal heads and eclectic clutter everywhere. Open Tues.-Sun. for lunch and dinner.

NORTH VALLEY WILDLIFE REFUGES

Unless the tule fog is thick, even beginning birders will have little trouble spotting ducks, geese, cranes, egrets, and swans—a total of 236 identified species—at the state's 8,400-acre **Gray Lodge Wildlife Area** just west of Gridley. On hunting days (three days a week during the season) up to a half-million birds huddle together at one end of the reserve while hunters hunker down in the cold water and mud elsewhere. Named for the old gray duck club once on the property, Gray Lodge is open daily to birdwatchers, small fee, best winter bird show from late November into February. For more information, contact Gray Lodge Wildlife Area, P.O. Box 37, Gridley 95948, tel. (916) 846-3315. To get there, from Gridley head west on Sycamore Rd. about six miles to Pennington Rd.; turn south and continue a few more miles to Rutherford Rd.; head west on Rutherford for two miles to reach the wildlife reserve's headquarters. Recently purchased by the Trust for Public Lands and the State of California Wildlife Conservation Board is a major portion of the old Schohr Ranch, some of which is already managed in conjunction with adjacent Gray Lodge.

Scattered to the south, north, and west of the Sutter Buttes are five separate areas comprising the **Sacramento Valley National Wildlife Refuges.** Of these, four are open to the public. The largest refuge, Sacramento National Wildlife Refuge, includes 10,783 acres first set aside in 1933 to provide feeding and resting areas for migrating waterfowl. As valley farming expanded and the natural wetlands disappeared, waterfowl damage to crops increased—the reason behind creating the smaller Colusa and Sutter refuges (named after the nearby towns to the east and north, respectively) toward the end of World War II. In 1962, the Delevan Refuge was established southwest of Princeton and east of Maxwell.

Though birds are present at all refuges year-round, the best time to come is in winter, usually November and December. Areas available for public use are open daily during daylight hours, though these access hours are sometimes modified during hunting season. The **Sacramento National Wildlife Refuge,** flanking I-5 between Willows and Maxwell, offers a short hiking trail, a photography blind for birders, and a six-mile auto tour route. The **Sutter Refuge** is open seasonally to hunters and fishing enthusiasts. The **Colusa Refuge** (entrance south off Hwy. 20, just west of town) features a five-mile auto tour and abundant ducks and geese. The **Delevan Refuge,** with over 5,600 acres of marsh and croplands, is another prime waterfowl wallow.

With advance notice, special programs and guided tours of all federal north valley wildlife refuges are available for clubs, schools, and other groups. For more information—including current fishing and hunting regulations and schedules—contact headquarters at Sacramento National Wildlife Refuge, Rt. 1 Box 311, Willows 95988, tel. (916) 934-2801.

THE LESSON OF BIRDS: SEVEN

Egrets, delicate and pure
white, are more

like a Chinese poet's
precise and intricate

words about his sullied
impure world

gone mad,
than birds.

—Gary Thompson

GRIDLEY AND COLUSA

Gridley, on Hwy. 99 north of Yuba City, claims the title of Kiwi Capital of the World; come in August for the **Butte County Fair.** Just west of town is the Gray Lodge wildlife refuge (see above). If you plan to visit Gray Lodge, also plan to stay at **McCrackin's Inn** bed and breakfast at 1835 Sycamore Ln., tel. (916) 846-2108—reasonably priced, friendly, and right on the way. The proprietor is an expert on Gray Lodge, a former employee. If just passing through, stop for magnificent mandarin oranges at roadside stands, usually from December into February.

Across the valley is **Colusa,** a small rice-farming center. Flanking the community on the east but almost invisible is the **Colusa-Sacramento River State Recreation Area,** P.O. Box 207, Colusa 95932, tel. (916) 458-4927, once the city dump and now a tangle of riparian vegetation fine in spring, summer, and fall for fishing, swimming (beach at the end of trail from parking lot), picnicking, and camping. Developed campsites (with hot showers) are $14, reservations through Mistix, tel. (800) 444-7275. The park usually floods in winter, and mosquitos torture visitors in spring and summer (bring repellent). To get there, head east over the levee from the Hwy. 20/Hwy. 45 intersection.

Just north of Colusa on Hwy. 45 is the new Wintun **Colusa Indian Bingo** palace, with high-stakes legal bingo on weekend nights and Sunday afternoons, tel. (916) 458-8844 or toll-free (800) 225-8393. One of the area's annual events is the **Colusa Rice and Waterfowl Festival,** usually held in early November at the fairgrounds. Another is the **California State Duck Calling Contest.**

Colusa itself is a bit short on amenities. But just southeast of town, off Hwy. 20, near the Meridian Bridge, is the marvelous **El Rio Club,** tel. (916) 696-0900, which serves decent dinners in a moosehead-decorated bar. To the west, in Williams, is **Granzella's,** tel. 473-5496, with wonderful deli fare, marinated olives to go, and simple meals for breakfast, lunch, and dinner.

If heading up-valley from Colusa via Hwy. 45, the "back way" to Chico and vicinity, consider fording the Sacramento River via the **Princeton Ferry,** one of only a few functioning farmland ferry systems remaining in California (a few moments' cheap thrill, small fee). Almost closed for good in 1986, the ferry was recently refurbished and resurrected. To find it: head north from Princeton proper, turn right just outside town as the highway climbs onto the levee (follow the signs); coming from Chico, take the turnoff to Afton then follow the signs. And if you should find yourself in Richvale, stop in at the **Richvale Cafe,** de facto city hall, since the town itself owns the restaurant. Civic leaders wait tables and do dishes.

Wilbur Hot Springs

West from Colusa and past Williams, an overgrown I-5 rest stop, Hwy. 20 winds up into the eastern foothills of the coast range. A surprise pleasure for bone-tired travelers there is Wilbur Hot Springs, Williams 95987, tel. (916) 473-2306 or 473-2326, a clothing-optional, relaxed resort and spa tucked back in the hills. To get there the official way, turn north at the intersec-

tion of Hwy. 20 and Hwy. 16 (onto an unpaved old stage road) and continue for four miles, then turn left at the silver bridge; the elegant old Victorian hotel and spa are about a mile farther. There's no electricity (the 17 private rooms and 20-person community bedroom are lit with kerosene lanterns), no traffic (park in the lot and walk the quarter mile in), and no particular concern with the concerns of the outside world. And when you get here, take your shoes off. Once inside the lodge, no shoes allowed. (Strip off everything else at the bathhouse.)

Though Wilbur Hot Springs offers massage, yoga classes, volleyball, the option of sleeping under the stars, and a community kitchen (bring your own food, cooking and eating utensils supplied), the main attraction is the rustic bathhouse itself. The four covered mineral water pools run warm to hot. Outside below the sundeck is a larger mineral pool—cold in summer, warm in winter. For overnight guests, the baths and other facilities are available 24 hours a day. Rates: $90 per couple overnight, $35 pp dorm space, $20 for day use (10-5). Children welcome, but pets are not. Advance reservations required.

CHICO AND VICINITY

Though the up-valley university town of Chico has been on the map for quite some time, it took *San Francisco Chronicle* columnist Herb Caen to remind the rest of California. Caen's original 1970s comment on Chico, that it was "the kind of place where you find Velveeta in the gourmet section at the supermarket," didn't offend anyone. In fact, good-humored locals started sending him similar examples of high culture, Chico-style—enough to keep Caen busy printing punchy one-liners for well over a decade (and still counting).

Chico is equally famous for the local university's ranking by *Playboy* magazine as the nation's number-one party school, a dubious honor indirectly connected to the drunken debauchery of CSU Chico's now-dead Pioneer Days celebration. Over the years, the students' "fun" has ceased to amuse the rest of the community, concerned with increased alcohol-related deaths and violence. When notified in 1987 of the most recent nationwide honors, former university president Robin Wilson—a one-time CIA operative and part-time writer—said he was "appalled, horrified, disgusted" by *Playboy*'s epithet. Trying to make the best of a bad situation, he added: "It's nice to be number one at something." But Wilson's most quoted remark was his warning that if Pioneer Days continued true to form he would personally "take it out in the backyard and shoot it in the head." He kept his word. And he retired in 1993.

CHICO SIGHTS

Remnants Of The Bidwell Legacy

The **Bidwell Mansion,** now a state historic park at 525 The Esplanade, tel. (916) 895-6144, was the center of valley social life from the 1860s until the turn of the century. An elegant three-story Victorian designed by Henry W. Cleveland (architect of San Francisco's Palace Hotel) in the style of an Italian villa, it was outfitted in the finery of the day and boasted newfangled technology (including the first indoor bathroom ever installed in California). The mansion is open daily 10-5 for docent-led tours (last

tour at 4 p.m.). Small fee. Well worth a stop. The new visitor center adjacent features exhibits about the women's suffrage movement, the temperance movement, Chico's Chinese, goldmining, agricultural history, and the mansion's most famous guests.

Even more impressive is 2,400-acre **Bidwell Park,** reportedly the third-largest city park in the nation. World famous while it lived was the magnificent old **Hooker Oak,** a majestic valley oak believed to be 1,000 years old and named after the famed British botanist Sir Joseph Hooker, who declared it the world's largest. Hooker Oak was felled by the fates in 1977 during a spring storm, whereupon it was discovered that the tree was actually two fused together and only a few centuries old. But the Hooker Oak was just one feature of wooded Bidwell Park which prompted Warner Brothers to come to town in 1937 to film *The Adventures of Robin Hood,* starring Errol Flynn and Olivia de Havilland. (The small **Chico Museum** in the old Carnegie library building at the corner of 2nd and Salem, tel. 916-891-4336, open Wed.-Sun. noon-4 p.m., sometimes features memorabilia of that particular event plus other locally focused rotating exhibits.)

In the narrow creekside section known as Lower Park, closest to downtown, are the **Chico Creek Nature Center,** 1968 E. 8th St., tel. (916) 891-4671, and both the **One-Mile** and **Five-Mile** Chico Creek public swimming areas, with shade trees, cool lawns, picnic tables, playground facilities. (The creek is dammed for "pool" use during summers only.) The popular **Chico Municipal Golf Course** is in the otherwise undeveloped foothill wildness of Upper Park, known for its fine natural (sometimes *au naturel*) swimming holes and ridgetop trail for hiking and mountain biking. Except for golfing fees, access to Bidwell Park is free. At last report.

Commercial Chico Sights

Worth noting in Chico is the accomplished creativity of its business community. With the university's central location and its substantial student consumer power, Chico is one of those rare valley towns which still has an economically viable

the Hooker Oak in 1973, while still considered the world's largest oak tree

WES DEMPSEY

downtown business district, one not yet choked off by the California shopping mall syndrome. Downtown (more or less defined by Wall and Salem streets to the east and west, respectively, and by 1st and 6th streets to the north and south) are contemporary cafes, coffeehouses, restaurants, and unusual shops, like **Grace Jr.** at 331 W. 5th St., wonderful for eclectic jewelry and odd greeting cards, the **Nature Walk** at 228 Main, and **Zucchini and Vine** at 2nd and Main. Across the street is **Tower Books** and adjacent record shop. A fabulous used bookstore, especially if you have time to dig a bit, is **The Bookstore** at 118 Main, tel. (916) 345-7441. Also downtown is one of the best old-time hardware stores anywhere, helpful and friendly **Collier Hardware** at 105 Broadway, tel. (916) 342-0195, which sells just about every useful doodad imaginable—and which provides friendly personnel to help you find it. (Chico also has two major shopping malls: the North Valley Plaza north of town—reached via the Mangrove-Cohasset traffic corridor—and the new Chico Mall just south of town via Hwy. 99 and E. 20th Street.)

And for all of you fly-fishing enthusiasts, no trip to Chico is complete without a stop at **Powell Fly Shop** just off The Esplanade at 1154 W. 8th Ave., tel. (916) 345-3396. Powell makes some of the finest fishing rods in the world—handmade works of art featured quite recently (and quite rightly) in the film *A River Runs Through It,* based on Norman Maclean's wonderful book.

A surprising number of local businesses are actually at the top of their respective art or craft

nationally and/or internationally. Since these *are* businesses, call first before dropping by. Most widely recognized is **Orient and Flume Art Glass,** 2161 Park Ave., tel. (916) 893-0373, with its handblown glasswares sold in places like Gump's and the Smithsonian's National Museum of American History. A showroom fronts the large warehouse studio just across the railroad tracks. Open Mon.-Fri. 9-5, weekends 10-5. Also well-known is **Caribou Mountaineering,** 46 Loren Ave., tel. 891-6415, which manufactures high-quality backpacks, daypacks, softsided luggage, even "walking wallets" perfect for travelers. Some good bargains, too, on "factory outlet" days. Here and in England, industry leader **AVL Looms** at 601 Orange, tel. 893-4915, manufactures exceptional dobby looms for worldwide cottage industries as well as home weavers, including its Apple computer-interfaced models popular with fabric designers. **Cruces Classic Auto Sales** downtown at 720 Main, tel. 345-9772, is the streetside showroom for the restored (and unrestored) classic cars which are Cruces's passion. Renowned for his work worldwide, Cruces displays some of these beauties in his walk-through museum of old cars. Most people just look, but some buy.

The very fine **Sierra Nevada Brewing Company,** in new headquarters adjacent to its brewpub at 1075 E. 20th St., tel. (916) 893-3520, is among America's hottest microbreweries, producing popular brews like its pale ale (grand-prize winner at the 1983 American Beer Festival

in Boulder, Colorado), porter (which took second prize), stout, and Bigfoot Barleywine Ale, not to mention its newer German-style lager and various seasonal and special-event brews. The *Home Fermenter's Digest* acclaimed Sierra Nevada's brews as "the finest American beer ever made." Locally produced but international in focus is Chico's *Videomaker* magazine, tel. 891-8410, the state-of-the-art publication for home video devotees. Also worldwide in perspective is **Moon Publications, 330 Wall St.,** tel. 345-5473 or toll-free (800) 345-5473, publisher of acclaimed domestic and international travel books.

CHICO AREA ACCOMMODATIONS

A drawback to Chico is its lack of camping, though many of the local homeless and others ignore laws banning campouts in Bidwell Park. (Since rapes, rip-offs, and other wretched events are not unknown in this very large, secluded park, this option is not recommended.) Head out to the hinterlands (Woodson Bridge along the Sacramento River or Lake Oroville) for good state campsites. Other almost-nearby camping possibilities include **Black Butte Lake** west of Orland via Hwy. 32, Star Rt. Box 30, Orland 95963, tel. (916) 865-4781, with developed Buckhorn Campground sites for $8. The **Stony Gorge Reservoir** west of Willows, 1140 West Wood St., Willows 95988, tel. 934-7066, has 150 free campsites, no drinking water. (By the way, for steaks and seafood and country-western music on weekends, *the* place is **Femino's Blue Gum Restaurant** five miles north of Willows on old Hwy. 99, tel. 934-3435.) In Orland get very inexpensive and authentic Mexican food at funky **Casa Blanca** downtown at 403 Colusa St., tel. 865-9816.

Motels, Hotels
Since Chico is no tourist town, finding a motel room is easy most times of the year—exceptions being homecoming and graduation celebrations at CSU Chico. Not particularly convenient to downtown but inexpensive is **Motel 6** just off Hwy. 99 next to the Holiday Inn at 665 Manzanita Court, tel. (916) 345-5500, $26 s, $32 d. Right next door is **Motel Orleans,** 655 Manzanita Court, tel. 345-2533, with rooms for similar rates. The **Holiday Inn,** 685 Manzanita Court, tel. 345-2491, has more amenities (including whirlpool and exercise room), $70-85. In the same general category but newer is the **Best Western Heritage Inn,** 25 Heritage Ln. just off Cohasset Rd., tel. 894-8600, with rooms $55 and up. There are also a few motels downtown on Main and Broadway, more north of town on The Esplanade (an extension of both Main and Broadway).

Area Bed And Breakfasts
Two Chico bed and breakfasts are convenient to the downtown area. **The Palms of Chico** at 1525 Dayton Rd., Chico 95928, tel. (916) 343-6868, is a "contemporary art inn" furnished Pacific Basin-style, a huge old house cloistered by palms and other park-type trees—an arboretum gone native—on 40 acres of farmland and orchards. Inside are fresh airy rooms without antiques, phones, or TV; ongoing art exhibits; and natural and organic foods at breakfast (including delicious breads from Chico's Poncé Bakery), if there is breakfast. (Sometimes you're on your own for meals, a fact reflected in the rates: $70 d without breakfast, $85 d with, $10 less for singles, $10 less for rooms with shared bathroom.) This dignified home, built in 1900 by Henry Butters, who founded the Sacramento-Northern Electric Railroad, has been transformed into an "eco-farm lodge" by the artist-owner in residence, a veritable alchemist of ideas (a habit dating back to the Berkeley Free Speech Movement). The Palms is popular with European travelers and generally attracts eclectic and sophisticated individuals, though all five rooms are available for groups, family gatherings, and retreats. Animated conversations about art and artists, organic gardening, and the politics of the solar age are free.

The O'Flaherty House, two blocks west of The Esplanade via W. 5th Ave., at 1462 Arcadian

HIGH-MINDED MAVERICKS: THE BIDWELL LEGACY

That Chico is known nowadays for its bad behavior and beer consumption is quite the irony, since city founders General John Bidwell and Annie E.K. Bidwell were politically progressive, active prohibitionists. It's no accident that Lincoln and Frances Willard, a well-known prohibitionist, suffragette, and friend of the Bidwells, are among the streets laid out directly west of the adobe-pink Bidwell Mansion. Chico's founding couple was also civic-minded on the local level: they laid out the city's streets and gave lots away to anyone who wanted one. To start a teacher's college, they donated land for the Chico Normal School (now California State University at Chico). And they preserved the most beautiful creekside acres of their massive landholdings in a natural state, land Annie deeded to the city as a park after John's death. Even Chico's abundant street trees are part of the Bidwells' legacy.

Among the first party of overland settlers to arrive in California in 1841, John Bidwell first worked for John Sutter as his bookkeeper and business manager (leaving temporarily to join Frémont and the bear flaggers at Sonoma). He then helped confirm the Sutter's Mill gold find, later discovering gold himself on the Feather River. With his gold rush earnings, Bidwell started a new career as an innovative farmer and horticulturalist on his 28,000-acre Rancho del Arroyo Chico—the most admired agricultural enterprise in the state—where he grew wheat and other grains, nuts, olives, raisins, and over 400 other varieties of fruit.

Always active in politics yet considered a high-minded maverick, Bidwell met the serious-minded Annie Ellicott Kennedy while serving a term in the U.S. Congress from 1865 to 1867. Bidwell's first bid for the California governorship was derailed by the state's powerful railroad lobby and, despite his incredible public popularity, he lost again in the 1870s. The Bidwells' farsighted beliefs, including support for election reforms, control of business monopolies, and women's rights, were quite controversial during the 19th century but have proved their worth to subsequent generations. Some of John Bidwell's biographical reminiscences (including "Life in California before the Gold Discovery," first published in 1890 in *The Century Illustrated* magazine) are available in the state parks' facsimile reprint, *Echoes of the Past*.

Ave., Chico 95926, tel. (916) 893-5494, pays tongue-in-cheek homage to the proprietors' imaginary aunt, "Dirty Mary" O'Flaherty, who purportedly operated a notorious gold rush-era cathouse in the Sierra Nevada before "retiring" here to cultivate local business. According to the story, Dirty Mary lived to be 92 and was entertaining a gentleman caller when she passed on to that Big Brocade Room in the Sky. This lighthearted hostelry is a refurbished 1905 Victorian featuring four upstairs guest rooms with shared baths, rates $48-82. The Carriage House out back, complete with living room and kitchen, is a great set up for families ($125 per night). Expanded continental breakfast. For a more straightlaced stay, in a large, fairly modern complex with easy access to the Hwy. 99 freeway via Hwy. 32, consider the **Music Express Inn** at

1091 El Monte Ave., Chico 95928, tel. 891-9833. Seven rooms and one suite, all with private baths, run $62-72.

Worth the drive, both for the price and the country-style quiet, is **The Inn at Shallow Creek Farm** about three miles west of I-5 on County Road DD (Rt. 3, Box 3176, Orland 95963), tel. (916) 865-4093, a small ivy-covered farmhouse surrounded by orchards and fields—and an impressive flock of poultry. Rooms are restful, tastefully decorated (the two upstairs share a bath). Downstairs there's a sunporch, a roomy living area with well-worn leather sofas in front of the fireplace, and a welcoming formal country dining room. Perhaps the best escape of all, though, and a bargain by B&B standards, is The Cottage near the barn—the one-time groundskeeper's quarters with four rooms, fully equipped kitchen, sunporch, and wood-burning stove. Rates: $45-75. Also within reasonable reach, at least by urban driving standards, is **McCracken's Inn** south of Chico in Gridley (see "Gridley and Colusa" above).

Camelot

Since Chico is almost in Paradise—that town is just to the east, up the hill via the Skyway—it's no surprise that Camelot is also nearby. Not exactly a bed and breakfast, this remarkable retreat on the rim of Butte Creek Canyon about a half-mile east of the Covered Bridge offers spectacular views and utter serenity. Camelot is a small handcrafted house, an escape from everything but nature and comfort. Meticulous craftsmanship includes subtle woodworking design motifs, a dining niche for two (with handcarved table and chairs, even handwoven placemats), and a handmade bed. Other nice touches include the interior rock waterfall, the similar "Garden of Eden" shower, a fully stocked modern kitchen, and a private deck with hot tub overlooking the canyon and sheltered by an oak tree. The living room fireplace is shared with the bedroom, one of many romantic touches. Romance, really, is the whole point of this place. Once arrived at Camelot, guests won't see another soul unless they want to. There's no check-in or check-out. Pay in advance, by check, and the key is left just outside the front door for arriving guests. Rates: $165 weekdays, $185 on weekend nights. Couples only. For more information (including exactly how to get here), contact: Camelot, 2803 Eskin Maidu Trail, Chico 95928, tel. (916) 343-9164.

GOOD FOOD CHICO STYLE

Chico's Velveeta cheese connection is a myth, since the city has more excellent, reasonably priced food choices per capita than most places in the state. For an excellent all-vegetarian grocery selection year-round, head for **Chico Natural Foods** at 818 Main St., tel. (916) 891-1713. Drawing rave reviews from *East West Journal* for its traditional European-style breads (made with fresh-ground organic whole grains and natural ingredients, all leavened without yeast) is **Poncé Bakery and Boulangerie**, 116 W. 12th St., tel. 891-8354. Try a loaf of the almond-raisin whole wheat to go. Also quite wonderful, for natural sourdough breads (no yeast) is **Chico Bread Works** on 14th St., well-distributed around town.

Coffee, Breakfast, Sweets

Downtown at least, Chico is short on breakfast eateries—unless you count all the coffee shops and bakeries. The Eurostyle **Caffe Siena** at 128 Broadway, tel. (916) 345-7745, features oak-roasted coffees and great muffins at breakfast, folk music some afternoons, and live classical music or jazz five nights a week. Another (very tiny) coffeehouse, this one also a gelato and light breakfast-lunch place by day and live music venue at night, is **Perchè No!** nearby at 119 W. 2nd St., tel. 893-4210. Truly loved downtown for its decadent pastries, baked goods, and good coffees is **The Upper Crust,** 130 Main St., tel. 895-3866. **Cory's Sweet Treats and Gallery** at 230 W. 3rd St., tel. 345-2955, serves good coffee, wonderful pastries, and breakfast entrees from Belgian waffles to veggie scramble. Open 6 a.m.-4 p.m. daily, except Sun. and Monday. For Sunday brunch, try the **Kramore Inn** (see below). For homemade candies and ice cream, **Shubert's** at 178 E. 7th St. is the local tradition.

Lunch, Simple Dinners

Speedy Burrito, next to Swensen's Ice Cream Parlor in the Phoenix Building at 300 Broadway (there's another west of town at 1031 Nord Ave.), tel. (916) 894-1178, makes an endless variety of burritos and tacos, vegetarian and otherwise, starting with whole pink and black turtle beans cooked with *kombu* (a "secret ingredient" from Japan that makes them gasless) and served with Jerseyland cheese from nearby Orland and locally grown Lundberg rice. **Tacos Cortes** is also good (and cheap) for burritos and such, and more authentic in the Mexican tradition—a family operation dishing up great food at a stucco sit-down restaurant at 1100 Dayton Rd., tel. 342-4189. (Bring your own beer.) The chimichanga is a meal in itself. **Juanita's** downtown at 126 W. 2nd St., tel. 893-4215, is another inexpensive eatery, new and already famous for its burritos—stuffed with beans and rice, braised tofu, chicken, or beef. Very casual, with Tex Mex leather tables and chairs, old brick walls, high ceilings.

A local hot spot for vegetarians, and quite reasonable, is hole-in-the-wall **Cafe Sandino** across from Chico Natural Foods at 817 Main St., tel. (916) 894-6515, noted for its homemade and wholesome Mexican and South American fare. The tamales here are justifiably popular.

For pizza—and Chico is full of pizza palaces—try **Woodstock's** at 22½ Normal, tel. (916) 893-1500, with homemade sauce and fresh ingredients on hand-thrown pizzas with either whole wheat or white crust. Great, too, is **Gashouse Pizza** at 2359 Esplanade, tel. 345-3621, or 1444 Park Ave., tel. 345-6602. **Caffé Malvina,** 232 W. 3rd St., tel. 895-1614, serves light lunches, including pizza by the slice, Italian dinners, and fine coffees. Great for burgers is the **Madison Bear Garden** right next to the CSU Chico campus, 316 W. 2nd St., tel. 891-1639, a bizarre beer hall most popular with the college crowd.

Fondue is the specialty of the house at **Rubino's** at 133½ Broadway (above Las Tapas), but the salads and sandwiches are also great. Call (916) 891-5140 for hours and reservations. There's another Rubino's about two miles north of town, just across the highway from the Philadelphia Square office complex, at 3221 The Esplanade, tel. 894-2380, actually the main operation now, with a wide selection of sandwiches and salads plus—for those in a hurry at lunch—the "Bino Express" buffet upstairs. Open Tues.-Sun. for lunch and dinner.

The best lunch spot around—also wonderful for breakfast—is casual and cheerful **Cory's Sweet Treats & Gallery** between Broadway and Salem at 230 W. 3rd St., tel. (916) 345-2955, usually so busy that patrons don't object to the necessity of sharing tables. The menu is quite simple, including unbelievable lumberjack-size sandwiches built from thick slices of fresh-baked bread and house-baked ham, smoked turkey, or vegetarian fillings. Also hearty and homestyle are the soups, salads, quiche, and daily specials. "Gallery" refers to the fine local artwork on the walls; once each month, Cory's usually hosts an evening reception for the artist and current show. Very popular and serving good, inexpensive vegetarian meals in addition to its meateater selections is the **Kramore Inn,** 1903 Park Ave., tel. 343-3701, which specializes in crepes—over 20 different kinds—at breakfast, lunch, and dinner. **The Redwood Forest** at 121 W. 3rd St., tel. 343-4315, is also time-honored for lunch—good homemade food, from quiche to chicken pot pie, also sandwiches and salads.

More Exotic, More Expensive

Chico's famous locally brewed beer now has a new home at **Sierra Nevada Brewing Co. Taproom & Restaurant** just west of Hwy. 99 via the 20th St. exit, 1075 E. 20th St., tel. (916) 345-2739. This very respectable brewpub, light and airy, with a contemporary spit-polished brass and wood decor, serves good sandwiches at lunch, homemade and wholesome entrees at dinner—everything from eggplant parmesan to pastas, chicken, and steak selections. Sierra Nevada's beer-and-blues dinners are worth it. During the day, tour the brewing facilities. Free tours are scheduled Tues.-Fri. at 2:30 p.m., and on Saturday every half-hour from noon to 3 p.m. Call in advance to arrange large group tours.

La Hacienda north of town at 2635 The Esplanade, tel. (916) 893-8270, is the area's oldest Mexican restaurant—full bar, quite attractive—serving generous, sometimes imaginative, entrees. Reservations often mandatory. Also good for Mexican and downtown is **La Fonda,** downstairs at 2nd and Salem streets, tel. 345-5289, with a wonderful tostada-bar lunch special, good dinners, massive margaritas. **Las Tapas** nearby at 131 Broadway, tel. 894-6623, is tops for Mediterranean dishes. The **Gen Kai Japanese Restaurant & Sushi Bar** in the small Almond Orchard mall, 2201 Pillsbury Rd., tel. 345-7226, is also quite good. Locally popular for Chinese is **Peter Chu's Mandarin Restaurant** across from the North Valley Plaza Mall at 2424 Cohasset Rd., tel. 894-8276, open after 5 p.m. for dinner. (The original Peter Chu's is above Paradise, in Magalia.) For good Thai, over 100 items on the menu (many vegetarian), head out to **Ni Yom** at 2574 The Esplanade, tel. 899-1055, open weekdays for lunch, daily for dinner. For Basque food, the place is **Basque Norte,** 3355 The Esplanade, tel. 891-5204.

For a bit of Italy in this notoriously WASPish wonderland, try **The Sicilian Cafe** just south of downtown between W. 9th and W. 11th streets, 1020 Main St., tel. (916) 345-2233. Settle in next to the imposing old-country vineyard mural and order any of the handmade pastas (served with your choice of three different sauces, one for vegetarians). Typical of the daily-changing specials: salmon carbonara, clam fettuccine, and chicken and prosciutto. For dessert, try the homemade ricotta cheesecake or cannoli. Wine (some Italian) and beer. Open Tues.-Sat. for dinner only.

All too easy to miss even in a tiny town like Chico is the area's finest restaurant, **Zephyr's 3rd Street Grill** at 192 E. 3rd St. (corner of Wall and 3rd), tel. (916) 895-1328, as noted for its casual yet elegant ambience and creative California cuisine as its attentive, friendly service. The menu here changes seasonally— also daily, for specials. At lunch, specials (usually under $10) might include Thai-style chicken stir fry or lasagna Bolognese, even gazpacho. Dinner features entrees like mesquite-grilled Ahi salad, spinach fettuccine with fresh local pasta, and rib-eye steak. And don't skip dessert —also ever-changing, seductive sweets like lemon custard cheesecake, chocolate ganache torte, or homemade shortbread layered with Creme Chantilly and fresh berries. At Sunday brunch, expect pancakes, crepes, specialty omelettes (and other egg dishes, like Caribbean-style huevos rancheros) and side dishes from peppered bacon to pork-apple sausage. Open weekdays only for lunch, Wed.-Sun. for dinner, Sunday for brunch.

One of Chico's favorites in the dinner department is **The Hatch Cover,** 1720 Esplanade, tel. (916) 345-5862, for prime rib, steaks, fresh seafood, chicken. **The Albatross,** north of town at 3312 Esplanade, tel. 345-6037, features wonderful seafood—quite popular, reservations mandatory. But the oldest restaurant in town is down-home **Wasney's Barbecue** in a little house at 1228 Dayton Rd., tel. 342-5723, open daily after 5 p.m. (except Tuesdays) for excellent chicken, lamb, steaks, and ribs cooked over a wood fire. At the end of the meal, Mama Wasney might come out to deliver the check personally— along with some of her famous fudge.

EVENTS, ENTERTAINMENT, AND INFORMATION

Events
The biggest local event is still the long-running **Silver Dollar Fair** held at the fairgrounds in south Chico over the Memorial Day weekend; call (916) 895-4666 for information. It's noted for family- and farm-style fun: carnival rides, car races, country-western headliners, 4-H livestock competitions, and rodeo. In September comes Chico's **Concours d'Elegance,** usually held at the CSU Chico campus, a celebration of fine cars spiced up by the community presence of Cruces Classic Cars. This being a diehard beer town, of course Chico has an **Oktoberfest** in October. Chico also has many outdoor events, including the **Bidwell Classic** marathon usually scheduled in March; the Chico Velo bicycle club's **Feather-Yuba Foothills Century** and **Wildflower Century** rides in March and April, respectively; and the ever-popular **Endangered Species Faire** each May, quite an eclectic interspecies celebration.

The Arts And Entertainment
Summer high life, Chico-style, is climbing into a well-inflated tractor tire inner tube with a six-pack of beer and floating slowly down the Sacramento River to Scotty's Landing. (But this thrill isn't free anymore, now that state park rangers charge a "launch fee" at Irvine Finch Park, a popular starting point.) And on most Friday evenings in summer, strollers can enjoy the free outdoor concerts in the downtown city plaza. But even in summer, when the student population thins out, the arts and entertainment scene is incredibly diverse. (Quite wonderful, for example, are "Shakespeare in the Park" productions.) For a current rundown on what's going on and where, anytime of year, pick up a free copy of the *Chico News & Review* for its calendar section.

Through the university's performing arts programs and other sponsors, Chico attracts fairly big musical acts, from rock 'n' roll to country-western and folk, from classical, jazz, and blues to world beat. And talented local musicians, in ever-evolving new combinations or in long-running bands still take the stage in bars and clubs all over town. Local coffeehouses are cool places, with live entertainment like bluegrass and Celtic folk music. **Las Tapas Restaurant** (see above) hosts occasional concerts of the **Chico Jazz Society.** Hot local clubs include the **Sierra Nevada Taproom & Restaurant** on E. 20th St., tel. (916) 345-2739, for blues and blues-rock dinner and dancing shows (but you can skip dinner and just come for the show, if there's room); the true-blue country **Jolly Fox** at 2601 The Esplanade, tel. 895-9518, complete with cowboy card room; and **Stevens' Hofbrau** way out on The Esplanade, noted for its prime rib weekend specials and acoustic music. A variety of restaurants and bars downtown, from **Duffy's Tavern, Juanita's** and **LaSalles** to wet-T-shirt-contest-happy **Madison Bear Garden,** also do the music and dancing thing. **Lollipops** in the Almond Orchard mall at 2201 Pillsbury Rd., tel. 343-2267, is a Top 40/golden oldies venue, popular with baby boomers, something of a singles scene. For a real good time—for any age, any time—get out of town and head to **Scotty's Boat Landing** on the Sacramento River, tel. 983-2020, a beer-and-burger joint with weekend rock or blues shows.

The community also features an impressive number of independent, even adventurous art galleries. Though there are several UA cinemas in Chico (the El Rey the most interesting), funky and fun for foreign and avant-garde films is the casual **Pageant Theater** at 351 E. 6th St., tel. (916) 343-0663. To find out what's showing there, pick up a flier from the rack at the door.

Information

The best source of information, bar none, is the **Chico News & Review,** published on Thursdays and available free in distribution racks all over town. Another possibility is the **Chico Chamber of Commerce** office downtown at 500 Main St., tel. (916) 891-5556, open weekdays 9-5, a good source for maps and brochures. (For AAA members, there's an office in town with free local maps, just off the freeway at 2221 Forest Ave., tel. 891-8601.)

TRANSPORTATION

Public transportation is fairly limited in Chico, which is big on bicycling (and cars). The community's **CATS** buses, tel. (916) 893-5252, provide get-around-town service to major destinations (like shopping centers and hospitals) during the day and into early evening on weekdays and Saturdays, and **Butte County Transit,** tel. 893-4229, runs to Paradise, Oroville, Gridley, and Biggs.

The cheapest get-out-of-town technique is taking phone numbers from the **Ride Board** in the lobby of the Bell Memorial Union on campus. With luck, you can hook up with someone going your way for the price of filling the gas tank. **Greyhound** at 717 Wall St., tel. (916) 343-8266, or (800) 531-5332 for Spanish information, usually has five north-south buses per day; the depot schedule can be erratic. At hideous hours in the middle of the night **Amtrak** stops in Chico at the "depot" at 5th and Orange, with one train north to Seattle and another south to Los Angeles daily. (Women, do not wait for the train alone.) There's no ticket office locally (though any travel agency can issue Amtrak tickets); call Amtrak Central, (800) 872-7245, for schedule information.

Though the **Chico Municipal Airport** is served by United Express (call 800-241-6522 for information and reservations but call 916-893-6722 for flight arrival and departure verification), to connect with cheaper flights the **Airport Transportation Service** van shuttle, tel. 891-1219, runs from Paradise, Oroville, Chico, and Marysville-Yuba City south to the Sacramento Metropolitan Airport (and the same trip in reverse) on a regular schedule, $25 one way.

NEAR CHICO:
SIGHTS AND OUTINGS

South of town are almond orchards, scattered rice fields, and farm communities, including down-home Durham and Richvale (where the **Richvale Cafe** serves as unofficial community center) and, farther east, the boom-and-bust town of Oroville, with its own unique sights (see

THE VINA CEMETERY

This is only cultural
I tell myself
as we walk from marker to marker,
hands held.
She's an archaeologist,
of sorts, a meticulous eye
working a startling new find—
this graveyard.
We move from stone
to weather–cracked stone
that must be touched
and catalogued in her memory
of gravestones.
She is an archaeologist
with a gentle touch and gentle
step, as we move
over this soil that will mother
us, too, into the next
millennium,
hands held.

—Gary Thompson

below). Closer to Chico and pleasant for pic-nicking is the restored 1887 **Honey Run Covered Bridge** in Butte Creek Canyon to the southeast, reached via Humbug Rd. (nice bike ride for the brave—narrow road, fast traffic) from the Skyway and restored by local volunteers. This bridge is unique primarily because of its tri-level roofline, one roof for each intercon-nected span. From the bridge, snaking Honey Run Rd. climbs almost vertically up the craggy canyon walls, the hair-raising back-door route to **Paradise,** a large ridgetop retirement and resi-dential community. Humbug Rd., which forks to the left from the covered bridge, continues up the canyon to the remains of old Centerville and the small **Colman Museum** (open week-ends) next to the Centerville School and pio-neer cemetery.

Past the municipal airport north of town via Cohasset Rd. is the one-time luxury mineral springs spa and resort of Richardson Springs, now privately owned. Just southwest of the

Richardson Springs turnoff, almost visible from Cohasset Rd., are remnants of the old Titan Missile Base built here in the 1950s but never actually operational (though an explosion in one of the missile silos brought national media at-tention). It's a pleasant drive on to Cohasset, a foothill town with a general store and church but most famous for **Vose's Shopping Center,** tel. (916) 342-5214, a fabulous if funky an-tique store with great bargains on refurbished furniture. Continuing on, soon the paved road disappears. With any luck at all, adventurers might end up in the Ishi Wilderness Area.

North of Chico via Hwy. 99 is the Nature Con-servancy's **Vina Plains Preserve,** noted for its native grasslands and fine springtime display of vernal pool wildflowers. For more information on guided tours and for specific directions, call (916) 343-3185. The **Our Lady of New Clair-vaux Trappist Monastery** and farm along the Sacramento River 17 miles north of town near Vina, on part of Leland Stanford's one-time vine-yard and ranch, has some guest facilities for spiritual seekers; call 839-2161 for information.

The Sacramento River

West of Chico is the Sacramento River, with some rare stretches where much of the native ri-parian vegetation has been preserved. The large-ly undeveloped **Bidwell River Park** directly west of Chico offers day-use access and picnic facil-ities from 6 a.m. to 10 p.m.; stop by Bidwell Man-sion in town or call (916) 895-6144 for more in-formation. About 12 miles east of Willows is the Nature Conservancy's small **Sacramento River Oxbow Preserve,** an island jungle of cotton-woods and willows and remarkable birdlife, ac-cessible by advance permission only; to make arrangements, call 343-3185. In response to the popularity of summertime tubing, the state of California installed the **Irvine Finch River Ac-cess** tube launch site at the Hwy. 32 bridge over the river (pay attention to the No Parking signs along the highway). Fee.

The **Woodson Bridge** area near Corning northwest of Chico, also along the Sacramento, offers camping, picnicking, fishing, and a unique experimental program of "palisading" to protect riverbanks from erosion without resorting to the Army Corps of Engineers' riprapping techniques. The 46 Woodson Bridge campsites are available year-round, with Mistix reservations wise from

the Temple of Assorted
Deities in Oroville

CALIFORNIA DEPARTMENT OF PARKS & RECREATION

Memorial Day to Labor Day, tel. (800) 444-7275. Six-hour "A River Experience" canoe trips are offered weekly by rangers during the Sacramento's tamer seasons, for the price of canoe rental (or bring your own). On July 4th, Woodson Bridge usually has a good fireworks show too. For more information, contact: Woodson Bridge State Recreation Area, 25340 South Ave., Corning 96021, tel. (916) 839-2112.

The Llano Seco Rancho Wildlife Preserve

A major portion of a one-time Mexican land grant, most of the old Parrott Ranch along the Sacramento River southwest of Chico is now included in an 18,000-acre riparian wildlife preserve—a major acquisition engineered by the Nature Conservancy in cooperation with Parrott Ranch heirs. Sections of this huge riverside tract not already "native"—and much of it is, since prior to its acquisition this was the largest officially unprotected riparian forest remaining along the Sacramento—will be allowed to revert to a natural state, under joint land-use management by the U.S. Fish and Wildlife Service, the California Department of Fish and Game, and the state Wildlife Conservation Board. The ultimate result will be a major wildlife and waterfowl preserve. (One-fifth of the state's wintering mallards, and one-fifth of the wood ducks and sandhill cranes, already arrive here. Numbers of waterfowl and other migrating bird are expected to increase here, as their habitats decrease elsewhere.)

Llano Seco, southwest of Durham and bordered on the north by Ord Ferry Road, on the east by Seven-Mile Lane (with a seven-mile border with the Sacramento River on its western edge), is twice the size of the Gray Lodge Wildlife Area near Gridley. The ranch is expected to be back in "pristine" natural condition within 10-15 years. But before that time arrives, the area will also be available to the public—for birdwatching and hiking, for example, both on a guided-tour basis. For more information, contact: **The Nature Conservancy,** California Regional Office, 785 Market St., San Francisco 94103, tel. (415) 777-0487.

IN AND AROUND OROVILLE

The first thing most people notice about Oroville is the assortment of desolate gravel heaps surrounding the town—remaining dredge piles from placer miners who literally stripped away the fertile Feather River floodplain in search of gold. Still something of a rough-and-tumble foothill outlaw town, Oroville's historic boom-and-bust economic style has hounded the community into this century. When Oroville got a 20th-century boost in the form of state money and jobs for constructing the massive earth-filled Oroville Dam that created Lake Oroville, things were almost rosy for a while. But when the job was done, the town was busted flat again. Even the recreational possibilities of the lake and surrounding areas have done little to help Oroville break its bad-luck streak. Worse for the community's self-confidence (and image) are ongoing controversies over the long-term health effects of the local Koppers Wood Treatment Plant's dioxin contamination of soil and water. So give Oroville a break—stop, look around.

Spectacular in spring is the lava cap wildflower display on flat-topped **Table Mountain** near the one-time mining town of Cherokee (the tiny **Cherokee Museum** is in the old boarding house) just north of Oroville. Surprising in Oroville is the **George Ohsawa Macrobiotic Foundation** and Vega Study Center at 1511 Robinson St., tel. (916) 533-7702, one of the most complete macrobiotic facilities in the world, sponsoring cooking classes, workshops, and retreats. Or come to good-time events like the **California State Old Time Fiddler's Association** regional championship competition in March and the **Wild Mountain Faire** usually in June, a full day of mountain music and merriment in nearby Concow.

The Temple Of Assorted Deities

A reminder that many of those who created California's Old West were non-Western is Oroville's **Liet Sheng Kong,** the Temple of Assorted Deities (or "Many Gods"), 1500 Broderick St. off 1st, tel. (916) 538-2496, built by local Chinese (with financial support from the Chinese emperor) in 1863 for worshippers of three different faiths: Confucianism, Buddhism, and Taoism. A state historic landmark also listed on the National Register of Historic Places, Oroville's Chinese temple is both a place of worship and a museum. Rich with artifacts throughout, on the main temple's altar sit the Queen of Heaven and Goddess of the Sea and Travel, Sing Moe or Tien How; God of Literature and Courage, Kwan Kung or Kuan Yu; and Guardian of the Monastery and Protector of the Law of Buddhism, Wei T'o. Call for current hours. Small fee.

Lake Oroville State Recreation Area

Completed in 1967, the **Oroville Dam** supplies water to local farmers, the San Joaquin Valley, and Southern California and also provides some flood control and generates electricity. The dam's construction created a large, many-fingered lake—and the necessity of the downstream **Feather River Fish Hatchery** at 5 Table Mountain Blvd., tel. (916) 538-2222,

to artificially perpetuate the salmon and steelhead spawn. (The best time to watch the salmon and steelhead run, throwing themselves in vain against the below-dam barrier, is in the fall.) In addition to good views from the 47-foot observation tower, the **visitor center and museum** atop Kelly Ridge offers both gold rush history and natural history, exhibits chronicling the development of the California Water Project, and films.

The lake itself, with a receding summertime water line, is popular for boating, fishing, and housebuilding. Camping facilities at Loafer Creek include picnic tables and outdoor stoves plus flush toilets, laundry tubs, and hot showers, $14 basic fee. Bidwell Canyon Campground has RV hookups. Reserve campsites in advance through Mistix, tel. (800) 444-7275. Also available: over 100 boat-in campsites and group camps. For more information, contact: Lake Oroville State Recreation Area, 400 Glenn Dr., Oroville 95965, tel. (916) 534-2324 (visitors center, tel. 538-2219).

Feather Falls

Feather Falls, just above Lake Oroville in Plumas National Forest, is fabulous for a day hike. The highest waterfall in California (outside Yosemite) and the sixth highest in the continental U.S., Feather Falls is best from March through May, when Sierra Nevada snow melt surges through the middle fork of the Feather River then plummets over the steep granite precipice, creating roaring whitewater and rainbow mist. The firs, ferns, and wildflowers are best in spring too. (In January and February, snow may line the trail; in summer, the trip is surprisingly hot.) Wear good walking shoes (the trail is steep in places) and layered clothing; bring plenty of drinking water, a picnic lunch, and any valuables (since vandalism and theft are an occasional problem in the parking lot). Sadly, too, the trail is open to motorbikes, so exhaust fumes and street-style noises may disturb the peace. Walking at a moderate pace, with time out for a picnic and a short scramble to get closer to the falls, the seven-mile roundtrip takes about six hours. The last mile out is the hardest, so save some strength—and some water. For more information, contact Plumas National Forest's Challenge Ranger District office, tel. (916) 675-2462, P.O. Drawer 369, Challenge, CA 95925.

RED BLUFF AND VICINITY

Named for the color of the riverbanks, Red Bluff often gains national notoriety in summer for being the hottest spot in the nation—with an all-time high temperature of 121 degrees in 1981—though it's famous locally for the annual **Red Bluff Bull and Gelding Sale** in January, the **Red Bluff Round-up** parade and rodeo in April, and the downtown **Cowtown Shopping Center.** The **William B. Ide Adobe State Historic Park** two miles northeast of town on the Sacramento River at 21659 Adobe Rd., Red Bluff 96080, tel. (916) 527-5927, features remnants of the rustic adobe homestead of the first (and only) president of the Bear Flag Republic, also picnic tables, and fishing. Open 8 a.m.-sunset daily, free. **Ide Adobe Day** in August includes demonstrations of adobe brick-making, candle-making, and old-time log sawing.

The Gray Davis Dye Creek Ranch Preserve

The 37,000-acre Gray Davis Dye Creek Ranch Preserve bordering the Tehama Wildlife Area east of Hwy. 99 and 10 miles southeast of Red Bluff on Cone Grove Road, is a working cattle ranch and cooperative "habitat enhancement" venture uniting ecologists and hunters. Jointly managed by the Nature Conservancy and Multiple Use Management, Inc., the goal is improving wildlife habitat while improving and maintaining healthy deer, duck, and other wildlife populations. Nature talks and walks into Dye Creek Canyon and the heart of Ishi country are offered periodically. (Call for information and reservations. Access to the preserve is only on a guided-tour basis.) Family recreation memberships are available, as are guided hunting trips. A pleasure in and of itself is a stay at the Dye Creek Lodge, including meals, lodging, and access to all recreational facilities.

For hike schedule and reservations, and for more information about other Dye Creek activities, contact Preserve Manager, c/o McCloud River Preserve, P.O. Box 409, McCloud 96057, tel. (916) 926-4366.

Red Bluff Area Practicalities

At the junction of I-5 and Hwy. 99, Red Bluff offers the usual array of roadside motels and fast-food eateries. Alternative accommodations include **The Faulkner House Bed and Breakfast,** 1029 Jefferson St., tel. (916) 529-0520, with rooms for $53-80. Of the four upstairs rooms in this very Victorian house—all have private baths—two of the loveliest also happen to be the smallest: the corner Tower Room, with quaint antique florals in tan tones, and the Wicker Room, cooled both by its tree-shaded window views and the aqua leaf motif. The **Buttons and Bows Bed and Breakfast** at 427 Washington, tel. 527-6405, is equally inviting, an 1880s estate Victorian on a tree-lined street just blocks from downtown. All three upstairs rooms share a generous bathroom and are light and airy, with old-fashioned decorating touches. The Rose Room comes with a wonderful balcony. Rates $53-65. And just down the street—well worth a stop—is the **Kelley Briggs House Museum.** Taking the local Victorian House walking tour is also worthwhile.

Blondie's Diner, a slightly self-concious 1950s throwback right downtown at Main and Antelope, tel. (916) 529-1668, isn't what people expect to find in Red Bluff. Blondie's serves good food California style, from a frisky tortellini to fettuccine tossed with red peppers and scallops in curry cream sauce, fine chicken dishes, good wines, even chocolate cake and hot apple crisp. Good burgers and basics, too. Nearby and very popular, **The China Panda** at 628 Main St., tel. 529-1298, serves an impressive selection of Chinese dishes at lunch and dinner (Tues.-Sun.), with lunch specials under $5. Good, too, and especially popular at lunch is the **Snack Box** at 257 Main, tel. 529-0227. A time-honored local institution (though this is a new place, since the original burned down some years back) is **The Green Barn** restaurant and bar on Hwy. 99 at Chestnut, tel. 527-7390, styled after an English pub and serving prime rib dinners and other meat-and-potatoes standards. Also good for dinner—and definitely best for views of the Sacramento River—is the **Riverside** restaurant and bar at 500 Riverside Way, tel. 529-1668.

For the best coffee anywhere around, stop by the **Delectables and Collectibles** coffeehouse and gift shop on Walnut. **Facts and Fiction,** on Walnut near the post office, is a decent bookstore. For more information about the north valley's hotspots, particularly recreation opportunities, contact the **Red Bluff-Tehama County Chamber of Commerce,** 100 Main St. (P.O. Box 100), Red Bluff 96080, tel. (916) 527-6220.

THE SAN JOAQUIN VALLEY

Californians may make fun of Sacramento, but they dismiss and demean the San Joaquin Valley. Here, truly, is the Other California. The Kingston Trio started the public insults with: "How many of you are from San Francisco? How many are from someplace else? How many are from Modesto and don't understand the first two questions?" More recently, a San Francisco newspaper columnist quipped that Fresno is "just like Modesto but without all the glitter," a meaningless insult except to those who have searched for Modesto nightlife. Late-night talker Johnny Carson did it too, referring to Fresno as "the Gateway to Bakersfield." So most people travel through the long, hot landscape between Los Angeles and parts north with barely a blink.

Yet people in Modesto, Fresno, and Bakersfield enjoy life in California's salad bowl. By way of explanation, Fresno's most famous son William Saroyan says, "We made this place of streets and dwellings in the stillness and loneliness of the desert." And Sacramento native Joan Didion says: "Valley towns understand one another, share a peculiar spirit." But the best explanation to date is still inscribed on the Modesto Arch stretched across the old highway: Water Wealth Contentment Health.

MODESTO

The biggest thing in Modesto is giant **Gallo Winery,** which produces one-fourth of all wine consumed in the U.S., 113 million gallons or so each year. Nearby Turlock is most famous for its long-time "Turkeys From Turlock" slogan, a radio advertising jingle stuffed into California's consciousness decades ago, though Livingston is Foster Farms headquarters. (Livingston is also famous as the site of the last stop light on the San Joaquin stretch of Hwy. 99—a distinction recently removed by progress.)

Despite the jokes, there *is* high culture in and around Modesto, including the Modesto Civic Theatre's "Shakespeare in the Park" performances and concerts by the Modesto Symphony and the Townsend Opera Players. More typical of the area, though: the **Modesto Model A's Swap Meet** at the fairgrounds in January, the **Ripon Almond Blossom Festival** in February, and the **Oakdale Rodeo** in April, followed in May by the **Patterson Apricot Fiesta.** But don't miss the **Stanislaus County Fair** in Turlock every August, the **Delicato Vineyards Grape Stomp** in September, and the **Manteca Pumpkin Fair** in October.

Once arrived in Modesto, stop for a tour of **The McHenry Mansion** at 906 15th St., tel. (209) 577-5341, an astounding restoration of the 1883 Italianate Victorian home of local banker Robert McHenry and his pioneering family. To achieve period authenticity, and the Anglo-Japanese style popular at the time, wallpapers here have been reproduced to exacting artistic specifications—some stenciling done by hand—and the carpets were woven on 19th-century looms by Stourvale Mills in England. Very unusual is the rose brass chandelier in the parlor, still lit by gas. Though restoration funds—over $2 million to date—have been collected and administered by the McHenry Mansion Foundation, the home itself was purchased in 1976 by the Julio Gallo Foundation and presented to the city of Modesto. Usually open Tues.-Thurs. and Sun. 1-4 p.m.; call to arrange individual or group tours (free) at other times. For information on renting the facility for luncheons, weddings, and other group functions, call the city Parks and Recreation Department at 577-5344.

Other area diversions include the **McHenry Museum** at 1402 I St., tel. (209) 577-5366, for a look at local history (free, open Tues.-Sun. noon-4 p.m.), and the **Great Valley Museum of Natural History** at 1100 Stoddard Ave., tel. 575-6196, for a look at native animals, plants, and natural ecosystems (free, open Tues.-Fri. noon-4:30 p.m., Sat. 10-4, closed in August). Or take a trip to Oakdale and indulge yourself at the **Hershey Visitors Center,** tel. 848-8126, with free chocolate factory tours on weekdays, or the **Bloomingcamp Apple Ranch,** tel. 847-1412, for ciders, pies, and apples (call for current days and times). Almond lovers, head to Salida and the **Blue Diamond Growers Store,** tel. 545-3222.

For a complete listing of accommodations, activities, and restaurants (also a current copy of the local harvest trails guide), contact the **Modesto Chamber of Commerce,** 1114 J St., P.O. Box 844, Modesto 95353, tel. (209) 577-5757. Another good source of local information is the daily *Modesto Bee* newspaper.

Modesto Area Camping
Camp at nearby **Modesto Reservoir,** 18139 Reservoir Rd., Waterford 95386, tel. (209) 874-9540, or at **Turlock Lake** farther south, 22600 Lake Rd., La Grange 95329, tel. 874-2008. **Caswell Memorial State Park** to the west along the banks of the Stanislaus River, 28000 S. Austin Rd., Ripon 95366, tel. 599-3810, is more noted for its 138-acre stand of valley oak forest and nature trail than for its swimming. Good campsites with hot showers and all, $14. Another possibility, just west of Santa Nella and I-5 via Hwy. 152, is the **San Luis Reservoir State Recreation Area,** tel. 826-1196. Farther south and 13 miles west of I-5 on Little Panoche Rd. is funky old **Mercey Hot Springs,** P.O. Box 1363, Los Banos 93635, no phone, with individual indoor hot tubs, plus campground and lodgings.

Other Modesto Accommodations
Modesto's **Motel 6** is just off Hwy. 99 at 722 Kansas Ave., tel. (209) 524-3000, with pool and a/c, rooms from $24. Near-

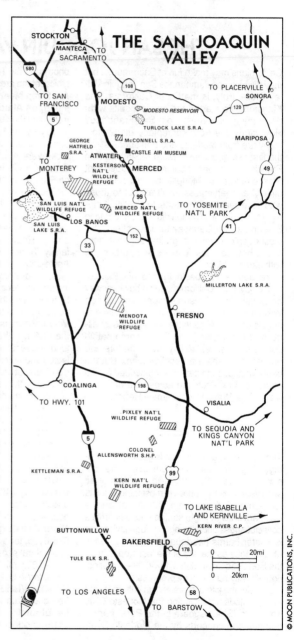

THE SAN JOAQUIN VALLEY

© MOON PUBLICATIONS, INC.

MODESTO CONVENTION & VISITORS BUREAU

The Hershey Chocolate Company in Oakdale, 15 miles east of Modesto, offers free public tours.

by at 500 Kansas is **Motel Orleans,** tel. 578-5400, the usual plus coin laundry, rooms slightly more. Motel row in Modesto proper is on McHenry Avenue. One possibility is the **Vagabond Inn,** 1525 McHenry, tel. 521-6340, with rooms for $38-62. Modesto even has a **Holiday Inn,** 1612 Sisk Rd., tel. 521-1612, with two pools, whirlpool, sauna, putting green, even lighted tennis courts. Rooms are $65. Newly remodeled.

Quite exceptional in the upscale motel genre is the **Best Western Mallard's Inn,** a ducky place just off the highway at 1720 Sisk Rd., tel. (209) 577-DUCK or toll-free for reservations (800) 528-1234. Bedspread, carpet, and towel colors all key off the "mallard" theme, as do the small bathroom baskets containing soaps and sundries. Rooms are generous, with queen beds and vanities, in-room brewed coffee, TV, and HBO. Some suites available. Pool and spa. Milk and cookies are delivered to your room in the evening. Breakfast, either continental buffet-style or cooked to order, is available downstairs in the Mallard's Grill restaurant. Since Mallard's caters to the business traveler, weekend rates are lowest—great for everyone else. Rates: $60-110. Also top of the line in Modesto (and a weekend bargain) is the **Red Lion Hotel** at Convention Center Plaza, 1150 9th St., tel. 526-6000, $93-124 Sun.-Thurs., $71 s or d on weekend nights.

In the bed and breakfast category, the **Malaga House,** 2828 Malaga Way, tel. (209) 529-

9269, is contemporary and friendly, pool, full breakfast. Rates: $50-60.

Modesto Area Restaurants

A surprise in Modesto is **St. Stan's Brewery, Pub, & Restaurant** at 821 L St., tel. (209) 524-4PUB, open daily for lunch and dinner. The main attraction at St. Stan's is the "alt bier," or old-style (pre-lager) beer, brewed and served here. (Since St. Stan's brews are high in alcohol content, in California they're considered malt liquors.) The Black Forest bar ambience includes 15-foot-tall faux fir trees. Upstairs is the elegant yet relaxed dining room. On the menu: plentiful pasta chices and dinner entrees from baked stuffed eggplant and Belgium beef stew to broiled New York steak. Jazz and dinner theater, too.

Modesto also has a **Chevy's,** 1700 Standiford Ave., tel. (209) 544-2144, a **Sizzler** at 3416 Dale Rd., tel. 578-5099, and an **A & W Root Beer** stand that's been here since 1957 (complete with carhops on roller skates), 14th and G Sts., tel. 522-7700. A bit fancier is the **Bon Appetit Cafe** at 500 9th St., tel. 526-7000, not to mention **Maxi's** at the Red Lion Hotel on 9th, tel. 526-6000. Locally recommended **Hazel's,** at 513 12th St., tel. 578-3463, serves elegant seven-course meals. Reservations must be made well in advance. Popular, too, for American standards is the dining room at the **Sundial Lodge,** open for dinner only, 808 McHenry Ave., tel. 524-4375.

the Castle
Air Museum near
Merced

KIM WEIR

MERCED AND VICINITY

The town's pride and joy is the **Castle Air Museum** adjacent to Castle Air Force Base just north of town, P.O. Box 488, Atwater 95301, tel. (209) 723-2178. Though the air base, a training facility for Strategic Air Command crews, is scheduled for closure by 1995 under current U.S. plans to downsize the military, the museum will remain. Castle's indoor museum features an impressive collection of wartime mementos, from vintage military uniforms and a Congresssional Medal of Honor to a once-top-secret Norden Bomb Sight. The big show's outside, though—a meticulously restored open-air collection of World War II aircraft and planes from the Korean and Vietnam wars: the B-17 Flying Fortress, a B-24 Liberator (one of only 15 still in existence), a B-25 Mitchell Bomber, a B-29 Superfortress (like the one that dropped the atomic bomb on Hiroshima), even an SR-71 spy plane. Quite an aviary of war birds. The museum complex is open daily 10-4 except major holidays. Guided tours are available, with advance notice. And if you're hungry, the basics—the "bomber burgers" are impressive examples of American culinary art—are available in the Flights of Fancy cafeteria. (Worth attending, the first Sunday in May or December, is the museum's fundraising **Omelette Breakfast** at the cafeteria—good food, good fun, just $5.) Also plan to show up for area air shows, including the **Antique Fly-In** in early June, held at the Merced Municipal Airport.

If you've got extra time on your hands, stop by the **Yosemite Wildlife Museum** off Hwy. 99 at 2040 Yosemite Parkway (Hwy. 140), tel. (209) 383-1052, a private natural history museum. (Group tours welcome.) Admission fee. Or take the tour of the **Old Courthouse,** now the Merced County Museum at 21st and N streets, a striking 1875 Italianate Renaissance Revival building designed by A.A. Bennett (also architect of the state Capitol) and open to the public Wed.-Sun. 1-4 p.m. Note the statues up top, all hand-carved from redwood. The three on the sides of the roof represent Justica, the Roman Goddess of Justice (without blindfold). Above them, on the cupola, is Minerva, Goddess of Wisdom.

Notable in the valley southeast of Merced is **The Grasslands,** a 25-square-mile area containing five national wildlife refuges—including the notorious Kesterson National Wildlife Area—160 hunt clubs, and altogether about 25% of the state's remaining wetlands, essential to the survival of migrating waterfowl. Elk graze, inside a fenced enclosure, in the San Luis National Wildlife Refuge, also popular for bird-watching and hunting (peak season: October through April). Ask locally for directions and current information; some refuges are more accessible from the other side of the valley.

Merced Practicalities
The Mansion House Restaurant at 455 W. 20th St. (20th and Canal), tel. (209) 383-2744, offers citified cuisine in a graceful but casual Victorian with multiple downstairs dining rooms,

upstairs banquet rooms. Open Mon.-Sat. for lunch and dinner, very popular for Sunday brunch. Very Merced is **The Branding Iron,** 640 W. 16th St., tel. 722-1822, with local brands dominating the decor. Open for lunch weekdays, for dinner daily. **The Eagles Nest** at the **Merced Travelodge,** 2000 E. Childs Ave., tel. 723-1041, serves contemporary California-style cuisine in a family atmosphere (children's menu), open daily 6 a.m.-10 p.m. Rooms at the motel, tel. 723-3121, run $45 and up. Other accommodations choices include the **Best Western Pine Cone Inn** at 1213 V St., tel. 723-3711, rates $55 and up, and the **Best Western Inn** at 1033 Motel Dr., tel. 723-2163, $38-56.

For more information about the area, contact the **Merced Convention and Visitors Bureau,** 690 W. 16th St., Merced 95344, tel. (209) 384-3333 or toll-free (800) 446-5353.

FRESNO AND VICINITY

Johnny Carson may consider Fresno the Gateway to Bakersfield, but the city prefers being recognized as the gateway to three Sierra Nevada national parks: Yosemite, Sequoia, and Kings Canyon. California's sixth-largest city, now larger than Sacramento, Fresno has become much more than the Raisin Capital of the World. Though it sprawls out in all directions, the city has a distinct and walkable downtown where the newer, taller buildings haven't yet crowded out the old; it also has a full cultural calendar, a state university and city college, worthwhile sights, and culinary diversions.

For more information, contact the **Fresno Convention and Visitors Bureau** (see "Fresno Area Accommodations" below). For information on nearby Hanford—a worthwhile side trip—contact the **Hanford Chamber of Commerce/Visitor Agency** at 213 W. 7th St., Hanford 93230, tel. (209) 582-0483.

Fresno Sights

The **Fresno Metropolitan Museum of Art, History, and Science** in the old *Fresno Bee* building, 1555 Van Ness at Calaveras, tel. (209) 441-1444, features a permanent collection of (former Fresnoan) Ansel Adams's photographs, Dutch Old Masters, an Asian Gallery, plus special rotating exhibits on local culture and natur-

F R E S N O ▲RT MUSEUM

al history. Open Tues.-Fri. 11 a.m.-5 p.m., weekends noon-5. Small admission fee. Among other local sights is the exceptional **Fresno Art Museum,** 2233 N. 1st St., tel. 485-4810, open Tues.-Sun. 10-5, featuring each year over 20 changing exhibits of Mexican and American art in six contemporary galleries. Museum gift shop, auditorium for films and plays. Handicapped-accessible. Small admission fee, free for children under age 16. Guided group tours available upon request.

The **Shin-Zen Japanese Friendship Gardens** in Woodward Park (Audubon Dr. and Friant Rd.), tel. (209) 488-1551, are a wonderful respite for the road weary, with acres of gardens, koi ponds, bridges, and Japanese sculptures representing the four seasons, even a Japanese teahouse (open only on special occasions). Docent-led tours are available. Call for current hours. More mainstream and quite popular is Fresno's 157-acre **Roeding Park,** 894 W. Belmont Ave., cool and green and complete with the decent Fresno Zoo, tel. 498-1551, as well as Playland and Storyland for the kiddies.

The **Kearney Mansion Museum** in Kearney Park seven miles west of downtown, 7160 W. Kearney Blvd., tel. (209) 441-0862, was once the center of M. Theo Kearney's Fruit Vale Estate. This 1900s mansion, listed on the National Register of Historic Places, has been lovingly restored—down to exact replicas of original wallpapers and carpets—and now honors the memory of "The Raisin King of California." Admission $3 adults, $2 teenagers, $1 children age 5-12. (No fee to use the surrounding 225-acre park if you tour the mansion.) Open for tours Fri.-Sun. 1-4 p.m. The **Meux Home Museum** in town at Tulare and R streets, tel. 233-8007, is the last remaining example of Victorian homes built earlier in Fresno's settlement history, restored and authentically furnished. Guided tours Fri.-Sun. noon-3:30 p.m., small fee. Pick up the local historical society's free "A Guide to Historic Architecture—Tower District" to more fully appreciate the community's architectural heritage.

Other worthwhile stops in and around Fresno include the **Mennonite Quilting Center** at 1010

KIM WEIR

*Shin-Zen Japanese Friendship Garden
in Woodward Park*

G St. in Reedley, tel. (209) 638-6911, with demonstrations and displays on the folk art of quilting (free), **Sun-Maid Growers** raisin-processing plant and store in Kingsburg, tel. 896-8000, and—also paying commercial homage to local agriculture—both **Simonian Farms** and **Sierra Nut House** in Fresno.

Fresno Area Accommodations

Camp at **Millerton Lake State Recreation Area,** P.O. Box 205, Friant 93626, tel. (209) 822-2225. For information about camping in nearby **Sierra National Forest,** stop by headquarters in the federal building at 1130 O St., tel. 487-5155. For information about other accommodations, the **Fresno Convention and Visitors Bureau,** 808 M St., Fresno 93721, tel. 233-0836 or toll-free (800) 543-8488, is quite accommodating. Besides providing current motel and hotel rates, the bureau will book and reserve rooms in advance (by mail only).

For travelers who don't plan much, and don't plan to spend much **Motel 6** is in three locations.

The first, at 933 N. Parkway Dr. just off Hwy. 99 (and just across the freeway from Roeding Park), tel. (209) 233-3913, has pool, a/c, rooms from $20. The second is on the same street but south of Belmont Ave. (take the Belmont exit from Hwy. 99) at 445 N. Parkway Dr., tel. 485-5011, rooms $22 and up. (Lots of other cheapies in the neighborhood.) The third, at 4245 N. Blackstone Ave., tel. 221-0800, is south of Shaw Ave. and just north of the Hwy. 99-Hwy. 41 intersection, same amenities as always, from $22. Nearby is the **Best Western Water Tree Inn,** 4141 N. Blackstone, tel. 222-4445, with rooms from $50. The top raisin in Fresno hotel-motel lodging, though, is the lushly landscaped Sheraton **Smuggler's Inn,** 3737 N. Blackstone Ave., tel. 226-2200, recent recipient of Mobil's four-star rating, with rooms for $75-100. But Fresno has some other juicy choices, including (with comparable room rates) the **Piccadilly Inn—Shaw** at 2305 Shaw Ave., tel. 226-3850, and the **Piccadilly Inn—University** northeast of town at 4961 N. Cedar, tel. 224-4200. Fresno has four Best Westerns, two Holiday Inns, a Marriott, and a Howard Johnson, in addition to many decent unaffiliated local motels. Contact the visitors bureau for more help in reserving accommodations.

The **Country Victorian Bed and Breakfast,** 1003 S. Orange Ave., tel. (209) 233-1988, offers four rooms (two with shared baths) and continental breakfast, $45-75. In nearby Hanford is the **Irwin Street Inn,** 522 N. Irwin, tel. 584-9286, four restored Victorians with rooms $70 and up.

Fresno Area Restaurants

Worth a stop is the **Farmer's Market** downtown at 2736 Divisadero at Tulare, tel. (209) 441-1009, an enclosed mall with over a dozen ethnic restaurants (shared dining area), family-run produce stalls (best selection on Saturdays, usually), health-food stores, bookshops, and florists. Even more genuine is the outdoor **produce market** convention on Tues., Thurs., and Sat. 7 a.m.-3 p.m. at the corner of Merced and N streets.

For inexpensive ethnic food, mostly Japanese and Mexican, head to old Chinatown, west of the railroad tracks in the vicinity of Kern and G streets. **George's** at 2405 Capitol St., tel. (209) 264-9433, has that California-cuisiney look but in fact dishes up wonderful Armenian authenticity, from peasant soup to shish kebab. Quite reasonable.

The **Butterfield Brewing Company Bar & Grill** at 777 E. Olive, tel. (209) 264-5521, is open for lunch and dinner daily, serving its award-winning handcrafted Bridalveil, Tower Dark, and San Joaquin ales, plus specialty beers. A restaurant more than a pub, at lunch Butterfield offers salads and sandwiches, "stout" chili, and barbecued ribs or chicken, most in the just-over-$5 range. Dinner entrees include more of the same plus pastas, the brewhouse platter (an assortment of sausages to complement the beer), and a good selection of chicken, beef, and seafood. Brunch features quiche, specialty omelettes, scrambles, and classic eggs Benedict. Specialty coffees available, too. Also good at lunch and dinner: **Livingstone's Restaurant And Pub** at 831 E. Fern, tel. 485-5198. For a quick meal, there's always **Fatburger** at 46 E. Herndon, tel. 439-2747.

Famous in Fresno is the **Basque Hotel** at 1102 F St., tel. (209) 233-2286, with inexpensive and incredibly generous portions of peasant fare served up family style; entrees change nightly. Traditional in Fresno is the family-style Basque fare at the old yellow-brick **Hotel Santa Fe**, 935 Santa Fe Ave. at Tulare, tel. 266-2170. Plenty of good food at a fair price. Very good for Italian and seafood is **Nicola's**, four blocks west of Hwy. 41 (Shields Ave. exit) at 3075 N. Maroa Ave., tel. 224-1660. **Harland's**, tel. 225-7100, Fresno's hot haute place in the untraditional California cuisine tradition (elegant and expensive), is located at 722 W. Shaw Avenue. For exceptional French country classics with a San Joaquin touch (also expensive), the place is **The Ripe Tomato**, 5064 N. Palm Ave., tel. 225-1850. Of course **The Daily Planet** 1211 N. Wishon, tel. 266-4259, is out of this world. Art deco and delightful, with a weekly-changing menu featuring very contemporary American cuisine, starting with lobster quesadillas for appetizers.

Out there in Hanford southeast of Fresno is another surprise, the impeccable **Imperial Dynasty,** adjacent to the Taoist Temple at 2 China Alley, tel. (209) 582-0196. Middle of nowhere, perhaps, and not a Chinese restaurant, people jet in from everywhere for the gourmet fare. You can drop in for regular dinners but reservations are necessary well in advance for the daily-changing nine-course dinners that run from $50. The **Superior Dairy** ice cream parlor in Hanford is also worth a stop for its real ice cream, milkshakes, sodas, and sundaes. Try the S-O-S, truly excessive! And if you have the time, take in a movie or a show at the fabulous **Hanford Fox Theatre**, tel. 584-7423, worth the price of admission just to see the interior.

Fresno Events
And Entertainment
Fresno attracts some big-league entertainment, so the local events calendar is constantly changing. Fairly predictable area events include the **Fresno County Blossom Trail** tour in February, a self-guided motor tour of area orchards in bloom, plus other events and festivities. The annual **"Viva El Mariachi" Mexican Folk Music Festival** is held at the convention center in March. The two-day **Clovis Rodeo** in April includes bronc and bull riding plus a barbecue and dance. In early May, sometimes stretching out all month, is the **William Saroyan Festival**, honoring Fresno's own Pulitzer Prize winner with films, exhibits, walking tours, and Armenian food and dancing. Also in May, in nearby communities: the **Selma Raisin Festival** and the **Kingsburg Swedish Festival**. In late May or early June comes Selma's **Portuguese Festival**. The **Obon Odori Festival** is scheduled for July. But if you like county fairs, don't miss **The Fresno Fair** in September, one of the world's largest, lasting over two weeks.

Fresno's recently restored **Tower Theater**, 815 E. Olive, tel. (209) 485-9050, with its mural of "Leda and the Swan" and glass bas-relief of "The Huntsman," is a fabulous venue for local theater and other performances. The **Fresno Public Theater** presents most of its performances at the Bonner Auditorium inside the **Fresno Museum of Art**. The Good Company Players hold forth, theatrically, from their **Second Space Theatre** at 928 E. Olive, tel. 266-0660. The same troupe performs Broadway musicals for dinner theater at **Roger Rocka's Music Hall** at the corner of Olive and Wishon, 1226 N. Wishon, tel.

266-9494. (Cost for dinner and a show, $25 and up.) The **Fresno Dance Repertory Association,** 1432 E. Fulton, tel. 23-DANCE, is actually two local dance groups: The Fresno Ballet and the Aloha Polynesian Dance Troupe. The **Fresno Philharmonic Orchestra** performs a season of subscription concerts with occasional guests like Claudio Arrau, Roberta Peters, and Isaac Stern, in the William Saroyan Theatre in the city's Convention Center complex, tel. 485-3020. For current events and nightlife, pick up a copy of the *Fresno Bee.*

Visalia

This, officially, is Middle America. Not only is Visalia (like Fresno) located near the state's geographic center, market researchers have discovered that the likes and dislikes of Visalians are a microcosm of West Coast consumer preference. The best inexpensive place to stay here is the hard-to-find **Oak Tree Inn** shaded by oaks at 401 Woodland Dr., a block west of Mooney Blvd. and just south of the Hwy. 198 overpass, tel. (209) 732-8861. Rooms with a/c, pool, laundry facilities, refrigerators, from $30. The **Holiday Inn Plaza Park** is next to the airport, 9000 W. Airport Dr., tel. 651-5000, with rooms from $66, but the new **Visalia Radisson Hotel** on the corner of Mineral King and Court St., tel. 636-1111 or toll-free for reservations (800) 333-3333, is in the same general price range (some suites). Ask about specials.

Mearle's Drive-In at 604 S. Mooney Blvd., tel. (209) 734-4447, no longer has carhops but just hop inside for the 1950s ambience and burgers, fries, milkshakes, and 15 flavors of ice cream. A classic in the genre. **Kay's Kafe** at 215 N. Giddings, tel. 732-9036, is locally famous for its farm-style breakfast and hearty lunches. For good sandwiches and deli-style Greek food, stop by the **Mediterranean Grill** at 225 W. Main, tel. 738-1212, though the **Valley Bakery** at 502 M St., tel. 485-2700, is the place to pick up traditional Armenian pastries and breads. (For more of Visalia's homegrown, ask at the visitors bureau for a copy of the current "Tulare County Harvest Trail Guide," which also lists locations of area Certified Farmers' Markets.) For Visalia-style fine dining the place is **Vintage Press** at 216 N. Willis St., tel. 733-3033, with daily specials (predominantly seafood) and glorious desserts.

For more information about what's going on in Middle America, contact the **Visalia Convention and Visitors Bureau,** 70 W. Mineral King, Visalia 93291, tel. (209) 734-5876.

BAKERSFIELD

The center of the southern San Joaquin's oil field development, it's somehow appropriate that a pall of dingy gray smog almost always hangs over Bakersfield these days. In addition to working in the cotton fields and just plain living day to day, locals spend time at the mall south of town. Even on a Sunday, everyone seems to be there.

Another place to go, though, is the **Bakersfield Museum of Art** at 1930 R St. (P.O. Box 1911), Bakersfield 93303-1911, tel. (805) 323-7219, which served as artistic headquarters for Christo's 1991 *The Umbrellas* environmental art extravaganza, which marched up to and over Tejon Pass. Stop here to get a feel for the complexity of that adventure into temporary contemporary outdoor art—and to appreciate current shows, which emphasize Southern California artists.

Other diversions include the **Kern County Museum** at 3801 Chester Ave., tel. (805) 861-2132, the nearby 14-acre **Pioneer Village** (an excellent outdoor "museum" of buildings and other history from the 1860s), and the adjacent hands-on **Lori Brock Junior Museum.** Family oriented, too, is the **California Living Museum (CALM)** at 14000 Alfred Harrel Hwy., tel. 872-TOUR. Otherwise, show up for the two-week-long **Great Kern County Fair** from late August into September. Bakersfield and vicinity also features a symphony orchestra, theater troupes, country-western music and rodeos, and agricultural festivals celebrating everything from cotton and grapes to tomatoes and potatoes. (A fine diversion, anytime, is the you-pick **Al Bussell Ranch** 12 miles west of town on Stockdale Hwy., tel. 589-2677, California's largest direct market farm.) For more information about the area, contact the **Kern County Board of Trade,** 2101 Oak St., P.O. Bin 1312, Bakersfield 93302, tel. 861-2367.

Sights Near Bakersfield

To the east in the smogbound Sierra Nevada foothills is **Lake Isabella** in the Kern River Valley,

KIM WEIR

the schoolhouse at
Colonel Allensworth State Historic Park

tel. (619) 379-2742, popular for camping, fishing, and water sports. If heading through the area in mid-February, stop off in **Kernville** for Whiskey Flat Days, a celebration of the area's ripsnorting gold rush history. But stop anytime at **Paisano's,** 13428 Sierra Way, tel. 376-6028, for fabulous pancake breakfasts and French toast or the specialty, fresh pizzas and pastas. Other campable recreation lakes closer to Bakersfield proper include **Lake Webb** and adjacent, smaller Lake Evans just southeast of town, as well as **Ming Lake** and **Hart Lake** in Kern River Park to the northeast; they're all part of the Kern County Park system, 1110 Golden State, tel. (805) 861-2345.

Though the best outdoor destination around is the Nature Conservancy's huge **Carrizo Plain Preserve** west of Taft and Maricopa, there are other small preserves in and around Bakersfield, including the **Kern River Preserve** along the South Fork of the Kern River 60 miles northeast of the city, a nesting area for the rare yellow-billed cuckoo; call (619) 378-2531 for permission and directions. Farther north near Visalia

are the conservancy's **Creighton Ranch** and **Kaweah Oaks** preserves; call (209) 627-3428 for information and access permission.

An economically famous if somewhat frumpy outpost of oil history is **Taft,** home of the **West Kern Oil Museum, Inc.** on Wood St. west of Hwy. 33, tel. (805) 765-6664 or 765-7371, open just Sat., Sun., and Wed. 1-4 p.m. Farther north— to the east of I-5 and across the valley from Visalia, and just as significant for its role in California's oil development since the 1890s—is **Coalinga,** where the **R.C. Baker Memorial Museum** at 297 W. Elm Ave., tel. (209) 935-1914, tells a more detailed story about the area's cultural, economic, and geologic history. Coalinga hosts the longest-running hot air balloon rally in the United States. And if you're anywhere near Coalinga and I-5, stop at **Harris Ranch,** tel. (209) 935-0717, noted for its decent American food and very comfortable accommodations.

On the way to Taft a slight detour off Hwy. 33 via Stockdale and Morris roads leads to the disappointing **Tule Elk State Reserve,** Rt. 1, Box 42, Buttonwillow 93206, tel. (805) 765-5004, with herds of native tule elk confined in protective pastures since their native grassland range is now under the plow. Picnic areas and a five-acre viewing field for the public.

Also disappointing, but only for its apparent low priority in the state parks system, is nearby **Colonel Allensworth State Historic Park,** west of Hwy. 99 near Earlimart, the remnants of the only town in California founded by black Americans. Determined to develop a pragmatic yet utopian community, one dedicated to the values of education and economic independence and to the idea that blacks could live in equality with whites, Colonel Allen Allensworth (a former slave who won his freedom during the Civil War) arrived in the area in 1908 to stake a claim to a piece of the American dream. As the community grew, its early farming and other successes attracted more residents. In addition to the community schoolhouse (like some of the other buildings, beautifully restored), Allensworth dreamed of starting a major technical institute for black students—a proposal rejected by the state Legislature. Soon after his accidental death in L.A. in 1914, Allensworth's dreams turned to dust, as agricultural development elsewhere in the valley created a water shortage that choked off community progress.

In May come to the park for its annual **Allensworth Old Time Jubilee,** complete with living history programs, historic games, and special guided tours. In October is the park's annual rededication ceremony. With advance arrangements, visitors can stay overnight 1900s-style in the restored **Hindsman House** as part of Allensworth's environmental living program. In the works: a new **hotel-style bed and breakfast** with limited food service and the possibility of arrivals and departures via Amtrak trains. Otherwise, stay here at the open prairie campground just north of Allensworth proper, fairly new and as yet unshaded by its small trees, $8. For more information, contact: Colonel Allensworth State Historic Park, Star Rt. 1, Box 148, Earlimart 93219, tel. (805) 849-3433. To get there from Earlimart, turn right on J22 and take it five miles to Hwy. 43 (heading south)—two miles to Allensworth.

Bakersfield Accommodations

There are four **Motel 6** choices in Bakersfield: the first near downtown at 350 Oak St. off Brundage Ln. (California Ave. exit), adjacent to the highway, tel. (805) 326-1222, with the same usual features, $24-30; another south of town at 2727 White Ln. just off Hwy. 99, tel. 834-2828, same amenities, lower price. To locate the others, call 392-9700 or 366-7231. Other motel choices include Bakersfield's **Plaza Inn Travelodge,** 1030 Wible Rd. (Ming Ave. exit off Hwy. 99), tel. 834-3377, with the usual valley necessities (a/c, pool, TV, movies, phones) plus coin laundry, rooms $34-40. The **Best Western Oak Inn** at 889 Oak St., tel. 324-9686, has rooms from $50. Plusher is the **Sheraton Valley Inn,** 5101 California Ave., tel. 325-9700, with whirlpool and exercise room, $65-120. Other better accommodations include **Best Western Hill**

House, tel. 327-4064, and Marriott's **Courtyard,** tel. 324-6660.

Bakersfield Area Restaurants

One popular place for Basque fare is the **Wool Growers,** 620 E. 19th St., tel. (805) 327-9584. Excellent but more expensive is **Chalet Basque,** 200 Oak St., tel. 327-2915, featuring seven-course dinners—choose from seafood, beef, chicken, or lamb—including wonderful sourdough bread, pink beans and salsa, well-spiced green beans, fabulous French fries (the potatoes peeled by hand), Basque pudding for dessert. Popular for its early-bird specials and 12-course Basque meals is the contemporary **Maitia's Basque Restaurant** at 3535 N. Union St., tel. 324-4711 (entrees available without the full family-style setup). Then there's the **Noriega Hotel** at 525 Sumner St., tel. 322-8419, another good choice for family-style Basque dining. Everyone waits in the bar—fascinating place in its own right—until the dining room doors open and dinner begins. Call for current seating time.

Bakersfield also has more than its share of exceptional Mexican restaurants; ask around for local recommendations. For another cultural change-up, consider the very contemporary **Blue Note Restaurant** at the corner of Stine and Planz (4705 Planz Rd.), tel. (805) 835-0463, noted for its California cuisine with French and Northern Italian influences, served up with some light jazz. Very reasonable early dinner specials. Fabulous desserts. Open for lunch weekdays, for dinner daily. Or try **Jassaud's** at 1001 S. Union St., tel. 327-9810, noted for its continental fare and French atmosphere, open 9-5. **Mama Tosca's** at 6631 Ming Ave., tel. 831-1242, is the place for fine Italian food, including homemade pastas and desserts.

BOB RACE

THE DELTA

The ancient tule marshes created by the confluence of the Sacramento and San Joaquin rivers are long gone in California's great delta. The Sacramento-San Joaquin Delta is the largest estuary on the West Coast, and the second largest in the country, overshadowed only by Chesapeake Bay. But by contemporary California standards there's really nothing to *do* in the delta—no world-class sights, amusement parks, or zoos, no big-name entertainment, nightclubs, coffeehouses. This fact is the main attraction of the lazy labyrinth of backwater sloughs, canals, lakes, lagoons, and meandering rivers and streams. The personality and pace of the Deep South seep up throughout the delta; no one here was surprised when Samuel Goldwyn, Jr. picked it as the filming location for *Huckleberry Finn*. People come here to drive along the levees and count great blue herons, to watch drawbridges go up and down and ferries and freighters pass, to windsurf and sail and water-ski, or to houseboat like modern-day Huck Finns down unknown waterways in search of nothing in particular.

THE LAND

Since the last ice age and until the last century the delta was a jungle of oaks, sycamores, willows, and vines punctuated by thickets of tules and teeming with life: herds of tule elk, pronghorn, and deer; beavers, river otters, and foxes; migrating waterfowl and songbirds; rivers of fish and the grizzlies who fished for them. Life went on, eon after eon, and however much water flowed through the delta—and then, as now, the mighty Sacramento River contributed 70-80%—it was always enough. But the situation soon changed, beginning in the 1860s when California leaders urged settlers to come and save the delta from its own wildness, to "reclaim" it for productive use. The wetlands were sold off for $1 an acre to anyone willing to dike and drain them.

The land in California's great delta—whether agricultural or recreational—isn't really *land,* not in the usual sense of the word. Before completion of the delta's complex system of levees and

THE DELTA

© MOON PUBLICATIONS, INC.

dredged canals, the annual winter-spring flooding of the area was as predictable as rain and Sierra Nevada snow melt. Some islands emerged in summer and fall, or appeared only in dry years—a fact acceptable to the 30,000 or so native people who once lived off the region's natural bounty but too unpredictable for settlers determined to stake their ownership claims.

The delta is the largest water engineering network in the world, its century-old levee system built by Chinese laborers just finished with the transcontinental railroad. Before the advent of the clamshell dredge in the 1930s, hundreds of windmills once dotted the landscape, powering the pumps that first drained the area. Almost all Northern California river water eventually arrives in the delta; today up to 85% is channeled, diverted, and pumped south to irrigate farmland and to provide drinking water for some 20 million urbanites in the Bay Area and Los Angeles.

But even with levees and modern water-pumping stations in place, the struggle to control life and water here is difficult.

Out of that struggle has come innovation, such as snowshoe-like horseshoes for draft animals to keep them from sinking into mushy delta soils. With the arrival of agricultural machinery the same problem called for an equally novel solution. Thus delta resident Ben Holt devised the caterpillar tread tractor shortly after the turn of the century, just in time for the British to buy the idea and convert it to military use, producing tanks that would roll ahead with ensuing world wars, mucky ground or no.

DELTA SIGHTS

Only five of the delta's 70 major islands feature sizable development or towns. These include Bethel Island and its namesake subdivision; Byron Tract, home to Discovery Bay; Brannan-Andrus Island, with Brannan Island State Recreation Area and the town of Isleton; New Hope Tract and the town of Thornton; Hotchkiss Tract and Oakley. About halfway between Dixon and Rio Vista is Hastings Island, the largest private pheasant-hunting club in the U.S., tel. (916) 678-3325, which includes a small trailer park (five-year waiting list for spaces) and a full-service restaurant open only during pheasant season.

Many of the area's tiny towns and attractions are scattered around the delta's edges. The port city of Stockton, itself missable, is nonetheless a major jumping-off point for the southern delta. Rio Vista (via Hwy. 12) is a good place to start from in the north, Sacramento (via scenic Hwy. 160) in the east, and Antioch (over the Antioch Bridge via Hwy. 160) in the west.

STOCKTON

Billing itself as both "cosmopolitan and country," Stockton is mostly a bit strange, a hodge-podge of comfortable subdivisions and depressed ethnic neighborhoods, modern shopping centers, and a harbor district and partially devastated downtown now undergoing commercial redevelopment. But Stockton has its history. This place, after all, was the inspiration for the baseball poem "Casey at the Bat," first published in the *San Francisco Examiner*. Poetically speaking, this is Mudville.

Once known as Tuleberg, Stockton is now home to the University of the Pacific, which shares a campus with Delta College. In addition to its community ballet, civic theater, chorale group, opera, symphony, and art galleries, the city also boasts the fine art-and-history **Haggin Museum** (open 1:30-5 p.m., closed Mondays) in Victory Park and the indoor-outdoor San Joaquin County Historical Museum (largely an ode to agriculture) in nearby Micke Grove County Park.

Odd but fun is **Pollardville** and its **Palace Showboat Theatre** just off Hwy. 99 between Stockton and Lodi, a somewhat garish decades-old "ghost town," with a "chicken kitchen" restaurant—you can't miss the huge rooster on the sign—and theater featuring old-time melodramas (like "The Drunkard") and vaudeville acts. The shows, which are surprisingly good, usually run from mid-May through October; adult admission is $20 or so with dinner (optional), lower without. Most other facilities, attractions, and events are open (Sun.-Thurs. 11-9, Fri. and Sat. 11-10) or are scheduled year-round, such as the **Pollardville Gunfighters Shoot-Outs** on Main St. and rides on **Pollard's Chicken Kitchen Railroad**. For more information, contact: Pollardville, 10480 N. Hwy. 99, Stockton 95212, tel. (209) 931-0272. For theater information and reservations, contact: The Palace Showboat Theatre at Pollardville, tel. 931-0274 or toll-free (800) 339-0274.

A complete listing of area attractions and events, plus accommodations, restaurants, and nightclubs, is available through the local visitors bureau. A series of area brochures, about antique shops, the delta, the greater Stockton area, and San Joaquin County gold-rush stops, is especially worthwhile.

For more information about Stockton and vicinity, contact the **Stockton-San Joaquin Convention and Visitors Bureau** at 46 W. Fremont St., Stockton 95202, tel. (209) 943-1987 or toll-free (800) 888-8016.

Stockton Area Accommodations
Stockton has two **Motel 6** choices, the first east of town just off I-5 at Hwy. 88, 4100 Waterloo Rd., tel. (209) 931-9511, with rooms for $27, and the second to the west of town just off I-5 at Hwy. 4 (Charter Way), 1625 French Camp Turnpike Rd., tel. 467-3600, $22 and up. **Motel Orleans** at 3951 E. Budweiser Ct., tel. 931-9341, charges prices in the same range. Also in that neighborhood is the very nice **Stockton Inn Best Western**, 4219 Waterloo Rd., tel. 931-3131, with large rooms $60-85, some suites, whirlpool, pool. (There's another Best Western on Charter Way, tel. 948-0321.)

Near the Civic Center is Stockton's **Comfort Inn**, 1005 N. El Dorado St., tel. (209) 466-2711,

WHEN THE LEVEE BREAKS

Like the lyrics from a traditonal blues song—"When the levee breaks I'll have no place to stay"—in an area dependent on its dikes and levees for its very existence, what happens when this system becomes unreliable? No one knows. But one of these days we'll probably find out.

For one thing, the levees themselves never were strong. Built of the area's loose peat soils and vulnerable even to gophers, they break when floodwaters threaten—more frequently all the time, despite increasing water diversions. During the past 100 years, each of the delta's 70 major islands and tracts has flooded at least once and since 1930 some have flooded several times. Meanwhile delta islands have been steadily "sinking" at a rate of three to five inches per year. And as they do, internal water pressure against the levees increases. When

a break occurs under these circumstances, ocean water from the Bay Area flows into the resulting water-pressure vacuum, adding salinity to the delta's freshwater ecosystem and, potentially, all interconnected federal and state water projects. Also, delta levees—in an area with five separate known fault lines—are unusually vulnerable to earthquakes. The peat soil itself is a particular problem, since it tends to amplify quake vibrations.

These problems are compounded by others, such as soil erosion. Since 1976, the dollar value of delta crops has plummeted by two-thirds; the fact that agricultural islands have the weakest levees has also affected agricultural productivity. Estimates of how much it will cost to repair or rebuild the Sacramento-San Joaquin levee system range to $4-10 billion or more. For some reason no one wants to pick up that tab.

reasonably priced rooms. The **Hotel Inn Plum Tree Plaza,** formerly the Plaza Hotel, on the corner of El Dorado at 111 E. March Ln., tel. 474-3301, offers rooms from $80. (Inquire about specials.) Also north of Stockton proper is the **Stockton Hilton** hotel off March Ln. at 2323 Grand Canal Blvd., tel. 957-9090, with rooms from $75-127.

Quite nice near Stockton is the **Wine and Roses Country Inn** at 2505 W. Turner Rd., Lodi 95242, tel. (209) 334-6988, an elegant country-style bed and breakfast, $85-95 weekdays, $105-115 on weekends. Country French dinners on Fri. and Sat., also Sunday brunch.

Stockton Food

Well worth a stop for early risers is the **Stockton Farmers Market** downtown under the freeway every Saturday morning from 7 a.m.-noon (though the show's really over by 9 or so), an amazing multicultural convention of San Joaquin farmers and international produce (some varieties with no name in the English language). Stockton even offers some ethnic variety in its restaurants, from (for Mexican) **Chevy's Fresh Mex** at 29 E. March Ln., tel. (209) 951-9915, and **Chili Pepper** at 235 N. Center St., tel. 467-3636, to **Bagatelle** (French) at 295 Lincoln Center, tel. 473-3227, and **De Parsia's** (Italian) at 3404 N. Delaware, tel. 944-9196. Time-honored in Stockton (since 1898) for reasonable

Cantonese fare is **On Lock Sam** downtown at 333 S. Sutter St., tel. 466-4561, full bar, reservations wise.

Another local tradition is the popular **Ye Olde Hoosier Inn** family restaurant at 1537 N. Wilson Way, tel. (209) 463-0271, open daily 7 a.m.-10 p.m. for American standards (most not quite living up to the Hoosier's reputation). Part of the popular chain, **La Boulangerie** near the Hilton at 2324 Grand Canal Blvd., tel. 478-4780, is a French bakery-style establishment with excellent coffee, croissants (try the raisin custard), and sandwiches (such as Swiss cheese with pesto). **Alberts** at 8103 N. Hwy. 99, tel. 476-1763, is refined and unusual, serving primarily Portuguese fare. Dress code. Reservations.

Shannon's Seafood just across from the Quail Lakes Shopping Center at 4722 Quail Lakes Dr., tel. (209) 952-1637, is a safe bet for lunch, dinner, and Sunday brunch. On the waterfront is **The Fish Market,** 445 W. Weber Ave., tel. 946-0991, with a good selection of fresh seafood, from crab salad and oysters on the half shell to grilled sea bass. Reservations advisable. Continental and French, excellent, and upscale by Stockton standards is **Le Bistro** north of town in the Village Square Shopping Center, 3121 W. Benjamin Holt Dr., tel. 951-0885, specializing in seafood and open weekdays for lunch and dinner, Sat. and Sun. for dinner only. Opera performances seasonally.

OTHER DELTA DESTINATIONS

Locke

The Chinese community of Locke sprang to life in 1915 shortly after nearby Walnut Grove's Chinatown burned to the ground. America's last rural Chinatown and listed on the National Register of Historic Places, today Locke has the look of a faded frontier town and consists of little more than levee-bound Main Street, one block long, with weatherbeaten wood frames leaning out over the narrow, pickup-lined street. But Locke in its prime was home to 2,000 or so Chinese and had general stores, herb shops, fish markets, a hotel, a dozen boarding houses, even the Star Theatre, where Chinese opera was performed. In the roaring twenties and through the Depression, Locke was also known for its Caucasian brothels and speak-easies and Chinese gambling houses and opium dens —attractive to both bone-tired field workers seeking escape from their dismal lives and big-city sophisticates out slumming.

Locke, the last rural Chinatown in America

DAVE HURST

Open on weekends only, the **Dai Loy Museum** is a former gambling house which was in business from 1916 to 1950. Displays include gamblers' artifacts, old photos, and gaming tables set up for fan-tan and flying bull, as well as testimony to the vital role of the Chinese in delta development. Almost a museum is **Al the Wop's** bar and restaurant, exuding delta cultural history (and crammed with farmers, ranch hands, and tourists), with local wisdom behind the bar and jars of peanut butter and jelly on every table.

Locke, itself a museum, is the center of various commercial-development proposals which preservationists fear will destroy its historic Chinese character. An excellent book about Locke is *Bitter Melon: Stories from the Last Rural Chinese Town in America* by Jeff Gillenkirk and James Motlow, published by The University of Washington Press.

Near Locke is **Delta Meadows River Park,** a portion of California's everglades—tule marshes and shady sloughs with water hyacinths and pond lilies, particularly popular with houseboaters for overnight anchorage. To get there from Locke head south, turn left off Hwy. 160 at the Tigas Company (onto Twin Cities Road).

Walnut Grove

Three miles from Ryde and a hop across the Delta Cross Channel from Locke is tiny Walnut Grove, the only town south of Red Bluff to occupy both banks of the Sacramento River. Reputed to be a lair for riverboat bandits in its early days, the town today is serene and sleepy, a farm community with little left of its Chinese past except a block-long strip of boarded-up bareboard buildings, a ghost town Chinatown sprinkled with Chinese-American groceries. Walnut Grove's modern claim to fame is football, since three NFL players—including Tony Eason, the New England Patriots' quarterback who got the team to the 1986 Super Bowl—grew up here, starting their football careers at Delta High School in Clarksburg. (Somewhat baffled about this, some people here say it's the delta water that grows so many big bruisers.)

Isleton

Another delta town with a Chinatown past is Isleton on Andrus Island, today a tin-sided shadow of its former self. In the 1930s, Isleton billed itself as The Asparagus Center of the World, since 90% of the world's canned asparagus was grown and processed in the area. During post-fire rebuilding in the 1920s and '30s, Japanese-Americans also became an integral part of the community. Gambling and prostitution once flourished along today's boarded-up Main Street. During World War II the population declined when residents of Japanese descent were shipped off to California internment camps; after the war the decline continued as area canneries relocated elsewhere.

Isleton only really comes to life these days during the community's Crawdad Festival, but a mix of old and new businesses, including the **Quong Wo Sing Co.** hardware and general store, the **Dragon Lady** art gallery, and **The Harmony Shop** porcelain doll emporium, are scattered among abandoned storefronts and two decent local restaurants. A good place to picnic just north of Isleton is **Hogback Island County Park** (free). To get there, from Hwy. 160 take Poverty Rd. north to its intersection with Walker Landing Rd., then turn left and continue on to the levee and Walker Landing's intersection with Grand Island Rd.; facilities include barbecues, picnic tables, and restrooms.

Rio Vista And Humphrey The Whale

Rio Vista, a small town astride Hwy. 12 just across the drawbridge from Brannan-Andrus Island, is most famous for a 45-ton celebrity humpback whale named Humphrey, who swam into the delta and up the Sacramento River in the fall of 1985, apparently determined to become the first whale to live in the community. Lost for weeks in nearby backwaters and sloughs after taking a wrong turn through the Golden Gate on his way to Mexico, Humphrey was an endangered individual of an endangered species.

His official rescuers at first maintained a hands-off policy, hoping the whale would realize his error, turn around, and swim the 55 miles back to sea. When it became clear that Humphrey couldn't or wouldn't make the trip on his own, marine biologists attempted to herd him with boats, lure him back to sea with recorded sounds of whales eating, or scare him downriver with killer whale sounds and by pounding on underwater pipes. But Humphrey the wrongway whale didn't budge until he was good and ready—which was after he was treated to the

sounds of whales mating—and even then he kept changing his mind and swimming back upriver. Prodded almost all the way out to the ocean, at one point Humphrey was the focus of 11 Navy vessels included in a flotilla of 30 boats determined to keep him going through San Pablo Bay. The world cheered when Humphrey finally swam—this time in the right direction—under the Golden Gate Bridge.

Humphrey made it home, and has survived. But that Humphrey is/was one travelin' fool. He's been spotted in some 25 different places since 1985, usually headed for land. The following year, the whale made another big splash when he was spotted near the Farallon Islands outside the Golden Gate. He was spotted again in 1987 and 1988, cavorting and feeding with other humpbacks near Bodega Bay. He beached himself in Bodega Bay on one outing. Then he came back to the Bay Area again, in 1990, apparently determined to finish his vacation. On that trip he skipped the delta and instead dawdled away a day or so, stuck in the rocks near Candlestick Park before another Coast Guard rescue. A short poem by 12-year-old Rio Vista resident Richard Fonbuena, inscribed on the town's monument to Humphrey, summarizes the event for all time:

> *Humphrey the Humpback whale,*
> *a mighty whale was he.*
> *He swam into the Delta to see*
> *what he could see.*
> *The people stood and stared.*
> *The fish was scared.*
> *He was famous across the nation*
> *until they ended his vacation.*

Sightseeing humans might peek into the **Rio Vista Museum** at 16 N. Front St., tel. (707) 374-5169, open 1:30-4:30 p.m. weekends only—a one-time blacksmith shop with several rooms of area memorabilia telling the story of Rio Vista. One wall is covered with old license plates and newspaper front pages.

Sailboarding is particularly popular in the open expanses of the Sacramento River near Rio Vista. Other Rio Vista diversions include the Bay Area Electric Railroad Association's **Western Railway Museum** at the Hwy. 12-Rio Vista Junction, featuring over 100 street-

KIM WEIR

Isleton is famous these days for its annual Crawdad festival—and the infamous Isleton Ike Sextet: "We ain't good, but we're cheap."

cars and railroad cars, also a small looping track for 15-minute rides. Open weekends and holidays from 11 a.m.-5 p.m., small fee. Or ride the *Nostalgia Train* for an 18-mile roundtrip, weekends only from October to December— very popular, so reservations are advisable. Pullman lounge car service aboard a 1930s lounge car includes deluxe "accommodations" and continental breakfast (with juices, coffee, tea, and Mimosas) served by uniformed museum volunteers; adults $25, children $12. Coach service aboard 1920s Suburban cars is perfect for picnicking; adults $10, children $6. Groups of up to 15 can opt for caboose service and have the whole kit and kaboodle for $175. Special family-oriented runs include *The Ghost Train,* a safe alternative to trick-or-treating just before Halloween (coach service only), and *The Santa Claus Limited* scheduled for two consecutive weekends prior to Christmas. For more information, contact the Western Railway Museum, P.O. Box 8136, Berkeley 94707-8136, tel. (510) 456-2166.

From Rio Vista, head north for a free ride on one of the delta's few remaining ferries, this one an authentic passenger ship requiring a licensed navigator at the helm. The **Ryer Island Ferry** *Real McCoy* navigates Cache Slough from Ryer Island Rd. off Hwy. 160 to Ryer Island. For another down-home delta crossing, turn right and follow the levee road to Steamboat Slough and the *J-Mack* cable-driven ferry, which runs to Grand Island and its landmark 1917 **Grand Island Mansion.**

Brannan Island State Recreation Area

Not a natural environment by any means, open, often wind-blown Brannan Island State Recreation Area several miles south of Rio Vista is nonetheless an ideal spot for picnicking, year-round camping, and recreational pursuits from boating and sailboarding to fishing and swimming. Flanked on three sides by the Sacramento River, Seven Mile Slough, and Three Mile Slough and accessible via Hwy. 160, Brannan Island's facilities include two family camping areas (the Willow and Cottonwood campgrounds); six group camps; 32 boat-in campsites with boat berths; boat-launching ramps; a public swimming beach and picnic area; a rally site for RVs; a sanitation station (but no RV hookups).

Accessible only by boat across Piper Slough from Bethel Island, **Franks Tract State Recreation Area** five miles southeast of Brannan Island is now largely underwater due to levee breakage. The large "lake" here offers exceptional fishing. **Little Franks Tract** is a marsh area rich in natural vegetation and wildlife (no hunting, no fires) and still protected by the levees.

Camping at Brannan Island is popular, $14 basic fee, cold showers only (outside restrooms). Camping reservations through Mistix, tel. (800) 444-7275, are usually necessary from March through October. The basic day-use fee for Brannan Island is $5. To help celebrate National Fishing Week in June, the park sponsors a children's fishing derby. For more information, contact: Brannan Island/Franks Tract State

Recreation Areas, 17645 Hwy. 160, Rio Vista 95471, tel. (916) 777-6671.

Grizzly Island State Recreation Area

Adjacent to privately owned portions of Solano County's Suisin Marsh is Grizzly Island State Recreation Area. Now only semi-vast after a century of reclamation but still one of the world's richest estuarine marshes, the marsh has no grizzlies these days, but tule elk, "the little elk of the prairie," have come home again. Believed extinct over 100 years ago, California's tule elk population is making quite a comeback everywhere the species has been reintroduced. (March and April are the best months for observing the matriarchal tule elk during calving season, also for watching river otters.)

Corraled by delta levees, the Grizzly Island area includes 1,887-acre Joice Island near the on-site headquarters and 8,600-acre Grizzly Island proper. Waterfowl hunting (by permit only, these issued at the headquarters on Wednesdays and weekends only in season) is popular here, as is fishing. With over a million birds wintering here, birdwatchers and hikers rule the roost when hunters aren't afield. For more information, contact: Grizzly Island, Region 3 Headquarters, Dept. of Fish and Game, P.O. Box 47, Yountville 94599, tel. (707) 944-2443.

Also popular with waterfowl hunters and fisherfolk is the state's **Lower Sherman Island Wildlife Area** at the confluence of the Sacramento and San Joaquin rivers, a delta island reclaimed by the forces of nature, with boat access only beyond the parking lot—fun to explore by canoe outside hunting season but only with great care, due to the area's strong tidal currents and sudden high winds (usually in the afternoon). For more information, call (916) 355-7010 during regular business hours.

DELTA PRACTICALITIES

Delta Accommodations

Most popular for overnights in the delta is houseboating. The cost for houseboat rentals is almost reasonable for groups and families when calculated per person, and summer reservations are necessary many months in advance. (Count on better rates and less advance planning, depending on weather trends, in the spring and autumn off-season.) For houseboat rental sources, see "Information" below.

Camping at **Brannan Island State Recreation Area** (see above) for both boaters and landlubbers is another popular option, though campers can also try **Sandy Beach County Park** on Beach Dr. in Rio Vista, tel. (707) 374-2097, tent sites, RVs OK but no hookups. The delta is dotted with private campground-cabin complexes as well, with motel accommodations also available at some local resorts. For local listings, refer to Hal Schell's "Delta Map and Guide" (see "Information" below). The former Ryde Hotel, now the **Grand Island Inn,** offers reasonable to moderately expensive hotel rooms (see restaurant listing below). The **River Rose, A Country Inn** at 8201 Freeport Blvd., Freeport 95832, tel. (916) 665-1998, is a new Early American-style B&B across the road from the Sacramento River. (One of these days, when the route for the Old Sac line extends this far, you may be able to come and go from Sacramento by steam train.) All 10 rooms are countrified and quiet, yet feature modern comforts such as private bathrooms and two-person whirlpool tubs. Full breakfast. Rates: $105-145. Rooms at the **The Delta Daze Inn** bed and breakfast in Isleton, tel. (916) 777-7777, all feature private baths—and free ice-cream parlor privileges.

Good Food Delta Style

Just south of Sacramento in Freeport, a popular stop is the original **A.J. Bump's Saloon** and restaurant, tel. (916) 665-2251. Also here on the edge of the delta is **Peter B's Freeport Inn,** tel. 665-1169, open for breakfast, lunch, and dinner, known for the chicken, seafood, and steaks (especially the New York strip) carefully cooked up in the restaurant's smoker. Lighter menu items and nightly specials, too. The **Courtland Docks** on Hwy. 160 in Courtland, tel. 775-1172, is a great stop for breakfast or lunch (homemade soups, good burgers, excellent apple pie), dinners on Fri. and Sat. nights only. Funky and fun. Try the World Famous Pear Na Colada. Closed Tuesdays.

Especially in smaller areas, even popular restaurants are open only seasonally, spring through fall.

Among the delta's most historically notorious stops is the **Ryde Hotel** on Hwy. 160 in Ryde, which housed a password-only speak-easy casino and dancehall in its basement during Prohibition. Later a popular bikers' bar and flophouse, the Ryde Hotel has since been restored to its grand 1920s style when people like Al Jolson and Herbert Hoover used to drop by. Now painted pink outside and art deco gray and pink inside, it's known as the **Grand Island Inn** (though it still says "Ryde Hotel" on the neon sign), tel. (916) 776-1318, and offers standard rooms with shared baths for $50, suites $80-99 (and the summer season books early). Dinners (full bar) include California country-style entrees like pan-fried catfish and Cajun-spiced pork tenderloin. Breakfast, lunch, and Sunday brunch also served. Seasonal. Restaurant open weekends April through October.

The place to stop in Locke is known locally as **Al The Wop's** (but officially called Al's Place in these more ethnically respectful times), tel. (916) 776-1800, noted for its very good grilled steak sandwiches, music video jukebox, and stuffed moose heads and ostrich. A small bribe may be all it takes to get the bartender to share the secret of how all those dollar bills got thumbtacked to the ceiling. (Hint: experiment origami-style with a dollar bill, a silver dollar, and a thumbtack.) Once a year management cleans the money off the ceiling to finance employee vacations *and* the world-famous Al the Wop's free liver-and-onions feed (usually held in February). Otherwise open spring through fall.

Popular and quite good in Walnut Grove is **Tony's**, tel. (916) 776-1317, which serves only two entrees at dinner: 20-ounce grilled New York steaks or breaded veal cutlets with Mornay sauce, both with all the trimmings. Outside Walnut Grove, on Walnut Grove Rd. near the Miller's Ferry Bridge over the north fork of the Mokelumne River, is **Giusti's**, tel. 776-1808, one of Erle Stanley Gardner's favorite places and fine for country-style Italian fare. (Note the hundreds of baseball and tractor caps on the walls.) Excellent California wine list. Reservations usually necessary weeks in advance for weekends. Open seasonally.

Just east of Giusti's is **Wimpy's Marina**, tel. (209) 794-2544, a homey American cafe with coffeecake and apple pie, hearty breakfasts and burgers, and an all-you-can-eat fried chicken dinner on Saturday nights from 5-9 p.m. Also near Walnut Grove is the four-story **Grand Island Mansion**, a 58-room Southern-style

---

UNIQUE DELTA ENTERTAINMENT: POKER RUNS

Entertainment in the delta falls into two basic categories: outdoor recreation and barhopping. Ever ingenious, delta residents have long combined the two into periodic "poker runs," unique barhopping-by-boat events where up to 500 or so boaters stop off at participating waterside watering holes to pick up playing cards for "the game." Among locally favorite runs is **Moore's Riverboat Poker Run** in May and **Wimpy's Poker Run** in June. Poker run or no, a perennially popular delta-style bar is **Lost Isle** at the Lost Isle Marina, a thatched-roof hideout accessible only by boat which hosts the **Lost Isle Luau** in August.

---

palace on the banks of Steamboat Slough popular for business retreats, private parties, and weddings but also for its $17 Sunday brunch, 10:30 a.m.-2 p.m. Reservations usually necessary, tel. (916) 775-1705.

Rogelio's on Main St. in Isleton, tel. (916) 777-6606, is popular for both Chinese and Mexican fare. Lunch and dinner daily, plus 24-hour card room. Also here is the **Croissanterie,** 7 Main St., tel. 777-6170, a light, airy, pleasant place open 7 a.m.-10 p.m. and a citified sign of the delta's changing times: everything from croissants and breakfast quiche to sandwiches and light suppers. Try the crawfish étouffée with hot French bread. **Ernie's,** 212 2nd St., tel. 777-6510, a venerable cafe and saloon going upscale but still specializing in asparagus and crawdads, is also open for breakfast, lunch, and dinner. Well south of Isleton at 106 W. Brannan Island Rd. is **Moore's Riverboat,** tel. 777-6545, the 1931 vessel *Fort Sutter* refitted as a restaurant and serving up some of the area's best crawdads (plastic bibs provided) and other seafood specialties like grilled calamari and baked red snapper. Live rock 'n' roll on weekend nights. Open weekends-only in the off-season.

Wild in Rio Vista is the non-vegetarian **Foster's Big Horn** on Main St., tel. (707) 374-2511, noted for its 250 big-game "trophies," including a 13-foot-tall bull elephant, part of one of the world's largest private collections (reputed to be worth $1.5 million and reputed to be for sale; call if decor matters). **The Point Restaurant,** at

120 Marina Dr., tel. 374-5400, a half-mile south of Hwy. 12 and Rio Vista proper via Main then 2nd St., offers American fare and riverside views at both lunch and dinner, open daily except Mondays and the week between Christmas and New Year's. Reservations wise at dinner.

On Miner Slough a few miles from the Ryer Island Ferry is the **Golden Gate Island Resort** (no phone, accessible only by boat) which serves snacks and beer aboard a huge dredge now doing duty as an art gallery, flea market, and de facto museum. Behind the Dutch Slough levee near Bethel Island is **The Artist Table** restaurant, tel. (510) 684-3414, a humble-looking cottage serving excellent food. Reservations mandatory.

Delta Events

The **Frozen Bun Run** water-skiing challenge on New Year's morning at Boyd's Harbor on Bethel Island is (they say) unforgettable, though those who miss it due to hangovers can participate in the similar **Polar Freeze** at Windmill Cove, usually held on the first Sunday of the new year. Also in January comes the next best thing to Christmas for delta folks: Stockton's annual **Ag Expo,** with row upon row of agricultural equipment, products, and services on display.

The **Miss San Joaquin County Regatta** is a boat parade sponsored in early March by the Stockton Yacht Club. The artsy-craftsy **Stockton Asparagus Festival** in Oak Grove Regional Park usually comes in late April. May's traditional **Portuguese Festa** in Clarksburg includes an auction, dances, food, and a parade. In mid-May, Rio Vista holds its popular **Trans-Delta Hobie Cat Race.** Also in May Stockton hosts the **San Joaquin County Spring Festival** celebration of ethnic diversity, as well as its annual **Arts Festival,** but the big deal is big-time boat and drag-boat racing on tap at the **Budweiser Boat Races** in June.

An even bigger draw, though, is Isleton's June **Crawdad Festival,** a weekend-long shindig featuring crawdads (also known as crayfish and crawfish) boiled alive and spiced Louisiana Cajun style, a fairly new food fest attracting upwards of 125,000 people. In June, too, is the **Bethel Island Boat Show,** a showcase also featuring crawdad races and other entertainment. (Boat shows, parades, and regattas abound year-round.) Celebrating Independence Day is also a major event in the delta, with Venice Island July 4th fireworks the most impressive. Also in July comes Courtland's **Pear Fair,** with pear-peeling and pear pie-eating contests, and the crowning of the community's much-admired Queen of the Pears. In August comes the **San Joaquin County Fair** in Stockton and the **Alligator Races** at Haven Acres Resort, where inflatable reptiles ply the waters in good-natured competition, not to mention the **Tracy Dry Bean Festival** and the **Filipino Barrio Festival.** In fall (usually the first week in October) is the famous four-day **Rio Vista Bass Derby,** billed as California's oldest bass-fishing competition. Come December, don't miss the **Oxbow Marina Lighted Boat Christmas Parade.**

Information

Fans of Perry Mason might poke around in delta-area stores, old bookshops, and libraries for copies of the three books Erle Stanley Gardner wrote about his delta experiences. Though good books, maps, and pamphlets are locally available, the best basic source of information about what to do and where to go in the delta—with everything from houseboat rental listings and tour boat information to ferry facts; from anchorage, marina, and fishing tips to tide corrections and water depths—is "Hal Schell's Delta Map and Guide," available at marinas, stores, information centers, and the Brannan Island State Recreation Area visitor center.

For more detailed local information, contact the **Stockton Visitors and Convention Bureau** (see "Stockton," above) or any of the chambers of commerce from the following locales: **Bethel Island,** P.O. Box 263, 94511, tel. (510) 684-3220; **Byron,** P.O. Box 368, 94514, tel. (510) 634-2860; **Isleton,** P.O. Box 758, 95641, tel. (916) 777-5880; **Rio Vista,** 60 Main St., 94571, tel. (707) 374-2700; **Sacramento,** 917 7th St., 95814, tel. (916) 443-3771; and **Tracy,** P.O. Box 891, 95376, tel. (209) 835-2131.

For information on delta cruises, some of which depart from West Sacramento, see "Transport" in the Sacramento chapter.

BOB RACE

THE MONTEREY BAY AREA
INTRODUCTION

The only remembered line of the long-lost Ohlone people's song of world renewal, "dancing on the brink of the world," has a particularly haunting resonance around Monterey Bay. Here, in the unfriendly fog and ghostly cypress along the untamed coast, the native "coast people" once danced. Like the area's vanished dancers, Monterey Bay is a mystery: everything seen, heard, tasted, and touched only hints at what remains hidden.

The first mystery is magnificent Monterey Bay itself, almost 60 miles long and 13 miles wide. Its offshore canyons, grander than Arizona's Grand Canyon, are the area's most impressive (if unseen) feature: the bay's largest submarine valley dips to 10,000 feet, and the adjacent tidal mudflats teem with life.

A second mystery is how two cities as different as Santa Cruz and Monterey could both take root and thrive on the shores of Monterey Bay.

One Bay, Many Worlds
Working-class Santa Cruz has the slightly seedy Boardwalk, sandy beaches, good swim-

ming, surfers, and—helped along by the presence of UC Santa Cruz—an intelligent and open-minded social scene. Nearby are the redwoods, waterfalls, and mountain-to-sea hiking trails of Big Basin, California's first state park, plus the Año Nuevo coastal area, the world's only mainland mating ground for the two-ton northern elephant seal. The monied Monterey Peninsula to the south is fringed by shifting sand dunes and some of the state's most ruggedly wild coastline. Near Monterey is peaceful Pacific Grove (where alcohol has been legal only since the 1960s), Carmel-by-the-Sea (where Clint Eastwood recently made everybody's day as mayor), and inland Carmel Valley (a tennis pro playground abounding in shopping centers). The Carmel Highlands hug the coast on the way south to Big Sur.

Just inland is the agriculturally rich Salinas Valley, boyhood stomping grounds of John Steinbeck. Steinbeck's focus on Depression-era farm workers unleashed great local wrath—all but forgotten and forgiven since his fame has subsequently benefited area tourism. Not far

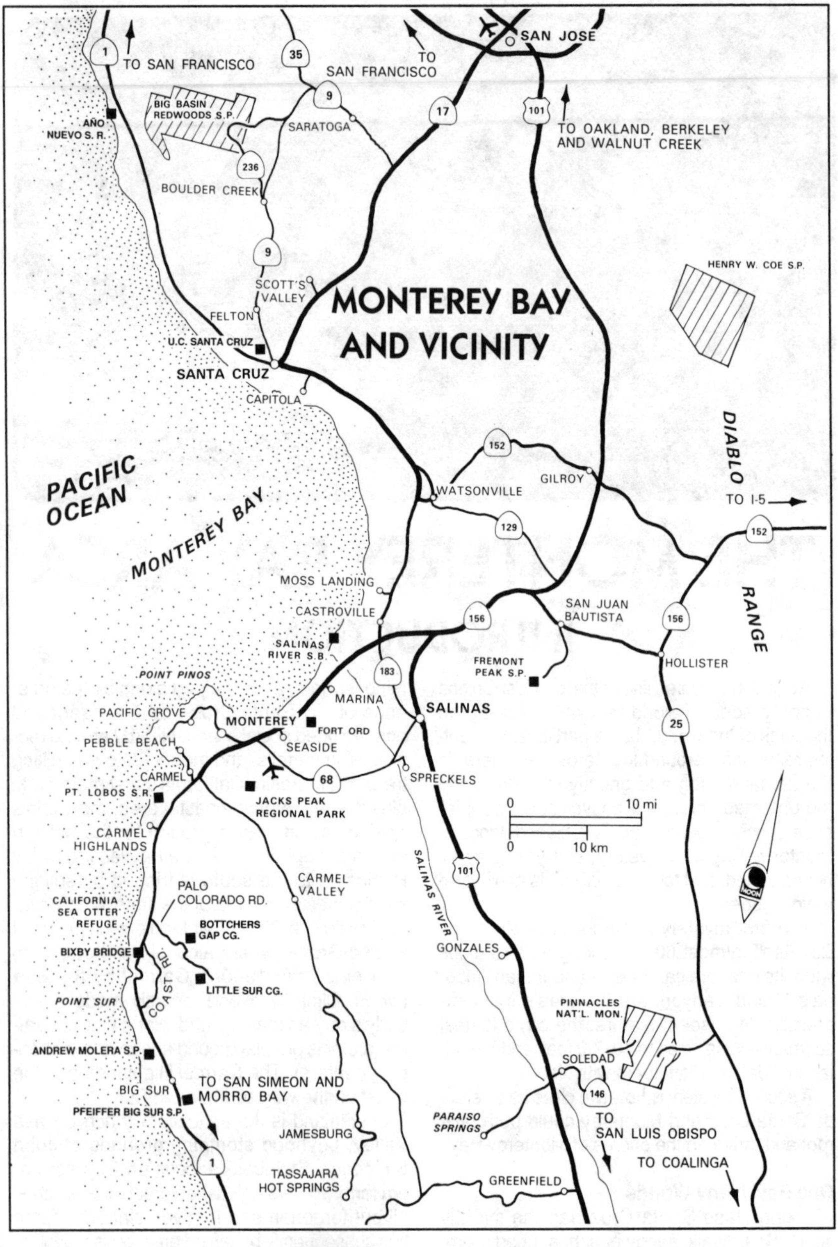

MONTEREY BAY AND VICINITY
PACIFIC OCEAN
MONTEREY BAY
TO SAN FRANCISCO
TO SAN FRANCISCO
SAN JOSE
TO OAKLAND, BERKELEY AND WALNUT CREEK
BIG BASIN REDWOODS S.P.
AÑO NUEVO S. R.
SARATOGA
BOULDER CREEK
SCOTT'S VALLEY
FELTON
U.C. SANTA CRUZ
SANTA CRUZ
CAPITOLA
HENRY W. COE S.P.
DIABLO RANGE
GILROY
WATSONVILLE
TO I-5
MOSS LANDING
CASTROVILLE
SALINAS RIVER S.B.
SAN JUAN BAUTISTA
HOLLISTER
FREMONT PEAK S.P.
POINT PINOS
PACIFIC GROVE
MONTEREY
FORT ORD
MARINA
SALINAS
SEASIDE
PEBBLE BEACH
CARMEL
PT. LOBOS S.R.
JACKS PEAK REGIONAL PARK
SPRECKELS
CARMEL HIGHLANDS
0 10 mi
0 10 km
CARMEL VALLEY
SALINAS RIVER
CALIFORNIA SEA OTTER REFUGE
PALO COLORADO RD.
BOTTCHERS GAP CG.
BIXBY BRIDGE
COAST RD.
LITTLE SUR CG.
POINT SUR
GONZALES
PINNACLES NAT'L. MON.
ANDREW MOLERA S.P.
SOLEDAD
BIG SUR
TO SAN SIMEON AND MORRO BAY
PFEIFFER BIG SUR S.P.
PARAISO SPRINGS
TO SAN LUIS OBISPO
JAMESBURG
TO COALINGA
TASSAJARA HOT SPRINGS
GREENFIELD
1
35
9
17
101
236
9
152
129
152
156
156
183
25
68
101
146
1
MOON
© MOON PUBLICATIONS, INC.

north, right on the San Andreas Fault, is Mission San Juan Bautista (where Jimmy Stewart and Kim Novak fought about his fear of heights in Hitchcock's *Vertigo*). Nearby are the headwaters of San Benito Creek, where lucky rockhounds might stumble upon some gem-quality, clear or sapphire-blue samples of the state's official gemstone, benitoite, found only here. Also in the neighborhood is Gilroy, self-proclaimed garlic capital of the world.

South of Salinas and east of Soledad is Pinnacles National Monument, the least visited of all national parks yet a fascinating volcanic jumble and almost "the peak" for experienced rock climbers.

THE LAND

Much of the redwood country from San Francisco to Big Sur resembles the boulder-strewn, rough-and-tumble north coast. Here the Pacific Ocean is far from peaceful; posted warnings about dangerous swimming conditions and undertows are no joke. Inland, the San Andreas Fault menaces, veering inland from the eastern side of the Coast Ranges through the Salinas Valley and on to the San Francisco Bay Area.

The Monterey Peninsula

Steinbeck captured the mood of the Monterey Peninsula in *Tortilla Flats*—"The wind . . . drove the fog across the pale moon like a thin wash of watercolor. . . . The treetops in the wind talked huskily, told fortunes and foretold deaths." The peninsula juts into the ocean 115 miles south of San Francisco and forms the southern border of Monterey Bay. The north shore sweeps in a crescent toward Santa Cruz and the Santa Cruz Mountains; east is the oak- and pine-covered Santa Lucia Range, rising in front of the barren Gabilan ("Sparrow Hawk") Mountains beloved by Steinbeck. Northward are the ecologically delicate Monterey Bay Dunes, now threatened by off-road vehicles and development. To the south the piney hills near Point Pinos and Asilomar overlook rocky crags and coves dotted with wind-sculpted trees; farther south, beyond Carmel and the Pebble Beach golf mecca, is Point Lobos, Robert Louis Stevenson's inspiration for Spyglass Hill in *Treasure Island*.

Monterey "Canyon"

Discovered in 1890 by George Davidson, Monterey Bay's submerged valley teems with sealife: bioluminescent fish glowing vivid blue to red,

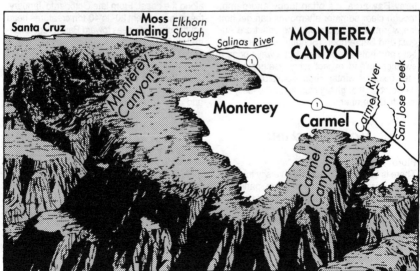

squid, tiny rare octopi, tentacle-shedding jellyfish, and myriad microscopic plants and animals—one of the most biologically prolific spots on the planet. Swaying with the ocean's motion, dense kelp thickets are home to sea lions, seals, sea otters, and giant Garibaldi "goldfish." Opal-eyed perch in schools of hundreds swim by leopard sharks and bottom fish. In the understory near the rocky ocean floor live abalones, anemones, crabs, sea urchins, and starfish.

Students of Monterey Canyon geology quibble over the origins of this unusual underwater valley. Computer-generated models of canyon creation suggest that the land once used to be near Bakersfield and was carved out by the Colorado River; later it shifted westward due to plate tectonics. More conventional speculation focuses on the creative forces of both the Sacramento and San Joaquin rivers, which perhaps once emptied at Elkhorn Slough, Monterey Canyon's principal "head."

Climate

The legendary California beach scene is almost a fantasy here—almost but not quite. Sunshine warms the sands (between storms) from fall to early spring, but count on fog from late spring well into summer. Throughout the Monterey Bay area, it's often foggy and damp, though clear summer afternoons can get hot; the warmest months along the coast are August and September. (Sunglasses, suntan lotion, and hats are prudent, but always bring a sweater.) Inland, expect hotter weather in summer, colder in winter. Rain is possible as early as October, though big storms don't usually roll in until December.

FLORA AND FAUNA

Flora

There is tremendous botanic diversity throughout California's central coast region, particularly near Monterey. Among the varied vascular plant species found regionally is the Monterey pine, an endemic tree once confined to the hills and slopes near Monterey, Cambria, and Año Nuevo as well as Guadalupe and Cedros islands off the coast of Baja, Mexico—now a common landscaping tree. The unusual Monterey cypress is a relict, a very specialized tree

which can't survive beyond the Monterey Peninsula. The soft green Sargent cypress is more common, ranging south to Santa Barbara along the coast and inland. The Macnab cypress is found only on poor serpentine soil, as are Bishop pines, which favor swamps and the slopes from "Huckleberry Hill" near Monterey south to the San Luis Range near Point Buchon and Santa Barbara County.

Coastal redwoods thrive near Santa Cruz and south through Big Sur. Not as lusty as those on the north coast, these redwoods often keep company with Douglas fir, pines, and a dense understory of shade-loving shrubs. Other central coast trees include the Sitka spruce and beach pines. A fairly common inland tree is the chaparral-loving knobcone pine, with its tenaciously closed "fire-climax" cones. Other regional trees include the California wax myrtle, the aromatic California laurel or "bay" tree, the California nutmeg, the tan oak (and many other oaks), plus alders, big-leaf maples, and occasional madrones. Eucalyptus trees thrive in the coastal locales where they've been introduced.

Whales And Sharks

The annual migrations of California gray whales, the state's official mammal, are big news all along the coast. From late October to January, these magnificent 20- to 40-ton creatures head south from Arctic seas toward Baja (pregnant females first). Once the mating season ends, males, newly pregnant females, and juveniles start their northward journey from February to June. Females with calves, often traveling close to shore, return later in the year, between March and July. (See "The North Coast" chapter for more information.) Once in a blue moon, when the krill population mushrooms in winter, rare blue whales will feed in and around Monterey Bay and north to the Farallon Islands.

A wide variety of harmless sharks are common in Monterey Bay. Occasionally, 20-foot-long great white sharks congregate here to feed on sea otters, seals, and sea lions. Unprovoked attacks on humans do occur (to surfers more often than scuba divers) but are very rare. The best protection is avoiding ocean areas where great whites are common, such as Año Nuevo Island at the north end of the bay; don't go into the water alone and never where these sharks have been recently sighted.

Seals And Sea Lions

Common in these parts is the California sea lion (the females are the barking "seals" popular in aquatic amusement parks). True seals don't have external ears, and the gregarious, fearless creatures swimming in shallow ocean waters or lolling on rocky jetties and docks usually do. Also here are northern or Steller's sea lions—which roar instead of bark and are usually lighter in color. Chunky harbor seals (no ear flaps, usually with spotted coats) more commonly haul out on sandy beaches, since they're awkward on land. Uncommon—but viewable at the Año Nuevo rookery during the winter mating and birthing season—are the massive northern elephant seals, the largest pinnipeds (fin-footed mammals) in the Western Hemisphere. One look at the two- or three-ton, 18-foot-long males explains the creatures' common name: their long, trunk-like noses serve no real purpose beyond sexual identification.

Sea Otters

The California sea otter population is making a comeback these days, after an estimated one-time population of almost 16,000 was decimated by eager fur hunters in centuries past. A single otter pelt was worth upwards of $1700 in 1910, when it was generally believed that sea otters were extinct in California. But a small pod survived off the coast near Carmel, a secret well guarded by biologists until the Big Sur Highway opened in 1938. Those counted today are fully protected. Sea otters frolic north along the coast to Jenner in Sonoma County, and south to Cambria. Watching otters eat is quite entertaining (binoculars are usually necessary). Carrying softball-sized rocks in their paws, they dive deep to dislodge abalone, mussels, and other shellfish, then leisurely smash the shells and dine while floating on their backs, "rafting" at anchor in forests of seaweed.

The otters' resurgence is something abalone fishermen are none too thrilled about, however, judging from heated public arguments up and down the coast. Now that the state's abalone populations are declining, fishermen assign the blame to these playful sea creatures (and they do feed heartily, each otter consuming about 2½ tons of seafood per year). But naturalists respond that, in the absence of their natural predators, California's abalone population ballooned enormously during this century, temporarily sa-

tiating an ever-increasing human appetite. The non-economically interested also point out that otters are not yet reestablished in prime abalone fishing grounds and therefore shouldn't take all the blame; young abalone are also consumed at a tender age by cabezon. Besides, sea otters also eat bothersome sea urchins.

Brown Pelicans

The ungainly looking, web-footed brown pelicans are actually incredibly graceful when diving for their dinners. Most noticeable in and around harbors perched on pilings or near piers, a squadron of 25 or more pelicans "gone fishin'" first glide above the water then, one by one, plunge dramatically to the sea. Brown pelicans are another back-from-the-brink success story, their numbers increasing dramatically since DDT (highly concentrated in fish) was banned. California's pelican platoons are often accompanied by greedy gulls somehow convinced they can snatch fish from the fleshy pelican pouches if they just try harder.

MONTEREY BAY AQUARIUM

The California sea otter, once thought extinct, is making a comeback.

Other Seabirds

Seabirds are the most obvious seashore fauna: long-billed curlews, ashy petrels nesting on cliffs, rare brown pelicans, surf divers like grebes and scooters, and various gulls. Pure white California gulls are seen only in winter here (they nest inland), but yellow-billed western gulls and the scarlet-billed, white-headed Herrman's gulls are common seaside scavengers. Look for the hyperactive, self-important sandpipers along the shore, also dowitchers, plovers, godwits, and avocets. Killdeers—so named for their "ki-dee" cry—lure people and other potential predators away from their clutches of eggs by feigning serious injury.

Tidepool Life

The twice-daily ebb of ocean tides reveals an otherwise hidden world. Tidepools below rocky headlands are nature's aquariums, sheltering abalone, anemones, barnacles, mussels, hermit crabs, starfish, sea snails, sea slugs, and tiny fish. Distinct zones of marine life are defined by the tides. The highest, or "splash" zone, is friendly to creatures naturally protected by shells from desiccation, including black turban snails and hermit crabs. The intertidal zones (high and low) protect spiny sea urchins and the harmless sea anemone. The "minus tide" or surf zone (farthest from shore and almost always underwater) is home to hazardous-to-human-health stingrays (particularly in late summer, watch where you step) and jellyfish.

HISTORY

Cabrillo spotted Point Pinos and Monterey Bay in 1542. Sixty years later, Vizcaino sailed into the bay and named it for the viceroy of Mexico, the count of Monte-Rey. A century later came Portola and Father Crespi who, later joined by Father Junipero Serra, founded both Monterey's presidio and the mission at Carmel. Monterey would later boast the state's first capital, first government building, first federal court, first newspaper, and (though other towns also claim the honor) first theater.

The quiet redwood groves near Santa Cruz remained undisturbed by civilization until the arrival of Portola's expedition in 1769. The sickly Spaniards made camp in the Rancho de Osos section of what is now Big Basin, experiencing an almost miraculous recovery in the valley they called Cañada de Salud or "Canyon of Health." A Spanish garrison and mission were soon established on the north end of Monterey Bay.

By the end of the 1700s, the entire central California coast was solidly Spanish, with missions, pueblos, and military bases or presidios holding the territory for the king of Spain. With the Mexican revolution, Californio loyalty went with the new administration closer to home. But the people here carried on their Spanish cultural heritage despite the secularization of the missions, the increasing influence of cattle ranches, and the foreign flood (primarily American) which threatened "tradition" in California. Along the rugged central coast just south of the boisterous and booming gold rush port of San Francisco, the influence of this new wave of "outsiders" was felt only later and locally, primarily near Monterey and Salinas.

Monterey: Capital Of Alta California

In addition to being the main port city for both Alta and Baja California, from 1775 to 1845 Monterey was the capital of Alta California—and naturally enough, the center of much political intrigue and scheming. Spared the devastating earthquakes that plagued other areas, Monterey had its own bad times, being burned and ransacked by the French pirate Hippolyte Bouchard in 1818. In 1822, Spanish rule ended in California. In 1845, Monterey lost part of its political prestige when Los Angeles temporarily became the territory's capital city. When the rancheros surrendered to Commodore Sloat in July 1846, the area became officially American, though the town's distinctive Spanish tranquility remained relatively undisturbed until the arrival of farmers, fishing fleets, fish canneries, and whalers. California's first constitution was drawn up in Monterey, at Colton Hall, in 1849.

Santa Cruz And
The Bad Boys Of Branciforte

Santa Cruz, the site of Mission Exaltacion de la Santa Cruz and a military garrison on the north end of Monterey Bay, got its start in 1791. But the 1797 establishment of Branciforte—a "model colony" financed by the Spanish government just across the San Lorenzo River—made life hard for the mission fathers. The rowdy, quasi-criminal culture of Branciforte so intrigued the native peoples that Santa Cruz men of the cloth had to use leg irons to keep the Ohlone home. And things just got worse. In 1818 the threat of pirates at nearby Monterey sent the mission folk into the hills, with the understanding that Branciforte's bad boys would pack up the mission's valuables and cart them inland for safekeeping. Instead, they looted the place and drank all the sacramental wine. The mission was eventually abandoned, then demolished by an earthquake in 1857. A small port city grew up around the plaza and borrowed the mission's name—Santa Cruz—while Branciforte, a smuggler's haven, continued to flourish until the late 1800s.

Economy

The livestock-grazing tradition of the ranchos, inherited from the Spanish, is still strong: cattle and sheep dot the hillsides in winter and spring. Modern agriculture is stronger here, though, with localized field crops including artichokes, broccoli, strawberries, pumpkins, garlic, carrots, lettuce, tomatoes, peppers, sweet corn—even fields of flowers grown for seed. Vineyards and local wineries are an up-and-coming economic item. Tree crops include almonds, apples, apricots, cherries, grapes, pears, plums, prunes, and walnuts. Tourism is an increasingly significant economic fact of life—some locals would say "overwhelming" fact of life.

THE NATIVE PEOPLE

Today, more than half a million people inhabit the central coast from Monterey Bay to Santa Barbara, where thousands of native people once shared the same territory. The Ohlone once flourished from the San Francisco peninsula to Monterey Bay and inland. Farther south, the Esselen people lived along the Big Sur coast and the Carmel River drainage; the Salinan along the coast and inland along the upper two-thirds of the Salinas River; and the Chumash south to Los Angeles and the Channel Islands.

The Ohlone

The Monterey-Santa Cruz area Ohlone people, often criticized by colonizing whites for being apathetic, squalid, and "surly," were nonethe-

---

SERRA: SAINT OR SINNER?

Declared "blessed" by Pope John Paul II in 1988 and a man who "lived a life of heroic virtue," the asthmatic, lame Franciscan priest Father Junipero Serra seems destined for Catholic sainthood, the first Californian and one of only a few Americans beatified.

Virtually unknown beyond California, Serra's contribution here is controversial. Does he deserve canonization? Did he perform a miracle or two? Many historians believe his efforts to Christianize and "civilize" native peoples was a cultural disaster amounting to genocide. Serra, they say, was disliked by the enslaved and overworked people he sought to save; his attitude toward his mission wards was reactionary even for his time. But Serra's defenders say he was benevolent, sincere in his concern for the "mission Indians," and not responsible for others' atrocities.

Cynical observers of Catholic saint-making suggest too that Serra's nomination is political, an attempt to create balance within the church, as do choices of campaign running mates in secular politics. From the point of view of the Catholic hierarchy, he's a perfect "affirmative action" candidate, since he represents the U.S., California, Hispanics, and evangelistic zeal all at once. But true believers see Serra's likely sainthood as simply recognition of his enlightened work on behalf of the poor and downtrodden.

---

less assimilated into the life of the Franciscan missions—though many of the mission Indians here were brought from the San Joaquin Valley. Because contact with whites came so early (and because mission fathers generally paid little attention to native culture), very little actual knowledge of the Ohlone was recorded, though the excellent The Ohlone Way by Malcolm Margolin points the way to an understanding of this indigenous culture. Shell mounds fringing bays and shorelines, particularly around San Francisco, testify to the importance of mussels and other seafood as a traditional food source. Beached whales, sea lions, and salmon, plus acorns and other gathered foods rounded out Ohlone diets. Dwellings may have commonly been built of redwood slabs; tule rafts capable of crossing San Francisco Bay were typical.

Fragmentary Ohlone myths say that the world was covered with water, above which arose a single mountain peak. Depending on the version of the tale, Coyote married the first woman here (or, Eagle, Coyote, and Hummingbird got things started, with tricky Hummingbird getting the girl). Besides totem animals, things sacred to the Ohlone included the sun, redwood trees, and possibly the ceremonial number five. As reported by anthropologist A.L. Kroeber in the classic *Handbook of the Indians of California,* "marriage was loose and divorce easy" and "songs of insult or vengeance were common." But there were other songs. The wood rat sang: "I dream of you, I dream of you jumping, rabbit, jack rabbit, and quail." A lover sang: "Come! Come! I mean you with the brown hat." Dancing was transformative, a way to transcend time and space, fear and disorder, and to enter the spirit world. And in the midst of the dance the people were "dancing on the brink of the world."

EVENTS AND RECREATION

Entertainment And Events

Lively nightclubs and bars are plentiful in both Santa Cruz and Monterey (more so in Monterey) though both cities and surrounding communities also offer the arts, theater, fine galleries, and more highbrow entertainment. Some of the area's "serious" annual events include the famed **Monterey Jazz Festival,** Carmel's **Bach Festival,** the Santa Cruz area **Cabrillo Music Festival,** and the traditional Christmas play *La Virgen del Tepeyac* in San Juan Bautista. (At least several months' advance planning is wise for these and other "big" events.)

Other Unique Events

Among the less serious regional happenings are the Santa Cruz **Great Monarch Poetry Read-Off,** and **Fungus Fair,** the Capitola **Sandcastle Contest,** Aptos's **World's Shortest Parade,** the Moss Landing **Shark Derby,** and the Castroville **Artichoke Festival.** Monterey's annual and **Great Monterey Squid Festival,** Carmel's **Surfabout,** the famous **Gilroy Garlic Festival,** and Watsonville's **West Coast Antique Fly-in** are also fun.

Outdoor Recreation

Except for the cyclists' suicide route along Hwy. 1 through Big Sur, the entire central coast area is excellent for bicycling: quiet roads and Victorian-lined streets, peaceful canyons and farmlands, dazzling ocean vistas. Foggy weather and coastal valley winds are the main potential drawbacks, so February to June is prime time. Cycling is serious business in most area communities, with bike clubs in Santa Cruz, Monterey, and Carmel. Big Basin Redwoods, Henry Cowell Redwoods, New Brighton, and state parks farther south all have designated overnight hiker/biker campsites. Hiking, backpacking, and rock climbing are other popular no-fee pastimes.

Monterey Peninsula Golfing

Golfers from around the world somehow can't help arriving on the Monterey Peninsula, clubs in tow, at some time in their lives. Something of an international golfing mecca, the Pebble Beach area between Carmel and Pacific Grove is the most famous, largely due to "The Crosby," which is now the AT&T Pebble Beach National Pro Am Golf Tournament. It may cost a pretty penny— up to $200 in greens fees—but the public is welcome at the following Pebble Beach private courses: **Pebble Beach Golf Links,** the **Links at Spanish Bay, Spyglass Hill Golf Course,** and the **Peter Hay Par 3,** all affiliated with The Lodge at Pebble Beach, tel. (408) 624-3811 or 624-6611 or toll-free (800) 654-9300; the **Poppy Hills Golf Course** just off 17 Mile Dr., tel. 624-2035; and the **Pacific Grove Municipal Golf Links,** great for beginners and quite reasonable, price-wise, tel. 648-3177.

Though Pebble Beach is world renowned for its golf courses and golf events, Carmel Valley and vicinity has nearly as many courses—most of them private in the country-club model, most recognizing reciprocal access agreements with other clubs. The **Rancho Canada Golf Club** about a mile east of Hwy. 1 via Carmel Valley Rd., tel. (408) 624-3811, is open to the public, however. As part and parcel of accommodations packages, nonmembers can golf at **Carmel Valley Ranch** on Old Ranch Rd. in Carmel, tel. toll-free (800) 422-7635, two nights and two rounds of golf for $600 or so (for two), and the **Quail Lodge Resort** on Valley Greens Dr., tel. 624-1581.

Other accessible area golf courses include the **Del Monte Golf Course** affiliated with the Hyatt Regency Monterey, tel. (408) 373-2436, and the **Laguna Seca Golf Club** on York Rd.

just off Hwy. 68 between Monterey and Salinas, tel. 373-3701.

Ocean Adventures

Ocean swimming is great fun, but dangerous in some areas: *never* swim alone, and pay attention to posted warnings about undertows and heavy surf. Beaches near Santa Cruz offer the safest swimming, but cold water, fog, and overcast weather can dampen swimmers' enthusiasm during the central coast summer. Surfers in wetsuits, a reliable indication that "surf's up," are a common sight in Santa Cruz, Carmel, and more remote areas. Scuba diving is popular on the Monterey Peninsula, particularly near Cannery Row, Asilomar, Carmel River state beaches, and Point Lobos Underwater Park. Sailing and sailboarding are other popular sea sports (though sand-castle-building is a definite first among landlubbers).

Beachcombing

Beachcombing is finest in February and March after winter storms—especially if searching for driftwood, agates, jasper, and jade—and best near the mouths of creeks and rivers. While exploring tidepools, refrain from taking or turning over rocks, which provide protective habitat for sea critters (the animals, too, don't like being molested). Since low tide is the time to "do" the coast, coastwalkers, beachcombers, and clammers need a current tide table (useful for a range of about 100 coastal miles), available at local sporting goods stores and dive shops. Also buy a California fishing license, since a permit is necessary for taking mussels, clams, and other sealife. But know the rules. Many regulations are enforced to protect threatened species, others for *human* well-being. There's an annual quarantine on mussels, for example, usually from May through October, to protect omnivores from nerve paralysis caused by the seasonal "red tide."

TRANSPORT

Getting There By Bus or Train

Greyhound bus connections are fairly good to the Monterey Bay area, especially from major cities north and south, with service to Santa Cruz, Monterey, Salinas, San Luis Obispo, and Santa Barbara (and points in between) supple-mented by local transit lines. **Peerless Stages,** tel. (415) 444-2900, connects Oakland, San Jose, and Santa Cruz. **SurTreks/Coastlines,** tel. (408) 649-4700, provides bus service between Monterey and San Luis Obispo. Amtrak's *Coast Starlight* runs from Los Angeles to Seattle with central coast stops in Oxnard, Santa Barbara, San Luis Obispo, and Salinas. For information and reservations, call Amtrak toll-free at (800) USA-RAIL. (The coast route connects in L.A. and Oakland with other Amtrak trains, in San Jose with the San Francisco-San Jose *Caltrain,* tel. 415-557-8661.)

Getting There By Air

Flying is considerably more expensive. Commuter flights connect central coast cities with major urban areas. The Monterey Airport offers common carrier service. San Jose Airport, the closest major airport in the north and not far from Santa Cruz, is served by commuter and major airlines.

Getting There By Car

This being California, most people drive cars, zipping close to the central coast on north-south Interstate 5 in the eastern San Joaquin, or traveling the historic El Camino Real (the "Royal Road" of the mission days), now modern Hwy. 101 which connects San Jose and points north with the Monterey Peninsula, Salinas, San Luis Obispo, Santa Barbara, and Los Angeles. Almost any route to the Monterey Bay area is faster than scenic Hwy. 1 along the coast. But they don't call it "1" for nothing. This hilly, treacherously twisting, mostly two-lane coast route offers spectacular scenery and lots of it, particularly along the Big Sur stretch between the Monterey Peninsula and San Luis Obispo. Driving the Big Sur route—plan carefully for walking or biking it—takes presence of mind as well as plenty of time. (The section between Carmel and Morro Bay is occasionally closed during winter due to landslides; call 800-952-7623 for current road conditions.) If possible, travel Hwy. 1 from north to south to take advantage of turnouts.

To avoid freeway traffic on the way to Monterey Bay, a multitude of smaller highways and decent local roads are good choices. From L.A., for example, take Hwy. 150 from 101, then Hwy. 33 into Ojai and up the coast. Or, also from Hwy. 101, skirt Lake Cachuma via Hwy. 154 en route to

Solvang. From the San Francisco Bay area, I-880 (then Hwy. 17) from San Jose is the preferred (if congested and treacherously twisting) local route connecting Santa Cruz, the only main alternative to Hwy. 1. Near Monterey, two-lane Hwy. 156 connects Highways 1 and 101 north of Monterey; Hwy. 68 makes the same connection between Monterey and Salinas. Take Laureles Canyon Rd. (G20) for a shortcut to Carmel Valley from Hwy. 68; Carmel Valley Rd. (G16) is the "back way" to head south from the Monterey Peninsula—scenic but slow.

Getting Around

Bicycles are viable transportation. You can even hike and walk throughout the area without difficulty. Both the Monterey and Santa Cruz areas are served by good local bus systems, which in addition to Greyhound and other bus lines offer some between-city connections.

MONTEREY

In his novel by the same name, local boy John Steinbeck described Monterey's Cannery Row as "a poem, a stink, a grating noise, a quality of light, a tune, a habit, a nostalgia, a dream," also a corrugated collection of sardine canneries, restaurants, honky-tonks, whorehouses, and waterfront laboratories. The street, he said, groaned under the weight of "silver rivers of fish." People here liked his description so much that they eventually put it on a plaque and planted it in today's touristy Cannery Row, among the few Steinbeck-era buildings still standing.

Local promoters claim that the legendary local writer would be proud of what the tourist dollar has wrought here, but this seems unlikely. When Steinbeck returned here in 1961 from his self-imposed exile, he noted the clean beaches, "where once they festered with fish guts and flies. The canneries which once put up a sickening stench are gone, their places filled with restaurants, antique shops, and the like. They fish for tourists now, not pilchards, and that species they are not likely to wipe out."

A City "Under Siege"

An early port for overland California immigrants (California's first pier was built here) and now a bustling tourist mecca, Monterey (literally, "The King's Wood") is trying hard to hang onto its once-cloistered charm. The recently hatched but justifiably popular Monterey Bay Aquarium is often blamed for the hopeless summer traffic snarls, though tourism throughout the Monterey Peninsula is the actual culprit. (The scheduled closure of Fort Ord, which will have a substantial impact on the local economy, may also reduce the local permanent population. For a time.) *Creative States Quarterly* editor Raymond Mungo described Monterey as a city "under siege," asking rhetorically: "How do you describe the difference a tornado makes in a small town, or the arrival of sudden prosperity in a sleepy backwater?" How, indeed?

THE MONTEREY BAY AQUARIUM

The fish are back on Cannery Row, at least at the west end. Doc's Western Biological Laboratory and the canneries immortalized by Steinbeck may be long gone, but Monterey now has an aquarium that the bohemian biologist would love.

Located just down the street from Doc's infamous marine lab, the Monterey Bay Aquarium on Cannery Row is a world-class cluster of fish tanks built into the converted Hovden Cannery. Luring 2.35 million visitors in 1984, its first year, Monterey's newest and best attraction is the brainchild of marine biologist Nancy Packard and her sister, aquarium director Julie Packard. Much help came from Hewlett-Packard computer magnate David Packard, who supported this nonprofit, public-education endeavor with a $40 million donation to his daughters' cause. Not coincidentally, Packard also designed many of the unique technological features of the major exhibits here. The facility also conducts its own research and environmental education and wildlife rescue programs, through the aquarium's foundation. The aquarium's trustees, for example, have allocated $10 million for a five-year unmanned underwater exploration and research project in the bay's Monterey Canyon.

The philosophy of the folks at the Monterey Bay Aquarium, most simply summarized as

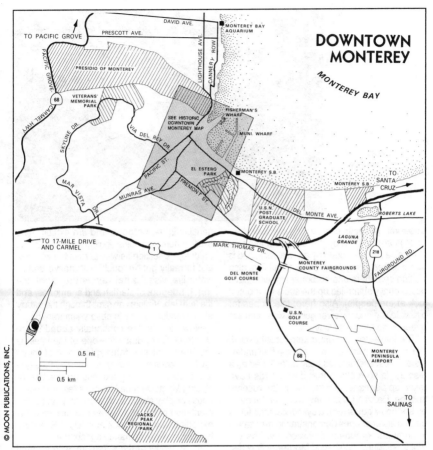

DOWNTOWN MONTEREY

"endorsing human interaction" with the natural world, is everywhere apparent, once inside. From a multilevel view of kelp forests in perpetual motion to face-to-face encounters with sharks and wolf eels, from petting velvety bat rays and starfish in "touch pools" to watching sea otters feed and frolic, here people can observe the native marine plants and wildlife of Monterey Bay up close and personal. More than 6,500 creatures representing hundreds of seagoing species are displayed together in environments closely approximating their natural underwater communities. Volunteer guides, dressed in rust-colored jackets or navy or gray aprons, are available throughout the aquarium

and are only too happy to share their knowledge about the natural history of Monterey Bay.

Aquarium Sights

Just inside the aquarium's entrance is the 30-foot-deep split-level **Sea Otter Tank**. These sleek aquatic clowns consume 25 percent of their body weight in seafood daily. If they're not eating or playing with toys, they're grooming themselves—and with 600,000 hairs per square inch on their pelts, it's easy to understand why otters were so prized by furriers (and hunted almost to extinction). To spot an occasional otter or two slipping into the aquarium over the seawall, or to watch for whales, head for the outdoor

the aquarium's moon jellies

MONTEREY BAY AQUARIUM, RICK BROWNE

observation decks nearby. The **outdoor tide-pool** is surrounded by the aquarium itself on three sides, on the fourth by artificial rock, and is home to sea stars, anemones, small fish, also visiting sea otters and harbor seals (who have occasionally shimmied up the stairs for a better look at the people). Also here: telescopes for birdwatching and a viewer-guided video camera overlooking Monterey Bay.

The three-story-tall **giant kelp forest** exhibit, the aquarium's centerpiece and the first under-water forest ever successfully established as a display, is so realistic that diving birds have taken up permanent residence on the "ocean" surface. Dazzling is the only word for the near-by **anchovy aquarium,** a cylindrical tank full of darting silver shapes demonstrating the "safety in numbers" group-mind philosophy. The 90-foot-long hourglass-shaped **Monterey Bay** display is a simulated underwater slice of sea life. Sharks roam the deep among the colorful anemones and sea slugs, bat rays glide under the pier with the salmon and mackerel, accompanied by octopi and wolf eels. The craggy-shored indoor-outdoor **coastal stream** exhibit has a steady rhythm all its own and provides a small spawning ground for salmon and steel-head. In the huge **marine mammals gallery** are models of a 43-foot-long barnacled gray whale and her calf, killer whales, dolphins, sea lions, and seals. Also here: a variety of educational videos and slide shows.

Unusual among the predominantly bay-relat-ed exhibits, but popular, is the live chambered

nautilus in the **octopus and kin** exhibit. Also exciting here, in a spine-tingling way, is watching an octopus suction its way across the window. But to really get "in touch" with native under-water life, visit the **bat ray petting pool,** the **touch tidepool** of starfish and anemones, and the **kelp lab.** Visitors can stroll through the **sandy shore** outdoor aviary to observe shorebirds.

New exhibits are continually added to the Monterey Bay Aquarium—one of the latest is the **Planet of the Jellies,** in honor of those mythic medusae of the deep—and various gal-leries have changing exhibits on themes in-cluding Monterey area history (a restored boiler house display about sardine canning, and docu-mentation of the 1940 Sea of Cortez scientific expedition by Steinbeck and "Doc" Ricketts), bay ecology, even marine agriculture.

In the works at the aquarium, with a grand opening scheduled for 1996, is an entirely new wing devoted to marinelife of the deep sea and open ocean—including a one-million-gallon aquatic exhibit with a seven-foot sunfish, sharks, and schooling albacore and bonito. Jellyfish and otherwise seldom-seen underwater creatures will also be on permanent display.

Tickets And Practicalities

To avoid the worst of the human crush, come in the off-season (weekdays if at all possible) and use the free Monterey and Salinas Transit shut-tle from downtown parking areas. All exhibits are wheelchair-accessible. The aquarium is open daily except Christmas, 10 a.m.-6 p.m.

(from 9:30 a.m. in summer). Admission is $9.75 adults, $7.25 students, seniors, and active-duty military, $4.50 for children under age 12. Advance reservations are a must most of the year. For group tour information and reservations, call (408) 648-4860.

To reserve tickets for a particular day and time, call toll-free (800) 756-3737 (small service charge). You can buy tickets at the aquarium on a just-show-up-and-take-your-chances basis. The aquarium's restaurant and gift/bookstores are worthwhile. The **Portola Cafe** has very good food and an oyster bar (the very idea itself surely a shock to the aquarium's permanent residents) and is fine for a glass of wine at sunset; open 10-5. Along with good books, educational toys, and nature art, the aquarium gift shops have some touristy bric-a-brac and forgettable edibles like chocolate sardines.

Tours And Information
Free self-guided tour scripts with maps, in Spanish, French, German, and Japanese, are available at the aquarium's information desk. All aquarium facilities and exhibits are accessible to the disabled; an explanatory brochure is available at the information desk. Members of the California State Automobile Association are eligible for special behind-the-scenes "fish-eye" aquarium tours; contact any AAA office for information and reservations. For general information, contact: Monterey Bay Aquarium, 886 Cannery Row, Monterey 93940-1085, tel. (408) 648-4888. To find out about "supporting memberships," which include privileges such as unlimited aquarium admission and the quarterly *Shorelines* newsletter, and for information about group visits, special educational programs for school children, and renting the aquarium for evening events, contact the aquarium office.

CANNERY ROW, FISHERMAN'S WHARF

Searching For Steinbeck On Cannery Row
Today the strip is reminiscent of Steinbeck's Cannery Row only when you consider how tourists are packed in here: like sardines. Of all the places the Nobel Prize-winning author immortalized, only "Doc's" marine lab (now a pri-

PUTTING THE BAY ON DISPLAY

The engineering feats shoring up the amazingly "natural" exhibits in the 177,000-square-foot Monterey Aquarium are themselves impressive. Most remarkable are the aquatic displays, concrete tanks with unbreakable one-ton acrylic windows over seven inches thick. The exhibits' "wave action" is simulated by a computer-controlled surge machine and hidden water jets. More than a half-million gallons of seawater are filtered and pumped through the various aquarium tanks daily to keep these habitats healthy. Six huge "organic" water filters screen out microorganisms which would otherwise cloud the water. In the event of an oil spill or other oceanic disaster, the aquarium's 16-inch intake pipes can be shut down on a moment's notice and the aquarium can operate as a "closed system" for up to two weeks.

vate social/drinking club) at 800 Cannery Row still stands unchanged—a humble brown shack almost as unassuming as it was in 1948, when marine biologist Ed Ricketts's car was smashed by the *Del Monte Express* train just a few blocks away. Wing Chong market, Steinbecked as "Lee Chong's Heavenly Flower Grocery," is across the street, now the Row's **General Store.** The fictional "La Ida Cafe" cathouse still survives, in actuality the most famous restaurant and salon on the Monterey Peninsula: **Kalisa's.**

Fairly new—connected to Steinbeck only by allusion, in appreciation of the author's fondness for drink—is the exceptional **Paul Masson Tasting Room and Museum** upstairs at 700 Cannery Row, tel. (408) 375-8755, with free winetasting in a 7,000-square-foot room overlooking the bay. Fabulous views. Premium varietals are also served by the glass. Enthusiasts, also tour the **Museum of California Wine History** here. The gift shop features wines and accessories, of course, as well as odder items like chardonnay mustard and cabernet hot fudge sauce. Open daily 10-6. There are several other winetasting facilities along the row, including **Bargetto Winery** downstairs.

For more information about Cannery Row, and to seriously trace Steinbeck's steps through the local landscape, contact the **Cannery Row Promotional District,** P.O. Box 9214, Monterey 93942, tel. (408) 373-1902, or stop by the

HISTORIC DOWNTOWN MONTEREY

ARTILLERY ST.

PRESIDIO OF MONTEREY

MONTEREY BAY

SHORELINE PARK

FISHERMAN'S WHARF

MUNICIPAL WHARF

VIZCAINO-SERRA LANDING SITE

SEENO ST.

FIRST BRICK HOUSE

OLD WHALING STATION

SCOTT ST.

MONTEREY MARINA

LARKIN ST.

CUSTOM HOUSE

CALIFORNIA'S FIRST THEATER

OLIVER ST.

PACIFIC HOUSE

HEADQUARTERS, MONTEREY STATE HISTORIC PARK

VAN BUREN ST.

CASA SOBERANES

LIGHTHOUSE AVE.

FRANKLIN ST.

GREYHOUND

MONTEREY INST. OF INTERNATIONAL STUDIES

MONTEREY PENINSULA CHAMBER OF COMMERCE

DEL MONTE AVE.

PACIFIC ST.

CASA SERRANO

CALLE PRINCIPAL

ALVARADO ST.

TYLER ST.

WASHINGTON ST.

ADAMS ST.

JEFFERSON ST.

FIRST FRENCH CONSULATE

LARKIN HOUSE

JACK'S PARK

COLTON HALL

PEARL ST.

MADISON ST.

MARITIME MUSEUM

POLK ST.

COOPER-MOLERA ADOBE

HOUSTON ST.

ABREGO ST.

CORTES ST.

CAMINO EL ESTERO

MONTEREY PENINSULA MUS. OF ART

STEVENSON HOUSE

WEBSTER ST.

FIGUEROA ST.

EL ESTERO

FREMONT'S HEADQUARTERS

MUNRAS AVE.

CHURCH ST.

EL ESTERO PARK

HARTNELL ST.

P.O.

ROYAL PRESIDIO CHAPEL

FREMONT ST.

0   0.1 mi

0   0.1 km

ELDORADO ST.

ABREGO ST.

© MOON PUBLICATIONS, INC.

group's office and information center in the railroad car at Edgewater Packing Company at 640 Wave Street. Guided tours of Cannery Row are also available.

Fisherman's Wharf

Tacky and tawdry, built up and beat up, Fisherman's Wharf is no longer a working wharf by any account. Still, a randy ramshackle charm more honest than Cannery Row surrounds this 1846 pier full of cheap shops, food stalls, decent restaurants, and stand-up bars indiscriminately frosted with gull guano and putrid fish scraps (the latter presumably leftovers from the 50-cent bags tourists buy to feed the sea lions). Built of stone by enslaved natives, convicts, and military deserters when Monterey was Alta California's capital, Fisherman's Wharf was originally a pier for cargo schooners. Later used by whalers and Italian-American fishing crews to unload their catch, the wharf today is bright and bustling, full of eateries and eaters. Come early

KIM WEIR

Searching for Steinbeck on Cannery Row: this inconspicuous private social club was once Doc's marine laboratory.

in the morning to beat the crowds, then launch yourself on a summer sightseeing tour of Monterey Bay or a winter whalewatching cruise.

MONTEREY STATE HISTORIC PARK

The Monterey State Historic Park, with headquarters at 20 Customs House Plaza, Monterey 93940, tel. (408) 649-2836, includes fine old adobes protected and preserved by the state, most of them once surrounded by enclosed gardens and adobe walls draped with bougainvillea vines. (At last report, the visitor center and most buildings were open daily in summer, otherwise closed on Mondays and Tuesdays—a cut-back trend that may worsen. Call ahead to avoid disappointment.) Definitely worth seeing are the Cooper-Molera, Stevenson, and Larkin homes, as well as Casa Soberanes. The museum displays at both the **Pacific** and **Custom House** buildings are free, open 10 a.m.-4 p.m. (until 5 in summer). An all-day admission fee of $4 adults, $2 children will get you into all other state park-maintained buildings. Many offer hourly tours, and can be seen separately ($2 adults, $1 children). Pick up the $2 "Historic Monterey: Path of History" self-guided tour map before setting out, to appreciate dozens of other historic sights near the bay and downtown.

The Pacific House building is scheduled for renovation, possibly in 1993, but exact dates—even the actual year—are uncertain, largely due to the state's current fiscal crisis. Whether or not the museum and information center here are closed during your visit, head across the plaza to the Monterey State Historic Park Information Center inside the colossal new Stanton Center built to house the Maritime Museum. A new attraction for visitors is the 14-minute film about the area's historical heritage.

Monterey Architecture

The Larkin House, a two-story redwood frame with low shingled roof, adobe walls, and wooden balconies skirting the second floor, and the recently restored Cooper-Molera Adobe, are good examples of the "Monterey Colonial" architectural style—a marriage of Yankee woodwork and Mexican adobe—which evolved here.

Most traditional Monterey adobes have south-facing patios to absorb sun in winter and a northern veranda to catch cool summer breezes. On the first floor were the kitchen, storerooms, dining room, living room, sometimes even a ballroom. The bedrooms on the second floor were entered from outside stairways, a tradition subsequently abandoned. That so many fine homes remain in Monterey today is mostly due to genteel local poverty: until recently, few developers with grandiose plans came knocking on the door. Also distinctive in Monterey are the "swept gardens"—dirt courtyards surrounded by colorful flowers under pine canopies—which were an adaptation to the originally barren home sites.

For an even better look at traditional local gardens, come to the **Monterey Garden Tour** in May, when many private gardens open for public tours. For info, contact the **Monterey History and Art Association,** 412 Pacific St. (P.O. Box 805), Monterey 93940, tel. (408) 372-2608.

Custom House And Pacific House

On July 7, 1846, Commodore John Drake Sloat raised the Stars and Stripes here at Alvarado and Waterfront streets, commemorating California's passage into American rule. The Custom House Building is the oldest government building on the West Coast—and quite multinational, since it has flown at one time or another the flags of Spain, Mexico, and the U.S. Until 1867, customs duties from foreign ships were collected here. Today you can inspect typical 19th-century cargo and try to reason with the parrot in residence.

Once a hotel, then a military supply depot, the building at Scott and Calle Principal was called Pacific House when it housed a public tavern in 1850. Later came law offices, a newspaper, a ballroom for "dashaway" temperance dances, and various small shops. Now it's an excellent museum of Native American artifacts, with special attention given to the Ohlone people, also the city's Spanish whaling industry and pioneer/logging periods.

The Customs House Plaza, between the Customs House and Pacific House, is now undergoing major construction and reconstruction, primarily to accommodate the Monterey History and Art Association's new **Stanton Center** and its **Maritime Museum and History Center.** Scheduled to open by late fall or winter 1993, this spacious new facility—with a $6.3 million price tag, financed through private and business contributions, foundations, and both the city of Monterey and the state of California—will display the ever-expanding local maritime history collection. The association's maritime research library, acclaimed ship photography collection, and scrimshaw collection will all become more accessible to the public. The new museum's permanent major exhibits—with themes including Commerce and Trade, Charts and Navigation, Discovery and Development, Pacific Station, Fishing and Canning, and The Changing Bay—will be accompanied by special revolving exhibits. The Stanton Center will also include a permanent visitors center for Monterey State Historic Park—the park's only visitor facility while the Pacific House is renovated (possibly in 1993).

Larkin House And Others

Built of adobe and wood in 1835 by Yankee merchant Thomas Oliver Larkin, later the only U.S. consul in the territory during Mexican rule, this home at Jefferson and Calle Principal, tel. (408) 646-3851, became the American consulate, then later military headquarters for Kearny, Mason, and Sherman. A fine pink Monterey adobe and the model for the local Colonial style, Larkin House is furnished with over $6 million in antiques and period furnishings. The home and headquarters of William Tecumseh Sherman is next door, now a museum focusing on both Larkin and Sherman. Around the corner at 540 Calle Principal is another Larkin building, the **House of the Four Winds,** a small adobe built in the 1830s and named for its weathervane. **The Gutierrez Adobe,** a typical middle-class Monterey "double adobe" home at 580 and 590 Calle Principal, was built in 1841 and later donated to the state by the Monterey Foundation.

The Cooper-Molera Adobe

The long, two-story Monterey Colonial adobe *casa grande* or "big house" at 508 Munras Ave. was finished in pinkish plaster when constructed in 1829 by Capt. John Bautista Rogers Cooper for his young bride Encarnacion (of California's influential Vallejo clan). The 2½-acre complex, which includes a neighboring home, two barns, and a visitor center, has been restored to its 19th-century authenticity.

Robert Louis Stevenson House

The sickly Scottish storyteller and poet lived at the French Hotel adobe boarding house at 530 Houston St. for several months in 1879 while courting his American love (and later wife), Fanny Osbourne. In a sunny upstairs room is the small portable desk at which he reputedly wrote *Treasure Island*. While in Monterey, Stevenson collected *Treasure* material on his convalescing coast walks and worked on "Amateur Immigrant," "The Old Pacific," "Capital," and "Vendetta of the West." He also worked as a reporter for the local newspaper—a job engineered by his friends, who, in order to keep the flat-broke Stevenson going, secretly paid the paper $2 a week to cover his wages. The restored downstairs is stuffed with period furniture. Several upstairs rooms are dedicated to Stevenson's memorabilia, paintings, and first editions. Local rumor has it that a 19th-century ghost—Stevenson's spirit, according to a previous caretaker—lives upstairs in the children's room.

Casa Soberanes

This is an 1830 Mediterranean-style adobe with tile roof and cantilevered balcony, hidden by thick hedges at 336 Pacific. Home to the Soberanes family from 1860 to 1922, it was later donated to the state. Take the tour or just stop to appreciate the garden and abalone-bordered flower beds, some encircled by century-old glass bottles buried bottoms up.

California's First Theater

First a sailors' saloon and lodging house, this small 1844 weathered wood and adobe at Scott and Pacific was built by the English sailor Jack Swan and is now Jack Swan's Tavern (simple meals and libations available). Commandeered by soldiers in 1848 for a makeshift theater, later—with a lookout station added to the roof—the tavern became a whaling station. Wander through the place and take a trip into the bawdy past, complete with the requisite painting of a reclining nude over the bar, brass bar rail and cuspidor, oil lamps, ancient booze bottles, and old theatrical props and paraphernalia. A modern postscript is the garden out back.

Casa Del Oro

Built by Thomas Larkin at the corner of Scott and Olivier as part of his business empire, this two-story chalk and adobe building was later a barracks for American troops, the Joseph Boston & Co. general store, a saloon, even a private residence. Rumors have it that this "house of gold" was once a mint, or that (when a saloon) it accepted gold dust in payment for drinks—thus the name.

Whaling Station

The old adobe Whaling Station at 391 Decatur St. near the Custom House was a two-story adobe flophouse for Portuguese whalers in the 1850s. Now a private home, tours are offered Fri. only 10 a.m.-2 p.m., including access to the walled garden (enter through the gate at the left of the house). Whale lovers, walk softly: the sidewalk in front of the house is made of whalebone.

California's First Brick House

This building nearby at 351 Decatur was started by Gallant Duncan Dickenson in 1847, built with bricks fashioned and fired in Monterey. The builder left for the gold fields before the house was finished, so the home—the first brick house built in California—and 60,000 bricks were auctioned off by the sheriff in 1851 for just over $1000.

OTHER MONTEREY SIGHTS

Colton Hall

California's constitutional convention took place here during September and October of 1849, and the state constitution was drafted upstairs in Colton Hall. The Reverend Walter Colton, Monterey's first American *alcalde,* or local magistrate, built this impressive, pillared "Carmel Stone" structure as a schoolhouse and public hall on Pacific between Madison and Jefferson. Colton and Robert Semple published the first American newspaper in California here, cranking up the presses on August 15, 1846. Next door is the 1854 **Monterey jail** (entrance on Dutra St.), a dreary, slot-windowed prison once home to gentleman-bandit Tiburcio Vasquez and killer Anastacio Garcia, who "went to God on a rope" pulled by his buddies.

Allen Knight Maritime Museum

If you're curious about Monterey's sailing and whaling days, this small museum at 550 Calle Principal, tel. (408) 375-2553, is a good stop:

compasses, bells, ship models, local naval history, and general maritime photos and displays. (Most of the museum collection is destined for the **Stanton Center** in Customs House Plaza, so check on the museum's current status before setting out.) The library here is available to scholars and writers by special arrangement. In summer, open Tues.-Fri. 10 a.m.-4 p.m., Sat. and Sun. 2-4 p.m. Otherwise open Tues.-Fri. 1-4 p.m., weekends 2-4. Free, but donations to the sponsoring Monterey History and Art Association always appreciated.

Monterey Peninsula Museum Of Art

This fine museum at 559 Pacific, tel. (408) 372-5477, is near many local historic sites and offers an excellent collection of Western art, including bronze cowboy-and-horse statues by Charles M. Russell. The Fine Arts collection includes photography and Asian art and artifacts. Also here: folk art plus high-concept graphics, photography, paintings, sculpture, and other contemporary art in changing exhibits. Open Tues.-Sat. 10 a.m.-4 p.m., Sun. 1-4 p.m., closed holidays. Free, technically, but a $2 donation is requested. Associated with the art museum is the amazing **La Mirada** (see below).

Casa Amesti And La Mirada

If you're in Monterey on a weekend, be sure to tour **Casa Amesti** at 516 Polk Street, a genteel Monterey colonial stylishly updated in the 1920s by Frances Adler Elkins, a noted West Coast interior designer whose other projects included the International House at UC Berkeley and the Royal Hawaiian Hotel in Honolulu. The sensibility here is royal, relaxed, and European without the velvet and gilt—furniture upholstered in linen and cotton, the woodwork in the library painted French provincial blue. Since 1954, Casa Amesti has served as a luncheon venue for upper-crust members of the Old Capital Club, who contribute to its maintenance. But just plain folks can come have a look-see on Saturday and Sunday, 2-4 p.m. Small admission fee, children under age 12 free. For information, contact the Monterey History and Art Association, tel. (408) 372-2608.

Another impressive Monterey-style adobe, also private but open to the public on a limited basis, is **La Mirada**, the Castro Adobe and Frank Work Estate at 720 Via Mirada, tel. (408)

372-3689, affiliated with the Monterey Peninsula Museum of Art. The home is exquisite. The original adobe portion was the residence of Jose Castro, one of the most prominent citizens in California during the Mexican period. Purchased in 1919 by Gouverneur Morris—author/playwright and descendant of the same-named Revolutionary War figure—the adobe was restored and expanded with the addition of a two-story wing and huge drawing room, to host artists and Hollywood stars.

These days, the two-and-a-half-acre estate overlooking El Estero still reflects the elegance of a bygone era, the house itself furnished in antiques and early California art. The gardens are perhaps even more elegant, at least in season, with a walled rose garden (old and new varieties), traditional herb garden (with medicinal, culinary, fragrant, and "beautifying" herbs), and a rhododendron garden with over 300 camellias, azaleas, rhododendrons, and other flowering perennials and trees. Public tours are scheduled only on Wed. and Sat. at 1, 2, and 3 p.m., $5 donation. Usually in May, **Springtime at La Mirada** features art, floral, and garden exhibits as well as gardening lectures and workshops and a ladies bridge festival. There's no on- or off-street parking here, so park at Monterey Peninsula College and take the shuttle.

Monterey Institute Of International Studies

A prestigious, private, and nonprofit graduate-level college headquartered at 425 Van Buren, tel. (408) 647-4100, specializing in foreign-language instruction and preparation for careers in international business and government. Fascinating and unique is the 200-seat auditorium here, which is set up for simultaneous translations of up to four languages. Visitors are welcome Mon.-Fri., 8:30 a.m.-5 p.m., and most of the institute's programs—including the film series—are open to the public.

The Presidio

One of the oldest military posts in the U.S., the Presidio of Monterey is the physical focal point of most local history—monuments galore—though the original complex, founded by Portola in 1770, was located in the area now defined by Webster, Fremont, Abrego, and El Estero streets. History buffs, note the commemorative monuments of

Portola, Junipero Serra, Vizcaino, and Commodore Sloat, plus late-in-the-game acknowledgement of native peoples. (When Lighthouse Ave. was widened through here, most of what remained of a 2,000-year-old Rumsen village was destroyed, leaving only a ceremonial rain rock, a rock mortar for grinding acorns, and an ancient burial ground marked by a tall wooden cross.) Also here: incredible panoramic views of Monterey Bay.

The **U.S. Army Museum,** in Building 113, tel. (408) 242-8414, once a tack house, is now filled with cavalry artifacts, uniforms, pistols, cannons, photos, posters, and dioramas about Army and Presidio history. (Open Mon.-Fri. 9 a.m.-4 p.m.) The main gate at Pacific and Artillery streets leads to the **Defense Language Institute.** Accompanied by the "Walk Through History" brochure, visit the earthen ruins and cannons of the **Fort Mervine** battlements, built by Commodore Sloat then dismantled in 1852. Fort Mervine's log huts were built during the Civil War.

The Royal Presidio Chapel

Originally established as a mission by Father Serra in June, 1770, this building at 555 Church St. near Figueroa became the Royal Presidio Chapel of San Carlos Borromeo when the mission was relocated to Carmel. The chapel, rebuilt from stone in 1791, became the San Carlos Cathedral, a parish church, after secularization in 1835. The cathedral's interior walls are decorated with Native American and Mexican folk art. Above, the upper gable facade is the first European art made in California, a chalk-carved Virgin of Guadalupe tucked into a shell niche. To get here, turn onto Church St. just after Camino El Estero ends at Fremont—a district once known as Washerwoman's Gulch.

MONTEREY OUTDOORS

Beaches And Parks

The 14-acre **Monterey Beach** is not very impressive (day use only) but you can stroll the rocky headlands on the peninsula's north side without interruption, traveling the Monterey Bay Recreation Trail past the **Pacific Grove Marine Gardens Fish Refuge** and **Asilomar State Beach**—tidepools, rugged shorelines, and thick carpets of brightly flowered (but nonnative) ice

plant. For ocean swimming head south to **Carmel River State Beach,** which includes a lagoon and bird sanctuary, or to **China Cove** at Point Lobos. **El Estero Park** in town—bounded by Del Monte Ave., Fremont Blvd., and Camino El Estero—has a small lagoon with ducks, pedalboat rentals, picnic tables, a par course, hiking and biking trails, and the **Dennis the Menace Playground** designed by cartoonist Hank Ketcham (particularly fun here is the hedge maze). Also at El Estero is the area's first **French Consulate,** built in 1830 and moved here in 1931, now the local Girl Scout headquarters. The **Don Dahvee Park** on Munras Ave. (a.k.a. motel row) is a secret oasis of picnic tables with a hiking/biking trail.

Jacks Peak/County Parks

The highest point on the peninsula (but not *that* high: 1,068 feet) and the focal point of a 525-acre regional park, Jacks Peak offers great views, good hiking and horseback trails, picnicking, plus fascinating flora and wildlife. Named after the land's former owner—Scottish immigrant and entrepreneur David Jacks, best known for his local dairies and their "Monterey Jack" cheese—the park has 4½ miles of marked trails, including the self-guided **Skyline Nature Trail.** From Jacks Peak amid the Monterey pines, you'll have spectacular views of both Monterey Bay and Carmel Valley—and possibly the pleasure of spotting American kestrels or red-shouldered hawks soaring on the wind currents. The park's first 55 acres were purchased by the Nature Conservancy, the rest bought up with county, federal, and private funds. To get here, take Olmstead County Rd. (from Hwy. 68 near Monterey Airport) for two miles. For more info, contact the **Monterey County Parks Dept.,** P.O. Box 367, Salinas 93902, tel. (408) 424-1971.

Other Outdoor Activities

Monterey and vicinity is most famous, of course, as an elite golfing oasis. For information on public access to area courses, which are primarily private, see this chapter's Introduction.

Otherwise, get some fresh air and see the sights by bicycle. Either bring your own or rent one, at any of several local bike rental outfits (see "Practicalities" below). Or tool around on a moped, available for rent through **Monterey Moped Adventures,** 1250 Del Monte Ave.,

*the Monterey Bay
Recreation Trail*

KIM WEIR

tel. (408) 373-2696, which also rents bikes—tandem bikes, bikes with child trailers, and "beach cruzers," plus the standards—and offers ample parking and easy acess to the bayside bike/hike trail.

Another way to "see" Monterey Bay is by getting right in it, by kayak. **Monterey Bay Kayaks** at 693 Del Monte Ave., tel. (408) 373-KELP, offers tours—bay tours and sunset tours, even trips into Elkhorn Slough and along the Salinas River—as well as classes and rentals of both open and closed kayaks. Everything is included in the basic all-day rental price ($20 for singles, $40 for doubles): wetsuits, paddling jackets, life jackets, water shoes. **Adventures by the Sea,** headquartered at the Doubletree Hotel downtown but also at 299 Cannery Row, tel. (408) 372-1807, also rents kayaks and offers kayak tours—in addition to bike rentals (bikes delivered to your hotel room and picked up again at no charge), bike trips (including a Pt. Pinos Lighthouse tour), and rollerblade rentals. The company's "Land & Sea Package" includes kayaking in the morning, mountain-bike touring in the afternoon, $60 for two.

More traditional boating companies also offer bay tours (including cocktail cruises), winter whalewatching, and fishing trips (discount coupons often available at the visitors bureau). Good choices: **Monterey Sport Fishing,** located at Fisherman's Wharf, tel. (408) 372-2203; **Princess Monterey Cruises,** tel. 372-2628; and **Randy's Fishing Trips,** tel. 372-7440, which even offers Point Sur fishing charters.

Another way to see the bay, of course, is to get a fish-eye view. The **Aquarius Dive Shop** at two Monterey locations, 32 Cannery Row and 2240 Del Monte Ave., tel. (408) 375-1933 or 375-5505 (toll-free 800-833-9992 for dive packages), is the best place around for rentals, instruction, equipment, and repairs. Aquarius also offers guided underwater tours (specializing in photography and video) and can provide tips on worthwhile dives worldwide. **Twin Otters, Inc.,** P.O. Box 8744, Monterey 93943, tel. (408) 394-4235, offers **scuba diving charters** of the bay's offshore reefs, also of Carmel bay and highlands, and from Yankee Point south to Granite Canyon. All hands are experienced divers; full replacement tanks available on the boat, the *Silver Prince,* which can carry small groups of up to 20. Private group charters, for whalewatching and sightseeing, are also available.

For a bird's-eye view—from a hot air balloon —contact **Ballooons-by-the-Sea,** tel. (408) 424-0111 or toll-free (800) 464-6420.

THE SAND DUNE CITIES

With the population of Fort Ord included in the census of **Marina,** this sad-sack sand dune city was once destined to become the largest community on the Monterey Peninsula. When the base closes in late 1993, it may become the smallest, eliminating most of the peninsula's most inexpensive lodgings and restaurants to boot. Besides surfing, the big deal at the beach here is hang-gliding. On the ground, explore the nearby dunes, serene in a simple stark way, with fragile shrubs and wildflowers (some quite rare, don't pick). The Monterey Peninsula's low-income inhabitants live in **Seaside** and **Sand City.** From Santa Cruz, head inland on Canyon del Rey Rd. to **Work Memorial Park** and the nearby **Frog Pond Natural Area** (entrance in the willows near the Del Rey Oaks City Hall), a seasonal freshwater marsh home to birds and the elusive inchlong Pacific tree frog. Or, take Del Monte Ave. off Hwy. 1 to **Del Monte Beach,** one of the least-bothered beaches of Monterey Bay (no facilities).

Del Monte Ave. also takes you past the **U.S. Naval Post-Graduate School,** a Navy preflight training school during World War II and now a military university offering doctorates, housed on the grounds of the stately 1880 Spanish-style **Del Monte Hotel.** The state's oldest large resort and queen of American watering holes for California's nouveau riche, the Del Monte was built by Charles Crocker and the rest of the railroading Big Four. Tour the grounds 8 a.m.-4:30 p.m. daily, and stop by **Herrmann Hall** in the old hotel. Downstairs is the school's **museum,** with memorabilia from the Del Monte's heyday, open Mon.-Fri 11 a.m.-2 p.m., closed on major holidays.

Worth stopping for in Seaside is the tranquil **Monterey Peninsula Buddhist Temple** at 1155 Noche Buena, tel. (408) 394-0119—beautiful Asian-style gardens, carp-filled ponds. Come in May for the bonsai show.

MONTEREY ACCOMMODATIONS

Monterey is so close to the neighboring communities of Pacific Grove, Carmel, and Carmel Valley, not to mention its own sand-dune suburbs, that peninsula visitors with cars can conveniently plan to stay and eat throughout the area. Current complete listings of accommodations (including prices) and restaurants in Monterey proper are available free from the convention and visitors bureau. Discounts of 50% or more are available at many inns, hotels, and motels during winter "Holiday Bounty" and other off-season promotions.

Camping, AYH Hostel, Asilomar
Outside town on the way to Salinas is **Lake Laguna Seca** at the Laguna Seca Raceway just off Hwy. 68, with 93 tent sites and 87 spots for RVs, $10-15 per night. (Not recommended for light sleepers when the races are on.) For information and reservations, contact Laguna Seca Recreation Area, P.O. Box 367, Salinas 93905, tel. (408) 647-7799. In Monterey, if you're desperate, try pitching a tent in year-round **Veterans Memorial Park** on Via del Rey adjacent to the presidio, tel. 646-3865. First-come, first-camped; $2 for hikers/bikers, $10 for others, including hot showers. (Arrive before 3 p.m. and get a permit from the attendant.)

Best bet for budget travelers (but only open in summer, mid-June to late August) is the AYH **Monterey Peninsula Hostel.** Sharing space with the Monterey High School at the south end of Larkin St. (on Hermann), tel. (408) 649-0375, this temporary stopgap effort is a mattresses-on-the-gymnasium-floor operation with no kitchens ($6 members, $9 nonmembers) and hopefully will one day become something more stable and permanent. For information, contact Monterey Peninsula AYH Hostel, c/o AYH Central California Council, P.O. Box 28148, San Jose 95159, tel. 298-0670. The state-run **Asilomar Conference Center** in Pacific Grove, tel. 372-8016, can also be a fairly inexpensive choice (in an incredibly beautiful setting) when not completely booked with businesspeople and other groups: $50 and up. Architect Julia Morgan designed many of the resort's pine lodges. Call ahead for reservations, up to 30 days in advance, or hope for last-minute cancellations.

Inexpensive Motels
"True value" motel and hotel lodging is scarce in these parts but not completely unavailable. If you're here for the Jazz Festival, plan to stay at a motel in Marina and vicinity or on Fremont St. (motel and fast-food row) just a block from the fairgrounds. Motels on Munras are generally pricier. Be careful, especially during high season, for "floating" motel rates. The price may double or triple even after you've made your reservation!

Always predictable, and predictably inexpensive in Monterey (clean, with pool, and not far from the downtown action) is **Motel 6** at 2124 Fremont, tel. (408) 646-8585, reachable on any eastbound bus (take bus No. 1), but popular: make reservations six months or more in advance or stop by at 11 a.m. or so to check for cancellations. Rates are $36, $8 for each additional person. (In Salinas, 15-20 minutes away by car, there are two Motel 6 facilities to choose from. There's another just outside Monterey proper, at 100 Reservation Rd. in Marina, tel. 384-1000). Other fairly inexpensive alternatives, particularly in the off-season, include the **Californian Motel** on Fremont near Motel 6, tel. 372-5851, the **Driftwood Motel,** also on Fremont, tel. 372-5059, as well as the **El Dorado Inn,** tel. 373-2921, and the **Carmel Hill Motor Lodge,** tel. 373-3252, both on Munras.

Moderate To Expensive Motels And Hotels

For assistance in booking mid-range to high-end accommodations in and around Monterey, for individuals or groups, contact **Resort II Me,** 140 Franklin St., Suite 204, Monterey 93940, tel. (408) 646-9250, a firm with a good track record in matching peninsula visitors with appropriate local lodgings. Travel agents can also help arrange good-value travel packages. But you can also shop around for bargains on your own since the entire area, from Santa Cruz south to the Monterey Peninsula, was overbuilt in the 1980s to accommodate the tourist trade.

Most of Monterey's many decent motels fall into a "mid-range" price category of between $70 and $150, at least during summer and for major events, and offer modern amenities. Some establishments provide complimentary breakfast and other extra services. Best bets include the **Best Western Park Crest Motel** at 1100 Munras, tel. (408) 372-4576 or (800) 528-1234, with regular rates of $69-159, off-season specials as low as $39 s from November through May, and the **Bay Park Hotel** at 1425 Munras, tel. 649-1020 or (800) 338-3564, with rates $72-109, lower in the off-season, 25% weekday discount, other occasional specials. Also offering good value in very comfortable, historic accommodations (on acres of lovely landscape) is the **Casa Munras Garden Hotel** at 700 Munras, tel. 375-2411 or toll-free (800) 222-2446 in California, (800) 222-2558 nationwide, rates $71-121 but some rooms (as available) as low as $55. Exceptionally nice, with spacious rooms and lower rates in the off-season, is the **Best Western Monterey Inn** at 825 Abrego, tel. 373-5345, $78-103 ($98-118 for rooms with fireplaces). A great deal downtown is the very attractive and accommodating **Colton Inn,** 707

Pacific, tel. 649-6500 or (800) 848-7007, with regular rates $89-104 (lower in the off-season).

The area's major hotels, at least downtown, are geared toward the convention crowds. Look for bargains when business is a bit slow. The **Doubletree Hotel** adjacent to the Convention Center downtown at Pacific and Del Monte, tel. (408) 649-4511 or (800) 528-0444, is convenient to just about everything but fairly expensive without specials (standard rates $150-200 during summer).

Expensive And Luxury Hotels

The **Monterey Bay Inn** at 242 Cannery Row, tel. (408) 373-6242 or (800) 424-6242, offers contemporary accommodations right on the bay (many view rooms with balconies) at $129-269. Near the Row, at 487 Foam St., tel. 373-8000, is the **Best Western Victorian Inn,** $139 and up for rooms and suites with gas fireplaces, other amenities.

For absolute bayside luxury, head for the 290-room, Craftsman-style **Monterey Plaza Hotel** located at 400 Cannery Row, tel. 646-1700, or toll-free (800) 334-3999 in California, (800) 631-1339 from elsewhere in the U.S. Owned by the British Trusthouse Forte Group in conjunction with the Japanese Town Development Company (thus the multiple flags), the Monterey Plaza's fine accommodations include Italian Empire and 18th-century Chinese furnishings, every convenience (even a complete fitness center with six Nautilus stations), and exceptional food service, including one of the area's finer restaurants. The 15 Grand Suites feature a grand piano. Regular room rates range from $150 to $280, suites start at $300. But do inquire about special packages, substantial bargains starting from $57-87 per person per night.

Also deluxe, downtown, is the adobe-style **Hotel Pacific** at 300 Pacific, tel. (408) 373-5700. All rooms have balconies or decks, fireplaces, wet bars, and refrigerators; some have a view. Regular rates run $144-214, corporate rates start at $109. Ask about specials.

The huge (575-room) **Hyatt Regency Monterey Resort and Conference Center** at 1 Old Golf Course Rd., tel. 372-1234 or toll-free (800) 824-2196, is definitely a resort, the spacious grounds here including an 18-hole golf course, six tennis courts (extra fee for both), two pools, whirlpools, fitness center, the works. There's a sports bar here, **Knuckles,** with 200 satellite channels and 11 TV monitors. Rates run $150-250, but inquire about packages.

The Monterey Hotel

With a delightful Old World ambience, right downtown, the refurbished and fashionable Monterey Hotel at 406 Alvarado St., Monterey 93940, tel. (408) 375-3184 or toll-free for reservations (800) 727-0960, comfortably combines the best features of hotels with a bed and breakfast feel. This graceful 1904 Victorian is classic yet quite contemporary. The large breakfast room downstairs is reserved for complimentary breakfast (even morning news programs on the TV). There's a wonderful small garden in back, just outside the cozy lobby. Wine and cheese are served on the sideboard here every afternoon, 5-7:30 p.m., and cookies and milk are served 8-11 p.m.

Standard rooms feature custom-made armoires with TV sets, telephones, private baths with tub showers, antiques, queen-sized beds, and tasteful yet subtle decorating touches, all individualized. Only two rooms, smaller than standard, feature double beds. One suite (Room 217) features two separate entrances, a feather bed in the bedroom, sofa bed in the sitting area, and an interior garden plot between. Street-facing suites, like Room 309, feature fabulous fan-shaped windows, fireplace, wet bar and refrigerator, jacuzzi-style tubs, and queen-sized beds with down comforters. (Though every floor features an outdoor landing and deck area, on the third floor interior landing there's an intimate atrium parlor, lit by the skylight overhead.) Back-landing suites, such as Room 402, include many of the same amenities plus special touches like marble countertops and antique sinks. The only inconvenience presented by a stay at the Monterey Hotel is lack of on-site parking. But an inexpensive city lot (rarely full) is quite nearby. Regular rates begin at $99 for standard rooms, $185 for a two-room suite with featherbed. But do inquire about off-season, midweek, and other specials (often advertised in major Bay Area newspapers), with rooms available for as low as $49-79.

Bed And Breakfasts

Reasonable is the **Del Monte Beach Inn,** 1110 Del Monte Ave., Monterey 93949, tel. (408) 649-4410 or (800) 727-4410, with rooms $40-75. A stay at this European-style inn includes continental breakfast. **The Jabberwock** at 598 Laine St., tel. 372-4777, is a "post-Victorian" with a Victorian name. Some shared baths. Full breakfasts (imaginative and good) plus cookies and milk at night, rooms $95-170. The historic **Merritt House** downtown at 386 Pacific St., tel. 646-9686, has charming modern rooms in an old adobe, $120-225. The 1929 English Tudor **Old Monterey Inn** at 500 Martin St., tel. 375-8284, has 10 rooms (most with fireplaces), serves full breakfasts and dinners, plus lunch on weekends. Rates: $160-220.

GOOD FOOD

In Monterey, eating well (and almost inexpensively) is easier than finding lodgings. Hard to beat is picnicking at the beaches or local parks. Happy hour, at the wharf and on "the Row" and elsewhere, is a big deal in the area. In addition to cheap drinks, many bars serve great (free) food from 4-7 p.m. With an abundance of reasonably priced (and generous) breakfast places, an inexpensive alternative to three meals is skipping lunch then shopping around for early-bird dinners, a mainstay at many local restaurants. But if you're in the area, do attend the **Historic Downtown Farmer's Market** on Alvarado St. (between Franklin and Del Monte) every Tuesday night 4:30-8 p.m. Great food, great fun.

Inexpensive Eating

Scout around in the communities surrounding Fort Ord for some real finds in the cheap eatery category—such as the exceptional Salvadoran **El Migueleño** a 1066 Broadway in Seaside, tel. (408) 899-2199. Their specialty, Playa Azul, combines six different kinds of seafood with ranchera sauce, white wine, and mushrooms, also white rice and beans. Also good for quick and interesting seafood and pastas, even house-made desserts, is **The Fishwife Seafood Cafe** at 789 Trinity (at Fremont), tel. 394-2027. Try the **Thai Hut** at 580 Broadway, tel. 899-1191, for some great deals at lunch and dinner, like the $5 all-you-can-eat buffet on Mon., Wed., and Fri. at lunch. **Yeng Ching** at 1868 Fremont (also over the border in Seaside), tel. 899-7801, is the place for Chinese. For great Vietnamese and a few Filipino dishes, head to tiny **Camvan's**

haggling over fresh strawberries at the Alvarado Street Farmer's Market

KIM WEIR

in Marina at Towne Plaza, 328-C Reservation Rd., tel. 883-0350—with 85 choices on the menu. Open daily for lunch and dinner.

Back in Monterey proper, **Rosine's** downtown at 434 Alvarado, tel. (408) 375-1400, is locally loved at breakfast, lunch, and dinner. In addition to good pancakes, waffles, and other standards, at breakfast here you can get veggie Benedict (with avocado, sauteed mushrooms, and tomatoes on the English muffin instead of Canadian bacon). Lunch features homemade soups, salads, sandwiches, and burgers. An array of pastas plus chicken, seafood, and steaks is on the menu at dinner, prime rib on Friday and Saturday nights. Adjacent is **The Poppy** at 444 Alvarado St., tel. 372-9496, with good down-home breakfasts—try the pecan waffles—and cheap lunch specials, okay dinners. A friendly family-style place (the waitstaff's banter is as good as the food), this was Steinbeck's model for the Golden Poppy Cafe in *Sweet Thursday.*

The **Old Monterey Cafe** at 489 Alvarado, tel. (408) 646-1021, serves 40 different kinds of omelettes at breakfast plus unusual choices like calamari and eggs, lingüiça and eggs, even pigs in a blanket. Just about everything is good at lunch, too, from hearty shrimp Louie and the Athenian Greek salad (with feta cheese, Greek olives, shrimp, and veggies) to the ¾-pound burgers and steak or calamari sandwiches. Open for breakfast and lunch Wed.-Mon. only.

Still reasonable (and delicious) is **Kathy's** at 700 Cass St. near the post office, tel. (408) 647-9540. Pick any three items for a fluffy omelette; includes home fries, cheese sauce, bran muffins, and homemade strawberry jam for under $5. Sandwiches $3-4, best when eaten on the patio. Open Mon.-Sat. for breakfast and lunch.

More Good Food And Fine Dining

For a casual lunch or Sunday brunch, the **Clock Garden,** 565 Abrego, tel. (408) 375-6100, seats guests outside amid the antique clocks planted in the garden, weather permitting. Especially attractive in these recessionary times are the various early bird specials. Try lunch or dinner at cozy **Triples,** 220 Olivier, tel. 372-4744, for friendly European elegance in an alley behind the Doubletree Inn. Call for reservations.

Bindel's at 500 Hartnell, tel. (408) 373-3737, is famous for its Sunday brunch and jazz on weekends. Lunch features selections like black bean soup with sour cream and rum or salads such as rock shrimp on spinach with macadamia nuts and vinaigrette dressing. Other fairly light fare: smoked pork quesadillas with black beans and rice, quiche of the day, or steamed Pacific salmon with dill chardonnay sauce. Everything under $10. Dinner entrees, all served with Bindel's famous Monterey Jack cheese bread and artichoke cream soup, include linguini with central coast vegetables and sweet basil in herb cream sauce, or seafood, steaks, and poultry. **Fresh Cream** upstairs at Heritage Harbor, 99 Pacific St., tel. 375-9798, has wonderful French country cuisine lightened by that fresh California touch. Expensive, but even travelers light in the pocketbook can afford dessert and coffee. Open for dinner, menu changes daily. Call for information and reservations. **Delfino's** at the Monterey Plaza on Cannery Row has *the* reputation for fine Italian food. A new contender is **Cibo** at 301 Alvarado, tel. 649-8151, serving stylish but more rustic Sicilian fare. Open for dinner nightly after 5 p.m.

Eating At The Wharf

Named for tender squid breaded then sauteed in butter, **Abalonetti** at 57 Fisherman's Wharf, tel. (408) 373-1851, offers relaxed lunch and dinner, primarily seafood and standard Italian fare. Fairly inexpensive, nice view. Out on the end of the secondary pier at the wharf is **Rappa's** outdoor cafe, tel. 372-7562, an oceanside oasis, quite reasonable, quite good, wonderful atmosphere. Good early-bird dinners.

The big news these days is **Cafe Fina** at 1 Fisherman's Wharf, tel. (408) 372-5200, very Italian, very lively and lighthearted, serving everything from mesquite-barbecued fish or smoked salmon on fettuccine with shallot cream sauce to goat cheese and black olive ravioli. People go crazy over Cafe Fina's "pizzettes," little eight-inch pizzas popped hot out of the restaurant's wood-burning oven.

Absolutely excellent (and expensive) is **Domenico's on the Wharf,** 50 Fisherman's Wharf, tel. (408) 372-3655, famous for its Southern Italian accent. Fresh seafood, homemade pasta, plus chicken, steak, veal dishes, and a long, very California wine list. Oyster bar open from 10 a.m. daily.

Eating On Cannery Row

Nick's at 700 Cannery Row is the place for breakfast, served daily until 3 p.m., especially enjoyable out on the patio in good weather. Also on the menu: burgers, sandwiches, and seafood platters at lunch, seafood entrees and such at dinner.

If you're spending most of the day at the **Monterey Aquarium,** try the oyster bar and restaurant there. Most of the places along Cannery Row offer early-bird dinners, so before you get hungry, go bargain shopping. **Beau Thai** at 807 Cannery Row, tel. (408) 373-8811, is a local hotspot for good Thai food. Another locally popular dinner house is the **Whaling Station Inn** at 763 Wave, tel. 373-3778, with everything from

seafood and house-made pastas to mesquite-grilled Black Angus steaks. Also in the neighborhood and famous for fine dining is **Delfino's** in the Monterey Plaza Hotel, 400 Cannery Row, tel. 646-1706. The view from the dining room is magnificent—both out toward the bay and into the open Genovese kitchen, where the elegant and exciting edibles come from. Extensive wine list (both Californian and Italian), outdoor dining in summer. Expensive.

Kalisa's

Legendary on the Row, though, is that survivor of the Steinbeck era, **Kalisa's,** at 851 Cannery Row, tel. (408) 372-8512, "A Cosmopolitan Gourmet Place," but really an eclectic people's eatery. Reasonable for lunch and dinner (and open till the wee hours on weekends), wonderful for Sunday brunch. The coffeehouse below features deli fare and ice cream in the daytime, suppers at night; meals are sometimes served in the garden out back. The "international" fare includes Greek-style pizza, northern Thai beef salad, rock cod roulade, and fresh fish. Live entertainment on Friday and Saturday nights is varied, too: belly dancers, magicians, and musicians. Jazz goes with upstairs dinners on weekend nights.

EVENTS

In March, show up for the **Monterey Wine Festival,** with more than 200 wineries strutting their stuff plus educational programs and workshops by industry pros, and for **Dixieland Monterey.** Usually held in April, the **Formula One International Motorcycle Races** at Laguna Seca draw a major audience. Traditionally, though, April is adobe month in Monterey, with the popular **Adobe Tour** through public and private historic buildings. In May is the **Great Monterey Squid Festival,** chic culinary indulgence for those with calamari cravings, plus arts, crafts, and entertainment. June is **Merienda,** Monterey's birthday party, also the **Monterey Bay Blues Festival.** The **Fourth of July** celebration here is fun, with fireworks off the Coast Guard Pier. On weekends only through July and August is the **Monterey Bay Theatrefest** at Custom House Plaza, followed by the August **Scottish Festival and Highland Games** at the fairgrounds.

Most famous of all, of course, is the **Monterey Jazz Festival,** the oldest continuous jazz fest in the nation—not as daring as others but hosting legendary greats and up-and-coming talent. This is the biggest party of the year here, usually held in late September, so get tickets and reserve rooms well in advance (four to six months). For info and tickets, contac:t Monterey Jazz Festival, 444 Pearl St., Monterey 93940, tel. (408) 373-3366 or 775-2021.

All you race car fans, plan to zoom into town for the long-running, three-day **Monterey Grand Prix** in October. In November comes the **Robert Louis Stevenson Un-Birthday Party** at the Stevenson House. The **Christmas in the Adobes** yuletide tour in mid-December is another big event, with luminaria-lit historic tours of 15 adobes, each dressed up in period holiday decorations, and the festivities accompanied by music and carolers. Fee. For information, contact the Monterey State Historic Park, tel. (408) 649-7118.

PRACTICALITIES

Information

The main **Monterey Peninsula Chamber of Commerce And Visitors and Convention Bureau** is at 380 Alvarado St., P.O. Box 1770, Monterey 93940, tel. (408) 649-1770. On weekends (when the chamber is closed) you can get good maps, brochures, and general info at the **visitor center** at Monterey State Historic Park near the Conference Center, 210 Olivier St., tel. 649-2836. The **Monterey History and Art Association,** 412 Pacific St., tel. 372-2608, has info on the annual adobe and garden tours. For information about Monterey County parks and area hiking trails, contact **Monterey County Parks and Recreation,** P.O. Box 5279, Salinas 93915, tel. 755-4899 (or inquire at the local **Sierra Club** chapter in Carmel).

The *Monterey Peninsula Herald* is the mainline community news source, but pick up free local publications for dinner specials and current activities and entertainment. Pick up the weekly *Coasting: The Easygoing Entertainment Guide* to all peninsula events and activities. Even better, for something of an alternative view of things, is the *Coast Weekly,* free, also offering entertainment and events information. Quite good, too, for visitors is the *Entertainment & Dining Review,* just what it says it is, also free. Specifically for seniors: the local edition of the *Senior Spectrum.* Other worthwhile local publications include the glossy *This Month on the Monterey Peninsula, Monterey Bay: The Magazine,* and the Monterey Peninsula/Salinas Valley *Adventures in Dining* magazine.

Parking And Transportation

Hitching into, out of, and around the Monterey Peninsula is difficult. Even getting around by car is a problem; finding streets is confusing due to missing signs, complex traffic signals, and one-way routes. Local traffic jams can be horrendous. Drivers, park at the 12-hour meters near Fisherman's Wharf—the cheapest lots are downtown—and walk or take the bus. (For more specific parking advice, pick up the free "Smart Parking in Monterey: How to Find Affordable Legal Public Parking" brochure at the visitors bureau.)

Bicycling is the other way to go—narrow local roads and few real bike paths, but you can get just about everywhere by bike if you're careful. Rent bikes at **Free-wheeling Cycles,** 188 Webster St. north of downtown, tel. (408) 373-3855, or—down on Cannery Row—**Bay Bikes,** 640 Wave St., tel. 646-9090, where in addition to mountain and tour bikes, you can rent those four-wheel covered surreys or "pedalinas" here. (Bay Bikes is also in downtown Carmel, tel. 625-BIKE, though only the Monterey shop has surreys.) Two other bike rental firms: **Monterey Moped Adventures** and **Adventures by the Sea** (for more about both, see "Other Outdoor Activities" above). (Get information on scheduled rides with the local **Velo Club Monterey** at either place.)

Once parked, from Memorial Day through Labor Day ride the **WAVE,** Monterey's "Waterfront Area Visitor Express," a shuttle bus system connecting The Tin Cannery shopping center (at the edge of Pacific Grove), the Monterey Bay Aquarium, Cannery Row, Fisherman's Wharf, and the town's historic downtown adobes with the downtown conference center, nearby motels and hotels, and parking garages. WAVE's Monterey-Salinas transit buses are identified by a wave logo. Buses run every 15 minutes. All-day fare (9 a.m.-9 p.m.) is 50 cents; transfers are accepted from other local buses. For more information, contact Monterey-Salinas Transit.

To get around on public buses otherwise, contact **Monterey-Salinas Transit** at 1 Ryan Ranch Rd., tel. (408) 899-2555 or 424-7695. "The Bus" serves the entire area, including Pacific Grove, Carmel, and Carmel Valley, from Watsonville south to Salinas. Local buses can get you just about anywhere, but some run sporadically. Pick up the free "Rider's Guide" schedule at the downtown **Transit Plaza** (where most buses stop and where Alvarado, Polk, Munras, Pearl, and Tyler streets converge) or at motels, the chamber of commerce, and the library. Fares for each transit zone are $1.25, exact change required, free transfers. Seniors, the disabled, and children can ride for 50 cents with the transit system's courtesy card. A day pass for a single zone is $3.75, for all zones $7.50. From late May through mid-October, bus No. 22 runs south to famous Nepenthe in Big Sur (five buses per day, $2.50). You can also connect to **Amtrak** in Salinas, tel. 422-7458.

Amtrak is in Salinas at 40 Railroad Ave., tel. (408) 422-7458, but call (800) USA-RAIL for train information—including information on Amtrak's Thruway bus connections from Monterey and vicinity, a service included in some fares—and reservations. **Greyhound** is at 351 Del Monte Ave., tel. 373-4735, close to the sights and just four blocks from the Alvarado St. city bus depot, open daily 8 a.m.-7:30 p.m.

Other Transportation And Tours

An unusual thrill: cruising town in a facsimile 1929 Model A, some with rumble seats, and a red Phaeton that seats five, from **Rent-A-Road-**ster at 756 Foam St., tel. (408) 647-1929. The basic rate is about $30 an hour but you can arrange half-day and full-day tours, too—and head south to Big Sur and San Simeon in style. **Adventure Tours Unlimited,** 99 Pacific St., tel. 375-9334, with a fleet of air-conditioned Ford vans, also doubles as an airport shuttle service, with delivery and pick-up at the local airport and as far afield as San Jose, San Francisco, and Oakland. (Advance notice and reservations are required for out-of-town pick-ups.) **Otter-Mobile Tours & Charters** located just south of town in Carmel, tel. 625-9782, offers van tours of local sights ("Peninsula Highlights") as well as trips to Pt. Lobos, Big Sur, San Simeon and Hearst Castle, and wineries in the Salinas Valley. The company designs personalized tours around specific interests, from nature hikes to hunting down Steinbeck's haunts. Also based in Carmel: **On-The-Loose Secret Tours,** tel. 624-1003, and **Steinbeck Country Tours,** tel. 625-5107. **Pelican Eco-Tours,** 14925 Joanne Ave., San Jose 95127, tel. 729-4083, offers small group naturalist-guided daytrips throughout the Monterey/Big Sur area and elsewhere, plus custom birdwatching and photography tours.

Almost a local institution, and particularly popular as an adjunct to corporate meetings and conventions, is **California Heritage Guides,** at last report inside Pacific House on Customs House Plaza, tel. (408) 373-6454, which organizes large group tours, teas, and shopping expeditions.

CARMEL AND VICINITY

Vizcaíno named the river here after Palestine's Mount Carmel (probably with the encouragement of several Carmelite friars accompanying his expedition). Carmel-by-the-Sea distinguishes this postcard-pretty, almost too-cute coastal village of 5,000 souls from affluent Carmel Valley 10 miles inland and Carmel Highlands just south of Point Lobos on the way to Big Sur. Everything about all the Carmels, though, says one thing quite loudly: money. Despite its bohemian beginnings, these days Carmel crankily guards its quaintness while cranking up the commercialism. (Shopping is the town's major draw.) Still free at last report are the beautiful city beaches and visits to the elegant old Carmel Mission. Almost free: tours of Robinson Jeffers's **Tor House** and fabulous **Point Lobos** just south of town.

Carmel hasn't always been so crowded or so crotchety. Open-minded artists, poets, writers, and other oddballs were the community's original movers and shakers—most of them shaken up and out of San Francisco after the 1906 earthquake. Upton Sinclair, Sinclair Lewis, Robinson Jeffers, and Jack London were some of the literary lights who once twinkled in this town. Master photographers Ansel Adams and Edward Weston were more recent residents. But (as often happens in California) land values shot up and the original bohemians were priced right out of the neighborhood.

Carmel-by-the-Sea is facing trying times. Sinclair Lewis predicted the future in 1933 when he said to Carmelites: "For God's sake, don't let the Babbits run the town. You've got every other city in the country beat." Growth—how much and what kind—is always the issue here. Lowlife tourists (locals refer to them as "the T-shirt and ice cream people") who come here to stroll and shop are both loved and hated.

In summer and on most warm-weather weekends, traffic on Hwy. 1 is backed up for a mile or more in either direction by the Carmel "crunch." Sane people take the bus, ride bikes, or walk to get here. This overly quaint community is so congested much of the time, parking is nonexistent. (If visitors do find a parking slot in downtown Carmel, it's only for an hour, and there's a steep fine if you're late getting back.) Other scarce items in Carmel: streetlights, traffic signals, sidewalks, street signs, house numbers, neon signs, and jukeboxes.

SIGHTS

Out And About
To get oriented, take a walk. Carmel has a few tiny parks hidden here and there, one especially for walkers. The **Mission Trails Park** has trails (five miles or so) winding through redwoods, willows, and wildflowers (in season). Finding it is challenging, of course, since Carmel doesn't believe in signs. To do it the easy way, start at the cleverly concealed Flanders Dr. entrance off Hatton Rd. (appreciate the **Lester Rowntree Memorial Arboretum** just inside) before strolling downhill to the Rio Rd. trailhead near the mission. Then visit the mission or head downtown. Carmel's shops and galleries alone are an easy day-long distraction for true shoppers, but local architecture is also intriguing. The area between 5th and 8th streets and Junipero and the city beach is packed with seacoast cottages, Carmel gingerbread "dollhouses," and adobe-and-post homes typical of the area.

Carmel Beaches
The downtown crescent of **Carmel Beach City Park** is beautiful—steeply sloping, blinding-white sands and aquamarine waters—but too cold and dangerous for swimming and a tourist zoo in summer. (A winter sunset stroll is wonderful, though.) A better alternative is to take Scenic Rd. (or Carmelo St.) south from Santa Lucia off Rio Rd. to **Carmel River State Beach,** fringed with eucalyptus and cypress and often uncrowded (but dangerous in high surf). This is where locals go to get away. There's a bird sanctuary in the marsh nearby, home for hawks, kingfishers, cormorants, herons, pelicans, sandpipers, snowy egrets, and sometimes flocks of migrating ducks and geese. **Middle Beach** beyond is almost a secret: a curving sandy crescent

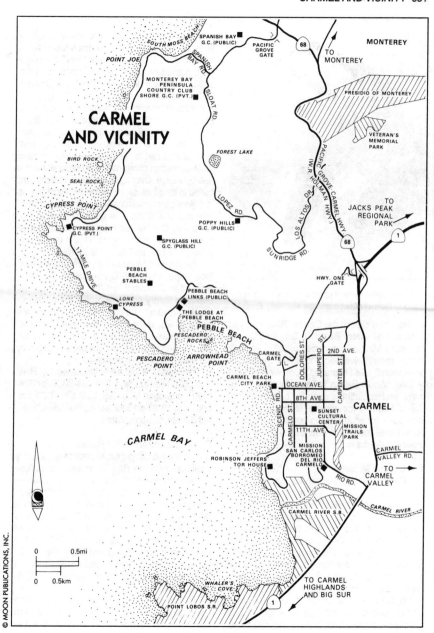

CARMEL AND VICINITY

CALIFORNIA DEPARTMENT OF PARKS & RECREATION

Father Serra, current candidate for sainthood, founded Carmel Mission and the Monterey Presidio.

on the south side of the Carmel River and just north of **Monastery Beach** at San Jose Creek. To get to Middle in summer or fall, just walk across the dry riverbed and follow the trail or (year-round) take Ribera Rd. from Hwy. 1. Safety note: Middle Beach is hazardous for swimming, and sometimes even for beachwalking, due to freak 10-foot waves. Monastery Beach is popular for scuba diving but the surf conditions here, too, are treacherous (almost 50 drowning deaths in the past couple of decades).

The Carmel Mission

The Carmel Mission or, properly, Mission Basilica San Carlos Borromeo del Rio Carmelo, is wonderful, well worth a visit. California's second mission, it was originally established at the Monterey Presidio in 1770, then moved here the following year. One-time headquarters and favorite foreign home of Father Junipero Serra (whose remains are buried at the foot of the altar in the sanctuary), the mission's magnificent vine-draped cathedral is the first thing to catch the eye. The romantic baroque stone church, one of the most graceful buildings in the state (complete with four-bell Moorish tower, arched roof, and star-shaped central window),

was completed in 1797.

Most of the buildings here are reconstructions, however, since the Carmel Mission fell to ruins in the 1800s. But these "new" old buildings, painstakingly rebuilt and restored in the 1930s under the direction of Sir Harry Downie, fail to suggest the size and complexity of the original bustling mission complex: an odd-shaped quadrangle with a central fountain, gardens, kitchen, carpenter and blacksmith shops, soldiers' housing, and priests' quarters. The native peoples attached to the mission—a labor force of 4,000 Christian converts—lived separately in a nearby village. Over 3,000 "mission Indians" are buried in the silent, simple cemetery, most graves in these gardens unmarked, some decorated with abalone shells. The gardens themselves, started by Downie, are fabulous: old-fashioned plant varieties, from bougainvillea to bird of paradise, fuchsias, and "tower of jewels."

The Carmel Mission has three museums. Note especially the 600 volumes Padre Serra brought to California in 1769, California's first unofficial library and now part of the mission's "book museum." The silver altar furnishings are also originals, as are the ornate vestments, Spanish and native artifacts, and other mission memorabilia. Serra's simple priest's cell is a lesson by contrast in modern materialism.

The mission is just a few blocks west of Hwy. 1 at 3080 Rio Rd., tel. (408) 624-3600 (or 624-1271), and open Mon.-Sat. 9:30 a.m.-4:30 p.m. and Sun. 10:30-4:15 for self-guided tours. Free, but donations appreciated.

Robinson Jeffers's Tor House

A medieval-looking granite retreat on a rocky knoll above Carmel Bay, Tor House was built by family-man poet Robinson Jeffers, who hauled the huge stones up from the beach below with horse teams. The manual labor, he said, cleared his mind and "my fingers had the art to make stone love stone." California's dark prince of poetry, Jeffers was generally aloof from the peninsula's other "seacoast bohemians." On the day he died here, January 20, 1961, it snowed—a rare event along any stretch of California's coast.

You can only begin to appreciate Tor House from the outside (it's just a short walk up from Carmel River Beach on Ocean View Ave. between Scenic Rd. and Stewart Way). Jeffers built the three-story Hawk Tower (complete with secret passageway) for his wife Una. The mellow redwood paneling, warm oriental rugs, and lovely gardens here soften the impact of the home's bleak tawny exterior, the overall effect somehow symbolizing Robinson Jeffers' hearth-centered life far removed from the world's insanity. Almost whimsical is the collection of 100-plus unicorns the poet gathered. One of Jeffers's twin sons, Donnan, and family still live at Tor House, so don't go snooping around. Small-group guided tours are offered on Fri. and Sat., advance reservations required. Write Jeffers's Tor House, P.O. Box 1887, 26304 Ocean View Ave., Carmel 93921, or call (408) 624-1813. Adults $5, college students $3.50, high school students $1.50, no children under 12.

ACCOMMODATIONS

Mary Austin's observation that "beauty is cheap here" may apply to the views, but little else. Camp southeast of Carmel Valley at **White Oaks campground,** seven sites, $3 or **China Camp,** six sites; both are first-come, first-camped. Farther on there's **Tassajara Hot Springs** in sum-

CALIFORNIA DEPARTMENT OF PARKS & RECREATION

Robinson Jeffers

mer (advance reservations required) and nearby **Arroyo Seco,** 46 sites. Call (408) 385-5434 for info. Or head south to Big Sur.

There are dozens of motels in Carmel and vicinity. The reasonable **Carmel River Inn,** 26600 Oliver Rd., Carmel 93921, tel. (408) 624-1575 or (800) 882-8142, is a 10-acre riverside spread with heated pool and cozy cottages, most with fireplaces and kitchens, also motel rooms, $50-110. The lovely **Carmel Wayfarer Inn** at 4th Ave. and Mission St., P.O. Box 1896, tel. 624-2711 or (800) 533-2711, has rooms (some with ocean views, some with fireplace and kitchen) $59-118. Breakfast included.

Other above-average Carmel accommodations—and there are plenty to choose from—include the **Carmel Studio Lodge** at 5th and Junipero, P.O. Box 2388, tel. (408) 624-8515, 19 rooms, some with kitchens (rates: $90-130); the **Carmel Oaks Inn** at 5th and Mission, tel. 624-5547 or (800) 266-5547, attractive and convenient, a bargain by local standards at $89-121; and the new **Lobos Lodge** at Monte Verde and Ocean, tel. 624-3874, $87-160. Bargains at most motels are available in the off-season, especially on weekdays.

Wonderful is the only word for the **Pine Inn** downtown on Ocean between Monte Verde and Lincoln, P.O. Box 250, tel. (408) 624-3851 or (800) 228-3851. This small hotel offers comfortable "Carmel Victorian" accommodations, $85-205, also fine dining (there's even a gazebo with rollback roof for eating al fresco, fog permitting). Even if you don't stay, sit on the terrace, act affluent, and sip Ramos fizzes.

The landmark 1929 **Cypress Inn** downtown at Lincoln and 7th, P.O. Box Y, Carmel 93921, tel. (408) 624-3871 or (800) 443-7443, is partially owned by Doris Day. It's a gracious and intimate place, another small hotel with a bed-and-breakfast sensibility. Pets allowed, for a price. Rates: $85-185. The **Sundial Lodge** at Monte Verde and 7th, P.O. Box J, tel. 624-8578, is a cross between small hotel and bed and breakfast. All 19 antique-furnished rooms have private baths, TV, telephones. Lovely English gardens and courtyard. Continental breakfast, afternoon tea. Rates: $99-165.

Très Carmel (and a historic treasure) is the Mediterranean-style **La Playa Hotel** at Camino Real and 8th, P.O. Box 900, tel. (408) 624-6476 or (800) 582-8900, lush gardens outside, guest rooms and cottages with fireplaces, ocean-view decks, and separate living areas. Rates: $100-200.

The **Adobe Inn** at Dolores and 8th, P.O. Box 4115, tel. 624-3933, is quite luxurious—just about every amenity, including wood-burning fireplaces, wet bars and refrigerators, patio or decks, color TV, phones, sauna, heated pool, some ocean views—in the $85-265 range. Ask about special winter rates.

Clint Eastwood's Carmel Mission Ranch

The traditional place to stay (and reasonable by local standards), just outside town, is the **Carmel Mission Ranch** bed and breakfast at 26270 Dolores, Carmel 93921, tel. (408) 624-6436. A quiet, 40-acre ranch overlooking the Carmel River with views of Carmel Bay and Point Lobos, the inn has B&B accommodations in the ranch house plus 15 cottages and a handful of motel rooms. The bunkhouse, farmhouse, old creamery (now the dining room/bar) and the dancehall (once a cow barn) are over a century old. And the mission *is* nearby. Regular rates are $95-250 (off-season discounts).

An interesting political P.S.: there are advantages to having a wealthy mayor. When developers recently proposed a condominium development at Mission Ranch, locals were up in arms. So former Mayor Clint Eastwood himself bought the place for about $5 million, with the promise to preserve it in perpetuity.

Bed And Breakfasts

Local inns offer an almost overwhelming amount of choice. (Keep in mind, of course, that "inn" in Carmel may be a code word for motel.) Local bed and breakfast inns are comparable, in price, to most Carmel area motels (and so much homier). The Victorian **Sea View Inn** on Camino Real between 11th and 12th, tel. (408) 624-8788, is $80-100, with continental breakfast and tea and cookies in the afternoon. The **Stonehouse Inn** at 8th and Monte Verde, P.O. Box 2517, Carmel 93921, tel. 624-4569, was built by local Indians. Full breakfast, wine and sherry, hors d'oeuvres, $90-125. Most rooms at the **Vagabond House** at 4th and Dolores, tel. 624-7738 or (800) 262-1262, have fireplaces. Continental breakfast served in rooms, $79-135. **The Cobblestone Inn** on Junipero near 8th, tel. 625-5222 or toll-free (800) 222-INNS, is a traditional Carmel home with cobblestone courtyard, fireplaces, and English country-house antiques. Rates include full breakfast buffet, complimentary tea, hors d'oeuvres, rooms $95-175. Other possibilities include the **Green Lantern** at 7th and Casanova, P.O. Box 1114, tel. 624-4392, with rustic multi-unit cottages (some with lofts) not far from town, $60-100, and **The Homestead** at Lincoln and 8th, P.O. Box 1285, tel. 624-4119: rooms with baths, and cottages for $50-80.

Staying In Carmel Highlands

The swanky and well-known 1916 **Highlands Inn** in Carmel Highlands is indeed beautiful, even more so after its recent refurbishing. Most people would have to forfeit their rent or house payments to stay here ($225-650 for rooms, many with fireplaces, some with whirlpool baths), but stroll through the Grand Lodge to appreciate the oak woodwork, twin yellow granite fireplaces, gorgeous earthy carpet, leather sofas and chairs, and granite tables. For info: Highlands Inn, P.O. Box 1700, Carmel 93921, tel. (408) 624-3801 or toll-free (800) 682-4811 in California, (800) 538-9525 elsewhere in the U.S. The nearby (hot pink) **Tickle Pink Motor Inn** just south of the Highlands Inn, 155 Highland Dr., 93923, tel. 624-1244, offers equally spectacular views—but it's hardly inexpensive at $109-209 per night, two-day weekend minimum.

Staying In Carmel Valley

Robles Del Rio Lodge, perched atop a hill overlooking Carmel Valley, is hard to find the first time, but it's well worth the trip. Rustic pine-paneled rooms in the lodge or in outlying cabins are $80-160, and include fabulous continental breakfasts by the lodge fireplace: homemade muffins and pastries, fresh fruit, juices, coffee, soft-cooked eggs. Other amenities include a pool, sauna, whirlpool, and tennis court. Affiliated with the lodge is the excellent **The Ridge** restaurant (classic French and California cuisine), tel. (408) 659-0170, serving lunch and dinner, closed Mondays. For room reservations (and directions), contact Robles Del Rio, 200 Punta Del Monte, Carmel Valley 93924, tel. 659-3705 or toll-free (800) 883-0843. Also rustic, and a local tradition, is **Los Laureles Lodge** on Carmel Valley Rd., tel. 659-2233 or toll-free (800) 533-4404, once part of the Boronda Spanish land grant and later a Del Monte ranch. Rooms $95-125, suites $150-350, excellent restaurant also.

A great choice, too, is the **Valley Lodge** on Carmel Valley Rd. at Ford, P.O. Box 93, tel. (408) 659-2261 or (800) 641-4646. After all, who can resist "Come listen to your beard grow" as an advertising slogan? The Lodge features rooms fronting the lovely gardens plus one- and two-bedroom cottages with fireplaces and kitchens. Pool, sauna, hot tub, fitness center. Rates: $85-215.

But if you must go see how the other one percent lives, head for the five-star **Quail Lodge** at the Carmel Valley Golf and Country Club, 8205 Valley Greens Dr., tel. (408) 624-1581 or (800) 538-9516, with elegant contemporary rooms and suites with fireplaces, plus access to private tennis and golf facilities and fine dining at The Covey restaurant. Rates: $215-345 (ask about off-season and special packages). Pricey, too, in the same vein is **Carmel Valley Ranch Resort,** 1 Old Ranch Rd. (off Robinson Canyon Rd.), tel. 625-9500 or (800) 4-CARMEL, a gated resort with 100 suites, all individually decorated, with wood-burning fireplaces, private decks. Private golf course, 12 tennis courts, pools, saunas, whirlpools. Rates: $235-295, suites with private outdoor hot tub/whirlpools $395-700.

You'll spend more, but avoid the country clubs and other "too new" places at the luxurious **Stonepine Estate Resort** at 150 E. Carmel Valley Rd., tel. (408) 659-2245, once the Crocker family's summer home. A Carmel version of a French chateau, Stonepine has eight luxury suites in the main house, another four in the equestrian center near (but not too near) the stables where fine carriage-trained draft horses live: Clydesdales, Belgians, and Percherons. Rates: $175-550. For more information about Carmel Valley lodgings and restaurants, contact: Carmel Valley Chamber of Commerce, tel. (408) 659-4000.

FOOD, ENTERTAINMENT, AND INFORMATION

Good Basic Meals

For a perfect omelette with home fries and homemade valley pork sausage, try **Katy's Cottage** (a satellite of Katy Curry's down-home Wagon Wheel in Carmel Valley) located on Lincoln between Ocean and 7th, tel. (408) 625-626. The

Tuck Box tearoom on Dolores near 7th, tel. 624-6365, is the place all the tourists stop to photograph. Famous for its pecan pie, shepherd's pie, and Welsh rarebit at lunch, the Box also makes hot scones and homemade preserves great for breakfast or afternoon tea. Breakfast of bacon and eggs, scones or muffins, and fresh-squeezed orange juice for under $5. (No reservations, so stop by if the line's not already out the door.)

Also great for breakfast is the **Carmel Cafe** on the west side of Mission between 5th and 6th, tel. (408) 624-1922, another quaint cottage, this one serving fresh baked breads and rolls, applewood smoked bacon from Corralitos, and genuine Vermont maple syrup on pancakes and waffles—not to mention the fresh-squeezed orange juice and fresh-ground coffee. Open daily for breakfast and lunch. Also cozy and crowded is **Em Le's** at Dolores and 5th, tel. 624-6780. Try the buttermilk waffles, available for lunch or dinner. For seafood dinner, consider the **Clam Box** at Mission and 5th, tel. 624-8597, a favorite locals' hangout.

The Hog's Breath Inn

The peaceful courtyard outside half-partner Clint Eastwood's **Hog's Breath Inn** on San Carlos between 5th and 6th, tel. (408) 625-1044, has a hog's head presiding. There's another inside, plus you'll get to look down the rifle barrel of a billboard-sized image of Eastwood. Mayor Eastwood fought with the former city council (ultimately suing) to add on the adjacent office complex; that controversy over "village atmosphere" launched his political career. Burgers ("Dirty Harry Hamburger") and better for lunch. Dinner is the usual steak and seafood fare, occasional wild pig, also vegetarian choices. Open for lunch 11:30 a.m.-3 p.m., for dinner 5-10 p.m., and for Sunday brunch, 11-3. Full bar.

More Good Food

Even if you can't afford to stay there, you can afford to eat at the Highlands Inn south of Carmel. The inn's **California Market** restaurant, tel. (408) 624-3801, serves California regional dishes with fresh local ingredients. The specialty here is Pizelle Monterey, with heaps of shrimp, avocado, artichokes, tomatoes, and—of course—Monterey Jack cheese served on a crisp flour tortilla. Ocean-view and deck dining, fabulous scenery. Open for breakfast, lunch, and dinner daily. (In the pricier category at the Highlands is the elegant **Pacific's Edge** restaurant, same telephone, open for lunch, dinner, and Sunday brunch.) Inexpensive **Ciao Mein** at 26344 Carmel Rancho Ln., tel. 625-5595, serves fascinating Italian-Chinese fare. Open Mon.-Sat. after 11:30 a.m.—complimentary pizza is served during happy hour Mon.-Friday.

The **Rio Grill** at The Crossroads (Hwy. 1 at Rio Rd.), tel. (408) 625-5436, is a long-running favorite for innovative American fare, everything fresh and/or made from scratch. Many entrees are served straight from the oakwood smoker. Open for lunch and dinner daily, great Sunday brunch. Interesting, too, is inexpensive **From Scratch** restaurant at The Barnyard Shopping Center, tel. 625-2448, casual and eclectic—local art on the walls—and open for breakfast and lunch daily, for dinner Tues.-Sat., and for brunch on Sunday.

Special Dining
All the Carmels are crowded with "cuisine." Ask around if you're looking for the elite and/or truly expensive experience. Among the hottest haute places in and around Carmel these days is **Anton & Michel**, in the Court of the Fountains on Mission between Ocean and 7th, tel. (408) 624-2406, not really that expensive considering the setting and exceptional continental fare. Open daily for lunch and dinner, reservations definitely recommended. Simple and superb **Creme Carmel** on San Carlos between Ocean and 7th, tel. 624-0444, is the place for classic yet California-style French cuisine. The list of daily specials is almost as long as your arm, and certainly as long as the regular menu. Don't miss this place. Dinner daily after 5:30 p.m.

Casanova at 5th and Mission, tel. (408) 625-0501, serves both country-style French and Italian cuisine in a landmark local Mediterranean-style house (complete with heated garden seating for you temperature-sensitive romantics). House-made pastas here are exceptional, as are the desserts. Impressive wine list. Open daily for breakfast, lunch, and dinner. Equally popular, for its Northern Italian fare, is **Giuliano's** at Mission and 5th, tel. 625-5231, where most dishes are reminiscent of Italy's Piedmont region. Italian and California wines, sophisticated yet friendly setting. Open for lunch Tues.-Sat., for dinner nightly. Sophisticated yet simple too is **La Bo-**heme, Dolores and 7th, tel. 624-7500, a tiny, family-style place with French cuisine and European peasant fare for dinner. No reservations; call for the day's menu. Open daily for dinner.

Entertainment
Sunsets from the beach or from craggy Point Lobos are entertainment enough for anyone. But the **Sierra Club** folks above the shoe store, on Ocean near Dolores, tel. (408) 624-8032, provide helpful information on hikes, sights, and occasional bike rides, open Mon.-Sat. 12:30-4:30 p.m. For live drama, the outdoor **Forest Theater** at Santa Rita and Mountain View, tel. 626-1681, offers light drama and musicals, Shakespeare, concerts. (There's also an *indoor* **Forest Theater**—with separate casts and productions.) For rowdy rock 'n' roll, head for the **Mission Ranch** 11 blocks out of town on Dolores (Carmel proper has laws about live music and leg-shaking downtown), tel. 624-6436, or try the **Hatchcover** in Carmel Valley. The least sentimental places to barhop are the **Hog's Breath** and the **General Store** at 5th and Junipero.

Events
Johann Sebastian Bach never knew a place like Carmel, but his spirit lives here nonetheless. From mid-July to August, Carmel sponsors its traditionally understated **Bach Festival,** honoring J.S. and other composers of his era, with daily concerts, recitals, and lectures at the mission and elsewhere. If you're going, get your tickets *early*. For information: Carmel Bach Festival, P.O. Box 575, Carmel 93921, tel. (408) 624-1521. For tickets call 624-2046. Closer to performance dates, stop by the festival office at the Sunset Cultural Center, San Carlos at 9th, 11 a.m.-3 p.m.

In June there's a **Surfabout** at Carmel Beach. Also at Carmel Beach, usually on a Sunday in late September or early October, the **Great Sandcastle Building Contest** gets underway. Events include "Novice" and "Advanced Sandbox." (Try getting the date from the Monterey Chamber of Commerce, as Carmel locals generally "don't know," just to keep the tourists away.) Also in October: the **Tor House Festival.** In December, the **Music for Christmas** series held at the Carmel Mission is quite nice. If in town for the holidays, try out the **Renaissance** and **Christmas Crafts** fairs.

Point Lobos

Information, Transport
The very local *Carmel Pine Cone* covers local events and politics. The *Carmel Valley Sun* is free, as are local street maps available at any Carmel motel. The **Carmel Business Association** is upstairs in the Eastwood Building (next to the Hog's Breath Inn) on San Carlos between 5th and 6th, P.O. Box 4444, Carmel 93921, tel. (408) 624-2522. The annual *Guide to Carmel-by-the-Sea* includes just about everything, from shopping hot spots to accommodations and eateries. The **Tourist Information Center** at Ocean and Mission, P.O. Box 7430, tel. 624-1711, is quite helpful and will make lodging reservations. There's an **Information Center** at the Thunderbird Bookstore and Cafe in The Barnyard on Hwy. 1 near Rio Rd. just south of town. The **Carmel Valley Chamber of Commerce** is in the Oak Building on Carmel Valley Rd., P.O. Box 288, Carmel Valley 93924, tel. 659-4000. To get to Carmel from Monterey without car or bike, take Monterey-Salinas Transit bus No. 52 (24 hours), tel. 899-2555.

POINT LOBOS

Point Lobos State Reserve is a 1,250-acre coastal wonderland about four miles south of Carmel and the crown jewel of California's state parks. Pack a picnic; this is the best the Monterey area has to offer. The relentless surf and wild winds have pounded these reddish shores for millennia, sculpting six miles of shallow aquamarine coves, wonderful tidepools, aptly named Bird Island, and jutting points: Granite, Coal, Chute, China, Cannery, Pinnacle, Pelican, and of course Lobos itself. From here, look to the sea, as Santa Cruz poet William Everson has, "standing in cypress and surrounded by cypress, watching through its witchery as the surf explodes in unbelievable beauty on the granite below." Local lore has it that Point Lobos inspired Robert Louis Stevenson's Spyglass Hill in *Treasure Island*. The muse for Robinson Jeffers's somber "Tamar" definitely lived (and lives) here.

Sights
From the dramatic headlands you can watch for whales in winter. Many other marine mammals are year-round residents. Brown pelicans and cormorants preen themselves on offshore rocks. Here, the sea otters aren't shy: they boldly crack open abalone and dine in front of visitors. (The entire area, south beyond Big Sur is now protected as part of the **Monterey Bay National Marine Sanctuary.** If heading south into Big Sur country, watch offshore otter antics—best with binoculars—from highway turnouts.) Harbor seals hide in the coves. The languorous, loudly barking sea lions gave rise to the original Spanish name Punta de los Lobos Marinos ("Point of the Sea Wolves"). Follow the crisscrossing reserve trails for a morning walk through groves of naturally bonsaied Monterey cypress and pine, seasonal wildflowers (300 species, best in April). Watch

for poison oak, which thrives here, too. Whaler's Cove near the picnic and parking area was once a granite quarry, then a whaler's cove—the cabin and cast-iron rendering pot are still there—and an abalone cannery. It's something of a miracle that the Point Lobos headland exists almost unscarred, as cattle grazed here for decades. Fortunately for us all, turn-of-the-century housing subdivision plans for Point Lobos were scuttled.

Safety First
Point Lobos is considered one of the state's "underwater parks," in recognition of its aquatic beauty. Scuba diving is popular but by permit only. Diver safety is a major concern of park staff. Get permits and current information about what to expect down below before easing into the water. Safety first for landlubbers, too: people aren't kidding when they mention "treacherous cliff and surf conditions" here, so think first before scrambling off in search of bigger and better tidepools. Particularly dangerous, even in serene surf, is the Monastery Beach area near San Jose Creek just beyond the reserve's northern border: there's a steep offshore drop-off into submarine Carmel Canyon and unstable sand underfoot. Children should be carefully supervised, and even experienced divers and swimmers might think twice before going into the water.

Information And Practicalities
Point Lobos is beautiful—and popular. It can be crowded in summer and sometimes on spring and fall weekends. Since only 450 people are allowed into the park at one time, plan your trip accordingly and come early in the day (or wait in long lines along Hwy. 1—not fun). Open for day use only, sunrise till sunset (9 a.m.-7 p.m. in summer, until 5 in winter), $6 per car.

You can also get to Point Lobos on Monterey Transit's bus No. 22 (to Big Sur). From Carmel, it's a fairly easy bike ride. The weather can be cold, damp, and windy even in summer, so bring a sweater or jacket in addition to good walking shoes (and, if you have them, binoculars). The park's informative brochure is printed in five languages. Guided tours are offered daily. To better appreciate the 200-plus species of birds spotted at Point Lobos, pick up the bird list at the ranger station, also the plant list. Bike riding is allowed but only on paved roads. In May, the Dept. of Fish and Game's **Marine Resources and Marine Pollution Studies Laboratory** at Granite Canyon sponsors an open house; contact the reserve office for information: Point Lobos State Reserve, Rt. 1 Box 62, Carmel 93923, tel. (408) 624-4909.

NEAR CARMEL

Carmel Valley Village
The sunny (and warmer) sprawling "village" of Carmel Valley is about 14 miles inland via Carmel Valley Rd., a well-designed but hellacious highway, at least between Carmel and these affluent suburbs and golf and tennis farms (including John Gardiner's Tennis Ranch). Locals curse tourists and others who drive the speed limit. Carmel Valley has definite diversion-value for the wealthy (or the wannabes), plus the **Garland Ranch Regional Park** north of town: hiking trails on 2,000 hilly acres with an astounding view from the top of Snively's Ridge; call (408) 659-4488 for info. Otherwise, skip it except for a mandatory stop at **Rosie's Cracker Barrel** (south of Carmel Valley Village then west on Equiline Rd.) for picnic supplies and whatnot. This is a *real* general store and the valley's unofficial community center since 1939. There's even a bar out back—definitely not a tourist joint.

Carmel Valley
And Peninsula Wineries
Not surprising in such a moderate Mediterranean climate, vineyards do well here. So do wineries. To keep up with them all pick up the "Monterey Wine Country Associates" brochure at area visitors centers. The very small **Chateau Julien** winery (its Chardonnay and merlot both honored as the best in the U.S. at the American Wine Championships in New York), is housed in a French-style Chateau at 8940 Carmel Valley Rd., Carmel 95923, tel. (408) 624-2600 and is open daily with tours on weekdays. Southwest of Carmel Valley and bordering Los Padres National Forest is the remote spring-fed "boutique" **Durney Winery,** owned by William Durney and his wife, screenwriter Dorothy Kingsley. Not open to the public, but the wines are widely available in Carmel, Mon-

terey, and vicinity. Also look around for other premium small-production wines, such as **La Reina Winery**'s hand-crafted chardonnay, and cabernet sauvignon from **Joullian Vineyards** and **Zabala Vineyards.**

Between Greenfield and Soledad along the inland Hwy. 101 corridor are a handful of good wineries. The 1978 private reserve cabernet sauvignon of **Jekel Vineyards,** 40155 Walnut Ave., Greenfield 93927, tel. (408) 674-5522, washed out Lafite-Rothschild and other international competitors in France in 1982; its 1982 chardonnay has also been a winner. Tasting daily 10-5 (appointments needed for tours or for groups of six or more). **Smith & Hook,** a one-time quarterhorse ranch at 37700 Foothill Blvd., Soledad 93960, tel. 678-2132, is known for its cabernet sauvignon—also for the amazing view across the Salinas Valley to the Gabilan Mountains. Open daily 10-6. Sharing space here is a separate label, **San Saba Vineyard,** tel. (214) 821-4044, which primarily produces an unusual red wine blending cabernet sauvignon and merlot (in addition to both). Also in the area: **Chalone Vineyard** on Stonewall Canyon Rd. (Hwy. 146), tel. (408) 678-1717, the county's oldest vineyard and winery, known for its estate-bottled varietals, and noted **Paraiso Springs Vineyard** at 38060 Paraiso Springs Rd., tel. 678-1592, at last report not yet open for tasting or tours. Call for current information.

Farther north along Hwy. 101 is Seagram's **Monterey Vineyard,** a massive mission-style operation at 800 S. Alta St., Gonzales 93926, tel. (408) 675-2316, open daily 10-5 for tasting and hourly tours. Monterey has award-winning chardonnay and Chenin Blanc, a new tasting room, nice picnic facilities, also a gallery show of Ansel Adams photography entitled "Birth of a Winery." Also here is an outpost of **Paul Masson Vineyards,** tel. 675-2481, most popular, though, for its Cannery Row tasting.

Worth popping into in Salinas is **Lockwood Vineyard** at Steinbeck Station, tel. (800) 753-1424, which uses only Southern Monterey County grapes in its wines—available only here and through restaurants. Tours by appointment only. **Morgan Winery** at 526 Brunken Ave., tel. (408) 422-9855, has garnered a glut of gold medals and other recognition for its Chardonnays. Winners here, too, are the cabernet, Pinot Noir, and sauvignon blanc.

True wine fanatics must make one more stop, of course—at America's most award-winning vineyard, **Ventana Vineyards** near the Monterey Airport just outside Monterey on Highway 68. For those looping back toward (or starting from) Monterey, stop by the **Monterey Peninsula Winery** also at home on the row, 786 Wave St., tel. 372-4949.

Jamesburg Earth Station

Open to visitors only on Wed. 1-3 p.m., the Jamesburg Earth Station is a popular stop for space technology fans. The impressive parabolic COMSAT dish antenna here transmits information to and from an orbiting communications satellite. There's a movie, lecture, and chance to peek into the control room. Call before you go, tel. (408) 659-2293. To get here, head southeast into the hills on Carmel Valley Rd. (20 miles east of Hwy. 1) which becomes Tularcitos Road. About 10 miles from Carmel Valley Village, turn right on Cachagua Rd. and hold onto your hat (and/or head) for the next five miles. After (or instead of) the Jamesburg tour, continue on Tularcitos until it joins Arroyo Seco Rd. then jog southwest toward the backside of Big Sur and the Arroyo Seco River canyon: camping and picnicking, trails, and the remote, undeveloped **Syke's Hot Springs** near Horse Bridge Camp.

Tassajara Hot Springs

Not far beyond the COMSAT station, Tassajara Hot Springs, a respected old resort since 1869, is now a monastic community operated by the **Zen Mountain Center** and open to the public only from May 1 until early September. Most people come here for the hot springs (bathing suits required), but marvelous vegetarian meals are also available. You can even camp here, but reservations are a must. The center will send a map and directions.

According to legend, these curative springs first flowed from the eyes of a young chief seeking help for his dying sister. Offering himself as a sacrifice to the sun, he turned to stone and his tears became the hot springs. Also here: serene surroundings, swimming pool, picnicking. Feel free to join in the monastery's prayers and meditations. For information, write Tassajara Hot Springs, Carmel Valley 93924. (No phone; also no radios, tape players, TVs, or cars.) The

Tassajara Rd. turnoff is off Cachagua Rd. near the southward intersection with Tularcitos.

MIRA Observatory
Not officially open to the public, but if for some reason you decide to drive the last six miles of unpaved Tassajara Rd., this is where you'll end up. The MIRA Observatory is a brand-new, barrel-shaped, rolltop professional observatory 12 miles inland from Big Sur, built by the Monterey Institute for Research in Astronomy (MIRA). MIRA's earth-tone, two-story corrugated Oliver Observing Station (named after a retired Hewlett-Packard vice president who kicked in some cash, some advanced electronics, and a 36-inch telescope) includes office and living space and has earned design awards from the American Institute of Architects.

PACIFIC GROVE AND VICINITY

Pacific Grove began as a prim, proper tent city founded in 1875 by Methodists who, Robert Louis Stevenson observed, "come to enjoy a life of teetotalism, religion, and flirtation." No boozing, waltzing, zither playing, or reading Sunday newspapers was allowed. Dedicated inebriate John Steinbeck lived here for many years but had to leave town to get drunk. Pacific Grove was the last "dry" town in California: alcohol has been legal here only since 1969. The first chautauqua in the western states was held here—bringing "moral attractions" to heathen Californians—and the hall where the summer meeting tents were stored still stands at 16th and Central avenues.

Nicknamed "Butterfly City U.S.A." in honor of migrating monarchs (a big fine and/or six months in jail is the penalty for "molesting" one), Pacific Grove has Victorians and modest seacoast cottages, community pride, a rocky shoreline and wonderful tidepools, and an absolutely uncommercial Butterfly Parade in October. Also here: Asilomar, a well-known state-owned conference center with its own beautiful beach.

SIGHTS

From Pacific Grove, embark on the too-famous 17-Mile Drive in adjacent Pebble Beach. But better (and free), tour the surf-pounded peninsula as a populist. The city of Pacific Grove is one of few in California owning its own beaches and shores, all dedicated to public use. Less crowded and hoity-toity than the 17-Mile Drive, just as spectacular, and absolutely free is a walk, bike ride, or drive along Ocean View Blvd.; the paved Monterey Bay Recreation Trail now extends all the way to Asilomar. Or cycle from here to Carmel on the Del Monte Forest ridge via Hwy. 68 (the Holman Hwy.) for a spectacular view of the bay, surrounding mountains, and the "17-Mile" coastline to the south. Walkers, take heart: the Monterey Peninsula Regional Parks people are completing the recreation trail from downtown Monterey to Asilomar and Pebble Beach via an old Southern Pacific right-of-way. Runners, the YMCA here, tel. (408) 373-4166, sponsors a **Sunday morning run** at 8 a.m. at Lovers Point most weekends.

The "Three-Mile Drive"—Or Walk
Along the Ocean View route are Berwick Park, Lovers Point, and Perkins Park (altogether, Pacific Grove has 13 community parks). These areas (and points in between) offer spectacular sunsets, crashing surf, craggy shorelines, swimming, sunbathing, picnicking, plus whalewatching in season, sea otters, sea lions, seals, shorebirds, even autumn flurries of monarch butterflies. Stanford University's **Hopkins Marine Station** on Point Cabrillo (China Point) is also along the way, the crystal offshore waters and abundant marinelife attracting scientists and students from around the world. This is the first marine laboratory on the Pacific coast. (Steinbeck fans, please note: this was the location of Chin Kee's Squid Yard in *Sweet Thursday.)* As for **Lovers Point,** no, Pacific Grove hasn't gone *sexual.* Romantics should restrain themselves, since the name is actually an abbreviation for "Lovers of Jesus Point." Picnic at **Perkins Point,** or wade or swim (safe beach). **Marine Gardens Park** is an aquatic park stretching along Ocean View, a good spot for watching sea otters frolic in the seaweed just offshore; wonderful tidepools.

Museum Of Natural History

Pacific Grove's Museum of Natural History at Forest and Central showcases *local* wonders of nature: sea otters, seabirds (over 400 specimens, a huge collection), rare insects, native plants. A fine array of Native American artifacts is on rotating display. Particularly impressive is the relief map of Monterey Bay, though youngsters will probably vote for "Sandy," the gray whale sculpture right out front. Besides the facsimile butterfly tree, the blazing feathery dried seaweed exhibit is a must-see. Many traveling exhibits visit this museum throughout the year, and the annual **Wildflower Show** on the third weekend in April is excellent. For information, contact the museum at 165 Forest Ave., Pacific Grove 93950, tel. (408) 648-3116. Open Tues.-Sun. 10-5. Free (donations greatly appreciated).

Point Pinos Lighthouse

This is the oldest operating lighthouse on the Pacific coast, built of local granite. The beacon here and the mournful foghorn have been warning

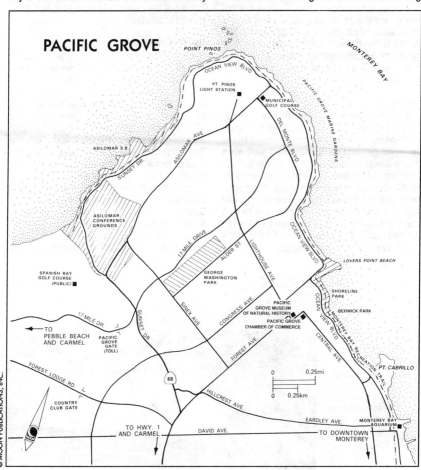

PACIFIC GROVE

© MOON PUBLICATIONS, INC.

seagoing vessels away from the point since the 1850s. Rebuilt in 1906, the original French Fresnel lenses and prisms are still in use, though the lighthouse is powered by electricity and a 1,000-watt lamp instead of whale oil. The **U.S. Coast Guard Museum** inside is free and open weekends 1-4 p.m. **Doc's Great Tidepool,** yet another Steinbeck-era footnote, is near the foot of the lighthouse.

Across from the lighthouse parking lot is fascinating **El Carmelo Cemetery,** a de facto nature preserve for deer and birds. (For more birdwatching, amble down to freshwater **Crespi Pond** near the golf course at Ocean View and Asilomar boulevards.) The Point Pinos Lighthouse is two blocks north of Lighthouse Ave. on Asilomar Boulevard. For info about the lighthouse and Coast Guard Museum, call (408) 372-4212.

Asilomar

The ladies of the Young Women's Christian Association's national Board of Directors coined this Spanish-sounding nonword from the Greek *asilo* ("refuge") and the Spanish *mar* ("sea") when they established this as a YWCA retreat in 1913. **Asilomar State Beach** has tidepools and wonderful white-sand beaches, shifting sand dunes, wind-sculpted forests, spectacular sunsets, and sea otters and gray whales offshore. Inland, many of Asilomar's original buildings (designed by architect Julia Morgan, best known for Hearst's San Simeon estate) are now historical landmarks.

Primarily a conference center with meeting rooms and accommodations for groups, Asilomar is now a nonprofit unit of the California state park system. Guest or not, anyone can fly kites or build sandcastles at the beach, stop to appreciate the forest of Monterey pine and cypress, and watch for deer, raccoons, gray ground squirrels, hawks, and owls. For info, contact: Asilomar Conference Center, 800 Asilomar Blvd., P.O. Box 537, Pacific Grove 93950, tel. (408) 372-8016. To stay here, make reservations up to two months in advance or call (not more than a week in advance) to inquire about cancellations.

The 17-Mile Drive

Technically in Pebble Beach, the best place to start off on the famed 17-Mile Drive is in Pacific Grove (or, alternatively, the Carmel Hill gate off Hwy. 1). Not even 17 miles long anymore since it no longer loops up to the old Del Monte Hotel, the "drive" still skirts plenty of ritzy digs in the 5,300-acre, privately owned Del Monte Forest of the four-gated town of Pebble Beach. Note the Byzantine castle of the banking/railroading Crocker family, which (believe it or not) includes a private beach heated with underground pipes.

From **Shepherd's Knoll,** there's a great panoramic view of both Monterey Bay and the Santa Cruz Mountains. **Huckleberry Hill** does have huckleberries, but botanically more fascinating is the unusual coexistence of Monterey pines, Bishop pines, and both Gowen and Mon-

beachcombing at
sunset, Asilomar

THE MONARCH BUTTERFLIES AND BUTTERFLY TREES

Pacific Grove is the best known of the 20 or so places where monarch butterflies overwinter. Once partial to Monterey pine or cypress trees for perching, monarchs these days prefer eucalyptus introduced from Australia. Adults arrive in late October and early November, their distinctive orange-and-black Halloweenish wings sometimes tattered and torn after migrating thousands of miles. But they still have that urge to merge, first alighting on low shrubs then meeting at certain local trees to socialize and sun themselves during the temperate Monterey Peninsula winter before heading north to Canada to mate in the spring and then die. Their offspring metamorphose into adult butterflies the following summer or fall and—mysteriously—make their way back to the California coast without ever having been here. Milkweed eaters, the monarchs somehow figured out this diet made them toxic to bug-loving birds—who subsequently learned to leave them alone.

The **Butterfly Grove Inn** at 1073 Lighthouse Ave. and the undeveloped area of **Washington Park** between Alder, Melrose, Sinex, and Short streets have the densest clusters of monarchs. Even when massed in hundreds, the butterflies may be hard to spot: with wings folded, their undersides provide neutral camouflage. But if fog-damp, monarchs will spread their wings to dry in the sun and "flash"—a priceless sight for any nature mystic.

KIM WEIR

Pacific Grove loves its Monarch Butterflies.

terey cypress. **Spanish Bay**, a nice place to picnic, is named for Portola's confused land expedition from Baja in 1769 to search for Monterey Bay. (He didn't find it until his second trip.) **Point Joe** is a treacherous, turbulent convergence of conflicting ocean currents, wet and wild even on calm days. ("Joe" has been commonly mistaken by mariners as the entrance to Monterey Bay, so countless ships have gone down on these rocks.) Both **Seal Rock** and **Bird Rock** are aptly named. **Fanshell Beach** is secluded for picnics (good fishing, but swimming is dangerous).

Most famous of all is the landmark **Lone Cypress** at the route's midpoint, the unofficially official emblem of the Monterey Peninsula. (No longer lonely—visited by millions each year—this craggy old-timer is now "posed" with supporting guy wires and is fed and watered in summer.) At **Pescadero Point**, note the cypress bleached ashen and ghost-like by sun, salt spray, and wind.

From Pacific Grove (or from other entrances), it won't cost you a cent on weekdays to travel the 17-Mile Drive by bike (the only way to go, anyway, but some steep grades). By car "the drive" costs $6.75, refundable if you eat at The Lodge. A map is available at any entrance. For info, call (408) 649-8500. The drive is open for touring from sunrise to sunset.

Pebble Beach

Very private Pebble Beach has seven world-class golf courses made famous by Bing Crosby's namesake tournament, "The Crosby," now called the **AT&T Pebble Beach National Pro Am Golf Tournament** and held each year in late January or early February. Also here and open to the public: jogging paths and beautiful horse trails. Just about everything else—country clubs, yacht clubs, tennis courts, swimming pools—is private (and well-guarded) though the public is welcome for a price. (See "Events and

Recreations" in this chapter's Introduction.) However, if you're here in August, join in the **Scottish Highland Games** or see how the rich get around at the **Concours d'Elegance** classic car fest at The Lodge.

PRACTICALITIES

Motel And Hotels

To maintain its "hometown America" aura, Pacific Grove has limited its motel development. The local chamber of commerce provides accommodations listings. Especially if the monarchs are in town, consider a stay at the **Butterfly Grove Inn,** 1073 Lighthouse Ave., Pacific Grove 93950, tel. (408) 373-4921. Butterflies are partial to some of the trees here. Quiet, with pool, spa, some kitchens and fireplaces. Choose rooms in a comfy old house or motel units, $55-90. The new **Lighthouse Lodge** down the road at 1249 Lighthouse Ave., tel. 655-2111, replaces the funky predecessor. Whirlpools and fireplaces, every luxury, $130-285. Most near-the-beach cottages at the 1930s-style **Bide-a-Wee-Motel,** 221 Asilomar Blvd., tel. 372-2330, have kitchenettes, $45-89.

Quite comfortable also are the woodsy **Andril Fireplace Cottages** (yes, they do have fireplaces) at 569 Asilomar Blvd., tel. (408) 375-0994—from $58-96. Or stay at **Asilomar** if there's room—quite reasonable, $50 and up. Asilomar has a heated pool, horseshoe pits, exercise trail, and volleyball for its guests. Cheapest are the older, rustic cottages. Some units have kitchens and fireplaces. (For more information, see "Monterey—Accommodations" or "Asilomar," under "Pacific Grove and Vicinity—Sights.")

New and near Asilomar is **Pacific Gardens Inn,** 701 Asilomar Blvd., tel. (408) 646-9414 or toll-free (800) 262-1566 in California, $88-98 (lower in winter) for contemporary rooms with wood-burning fireplaces, refrigerators, TV and phones—even popcorn poppers and coffee makers. Suites feature full kitchens and living rooms. Complimentary continental breakfast and evening wine and cheese. Full breakfast included. Very nice. Right across from Asilomar is the all-suites **Rosedale Inn,** 775 Asilomar Blvd., tel. 655-1000 or (800) 822-5606, all rooms with fireplace, large Jacuzzi, wet bar, refrigerator, microwave, remote-control color TV, VCR,

even hair dryer. Some suites have two or three TVs and/or private patio. Rates: $105-175.

Definitely beyond the reach of most people's pocketbooks is luxurious **The Inn at Spanish Bay** resort at the Scottish Links Golf Course in adjacent Pebble Beach, accessible via 17-Mile Dr., tel. (408) 647-7500. Rooms here are definitely deluxe, with gas-burning fireplaces, patios, balconies with views. The facilities include beach access, pool, saunas, whirlpools, health club, tennis courts, putting green. A stay here runs $230 to $335 sans specials. Also an unlikely choice for most travelers is **The Lodge at Pebble Beach:** rich folks drop up to $425 a day for a room. (If you don't stay, peek into the *very* exclusive shops here.)

Bed And Breakfasts

Bed and breakfast inns are popular in Pacific Grove; these comfortable, often luxurious home lodgings are comparable in price to much less pleasant alternatives elsewhere on the peninsula.

New and delightful is the 1907 **Maison Bleu Inn Country French Bed and Breakfast Inn,** 157 15th St., tel. (408) 373-2993 or 373-1358, an intimate inn both Victorian and Edwardian, with just five rooms (four share two baths), full breakfast (in your room if you'd like), even cookies and fruit. A great choice. Rates: $85-115. A real deal, too, is the historic three-story (no elevator) **Pacific Grove Inn** at 581 Pine, tel. 375-2825, offering genuine charm and true value. Some rooms and suites in this 1904 Queen Anne have ocean views, most have fireplaces, all have private baths and modern amenities like color TV, radios, telephones. Breakfast buffet every morning. Regular rates range from $47 to $107.50 (two-bedroom suites $87.50-147.50), lower on weekdays; off-season rates dip as low as $47.50-87.50.

Also among the nicest is the **Green Gables Inn,** 104 5th St., Pacific Grove 93950, tel. (408) 375-2095 or (800) 841-5252, a romantic gabled Queen Anne seaside "summer house" with marvelous views, five rooms upstairs, suite downstairs, and five rooms in the carriage house, $100-145 ($160 for the suite) including continental breakfast. Full of fine Victoriana and old books is the **Martine Inn,** 255 Oceanview Blvd., tel. 373-3388, with full breakfasts, hors d'oeuvres, whirlpool, spa, game room, $115-225. Or try the **Gosby House Inn,** 643 Lighthouse Ave., tel. 375-1287 or (800) 342-4888, a charming (and huge) Queen Anne with fine antiques, restful garden, homemade food, and fresh flowers, $85-125 per room. All have great bayside views and access.

The 1888 **Centrella Hotel** at 612 Central Ave., tel. (408) 372-3372 or (800) 233-3372, is newly renovated with 20 rooms, some cottages, $90-180, including complimentary morning newspaper, full buffet breakfast, and a social hour in the afternoon (wine, hors d'oeuvres). Some rooms with shared baths. "Remember the Romance" packages as low as $129. The **House of Seven Gables** at 555 Ocean View Blvd., tel. 372-4341, has ocean views from all 14 rooms ($95-185, includes breakfast and 4 p.m. tea), as does the **Roserox Country Inn by the Sea** next door at 557 Ocean View, tel. 373-ROSE, $105-205; breakfast, cheese/wine social in the afternoon.

Good Food

You can get marvelous crepes for breakfast or lunch, also good waffles and homemade soups, at **Toastie's Cafe,** 702 Lighthouse Ave., tel. (408) 373-7543, open daily 7 a.m.-2 p.m. Another cheap but good choice is the **Bagel Bakery** at 201 Lighthouse, where you can get a full meal anytime for $5 or less. Fresh-baked bagels, homemade soups, salad bar for lunch or dinner. Open daily 7:30 a.m.-9 p.m., until 7 p.m. on Sunday. Or try the vegetarian dishes and cheesecake at **Tillie Gort's Coffee House** and art gallery at 111 Central, tel. 373-0335.

Anna's Ristorante Italiano at 209 Forest Ave., tel. (408) 375-7997, with another location in Seaside, is a funky little hole-in-the-wall with formica tables and paper placemats, a great place for good homemade pastas and other Italian fare without all the fuss. Quite reasonable, open for lunch and dinner. The **Pacific Grove Coffee Roasting Company** at 510 Lighthouse Ave., tel. 655-5633, is the place for lattes, cappuccino, espresso, and wonderful pastries, but simple lunches—with soups, salads, and sandwiches from Central 159—are also available.

More Good Food

Central 159 at 159 Central Ave. in Pacific Grove, tel. (408) 372-2235, is an innovative California-style cafe, fresh and fun, moderately priced but definitely superb. The new kid in the neighborhood is **El Cocodrillo Rotisserie & Seafood Grill** at 701 Lighthouse Ave. (at Congress), tel. 655-3311, with eclectic and exotic decor to match its Central American-style contemporary cuisine. Just to get into the spirit here, try the housemade mango cheesecake for dessert.

A kick for art deco aficionados is the **Cafe Belvedere** up on the roof in the one-time penthouse at Ford's, 542 Lighthouse, tel. (408) 372-7131, serving California cuisine at lunch only, Mon.-Sat. 11-3, Sun. noon-3. Good food, and the view of the bay through the arched windows is fabulous. **Allegro Gourmet Pizzeria,** near Prescott at 1184 Forest, tel. 373-5656, offers innovative pizzas and exceptional calzones—people come from far and wide for the latter—but you can also enjoy pasta and risotto dishes, Italian-style sandwiches, and salads.

Popular with locals (and a favorite of the late, great Ansel Adams) is **Pablo's** at 1184 Forest Ave., tel. (408) 646-8888, featuring *real* Mexican food, even *mariscos*. Open 11 a.m.-9 p.m. Locals say the chiles rellenos at **Pepper's** at 170 Forest Ave., tel. 373-6892, are the best on the peninsula. For boisterous Basque food, **Fandango** in the stone house at 223 17th St. off Lighthouse Ave., tel. 372-3456, serves up wonderful Mediterranean meals in several separate dining rooms warmed by fireplaces. Lunch is fairly inexpensive, dinners $15 and up. Try the chocolate nougatine pie or *vacherin* for dessert. Sunday brunch here is superb. Formal dress prevails at dinner in the smaller dining rooms, but everything is casual in the Terrace Room. Open for lunch and dinner daily, for brunch on Sunday.

Another upscale choice: fine fixed-price Austrian and European dinners at **Gernot's Victorian House,** in an 1892 Victorian at 649 Lighthouse, tel. (408) 646-1477, open Tues.-Sun. after 5:30 p.m. (reservations advised). One of the best restaurants on the entire Monterey Peninsula, some say, **The Old Bath House** at 620 Ocean View, tel. 375-5195, is elegant and expensive, featuring northern Italian and French fare, exceptional desserts, appetizing views.

Entertainment, Events

More than 75 local galleries will keep anyone busy. The **Peninsula Potters Gallery** at 2078 Sunset Dr., tel. (408) 372-8867, is open Mon.-Sat. 10 a.m.-4 p.m.—the place to appreciate the potter's art. Also worth stopping for is the **Pacific Grove Art Center** at 568 Lighthouse, tel. 375-2208. For drama, see what's playing at the professional **California Repertory Theatre** at the American Tin Cannery, 125 Ocean View Blvd., tel. 372-0750 (box office 372-4373), tickets $9-13.

The renowned Pacific Grove **Wildflower Show** is in April, with over 500 native species (150 outdoors) in bloom at the Pacific Grove Natural History Museum, tel. (408) 372-4212. In March or April there's the **Good Old Days** celebration with parade, Victorian home tours, and arts and crafts galore. Come June, there's an **Antique Classic and Vintage Car Show** in Pacific Grove, followed by July's **Feast of Lanterns,** a traditional boat parade and fireworks ceremony that started when Chinese fishermen lived at China Point (their village was torched in 1906). But Pacific Grove's biggest party comes in October with **Welcome Back Monarch Day.** This native naturalistic, and noncommercial bash includes the **Butterfly Parade,** carnival, and bazaar, all to benefit the PTA.

Information, Transport

For events, accommodations, restaurants, and other current information, stop by the **Pacific Grove Chamber of Commerce** at Forest and Central, P.O. Box 167, Pacific Grove 93950, tel. (408) 373-3304. Local newspapers include the daily *Monterey Peninsula Herald* and two weeklies. The **Pacific Grove Public Library** at the corner of Fountain and Central is open Mon.-Thurs. 10 a.m.-8 p.m., Fri. and Sat. 10-5. The **Greyhound** station is at 613 Lighthouse, tel. 649-1121. Pacific Grove is well served by Monterey-Salinas Transit buses (see "Monterey—Transport").

SANTA CRUZ

Still in tune with its gracefully aging Boardwalk, Santa Cruz is a middle-class tourist town enlightened and enlivened by retirees and the local University of California campus. Here, people can exist even if they don't have lots of money— quite a different world from the affluent and staid Monterey Peninsula.

The Santa Cruz attitude has little to do with its name, taken from a nearby stream called Arroyo de Santa Cruz ("Holy Cross Creek") by Portola. No, the town's relaxed good cheer must be karmic compensation for the morose mission days and the brutishness of nearby Branciforte. The Gay Nineties were happier here than anywhere else in Northern California, with trainloads of Bay Area vacationers in their finest summer whites stepping out to enjoy the Santa Cruz waterfront, the Sea Beach Hotel, and the landmark Boardwalk and amusement park, with its fine merry-go-round, classic wooden roller coaster, pleasure pier, natatorium (indoor pool), and dancehall casino. (More decadent fun lovers visited the ship anchored offshore to gamble or engage the services of prostitutes.)

Santa Cruz today still welcomes millions of visitors each year, yet somehow manages to retain its dignity—except when embroiled in hot local political debates or when inundated by college students during the annual rites of spring. A tourist town it may be, but some of the best things here are free: watching the sunset from East, West, or Cliff drives, beachcombing, bike riding (excellent local bike lanes), swimming, and sunbathing.

The "People's Republic Of Santa Cruz"

Old-timers weren't ready for the changes in community consciousness which arrived in Santa Cruz along with the idyllic UC Santa Cruz campus in the 1960s. More outsiders came when back-to-the-landers fled San Francisco's Haight Ashbury for the hills near here, and when Silicon Valley electronics wizards started moving in. The city's boardwalk-and-beach hedonism may be legendary—massage parlors in town do a brisk business—but so are the Santa Cruz City Council's foreign policy decisions opposing contra aid, proclaiming the city a "free port" for Nicaragua, and calling for the divestiture of investments in South Africa.

Though there's always some argument, the city's progressive politics are now firmly entrenched, as are other "dancing-on-the-brink" attitudes. The People's Republic of Santa Cruz is also a way station for the spiritually weary, with its own unique evangelical crusade for higher consciousness. Dreams and dreamers run the show.

History

The charming Santa Cruz blend of innocence and sleaze has roots in local history. The area's earliest residents were the Ohlone people, who avoided the sacred redwood forests and subsisted on seafood, small game, acorns, and other foods gathered in woodland areas. Then came the mission and missionaries, a Spanish military garrison, and the den-of-thieves culture of Branciforte, an active threat to the holy fathers' attempted good works among the heathens. Mission Exaltacion de la Santa Cruz declined, was abandoned, then collapsed following an earthquake in 1857.

A small trading town, borrowing the mission's name, grew up around the old mission plaza in the 1840s to supply whalers with fruit and vegetables. Nearby Branciforte became a smugglers' haven, hosting bullfight festivals and illicit activities until 1867. But the "education" and excitement imported by foreigners proved to be too much for the Ohlone; the only traces of their culture today are burial grounds.

Branciforte disappeared, too, absorbed as a suburb when redwood loggers arrived to harvest the forests during the gold rush. ("Barkstrippers" went after tan oaks, extracting tannin for processing leather.) By the late 1800s, when the city was well established as a resort town, the local lumber industry was ready to log Big Basin itself. But those plans went awry due to the intervention of the Sempervirens Club early in the 20th century.

THE BOARDWALK

The Santa Cruz Beach Boardwalk

The Boardwalk may be old, but it's certainly lively, with a million visitors per year. This is the West Coast's answer to Atlantic City. The original wood planking is now paved over with asphalt, stretching from 400 Beach St. for a half mile along one of Northern California's finest swimming beaches. A recent multimillion-dollar face lift hasn't diminished the Boardwalk's charms one iota. Open daily from Memorial Day to Labor Day each year, otherwise just on weekends, the amusement park atmosphere here is authentic, with 27 carnival rides, odd shops and eateries, good-time arcades, even a big-band ballroom. Ride the **Sky Glider** to get a good aerial view of the Boardwalk and beach scene.

None other than the *New York Times* has declared the 1924 **Giant Dipper** roller coaster here one of the nation's 10 best. A gleaming white wooden rocker 'n' roller, the Dipper's quite a sight any time but truly impressive when lit up at night. The 1911 **Charles Looff carousel,** one of only six Looff creations still operating in the U.S., has 70 handcrafted horses, two chariots, and a circa 1894 Ruth Band pipe organ—all now lovingly restored to the merry-go-round's original glory. (Both the Dipper and the carousel are national historic landmarks.)

New rides feature more terror, of course. The bright lights and unusual views offered by the

sailing on Monterey Bay
near Santa Cruz

KIM WEIR

SANTA CRUZ AND VICINITY

© MOON PUBLICATIONS, INC.

Italian-made **Typhoon** are just part of the joys of being suspended upside down in midair. The **Hurricane** is the Boardwalk's new roller coaster, a two-minute high-tech ride with two trains (each with three cars seating four), maximum gravitational force of 4.7 G's, and a banking angle of 80 degrees. There's only one other of its kind in the U.S., on the east coast. Also state of the art in adrenaline inducement at the Boardwalk is the **Wave Jammer**.

The antique fun technologies in the penny arcades at the Boardwalk's west end cost a bit more these days, but it could be worth it to Measure the Thrill of Your Kisses or Find Your Ideal Mate. Playing miniature golf at the new, two-story, $5.2-million **Neptune's Kingdom** amusement center—housed in the Boardwalk's original "plunge" building or natatorium, that era well illustrated by the impressive display of historical photography in the "historium" here—

the Boardwalk's restored Charles Looff carousel

sporting events like the Sprout Toss and Sprout Putt for people who don't); and the **Santa Cruz Christmas Craft and Gift Festival** held at the Cocoanut Grove during Thanksgiving weekend (Friday through Sunday).

Admission to the Boardwalk is free, though enjoying its amusements is not. The best deal is the all-day ride ticket, $16 at last report. For current complete information, contact the **Santa Cruz Seaside Company,** 400 Beach St., Santa Cruz 95060-5491, tel. (408) 423-5590. While you're at it, inquire about special vacation packages, including accommodations at the Holiday Inn, the Sea & Sand Inn, or the Carousel Motel—the latter a particularly good deal for families in summer (on weekdays).

For current hours, call (408) 426-7433. For information on special Boardwalk activities, call 423-5590. To find out what's happening at the Cocoanut Grove, call 423-2053.

The Santa Cruz Wharf
The pier at the western end of Santa Cruz Beach, once a good place to buy cheap, fresh fish, did booming business during the state's steamship heyday. Today, the place is packed instead with tourists, and most fish markets, restaurants, and shops charge a pretty penny. Still, the wharf's worth a sunset stroll. (Peer down into the fenced-off "holes" to watch the sea lions.) A few commercial fishing boats still haul their catch of salmon and cod ashore in summer, doubling as whalewatching tour boats in winter. Worth a look, too, are the kiosk displays on wharf and fishing history.

is a nautically themed adventure in special effects, with an erupting volcano, firing cannons, and talking pirates. Perfect diversion for the video-game generation and their awestruck parents. Though the rest of the Boardwalk's attractions are seasonal, Neptune's Kingdom and the arcade are open daily. Nearby is the esteemed **Cocoanut Grove** casino and ballroom, a dignified old dancehall that still swings with nostalgic tunes from the 1930s and '40s at special shindigs put on by the Glenn Miller Orchestra, Harry James, and Nelson Riddle. Sunday brunch in the Grove's Sun Room, with its Victorian-modern decor and galleria-style retracting glass roof, is a big event.

To fully appreciate the Boardwalk then and now, pick up the "Walking Tour of the Historical Santa Cruz Boardwalk" brochure, as well as a current attractions map/listing. Both will help you locate yourself, then and now. Annual Santa Cruz events held here include the **Clam Chowder Cook-Off and Festival,** in late February; the **Brussels Sprout Festival** in mid-October (plenty of food for people who like them, special

BEACHES

Most of the outdoor "action" most of the time is at local beaches: swimming, surfing, and fishing are all big, as well as tamer pastimes like beachcombing, building sandcastles, and sunbathing. The in-town **Santa Cruz Beach** at the Boardwalk, with fine white sand and towel-to-towel baking bodies in summer, is "the scene"—especially for outsiders from San Jose, locals say. For more privacy, head east to the mouth of the San Lorenzo River. **Cowell Beach** to the southwest of the pier, where Huey Lewis and the News filmed one of their music videos, is a surfing beach. Just before **Lighthouse Field State**

Beach on W. Cliff is the new, one-of-its-kind Santa Cruz Surfing Museum, an eclectic lighthouse collection of surf's-up memorabilia keeping watch over the hotdoggers in churning Steamer Lane (see below). **Natural Bridges State Beach,** farther southwest at the end of W. Cliff Dr., attracts the mythic monarch butterflies each year from October to May. Though Pacific Grove near Monterey proudly proclaims itself *the* destination of choice for these regal insects, Santa Cruz people claim they get the most monarchs. Sadly, generations of people walking across the sandstone "natural bridge" here finally caused the center arch to collapse. Leathery green fields of Brussels sprouts fringe the fragile sandy cliffs. For information on guided butterfly walks and tidepool tours, stop by the visitor center or call (408) 423-4609. Come in February for the annual **Migration Festival,** a park fundraiser sponsored by the Monterey Bay Natural Historical Association. (Day-use fee at Natural Bridges, $3.)

Davenport Beach at Davenport Landing up the coast toward Año Nuevo is a hot spot for sailboarders, often relatively uncrowded. The **Red White and Blue Beach** just south of Davenport is a popular nude beach (too popular, some say: women shouldn't go alone), $7 per car for the privilege of an allover tan. Nearby is trash-strewn **Bonny Doon Beach,** up the coast from Santa Cruz at the intersection of Hwy. 1 and Bonny Doon Rd. south of Davenport, free but even wilder for sunbathing sans swimsuit.

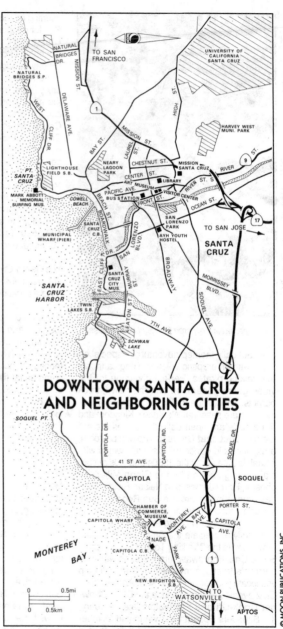

DOWNTOWN SANTA CRUZ AND NEIGHBORING CITIES

© MOON PUBLICATIONS, INC.

onboard the Giant Dipper at the Santa Cruz Beach Boardwalk

SANTA CRUZ SEASIDE COMPANY, ANN T. PARKER

Popular with surfers. For beaches between Santa Cruz and Monterey, see "Near Santa Cruz" below.

Locals' Beaches

Near the city museum, along E. Cliff Dr., is **Tyrell Park** and more inaccessible sandy beaches. **Twin Lakes Beach** near the Santa Cruz Yacht Harbor, on the eastern extension of E. Cliff before it becomes Portola, is a popular locals' beach, usually quite warm. Beyond the Santa Cruz Yacht Harbor, various small, locally popular beaches line E. Cliff Drive; the unofficially named **26th St. Beach** (at the end of 26th St., naturally enough) is probably tops among them. Hot for local surfing is the **Pleasure Point,** E. Cliff at Pleasure Point Drive.

Santa Cruz Surfing Museum

Cowabunga! Instead of a ribbon-cutting ceremony, they snipped a hot-pink surfer's leash when they opened the world's first surfing museum here in May 1986. This historical exhibit reaches back to the 1930s and features displays like the evolution of surfboards—including the Model T of boards, a 15-foot redwood plank weighing 100 pounds—and an experimental Jack O'Neill wetsuit made of nylon and foam, the forerunner to the Neoprene "shortjohn." Some say two Polynesian princes introduced surfing to Santa Cruz in 1885. True or not, by 1912 local posters announced the surfing exploits of Olympic swimmer and "Father of Surfing," Duke Kahanamoku.

The museum's location on the ground floor of the brick lighthouse on W. Cliff Drive northwest of town near Steamer's Lane, prime surf turf, seems the most fitting place for official homage to life in pursuit of the perfect wave. The lighthouse was built by the family of Mark Abbott, a surfer killed nearby. Conspicuously absent here are displays of beer cans, dope roaches, and other historical paraphernalia of beach culture. If you care to support the Surfrider Foundation, an environmental group dedicated to protecting primo coastlines, buy one of the T-shirts declaring "Real surfers don't have real jobs." The museum is free. For information and current hours, call (408) 429-3429.

SEEING THE SIGHTS FROM SEASIDE

Sailing Santa Cruz And The Bay

For an unusual view of the Boardwalk and the bay, take a boat ride. One of the best going—definitely not just any boat—is the ***Chardonnay II,*** a 70-foot ultra-light sailing yacht offering special-emphasis cruises such as winetasting (usually on Saturdays), marine ecology (usually on Sundays), whalewatching (winter and spring), even a Wednesday night Boat Race Cruise in the company of almost every other boat from the Santa Cruise Yacht Harbor. This sleek albino seal of a sailboat can hold up to 49 passengers and features every imaginable

AFTER THE EARTHQUAKE: VISION SANTA CRUZ

The October 17, 1989 Loma Prieta earthquake essentially demolished much of downtown Santa Cruz—and certainly a majority of historical buildings, a fact which led to the city's erasure from the National Register of Historic Places. Though the damage and death toll in San Francisco and Oakland received more media attention, the quake's epicenter was here, or nearby, at Forest of Nisene Marks State Park.

Domed tents or pavilions have taken the place of buildings toppled along the downtown Pacific Garden Mall, once the undisputed center of local shopping, social life, and cultural curiosity. Surviving businesses that haven't already relocated to Capitola or elsewhere—an exodus which now includes the mall's major department stores—may one day move back into more permanent quarters here or elsewhere downtown. Just when that might be is as yet unknown, due to community wrangles and lawsuits over exactly what to do, where, and how. Major battles have been waged, for example, over whether property owners of surviving but severely damaged historic buildings should be allowed to demolish them and start over. Many of these buildings were destroyed by "mysterious" arson fires before such issues could be settled.

Years after the quake, Santa Cruz is just starting to rebuild—a fact that makes finding one's way through and around downtown construction areas and traffic detours something like a fast trip through an experimental rat maze. Other than that, though—especially since the Boardwalk, the beaches, the parks, and most restaurants and motels were largely unaffected by the quake—Santa Cruz is still Santa Cruz.

To get an idea of just what was lost, and how it may one day be replaced, stop in at the "Vision Santa Cruz" information center downtown, sharing space in the new Santa Cruz Chamber of Commerce office (formerly PG&E) at 1543 Pacific Ave., tel. (408) 459-0900, free admission and open daily noon-5 p.m. Vision Santa Cruz includes a huge model of the entire downtown district—a representation of how things might look after reconstruction—as well as local history displays and earthquake exhibits. The small museum store features a good selection of history and natural history books.

amenity, from CD player, TV/VCR, cellular phones, plus built-in bar and plenty of below-deck space, making it fun (and affordable, at a basic rate of $500 per hour) as a private group charter for personally designed adventures (two-hour minimum from Santa Cruz, three-hour from Monterey). For more information and to make reservations (required) contact **Chardonnay Sailing Charters,** Santa Cruz Seaside Company (at the Boardwalk), tel. (408) 423-5590, or call 423-1213.

There are other boat and charter companies at or near the city's yacht harbor, including **Pacific Yachting** at 333 Lake Ave., tel. (408) 476-2370, which offers similar boat rides on smaller yachts as well as sailing lessons, even a six-day sea going instruction vacation. Probably the best deal going, though, is through the University of California at Santa Cruz Sailing Club and the university's office of Physical Education, tel. 459-2531. In summer, UCSC sailing and boating courses are open to the public. If you qualify for membership—by enrolling in the alumni association and buying a current UCSC recreation card—you can use the boats all year. The local **Coast Guard Auxiliary,** tel. 423-7119, also offers sailing, boating skills, seamanship, and coastal navigation courses, evenings only.

Fishing Charters, Other Ocean Adventures

For more traditional boat tours, whalewatching trips, and fishing charters, contact **Stagnaro's Fishing Trips** at the municipal wharf, tel. (408) 425-7003, or **Shamrock Charters** at the yacht harbor, tel. 476-2648.

Kayaking is great sport in these parts. **Venture Quest** at 931 Pacific Ave., tel. (408) 427-2267, offers kayaks and accessories for sale but also lessons and guided tours. **Kayak Connection** at the Santa Cruz Yacht Harbor, 413 Lake Ave., tel. 479-1121, also rents and sells equipment, in addition to offering birdwatching, fishing, and moonlight guided tours. At the municipal wharf (May through September only) contact the **Kayak Shack,** tel. 429-5066, for information on rentals and bay tours.

Scubadventures at 2222 E. Cliff Dr., tel. (408) 476-5201, is a full-service dive center and specialty shop, providing complete current information on local diving conditions as well as instruction, rentals, and sales. **Club Ed** at Cowell

the Santa Cruz Beach Boardwalk as seen from Monterey Bay

Beach, tel. 462-6083, rents surfboards, boogieboards, skimboards, and sailboards, and offers lessons in riding all of the above. Or you can "do" the bay from the air, with a little help from **Pacific Parasail** at the municipal wharf, tel. 423-3545, open daily in summer, only on weekends and holidays otherwise.

HISTORY, NATURAL HISTORY, AND THE SUPERNATURAL

Santa Cruz City Tour

If over- or underwhelmed by the Boardwalk, take the Santa Cruz walking tour. This expedition is a lot quicker than it used to be, with so many of the city's unusual Victorians—with frilly wedding-cake furbelows and "witch's hat" towers on the Queen Annes—now departed to that great Historical Register in the Sky. But some grande dames remain. To find them, stop by the visitors council and pick up a copy of the "Historic Santa Cruz Walking Tours and Museum Guide" brochure. (Most houses are private homes or businesses, so don't trespass.) To find out more about the county's historical heritage, stop by the **Art Museum of Santa Cruz County** at 1543 Pacific Avenue, or contact the **Santa Cruz County Historical Trust** at the same location, Suite 200, tel. (408) 425-3499, a program-oriented umbrella organization filling in for the county museum (not yet replaced after the 1989 earthquake). Ask if small regional museums—including the **Davenport Jail** up the coast in Davenport, and **Rancho del Oso** nearby—are currently open.

Newly restored in town and open to the public is the **Santa Cruz Mission Adobe,** a state historical park just off Mission Plaza at the end of School St., tel. (408) 425-5849, open to the public Thurs.-Sun. 10-4. This is one of the county's last remaining original adobes, built by and for Native Americans "employed" at Mission Santa Cruz. Once a 17-unit "home for new citizens," only seven units remain, these now comprising a California history museum circa the 1840s. Restored rooms illustrate the reality of how Native American, Californio, and Irish-American families once lived. Call for current information about guided tours and "living history" demonstrations (usually sponsored on Sundays, the latter just in March). School groups welcome—Thursdays and Fridays—by advance reservation only. But plan a picnic here anytime; bring your own water.

Nearby, at 126 High St., is what's left of the original mission: just a memory, really. The chosen original site of the **Misión de Exaltacion de la Santa Cruz** was at High and Emmet streets, too close to the San Lorenzo River, as it turned out. The move to higher ground left only the garden at the lower level. The original Santa Cruz mission complex was finished in 1794 but was completely destroyed by earthquakes in the mid-19th century. The replica church, scaled down by two-thirds and built in 1931 on the upper level, seems to have lost more than just stature. Open daily 9-5.

The Santa Cruz City Museum

This museum is at home in The Octagon, an eight-sided 1882 brick building at 1305 East Cliff Dr., tel. (408) 429-3773. On display here is local history, including native and natural history, a tidepool aquarium, an impressive seashell collection, and an outdoor climbable whale. Donation. Call for current hours, and for information about other area museums.

The Santa Cruz Mystery Spot

The much bumpersticker-ballyhooed Mystery Spot is a place where "every law of gravitation has gone haywire." Or has it? Trees, people, even the Spot's rustic shack and furnishings seem spellbound by "the force"—though people wearing slick-soled shoes seem to have the hardest time staying with the mysterious program. Hard-core tourists tend to love this place (Mom or Dad or the kids can *literally* climb the walls) but others leave wondering why they spent the small fee to get in.

The Mystery Spot is at 1953 Branciforte Dr. (follow Market St. north from Water St. for a few miles; it becomes Branciforte), tel. (408) 423-8897. Open daily 9:30 a.m.-4:30 p.m.

Some Santa Cruz
Spiritual/Supernatural Attractions

Perhaps more interesting even than The Spot are two other oddball attractions: the **Shroud of Turin Museum** at St. Joseph's Shrine, 544 W. Cliff Dr., tel. (408) 423-7658, and the life-sized wax interpretation of **The Last Supper** at the Santa Cruz Memorial Park & Funeral Home, 1927 Ocean Street Extension, tel. 426-2601.

About the shroud shrine: the displays here attempt to rekindle the controversy over that renowned piece of linen—purported to show Christ's after-death visage—and to challenge the conclusions of carbon tests declaring the shroud a fake. As if to underscore the seriousness of this issue, the 15-minute documentary video on the 1978 test series is narrated by none other than Geraldo Rivera. Open Sat. and Sun. noon to 5 p.m. (call in advance to arrange midweek visits).

The Last Supper, an interpretation of Da Vinci's famous painting in life-sized wax figures, is the original work of two Katherine Struberghs from Los Angeles, mother and daughter, who spared themselves no trial or trouble in this endeavor. (Each hair on every wax head was implanted by hand—that task alone requiring eight months.) But after some 40 years' residence at the Santa Cruz Art League, Jesus and his disciples were in a sad state of disrepair. That was before the funeral home and local Oddfellows Lodge took on the task of financing something of a resurrection. The job involved patching the cracks in the figures' heads, washing and setting their hair and beards, replacing fingers (and fingernails and toenails), even polishing their glass eyeballs.

To find other attractions of a spiritualistic (usually New Age) stripe, peruse local newspapers for current listings of scheduled speakers and other events.

UC SANTA CRUZ

When the doors of UC Santa Cruz opened in the 1960s, few California students could gain admission to the close-knit, redwood-cloistered campus on the hill. The selection process (complete with essay) was weighted in favor of unusual abilities, aptitudes, and attitudes to recruit students not likely to thrive within the traditional university structure. So many children of movie stars and other members of California's monied upper classes attended UC Santa Cruz at one time that it was often playfully dubbed California's public finishing school. With grandiose plans of attracting an enrollment of 27,000 one day, the university's student body has so far remained relatively small (7,000-8,000), though growth is on the agenda.

Sights

On a clear day, the view of Monterey Bay (and of whales passing offshore in winter and spring) from the top of the hill at 2,000-acre UC Santa Cruz is marvelous. Once the Henry Cowell Ranch, the University of California regents set about transforming the redwood-forested rangeland here into California's educational Camelot in 1961. They hired some of the state's finest architects, whose designs ranged from modern Mediterranean to "Italian hill village" (Kresge College). The official explanation for the Santa Cruz "college cluster" concept was to avoid the depersonalization common to large UC campuses, but another reason was alluded to when

THE SANTA CRUZ SLUGS

Refreshingly out of step with current careerism, the UC Santa Cruz student body convinced then-Chancellor Robert Sinsheimer in 1986 to declare the noble banana slug (a common on-campus companion) their school mascot—instead of the more acceptable sea lion—after a hard-fought, five-year campaign. When the chancellor declared the Santa Cruz Sea Lions the official choice in 1981, students protested that the banana slug would more appropriately be "a statement about the ideology of Santa Cruz," a philosophy with no room for football teams, cheerleaders, fraternities, and sororities.

Finally acceding to the students' preference for a slimy, spineless, sluggish, yellow gastropod (defended as "flexible, golden, and deliberate" by one professor), Sinsheimer said that students should have a school mascot "with which they can empathize." He also proposed genetic engineering research on slugs to "improve the breed" because "the potential seems endless."

then-Governor Ronald Reagan declared the campus "riot-proof."

Wander the campus hiking trails and paths (but not alone) to appreciate the place. Some of the old converted ranch buildings are also worth noting: the lime kilns, blacksmith's shop, cookhouse, horse barn, bull barn, slaughterhouse, cookhouse, workers' cabins, cooperage. For information and guided campus tours, stop by the wood-and-stone Cook House near the entrance or write: UCSC, Admissions Office/Cook House, Santa Cruz 95064, or call (408) 429-4008.

The Long Marine Lab and Aquarium is a UC Santa Cruz facility on the western edge of town, just off Delaware Ave. near Natural Bridges State Beach, open to the public Tues.-Sun. afternoons. For aquarium info, call (408) 429-4308.

SANTA CRUZ ACCOMMODATIONS

Beach Camping

Best for nearby tent camping is **New Brighton State Beach** in Capitola. It has 115 developed campsites, with especially nice ones on the cliffs, and provides a good base camp for the en-

tire Santa Cruz area. There's a small beach and some sheltered picnic tables. (Accessible via local bus—take No. 58 or the "Park Avenue" route—but very popular, so reserve for summer at least six months ahead.) "New Bright" was once called China Beach or China Cove, after the Chinese fishermen who built a village here in the 1870s. Day-use fee. Camping $16 in summer, $14 in winter.

Seacliff State Beach near Aptos (24 sites) is a better beach but camping is a disappointment: just for RVs, $16 includes hookups. **Sunset State Beach**, 15 miles south of Santa Cruz in the Pajaro Dunes four miles west of Watsonville (take bus No. 54B from Santa Cruz), has 90 campsites, 60 picnic sites, nice beaches, but way too many RVs and not much privacy. Even so, advance reservations are necessary. Call (408) 688-3241 for info about beach parks and Mistix at (800) 444-7275 for camping reservations.

Redwoods Camping And "Tent Cabins"

New at nearby **Big Basin State Park** are 36 year-round "tent cabins"—two double beds, a camp lamp, and woodstove in each cabin—for uptown campers, $29 per night for up to eight people plus $9 for linens-and-blanket rental in lieu of sleeping bags. Regular campsites are available sometimes at the last minute, even in summer and on warm-season weekends, at both Big Basin near Boulder Creek (190 campsites, many with trailer hookups, some tents-only walk-ins; call 408-338-6132 for info) and **Henry Cowell Redwoods** just north of the UC campus (150 sites, 105 "developed"; call 335-9145 for info), but make reservations to guarantee a space. All are quite civilized, at least in developed areas: hot showers, flush toilets, also tables, barbecues, and cupboards, $14-16. To reserve Big Basin tent cabins or campsites at any of these year-round parks, contact Mistix up to eight weeks in advance: P.O. Box 85705, San Diego 92138-5705, tel. (800) 444-7275.

Other Campgrounds

Private campgrounds and trailer parks are always a possibility (complete current listing available at the local chamber of commerce). Possibilities include **Cotillion Gardens** at 300 Old Big Tree Rd., Felton 95018, tel. (408) 335-7669;

Carbonero Creek, 917 Disc Dr., Scotts Valley 95066, tel. 438-1288; and the **Santa Cruz KOA Kampground,** 1186 San Andreas Rd., Watsonville 95076, tel. 722-0551.

AYH Hostels

Santa Cruz finally has its permanent American Youth Hostels facility. Located in a five-bedroom Victorian on Broadway, visitors are told to arrive "by foot, bicycle, or public transportation" because no auto parking is available. Open year-round, for AYH or IVF members only, $12. Reservations necessary. For info, contact: **Santa Cruz AYH Hostel,** P.O. Box 1241, 511 Broadway, Santa Cruz 95061, tel. (408) 423-8304. Other nearby AYH choices include the **Pigeon Point** and **Point Montara** lighthouse hostels up the coast toward San Francisco (see "Año Nuevo"), both unique and incredibly cheap for on-the-beach lodgings. Or try the **Sanborn Park** hostel just over the hills in Saratoga, tel. 741-9555. If you're heading that way, spartan summer-only, school-floor hostel facilities are available down the coast at the **Monterey Peninsula Hostel.**

UC Santa Cruz Student Housing

Students and nonstudents alike in summer can stay at UC Santa Cruz, tel. (408) 429-2611, which offers 2,500 beds on the American plan (including use of the shuttle bus and all campus recreation facilities), late June through August: $45 s ($62 s with meals), $36 pp d ($52 pp d with meals).

Reasonable Motels And More

As a general rule, motels closer to the freeway are cheaper, while those on the river are seedier. There are some fairly inexpensive motels near the beach (some with kitchens, Jacuzzis, pools, cable TV, etc.). Rates in Santa Cruz can sometimes mysteriously increase in summer and on weekends and holidays, so ask before you sign in.

Inexpensive by local standards, especially in the low season, is the **Sunset Inn** at 2424 Mission St., tel. (408) 423-3471, decent rooms with TV and phone, rates $45-75. Also reasonable is the **Pacific Inn,** 330 Ocean St., tel. 425-3722, regular rates $69-99, almost half that on weekdays in winter. Another good deal is the **Sandpiper Lodge** at 111 Ocean, tel. 429-8244, a small motel with rooms and suites $59-99.

If you're going to spend substantially more, for value nothing·much in the motel/resort category beats **Chaminade.** (See below.) Otherwise, and closer to Santa Cruz attractions, the **Dream Inn** overlooking the beach at 175 W. Cliff Dr., tel. (408) 426-4330, has rooms with balconies and patios, most modern amenities, $159-205. Similar and less expensive is the **Comfort Inn** at 110 Plymouth, tel. 426-6224, rates $79-119. The **Best Western All Suites Inn** at 500 Ocean, tel. 458-9898, offers rooms with in-room whirlpools and microwaves, some gas fireplaces, other amenities. Indoor heated pool and sauna. Rates: $95-175, better deals in the low season. Decent too are the **Best Western Inn** at 126 Plymouth, tel. 425-4717, with high-season rates of $65-95,

Pigeon Point Hostel

BOB NILSEN

and the **Best Western Torch-Lite Inn,** 500 Riverside Ave., tel. 426-7575, rates $68-79.

Santa Cruz Bed And Breakfasts

Legendary is the been-there-forever local landmark, **The Babbling Brook Inn,** 1025 Laurel, tel. (408) 427-2437 or (800) 866-1131, rooms $85-125. This place was once a log cabin, added to and otherwise spruced up by the Countess Florenzo de Chandler. All 12 rooms are quite romantic, with Country French decor, private bathrooms, phone, and TV. Most have fireplaces, private deck, and outside entrance. Two feature one-person whirlpool bathtubs. Breakfast for two included. Also here: a babbling brook, waterfalls, and a garden gazebo.

Other Santa Cruz inns tend to cluster near the ocean. The 1910 **Darling House** seaside mansion at 314 W. Cliff Dr., tel. (408) 458-1958, features eight rooms (two with private baths, two with fireplaces), telephones, spa, TV on request. Continental breakfast, complimentary evening beverages. On weekdays in the off-season, complimentary gourmet dinners are also included. High season rates: $85-195. Low season: $50-195. **The Pleasure Point Inn** on E. Cliff Dr., tel. 475-4657, overlooks the surf and surfers, three rooms with private baths, one with private deck and fireplace. Continental breakfast. Yacht available. Rates: $95-125. Another choice is the **Cliff Crest** at 407 Cliff St., a Queen Anne by the beach and Boardwalk, tel. 427-2609, rooms $85-135. Some of the rooms at the **Chateau Victorian,** 118 1st St., tel. 458-9458, have fireplaces. Local Santa Cruz Mountains wines served, also generous continental breakfasts. Rates: $99-131.

Other Bed And Breakfasts

If you're heading up the coast from Santa Cruz, consider a meal stop or a stay at the **New Davenport Cash Store Restaurant & Bed and Breakfast Inn** on Hwy. 1, P.O. Box J, Davenport 95017, tel. (408) 425-1818. The comfortable rooms are upstairs, with rates $55-105, and the food here is very good, at breakfast, lunch, and dinner. (Some of the pastries served here are made just up the road at **Whale City Bakery,** where a wide variety of homemade treats and very good coffee are worth a stop.)

Aside from the fine inns in nearby Soquel, Aptos, and Capitola (see below), other choices near Santa Cruz include the three-room 1879

Victorian **Chateau des Fleurs** in Ben Lomond, tel. (408) 336-8943, with rates $90-100, and the lovely **Fairview Manor,** also in Ben Lomond, tel. 336-3355, rates $89-99.

Soquel And Aptos Accommodations

A pleasant surprise here is the **Best Western Seacliff Inn** in Aptos just off the highway at 7500 Old Dominion Court, tel. (408) 688-7300 or toll-free (800) 367-2003, a cut or two above the usual and an easy stroll to the beach. Rooms here are large and comfortable, with private balconies, clustered village-style around the large outdoor pool and Jacuzzi area. Suites have in-room spas. But the best surprise of all is the restaurant, **Severino's,** good food (outdoor dining too, by the koi pond) and great "sunset dinner" specials, served Sun.-Thurs. 5-6:30 p.m. Rooms run $79-149, suites $99-215. But do inquire about off-season specials. A good deal anytime but especially on weekdays is the **Rio Sands Motel,** 116 Aptos Beach Dr., tel. 688-3207 or toll-free (800) 826-2077, decent rooms not far from the beach, heated pool and spa, rooms $50-90, suites $65-100.

The **Blue Spruce Bed & Breakfast Inn,** 2815 S. Main St., Soquel 95073, tel. (408) 464-1137, is a romantic and spruced-up 1875 Victorian farmhouse just a few miles from downtown Santa Cruz, its six rooms all featuring private baths and entrances, unique antique room decor color-keyed to the handmade Lancaster County quilts. Five rooms have private spas; two have gas fireplaces. Rates: $80-125.

The elegant Southern-style **Mangels House Bed & Breakfast Inn** at 570 Aptos Creek Rd., P.O. Box 302, Aptos 95001, tel. (408) 688-7982, is a landmark local mansion, an 1886 Italianate Victorian situated on four secluded acres at the edge of Forest of Nisene Marks State Park. One room has a fireplace; some have balconies and shared bathrooms. Rates: $100-125.

Exceptional, too, is the **Bayview Hotel Bed and Breakfast Inn** at 8041 Soquel Dr., Aptos 95003, tel. (408) 688-8654, an 1878 Victorian hotel with seven elegant rooms with private baths downstairs, and The Veranda restaurant upstairs. Rates: $75-115.

Capitola Accommodations

Almost legendary almost overnight, Capitola's **The Inn at Depot Hill** at 250 Monterey Ave.,

Capitola 95010, tel. (408) 462-DEPO, is a luxurious bed and breakfast, essentially a small luxury hotel housed in the one-time railroad depot. Each of the eight rooms features its own unique design motif, keyed from international themes (the Delft Room, Stratford-on-Avon, the Paris Room, and Portofino, for example), plus private garden and entrance, fireplace, telephone with modem/fax capability, and state-of-the-art TV/VCR and stereo system. The private white-marble bathrooms are supplied with bathrobes, hair dryers, and other little luxuries. Bathrooms have double showers, so two isn't necessarily a crowd. The pure linen bedsheets are hand-washed and hand-ironed daily. Rates: $155-250, breakfast, afternoon tea or wine, after-dinner dessert, and off-street parking included.

A long-standing local jewel, though, is the **Capitola Venetian Hotel,** 1500 Wharf Rd., tel. (408) 476-6471 or toll-free (800) 332-2780, California's first condominium complex, built in the 1920s. These clustered Mediterranean-style stucco apartments are relaxed and relaxing, close to the beach. All have kitchens; some have balconies, ocean views, and fireplaces. Rates: $60-200, two-night minimum on most weekends.

GOOD FOOD IN AND AROUND SANTA CRUZ

Brown-bag it to avoid junk food and/or tourist-trap prices near the beach. To do Santa Cruz area farm trails, pick up a copy of the "Country Crossroads" map and brochure, a joint venture with Santa Clara County row-crop farmers and orchardists, great for hunting down strawberries, raspberries, apples, and homegrown veggies of all kinds. Ask about the current times and place for the Santa Cruz **Farmer's Market.**

Near The Beach

Unforgettable for breakfast or lunch is funky **Aldo's,** tel. (408) 426-3736, at the west end of the yacht harbor (616 Atlantic Ave.), with various egg and omelette combinations. Best of all, though, is the raisin toast, made with Aldo's homemade *fugasa bread.* Eat outdoors on the old picnic tables covered with checkered plastic tablecloths to enjoy the sun, sea air, and seagulls. (If Buffalo, the restaurant's dog, is still around, he'll make the rounds to greet you.)

Homemade pastas and fresh fish at lunch and dinner. The Boardwalk alone features about 20 restaurants and food stands. The best Sunday brunch experience around is also here, at the historic **The Cocoanut Grove,** a veritable feast for the eyes as well as the stomach. And if the weather's good, you'll enjoy the sunny atmosphere created by the sunroof. Nearby, along streets near the beach and Boardwalk, are a variety of restaurants, everything from authentic and casual ethnic eateries to sit-down dining establishments. Head to the municipal wharf to see what's new in the fresh-off-the-boat seafood department.

India Joze

A noted local institution is **India Joze,** 1001 Center St., tel. (408) 427-3554, featuring unusual and imaginative dishes from Indonesia, east India, and Asia daily, also fine pastries. Open for breakfast and lunch, then dinner and dessert, Sun.-Fri., Sat. for brunch and dinner. Reservations strongly suggested. India Joze is also the home of (or at least the inspiration for) the August **International Calamari Festival,** a month-long feast featuring 80-plus international dishes served up at the restaurant and other locations, plus a squid-kissing booth, the Squid Olympics, sometimes even sermons on squid sal(i)vation.

Veggie Fare And Other Cheap Eats

The Crepe Place at 2027 N. Pacific Ave. north of Water St., tel. (408) 429-6994, has good inexpensive breakfasts, dessert crepes (and every other kind), good but unpretentious lunches, and dinners into the wee hours. Open daily for lunch and dinner, on weekends for brunch, best late night spot. The **Saturn Cafe** at 1230 Mission, tel. 429-8505, has inexpensive and wonderful vegetarian meals for lunch, dinner, and beyond. Open daily for lunch and dinner, and until late for desserts and coffee.

For "natural fast foods," don't miss **Dharma's** —now in Capitola at 4250 Capitola Rd., tel. (408) 462-1717—and savor a Brahma Burger, Dharma Dog, or Nuclear Sub sandwich (baked tofu, guacamole, cheese, lettuce, olives, pickle, and secret sauce on a roll).

The **Santa Cruz Brewing Co. and Front Street Pub** at 516 Front St., tel. (408) 429-8838, is a local microbrewery (tours available) featuring homemade root beer as well as handcrafted seasonal brews and perennial favorites like Lighthouse Amber, Lighthouse Lager, and Pacific Porter. The **Seabright Brewery** brewpub at 519 Seabright Ave., Suite 107, tel. 426-2739, is popular for its Seabright Amber and Pelican Pale—not to mention casual dining out on the patio. (Beer fans, if you're heading toward Boulder Creek, stop by the **Boulder Creek Brewery and Cafe** on the highway, tel. 338-7882.)

The Santa Cruz Coffee Roasting Company at the Palomar Inn, 1330 Pacific Ave., tel. (408) 459-0100, excellent coffee, also a bistro-style cafe lunch. Not far away and absolutely wonderful is **Zoccoli's Delicatessen** at 1334 Pacific Ave., tel. 423-1711, where it's typical to see people lining up for sandwiches, salads, and genuine "good deal" lunch specials, usually under $5. Fresh homemade pastas. Open Mon.-Sat. 9 a.m.-5:30 p.m.

The Whole Earth Restaurant
A visit to Santa Cruz wouldn't be complete without feasting at the **Whole Earth Restaurant** at the UC Santa Cruz campus on Redwood Blvd. next to the library, tel. (408) 426-8255. A quiet, comfortable place, this very fine organic eatery was the inspiration and training ground for Sharon Cadwallader's well-known *Whole Earth Cookbook* and its sequel. After all these years, the food is still good and still reasonable. Happy hour Friday 4:30-6:30 p.m., live music during the school year.

Chaminade
The old Chaminade Brothers Seminary and Monastery, on Chaminade Ln. just off Paul Sweet Rd., P.O. Box 2788, Santa Cruz 95603, tel. (408) 475-5600, fell into the hands of developers and is now Chaminade, a conference center and resort. But as part of the deal, the new owners had to include a public restaurant or two in their development plans. So this is the place to come on Friday nights for what is no doubt the best seafood buffet in Santa Cruz County—15 types of fish and seafood, outdoor grill, and a spectacular view of Monterey Bay, worth every penny of the (fairly high) price. The **Sunset Dining Room at Chaminade** also serves appetizing breakfast, lunch, and dinner buffets, and a brunch buffet on weekends. Outdoor dining is available, weather permitting. Open daily. Also at

Chaminade is the elegant **Library at Chaminade,** considerably more sedate and noted for its fine continental fare. Open only on Friday and Saturday, dinners only. Reservations.

You can also sign on for a stay here, toll-free tel. (800) 283-6569 for reservations. Facilities include health club (with massage and men's and women's "therapy pools"), jogging track, heated pool, saunas, whirlpools. Valet parking, airport transportation available. Rates: $125-145 (lower on weekdays). Six-course intimate dinners nightly, also wonderful Sunday brunches with seatings at 10:30 a.m. and 12:30 p.m. Very special, reservations wise.

Capitola Food
Dharma's Natural Foods Restaurant, a Santa Cruz institution now at home at 4250 Capitola Rd., tel. (408) 462-1717, is purported to be the oldest completely vegetarian restaurant in the country. Open daily for breakfast, lunch, and dinner. Near the beach, on or near the Esplanade, is an endless variety of inexpensive eateries. A good bet among them is the **Coyote Cafe Grill y Taqueria** at 201 Esplanade, tel. (408) 479-HOWL, serving wonderful soft tacos and burritos, delicious and authentic (with cabbage instead of lettuce, for example). Fillings include some vegetarian selections plus marinated meats—pork (al pastor or chile verde), beef (carne asada or chile colorado) and chicken (primavera, colorado, or asado). Try the unusual "Chicken Itza," available as either a taco or burrito and featuring chicken breast marinated in citrus-cilantro sauce then charbroiled, topped with spicy peanut, salsa fresca, and creamy avocado sauces. All entrees $5 or less. Also available: a good selection of beers and ales, imported and domestic, plus wines by the glass.

There are more expensive restaurant possibilities, too. **Seabonne** in Capitola at 231 Esplanade, tel. (408) 462-1350, is one of the area's better restaurants, serving up imaginative seafood and romantic views. Open for dinner nightly. Reservations wise. Also exceptional is **Antoine's Restaurant** near the beach at 200 Monterey Ave., tel. 479-1974, a dress-up place known for its Cajun Creole food.

Unbeatable for pastries and decadent desserts is **Gayle's Bakery and Rosticceria** at 504 Bay Ave. in Capitola, tel. (408) 462-1127 (bakery), tel. 462-4747 (deli). The "rosticceria" has a wonderful selection of salads and home-made pastas, soups, sandwiches, pizza, spit-roasted meats, even "dinner-to-go" and heat-and-serve casseroles. Nothing here is exactly in the budget category. But the aromas drifting in from Gayle's Bakery are the real draw. Breakfast pastries include various cheese Danishes, crois-sants, chocolatine, lemon tea bread, muffins, pecan rolls, apple-nut turnovers, even a Sch-necken ring smothered in walnuts. The apple crumb and ollalieberry pies are unforgettable, not to mention the praline cheesecake or the two dozen cakes—chocolate mousse, hasselnuss, raspberry, poppyseed, mocha. (All pies and cakes also served by the slice.)

And for decadence-to-go, try Grand Marnier truffles, florentines, éclairs, or Napoleons. Gayle's also has over two dozen types of fresh-baked bread. The Capitola sourdough bread and sour baguette are good for picnics, and a two-pound loaf of the excellent Pain de Compagne costs $2.50. (If you're heading back toward the Bay or San Jose the back way via Corralitos, stop by the **Corralitos Market and Sausage Co.,** 569 Cor-ralitos Rd. via Freedom Blvd., Watsonville 95076, tel. 408-722-2633, for homemade sausages, smoke-cured ham and turkey breast, other spe-cialty meats—all great with Gayle's breads.) Gayle's is open daily 7 a.m.-7 p.m.

Most famous of them all in Capitola, though, is the **Shadowbrook Restaurant,** 1750 Wharf Rd. at Capitola Rd, tel. (408) 475-1511, known for its romantic garden setting—ferns, roses, ivy outside, a Monterey pine and plants inside—and the tram ride down the hill to Soquel Creek. The Shadowbrook is open for "continental-fla-vored American" dinners nightly. Extensive wine list. Brunch, with choices like apple and cheddar omelettes, is served on weekends. Reserva-tions recommended.

Aptos Food

Reasonably priced and unusually imaginative for breakfast is **The Broken Egg** at 7887 So-quel Dr. (across from the Rancho Del Mar Shopping Center), tel. (408) 688-4322. Of course egg dishes are a major attraction, from create-your-own omelettes, scrambles, and huevos rancheros to truly unique creations like "breakfast pie" and "eggs in a basket." But the crepes here are also good, along with pan-cakes, French toast, and potato specialties.

(Breakfast served anytime, and anything can be ordered for takeout.) You can also order burgers and sandwiches and fruit or shrimp salad. Espresso bar, good selection of teas and fresh-squeezed juices. Open daily for breakfast and lunch (7 a.m.-3 p.m.), and Thurs. through Sunday for dinner, too.

The best place around for Thai food, locals say, is **Bangkok West** at 2505 Cabrillo College Dr., tel. (408) 479-8297, open daily for lunch and dinner. Exceptional, too, is **The Veranda** up-stairs at the Bayview Hotel, 8041 Soquel Dr., tel. 685-1881, beloved for its very good Ameri-can fare and seasonally changing menu, every-thing served up with a helping of the inn's historic 1878 charm. Open weekdays for lunch, nightly for dinner. Reservations advisable.

Soquel Food

The **Little Tampico** in Soquel, 2605 Main St., tel. (408) 475-2218, isn't exactly inexpensive. A real bargain here, though, is the specialty "Otila's Plate": a mini-taco, enchilada, tostada, and taqui-to, plus rice and beans. Another good choice: nachos with everything. (Various Tampico restau-rant relatives dot the county, too.) The family-run **Ranjeet's,** in an old converted house at 3051 Porter St. off Old San Jose Rd. in Soquel, tel. 475-6407, is unusual for "lightly continental" cui-sine with a Polynesian flair. Fine dining featuring pasta, seafood, steak. Good wine list, fabulous desserts. Open daily after 5:30 p.m.

ARTS AND ENTERTAINMENT

Entertainment

Santa Cruz has more than its fair share of good movie theaters and film series. To get an idea of what's playing where, scan local entertaiment papers and/or pick up a current copy of the free bimonthly *Santa Cruz Movie Times*. Local coffee-houses—a phenomenon extending south into Capitola—also offer casual, relaxed, sometimes highbrow entertainment (like poetry readings). Clubs and night spots abound, too.

Clubs

If you're into big-band swing, ticket prices for **Cocoanut Grove** dances (call 408-423-5590 for info) run $15 and up. **The Kuumbwa Jazz Center** at 320 Cedar St., tel. 427-2227, is a no-booze, no-cigarettes, under-21-welcome place with great jazz, often big names, rarely packed. Most shows at 8 p.m., tickets $3-12. The **Catalyst** at 1011 Pacific Garden Mall, tel. 423-1336, is legendary for its Friday afternoon happy hour in the Garden Room—seems like *everybody's* here 5-7 p.m., drinking beer and making the scene, sometimes presided over by the house Dixieland band, Jake and the Abalone Stompers. The 700-seat theater (massive dance floor) hosts good local bands or national acts nightly (cover charge). Sometimes poetry readings and political events are held here, too. For women's music on Wednesday nights, head for the **Saturn Cafe** at 1230 Mission St., tel. 429-8505.

Events And The Arts

Judging by the events people turn out for in Santa Cruz—the **Welcome Back Monarchs Day,** the **Calamari Festival** (with the world's first Squid Olympics), the **Brussels Sprouts Festival,** and the banana slug beauty contest and truck rodeo at **Scott Valley Days**—locals have a strange, naturalistic sense of humor. For an up-to-date quarterly calendar of city and county events, contact the local visitors council (see "Information and Services" below). Bike races have prominent local appeal, though professional volleyball competitions are also held year-round. Whalewatching in winter is another popular draw.

Kicking off the year's major events, in January come for the **Northwest Surfing Association Surf Contest** at Steamer Lane. (Bring your own wet suit.) For wine lovers, January also features the county-wide **Vintners Passport Saturday.** Head for the Boardwalk in February for the annual **Clam Chowder Cook-Off.** In March, Felton holds its **Great Train Robberies** festival; Watsonville its **Folk Art Fair.** Head to Felton in April (usually) for the **Amazing Egg Hunt,** or in May for its big **Bluegrass Festival.** Definitely different over Memorial Day weekend is the annual **Civil War Reenactment** at Roaring Camp. Felton's **Pops for Pops** Father's Day symphony concert and festival in June also includes family-oriented fun, like taking the narrow-gauge train to Roaring Camp. Also in June: Ben Lomond's **Redwood Mountain Faire,** and Watsonville's **Strawberry Festival.**

The very fast annual **Santa Cruz to Capitola Wharf to Wharf Race** in July is a major event for runners, with more than half of the usual number of applicants turned away due to its immense popularity—a popularity only increasing with the recent added inducement of a $20,000 total prize purse. (For information, call the "race hotline," tel. 408-475-2196.) In August comes the **International Calamari Festival,** a celebration of the noble squid. The **Shakespeare Santa Cruz Festival** is also held in August, along with **1907 Week** at the Boardwalk—with almost everything (especially the prices) scaled back accordingly.

In September, Capitola's annual **Art & Wine Festival** has become incredibly popular, almost overshadowing the community's traditional **Begonia Festival.** In October, come for the county-wide artists' **Open Studio,** with open-house art shows held everywhere, from private homes and studios to galleries and museums. Wonderful exposure for artists, great pleasure for aficionados.

There's another **Vintners Passport Weekend** in November, accompanied by Felton's **Mountain Man Rendezvous** and the **Christmas Crafts Faire** and gift show at the Boardwalk's Cocoanut Grove. In December, Felton sponsors its **Pioneer Christmas** festivities. Not to be outdone, Santa Cruz celebrates its **Fungus Fair.**

The June Miss California Pageant was moved from its traditional Santa Cruz locale to San Diego some time ago. Apparently the show's promoters thought the predominantly "progressive" ambience here was a tad too negative. But you can't lose 'em all: after 20-some years, the famed July-August **Cabrillo Music Festival** (described by *The New Yorker* as one of the most adventurous and attractive in America) is still going strong, with performances at UC Santa Cruz, Mission San Juan Bautista, and Watsonville. For information—and do make your plans well in advance—contact the Cabrillo Music Festival, 9053 Soquel Dr., Aptos 95003, tel. (408) 662-2701. To reserve tickets, call 429-3444.

Truly tragic is the demise of one of the area's all-time best events, the September Festival of Saws, a unique musical experience once attracting saw players from around the globe. Who could resist sentimental tunes like "What Do Clones Do On Mother's Day" by the Cheap Suit Serenaders?

Even on a smaller scale, local performing arts are always an adventure. Check local news-

Judging by the eccentric array of local events, Santa Cruz residents have a refreshingly strange sense of humor.

SANTA CRUZ CONFERENCE & VISITORS COUNCIL

papers or call the **Performing Arts Alliance hotline** at tel. (408) 459-7989 for what's current if you just happen to be in Santa Cruz. But if you're coming for culture and can plan ahead, contact groups such as the **Santa Cruz Chamber Players,** with its September-to-March series of family-oriented concerts, tel. 426-0865; the **Santa Cruz Baroque Festival,** with February-to-May concerts of early music masterworks, tel. 336-5731; the year-round **Santa Cruz County Symphony,** tel. 462-0553; the noted **Tandy Beal & Company** dance troupe (local performances when not touring internationally, tel. 429-1324; and the year-round **Actors Theatre,** tel. 425-1003 or (for tickets and reservations) 425-7529. For performance arts at UCSC, see "Information and Services" below.

Stop by **The Art Museum of Santa Cruz County** at 705 Front St., tel. (408) 429-1964, most noted for its Rental Gallery—an impressive array of local art both for sale and for rent—and the mobile Art Box museum on wheels, for community arts education. Ask here, too, about local private galleries and university installations. Open Tues.-Fri. 10-4. Possibly open by now is the **Santa Cruz Art and History Project,** a new museum in the old jail.

GETTING ORIENTED

Drivers, be warned: parking can be impossible, especially in summer, especially at the beach. There's a charge for parking at the Boardwalk (in lots with attendants), metered parking elsewhere. Best bet: park elsewhere and take the shuttle. Second best: drive to the beach, unload passengers and beach paraphernalia, then park a mile or so away. By the time you walk back, your companions should be done battling for beach towel space.

You can usually find free parking on weekends in the public garage at the county government center at 701 Ocean Street, conveniently also a stop for the summer weekends-only **beach shuttle** to the Boardwalk and vicinity. Another possibility is the River Street parking garage at River and Front streets.

Information And Services
The best all-around source for city and county information is the **Santa Cruz County Conference and Visitors Council** downtown at 701 Front St., Santa Cruz 95060, tel. (408) 425-1234 or toll-free (800) 833-3494, open 9-5 weekdays. (There's also a visitor information kiosk downtown on Ocean between Soquel and Water, open daily in summer, tel. 458-0800.) Definitely request the current accommodations, dining, and visitor guides.

If you've got time to roam farther afield, also pick up a current copy of the "County Crossroads" farm trails map, and ask about area wineries. Cyclists, request the "Santa Cruz County Bikeway Map," antiquers, the current "Antiques, Arts, & Collectibles" directory for Santa Cruz and Monterey counties, published every June—not a complete listing, by far, but certainly a good start. And if you once were familiar with Santa Cruz and—post-quake—now find yourself lost, pick up the "Downtown Santa Cruz Directory" brochure.

For current listings and features on the local arts and entertainment scene, pick up the monthly *Santa Cruz Magazine.* Another valuable source of performing arts information, focused on the university, is the **UCSC Performing Arts calendar,** usually published bimonthly and available around town, or call (408) 459-ARTS for information (Arts and Lectures, tel. 459-2826; Theatre Arts, tel. 459-2974; Music Board, tel. 459-2292). To order performance tickets by phone ($2 service charge), call the UCSC Ticket Office at 459-2159 (voice or TDD).

City on a Hill is the UC Santa Cruz paper, an excellent local publication but, sadly, published only during the regular school year. The free *Santa Cruz Good Times* is a good, long-running weekly local paper with an entertainment guide and sometimes entertaining political features. The free *Student Guide* comes out seasonally, offering lots of ads and some good entertaining reading about Santa Cruz. The local women's publication is the monthly *Matrix.* The quarterly *Lavender Reader* is a good local lesbian and gay publication, published by the **Lesbian and Gay Community Center,** 1332 Commerce Ln., tel. (408) 425-5422. The *Santa Cruz Sentinel* and the *Watsonville Register-Pajaronian* are the traditional area papers. The **Santa Cruz Parks and Recreation Dept.** at Harvey West Park, tel. 429-3663, open weekdays 8 a.m.-noon and 1-5 p.m., usually publishes a *Summer Activity Guide* (especially useful for advance planning).

The Santa Cruz **post office** is at 850 Front St., tel. (408) 426-5200, open weekdays 8-5. The **Santa Cruz Public Library** is at 224 Church St., tel. 429-3526 or 429-2533. (If you want to hobnob with the people on the hill, visit the **Dean McHenry Library** on campus, tel. 429-2801.) For senior information, stop by the **Senior Center** at 222 Market, tel. 423-6640, or at 1777 Capitola Rd., tel. 462-1433.

Getting Here
The **Greyhound/Peerless** bus company is at 425 Front St., tel. (408) 423-1800, open weekdays 7:30 a.m.-8 p.m., and provides service from San Francisco to Santa Cruz, Fort Ord, Mon-

terey, also connections south: to L.A. via Salinas, to L.A. via San Jose. From the East Bay and South Bay, take AMTRAK, tel. (800) USA-RAIL, now offering bus connections from Salinas.

Getting Around
The **Santa Cruz Beach Shuttle** is the way to avoid parking nightmares, with regular service between the County Government Center and the wharf area June through Labor Day. Bicyclists will be in hog heaven here, with everything from excellent bike lanes to locking bike racks at bus stops. (There's even a free "bicycle loan" program in Capitola to get people out of their cars; lost bikes found by police are renovated for free public use.)

The **Santa Cruz Metropolitan Transit District,** "the Metro," at 920 Pacific Ave., tel. (408) 425-8600 or 688-8600, provides superb public transit throughout the northern Monterey Bay area. The Metro has a "bike and ride" service for bicyclists who want to hitch a bus ride part way (bike racks onboard). For current route info, call 425-8600 or 688-8600, or pick up a free copy of the excellent "Headways" (which includes Spanish translations). Buses will get you anywhere you want to go in town and considerably beyond for $1 ($2 for an all-day pass), exact coin change only. Here, bus riders don't have to miss the nightlife, either; the most popular routes run daily 6:30 a.m.-midnight.

You can also rent a car, of course, from local agencies like **Pacific Coast Enterprises,** tel. (408) 423-5820, or from **Enterprise Rent-A-Car,** tel. 426-7799 or toll-free (800) 325-8007, or local branches of the nationals: **Avis,** tel. 423-1244, and **Budget,** tel. 425-1808, both located on Ocean Street. **Yellow Cab** is at 224 Walnut Ave., tel. 423-1234, also home to the **Santa Cruz Airporter,** tel. 423-1214 or toll-free in California (800) 223-4142, which provides shuttle van service to both the San Francisco and San Jose airports as well as to *CalTrain* and the Amtrak station in San Jose. (See also "Getting Away" below.)

For some guided assistance in seeing the sights, contact **Earth, Sea and Sky Tours,** P.O. Box 1630, Aptos 95001, tel. (408) 688-5544. **Pelican Eco-Tours** based in San Jose, tel. 729-4083, offers small-group naturalist-guided tours around Monterey Bay—including Año Nuevo—and down into Big Sur. Most organized tours depart from San Jose or Monterey, but they may pick you up in Santa Cruz with advance arrangements. You can also custom-design your own tour. On top of that, a percentage of all proceeds is donated to the Nature Conservancy.

Getting Away
You can get to Boulder Creek, Big Basin State Park, Ben Lomond, Felton, north coast beaches, *almost* all the way to Año Nuevo State Reserve just across the San Mateo County line, also to south coast beaches and towns via The Metro buses. (**Monterey-Salinas Transit** from Wat-

sonville provides good service in Monterey County.) For ridesharing out of town, check the ride board at UC Santa Cruz and local classifieds.

Another way to get out of town is via Santa Cruz Metro's *Cal Train Connector* buses to the San Jose train station, nine trips daily (eight on weekends or holidays) which directly connect with the *CalTrain* (to San Francisco) and Amtrak (to Oakland, Berkeley, and Sacramento), just $5. For information on the Connector, call (408) 425-8600; on *CalTrain* fares and schedules, (800) 558-8661; on Amtrak, (800) USA-RAIL.

NEAR SANTA CRUZ

AÑO NUEVO RESERVE

About 20 miles north of Santa Cruz and just across the county line is the Año Nuevo State Reserve, breeding ground and rookery for sea lions and seals—particularly the unusual (and once nearly extinct) northern elephant seals. The pendulous proboscis of a "smiling" two- to three-ton alpha bull dangles down like a fire-hose, so the name is apt.

At first glance, windswept, cold Año Nuevo seems almost desolate, inhospitable to life. This is far from the truth, however. Año Nuevo is the only place in the world where people can get off their bikes or the bus or get out of their cars and walk out among aggressive, wild northern elephant seals in their natural habitat. Especially impressive is that first glimpse of hundreds of these huge seals nestled like World War II torpedos among the sand dunes. A large number of other animal and plant species also consider this area home; to better appreciate the ecologically fascinating animal and plantlife of the entire area, *The Natural History of Año Nuevo,* by Burney J. Le Boeuf and Stephanie Kaza, is well worth buying.

**The Survival Of
The Northern Elephant Seal**
Hunted almost to extinction for their oil-rich blubber, at the turn of the century there were only 20-100 northern elephant seals remaining on Isla de Guadalupe west of Baja. Descendants of these survivors recently began migrating north again to

California. In the 1950s a few arrived at Año Nuevo Island, attracted to its rocky safety. The first pup was born on the island in the 1960s. By 1975, the mainland dunes had slowly been colonized by seals crowded off the island rookery, and the first pup was born onshore. By 1988, 800 northern elephant seals were born on the mainland, part of a total known population of more than 80,000 and an apparent ecological success story. (Only time will tell, though, since the species' genetic diversity has been eliminated by their swim at the brink of extinction.)

The Año Nuevo Mating Season
Male northern elephant seals start arriving in December. Who arrives first and who remains dominant among the males during the long mating season is important because the "alpha bull" gets to breed with most of the females. Though the males are biologically committed to conserving their energy for sex—lying about as if dead, in or out of the water, often not even breathing for stretches of up to a half-hour—the bellowing, often bloody nose-to-nose battles of two challengers are some sight. Arching up with heads back and canine teeth ready to tear flesh, the males bellow and bark and bang their chests together.

Then, usually in January, the females start to arrive, ready to bear offspring conceived the previous year. They give birth to their pups within the first few days of their arrival. The males continue to wage war, the successful alpha bull now frantically trying to protect his harem of 50 or so females from marauders. For every two pounds

the northern
elephant seal

BOB NILSEN

in body weight a pup gains, its mother loses a pound. Within 28 days, she loses about half her weight, then, almost shriveled, she leaves. Her pup, about 60 pounds at birth, weighs 300-500 pounds a month later. Although inseminated by the bull before leaving the rookery, the emaciated female is in no condition for another pregnancy, so "conception" is actually delayed for several months, allowing the female to feed and regain her strength. Then, after an eight-month gestation period, the cycle starts all over again.

Año Nuevo Etiquette

The Marine Mammal Act of 1972 prohibits people from harassing or otherwise disturbing these magnificent sea mammals, so be respectful. While walking among the elephant seals, remember that these seemingly slug-like creatures *are* wild beasts and can move as fast as any human across the sand, though for shorter distances. For this reason, keeping a 20-foot minimum distance between you and the seals (especially during the macho mating season) is important. No food or drinks are allowed on the reserve, and nothing in the reserve may be disturbed. The first males often begin to arrive in November before the official docent-led tours begin, so it's possible to tour the area unsupervised. Visit the dunes without a tour guide in spring and summer also, when many elephant seals return here to molt.

New since 1990 is the reserve's "equal access boardwalk" across the sand, making it possible for physically challenged individuals to see the seals.

Information And Tours

Official 2½-hour guided tours of Año Nuevo begin in December and continue through March, rain or shine, though January and February is prime time and reservations are necessary. The reserve is open from 8 a.m. until sunset, day-use fee $5. Tour tickets ($4 plus surcharge for credit card reservations) are available only through Mistix, tel. (800) 444-7275. Mistix also handles reservations for school groups. Reservations cannot be made before November 1. To take a chance on no-shows, arrive at Año Nuevo before scheduled tours and get on the waiting list. Organized bus tours are available through **San Mateo Transit,** 945 California Dr., Burlingame 94010, tel. (800) 660-4287, or (415) 508-6441, and **Santa Cruz Metropolitan Transit District** (see "Santa Cruz—Getting Around"). And if you're staying at the nearby AYH Pigeon Point Hostel, they sometimes have extra tickets for hostelers. For more information, and to make reservations for groups of disabled persons contact: Año Nuevo State Reserve, New Year's Creek Rd., Pescadero 94060, tel. (415) 879-0595 or 879-0227.

COASTAL HOSTELS

The Pigeon Point Lighthouse Hostel

The AYH Pigeon Point Lighthouse Hostel, Pigeon Point Rd., Pescadero 94060, tel. (415) 879-0633, about five miles south of the Pescadero turnoff and six miles north of Año

WILDER RANCH STATE PARK

Open to the public since mid-1989, Wilder Ranch State Park is best summed up as "a California coastal dairy-farm museum," a remnant of the days when dairies were more important to the local economy than tourists. Though damaged by the 1989 earthquake, the old Victorian ranch house is open again decked out in period furnishings, and the grounds include an elaborate 1890s stable, a dairy barn, and a bunkhouse-workshop with water-driven machinery. Seasoned vehicles and farm equipment, from a 1916 Dodge touring sedan to seed spreaders and road graders, are scattered throughout the grounds.

Even more attractive, though, are the park's five miles of coastline and thousands of acres of forest, creeks, and canyons. Wilder Ranch is two miles north of Santa Cruz on the west side of Hwy. 1 (1401 Coast Rd.), tel. (408) 426-0505, open for day-use only, $6 per car. (To get here by bus, take Santa Cruz Metro No. 40 and ask the driver to drop you at the ranch.) General ranch tours, led by docents dressed in period attire, are offered every Saturday and Sunday, usually at 1 p.m. Historical games are played on the lawn—hoop 'n' stick, bubbles, stilts—on weekends as well, 10 a.m.-4 p.m. A variety of other history- and natural history-oriented events are sponsored throughout the year, from demonstrations on making corn-husk dolls or quilts to mastering cowboy-style roping, plus guided hikes and bird walks. Usually on the first Saturday in May is the park's **annual open house,** a full day of old-fashioned family fun and fundraising, including a barn dance and country barbecue (complete with hand-cranked ice cream, even fresh-baked pies from Gizdich Ranch near Watsonville).

Nuevo, is *the* place to stay while visiting the elephant seals. Named after the clipper ship *Carrier Pigeon,* one of many notorious shipwrecks off the coastal shoals here, the 1872 lighthouse is now automated but still impressive with its Fresnel lens and distinctive 10-second flash pattern. (Lighthouse tours are offered every Sunday, small donation, advance reservations usually necessary.)

The hostel itself is four former family residences for the U.S. Coast Guard, basic male or female bunkrooms, plus a few spartan couples' rooms. The old Fog Signal Building is now a rec room; there's also a hot tub perched on rocky cliffs above surging surf. Fabulous sunset views, wonderful tidepools. Rates: $8 AYH members, $11 nonmembers, $4 extra for couples' rooms ($1 extra for linen rental without sleep sack or sleeping bag), simple clean-up chores required. Get groceries in Pescadero and prepare meals in the well-equipped communal kitchens, or ask for local restaurant suggestions. Open to travelers of all ages. For info and/or to check in, the hostel office is open 7:30-9:30 a.m. and 4:30-9:30 p.m. only. Very popular, so reserve well in advance.

The Point Montara Lighthouse Hostel
Farther up the coast, 25 miles north of Pigeon Point and 25 miles south of San Francisco, is the very fine American Youth Hostels' Point Montara Lighthouse Hostel, 16th St. at Hwy. 1, Montara 94037, tel. (415) 728-7177, popular—like Pigeon Point—with bicyclists and accessible via bus from the Bay Area. The 1875 lighthouse itself is no longer in operation, and the Fog Signal Building here is now a roomy woodstove-heated community room. Hostel facilities include kitchens, dining rooms, laundry, bunkrooms, couples' and family quarters. Volleyball court, outdoor hot tub, and bicycle rentals also available. Open to travelers of all ages. Reserve in advance: $8 AYH members, $11 nonmembers, $4 extra for couples or family accommodations. Ask at the office for referrals to local restaurants.

BIG BASIN REDWOODS STATE PARK

California's first state park was established here about 24 miles upcanyon from Santa Cruz. To save Big Basin's towering *Sequoia sempervirens* coast redwoods from lumbermen, 60-some conservationists led by Andrew P. Hill camped at the base of Slippery Rock on May 15, 1900, and formed the Sempervirens Club. Just two years later, in September 1902, 3,800 acres of primeval forest were deeded to the state, the beginning of California's state park system.

Big Basin Flora and Fauna
Today, Big Basin Redwoods State Park includes 16,000 acres on the ocean-facing slopes of the Santa Cruz Mountains, and efforts to

protect (and expand) the park still continue under the auspices of the Sempervirens Fund and the Save-the-Redwoods League. (Donations are always welcome.) Tall coast redwoods and Douglas fir predominate. Wild ginger, violets, and milkmaids are common in spring, also a few rare orchids grow here. Native azaleas bloom in early summer, and by late summer huckleberries are ready for picking. In the fall and winter rainy season, mushrooms and other forest fungi "blossom."

At one time, the coast grizzly (one of seven bear species which roamed the state's lower regions) thrived between San Francisco and San Luis Obispo. The last grizzly was spotted here in 1878. Common are black-tailed deer, raccoons, skunks, and gray squirrels. Rare are mountain lions, bobcats, coyotes, foxes, and opossum. There are, however, various fascinating reptiles in Big Basin, including the endangered western skink. Predictably, rattlers are fairly common in chaparral areas, but other snakes are shy. Squawking Steller's jays are ever-present; acorn woodpeckers, dark-eyed juncos, owls, and hummingbirds—altogether about 250 bird species—also haunt Big Basin. Spotting marbled murrelets (shorebirds which nest 200 feet up in the redwoods) is a birding challenge.

Hikes And Sights

The best time to be in Big Basin is in the fall, when the weather is perfect and most tourists have gone home. Winter and spring are also prime times, though rainier (at least in some years). Roadcuts into the park offer a peek into local geology—tilted, folded, twisted layers of thick marine sediments. Big Basin's **Nature Lodge** and museum has good natural history exhibits, also many fine books including *Short Historic Tours of Big Basin* by Jennie and Denzil Verado. The carved-log seating and the covered stage at the amphitheater attract impromptu human performances (harmonica concerts, freestyle softshoe, joke routines) when no park campfires or other official events are scheduled.

Also here: over 100 miles of hiking trails. Take the half-mile **Redwood Trail** loop to stretch your legs (and see one of the park's most impressive stands of virgin redwoods). Or hike the more ambitious **Skyline-to-the-Sea** trail, at least an overnight trip. It's 11 miles from the basin rim to the seabird haven of Waddell Beach, with

SEQUOIA: WHAT'S IN A NAME?

The name *Sequoia* honoring these magnificent trees is the Latinized form of "Sequoyah," the name of the great Cherokee intellectual. Though he never achieved his ultimate goal of uniting all Native American peoples with one common language, Sequoyah single-handedly created a written language for his tribe before dying at age 70 in the Mexican Sierra. Tormented by the injustices suffered by his people and impressed by the whites' "talking leaves," at the age of 49 Sequoyah set out to create an alphabet for the Cherokees. At first he made a symbol for every word of the Cherokee language until there were thousands—an unworkable system. So Sequoyah started again, dividing Cherokee speech into individual sounds with a written sign for each. After 12 years of work, the Cherokee language was rendered into 85 symbols. After initial scorn, the Cherokees accepted Sequoyah's work, and life for the Cherokees changed quickly. Most learned to read within a few months, and the tribe eventually published its own newspaper.

trail camps along the way (camping and fires allowed only in designated areas). Hikers, bring food and water: Waddell Creek flows with reclaimed waste water.

Another popular route is the **Pine Mountain Trail,** but most dramatic in Big Basin are the waterfalls. **Berry Creek Falls** is a particularly pleasant destination: rushing water, redwood mists, and glistening rocks fringed with delicate ferns. Nearby are both **Silver Falls** and the **Golden Falls Cascade.**

Information And Practicalities

For park info, contact Big Basin Redwoods State Park, 21600 Big Basin Way, Boulder Creek 95006, tel. (408) 338-6132. Big Basin has 190 campsites ($14) plus five group camps (reserve all campsites through Mistix, tel. 800-444-7275 during summer, otherwise first-come, first-camped). An unusual "outdoor" option: the park's tent cabins, each of which includes one or more platform beds with mattresses, a woodstove, a bench and table inside, and a picnic table and fireplace ring/grill outside. Basic rate $29, linen

THE ROARING CAMP AND BIG TREES RAILROAD

F. Norman Clark, the self-described "professional at oddities" who also owns the narrow-gauge railroad in Felton, bought the Southern Pacific rails connecting Santa Cruz and nearby Olympia to make it possible for visitors to get to Henry Cowell Redwoods State Park and Felton (*almost* to Big Basin) by train. During logging's commercial heyday here in the 1900s, 20 or more trains passed over these tracks every day.

That route into the woods from Santa Cruz has been discontinued. But you can still take the Felton ride and visit Roaring Camp. Round-trip for adults $11, children $8. For information on the narrow-gauge route from Felton (with optional Chuckwagon Bar-B-Q on weekends and Moonlight Parties on moonlit Saturday nights), contact: Roaring Camp and Big Trees Narrow-Gauge Railroad, P.O. Box G-1, Felton 95018, tel. (408) 335-4484.

and lantern rental extra. Reserve through Mistix. To reserve backpacker campsites at the park's six trail camps, contact park headquarters. It costs $5 to park here (day-use fee), small fee for the map/brochure showing all trails and major park features.

NEAR BIG BASIN

Henry Cowell Redwoods State Park
The Redwood Grove in the dark San Lorenzo Canyon here is the park's hub and one of the most impressive redwood groves along the central coast, with the "Neckbreaker," the "Giant," and the "Fremont Tree" all standouts. You can camp at Graham Hill, picnic near the grove, or head out on the 15-mile-web of hiking and horseback trails. Henry Cowell has 150 campsites. For information about Henry Cowell Redwoods State Park, call (408) 335-9145.

Other Parks
Between Big Basin and Saratoga is **Castle Rock**, an essentially undeveloped state park and a hiker's paradise. Ask at Big Basin for current trail information. **Highlands County Park** at

8500 Hwy. 9 in Ben Lomond, tel. (408) 336-8551, is open daily from 9 a.m.-dusk, the pool from 12:30-5 p.m. in spring and summer ($1 parking and pool fee). This old estate, transformed into a park with picnic tables and nature trails, also has a sandy beach along the river. Another swimming spot is at **Ben Lomond County Park** on Mill St., tel. 336-9962—free, open daily in summer. Shaded picnic tables and barbecue facilities; the rope swing at the beach makes for good river swimming. Closer to Big Basin is **Boulder Creek Park** on Middleton Ave. east of Hwy. 9 in Boulder Creek, also free. The swimming hole here has both shallows and deeps, plus there's a sandy beach, picnic tables, and barbecue pits in the shade.

SOUTH FROM SANTA CRUZ

Beaches And State Parks
About six miles down the coast from Santa Cruz City Beach and just south of the Capitola suburbs is **New Brighton State Beach,** tel. (408) 475-4850—65 often-sunny acres protected by headlands, with nature trails and good bird-watching, also a dazzling nighttime view of Monterey Bay from the wooded plateau. Several miles farther south, two-mile-long **Seacliff State Beach,** tel. 688-3222, is so popular you may not be able to stop. Nice for hiking, pelican-watching, fossil appreciation, swimming, sunbathing. The pier here is wheelchair-accessible, reaching out to the pink concrete carcass of the doomed WW I-vintage *Palo Alto,* sunk here after seeing no wartime action and now a long-abandoned amusement pier. Birds live in the prow these days, and people enjoy the pier's more mundane pleasures: people-watching, fishing (no license required), strolling. To reserve space for the park's guided walks—ship walks on Saturday at 2 p.m., fossil walks on Sunday at noon—call 688-7146. As the name suggests, **Rio del Mar** beach is where Aptos Creek meets the sea—restrooms, miles of sand, free, limited parking.

The next sandy stop is **Manresa Beach State Park,** tel. (408) 761-1795, with stairways to the surf from the main parking lot, also off Sand Dollar Dr. (restrooms, outdoor shower, tent camping available). The fastest way to get here is via rural San Andreas Rd., which also takes you to **Sunset Beach State Park**—3½ miles of sand and at least off-season seclusion, plus picnicking on the bluff above the beach as well as tent camping. Call 724-1266 for information. Parking for pretty **Palm Beach** near Pajaro Dunes—a great place to find sand dollars—is near the end of Beach St. (also here: picnic facilities, a par course, restrooms). **Zmudowski Beach State Park** is near where the Pajaro River reaches the sea: good hiking and surf fishing, rarely crowded. Next, near Moss Landing, are **Salinas River State Beach** and **Jetty State Beach.** "En route camping" for self-contained RVs is now available at **Moss Landing State Beach.**

To reserve campsites at all state beaches and parks, call Mistix toll-free, (800) 444-7275.

Santa Cruz Suburbs

The wharf in **Capitola** has stood since 1857, when the area was known as Soquel Landing. The name "Camp Capitola" was an expression of Soquel locals' desire to be the state capital, the closest they ever came. Capitola was, however, the state's first seaside resort. Nowadays, Capitola is big on art galleries and fine craft shops—take a stroll along Capitola Ave. from the trestle to the creek—but most famous for its begonias. The year's big event is the **Begonia Festival,** usually held early in September. Stop by **Antoneiii Brothers' Begonia Gardens** at 2545 Capitola, tel. (408) 475-5222, for a 10,000-square-foot greenhouse display of begonias, best in August and September.

Aptos, just on the other side of the freeway, is more or less the same as Capitola but home to Cabrillo College and the **World's Shortest Parade,** usually sponsored on the July 4th weekend by the Aptos Ladies' Tuesday Evening Society. High-rent **Soquel,** once a booming lumber town and the place where Portola and his men were awestruck by their first sight of coastal redwoods, is now noted for antiques and oaks.

Forest Of Nisene Marks

Nisene Marks is part of Nature Conservancy lands recently deeded to the state and is definitely a hiker's park. Named for the Danish immigrant who hiked here until the age of 96 and whose family donated the land for public use, this is an oasis of solitude. (This is also the epi-

the Roaring Camp and Big Trees Railroad

SAN JOSE CONVENTION & VISITORS BUREAU

center of the 1989 earthquake that brought down much of Santa Cruz.) Lots to see, but little more than birdsong, rustling leaves, and babbling brooks to listen to. Nisene Marks includes 10,000 acres of hefty second-growth redwoods on the steep southern range of the Santa Cruz Mountains, six creeks, lovely Maple Falls, alders, maples, and more rugged trails than anyone can hike in a day. There's also an old mill site, abandoned trestles and railroad tracks, and logging cabins.

To get here from the coast, take the Aptos-Seacliff exit north from Hwy. 1, and turn right on Soquel Drive. At the first left after the stop sign, drive north on Aptos Creek Rd. and across the railroad tracks. (Bring water and food for day trips. No fires allowed.) The park is open daily 6 a.m.-sunset.

For info and a trail map, contact: Forest of Nisene Marks State Park, Aptos Creek Rd., Aptos 95003, tel. (408) 335-9145. To reserve the trail camp (a six-mile one-way hike), just six sites, primitive, call Mistix, toll-free (800) 444-7275.

WATSONVILLE

Watsonville, an agriculturally rich city of over 25,000, is the mushroom capital of the U.S., though the town calls this lovely section of the Pajaro Valley the "Strawberry Capital of the World," also "Apple City of the Ives." Farming got off to a brisk clod-busting start during the gold rush, when produce grown here was in great demand. Among the early settlers were Chinese, Germans, Slavs, and immigrants from the Sandwich Islands and the Azores, though none gained as much notoriety as Watsonville stagedriver Charlie Parkhurst, one of the roughest, toughest, most daring muleskinners in the state—a "man" later unveiled as a woman, the first to ever vote in California.

For the local "Country Crossroads" farm trails map, and other information, contact the **Pajaro Valley Chamber of Commerce**, P.O. Box 470, Watsonville 95077, tel. (408) 724-3900. Or stop by Country Crossroads headquarters at the farm bureau office, 600 Main, Suite 2.

An almost mandatory stop, from May through January, is **Gizdich Ranch** at 55 Peckham Rd., tel. 722-1056, fabulous from late summer through fall for its fresh apples, homemade apple pies, and fresh-squeezed natural apple juices. Earlier in the season this is a "Pik-Yor-Sef" berry farm, with raspberries, olallieberries, and strawberries (usually also available in pies, fritters, and pastries). Also worth seeking in Watsonville are Mexican and Filipino eateries, many quite good, most inexpensive. Watsonville also has its share of motels, in addition to camping at Pinto Lake (see below) and at the Santa Cruz KOA.

The area also offers unusual diversions. The biggest event here is the annual **West Coast Antique Fly-In** each May, when over 50,000 people show up to appreciate the hundreds of classic, antique, and home-built airplanes on the ground and in the air. In June is the annual **Strawberry Festival,** also the **"Almost Annual" Fats Waller Memorial Jazz Festival,** a three day festival of food, foot-stompin', and crawdad cuisine. In September comes the **Santa Cruz County Fair.**

Sights

Just a few miles northwest of Watsonville at 451 Green Valley Rd., tel. (408) 722-8129, is tiny **Pinto Lake City Park,** with swimming, sailing, sailboarding, fishing, and camping, plus a 180-acre urban nature refuge and picnic area. The **Ellicott Slough National Wildlife Refuge,** another 180-acre ecological reserve of coastal uplands for the Santa Cruz long-toed salamander, is four miles west along San Andreas Rd.; to get there, turn west off Hwy. 1 at the Larkin Valley Rd. exit and continue west on San Andreas Rd. to the refuge, which is next to the Santa Cruz KOA.

The Glass House

This is the "Mother House" of California's Vallejo clan, built in the 1820s. General Mariano Guadalupe Vallejo (see "Sonoma" under "The Valley of the Moon—Sonoma Valley" in "The Wine Country" chapter) was one of five sons and eight daughters born to his parents here, $2\frac{1}{2}$ miles southeast of Watsonville near Hwy. 1. Called the "House of Glass," the Vallejo home has 20-inch-thick walls, handhewn redwood window frames and joists, and—legend has it—a completely glassed-in second story veranda because Don Ignacio Vincente Ferrer Vallejo got a shipment of 12 dozen windows instead of one dozen. From the Vallejo ranch, Jose Castro, Juan Bautista Alvarado, and their rebel troops launched their 1835 attack on Monterey to create the free state of Alta California. The victorious single shot (fired by a lawyer who consulted a book to figure out how to work the cannon) hit the governor's house, and he surrendered immediately.

MOSS LANDING AND VICINITY

Moss Landing is a crazy quilt of weird shops and roadside knickknack stands near the mouth of Elkhorn Slough. The PG&E steam power plant here, circa 1948, is the second largest in the world. All this plus, the Kaiser firebrick-making plant, makes for an odd-looking community. First a Salinas Valley produce port then a whaling harbor until 1930, modern Moss Landing is surrounded by artichoke and broccoli fields. The busy fishing harbor and adjoining slough are home to hundreds of bird and plant species, making this an important center for marinelife studies. These days the area is also noted for its indoor recreational opportunities, with over two dozen antique and junque shops along Moss Landing Road. Show up on the last Sunday in

July for the annual **Antique Street Fair,** which draws more than 350 antique dealers and at least 12,000 civilian antiquers.

Time-honored people's eateries abound, particularly near the harbor, most serving chowders and seafood and/or ethnic specials. Declared by none other than the *New York Times* as one of the Monterey Peninsula's six best restaurants is the **Moss Landing Oyster Bar & Company** at 413 Moss Landing Rd., tel. (408) 633-5302, noted for its exceptional fresh seafood and house-made pastas and desserts. (Outdoor patio dining in good weather.) New and quite good, right on the highway, is **The Whole Enchilada,** tel. 633-3038, open for lunch and dinner daily and specializing in Mexican seafood entrees. (The "whole enchilada," by the way, is filet of red snapper wrapped in a corn tortilla and smothered in enchilada sauce and melted cheese.) The Enchilada's associated **Moss Landing Inn and Jazz Club,** tel. 633-9990, is a bar featuring live jazz on Sundays 4:30-8:30 p.m.

Moss Landing Marine Laboratory

The laboratory here, jointly operated by nine campuses of the California State Universities and Colleges (CSUC) system, studies local marinelife, birds, and tidepools, but particularly Monterey Bay's spectacular underwater submarine canyons, which start where Elkhorn Slough enters the bay at Moss Landing. You can stop for a visit and quick look around, but don't disturb classes or research projects. Best to come in spring, usually the first Sunday after Easter, for the big open house: a complete tour, a chance to explore the "touch tank" full of starfish, sea cucumbers, sponges, snails, and anemones, also slide shows, movies, and marinelife dioramas.

The Elkhorn Slough Reserve

Most people come here to hike and birdwatch, but the fish life in this coastal estuary, the second largest in California, is also phenomenal. No wonder the Ohlone people built villages here some 5,000 years ago. Wetlands like this, oozing with life and nourished by rich bay sediments, are among those natural environments most threatened by "progress." Thanks to the Nature Conservancy, the Elkhorn Slough (originally the mouth of the Salinas River until a 1908 diversion) is now protected as a federal and state estuarine sanctuary and recognized as a National Estuarine Research Reserve. California's first. Elkhorn Slough is managed by the California Department of Fish and Game.

These meandering channels along an old, seven-mile-long river are thick with marshy grasses and wildflowers beneath a plateau of oaks and eucalyptus. In winter, an incredible variety of shorebirds (not counting migrating waterfowl) call this area home. Endangered birds like the brown pelican, the California clapper rail, and the California least tern thrive here. The tule elk once hunted by the Ohlone are long gone, but harbor seals bask on the mudflats, and bobcats, gray foxes, muskrats, otters, and black-tailed deer are still here.

Though this is a private nature sanctuary, not a park, the public can visit; 4½ miles of trails pass by tidal mudflats, salt marshes, and an old abandoned dairy. But there's no better way to see the slough than from the seat of a kayak; stop at the visitors' center at the entrance (Wed.-Sun. 9-5) to arrange a guided tour, or contact: **Elkhorn Slough Foundation,** 1700 Elkhorn Rd., Watsonville 95076, tel. (408) 728-2822 or 728-0560. Arrange kayak tours through the foundation or through **Monterey Bay Kayaks,** 693 Del Monte Ave., Monterey 93940, tel. 373-5357. (See "Monterey.")

Castroville

Calling itself "Artichoke Capital of the World" (though that delicious leathery thistle grows throughout Santa Cruz and Monterey counties), Castroville hosts the annual **Artichoke Festival** every September, call (408) 633-3402 for information. Some party: artichokes fried, baked, mashed, and boiled, also added as colorful ingredients to cookies and cakes. According to local lore, Marilyn Monroe reigned as Miss Artichoke in 1947. The heart of Castroville is Swiss-Italian, which hardly explains the appearance of **The Giant Artichoke** on Hwy. 1, tel. 633-3204, a bizarre restaurant and good rest stop. Get picnic supplies or nibble on french-fried artichokes with mayo dip, artichoke soup, artichoke nut cake, and steamed artichokes. **The Franco Restaurant** at 10639 Merritt, tel. 633-2090, sponsors a Marilyn Monroe look-alike contest in June. But come by anytime to grab a burger—considered the best in the county—and ogle the Marilyn memorabilia. Open Wed.-Sun. for lunch and dinner.

SALINAS AND VICINITY

The sometimes bone-dry Salinas River starts in the mountains above San Luis Obispo and flows north through the Salinas Valley, much of the time underground, unseen. Named for the salt marshes or *salinas* near the river's mouth, the Salinas River is the longest underground waterway in the United States. The 100-mile-long Salinas Valley, with its fertile soil and lush lettuce fields, is sometimes referred to as the nation's Salad Bowl. To the west is the Santa Lucia Range, to the east, the Gabilan and Diablo mountains. Cattle graze in the hills. A Salinas tradition (since 1911) is the four-day **California Rodeo** in July, the world's fourth largest, with broncobusting and bull riding, roping and tying, barrel racing, even a big Western dance on Saturday night. The rowdiness here rivals Mardi Gras (cowboy-style, of course). For information, contact the California Rodeo, P.O. Box 1648, Salinas 93902, tel. (408) 757-2951 or 424-7355. There's high art too: if you make it to the rodeo grounds, you'll see three massive sculptures by Claes Oldenberg, *Hats in Three Stages of Landing.*

No longer such a small town, Salinas is the blue-collar birthplace of novelist John Steinbeck, who chronicled the lives and hard times of California's down-and-out. Some things don't change much. More than 50 years after the 1939 publication of Steinbeck's Pulitzer Prize-winning *The Grapes of Wrath,* the United Farm Workers (UFW) are still attempting to organize the primarily Hispanic farm laborers and migrant workers. The idea of a unionized agricultural labor force has never been popular in the U.S., and certainly not with Salinas Valley growers. In 1936, during a lettuce workers' strike, Salinas was the center of national attention. Reports to the California Highway Patrol that communists were advancing on the town—"proven" by red flags planted along the highway, some of which were sent as evidence to politicians in Sacramento—led to tear gas and tussling between officers, growers, and strikers. (The state highway commission later insisted that the construction warning banners be returned to the area's roadsides.)

Sights

The **Boronda Adobe** is an outstanding example of a Mexican-era "Monterey Colonial" adobe—the building recently refurbished and now including museum displays and exhibits. This tiny one at Boronda Rd. and W. Laurel, built between 1844 and 1848 by Jose Eusebio Boronda and virtually unaltered since, has many handsome, original furnishings. Open daily 9-3 or by appointment, tel. (408) 757-8085. **Toro Park,** on the way to Monterey via Hwy. 68, is a pleasant regional park with good hiking, also bike and horse trails. For an invigorating walk and for views of both Monterey Bay and Salinas Valley, take the 21½-mile trail to Eagle Rock. If horseback riding sounds easier, stop by the **Toro Regional Park Stables,** tel. 484-9932. The park is open daily 8 a.m.-dusk, day-use fee.

The town of **Spreckels** is a satellite community southeast of Salinas, developed by Claus Spreckels in the late 1890s to house employees of his sugar beet factory—a real "company town," including "sugar beet" architectural motifs in the roof gables of many homes. **Natividad** is a one-time stage station about seven miles north of Salinas and the site of the 1846 **Battle of Natividad,** where Californios attacked Yankee invaders herding 300 horses to Frémont's troops in Monterey.

THE STEINBECK LEGACY

Salinas Valley's Despised Star

The Grapes of Wrath didn't do much for Steinbeck's local popularity. Started as a photojournalism project chronicling the "Okie" Dust Bowl migrations to California during the Depression, Steinbeck's *Grapes* instead became fiction. The entire book was a whirlwind, written between June and October 1938. After publication it became, and remained, a bestseller through 1940. Steinbeck was unhappy about the book's incredible commercial success; he believed there was something wrong with books that became so popular.

p.m. Inside is the Steinbeck Room, with a collection of over 30,000 items, including original letters and first editions. Listen to the taped "oral history" interviews with local people who remember Steinbeck. Some of the barbed remarks, made decades after the publication of *The Grapes of Wrath,* make it clear that local wrath runs at least as deep as the Salinas River.

To visit some of the actual places Steinbeck immortalized in his fiction, buy the 37-page *A Guide to Steinbeck Country,* on sale at the Salinas Library for $5. If you can't find it locally, "The John Steinbeck Map" of America is available from Aaron Blake Publishers, 1800 S. Robertson Blvd., Suite 130, Los Angeles 90035, tel. (213) 553-4535.

In August, there's a **Steinbeck Festival** here, three days of films, lectures, tours, and social mixers; tel. (408) 758-7314. In February or March, there's a Piscean **Steinbeck Birthday Party.**

PRACTICALITIES

Accommodations

Camp at the **Laguna Seca Raceway** facility near Monterey (see "Monterey" above). **Fremont Peak State Park** on the way to San Juan Bautista has some first-come, first-camped primitive campsites. **Arroyo Seco,** 20 miles to the southwest, has several campgrounds. **San Lorenzo Regional Park** on the Salinas River near King City has about 200 campsites with hot showers, picnic tables, even a historical museum about agriculture. For San Lorenzo info, contact: Monterey County Parks, the Courthouse, P.O. Box 367, Salinas 93902, tel. (408) 424-1971. Or, farther south, camp at **Los Coches Wayside Camp** just south of Soledad or **Paraiso Hot Springs** nearby. Both **Lake San Antonio** (north and south shore) and **Lake Nacimiento** on the way to San Luis Obispo have abundant campsites.

In Salinas, there are two **Motel 6**'s to choose from, both just off Hwy. 101, both with pool and color TV: 1010 Fairview Ave., tel. (408) 758-2122, $23 s, $29 d, and a newer one at 1257 De La Torr Blvd. (from Hwy. 101, take the Airport Blvd. exit), tel. 757-3077, $25 s, $31 d. A bit more on the upscale side are most other motels lining Hwy. 101.

Salinas native John Steinbeck

Vilified here as a left-winger and Salinas Valley traitor during his lifetime, Steinbeck never came back to Salinas. (The only way the town would ever take him back, he once said, was in a six-foot wooden box. And that's how he arrived.) Most folks here have long since forgiven their local literary light for his political views, however, so now you'll find his name and book titles at least mentioned, if not prominently displayed, around town. An example of this, and something of a backhanded honor, considering the surly author's dedication to drink, is the **Steinbeck Drug and Alcohol Treatment Center.**

Steinbeck's Rehabilitation

But some people are trying to make it up to Steinbeck. After all, he is the only American ever to win both the Pulitzer and Nobel prizes for literature. Efforts are underway to start a (permanent) local Steinbeck Center. There's a Steinbeck statue outside the **John Steinbeck Library** at 110 W. San Luis St., tel. (408) 758-7311, open Mon.-Thurs. 10 a.m.-9 p.m., Fri. and Sat. 10 a.m.-6

Good Food, Entertainment

Cheap and good (near the Greyhound station) is the locally popular **Rosita's Armory Cafe** at 231 Salinas St., tel. (408) 424-7039. For an authentic Mexican feast, another bargain is **Los Arcos de Alisal** at 504 E. Alisal, tel. 422-6886, open daily for lunch and dinner. Family-friendly **Dudley's Bar & Grill** at 1420 S. Main, tel. 754-2211, is great for Sunday brunch, not to mention lunch or dinner daily; try the salmon salad with dill dressing. **Smalley's Roundup** at 700 W. Market, tel. 758-0511, is locally famous for its oakwood barbecue and other cowboy-style fine dining. (Reservations wise at dinner.) Good for more of the same, also early-bird dinners, is the **Italian Villa** two miles southwest of town on Hwy. 68, tel. 424-6266.

The Salinas Valley Guild serves up gourmet lunches for Steinbeck fans and literary ghosts weekdays at the Victorian **Steinbeck House,** the author's birthplace and "a living museum" at 132 Central St.; call (408) 424-2735 for reservations. (Two seatings, 11:45 a.m. and 1:15 p.m.) The house is open 1-3 p.m. for visits, and there's a "Best Cellar" gift shop in the basement. For Salinas-flavored theater, both the **Western Stage** and the **Studio Theatre** schedule popular productions on the Hartnell College campus, 156 Homestead Ave. in Salinas; call 758-1220 for reservations. Tickets $6-7 weekends, $3-5 weekdays.

Information And Transportation

The **Salinas Area Chamber of Commerce,** 119 E. Alisal, P.O. Box 1170, Salinas 93902, tel. (408) 424-7611, has info on accommodations and sights, also a great little brochure: "Steinbeck Country Starts in Salinas." **Amtrak** is at 40 Railroad Ave., tel. 422-7458 or (800) USA-RAIL for fare and schedule information. There's no train station in Monterey, but you can connect via **Monterey-Salinas Transit** bus No. 20 or 21 (or via the Amtrak Thruway bus as part of your train fare). For more information, contact Monterey-Salinas Transit, 1 Ryan Rd. in Monterey, tel. 424-7695 or 899-2555. **Greyhound** is at 19 W. Gabilan St., tel. 426-1626. The **Salinas Municipal Airport** is on Airport Blvd., tel. 758-7214.

SAN JUAN BAUTISTA AND VICINITY

The tiny town of San Juan Bautista is charming and charmed, as friendly as it is sunny. (People here say the weather in this pastoral valley is "salubrious." Take their word for it.) Named for John the Baptist, the 1797 Spanish mission of San Juan Bautista is central to this serene community at the foot of the Gabilan Mountains. But the historic plaza, still bordered by old adobes and now a state historic park, is the true center of San Juan—rallying point for two revolutions, one-time home of famed bandit Tiburcio Vasquez, and the theatrical setting for David Belasco's *Rose of the Rancho.* Movie fans may remember Jimmy Stewart and Kim Novak in the mission scenes from Alfred Hitchcock's *Vertigo,* which were filmed here.

But one of the most colorful characters ever to stumble off the stage in San Juan Bautista was one-eyed stagecoach driver Charley Parkhurst, a truculent, swaggering, tobacco-chewing tough. "He," however, was a woman, born Charlotte Parkhurst in New Hampshire. (Charley voted in Santa Cruz in 1866, more than 50 years before American women's suffrage.)

In addition to history, San Juan Bautista has galleries, antique and craft shops, and an incredible local theater troupe. To get oriented, pick up a walking tour brochure at the **San Juan Bautista Chamber of Commerce** office, 402-A 3rd St., P.O. Box 1037, San Juan Bautista 95045, tel. (408) 623-2454, or elsewhere around town. In June, experience mid-1800s mission days at **Early Days in San Juan Bautista,** a traditional celebration complete with horse-drawn carriages, period dress, music, fandango. The barroom at the Plaza Hotel is even open for card games. The **Flea Market** here in August is one of the country's best. Later in the month, "San Juan Fiesta Day" is the most popular venue of the wandering **Cabrillo Music Festival** (see "Santa Cruz"). But the event of the year is *La Virgen del Tepeyac* or *La Pastorela* (they alternate yearly), traditional Christmas musicals which attract visitors from around the world. (See "El Teatro Campesino" below.)

Historic San Juan Bautista

Partly destroyed by earthquakes in 1800 and 1906 (the San Andreas Fault is just 40 feet away), **Mission San Juan Bautista** has been restored many times. The 15th and largest of the Franciscan settlements in California, the mission here is not as architecturally spectacular as others in the Catholic chain. Visitors can tour sections of the mission—it's still an active parish church—though it's not really part of the adjacent state historic park. After visiting the small museum and gardens, note the old dirt road beyond the wall of the mission cemetery. This is an unspoiled, unchanged section of the original 650-mile El Camino Real which once connected all the California missions.

San Juan Bautista's oldest building is the **Plaza Hotel** at Second and Mariposa streets on the west side of the plaza (originally barracks built for Spanish soldiers in 1813). In horse and buggy days San Juan Bautista was a major stage stop between San Francisco and Los Angeles, and the hotel was famous statewide. (Note the two-story outhouse out back.) Also fascinating is the stable—with its herd of fine old horse-drawn vehicles and the "Instructions for Stagecoach Passengers" plaque out front—and the restored **blacksmith shop.** Also worth a peek: the **jail, washhouse,** and **cabin.**

Above the town of San Juan Bautista is **Pagan Hill.** There's a giant concrete cross today where mission fathers once put up a wooden one, intended to ward off evil spirits supposedly summoned by Indian neophytes secretly practicing their traditional earth religion. The park is open 9:30 a.m.-4 p.m. daily, until 5 in summer. For information, contact: San Juan Bautista State Historic Park, P.O. Box 116, San Juan Bautista 95045, tel. (408) 623-4881.

El Teatro Campesino

Don't pass through San Juan Bautista without enjoying a performance by San Juan Bautista's El Teatro Campesino. Hispanic playwright Luis Valdez founded this small theater group as guerrilla theater on the United Farm Workers' picket lines more than two decades ago. But Valdez's smash-hits *Zoot Suit* and *Corridos* have since brought highly acclaimed nationwide tours and the birth of other Chicano *teatros* throughout the American Southwest. El Teatro's *La Pastorella*, the shepherd's story that alternates with the miracle play *La Virgen del Tepeyac,* is a hilarious and deeply poetic spectacle, a musical folk pageant about shepherds trying to get past comic yet terrifying devils to reach the Christ child. Besides Spanish-language plays, the company also presents contemporary and traditional theater in English. El Teatro Campesino's permanent playhouse is at 705 4th St., tel. (408) 623-2444 (theater) and 623-4995 (store).

Practicalities

There are tent sites (and RV hookups) at the private **Mission Farm Campground and R.V. Park** in a walnut orchard at 400 San Juan-Hollister Rd., tel. (408) 623-4456, as well as the **KOA Campground-San Juan Bautista** on Anzar Rd., tel. 623-4263. A considerable change-up is the **San Juan Inn** at Hwy. 156 and Alameda, tel. 623-4380, with rooms from $42. Another possibility is the **Posada de San Juan Hotel/Inn** at 310 4th St., tel. 623-4030, with fireplace and whirlpool tubs in every room. Call **Bed and Breakfast San Juan,** 315 The Alameda, tel. 623-4101, to arrange overnight stays in local historic homes.

Get groceries at the **Plaza Market** on 3rd Street. For farm-fresh produce, pick up a copy of "San Benito County Cornucopia Guide" to nearby family farms and ranches. (Fresh cherries in June, apricots in July, summer vegetables, apples, walnuts, and kiwis in the fall.)

The **Mission Coffee Shop** at 300 3rd St., tel. (408) 623-9994, is good for families at breakfast and lunch. Try **Felipe's** at 313 3rd, tel. 623-2161, for Mexican and Salvadoran food.

La Casa Rosa, 107 3rd St., tel. (408) 623-4563, is famous for its butter lettuce salads with fresh herb dressing, fresh rolls, and hearty Peruvian-style casseroles (a Californio favorite). **Doña Esther** at 25 Franklin, tel. 623-2518, serves Mexican fare—and the best margaritas in town. Despite the ominously accurate name, well worth a stop for continental-style lunch and dinner (and the view of the San Juan Valley) is the **Fault Line Restaurant** nearby at 11 Franklin, tel. 623-2117.

Fremont Peak

In March 1846, General John C. Frémont and Kit Carson built a "fort" here in defiance of the Mexican government, unfurled their flags on Gabilan Peak, now Fremont Peak, and waited for the supposedly imminent attack of Californio troops. But when no battle came, they broke camp and took off for Oregon. **Fremont Peak State Park,** a long, narrow, isolated strip in the Gabilan Mountains northeast of Salinas, has rolling hills with oaks, madrones, Coulter pines, and spring wildflowers that attract hundreds of hummingbirds. Good hiking in spring, good views from the top of Fremont Peak. Brand new at Fremont Peak is an observatory with a 30-inch Challenger reflecting telescope, open to the public at least twice monthly, free programs; call (408) 623-2465 for details.

There are about 25 primitive campsites (some in the picnic area), also a group camp. To get to the park, from Hwy. 156 head 11 miles south on San Juan Canyon Rd. (County Rd. G1)—paved but steep and winding. For info, contact: Fremont Peak State Park, P.O. Box 1110, San Juan Bautista 95045, tel. (408) 623-4255.

GILROY AND VICINITY

Gilroy And Garlic

Will Rogers supposedly described Gilroy as "the only town in America where you can marinate a steak just by hanging it out on the clothesline." But Gilroy, the "undisputed garlic capital of the world," dedicates very few acres to growing the stinking rose these days. The legendary local garlic farms have been declining due to soil disease since 1979—ironically, the first year of the now-famous and phenomenally successful Gilroy Garlic Festival. Gilroy now grows housing subdivisions (*San Francisco Chronicle* columnist Herb Caen defines modern Gilroy as the place "where the carpet ends and the linoleum begins"), and the San Joaquin Valley grows most of California's garlic. Nonetheless, that unmistakable oily aroma still permeates the air in summer, since over 90% of the world's garlic is processed or packaged here.

The Gilroy Garlic Festival

It's chic to reek in Gilroy. Every July, 150,000 or more garlic lovers descend on the town for several dusty days of sampling garlic perfume, garlic chocolate, and all-you-can-eat garlic ice cream (for some reason, just a few gallons of the stuff takes care of the entire crowd). Who wouldn't pay the $5 admission for belly dancing, big bands, and the crowning of the Garlic Queen? To avoid the crushing, garlic-loving crowds on bumper-to-bumper Hwy. 101, if possible come from Santa Cruz via Corralitos and Hecker Pass on Hwy. 152. For more information, contact the Gilroy Garlic Festival Association, P.O. Box 2311, Gilroy 95021, tel. (408) 842-1625.

Gilroy Wineries

Besides sniffing out local Italian scallions, tour the Gilroy "wine country." Most of the area's wineries are tucked into the Santa Cruz Mountain foothills west of the city, seven of these along Hwy. 152's Hecker Pass. The hearty, full-flavored red wines produced here are still made by hand. The family-run **Conrotto Winery** flourished even during Prohibition in a prune-drying shed. The **Live Oaks Winery** has a fine aged burgundy. **Summerhill Vineyards** is more modern, with occasional winetasting brunches. Come by **Sarah's Winery** (by appointment only) to meet delightful proprietor Marilyn Otteman, who refers to her fine white wines as "ladies," or visit the nearby **Thomas Kruse Winery,** with its eclectic collection of old equipment presided over by philosopher-winemaker Thomas Kruse. His Gilroy Red and other wines sport handwritten, offbeat labels. The **Fortino** and **Hecker Pass** wineries are run by the Fortino family and specialize in old-country hearty red wines.

Casa De Fruta And Coyote Reservoir

Unforgettable is one word for Casa de Fruta, 9840 Pacheco Pass Hwy., tel. (408) 637-7775, a sprawl of neon-lit truckstop-type buildings complete with trailer park and swimming pool, motel, petting zoo, merry-go-round, and miniature train and tunnel. Stop off at the Casa de Fruta Coffee Shop (open 24 hours) and read about the Casa de Fruta Country Store, Casa de Fruta Gift Shop, Casa de Fruta Fruit Stand, Casa de Burger, Casa de Sweets Bakery and Candy Factory, Casa de Choo-Choo, and Casa de Merry-Go-Round on the "mail me" souvenir paper placemats. (To see the coffee cups "flip," ask the coffee shop staff for a show.)

Coyote Reservoir, eight miles north of Gilroy, is great for sailboarding, sailing, and fishing. Open year-round from 8 a.m. to sunset for day use; 75 campsites. For info, contact **Coyote Lake Park,** 10840 Coyote Lake Rd., Gilroy 95020, tel. (408) 842-7800. To get to Coyote Lake, take the Leavesley Rd./Hwy. 152 exit east from Hwy. 101; after two to three miles head north on New Ave. then east on Roop Rd. to Gilroy Hot Springs Road. The Coyote Reservoir Rd. turnoff is about a mile farther, the campground two miles more.

Hollister

If Gilroy is the garlic capital of the world, then Hollister is the earthquake capital. Because of the region's heavy faulting, some say this San Benito County town moves every day, however imperceptibly. (A small 1985 quake, for example, shook loose a 20,000-gallon oak wine cask and flooded the Almaden Winery just south of town.) Agricultural Hollister is as historic as San Juan Bautista, but the "feel" here is straight out of the Old West. Stop by the **San Benito County Historical Museum** at West and Ann streets (open Sat. and Sun.), then wander through Old Town (particularly along 5th St.) to appreciate Hollister's old Victorians.

Traditional cowboy events and some unique competitions are the name of the game during June's **San Benito County Rodeo** here, an event dedicated to the vaquero. The **Fiesta-Rodeo** in July dates back to 1907, when it was first held to raise funds for rebuilding Mission San Juan Bautista after the big quake in 1906.

PINNACLES NATIONAL MONUMENT AND VICINITY

Exploring these barren 1,600 acres of volcanic spires and ravines is a little like rock climbing on the moon. The weird dark-red rocks are bizarrely eroded, unlike anywhere else in North America, forming gaping gorges, crumbling caverns, terrifying terraces. Rock climbers' heaven (not for beginners), this stunning old volcano offers excellent trails, too, with pebbles the size of houses to stumble over. Visitors afraid of earthquakes should know that the Pinnacles sit atop an active section of the San Andreas Fault. Spring is the best time to visit,

when wildflowers brighten up the chaparral, but sunlight on the rocks throughout the day creates rainbows of colors year-round. Climbers come during the cool weather. In winter, also watch the raptors: golden eagles, red-shouldered hawks, kestrels, prairie falcons.

Hikes

Trails alone connect the park's east and west sides. Pinnacles has four self-guided nature trails; the **Geology Hike** and **Balconies Trail** are quite fascinating. The short **Moses Spring Trail** is one of the best. Longest is the trek up the **Chalone Peak Trail,** 11 miles roundtrip, passing fantastic rock formations (quite a view of Salinas once you get to the top of North Chalone Peak). Less ambitious is the **Condor Gulch Trail,** a two-mile easy hike into Balconies Caves from the Chalone Creek picnic area. Various interconnecting trails encourage creativity on foot. Since the best camping and caves are on the park's east side, as well as the most fascinating rock formations and visitor center displays, the fit, fast, and willing can hike east to west and back in one (long) day. Easiest return trip is via the Old Pinnacles Trail, rather than the steep Juniper Canyon Trail. Pack plenty of water.

Practicalities

Good rules of thumb in the Pinnacles: carry water at all times, and watch out for poison oak, stinging nettles, and rattlesnakes. Spelunkers, bring good flashlights and helmets. Pick up guides to the area's plant life and natural history, also topo maps, at the visitors centers. Rock climbers can thumb through old guides there for climbing routes. For info, contact: Pinnacles National Monument, Paicines 95043, tel. (408) 389-4485.

Though private camping outside the park's western border may be available—call park headquarters for current information—the private **Pinnacles Campground, Inc.** to the east, 2400 State Hwy., Paicines 95043, tel. (408) 389-4462, is quite nice: flush toilets, hot showers, fire rings, picnic tables, swimming pool, some RV hookups and group facilities. Pinnacles is most accessible from the coast via Hwy. 146 from Soledad, but it's a narrow road, not recommended for camper and trailers. To reach the eastern side, head west from Hwy. 25. From

Hollister, it's about 34 miles south then about five miles west to the park entrance.

Soledad

Soledad is a sleepy town where no one hurries, and the oldest settlement in the Salinas Valley. Stop by the local bakery or *panaderia* on Front St. for fresh Mexican pastries and hot tortillas. **Mission Nuestra Senora de La Soledad** was founded here in 1791 to minister to the Salinas Valley natives. Our Lady of Solitude Mission three miles southwest of town was quite prosperous until 1825. But this, the 13th in California's mission chain, was beset by problems ranging from raging Salinas River floods to disease epidemics before it crumbled into ruin. The chapel was reconstructed and rededicated, and another wing has since been restored. The original 1799 mission bell still hangs in the courtyard of this active parish church. Lovely garden. Open daily 10 a.m-4 p.m., museum open same hours but closed Tues., tel. (408) 678-2586. Just three miles south of Soledad (west at the Arroyo Seco interchange from Hwy. 101) is the 1843 **Richardson Adobe** at Los Coches Rancho Wayside Campground.

Paraiso Hot Springs

Nestled in a grove of lovely old palm trees, with a sweeping valley view, this serene, scenic 240-acre resort a few miles southwest of Soledad has an indoor hot mineral bath (suits required), outdoor pools, picnic tables and barbecues, campgrounds, Victorian cabins—a genuinely restful getaway, rarely crowded. There's not much to do here but loll around in the waters and soak up the sun, but visitors can use the lending library, recreation room, and enjoy free coffee and cookies. Nothing much happens after 6 p.m. but the sunset and moonrise. Facilities include indoor and outdoor baths and pools, tent cabins, and furnished cabins. Weekly and monthly rates available. For more information and reservations, contact: Paraiso Hot Springs, Soledad 93960, tel. (408) 678-2882.

ROBERT RACE

THE CENTRAL COAST
INTRODUCTION

Along this swath of coastline where north becomes south, something in the air eventually transforms people into curmudgeons. The prevailing attitude is quite straightforward: *go away*. Henry Miller, one of the coast's crustiest and lustiest curmudgeons, believed the source of this sentiment was the land itself, speaking through its inhabitants. "And so it happens," he wrote from his home in Big Sur, "that whoever settles in this region tries to keep others from coming here. Something about the land makes one long to keep it intact—and strictly for oneself." And so it happens, like children denied candy or toys or the latest fashion fad, we want it all the more, the desire becomes altogether too great. The rest of us can't stay away. The central coast's inherent inaccessibility is its greatest attraction.

THE LAND

The land itself is unfriendly, at least from the human perspective. Especially in the north, the indomitable unstable terrain—with its habit of sliding out from under whole hillsides, houses, highways, and hiking trails at the slightest provocation—has made the area hard to inhabit. But despite its contrariness the central coast, that unmistakable pivotal point between California's north and south, successfully blends both.

The Great Transition
Though the collective Coast Ranges continue south through the region, here the terrain takes on a new look. The redwoods thin out, limiting themselves to a few large groves in Big Sur country and otherwise straggling south a short distance beyond San Simeon, tucked into hidden folds in the rounded coastal mountains. Where redwood country ends either the grasslands of the dominant coastal oak woodlands begin or the chaparral takes over, in places almost impenetrable. Even the coastline reflects the transition—the rocky rough-and-tumble shores along the Big Sur coast transform into tamer beaches and bluffs near San Simeon and points south.

Los Padres National Forest inland from the coast is similarly divided into two distinct sections.

The northernmost (and largest) Monterey County section includes most of the rugged 100-mile-long Santa Lucia Range and its Ventana Wilderness. The southern stretch of Los Padres, essentially the San Luis Obispo and Santa Barbara backcountry, is often closed to hikers and backpackers during the summer due to high fire danger. This area includes the southern extension of the Santa Lucias, the La Panza Range, the Sierra Madre Mountains, also the San Rafael Wilderness and a portion of the San Rafael Mountains. Farther south but still in Los Padres National Forest are the Santa Ynez Mountains east of Santa Barbara, angling northwest to Point Arguello near Lompoc, and part of the unusual east-west Transverse Ranges which create the geographic boundary between northcentral and Southern California.

Another clue that the north-south transition occurs here is water or, moving southward, the increasingly obvious lack of it. Though both the north and south forks of the Little Sur River, the Big Sur River a few miles to the south, and other northern waterways flow to the sea throughout the year, as does the Cuyama River in the south (known as the Santa Maria River as it nears the ocean), most of the area's streams are seasonal. But off-season hikers, beware: even inland streams with a six-month flow are not to be dismissed during winter and spring, when deceptively dinky creekbeds can become death-dealing torrents overnight.

Major lakes throughout California's central coast region are actually water-capturing reservoirs, including Lake San Antonio, known for its winter bald eagle population, Lake Nacimiento on the other side of the mountains from San Simeon, and Santa Margarita Lake east of San Luis Obispo near the headwaters of the Salinas River. Other popular regional reservoirs include Lopez Lake southeast of San Luis Obispo and Lake Cachuma near Santa Barbara.

BIG SUR AND VICINITY

The poet Robinson Jeffers described this redwood-and-rock coast as "that jagged country which nothing but a falling meteor will ever plow." It's only fitting, then, that this area was called Jeffers Country long before it became known as Big Sur. Sienna-colored sandstone and granite, surly waves, and the sundown sea come together in a never-ending dance of creation and destruction. Writer Henry Miller said Big Sur was "the face of the earth as the creator intended it to look," a point hard to argue. But Big Sur as a specific *place* is difficult to locate. It's not only a town, a valley, and a river—the entire coastline from just south of Carmel Highlands to somewhere north of San Simeon (some suggest the southern limit is the Monterey County line) is considered Big Sur country.

Once "in" Big Sur, wherever that might be, visitors soon notice some genuine oddities—odd at least by California standards. People here don't have much money and don't seem to care. They build unusual dwellings—glass tepees and geodesic domes, round redwood houses with the look of wine barrels ready to roll into the sea—both to fit the limited space available and to express that elusive Big Sur sense of *style*.

Because the terrain itself is so tormented and twisted, broadcast signals somehow never arrive in Big Sur. There's no TV, and electricity and telephones with dial service have only been available in Big Sur since the 1950s, though some people along the south coast and in more remote areas still have neither.

Social life in Big Sur consists of bowling at the naval station, attending a poetry reading or the annual Big Sur Potluck Revue at the Grange Hall in the valley, driving into "town" (Monterey) for a few movie cassettes, or—for a really wild night—drinks on the deck at sunset and dancing cheek to cheek at Nepenthe. Big Sur is a very *different* California, where even the chamber of commerce urges visitors "to slow down, meditate," and "catch up with your soul."

It's almost impossible to catch up with your soul, however, when traffic is bumper-to-bumper. Appreciating Big Sur while driving or (only for the brave) bicycling in a mile-long coastline convoy is akin to honeymooning in Hades—a universal impulse but the wrong ambience. As it

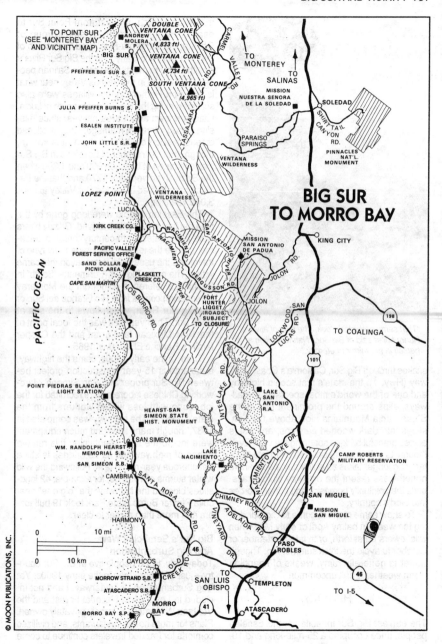

BIG SUR
TO MORRO BAY

PACIFIC OCEAN

TO POINT SUR
(SEE "MONTEREY BAY
AND VICINITY" MAP)

DOUBLE
VENTANA CONE
(4,833 ft)

VENTANA CONE
(4,734 ft)

SOUTH VENTANA CONE
(4,965 ft)

ANDREW
MOLERA
S. P.

BIG SUR

PFEIFFER BIG SUR S. P.

JULIA PFEIFFER BURNS S. P.

ESALEN INSTITUTE

JOHN LITTLE S.R.

LOPEZ POINT

LUCIA

KIRK CREEK CG.

PACIFIC VALLEY
FOREST SERVICE OFFICE

SAND DOLLAR
PICNIC AREA

PLASKETT
CREEK CG.

CAPE SAN MARTIN

POINT PIEDRAS BLANCAS
LIGHT STATION

HEARST-SAN
SIMEON STATE
HIST. MONUMENT

SAN SIMEON

WM. RANDOLPH HEARST
MEMORIAL S.B.

SAN SIMEON S.B.

CAMBRIA

HARMONY

MORROW STRAND S.B.

ATASCADERO S.B.

MORRO BAY S.P.

MORRO
BAY

CAYUCOS

CARMEL
VALLEY
RD.

TO
MONTEREY

TO
SALINAS

MISSION NUESTRA SENORA
DE LA SOLEDAD

SOLEDAD

SHIRT TAIL
CANYON
RD.

PARAISO
SPRINGS

PINNACLES
NAT'L.
MONUMENT

VENTANA
WILDERNESS

VENTANA
WILDERNESS

TASSAJARA RD.

NACIMIENTO RD.

NACIMIENTO RIVER

LOS BURROS RD.

SAN ANTONIO RIVER

FERGUSSON RD.

MISSION
SAN ANTONIO
DE PADUA

KING CITY

FORT
HUNTER
LIGGETT
(ROADS
SUBJECT
TO CLOSURE)

JOLON

JOLON RD.

LOCKWOOD - SAN

LUCAS RD.

198

TO COALINGA

101

INTER LAKE RD.

LAKE
SAN ANTONIO
R.A.

NACIMIENTO LAKE DR.

LAKE
NACIMIENTO
R.A.

CAMP ROBERTS
MILITARY RESERVATION

SANTA ROSA CREEK RD.

CHIMNEY ROCK RD.

ADELAIDA DR.

SAN MIGUEL

MISSION
SAN MIGUEL

VINEYARD DR.

OLD CREEK RD.

46

TO
SAN LUIS
OBISPO

PASO
ROBLES

TEMPLETON

46

TO I-5

41

ATASCADERO

0   10 mi

0   10 km

© MOON PUBLICATIONS, INC.

1

KIM WEIR

"That same prehistoric look. The look of always," Henry Miller said of Big Sur. "Nature smiling at herself in the mirror of eternity."

snakes through Big Sur, California's Coast Highway (Hwy. 1), the state's first scenic highway and one of the world's most spectacular roadways, slips around the prominent ribs of the Santa Lucia Mountains high above the sea, slides into dark wooded canyons, and soars across graceful bridges spanning the void. Even though its existence means that a trip into Monterey no longer takes an entire day, people here nonetheless resent the highway which transports the spiritually homesick and hungry hordes into God's country.

To show some respect, come to Big Sur during the week, in balmy April or early May when wildflowers burst forth, or in late September or October to avoid the thick summer fog. Though winter is generally rainy, weeks of sparkling warm weather aren't uncommon.

HISTORY

The earliest Big Sur inhabitants, the Esselen people, once occupied a 25-mile-long and 10-mile-wide stretch of coast from Point Sur to near Lucia in the south. A small group of Ohlone, the Sargenta-Ruc, lived from south of the Palo Colorado Canyon to the Big Sur River's mouth. Though most of the area's Salinan peoples lived inland in the Salinas Valley near what is now Fort Hunter-Liggett, villages were also scattered along the Big Sur coast south of Lucia. Little is known about area natives, since mission-forced intertribal marriages and introduced diseases soon obliterated them. It is known, though, that the number of Esselens in Big Sur was estimated at between 900 and 1,300 when the Spanish arrived after 1770 and that the Esselen people lived in the Big Sur Valley at least 3,000 years ago.

The Esselen people were long gone by the time the first area settlers arrived. Grizzly bears were the greatest 18th-century threat to settlement, since the terrain discouraged any type of travel and the usual wildlife predation that came with it. The name Big Sur (Sur means "South" in Spanish, a reference point from the Monterey perspective) comes from Rio Grande del Sur, or the Big Sur River, which flows to the sea at Point Sur. The river itself was the focal point of the 1834 Mexican land grant and the Cooper family's Rancho El Sur until 1965.

Then, in the early 1900s, came the highway, a hazardous 15-year construction project between Big Sur proper and San Simeon. Hardworking Chinese laborers were recruited for the job along with less willing workers from the state's prisons. The highway was completed in 1937, though many lives and much equipment were lost to the sea. Maintaining this remote ribbon of highway and its 29 bridges is still a treacherous year-round task. Following the wild winter storms of 1982-83, for example, 42 landslides blocked the highway; the "big one" near Julia Pfeiffer Burns State Park took 19 bulldozers and more than a year to clear.

Big Sur's Semi-civil Wars And Big Surbanization

Today only 1,300 people live in Big Sur country—just 300 more than in the early 1900s. Yet "Big Surbanization" is underway. Land not included in Los Padres National Forest and the Ventana Wilderness is largely privately owned. Plans for more hotels, restaurants, and civilized comforts for frazzled travelers continue to come

THE ESALEN INSTITUTE

The Esselen and Salinan peoples frequented the hot springs here, supposedly called *tok-i-tok*, "hot healing water." In 1939 Dr. H.C. Murphy (who presided at John Steinbeck's birth in Salinas) opened Slate's Hot Springs resort on the site. The hot springs were transformed by grandson Michael Murphy into the famed Esalen Institute, where human-potential practitioners and participants including Joan Baez, Gregory Bateson, the Beatles, Jerry Brown, Carlos Castaneda, Buckminster Fuller, Aldous Huxley, Linus Pauling, B.F. Skinner, Hunter S. Thompson, and Alan Watts taught or learned in residential workshops.

Esalen is the Cadillac of New Age retreats, according to absurdist/comedian/editor Paul Krassner. Even writer Alice Kahn who, before arriving at Esalen, considered herself the "last psycho-virgin in California" and "hard-core unevolved," eventually admitted that there was something about the Esalen Institute that defied all cynicism.

Esalen's magic doesn't necessarily come cheap. The introductory "Experiencing Esalen" weekend workshop runs $300 or so, including simple but pleasant accommodations and wonderful meals. Five-day workshops (like "Pleasure and Addiction" and "Using Risk to Effect Change") are substantially more. But Esalen tries to accommodate even the less affluent with scholarships, a work-study program, senior citizen discounts, family rates, and bunk bed or sleeping bag options. You can also arrange just an overnight or weekend stay (sans enlightenment) assuming space is available. The massages at Esalen are world-renowned, from $50 an hour. Entrance to the facilities here are by reservation only; for information on workshops and lodgings and a copy of Esalen's current catalog of events, contact: Esalen Institute, Big Sur 93920, tel. (408) 667-3000.

up, and the eternal, wild peace Robinson Jeffers predicted would reign here forever has at last been touched by ripples of civilization. Nobody wants the character of Big Sur to change, but people can't agree on how best to save it.

As elsewhere in California, some Big Sur landowners believe that private property rights are sacrosanct, beyond the regulation of God or the government. Others argue that state and local land-use controls are adequate. Still others contend that federal intervention is necessary, possibly granting the region "scenic area" or national park status—an idea fought sawtooth and nail by most residents. The reason Big Sur is still ruggedly beautiful, they say, is because local people have kept it that way. A favorite response to the suggestion of more government involvement: "Don't Yosemitecate Big Sur." In March of 1986, both of California's senators proposed that the U.S. Forest Service take primary responsibility for safeguarding Big Sur's scenic beauty—with no new logging, mining claims, or grazing privileges allowed. The final result, which limits but doesn't eliminate new development, seems to please almost everyone.

BIG SUR RECREATION

The ultimate activity in Big Sur is just bumming around: scrambling down to beaches to hunt for jade and look at tidepools or scuba dive or surf where it's possible, also cycling, sightseeing, and watching the sun set. Along the coastline proper there are few long hiking trails, since much of the terrain is treacherous and much of the rest privately owned, but the Big Sur backcountry offers good hiking and backpacking.

The Ventana Wilderness

Local lore has it that a natural land bridge once connected two mountain peaks at Bottchers Gap, creating a window (or *ventana* in Spanish) until the 1906 San Francisco earthquake brought it all tumbling down. The Big Sur, Little Sur, Arroyo Seco, and Carmel rivers all cut through this 161,000-acre area, creating dramatic canyon gorges and wildlands well worth exploring. Steep, sharp-crested ridges and serrated V-shaped valleys are clothed mostly in oaks, madrones, and dense chaparral. Redwoods grow on north-facing slopes near the fog-cooled coast, pines at higher elevations. The gnarly spiral-shaped bristlecone firs found only here are in the rockiest, most remote areas, their total range only about 12 miles wide and 55 miles long.

Most of all, the Ventana Wilderness provides a great escape from the creeping coastal traffic (a free visitor permit is required to enter), and offers great backpacking and hiking when the Sierra Nevada, Klamath Mountains, and Cas-

the "Rainbow Bridge," now Bixby Creek Bridge, where Lady Bird Johnson stood in 1966 to dedicate Highway 1 as the state's first scenic highway

CALIFORNIA DEPARTMENT OF PARKS & RECREATION

cades are still snowbound—though roads here are sometimes impassible during the rainy season. Hunting, fishing, and horseback riding are also permitted. Crisscrossing Ventana Wilderness are nearly 400 miles of backcountry trails and 82 vehicle-accessible campgrounds (trailside camping possible with a permit).

The wilderness trailheads are at Big Sur Station, Carmel River, China Camp, Arroyo Seco, Memorial Park, Bottchers Gap, and Cone Peak Road. The Ventana Wilderness recreation map, available for $3 from ranger district offices, shows all roads, trails, and campgrounds. Fire-hazardous areas, routinely closed to the public after July 1 (or earlier), are coded yellow on maps.

Trail and campground traffic fluctuates from year to year, so solitude seekers should ask rangers about more remote routes and destinations. Since the devastating Marble Cone fire of 1978 (and other more recent fires), much of what once was forest is now chaparral and brushland. As the natural succession progresses, dense undergrowth obliterates trails not already erased by erosion. Despite dedicated volunteer trail work, lack of federal trail maintenance has also taken its toll.

Backcountry travelers should also heed fire regulations. Because of the high fire danger in peak tourist season, using a campstove or building a fire outside designated campgrounds requires a fire permit. Also, bring water—but think twice before bringing Fido along, since flea-transmitted plague is a possibility. Other bothersome realities include ticks (especially in winter and early spring), rattlesnakes, poison oak, and fast-rising rivers and streams following rainstorms.

Big Sur Hikes

The grandest views of Big Sur come from the ridges just back from the coast. A great companion is *Hiking the Big Sur Country* by Jeffrey P. Schaffer (Wilderness Press). The short but steep **Valley View Trail** from Pfeiffer-Big Sur State Park is usually uncrowded, especially midweek (there are benches up top for sitting and staring off the edge of the world). But for those *serious* about coastal hiking, walk all the way from Pfeiffer-Big Sur to Salmon Creek near the southern Monterey County line. The trip from Bottchers Gap to Ventana Double Cone via **Skinner Ridge Trail** is about 16 miles one way and challenging, with a variety of possible campsites, dazzling spring wildflowers, and oak and pine forests.

Or, take either the nine-mile **Pine Ridge Trail** from Big Sur or the 15-mile trail from China Camp on Chews Ridge to undeveloped Sykes Hot Springs, just 400 yards from Sykes Camp (very popular these days). Another good, fairly short *visual* hike is the trip to nearby Mount Manuel, a nine-mile round trip. The two-mile walk to **Pfeiffer Beach** is also worth it—miles from the highway, fringed by forest, with a wading cove and meditative monolith.

Big Sur Back Roads

For an unforgettable dry-season side trip, a true joy ride, take the **Old Coast Road** from just north of the Bixby Bridge inland to the Big Sur Valley: barren granite, a thickly forested gorge, and good views of sea and sky before the road loops back to Hwy. 1 south of Point Sur near the entrance to Andrew Molera State Park. **Palo Colorado Road**, mostly unpaved and narrow, winds through a canyon of redwoods and ferns and summer homes, up onto hot and dry Las Piedras Ridge, then down into the Little Sur watershed. Near the Palo Colorado intersection with the highway is the **Coastanoan Winery** in the historic three-story squared-log redwood home at the Grimes Ranch, with invitation-only winetasting, tel. (408) 624-8368.

Marvelous for the sense of adventure and the views is a drive along the **Nacimiento-Fergusson Road** from the coast inland to what's left of old Jolon and the fabulous nearby mission, both included within the Fort Hunter-Liggett Military Reservation. (Taking this route is always somewhat risky, particularly on weekends, since all roads through Hunter-Liggett are closed when military exercises are underway—less common these days.) Even more thrilling is driving rough-and-ready **Los Burros Rd.** farther south, an unmarked turnoff just south of Willow Creek and Cape San Martin which leads to the long-gone town of Manchester in the Los Burros gold mining district (an indestructible vehicle and plenty of time is required for this route, and it's often closed to traffic after winter storms).

Big Sur back roads leading to the sea are rarer and easy to miss. About one mile south of the entrance to Pfeiffer-Big Sur State Park is **Sycamore Canyon Road**, which winds its way downhill for two exciting miles before the parking lot near Pfeiffer Beach. At Willow Creek there's a road curling down from the vista point to the rocky beach below, and just south of Willow Creek a dirt road leads to Cape San Martin (good for views any day but especially fine for whalewatching).

HEADING SOUTH: BIG SUR SIGHTS

Garrapata State Park

Garrapata State Park stretches north along the coast from Soberanes Point, where the Santa Lucia Mountains first dive into the sea. South-ward, the at-first unimpressive **Point Sur** and its lighthouse beacon stand out beyond Garrapata State Park and beach, named after the noble wood tick and featuring a crescent of creek-veined white sand, granite arches, caves and grottos, and sea otters. Ticks or no ticks, the unofficial nude beach here is one of the best in Northern California. Winter whalewatching is usually good from high ground. On weekends in January, ranger-led whalewatch programs are held at Granite Canyon. Or, if it's not foggy, take the two-mile loop trail from the turnout for the view.

South of Garrapata and inland is private **Palo Colorado Canyon**, reached via the road of the same name. Dark and secluded even in summer, the canyon is often cut off from the rest of the world when winter storms stomp through. The name itself is Spanish for "tall redwood." About eight miles in at the end of the road is isolated **Bottchers Gap Campground**, complete with restrooms, picnic tables, and multiple trailheads into the Ventana Wilderness. A few miles farther south on the highway is the famous **Rainbow Bridge** (now called Bixby Creek Bridge), 260 feet high and 700 feet long, the highest single-arch bridge in the world when constructed in 1932 and still the most photographed of all Big Sur bridges.

Point Sur Lighthouse State Park

Up atop Point Sur stands the Point Sur Lighthouse, an 1889 sandstone affair still standing guard at this shipwreck site once known as the Graveyard of the Pacific. In the days when the only way to get here was on horseback, 395 wooden stair steps led to the lighthouse, originally a giant multi-wick kerosene lantern surrounded by a Fresnel lens with a 16-panel prism. The Point Sur Lighthouse is now computer operated and features an electrical aerobeacon, radio-beacon, and fog "diaphone." This 34-acre area and its central rocky mound (good views and whalewatching) is now a state park, though the Coast Guard still maintains the lighthouse. Current information about ranger-guided lighthouse tours ($2) is posted throughout Big Sur or call (408) 625-4419. For information about winter whalewatching programs here and at both Garrapata and Julia Pfeiffer Burns state parks, call 667-2315.

Andrew Molera State Park

Inland and up, past what remains of the pioneering Molera Ranch (part of the original Rancho El Sur), is marvelous Andrew Molera State Park, a 2,100-acre park first donated to the Nature Conservancy by Frances Molera in honor of her brother, then deeded to the state for management. There's no pavement here, just a rundown dirt parking lot and a short trail winding through sycamores, maples, and a few redwoods along the east fork of the Big Sur River to the two-mile beach and adjacent seabird-sanctuary lagoon below. (The big breakers cresting along the coast here are created by the Sur Breakers Reef.) The trail north of the river's mouth leads up a steep promontory to Garnet Beach, noted for its colorful pebbles.

Worthwhile, too, is the two-hour trek across the sand and up the ridges on horseback with former Esalen psychologist and wrangler Nevada Robertson as guide. (She also takes Big Sur travelers into the Ventana Wilderness for one- or two-day trips.) The Andrew Molera horseback route has changed somewhat following the devastating 1989 summer fire that blackened most of the park on the east side of the highway. Except when firefighting crews are camped here and on major holiday weekends, it's usually uncrowded at Andrew Molera.

Among its other attractions, the park also features a primitive yet peaceful 50-site walk-in campground just one-quarter mile from the parking lot (three-night limit, dogs allowed only with proof of current rabies vaccination). For more in-

formation about the park, contact: Andrew Molera State Park, P.O. Box A, Big Sur 93920, tel. (408) 667-2315. For information about seeing Big Sur on horseback, contact: **Big Sur Trail Rides,** P.O. Box 111, Big Sur 93920, tel. 667-2666. By reservation only.

Pfeiffer-Big Sur State Park

Inland on the other side of the ridge from Andrew Molera State Park is protected, sunny Big Sur Valley, a visitor-oriented settlement surrounding picnic and camping facilities at 821-acre Pfeiffer-Big Sur State Park adjoining the Ventana Wilderness. Take the one-mile nature trail or meander up through the redwoods to **Pfeiffer Falls,** a verdant, fern-lined canyon at its best in spring and early summer, then on up to **Valley View** for a look at the precipitous Big Sur River gorge below. Redwoods, sycamores, big-leaf maples, cottonwoods, and willows hug the river, giving way to oaks, chaparral, and Santa Lucia bristlecone fir at higher elevations. Abundant poison oak. Raccoons can be particularly pesky here, like the begging birds, so keep food out of harm's way.

To hike within the Ventana Wilderness, head south on the highway one-half mile to the U.S. Forest Service office (where trails begin), tel. (408) 667-2423, for a permit and current information. About a mile south of the entrance to Pfeiffer-Big Sur is the road to Los Padres National Forest's **Pfeiffer Beach** (take the second right-hand turnoff after the park), mauve and white sands streaked with black, cypresses, and craggy caves. It's heaven here on a clear,

Point Sur Lighthouse

calm day, but the hissing sand stings mercilessly when the weather is up. And any day, forget the idea of an ocean swim. The water's cold, the surf capricious, and the currents tricky; even expert divers need to register with rangers before jumping in. Pfeiffer Beach is open to the public from 6 a.m. to sunset.

The outdoor amphitheater at Pfeiffer-Big Sur State Park (which hosts many of the park's educational summer campfires and interpretive programs) and lagoons were built by the Civilian Conservation Corps during the Depression. The large developed year-round campground has over 200 campsites with picnic tables and hot showers ($16 per night; advance reservations through Mistix, tel. 800-444-7275, are advisable in summer and good-weather weekends). The day-use fee for short park hikes and picnicking is $5. The park is crowded in summer. For more information, contact: Pfeiffer-Big Sur State Park, Big Sur 93920, tel. (408) 667-2315.

Urban Big Sur

Nowhere in Big Sur country are visitors really diverted from the land because big-time boutiques, gaudy gift shops, even movie theaters don't exist. But urban Big Sur starts at Big Sur Valley and stretches south past the post office and Forest Service office to Deetjen's Big Sur Inn. This "big city" part of Big Sur includes the area's most famous inns and restaurants: the Ventana Inn, Nepenthe, and Deetjen's (see "Big Sur Practicalities" below). Fascinating about Nepenthe is the fact that although cinematographer Orson Welles was persona non grata just down the coast at San Simeon (for his too-faithful portrayal of William Randolph Hearst in *Citizen Kane*), when he bought what was then the Trails Club Log Cabin in Big Sur for his wife Rita Hayworth in 1944, he was able to haunt Hearst from the north. Welles's place became Nepenthe ("surcease from sorrows") shortly after he sold it in 1947.

South of Deetjen's is the noted **Coast Gallery** at Lafler Canyon (named for editor Henry Lafler, a friend of Jack London), tel. (408) 667-2301, open daily 9 a.m.-5 p.m. Rebuilt from redwood water tanks in 1973, the Coast Gallery offers fine local arts and crafts, from jewelry and pottery to paintings (including watercolors by Henry Miller), sculpture, and woodcarvings. Nearby is the **Henry Miller Memorial Library,** a collection of friendly clutter about the writer and his life's work located on the highway about one mile south of the Ventana Inn but almost hidden behind redwoods and an unassuming redwood double gate; call 667-2574 or the county library at 667-2537 for information. Emil White, Miller's friend, says he started the library in his own home "because I missed him." Usually open daily.

Julia Pfeiffer Burns State Park

Partington Cove is about one mile south of Partington Ridge, the impressive northern boundary of Julia Pfeiffer Burns State Park. To get down to the cove, park on the east side of the highway and head down the steep trail which starts near the fence (by the black mailbox) on the west side of the road. The branching trail leads back into the redwoods to the tiny beach at the stream's mouth, or across a wooden footbridge, through a rock tunnel hewn in the 1880s by pioneer John Partington, and on to the old dock where tan bark was once loaded onto seagoing freighters. A fine place for a smidgeon of inspirational solitude.

There's a stone marker farther south at the park's official entrance, about seven miles south of Nepenthe. These spectacular 4,000 acres straddling the highway also include a large underwater park offshore. Picnic in the coast redwoods by McWay Creek (almost the southern limit of their range) or hike up into the chaparral and the Los Padres National Forest. After picnicking, take the short walk along McWay Creek (watch for poison oak) then through the tunnel under the road to **Saddle Rock** and the cliffs above **Waterfall Cove,** the only California waterfall that plunges directly into the sea. The cliffs are rugged here; it's a good place to view whales and otters. Only experienced divers, by permit, are allowed to scuba offshore.

The park also features limited year-round camping at walk-in environmental sites and group campgrounds only. For more information about the park, including winter whalewatching programs held here on weekends, contact: Julia Pfeiffer Burns State Park, Big Sur 93920, tel. (408) 667-2315.

The still raw 1,400-foot-wide slash of earth just north of Julia Pfeiffer Burns State Park, which stopped traffic through Big Sur for over a year, has earned the area's landslide-of-all-time award (so far). Heading south from the park, the highway crosses Anderson Creek and rugged Anderson Canyon, where an old collection of highway construction cabins for convicts sheltered such bohemians as Henry Miller and his friend Emil White in the 1940s. A few human residents and a new population of bald eagles now call Anderson Canyon home.

Landels-Hill Big Creek Reserve

Just south of the Esalen Institute is the **John Little State Reserve,** 21 acres of coast open to the public for day use (frequently foggy). About five miles south of Esalen, beyond the Dolan Creek and dramatic Big Creek bridges, is the entrance to the Nature Conservancy's **Landels-Hill Big Creek Reserve,** more than 4,000 acres cooperatively managed by the Conservancy, the Save-the-Redwoods League, and the University of California. Safe behind these rusted cast-iron gates are 11 different plant communities, at least 350 plant species, 100 varieties of birds, and 50 types of mammals. A 10-acre area is open as a public educational center, groups welcome. For more information, contact: Landels-Hill Big Creek Preserve, UC Environmental Field Program, attention John Smiley, 231 Clark Kerr Hall, Santa Cruz 95064.

Lucia And The New Camaldali Hermitage

The tiny "town" of Lucia is privately owned, with gas station and a good down-home restaurant open after 7 a.m. until dark, when they shut off the generator. Try the homemade split pea soup. Different, too, is a stay in one of the 10 rustic cabins on the coast. Come nightfall, kerosene lanterns provide the ambience. A simple yet spectacular spot, call (408) 667-2391 for information and reservations.

South of Lucia (at the white cross), the road to the left leads to the New Camaldoli Hermitage, a small Benedictine monastery at the former Lucia Ranch. The sign says that the monks "regret we cannot invite you to camp, hunt, or enjoy a walk on our property" due to the hermitage's customary solitude and avoidance of "unnecessary speaking." But visitors *can* come to buy crafts and homemade fruitcake and to attend daily mass.

In addition, the hermitage is available for very serene retreats of up to several days (few outsiders can stand the no-talk rules for much longer than that), simple meals included (suggested offering $30 a day). For more information contact: New Camaldoli Hermitage, Director of Vocations, Big Sur 93920, tel. (408) 667-2456 or 667-2341.

Pacific Valley And Gorda

The four-mile marine terrace of Pacific Valley south of Wild Cattle Creek Bridge and north of Willow Creek offers good coastal access and jade, the closest thing to big business in these parts. **Sand Dollar Beach** is a crescent of rocky beach, perfect for picnics and hang gliding; jade hunting is particularly good at **Jade Cove,** actually a series of coves between Plaskett Point and Willow Creek under striking serpentine cliffs shaped by the sea. Take the path down to the rocky cove and look for the rare and valuable harder-than-steel blue-green nephrite jade, one of two types of true jade, though most people find only mediocre gray-green Monterey jade. (But think big: in 1971, several offshore divers dragged up an eight-foot-long, 9,000-pound boulder of solid nephrite jade valued at $180,000.)

Willow Creek (there's a road heading down just south of the bridge) is more accessible for jade hunters, another rocky beach with crashing surf, good rock fishing, restrooms. From **Cape San Martin** just south (rough dirt road hidden behind the bluff, easy to miss) take in the spectacular 360-degree coastal views.

Stop by the **Pacific Valley Center** restaurant, tel. (805) 927-8655, for great homemade pie. And stop by the U.S. Forest Service office, also in Pacific Valley, to get wilderness and fire permits, then take the short hike to **Salmon Creek Falls,** a 75-foot cascade of crystal water just 200 yards off the highway. (From the Forest Service office, work your way up the creek, then climb along the notch behind the falls for a view from the inside out.) This is also just about the end of redwood country; there are a few lost-looking loners near the creek.

Gorda (Spanish for "fat girl," nicknamed "Sorta Gorda" by locals) south of Pacific Valley is another tiny, privately owned spot in the road, casual and friendly, gas and a general store.

BIG SUR PRACTICALITIES

Public Camping

In the accommodations category nothing but camping is truly inexpensive in Big Sur, so to travel on the cheap make Mistix reservations *early* (where applicable) and stock up on groceries and sundries in Monterey up north or in San Luis Obispo to the south. The U.S. Forest Service **Bottchers Gap Campground** on Palo Colorado Canyon Rd. has primitive, walk-in tent sites (first-come, first-served, rough road). The Forest Service's **Kirk Creek Campground** is far south of urban Big Sur and just north of the intersection with Nacimiento-Fergusson Rd.: 33 first-come, first-served campsites, picnic tables, and grills all situated on a grassy seaside bluff. (Inland, halfway to Jolon, are two small creekside campgrounds managed by Los Padres National Forest, free since there's no reliable drinking water but popular with deer hunters.)

Also Forest Service and even farther south is **Plaskett Creek Campground,** $8. For more information on the area's national forest campgrounds and for free visitor permits, fire permits, maps, and other information about Los Padres National Forest and the Ventana Wilderness, stop by the **Big Sur Station Ranger District** office at Pfeiffer-Big Sur State Park, open daily 8 a.m.-4:30 p.m., tel. (408) 667-2423; the district office farther south at **Pacific Valley**, tel. (805) 927-4211; or the **Monterey Ranger District** office at 406 South Mildred Ave., King City 93930, tel. (408) 385-5434.

For secluded camping, try **Andrew Molera State Park,** with 50 walk-in tent sites not far from the dusty parking lot, $3, or **Julia Pfeiffer Burns State Park,** almost as nice, with two separate environmental campgrounds (far from RVs). More comforts (including flush toilets and hot showers) are available at the attractive redwoods-and-river family campground at **Pfeiffer-Big Sur State Park,** 200-plus tents-only campsites plus a regular summer schedule of educational and informational programs, $16 per night. For information about any of the area's state park campgrounds, stop by the office at Pfeiffer-Big Sur State Park or call (408) 667-2315. For Mistix reservations (usually necessary from May through early September and on warm-weather weekends), call (800) 444-7275.

Private Camping

Not far from the state campgrounds at Pfeiffer-Big Sur State Park is the private riverside **Big Sur Campground,** Hwy. 1, Big Sur 93920, tel. (408) 667-2322, with tent sites at $19 and up, RV hookups, also tent cabins and cabins. Also on the Big Sur River is the **Riverside Campground,** Hwy.. 1, tel. 667-2414: 38 tent or RV sites, plus cabins. The private **Ventana Campground** near the Ventana Inn, Hwy. 1, tel. 667-2331, has 100 sites near a stream in a very scenic redwood setting, some RV hookups, hot showers, fireplaces, picnic tables. Down the coast south of Lucia is the postcard-pretty and private **Lime Kiln Beach Redwood Campground,** Hwy. 1, tel. 667-2403, which takes up most of the steep canyon and offers some good hiking in addition to tent and RV sites for $15 and up.

The Ventana Inn

Perhaps tuned into the same philosophical frequency as Henry Miller ("There being nothing to improve on in the surroundings, the tendency is to set about improving oneself"), the Ventana Inn people don't provide distractions like tennis courts and TV (though the desperately undiverted can make telephone calls and watch movies). But the woodsy, world-class Ventana Inn high up on the hill in Big Sur, tel. (408) 624-4812, does offer luxurious and relaxed contemporary lodgings on 1,000 acres overlooking the sea, outdoor Japanese hot tubs, a clothing-optional heated pool, even a chauffered Mercedes bus. This rough-hewn and handbuilt hostelry, with unfinished cedar interiors, parquet floors, and down-home luxuries like king-size beds with handmade quilted spreads and six pillows, even offers breakfast in bed. For a little extra, rooms come with a fireplace and Jacuzzi. The Ventana Inn also has a library, not to mention the hiking trails and hammocks. In the afternoon 4:30-6 p.m. there's a complimentary Fetzer wine and cheese buffet in the main lodge. Rooms run $170-775, reservations wise. (If a stay here seems just *too rich,* try drinks-with-a-view or a bite of the California cuisine in the lovely two-tiered restaurant.)

Deetjen's Big Sur Inn

Just south of the noted Nepenthe restaurant and the Henry Miller Library is the landward Norwegian-style Deetjen's Big Sur Inn in Castro

Canyon, tel. (408) 667-2377, a rambling ever-blooming inn with redwood rooms. Reservations advised. *Very* Big Sur. Rooms run $50-110. Reservations are also taken for meals. Eating at Deetjen's is as big a treat as an overnight. Wonderful breakfasts served from 8-11:30 a.m., and dinner starts at 6:15 p.m.

Other Accommodations

The **River Inn** on Hwy. 1 in Big Sur Valley, Big Sur 93920, tel. (408) 667-2700 or toll-free (800) 328-2884 in California, (800) 548-3610 in the U.S., is a motel-restaurant-bar popular with locals and featuring views of the river and live music most weekends; rooms run $55-120. Rooms at

the adobe **Glen Oaks Motel,** Hwy. 1, tel. 667-2623, are $40-44 d, $48-54 for four. Rooms at the **Fernwood Motel,** Hwy. 1, tel. 667-2422, are $50 (up to four people). The **Big Sur Lodge** nearby, just inside the park's entrance, P.O. Box 190, tel. 667-2171, is quiet, with pool, sauna, restaurant, and a circle of cabins, $90 and up for two (fireplaces and kitchens extra).

Food

The best bet for fairly inexpensive fare is in and around the Big Sur Valley. Get decent inexpensive sandwiches and groceries at the **Fernwood Burger Bar** on Hwy. 1, tel. (408) 667-2422, open daily 11:30 a.m.-midnight. (Gas is cheaper here than elsewhere, too.) Tasty home-baked pies are an after-meal specialty at the **Big Sur Lodge** dining room overlooking the river, also known for red snapper and such (no alcohol served), tel. 667-2171, open April to December. But **Deetjen's,** tel. 667-2377, is best for breakfast, comfortable and cozy with fireplace blazing in the open-beamed hobbit-style dining rooms. Dinner is more formal (classical music, two seatings, by reservation only), with entrees including steaks, fish, California country cuisine, and vegetarian dishes.

Big Sur's new haute cuisine hotspot is the **Glen Oaks Restaurant,** north of Pfeiffer-Big Sur, tel. (408) 667-2623, with fine music, flowers, a copper fireplace, and French elegance à la Big Sur, with entrees including crepes and pastas and mushroom stroganoff. Open for dinner Tues.-Sun. nights. The Glen Oaks also serves a fine Sunday brunch, with omelettes and eggs Benedict and cornmeal hotcakes. But the best of them is up there on top of the world—the casual and very California **Ventana Inn Restaurant,** tel. 667-2331, more reasonable at lunch than dinner but equally good; $10 minimum orders. No reservations taken for lunch, served Mon.-Fri. noon-3 p.m., Sat. and Sun. 11-3, but sign up for dinner (served 6-9:30 p.m.) anytime after 10 a.m. Reservations are required at dinner (served 6-9 or 6-9:30 p.m.).

A quarter-mile north of Palo Colorado Rd. on Hwy. 1 is **Rocky Point Restaurant,** tel. (408) 624-2933, a well-heeled roadhouse overlooking the ocean. Open for lunch from 11:30 a.m. to 3 p.m., for dinner after 5:30 p.m. Reservations necessary.

NEPENTHE

Nepenthe, about a mile south of the Ventana Inn, was built almost exactly on the site of the cabin Orson Wells bought for Rita Hayworth. So it's not too surprising that the restaurant is almost as legendary as Big Sur itself. A striking multilevel structure complete with an arts and crafts center, the restaurant was named for an ancient Egyptian drug taken to help people forget. Naturally enough, the bar here does a brisk business. As is traditional at Nepenthe, relax on the upper deck (the "gay pavilion," presided over by a sculpted bronze and redwood phoenix) with drink in hand to salute the sea and setting sun. Surreal views. But the open-beamed restaurant and its outdoor above-ocean terrace isn't nearly as rowdy these days as all those bohemian celebrity stories would suggest. Nonetheless, thrill-seekers insist on sitting on the top deck, even though there's often more room available downstairs at the Cafe Amphora health food deli and deck.

The fare here is good but not as spectacular as the views. Try the homemade soups, the hefty chef's salad, any of the vegetarian selections, or the world-famous Ambrosia burger (an excellent cheeseburger on French roll with pickles and a salad for a hefty price) accompanied by a Basket o' Fries. Good pies and cakes for dessert. To avoid the worst of the tourist traffic and to appreciate Nepenthe at its best, come later in September or October. And although Nepenthe is casual any time of year, it's not that casual: John F. Kennedy was once turned away because he showed up barefoot. Nepenthe is open for lunch and dinner daily, with music and dancing around the hearth at night.

Events

There aren't many organized activities in Big Sur. But in April Big Sur hosts the annual **Big Sur International Marathon,** with 1,600 or more runners hugging the highway curves from the village to Carmel. The **River Run** through the redwoods in October is also quite the cultural event; musical groups provide entertainment for runners throughout the course.

Information, Services, Transport

For general information about the area, contact the **Big Sur Chamber of Commerce,** P.O. Box 87, Big Sur 93920, tel. (408) 667-2111. (Send a stamped, self-addressed legal-sized envelope for a free guide to Big Sur.) Headquarters for the state parks is at **Pfeiffer-Big Sur** on Hwy. 1, Big Sur 93920, tel. 667-2315, open daily. Also at Pfeiffer-Big Sur is the **Big Sur Station** office of Los Padres National Forest, tel. 667-2423, open daily 8 a.m.-4:30 p.m., the place to go in search of forest and wilderness maps, permits, and backcountry camping and recreation information. There's a **laundromat** at Pfeiffer-Big Sur State Park in the Big Sur Lodge complex.

Bicycling Big Sur can be marvelous but less than fun when fighting RVs and weekend speedsters for road space. Forewarned, fearless cyclists should plan to ride from north to south to take advantage of the tailwind. (Driving south makes sense, too, since most vistas and turnouts are seaward.) It takes *at least* five hours by car to drive the 150 miles of Hwy. 1 between Monterey and San Luis Obispo.

Hitchhiking is almost as difficult as safely riding a bicycle along this stretch of Hwy. 1, so don't count on thumbs for transportation. More reliable is **Monterey-Salinas Transit's** Bus No. 22, which runs to and from Big Sur daily mid-April-Oct., stopping at Point Lobos, Garrapata State Park, the Bixby Creek Bridge, Point Sur Lighthouse, Pfeiffer-Big Sur and the River Inn, Pfeiffer Beach, the Ventana Inn, and Nepenthe; call (408) 899-2555 for information.

SAN SIMEON AND VICINITY

The **Hearst San Simeon State Historic Monument** is California's number two tourist attraction, second only to Disneyland. Somehow that fact alone puts the place into proper perspective. Media magnate William Randolph Hearst's castle is a rich man's playground filled to overflowing with artistic diversions and other expensive toys, a monument to one man's monumental ego and equally impressive poor taste.

In real life, of course, Hearst was a wealthy and powerful man, the subject of the greatest American movie ever made, Orson Welles's 1941 *Citizen Kane.* "Pleasure," Hearst once wrote, "is worth what you can afford to pay for it." (And that attitude showed itself quite early: on his 10th birthday little William asked for the Louvre as a present.) One scene in the movie, where Charles Foster Kane shouts across the cavernous living room at Xanadu to attract the attention of his bored young mistress, endlessly working jigsaw puzzles while she sits before a fireplace as big as the mouth of Jonah's whale, won't seem so surreal once you see San Simeon.

Designed by Berkeley architect Julia Morgan, the buildings themselves are odd yet handsome hallmarks of Spanish Renaissance architecture. The centerpiece La Casa Grande alone has 100 rooms (including a movie theater, a billiards room, two libraries, and 31 bathrooms) adorned with silk banners, fine Belgian and French tapestries, Norman fireplaces, European choir stalls, and ornately carved ceilings virtually stolen from continental monasteries. The furnishings and art Hearst collected from around the world complete the picture, one that includes everything but humor, grace, warmth, and understanding.

The notably self-negating nature of this rich but richly disappointed man's life is somehow fully expressed here in the country's most ostentatious and theatrical temple to obscene wealth. In contrast to Orson Welles's authentic artistic interpretation of Hearst's life, William Randolph's idea of hearth, home, and humanity was full-flown fantasy sadly separated from heart and vision.

THE CAST OF CHARACTERS

Orson Welles, his brilliant film career essentially destroyed by William Randolph Hearst's vengeful media and movie industry machinations, was probably never invited to the famous celebrity encounters staged at La Cuesta Encantada, The Enchanted Hill. Hearst's wife, who refused to divorce him despite his insistence, never socialized here either (though she did come to the castle on occasion when summoned to preside over meetings with presidents and such). But those attending Hearst's flamboyant parties, carefully orchestrated by the lord of the manor and his lady and mistress, Ziegfeld Follies showgirl Marion Davies, included characters like Charlie Chaplin, Greta Garbo, Clark Gable, Vivien Leigh, Laurence Olivier, Shirley Temple, Mary Pickford, and Rudolph Valentino. Even Hollywood moguls like Louis B. Mayer, Jack Warner, and Darryl Zanuck got through the gates, as did garrulous professional gossips like Hedda Hopper and Louella Parsons. Celebrities from farther afield, including Winston Churchill, President Calvin Coolidge, Charles Lindbergh, and George Bernard Shaw, also helped Hearst stave off the inevitable loneliness at the top. Cary Gary, who was a regular at "the ranch," said it was "a great place to spend the Depression."

Among Hearst's numerous house rules (informal dress only, no dirty jokes, no drinking in excess, and—ironically—no accompaniment by anyone other than one's spouse), perhaps his most revealing was: "Never mention death." But in the movie, only on his deathbed does Charles Foster Kane finally recognize the true worth and wreckage of his life. The word he whispers at the end—remembering the only thing he had ever really loved, his little sled—almost echoes through the great halls of San Simeon: *Rosebud*....

Citizen Hearst

The name San Simeon was originally given to a rancho attached to Mission San Miguel, 40,000 acres bought by mining scion George Hearst in the late 1800s. The first millionaire Hearst owned Nevada's Ophir silver mine and the rich Homestake gold mine in South Dakota, and staked-out territory in California's gold fields.

George Hearst later expanded the family holdings to 275,000 acres (including 50 miles of coastline) for the family's "Camp Hill" Victorian retreat and cattle ranch. With his substantial wealth, he was even able to buy himself a U.S. Senate seat.

But young William Randolph had even more ambitious plans—personally and for the property. The only son of the senator and San Francisco school teacher, socialite, and philanthropist Phoebe Apperson, the high-rolling junior Hearst took a fraction of the family wealth and his daddy's failing *San Francisco Examiner* and created a successful yellow-journalism chain, eventually adding radio stations and movie production companies.

Though he was described by employee Ambrose Bierce as a "shrinking violet," Hearst projected an altogether different image to the world at large. Putting his new-found power of propaganda to work in the political arena, Hearst (primarily for the headlines) goaded Congress into launching the Spanish-American War in 1898. But unlike his father, William Randolph Hearst was unable to buy much personal political power. Though he aspired to the presidency, he had to settle for two terms as a congressmember from New York.

Following his parents' death, William Randolph Hearst decided to build a house at "the ranch," partly as a place to store his already burgeoning art collection. Architect Julia Morgan, a family favorite, signed on for the project in 1919—for her, the beginning of a 28-year architectural collaboration. Morgan and Hearst planned the ever-evolving Enchanted Hill as a Mediterranean hill town, with La Casa Grande, the main house, as the "cathedral" facing the sea. Three additional palaces were clustered in front, the whole town surrounded by lavish terraced gardens.

Julia Morgan

Julia Morgan, San Simeon's architect, supervised the execution of almost every detail of Hearst's rambling 144-room pleasure palace. This 95-pound, teetotaling, workaholic woman was UC Berkeley's first female engineering graduate (at a time when a total of two dozen women were enrolled there) and the first woman to graduate from the École des Beaux-Arts in Paris. Her eccentric mentor Bernard Maybeck, whose California redwood homes characteristically "climb the hill" on steep lots to blend into the landscape, encouraged her career, as did John Galen Howard of New York.

Though credited only after her death for her accomplishments, Julia Morgan deserved at least as much recognition for her work as Edith Wharton in American literature and Mary Cassatt in painting, irate architecture and art historians have pointed out. But if acclaim came late for Morgan, it was partly her preference. She loathed publicity, disdained the very idea of celebrity, and believed that architects should be like anonymous medieval masters and let the work speak for itself.

Julia Morgan's work with William Randolph Hearst departed dramatically from her belief that buildings should be unobtrusive, the cornerstone of her brilliant but equally unobtrusive career. "My style," she said to those who seemed bewildered by the contradiction, "is to please my client." Pleasing her client in this case was quite a task. Hearst arbitrarily and habitually changed his mind, all the while complaining about slow progress and high costs. And she certainly didn't do the job for money, though Hearst and her other clients paid her well. Morgan divided her substantial earnings among her staff, keeping only about $10,000 annually to cover office overhead and personal expenses.

The perennially private Morgan, who never allowed her name to be posted at construction sites, designed almost 800 buildings in California and the West, among them the original Asilomar, the Berkeley City Club, the Oakland YWCA, and the bell tower, library, social hall, and gym at Oakland's Mills College. She also designed and supervised the reconstruction of San Francisco's Fairmont Hotel following its devastation in the 1906 earthquake. Other Hearst commissions included the family's Wyntoon retreat near Mount Shasta as well as the *Los Angeles Herald-Examiner* building.

THE SET: LIGHTS, ACTION, CAMERAS

Though the family, through the $3.5 billion Hearst Corporation, gave the white elephant San Simeon to the state in 1958 in memory of William Randolph, descendants still own most of the surrounding land (and Hearst's art). Hearst's

CALIFORNIA DEPARTMENT OF PARKS & RECREATION

on Hearst's enchanted hill

obsession was never satisfied and the project never technically finished, but most of La Casa Grande and adjacent buildings, pools, and grand gardens graced La Cuesta Encantada by the time major construction ceased in 1947 when Hearst became ill and moved away. He died four years later.

In spring when the hills are emerald green, from the faraway highway Hearst's castle appears as if by magic up on the hill. (Before the place opened for public tours in the 1950s, the closest view commoners could get was from the road, with the assistance of coin-operated telescopes.) One thing visitors *don't* see on the shuttle up the enchanted hill is William Randolph Hearst's 2,000-acre zoo—"the largest private zoo since Noah," as Charles Foster Kane would put it—once the country's largest. The inmates have long since been dispersed though survivors of Hearst's exotic elk, zebras, Barbary sheep, and Himalayan goat herds still roam the grounds.

There are four separate tours of the Hearst San Simeon State Historic Monument, each taking approximately two hours. Theoretically the San Simeon tours could all be taken in a day, but don't try it. So much Hearst in the short span of a day could be detrimental to one's well-being. A dosage of two tours per day makes the trip here worthwhile yet not overwhelming. Visitors obsessed with seeing it all should plan a two-day stay in the area or come back again some other time. Whichever tour or combination of tours you select, be sure to wear comfortable walking shoes. Lots of stairs.

Tour One is a good first-time visit, taking in the castle's main floor, one guesthouse, and some of the gardens—a total of 150 steps and a half mile of walking. Included on the tour is a short showing in the theater of some of Hearst's "home movies." Particularly impressive in a gloomy Gothic way is the dining room, where silk Siennese banners hang over the lord's table. The poolroom and mammoth great hall, with Canova's *Venus,* are also unforgettable. All the tours include both the Greco-Roman Neptune Pool and statuary and the indoor Roman Pool with its mosaics of lapis lazuli and gold leaf. It's hard to imagine Churchill, cigar in mouth, cavorting here in an inner tube.

Tour Two requires more walking, covering the mansion's upper floors, the kitchen, and Hearst's Gothic Suite (from which he ran his 94 separate business enterprises), with its frescoes and rose-tinted Venetian glass windows. The delightfully lit Celestial Suite was the nonetheless depressing extramarital playground of Hearst and Marion Davies. **Tour Three** covers one of the guesthouses plus the "new wing," with 36 luxurious bedrooms, sitting rooms, and marble bathrooms furnished with fine art.

Gardeners will be moved to tears by **Tour Four** (April-Aug. only), which includes a long stroll through the San Simeon grounds but does not go inside the castle itself. Realizing that all the rich topsoil here had to be manually carried up the hill makes the array of exotic plant life, including unusual camellias and some 6,000 rosebushes, all the more impressive—not to mention the fact that gardeners at San Simeon worked only at night because Hearst couldn't stand watching them. Also included on the fourth tour is the lower level of the elegant, 17-room Casa del Mar guesthouse (where Hearst spent much of his time), the recently redone underground Neptune Pool dressing rooms, the never-finished bowling alley, and Hearst's wine cellar.

David Niven once remarked that, with Hearst as host, the wine flowed "like glue." Subsequently, Niven was the only guest allowed free access to the castle's wine cellar.

Features And Coming Attractions
Someone should have called upon one of Julia Morgan's architectural disciples to design San Simeon's $7 million **visitor center** at the foot of The Enchanted Hill. Far from enchanting itself, the Spanish-style stucco and tile structure is actually more reminiscent of a Taco Bell-cum-urban transport terminal, with four separate loading docks for people trucked off on the various tours. One redeeming feature of the new center, however, is the exhibition room, which offers over an hour's worth of very good information about William Randolph Hearst's life and times, as well as Julia Morgan's. Another special feature is the conservation area, where visitors can watch artisans in their monumental daily work of maintaining and preserving Hearst's monument to himself.

San Simeon is open daily except Thanksgiving, Christmas, and New Year's Day, with the regular two-hour tours leaving the visitor center area on the hour from 8 a.m. through 4 p.m. Special tours of San Simeon are scheduled for people with disabilities. (Write the park for more information.) In addition, a special brochure for international travelers (printed in Japanese, Korean, French, German, Hebrew, Italian, and Spanish) is available. With a little forethought (see "Near San Simeon" below), visitors can avoid eating the concession-style food here.

Fairly new at San Simeon are the **Hearst Castle Evening Tours,** two-hour adventures featuring the highlights of other tours—with the added benefit of allowing you to pretend to be some Hollywood celebrity, just arrived and in need of orientation. (Hearst himself handed out tour maps, since newcomers often got lost.) Guides dress in period costume and show you around. It's worth it just to see the castle in lights.

But **Christmas at the Castle** is a special treat for those who come during the otherwise downtime month of December. Holiday visitors are treated to the palace in all its yuletide splendor: access to the castle's most popular features plus towering tinsel-and-twinkle Christmas trees, an exact replica of the Hearst family's traditional nativity scene, tour guides dressed in period costume—experiences once shared only by friends and by celebrity guests. Regular admission to each of the four San Simeon tours is $14 adults, $8 children. Evening tour rates: $25 adults, $13 children.

Reservations (which can be made up to two months in advance but should be assured at least one month ahead of time) can be made through Mistix, tel. (800) 444-7275, all major credit cards accepted. (The chance of getting tickets on a drop-in, last-minute basis is quite small.) For mail-in reservation forms and other information, call (800) 452-1950. To make reservations for wheelchair-accessible tours, contact the monument directly at (805) 927-2020. For other information, write Hearst San Simeon State Historical Monument, P.O. Box 8, San Simeon 93452, or call 927-2000 for a current recorded message.

NEAR SAN SIMEON

San Simeon:
The Town And Beaches

Done with the display of pompous circumstance on the hill, head for the serene sandy beaches nearby for a long coast walk to clear out the clutter. Good ocean swimming. Nude sunbathers sometimes congregate at the north end of **William Randolph Hearst Memorial State Beach** near San Simeon, indulging in a healthy hedonism Hearst would absolutely hate, but other-

wise it's a family-style stop with good picnicking, restrooms, and a public pier popular for fishing. Day-use fee, $3. Another picnicking possibility, especially for whalewatchers, is **Piedras Blancas Lighthouse** up the coast. The lighthouse, built in 1874, is now automated and off-limits to the public. Wonderful tidepools and good abalone diving are characteristics of the coast near here. **San Simeon State Beach** farther south near Cambria is larger and rockier, with fishing, picnicking, and campsites off San Simeon Creek Rd. (1½ miles south of San Simeon on Hwy. 1), tel. (805) 927-2037.

The "town" of San Simeon is actually two tiny towns: the original Spanish-style, red-tile-roofed village built for Hearst employees and "San Simeon Acres," the highway's motel row. The old **Sebastian's General Store** in the real San Simeon is a state historic monument and a great picnic supply stop with old-time post office and more modern garden cafe. Quite casual and comfortable, with whaling implements on the wall. Party boats powered by **Virg's Fish'n,** tel. (805) 927-4676 or 927-4677, set out from the harbor March to October for fishing. Ask about whalewatching tours.

Cambria

Its borders blending into San Simeon about eight miles south of Hearst's castle, the artsy coastal town of Cambria now bears the Roman name for ancient Wales but was previously called Rosaville, San Simeon, and (seriously) Slabtown. In some ways, Cambria is becoming the Carmel of southern Big Sur, with its glut of galleries and other come-hither shops, but without the smog and crowds. Several of the area's historic buildings remain, including the 1877 Squibb-Darke home, the Brambles restaurant on Burton Dr. in Old Town to the east, and the restored Santa Rosa Catholic Church on Bridge St. (across Main, past the library and post office).

Though the cliffs and No Trespassing signs across Santa Rosa Creek tend to slow people down, **Moonstone Beach** offers miles of walking, sea otters, sunsets, and good surfing.

Just outside Cambria in Cambria Pines is Arthur Beal's beautifully bizarre **Nit Wit Ridge,** a middle-class San Simeon. A handsome multilevel, sand castle-like cement structure lovingly built by Captain Nitwit (also known as Dr. Tinkerpaw), construction started in 1928 with a

---

HARMONY

Start wedded life auspiciously by getting married at the chapel in Harmony. This privately owned one-time dairy town is also growing into an artsy enclave, with pottery and glass-blowers' shops, an artists' studio, gift shop, and restaurant. As the story goes, Harmony (population 18, more or less) got its name in the 1890s when feuding neighbors put aside their differences to build a school; when it was finished, they called it Harmony Valley Schoolhouse. The old **Harmony Valley Creamery,** where none other than William Randolph Hearst once stopped for provisions on the way to his castle, is now an arts and crafts complex and restaurant with "country continental cuisine."

one-room shack architecturally enhanced with leftover construction cement, abalone shells, glass, discarded car parts, and beer cans, with later additions of bones, driftwood, feathers, and rock. (Look but don't touch. It's a private home.) To get there, in Cambria head south on Main St., turn left on Sheffield, left again on Cornwall, then right on Hillcrest and head uphill.

SAN SIMEON AREA PRACTICALITIES

San Simeon and the stretch of shoreline it dominates is so close to San Luis Obispo and Morro Bay that people often make day trips here from those communities. For San Simeon visitors who have reserved all four tours over a several-day period or who prefer more isolated accommodations and eateries, there are some decent choices near San Simeon and Cambria. For current information about local practicalities, contact the **San Simeon Chamber of Commerce,** 9255 Hearst Dr., P.O. Box 1, San Simeon 93452, tel. (805) 927-3500, or the **Cambria Chamber of Commerce,** 767 Main, Cambria 93428, tel. 927-3624.

Accommodations
Most motels near San Simeon and Cambria are fairly pricey and often stuffed with groups assembled for castle tours, so camping up or down the coast is a sensible option. (But as with motels, make reservations well in advance.) Public camping is available at **San Simeon State Beach,** 116 developed sites with hot showers near the beach, $16, also primitive hillside sites at the park's **Washburn** area; call (805) 927-4509 or 927-4621 for information. Or camp farther south at either **Atascadero State Beach** (summer only), tel. 543-2161, or mighty fine **Morro Bay State Park,** tel. 772-2560. Year-round, make Mistix reservations for all three, tel. (800) 444-7275.

From October or November into mid-spring, even the more expensive motels in San Simeon proper feature cheaper rates. The beachfront **Piedras Blancas Motel** seven miles north of Hearst's house on Hwy 1., P.O. Box 97, San Simeon 93452, tel. (805) 927-4202, has views of the castle on sunny days and often has vacancies when places closer to San Simeon are full.

Rates: $45-95, depending upon the season. Another possibility is the remote **Ragged Point Inn,** 15 miles north of San Simeon on Hwy. 1, P.O. Box 110, San Simeon 93452, tel. 927-4502. South of San Simeon, **Cayucos** also has decent, less expensive motels.

Sometimes offering great bargains in the off-season—like the $29 special, single or double, available September into May with holiday and other exceptions—is the **Silver Surf Motel** on the frontage road parallel to the highway, 9390 Castillo Dr., tel. (805) 927-4661 or toll-free (reservations only) (800) 736-1353. Some rooms have ocean views and balconies, fireplaces, also phones, TV, complimentary coffee and tea, plus pool and spa. Regular rates: $55-75. Also a bargain by San Simeon standards is the **San Simeon Lodge** south of the monument at 9520 Castillo Dr., tel. (805) 927-4601, basic but decent rooms with TV and phones, rates $50-75 (lower in the off-season). The nearby **El Rey Inn,** 9260 Castillo Dr., tel. 927-3998 or toll-free (800) 322-8029, offers something close to luxury for $69-89, large rooms with amenities (TV, movies, phones), some gas fireplaces and refrigerators. Both also have heated swimming pools. The large **Best Western Green Tree Inn** on the highway, tel. 927-4691, toll-free (800) 231-6461 in California or (800) 992-9240 from elsewhere in the U.S., offers more of the same plus heated indoor pool, whirlpool. Rates: $75-80. Ask about special two- or three-day packages, including a bottle of Central Coast wine, continental breakfast, candle-light dinner, and tour tickets to Hearst castle.

In general, accommodations in Cambria are cheaper than in San Simeon. For cabins, try the **Cambria Pines Lodge** at 2905 Burton Dr., P.O. Box 1356, Cambria 93428, tel. (805) 927-4200 or (800) 727-8557, with indoor pool, sauna, and whirlpool, rates $60-100. Cheaper cottages with kitchenettes are available at the **Small Hotel by the Sea** off the highway at the south end of town, 2601 Main St., tel. 927-4305, rooms $55, less in winter. The **Blue Bird Motel** at 1880 Main, tel. 927-4634, has rooms $42-78. The **San Simeon Pines Resort Motel,** on Hwy. 1 in Cambria, P.O. Box 115, San Simeon 93422, tel. 927-4648, is woodsy and right across the street from Moonstone Beach, with rooms $70-98. Or try the **White Water Inn,** 6790 Moonstone Beach Dr., Cambria 93428, tel. 927-1066. A good bargain, too, by local standards is the

Near San Luis Obispo is the coastal town of Morro Bay, noted among other things for its outdoor chess board.

Sea Otter Inn at 6656 Moonstone Beach Dr., tel. 927-5888, with rates $65-110. Top of the line, though, is the European-style **Sand Pebbles Inn** also on Moonstone, tel. 927-5600, French country decor, views, gas fireplaces, some whirlpools. Rates: $75-125.

Bed And Breakfasts

Cambria offers options for the bed and breakfast set. The new **Blue Whale Inn** at 6736 Moonstone Beach Dr., Cambria 93428, tel. (805) 927-4647, features six striking country-French "mini-suites" with ocean views, separate entrances, gas fireplaces, refrigerators. Full breakfast. Rates: $115-165.

The Early American **J. Patrick House Bed and Breakfast Inn** at 2990 Burton Dr., tel. (805) 927-3812, is an interesting log home, with a fireplace and private bath in each room and comfortable common room, $90-110. The **Pickford House** bed and breakfast is a new old-looking place at 2555 McLeod Ave., tel. 927-8619, with rooms named—and decorated—after some of Hearst Castle's most noted guests, including Lillian Gish and Rudolph Valentino. Breakfast of omelettes, Danish *aebleskivers,* fresh fruit. Rates $70-120. Authentically old (by California standards) and furnished with turn-of-the-century antiques is the two-story 1870s **Olallieberry Inn,** 2476 Main, tel. 927-3222, six rooms with private baths, $75-100. Other bed and breakfast choices: the three-story, seven-room **Beach House** at 6360 Moonstone Beach Dr., tel. 927-3136, all rooms with private baths, two with fire-

places, even telescopes and binoculars provided for watching dolphins and whales (and surfers), rates $100-135; and **Windrush** down the road at 6820 Moonstone, tel. 927-8844, with just two rooms, each with separate entrance and private bath, rates $75.

Good Food

Stop at **Sebastian's General Store** in San Simeon, tel. (805) 927-4217, to stock up on picnic supplies or enjoy burgers and such in the outdoor cafe. (Migrating monarch butterflies flutter to these cypress and eucalyptus trees in winter.)

Most of the restaurants are in Cambria. **Rosa's Cantina** at 2336 Main St., tel. (805) 927-0143, serves Southwestern-style Mexican at lunch and dinner, from fish tacos to homemade tamales. Full bar, good margaritas. A cheap-eats Cambria hotspot is the **Chuck Wagon** on Moonstone Dr. (at the only stoplight in town), tel. 927-4644, open daily in summer 7 a.m.-9 p.m., 11 a.m.-8 p.m. the rest of the year for all-you-can-eat breakfast, lunch, and dinner. **Canozzi's Saloon,** 2226 Main, tel. 927-8941, is a rusty old tavern and pool hall with weird signs and memorabilia hanging from the ceiling. This is *the* place for listening to live music on weekends and making the scene, Cambria-style.

Casual but quite good for American fare from pastas to seafood, and famous for its fresh-baked breads and pastries, is the small **Sow's Ear** restaurant at 2248 Main St. in Cambria, tel. (805) 927-4865. Try **Mustache Pete's** at 4090 Burton

Dr., tel. 927-8589, for Italian, early-bird dinners. Diners *can* get a good hamburger for dinner at the English-style **Brambles Dinner House** at 4005 Burton Dr. in Cambria, tel. 927-4716, but even better are the homemade soups, breads, and oakwood-broiled salmon. The Brambles is famous for its prime rib with Yorkshire pudding, excellent roast rack of lamb, and brandy ice cream for dessert. Reservations almost essential.

Also exceptional is **Ian's** at 2150 Center St. in Cambria, tel. (805) 927-8649, with a changing menu featuring grilled quail and sausage, broiled sea bass, broiled oysters with cilantro, vegetarian fare, and homemade ice cream for dessert. Open nightly 5-9 p.m., Sat. 5:30-9, reservations a must. The **Europa Restaurant** at 9240 Castillo Dr. in San Simeon, tel. 927-3087, features classical Lebanese, Hungarian, and American fare at dinner plus specialties like fresh seafood and pastas. Open daily for dinner after 5:30 p.m., closed on Sundays in winter. Reservations advised.

THE CENTRAL COAST: SAN LUIS OBISPO TO SANTA BARBARA

The biggest city immediately south from San Simeon is **San Luis Obispo,** a convenient stop halfway between L.A. and San Francisco along Hwy. 101 and most famous for creating both the word and the modern-concept "motel," a contraction of "motor hotel." The town's (and the world's) first motel, the **Motel Inn** on Monterey St., still stands, at last report undergoing a complete renovation. Stop by the visitors bureau downtown for current city and county information, including a copy of the new "Bounty of the County" self-guided tour brochure. Agriculture is big business around here, a fact reflected in the prominent presence of the well-respected **California State Polytechnic University,** also known as Cal Poly or (snidely) "Cow Poly." Pick up an "Ag's My Bag" bumpersticker as a souvenir or—if you can time your trip appropriately—roll into town on a Thursday evening to enjoy the Higuera Street farmer's market, one of the best anywhere (cancelled only in the event of rain).

Well worth going out of your way for (inland from the coast and north of San Luis Obispo) is **Mission San Antonio de Padua,** smack-dab in the middle of Fort Hunter-Liggett (security check at the base gate), not the grandest or most spruced-up but perhaps the most genuinely evocative of all the California missions. (From here, you can take narrow Nacimiento-Fergusson Rd. back over the coastal mountains to Big Sur.) Nearby **Lake San Antonio** is popular in winter for guided bald eagle-watching tours.

Off in the other direction, via Hwy. 58, is the Nature Conservancy's **Carrizo Plain Preserve,** earthquake territory once sacred to the Chumash people. The native grasses and shrub lands surrounding Soda Lake offer refuge to some of the state's most endangered animal species. And if you head east from Paso Robles toward the San Joaquin Valley via Hwy. 46, you'll come to the shrine (outside Aggie's restaurant) marking (almost) the spot where actor James Dean *(Rebel Without A Cause, Giant,* and *East of Eden)* died in a head-on car accident in 1955.

Morro Rock, California's little Gibraltar, spotted by Cabrillo in 1542, is the first thing people notice at **Morro Bay** over on the coast. But the Morro Bay Chess Club has its **giant outdoor chessboard** downtown. **Morro Bay State Park, Montana de Oro State Park,** and area beaches are all worth exploring. The one-time port towns and piers along **San Luis Obispo Bay** to the south also have their attractions, including **Great American Melodrama and Vaudeville** in Oceano and the famous **F. McClintock's Saloon and Dining House** on Hwy. 101 in Pismo Beach, famous for its performance art, courtesy of the wait staff, who fill your glasses (without spilling, usually) pouring from a pitcher held several feet in the air—and infamous for its fried turkey nut appetizers.

Still heading south, **Santa Maria** is most noted for its own unique culinary heritage, this one preserved since the days of the vaqueros. This is the hometown of "Santa Maria Barbecue," a complete meal which traditionally includes slabs of prime sirloin barbecued over a slow red-oak fire, then sliced as thin as paper and served with *salsa cruda,* pinquito beans, salad, toasted garlic bread, and dessert. Near town is the Nature Conservancy's **Nipomo Dunes Preserve,** a coastal wildlife and plant preserve also protecting the remains of Cecil B. DeMille's *The Ten Commandments* movie set, buried under the sand here once filming was finished.

Lompoc is noted for its blooming flower fields —this is a major seed-producing area—and is home to Vandenberg Air Force Base as well as **Mission La Purisima State Historic Park** four miles east of town, California's only complete mission compound.

Farther south, **Solvang** is a Danish-style town founded in 1911 and now a well-trod tourist destination. If you've got time, worth exploring nearby are the towns of **Los Olivos** and **Los Alamos.**

Technically speaking, Point Conception just below Vandenberg marks the spot where California turns on itself—that pivotal geographical point where Northern California becomes Southern California. The subtle climatic and terrain changes are unmistakable by the time you arrive in **Santa Barbara,** a richly endowed city noted for its gracious red-tile-roofed California Spanish-style buildings—for the most part an architectural affectation subsequent to the devasting 1929 earthquake here. Even if you have time for nothing else, stop to see the **Santa Barbara County Courthouse** one block up from State Street at Anapamu and Anacapa, an L-shaped Spanish-Moorish castle and quite possibly the most beautiful public building in all of California. Other attractions are abundant, from **Mission Santa Barbara,** "Queen of the Missions," to the **Santa Barbara Museum of Natural History** and the **Santa Barbara Botanic Gardens.** Despite the presence of offshore oil wells, public beaches in the area are sublime.

Continue south from Santa Barbara to **Ventura** to set off on whalewatching trips and guided boat tours of California's **Channel Islands** (with Island Packers, tel. 805-642-3193), a national park often visible from Santa Barbara and vicinity.

BOOKLIST

The virtual "publisher of record" for all things Californian is the **University of California Press,** 2120 Berkeley Way, Berkeley 94720, tel. (415) 642-4247 or (800) 822-6657 to order, which publishes hundreds of titles on the subject —all excellent, some included below.

Other publishers specializing in California (including contemporary and regional travel) include **Chronicle Books,** Division of Chronicle Publishing Co., 275 Fifth St., San Francisco 94103, tel. (415) 777-7240; **Lane Publishing (Sunset Books),** 80 Willow Rd., Menlo Park 94025, tel. (415) 321-3600 or toll-free (800) 227-7346; **Presidio Press,** 31 Pamaron Way, Novato 94947, tel. (415) 883-1373; and **Heyday Books,** P.O. Box 9145, Berkeley 94709, tel. (510) 549-3564.

Foghorn Press, P.O. Box 77845 (555 De Haro St., Suite 220), San Francisco 94107, tel. (415) 241-9550 or (800) 842-7477 for orders, publishes a generous list of unusual and unusually thorough, California books, including Tom Stienstra's camping, fishing, and "getaways" guides as well as Laurel Cook's new *California Spas.*

Among the best guidebooks around for serious regional travel in Northern California are those informative and entertaining titles *(The Best of the Wine Country* and *The Best of the Gold Country,* for example) offered by Don and Betty Martin's **Pine Cone Press,** P.O. Box 1494, Columbia 95310, tel. (209) 532-2699.

To sample a very tasty special-interest list, wine aficionados should contact **The Wine Appreciation Guild,** 155 Connecticut St., San Francisco 94107, tel. (415) 864-1202 or (to order) tel. (800) 231-WINE in California or (800) 242-9462 from outside California.

Sierra Club Books, 730 Polk St., San Francisco 94109, tel. (415) 923-5600, and **Wilderness Press,** 2440 Bancroft Way, Berkeley 94704, tel. (415) 843-8080 or (to order) (800) 443-7227, are the two top publishers of wilderness guides and maps for California. Wilderness Press updates its guides frequently, to keep up with changing trail conditions, and also publishes update supplements for all guides.

For those planning a serious Sierra Nevada backpacking trek or other adventure, the "High Sierra Hiking Guides" published by Wilderness Press present accurate trail and other information for specific U.S. Geological Survey 15-minute quadrangles and also include a four-color topographical map (available separately).

Contact these and other publishers listed below for a complete list of current titles relating to California.

Though the titles listed below at least represent a good introduction to California history, natural history, literature, recreation, and travel, the author would appreciate receiving any and all suggestions about other books that should be included. Send the names of new booklist candidates (or actual books, if you're either a publisher or an unusually generous person) for *Northern California Handbook,* along with other possible text additions, corrections, and suggestions, to: Kim Weir, Moon Publications, P.O. Box 3040, 330 Wall St., Chico, CA 95927.

COMPANION READING, GENERAL TRAVEL

Baldy, Marian. *The University Wine Course.* San Francisco: The Wine Appreciation Guild, 1993. Destined to be a classic and designed for both instructional and personal use, this friendly book offers a comprehensive education about wine. *The University Wine Course* explains it all, from viticulture to varietals. And the lips-on lab exercises and chapter-by-chapter examinations help even the hopelessly déclassé develop the subtle sensory awareness necessary for any deeper appreciation of the winemaker's art. Special sections and appendixes on reading (and understanding) wine labels, combining wine and food, and understanding wine terminology make it a life-long personal library reference. Definitely "do" this book before doing the California wine country. For college wine appreciation instructors and winery personnel, the companion *Teacher's Manual for The University Wine Course* may also come in handy.

Browning, Peter. *Place Names of the Sierra Nevada.* Berkeley: Wilderness Press, 1991. The first since Francis Farquhar's 1926 classic of the same title, the author used Farquhar's revision notes in addition to original source material to gather up this collection of lore.

Callenbach, Ernest. *Ecotopia.* Berkeley: Banyan Tree, 1975. Also worthwhile, from the perspective that northernmost Northern California belongs in its own utopian state, is Callenbach's *Ecotopia Emerging.*

Crain, Jim. *Historic Country Inns of California.* San Francisco: Chronicle Books, 1984.

Gebhard, David, and Scott Zimmerman. *Romanza: The California Architecture of Frank Lloyd Wright.* San Francisco: Chronicle Books, 1988. Accompanied by color photographs, architectural renderings, and floor plans, this book provides an analysis of 24 California buildings—public and private—designed by the noted American architect.

Gleeson, Bill. *Back Road Wineries of California.* San Francisco: Chronicle Books, 1989. Also by Gleeson: *Small Hotels of California* (OP); *Weekends for Two in Northern California;* and *The Great Family Getaway Guide.*

Gudde, Erwin G. *1000 California Place Names: Their Origin and Meaning.* Berkeley: University of California Press, 1969. A convenient, alphabetically arranged pocketbook perfect for travelers, explaining the names of mountains, rivers, and towns throughout California.

Gunsky, Frederic, ed. *South of Yosemite; Selected Writings of John Muir.* Berkeley: Wilderness Press, 1988. The first collection of Muir's writings to explore what is now the Sequoia and Kings Canyon region fulfills the famed naturalist's dream of a book he intended to title *The Yosemite and the Other Yosemites.* This "Other Yosemite" anthology includes some of Muir's best work.

Hansen, Gladys. *San Francisco Almanac.* Second ed. San Francisco: Presidio Press, 1980. Out of print, but worth looking for. Easy-to-use source for San Francisco facts, written by the city archivist. Contains a detailed chronology, maps, and bibliography. Also fun: what some famous people have said about San Francisco. Fascinating, too, is the author's *Denial of Disaster: The Untold Story & Unpublished Photographs of the San Francisco Earthquake & Fire of 1906,* co-authored by Emmet Condon, 1989.

Hart, James D. *A Companion to California.* Berkeley: University of California Press. Revised and expanded, 1987. Another very worthy book for Californiacs to collect, with thousands of brief entries on all aspects of California and more in-depth pieces on subjects such as literature.

Herron, Don. *The Literary World of San Francisco and its Environs.* San Francisco: City Lights Books, 1985. A well-mapped "pocket guide" for do-it-yourself walking and driving tours to sites where literary lights shine in and around San Francisco, their homes and haunts. This is the companion guide to the excellent *Literary San Francisco* by Lawrence Ferlinghetti and Nancy J. Peters. Also by Herron: *The Dashiell Hammet Tour: A Guidebook.*

Houston, James D. *Californians: Searching for the Golden State.* Berkeley: Creative Arts Book Company, 1985. Good prose, good points in this collection of personal essays about Californians in their endless search for the meaning of their own dream.

Kael, Pauline, Herman J. Mankiewicz, and Orson Welles. *The Citizen Kane Book: Raising Kane.* New York: Limelight Editions, 1984. Includes an excellent essay on the classic American film, plus script and stills.

Kahrl, William. *Water and Power: The Conflict Over Los Angeles' Water Supply in the Owens Valley.* Berkeley: University of California Press, 1982. Perhaps the best book available for anyone who wants to understand the politics of water and power in California, and how water and political power have transformed the state's economy and land. To keep up with new twists and turns in this meandering tale, read the *Sacramento Bee* (where Kahrl is now an editor).

Kirker, Harold. *California's Architectural Frontier.* San Marino, CA: The Huntington Library, 1970

(OP). Perhaps more useful and easier to find is Kirker's 1991 Old Forms on a New Land: California Architecture in Perspective.

Le Guin, Ursula K. Always Coming Home. Ms. Le Guin gained fame as a science fiction writer, for novels including The Left Hand of Darkness and The Dispossessed. Her formal literary recognition includes the Hugo, Gandalf, Kafka, Nebula, and National Book awards. Always Coming Home is perhaps Le Guin's masterwork, and a special treat for those who love California—particularly Northern California (sometimes referred to, in a regionally chauvinistic sense, as "Superior California"). The geographical borders of the land she describes (and maps) in this imaginative exploration of "futuristic anthropology" just happen to coincide with those in Northern California Handbook. Must reading for anyone helping to remake the California dream.

Le Guin, Ursula K. Dancing at the Edge of the World: Thoughts on Words, Women, Places. New York: Grove Press, 1989. This delightful collection of essays includes some rare sidelong glances into the soul of the northstate—and why not? The daughter of UC Berkeley anthropologist Alfred L. Kroeber and Ishi's biographer Theodora Kroeber, Le Guin offers a unique perspective on California as a place, then, now, and in the times to come. Particularly enjoyable in this context: "A Non-Euclidian View of California as a Cold Place to Be"; "The Fisherwoman's Daughter" (about, among other things, her mother); and "Woman/Wilderness." In addition, the foreword to Northern California Handbook, "World-Making," appeared here first.

Michaels, Leonard, David Reid, and Raquel Scherr, eds. West of the West: Imagining California. New York: HarperCollins Publishers, 1991. Though any anthology about California is destined to be incomplete, this one is exceptional—offering selections by Maya Angelou, Simone de Beauvoir, Joan Didion, Umberto Eco, Gretel Ehrlich, M.F.K. Fisher, Aldous Huxley, Jack Kerouac, Maxine Hong Kingston, Rudyard Kipling, Henry Miller, Ishmael Reed, Kenneth Rexroth, Richard Rodriguez, Randy Shilts, Gertrude Stein, John Steinbeck, Octavio Paz, Amy Tan, Gore Vidal, Walt Whitman, and Tom Wolfe.

Muscatine, Doris. The University of California/Sotheby Book of California Wine. Berkeley: University of California Press, 1984. An expensive companion ($65) but worthwhile for wine lovers.

Olmstead, R., and T.H. Watkins. Here Today: San Francisco Architectural Heritage. San Francisco: Chronicle Books, 1978.

Reece, Daphne. Historic Houses of California. San Francisco: Chronicle Books, 1983.

Reid, Robert Leonard, ed. A Treasury of the Sierra Nevada. Berkeley: Wilderness Press, 1983. Words by Mark Twain, Robert Louis Stevenson, Walt Whitman, and John Muir are included in this anthology, the first and only Sierra Nevada literary compilation.

Robertson, David. A History of the Art and Literature of Yosemite. Berkeley: Wilderness Press, 1984. A fully illustrated history and a thoughtful Yosemite travel companion.

WPA Guide to California: The Federal Writers Project Guide to 1930s California. New York: Pantheon Press (an imprint of Random House), 1984. The classic travel guide to California, first published during the Depression, is somewhat dated as far as contemporary sights but excellent as a companion volume and background information source.

HISTORY AND PEOPLE

Adams, Ansel, with Mary Alinder. Ansel Adams: An Autobiography. Boston: Bulfinch Press, 1990. A compelling, expansive, enlightening sharing of self by the extraordinary photographer—not coincidentally also a generous, extraordinary human being.

Atherton, Gertrude. My San Francisco, A Wayward Biography. Indianapolis and New York: The Bobbs-Merrill Company, 1946. The 56th book—written at the age of 90—by the woman Kevin Starr has called "the daughter of the elite" whose career of historical fiction "document[ed] . . . itself . . . in a careless but vivid output. . . ." A delightfully chatty browse through the past, filled with dropped names and accounts of Atherton's own meetings with historic figures.

Bronson, William. *The Earth Shook, the Sky Burned: A Moving Record of America's Great Earthquake & Fire: San Francisco, April 18, 1906*. San Francisco: Chronicle Books, 1986. Originally published by Doubleday, 1959.

California Inventory of Historic Resources. Sacramento: California Department of Parks and Recreation, 1976. Compiled in response to the National Historic Preservation Act of 1966 directing all states to identify all properties "possessing historical, architectural, archaeological, and cultural value." Organized by category—sites of aboriginal, economic, or government interest, for example—and indexed by county. (A wide variety of other publications is available from the Department of Parks and Recreation; see "Introduction" for more information.)

Clarke, James Mitchell. *The Life and Adventures of John Muir*. San Francisco: Sierra Club Books (OP).

Cleland, Robert Glass. *A History of California: The American Period*. Westport, CT: Greenwood Press, 1975. Originally published in 1922.
Cleland, Robert Glass. *From Wilderness to Empire: A History of California*. New York: Alfred Knopf, 1944 (OP).

Cole, Tom. *A Short History of San Francisco*. Lagunitas, CA: Lexikos, 1986. Very accessible, thoroughly entertaining overview, with clean design and some great old photos and illustrations.

d'Azevedo, Warren. *Straight with the Medicine: Narratives of Washoe Followers of the Tipi Way*. Berkeley: Heyday Books, 1985. Cultural and spiritual insights shared by those involved in the peyote religious practices adopted in and around the eastern Sierra Nevada in the 1930s.

Dreyer, Peter. *A Gardener Touched With Genius: The Life of Luther Burbank*. Berkeley: University of California Press, 1985.
Ellison, William Henry. *A Self-Governing Dominion, California 1849-1860*. Berkeley: University of California Press, 1978.

Farquhar, Francis P. *History of the Sierra Nevada*. Berkeley: University of California Press, 1965.

Fremont, John Charles. *Memoirs of My Life*. New York: Penguin, 1984. Originally published in Chicago, 1887. The old Bearflagger himself tells the story of early California—at least some of it.

Gudde, Erwin Gustav. *California Gold Camps*. Berkeley: University of California Press, 1975.
Harte, Bret. *The Writings of Bret Harte*. New York: AMS Press, 1903.

Heizer, Robert F., and M.A. Whipple. *The California Indians*. Berkeley: University of California Press, 1971. A worthwhile collection of essays about California's native peoples, covering general, regional, and specific topics—a good supplement to the work of A.L. Kroeber (who also contributed to this volume).

Heizer, Robert F. *The Destruction of the California Indians*. Utah: Gibbs Smith Publishing, 1974.

Heizer, Robert F. *Prehistoric Rock Art of Nevada and Eastern California*. Berkeley: University of California Press, 1976.

Holiday, James. *The World Rushed In: The California Gold Rush Experience: An Eyewitness Account of a Nation Heading West*. New York: Simon and Schuster, 1981. Reprint of a classic history, made while new Californians were busy making up the myth.

Horton, Tom. *Super Span: The Golden Gate Bridge*. San Francisco: Chronicle Books, 1983. How the Golden Gate Bridge came to be, illustrated with anecdotes and photographs—a very compelling history of an inanimate object.

Houston, James, and Jeanne Houston. *Farewell to Manzanar*. New York: Bantam Books, 1983. A good goodbye to California's World War II internment of Japanese Americans.

Hutchinson, W.H. *California: The Golden Shore by the Sundown Sea*. Belmont, CA: Star Publishing Company, 1988. The late author, a professor emeritus of history at CSU Chico known as Old Hutch to former students, presents a dizzying amount of historical, economic, and political detail from his own unique perspective in this analysis of California's past and present. Hutchinson saw the state from many sides during a lifetime spent as "a horse wrangler, cowboy, miner, boiler fireman, merchant seaman, corporate bureaucrat, rodeo and horse show announcer, and freelance writer."

Jackson, Mrs. Helen Hunt. *Century of Dishonor: A Sketch of the US Government's Dealings (with some of the Indian tribes).* Irvine, CA: Reprint Services, 1988. Originally published in Boston, 1881.

Jackson, Joseph Henry. *Anybody's Gold: The Story of California's Mining Towns.* San Francisco: Chronicle Books, 1970. A lively history back in print after a 30-year hiatus.

Kroeber, Alfred L. *Handbook of the Indians of California.* New York: Dover Publications, 1976 (unabridged facsimile version of the original work, *Bulletin 78* of the Bureau of American Ethnology of the Smithsonian Institution, published by the U.S. Government Printing Office). The classic compendium of observed facts about California's native peoples by the noted UC Berkeley anthropologist who befriended Ishi.

Kroeber, Theodora. *Ishi in Two Worlds: A Biography of the Last Wild Indian in North America.* Berkeley: University of California Press, 1961. The classic biography of Ishi, an incredible 20th-century story well told by A.L. Kroeber's widow, also available in an illustrated edition. Also worthwhile by Kroeber: *Inland Whale: California Indian Legends.*

Lennon, Nigey. *Mark Twain in California.* San Francisco: Chronicle Books, 1982. An entertaining, enlightened, easy-reading biography from a true lover of Samuel Clemens's writings as Mark Twain.

Lewis, Oscar. *The Big Four.* Sausalito, CA: Comstock Editions, 1982. Originally published in New York, 1938.

Margolin, Malcolm. *The Way We Lived.* Berkeley: Heyday Books, 1981. A wonderful collection of California native peoples' reminiscences, sto-

ries, and songs. Also by Margolin: *The Ohlone Way,* about the life of California's first residents of the San Francisco-Monterey Bay Area.

Milosz, Czeslaw. *Visions from San Francisco Bay.* New York: Farrar, Straus & Giroux, 1982. Essays on emigration from the Nobel Prize winner in literature. Originally published in Polish, 1969.

Murray, Keith A. *The Modocs and Their War.* Norman, OK: University of Oklahoma Press, 1976.

Perry, Charles. *The Haight-Ashbury: A History.* New York: Rolling Stone Press (an imprint of Random House), 1984. A detailed chronicle of events which began in 1965 and led up to the Summer of Love, with research, writing, and some pointed observations by the author, a *Rolling Stone* editor.

Powers, Stephen. *Tribes of California.* Berkeley: University of California Press, 1977.

Ridge, John. *The Life and Adventures of Joaquin Murrieta.* Norman, OK: University of Oklahoma Press, 1986.

Robertson, David. *West of Eden: History of Art and Literature of Yosemite.* Berkeley: Wilderness Press, 1984.

Royce, Josiah. *California from the Conquest in 1846 to the Second Vigilance Committee in San Francisco 1856.* New York: AMS Press. Originally published in Boston, 1886.

St. Pierre, Brian. *John Steinbeck: The California Years.* San Francisco: Chronicle Books, 1983. Saunders, Richard. *Ambrose Bierce: The Making of a Misanthrope.* San Francisco: Chronicle Books, 1984.

Sinclair, Upton. *American Outpost: A Book of Reminiscences.* New York: 1932.

Starr, Kevin. *Americans and the California Dream: 1850-1915.* New York: Oxford University Press, 1973. A cultural history, written by a native San Franciscan, former newspaper columnist, one-time head of the city's library system, .

and current professor and historian. The focus on Northern California taps an impressively varied body of sources as it seeks to "suggest the poetry and the moral drama of social experience" from California's first days of statehood through the Panama-Pacific Exposition of 1915 when, in the author's opinion, "California came of age." (Starr's 1985 *Inventing the Dream: California Through the Progressive Era,* second in a projected five-part series, addresses Southern California. Annotations in both suggest rich possibilities for further reading.)

Steinbeck, John. *Working Days: The Journals of the Grapes of Wrath 1938-1941.* New York: Penguin, 1989. Less an explanation for *The Grapes of Wrath* than a portrait of a writer possessed—and therefore quite interesting.

Stevenson, Robert Louis. *From Scotland to Silverado.* Cambridge, MA: The Belknap Press of Harvard University Press, 1966. An annotated collection of the sickly and lovelorn young Stevenson's travel essays, including his first impressions of Monterey and San Francisco, and the works that have come to be known as *The Silverado Squatters.* Contains considerable text—marked therein—that the author's family and friends had removed from previous editions. A useful introduction by James D. Hart details the journeys and relationships behind the essays.

Stone, Irving. *Jack London: Sailor on Horseback.* New York: Doubleday, 1986. Originally published in Boston, 1938.

Stone, Irving. *Men to Match My Mountains.* New York: Berkeley Publishers, 1987. A classic California history, originally published in 1956.

Turner, Frederick. *Rediscovering America.* New York: Penguin, 1985. A fascinating cultural history and biography of John Muir—the man in his time and ours—generally more interesting reading than much of Muir's own work.

van der Zee, John, and Boyd Jacobson. *The Imagined City: San Francisco in the Minds of its Writers.* San Francisco: California Living Books, 1980 (OP). Quotes about San Francisco pulled from the works—mostly fiction—of 37 writers, both widely known and locally celebrated. Accompanied by photos and a page-long biography of each author, as well as historical photographs.

NATURE AND NATURAL HISTORY

Adams, Ansel. *Yosemite and the Range of Light.* Boston: Bulfinch Press, 1982. A coffee table photography art book—worth buying a coffee table for—from the master of Sierra Nevada photography.

Alt, David, and Donald Hyndman. *Roadside Geology of Northern California.* Missoula, MT: Mountain Press, 1975. The classic glovebox companion guide to the northstate landscape.

Bakker, Elna. *An Island Called California: An Ecological Introduction to its Natural Communities.* Berkeley: University of California Press, 1985. An excellent, time-honored introduction to the characteristics of, and relationships between, California's natural communities.

Berry, William, and Elizabeth Berry. *Mammals of the San Francisco Bay Region.* Berkeley: University of California Press, 1959. Among other regional titles available: *Evolution of the Landscapes of the San Francisco Bay Region,* by Arthur David Howard; *Introduction to the Natural History of the San Francisco Bay Region,* by Arthur Smith; *Native Shrubs of the San Francisco Bay Region,* by Roxana S. Ferris; *Native Trees of the San Francisco Bay Region,* by Woodbridge Metcalf; *Rocks and Minerals of the San Francisco Bay Region,* by Oliver E. Bowen, Jr.; *Spring Wildflowers of the San Francisco Bay Region,* by Helen Sharsmith; and *Weather of the San Francisco Bay Region,* by Harold Gilliam.

California Coastal Commission, State of California. *California Coastal Resource Guide.* Berkeley: University of California Press, 1987. The indispensable guide to the California coast and its wonders—the land, marine geology, biology—as well as parks, landmarks, and amusements.

California Department of Parks and Recreation, State of California. *A Visitor's Guide to Califor-*

nia's State Parks, 1990. This large-format, very pretty book includes abundant full-color photography and brief, accessible basic information about the features and facilities of the state's parks and recreation areas. A Visitor's Guide is available at retail bookstores and at the state parks themselves, and can also be ordered by mail or by phone. By mail, send a check ($17, includes postage and handling) made out to Department of Parks and Recreation to Publications, Department of Parks and Recreation, P.O. Box 942896, Sacramento 94296-0001. If you'll be making campground reservations anyway, you can order A Visitors' Guide simultaneously by calling Mistix, tel. (800) 444-7275 (major credit card required).

Carville, Julie Stauffer. Lingering in Tahoe's Wild Gardens: A Guide to Hundreds of the Most Beautiful Wildflower Gardens of the Lake Tahoe Region. Berkeley: Mountain Gypsy Press (distributed by Wilderness Press), 1990. A hiking guide offering 30 backcountry explorations and the 280 types of flowers you may find along the way (in late spring and summer).

Clarke, Charlotte. Edible and Useful Plants of California. Berkeley: University of California Press, 1978.

Cogswell, Howard. Water Birds of California. Berkeley: University of California Press, 1977. Dawson, Vale, and Michael Foster. Seashore Plants of California. Berkeley: University of California Press, 1982.

DeSante, David, and Peter Pyle. Distributional Checklist to North American Birds. The most accurate and up-to-date information ever assembled on the abundance and status of birds north of Mexico—indispensable to serious birders—but hard to find. A reliable source is the Mono Lake Committee (mail orders accepted). For more information, see "Sierra Nevada" chapter.

Duremberger, Robert. Elements of California Geography. Out of print but worth searching for. This is the classic work on California geography. Fitch, John. Tidepool and Nearshore Fishes of California. Berkeley: University of California Press, 1975.

Farrand, John Jr. Western Birds. New York: McGraw-Hill Book Co., 1988. This birding guide includes color photographs instead of art work for illustrations; conveniently included with descriptive listings. Though the book contains no range maps, the "Similar Species" listing helps eliminate birds with similar features.

Gaines, David. Birds of Yosemite and the East Slope. Berkeley: Artemesia Press (distributed by Wilderness Press), 1992. This book describes the 343 species of birds in the Yosemite and Mono Lake regions, emphasizing their ecological relationships and survival status rather than serving as a birder's identification guide.

Gaines, David, and the Mono Lake Committee. Mono Lake Guidebook. Berkeley: Wilderness Press, 1989. The guidebook to Mono Lake and the eastern Sierra Nevada, now out in a new edition, emphasized the region's natural history.

Garth, John S., and J.W. Tilden. California Butterflies. Berkeley: University of California Press, 1986. At long last, the definitive field guide and key to California butterflies (in both the larval and adult stages) is available, and in paperback; compact and fairly convenient to tote around.

Geologic Society of the Oregon Country. Roadside Geology of the Eastern Sierra Nevada. Informative pamphlet-sized book including Devil's Postpile, Mono Lake, the White Mountains, and Yosemite, available from the Mono Lake Committee (see "Sierra Nevada" chapter).

Grillos, Steve. Fern and Fern Allies of California. Berkeley: University of California Press, 1966.

Grinnell, Joseph, and Alden Miller. The Distribution of the Birds of California. Out of print but available through the Mono Lake Committee (see "Sierra Nevada" chapter), this is the definitive California birder's guide—for those interested in serious study.

Harris, Stephen. Fire Mountains of the West: The Cascade and Mono Lake Volcanoes. Missoula, MT: Mountain Press, 1988. Heizer, Robert F. The Natural World of the California Indians. Berkeley: University of California Press, 1962.

Hickman, Jim, ed. *The Jepson Manual: Higher Plants of California.* Berkeley: University of California Press (with cooperation and support from the California Native Plant Society and the Jepson Herbarium), 1993. Hot off the presses but at least 10 years in the making, *The Jepson Manual* is already considered the bible of California botany. The brainchild of both Jim Hickman and Larry Heckard, curator of the Jepson Herbarium, this book is a cumulative picture of the extraordinary flora of California, and the first comprehensive attempt to fit it all into one volume since the Munz *A California Flora* was published in 1959. The best work of almost 200 botanist-authors has been collected here, along with exceptional line drawings and illustrations (absent from the Munz flora) that make it easier to identify and compare plant species. This book is the botanical reference book for a California lifetime—a hefty investment for a hefty tome, especially essential for serious ecologists and botanists, amateur and otherwise.

Hill, Mary. *California Landscape: Origin and Evolution.* Berkeley: University of California Press, 1984. An emphasis on the most recent history of California landforms. Also by Hill: *Geology of the Sierra Nevada.*

Klauber, Laurence. *Rattlesnakes.* Berkeley: University of California Press, 1982.

Leatherwood, Stephen, and Randall Reeves. *The Sierra Club Handbook of Whales and Dolphins.* San Francisco: Sierra Club Books, 1983.

Le Boeuf, Burney J., and Stephanie Kaza. *The Natural History of Año Nuevo.* Pacific Grove, CA: The Boxwood Press, 1981. An excellent, very comprehensive guide to the natural features of the Año Nuevo area just north of Santa Cruz.

Lederer, Roger. *Pacific Coast Bird Finder.* Berkeley: Nature Study Guild, 1977. A handy, hip-pocket-sized guide to birding for beginners. Also available: *Pacific Coast Tree Finder* by Tom Watts, among similar titles. All titles now available through Wilderness Press.

McGinnis, Samuel. *Freshwater Fishes of California.* Berkeley: University of California Press, 1985. Including a simple but effective method of identifying fish, this guide also offers fisherfolk help in developing better angling strategies, since it indicates when and where a species feeds and what its food preferences are.

Miller, Crane S., and Richard S. Hyslop. *California: The Geography of Diversity.* Palo Alto, CA: Mayfield Publishing Company, 1983.

Muir, John. *The Mountains of California.* Berkeley: Ten Speed Press, 1988. Very enjoyable facsimile reprint of the noted mountaineer's musings and observations.

Munz, Phillip A., and David D. Keck. *A California Flora and Supplement.* Berkeley: University of California Press, 1968. Until quite recently this was it, the California botanist's bible—a complete descriptive "key" to every plant known to grow in California—but quite hefty to tote around on pleasure trips. More useful for amateur botanists are Munz's *California Mountain Wildflowers, Shore Wildflowers,* and *California Desert Wildflowers,* as well as other illustrated plant guides published by UC Press. Serious amateur and professional botanists and ecologists are more than ecstatic these days about the recent publication of the *new* California plant bible: *The Jepson Manual,* edited by Jim Hickman. (For more information, see above.)

National Geographic Society Field Guide to the Birds of North America. National Geographic Society (OP). One of the best guides to bird identification available, but hard to find. One sure source (mail orders accepted) is the Mono Lake Committee (see "Sierra Nevada" chapter).

Neihaus, Theodore. *Sierra Wildflowers.* Berkeley: University of California Press, 1974.

Orr, Robert. *Marine Mammals of California.* Berkeley: University of California Press, 1972. Orr, R.T., and D.B. Orr. *Mushrooms of Western North America.* Berkeley: University of California Press, 1979.

Peterson, Roger Tory. *A Field Guide to Western Birds.* Boston: Houghton Mifflin Co., 1990. The third edition of this birding classic has striking new features, including new full-color illustrations (including juveniles, females, and in-flight birds) facing the written descriptions. The only thing you'll have to flip around for are the range maps, tucked away in the back.

Peterson, Victor. *Native Trees of the Sierra Nevada.* Berkeley: University of California Press, 1974.

Powell, Jerry. *California Insects.* Berkeley: University of California Press, 1980.

Rinehart, Dean, and Ward Smith. *Earthquakes and Young Volcanoes along the Eastern Sierra Nevada.* Palo Alto, CA: Genny Smith Books, 1982.

Robbins, Chandler, Bertel Brown, Herbert Zim, and Arthur Singer. *Birds of North America.* New York: Western Publishing, 1983. A good field guide for California birdwatching.

Sale, Kirkpatrick. *Dwellers in the Land.* San Francisco: Sierra Club Books, 1985. One of the first books putting forth the bioregional philosophy, envisioning a world based not on political borders but on natural geographic regions.

Schmitz, Marjorie. *Growing California Native Plants.* Berkeley: University of California Paree, 1980. A handy guide for for those interested in planting, growing, and otherwise supporting the success of California's beleaguered native plants.

Schoenherr, Allan A. *A Natural History of California.* Berkeley: University of California Press, 1992. With introductory chapters on ecology and geology, *A Natural History* covers California's climate, geology, soil, plant life, and animals based on distinct bioregions, with almost 300 photographs and numerous illustrations and tables. An exceptionally readable and well illustrated introduction to California's astounding natural diversity and drama written by an ecology professor from CSU Fullerton, this 700-some page reference belongs on any Californiac's library shelf.

The Sierra Club Guide to the National Parks: Pacific Southwest and Hawaii. New York: Stewart, Tabori & Chang (distributed by Random House), 1984. A well-written, informative, and beautifully illustrated guide to the natural history and sights of California's national parks, including Channel Islands, Lassen, Redwood, Sequoia, Kings Canyon, and Yosemite. Color photos.

Stebbins, Robert. *California Amphibians and Reptiles.* Berkeley: University of California Press, 1972.

Storer, Tracy I., and Robert L. Usinger. *Sierra Nevada Natural History: An Illustrated Handbook.* Berkeley: University of California Press, 1970. The indispensable, all-in-one natural history companion volume, compact and packable, for appreciating and understanding the Sierra Nevada.

Wallace, David Rains. *The Klamath Knot.* San Francisco: Sierra Club Books, 1983.

Weeden, Norman. *A Sierra Nevada Flora.* Berkeley: Wilderness Press, 1986. Perhaps *the* definitive field guide to Sierra Nevada plants, this one includes trees, shrubs, and ferns in addition to wildflowers. Complete, accurate, and quite compact, with hundreds of illustrations.

Whitley, Stephen. *Sierra Club Naturalist's Guide to the Sierra Nevada.* San Francisco: Sierra Club Books, 1979.

Williams, H., and G.H. Curtis. *The Sutter Buttes of California: A Study of Plio-Pleistocene Volcanism.* Berkeley: University of California Press, 1979 (OP).

Wilson, Lynn, Jim Wilson, and Jeff Nichols. *Wildflowers of Yosemite.* Berkeley: The Sierra Press (distributed by Wilderness Press), 1987. A useful guide to most of the wildflowers common to Yosemite and the central Sierra Nevada, with descriptions in everyday English, color photographs, and species-specific road and trail wildflower tours.

Wiltens, James. *Thistle Greens and Mistletoe: Edible and Poisonous Plants of Northern California.* Berkeley: Wilderness Press, 1988. How to eat cactus and pine cones and make gourmet weed salads are just a few of the fascinating and practical facts shared here about common northstate plants.

ENJOYING THE OUTDOORS, RECREATION, TRAVEL

Bakalinsky, Adah. *Stairway Walks in San Francisco* Berkeley: Lexikos, 1992 (also distributed by Wilderness Press). Twenty-six neighborhood walks connecting San Francisco's 200-plus stairways, choreographed by a veteran city walker and walking tour guide.

Blue, Anthony Dias, ed. *Zagat San Francisco Bay Area Restaurant Survey.* New York: Zagat Survey, 1993. This annually updated collection, a compilation of "people's reviews" of regional restaurants, is a fairly reliable guide to what's hot and what's not.

Brant, Michelle. *Timeless Walks in San Francisco: A Historical Walking Guide.* Berkeley: Brant, 1986.

Braun, Randall Gray. *Cyclists' Route Atlas: A Guide to the Delta, Farm, and Wine Country.* Berkeley: Heyday Books, 1986. An excellent, detailed route guide for cyclists, complete with firsthand tips, maps, and photographs. Also by Braun: *Cyclists' Route Atlas: A Guide to the Gold Country & High Sierra/North* and *Cyclists' Route Atlas: A Guide to the Gold Country & High Sierra/South.*

Bridge, Raymond. *Bike Touring.* San Francisco: Sierra Club Books, 1979.

Cassady, Jim, and Fryar Calhoun. *California White Water: A Guide to the Rivers.* Berkeley: Cassady & Calhoun, 1985. Also available: "California River Maps" and "White Water Guides."

Cook, Laurel. *California Spas.* San Francisco: Foghorn Press, 1992. Designed for the serious aficionado, this book includes relevant facts about more than 50 spas, from specific features, accommodations, and prices to special workshops. Also helpful is information about how to receive a massage—and how to evaluate massage practitioners.

Culliney, John, and Edward Crockett. *Exploring Underwater.* San Francisco: Sierra Club Books, 1980.

Cutter, Ralph. *Sierra Trout Guide.* Berkeley: Wilderness Press, 1991. Expanded and revised, this is a comprehensive introduction to the sport of trout fishing.

Darvil, Fred Jr., M.D. *Mountaineering Medicine: A Wilderness Medical Guide.* Berkeley: Wilderness Press, 1992. Written specifically for mountaineers, this small manual is indispensable for all outdoorsfolk and wilderness travelers.

Doan, Marilyn. *Starting Small in the Wilderness.* San Francisco: Sierra Club Books, 1979.

Doss, Margot Patterson. *New San Francisco at Your Feet.* New York: Grove Press, 1990. One of a series of popular Bay Area walking guides by the same author, including: *The Bay Area at Your Feet,* 1987; *There, There: East San Francisco Bay at Your Feet* (OP); and *A Walker's Yearbook: 52 Seasonal Walks in the San Francisco Bay Area,* 1983 (OP).

Felzer, Ron. *Hetch Hetchy.* Berkeley: Wilderness Press, 1983. Revised and updated 1992. Other detailed backpacking guides by Felzer: *Mineral King* and *Devil's Postpile.*

Fong-Torres, Shirley. *San Francisco Chinatown: A Walking Tour.* San Francisco: China Books, 1991. Definitely an insider's guide to Chinatown, escorting visitors through the neighborhood almost step by step while filling in fascinating details about the history and culture of the Chinese in California. Fong-Torres also includes a culinary education, even abundant recipes for simple and authentic Chinese cuisine. (For information on "Wok Wiz" culinary tours led by the author and her staff, see this book's Walking Tours section in "San Francisco.")

Freeman, Jim. *California Steelhead Fishing.* San Francisco: Chronicle Books, 1984. An outdoor bible for California fisherfolk, with firsthand tips on how and where to fish for steelhead. Also by Freeman: *California Trout Fishing.*

Green, David. *Marble Mountain Wilderness.* Berkeley: Wilderness Press, 1980 (OP). Also by Green: *A Pacific Crest Odyssey.*

Greenwald, John A. *Saddleback Sightseeing in California: A Guide to Rental Horses, Trail Rides, and Guest Ranches*. Baldwin Park, CA: Gem Guides Book Co., 1992. For modern-day dudes and dudettes, everything from hourly rental riding opportunities to guest ranch riding and pack trips is included here.

Hagar, Laura, and Stephanie Irving, eds. *Northern California Best Places*. Seattle: Sasquatch Books, 1992. Though this reviewer also contributed to *Best Places* and therefore isn't entirely objective, this massive compilation of detailed restaurant and accommodation reviews offers some entertaining insights as well as great local guidance in all price categories—always a plus. Hart, John. *Walking Softly in the Wilderness*. San Francisco: Sierra Club Books, 1984. Also by Hart: *Hiking the Bigfoot Country* and *Hiking the Great Basin*.

Holing, Dwight. *California Wild Lands: A Guide to the Nature Conservancy Preserves*. San Francisco: Chronicle Books, 1988. An exceptionally informative, readable guide to Nature Conservancy preserves throughout California—definitely a worthwhile purchase.

Jardine, Ray. *The Pacific Crest Trail Handbook*. Berkeley: Adventure Lore Press (distributed by Wilderness Press), 1992. The author and his wife have hiked the entire 2,500-mile route between Mexico and Canada *twice*, so the information included here—on everything from equipment and clothing to mosquitos, ticks, and bears—is all a serious hiker needs to know.

Jeffrey, Nan, and Kevin Jeffrey. *Adventuring with Children: The Family Pack-Along Guide to the Outdoors and the World*. San Francisco: Foghorn Press, 1992. This enthusiastic guide to getting out and about with children—and without fear and loathing—is invaluable for those who are determined to see the world, as sanely as possible.

Jenkins, J.C., and Ruby Johnson Jenkins. *Exploring the Southern Sierra: East Side*. Berkeley: Wilderness Press, 1992. Originally entitled *Self Propelled in the Southern Sierra, Volume 1*. This newly updated outdoor guide includes 150 adventures in one of the state's remaining sanctuaries of solitude. Includes a four-color foldout map. Also by Jenkins, (also destined to be retitled): *Self-Propelled in the Southern Sierra, Volume 2: The Great Western Divides*.

Kirkendall, Tom, and Vicky Springs. *Bicycling the Pacific Coast*. Seattle: The Mountaineers, 1990. A very good, very practical mile-by-mile guide to the tricky business of cycling along the California coast (and north).

Larson, Lane, and Peggy Larson. *Caving*. San Francisco: Sierra Club Books, 1982.

Libkind, Marcus. *Ski Tours in Lassen Volcanic National Park*. Berkeley: Bittersweet Enterprises (distributed by Wilderness Press), 1989. This tour-by-tour guide includes options for beginners and accomplished cross-country skiers. Special features are highlighted; topo maps and mileage logs included. Libkind has also written four Sierra Nevada ski tour guides: *Covering the Lake Tahoe Area; Carson Pass, Bear Valley, and Pinecrest; Yosemite, Kings Canyon, Sequoia, and Vicinity;* and *The Eastern Sierra Nevada*.

Linkhart, Luther. *The Trinity Alps: A Hiking and Backpacking Guide*. Berkeley: Wilderness Press, 1986.

Loam, Jayson, and Marjorie Gersg. *Hot Springs and Hot Pools of the Southwest*. Berkeley: Aqua Thermal Press (distributed by Wilderness Press), 1992. A useful guide to California's commercial as well as unimproved (natural) yet accessible hot springs, including those in Arizona, Nevada, New Mexico, Texas, and Baja Mexico.

Lorentzen, Bob. *The Hiker's Hip Pocket Guide to the Mendocino Highlands*. Berkeley: Bored Feet Publications, updated in 1992 (distributed by Wilderness Press). The latest in Lorentzen's excellent hiking series, this one selects day hikes and overnight trips in inland Mendocino and Lake counties, including the Yolla Bolly-Middle Eel and Snow Mountain wildernesses. And Lorentzen's guides really *do* fit in your pocket—quite handy.

Lorentzen, Bob. *The Hiker's Hip Pocket Guide to the Mendocino Coast*. Berkeley: Bored Feet Publications, 1992 (updated distributed by

Wilderness Press). Another very good, easy to follow local hiking guide. Also by Lorentzen: *The Hiker's Hip Pocket Guide to the Humboldt Coast* and *The Hiker's Hip Pocket Guide to Sonoma County.*

Margolin, Malcolm. *East Bay Out.* Second ed., Berkeley: Heyday Books, 1988. Published with the cooperation and sponsorship of the East Bay Regional Parks District, this excellent guide focuses as much on the *feeling* as the facts of the East Bay's remaining wildlands, also urban parks and diversions. Highly recommended.

Martin, Don W., and Betty Woo Martin. *Inside San Francisco: A Witty, Opinionated, and Remarkably Useful Pocket Guide to Everybody's Favorite City.* Columbia, CA: Pine Cone Press, 1991. Once again, the Martins manage to pack almost everything an intelligent, thoughtful traveler might need into one tiny suitcase—all the practicalities, informed listings of worthwhile diversions, and enough trivia to educate even the experts. By the same authors and also worth picking up if you're new to San Francisco and vicinity and/or planning a long stay: *San Francisco's Ultimate Dining Guide* (especially if it's been updated) and *The Best of San Francisco,* Second ed., Chronicle Books, 1990.

Martin, Don W., and Betty Woo Martin. *The Best of the Gold Country: A Complete, Witty, and Remarkably Useful Guide to California's Sierra Foothills and Historic Sacramento.* Columbia, CA: Pine Cone Press, (revised edition): 1992. Now that the authors have made their home in California's historic gold country, this book has gotten even better. Thoughtfully organized, the text exploring the western Sierra Nevada foothills from south to north, this particular guidebook makes it easy to find—and enjoy—every area's best attractions, diversions, accommodations, and restaurants. The history and background information is exceptionally well presented, in a lighthearted style, and the how-to "For the Love of Gold" chapter will help anyone fulfill those new gold dreams.

Martin, Don W., and Betty Woo Martin. *The Best of the Wine Country: A Witty, Opinionated, and Remarkably Useful Guide to California's Vinelands.* Columbia, CA: Pine Cone Press,

1991. Among the most recent regional guidebooks by the indefatigable Martins, this one follows the authors' trademark, comprehensive-yet-highly-selective style, as practical as it is entertaining.

McConnaughey, Bayard H., and Evelyn McConnaughey. *Pacific Coast.* New York: Alfred A. Knopf, Inc., 1986. One of the Audubon Society Nature Guides. Over 600 color plates, keyed to region and habitat type, make it easy to identify marine mammals, shorebirds, seashells, and other inhabitants and features of the West Coast, from Alaska to California.

McMillon, Bill, and Kevin McMillon. *Best Hikes With Children: San Francisco's North Bay.* Seattle: The Mountaineers, 1992.

Meyers, Carole Terwilliger. *Eating Out with the Kids in San Francisco and the Bay Area.* Albany, CA: Carousel Press, 1985. A bona fide parent writes about more than 200 restaurants—not just pizza and ice cream parlors—where you can take children *and* have a decent meal. Some reviews are accompanied by suggestions for nearby outings. By the same author and equally helpful for parents: *San Francisco Family Fun.*

Mitchell, Linda, and Allen Mitchell. *California Parks Access.* Berkeley: Cougar Pass Publications (distributed by Wilderness Press). A very useful guide to national and state parks in California for visitors with limited mobility. Both challenges and wheelchair-accessible features are listed. Informationally accessible appendixes are helpful, too.

Neumann, Phyllis. *Sonoma County Bike Trails.* Second ed. Penngrove, CA: Sonoma County Bike Trails, 1989. The long-running, ever-popular cycling guide to Sonoma County.

Olmsted, Gerald W. *The Best of the Sierra Nevada.* New York: Crown Publishers, Inc., 1991. A fascinating and useful guidebook and companion volume, especially generous with history, natural history, and outback recreational information.

Parr, Barry. *San Francisco and the Bay Area.* Oakland: Compass American Guides, 1992.

With its dazzling prose and impressive intellectual intimacy, Parr's general guide to The City and vicinity is one of the best available, enjoyable, too, even for California natives, as companion reading.

Paul, Bill. *The Pacific Crest Bicycle Trail.* Berkeley: Bittersweet Enterprises, 1991 (distributed by Wilderness Press). This is a handy guide for adventurers on wheels, covering a 2,500-mile road (not trail) route from Canada to Mexico, with elevations, campgrounds, and detailed maps included.

Perry, John, and Jane Greverus Perry. *The Sierra Club Guide to the Natural Areas of California.* San Francisco: Sierra Club Books, 1983. A just-the-facts yet very useful guide to California's public lands and parks. Organized by regions, also indexed for easy access.

Pitcher, Don. *Berkeley Inside/Out.* Berkeley: Heyday Books, 1989. The definitive general guide to Berkeley, featuring an abundance of practical facts and insider insights as well as Malcolm Margolin's "Historical Introduction."

Pomada, Elizabeth. *Places to go with Children in Northern California.* San Francisco: Chronicle Books, 1989. As important as finding a place to eat with kids is finding appropriate places to take them before and after meals. For aficionados of California's Victorian homes and buildings, the author's "Painted Ladies" series, co-authored with Michael Larsen, is quite charming too.

Recreation Lakes of California. Sail Sales Publishing, 1988. A very useful guide to the endless recreation lakes in California, complete with general maps (not to scale) and local contact addresses and phones. A worthwhile investment for boaters and fisherfolk.

Riegert, Ray. *Hidden San Francisco and Northern California.* Fifth ed. Berkeley: Ulysses Press, 1992. Written for San Francisco visitors by a local whose sense of adventure comes through in his writing, this guidebook is one of the best for revealing points of interest that only neighborhood residents are likely to know about. Among Riegert's ever-growing list of other titles: *Hidden Coast of California.*

Roper, Steve. *The Climbers' Guide to the High Sierra.* San Francisco: Sierra Club Books, 1976. Also by Roper: *The Climbers' Guide to Yosemite Valley.*

Rowell, Galen, ed. *The Vertical World of Yosemite: A Collection of Writings and Photographs on Rock Climbing in Yosemite.* Berkeley: Wilderness Press, 1974; re-released in 1991. Rowell's first book, back in print with a new introduction, shares the Yosemite mountain high in the words of 14 climbers. Abundant astounding photographs, some color.

Rusmore, Jean, and Frances Spangle. *Peninsula Trails.* Berkeley: Wilderness Press, 1989. By the same authors: *South Bay Trails: Outdoor Adventures Around the Santa Clara Valley.* Schaffer, Jeffrey. *Hiking the Big Sur Country: The Ventana Wilderness.* Berkeley: Wilderness Press, 1988. Other good hiking and backpacking guides by this prolific pathfinder include: *The Carson-Iceberg Wilderness; Desolation Wilderness and the South Lake Tahoe Basin; Lassen Volcanic National Park; The Pacific Crest Trail Volume 1: California; Sonora Pass; The Tahoe Sierra;* and *Yosemite National Park.* Schifrin, Ben. *Emigrant Wilderness.* Berkeley: Wilderness Press, 1990.

Selters, Andy, and Michael Zanger. *The Mt. Shasta Book: A Guide to Hiking, Climbing, Skiing, and Exploring the Mountain and Surrounding Area.* Berkeley: Wilderness Press, 1989.

Silverman, Goldie. *Backpacking with Babies and Small Children.* Berkeley: Wilderness Press, 1986. Everything adventurous parents need to know, or consider, before heading to the woods with youngsters in tow.

Stienstra, Tom. *California Camping: The Complete Guide.* San Francisco: Foghorn Press, 1992. This is undoubtedly the ultimate reference to California camping and campgrounds, federal, state, and local. Included in the 1992-93 edition is Stienstra's compilation of "Secret Campgrounds," an invaluable assist when you truly need to get away from it all. In addition to a thorough practical introduction to the basics of California camping, this guidebook is meticulously organized by area, starting with the general subdivisions of Northern, Central, and Southern California. Even accidental outdoorspeople should carry this one along at all times.

Stienstra, Tom. *California Fishing: The Complete Guide.* San Francisco: Foghorn Press, 1992. This is it, *the* guide for people who think finding God has something to do with strapping on rubber waders or climbing into a tiny boat, making educated fish-eyed guesses about lures, ripples, or lake depths, and generally observing a strict code of silence in the outdoors. As besieged as California's fisheries have been by the state's 30 million-plus population and other attendant devastations and distractions of modern times, fisherfolk can still enjoy some world-class sport in Northern California. This 768-page tome contains just about everything novices and masters need to know to figure out what to do as well as where and when to do it.

Stienstra, Tom. *Great Outdoor Getaways to the Bay Area and Beyond.* San Francisco: Foghorn Press, 1991. A gem for anyone who needs to get outdoors and who prefers areas not already tramped by everyone else in California. The book's organization is unique, too, allowing readers to locate that great escape by map, activity, and specific destination (particular forest, mountain, or park). Usually updated annually.

Sunderland, Bill, and Dale Lackey. *California Blue Ribbon Trout Streams.* Berkeley: Amato Publications (distributed by Wilderness Press), 1991. This good angling guide includes world-class fishing sites accessible by car plus all the particulars, including best baits, flies, and lures. Tejada-Flores, Lito. *Backcountry Skiing.* San Francisco: Sierra Club Books, 1981.

Wallace, David Rains. *The Klamath Knot.* San Francisco: Sierra Club Books, 1983. Worthwhile and readable natural history of California's Klamath Mountains.

Wayburn, Peggy. *Adventuring in the San Francisco Bay Area.* San Francisco: Sierra Club Books, 1987. A fine guide to outdoor activities in the nine Bay Area counties, as well as the islands of the bay. Appendixes list frequent and occasional bird visitors, as well as California state parks, environmental organizations, and nature classes, all with addresses and phones.

Whitnah, Dorothy L. *An Outdoor Guide to the San Francisco Bay Area.* Berkeley: Wilderness Press, 1989. A well-worth-it, nuts-and-bolts guide to Bay Area open space. Includes distances and grades for trail hikes as well as directions for getting there. Especially handy for those without a car, because it discusses public transit options for each destination. Another useful book by Whitnah: *Point Reyes,* a comprehensive guide including trails, campgrounds, and picnic areas.

Winnett, Thomas. *The John Muir Trail.* Berkeley: Wilderness Press, 1984. Other books by Winnett include *The Tahoe-Yosemite Trail,* 1987. Very worthwhile, co-authored by Jason Winnett and Thomas Winnett, are: *Sierra North: 100 Back-Country Trips* and *Sierra South: 100 Back-Country Trips.*

Winnett, Thomas, and Melanie Findling. *Backpacking Basics.* Berkeley: Wilderness Press, 1988. Everything you need to know about going the distance on foot—with an emphasis on getting (and staying) in shape, the principles of low-impact camping, and how to save money on just about everything you'll need.

INDEX

Page numbers in **boldface** indicate the primary reference. *Italicized* page numbers indicate
information in captions, special topics, charts, illustrations, or maps.

ABOUT THE AUTHOR

Kim Weir is a California native. She is also a journalist and writer. A curious generalist by nature, Weir is most happy when turning over rocks—literally and figuratively—and churning through detritus or poking into this and that to discover what usually goes unnoticed. At last report, she was living near the Ishi Wilderness in California's far north.

Weir's formal study of environmental issues began at the University of California at Santa Barbara and continued at California State University, Chico, where she studied biology and obtained a bachelor's degree in environmental studies and analysis. Since all things are interconnected, as a journalist Weir covered the political environment and the natural and unnatural antics of politicians. Before signing on with Moon Publications, she also held an editorial post with a scholarly publishing company.

Kim Weir is a member of the Society of American Travel Writers (SATW). Her award–winning essay—"Ecotourism is Popular—But is it Populist? And Will it Save the World?"—was published in the 1993 international *American Express Annual Review of Travel*.

In addition to her "Out There" California travel column and occasional freelance assignments, Weir is currently at work on additional titles for Moon Publications. As a writer her interests are still expanding exponentially, and may one day invade the entire world. She is currently developing a collection of essays about America, for example, and threatens to write fiction.

NOW DISAPPEARING AT A LOCATION NEAR YOU.

The fact is, it's already too late to save at least 48 California plants and animals.

It's not too late, however, for another 800 that are on the brink of extinction.

From the diminutive kit fox (pictured above) to the majestic desert bighorn sheep, there's still time…but only if we act now.

Since 1959, the California Nature Conservancy has saved 277,000 acres of wild land. And it's been done by using a novel approach—we've bought it.

You see, our philosophy is to use the money we receive to buy land and therefore save valuable, irreplaceable plant and animal life.

We can't do it alone. Please help us by sending a tax-deductible contribution to The Nature Conservancy at 785 Market St., San Francisco, California 94103 or call 800-582-2273 for more information. You'll be saving some of California's most important resources.

Remember, the loss of another species is a loss for all generations who follow us.

The Nature Conservancy

To Protect and Preserve

MOON HANDBOOKS—THE IDEAL TRAVELING COMPANIONS

Open a Moon Handbook and you're opening your eyes and heart to the world. Thoughtful, sensitive, and provocative, Moon Handbooks encourage an intimate understanding of a region, from its culture and history to essential practicalities. Fun to read and packed with valuable information on accommodations, dining, recreation, plus indispensable travel tips, detailed maps, charts, illustrations, photos, glossaries, and indexes, Moon Handbooks are ideal traveling companions: informative, entertaining, and highly practical.

To locate the bookstore nearest you that carries Moon Travel Handbooks or to order directly from Moon Publications, call: (800) 345-5473, Monday-Friday, 9 a.m.-5 p.m. PST.

THE PACIFIC/ASIA SERIES

BALI HANDBOOK   by Bill Dalton
Detailed travel information on the most famous island in the world. 428 pages.   **$12.95**

BANGKOK HANDBOOK   by Michael Buckley
Your tour guide through this exotic and dynamic city reveals the affordable and accessible possibilities. Thai phrasebook. 214 pages.   **$10.95**

BLUEPRINT FOR PARADISE: How to Live on a Tropic Island   by Ross Norgrove
This one-of-a-kind guide has everything you need to know about moving to and living comfortably on a tropical island. 212 pages.   **$14.95**

FIJI ISLANDS HANDBOOK   by David Stanley
The first and still the best source of information on travel around this 322-island archipelago. Fijian glossary. 198 pages.   **$11.95**

INDONESIA HANDBOOK   by Bill Dalton
This one-volume encyclopedia explores island by island the many facets of this sprawling, kaleidoscopic island nation. Extensive Indonesian vocabulary. 1,000 pages.   **$19.95**

JAPAN HANDBOOK   by J.D. Bisignani
In this comprehensive new edition, award-winning travel writer J.D. Bisignani offers to inveterate travelers, newcomers, and businesspeople alike a thoroughgoing presentation of Japan's many facets. 950 pages.   **$22.50**

MICRONESIA HANDBOOK: Guide to the Caroline, Gilbert, Mariana, and Marshall Islands
by David Stanley
Micronesia Handbook guides you on a real Pacific adventure all your own. 345 pages.   **$11.95**

NEW ZEALAND HANDBOOK   by Jane King
Introduces you to the people, places, history, and culture of this extraordinary land. 571 pages.
$18.95

OUTBACK AUSTRALIA HANDBOOK   by Marael Johnson
Australia is an endlessly fascinating, vast land, and *Outback Australia Handbook* explores the cities and towns, sheep stations, and wilderness areas of the Northern Territory, Western Australia, and South Australia. Full of travel tips and cultural information for adventuring, relaxing, or just getting away from it all. 355 pages.   **$15.95**

PHILIPPINES HANDBOOK   by Peter Harper and Evelyn Peplow
Crammed with detailed information, *Philippines Handbook* equips the escapist, hedonist, or business traveler with thorough coverage of the Philippines's colorful history, landscapes, and culture. 600 pages.   **$17.95**

SOUTHEAST ASIA HANDBOOK   by Carl Parkes
Helps the enlightened traveler discover the real Southeast Asia. 873 pages.   **$16.95**

SOUTH KOREA HANDBOOK   by Robert Nilsen
Whether you're visiting on business or searching for adventure, *South Korea Handbook* is an invaluable companion. Korean glossary with useful notes on speaking and reading the language. 548 pages.   **$14.95**

SOUTH PACIFIC HANDBOOK   by David Stanley
The original comprehensive guide to the 16 territories in the South Pacific. 740 pages.   **$19.95**

TAHITI-POLYNESIA HANDBOOK   by David Stanley
All five French-Polynesian archipelagoes are covered in this comprehensive guide by Oceania's best-known travel writer. 235 pages.   **$11.95**

THAILAND HANDBOOK   by Carl Parkes
Presents the richest source of information on travel in Thailand. 568 pages.   **$16.95**

THE HAWAIIAN SERIES

BIG ISLAND OF HAWAII HANDBOOK   by J.D. Bisignani
An entertaining yet informative text packed with insider tips on accommodations, dining, sports and outdoor activities, natural attractions, and must-see sights. 347 pages.   **$11.95**

HAWAII HANDBOOK   by J.D. Bisignani
Winner of the 1989 Hawaii Visitors Bureau's Best Guide Award and the Grand Award for Excellence in Travel Journalism, this guide takes you beyond the glitz and high-priced hype and leads you to a genuine Hawaiian experience. Covers all 8 Hawaiian Islands. 879 pages.   **$15.95**

KAUAI HANDBOOK   by J.D. Bisignani
Kauai Handbook is the perfect antidote to the workaday world. Hawaiian and pidgin glossaries. 236 pages.   **$9.95**

MAUI HANDBOOK   by J.D. Bisignani
"No fool-'round" advice on accommodations, eateries, and recreation, plus a comprehensive introduction to island ways, geography, and history. Hawaiian and pidgin glossaries. 350 pages.   **$11.95**

OAHU HANDBOOK by J.D. Bisignani
A handy guide to Honolulu, renowned surfing beaches, and Oahu's countless other diversions.
Hawaiian and pidgin glossaries. 354 pages.   **$11.95**

THE AMERICAS SERIES

ALASKA-YUKON HANDBOOK by Deke Castleman and Don Pitcher
Get the inside story, with plenty of well-seasoned advice to help you cover more miles on less
money. 384 pages.   **$13.95**

ARIZONA TRAVELER'S HANDBOOK by Bill Weir
This meticulously researched guide contains everything necessary to make Arizona accessible
and enjoyable. 505 pages.   **$14.95**

BAJA HANDBOOK by Joe Cummings
A comprehensive guide with all the travel information and background on the land, history, and
culture of this untamed thousand-mile-long peninsula. 356 pages.   **$13.95**

BELIZE HANDBOOK by Chicki Mallan
Complete with detailed maps, practical information, and an overview of the area's flamboyant
history, culture, and geographical features, *Belize Handbook* is the only comprehensive guide
of its kind to this spectacular region. 263 pages.   **$14.95**

BRITISH COLUMBIA HANDBOOK by Jane King
With an emphasis on outdoor adventures, this guide covers mainland British Columbia,
Vancouver Island, the Queen Charlotte Islands, and the Canadian Rockies. 381 pages.
$13.95

CANCUN HANDBOOK by Chicki Mallan
Covers the city's luxury scene as well as more modest attractions, plus many side trips to
unspoiled beaches and Mayan ruins. Spanish glossary. 257 pages.   **$12.95**

CATALINA ISLAND HANDBOOK: A Guide to California's Channel Islands
by Chicki Mallan
A complete guide to these remarkable islands, from the windy solitude of the Channel Islands
National Marine Sanctuary to bustling Avalon. 245 pages.   **$10.95**

COLORADO HANDBOOK by Stephen Metzger
Essential details to the all-season possibilities in Colorado fill this guide. Practical travel tips
combine with recreation—skiing, nightlife, and wilderness exploration—plus entertaining
essays. 416 pages.   **$17.95**

COSTA RICA HANDBOOK by Christopher P. Baker
Experience the many wonders of the natural world as you explore this remarkable land.
Spanish-English glossary. 700 pages.   **$17.95**

IDAHO HANDBOOK by Bill Loftus
A year-round guide to everything in this outdoor wonderland, from whitewater adventures to
rural hideaways. 275 pages.   **$12.95**

JAMAICA HANDBOOK   by Karl Luntta
From the sun and surf of Montego Bay and Ocho Rios to the cool slopes of the Blue Mountains, author Karl Luntta offers island-seekers a perceptive, personal view of Jamaica. 230 pages. **$14.95**

MONTANA HANDBOOK   by W.C. McRae and Judy Jewell
The wild West is yours with this extensive guide to the Treasure State, complete with travel practicalities, history, and lively essays on Montana life. 393 pages.   **$13.95**

NEVADA HANDBOOK   by Deke Castleman
Nevada Handbook puts the Silver State into perspective and makes it manageable and affordable. 400 pages.   **$14.95**

NEW MEXICO HANDBOOK   by Stephen Metzger
A close-up and complete look at every aspect of this wondrous state. 375 pages.   **$13.95**

NORTHERN CALIFORNIA HANDBOOK   by Kim Weir
An outstanding companion for imaginative travel in the territory north of the Tehachapis. 780 pages.   **$19.95**

OREGON HANDBOOK   by Stuart Warren and Ted Long Ishikawa
Brimming with travel practicalities and insiders' views on Oregon's history, culture, arts, and activities. 461 pages.   **$15.95**

PACIFIC MEXICO HANDBOOK   by Bruce Whipperman
Explore 2,000 miles of gorgeous beaches, quiet resort towns, and famous archaeological sites along Mexico's Pacific coast. Spanish-English glossary. 428 pages.   **$15.95**

TEXAS HANDBOOK   by Joe Cummings
Seasoned travel writer Joe Cummings brings an insider's perspective to his home state. 483 pages.   **$13.95**

UTAH HANDBOOK   by Bill Weir
Weir gives you all the carefully researched facts and background to make your visit a success. 445 pages.   **$14.95**

WASHINGTON HANDBOOK   by Dianne J. Boulerice Lyons and Archie Satterfield
Covers sights, shopping, services, transportation, and outdoor recreation, with complete listings for restaurants and accommodations. 433 pages.   **$13.95**

WYOMING HANDBOOK   by Don Pitcher
All you need to know to open the doors to this wide and wild state. 495 pages.   **$14.95**

YUCATAN HANDBOOK   by Chicki Mallan
All the information you'll need to guide you into every corner of this exotic land. Mayan and Spanish glossaries. 391 pages.   **$14.95**

THE INTERNATIONAL SERIES

EGYPT HANDBOOK   by Kathy Hansen
An invaluable resource for intelligent travel in Egypt. Arabic glossary. 522 pages.   **$18.95**

MOSCOW-ST. PETERSBURG HANDBOOK   by Masha Nordbye
Provides the visitor with an extensive introduction to the history, culture, and people of these
two great cities, as well as practical information on where to stay, eat, and shop. 260 pages.
$13.95

NEPAL HANDBOOK   by Kerry Moran
Whether you're planning a week in Kathmandu or months out on the trail, *Nepal Handbook* will
take you into the heart of this Himalayan jewel. 378 pages.   **$12.95**

NEPALI AAMA   by Broughton Coburn
A delightful photo-journey into the life of a Gurung tribeswoman of Central Nepal. Having lived
with Aama (translated, "mother") for two years, first as an outsider and later as an adopted
member of the family, Coburn presents an intimate glimpse into a culture alive with humor,
folklore, religion, and ancient rituals. 165 pages.   **$13.95**

PAKISTAN HANDBOOK   by Isobel Shaw
For armchair travelers and trekkers alike, the most detailed and authoritative guide to Pakistan
ever published. Urdu glossary. 478 pages.   **$15.95**

STAYING HEALTHY IN ASIA, AFRICA, AND LATIN AMERICA
by Dirk G. Schroeder, Sc D, MPH
Don't leave home without it! Besides providing a complete overview of the health problems that
exist in these areas, this book will help you determine which immunizations you'll need
beforehand, what medications to take with you, and how to recognize and treat infections and
diseases. Includes extensively illustrated first-aid information and precautions for heat, cold,
and high altitude. 200 pages.   **$10.95**

New travel handbooks may be available that are not on this list.
To find out more about current or upcoming titles,
call us toll-free at (800) 345-5473.

MOONBELTS

Made of heavy-duty Cordura nylon, the Moonbelt offers maximum protection for your money
and important papers. This all-weather pouch slips under your shirt or waistband, rendering it
virtually undetectable and inaccessible to pickpockets. One-inch-wide nylon webbing, heavy-
duty zipper, one-inch quick-release buckle. Accommodates traveler's checks, passport, cash,
photos. Size 5 x 9 inches. Black.   **$8.95**

IMPORTANT ORDERING INFORMATION

FOR FASTER SERVICE: Call to locate the bookstore nearest you that carries Moon Travel Handbooks or order directly from Moon Publications:

(800) 345-5473 • **Monday-Friday** • **9 a.m.-5 p.m. PST** • fax **(916) 345-6751**

PRICES: All prices are subject to change. We always ship the most current edition. We will let you know if there is a price increase on the book you ordered.

SHIPPING & HANDLING OPTIONS: 1) Domestic UPS or USPS first class (allow 10 working days for delivery): $3.50 for the first item, 50 cents for each additional item.

Exceptions:
• **Moonbelt** shipping is $1.50 for one, 50 cents for each additional belt.
• Add $2.00 for same-day handling.
• UPS 2nd Day Air or Printed Airmail requires a special quote.
• International Surface Bookrate (8-12 weeks delivery):
   $3.00 for the first item, $1.00 for each additional item. Note: Moon Publications cannot guarantee international surface bookrate shipping.

FOREIGN ORDERS: All orders that originate outside the U.S.A. must be paid for with either an International Money Order or a check in U.S. currency drawn on a major U.S. bank based in the U.S.A.

TELEPHONE ORDERS: We accept Visa or MasterCard payments. Minimum order is US$15.00. Call in your order: (800) 345-5473, 9 a.m.-5 p.m. Pacific Standard Time.

ORDER FORM

Be sure to call (800) 345-5473 for current prices and editions or for the name of the bookstore
nearest you that carries Moon Travel Handbooks • 9 a.m.–5 p.m. PST
(See important ordering information on preceding page)

Name: _____ Date: _____

Street: _____

City: _____ Daytime Phone: _____

State or Country: _____ Zip Code: _____

QUANTITY	TITLE	PRICE

Taxable Total_____

Sales Tax (7.25%) for California Residents_____

Shipping & Handling_____

TOTAL_____

Ship: ☐ UPS (no PO Boxes) ☐ 1st class ☐ International surface mail

Ship to: ☐ address above ☐ other _____

_____

Make checks payable to: **MOON PUBLICATIONS, INC**. P.O. Box 3040, Chico, CA 95927-3040
U.S.A. We accept Visa and MasterCard. **To Order**: Call in your Visa or MasterCard number, or send
a written order with your Visa or MasterCard number and expiration date clearly written.

Card Number: ☐ **Visa** ☐ **MasterCard**

☐ ☐ ☐ ☐ ☐ ☐ ☐ ☐ ☐ ☐ ☐ ☐ ☐ ☐ ☐ ☐

Exact Name on Card: _____

expiration date:_____

signature_____

W/94

THE METRIC SYSTEM

1 inch = 2.54 centimeters (cm)
1 foot = .304 meters (m)
1 mile = 1.6093 kilometers (km)
1 km = .6124 miles
1 fathom = 1.8288 m
1 chain = 20.1168 m
1 furlong = 201.168 m
1 acre = .4047 hectares
1 sq km = 100 hectares
1 sq mile = 2.59 square km
1 ounce = 28.35 grams
1 pound = .4536 kilograms
1 short ton = .90718 metric ton
1 short ton = 2000 pounds
1 long ton = 1.016 metric tons
1 long ton = 2240 pounds
1 metric ton = 1000 kilograms
1 quart = .94635 liters
1 US gallon = 3.7854 liters
1 Imperial gallon = 4.5459 liters
1 nautical mile = 1.852 km

To compute centigrade temperatures, subtract 32 from Fahrenheit and divide by 1.8. To go the other way, multiply centigrade by 1.8 and add 32.

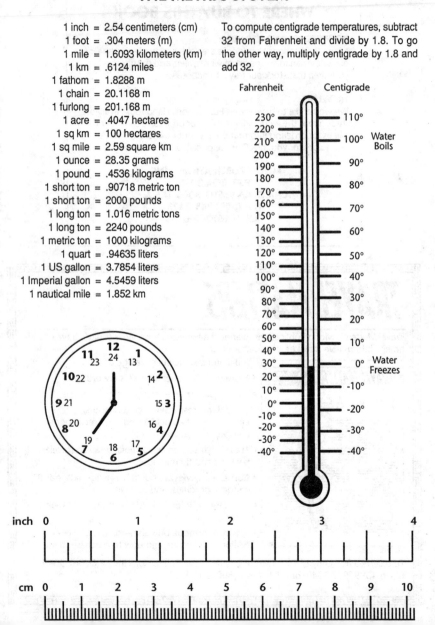